Plays Of Hen

Table Of Contents

Henrik Ibsen - Hedda Gabler

Index Of Contents

CHARACTERS.

GEORGE TESMAN.

HEDDA TESMAN, his wife.

MISS JULIANA TESMAN, his aunt.

MRS. ELVSTED.

JUDGE BRACK.

EILERT LOVBORG.

BERTA, servant at the Tesmans.

The scene of the action is Tesman's villa, in the west end of Christiania.

ACT FIRST.

A spacious, handsome, and tastefully furnished drawing room, decorated in dark colours. In the back, a wide doorway with curtains drawn back, leading into a smaller room decorated in the same style as the drawing-room. In the right-hand wall of the front room, a folding door leading out to the hall. In the opposite wall, on the left, a glass door, also with curtains drawn back. Through the panes can be seen part of a verandah outside, and trees covered with autumn foliage. An oval table, with a cover on it, and surrounded by chairs, stands well forward. In front, by the wall on the right, a wide stove of dark porcelain, a high-backed arm-chair, a cushioned foot-rest, and two footstools. A settee, with a small round table in front of it, fills the upper right-hand corner. In front, on the left, a little way from the wall, a sofa. Further back than the glass door, a piano. On either side of the doorway at the back a whatnot with terra-cotta and majolica ornaments. Against the back wall of the inner room a sofa, with a table, and one or two chairs. Over the sofa hangs the portrait of a handsome elderly man in a General's uniform. Over the table a hanging lamp, with an opal glass shade. A number of bouquets are arranged about the drawing-room, in vases and glasses. Others lie upon the tables. The floors in both rooms are covered with thick carpets. Morning light. The sun shines in through the glass door.

MISS JULIANA TESMAN, with her bonnet on a carrying a parasol, comes in from the hall, followed by BERTA, who carries a bouquet wrapped in paper. MISS TESMAN is a comely and pleasant- looking lady of about sixty-five. She is nicely but simply dressed in a grey walking-costume. BERTA is a middle-aged woman of plain and rather countrified appearance.

MISS TESMAN. [Stops close to the door, listens, and says softly:] Upon my word, I don't believe they are stirring yet!

BERTA. [Also softly.] I told you so, Miss. Remember how late the steamboat got in last night. And then, when they got home! good Lord, what a lot the young mistress had to unpack before she could get to bed.

MISS TESMAN. Well well, let them have their sleep out. But let us see that they get a good breath of the fresh morning air when they do appear.

[She goes to the glass door and throws it open.

BERTA. [Beside the table, at a loss what to do with the bouquet in her hand.]

I declare there isn't a bit of room left. I think I'll put it down here, Miss.

[She places it on the piano.

MISS TESMAN. So you've got a new mistress now, my dear Berta. Heaven knows it was a wrench to me to part with you.

BERTA. [On the point of weeping.] And do you think it wasn't hard for me, too, Miss? After all the blessed years I've been with you and Miss Rina.

MISS TESMAN. We must make the best of it, Berta. There was nothing else to be done. George can't do without you, you see-he absolutely can't. He has had you to look after him ever since he was a little boy.

BERTA. Ah but, Miss Julia, I can't help thinking of Miss Rina lying helpless at home there, poor thing. And with only that new girl too! She'll never learn to take proper care of an invalid.

MISS TESMAN. Oh, I shall manage to train her. And of course, you know, I shall take most of it upon myself. You needn't be uneasy about my poor sister, my dear Berta.

BERTA. Well, but there's another thing, Miss. I'm so mortally afraid I shan't be able to suit the young mistress.

MISS TESMAN. Oh well, just at first there may be one or two things

BERTA. Most like she'll be terrible grand in her ways.

MISS TESMAN. Well, you can't wonder at that, General Gabler's daughter! Think of the sort of life she was accustomed to in her father's time. Don't you remember how we used to see her riding down the road along with the General? In that long black habit, and with feathers in her hat?

BERTA. Yes, indeed, I remember well enough! But, good Lord, I should never have dreamt in those days that she and Master George would make a match of it.

MISS TESMAN. Nor I. But by-the-bye, Berta, while I think of it: in future you mustn't say Master George. You must say Dr. Tesman.

BERTA. Yes, the young mistress spoke of that too, last night, the moment they set foot in the house. Is it true then, Miss?

MISS TESMAN. Yes, indeed it is. Only think, Berta, some foreign university has made him a doctor while he has been abroad, you understand. I hadn't heard a word about it, until he told me himself upon the pier.

BERTA. Well well, he's clever enough for anything, he is. But I didn't think he'd have gone in for doctoring people.

MISS TESMAN. No no, it's not that sort of doctor he is. [Nods significantly.] But let me tell you, we may have to call him something still grander before long.

BERTA. You don't day so! What can that be, Miss?

MISS TESMAN. [Smiling.] H'm, wouldn't you like to know! [With emotion.] Ah, dear dear, if my poor brother could only look up from his grave now, and see what his little boy has grown into! [Looks around.] But bless me, Berta, why have you done this? Taken the chintz covers off all the furniture.

BERTA. The mistress told me to. She can't abide covers on the chairs, she says.

MISS TESMAN. Are they going to make this their everyday sitting-room then?

BERTA. Yes, that's what I understood from the mistress. Master George, the doctor, he said nothing.

GEORGE TESMAN comes from the right into the inner room, humming to himself, and carrying an unstrapped empty portmanteau. He is a middle-sized, young-looking man of thirty-three, rather stout, with a round, open, cheerful face, fair hair and beard. He wears spectacles, and is somewhat carelessly dressed in comfortable indoor clothes.

MISS TESMAN. Good morning, good morning, George.

TESMAN. [In the doorway between the rooms.] Aunt Julia! Dear Aunt Julia! [Goes up to her and shakes hands warmly.] Come all this way so early! Eh?

MISS TESMAN. Why, of course I had to come and see how you were getting on.

TESMAN. In spite of your having had no proper night's rest?

MISS TESMAN. Oh, that makes no difference to me.

TESMAN. Well, I suppose you got home all right from the pier? Eh?

MISS TESMAN. Yes, quite safely, thank goodness. Judge Brack was good enough to see me right to my door.

TESMAN. We were so sorry we couldn't give you a seat in the carriage. But you saw what a pile of boxes Hedda had to bring with her.

MISS TESMAN. Yes, she had certainly plenty of boxes.

BERTA. [To TESMAN.] Shall I go in and see if there's anything I can do for the mistress?

TESMAN. No thank you, Berta, you needn't. She said she would ring if she wanted anything.

BERTA. [Going towards the right.] Very well.

TESMAN. But look here, take this portmanteau with you.

BERTA. [Taking it.] I'll put it in the attic. [She goes out by the hall door.

TESMAN. Fancy, Auntie, I had the whole of that portmanteau chock full of copies of the documents. You wouldn't believe how much I have picked up from all the archives I have been examining, curious old details that no one has had any idea of -

MISS TESMAN. Yes, you don't seem to have wasted you time on your wedding trip, George.

TESMAN. No, that I haven't. But do take off your bonnet, Auntie. Look here! Let me untie the strings, eh?

MISS TESMAN. [While he does so.] Well well, this is just as if you were still at home with us.

TESMAN. [With the bonnet in his hand, looks at it from all sides.] Why, what a gorgeous bonnet you've been investing in!

MISS TESMAN. I bought it on Hedda's account.

TESMAN. On Hedda's account? Eh?

MISS TESMAN. Yes, so that Hedda needn't be ashamed of me if we happened to go out together.

TESMAN. [Patting her cheek.] You always think of everything, Aunt Julia. [Lays the bonnet on a chair beside the table.] And now, look here, suppose we sit comfortably on the sofa and have a little chat, till Hedda comes. [They seat themselves. She places her parasol in the corner of the sofa.

MISS TESMAN. [Takes both his hands and looks at him.] What a delight it is to have you again, as large as life, before my very eyes, George! My George, my poor brother's own boy!

TESMAN. And it's a delight for me, too, to see you again, Aunt Julia! You, who have been father and mother in one to me.

MISS TESMAN. Oh yes, I know you will always keep a place in your heart for your old aunts.

TESMAN. And what about Aunt Rina? No improvement, eh?

MISS TESMAN. Oh, no, we can scarcely look for any improvement in her case, poor thing. There she lies, helpless, as she has lain for all these years. But heaven grant I may not lose her yet awhile! For if I did, I don't know what I should make of my life, George, especially now that I haven't you to look after any more.

TESMAN. [Patting her back.] There there there!

MISS TESMAN. [Suddenly changing her tone.] And to think that here are you a married man, George! And that you should be the one to carry off Hedda Gabler, the beautiful Hedda Gabler! Only think of it, she, that was so beset with admirers!

TESMAN. [Hums a little and smiles complacently.] Yes, I fancy I have several good friends about town who would like to stand in my shoes, eh?

MISS TESMAN. And then this fine long wedding-tour you have had! More than five, nearly six months

TESMAN. Well, for me it has been a sort of tour of research as well. I have had to do so much grubbing among old records and to read no end of books too, Auntie.

MISS TESMAN. Oh yes, I suppose so. [More confidentially, and lowering her voice a little.] But listen now, George, have you nothing, nothing special to tell me?

TESMAN. As to our journey?

MISS TESMAN. Yes.

TESMAN. No, I don't know of anything except what I have told you in my letters. I had a doctor's degree conferred on me, but that I told you yesterday.

MISS TESMAN. Yes, yes, you did. But what I mean is, haven't you any, any, expectations?

TESMAN. Expectations?

MISS TESMAN. Why you know, George, I'm your old auntie!

TESMAN. Why, of course I have expectations.

MISS TESMAN. Ah!

TESMAN. I have every expectation of being a professor one of these days.

MISS TESMAN. Oh yes, a professor

TESMAN.

Indeed, I may say I am certain of it. But my dear Auntie, you know all about that already!

MISS TESMAN.

[Laughing to herself.] Yes, of course I do. You are quite right there. [Changing the subject.] But we were talking about your journey. It must have cost a great deal of money, George?

Tesman. Well, you see, my handsome travelling-scholarship went a good way.

MISS TESMAN. But I can't understand how you can have made it go far enough for two.

TESMAN. No, that's not easy to understand, eh?

MISS TESMAN. And especially travelling with a lady, they tell me that makes it ever so much more expensive.

TESMAN. Yes, of course, it makes it a little more expensive. But Hedda had to have this trip, Auntie! She really had to. Nothing else would have done.

MISS TESMAN. No no, I suppose not. A wedding-tour seems to be quite indispensable nowadays. But tell me now, have you gone thoroughly over the house yet?

TESMAN. Yes, you may be sure I have. I have been afoot ever since daylight.

MISS TESMAN. And what do you think of it all?

TESMAN. I'm delighted! Quite delighted! Only I can't think what we are to do with the two empty rooms between this inner parlour and Hedda's bedroom.

MISS TESMAN. [Laughing.] Oh my dear George, I daresay you may find some use for them, in the course of time.

TESMAN. Why of course you are quite right, Aunt Julia! You mean as my library increases, eh?

MISS TESMAN. Yes, quite so, my dear boy. It was your library I was thinking of.

TESMAN. I am specially pleased on Hedda's account. Often and often, before we were engaged, she said that she would never care to live anywhere but in Secretary Falk's villa.

MISS TESMAN. Yes, it was lucky that this very house should come into the market, just after you had started.

TESMAN. Yes, Aunt Julia, the luck was on our side, wasn't it, eh?

MISS TESMAN. But the expense, my dear George! You will find it very expensive, all this.

TESMAN. [Looks at her, a little cast down.] Yes, I suppose I shall, Aunt!

MISS TESMAN. Oh, frightfully!

TESMAN. How much do you think? In round numbers? Eh?

MISS TESMAN. Oh, I can't even guess until all the accounts come in.

TESMAN. Well, fortunately, Judge Brack has secured the most favourable terms for me, so he said in a letter to Hedda.

MISS TESMAN. Yes, don't be uneasy, my dear boy. Besides, I have given security for the furniture and all the carpets.

TESMAN. Security? You? My dear Aunt Julia, what sort of security could you give?

MISS TESMAN. I have given a mortgage on our annuity.

TESMAN. [Jumps up.] What! On your and Aunt Rina's annuity!

MISS TESMAN. Yes, I knew of no other plan, you see.

TESMAN. [Placing himself before her.] Have you gone out of your senses, Auntie? Your annuity, it's all that you and Aunt Rina have to live upon.

MISS TESMAN. Well well, don't get so excited about it. It's only a matter of form you know, Judge Brack assured me of that. It was he that was kind enough to arrange the whole affair for me. A mere matter of form, he said.

TESMAN. Yes, that may be all very well. But nevertheless

MISS TESMAN. You will have your own salary to depend upon now. And, good heavens, even if we did have to pay up a little! To eke things out a bit at the start! Why, it would be nothing but a pleasure to us.

TESMAN. Oh Auntie, will you never be tired of making sacrifices for me!

MISS TESMAN. [Rises and lays her hand on his shoulders.] Have I any other happiness in this world except to smooth your way for you, my dear boy. You, who have had neither father nor mother to depend on. And now we have reached the goal, George! Things have looked black enough for us, sometimes; but, thank heaven, now you have nothing to fear.

TESMAN. Yes, it is really marvellous how every thing has turned out for the best.

MISS TESMAN. And the people who opposed you, who wanted to bar the way for you, now you have them at your feet. They have fallen, George. Your most dangerous rival, his fall was the worst. And now he has to lie on the bed he has made for himself, poor misguided creature.

TESMAN. Have you heard anything of Eilert? Since I went away, I mean.

MISS TESMAN. Only that he is said to have published a new book.

TESMAN. What! Eilert Lovborg! Recently, eh?

MISS TESMAN. Yes, so they say. Heaven knows whether it can be worth anything! Ah, when your new book appears that will be another story, George! What is it to be about?

TESMAN. It will deal with the domestic industries of Brabant during the Middle Ages.

MISS TESMAN. Fancy, to be able to write on such a subject as that!

TESMAN. However, it may be some time before the book is ready. I have all these collections to arrange first, you see.

MISS TESMAN. Yes, collecting and arranging, no one can beat you at that. There you are my poor brother's own son.

TESMAN. I am looking forward eagerly to setting to work at it; especially now that I have my own delightful home to work in.

MISS TESMAN. And, most of all, now that you have got the wife of your heart, my dear George.

TESMAN. [Embracing her.] Oh yes, yes, Aunt Julia! Hedda, she is the best part of it all! I believe I hear her coming, eh?

HEDDA enters from the left through the inner room. Her face and figure show refinement and distinction. Her complexion is pale and opaque. Her steel-grey eyes express a cold, unruffled repose. Her hair is of an agreeable brown, but not particularly abundant. She is dressed in a tasteful, somewhat loose-fitting morning gown.

MISS TESMAN. [Going to meet HEDDA.] Good morning, my dear Hedda! Good morning, and a hearty welcome!

HEDDA. [Holds out her hand.] Good morning, dear Miss Tesman! So early a call! That is kind of you.

MISS TESMAN. [With some embarrassment.] Well, has the bride slept well in her new home?

HEDDA. Oh yes, thanks. Passably.

TESMAN. [Laughing.] Passably! Come, that's good, Hedda! You were sleeping like a stone when I got up.

HEDDA. Fortunately. Of course one has always to accustom one's self to new surroundings, Miss Tesman, little by little. [Looking towards the left.] Oh, there the servant has gone and opened the veranda door, and let in a whole flood of sunshine.

MISS TESMAN. [Going towards the door.] Well, then we will shut it.

HEDDA. No no, not that! Tesman, please draw the curtains. That will give a softer light.

TESMAN. [At the door.] All right, all right. There now, Hedda, now you have both shade and fresh air.

HEDDA. Yes, fresh air we certainly must have, with all these stacks of flowers. But, won't you sit down, Miss Tesman?

MISS TESMAN.

No, thank you. Now that I have seen that everything is all right here, thank heaven! I must be getting home again. My sister is lying longing for me, poor thing.

TESMAN. Give her my very best love, Auntie; and say I shall look in and see her later in the day.

MISS TESMAN. Yes, yes, I'll be sure to tell her. But by-the-bye, George [Feeling in her dress pocket] I had almost forgotten, I have something for you here.

TESMAN. What is it, Auntie? Eh?

MISS TESMAN. [Produces a flat parcel wrapped in newspaper and hands it to him.] Look here, my dear boy.

TESMAN. [Opening the parcel.] Well, I declare! Have you really saved them for me, Aunt Julia! Hedda! isn't this touching, eh?

HEDDA. [Beside the whatnot on the right.] Well, what is it?

TESMAN. My old morning-shoes! My slippers.

HEDDA. Indeed. I remember you often spoke of them while we were abroad.

TESMAN. Yes, I missed them terribly. [Goes up to her.] Now you shall see them, Hedda!

HEDDA. [Going towards the stove.] Thanks, I really don't care about it.

TESMAN. [Following her.] Only think ill as she was, Aunt Rina embroidered these for me. Oh you can't think how many associations cling to them.

HEDDA. [At the table.] Scarcely for me.

MISS TESMAN. Of course not for Hedda, George.

TESMAN. Well, but now that she belongs to the family, I thought

HEDDA. [Interrupting.] We shall never get on with this servant, Tesman.

MISS TESMAN. Not get on with Berta?

TESMAN. Why, dear, what puts that in your head? Eh?

HEDDA. [Pointing.] Look there! She has left her old bonnet lying about on a chair.

TESMAN. [In consternation, drops the slippers on the floor.] Why, Hedda

HEDDA. Just fancy, if any one should come in and see it!

TESMAN. But Hedda that's Aunt Julia's bonnet.

HEDDA. Is it!

MISS TESMAN. [Taking up the bonnet.] Yes, indeed it's mine. And, what's more, it's not old, Madam Hedda.

HEDDA. I really did not look closely at it, Miss Tesman.

MISS TESMAN. [Trying on the bonnet.] Let me tell you it's the first time I have worn it, the very first time.

TESMAN. And a very nice bonnet it is too, quite a beauty!

MISS TESMAN. Oh, it's no such great things, George. [Looks around her.] My parasol? Ah, here. [Takes it.] For this is mine too [mutters] not Berta's.

TESMAN. A new bonnet and a new parasol! Only think, Hedda.

HEDDA. Very handsome indeed.

TESMAN. Yes, isn't it? Eh? But Auntie, take a good look at Hedda before you go! See how handsome she is!

MISS TESMAN. Oh, my dear boy, there's nothing new in that. Hedda was always lovely. [She nods and goes toward the right.]

TESMAN. [Following.] Yes, but have you noticed what splendid condition she is in? How she has filled out on the journey?

HEDDA. [Crossing the room.] Oh, do be quiet!

MISS TESMAN. [Who has stopped and turned.] Filled out?

TESMAN. Of course you don't notice it so much now that she has that dress on. But I, who can see

HEDDA. [At the glass door, impatiently.] Oh, you can't see anything.

TESMAN. It must be the mountain air in the Tyrol

HEDDA. [Curtly, interrupting.] I am exactly as I was when I started.

TESMAN. So you insist; but I'm quite certain you are not. Don't you agree with me, Auntie?

MISS TESMAN. [Who has been gazing at her with folded hands.] Hedda is lovely, lovely, lovely. [Goes up to her, takes her head between both hands, draws it downwards, and kisses her hair.] God bless and preserve Hedda Tesman for George's sake.

HEDDA. [Gently freeing herself.] Oh! Let me go.

MISS TESMAN. [In quiet emotion.] I shall not let a day pass without coming to see you.

TESMAN. No you won't, will you, Auntie? Eh?

MISS TESMAN. Good-bye, good-bye! [She goes out by the hall door. TESMAN accompanies her. The door remains half open. TESMAN can be heard repeating his message to Aunt Rina and his thanks for the slippers. [In the meantime, HEDDA walks about the room, raising her arms and clenching her hands as if in desperation. Then she flings back the curtains from the glass door, and stands there looking out. [Presently, TESMAN returns and closes the door behind him.

TESMAN. [Picks up the slippers from the floor.] What are you looking at, Hedda?

HEDDA. [Once more calm and mistress of herself.] I am only looking at the leaves. They are so yellow, so withered.

TESMAN. [Wraps up the slippers and lays them on the table.] Well, you see, we are well into September now.

HEDDA. [Again restless.] Yes, to think of it! already in, in September.

TESMAN. Don't you think Aunt Julia's manner was strange, dear? Almost solemn? Can you imagine what was the matter with her? Eh?

HEDDA. I scarcely know her, you see. Is she not often like that?

TESMAN. No, not as she was to-day.

HEDDA. [Leaving the glass door.] Do you think she was annoyed about the bonnet?

TESMAN. Oh, scarcely at all. Perhaps a little, just at the moment

HEDDA. But what an idea, to pitch her bonnet about in the drawing-room! No one does that sort of thing.

TESMAN. Well you may be sure Aunt Julia won't do it again.

HEDDA. In any case, I shall manage to make my peace with her.

TESMAN. Yes, my dear, good Hedda, if you only would.

HEDDA. When you call this afternoon, you might invite her to spend the evening here.

TESMAN. Yes, that I will. And there's one thing more you could do that would delight her heart.

HEDDA. What is it?

TESMAN. If you could only prevail on yourself to say *du* to her. For my sake, Hedda? Eh?

HEDDA. No, no, Tesman, you really mustn't ask that of me. I have told you so already. I shall try to call her "Aunt"; and you must be satisfied with that.

TESMAN. Well well. Only I think now that you belong to the family, you

HEDDA. H'm, I can't in the least see why [She goes up towards the middle doorway.

TESMAN. [After a pause.] Is there anything the matter with you, Hedda? Eh?

HEDDA. I'm only looking at my old piano. It doesn't go at all well with all the other things.

TESMAN. The first time I draw my salary, we'll see about exchanging it.

HEDDA. No, no, no exchanging. I don't want to part with it. Suppose we put it there in the inner room, and then get another here in its place. When it's convenient, I mean.

TESMAN. [A little taken aback.] Yes, of course we could do that.

HEDDA. [Takes up the bouquet from the piano.] These flowers were not here last night when we arrived.

TESMAN. Aunt Julia must have brought them for you.

HEDDA. [Examining the bouquet.] A visiting-card. [Takes it out and reads:] "Shall return later in the day." Can you guess whose card it is?

TESMAN. No. Whose? Eh?

HEDDA. The name is "Mrs. Elvsted."

TESMAN. Is it really? Sheriff Elvsted's wife? Miss Rysing that was.

HEDDA. Exactly. The girl with the irritating hair, that she was always showing off. An old flame of yours I've been told.

TESMAN. [Laughing.] Oh, that didn't last long; and it was before I met you, Hedda. But fancy her being in town!

HEDDA. It's odd that she should call upon us. I have scarcely seen her since we left school.

TESMAN. I haven't see her either for heaven knows how long. I wonder how she can endure to live in such an out-of-the way hole, eh?

HEDDA. [After a moment's thought, says suddenly.] Tell me, Tesman, isn't it somewhere near there that he, that, Eilert Lovborg is living?

TESMAN. Yes, he is somewhere in that part of the country.

BERTA enters by the hall door.

BERTA. That lady, ma'am, that brought some flowers a little while ago, is here again. [Pointing.] The flowers you have in your hand, ma'am.

HEDDA. Ah, is she? Well, please show her in.

BERTA opens the door for MRS. ELVSTED, and goes out herself. MRS. ELVSTED is a woman of fragile figure, with pretty, soft features. Her eyes are light blue, large, round, and somewhat prominent, with a startled, inquiring expression. Her hair is remarkably light, almost flaxen, and unusually abundant and wavy. She is a couple of years younger than HEDDA. She wears a dark visiting dress, tasteful, but not quite in the latest fashion.

HEDDA. [Receives her warmly.] How do you do, my dear Mrs. Elvsted? It's delightful to see you again.

MRS. ELVSTED. [Nervously, struggling for self-control.] Yes, it's a very long time since we met.

TESMAN. [Gives her his hand.] And we too, eh?

HEDDA. Thanks for your lovely flowers

MRS. ELVSTED. Oh, not at all. I would have come straight here yesterday afternoon; but I heard that you were away

TESMAN. Have you just come to town? Eh?

MRS. ELVSTED. I arrived yesterday, about midday. Oh, I was quite in despair when I heard that you were not at home.

HEDDA. In despair! How so?

TESMAN. Why, my dear Mrs. Rysing, I mean Mrs. Elvsted

HEDDA. I hope that you are not in any trouble?

MRS. ELVSTED. Yes, I am. And I don't know another living creature here that I can turn to.

HEDDA. [Laying the bouquet on the table.] Come, let us sit here on the sofa

MRS. ELVSTED. Oh, I am too restless to sit down.

HEDDA. Oh no, you're not. Come here. [She draws MRS. ELVSTED down upon the sofa and sits at her side.

TESMAN. Well? What is it, Mrs. Elvsted?

HEDDA. Has anything particular happened to you at home?

MRS. ELVSTED.

Yes and no. Oh, I am so anxious you should not misunderstand me

HEDDA. Then your best plan is to tell us the whole story, Mrs. Elvsted.

TESMAN. I suppose that's what you have come for, eh?

MRS. ELVSTED. Yes, yes, of course it is. Well then, I must tell you, if you don't already know that Eilert Lovborg is in town, too.

HEDDA. Lovborg!

TESMAN. What! Has Eilert Lovborg come back? Fancy that, Hedda!

HEDDA. Well well, I hear it.

MRS. ELVSTED. He has been here a week already. Just fancy, a whole week! In this terrible town, alone! With so many temptations on all sides.

HEDDA. But, my dear Mrs. Elvsted, how does he concern you so much?

MRS. ELVSTED. [Looks at her with a startled air, and says rapidly.] He was the children's tutor.

HEDDA. Your children's?

MRS. ELVSTED. My husband's. I have none.

HEDDA. Your step-children's, then?

MRS. ELVSTED. Yes.

TESMAN. [Somewhat hesitatingly.] Then was he, I don't know how to express it, was he, regular enough in his habits to be fit for the post? Eh?

MRS. ELVSTED. For the last two years his conduct has been irreproachable.

TESMAN. Has it indeed? Fancy that, Hedda!

HEDDA. I hear it.

MRS. ELVSTED. Perfectly irreproachable, I assure you! In every respect. But all the same, now that I know he is here, in this great town and with a large sum of money in his hands, I can't help being in mortal fear for him.

TESMAN. Why did he not remain where he was? With you and your husband? Eh?

MRS. ELVSTED. After his book was published he was too restless and unsettled to remain with us.

TESMAN. Yes, by-the-bye, Aunt Julia told me he had published a new book.

MRS. ELVSTED. Yes, a big book, dealing with the march of civilisation, in broad outline, as it were. It came out about a fortnight ago. And since it has sold so well, and been so much read and made such a sensation

TESMAN. Has it indeed? It must be something he has had lying by since his better days.

MRS. ELVSTED. Long ago, you mean?

TESMAN. Yes.

MRS. ELVSTED. No, he has written it all since he has been with us, within the last year.

TESMAN. Isn't that good news, Hedda? Think of that.

MRS. ELVSTED. Ah yes, if only it would last!

HEDDA. Have you seen him here in town?

MRS. ELVSTED. No, not yet. I have had the greatest difficulty in finding out his address. But this morning I discovered it at last.

HEDDA. [Looks searchingly at her.] Do you know, it seems to me a little odd of your husband, h'm

MRS. ELVSTED. [Starting nervously.] Of my husband! What?

HEDDA. That he should send you to town on such an errand that he does not come himself and look after his friend.

MRS. ELVSTED. Oh no, no, my husband has no time. And besides, I-I had some shopping to do.

HEDDA. [With a slight smile.] Ah, that is a different matter.

MRS. ELVSTED. [Rising quickly and uneasily.] And now I beg and implore you, Mr. Tesman, receive Eilert Lovborg kindly if he comes to you! And that he is sure to do. You see you were such great friends in the old days. And then you are interested in the same studies, the same branch of science, so far as I can understand.

TESMAN. We used to be at any rate.

MRS. ELVSTED. That is why I beg so earnestly that you, you too, will keep a sharp eye upon him. Oh, you will promise me that, Mr. Tesman, won't you?

TESMAN. With the greatest of pleasure, Mrs. Rysing

HEDDA. Elvsted.

TESMAN. I assure you I shall do all I possibly can for Eilert. You may rely upon me.

MRS. ELVSTED. Oh, how very, very kind of you! [Presses his hands.] Thanks, thanks, thanks! [Frightened.] You see, my husband is so very fond of him!

HEDDA. [Rising.] You ought to write to him, Tesman. Perhaps he may not care to come to you of his own accord.

TESMAN. Well, perhaps it would be the right thing to do, Hedda? Eh?

HEDDA. And the sooner the better. Why not at once?

MRS. ELVSTED. [Imploringly.] Oh, if you only would!

TESMAN. I'll write this moment. Have you his address, Mrs., Mrs. Elvsted.

MRS. ELVSTED. Yes. [Takes a slip of paper from her pocket, and hands it to him.] Here it is.

TESMAN. Good, good. Then I'll go in [Looks about him.] By-the-bye, my slippers? Oh, here. [Takes the packet and is about to go.

HEDDA. Be sure you write him a cordial, friendly letter. And a good long one too.

TESMAN. Yes, I will.

MRS. ELVSTED. But please, please don't say a word to show that I have suggested it.

TESMAN. No, how could you think I would? Eh? [He goes out to the right, through the inner room.

HEDDA. [Goes up to MRS. ELVSTED, smiles, and says in a low voice.] There! We have killed two birds with one stone.

MRS. ELVSTED. What do you mean?

HEDDA. Could you not see that I wanted him to go?

MRS. ELVSTED. Yes, to write the letter

HEDDA. And that I might speak to you alone.

MRS. ELVSTED. [Confused.] About the same thing?

HEDDA. Precisely.

MRS. ELVSTED. [Apprehensively.] But there is nothing more, Mrs. Tesman! Absolutely nothing!

HEDDA. Oh yes, but there is. There is a great deal more, I can see that. Sit here, and we'll have a cosy, confidential chat. [She forces MRS. ELVSTED to sit in the easy-chair beside the stove, and seats herself on one of the footstools.

MRS. ELVSTED. [Anxiously, looking at her watch.] But, my dear Mrs. Tesman, I was really on the point of going.

HEDDA. Oh, you can't be in such a hurry. Well? Now tell me something about your life at home.

MRS. ELVSTED. Oh, that is just what I care least to speak about.

HEDDA. But to me, dear? Why, weren't we schoolfellows?

MRS. ELVSTED. Yes, but you were in the class above me. Oh, how dreadfully afraid of you I was then!

HEDDA. Afraid of me?

MRS. ELVSTED. Yes, dreadfully. For when we met on the stairs you used always to pull my hair.

HEDDA. Did I, really?

MRS. ELVSTED. Yes, and once you said you would burn it off my head.

HEDDA. Oh that was all nonsense, of course.

MRS. ELVSTED. Yes, but I was so silly in those days. And since then, too, we have drifted so far, far apart from each other. Our circles have been so entirely different.

HEDDA. Well then, we must try to drift together again. Now listen. At school we said *du* to each other; and we called each other by our Christian names

MRS. ELVSTED. No, I am sure you must be mistaken.

HEDDA. No, not at all! I can remember quite distinctly. So now we are going to renew our old friendship. [Draws the footstool closer to MRS. ELVSTED.] There now! [Kisses her cheek.] You must say *du* to me and call me Hedda.

MRS. ELVSTED. [Presses and pats her hands.] Oh, how good and kind you are! I am not used to such kindness.

HEDDA. There, there, there! And I shall say *du* to you, as in the old days, and call you my dear Thora.

MRS. ELVSTED. My name is Thea.

HEDDA. Why, of course! I meant Thea. [Looks at her compassionately.] So you are not accustomed to goodness and kindness, Thea? Not in your own home?

MRS. ELVSTED. Oh, if I only had a home! But I haven't any; I have never had a home.

HEDDA. [Looks at her for a moment.] I almost suspected as much.

MRS. ELVSTED. [Gazing helplessly before her.] Yes, yes, yes.

HEDDA. I don't quite remember, was it not as housekeeper that you first went to Mr. Elvsted's?

MRS. ELVSTED. I really went as governess. But his wife, his late wife, was an invalid, and rarely left her room. So I had to look after the housekeeping as well.

HEDDA. And then, at last, you became mistress of the house.

MRS. ELVSTED. [Sadly.] Yes, I did.

HEDDA. Let me see, about how long ago was that?

MRS. ELVSTED. My marriage?

HEDDA. Yes.

MRS. ELVSTED. Five years ago.

HEDDA. To be sure; it must be that.

MRS. ELVSTED. Oh those five years! Or at all events the last two or three of them! Oh, if you could only imagine

HEDDA. [Giving her a little slap on the hand.] De? Fie, Thea!

MRS. ELVSTED. Yes, yes, I will try. Well, if, you could only imagine and understand

HEDDA. [Lightly.] Eilert Lovborg has been in your neighbourhood about three years, hasn't he?

MRS. ELVSTED. [Looks at here doubtfully.] Eilert Lovborg? Yes, he has.

HEDDA. Had you known him before, in town here?

MRS. ELVSTED. Scarcely at all. I mean, I knew him by name of course.

HEDDA. But you saw a good deal of him in the country?

MRS. ELVSTED. Yes, he came to us every day. You see, he gave the children lessons; for in the long run I couldn't manage it all myself.

HEDDA. No, that's clear. And your husband? I suppose he is often away from home?

MRS. ELVSTED. Yes. Being sheriff, you know, he has to travel about a good deal in his district.

HEDDA. [Leaning against the arm of the chair.] Thea, my poor, sweet Thea, now you must tell me everything, exactly as it stands.

MRS. ELVSTED. Well, then you must question me.

HEDDA. What sort of a man is your husband, Thea? I mean, you know, in everyday life. Is he kind to you?

MRS. ELVSTED. [Evasively.] I am sure he means well in everything.

HEDDA. I should think he must be altogether too old for you. There is at least twenty years' difference between you, is there not?

MRS. ELVSTED. [Irritably.] Yes, that is true, too. Everything about him is repellent to me! We have not a thought in common. We have no single point of sympathy, he and I.

HEDDA. But is he not fond of you all the same? In his own way?

MRS. ELVSTED. Oh I really don't know. I think he regards me simply as a useful property. And then it doesn't cost much to keep me. I am not expensive.

HEDDA. That is stupid of you.

MRS. ELVSTED. [Shakes her head.] It cannot be otherwise, not with him. I don't think he really cares for any one but himself and perhaps a little for the children.

HEDDA. And for Eilert Lovborg, Thea?

MRS. ELVSTED. [Looking at her.] For Eilert Lovborg? What puts that into your head?

HEDDA. Well, my dear, I should say, when he sends you after him all the way to town [Smiling almost imperceptibly.] And besides, you said so yourself, to Tesman.

MRS. ELVSTED. [With a little nervous twitch.] Did I? Yes, I suppose I did. [Vehemently, but not loudly.] No, I may just as well make a clean breast of it at once! For it must all come out in any case.

HEDDA. Why, my dear Thea?

MRS. ELVSTED. Well, to make a long story short: My husband did not know that I was coming.

HEDDA. What! Your husband didn't know it!

MRS. ELVSTED. No, of course not. For that matter, he was away from home himself, he was travelling. Oh, I could bear it no longer, Hedda! I couldn't indeed, so utterly alone as I should have been in future.

HEDDA. Well? And then?

MRS. ELVSTED. So I put together some of my things, what I needed most, as quietly as possible. And then I left the house.

HEDDA. Without a word?

MRS. ELVSTED. Yes and took the train to town.

HEDDA. Why, my dear, good Thea, to think of you daring to do it!

MRS. ELVSTED. [Rises and moves about the room.] What else could I possibly do?

HEDDA. But what do you think your husband will say when you go home again?

MRS. ELVSTED. [At the table, looks at her.] Back to him?

HEDDA. Of course.

MRS. ELVSTED. I shall never go back to him again.

HEDDA. [Rising and going towards her.] Then you have left your home, for good and all?

MRS. ELVSTED. Yes. There was nothing else to be done.

HEDDA. But then, to take flight so openly.

MRS. ELVSTED. Oh, it's impossible to keep things of that sort secret.

HEDDA. But what do you think people will say of you, Thea?

MRS. ELVSTED. They may say what they like, for aught *I* care. [Seats herself wearily and sadly on the sofa.] I have done nothing but what I had to do.

HEDDA. [After a short silence.] And what are your plans now? What do you think of doing.

MRS. ELVSTED. I don't know yet. I only know this, that I must live here, where Eilert Lovborg is, if I am to live at all.

HEDDA. [Takes a chair from the table, seats herself beside her, and strokes her hands.] My dear Thea, how did this, this friendship, between you and Eilert Lovborg come about?

MRS. ELVSTED. Oh it grew up gradually. I gained a sort of influence over him.

HEDDA. Indeed?

MRS. ELVSTED. He gave up his old habits. Not because I asked him to, for I never dared do that. But of course he saw how repulsive they were to me; and so he dropped them.

HEDDA. [Concealing an involuntary smile of scorn.] Then you have reclaimed him, as the saying goes, my little Thea.

MRS. ELVSTED. So he says himself, at any rate. And he, on his side, has made a real human being of me, taught me to think, and to understand so many things.

HEDDA. Did he give you lessons too, then?

MRS. ELVSTED. No, not exactly lessons. But he talked to me, talked about such an infinity of things. And then came the lovely, happy time when I began to share in his work, when he allowed me to help him!

HEDDA. Oh he did, did he?

MRS. ELVSTED. Yes! He never wrote anything without my assistance.

HEDDA. You were two good comrades, in fact?

MRS. ELVSTED. [Eagerly.] Comrades! Yes, fancy, Hedda, that is the very word he used! Oh, I ought to feel perfectly happy; and yet I cannot; for I don't know how long it will last.

HEDDA. Are you no surer of him than that?

MRS. ELVSTED. [Gloomily.] A woman's shadow stands between Eilert Lovborg and me.

HEDDA. [Looks at her anxiously.] Who can that be?

MRS. ELVSTED. I don't know. Some one he knew in his, in his past. Some one he has never been able wholly to forget.

HEDDA. What has he told you about this?

MRS. ELVSTED. He has only once, quite vaguely, alluded to it.

HEDDA. Well! And what did he say?

MRS. ELVSTED. He said that when they parted, she threatened to shoot him with a pistol.

HEDDA. [With cold composure.] Oh nonsense! No one does that sort of thing here.

MRS. ELVSTED. No. And that is why I think it must have been that red-haired singing-woman whom he once

HEDDA. Yes, very likely.

MRS. ELVSTED. For I remember they used to say of her that she carried loaded firearms.

HEDDA. Oh, then of course it must have been she.

MRS. ELVSTE. [Wringing her hands.] And now just fancy, Hedda, I hear that this singing-woman, that she is in town again! Oh, I don't know what to do

HEDDA. [Glancing towards the inner room.] Hush! Here comes Tesman. [Rises and whispers.] Thea, all this must remain between you and me.

MRS. ELVSTED. [Springing up.] Oh yes, yes! For heaven's sake!

GEORGE TESMAN, with a letter in his hand, comes from the right through the inner room.

TESMAN. There now, the epistle is finished.

HEDDA. That's right. And now Mrs. Elvsted is just going. Wait a moment, I'll go with you to the garden gate.

TESMAN. Do you think Berta could post the letter, Hedda dear?

HEDDA. [Takes it.] I will tell her to.

BERTA enters from the hall.

BERTA. Judge Brack wishes to know if Mrs. Tesman will receive him.

HEDDA. Yes, ask Judge Brack to come in. And look here, put this letter in the post.

BERTA. [Taking the letter.] Yes, ma'am. [She opens the door for JUDGE BRACK and goes out herself. Brack is a main of forty-five; thick set, but well-built and elastic in his movements. His face is roundish with an aristocratic profile. His hair is short, still almost black, and carefully dressed. His eyebrows thick. His moustaches are also thick, with short-cut ends. He wears a well-cut walking-suit, a little too youthful for his age. He uses an eye-glass, which he now and then lets drop.

JUDGE BRACK. [With his hat in his hand, bowing.] May one venture to call so early in the day?

HEDDA. Of course one may.

TESMAN. [Presses his hand.] You are welcome at any time. [Introducing him.] Judge Brack, Miss Rysing

HEDDA. Oh!

BRACK.

[Bowing.] Ah, delighted

HEDDA. [Looks at him and laughs.] It's nice to have a look at you by daylight, Judge!

BRACK. So you find me altered?

HEDDA. A little younger, I think.

BRACK. Thank you so much.

TESMAN. But what do you think of Hedda, eh? Doesn't she look flourishing? She has actually

HEDDA. Oh, do leave me alone. You haven't thanked Judge Brack for all the trouble he has taken

BRACK. Oh, nonsense, it was a pleasure to me

HEDDA. Yes, you are a friend indeed. But here stands Thea all impatience to be off, so *au revoir,* Judge. I shall be back again presently. [Mutual salutations. MRS. ELVSTED and HEDDA go out by the hall door.

BRACK. Well, is your wife tolerably satisfied

TESMAN. Yes, we can't thank you sufficiently. Of course she talks of a little re-arrangement here and there; and one or two things are still wanting. We shall have to buy some additional trifles.

BRACK. Indeed!

TESMAN. But we won't trouble you about these things. Hedda say she herself will look after what is wanting. Shan't we sit down? Eh?

BRACK. Thanks, for a moment. [Seats himself beside the table.] There is something I wanted to speak to about, my dear Tesman.

TESMAN. Indeed? Ah, I understand! [Seating himself.] I suppose it's the serious part of the frolic that is coming now. Eh?

BRACK. Oh, the money question is not so very pressing; though, for that matter, I wish we had gone a little more economically to work.

TESMAN. But that would never have done, you know! Think of Hedda, my dear fellow! You, who know her so well! I couldn't possibly ask her to put up with a shabby style of living!

BRACK. No, no, that is just the difficulty.

TESMAN. And then, fortunately, it can't be long before I receive my appointment.

BRACK. Well, you see, such things are often apt to hang fire for a long time.

TESMAN. Have you heard anything definite? Eh?

BRACK. Nothing exactly definite. [Interrupting himself.] But by-the-bye, I have one piece of news for you.

TESMAN. Well?

BRACK. Your old friend, Eilert Lovborg, has returned to town.

TESMAN. I know that already.

BRACK. Indeed! How did you learn it?

TESMAN. From that lady who went out with Hedda.

BRACK. Really? What was her name? I didn't quite catch it.

TESMAN. Mrs. Elvsted.

BRACK. Aha, Sheriff Elvsted's wife? Of course, he has been living up in their regions.

TESMAN. And fancy, I'm delighted to hear that he is quite a reformed character.

BRACK. So they say.

TESMAN. And then he has published a new book, eh?

BRACK. Yes, indeed he has.

TESMAN. And I hear it has made some sensation!

BRACK. Quite an unusual sensation.

TESMAN. Fancy, isn't that good news! A man of such extraordinary talents.I felt so grieved to think that he had gone irretrievably to ruin.

BRACK. That was what everybody thought.

TESMAN. But I cannot imagine what he will take to now! How in the world will he be able to make his living? Eh? [During the last words, HEDDA has entered by the hall door.

HEDDA. [To BRACK, laughing with a touch of scorn.] Tesman is for ever worrying about how people are to make their living.

TESMAN. Well you see, dear, we were talking about poor Eilert Lovborg.

HEDDA. [Glancing at him rapidly.] Oh, indeed? [Sets herself in the arm-chair beside the stove and asks indifferently:] What is the matter with him?

TESMAN. Well, no doubt he has run through all his property long ago; and he can scarcely write a new book every year, eh? So I really can't see what is to become of him.

BRACK. Perhaps I can give you some information on that point.

TESMAN. Indeed!

BRACK. You must remember that his relations have a good deal of influence.

TESMAN. Oh, his relations, unfortunately, have entirely washed their hands of him.

BRACK. At one time they called him the hope of the family.

TESMAN. At one time, yes! But he has put an end to all that.

HEDDA. Who knows? [With a slight smile.] I hear they have reclaimed him up at Sheriff Elvsted's

BRACK. And then this book that he has published

TESMAN. Well well, I hope to goodness they may find something for him to do. I have just written to him. I asked him to come and see us this evening, Hedda dear.

BRACK. But my dear fellow, you are booked for my bachelor's party this evening. You promised on the pier last night.

HEDDA. Had you forgotten, Tesman?

TESMAN. Yes, I had utterly forgotten.

BRACK. But it doesn't matter, for you may be sure he won't come.

TESMAN. What makes you think that? Eh?

BRACK. [With a little hesitation, rising and resting his hands on the back of his chair.] My dear Tesman and you too, Mrs. Tesman, I think I ought not to keep you in the dark about something that, that

TESMAN. That concerns Eilert?

BRACK. Both you and him.

TESMAN. Well, my dear Judge, out with it.

BRACK. You must be prepared to find your appointment deferred longer than you desired or expected.

TESMAN. [Jumping up uneasily.] Is there some hitch about it? Eh?

BRACK. The nomination may perhaps be made conditional on the result of a competition

TESMAN. Competition! Think of that, Hedda!

HEDDA. [Leans further back in the chair.] Aha, aha!

TESMAN. But who can my competitor be? Surely not?

BRACK. Yes, precisely, Eilert Lovborg.

TESMAN. [Clasping his hands.] No, no, it's quite impossible! Eh?

BRACK. H'm, that is what it may come to, all the same.

TESMAN. Well but, Judge Brack, it would show the most incredible lack of consideration for me. [Gesticulates with his arms.] For, just think, I'm a married man! We have married on the strength of these prospects, Hedda and I; and run deep into debt; and borrowed money from Aunt Julia too. Good heavens, they had as good as promised me the appointment. Eh?

BRACK. Well, well, well, no doubt you will get it in the end; only after a contest.

HEDDA. [Immovable in her arm-chair.] Fancy, Tesman, there will be a sort of sporting interest in that.

TESMAN. Why, my dearest Hedda, how can you be so indifferent about it?

HEDDA. [As before.] I am not at all indifferent. I am most eager to see who wins.

BRACK. In any case, Mrs. Tesman, it is best that you should know how matters stand. I mean before you set about the little purchases I hear you are threatening.

HEDDA. This can make no difference.

BRACK. Indeed! Then I have no more to say. Good-bye! [To TESMAN.] I shall look in on my way back from my afternoon walk, and take you home with me.

TESMAN. Oh yes, yes, your news has quite upset me.

HEDDA. [Reclining, holds out her hand.] Good-bye, Judge; and be sure you call in the afternoon.

BRACK. Many thanks. Good-bye, good-bye!

TESMAN. [Accompanying him to the door.] Good-bye my dear Judge! You must really excuse me [JUDGE BRACK goes out by the hall door.

TESMAN. [Crosses the room.] Oh Hedda, one should never rush into adventures. Eh?

HEDDA. [Looks at him, smiling.] Do you do that?

TESMAN. Yes, dear, there is no denying, it was adventurous to go and marry and set up house upon mere expectations.

HEDDA. Perhaps you are right there.

TESMAN. Well at all events, we have our delightful home, Hedda! Fancy, the home we both dreamed of the home we were in love with, I may almost say. Eh?

HEDDA. [Rising slowly and wearily.] It was part of our compact that we were to go into society to keep open house.

TESMAN. Yes, if you only knew how I had been looking forward to it! Fancy, to see you as hostess, in a select circle! Eh? Well, well, well for the present we shall have to get on without society, Hedda, only to invite Aunt Julia now and then. Oh, I intended you to lead such an utterly different life, dear!

HEDDA. Of course I cannot have my man in livery just yet.

TESMAN. Oh, no, unfortunately. It would be out of the question for us to keep a footman, you know.

HEDDA. And the saddle-horse I was to have had

TESMAN. [Aghast.] The saddle-horse!

HEDDA. I suppose I must not think of that now.

TESMAN. Good heavens, no! that's as clear as daylight!

HEDDA. [Goes up the room.] Well, I shall have one thing at least to kill time with in the meanwhile.

TESMAN. [Beaming.] Oh thank heaven for that! What is it, Hedda. Eh?

HEDDA. [In the middle doorway, looks at him with covert scorn.] My pistols, George.

TESMAN. [In alarm.] Your pistols!

HEDDA. [With cold eyes.] General Gabler's pistols. [She goes out through the inner room, to the left.

TESMAN. [Rushes up to the middle doorway and calls after her:] No, for heaven's sake, Hedda darling, don't touch those dangerous things! For my sake Hedda! Eh?

Act Second

The room at the TESMANS' as in the first Act, except that the piano has been removed, and an elegant little writing-table with the book-shelves put in its place. A smaller table stands near the sofa on the left. Most of the bouquets have been taken away. MRS. ELVSTED'S bouquet is upon the large table in front. It is afternoon.

HEDDA, dressed to receive callers, is alone in the room. She stands by the open glass door, loading a revolver. The fellow to it lies in an open pistol-case on the writing- table.

HEDDA. [Looks down the garden, and calls:] So you are here again, Judge!

BRACK. [Is heard calling from a distance.] As you see, Mrs. Tesman!

HEDDA. [Raises the pistol and points.] Now I'll shoot you, Judge Brack!

BRACK. [Calling unseen.] No, no, no! Don't stand aiming at me!

HEDDA. This is what comes of sneaking in by the back way. [She fires.]

BRACK. [Nearer.] Are you out of your senses!

HEDDA. Dear me, did I happen to hit you?

BRACK. [Still outside.] I wish you would let these pranks alone!

HEDDA. Come in then, Judge.

JUDGE BRACK, dressed as though for a men's party, enters by the glass door. He carries a light overcoat over his arm.

BRACK. What the deuce, haven't you tired of that sport, yet? What are you shooting at?

HEDDA. Oh, I am only firing in the air.

BRACK. [Gently takes the pistol out of her hand.] Allow me, madam! [Looks at it.] Ah, I know this pistol well! [Looks around.] Where is the case? Ah, here it is. [Lays the pistol in it, and shuts it.] Now we won't play at that game any more to-day.

HEDDA. Then what in heaven's name would you have me do with myself?

BRACK. Have you had no visitors?

HEDDA. [Closing the glass door.] Not one. I suppose all our set are still out of town.

BRACK. And is Tesman not at home either?

HEDDA. [At the writing-table, putting the pistol-case in a drawer which she shuts.] No. He rushed off to his aunt's directly after lunch; he didn't expect you so early.

BRACK. H'm, how stupid of me not to have thought of that!

HEDDA. [Turning her head to look at him.] Why stupid?

BRACK. Because if I had thought of it I should have come a little earlier.

HEDDA. [Crossing the room.] Then you would have found no one to receive you; for I have been in my room changing my dress ever since lunch.

BRACK. And is there no sort of little chink that we could hold a parley through?

HEDDA. You have forgotten to arrange one.

BRACK. That was another piece of stupidity.

HEDDA. Well, we must just settle down here and wait. Tesman is not likely to be back for some time yet.

BRACK. Never mind; I shall not be impatient.

HEDDA seats herself in the corner of the sofa. BRACK lays his overcoat over the back of the nearest chair, and sits down, but keeps his hat in his hand. A short silence. They look at each other.

HEDDA. Well?

BRACK. [In the same tone.] Well?

HEDDA. I spoke first.

BRACK. [Bending a little forward.] Come, let us have a cosy little chat, Mrs. Hedda.

HEDDA. [Leaning further back in the sofa.] Does it not seem like a whole eternity since our last talk? Of course I don't count those few words yesterday evening and this morning.

BRACK. You mean since out last confidential talk? Our last *tete-a-tete*?

HEDDA. Well yes, since you put it so.

BRACK. Not a day passed but I have wished that you were home again.

HEDDA. And I have done nothing but wish the same thing.

BRACK. You? Really, Mrs. Hedda? And I thought you had been enjoying your tour so much!

HEDDA. Oh yes, you may be sure of that!

BRACK. But Tesman's letters spoke of nothing but happiness.

HEDDA. Oh, Tesman! You see, he thinks nothing is so delightful as grubbing in libraries and making copies of old parchments, or whatever you call them.

BRACK. [With a smile of malice.] Well, that is his vocation in life or part of it at any rate.

HEDDA. Yes, of course; and no doubt when it's your vocation. But *I*! Oh, my dear Mr. Brack, how mortally bored I have been.

BRACK. [Sympathetically.] Do you really say so? In downright earnest?

HEDDA. Yes, you can surely understand it! To go for six whole months without meeting a soul that knew anything of our circle, or could talk about things we were interested in.

BRACK. Yes, yes, I too should feel that a deprivation.

HEDDA. And then, what I found most intolerable of all

BRACK. Well?

HEDDA. was being everlastingly in the company of one and the same person

BRACK. [With a nod of assent.] Morning, noon, and night, yes, at all possible times and seasons.

HEDDA. I said "everlastingly."

BRACK. Just so. But I should have thought, with our excellent Tesman, one could

HEDDA. Tesman is a specialist, my dear Judge.

BRACK. Undeniable.

HEDDA. And specialists are not at all amusing to travel with. Not in the long run at any rate.

BRACK. Not even the specialist one happens to love?

HEDDA. Faugh, don't use that sickening word!

BRACK. [Taken aback.] What do you say, Mrs. Hedda?

HEDDA. [Half laughing, half irritated.] You should just try it! To hear of nothing but the history of civilisation, morning, noon, and night

BRACK. Everlastingly.

HEDDA. Yes yes yes! And then all this about the domestic industry of the middle ages! That's the most disgusting part of it!

BRACK. [Looks searchingly at her.] But tell me, in that case, how am I to understand your? H'm

HEDDA. My accepting George Tesman, you mean?

BRACK. Well, let us put it so.

HEDDA. Good heavens, do you see anything so wonderful in that?

BRACK. Yes and no, Mrs. Hedda.

HEDDA. I had positively danced myself tired, my dear Judge. My day was done [With a slight shudder.] Oh no, I won't say that; nor think it either!

BRACK. You have assuredly no reason to.

HEDDA. Oh, reasons [Watching him closely.] And George Tesman, after all, you must admit that he is correctness itself.

BRACK. His correctness and respectability are beyond all question.

HEDDA. And I don't see anything absolutely ridiculous about him. Do you?

BRACK. Ridiculous? N-no, I shouldn't exactly say so

HEDDA. Well, and his powers of research, at all events, are untiring. I see no reason why he should not one day come to the front, after all.

BRACK. [Looks at her hesitatingly.] I thought that you, like every one else, expected him to attain the highest distinction.

HEDDA. [With an expression of fatigue.] Yes, so I did. And then, since he was bent, at all hazards, on being allowed to provide for me. I really don't know why I should not have accepted his offer?

BRACK. No, if you look at it in that light

HEDDA. It was more than my other adorers were prepared to do for me, my dear Judge.

BRACK. [Laughing.] Well, I can't answer for all the rest; but as for myself, you know quite well that I have always entertained a, a certain respect for the marriage tie, for marriage as an institution, Mrs. Hedda.

HEDDA. [Jestingly.] Oh, I assure you I have never cherished any hopes with respect to you.

BRACK. All I require is a pleasant and intimate interior, where I can make myself useful in every way, and am free to come and go as, as a trusted friend

HEDDA. Of the master of the house, do you mean?

BRACK. [Bowing.] Frankly of the mistress first of all; but of course of the master too, in the second place. Such a triangular friendship, if I may call it so, is really a great convenience for all the parties, let me tell you.

HEDDA. Yes, I have many a time longed for some one to make a third on our travels. Oh, those railway-carriage *tete-a-tetes*!

BRACK. Fortunately your wedding journey is over now.

HEDDA. [Shaking her head.] Not by a long, long way. I have only arrived at a station on the line.

BRACK. Well, then the passengers jump out and move about a little, Mrs. Hedda.

HEDDA. I never jump out.

BRACK. Really?

HEDDA. No, because there is always some one standing by to

BRACK. [Laughing.] To look at your ankles, do you mean?

HEDDA. Precisely.

BRACK. Well but, dear me

HEDDA. [With a gesture of repulsion.] I won't have it. I would rather keep my seat where I happen to be, and continue the *tete-a-tete*.

BRACK. But suppose a third person were to jump in and join the couple.

HEDDA. Ah, that is quite another matter!

BRACK. A trusted, sympathetic friend

HEDDA. - with a fund of conversation on all sorts of lively topics

BRACK. - and not the least bit of a specialist!

HEDDA. [With an audible sigh.] Yes, that would be a relief indeed.

BRACK. [Hears the front door open, and glances in that direction.] The triangle is completed.

HEDDA. [Half aloud.] And on goes the train.

GEORGE TESMAN, in a grey walking-suit, with a soft felt hat, enters from the hall. He has a number of unbound books under his arm and in his pockets.

TESMAN. [Goes up to the table beside the corner settee.] Ouf, what a load for a warm day, all these books. [Lays them on the table.] I'm positively perspiring, Hedda. Hallo, are you there already, my dear Judge? Eh? Berta didn't tell me.

BRACK. [Rising.] I came in through the garden.

HEDDA. What books have you got there?

TESMAN. [Stands looking them through.] Some new books on my special subjects, quite indispensable to me.

HEDDA. Your special subjects?

BRACK. Yes, books on his special subjects, Mrs. Tesman. [BRACK and HEDDA exchange a confidential smile.

HEDDA. Do you need still more books on your special subjects?

TESMAN. Yes, my dear Hedda, one can never have too many of them. Of course one must keep up with all that is written and published.

HEDDA. Yes, I suppose one must.

TESMAN. [Searching among his books.] And look here, I have got hold of Eilert Lovborg's new book too. [Offering it to her.] Perhaps you would like to glance through it, Hedda? Eh?

HEDDA. No, thank you. Or rather, afterwards perhaps.

TESMAN. I looked into it a little on the way home.

BRACK. Well, what do you think of it, as a specialist?

TESMAN. I think it shows quite remarkable soundness of judgment. He never wrote like that before. [Putting the books together.] Now I shall take all these into my study. I'm longing to cut the leaves! And then I must change my clothes. [To BRACK.] I suppose we needn't start just yet? Eh?

BRACK. Oh, dear no, there is not the slightest hurry.

TESMAN. Well then, I will take my time. [Is going with his books, but stops in the doorway and turns.] By-the-bye, Hedda. Aunt Julia is not coming this evening.

HEDDA. Not coming? Is it that affair of the bonnet that keeps her away?

TESMAN. Oh, not at all. How could you think such a thing of Aunt Julia? Just fancy! The fact is, Aunt Rina is very ill.

HEDDA. She always is.

TESMAN. Yes, but to-day she is much worse than usual, poor dear.

HEDDA. Oh, then it's only natural that her sister should remain with her. I must bear my disappointment.

TESMAN. And you can't imagine, dear, how delighted Aunt Julia seemed to be, because you had come home looking so flourishing!

HEDDA. [Half aloud, rising.] Oh, those everlasting Aunts!

TESMAN. What?

HEDDA. [Going to the glass door.] Nothing.

TESMAN. Oh, all right. [He goes through the inner room, out to the right.

BRACK. What bonnet were you talking about?

HEDDA. Oh, it was a little episode with Miss Tesman this morning. She had laid down her bonnet on the chair there [Looks at him and smiles.] and I pretended to think it was the servant's.

BRACK. [Shaking his head.] Now my dear Mrs. Hedda, how could you do such a thing? To the excellent old lady, too!

HEDDA. [Nervously crossing the room.] Well, you see, these impulses come over me all of a sudden; and I cannot resist them. [Throws herself down in the easy-chair by the stove.] Oh, I don't know how to explain it.

BRACK. [Behind the easy-chair.] You are not really happy, that is at the bottom of it.

HEDDA. [Looking straight before her.] I know of no reason why I should be happy. Perhaps you can give me one?

BRACK. Well-amongst other things, because you have got exactly the home you had set your heart on.

HEDDA. [Looks up at him and laughs.] Do you too believe in that legend?

BRACK. Is there nothing in it, then?

HEDDA. Oh yes, there is something in it.

BRACK. Well?

HEDDA. There is this in it, that I made use of Tesman to see me home from evening parties last summer

BRACK. I, unfortunately, had to go quite a different way.

HEDDA. That's true. I know you were going a different way last summer.

BRACK. [Laughing.] Oh fie, Mrs. Hedda! Well, then, you and Tesman?

HEDDA. Well, we happened to pass here one evening; Tesman, poor fellow, was writhing in the agony of having to find conversation; so I took pity on the learned man

BRACK. [Smiles doubtfully.] You took pity? H'm

HEDDA. Yes, I really did. And so to help him out of his torment I happened to say, in pure thoughtlessness, that I should like to live in this villa.

BRACK. No more than that?

HEDDA. Not that evening.

BRACK. But afterwards?

HEDDA. Yes, my thoughtlessness had consequences, my dear Judge.

BRACK. Unfortunately that too often happens, Mrs. Hedda.

HEDDA. Thanks! So you see it was this enthusiasm for Secretary Falk's villa that first constituted a bond of sympathy between George Tesman and me. From that came our engagement and our marriage, and our wedding journey, and all the rest of it. Well, well, my dear Judge as you make your bed so you must lie, I could almost say.

BRACK. This is exquisite! And you really cared not a rap about it all the time?

HEDDA. No, heaven knows I didn't.

BRACK. But now? Now that we have made it so homelike for you?

HEDDA. Uh, the rooms all seem to smell of lavender and dried rose-leaves. But perhaps it's Aunt Julia that has brought that scent with her.

BRACK. [Laughing.] No, I think it must be a legacy from the late Mrs. Secretary Falk.

HEDDA. Yes, there is an odour of mortality about it. It reminds me of a bouquet the day after the ball. [Clasps her hands behind her head, leans back in her chair and looks at him.] Oh, my dear Judge, you cannot imagine how horribly I shall bore myself here.

BRACK. Why should not you, too, find some sort of vocation in life, Mrs. Hedda?

HEDDA. A vocation, that should attract me?

BRACK. If possible, of course.

HEDDA. Heaven knows what sort of a vocation that could be. I often wonder whether [Breaking off.] But that would never do either.

BRACK. Who can tell? Let me hear what it is.

HEDDA. Whether I might not get Tesman to go into politics, I mean.

BRACK. [Laughing.] Tesman? No really now, political life is not the thing for him, not at all in his line.

HEDDA. No, I daresay not. But if I could get him into it all the same?

BRACK. Why, what satisfaction could you find in that? If he is not fitted for that sort of thing, why should you want to drive him into it?

HEDDA. Because I am bored, I tell you! [After a pause.] So you think it quite out of the question that Tesman should ever get into the ministry?

BRACK. H'm, you see, my dear Mrs. Hedda to get into the ministry, he would have to be a tolerably rich man.

HEDDA. [Rising impatiently.] Yes, there we have it! It is this genteel poverty I have managed to drop into! [Crosses the room.] That is what makes life so pitiable! So utterly ludicrous! For that's what it is.

BRACK. Now *I* should say the fault lay elsewhere.

HEDDA. Where, then?

BRACK. You have never gone through any really stimulating experience.

HEDDA. Anything serious, you mean?

BRACK. Yes, you may call it so. But now you may perhaps have one in store.

HEDDA. [Tossing her head.] Oh, you're thinking of the annoyances about this wretched professorship! But that must be Tesman's own affair. I assure you I shall not waste a thought upon it.

BRACK. No, no, I daresay not. But suppose now that what people call, in elegant language, a solemn responsibility were to come upon you? [Smiling.] A new responsibility, Mrs. Hedda?

HEDDA. [Angrily.] Be quiet! Nothing of that sort will ever happen!

BRACK. [Warily.] We will speak of this again a year hence, at the very outside.

HEDDA. [Curtly.] I have no turn for anything of the sort, Judge Brack. No responsibilities for me!

BRACK. Are you so unlike the generality of women as to have no turn for duties which -?

HEDDA. [Beside the glass door.] Oh, be quiet, I tell you! I often think there is only one thing in the world I have any turn for.

BRACK. [Drawing near to her.] And what is that, if I may ask?

HEDDA. [Stands looking out.] Boring myself to death. Now you know it. [Turns, looks towards the inner room, and laughs.] Yes, as I thought! Here comes the Professor.

BRACK. [Softly, in a tone of warning.] Come, come, come, Mrs. Hedda!

GEORGE TESMAN, dressed for the party, with his gloves and hat in his hand, enters from the right through the inner room.

TESMAN. Hedda, has no message come from Eilert Lovborg? Eh?

HEDDA. No.

TESMAN. Then you'll see he'll be here presently.

BRACK. Do you really think he will come?

TESMAN. Yes, I am almost sure of it. For what you were telling us this morning must have been a mere floating rumour.

BRACK. You think so?

TESMAN. At any rate, Aunt Julia said she did not believe for a moment that he would ever stand in my way again. Fancy that!

BRACK. Well then, that's all right.

TESMAN. [Placing his hat and gloves on a chair on the right.] Yes, but you must really let me wait for him as long as possible.

BRACK. We have plenty of time yet. None of my guests will arrive before seven or half-past.

TESMAN. Then meanwhile we can keep Hedda company, and see what happens. Eh?

HEDDA. [Placing BRACK'S hat and overcoat upon the corner settee.] And at the worst Mr. Lovborg can remain here with me.

BRACK. [Offering to take his things.] Oh, allow me, Mrs. Tesman! What do you mean by "At the worst"?

HEDDA. If he won't go with you and Tesman.

TESMAN. [Looks dubiously at her.] But, Hedda dear, do you think it would quite do for him to remain here with you? Eh? Remember, Aunt Julia can't come.

HEDDA. No, but Mrs. Elvsted is coming. We three can have a cup of tea together.

TESMAN. Oh yes, that will be all right.

BRACK. [Smiling.] And that would perhaps be the safest plan for him.

HEDDA. Why so?

BRACK. Well, you know, Mrs. Tesman, how you used to gird at my little bachelor parties. You declared they were adapted only for men of the strictest principles.

HEDDA. But no doubt Mr. Lovborg's principles are strict enough now. A converted sinner [BERTA appears at the hall door.

BERTA. There's a gentleman asking if you are at home, ma'am

HEDDA. Well, show him in.

TESMAN. [Softly.] I'm sure it is he! Fancy that!

EILERT LOVBORG enters from the hall. He is slim and lean; of the same age as TESMAN, but looks older and somewhat worn-out. His hair and beard are of a blackish brown, his face long and pale, but with patches of colour on the cheeks. He is dressed in a well-cut black visiting suit, quite new. He has dark gloves and a silk hat. He stops near the door, and makes a rapid bow, seeming somewhat embarrassed.

TESMAN. [Goes up to him and shakes him warmly by the hand.] Well, my dear Eilert, so at last we meet again!

EILERT LOVBORG. [Speaks in a subdued voice.] Thanks for your letter, Tesman. [Approaching HEDDA.] Will you too shake hands with me, Mrs. Tesman?

HEDDA. [Taking his hand.] I am glad to see you, Mr. Lovborg. [With a motion of her hand.] I don't know whether you two gentlemen?

LOVBORG. [Bowing slightly.] Judge Brack, I think.

BRACK. [Doing likewise.] Oh yes, in the old days

TESMAN. [To LOVBORG, with his hands on his shoulders.] And now you must make yourself entirely at home, Eilert! Mustn't he, Hedda? For I hear you are going to settle in town again? Eh?

LOVBORG. Yes, I am.

TESMAN. Quite right, quite right. Let me tell you, I have got hold of your new book; but I haven't had time to read it yet.

LOVBORG. You may spare yourself the trouble.

TESMAN. Why so?

LOVBORG. Because there is very little in it.

TESMAN. Just fancy, how can you say so?

BRACK. But it has been very much praised, I hear.

LOVBORG. That was what I wanted; so I put nothing into the book but what every one would agree with.

BRACK. Very wise of you.

TESMAN. Well but, my dear Eilert!

LOVBORG. For now I mean to win myself a position again to make a fresh start.

TESMAN. [A little embarrassed.] Ah, that is what you wish to do? Eh?

LOVBORG. [Smiling, lays down his hat, and draws a packet wrapped in paper, from his coat pocket.] But when this one appears, George Tesman, you will have to read it. For this is the real book, the book I have put my true self into.

TESMAN. Indeed? And what is it?

LOVBORG. It is the continuation.

TESMAN. The continuation? Of what?

LOVBORG. Of the book.

TESMAN. Of the new book?

LOVBORG. Of course.

TESMAN. Why, my dear Eilert, does it not come down to our own days?

LOVBORG. Yes, it does; and this one deals with the future.

TESMAN. With the future! But, good heavens, we know nothing of the future!

LOVBORG. No; but there is a thing or two to be said about it all the same. [Opens the packet.] Look here

TESMAN. Why, that's not your handwriting.

LOVBORG. I dictated it. [Turning over the pages.] It falls into two sections. The first deals with the civilising forces of the future. And here is the second [running through the pages towards the end] forecasting the probable line of development.

TESMAN. How odd now! I should never have thought of writing anything of that sort.

HEDDA. [At the glass door, drumming on the pane.] H'm. I daresay not.

LOVBORG. [Replacing the manuscript in its paper and laying the packet on the table.] I brought it, thinking I might read you a little of it this evening.

TESMAN. That was very good of you, Eilert. But this evening? [Looking back at BRACK.] I don't see how we can manage it

LOVBORG. Well then, some other time. There is no hurry.

BRACK. I must tell you, Mr. Lovborg, there is a little gathering at my house this evening, mainly in honour of Tesman, you know

LOVBORG. [Looking for his hat.] Oh, then I won't detain you

BRACK. No, but listen, will you not do me the favour of joining us?

LOVBORG. [Curtly and decidedly.] No, I can't, thank you very much.

BRACK. Oh, nonsense, do! We shall be quite a select little circle. And I assure you we shall have a "lively time," as Mrs. Hed-, as Mrs. Tesman says.

LOVBORG. I have no doubt of it. But nevertheless

BRACK. And then you might bring your manuscript with you, and read it to Tesman at my house. I could give you a room to yourselves.

TESMAN. Yes, think of that, Eilert,why shouldn't you? Eh?

HEDDA. [Interposing.] But, Tesman, if Mr. Lovborg would really rather not! I am sure Mr. Lovborg is much more inclined to remain here and have supper with me.

LOVBORG. [Looking at her.] With you, Mrs. Tesman?

HEDDA. And with Mrs. Elvsted.

LOVBORG. Ah [Lightly.] I saw her for a moment this morning.

HEDDA. Did you? Well, she is coming this evening. So you see you are almost bound to remain, Mr. Lovborg, or she will have no one to see her home.

LOVBORG. That's true. Many thanks, Mrs. Tesman, in that case I will remain.

HEDDA. Then I have one or two orders to give the servant [She goes to the hall door and rings. BERTA enters. HEDDA talks to her in a whisper, and points towards the inner room. BERTA nods and goes out again.

TESMAN. [At the same time, to LOVBORG.] Tell me, Eilert, is it this new subject, the future, that you are going to lecture about?

LOVBORG. Yes.

TESMAN. They told me at the bookseller's that you are going to deliver a course of lectures this autumn.

LOVBORG. That is my intention. I hope you won't take it ill, Tesman.

TESMAN. Oh no, not in the least! But?

LOVBORG. I can quite understand that it must be very disagreeable to you.

TESMAN. [Cast down.] Oh, I can't expect you, out of consideration for me, to

LOVBORG. But I shall wait till you have received your appointment.

TESMAN. Will you wait? Yes but, yes, but are you not going to compete with me? Eh?

LOVBORG. No; it is only the moral victory I care for.

TESMAN. Why, bless me, then Aunt Julia was right after all! Oh yes, I knew it! Hedda! Just fancy, Eilert Lovborg is not going to stand in our way!

HEDDA. [Curtly.] Our way? Pray leave me out of the question. [She goes up towards the inner room, where BERTA is placing a tray with decanters and glasses on the table. HEDDA nods approval, and comes forward again. BERTA goes out.

TESMAN. [At the same time.] And you, Judge Brack, what do you say to this? Eh?

BRACK. Well, I say that a moral victory, h'm, may be all very fine

TESMAN. Yes, certainly. But all the same

HEDDA. [Looking at TESMAN with a cold smile.] You stand there looking as if you were thunderstruck

TESMAN. Yes, so I am, I almost think

BRACK. Don't you see, Mrs. Tesman, a thunderstorm has just passed over?

HEDDA. [Pointing towards the room.] Will you not take a glass of cold punch, gentlemen?

BRACK. [Looking at his watch.] A stirrup-cup? Yes, it wouldn't come amiss.

TESMAN. A capital idea, Hedda! Just the thing! Now that the weight has been taken off my mind

HEDDA. Will you not join them, Mr. Lovborg?

LOVBORG. [With a gesture of refusal.] No, thank you. Nothing for me.

BRACK. Why bless me, cold punch is surely not poison.

LOVBORG. Perhaps not for everyone.

HEDDA. I will keep Mr. Lovborg company in the meantime.

TESMAN. Yes, yes, Hedda dear, do. [He and BRACK go into the inner room, seat themselves, drink punch, smoke cigarettes, and carry on a lively conversation during what follows. EILERT LOVBORG remains standing beside the stove. HEDDA goes to the writing-table.

HEDDA. [Raising he voice a little.] Do you care to look at some photographs, Mr. Lovborg? You know Tesman and I made a tour in they Tyrol on our way home? [She takes up an album, and places it on the table beside the sofa, in the further corner of which she seats herself. EILERT LOVBORG approaches, stops, and looks at her. Then he takes a chair and seats himself to her left.

HEDDA. [Opening the album.] Do you see this range of mountains, Mr. Lovborg? It's the Ortler group. Tesman has written the name underneath. Here it is: "The Ortler group near Meran."

LOVBORG. [Who has never taken his eyes off her, says softly and slowly:] Hedda Gabler!

HEDDA. [Glancing hastily at him.] Ah! Hush!

LOVBORG. [Repeats softly.] Hedda Gabler!

HEDDA. [Looking at the album.] That was my name in the old days, when we two knew each other.

LOVBORG. And I must teach myself never to say Hedda Gabler again, never, as long as I live.

HEDDA. [Still turning over the pages.] Yes, you must. And I think you ought to practise in time. The sooner the better, I should say.

LOVBORG. [In a tone of indignation.] Hedda Gabler married? And married to George Tesman!

HEDDA. Yes, so the world goes.

LOVBORG. Oh, Hedda, Hedda, how could you throw yourself away!

HEDDA. [Looks sharply at him.] What? I can't allow this!

LOVBORG. What do you mean? [TESMAN comes into the room and goes towards the sofa.

HEDDA. [Hears him coming and says in an indifferent tone.] And this is a view from the Val d'Ampezzo, Mr. Lovborg. Just look at these peaks! [Looks affectionately up at TESMAN.] What's the name of these curious peaks, dear?

TESMAN. Let me see. Oh, those are the Dolomites.

HEDDA. Yes, that's it! Those are the Dolomites, Mr. Lovborg.

TESMAN. Hedda, dear, I only wanted to ask whether I shouldn't bring you a little punch after all? For yourself at any rate, eh?

HEDDA. Yes, do, please; and perhaps a few biscuits.

TESMAN. No cigarettes?

HEDDA. No.

TESMAN. Very well. [He goes into the inner room and out to the right. BRACK sits in the inner room, and keeps an eye from time to time on HEDDA and LOVBORG.

LOVBORG. [Softly, as before.] Answer me, Hedda, how could you go and do this?

HEDDA. [Apparently absorbed in the album.] If you continue to say *du* to me I won't talk to you.

LOVBORG. May I not say *du* even when we are alone?

HEDDA. No. You may think it; but you mustn't say it.

LOVBORG. Ah, I understand. It is an offence against George Tesman, whom you love.

HEDDA. [Glances at him and smiles.] Love? What an idea!

LOVBORG. You don't love him then!

HEDDA. But I won't hear of any sort of unfaithfulness! Remember that.

LOVBORG. Hedda, answer me one thing

HEDDA. Hush! [TESMAN enters with a small tray from the inner room.

TESMAN. Here you are! Isn't this tempting? [He puts the tray on the table.

HEDDA. Why do you bring it yourself?

TESMAN. [Filling the glasses.] Because I think it's such fun to wait upon you, Hedda.

HEDDA. But you have poured out two glasses. Mr. Lovborg said he wouldn't have any

TESMAN. No, but Mrs. Elvsted will soon be here, won't she?

HEDDA. Yes, by-the-bye Mrs. Elvsted

TESMAN. Had you forgotten her? Eh?

HEDDA. We were so absorbed in these photographs. [Shows him a picture.] Do you remember this little village?

TESMAN. Oh, it's that one just below the Brenner Pass. It was there we passed the night

HEDDA. - and met that lively party of tourists.

TESMAN. Yes, that was the place. Fancy, if we could only have had you with us, Eilert! Eh? [He returns to the inner room and sits beside BRACK.

LOVBORG. Answer me one thing, Hedda

HEDDA. Well?

LOVBORG. Was there no love in your friendship for me either? Not a spark not a tinge of love in it?

HEDDA. I wonder if there was? To me it seems as though we were two good comrades, two thoroughly intimate friends. [Smilingly.] You especially were frankness itself.

LOVBORG. It was you that made me so.

HEDDA. As I look back upon it all, I think there was really something beautiful, something fascinating, something daring, in, in that secret intimacy that comradeship which no living creature so much as dreamed of.

LOVBORG. Yes, yes, Hedda! Was there not? When I used to come to your father's in the afternoon and the General sat over at the window reading his papers with his back towards us

HEDDA. And we two on the corner sofa

LOVBORG. Always with the same illustrated paper before us

HEDDA. For want of an album, yes.

LOVBORG. Yes, Hedda, and when I made my confessions to you, told you about myself, things that at that time no one else knew! There I would sit and tell you of my escapades, my days and nights of devilment. Oh, Hedda, what was the power in you that forced me to confess these things?

HEDDA. Do you think it was any power in me?

LOVBORG. How else can I explain it? And all those, those roundabout questions you used to put to me

HEDDA. Which you understood so particularly well

LOVBORG. How could you sit and question me like that? Question me quite frankly

HEDDA. In roundabout terms, please observe.

LOVBORG. Yes, but frankly nevertheless. Cross-question me about, all that sort of thing?

HEDDA. And how could you answer, Mr. Lovborg?

LOVBORG. Yes, that is just what I can't understand in looking back upon it. But tell me now, Hedda, was there not love at the bottom of our friendship? On your side, did you not feel as though you might purge my stains away if I made you my confessor? Was it not so?

HEDDA. No, not quite.

LOVBORG. What was you motive, then?

HEDDA. Do think it quite incomprehensible that a young girl when it can be done, without any one knowing

LOVBORG. Well?

HEDDA. - should be glad to have a peep, now and then, into a world which?

LOVBORG. Which?

HEDDA. - which she is forbidden to know anything about?

LOVBORG. So that was it?

HEDDA. Partly. Partly, I almost think.

LOVBORG. Comradeship in the thirst for life. But why should not that, at any rate, have continued?

HEDDA. The fault was yours.

LOVBORG. It was you that broke with me.

HEDDA. Yes, when our friendship threatened to develop into something more serious. Shame upon you, Eilert Lovborg! How could you think of wronging your, your frank comrade.

LOVBORG. [Clenches his hands.] Oh, why did you not carry out your threat? Why did you not shoot me down?

HEDDA. Because I have such a dread of scandal.

LOVBORG. Yes, Hedda, you are a coward at heart.

HEDDA. A terrible coward. [Changing her tone.] But it was a lucky thing for you. And now you have found ample consolation at the Elvsteds'.

LOVBORG. I know what Thea has confided to you.

HEDDA. And perhaps you have confided to her something about us?

LOVBORG. Not a word. She is too stupid to understand anything of that sort.

HEDDA. Stupid?

LOVBORG. She is stupid about matters of that sort.

HEDDA. And I am cowardly. [Bends over towards him, without looking him in the face, and says more softly:] But now I will confide something to you.

LOVBORG. [Eagerly.] Well?

HEDDA. The fact that I dared not shoot you down

LOVBORG. Yes!

HEDDA. - that was not my arrant cowardice that evening.

LOVBORG. [Looks at her a moment, understands, and whispers passionately.] Oh, Hedda! Hedda Gabler! Now I begin to see a hidden reason beneath our comradeship! You and I! After all, then, it was your craving for life

HEDDA. [Softly, with a sharp glance.] Take care! Believe nothing of the sort! [Twilight has begun to fall. The hall door is opened from without by BERTA.

HEDDA. [Closes the album with a bang and calls smilingly:] Ah, at last! My darling Thea, come along!

MRS. ELVSTED enters from the hall. She is in evening dress. The door is closed behind her.

HEDDA. [On the sofa, stretches out her arms towards her.] My sweet Thea, you can't think how I have been longing for you! [MRS. ELVSTED, in passing, exchanges slight salutations with the gentlemen in the inner room, then goes up to the table and gives HEDDA her hand. EILERT LOVBORG has risen. He and MRS. ELVSTED greet each other with a silent nod.

MRS. ELVSTED. Ought I to go in and talk to your husband for a moment?

HEDDA. Oh, not at all. Leave those two alone. They will soon be going.

MRS. ELVSTED. Are they going out?

HEDDA. Yes, to a supper-party.

MRS. ELVSTED. [Quickly, to LOVBORG.] Not you?

LOVBORG. No.

HEDDA. Mr. Lovborg remains with us.

MRS. ELVSTED. [Takes a chair and is about to seat herself at his side.] Oh, how nice it is here!

HEDDA. No, thank you, my little Thea! Not there! You'll be good enough to come over here to me. I will sit between you.

MRS. ELVSTED.

Yes, just as you please. [She goes round the table and seats herself on the sofa on HEDDA'S right. LOVBORG re-seats himself on his chair.

LOVBORG. [After a short pause, to HEDDA.] Is not she lovely to look at?

HEDDA. [Lightly stroking her hair.] Only to look at!

LOVBORG. Yes. For we two, she and I, we are two real comrades. We have absolute faith in each other; so we can sit and talk with perfect frankness

HEDDA. Not round about, Mr. Lovborg?

LOVBORG. Well

MRS. ELVSTED. [Softly clinging close to HEDDA.] Oh, how happy I am, Hedda! For only think, he says I have inspired him too.

HEDDA. [Looks at her with a smile.] Ah! Does he say that, dear?

LOVBORG. And then she is so brave, Mrs. Tesman!

MRS. ELVSTED. Good heavens, am I brave?

LOVBORG. Exceedingly, where your comrade is concerned.

HEDDA. Exceedingly, where your comrade is concerned.

HEDDA. Ah, yes, courage! If one only had that!

LOVBORG. What then? What do you mean?

HEDDA. Then life would perhaps be liveable, after all. [With a sudden change of tone.] But now, my dearest Thea, you really must have a glass of cold punch.

MRS. ELVSTED. No, thanks, I never take anything of that kind.

HEDDA. Well then, you, Mr. Lovborg.

LOVBORG. Nor I, thank you.

MRS. ELVSTED. No, he doesn't either.

HEDDA. [Looks fixedly at him.] But if I say you shall?

LOVBORG. It would be of no use.

HEDDA. [Laughing.] Then I, poor creature, have no sort of power over you?

LOVBORG. Not in that respect.

HEDDA. But seriously, I think you ought to, for your own sake.

MRS. ELVSTED. Why, Hedda!

LOVBORG. How so?

HEDDA. Or rather on account of other people.

LOVBORG. Indeed?

HEDDA. Otherwise people might be apt to suspect that, in your heart of hearts, you did not feel quite secure, quite confident in yourself.

MRS. ELVSTED. [Softly.] Oh please, Hedda!

LOVBORG. People may suspect what they like for the present.

MRS. ELVSTED. [Joyfully.] Yes, let them!

HEDDA. I saw it plainly in Judge Brack's face a moment ago.

LOVBORG. What did you see?

HEDDA. His contemptuous smile, when you dared not go with them into the inner room.

LOVBORG. Dared not? Of course I preferred to stop here and talk to you.

MRS. ELVSTED. What could be more natural, Hedda?

HEDDA. But the Judge could not guess that. And I say, too, the way he smiled and glanced at Tesman when you dared not accept his invitation to this wretched little supper-party of his.

LOVBORG. Dared not! Do you say I dared not?

HEDDA. *I* don't say so. But that was how Judge Brack understood it.

LOVBORG. Well, let him.

HEDDA. Then you are not going with them?

LOVBORG. I will stay here with you and Thea.

MRS. ELVSTED. Yes, Hedda, how can you doubt that?

HEDDA. [Smiles and nods approvingly to LOVBORG.] Firm as a rock! Faithful to your principles, now and for ever! Ah, that is how a man should be! [Turns to MRS. ELVSTED and caresses her.] Well now, what did I tell you, when you came to us this morning in such a state of distraction

LOVBORG. [Surprised.] Distraction!

MRS. ELVSTED. [Terrified.] Hedda, oh Hedda!

HEDDA. You can see for yourself! You haven't the slightest reason to be in such mortal terror [Interrupting herself.] There! Now we can all three enjoy ourselves!

LOVBORG. [Who has given a start.] Ah, what is all this, Mrs. Tesman?

MRS. ELVSTED. Oh my God, Hedda! What are you saying? What are you doing?

HEDDA. Don't get excited! That horrid Judge Brack is sitting watching you.

LOVBORG. So she was in mortal terror! On my account!

MRS. ELVSTED. [Softly and piteously.] Oh, Hedda, now you have ruined everything!

LOVBORG. [Looks fixedly at her for a moment. His face is distorted.] So that was my comrade's frank confidence in me?

MRS. ELVSTED. [Imploringly.] Oh, my dearest friend, only let me tell you

LOVBORG. [Takes one of the glasses of punch, raises it to his lips, and says in a low, husky voice.] Your health, Thea! [He empties the glass, puts it down, and takes the second.

MRS. ELVSTED. [Softly.] Oh, Hedda, Hedda, how could you do this?

HEDDA. *I* do it? *I*? Are you crazy?

LOVBORG. Here's to your health too, Mrs. Tesman. Thanks for the truth. Hurrah for the truth! [He empties the glass and is about to re-fill it.

HEDDA. [Lays her hand on his arm.] Come, come, no more for the present. Remember you are going out to supper.

MRS. ELVSTED. No, no, no!

HEDDA. Hush! They are sitting watching you.

LOVBORG. [Putting down the glass.] Now, Thea, tell me the truth

MRS. ELVSTED. Yes.

LOVBORG. Did your husband know that you had come after me?

MRS. ELVSTED. [Wringing her hands.] Oh, Hedda, do you hear what his is asking?

LOVBORG. Was it arranged between you and him that you were to come to town and look after me? Perhaps it was the Sheriff himself that urged you to come? Aha, my dear, no doubt he wanted my help in his office! Or was it at the card-table that he missed me?

MRS. ELVSTED. [Softly, in agony.] Oh, Lovborg, Lovborg!

LOVBORG. [Seizes a glass and is on the point of filling it.] Here's a glass for the old Sheriff too!

HEDDA. [Preventing him.] No more just now. Remember, you have to read your manuscript to Tesman.

LOVBORG. [Calmly, putting down the glass.] It was stupid of me all this. Thea, to take it in this way, I mean. Don't be angry with me, my dear, dear comrade. You shall see, both you and the others, that if I was fallen once, now I have risen again! Thanks to you, Thea.

MRS. ELVSTED. [Radiant with joy.] Oh, heaven be praised! [BRACK has in the meantime looked at his watch. He and TESMAN rise and come into the drawing-room.

BRACK. [Takes his hat and overcoat.] Well, Mrs. Tesman, our time has come.

HEDDA. I suppose it has.

LOVBORG. [Rising.] Mine too, Judge Brack.

MRS. ELVSTED. [Softly and imploringly.] Oh, Lovborg, don't do it!

HEDDA. [Pinching her arm.] They can hear you!

MRS. ELVSTED. [With a suppressed shriek.] Ow!

LOVBORG. [To BRACK.] You were good enough to invite me.

JUDGE BRACK. Well, are you coming after all?

LOVBORG. Yes, many thanks.

BRACK. I'm delighted

LOVBORG. [To TESMAN, putting the parcel of MS. in his pocket.] I should like to show you one or two things before I send it to the printers.

TESMAN. Fancy, that will be delightful. But, Hedda dear, how is Mrs. Elvsted to get home? Eh?

HEDDA. Oh, that can be managed somehow.

LOVBORG. [Looking towards the ladies.] Mrs. Elvsted? Of course, I'll come again and fetch her. [Approaching.] At ten or thereabouts, Mrs. Tesman? Will that do?

HEDDA. Certainly. That will do capitally.

TESMAN. Well, then, that's all right. But you must not expect me so early, Hedda.

HEDDA. Oh, you may stop as long, as long as every you please.

MRS. ELVSTED. [Trying to conceal her anxiety.] Well then, Mr. Lovborg I shall remain here until you come.

LOVBORG. [With his hat in his hand.] Pray do, Mrs. Elvsted.

BRACK. And now off goes the excursion train, gentlemen! I hope we shall have a lively time, as a certain fair lady puts it.

HEDDA. Ah, if only the fair lady could be present unseen!

BRACK. Why unseen?

HEDDA. In order to hear a little of your liveliness at first hand, Judge Brack.

BRACK. [Laughing.] I should not advise the fair lady to try it.

TESMAN. [Also laughing.] Come, you're a nice one Hedda! Fancy that!

BRACK. Well, good-bye, good-bye, ladies.

LOVBORG. [Bowing.] About ten o'clock, then, [BRACK, LOVBORG, and TESMAN go out by the hall door. At the same time, BERTA enters from the inner room with a lighted lamp, which she places on the drawing-room table; she goes out by the way she came.

MRS. ELVSTED. [Who has risen and is wandering restlessly about the room.] Hedda, Hedda, what will come of all this?

HEDDA. At ten o'clock, he will be here. I can see him already with vine-leaves in his hair, flushed and fearless

MRS. ELVSTED. Oh, I hope he may.

HEDDA. And then, you see, then he will have regained control over himself. Then he will be a free man for all his days.

MRS. ELVSTED. Oh God! if he would only come as you see him now!

HEDDA. He will come as I see him so, and not otherwise! [Rises and approaches THEA.] You may doubt him as long as you please; *I* believe in him. And now we will try

MRS. ELVSTED. You have some hidden motive in this, Hedda!

HEDDA. Yes, I have. I want for once in my life to have power to mould a human destiny.

MRS. ELVSTED. Have you not the power?

HEDDA. I have not and have never had it.

MRS. ELVSTED. Not your husband's?

HEDDA. Do you think that is worth the trouble? Oh, if you could only understand how poor I am. And fate has made you so rich! [Clasps her passionately in her arms.] I think I must burn your hair off after all.

MRS. ELVSTED. Let me go! Let me go! I am afraid of you, Hedda!

BERTA. [In the middle doorway.] Tea is laid in the dining-room, ma'am.

HEDDA. Very well. We are coming

MRS. ELVSTED. No, no, no! I would rather go home alone! At once!

HEDDA. Nonsense! First you shall have a cup of tea, you little stupid. And then at ten o'clock Eilert Lovborg will be here with vine-leaves in his hair. [She drags MRS. ELVSTED almost by force to the middle doorway.]

Act Third

The room at the TESMANS'. The curtains are drawn over the middle doorway, and also over the glass door. The lamp, half turned down, and with a shade over it, is burning on the table. In the stove, the door of which stands open, there has been a fire, which is now nearly burnt out.

MRS. ELVSTED, wrapped in a large shawl, and with her feet upon a foot-rest, sits close to the stove, sunk back in the arm-chair. HEDDA, fully dressed, lies sleeping upon the sofa, with a sofa-blanket over her.

MRS. ELVSTED. [After a pause, suddenly sits up in her chair, and listens eagerly. Then she sinks back again wearily, moaning to herself.] Not yet! Oh God, oh God, not yet!

BERTA slips cautiously in by the hall door. She has a letter in her hand.

MRS. ELVSTED. [Turns and whispers eagerly.] Well, has any one come?

BERTA. [Softly.] Yes, a girl has just brought this letter.

MRS. ELVSTED. [Quickly, holding out her hand.] A letter! Give it to me!

BERTA. No, it's for Dr. Tesman, ma'am.

MRS. ELVSTED. Oh, indeed.

BERTA. It was Miss Tesman's servant that brought it. I'll lay it here on the table.

MRS. ELVSTED. Yes, do.

BERTA. [Laying down the letter.] I think I had better put out the lamp. It's smoking.

MRS. ELVSTED. Yes, put it out. It must soon be daylight now.

BERTA. [Putting out the lamp.] It is daylight already, ma'am.

MRS. ELVSTED. Yes, broad day! And no one come back yet!

BERTA. Lord bless you, ma'am I guessed how it would be.

MRS. ELVSTED. You guessed?

BERTA. Yes, when I saw that a certain person had come back to town and that he went off with them. For we've heard enough about that gentleman before now.

MRS. ELVSTED. Don't speak so loud. You will waken Mrs. Tesman.

BERTA. [Looks towards the sofa and sighs.] No, no, let her sleep, poor thing. Shan't I put some wood on the fire?

MRS. ELVSTED. Thanks, not for me.

BERTA. Oh, very well. [She goes softly out by the hall door.

HEDDA. [Is wakened by the shutting of the door, and looks up.] What's that?

MRS. ELVSTED. It was only the servant.

HEDDA. [Looking about her.] Oh, we're here! Yes, now I remember. [Sits erect upon the sofa, stretches herself, and rubs her eyes.] What o'clock is it, Thea?

MRS. ELVSTED. [Looks at her watch.] It's past seven.

HEDDA. When did Tesman come home?

MRS. ELVSTED. He has not come.

HEDDA. Not come home yet?

MRS. ELVSTED. [Rising.] No one has come.

HEDDA. Think of our watching and waiting here till four in the morning

MRS. ELVSTED. [Wringing her hands.] And how I watched and waited for him!

HEDDA. [Yawns, and says with her hand before her mouth.] Well, well, we might have spared ourselves the trouble.

MRS. ELVSTED. Did you get a little sleep?

HEDDA. Oh yes; I believe I have slept pretty well. Have you not?

MRS. ELVSTED. Not for a moment. I couldn't, Hedda! not to save my life.

HEDDA. [Rises and goes towards her.] There there there! There's nothing to be so alarmed about. I understand quite well what has happened.

MRS. ELVSTED. Well, what do you think? Won't you tell me?

HEDDA. Why, of course it has been a very late affair at Judge Brack's

MRS. ELVSTED. Yes, yes, that is clear enough. But all the same

HEDDA. And then, you see, Tesman hasn't cared to come home and ring us up in the middle of the night. [Laughing.] Perhaps he wasn't inclined to show himself either, immediately after a jollification.

MRS. ELVSTED. But in that case, where can he have gone?

HEDDA. Of course he has gone to his Aunts' and slept there. They have his old room ready for him.

MRS. ELVSTED. No, he can't be with them for a letter has just come for him from Miss Tesman. There it lies.

HEDDA. Indeed? [Looks at the address.] Why yes, it's addressed in Aunt Julia's hand. Well then, he has remained at Judge Brack's. And as for Eilert Lovborg, he is sitting, with vine leaves in his hair, reading his manuscript.

MRS. ELVSTED. Oh, Hedda, you are just saying things you don't believe a bit.

HEDDA. You really are a little blockhead, Thea.

MRS. ELVSTED. Oh yes, I suppose I am.

HEDDA. And how mortally tired you look.

MRS. ELVSTED. Yes, I am mortally tired.

HEDDA. Well then, you must do as I tell you. You must go into my room and lie down for a little while.

MRS. ELVSTED. Oh no, no, I shouldn't be able to sleep.

HEDDA. I am sure you would.

MRS. ELVSTED. Well, but you husband is certain to come soon now; and then I want to know at once

HEDDA. I shall take care to let you know when he comes.

MRS. ELVSTED. Do you promise me, Hedda?

HEDDA. Yes, rely upon me. Just you go in and have a sleep in the meantime.

MRS. ELVSTED. Thanks; then I'll try. [She goes off to the inner room. [HEDDA goes up to the glass door and draws back the curtains. The broad daylight streams into the room. Then she takes a little hand-glass from the writing-table, looks at herself in it, and arranges her hair. Next she goes to the hall door and presses the bell-button.

BERTA presently appears at the hall door.

BERTA. Did you want anything, ma'am?

HEDDA. Yes; you must put some more wood in the stove. I am shivering.

BERTA. Bless me, I'll make up the fire at once. [She rakes the embers together and lays a piece of wood upon them; then stops and listens.] That was a ring at the front door, ma'am.

HEDDA. Then go to the door. I will look after the fire.

BERTA. It'll soon burn up. [She goes out by the hall door. [HEDDA kneels on the foot-rest and lays some more pieces of wood in the stove.

After a short pause, GEORGE TESMAN enters from the hall. He steals on tiptoe towards the middle doorway and is about to slip through the curtains.

HEDDA. [At the stove, without looking up.] Good morning.

TESMAN. [Turns.] Hedda! [Approaching her.] Good heavens, are you up so early? Eh?

HEDDA. Yes, I am up very early this morning.

TESMAN. And I never doubted you were still sound asleep! Fancy that, Hedda!

HEDDA. Don't speak so loud. Mrs. Elvsted is resting in my room.

TESMAN. Has Mrs. Elvsted been here all night?

HEDDA. Yes, since no one came to fetch her.

TESMAN. Ah, to be sure.

HEDDA. [Closes the door of the stove and rises.] Well, did you enjoy yourselves at Judge Brack's?

TESMAN. Have you been anxious about me? Eh?

HEDDA. No, I should never think of being anxious. But I asked if you had enjoyed yourself.

TESMAN. Oh yes, for once in a way. Especially the beginning of the evening; for then Eilert read me part of his book. We arrived more than an hour too early, fancy that! And Brack had all sorts of arrangements to make so Eilert read to me.

HEDDA. [Seating herself by the table on the right.] Well? Tell me then

TESMAN. [Sitting on a footstool near the stove.] Oh, Hedda, you can't conceive what a book that is going to be! I believe it is one of the most remarkable things that have ever been written. Fancy that!

HEDDA. Yes yes; I don't care about that

TESMAN. I must make a confession to you, Hedda. When he had finished reading a horrid feeling came over me.

HEDDA. A horrid feeling?

TESMAN. I felt jealous of Eilert for having had it in him to write such a book. Only think, Hedda!

HEDDA. Yes, yes, I am thinking!

TESMAN. And then how pitiful to think that he, with all his gifts, should be irreclaimable, after all.

HEDDA. I suppose you mean that he has more courage than the rest?

TESMAN. No, not at all, mean that he is incapable of taking his pleasure in moderation.

HEDDA. And what came of it all in the end?

TESMAN. Well, to tell the truth, I think it might best be described as an orgie, Hedda.

HEDDA. Had he vine-leaves in his hair?

TESMAN. Vine-leaves? No, I saw nothing of the sort. But he made a long, rambling speech in honour of the woman who had inspired him in his work, that was the phrase he used.

HEDDA. Did he name her?

TESMAN. No, he didn't; but I can't help thinking he meant Mrs. Elvsted. You may be sure he did.

HEDDA. Well, where did you part from him?

TESMAN. On the way to town. We broke up, the last of us at any rate, all together; and Brack came with us to get a breath of fresh air. And then, you see, we agreed to take Eilert home; for he had had far more than was good for him.

HEDDA. I daresay.

TESMAN. But now comes the strange part of it, Hedda; or, I should rather say, the melancholy part of it. I declare I am almost ashamed on Eilert's account to tell you

HEDDA. Oh, go on!

TESMAN. Well, as we were getting near town, you see, I happened to drop a little behind the others. Only for a minute or two, fancy that!

HEDDA. Yes yes yes, but?

TESMAN. And then, as I hurried after them, what do you think I found by the wayside? Eh?

HEDDA. Oh, how should I know!

TESMAN. You mustn't speak of it to a soul, Hedda! Do you hear! Promise me, for Eilert's sake. [Draws a parcel, wrapped in paper, from his coat pocket.] Fancy, dear, I found this.

HEDDA. Is not that the parcel he had with him yesterday?

TESMAN. Yes, it is the whole of his precious, irreplaceable manuscript! And he had gone and lost it, and knew nothing about it. Only fancy, Hedda! So deplorably

HEDDA. But why did you not give him back the parcel at once?

TESMAN. I didn't dare to in the state he was then in

HEDDA. Did you not tell any of the others that you had found it?

TESMAN. Oh, far from it! You can surely understand that, for Eilert's sake, I wouldn't do that.

HEDDA. So no one knows that Eilert Lovborg's manuscript is in your possession?

TESMAN. No. And no one must know it.

HEDDA. Then what did you say to him afterwards?

TESMAN. I didn't talk to him again at all; for when we got in among the streets, he and two or three of the others gave us the slip and disappeared. Fancy that!

HEDDA. Indeed! They must have taken him home then.

TESMAN. Yes, so it would appear. And Brack, too, left us.

HEDDA. And what have you been doing with yourself since?

TESMAN. Well, I and some of the others went home with one of the party, a jolly fellow, and took our morning coffee with him; or perhaps I should rather call it our night coffee, eh? But now, when I have rested a little, and given Eilert, poor fellow, time to have his sleep out, I must take this back to him.

HEDDA. [Holds out her hand for the packet.] No, don't give it to him! Not in such a hurry, I mean. Let me read it first.

TESMAN. No, my dearest Hedda, I mustn't, I really mustn't.

HEDDA. You must not?

TESMAN. No, for you can imagine what a state of despair he will be in when he wakens and misses the manuscript. He has no copy of it, you must know! He told me so.

HEDDA. [Looking searchingly at him.] Can such a thing not be reproduced? Written over again?

TESMAN. No, I don't think that would be possible. For the inspiration, you see

HEDDA. Yes, yes, I suppose it depends on that [Lightly.] But, by-the-bye, here is a letter for you.

TESMAN. Fancy!

HEDDA. [Handing it to him.] It came early this morning.

TESMAN. It's from Aunt Julia! What can it be? [He lays the packet on the other footstool, opens the letter, runs his eye through it, and jumps up.] Oh, Hedda, she says that poor Aunt Rina is dying!

HEDDA. Well, we were prepared for that.

TESMAN. And that if I want to see her again, I must make haste. I'll run in to them at once.

HEDDA. [Suppressing a smile.] Will you run?

TESMAN. Oh, my dearest Hedda, if you could only make up your mind to come with me! Just think!

HEDDA. [Rises and says wearily, repelling the idea.] No, no don't ask me. I will not look upon sickness and death. I loathe all sorts of ugliness.

TESMAN. Well, well, then! [Bustling around.] My hat? My overcoat? Oh, in the hall. I do hope I mayn't come too late, Hedda! Eh?

HEDDA. Oh, if you run [BERTA appears at the hall door.

BERTA. Judge Brack is at the door, and wishes to know if he may come in.

TESMAN. At this time! No, I can't possibly see him.

HEDDA. But I can. [To BERTA.] Ask Judge Brack to come in. [BERTA goes out.

HEDDA. [Quickly, whispering.] The parcel, Tesman! [She snatches it up from the stool.

TESMAN. Yes, give it to me!

HEDDA. No, no, I will keep it till you come back. [She goes to the writing-table and places it in the bookcase. TESMAN stands in a flurry of haste, and cannot get his gloves on.

JUDGE BRACK enters from the hall.

HEDDA. [Nodding to him.] You are an early bird, I must say.

BRACK. Yes, don't you think so! [To TESMAN.] Are you on the move, too?

TESMAN. Yes, I must rush of to my aunts'. Fancy, the invalid one is lying at death's door, poor creature.

BRACK. Dear me, is she indeed? Then on no account let me detain you. At such a critical moment

TESMAN. Yes, I must really rush Good-bye! Good-bye! [He hastens out by the hall door.

HEDDA. [Approaching.] You seem to have made a particularly lively night of it at your rooms, Judge Brack.

BRACK. I assure you I have not had my clothes off, Mrs. Hedda.

HEDDA. Not you, either?

BRACK. No, as you may see. But what has Tesman been telling you of the night's adventures?

HEDDA. Oh, some tiresome story. Only that they went and had coffee somewhere or other.

BRACK. I have heard about that coffee-party already. Eilert Lovborg was not with them, I fancy?

HEDDA. No, they had taken him home before that.

BRACK. Tesman too?

HEDDA. No, but some of the others, he said.

BRACK. [Smiling.] George Tesman is really an ingenuous creature, Mrs. Hedda.

HEDDA. Yes, heaven knows he is. Then is there something behind all this?

BRACK. Yes, perhaps there may be.

HEDDA. Well then, sit down, my dear Judge, and tell your story in comfort. [She seats herself to the left of the table. BRACK sits near her, at the long side of the table.

HEDDA. Now then?

BRACK. I had special reasons for keeping track of my guests last night.

HEDDA. Of Eilert Lovborg among the rest, perhaps?

BRACK. Frankly, yes.

HEDDA. Now you make me really curious

BRACK. Do you know where he and one or two of the others finished the night, Mrs. Hedda?

HEDDA. If it is not quite unmentionable, tell me.

BRACK. Oh no, it's not at all unmentionable. Well, they put in an appearance at a particularly animated soiree.

HEDDA. Of the lively kind?

BRACK. Of the very liveliest

HEDDA. Tell me more of this, Judge Brack

BRACK. Lovborg, as well as the others, had been invited in advance. I knew all about it. But he had declined the invitation; for now, as you know, he has become a new man.

HEDDA. Up at the Elvsteds', yes. But he went after all, then?

BRACK. Well, you see, Mrs. Hedda, unhappily the spirit moved him at my rooms last evening

HEDDA. Yes, I hear he found inspiration.

BRACK. Pretty violent inspiration. Well, I fancy that altered his purpose; for we menfolk are unfortunately not always so firm in our principles as we ought to be.

HEDDA. Oh, I am sure you are an exception, Judge Brack. But as to Lovborg?

BRACK. To make a long story short, he landed at last in Mademoiselle Diana's rooms.

HEDDA. Mademoiselle Diana's?

BRACK. It was Mademoiselle Diana that was giving the soiree, to a select circle of her admirers and her lady friends.

HEDDA. Is she a red-haired woman?

BRACK. Precisely.

HEDDA. A sort of a - singer?

BRACK. Oh yes, in her leisure moments. And moreover a mighty huntress, of men, Mrs. Hedda. You have no doubt heard of her. Eilert Lovborg was one of her most enthusiastic protectors in the days of his glory.

HEDDA. And how did all this end?

BRACK. Far from amicably, it appears. After a most tender meeting, they seem to have come to blows

HEDDA. Lovborg and she?

BRACK. Yes. He accused her or her friends of having robbed him. He declared that his pocket-book had disappeared and other things as well. In short, he seems to have made a furious disturbance.

HEDDA. And what came of it all?

BRACK. It came to a general scrimmage, in which the ladies as well as the gentlemen took part. Fortunately the police at last appeared on the scene.

HEDDA. The police too?

BRACK. Yes. I fancy it will prove a costly frolic for Eilert Lovborg, crazy being that he is.

HEDDA. How so?

BRACK. He seems to have made a violent resistance, to have hit one of the constables on the head and torn the coat off his back. So they had to march him off to the police-station with the rest.

HEDDA. How have you learnt all this?

BRACK. From the police themselves.

HEDDA. [Gazing straight before her.] So that is what happened. Then he had no vine-leaves in his hair.

BRACK. Vine-leaves, Mrs. Hedda?

HEDDA. [Changing her tone.] But tell me now, Judge, what is your real reason for tracking out Eilert Lovborg's movements so carefully?

BRACK. In the first place, it could not be entirely indifferent to me if it should appear in the police-court that he came straight from my house.

HEDDA. Will the matter come into court then?

BRACK. Of course. However, I should scarcely have troubled so much about that. But I thought that, as a friend of the family, it was my duty to supply you and Tesman with a full account of his nocturnal exploits.

HEDDA. Why so, Judge Brack?

BRACK. Why, because I have a shrewd suspicion that he intends to use you as a sort of blind.

HEDDA. Oh, how can you think such a thing!

BRACK. Good heavens, Mrs. Hedda, we have eyes in our head. Mark my words! This Mrs. Elvsted will be in no hurry to leave town again.

HEDDA. Well, even if there should be anything between them, I suppose there are plenty of other places where they could meet.

BRACK. Not a single home. Henceforth, as before, every respectable house will be closed against Eilert Lovborg.

HEDDA. And so ought mine to be, you mean?

BRACK. Yes. I confess it would be more than painful to me if this personage were to be made free of your house. How superfluous, how intrusive, he would be, if he were to force his way into

HEDDA. - into the triangle?

BRACK. Precisely. It would simply mean that I should find myself homeless.

HEDDA. [Looks at him with a smile.] So you want to be the one cock in the basket that is your aim.

BRACK. [Nods slowly and lowers his voice.] Yes, that is my aim. And for that I will fight with every weapon I can command.

HEDDA. [Her smile vanishing.] I see you are a dangerous person when it comes to the point.

BRACK. Do you think so?

HEDDA. I am beginning to think so. And I am exceedingly glad to think that you have no sort of hold over me.

BRACK. [Laughing equivocally.] Well well, Mrs. Hedda, perhaps you are right there. If I had, who knows what I might be capable of?

HEDDA. Come come now, Judge Brack! That sounds almost like a threat.

BRACK. [Rising.] Oh, not at all! The triangle, you know, ought, if possible, to be spontaneously constructed.

HEDDA. There I agree with you.

BRACK. Well, now I have said all I had to say; and I had better be getting back to town. Good-bye, Mrs. Hedda. [He goes towards the glass door.

HEDDA. [Rising.] Are you going through the garden?

BRACK. Yes, it's a short cut for me.

HEDDA. And then it is a back way, too.

BRACK. Quite so. I have no objection to back ways. They may be piquant enough at times.

HEDDA. When there is ball practice going on, you mean?

BRACK. [In the doorway, laughing to her.] Oh, people don't shoot their tame poultry, I fancy.

HEDDA. [Also laughing.] Oh no, when there is only one cock in the basket [They exchange laughing nods of farewell. He goes. She closes the door behind him. [HEDDA, who has become quite serious, stands for a moment looking out. Presently she goes and peeps through the curtain over the middle doorway. Then she goes to the writing-table, takes LOVBORG'S packet out of the bookcase, and is on the point of looking through its contents. BERTA is heard speaking loudly in the hall. HEDDA turns and listens. Then she hastily locks up the packet in the drawer, and lays the key on the inkstand.

EILERT LOVBORG, with his greatcoat on and his hat in his hand, tears open the hall door. He looks somewhat confused and irritated.

LOVBORG. [Looking towards the hall.] and I tell you I must and will come in! There! [He closes the door, turns, sees HEDDA, at once regains his self- control, and bows.

HEDDA. [At the writing-table.] Well, Mr Lovborg, this is rather a late hour to call for Thea.

LOVBORG. You mean rather an early hour to call on you. Pray pardon me.

HEDDA. How do you know that she is still here?

LOVBORG. They told me at her lodgings that she had been out all night.

HEDDA. [Going to the oval table.] Did you notice anything about the people of the house when they said that?

LOVBORG. [Looks inquiringly at her.] Notice anything about them?

HEDDA. I mean, did they seem to think it odd?

LOVBORG. [Suddenly understanding.] Oh yes, of course! I am dragging her down with me! However, I didn't notice anything. I suppose Tesman is not up yet.

HEDDA. No, I think not

LOVBORG. When did he come home?

HEDDA. Very late.

LOVBORG. Did he tell you anything?

HEDDA. Yes, I gathered that you had had an exceedingly jolly evening at Judge Brack's.

LOVBORG. Nothing more?

HEDDA. I don't think so. However, I was so dreadfully sleepy

MRS. ELVSTED enters through the curtains of the middle doorway.

MRS. ELVSTED. [Going towards him.] Ah, Lovborg! At last!

LOVBORG. Yes, at last. And too late!

MRS. ELVSTED. [Looks anxiously at him.] What is too late?

LOVBORG. Everything is too late now. It is all over with me.

MRS. ELVSTED. Oh no, no, don't say that!

LOVBORG. You will say the same when you hear

MRS. ELVSTED. I won't hear anything!

HEDDA. Perhaps you would prefer to talk to her alone? If so, I will leave you.

LOVBORG. No, stay, you too. I beg you to stay.

MRS. ELVSTED. Yes, but I won't hear anything, I tell you.

LOVBORG. It is not last night's adventures that I want to talk about.

MRS. ELVSTED. What is it then?

LOVBORG. I want to say that now our ways must part.

MRS. ELVSTED. Part!

HEDDA. [Involuntarily.] I knew it!

LOVBORG. You can be of no more service to me, Thea.

MRS. ELVSTED. How can you stand there and say that! No more service to you! Am I not to help you now, as before? Are we not to go on working together?

LOVBORG. Henceforward I shall do no work.

MRS. ELVSTED. [Despairingly.] Then what am I to do with my life?

LOVBORG. You must try to live your life as if you had never know me.

MRS. ELVSTED. But you know I cannot do that!

LOVBORG. Try if you cannot, Thea. You must go home again

MRS. ELVSTED. [In vehement protest.] Never in this world! Where you are, there will I be also! I will not let myself be driven away like this! I will remain here! I will be with you when the book appears.

HEDDA. [Half aloud, in suspense.] Ah yes, the book!

LOVBORG. [Looks at her.] My book and Thea's; for that is what it is.

MRS. ELVSTED. Yes, I feel that it is. And that is why I have a right to be with you when it appears! I will see with my own eyes how respect and honour pour in upon you afresh. And the happiness, the happiness, oh, I must share it with you!

LOVBORG. Thea, our book will never appear.

HEDDA. Ah!

MRS. ELVSTED. Never appear!

LOVBORG. Can never appear.

MRS. ELVSTED. [In agonised foreboding.] Lovborg, what have you done with the manuscript?

HEDDA. [Looks anxiously at him.] Yes, the manuscript?

MRS. ELVSTED. Where is it?

LOVBORG. The manuscript. Well then, I have torn the manuscript into a thousand pieces.

MRS. ELVSTED. [Shrieks.] Oh no, no!

HEDDA. [Involuntarily.] But that's not

LOVBORG. [Looks at her.] Not true, you think?

HEDDA. [Collecting herself.] Oh well, of course, since you say so. But it sounded so improbable

LOVBORG. It is true, all the same.

MRS. ELVSTED. [Wringing her hands.] Oh God, oh God, Hedda, torn his own work to pieces!

LOVBORG. I have torn my own life to pieces. So why should I not tear my life- work too?

MRS. ELVSTED. And you did this last night?

LOVBORG. Yes, I tell you! Tore it into a thousand pieces and scattered them on the fiord far out. There there is cool sea-water at any rate, let them drift upon it, drift with the current and the wind. And then presently they will sink deeper and deeper, as I shall, Thea.

MRS. ELVSTED. Do you know, Lovborg, that what you have done with the book, I shall think of it to my dying day as though you had killed a little child.

LOVBORG. Yes, you are right. It is a sort of child-murder.

MRS. ELVSTED. How could you, then! Did not the child belong to me too?

HEDDA. [Almost inaudibly.] Ah, the child

MRS. ELVSTED. [Breathing heavily.] It is all over then. Well well, now I will go, Hedda.

HEDDA. But you are not going away from town?

MRS. ELVSTED. Oh, I don't know what I shall do. I see nothing but darkness before me. [She goes out by the hall door.

HEDDA. [Stands waiting for a moment.] So you are not going to see her home, Mr. Lovborg?

LOVBORG. I? Through the streets? Would you have people see her walking with me?

HEDDA. Of course I don't know what else may have happened last night. But is it so utterly irretrievable?

LOVBORG. It will not end with last night, I know that perfectly well. And the thing is that now I have no taste for that sort of life either. I won't begin it anew. She has broken my courage and my power of braving life out.

HEDDA. [Looking straight before her.] So that pretty little fool has had her fingers in a man's destiny. [Looks at him.] But all the same, how could you treat her so heartlessly.

LOVBORG. Oh, don't say that I was heartless!

HEDDA. To go and destroy what has filled her whole soul for months and years! You do not call that heartless!

LOVBORG. To you I can tell the truth, Hedda.

HEDDA. The truth?

LOVBORG. First promise me, give me your word, that what I now confide in you Thea shall never know.

HEDDA. I give you my word.

LOVBORG. Good. Then let me tell you that what I said just now was untrue.

HEDDA. About the manuscript?

LOVBORG. Yes. I have not torn it to pieces, nor thrown it into the fiord.

HEDDA. No, no. But where is it then?

LOVBORG. I have destroyed it none the less, utterly destroyed it, Hedda!

HEDDA. I don't understand.

LOVBORG. Thea said that what I had done seemed to her like a child-murder.

HEDDA. Yes, so she said.

LOVBORG. But to kill his child, that is not the worst thing a father can do to it.

HEDDA. Not the worst?

LOVBORG. Suppose now, Hedda, that a man, in the small hours of the morning, came home to his child's mother after a night of riot and debauchery, and said: "Listen, I have been here and there, in this place and in that. And I have taken our child with, to this place and to that. And I have lost the child, utterly lost it. The devil knows into what hands it may have fallen, who may have had their clutches on it."

HEDDA. Well, but when all is said and done, you know, this was only a book

LOVBORG. Thea's pure soul was in that book.

HEDDA. Yes, so I understand.

LOVBORG. And you can understand, too, that for her and me together no future is possible.

HEDDA. What path do you mean to take then?

LOVBORG. None. I will only try to make an end of it all, the sooner the better.

HEDDA. [A step nearer him.] Eilert Lovborg, listen to me. Will you not try to, to do it beautifully?

LOVBORG. Beautifully? [Smiling.] With vine-leaves in my hair, as you used to dream in the old days?

HEDDA. No, no. I have lost my faith in the vine-leaves. But beautifully nevertheless! For once in a way! Good-bye! You must go now and do not come here any more.

LOVBORG. Good-bye, Mrs. Tesman. And give George Tesman my love. [He is on the point of going.

HEDDA. No, wait! I must give you a memento to take with you. [She goes to the writing-table and opens the drawer and the pistol-case; then returns to LOVBORG with one of the pistols.

LOVBORG. [Looks at her.] This? Is this the memento?

HEDDA. [Nodding slowly.] Do you recognise it? It was aimed at you once.

LOVBORG. You should have used it then.

HEDDA. Take it, and do you use it now.

LOVBORG. [Puts the pistol in his breast pocket.] Thanks!

HEDDA. And beautifully, Eilert Lovborg. Promise me that!

LOVBORG. Good-bye, Hedda Gabler. [He goes out by the hall door. [HEDDA listens for a moment at the door. Then she goes up to the writing-table, takes out the packet of manuscript, peeps under the cover, draws a few of the sheets half out, and looks at them. Next she goes over and seats herself in the arm-chair beside the stove, with the packet in her lap. Presently she opens the stove door, and then the packet.

HEDDA. [Throws one of the quires into the fire and whispers to herself.] Now I am burning your child, Thea! Burning it, curly-locks! [Throwing one or two more quires into the stove.] Your child and Eilert Lovborg's. [Throws the rest in.] I am burning, I am burning your child.

Act Fourth

The same rooms at the TESMANS'. It is evening. The drawing- room is in darkness. The back room is light by the hanging lamp over the table. The curtains over the glass door are drawn close.

HEDDA, dressed in black, walks to and fro in the dark room. Then she goes into the back room and disappears for a moment to the left. She is heard to strike a few chords on the piano. Presently she comes in sight again, and returns to the drawing-room.

BERTA enters from the right, through the inner room, with a lighted lamp, which she places on the table in front of the corner settee in the drawing-room. Her eyes are red with weeping, and she has black ribbons in her cap. She goes quietly and circumspectly out to the right. HEDDA goes up to the glass door, lifts the curtain a little aside, and looks out into the darkness.

Shortly afterwards, MISS TESMAN, in mourning, with a bonnet and veil on, comes in from the hall. HEDDA goes towards her and holds out her hand.

MISS TESMAN. Yes, Hedda, here I am, in mourning and forlorn; for now my poor sister has at last found peace.

HEDDA. I have heard the news already, as you see. Tesman sent me a card.

MISS TESMAN. Yes, he promised me he would. But nevertheless I thought that to Hedda, here in the house of life, I ought myself to bring the tidings of death.

HEDDA. That was very kind of you.

MISS TESMAN. Ah, Rina ought not to have left us just now. This is not the time for Hedda's house to be a house of mourning.

HEDDA. [Changing the subject.] She died quite peacefully, did she not, Miss Tesman?

MISS TESMAN. Oh, her end was so calm, so beautiful. And then she had the unspeakable happiness of seeing George once more, and bidding him good-bye. Has he not come home yet?

HEDDA. No. He wrote that he might be detained. But won't you sit down?

MISS TESMAN. No thank you, my dear, dear Hedda. I should like to, but I have so much to do. I must prepare my dear one for her rest as well as I can. She shall go to her grave looking her best.

HEDDA. Can I not help you in any way?

MISS TESMAN. Oh, you must not think of it! Hedda Tesman must have no hand in such mournful work. Nor let her thought dwell on it either, not at this time.

HEDDA. One is not always mistress of one's thoughts

MISS TESMAN. [Continuing.] Ah yes, it is the way of the world. At home we shall be sewing a shroud; and here there will soon be sewing too, I suppose but of another sort, thank God!

GEORGE TESMAN enters by the hall door.

HEDDA. Ah, you have come at last!

TESMAN. You here, Aunt Julia? With Hedda? Fancy that!

MISS TESMAN. I was just going, my dear boy. Well, have you done all you promised?

TESMAN. No; I'm really afraid I have forgotten half of it. I must come to you again tomorrow. To-day my brain is all in a whirl. I can't keep my thoughts together.

MISS TESMAN. Why, my dear George, you mustn't take it in this way.

TESMAN. Mustn't? How do you mean?

MISS TESMAN. Even in your sorrow you must rejoice, as I do, rejoice that she is at rest.

TESMAN. Oh yes, yes, you are thinking of Aunt Rina.

HEDDA. You will feel lonely now, Miss Tesman.

MISS TESMAN. Just at first, yes. But that will not last very long, I hope. I daresay I shall soon find an occupant for Rina's little room.

TESMAN. Indeed? Who do you think will take it? Eh?

MISS TESMAN. Oh, there's always some poor invalid or other in want of nursing, unfortunately.

HEDDA. Would you really take such a burden upon you again?

MISS TESMAN. A burden! Heaven forgive you, child, it has been no burden to me.

HEDDA. But suppose you had a total stranger on your hands

MISS TESMAN. Oh, one soon makes friends with sick folk; and it's such an absolute necessity for me to have some one to live for. Well, heaven be praised, there may soon be something in this house, too, to keep an old aunt busy.

HEDDA. Oh, don't trouble about anything here.

TESMAN. Yes, just fancy what a nice time we three might have together, if?

HEDDA. If?

TESMAN. [Uneasily.] Oh nothing. It will all come right. Let us hope so, eh?

MISS TESMAN. Well well, I daresay you two want to talk to each other. [Smiling.] And perhaps Hedda may have something to tell you too, George. Good- bye! I must go home to Rina. [Turning at the door.] How strange it is to think that now Rina is with me and with my poor brother as well!

TESMAN. Yes, fancy that, Aunt Julia! Eh? [MISS TESMAN goes out by the hall door.

HEDDA. [Follows TESMAN coldly and searchingly with her eyes.] I almost believe your Aunt Rina's death affects you more than it does your Aunt Julia.

TESMAN. Oh, it's not that alone. It's Eilert I am so terribly uneasy about.

HEDDA. [Quickly.] Is there anything new about him?

TESMAN. I looked in at his rooms this afternoon, intending to tell him the manuscript was in safe keeping.

HEDDA. Well, did you find him?

TESMAN. No. He wasn't at home. But afterwards I met Mrs. Elvsted, and she told me that he had been here early this morning.

HEDDA. Yes, directly after you had gone.

TESMAN. And he said that he had torn his manuscript to pieces, eh?

HEDDA. Yes, so he declared.

TESMAN. Why, good heavens, he must have been completely out of his mind! And I suppose you thought it best not to give it back to him, Hedda?

HEDDA. No, he did not get it.

TESMAN. But of course you told him that we had it?

HEDDA. No. [Quickly.] Did you tell Mrs. Elvsted?

TESMAN. No; I thought I had better not. But you ought to have told him. Fancy, if, in desperation, he should go and do himself some injury! Let me have the manuscript, Hedda! I will take it to him at once. Where is it?

HEDDA. [Cold and immovable, leaning on the arm-chair.] I have not got it.

TESMAN. Have not got it? What in the world do you mean?

HEDDA. I have burnt it, every line of it.

TESMAN. [With a violent movement of terror.] Burnt! Burnt Eilert's manuscript!

HEDDA. Don't scream so. The servant might hear you.

TESMAN. Burnt! Why, good God! No, no, no! It's impossible!

HEDDA. It is so, nevertheless.

TESMAN. Do you know what you have done, Hedda? It's unlawful appropriation of lost property. Fancy that! Just ask Judge Brack, and he'll tell you what it is.

HEDDA. I advise you not to speak of it, either to Judge Brack or to anyone else.

TESMAN. But how could you do anything so unheard-of? What put it into your head? What possessed you? Answer me that, eh?

HEDDA. [Suppressing an almost imperceptible smile.] I did it for your sake, George.

TESMAN. For my sake!

HEDDA. This morning, when you told me about what he had read to you

TESMAN. Yes yes, what then?

HEDDA. You acknowledged that you envied him his work.

TESMAN. Oh, of course I didn't mean that literally.

HEDDA. No matter, I could not bear the idea that any one should throw you into the shade.

TESMAN. [In an outburst of mingled doubt and joy.] Hedda! Oh, is this true? But, but, I never knew you show your love like that before. Fancy that!

HEDDA. Well, I may as well tell you that, just at this time [Impatiently breaking off.] No, no; you can ask Aunt Julia. She well tell you, fast enough.

TESMAN. Oh, I almost think I understand you, Hedda! [Clasps his hands together.] Great heavens! do you really mean it! Eh?

HEDDA. Don't shout so. The servant might hear.

TESMAN. [Laughing in irrepressible glee.] The servant! Why, how absurd you are, Hedda. It's only my old Berta! Why, I'll tell Berta myself.

HEDDA. [Clenching her hands together in desperation.] Oh, it is killing me, it is killing me, all this!

TESMAN. What is, Hedda? Eh?

HEDDA. [Coldly, controlling herself.] All this, absurdity, George.

TESMAN. Absurdity! Do you see anything absurd in my being overjoyed at the news! But after all, perhaps I had better not say anything to Berta.

HEDDA. Oh, why not that too?

TESMAN. No, no, not yet! But I must certainly tell Aunt Julia. And then that you have begun to call me George too! Fancy that! Oh, Aunt Julia will be so happy, so happy!

HEDDA.

When she hears that I have burnt Eilert Lovborg's manuscript for your sake?

TESMAN. No, by-the-bye, that affair of the manuscript, of course nobody must know about that. But that you love me so much, Hedda, Aunt Julia must really share my joy in that! I wonder, now, whether this sort of thing is usual in young wives? Eh?

HEDDA. I think you had better ask Aunt Julia that question too.

TESMAN. I will indeed, some time or other. [Looks uneasy and downcast again.] And yet the manuscript, the manuscript! Good God! it is terrible to think what will become of poor Eilert now.

MRS. ELVSTED, dressed as in the first Act, with hat and cloak, enters by the hall door.

MRS. ELVSTED. [Greets them hurriedly, and says in evident agitation.] Oh, dear Hedda, forgive my coming again.

HEDDA. What is the matter with you, Thea?

TESMAN. Something about Eilert Lovborg again, eh?

MRS. ELVSTED. Yes! I am dreadfully afraid some misfortune has happened to him.

HEDDA. [Seized her arm.] Ah, do you think so?

TESMAN. Why, good Lord, what makes you think that, Mrs. Elvsted?

MRS. ELVSTED. I heard them talking of him at my boarding-house, just as I came in. Oh, the most incredible rumours are afloat about him to-day.

TESMAN. Yes, fancy, so I heard too! And I can bear witness that he went straight home to bed last night. Fancy that!

HEDDA. Well, what did they say at the boarding-house?

MRS. ELVSTED. Oh, I couldn't make out anything clearly. Either they knew nothing definite, or else. They stopped talking when the saw me; and I did not dare to ask.

TESMAN. [Moving about uneasily.] We must hope, we must hope that you misunderstood them, Mrs. Elvsted.

MRS. ELVSTED. No, no; I am sure it was of him they were talking. And I heard something about the hospital or

TESMAN. The hospital?

HEDDA. No, surely that cannot be!

MRS. ELVSTED. Oh, I was in such mortal terror! I went to his lodgings and asked for him there.

HEDDA. You could make up your mind to that, Thea!

MRS. ELVSTED. What else could I do? I really could bear the suspense no longer.

TESMAN. But you didn't find him either, eh?

MRS. ELVSTED. No. And the people knew nothing about him. He hadn't been home since yesterday afternoon, they said.

TESMAN. Yesterday! Fancy, how could they say that?

MRS. ELVSTED. Oh, I am sure something terrible must have happened to him.

TESMAN. Hedda dear, how would it be if I were to go and make inquiries?

HEDDA. No, no, don't you mix yourself up in this affair.

JUDGE BRACK, with his hat in his hand, enters by the hall door, which BERTA opens, and closes behind him. He looks grave and bows in silence.

TESMAN. Oh, is that you, my dear Judge? Eh?

BRACK. Yes. It was imperative I should see you this evening.

TESMAN. I can see you have heard the news about Aunt Rina?

BRACK. Yes, that among other things.

TESMAN. Isn't it sad, eh?

BRACK. Well, my dear Tesman, that depends on how you look at it.

TESMAN. [Looks doubtfully at him.] Has anything else happened?

BRACK. Yes.

HEDDA. [In suspense.] Anything sad, Judge Brack?

BRACK. That, too, depends on how you look at it, Mrs. Tesman.

MRS. ELVSTED. [Unable to restrain her anxiety.] Oh! it is something about Eilert Lovborg!

BRACK. [With a glance at her.] What makes you think that, Madam? Perhaps you have already heard something?

MRS. ELVSTED. [In confusion.] No, nothing at all, but

TESMAN. Oh, for heaven's sake, tell us!

BRACK. [Shrugging his shoulders.] Well, I regret to say Eilert Lovborg has been taken to the hospital. He is lying at the point of death.

MRS. ELVSTED. [Shrieks.] Oh God! oh God!

TESMAN. To the hospital! And at the point of death!

HEDDA. [Involuntarily.] So soon then

MRS. ELVSTED. [Wailing.] And we parted in anger, Hedda!

HEDDA. [Whispers.] Thea, Thea, be careful!

MRS. ELVSTED. [Not heeding her.] I must go to him! I must see him alive!

BRACK. It is useless, Madam. No one will be admitted.

MRS. ELVSTED. Oh, at least tell me what has happened to him? What is it?

TESMAN. You don't mean to say that he has himself. Eh?

HEDDA. Yes, I am sure he has.

BRACK. [Keeping his eyes fixed upon her.] Unfortunately you have guessed quite correctly, Mrs. Tesman.

MRS. ELVSTED. Oh, how horrible!

TESMAN. Himself, then! Fancy that!

HEDDA. Shot himself!

BRACK. Rightly guessed again, Mrs. Tesman.

MRS. ELVSTED. [With an effort at self-control.] When did it happen, Mr. Brack?

BRACK. This afternoon, between three and four.

TESMAN. But, good Lord, where did he do it? Eh?

BRACK. [With some hesitation.] Where? Well I suppose at his lodgings.

MRS. ELVSTED. No, that cannot be; for I was there between six and seven.

BRACK. Well then, somewhere else. I don't know exactly. I only know that he was found. He had shot himself in the breast.

MRS. ELVSTED. Oh, how terrible! That he should die like that!

HEDDA. [To BRACK.] Was it in the breast?

BRACK. Yes, as I told you.

HEDDA. Not in the temple?

BRACK. In the breast, Mrs. Tesman.

HEDDA. Well, well, the breast is a good place, too.

BRACK. How do you mean, Mrs. Tesman?

HEDDA. [Evasively.] Oh, nothing, nothing.

TESMAN. And the wound is dangerous, you say, eh?

BRACK. Absolutely mortal. The end has probably come by this time.

MRS. ELVSTED. Yes, yes, I feel it. The end! The end! Oh, Hedda!

TESMAN. But tell me, how have you learnt all this?

BRACK. [Curtly.] Through one of the police. A man I had some business with.

HEDDA. [In a clear voice.] At last a deed worth doing!

TESMAN. [Terrified.] Good heavens, Hedda! what are you saying?

HEDDA. I say there is beauty in this.

BRACK. H'm, Mrs. Tesman

MRS. ELVSTED. Oh, Hedda, how can you talk of beauty in such an act!

HEDDA. Eilert Lovborg has himself made up his account with life. He has had the courage to do the one right thing.

MRS. ELVSTED. No, you must never think that was how it happened! It must have been in delirium that he did it.

TESMAN. In despair!

HEDDA. That he did not. I am certain of that.

MRS. ELVSTED. Yes, yes! In delirium! Just as when he tore up our manuscript.

BRACK. [Starting.] The manuscript? Has he torn that up?

MRS. ELVSTED. Yes, last night.

TESMAN. [Whispers softly.] Oh, Hedda, we shall never get over this.

BRACK. H'm, very extraordinary.

TESMAN. [Moving about the room.] To think of Eilert going out of the world in this way! And not leaving behind him the book that would have immortalised his name

MRS. ELVSTED. Oh, if only it could be put together again!

TESMAN. Yes, if it only could! I don't know what I would not give

MRS. ELVSTED. Perhaps it can, Mr. Tesman.

TESMAN. What do you mean?

MRS. ELVSTED. [Searches in the pocket of her dress.] Look here. I have kept all the loose notes he used to dictate from.

HEDDA. [A step forward.] Ah!

TESMAN. You have kept them, Mrs. Elvsted! Eh?

MRS. ELVSTED. Yes, I have them here. I put them in my pocket when I left home. Here they still are

TESMAN. Oh, do let me see them!

MRS. ELVSTED. [Hands him a bundle of papers.] But they are in such disorder, all mixed up.

TESMAN. Fancy, if we could make something out of them, after all! Perhaps if we two put our heads together

MRS. ELVSTED. Oh yes, at least let us try

TESMAN. We will manage it! We must! I will dedicate my life to this task.

HEDDA. You, George? Your life?

TESMAN. Yes, or rather all the time I can spare. My own collections must wait in the meantime. Hedda, you understand, eh? I owe this to Eilert's memory.

HEDDA. Perhaps.

TESMAN. And so, my dear Mrs. Elvsted, we will give our whole minds to it. There is no use in brooding over what can't be undone, eh? We must try to control our grief as much as possible, and

MRS. ELVSTED. Yes, yes, Mr. Tesman, I will do the best I can.

TESMAN. Well then, come here. I can't rest until we have looked through the notes. Where shall we sit? Here? No, in there, in the back room. Excuse me, my dear Judge. Come with me, Mrs. Elvsted.

MRS. ELVSTED. Oh, if only it were possible! [TESMAN and MRS. ELVSTED go into the back room. She takes off her hat and cloak. They both sit at the table under the hanging lamp, and are soon deep in an eager examination of the papers. HEDDA crosses to the stove and sits in the arm- chair. Presently BRACK goes up to her.

HEDDA. [In a low voice.] Oh, what a sense of freedom it gives one, this act of Eilert Lovborg's.

BRACK. Freedom, Mrs. Hedda? Well, of course, it is a release for him

HEDDA. I mean for me. It gives me a sense of freedom to know that a deed of deliberate courage is still possible in this world, a deed of spontaneous beauty.

BRACK. [Smiling.] H'm, my dear Mrs. Hedda

HEDDA. Oh, I know what you are going to say. For you are a kind of specialist too, like, you know!

BRACK. [Looking hard at her.] Eilert Lovborg was more to you than perhaps you are willing to admit to yourself. Am I wrong?

HEDDA. I don't answer such questions. I only know that Eilert Lovborg has had the courage to live his life after his own fashion. And then the last great act, with its beauty! Ah! that he should have the will and the strength to turn away from the banquet of life so early.

BRACK. I am sorry, Mrs. Hedda, but I fear I must dispel an amiable illusion.

HEDDA. Illusion?

BRACK. Which could not have lasted long in any case.

HEDDA. What do you mean?

BRACK. Eilert Lovborg did not shoot himself voluntarily.

HEDDA. Not voluntarily?

BRACK. No. The thing did not happen exactly as I told it.

HEDDA. [In suspense.] Have you concealed something? What is it?

BRACK. For poor Mrs. Elvsted's sake I idealised the facts a little.

HEDDA. What are the facts?

BRACK. First, that he is already dead.

HEDDA. At the hospital?

BRACK. Yes, without regaining consciousness.

HEDDA. What more have you concealed?

BRACK. This, the event did not happen at his lodgings.

HEDDA. Oh, that can make no difference.

BRACK. Perhaps it may. For I must tell you, Eilert Lovborg was found shot in, in Mademoiselle Diana's boudoir.

HEDDA. [Makes a motion as if to rise, but sinks back again.] That is impossible, Judge Brack! He cannot have been there again to-day.

BRACK. He was there this afternoon. He went there, he said, to demand the return of something which they had taken from him. Talked wildly about a lost child

HEDDA. Ah, so that is why

BRACK. I thought probably he meant his manuscript; but now I hear he destroyed that himself. So I suppose it must have been his pocket- book.

HEDDA. Yes, no doubt. And there, there he was found?

BRACK. Yes, there. With a pistol in his breast-pocket, discharged. The ball had lodged in a vital part.

HEDDA. In the breast, yes?

BRACK. No, in the bowels.

HEDDA. [Looks up at him with an expression of loathing.] That too! Oh, what curse is it that makes everything I touch turn ludicrous and mean?

BRACK. There is one point more, Mrs. Hedda, another disagreeable feature in the affair.

HEDDA. And what is that?

BRACK. The pistol he carried

HEDDA. [Breathless.] Well? What of it?

BRACK. He must have stolen it.

HEDDA. [Leaps up.] Stolen it! That is not true! He did not steal it!

BRACK. No other explanation is possible. He must have stolen it. Hush!

TESMAN and MRS. ELVSTED have risen from the table in the back-room, and come into the drawing-room.

TESMAN. [With the papers in both his hands.] Hedda, dear, it is almost impossible to see under that lamp. Think of that!

HEDDA. Yes, I am thinking.

TESMAN. Would you mind our sitting at you writing-table, eh?

HEDDA. If you like. [Quickly.] No, wait! Let me clear it first!

TESMAN. Oh, you needn't trouble, Hedda. There is plenty of room.

HEDDA. No no, let me clear it, I say! I will take these things in and put them on the piano. There! [She has drawn out an object, covered with sheet music, from under the bookcase, places several other pieces of music upon it, and carries the whole into the inner room, to the left. TESMAN lays the scraps of paper on the writing-table, and moves the lamp there from the corner table. He and Mrs. Elvsted sit down and proceed with their work. HEDDA returns.

HEDDA. [Behind Mrs. Elvsted's chair, gently ruffling her hair.] Well, my sweet Thea, how goes it with Eilert Lovborg's monument?

MRS. ELVSTED. [Looks dispiritedly up at her.] Oh, it will be terribly hard to put in order.

TESMAN. We must manage it. I am determined. And arranging other people's papers is just the work for me. [HEDDA goes over to the stove, and seats herself on one of the footstools. BRACK stands over her, leaning on the arm-chair.

HEDDA. [Whispers.] What did you say about the pistol?

BRACK. [Softly.] That he must have stolen it.

HEDDA. Why stolen it?

BRACK. Because every other explanation ought to be impossible, Mrs. Hedda.

HEDDA. Indeed?

BRACK. [Glances at her.] Of course Eilert Lovborg was here this morning. Was he not?

HEDDA. Yes.

BRACK. Were you alone with him?

HEDDA. Part of the time.

BRACK. Did you not leave the room whilst he was here?

HEDDA. No.

BRACK. Try to recollect. Were you not out of the room a moment?

HEDDA. Yes, perhaps just a moment out in the hall.

BRACK. And where was you pistol-case during that time?

HEDDA. I had it locked up in

BRACK. Well, Mrs. Hedda?

HEDDA. The case stood there on the writing-table.

BRACK. Have you looked since, to see whether both the pistols are there?

HEDDA. No.

BRACK. Well, you need not. I saw the pistol found in Lovborg's pocket, and I knew it at once as the one I had seen yesterday and before, too.

HEDDA. Have you it with you?

BRACK. No; the police have it.

HEDDA. What will the police do with it?

BRACK. Search till they find the owner.

HEDDA. Do you think they will succeed?

BRACK. [Bends over her and whispers.] No, Hedda Gabler, not so long as I say nothing. HEDDA.

[Looks frightened at him.] And if you do not say nothing, what then?

BRACK. [Shrugs his shoulders.] There is always the possibility that the pistol was stolen.

HEDDA. [Firmly.] Death rather than that.

BRACK. [Smiling.] People say such things but they don't do them.

HEDDA. [Without replying.] And supposing the pistol was not stolen, and the owner is discovered? What then?

BRACK. Well, Hedda, then comes the scandal!

HEDDA. The scandal!

BRACK. Yes, the scandal of which you are so mortally afraid. You will, of course, be brought before the court, both you and Mademoiselle Diana. She will have to explain how the thing happened, whether it was an accidental shot or murder. Did the pistol go off as he was trying to take it out of his pocket, to threaten her with? Or did she tear the pistol out of his hand, shoot him, and push it back into his pocket? That would be quite like her; for she is an able-bodied young person, this same Mademoiselle Diana.

HEDDA. But *I* have nothing to do with all this repulsive business.

BRACK. No. But you will have to answer the question: Why did you give Eilert the pistol? And what conclusions will people draw from the fact that you did give it to him?

HEDDA. [Lets her head sink.] That is true. I did not think of that.

BRACK. Well, fortunately, there is no danger, so long as I say nothing.

HEDDA. [Looks up at him.] So I am in your power, Judge Brack. You have me at your beck and call, from this time forward.

BRACK. [Whispers softly.] Dearest Hedda, believe me, I shall not abuse my advantage.

HEDDA. I am in your power none the less. Subject to your will and your demands. A slave, a slave then! [Rises impetuously.] No, I cannot endure the thought of that! Never!

BRACK. [Looks half-mockingly at her.] People generally get used to the inevitable.

HEDDA. [Returns his look.] Yes, perhaps. [She crosses to the writing-table. Suppressing an involuntary smile, she imitates TESMAN'S intonations.] Well? Are you getting on, George? Eh?

TESMAN. Heaven knows, dear. In any case it will be the work of months.

HEDDA. [As before.] Fancy that! [Passes her hands softly through Mrs. Elvsted's hair.] Doesn't it seem strange to you, Thea? Here are you sitting with Tesman, just as you used to sit with Eilert Lovborg?

MRS. ELVSTED. Ah, if I could only inspire your husband in the same way!

HEDDA. Oh, that will come too in time.

TESMAN. Yes, do you know, Hedda I really think I begin to feel something of the sort. But won't you go and sit with Brack again?

HEDDA. Is there nothing I can do to help you two?

TESMAN. No, nothing in the world. [Turning his head.] I trust to you to keep Hedda company, my dear Brack.

BRACK. [With a glance at HEDDA.] With the very greatest of pleasure.

HEDDA. Thanks. But I am tired this evening. I will go in and lie down a little on the sofa.

TESMAN. Yes, do dear, eh? [HEDDA goes into the back room and draws the curtains. A short pause. Suddenly she is heard playing a wild dance on the piano.

MRS. ELVSTED. [Starts from her chair.] Oh, what is that?

TESMAN. [Runs to the doorway.] Why, my dearest Hedda, don't play dance-music to-night! Just think of Aunt Rina! And of Eilert too!

HEDDA. [Puts her head out between the curtains.] And of Aunt Julia. And of all the rest of them. After this, I will be quiet. [Closes the curtains again.]

TESMAN. [At the writing-table.] It's not good for her to see us at this distressing work. I'll tell you what, Mrs. Elvsted, you shall take the empty room at Aunt Julia's, and then I will come over in the evenings, and we can sit and work there, eh?

HEDDA. [In the inner room.] I hear what you are saying, Tesman. But how am *I* to get through the evenings out here?

TESMAN. [Turning over the papers.] Oh, I daresay Judge Brack will be so kind as to look in now and then, even though I am out.

BRACK. [In the arm-chair, calls out gaily.] Every blessed evening, with all the pleasure in life, Mrs. Tesman! We shall get on capitally together, we two!

HEDDA. [Speaking loud and clear.] Yes, don't you flatter yourself we will, Judge Brack? Now that you are the one cock in the basket [A shot is heard within. TESMAN, MRS. ELVSTED, and BRACK leap to their feet.

TESMAN. Oh, now she is playing with those pistols again. [He throws back the curtains and runs in, followed by MRS. ELVSTED. HEDDA lies stretched on the sofa, lifeless. Confusion and cries. BERTA enters in alarm from the right.

TESMAN. [Shrieks to BRACK.] Shot herself! Shot herself in the temple! Fancy that!

BRACK. [Half-fainting in the arm-chair.] Good God! people don't do such things.

THE END.

The Master Builder, By Henrik Ibsen

Index Of Contents

The Master Builder

Characters.
HALVARD SOLNESS, Master Builder.
ALINE SOLNESS, his wife.
DOCTOR HERDAL, physician.
KNUT BROVIK, formerly an architect, now in SOLNESS'S employment.
RAGNAR BROVIK, his son, draughtsman.
KAIA BROVIK, his niece, book-keeper.
MISS HILDA WANGEL.
Some Ladies.
A Crowd in the street.

The action passes in and about SOLNESS'S house.

Act First.

A plainly-furnished work-room in the house of HALVARD SOLNESS. Folding doors on the left lead out to the hall. On the right is the door leading to the inner rooms of the house. At the back is an open door into the draughtsmen's office. In front, on the left, a desk with books, papers and writing materials. Further back than the folding door, a stove. In the right- hand corner, a sofa, a table, and one or two chairs. On the table a water-bottle and glass. A smaller table, with a rocking-chair and arm-chair, in front on the right. Lighted lamps, with shades, on the table in the draughtmen's office, on the table in the corner, and on the desk.

In the draughtsmen's office sit KNUT BROVIK and his son RAGNAR, occupied with plans and calculations. At the desk in the outer office stands KAIA FOSLI, writing in the ledger. KNUT BROVICK is a spare old man with white hair and beard. He wears a rather threadbare but well-brushed black coat, with spectacles, and a somewhat discoloured white neckcloth. RAGNAR BROVIK is a well-dressed, light-haired man in his thirties, with a slight stoop. KAIA FOSLI is a slightly built girl, a little over twenty, carefully dressed, and delicate-looking. She has a green shade over her eyes. All three go on working for some time in silence.

KNUT BROVIK. [Rises suddenly, as if in distress, from the table; breathes heavily and laboriously as he comes forward into the doorway.] No, I can't bear it much longer!

KAIA. [Going up to him.] You are feeling very ill this evening, are you not, Uncle?

BROVIK. Oh, I seem to get worse every day.

RAGNAR. [Has risen and advances.] You ought to go home, father. Try to get a little sleep

BROVIK. [Impatiently.] Go to bed, I suppose? Would you have me stifled outright?

KAIA. Then take a little walk.

RAGNAR. Yes, do. I will come with you.

BROVIK. [With warmth.] I will not go till he comes! I and determined to have it out this evening with [in a tone of suppressed bitterness] with him, with the chief.

KAIA. [Anxiously.] Oh no, uncle, do wait awhile before doing that!

RAGNAR. Yes, better wait, father!

BROVIK. [Draws is breath laboriously.] Ha, ha! *I* haven't much time for waiting.

KAIA. [Listening.] Hush! I hear him on the stairs. [All three go back to their work. A short silence.

HALVARD SOLNESS comes in through the hall door. He is a man no longer young, but healthy and vigorous, with close-cut curly hair, dark moustache and dark thick eyebrows. He wears a greyish-green buttoned jacket with an upstanding collar and broad lappels. On his head he wears a soft grey felt hat, and he has one or two light portfolios under his arm.

SOLNESS. [Near the door, points towards the draughtsmen's office, and asks in a whisper:] Are they gone?

KAIA. [Softly, shaking her] No.

[She takes the shade off her eyes. SOLNESS crosses the room, throws his hat on a chair, places the portfolios on the table by the sofa, and approaches the desk again. KAIA goes on writing without intermission, but seems nervous and uneasy.

SOLNESS. [Aloud.] What is that you are entering, Miss Fosli?

KAIA. [Starts.] Oh, it is only something that

SOLNESS. Let me look at it, Miss Fosli. [Bends over her, pretends to be looking into the ledger, and whispers:] Kaia!

KAIA. [Softly, still writing.] Well?

SOLNESS. Why do you always take that shade off when I come?

KAIA. [As before.] I look so ugly with it on.

SOLNESS. [Smiling.] Then you don't like to look ugly, Kaia?

KAIA. [Half glancing up at him.] Not for all the world. Not in your eyes.

SOLNESS. [Strokes her hair gently.] Poor, poor little Kaia

KAIA. [Bending her head.] Hush, they can hear you!

[SOLNESS strolls across the room to the right, turns and pauses at the door of the draughtsmen's office.

SOLNESS. Has any one been here for me?

RAGNAR. [Rising.] Yes, the young couple who want a villa built, out at Lovstrand.

SOLNESS. [Growling.] Oh, those two! They must wait. I am not quite clear about the plans yet.

RAGNAR. [Advancing, with some hesitation.] They were very anxious to have the drawings at once.

SOLNESS. [As before.] Yes, of course, so they all are.

BROVIK. [Looks up.] They say they are longing so to get into a house of their own.

SOLNESS. Yes, yes, we know all that! And so they are content to take whatever is offered them. They get a, a roof over their heads, an address but nothing to call a home. No thank you! In that case, let them apply to somebody else. Tell them that, the next time they call.

BROVIK. [Pushes his glasses up on to his forehead and looks in astonishment at him.] To somebody else? Are you prepared to give up the commission?

SOLNESS. [Impatiently.] Yes, yes, yes, devil take it! If that is to be the way of it. Rather that, than build away at random. [Vehemently.] Besides, I know very little about these people as yet.

BROVIK. The people are safe enough. Ragnar knows them. He is a friend of the family.

SOLNESS. Oh, safe, safe enough! That is not at all what I mean. Good lord, don't you understand me either? [Angrily.] I won't have anything to do with these strangers. They may apply to whom they please, so far as I am concerned.

BROVIK. [Rising.] Do you really mean that?

SOLNESS. [Sulkily.] Yes I do. For once in a way. [He comes forward.

[BROVIK exchanges a glance with RAGNAR, who makes a warning gesture. Then BROVIK comes into the front room.

BROVIK. May I have a few words with you?

SOLNESS. Certainly.

BROVIK. [To KAIA.] Just go in there for moment, Kaia.

KAIA. [Uneasily.] Oh, but uncle

BROVIK. Do as I say, child. And shut the door after you.

[KAIA goes reluctantly into the draughtsmen's office, glances anxiously and imploringly at SOLNESS, and shuts the door.

BROVIK. [Lowering his voice a little.] I don't want the poor children to know how I am.

SOLNESS. Yes, you have been looking very poorly of late.

BROVIK. It will soon be all over with me. My strength is ebbing from day to day.

SOLNESS. Won't you sit down?

BROVIK. Thanks, may I?

SOLNESS. [Placing the arm-chair more conveniently.] Here, take this chair. And now?

BROVIK. [Has seated himself with difficulty.] Well, you see, it's about Ragnar. That is what weighs most upon me. What is to become of him?

SOLNESS. Of course your son will stay with me as long as ever he likes.

BROVIK. But that is just what he does not like. He feels that he cannot stay here any longer.

SOLNESS. Why, I should say he was very well off here. But if he wants more money, I should not mind

BROVIK. No, no! It is not that. [Impatiently.] But sooner or later he, too, must have a chance of doing something on his own account.

SOLNESS. [Without looking at him.] Do you think that Ragnar has quite talent enough to stand alone?

BROVIK. No, that is just the heartbreaking part of it. I have begun to have my doubts about the boy. For you have never said so much as, as one encouraging word about him. And yet I cannot but think there must be something in him, he can't be without talent.

SOLNESS. Well, but he has learnt nothing, nothing thoroughly, I mean. Except, of course, to draw.

BROVIK. [Looks at him with covert hatred, and says hoarsely.] You had learned little enough of the business when you were in my employment. But that did not prevent you from setting to work [breathing with difficulty] and pushing your way up, and taking the wind out of my sails, mine, and so may other people's.

SOLNESS. Yes, you see, circumstances favoured me.

BROVIK. You are right there. Everything favoured you. But then how can you have the heart to let me go to my grave, without having seen what Ragnar is fit for? And of course I am anxious to see them married, too, before I go.

SOLNESS. [Sharply.] Is it she who wishes it?

BROVIK. Not Kaia so much as Ragnar, he talks about it every day. [Appealingly.] You must help him to get some independent work now! I must see something that the lad has done. Do you hear?

SOLNESS. [Peevishly.] Hang it, man, you can't expect me to drag commissions down from the moon for him!

BROVIK. He has the chance of a capital commission at this very moment. A big bit of work.

SOLNESS. [Uneasily, startled.] Has he?

BROVIK. I you would give your consent.

SOLNESS. What sort of work do you mean?

BROVIK. [With some hesitation.] He can have the building of that villa out at Lovstrand.

SOLNESS. That! Why I am going to build that myself.

BROVIK. Oh you don't much care about doing it.

SOLNESS. [Flaring up.] Don't care! Who dares to say that?

BROVIK. You said so yourself just now.

SOLNESS. Oh, never mind what I say. Would they give Ragnar the building of that villa?

BROVIK. Yes. You see, he knows the family. And then, just for the fun of the thing, he has made drawings and estimates and so forth

SOLNESS. Are they pleased with the drawings? The people who will have to live in the house?

BROVIK. Yes. If you would only look through them and approve of them

SOLNESS. Then they would let Ragnar build their home for them?

BROVIK. They were immensely pleased with his idea. They thought it exceedingly original, they said.

SOLNESS. Oho! Original! Not the old-fashioned stuff that *I* am in the habit of turning out!

BROVIK. It seemed to them different.

SOLNESS. [With suppressed irritation.] So it was to see Ragnar that they came here, whilst I was out!

BROVIK. They came to call upon you and at the same time to ask whether you would mind retiring

SOLNESS. [Angrily.] Retire? I?

BROVIK. In case you thought that Ragnar's drawings

SOLNESS. I! Retire in favour of your son!

BROVIK. Retire from the agreement, they meant.

SOLNESS. Oh, it comes to the same thing. [Laughs angrily.] So that is it, is it? Halvard Solness is to see about retiring now! To make room for younger men! For the very youngest, perhaps! He must make room! Room! Room!

BROVIK. Why, good heavens! there is surely room for more than one single man

SOLNESS. Oh, there's not so very much room to spare either. But, be that as it may, I will never retire! I will never give way to anybody! Never of my own free will. Never in this world will I do that!

BROVIK. [Rise with difficulty.] Then I am to pass out of life without any certainty? Without a gleam of happiness? Without any faith or trust in Ragnar? Without having seen a single piece of work of his doing? Is that to be the way of it?

SOLNESS. [Turns half aside, and mutters.] H'm, don't ask more just now.

BROVIK. I must have an answer to this one question. Am I to pass out of life in such utter poverty?

SOLNESS. [Seems to struggle with himself; finally he says, in a low but firm voice:] You must pass out of life as best you can.

BROVIK. Then be it so. [He goes up the room.

SOLNESS. [Following him, half is desperation.] Don't you understand that I cannot help it? I am what I am, and I cannot change my nature!

BROVIK. No; I suppose that you can't. [Reels and supports himself against the sofa-table.] May I have a glass of water?

SOLNESS. By all means. [Fills a glass and hands it to him.

BROVIK. Thanks. [Drinks and puts the glass down again.
[SOLNESS goes up and opens the door of the draughtsmen's office.

SOLNESS. Ragnar, you must come and take your father home.

Ragnar rises quickly. He and KAIA come into the work-room.

RAGNAR. What is the matter, father?

BROVIK. Give me your arm. Now let us go.

RAGNAR. Very well. You had better put your things on, too, Kaia.

SOLNESS. Miss Fosli must stay, just for a moment. There is a letter I want written.

BROVIK. [Looks at SOLNESS.] Good night. Sleep well, if you can.

SOLNESS. Good night.
[BROVIK and RAGNAR go out by the hall-door. KAIA goes to the desk. SOLNESS stands with bent head, to the right, by the arm-chair.

KAIA. [Dubiously.] Is there any letter?

SOLNESS. [Curtly.] No, of course not. [Looks sternly at her.] Kaia!

KAIA. [Anxiously, in a low voice.] Yes!

SOLNESS. [Points imperatively to a spot on the floor.] Come here! At once!

KAIA. [Hesitatingly.] Yes.

SOLNESS. [As before.] Nearer!

KAIA. [Obeying.] What do you want with me?

SOLNESS. [Looks at her for a while.] Is it you I have to thank for all this?

KAIA. No, no, don't think that!

SOLNESS. But confess now, you want to get married!

KAIA. [Softly.] Ragnar and I have been engaged for four or five years, and so

SOLNESS. And so you think it time there were an end of it. Is not that so?

KAIA. Ragnar and Uncle say I must. So I suppose I shall have to give in.

SOLNESS. [More gently.] Kaia, don't you really care a little bit for Ragnar, too?

KAIA. I cared very much for Ragnar once, before I came here to you.

SOLNESS. But you don't now? Not in the least?

KAIA. [Passionately, clasping hands and holding them out towards him.] Oh, you know very well there is only one person I care for now! I shall never care for any one else.

SOLNESS. Yes, you say that. And yet you go away from me, leave me alone here with everything on my hands.

KAIA. But could I not stay with you, even if Ragnar?

SOLNESS. [Repudiating the idea.] No, no, that is quite impossible. If Ragnar leaves me and starts work on his own account, then of course he will need you himself.

KAIA. [Wringing her hands.] Oh, I feel as if I could not be separated from you! It's quite, quite impossible!

SOLNESS. Then be sure you get those foolish notions out of Ragnar's head. Marry him as much as you please [Alters his tone.] I mean, don't let him throw up his good situation with me. For then I can keep you too, my dear Kaia.

KAIA. Oh yes, how lovely that would be, if it could only be managed!

SOLNESS. [Clasps her head with his two hands and whispers.] For I cannot get on without you, you see. I must have you with me every single day.

KAIA. [In nervous exaltation.] My God! My God!

SOLNESS. [Kisses her hair.] Kaia, Kaia!

KAIA. [Sinks down before him.] Oh, how good you are to me! How unspeakably good you are!

SOLNESS. [Vehemently.] Get up! For goodness' sake get up! I think I hear some one.
[He helps her to rise. She staggers over to the desk].

MRS. SOLNESS enters by the door on the right. She looks thin and wasted with grief, but shows traces of bygone beauty. Blonde ringlets. Dressed with good taste, wholly in black. Speaks some-what slowly and in a plaintive voice.

MRS. SOLNESS. [In the doorway.] Halvard!

SOLNESS. [Turns.] Oh, are you there, my dear?

MRS. SOLNESS. [With a glance at KAIA.] I am afraid I am disturbing you.

SOLNESS. Not in the least. Miss Fosli has only a short letter to write.

MRS. SOLNESS. Yes, so I see.

SOLNESS. What do you want with me, Aline?

MRS. SOLNESS. I merely wanted to tell you that Dr. Herdal is in the drawing-room. Won't you come and see him, Halvard?

SOLNESS. [Looks suspiciously at her.]. H'm, is the doctor so very anxious to see me?

MRS. SOLNESS. Well, not exactly anxious. He really came to see me; but he would like to say how-do-you-do to you at the same time.

SOLNESS. [Laughs to himself.] Yes, I daresay. Well, you must ask him to wait a little.

MRS. SOLNESS. Then you will come in presently?

SOLNESS. Perhaps I will. Presently, presently, dear. In a little while.

MRS. SOLNESS. [Glancing again at KAIA.] Well now, don't forget, Halvard.
[Withdraws and closes the door behind her.

KAIA. [Softly.] Oh dear, oh dear, I am sure Mrs. Solness thinks ill of me in some way!

SOLNESS. Oh, not in the least. Not more than usual at any rate. But all the same, you had better go now, Kaia.

KAIA. Yes, yes, now I must go.

SOLNESS. [Severely.] And mind you get that matter settled for me. Do you hear?

KAIA. Oh, if it only depended on me

SOLNESS. I will have it settled, I say! And to-morrow too, not a day later!

KAIA. [Terrified.] If there's nothing else for it, I am quite willing to break off the engagement.

SOLNESS. [Angrily.] Break it off. Are you mad? Would you think of breaking it off?

KAIA. [Distracted.] Yes, if necessary. For I must, I must stay here with you! I can't leave you! That is utterly, utterly impossible!

SOLNESS. [With a sudden outburst.] But deuce take it, how about Ragnar then! It's Ragnar that I

KAIA. [Looks at him with terrified eyes.] It is chiefly on Ragnar's account, that, that you?

SOLNESS. [Collecting himself.] No, no, of course not! You don't understand me either. [Gently and softly.] Of course it is you I want to keep. You above everything, Kaia. But for that very reason, you must prevent Ragnar, too, from throwing up his situation. There, there, now go home.

KAIA. Yes, yes, good-night, then.

SOLNESS. Good night. [As she is going.] Oh, stop a moment! Are Ragnar's drawings in there?

KAIA. I did not see him take them with him.

SOLNESS. Then just go and find them for me. I might perhaps glance over them, after all.

KAIA. [Happy.] Oh yes, please do!

SOLNESS. For your sake, Kaia dear. Now, let me have them at once, please.
[KAIA hurries into the draughtsmen's office, searches anxiously in the table-drawer, finds a portfolio and brings it with her.

KAIA. Here are all the drawings.

SOLNESS. Good. Put them down there on the table.

KAIA. [Putting down the portfolio.] Good night, then. [Beseechingly.] And please, please think kindly of me.

SOLNESS. Oh, that I always do. Good-night, my dear little Kaia. [Glances to the right.] Go, go now!

MRS. SOLNESS and DR. HERDAL enter by the door on the right. He is a stoutish, elderly man, with a round, good-humoured face, clean shaven, with thin, light hair, and gold spectacles.

MRS. SOLNESS. [Still in the doorway.] Halvard, I cannot keep the doctor any longer.

SOLNESS. Well then, come in here.

MRS. SOLNESS. [To KAIA, who is turning down the desk-lamp.] Have you finished the letter already, Miss Fosli?

KAIA. [In confusion.] The letter?

SOLNESS. Yes, it was quite a short one.

MRS. SOLNESS. It must have been very short.

SOLNESS. You may go now, Miss Fosli. And please come in good time to-morrow morning.

KAIA. I will be sure to. Good-night, Mrs. Solness.
[She goes out by the hall door.

SOLNESS. Are you in a hurry, doctor?

DR. HERDAL. No, not at all.

SOLNESS. May I have a little chat with you?

DR. HERDAL. With the greatest of pleasure.

SOLNESS. Then let us sit down. [He motions the doctor to take the rocking- chair, and sits down himself in the arm-chair. Looks searchingly at him.] Tell me, did you notice anything odd about Aline?

DR. HERDAL. Do you mean just now, when she was here?

SOLNESS. Yes, in her manner to me. Did you notice anything?

DR. HERDAL. [Smiling.] Well, I admit, one couldn't well avoid noticing that your wife, h'm, that your wife is not particularly fond of this Miss Fosli.

SOLNESS. Is that all? I have noticed that myself.

DR. HERDAL. And I must say I am scarcely surprised at it.

SOLNESS. At what?

DR. HERDAL. That she should not exactly approve of your seeing so much of another woman, all day and every day.

SOLNESS. No, no, I suppose you are right there and Aline too. But it's impossible to make any change.

DR. HERDAL. Could you not engage a clerk?

SOLNESS. The first man that came to hand? No, thank you, that would never do for me.

DR. HERDAL. But now, if your wife? Suppose, with her delicate health, all this tries her too much?

SOLNESS. Even then, I might almost say, it can make no difference. I must keep Kaia Fosli. No one else could fill her place.

DR. HERDAL. No one else?

SOLNESS. [Curtly.] No, no one.

DR. HERDAL. [Drawing his chair closer.] Now listen to me, my dear Mr. Solness. May I ask you a question, quite between ourselves?

SOLNESS. By all means.

DR. HERDAL. Women, you see, in certain matters, they have a deucedly keen intuition

SOLNESS. They have, indeed. There is not the least doubt of that. But?

DR. HERDAL. Well, tell me now, if your wife can't endure this Kaia Fosli?

SOLNESS. Well, what then?

DR. HERDAL. - may she not have just, just the least little bit of reason for this instinctive dislike?

SOLNESS. [Looks at him and rises.] Oho!

DR. HERDAL. Now don't be offended but hasn't she?

SOLNESS. [With curt decision.] No.

DR. HERDAL. No reason of any sort?

SOLNESS. No other than her own suspicious nature.

DR. HERDAL. I know you have known a good many women in your time.

SOLNESS. Yes, I have.

DR. HERDAL. And have been a good deal taken with some of them, too.

SOLNESS. Oh yes, I don't deny it.

DR. HERDAL. But as regards Miss Fosli, then? There is nothing of that sort in this case?

SOLNESS. No; nothing at all, on my side.

DR. HERDAL. But on her side?

SOLNESS. I don't think you have any right to ask that question, doctor.

DR. HERDAL. Well, you know, we were discussing your wife's intuition.

SOLNESS. So we were. And for that matter [lowers his voice] Aline's intuition, as you call it, in a certain sense, it has not been so far astray.

DR. HERDAL. Aha! there we have it!

SOLNESS. [Sits down.] Doctor Herdal I am going to tell you a strange story if you care to listen to it.

DR. HERDAL. I like listening to strange stories.

SOLNESS. Very well then. I daresay you recollect that I took Knut Brovik and his son into my employment, after the old man's business had gone to the dogs.

DR. HERDAL. Yes, so I have understood.

SOLNESS. You see, they really are clever fellows, these two. Each of them has talent in his own way. But then the son took it into his head to get engaged; and the next thing, of course, was that he wanted to get married and begin to build on his own account. That is the way with all these young people.

DR. HERDAL. [Laughing.] Yes, they have a bad habit of wanting to marry.

SOLNESS. Just so. But of course that did not suit my plans; for I needed Ragnar myself and the old man too. He is exceedingly good at calculating bearing strains and cubic contents and all that sort of devilry, you know.

DR. HERDAL. Oh yes, no doubt that's indispensable.

SOLNESS. Yes, it is. But Ragnar was absolutely bent on setting to work for himself. He would hear of nothing else.

DR. HERDAL. But he has stayed with you all the same.

SOLNESS. Yes, I'll tell you how that came about. One day this girl, Kaia Fosli, came to see them on some errand or other. She had never been here before. And when I saw how utterly infatuated they were with each other, the thought occurred to me: if I cold only get her into the office here, then perhaps Ragnar too would stay where he is.

DR. HERDAL. That was not at all a bad idea.

SOLNESS. Yes, but at the time I did not breathe a word of what was in my mind. I merely stood and looked at her and kept on wishing intently that I could have her here. Then I talked to her a little, in a friendly way, about one thing and another. And then she went away.

DR. HERDAL. Well?

SOLNESS. Well then, next day, pretty late in the evening, when old Brovik and Ragnar had gone home, she came here again, and behaved as if I had made an arrangement with her.

DR. HERDAL. An arrangement? What about?

SOLNESS. About the very thing my mind had been fixed on. But I hadn't said one single word about it.

DR. HERDAL. That was most extraordinary.

SOLNESS. Yes, was it not? And now she wanted to know what she was to do here, whether she could begin the very next morning, and so forth.

DR. HERDAL. Don't you think she did it in order to be with her sweetheart?

SOLNESS. That was what occurred to me at first. But no, that was not it. She seemed to drift quite away from him when once she had come here to me.

DR. HERDAL. She drifted over to you, then?

SOLNESS. Yes, entirely. If I happen to look at her when her back is turned, I can tell that she feels it. She quivers and trembles the moment I come near her. What do you think of that?

DR. HERDAL. H'm, that's not very hard to explain.

SOLNESS. Well, but what about the other thing? That she believed I had said to her what I had only wished and willed, silently, inwardly, to myself? What do you say to that? Can you explain that, Dr. Herdal?

DR. HERDAL. No, I won't undertake to do that.

SOLNESS. I felt sure you would not; and so I have never cared to talk about it till now. But it's a cursed nuisance to me in the long run, you understand. Here have I got to go on day after day, pretending. And it's a shame to treat her so, too, poor girl. [Vehemently.] But I cannot do anything else. For if she runs away from me then Ragnar will be off too.

DR. HERDAL. And you have not told your wife the rights of the story?

SOLNESS. No.

DR. HERDAL. The why on earth don't you?

SOLNESS. [Looks fixedly at him, and says in a low voice:] Because I seem to find a sort of, of salutary self-torture in allowing Aline to do me an injustice.

DR. HERDAL. [Shakes his head.] I don't in the least understand what you mean.

SOLNESS. Well, you see it is like paying off a little bit of a huge, immeasurable debt

DR. HERDAL. To your wife?

SOLNESS. Yes; and that always helps to relieve one's mind a little. One can breathe more freely for a while, you understand.

DR. HERDAL. No, goodness knows, I don't understand at all

SOLNESS. [Breaking off, rises again.] Well, well, well, then we won't talk any more about it. [He saunters across the room, returns, and stops beside the table. Looks at the doctor with a sly smile.] I suppose you think you have drawn me out nicely now, doctor?

DR. HERDAL. [With some irritation.] Drawn you out? Again I have not the faintest notion of what you mean, Mr. Solness.

SOLNESS. Oh come, out with it; I have seen it quite clearly, you know.

DR. HERDAL. What have you seen?

SOLNESS. [In a low voice, slowly.] That you have been quietly keeping an eye upon me.

DR. HERDAL. That *I* have! And why in all the world should I do that?

SOLNESS. Because you think that I [Passionately.] Well devil take it, you think the same of me as Aline does.

DR. HERDAL. And what does she think about you?

SOLNESS. [Having recovered his self-control.] She has begun to think that I am, that I am ill.

DR. HERDAL. Ill! You! She has never hinted such a thing to me. Why, what can she think is the matter with you?

SOLNESS. [Leans over the back of the chair and whispers.] Aline has made up her mind that I am mad. That is what she thinks.

DR. HERDAL. [Rising.] Why, my dear fellow!

SOLNESS. Yes, on my soul she does! I tell you it is so. And she has got you to think the same! Oh, I can assure you, doctor, I see it in your face as clearly as possible. You don't take me in so easily, I can tell you.

DR. HERDAL. [Looks at him in amazement.] Never, Mr. Solness, never has such a thought entered my mind.

SOLNESS. [With and incredulous smile.] Really? Has it not?

DR. HERDAL. No, never! Nor your wife's mind either, I am convinced. I could almost swear to that.

SOLNESS. Well, I wouldn't advise you to. For, in a certain sense, you see, perhaps, perhaps she is not so far wrong in thinking something of the kind.

DR. HERDAL. Come now, I really must say

SOLNESS. [Interrupting, with a sweep of his hand.] Well, well, my dear doctor, don't let us discuss this any further. We had better agree to differ. [Changes to a tone of quiet amusement.] But look here now, doctor, h'm

DR. HERDAL. Well?

SOLNESS. Since you don't believe that I am ill, and crazy, and mad, and so forth

DR. HERDAL. What then?

SOLNESS. Then I daresay you fancy that I am an extremely happy man.

DR. HERDAL. Is that mere fancy?

SOLNESS. [Laughs.] No, no, of course not! Heaven forbid! Only think, to be Solness the master builder! Halvard Solness! What could be more delightful?

DR. HERDAL. Yes, I must say it seems to me you have had the luck on your side to an astounding degree.

SOLNESS. [Suppresses a gloomy smile.] So I have. I can't complain on that score.

DR. HERDAL. First of all that grim old robbers' castle was burnt down for you. And that was certainly a great piece of luck.

SOLNESS. [Seriously.] It was the home of Aline's family. Remember that.

DR. HERDAL. Yes, it must have been a great grief to her.

SOLNESS. She has not got over it to this day, not in all these twelve or thirteen years.

DR. HERDAL. But you, yourself, you rose upon the ruins. You began as a poor boy from a country village, and now you are at the head of your profession. Ah, yes, Mr. Solness, you have undoubtedly had the luck on your side.

SOLNESS. [Looking at him with embarrassment.] Yes, but that is just what makes me so horribly afraid.

DR. HERDAL. Afraid? Because you have the luck on your side!

SOLNESS. It terrifies me, terrifies me every hour of the day. For sooner or later the luck must turn, you see.

DR. HERDAL. Oh nonsense! What should make the luck turn?

SOLNESS. [With firm assurance.] The younger generation!

DR. HERDAL. Pooh! The younger generation! You are not laid on the shelf yet, I should hope. Oh no, your position here is probably firmer now than it has ever been.

SOLNESS. The luck will turn. I know it, I feel the day approaching. Some one or other will take it into his head to say: Give me a chance! And then all the rest will come clamouring after him, and shake their fists at me and shout: Make room, make room! Yes, just you see, doctor, presently the younger generation will come knocking at my door

DR. HERDAL. [Laughing.] Well, and what if they do?

SOLNESS. What if they do? Then there's an end of Halvard Solness.
[There is a knock at the door on the left.

SOLNESS. [Starts.] What's that? Did you not hear something?

DR. HERDAL. Some one is knocking at the door.

SOLNESS. [Loudly.] Come in.

HILDA WANGEL enters by the hall door. She is of middle height, supple, and delicately built. Somewhat sunburnt. Dressed in a tourist costume, with skirt caught up for walking, a sailor's collar open at the throat, and a small sailor hat on her head. Knapsack on back, plaid in strap, and alpenstock.

HILDA. [Goes straight up to SOLNESS, her eyes sparkling with happiness.] Good evening!

SOLNESS. [Looks doubtfully at her.] Good evening

HILDA. [Laughs.] I almost believe you don't recognise me!

SOLNESS. No, I must admit that, just for the moment

DR. HERDAL. [Approaching.] But *I* recognise you, my dear young lady

HILDA. [Pleased.] Oh, is it you that

DR. HERDAL. Of course it is. [To SOLNESS.] We met at one of the mountain stations this summer. [To HILDA.] What became of the other ladies?

HILDA. Oh, they went westward.

DR. HERDAL. They didn't much like all the fun we used to have in the evenings.

HILDA. No, I believe they didn't.

DR. HERDAL. [Holds up his finger at her.] And I am afraid it can't be denied that you flirted a little with us.

HILDA. Well, that was better fun than to sit there knitting stockings with all those old women.

DR. HERDAL. [Laughs.] There I entirely agree with you!

SOLNESS. Have you come to town this evening?

HILDA. Yes, I have just arrived.

DR. HERDAL. Quite alone, Miss Wangel?

HILDA. Oh yes!

SOLNESS. Wangel? Is your name Wangel?

HILDA. [Looks in amused surprise at him.] Yes, of course it is.

SOLNESS. Then you must be a daughter of the district doctor up at Lysanger?

HILDA. [As before.] Yes, who else's daughter should I be?

SOLNESS. Oh, then I suppose we met up there, that summer when I was building a tower on the old church.

HILDA. [More seriously.] Yes, of course it was then we met.

SOLNESS. Well, that is a long time ago.

HILDA. [Looks hard at him.] It is exactly ten years.

SOLNESS. You must have been a mere child then, I should think.

HILDA. [Carelessly.] Well, I was twelve or thirteen.

DR. HERDAL. Is this the first time you have ever been up to town, Miss Wangel?

HILDA. Yes, it is indeed.

SOLNESS. And don't you know any one here?

HILDA. Nobody but you. And of course, your wife.

SOLNESS. So you know her, too?

HILDA. Only a little. We spent a few days together at the sanatorium.

SOLNESS. Ah, up there?

HILDA. She said I might come and pay her a visit if ever I came up to town. [Smiles.] Not that that was necessary.

SOLNESS. Odd that she should never have mentioned it.
[HILDA puts her stick down by the stove, takes off the knapsack and lays it and the plaid on the sofa. DR. HERDAL offers to help her. SOLNESS stands and gazes at her.

HILDA. [Going towards him.] Well, now I must ask you to let me stay the night here.

SOLNESS. I am sure there will be no difficulty about that.

HILDA. For I have no other clothes than those I stand in, except a change of linen in my knapsack. And that has to go to the wash, for it's very dirty.

SOLNESS. Oh yes, that can be managed. Now I'll just let my wife know

DR. HERDAL. Meanwhile I will go and see my patient.

SOLNESS. Yes, do; and come again later on.

DR. HERDAL. [Playfully, with a glance at HILDA.] Oh that I will, you may be very certain! [Laughs.] So your prediction has come true, Mr. Solness!

SOLNESS. How so?

DR. HERDAL. The younger generation did come knocking at your door.

SOLNESS. [Cheerfully.] Yes, but in a very different way from what I meant.

DR. HERDAL. Very different, yes. That's undeniable.
[He goes out by the hall-door. SOLNESS opens the door on the right and speaks into the side room.

SOLNESS. Aline! Will you come in here, please. Here is a friend of yours, Miss Wangel.

MRS. SOLNESS. [Appears in the doorway.] Who do you say it is? [Sees HILDA.]. Oh, is it you, Miss Wangel?

SOLNESS. Miss Wangel has this moment arrived; and she would like to stay the night here.

MRS. SOLNESS. Here with us? Oh yes, certainly.

SOLNESS. Till she can get her things a little in order, you know.

MRS. SOLNESS. I will do the best I can for you. It's no more than my duty. I suppose your trunk is coming on later?

HILDA. I have no trunk.

MRS. SOLNESS. Well, it will be all right, I daresay. In the meantime, you must excuse my leaving you here with my husband, until I can get a room made a little more comfortable for you.

SOLNESS. Can we not give her one of the nurseries? They are all ready as it is.

MRS. SOLNESS. Oh yes. There we have room and to spare. [To HILDA.] Sit down now, and rest a little. [She goes out to the right.
[HILDA, with her hands behind her back, strolls about the room and looks at various objects. SOLNESS stands in front, beside the table, also with his hands behind his back, and follows her with his eyes.

HILDA. [Stops and looks at him.] Have you several nurseries?

SOLNESS. There are three nurseries in the house.

HILDA. That's a lot. Then I suppose you have a great many children?

SOLNESS. No. We have no child. But now you can be the child here, for the time being.

HILDA. For to-night, yes. I shall not cry. I mean to sleep as sound as a stone.

SOLNESS. Yes, you must be very tired, I should think.

HILDA. Oh no! But all the same. It's so delicious to lie and dream.

SOLNESS. Do you dream much of nights?

HILDA. Oh yes! Almost always.

SOLNESS. What do you dream about most?

HILDA. I sha'n't tell you to-night. Another time perhaps.
[She again strolls about the room, stops at the desk and turns over the books and papers a little.

SOLNESS. [Approaching.] Are you searching for anything?

HILDA. No, I am merely looking at all these things. [Turns.] Perhaps I mustn't?

SOLNESS. Oh, by all means.

HILDA. Is it you that writes in this great ledger?

SOLNESS. No, it's my book-keeper.

HILDA. Is it a woman?

SOLNESS. [Smiles.] Yes.

HILDA. One you employ here, in your office?

SOLNESS. Yes.

HILDA. Is she married?

SOLNESS. No, she is single.

HILDA. Oh, indeed!

SOLNESS. But I believe she is soon going to be married.

HILDA. That's a good thing for her.

SOLNESS. But not such a good thing for me. For then I shall have nobody to help me.

HILDA. Can't you get hold of some one else who will do just as well?

SOLNESS. Perhaps you would stay here and, and write in the ledger?

HILDA. [Measures him with a glance.] Yes, I daresay! No, thank you, nothing of that sort for me.
[She again strolls across the room, and sits down on the rocking-chair. SOLNESS too goes to the table.

HILDA. [Continuing.] For there must surely be plenty of other thing to be done here. [Looks smilingly at him.] Don't you think so, too?

SOLNESS. Of course. First of all, I suppose, you want to make a round of the shops, and get yourself up in the height of fashion.

HILDA. [Amused.] No, I think I shall let that alone!

SOLNESS. Indeed?

HILDA. For you must know I have run through all my money.

SOLNESS. [Laughs.] Neither trunk nor money, then?

HILDA. Neither one nor the other. But never mind, it doesn't matter now.

SOLNESS. Come now, I like you for that.

HILDA. Only for that?

SOLNESS. For that among other things. [Sits in the arm-chair.] Is your father alive still?

HILDA. Yes, father's alive.

SOLNESS. Perhaps you are thinking of studying here?

HILDA. No, that hadn't occurred to me.

SOLNESS. But I suppose you will be staying for some time?

HILDA. That must depend upon circumstances.
[She sits awhile rocking herself and looking at him, half seriously, half with a suppressed smile. Then she takes off her hat and puts it on the table in front of her.

HILDA. Mr. Solness!

SOLNESS. Well?

HILDA. Have you a very bad memory?

SOLNESS. A bad memory? No, not that I am aware of.

HILDA. Then have you nothing to say to me about what happened up there?

SOLNESS. [In momentary surprise.] Up at Lysanger? [Indifferently.] Why, it was nothing much to talk about it seems to me.

HILDA. [Looks reproachfully at him.] How can you sit there and say such things?

SOLNESS. Well, then, you talk to me about it.

HILDA. When the tower was finished, we had grand doings in the town.

SOLNESS. Yes, I shall not easily forget that day.

HILDA. [Smiles.] Will you not? That comes well from you.

SOLNESS. Comes well?

HILDA. There was music in the churchyard and many, many hundreds of people. We school-girls were dressed in white; and we all carried flags.

SOLNESS. Ah yes, those flags I can tell you I remember them!

HILDA. Then you climbed right up the scaffolding, straight to the very top; and you had a great wreath with you; and you hung that wreath right away up on the weather-vane.

SOLNESS. [Curtly interrupting.] I always did that in those days. It is an old custom.

HILDA. It was so wonderfully thrilling to stand below and look up at you. Fancy, if he should fall over! He the master builder himself!

SOLNESS. [As if to divert her from the subject.] Yes, yes, yes, that might very will have happened, too. For one of those white-frocked little devils, she went on in such a way, and screamed up at me so

HILDA. [Sparkling with pleasure.] "Hurrah for Master Builder Solness!" Yes!

SOLNESS. - and waved and flourished with her flag, so that I, so that it almost made me giddy to look at it.

HILDA. [In a lower voice, seriously.] That little devil, that was *I*.

SOLNESS. [Fixes his eyes steadily upon her.] I am sure of that now. It must have been you.

HILDA. [Lively again.] Oh, it was so gloriously thrilling! I could not have believed there was a builder in the whole world that could build such a tremendously high tower. And then, that you yourself should stand at the very top of it, as large as life! And that you should not be the least bit dizzy! It was that above everything that made one, made one dizzy to think of.

SOLNESS. How could you be so certain that I was not?

HILDA. [Scouting the idea.] No indeed! Oh no! I knew that instinctively. For if you had been, you could never have stood up there and sung.

SOLNESS. [Looks at her in astonishment.] Sung? Did *I* sing?

HILDA. Yes, I should think you did.

SOLNESS.

[Shakes his head.] I have never sung a note in my life.

HILDA. Yes, indeed, you sang then. It sounded like harps in the air.

SOLNESS. [Thoughtfully.] This is very strange all this.

HILDA. [Is silent awhile, looks at him and says in a low voice:] But then, it was after that, that the real thing happened.

SOLNESS. The real thing?

HILDA. [Sparking with vivacity.] Yes, I surely don't need to remind you of that?

SOLNESS. Oh yes do remind me a little of that, too.

HILDA. Don't you remember that a great dinner was given in your honour at the Club?

SOLNESS. Yes, to be sure. It must have been the same afternoon, for I left the place next morning.

HILDA. And from the Club you were invited to come round to our house to supper.

SOLNESS. Quite right, Miss Wangel. It is wonderful how all these trifles have impressed themselves on your mind.

HILDA. Trifles! I like that! Perhaps it was a trifle, too, that I was alone in the room when you came in?

SOLNESS. Were you alone?

HILDA. [Without answering him.] You didn't call me a little devil then?

SOLNESS. No, I suppose I did not.

HILDA. You said I was lovely in my white dress, and that I looked like a little princess.

SOLNESS. I have no doubt you did, Miss Wangel. And besides, I was feeling so buoyant and free that day

HILDA. And then you said that when I grew up I should be your princess.

SOLNESS. [Laughing a little.] Dear, dear, did I say that too?

HILDA. Yes, you did. And when I asked how long I should have to wait, you said that you would come again in ten years, like a troll, and carry me off, to Spain or some such place. And you promised you would buy me a kingdom there.

SOLNESS. [As before.] Yes, after a good dinner one doesn't haggle about the halfpence. But did I really say all that?

HILDA. [Laughs to herself.] Yes. And you told me, too, what the kingdom was to be called.

SOLNESS. Well, what was it?

HILDA. It was to be called the kingdom of Orangia,* you said.

*In the original "Appelsinia," "appelsin" meaning "orange."

SOLNESS. Well, that was an appetising name.

HILDA. No, I didn't like it a bit; for it seemed as though you wanted to make game of me.

SOLNESS. I am sure that cannot have been my intention.

HILDA. No, I should hope not, considering what you did next

SOLNESS. What in the world did I do next?

HILDA. Well, that's the finishing touch, if you have forgotten that too. I should have thought no one could help remembering such a thing as that.

SOLNESS. Yes, yes, just give me a hint, and then perhaps Well?

HILDA. [Looks fixedly at him.] You came and kissed me, Mr. Solness.

SOLNESS. [Open-mouthed.] *I* did!

HILDA. Yes, indeed you did. You took me in both your arms, and bent my head back, and kissed me many times.

SOLNESS. Now really, my dear Miss Wangel!

HILDA. [Rises.] You surely cannot mean to deny it?

SOLNESS. Yes, I do. I deny it altogether!

HILDA. [Looks scornfully at him.] Oh, indeed!
[She turns and goes slowly up to the stove, where she remains standing motionless, her face averted from him, her hands behind her back. Short pause.

SOLNESS. [Goes cautiously up behind her.] Miss Wangel!

HILDA. [Is silent and does not move.]

SOLNESS. Don't stand there like a statue. You must have dreamt all this. [Lays his hand on her arm.] Now just listen

HILDA. [Makes an impatient movement with her arm.]

SOLNESS. [As a thought flashes upon him.] Or! Wait a moment! There is something under all this, you may depend!

HILDA. [Does not move.]

SOLNESS. [In a low voice, but with emphasis.] I must have thought all that. I must have wished it, have willed it, have longed to do it. And then. May not that be the explanation.

HILDA. [Is still silent.]

SOLNESS. [Impatiently.] Oh very well, deuce take it all, then I did do it, I suppose.

HILDA. [Turns her head a little, but without looking at him.] Then you admit it now?

SOLNESS. Yes, whatever you like.

HILDA. You came and put your arms round me?

SOLNESS. Oh yes!

HILDA. And bent my head back?

SOLNESS. Very far back.

HILDA. And kissed me?

SOLNESS. Yes, I did.

HILDA. Many times?

SOLNESS. As many as ever you like.

HILDA. [Turns quickly toward him and has once more the sparkling expression of gladness in her eyes.] Well, you see, I got it out of you at last!

SOLNESS. [With a slight smile.] Yes, just think of my forgetting such a thing as that.

HILDA. [Again a little sulky, retreats from him.] Oh, you have kissed so many people in your time, I suppose.

SOLNESS. No, you mustn't think that of me. [HILDA seats herself in the arm-chair. SOLNESS stands and leans against the rocking-chair. Looks observantly at her.] Miss Wangel!

HILDA. Yes!

SOLNESS. How was it now? What came of all this, between us two.

HILDA. Why, nothing more came of it. You know that quite well. For then the other guests came in, and then, bah!

SOLNESS. Quite so! The others came in. To think of my forgetting that too!

HILDA. Oh, you haven't really forgotten anything: you are only a little ashamed of it all. I am sure one doesn't forget things of that kind.

SOLNESS. No, one would suppose not.

HILDA. [Lively again, looks at him.] Perhaps you have even forgotten what day it was?

SOLNESS. What day?

HILDA. Yes, on what day did you hang the wreath on the tower? Well? Tell me at once!

SOLNESS. H'm, I confess I have forgotten the particular day. I only know it was ten years ago. Some time in autumn.

HILDA. [Nods her head slowly several times.] It was ten years ago, on the 19th of September.

SOLNESS. Yes, it must have been about that time. Fancy your remembering that too! [Stops.] But wait a moment! Yes, it's the 19th of September today.

HILDA. Yes, it is; and the ten years are gone. And you didn't come as you had promised me.

SOLNESS. Promised you? Threatened, I suppose you mean?

HILDA. I don't think there was any sort of threat in that.

SOLNESS. Well then, a little bit of fun.

HILDA. Was that all you wanted? To make fun of me?

SOLNESS. Well, or to have a little joke with you. Upon my soul, I don't recollect. But it must have been something of that kind; for you were a mere child then.

HILDA. Oh, perhaps I wasn't quite such a child either. Not such a mere chit as you imagine.

SOLNESS. [Looks searchingly at her.] Did you really and seriously expect me to come again?

HILDA. [Conceals a half-teasing smile.] Yes, indeed! I did expect that of you.

SOLNESS. That I should come back to your home, and take you away with me?

HILDA. Just like a troll, yes.

SOLNESS. And make a princess of you?

HILDA. That's what you promised.

SOLNESS. And give you a kingdom as well?

HILDA. [Looks up at the ceiling.] Why not? Of course it need not have been an actual, everyday sort of a kingdom.

SOLNESS. But something else just as good?

HILDA. Yes, at least as good. [Looks at him a moment.] I thought, if you could build the highest church-towers in the world, you could surely manage to raise a kingdom of one sort or another as well.

SOLNESS. [Shakes his head.] I can't quite make you out, Miss Wangel.

HILDA. Can you not? To me it seems all so simple.

SOLNESS. No, I can't make up my mind whether you mean all you say, or are simply having a joke with me.

HILDA. [Smiles.] Making fun of you, perhaps? I, too?

SOLNESS. Yes, exactly. Making fun of both of us. [Looks at her.] Is it long since you found out that I was married?

HILDA. I have know it all along. Why do you ask me that?

SOLNESS. [Lightly.] Oh, well, it just occurred to me. [Looks earnestly at her, and says in a low voice.] What have you come for?

HILDA. I want my kingdom. The time is up.

SOLNESS. [Laughs involuntarily.] What a girl you are!

HILDA. [Gaily.] Out with my kingdom, Mr. Solness! [Raps with her fingers.] The kingdom on the table!

SOLNESS. [Pushing the rocking-chair nearer and sitting down.] Now, seriously speaking, what have you come for? What do you really want to do here?

HILDA. Oh, first of all, I want to go round and look at all the things that you have built.

SOLNESS. That will give you plenty of exercise.

HILDA. Yes, I know you have built a tremendous lot.

SOLNESS. I have indeed especially of late years.

HILDA. Many church-towers among the rest? Immensely high ones?

SOLNESS. No. I build no more church-towers now. Nor churches either.

HILDA. What do you build then?

SOLNESS. Homes for human beings.

HILDA. [Reflectively.] Couldn't you build a little, -a little bit of a church-tower over these homes as well?

SOLNESS. [Starting.] What do you mean by that?

HILDA. I mean, something that points, points up into the free air. With the vane at a dizzy height.

SOLNESS. [Pondering a little.] Strange that you should say that for that is just what I am most anxious to do.

HILDA. [Impatiently.] Why don't you do it, then?

SOLNESS. [Shakes his head.] No, the people will not have it.

HILDA. Fancy their not wanting it!

SOLNESS. [More lightly.] But now I am building a new home for myself, just opposite here.

HILDA. For yourself?

SOLNESS. Yes. It is almost finished. And on that there is a tower.

HILDA. A high tower?

SOLNESS. Yes.

HILDA. Very high?

SOLNESS. No doubt people will say it is too high, too high for a dwelling-house.

HILDA. I'll go out to look at that tower first thing to-morrow morning.

SOLNESS. [Sits resting his cheek on his hand, and gazes at her.] Tell me, Miss Wangel, what is your name? Your Christian name, I mean.

HILDA. Why, Hilda, of course.

SOLNESS. [As before.] Hilda? Indeed?

HILDA. Don't you remember that? You called me Hilda yourself, that day when you misbehaved.

SOLNESS. Did I really.

HILDA. But then you said "little Hilda"; and I didn't like that.

SOLNESS. Oh, you didn't like that, Miss Hilda?

HILDA. No, not at such a time as that. But "Princess Hilda" that will sound very well, I think.

SOLNESS. Very well indeed. Princess Hilda of, of, what was to be the name of the kingdom?

HILDA. Pooh! I won't have anything to do with that stupid kingdom. I have set my heart upon quite a different one!

SOLNESS. [Has leaned back in the chair, still gazing at her.] Isn't it strange? The more I think of it now, the more it seems to me as though I had gone about all these years torturing myself with, h'm

HILDA. With what?

SOLNESS. With the effort to recover something, some experience, which I seemed to have forgotten. But I never had the least inkling of what it could be.

HILDA. You should have tied a knot in your pocket-handkerchief, Mr. Solness.

SOLNESS. In that case, I should simply have had to go racking my brains to discover what the knot could mean.

HILDA. Oh yes, I suppose there are trolls of that kind in the world, too.

SOLNESS. [Rises slowly.] What a good thing it is that you have come to me now.

HILDA. [Looks deeply into his eyes.] Is it a good thing!

SOLNESS. For I have been so lonely here. I have been gazing so helplessly at it all. [In a lower voice.] I must tell you, I have begun to be afraid of the younger generation.

HILDA. [With a little snort of contempt.] Pooh, is the younger generation something to be afraid of?

SOLNESS. It is indeed. And that is why I have locked and barred myself in. [Mysteriously.] I tell you the younger generation will one day come and thunder at my door! They will break in upon me!

HILDA. Then I should say you ought to go out and open the door to the younger generation.

SOLNESS. Open the door?

HILDA. Yes. Let them come in to you on friendly terms, as it were.

SOLNESS. No, no, no! The younger generation, it means retribution, you see. It comes, as if under a new banner, heralding the turn of fortune.

HILDA. [Rises, looks at him, and says with a quivering twitch of her lips.] Can *I* be of any use to you, Mr. Solness?

SOLNESS. Yes, you can indeed! For you, too, come, under a new banner it seems to me. You marshalled against youth!

DR. HERDAL comes in by the hall-door.

DR. HERDAL. What-, you and Miss Wangel here still?

SOLNESS. Yes. We have had no end of things to talk about.

HILDA. Both old and new.

DR. HERDAL. Have you really?

HILDA. Oh, it has been the greatest fun. For Mr. Solness, he has such a miraculous memory. All the least little details he remembers instantly.

MRS. SOLNESS enters by the door on the right.

MRS. SOLNESS. Well, Miss Wangel, your room is quite ready for you now.

HILDA. Oh, how kind you are to me!

SOLNESS. [To MRS. SOLNESS.] The nursery?

MRS. SOLNESS. Yes, the middle one. But first let us go in to supper.

SOLNESS. [Nods to HILDA.] Hilda shall sleep in the nursery, she shall.

MRS. SOLNESS. [Looks at him.] Hilda?

SOLNESS. Yes, Miss Wangel's name is Hilda. I knew her when she was a child.

MRS. SOLNESS. Did you really, Halvard? Well, shall we go?
[She takes DR. HERDAL's arm and goes out with him to the right. HILDA has meanwhile been collecting her travelling things.

HILDA. [Softly and rapidly to SOLNESS.] Is it true, what you said? Can I be of use to you?

SOLNESS. [Takes the things from her.] You are the very being I have needed most.

HILDA. [Looks at him with happy, wondering eyes and clasps her hands.] But then, great heavens!

SOLNESS. [Eagerly.] What?

HILDA. Then I have my kingdom!

SOLNESS. [Involuntarily.] Hilda!

HILDA. [Again with the quivering twitch of her lips.] Almost, I was going to say.
[She goes out to the right, SOLNESS follows her.

Act Second.

A prettily furnished small drawing-room in SOLNESS'S house. In the back, a glass-door leading out to the verandah and garden. The right-hand corner is cut off transversely by a large bay-window, in which are flower-stands. The left- hand corner is similarly cut off by a transverse wall, in which is a small door papered like the wall. On each side, an ordinary door. In front, on the right, a console table with a large mirror over it. Well-filled stands of plants and flowers. In front, on the left, a sofa with a table and chairs. Further back, a bookcase. Well forward in the room, before the bay window, a small table and some chairs. It is early in the day.

SOLNESS sits by the little table with RAGNAR BROVIK'S portfolio open in front of him. He is turning the drawings over and closely examining some of them. MRS. SOLNESS moves about noiselessly with a small watering-pot, attending to her flowers. She is dressed in black as before. Her hat, cloak and parasol lie on a chair near the mirror. Unobserved by her, SOLNESS now and again follows her with his eyes. Neither of them speaks.

KAIA FOSLI enters quietly by the door on the left.

SOLNESS. [Turns his head, and says in an off-hand tone of indifference:] Well, is that you?

KAIA. I merely wished to let you know that I have come.

SOLNESS. Yes, yes, that's all right. Hasn't Ragnar come too?

KAIA. No, not yet. He had to wait a little while to see the doctor. But he is coming presently to hear

SOLNESS. How is the old man to-day?

KAIA. Not well. He begs you to excuse him; he is obliged to keep his bed to-day.

SOLNESS. Why, of course; by all means let him rest. But now, get to your work.

KAIA. Yes. [Pauses at the door.] Do you wish to speak to Ragnar when he comes?

SOLNESS. No, I don't know that I have anything particular to say to him.
[KAIA goes out again to the left. SOLNESS remains seated, turning over the drawings.

MRS. SOLNESS. [Over beside the plants.] I wonder if he isn't going to die now, as well?

SOLNESS. [Looks up at her.] As well as who?

MRS. SOLNESS. [Without answering.] Yes, yes, depend upon it, Halvard, old Brovik is going to die too. You'll see that he will.

SOLNESS. My dear Aline, ought you not to go out for a little walk?

MRS. SOLNESS. Yes, I suppose I ought to.
[She continues to attend the flowers.

SOLNESS. [Bending over the drawings.] Is she still asleep?

MRS. SOLNESS. [Looking at him.] Is it Miss Wangel you are sitting there thinking about?

SOLNESS. [Indifferently.] I just happened to recollect her.

MRS. SOLNESS. Miss Wangle was up long ago.

SOLNESS. Oh, was she?

MRS. SOLNESS. When I went in to see her, she was busy putting her things in order.
[She goes in front of the mirror and slowly begins to put on her hat.

SOLNESS. [After a short pause.] So we have found a use for one our nurseries after all, Aline.

MRS. SOLNESS. Yes, we have.

SOLNESS. That seems to me better than to have them all standing empty.

MRS. SOLNESS. That emptiness is dreadful; you are right there.

SOLNESS. [Closes the portfolio, rises and approaches her.] You will find that we shall get on far better after this, Aline. Things will be more comfortable. Life will be easier, especially for you.

MRS. SOLNESS. [Looks at him.] After this?

SOLNESS. Yes, believe me, Aline

MRS. SOLNESS. Do you mean because she has come here?

SOLNESS. [Checking himself.] I mean, of course, when once we have moved into the new home.

MRS. SOLNESS. [Takes her cloak.] Ah, do you think so, Halvard? Will it be better then?

SOLNESS. I can't think otherwise. And surely you think so too?

MRS. SOLNESS. I think nothing at all about the new house.

SOLNESS. [Cast down.] It's hard for me to hear you say that; for you know it is mainly for your sake that I have built it.
[He offers to help her on with her cloak.

MRS. SOLNESS. [Evades him.] The fact is, you do far too much for my sake.

SOLNESS. [With a certain vehemence.] No, no, you really mustn't say that, Aline! I cannot bear to hear you say such things!

MRS. SOLNESS. Very well, then I won't say it, Halvard.

SOLNESS. But I stick to what *I* said. You'll see that things will be easier for you in the new place.

MRS. SOLNESS. Oh, heavens, easier for me!

SOLNESS. [Eagerly.] Yes, indeed they will! You may be quite sure of that! For you see, there will be so very, very much there that will remind you of your own home

MRS. SOLNESS. The home that used to be father's and mother's and that was burnt to the ground

SOLNESS. [In a low voice.] Yes, yes, my poor Aline. That was a terrible blow for you.

MRS. SOLNESS. [Breaking out in lamentation.] You may build as much as ever you like, Halvard, you can never build up again a real home for me!

SOLNESS. [Crosses the room.] Well, in Heaven's name, let us talk no more about it then.

MRS. SOLNESS. We are not in the habit of talking about it. For you always put the thought away from you

SOLNESS. [Stops suddenly and looks at her.] Do I? And why should I do that? Put the thought away from me?

MRS. SOLNESS. Oh yes, Halvard, I understand you very well. You are so anxious to spare me and to find excuses for me too as much as ever you can.

SOLNESS. [With astonishment in his eyes.] You! Is it you, yourself, that your are talking about, Aline?

MRS. SOLNESS. Yes, who else should it be but myself?

SOLNESS. [Involuntarily to himself.] That too!

MRS. SOLNESS. As for the old house, I wouldn't mind so much about that. When once misfortune was in the air, why

SOLNESS. Ah, you are right there. Misfortune will have its way as the saying goes.

MRS. SOLNESS. But it's what came of the fire, the dreadful thing that followed! That is the thing! That, that, that!

SOLNESS. [Vehemently.] Don't think about that, Aline!

MRS. SOLNESS. Ah, that is exactly what I cannot help thinking about. And now, at last, I must speak about it, too; for I don't seem to be able to bear it any longer. And then never to be able to forgive myself

SOLNESS. [Exclaiming.] Yourself!

MRS. SOLNESS. Yes, for I had duties on both sides, both towards you and towards the little ones. I ought to have hardened myself not to have let the horror take such hold upon me, nor the grief for the burning of my home. [Wrings her hands.] Oh, Halvard, if I had only had the strength!

SOLNESS. [Softly, much moved, comes closer.] Aline, you must promise me never to think these thoughts any more. Promise me that, dear!

MRS. SOLNESS. Oh, promise, promise! One can promise anything.

SOLNESS. [Clenches his hands and crosses the room.] Oh, but this is hopeless, hopeless! Never a ray of sunlight! Not so much as a gleam of brightness to light up our home!

MRS. SOLNESS. This is no home, Halvard.

SOLNESS. Oh no, you may well say that. [Gloomily.] And God knows whether you are not right in saying that it will be no better for us in the new house, either.

MRS. SOLNESS. It will never be any better. Just as empty, just as desolate, there as here.

SOLNESS. [Vehemently.] Why in all the world have we built it then? Can you tell me that?

MRS. SOLNESS. No; you must answer that question for yourself.

SOLNESS. [Glances suspiciously at her.] What do you mean by that, Aline?

MRS. SOLNESS. What do I mean?

SOLNESS. Yes, in the devil's name! You said it so strangely as if you had some hidden meaning in it.

MRS. SOLNESS. No, indeed, I assure you

SOLNESS. [Comes closer.] Oh, come now, I know what I know. I have both my eyes and my ears about me, Aline, you may depend upon that!

MRS. SOLNESS. Why, what are you talking about? What is it?

SOLNESS. [Places himself in front of her.] Do you mean to say you don't find a kind of lurking, hidden meaning in the most innocent word I happen to say?

MRS. SOLNESS. *I* do you say? *I* do that?

SOLNESS. [Laughs.] Ho-ho-ho! It's natural enough, Aline! When you have a sick man on your hands

MRS. SOLNESS. [Anxiously.] Sick? Are you ill, Halvard?

SOLNESS. [Violently.] A half-mad man then! A crazy man! Call me what you will.

MRS. SOLNESS. [Feels blindly for a chair and sits down.] Halvard, for God's sake

SOLNESS. But you are wrong, both you and the doctor. I am not in the state that you imagine.
[He walks up and down the room. MRS. SOLNESS follows him anxiously with her eyes. Finally he goes up to her.

SOLNESS. [Calmly.] In reality there is nothing whatever the matter with me.

MRS. SOLNESS. No, there isn't, is there? But then what is it that troubles you so?

SOLNESS. Why this, that I often feel ready to sink under this terrible burden of debt

MRS. SOLNESS. Debt, do you say? But you owe no one anything, Halvard!

SOLNESS. [Softly, with emotion.] I owe a boundless debt to you, to you, to you, Aline.

MRS. SOLNESS. [Rises slowly.] What is behind all this? You may just as well tell me at once.

SOLNESS. But there is nothing behind it! I have never done you any wrong, not wittingly and willfully, at any rate. And yet, and yet it seems as though a crushing debt rested upon me and weighed me down.

MRS. SOLNESS. A debt to me?

SOLNESS. Chiefly to you.

MRS. SOLNESS. Then you are ill after all, Halvard.

SOLNESS. [Gloomily.] I suppose I must be, or not far from it. [Looks towards the door to the right, which is opened at this moment.] Ah! now it grows light.

HILDA WANGEL comes in. She has made some alteration in her dress, and let down her skirt.

HILDA. Good morning, Mr. Solness!

SOLNESS. [Nods.] Slept well?

HILDA. Quite deliciously! Like a child in a cradle. Oh, I lay and stretched myself like, like a princess!

SOLNESS. [Smiles a little.] You were thoroughly comfortable then?

HILDA. I should think so.

SOLNESS. And no doubt you dreamed, too.

HILDA. Yes, I did. But that was horrid.

SOLNESS. Was it?

HILDA. Yes, for I dreamed I was falling over a frightfully high, sheer precipice. Do you never have that kind of dream?

SOLNESS. Oh yes, now and then

HILDA. It's tremendously thrilling, when you fall and fall

SOLNESS. It seems to make one's blood run cold.

HILDA. Do you draw your legs up under you while you are falling?

SOLNESS. Yes, as high as ever I can.

HILDA. So do I.

MRS. SOLNESS. [Takes her parasol.] I must go into town now, Halvard. [To HILDA.] And I'll try to get one or two things that you may require.

HILDA. [Making a motion to throw her arms round her neck.] Oh, you dear, Mrs. Solness! You are really much too kind to me! Frightfully kind

MRS. SOLNESS. [Deprecatingly, freeing herself.] Oh, not at all. It's only my duty, so I am very glad to do it.

HILDA. [Offended, pouts.] But really, I think I am quite fit to be seen in the streets, now that I've put my dress to rights. Or do you think I am not?

MRS. SOLNESS. To tell you the truth, I think people would stare at you a little.

HILDA. [Contemptuously.] Pooh! Is that all? That only amuses me.

SOLNESS. [With suppressed ill-humour.] Yes, but people might take it into their heads that you were mad too, you see.

HILDA. Mad? Are there so many mad people here in town, then?

SOLNESS. [Points to his own forehead.] Here you see one at all events.

HILDA. You, Mr. Solness!

SOLNESS. Have you not noticed that yet?

HILDA. No, I certainly have not. [Reflects and laughs a little.] And yet, perhaps in one single thing.

SOLNESS. Ah, do you hear that, Aline?

MRS. SOLNESS. What is that one single thing, Miss Wangel?

HILDA. No, I won't say.

SOLNESS. Oh yes, do!

HILDA. No thank you, I am not so mad as that.

MRS. SOLNESS. When you and Miss Wangel are alone, I daresay she will tell you, Halvard.

SOLNESS. Ah, you think she will?

MRS. SOLNESS. Oh yes, certainly. For you have known her so well in the past. Ever since she was a child, you tell me.
[She goes out by the door on the left.

HILDA. [After a little while.] Does your wife dislike me very much?

SOLNESS. Did you think you noticed anything of the kind?

HILDA. Did you notice it yourself?

SOLNESS. [Evasively.] Aline has become exceedingly shy with strangers of late years.

HILDA. Has she really?

SOLNESS. But if only you could get to know her thoroughly! Ah, she is so good, so kind, so excellent a creature

HILDA. [Impatiently.] But if she is all that, what made her say that about her duty?

SOLNESS. Her duty?

HILDA. She said that she would go out and buy something for me, because it was her duty. Oh, I can't bear that ugly, horrid word!

SOLNESS. Why not?

HILDA. It sounds so could and sharp, and stinging. Duty, duty, duty. Don't you think so, too? Doesn't it seem to sting you?

SOLNESS. H'm, haven't thought much about it.

HILDA. Yes, it does. And if she is so good, as you say she is, why should she talk in that way?

SOLNESS. But, good Lord, what would you have had her say, then?

HILDA. She might have said she would do it because she had taken a tremendous fancy to me. She might have said something like that, something really warm and cordial, you understand.

SOLNESS. [Looks at her.] Is that how you would like to have it?

HILDA. Yes, precisely. [She wanders about the room, stops at the bookcase and looks at the books.] What a lot of books you have.

SOLNESS. Yes, I have got together a good many.

HILDA. Do you read them all, too?

SOLNESS. I used to try to. Do you read much?

HILDA. No, never! I have given it up. For it all seems so irrelevant.

SOLNESS. That is just my feeling.
[HILDA wanders about a little, stops at the small table, opens the portfolio and turns over the contents.

HILDA. Are all these your drawings yours?

SOLNESS. No, they are drawn by a young man whom I employ to help me.

HILDA. Some one you have taught?

SOLNESS. Oh yes, no doubt he has learnt something from me, too.

HILDA. [Sits down.] Then I suppose he is very clever. [Looks at a drawing.] Isn't he?

SOLNESS. Oh, he might be worse. For my purpose

HILDA. Oh yes, I'm sure he is frightfully clever.

SOLNESS. Do you think you can see that in the drawings?

HILDA. Pooh, these scrawlings! But if he has been learning from you

SOLNESS. Oh, so far as that goesthere are plenty of people here that have learnt from me, and have come to little enough for all that.

HILDA. [Looks at him and shakes her head.] No, I can't for the life of me understand how you can be so stupid.

SOLNESS. Stupid? Do you think I am so very stupid?

HILDA. Yes, I do indeed. If you are content to go about here teaching all these people

SOLNESS. [With a slight start.] Well, and why not?

HILDA. [Rises, half serious, half laughing.] No indeed, Mr. Solness! What can be the good of that? No one but you should be allowed to build. You should stand quite alone, do it all yourself. Now you know it.

SOLNESS. [Involuntarily.] Hilda!

HILDA. Well!

SOLNESS. How in the world did that come into your head?

HILDA. Do you think I am so very far wrong then?

SOLNESS. No, that's not what I mean. But now I'll tell you something.

HILDA. Well?

SOLNESS. I keep on, incessantly, in silence and alone, brooding on that very thought.

HILDA. Yes, that seems to me perfectly natural.

SOLNESS. [Looks somewhat searchingly at her.] Perhaps you have noticed it already?

HILDA. No, indeed I haven't.

SOLNESS. But just now, when you said you thought I was, off my balance? In one thing, you said

HILDA. Oh, I was thinking of something quite different.

SOLNESS. What was it?

HILDA. I am not going to tell you.

SOLNESS. [Crosses the room.] Well, well, as you please. [Stops at the bow- window.] Come here, and I will show you something.

HILDA. [Approaching.] What is it?

SOLNESS. Do you see over here in the garden?

HILDA. Yes?

SOLNESS. [Points.] Right above the great quarry?

HILDA. That new house, you mean?

SOLNESS. The one that is being built, yes. Almost finished.

HILDA. It seems to have a very high tower.

SOLNESS. The scaffolding is still up.

HILDA. Is that your new house?

SOLNESS. Yes.

HILDA. The house you are soon going to move into?

SOLNESS. Yes.

HILDA. [Looks at him.] Are there nurseries in that house, too?

SOLNESS. Three, as there are here.

HILDA. And no child.

SOLNESS. And there never will be one.

HILDA. [With a half-smile.] Well, isn't it just as I said?

SOLNESS. That?

HILDA. That you are a little, a little mad after all.

SOLNESS. Was that what you were thinking of?

HILDA. Yes, of all the empty nurseries I slept in.

SOLNESS. [Lowers his voice.] We have had children, Aline and I.

HILDA. [Looks eagerly at him.] Have you?

SOLNESS. Two little boys. They were of the same age.

HILDA. Twins, then.

SOLNESS. Yes, twins. It's eleven or twelve years ago now.

HILDA. [Cautiously.] And so both of them? You have lost both the twins, then?

SOLNESS. [With quiet emotion.] We kept them only about three weeks. Or scarcely so much. [Bursts forth.] Oh, Hilda, I can't tell you what a good thing it is for me that you have come! For now at last I have some one to talk to!

HILDA. Can you not talk to her, too?

SOLNESS. Not about this. Not as I want to talk and must talk. [Gloomily.] And not about so many other things, either.

HILDA. [In a subdued voice.] Was that all you meant when you said you need me?

SOLNESS. That was mainly what I meant at all events, yesterday. For to-day I am not so sure [Breaking off.] Come here and let us sit down, Hilda. Sit there on the sofa so that you can look into the garden. [HILDA seats herself in the corner of the sofa. SOLNESS brings a chair closer.] Should you like to hear about it?

HILDA. Yes, I shall love to sit and listen to you.

SOLNESS. [Sits down.] Then I will tell you all about it.

HILDA. Now I can see both the garden and you, Mr. Solness. So now, tell away! Begin!

SOLNESS. [Points towards the bow-window.] Out there on the rising ground, where you see the new house

HILDA. Yes?

SOLNESS. Aline and I lived there in the first years of our married life. There was an old house up there that had belonged to her mother; and we inherited it, and the whole of the great garden with it.

HILDA. Was there a tower on that house, too?

SOLNESS. No, nothing of the kind. From the outside it looked like a great, dark, ugly wooden box; but all the same, it was snug and comfortable enough inside.

HILDA. Then did you pull down the ramshackle old place?

SOLNESS. No, it was burnt down.

HILDA. The whole of it?

SOLNESS. Yes.

HILDA. Was that a great misfortune for you?

SOLNESS. That depends on how you look at it. As a builder, the fire was the making of me

HILDA. Well, but

SOLNESS. It was just after the birth of the two little boys

HILDA. The poor little twins, yes.

SOLNESS. They came healthy and bonny into the world. And they were growing too, you could see the difference day to day.

HILDA. Little children do grow quickly at first.

SOLNESS. It was the prettiest sight in the world to see Aline lying with the two of them in her arms. But then came the night of the fire

HILDA. [Excitedly.] What happened? Do tell me! Was any one burnt?

SOLNESS. No, not that. Every one got safe and sound out of the house

HILDA. Well, and what then?

SOLNESS. The fright had shaken Aline terribly. The alarm, the escape, the break-neck hurry and then the ice-cold night air, for they had to be carried out just as they lay, both she and the little ones.

HILDA. Was it too much for them?

SOLNESS. Oh no, they stood it well enough. But Aline fell into a fever, and it affected her milk. She would insist on nursing them herself; because it was her duty, she said. And both our little boys, they [Clenching his hands.] they, oh!

HILDA. They did not get over that?

SOLNESS. No, that they did not get over. That was how we lost them.

HILDA. It must have been terribly hard for you.

SOLNESS. Hard enough for me; but ten time harder for Aline. [Clenching his hands in suppressed fury.] Oh, that such things should be allowed to happen here the world! [Shortly and firmly.] From the day I lost them, I had no heart for building churches.

HILDA. Did you not like building the church-tower in our town?

SOLNESS. I didn't like it. I know how free and happy I felt when that tower was finished.

HILDA. *I* know that, too.

SOLNESS. And now I shall never, never build anything of that sort again! Neither churches nor church-towers.

HILDA. [Nods slowly.] Nothing but houses for people to live in.

SOLNESS. Homes for human beings, Hilda.

HILDA. But homes with high towers and pinnacles upon them.

SOLNESS. If possible. [Adopts a lighter tone.] But, as I said before, that fire was the making of me, as a builder, I mean.

HILDA. Why don't you call yourself an architect, like the others?

SOLNESS. I have not been systematically enough taught for that. Most of what I know I have found out for myself.

HILDA. But you succeeded all the same.

SOLNESS. Yes, thanks to the fire. I laid out almost the whole of the garden in villa lots; and there I was able to build after my own heart. So I came to the front with a rush.

HILDA. [Looks keenly at him.] You must surely be a very happy man, as matters stand with you.

SOLNESS. [Gloomily.] Happy? Do you say that, too, like all the rest of them?

HILDA. Yes, I should say you must be. If you could only cease thing about the two little children

SOLNESS. [Slowly.] The two little children, they are not so easy to forget, Hilda.

HILDA. [Somewhat uncertainly.] Do you still feel their loss so much, after all these years?

SOLNESS. [Looks fixedly at her, without replying.] A happy man you said

HILDA. Well, now, are you not happy in other respects?

SOLNESS. [Continues to look at her.] When I told you all this about the fire, h'm

HILDA. Well?

SOLNESS. Was there not one special thought that you, that you seized upon?

HILDA. [Reflects in vain.] No. What thought should that be?

SOLNESS. [With subdued emphasis.] It was simply and solely by that fire that I was enabled to build homes for human beings. Cosy, comfortable, bright homes, where father and mother and the whole troop of children can live in safety and gladness, feeling what a happy thing it is to be alive in the world and most of all to belong to each other, in great things and in small.

HILDA. [Ardently.] Well, and is it not a great happiness for you to be able to build such beautiful homes?

SOLNESS. The price, Hilda! The terrible price I had to pay for the opportunity!

HILDA. But can you never get over that?

SOLNESS. No. That I might build homes for others, I had to forego, to forego for all time, the home that might have been my own. I mean a home for a troop of children and for father and mother, too.

HILDA. [Cautiously.] But need you have done that? For all time, you say?

SOLNESS. [Nods slowly.] That was the price of this happiness that people talk about. [Breathes heavily.] This happiness, h'm, this happiness was not to be bought any cheaper, Hilda.

HILDA. [As before.] But may it not come right even yet?

SOLNESS. Never in this world, never. That is another consequence of the fire and of Aline's illness afterwards.

HILDA. [Looks at him with an indefinable expression.] And yet you build all these nurseries.

SOLNESS. [Seriously.] Have you never noticed, Hilda, how the impossible, how it seems to beckon and cry aloud to one?

HILDA. [Reflecting.] The impossible? [With animation.] Yes, indeed! Is that how you feel too?

SOLNESS. Yes, I do.

HILDA. Then there must be a little of the troll in you too.

SOLNESS. Why of the troll?

HILDA. What would you call it, then?

SOLNESS. [Rises.] Well, well, perhaps you are right. [Vehemently.] But how can I help turning into a troll, when this is how it always goes with me in everything, in everything!

HILDA. How do you mean?

SOLNESS. [Speaking low, with inward emotion.] Mark what I say to you, Hilda. All that I have succeeded in doing, building, creating all the beauty, security, cheerful comfort, ay, and magnificence too [Clenches his hands.] Oh, is it not terrible even to think of?

HILDA. What is so terrible?

SOLNESS. That all this I have to make up for, to pay for, not in money, but in human happiness. And not with my own happiness only, but with other people's too. Yes, yes, do you see that, Hilda? That is the price which my position as an artist has cost me and others. And every single day I have to look on while the price is paid for me anew. Over again, and over again, and over again for ever!

HILDA. [Rises and looks steadily at him.] Now I can see that you are thinking of, of her.

SOLNESS. Yes, mainly of Aline. For Aline she, too, had her vocation in life, just as much as I had mine. [His voice quivers.] But her vocation has had to be stunted, and crushed, and shattered in order that mine might force its way to, to a sort of great victory. For you must know that Aline, she, too, had a talent for building.

HILDA. She! For building?

SOLNESS. [Shakes his head.] Not houses and towers, and spires, not such things as I work away at

HILDA. Well, but what then?

SOLNESS. [Softly, with emotion.] For building up the souls of little children, Hilda. For building up children's souls in perfect balance, and in noble and beautiful forms. For enabling them to soar up into erect and full-grown human souls. That was Aline's talent. And there it all lies now, unused and unusable for ever, of no earthly service to any one, just like the ruins left by a fire.

HILDA. Yes, but even if this were so?

SOLNESS. It is so! It is so! I know it!

HILDA. Well, but in any case it is not your fault.

SOLNESS. [Fixes his eyes on her, and nods slowly.] Ah, that is the great, the terrible question. That is the doubt that is gnawing me, night and day.

HILDA. That?

SOLNESS. Yes. Suppose the fault was mine, in a certain sense.

HILDA. Your fault! The fire!

SOLNESS. All of it; the whole thing. And yet, perhaps, I may not have had anything to do with it.

HILDA. [Looks at him with a troubled expression.] Oh, Mr. Solness, if you can talk like that, I am afraid you must be, ill after all.

SOLNESS. H'm, I don't think I shall ever be of quite sound mind on that point.

RAGNAR BROVIK cautiously opens the little door in the left- hand corner. HILDA comes forward.

RAGNAR. [When he sees Hilda.] Oh. I beg pardon, Mr. Solness [He makes a movement to withdraw.

SOLNESS. No, no, don't go. Let us get it over.

RAGNAR. Oh, yes, if only we could.

SOLNESS. I hear your father is no better?

RAGNAR. Father is fast growing weaker and therefore I beg and implore you to write a few kind words for me on one of the plans! Something for father to read before he

SOLNESS. [Vehemently.] I won't hear anything more about those drawings of yours!

RAGNAR. Have you looked at them?

SOLNESS. Yes, I have.

RAGNAR. And they are good for nothing? And *I* am good for nothing, too?

SOLNESS. [Evasively.] Stay here with me, Ragnar. You shall have everything your own way. And then you can marry Kaia, and live at your ease and happily too, who knows? Only don't think of building on your own account.

RAGNAR. Well, well, then I must go home and tell father what you say, I promised I would. Is this what I am to tell father before he dies?

SOLNESS. [With a groan.] Oh tell him, tell him what you will, for me. Best to say nothing at all to him! [With a sudden outburst.] I cannot do anything else, Ragnar!

RAGNAR. May I have the drawings to take with me?

SOLNESS. Yes, take them, take them by all means! They are lying there on the table.

RAGNAR. [Goes to the table.] Thanks.

HILDA. [Puts her hand on the portfolio.] No, no; leave them here.

SOLNESS. Why?

HILDA. Because I want to look at them, too.

SOLNESS. But you have been [To RAGNAR.] Well, leave them here, then.

RAGNAR. Very well.

SOLNESS. And go home at once to your father.

RAGNAR. Yes, I suppose I must.

SOLNESS. [As if in desperation.] Ragnar, you must not ask me to do what is beyond my power! Do you hear, Ragnar? You must not!

RAGNAR. No, no. I beg you pardon
[He bows, and goes out by the corner door. HILDA goes over and sits down on a chair near the mirror.

HILDA. [Looks angrily at SOLNESS.] That was a very ugly thing to do.

SOLNESS. Do you think so, too?

HILDA. Yes, it was horribly ugly and hard and bad and cruel as well.

SOLNESS. Oh, you don't understand my position.

HILDA. No matter. I say you ought not to be like that.

SOLNESS. You said yourself, only just now, that no one but *I* ought to be allowed to build.

HILDA. *I* may say such things but you must not.

SOLNESS. I most of all, surely, who have paid so dear for my position.

HILDA. Oh yes, with what you call domestic comfort, and that sort of thing.

SOLNESS. And with my peace of soul into the bargain.

HILDA. [Rising.] Peace of soul! [With feeling.] Yes, yes, you are right in that! Poor Mr. Solness, you fancy that

SOLNESS. [With a quiet, chuckling laugh.] Just sit down again, Hilda, and I'll tell you something funny.

HILDA. [Sits down; with intent interest.] Well?

SOLNESS. It sounds such a ludicrous little thing; for, you see, the whole story turns upon nothing but a crack in the chimney.

HILDA. No more than that?

SOLNESS. No, not to begin with.
[He moves a chair nearer to HILDA and sits down.

HILDA. [Impatiently, taps on her knee.] Well, now for the crack in the chimney!

SOLNESS. I had noticed the split in the flue long, long before the fire. Every time I went up into the attic, I looked to see if it was still there.

HILDA. And it was?

SOLNESS. Yes; for no one else knew about it.

HILDA. And you said nothing?

SOLNESS. Nothing.

HILDA. And did not think of repairing the flue either?

SOLNESS. Oh yes, I thought about it but never got any further. Every time I intended to set to work, it seemed just as if a hand held me back. Not to-day, I thought, to-morrow; and nothing ever came of it.

HILDA. But why did you keep putting it off like that?

SOLNESS. Because I was revolving something in my mind. [Slowly, and in a low voice.] Through that little black crack in the chimney, I might, perhaps, force my way upwards as a builder.

HILDA. [Looking straight in front of her.] That must have been thrilling.

SOLNESS. Almost irresistible, quite irresistible. For at that time it appeared to me a perfectly simple and straightforward matter. I would have had it happen in the winter-time, a little before midday. I was to be out driving Aline in the sleigh. The servants at home would have made huge fires in the stoves.

HILDA. For, of course, it was to be bitterly cold that day?

SOLNESS. Rather biting, yes, and they would want Aline to find it thoroughly snug and warm when she came home.

HILDA. I suppose she is very chilly by nature?

SOLNESS. She is. And as we drove home, we were to see the smoke.

HILDA. Only the smoke?

SOLNESS. The smoke first. But when we came up to the garden gate, the whole of the old timber-box was to be a rolling mass of flames. That is how I wanted it to be, you see.

HILDA. Oh, why, why could it not have happened so!

SOLNESS. You may well say that, Hilda.

HILDA. Well, but now listen, Mr. Solness. Are you perfectly certain that the fire was caused by that little crack in the chimney!

SOLNESS. No, on the contrary, I am perfectly certain that the crack in the chimney had nothing whatever to do with the fire.

HILDA. What!

SOLNESS. It has been clearly ascertained that the fire broke out in a clothes- cupboard, in a totally different part of the house.

HILDA. Then what is all this nonsense you are talking about the crack in the chimney!

SOLNESS. May I go on talking to you a little, Hilda?

HILDA. Yes, if you'll only talk sensibly

SOLNESS. I will try to. [He moves his chair nearer.

HILDA. Out with it, then, Mr. Solness.

SOLNESS. [Confidentially.] Don't you agree with me, Hilda, that there exist special, chosen people who have been endowed with the power and faculty if desiring a thing, craving for a thing, willing a thing, so persistently and so, so inexorably, that at last it has to happen? Don't you believe that?

HILDA. [With an indefinable expression in her eyes.] If that is so, we shall see, one of these days, whether *I* am one of the chosen.

SOLNESS. It is not one's self alone that can do such great things. Oh, no, the helpers and the servers, they must do their part too, if it is to be of any good. But they never come of themselves. One has to call upon them very persistently, inwardly, you understand.

HILDA. What are these helpers and servers?

SOLNESS. Oh, we can talk about that some other time. For the present, let us keep to this business of the fire.

HILDA. Don't you think that fire would have happened all the same, even without your wishing for it?

SOLNESS. If the house had been old Knut Brovik's, it would never have burnt down so conveniently for him. I am sure of that; for he does not know how to call for the helpers, no, nor for the servers, either. [Rises in unrest.] So you see, Hilda, it is my fault, after all, that the lives of the two little boys had to be sacrificed. And do you think it is not my fault, too, that Aline has never been the woman she should and might have been and that she most longed to be?

HILDA. Yes, but if it is all the work of these helpers and servers?

SOLNESS. Who called for the helpers and servers? It was I! And they came and obeyed my will. [In increasing excitement.] That is what people call having the luck on your side; but I must tell you what this sort of luck feels like! It feels like a great raw place here on my breast. And the helpers and servers keep on flaying pieces of skin off other people in order to close my sore! But still the sore is not healed, never, never! Oh, if you knew how it can sometimes gnaw and burn!

HILDA. [Looks attentively at him.] You are ill, Mr. Solness. Very ill, I almost think.

SOLNESS. Say mad; for that is what you mean.

HILDA. No, I don't think there is much amiss with your intellect.

SOLNESS. With what then? Out with it!

HILDA. I wonder whether you were not sent into the world with a sickly conscience.

SOLNESS. A sickly conscience? What devilry is that?

HILDA. I mean that your conscience is feeble, too delicately built, as it were, hasn't strength to take a grip of things, to lift and bear what is heavy.

SOLNESS. [Growls.] H'm! May I ask, then, what sort of a conscience one ought to have?

HILDA. I should like your conscience to be, to be thoroughly robust.

SOLNESS. Indeed? Robust, eh? Is your own conscience robust, may I ask?

HILDA. Yes, I think it is. I have never noticed that it wasn't.

SOLNESS. It has not been put very severely to the test, I should think.

HILDA. [With a quivering of the lips.] Oh, it was no such simple matter to leave father, I am so awfully fond of him.

SOLNESS. Dear me! for a month or two

HILDA. I think I shall never go home again.

SOLNESS. Never? Then why did you leave him?

HILDA. [Half-seriously, half-banteringly.] Have you forgotten again that the ten year are up?

SOLNESS. Oh nonsense. Was anything wrong at home? Eh?

HILDA. [Quite seriously.] It was this impulse within me that urged and goaded me to come and lured and drew me on, as well.

SOLNESS. [Eagerly.] There we have it! There we have it, Hilda! There is the troll in you too, as in me. For it's the troll in one, you see, it is that that calls to the powers outside us. And then you must give in, whether you will or no.

HILDA. I almost think you are right, Mr. Solness.

SOLNESS. [Walks about the room.] Oh, there are devils innumerable abroad in the world, Hilda, that one never sees.

HILDA. Devils, too?

SOLNESS. [Stops.] Good devils and bad devils; light-haired devils and black- haired devils. If only you could always tell whether it is the light or dark ones that have got hold of you! [Paces about.] Ho-ho! Then it would be simple enough!

HILDA. [Follows him with her eyes.] Or if one had a really vigorous, radiantly healthy conscience, so that one dared to do what one would.

SOLNESS. [Stops beside the console table.] I believe, now, that most people are just as puny creatures as I am in that respect.

HILDA. I shouldn't wonder.

SOLNESS. [Leaning against the table.] In the sagas. Have you read any of the old sagas?

HILDA. Oh yes! When I used to read books, I

SOLNESS. In the sagas you read about vikings, who sailed to foreign lands, and plundered and burned and killed men

HILDA. And carried off women

SOLNESS. - and kept them in captivity

HILDA. - took them home in their ships

SOLNESS. - and behaved to them like, like the very worst of trolls.

HILDA. [Looks straight before her, with a half-veiled look.] I think that must have been thrilling.

SOLNESS. [With a short, deep laugh.] To carry off women, eh?

HILDA. To be carried off.

SOLNESS. [Looks at her a moment.] Oh, indeed.

HILDA. [As if breaking the thread of the conversation.] But what made you speak of these vikings, Mr. Solness?

SOLNESS. Why, those fellows must have had robust consciences, if you like! When they got home again, they could eat and drink, and be as happy as children. And the women, too! They often would not leave them on any account. Can you understand that, Hilda?

HILDA. Those women I can understand exceedingly well.

SOLNESS. Oho! Perhaps you could do the same yourself?

HILDA. Why not?

SOLNESS. Live, of your own free will, with a ruffian like that?

HILDA. If it was a ruffian I had come to love

SOLNESS. Could you come to love a man like that?

HILDA. Good heavens, you know very well one can't choose whom one is going to love.

SOLNESS. [Looks meditatively at her.] Oh no, I suppose it is the troll within one that's responsible for that.

HILDA. [Half-laughing.] And all those blessed devils, that you know so well, both the light-haired and the dark-haired ones.

SOLNESS. [Quietly and warmly.] Then I hope with all my heart that the devils will choose carefully for you, Hilda.

HILDA. For me they have chosen already, once and for all.

SOLNESS. [Looks earnestly at her.] Hilda, you are like a wild bird of the woods.

HILDA. Far from it. I don't hide myself away under the bushes.

SOLNESS. No, no. There is rather something of the bird of prey in you.

HILDA. That is nearer it, perhaps. [Very vehemently.] And why not a bird of prey? Why should not *I* go a-hunting, I, as well as the rest? Carry off the prey I want, if only I can get my claws into it, and do with it as I will.

SOLNESS. Hilda, do you know what you are?

HILDA. Yes, I suppose I am a strange sort of bird.

SOLNESS. No. You are like a dawning day. When I look at you, I seem to be looking towards the sunrise.

HILDA. Tell me, Mr. Solness, are you certain that you have never called me to you? Inwardly, you know?

SOLNESS. [Softly and slowly.] I almost think I must have.

HILDA. What did you want with me?

SOLNESS. You are the younger generation, Hilda.

HILDA. [Smiles.] That younger generation that you are so afraid of?

SOLNESS. [Nods slowly.] And which, in my heart, I yearn towards so deeply.
[HILDA rises, goes to the little table, and fetches RAGNAR BROVIK'S portfolio.

HILDA. [Holds out the portfolio to him.] We were talking of these drawings

SOLNESS. [Shortly, waving them away.] Put those things away! I have seen enough of them.

HILDA. Yes, but you have to write your approval on them.

SOLNESS. Write my approval on them? Never!

HILDA. But the poor old man is lying at death's door! Can't you give him and his son this pleasure before they are parted? And perhaps he might get the commission to carry them out, too.

SOLNESS. Yes, that is just what he would get. He has made sure of that, has my fine gentleman!

HILDA. Then, good heavens, if that is so, can't you tell the least little bit of a lie for once in a way?

SOLNESS. A lie? [Raging.] Hilda, take those devil's drawings out of my sight!

HILDA. [Draws the portfolio a little nearer to herself.] Well, well, well, don't bite me. You talk of trolls but I think you go on like a troll yourself. [Looks round.] Where do you keep your pen and ink?

SOLNESS. There is nothing of the sort in here.

HILDA. [Goes towards the door.] But in the office where that young lady is

SOLNESS. Stay where you are, Hilda! I ought to tell a lie, you say. Oh yes, for the sake of his old father I might well do that for in my time I have crushed him, trodden him under foot

HILDA. Him, too?

SOLNESS. I needed room for myself. But this Ragnar, he must on no account be allowed to come to the front.

HILDA. Poor fellow, there is surely no fear of that. If he has nothing in him

SOLNESS. [Comes closer, looks at her, and whispers.] If Ragnar Brovik gets his chance, he will strike me to the earth. Crush me, as I crushed his father.

HILDA. Crush you? Has he the ability for that?

SOLNESS. Yes, you may depend upon it he has the ability! He is the younger generation that stands ready to knock at my door, to make an end of Halvard Solness.

HILDA. [Looks at him with quiet reproach.] And yet you would bar him out. Fie, Mr. Solness!

SOLNESS. The fight I have been fighting has cost heart's blood enough. And I am afraid, too, that the helpers and servers will not obey me any longer.

HILDA. Then you must go ahead without them. There is nothing else for it.

SOLNESS. It is hopeless, Hilda. The luck is bound to turn. A little sooner or a little later. Retribution is inexorable.

HILDA. [In distress, putting her hands over her ears.] Don't talk like that! Do you want to kill me? To take from me what is more than my life?

SOLNESS. And what is that?

HILDA. The longing to see you great. To see you, with a wreath in your hand, high, high up upon a church-tower. [Calm again.] Come, out with your pencil now. You must have a pencil about you?

SOLNESS. [Takes out his pocket-book.] I have one here.

HILDA. [Lays the portfolio on the sofa-table.] Very well. Now let us two sit down here, Mr. Solness. [SOLNESS seats himself at the table. HILDA stands behind him, leaning over the back of the chair.] And now we well write on the drawings. We must write very, very nicely and cordially, for this horrid Ruar, or whatever his name is.

SOLNESS. [Writes a few words, turns his head and looks at her.] Tell me one thing, Hilda.

HILDA. Yes!

SOLNESS. If you have been waiting for me all these ten years

HILDA. What then?

SOLNESS. Why have you never written to me? Then I could have answered you.

HILDA. [Hastily.] No, no, no! That was just what I did not want.

SOLNESS. Why not?

HILDA. I was afraid the whole thing might fall to pieces. But we were going to write on the drawings, Mr. Solness.

SOLNESS. So we were.

HILDA. [Bends forward and looks over his shoulder while he writes.] Mind now, kindly and cordially! Oh how I hate, how I hate this Ruald

SOLNESS. [Writing.] Have you never really cared for any one, Hilda?

HILDA. For any one else, I suppose you mean?

SOLNESS. [Looks up at her.] For any one else, yes. Have you never? In all these ten years? Never?

HILDA. Oh yes, now and then. When I was perfectly furious with you for not coming.

SOLNESS. Then you did take an interest in other people, too?

HILDA. A little bit, for a week or so. Good heavens, Mr. Solness, you surely know how such things come about.

SOLNESS. Hilda, what is it you have come for?

HILDA. Don't waste time talking. The poor old man might go and die in the meantime.

SOLNESS. Answer me, Hilda. What do you want of me?

HILDA. I want my kingdom.

SOLNESS. H'm

He gives a rapid glance toward the door on the left, and then goes on writing on the drawings. At the same moment MRS. SOLNESS enters.

MRS. SOLNESS. Here are a few things I have got for you, Miss Wangel. The large parcels will be sent later on.

HILDA. Oh, how very, very kind of you!

MRS. SOLNESS. Only my simple duty. Nothing more than that.

SOLNESS. [Reading over what he has written.] Aline!

MRS. SOLNESS. Yes?

SOLNESS. Did you notice whether the, the book-keeper was out there?

MRS. SOLNESS. Yes, of course, she was there.

SOLNESS. [Puts the drawings in the portfolio.] H'm

MRS. SOLNESS. She was standing at the desk, as she always is, when *I* go through the room.

SOLNESS. [Rises.] Then I'll give this to her and tell her that

HILDA. [Takes the portfolio from him.] Oh, no, let me have the pleasure of doing that! [Goes to the door, but turns.] What is her name?

SOLNESS. Her name is Miss Fosli.

HILDA. Pooh, that sounds so cold! Her Christian name, I mean?

SOLNESS. Kaia, I believe.

HILDA. [Opens the door and calls out.] Kaia, come in here! Make haste! Mr. Solness wants to speak to you.

KAIA FOSLI appears at the door.

KAIA. [Looking at him in alarm.] Here I am?

HILDA. [Handing her the portfolio.] See her, Kaia! You can take this home; Mr. Solness was written on them now.

KAIA. Oh, at last!

SOLNESS. Give them to the old man as soon as you can.

KAIA. I will go straight home with them.

SOLNESS. Yes, do. Now Ragnar will have a chance of building for himself.

KAIA. Oh, may he come and thank you for all?

SOLNESS. [Harshly.] I won't have any thanks! Tell him that from me.

KAIA. Yes, I will

SOLNESS. And tell him at the same time that henceforward I do not require his services, nor yours either.

KAIA. [Softly and quiveringly.] Not mine either?

SOLNESS. You will have other things to think of now, and to attend to; and that is a very good thing for you. Well, go home with the drawings now, Miss Fosli. At once! Do you hear?

KAIA. [As before.] Yes, Mr. Solness. [She goes out.

MRS. SOLNESS. Heavens! what deceitful eyes she has.

SOLNESS. She? That poor little creature?

MRS. SOLNESS. Oh, I can see what I can see, Halvard. Are you really dismissing them?

SOLNESS. Yes.

MRS. SOLNESS. Her as well?

SOLNESS. Was not that what you wished?

MRS. SOLNESS. But how can you get on without her? Oh well, no doubt you have some one else in reserve, Halvard.

HILDA. [Playfully.] Well, *I* for one am not the person to stand at a desk.

SOLNESS. Never mind, never mind, it will be all right, Aline. Now all you have to do is think about moving into our new home as quickly as you can. This evening we will hang up the wreath [Turns to HILDA.] What do you say to that, Miss Hilda?

HILDA. [Looks at him with sparkling eyes.] It will be splendid to see you so high up once more.

SOLNESS. Me!

MRS. SOLNESS. For Heaven's sake, Miss Wangel, don't imagine such a thing! My husband! when he always gets so dizzy!

HILDA. He get dizzy! No, I know quite well he does not!

MRS. SOLNESS. Oh yes, indeed he does.

HILDA. But I have seen him with my own eyes right up at the top of a high church-tower!

MRS. SOLNESS. Yes, I hear people talk of that; but it is utterly impossible

SOLNESS. [Vehemently.] Impossible, impossible, yes! But there I stood all the same!

MRS. SOLNESS. O, how can you say so, Halvard? Why, you can't even bear to go out on the second-storey balcony here. You have always been like that.

SOLNESS. You may perhaps see something different this evening.

MRS. SOLNESS. [In alarm.] No, no, no! Please God I shall never see that. I will write at once to the doctor and I am sure he won't let you do it.

SOLNESS. Why, Aline!

MRS. SOLNESS. Oh, you know you're ill, Halvard. This proves it! Oh God, Oh God!
[She goes hastily out to the right.

HILDA. [Looks intently at him.] Is it so, or is it not?

SOLNESS. That I turn dizzy?

HILDA. That my master builder dares not, cannot, climb as high as he builds?

SOLNESS. Is that the way you look at it?

HILDA. Yes.

SOLNESS. I believe there is scarcely a corner in me that is safe from you.

HILDA. [Looks towards the bow-window.] Up there, then. Right up there

SOLNESS. [Approaches her.] You might have the topmost room in the tower, Hilda, there you might live like a princess.

HILDA. [Indefinably, between earnest and jest.] Yes, that is what you promised me.

SOLNESS. Did I really?

HILDA. Fie, Mr. Solness! You said I should be a princess, and that you would give me a kingdom. And then you went andWell!

SOLNESS. [Cautiously.] Are you quite certain that this is not a dream, a fancy, that has fixed itself in your mind?

HILDA. [Sharply.] Do you mean that you did not do it?

SOLNESS. I scarcely know myself. [More softly.] But now I know so much for certain, that I

HILDA. That you? Say it at once!

SOLNESS. that I ought to have done it.

HILDA. [Exclaims with animation.] Don't tell me you can ever be dizzy!

SOLNESS. This evening, then, we will hang up the wreath, Princess Hilda.

HILDA. [With a bitter curve of the lips.] Over your new home, yes.

SOLNESS. Over the new house, which will never be a home for me.
[He goes out through the garden door.

HILDA. [Looks straight in front of her with a far-away expression, and whispers to herself. The only words audible are:]frightfully thrilling

Act Third.

The large broad verandah of SOLNESS'S dwelling-house. Part of the house, with outer door leading to the verandah, is seen to the left. A railing along the verandah to the right. At the back, from the end of the verandah, a flight of steps leads down to the garden below. Tall old trees in the garden spread their branches over the verandah and towards the house. Far to the right, in among the trees, a glimpse is caught of the lower part of the new villa, with scaffolding round so much as is seen of the tower. In the background the garden is bounded by an old wooden fence. Outside the fence, a street with low, tumble-down cottages.

Evening sky with sun-lit clouds.

On the verandah, a garden bench stands along the wall of the house, and in front of the bench a long table. On the other side of the table, an arm-chair and some stools. All the furniture is of wicker-work.

MRS. SOLNESS, wrapped in a large white crepe shawl, sits resting in the arm-chair and gazes over to the right. Shortly after, HILDA WANGEL comes up the flight of steps from the garden. She is dressed as in the last act, and wears her hat. She has in her bodice a little nosegay of small common flowers.

MRS. SOLNESS. [Turning her head a little.] Have you been round the garden, Miss Wangel?

HILDA. Yes, I have been taking a look at it.

MRS. SOLNESS. And found some flowers too, I see.

HILDA. Yes, indeed! There are such heaps of them in among the bushes.

MRS. SOLNESS. Are there, really? Still? You see I scarcely ever go there.

HILDA. [Closer.] What! Don't you take a run down into the garden every day, then?

MRS. SOLNESS. [With a faint smile.] I don't "run" anywhere, nowadays.

HILDA. Well, but do you not go down now and then to look at all the lovely things there?

MRS. SOLNESS. It has all become so strange to me. I am almost afraid to see it again.

HILDA. Your own garden!

MRS. SOLNESS. I don't feel that it is mine any longer.

HILDA. What do you mean?

MRS. SOLNESS. No, no, it is not, not as it was in my mother's and father's time. They have taken away so much, so much of the garden, Miss Wangel. Fancy, they have parcelled it out and built houses for strangers, people that I don't know. And they can sit and look in upon me from their windows.

HILDA. [With a bright expression.] Mrs. Solness!

MRS. SOLNESS. Yes?

HILDA. May I stay here with you a little?

MRS. SOLNESS. Yes, by all means, if you care to.
[HILDA moves a stool close to the arm-chair and sits down.

HILDA. Ah, here one can sit and sun oneself like a cat.

MRS. SOLNESS. [Lays her hand softly on HILDA'S neck.] It is nice of you to be willing to sit with me. I thought you wanted to go in to my husband.

HILDA. What should I want with him?

MRS. SOLNESS. To help him, I thought.

HILDA. No, thank you. And besides, he is not in. He is over there with his workmen. But he looked so fierce that I did not dare to talk to him.

MRS. SOLNESS. He is so kind and gentle in reality.

HILDA. He!

MRS. SOLNESS. You do not really know him yet, Miss Wangel.

HILDA. [Looks affectionately at her.] Are you pleased at the thought of moving over to the new house?

MRS. SOLNESS. I ought to be pleased; for it is what Halvard wants

HILDA. Oh, not just on that account, surely?

MRS. SOLNESS. Yes, yes, Miss Wangel; for it is only my duty to submit myself to him. But very often it is dreadfully difficult to force one's mind to obedience.

HILDA. Yes, that must be difficult indeed.

MRS. SOLNESS. I can tell you it is when one has so many faults as I have

HILDA. When one has gone through so much trouble as you have

MRS. SOLNESS. How do you know about that?

HILDA. Your husband told me.

MRS. SOLNESS. To me he very seldom mentions these things. Yes, I can tell you I have gone through more than enough trouble in my life, Miss Wangel.

HILDA. [Looks sympathetically at her and nods slowly.] Poor Mrs. Solness. First of all there was the fire

MRS. SOLNESS. [With a sigh.] Yes, everything that was mine was burnt.

HILDA. And then came what was worse.

MRS. SOLNESS. [Looking inquiringly at her.] Worse?

HILDA. The worst of all.

MRS. SOLNESS. What do you mean?

HILDA. [Softly.] You lost the two little boys.

MRS. SOLNESS. Oh, yes, the boys. But, you see, that was a thing apart. That was a dispensation of Providence; and in such things one can only bow in submission, yes, and be thankful, too.

HILDA. Then you are so?

MRS. SOLNESS. Not always, I am sorry to say. I know well enough that it is my duty but all the same I cannot.

HILDA. No, no, I think that is only natural.

MRS. SOLNESS. And often and often I have to remind myself that it was a righteous punishment for me

HILDA. Why?

MRS. SOLNESS. Because I had not fortitude enough in misfortune.

HILDA. But I don't see that

MRS. SOLNESS. Oh, no, no, Miss Wangel do not talk to me any more about the two little boys. We ought to feel nothing but joy in thinking of them; for they are so happy, so happy now. No, it is the small losses in life that cut one to the heart, the loss of all that other people look upon as almost nothing.

HILDA. [Lays her arms on MRS. SOLNESS'S knees, and looks up at her affectionately.] Dear Mrs. Solness, tell me what things you mean!

MRS. SOLNESS. As I say, only little things. All the old portraits were burnt on the walls. And all the old silk dresses were burnt, what had belonged to the family for generations and generations. And all mother's and grandmother's lace, that was burnt, too. And only think, the jewels, too! [Sadly.] And then all the dolls.

HILDA. The dolls?

MRS. SOLNESS. [Choking with tears.] I had nine lovely dolls.

HILDA. And they were burnt too?

MRS. SOLNESS. All of them. Oh, it was hard, so hard for me.

HILDA. Had you put by all these dolls, then? Ever since you were little?

MRS. SOLNESS. I had not put them by. The dolls and I had gone on living together.

HILDA. After you were grown up?

MRS. SOLNESS. Yes, long after that.

HILDA. After you were married, too?

MRS. SOLNESS. Oh yes, indeed. So long as he did not see it. But they were all burnt up, poor things. No one thought of saving them. Oh, it is so miserable to think of. You mustn't laugh at me, Miss Wangel.

HILDA. I am not laughing in the least.

MRS. SOLNESS. For you see, in a certain sense, there was life in them, too. I carried them under my heart, like little unborn children.

DR. HERDAL, with his hat in his hand, comes out through the door, and observes MRS. SOLNESS. and HILDA.

DR. HERDAL. Well, Mrs. Solness, so you are sitting out here catching cold?

MRS. SOLNESS. I find it so pleasant and warm here to-day.

DR. HERDAL. Yes, yes. But is there anything going on here? I got a note from you.

MRS. SOLNESS. [Rises.] Yes, there is something I must talk to you about.

DR. HERDAL. Very well; then perhaps we better go in. [To HILDA.] Still in your mountaineering dress, Miss Wangel?

HILDA. [Gaily, rising.] Yes, in full uniform! But to-day I am not going climbing and breaking my neck. We two will stop quietly below and look on, doctor.

DR. HERDAL. What are we to look on at?

MRS. SOLNESS. [Softly, in alarm, to HILDA.] Hush, hush, for God's sake! He is coming! Try to get that idea out of his head. And let us be friends, Miss Wangel. Don't you think we can?

HILDA. [Throws her arms impetuously round MRS. SOLNESS'S neck.] Oh, if we only could!

MRS. SOLNESS. [Gently disengages herself.] There, there, there! There he comes, doctor. Let me have a word with you.

DR. HERDAL. Is it about him?

MRS. SOLNESS. Yes, to be sure it's about him. Do come in.

She and the doctor enter the house. Next moment SOLNESS comes up from the garden by the flight of steps. A serious look comes over HILDA'S face.

SOLNESS. [Glances at the house-door, which is closed cautiously from within.] Have you noticed, Hilda, that as soon as I come, she goes?

HILDA. I have noticed that as soon as you come, you make her go.

SOLNESS. Perhaps so. But I cannot help it. [Looks observantly at her.] Are you cold, Hilda? I think you look cold.

HILDA. I have just come up out of a tomb.

SOLNESS. What do you mean by that?

HILDA. That I have got chilled through and through, Mr. Solness.

SOLNESS. [Slowly.] I believe I understand

HILDA. What brings you up here just now?

SOLNESS. I caught sight of you from over there.

HILDA. But then you must have seen her too?

SOLNESS. I knew she would go at once if I came.

HILDA. Is it very painful for you that she should avoid you in this way?

SOLNESS. In one sense, it's a relief as well.

HILDA. Not to have her before your eyes?

SOLNESS. Yes.

HILDA. Not to be always seeing how heavily the loss of the little boys weighs upon her?

SOLNESS. Yes. Chiefly that.
[HILDA drifts across the verandah with her hands behind her back, stops at the railing and looks out over the garden.

SOLNESS. [After a short pause.] Did you have a long talk with her?
[HILDA stands motionless and does not answer.

SOLNESS. Had you a long talk, I asked? [HILDA is silent as before.

SOLNESS. What was she talking about, Hilda? [HILDA continues silent.

SOLNESS. Poor Aline! I suppose it was about the little boys.

HILDA.
[A nervous shudder runs through her; then she nods hurriedly once or twice.

SOLNESS. She will never get over it, never in this world. [Approaches her.] Now you are standing there again like a statue; just as you stood last night.

HILDA. [Turns and looks at him, with great serious eyes.] I am going away.

SOLNESS. [Sharply.] Going away!

HILDA. Yes.

SOLNESS. But I won't allow you to!

HILDA. What am I to do here now?

SOLNESS. Simply to be here, Hilda!

HILDA. [Measures him with a look.] Oh, thank you. You know it wouldn't end there.

SOLNESS. [Heedlessly.] So much the better!

HILDA. [Vehemently.] I cannot do any harm to one whom I know! I can't take away anything that belongs to her.

SOLNESS. Who wants you to do that?

HILDA. [Continuing.] A stranger, yes! for that is quite a different thing! A person I have never set eyes on. But one that I have come into close contact with! Oh no! Oh no! Ugh!

SOLNESS. Yes, but I never proposed you should.

HILDA. Oh, Mr. Solness, you know quite well what the end of it would be. And that is why I am going away.

SOLNESS. And what is to become of me when you are gone? What shall I have to live for then? After that?

HILDA. [With the indefinable look in her eyes.] It is surely not so hard for you. You have your duties to her. Live for those duties.

SOLNESS. Too late. These powers, these, these

HILDA. devils

SOLNESS. Yes, these devils! And the troll within me as well, they have drawn all the life-blood out of her. [Laughs in desperation.] They did it for my happiness! Yes, yes! [Sadly.] And now she is dead for my sake. And I am chained alive to a dead woman. [In wild anguish.] *I-I* who cannot live without joy in life! [HILDA moves round the table and seats herself on the bench, with her elbows on the table, and her head supported by her hands.

HILDA. [Sits and looks at him awhile.] What will you build next?

SOLNESS. [Shakes his head.] I don't believe I shall build much more.

HILDA. Not those cosy, happy homes for mother and father, and for the troop of children?

SOLNESS. I wonder whether there will be any use for such homes in the coming time.

HILDA. Poor Mr. Solness! And you have gone all these ten years and staked your whole life on that alone.

SOLNESS. Yes, you may well say so, Hilda.

HILDA. [With an outburst.] Oh, it all seems to me so foolish, so foolish!

SOLNESS. All what?

HILDA. Not to be able to grasp at your own happiness, at your own life! Merely because some one you know happens to stand in the way!

SOLNESS. One whom you have no right to set aside.

HILDA. I wonder whether one really has not the right! And yet, and yet. Oh! if one could only sleep the whole thing away!
[She lays her arms flat don on the table, rests the left side of her head on her hands, and shuts her eyes.

SOLNESS. [Turns the arm-chair and sits down at the table.] Had you a cosy, happy home, up there with your father, Hilda?

HILDA. [Without stirring, answers as if half asleep.] I had only a cage.

SOLNESS. And you are determined not to go back to it?

HILDA. [As before.] The wild bird never wants to go back to the cage.

SOLNESS. Rather range through the free air

HILDA. [Still as before.] The bird of prey loves to range

SOLNESS. [Lets his eyes rest on her.] If only one had the viking-spirit in life

HILDA. [In her usual voice; opens her eyes but does not move.] And the other thing? Say what that was!

SOLNESS. A robust conscience.

[HILDA sits erect on the bench, with animation. Her eyes have once more the sparkling expression of gladness.

HILDA. [Nods to him.] *I* know what you are going to build next!

SOLNESS. Then you know more than I do, Hilda.

HILDA. Yes, builders are such stupid people.

SOLNESS. What is it to be then?

HILDA. [Nods again.] The castle.

SOLNESS. What castle?

HILDA. My castle, of course.

SOLNESS. Do you want a castle now?

HILDA. Don't you owe me a kingdom, I should like to know?

SOLNESS. You say I do.

HILDA. Well, you admit you owe me this kingdom. And you can't have a kingdom without a royal castle, I should think.

SOLNESS. [More and more animated.] Yes, they usually go together.

HILDA. Good! Then build it for me! This moment!

SOLNESS. [Laughing.] Must you have that on the instant, too?

HILDA. Yes, to be sure! For the ten years are up now, and I am not going to wait any longer. So, out with the castle, Mr. Solness!

SOLNESS. It's no light matter to owe you anything, Hilda.

HILDA. You should have thought of that before. It is too late now. So [tapping the table] the castle on the table! It is my castle! I will have it at once!

SOLNESS. [More seriously, leans over towards her, with his arms on the table.] What sort of castle have you imagined, Hilda?
[Her expression becomes more and more veiled. She seems gazing inwards at herself.

HILDA. [Slowly.] My castle shall stand on a height, on a very great height, with a clear outlook on all sides, so that I can see far, far around.

SOLNESS. And no doubt it is to have a high tower!

HILDA. A tremendously high tower. And at the very top of the tower there shall be a balcony. And I will stand out upon it

SOLNESS. [Involuntarily clutches at his forehead.] How can you like to stand at such a dizzy height?

HILDA. Yes, I will! Right up there will I stand and look down on the other people, on those that are building churches, and homes for mother and father and the troop of children. And you may come up and look on at it, too.

SOLNESS. [In a low tone.] Is the builder to be allowed to come up beside the princess?

HILDA. If the builder will.

SOLNESS. [More softly.] Then I think the builder will come.

HILDA. [Nods.] The builder, he will come.

SOLNESS. But he will never be able to build any more. Poor builder!

HILDA. [Animated.] Oh, yes, he will! We two will set to work together. And then we will build the loveliest, the very loveliest thing in all the world.

SOLNESS. [Intently.] Hilda, tell me what that is!

HILDA. [Looks smilingly at him, shakes her head a little, pouts, and speaks as if to a child.] Builders, they are such very, very stupid people.

SOLNESS. Yes, no doubt they are stupid. But now tell me what it is, the loveliest thing in the world, that we two are to build together?

HILDA. [Is silent a little while, then says with an indefinable expression in her eyes.] Castles in the air.

SOLNESS. Castles in the air?

HILDA. [Nods.] Castles in the air, yes! Do you know what sort of thing a castle in the air is?

SOLNESS. It is the loveliest thing in the world, you say.

HILDA. [Rises with vehemence, and makes a gesture of repulsion with her hand.] Yes, to be sure it is! Castles in the air, they are so easy to build, too [looks scornfully at him] especially for the builders who have a, a dizzy conscience.

SOLNESS. [Rises.] After this day we two will build together, Hilda.

HILDA. [With a half-dubious smile.] A real castle in the air?

SOLNESS. Yes. One with a firm foundation under it.

RAGNAR BROVIK comes out from the house. He is carrying a large green wreath with flowers and silk ribbons.

HILDA. [With an outburst of pleasure.] The wreath! Oh, that will be glorious!

SOLNESS. [In surprise.] Have you brought the wreath Ragnar?

RAGNAR. I promised the foreman I would.

SOLNESS. [Relieved.] Ah, then I suppose you father is better?

RAGNAR. No.

SOLNESS. Was he not cheered by what I wrote?

RAGNAR. It came too late.

SOLNESS. Too late!

RAGNAR. When she came with it he was unconscious. He had had a stroke.

SOLNESS. Why, then, you must go home to him! You must attend to your father!

RAGNAR. He does not need me any more.

SOLNESS. But surely you ought to be with him.

RAGNAR. She is sitting by his bed.

SOLNESS. [Rather uncertainly.] Kaia?

RAGNAR. [Looking darkly at him.] Yes, Kaia.

SOLNESS. Go home, Ragnar, both to him and to her. Give me the wreath.

RAGNAR. [Suppresses a mocking smile.] You don't mean that you yourself?

SOLNESS. I will take it down to them myself [Takes the wreath from him.] And now you go home; we don't require you to-day.

RAGNAR. I know you do not require me any more; but to-day I shall remain.

SOLNESS. Well, remain then, since you are bent upon it.

HILDA. [At the railing.] Mr. Solness, I will stand here and look on at you.

SOLNESS. At me!

HILDA. It will be fearfully thrilling.

SOLNESS. [In a low tone.] We will talk about that presently, Hilda.
[He goes down the flight of steps with the wreath, and away through the garden.

HILDA. [Looks after him, then turns to RAGNAR.] I think you might at least have thanked him

RAGNAR. Thanked him? Ought I to have thanked him?

HILDA. Yes, of course you ought!

RAGNAR. I think it is rather you I ought to thank.

HILDA. How can you say such a thing?

RAGNAR. [Without answering her.] But I advise you to take care, Miss Wangel! For you don't know him rightly yet.

HILDA. [Ardently.] Oh, no one knows him as I do!

RAGNAR. [Laughs in exasperation.] Thank him, when he has held me down year after year! When he made father disbelieve in me, made me disbelieve in myself! And all merely that he might!

HILDA. [As if divining something.] That he might? Tell me at once!

RAGNAR. That he might keep her with him.

HILDA. [With a start towards him.] The girl at the desk.

RAGNAR. Yes.

HILDA. [Threateningly, clenching her hands.] That is not true! You are telling falsehoods about him!

RAGNAR. I would not believe it either until to-day when she said so herself.

HILDA. [As if beside herself.] What did she say? I will know! At once! at once!

RAGNAR. She said that he had taken possession of her mind, her whole mind, centred all her thoughts upon himself alone. She says that she can never leave him, that she will remain here, where he is

HILDA. [With flashing eyes.] She will not be allowed to!

RAGNAR. [As if feeling his way.] Who will not allow her?

HILDA. [Rapidly.] He will not either!

RAGNAR. Oh no, I understand the whole thing now. After this, she would merely be in the way.

HILDA. You understand nothing since you can talk like that! No, *I* will tell you why he kept hold of her.

RAGNAR. Well then, why?

HILDA. In order to keep hold of you.

RAGNAR. Has he told you so?

HILDA. No, but it is so. It must be so! [Wildly.] I will, I will have it so!

RAGNAR. And at the very moment when you came, he let her go.

HILDA. It was you, you that he let go! What do you suppose he cares about strange women like her?

RAGNAR. [Reflects.] Is it possible that all this time he has been afraid of me?

HILDA. He afraid! I would not be so conceited if I were you.

RAGNAR. Oh, he must have seen long ago that I had something in me, too. Besides—cowardly, that is just what he is, you see.

HILDA. He! Oh yes, I am likely to believe that!

RAGNAR. In a certain sense he is cowardly, he, the great master builder. He is not afraid of robbing others of their happiness as he has done both for my father and me. But when it comes to climbing up a paltry bit of scaffolding, he will do anything rather than that.

HILDA. Oh, you should just have seen him high, high up at the dizzy height where I once saw him.

RAGNAR. Did you see that?

HILDA. Yes, indeed I did. How free and great he looked as he stood and fastened the wreath to the church vane!

RAGNAR. I know that he ventured that, once in his life, one solitary time. It is a legend among us younger men. But no power on earth would induce him to do it again.

HILDA. To-day he will do it again!

RAGNAR. [Scornfully.] Yes, I daresay!

HILDA. We shall see it!

RAGNAR. That neither you nor I will see.

HILDA. [With uncontrollable vehemence.] I will se it! I will and I must see it!

RAGNAR. But he will not do it. He simply dare not do it. For you see he cannot get over this infirmity, master builder though he be.

MRS. SOLNESS comes from the house on to the verandah.

MRS. SOLNESS. [Looks around.] Is he not here? Where has he gone to?

RAGNAR. Mr. Solness is down with the men.

HILDA. He took the wreath with him.

MRS. SOLNESS. [Terrified.] Took the wreath with him! Oh God! oh God! Brovik, you must go down to him! Get him to come back here!

RAGNAR. Shall I say you want to speak to him, Mrs. Solness?

MRS. SOLNESS. Oh yes, do! No, no, don't say that *I* want anything! You can say that somebody is here, and that he must come at once.

RAGNAR. Good. I will do so, Mrs. Solness.
[He goes down the flight of steps and away through the garden.

MRS. SOLNESS. Oh, Miss Wangel, you can't think how anxious I feel about him.

HILDA. Is there anything in this to be terribly frightened about?

MRS. SOLNESS. Oh yes; surely you can understand. Just think, if he were really to do it! If he should take it into his head to climb up the scaffolding!

HILDA. [Eagerly.] Do you think he will?

MRS. SOLNESS. Oh, one can never tell what he might take into his head. I am afraid there is nothing he mightn't think of doing.

HILDA. Aha! Perhaps you too think he is well?

MRS. SOLNESS. Oh, I don't know what to think about him now. The doctor has been telling me all sorts of things; and putting it all together with several things I have heard him say

DR. HERDAL looks out, at the door.

DR. HERDAL. Is he not coming soon?

MRS. SOLNESS. Yes, I think so. I have sent for him at any rate.

DR. HERDAL. [Advancing.] I am afraid you will have to go in, my dear lady

MRS. SOLNESS. Oh no! Oh no! I shall stay out here and wait for Halvard.

DR. HERDAL. But some ladies have just come to call on you

MRS. SOLNESS. Good heavens, that too! And just at this moment!

DR. HERDAL. They say they positively must see the ceremony.

MRS. SOLNESS. Well, well, I suppose I must go to them after all. It is my duty.

HILDA. Can't you ask the ladies to go away?

MRS. SOLNESS. No, that would never do. Now that they are here, it is my duty to see them. But do you stay out here in the meantime and receive him when he comes.

DR. HERDAL. And try to occupy his attention as long as possible

MRS. SOLNESS. Yes, do, dear Miss Wangel. Keep as firm hold of him as ever you can.

HILDA. Would it not be best for you to do that?

MRS. SOLNESS. Yes; God knows that is my duty. But when one has duties in so many directions

DR. HERDAL. [Looks towards the garden.] There he is coming.

MRS. SOLNESS. And I have to go in!

DR. HERDAL. [To HILDA.] Don't say anything about my being here.

HILDA. Oh no! I daresay I shall find something else to talk to Mr. Solness about.

MRS. SOLNESS. And be sure you keep firm hold of him. I believe you can do it best.
[MRS. SOLNESS and DR. HERDAL go into the house. HILDA remains standing on the verandah. SOLNESS comes from the garden, up the flight of steps.

SOLNESS. Somebody wants me, I hear.

HILDA. Yes; it is I, Mr. Solness.

SOLNESS. Oh, is it you, Hilda? I was afraid it might be Aline or the Doctor.

HILDA. You are very easily frightened, it seems!

SOLNESS. Do you think so?

HILDA. Yes; people say that you are afraid to climb about on the scaffoldings, you know.

SOLNESS. Well, that is quite a special thing.

HILDA. Then it is true that you are afraid to do it?

SOLNESS. Yes, I am.

HILDA. Afraid of falling down and killing yourself?

SOLNESS. No, not of that.

HILDA. Of what, then?

SOLNESS. I am afraid of retribution, Hilda.

HILDA. Of retribution? [Shakes her head.] I don't understand that.

SOLNESS. Sit down, and I will tell you something.

HILDA. Yes, do! At once!
[She sits on a stool by the railing, and looks expectantly at him.

SOLNESS. [Throws his hat on the table.] You know that I began by building churches.

HILDA. [Nods.] I know that well.

SOLNESS. For, you see, I came as a boy from a pious home in the country; and so it seemed to me that this church-building was the noblest task I could set myself.

HILDA. Yes, yes.

SOLNESS. And I venture to say that I built those poor little churches with such honest and warm and heartfelt devotion that, that

HILDA. That? Well?

SOLNESS. Well, that I think that he ought to have been pleased with me.

HILDA. He? What he?

SOLNESS. He who was to have the churches, of course! He to whose honour and glory they were dedicated.

HILDA. Oh, indeed! But are you certain, then, that, that he was not pleased with you?

SOLNESS. [Scornfully.] He pleased with me! How can you talk so, Hilda? He who gave the troll in me leave to lord it just as it pleased. He who bade them be at hand to serve me, both day and might, all these, all these

HILDA. Devils

SOLNESS. Yes, of both kinds. Oh no, he mad me feel clearly enough that he was not pleased with me. [Mysteriously.] You see, that was really the reason why he made the old house burn down.

HILDA. Was that why?

SOLNESS. Yes, don't you understand? He wanted to give me the chance of becoming an accomplished master in my own sphere, so that I might build all the more glorious churches for him. At first I did not understand what he was driving at; but all of a sudden it flashed upon me.

HILDA. When was that?

SOLNESS. It was when I was building the church-tower up at Lysanger.

HILDA. I thought so.

SOLNESS. For you see, Hilda, up there, amidst those new surroundings, I used to go about musing and pondering within myself. Then I saw plainly why he had taken my little children from me. It was that I should have nothing else to attach myself to. No such thing as love and happiness, you understand. I was to be only a master builder, nothing else. and all my life long I was to go on building for him. [Laughs.] But I can tell you nothing came of that!

HILDA. What did you do then?

SOLNESS. First of all, I searched and tried my own heart

HILDA. And then?

SOLNESS. The I did the impossible, I, no less than he.

HILDA. The impossible?

SOLNESS. I had never before been able to climb up to a great, free height. But that day I did it.

HILDA. [Leaping up.] Yes, yes, you did!

SOLNESS. And when I stood there, high over everything, and was hanging the wreath over the vane, I said to him: Hear me now, thou Mighty One! From this day forward I will be a free builder, I too, in my sphere, just as thou in thine. I will never more build churches for thee only homes for human beings.

HILDA. [With great sparkling eyes.] That was the song that I heard through the air!

SOLNESS. But afterwards his turn came.

HILDA. What do you mean by that?

SOLNESS. [Looks despondently at her.] Building homes for human beings, is not worth a rap, Hilda.

HILDA. Do you say that now?

SOLNESS. Yes, for now I see it. Men have no use for these homes of theirs to be happy in. And I should not have had any use for such a home, if I had had one. [With a quiet, bitter laugh.] See, that is the upshot of the whole affair, however far back I look. Nothing really built; nor anything sacrificed for the chance of building. Nothing, nothing! the whole is nothing!

HILDA. Then you will never build anything more?

SOLNESS. [With animation.] On the contrary, I am just going to begin!

HILDA. What, then? What will you build? Tell me at once!

SOLNESS. I believe there is only one possible dwelling-place for human happiness and that is what I am going to build now.

HILDA. [Looks fixedly at him.] Mr. Solness, you mean our castles in the air.

SOLNESS. The castles in the air, yes.

HILDA. I am afraid you would turn dizzy before we got half-way up.

SOLNESS. Not if I can mount hand in hand with you, Hilda.

HILDA. [With an expression of suppressed resentment.] Only with me? Will there be no others of the party?

SOLNESS. Who else should there be?

HILDA. Oh, that girl, that Kaia at the desk. Poor thing, don't you want to take her with you too?

SOLNESS. Oho! Was it about her that Aline was talking to you?

HILDA. Is it so, or is it not?

SOLNESS. [Vehemently.] I will not answer such a question. You must believe in me, wholly and entirely!

HILDA. All these ten years I have believed in you so utterly, so utterly.

SOLNESS. You must go on believing in me!

HILDA. Then let me see you stand free and high up!

SOLNESS. [Sadly.] Oh Hilda, it is not every day that I can do that.

HILDA. [Passionately.] I will have you do it! I will have it! [Imploringly.] Just once more, Mr. Solness! Do the impossible once again!

SOLNESS. [Stands and looks deep into her eyes.] If I try it, Hilda, I will stand up there and talk to him as I did that time before.

HILDA. [In rising excitement.] What will you say to him?

SOLNESS. I will say to him: Hear me, Mighty Lord, thou may'st judge me as seems best to thee. But hereafter I will build nothing but the loveliest thing in the world

HILDA. [Carried away.] Yes, yes, yes!

SOLNESS. build it together with a princess, whom I love

HILDA. Yes, tell him that! Tell him that!

SOLNESS. Yes. And then I will say to him: Now I shall go down and throw my arms round her and kiss her

HILDA. - many times! Say that!

SOLNESS. - many, many times, I will say it!

HILDA. And then?

SOLNESS. Then I will wave my hat and come down to the earth and do as I said to him.

HILDA. [With outstretched arms.] Now I see you again as I did when there was song in the air!

SOLNESS. [Looks at here with his head bowed.] How have you become what you are, Hilda?

HILDA. How have you made me what I am?

SOLNESS. [Shortly and firmly.] The princess shall have her castle.

HILDA. [Jubilant, clapping her hands.] Oh, Mr. Solness! My lovely, lovely castle. Our castle in the air!

SOLNESS. On a firm foundation.
[In the street a crowd of people has assembled, vaguely seen through the trees. Music of wind-instruments is heard far away behind the new house.

MRS. SOLNESS, with a fur collar round her neck, DOCTOR HERDAL with her white shawl on his arm, and some ladies, come out on the verandah. RAGNAR BROVIK comes at the same time up from the garden.

MRS. SOLNESS. [To RAGNAR.] Are we to have music, too?

RAGNAR. Yes. It's the band of the Mason's Union. [To SOLNESS.] The foreman asked me to tell you that he is ready now to go up with the wreath.

SOLNESS. [Takes his hat.] Good. I will go down to him myself.

MRS. SOLNESS. [Anxiously.] What have you to do down there, Halvard?

SOLNESS. [Curtly.] I must be down below with the men.

MRS. SOLNESS. Yes, down below, only down below.

SOLNESS. That is where I always stand on everyday occasions.
[He goes down the flight of steps and away through the garden.

MRS. SOLNESS. [Calls after him over the railing.] But do beg the man to be careful when he goes up! Promise me that, Halvard!

DR. HERDAL. [To MRS. SOLNESS.] Don't you see that I was right? He has given up all thought of that folly.

MRS. SOLNESS. Oh, what a relief! Twice workmen have fallen, and each time they were killed on the spot. [Turns to HILDA.] Thank you, Miss Wangel, for having kept such a firm hold upon him. I should never have been able to manage him.

DR. HERDAL. [Playfully.] Yes, yes, Miss Wangel, you know how to keep firm hold on a man, when you give your mind to it.
[MRS. SOLNESS and DR. HERDAL go up to the ladies, who are standing nearer to the steps and looking over the garden. HILDA remains standing beside the railing in the foreground. RAGNAR goes up to her.

RAGNAR. [With suppressed laughter, half whispering.] Miss Wangel, do you see all those young fellows down in the street?

HILDA. Yes.

RAGNAR. They are my fellow students, come to look at the master.

HILDA. What do they want to look at him for?

RAGNAR. They want to see how he daren't climb to the top of his own house.

HILDA. Oh, that is what those boys want, is it?

RAGNAR. [Spitefully and scornfully.] He has kept us down so long, now we are going to see him keep quietly down below himself.

HILDA. You will not see that, not this time.

RAGNAR. [Smiles.] Indeed! Then where shall we see him?

HILDA. High, high up by the vane! That is where you will see him!

RAGNAR. [Laughs.] Him! Oh yes, I daresay!

HILDA. His will is to reach the top, so at the top you shall see him.

RAGNAR. His will, yes; that I can easily believe. But he simply cannot do it. His head would swim round, long, long before he got half-way. He would have to crawl down again on his hands and knees.

DR. HERDAL. [Points across.] Look! There goes the foreman up the ladders.

MRS. SOLNESS. And of course he has the wreath to carry too. Oh, I do hope he will be careful!

RAGNAR. [Stares incredulously and shouts.] Why, but it's

HILDA. [Breaking out in jubilation.] It is the master builder himself!

MRS. SOLNESS. [Screams with terror.] Yes, it is Halvard! Oh my great God! Halvard! Halvard!

DR. HERDAL. Hush! Don't shout to him!

MRS. SOLNESS. [Half beside herself.] I must go to him! I must get him to come down again!

DR. HERDAL. [Holds her.] Don't move, any of you! Not a sound!

HILDA. [Immovable, follows SOLNESS with her eyes.] He climbs and climbs. Higher and higher! Higher and higher! Look! Just look!

RAGNAR. [Breathless.] He must turn now. He can't possibly help it.

HILDA. He climbs and climbs. He will soon be at the top now.

MRS. SOLNESS. Oh, I shall die of terror. I cannot bear to see it.

DR. HERDAL. Then don't look up at him.

HILDA. There he is standing on the topmost planks! Right at the top!

DR. HERDAL. Nobody must move! Do you dear?

HILDA. [Exulting, with quiet intensity.] At last! At last! Now I see him great and free again!

RAGNAR. [Almost voiceless.] But this is im

HILDA. So I have seen him all through these ten years. How secure he stands! Frightfully thrilling all the same. Look at him! Now he is hanging the wreath round the vane!

RAGNAR. I feel as if I were looking at something utterly impossible.

HILDA. Yes, it is the impossible that he is doing now! [With the indefinable expression in her eyes.] Can you see any one else up there with him?

RAGNAR. There is no one else.

HILDA. Yes, there is one he is striving with.

RAGNAR. You are mistaken.

HILDA. Then do you hear no song in the air, either?

RAGNAR. It must be the wind in the tree-tops.

HILDA. *I* hear a song, a mighty song! [Shouts in wild jubilation and glee.] Look, look! Now he is waving his hat! He is waving it to us down here! Oh, wave, wave back to him! For now it is finished! [Snatches the white shawl from the Doctor, waves it, and shouts up to SOLNESS.] Hurrah for Master Builder Solness!

DR. HERDAL. Stop! Stop! For God's sake!
[The ladies on the verandah wave their pocket-handkerchiefs, and the shouts of "Hurrah" are taken up in the street. Then they are suddenly silenced, and the crowd bursts out into a shriek of horror. A human body, with planks and fragments of wood, is vaguely perceived crashing down behind the trees.

MRS. SOLNESS AND THE LADIES. [At the same time.] He is falling! He is falling!
[MRS. SOLNESS totters, falls backwards, swooning, and is caught, amid cries and confusion, by the ladies. The crowd in the street breaks down the fence and storms into the garden. At the same time DR. HERDAL, too, rushes down thither. A short pause.

HILDA. [Stares fixedly upwards and says, as if petrified.] My Master Builder.

RAGNAR. [Supports himself, trembling, against the railing.] He must be dashed to pieces, killed on the spot.

ONE OF THE LADIES. [Whilst MRS. SOLNESS is carried into the house.] Run down for the doctor

RAGNAR. I can't stir a root

ANOTHER LADY. Then call to some one!

RAGNAR. [Tries to call out.] How is it? Is he alive?

A VOICE. [Below, in the garden.] Mr. Solness is dead!

OTHER VOICES. [Nearer.] The head is all crushed. He fell right into the quarry.

HILDA. [Turns to RAGNAR, and says quietly.] I can't see him up there now.

RAGNAR. This is terrible. So, after all, he could not do it.

HILDA. [As if in quiet spell-bound triumph.] But he mounted right to the top. And I heard harps in the air. [Waves her shawl in the air, and shrieks with wild intensity.] My, my Master Builder!

Henrik Ibsen - A Doll's House

Index Of Contents

A Doll's House

DRAMATIS PERSONAE

Torvald Helmer.
Nora, his wife.
Doctor Rank.
Mrs. Linde.
Nils Krogstad.
Helmer's three young children.
Anne, their nurse.
A Housemaid.
A Porter.

(The action takes place in Helmer's house.)

ACT I

(SCENE. A room furnished comfortably and tastefully, but not extravagantly. At the back, a door to the right leads to the entrance-hall, another to the left leads to Helmer's study. Between the doors stands a piano. In the middle of the left-hand wall is a door, and beyond it a window. Near the window are a round table, arm-chairs and a small sofa. In the right-hand wall, at the farther end, another door; and on the same side, nearer the footlights, a stove, two easy chairs and a rocking-chair; between the stove and the door, a small table. Engravings on the walls; a cabinet with china and other small objects; a small book-case with well-bound books. The floors are carpeted, and a fire burns in the stove. It is winter.

A bell rings in the hall; shortly afterwards the door is heard to open. Enter NORA, humming a tune and in high spirits. She is in outdoor dress and carries a number of parcels; these she lays on the table to the right. She leaves the outer door open after her, and through it is seen a PORTER who is carrying a Christmas Tree and a basket, which he gives to the MAID who has opened the door.)

Nora. Hide the Christmas Tree carefully, Helen. Be sure the children do not see it until this evening, when it is dressed. (To the PORTER, taking out her purse.) How much?

Porter. Sixpence.

Nora. There is a shilling. No, keep the change. (The PORTER thanks her, and goes out. NORA shuts the door. She is laughing to herself, as she takes off her hat and coat. She takes a packet of macaroons from her pocket and eats one or two; then goes cautiously to her husband's door and listens.) Yes, he is in. (Still humming, she goes to the table on the right.)

Helmer (calls out from his room). Is that my little lark twittering out there?

Nora (busy opening some of the parcels). Yes, it is!

Helmer. Is it my little squirrel bustling about?

Nora. Yes!

Helmer. When did my squirrel come home?

Nora. Just now. (Puts the bag of macaroons into her pocket and wipes her mouth.) Come in here, Torvald, and see what I have bought.

Helmer. Don't disturb me. (A little later, he opens the door and looks into the room, pen in hand.) Bought, did you say? All these things? Has my little spendthrift been wasting money again?

Nora. Yes but, Torvald, this year we really can let ourselves go a little. This is the first Christmas that we have not needed to economise.

Helmer. Still, you know, we can't spend money recklessly. Nora. Yes, Torvald, we may be a wee bit more reckless now, mayn't we? Just a tiny wee bit! You are going to have a big salary and earn lots and lots of money.

Helmer. Yes, after the New Year; but then it will be a whole quarter before the salary is due.

Nora. Pooh! we can borrow until then.

Helmer. Nora! (Goes up to her and takes her playfully by the ear.) The same little featherhead! Suppose, now, that I borrowed fifty pounds today, and you spent it all in the Christmas week, and then on New Year's Eve a slate fell on my head and killed me, and Nora (putting her hands over his mouth). Oh! don't say such horrid things.

Helmer. Still, suppose that happened, what then?

Nora. If that were to happen, I don't suppose I should care whether I owed money or not.

Helmer. Yes, but what about the people who had lent it?

Nora. They? Who would bother about them? I should not know who they were.

Helmer. That is like a woman! But seriously, Nora, you know what I think about that. No debt, no borrowing. There can be no freedom or beauty about a home life that depends on borrowing and debt. We two have kept bravely on the straight road so far, and we will go on the same way for the short time longer that there need be any struggle.

Nora (moving towards the stove). As you please, Torvald.

Helmer (following her). Come, come, my little skylark must not droop her wings. What is this! Is my little squirrel out of temper? (Taking out his purse.) Nora, what do you think I have got here?

Nora (turning round quickly). Money!

Helmer. There you are. (Gives her some money.) Do you think I don't know what a lot is wanted for housekeeping at Christmas-time?

Nora (counting). Ten shillings, a pound, two pounds! Thank you, thank you, Torvald; that will keep me going for a long time.

Helmer. Indeed it must.

Nora. Yes, yes, it will. But come here and let me show you what I have bought. And all so cheap! Look, here is a new suit for Ivar, and a sword; and a horse and a trumpet for Bob; and a doll and dolly's bedstead for Emmy, they are very plain, but anyway she will soon break them in pieces. And here are dress-lengths and handkerchiefs for the maids; old Anne ought really to have something better.

Helmer. And what is in this parcel?

Nora (crying out). No, no! you mustn't see that until this evening.

Helmer. Very well. But now tell me, you extravagant little person, what would you like for yourself?

Nora. For myself? Oh, I am sure I don't want anything.

Helmer. Yes, but you must. Tell me something reasonable that you would particularly like to have.

Nora. No, I really can't think of anything unless, Torvald

Helmer. Well?

Nora (playing with his coat buttons, and without raising her eyes to his). If you really want to give me something, you might, you might

Helmer. Well, out with it!

Nora (speaking quickly). You might give me money, Torvald. Only just as much as you can afford; and then one of these days I will buy something with it.

Helmer. But, Nora

Nora. Oh, do! dear Torvald; please, please do! Then I will wrap it up in beautiful gilt paper and hang it on the Christmas Tree. Wouldn't that be fun?

Helmer. What are little people called that are always wasting money?

Nora. Spendthrifts, I know. Let us do as you suggest, Torvald, and then I shall have time to think what I am most in want of. That is a very sensible plan, isn't it?

Helmer (smiling). Indeed it is, that is to say, if you were really to save out of the money I give you, and then really buy something for yourself. But if you spend it all on the housekeeping and any number of unnecessary things, then I merely have to pay up again.

Nora. Oh but, Torvald

Helmer. You can't deny it, my dear little Nora. (Puts his arm round her waist.) It's a sweet little spendthrift, but she uses up a deal of money. One would hardly believe how expensive such little persons are!

Nora. It's a shame to say that. I do really save all I can.

Helmer (laughing). That's very true, all you can. But you can't save anything!

Nora (smiling quietly and happily). You haven't any idea how many expenses we skylarks and squirrels have, Torvald.

Helmer. You are an odd little soul. Very like your father. You always find some new way of wheedling money out of me, and, as soon as you have got it, it seems to melt in your hands. You never know where it has gone. Still, one must take you as you are. It is in the blood; for indeed it is true that you can inherit these things, Nora.

Nora. Ah, I wish I had inherited many of papa's qualities.

Helmer. And I would not wish you to be anything but just what you are, my sweet little skylark. But, do you know, it strikes me that you are looking rather, what shall I say, rather uneasy today?

Nora. Do I?

Helmer. You do, really. Look straight at me.

Nora (looks at him). Well?

Helmer (wagging his finger at her). Hasn't Miss Sweet Tooth been breaking rules in town today?

Nora. No; what makes you think that?

Helmer. Hasn't she paid a visit to the confectioner's?

Nora. No, I assure you, Torvald

Helmer. Not been nibbling sweets?

Nora. No, certainly not.

Helmer. Not even taken a bite at a macaroon or two?

Nora. No, Torvald, I assure you really

Helmer. There, there, of course I was only joking.

Nora (going to the table on the right). I should not think of going against your wishes.

Helmer. No, I am sure of that; besides, you gave me your word (Going up to her.) Keep your little Christmas secrets to yourself, my darling. They will all be revealed tonight when the Christmas Tree is lit, no doubt.

Nora. Did you remember to invite Doctor Rank?

Helmer. No. But there is no need; as a matter of course he will come to dinner with us. However, I will ask him when he comes in this morning. I have ordered some good wine. Nora, you can't think how I am looking forward to this evening.

Nora. So am I! And how the children will enjoy themselves, Torvald!

Helmer. It is splendid to feel that one has a perfectly safe appointment, and a big enough income. It's delightful to think of, isn't it?

Nora. It's wonderful!

Helmer. Do you remember last Christmas? For a full three weeks beforehand you shut yourself up every evening until long after midnight, making ornaments for the Christmas Tree, and all the other fine things that were to be a surprise to us. It was the dullest three weeks I ever spent!

Nora. I didn't find it dull.

Helmer (smiling). But there was precious little result, Nora.

Nora. Oh, you shouldn't tease me about that again. How could I help the cat's going in and tearing everything to pieces?

Helmer. Of course you couldn't, poor little girl. You had the best of intentions to please us all, and that's the main thing. But it is a good thing that our hard times are over.

Nora. Yes, it is really wonderful.

Helmer. This time I needn't sit here and be dull all alone, and you needn't ruin your dear eyes and your pretty little hands

Nora (clapping her hands). No, Torvald, I needn't any longer, need I! It's wonderfully lovely to hear you say so! (Taking his arm.) Now I will tell you how I have been thinking we ought to arrange things, Torvald. As soon as Christmas is over (A bell rings in the hall.) There's the bell. (She tidies the room a little.) There's some one at the door. What a nuisance!

Helmer. If it is a caller, remember I am not at home.

Maid (in the doorway). A lady to see you, ma'am, a stranger.

Nora. Ask her to come in.

Maid (to HELMER). The doctor came at the same time, sir.

Helmer. Did he go straight into my room?

Maid. Yes, sir.

(HELMER goes into his room. The MAID ushers in Mrs. LINDE, who is in travelling dress, and shuts the door.)
Mrs. Linde (in a dejected and timid voice). How do you do, Nora?

Nora (doubtfully). How do you do, Mrs. Linde. You don't recognise me, I suppose.

Nora. No, I don't know, yes, to be sure, I seem to (Suddenly.) Yes! Christine! Is it really you?

Mrs. Linde. Yes, it is I.

Nora. Christine! To think of my not recognising you! And yet how could I (In a gentle voice.) How you have altered, Christine!

Mrs. Linde. Yes, I have indeed. In nine, ten long years

Nora. Is it so long since we met? I suppose it is. The last eight years have been a happy time for me, I can tell you. And so now you have come into the town, and have taken this long journey in winter, that was plucky of you.

Mrs. Linde. I arrived by steamer this morning.

Nora. To have some fun at Christmas-time, of course. How delightful! We will have such fun together! But take off your things. You are not cold, I hope. (Helps her.) Now we will sit down by the stove, and be cosy. No, take this armchair; I will sit here in the rocking-chair. (Takes her hands.) Now you look like your old self again; it was only the first moment. You are a little paler, Christine, and perhaps a little thinner.

Mrs. Linde. And much, much older, Nora.

Nora. Perhaps a little older; very, very little; certainly not much. (Stops suddenly and speaks seriously.) What a thoughtless creature I am, chattering away like this. My poor, dear Christine, do forgive me.

Mrs. Linde. What do you mean, Nora?

Nora (gently). Poor Christine, you are a widow.

Mrs. Linde. Yes; it is three years ago now.

Nora. Yes, I knew; I saw it in the papers. I assure you, Christine, I meant ever so often to write to you at the time, but I always put it off and something always prevented me.

Mrs. Linde. I quite understand, dear.

Nora. It was very bad of me, Christine. Poor thing, how you must have suffered. And he left you nothing?

Mrs. Linde. No.

Nora. And no children?

Mrs. Linde. No.

Nora. Nothing at all, then.

Mrs. Linde. Not even any sorrow or grief to live upon.

Nora (looking incredulously at her). But, Christine, is that possible?

Mrs. Linde (smiles sadly and strokes her hair). It sometimes happens, Nora.

Nora. So you are quite alone. How dreadfully sad that must be. I have three lovely children. You can't see them just now, for they are out with their nurse. But now you must tell me all about it.

Mrs. Linde. No, no; I want to hear about you.

Nora. No, you must begin. I mustn't be selfish today; today I must only think of your affairs. But there is one thing I must tell you. Do you know we have just had a great piece of good luck?

Mrs. Linde. No, what is it?

Nora. Just fancy, my husband has been made manager of the Bank!

Mrs. Linde. Your husband? What good luck!

Nora. Yes, tremendous! A barrister's profession is such an uncertain thing, especially if he won't undertake unsavoury cases; and naturally Torvald has never been willing to do that, and I quite agree with him. You may imagine how pleased we are! He is to take up his work in the Bank at the New Year, and then he will have a big salary and lots of commissions. For the future we can live quite differently, we can do just as we like. I feel so relieved and so happy, Christine! It will be splendid to have heaps of money and not need to have any anxiety, won't it?

Mrs. Linde. Yes, anyhow I think it would be delightful to have what one needs.

Nora. No, not only what one needs, but heaps and heaps of money.

Mrs. Linde (smiling). Nora, Nora, haven't you learned sense yet? In our schooldays you were a great spendthrift.

Nora (laughing). Yes, that is what Torvald says now. (Wags her finger at her.) But "Nora, Nora" is not so silly as you think. We have not been in a position for me to waste money. We have both had to work.

Mrs. Linde. You too?

Nora. Yes; odds and ends, needlework, crotchet-work, embroidery, and that kind of thing. (Dropping her voice.) And other things as well. You know Torvald left his office when we were married? There was no prospect of promotion there, and he had to try and earn more than before. But during the first year he over-worked himself dreadfully. You see, he had to make money every way he could, and he worked early and late; but he couldn't stand it, and fell dreadfully ill, and the doctors said it was necessary for him to go south.

Mrs. Linde. You spent a whole year in Italy, didn't you?

Nora. Yes. It was no easy matter to get away, I can tell you. It was just after Ivar was born; but naturally we had to go. It was a wonderfully beautiful journey, and it saved Torvald's life. But it cost a tremendous lot of money, Christine.

Mrs. Linde. So I should think.

Nora. It cost about two hundred and fifty pounds. That's a lot, isn't it?

Mrs. Linde. Yes, and in emergencies like that it is lucky to have the money.

Nora. I ought to tell you that we had it from papa.

Mrs. Linde. Oh, I see. It was just about that time that he died, wasn't it?

Nora. Yes; and, just think of it, I couldn't go and nurse him. I was expecting little Ivar's birth every day and I had my poor sick Torvald to look after. My dear, kind father, I never saw him again, Christine. That was the saddest time I have known since our marriage.

Mrs. Linde. I know how fond you were of him. And then you went off to Italy?

Nora. Yes; you see we had money then, and the doctors insisted on our going, so we started a month later.

Mrs. Linde. And your husband came back quite well?

Nora. As sound as a bell!

Mrs. Linde. But the doctor?

Nora. What doctor?

Mrs. Linde. I thought your maid said the gentleman who arrived here just as I did, was the doctor?

Nora. Yes, that was Doctor Rank, but he doesn't come here professionally. He is our greatest friend, and comes in at least once everyday. No, Torvald has not had an hour's illness since then, and our children are strong and healthy and so am I. (Jumps up and claps her hands.) Christine! Christine! it's good to be alive and happy! But how horrid of me; I am talking of nothing but my own affairs. (Sits on a stool near her, and rests her arms on her knees.) You mustn't be angry with me. Tell me, is it really true that you did not love your husband? Why did you marry him?

Mrs. Linde. My mother was alive then, and was bedridden and helpless, and I had to provide for my two younger brothers; so I did not think I was justified in refusing his offer.

Nora. No, perhaps you were quite right. He was rich at that time, then?

Mrs. Linde. I believe he was quite well off. But his business was a precarious one; and, when he died, it all went to pieces and there was nothing left.

Nora. And then?

Mrs. Linde. Well, I had to turn my hand to anything I could find; first a small shop, then a small school, and so on. The last three years have seemed like one long working-day, with no rest. Now it is at an end, Nora. My poor mother needs me no more, for she is gone; and the boys do not need me either; they have got situations and can shift for themselves.

Nora. What a relief you must feel if

Mrs. Linde. No, indeed; I only feel my life unspeakably empty. No one to live for anymore. (Gets up restlessly.) That was why I could not stand the life in my little backwater any longer. I hope it may be easier here to find something which will busy me and occupy my thoughts. If only I could have the good luck to get some regular work, office work of some kind

Nora. But, Christine, that is so frightfully tiring, and you look tired out now. You had far better go away to some watering-place.

Mrs. Linde (walking to the window). I have no father to give me money for a journey, Nora.

Nora (rising). Oh, don't be angry with me!

Mrs. Linde (going up to her). It is you that must not be angry with me, dear. The worst of a position like mine is that it makes one so bitter. No one to work for, and yet obliged to be always on the lookout for chances. One must live, and so one becomes selfish. When you told me of the happy turn your fortunes have taken, you will hardly believe it, I was delighted not so much on your account as on my own.

Nora. How do you mean? Oh, I understand. You mean that perhaps Torvald could get you something to do.

Mrs. Linde. Yes, that was what I was thinking of.

Nora. He must, Christine. Just leave it to me; I will broach the subject very cleverly, I will think of something that will please him very much. It will make me so happy to be of some use to you.

Mrs. Linde. How kind you are, Nora, to be so anxious to help me! It is doubly kind in you, for you know so little of the burdens and troubles of life.

Nora. I? I know so little of them?

Mrs. Linde (smiling). My dear! Small household cares and that sort of thing! You are a child, Nora.

Nora (tosses her head and crosses the stage). You ought not to be so superior.

Mrs. Linde. No?

Nora. You are just like the others. They all think that I am incapable of anything really serious -

Mrs. Linde. Come, come

Nora. - that I have gone through nothing in this world of cares.

Mrs. Linde. But, my dear Nora, you have just told me all your troubles.

Nora. Pooh! those were trifles. (Lowering her voice.) I have not told you the important thing.

Mrs. Linde. The important thing? What do you mean?

Nora. You look down upon me altogether, Christine but you ought not to. You are proud, aren't you, of having worked so hard and so long for your mother?

Mrs. Linde. Indeed, I don't look down on anyone. But it is true that I am both proud and glad to think that I was privileged to make the end of my mother's life almost free from care.

Nora. And you are proud to think of what you have done for your brothers?

Mrs. Linde. I think I have the right to be.

Nora. I think so, too. But now, listen to this; I too have something to be proud and glad of.

Mrs. Linde. I have no doubt you have. But what do you refer to?

Nora. Speak low. Suppose Torvald were to hear! He mustn't on any account, no one in the world must know, Christine, except you.

Mrs. Linde. But what is it?

Nora. Come here. (Pulls her down on the sofa beside her.) Now I will show you that I too have something to be proud and glad of. It was I who saved Torvald's life.

Mrs. Linde. "Saved"? How?

Nora. I told you about our trip to Italy. Torvald would never have recovered if he had not gone there

Mrs. Linde. Yes, but your father gave you the necessary funds.

Nora (smiling). Yes, that is what Torvald and all the others think, but -

Mrs. Linde. But -

Nora. Papa didn't give us a shilling. It was I who procured the money.

Mrs. Linde. You? All that large sum?

Nora. Two hundred and fifty pounds. What do you think of that?

Mrs. Linde. But, Nora, how could you possibly do it? Did you win a prize in the Lottery?

Nora (contemptuously). In the Lottery? There would have been no credit in that.

Mrs. Linde. But where did you get it from, then? Nora (humming and smiling with an air of mystery). Hm, hm! Aha!

Mrs. Linde. Because you couldn't have borrowed it.

Nora. Couldn't I? Why not?

Mrs. Linde. No, a wife cannot borrow without her husband's consent.

Nora (tossing her head). Oh, if it is a wife who has any head for business, a wife who has the wit to be a little bit clever

Mrs. Linde. I don't understand it at all, Nora.

Nora. There is no need you should. I never said I had borrowed the money. I may have got it some other way. (Lies back on the sofa.) Perhaps I got it from some other admirer. When anyone is as attractive as I am

Mrs. Linde. You are a mad creature.

Nora. Now, you know you're full of curiosity, Christine.

Mrs. Linde. Listen to me, Nora dear. Haven't you been a little bit imprudent?

Nora (sits up straight). Is it imprudent to save your husband's life?

Mrs. Linde. It seems to me imprudent, without his knowledge, to -

Nora. But it was absolutely necessary that he should not know! My goodness, can't you understand that? It was necessary he should have no idea what a dangerous condition he was in. It was to me that the doctors came and said that his life was in danger, and that the only thing to save him was to live in the south. Do you suppose I didn't try, first of all, to get what I wanted as if it were for myself? I told him how much I should love to travel abroad like other young wives; I tried tears and entreaties with him; I told him that he ought to remember the condition I was in, and that he ought to be kind and indulgent to me; I even hinted that he might raise a loan. That nearly made him angry, Christine. He said I was thoughtless, and that it was his duty as my husband not to indulge me in my whims and caprices as I believe he called them. Very well, I thought, you must be saved and that was how I came to devise a way out of the difficulty

Mrs. Linde. And did your husband never get to know from your father that the money had not come from him?

Nora. No, never. Papa died just at that time. I had meant to let him into the secret and beg him never to reveal it. But he was so ill then alas, there never was any need to tell him.

Mrs. Linde. And since then have you never told your secret to your husband?

Nora. Good Heavens, no! How could you think so? A man who has such strong opinions about these things! And besides, how painful and humiliating it would be for Torvald, with his manly independence, to know that he owed me anything! It would upset our mutual relations altogether; our beautiful happy home would no longer be what it is now.

Mrs. Linde. Do you mean never to tell him about it?

Nora (meditatively, and with a half smile). Yes, someday, perhaps, after many years, when I am no longer as nice-looking as I am now. Don't laugh at me! I mean, of course, when Torvald is no longer as devoted to me as he is now; when my dancing and dressing-up and reciting have palled on him; then it may be a good thing to have something in reserve (Breaking off.) What nonsense! That time will never come. Now, what do you think of my great secret, Christine? Do you still think I am of no use? I can tell you, too, that this affair has caused me a lot of worry. It has been by no means easy for me to meet my engagements punctually. I may tell you that there is something that is called, in business, quarterly interest, and another thing called payment in installments, and it is always so dreadfully difficult to manage them. I have had to save a little here and there, where I could, you understand. I have not been able to put aside much from my housekeeping money, for Torvald must have a good table. I couldn't let my children be shabbily dressed; I have felt obliged to use up all he gave me for them, the sweet little darlings!

Mrs. Linde. So it has all had to come out of your own necessaries of life, poor Nora?

Nora. Of course. Besides, I was the one responsible for it. Whenever Torvald has given me money for new dresses and such things, I have never spent more than half of it; I have always bought the simplest and cheapest things. Thank Heaven, any clothes look well on me, and so Torvald has never noticed it. But it was often very hard on me, Christine, because it is delightful to be really well dressed, isn't it?

Mrs. Linde. Quite so.

Nora. Well, then I have found other ways of earning money. Last winter I was lucky enough to get a lot of copying to do; so I locked myself up and sat writing every evening until quite late at night. Many a time I was desperately tired; but all the same it was a tremendous pleasure to sit there working and earning money. It was like being a man.

Mrs. Linde. How much have you been able to pay off in that way?

Nora. I can't tell you exactly. You see, it is very difficult to keep an account of a business matter of that kind. I only know that I have paid every penny that I could scrape together. Many a time I was at my wits' end. (Smiles.) Then I used to sit here and imagine that a rich old gentleman had fallen in love with me

Mrs. Linde. What! Who was it?

Nora. Be quiet! that he had died; and that when his will was opened it contained, written in big letters, the instruction: "The lovely Mrs. Nora Helmer is to have all I possess paid over to her at once in cash."

Mrs. Linde. But, my dear Nora, who could the man be?

Nora. Good gracious, can't you understand? There was no old gentleman at all; it was only something that I used to sit here and imagine, when I couldn't think of any way of procuring money. But it's all the same now; the tiresome old person can stay where he is, as far as I am concerned; I don't care about him or his will either, for I am free from care now. (Jumps up.) My goodness, it's delightful to think of, Christine! Free from care! To be able to be free from care, quite free from care; to be able to play and romp with the children; to be able to keep the house beautifully and have everything just as Torvald likes it! And, think of it, soon the spring will come and the big blue sky! Perhaps we shall be able to take a little trip, perhaps I shall see the sea again! Oh, it's a wonderful thing to be alive and be happy. (A bell is heard in the hall.)

Mrs. Linde (rising). There is the bell; perhaps I had better go.

Nora. No, don't go; no one will come in here; it is sure to be for Torvald.

Servant (at the hall door). Excuse me, ma'am, there is a gentleman to see the master, and as the doctor is with him

Nora. Who is it?

Krogstad (at the door). It is I, Mrs. Helmer. (Mrs. LINDE starts, trembles, and turns to the window.)

Nora (takes a step towards him, and speaks in a strained, low voice). You? What is it? What do you want to see my husband about?

Krogstad. Bank business, in a way. I have a small post in the Bank, and I hear your husband is to be our chief now

Nora. Then it is -

Krogstad. Nothing but dry business matters, Mrs. Helmer; absolutely nothing else.

Nora. Be so good as to go into the study, then. (She bows indifferently to him and shuts the door into the hall; then comes back and makes up the fire in the stove.)

Mrs. Linde. Nora, who was that man?

Nora. A lawyer, of the name of Krogstad.

Mrs. Linde. Then it really was he.

Nora. Do you know the man?

Mrs. Linde. I used to, many years ago. At one time he was a solicitor's clerk in our town.

Nora. Yes, he was.

Mrs. Linde. He is greatly altered.

Nora. He made a very unhappy marriage.

Mrs. Linde. He is a widower now, isn't he?

Nora. With several children. There now, it is burning up. (Shuts the door of the stove and moves the rocking-chair aside.)

Mrs. Linde. They say he carries on various kinds of business.

Nora. Really! Perhaps he does; I don't know anything about it. But don't let us think of business; it is so tiresome.

Doctor Rank (comes out of HELMER'S study. Before he shuts the door he calls to him). No, my dear fellow, I won't disturb you; I would rather go in to your wife for a little while. (Shuts the door and sees Mrs. LINDE.) I beg your pardon; I am afraid I am disturbing you too.

Nora. No, not at all. (Introducing him). Doctor Rank, Mrs. Linde.

Rank. I have often heard Mrs. Linde's name mentioned here. I think I passed you on the stairs when I arrived, Mrs. Linde?

Mrs. Linde. Yes, I go up very slowly; I can't manage stairs well.

Rank. Ah! some slight internal weakness?

Mrs. Linde. No, the fact is I have been overworking myself.

Rank. Nothing more than that? Then I suppose you have come to town to amuse yourself with our entertainments?

Mrs. Linde. I have come to look for work.

Rank. Is that a good cure for overwork?

Mrs. Linde. One must live, Doctor Rank.

Rank. Yes, the general opinion seems to be that it is necessary.

Nora. Look here, Doctor Rank, you know you want to live.

Rank. Certainly. However wretched I may feel, I want to prolong the agony as long as possible. All my patients are like that. And so are those who are morally diseased; one of them, and a bad case too, is at this very moment with Helmer

Mrs. Linde (sadly). Ah!

Nora. Whom do you mean?

Rank. A lawyer of the name of Krogstad, a fellow you don't know at all. He suffers from a diseased moral character, Mrs. Helmer; but even he began talking of its being highly important that he should live.

Nora. Did he? What did he want to speak to Torvald about?

Rank. I have no idea; I only heard that it was something about the Bank.

Nora. I didn't know this, what's his name, Krogstad had anything to do with the Bank.

Rank. Yes, he has some sort of appointment there. (To Mrs. LINDE.) I don't know whether you find also in your part of the world that there are certain people who go zealously snuffing about to smell out moral corruption, and, as soon as they have found some, put the person concerned into some lucrative position where they can keep their eye on him. Healthy natures are left out in the cold.

Mrs. Linde. Still I think the sick are those who most need taking care of.

Rank (shrugging his shoulders). Yes, there you are. That is the sentiment that is turning Society into a sick-house.

(NORA, who has been absorbed in her thoughts, breaks out into smothered laughter and claps her hands.)

Rank. Why do you laugh at that? Have you any notion what Society really is?

Nora. What do I care about tiresome Society? I am laughing at something quite different, something extremely amusing. Tell me, Doctor Rank, are all the people who are employed in the Bank dependent on Torvald now?

Rank. Is that what you find so extremely amusing?

Nora (smiling and humming). That's my affair! (Walking about the room.) It's perfectly glorious to think that we have, that Torvald has so much power over so many people. (Takes the packet from her pocket.) Doctor Rank, what do you say to a macaroon?

Rank. What, macaroons? I thought they were forbidden here.

Nora. Yes, but these are some Christine gave me.

Mrs. Linde. What! I?

Nora. Oh, well, don't be alarmed! You couldn't know that Torvald had forbidden them. I must tell you that he is afraid they will spoil my teeth. But, bah! once in a way. That's so, isn't it, Doctor Rank? By your leave! (Puts a macaroon into his mouth.) You must have one too, Christine. And I shall have one, just a little one, or at most two. (Walking about.) I am tremendously happy. There is just one thing in the world now that I should dearly love to do.

Rank. Well, what is that?

Nora. It's something I should dearly love to say, if Torvald could hear me.

Rank. Well, why can't you say it?

Nora. No, I daren't; it's so shocking.

Mrs. Linde. Shocking?

Rank. Well, I should not advise you to say it. Still, with us you might. What is it you would so much like to say if Torvald could hear you?

Nora. I should just love to say Well, I'm damned!

Rank. Are you mad?

Mrs. Linde. Nora, dear!

Rank. Say it, here he is!

Nora (hiding the packet). Hush! Hush! Hush! (HELMER comes out of his room, with his coat over his arm and his hat in his hand.)

Nora. Well, Torvald dear, have you got rid of him?

Helmer. Yes, he has just gone.

Nora. Let me introduce you, this is Christine, who has come to town.

Helmer. Christine? Excuse me, but I don't know

Nora. Mrs. Linde, dear; Christine Linde.

Helmer. Of course. A school friend of my wife's, I presume?

Mrs. Linde. Yes, we have known each other since then.

Nora. And just think, she has taken a long journey in order to see you.

Helmer. What do you mean? Mrs. Linde. No, really, I -

Nora. Christine is tremendously clever at book-keeping, and she is frightfully anxious to work under some clever man, so as to perfect herself

Helmer. Very sensible, Mrs. Linde.

Nora. And when she heard you had been appointed manager of the Bank, the news was telegraphed, you know, she travelled here as quick as she could. Torvald, I am sure you will be able to do something for Christine, for my sake, won't you?

Helmer. Well, it is not altogether impossible. I presume you are a widow, Mrs. Linde?

Mrs. Linde. Yes.

Helmer. And have had some experience of book-keeping?

Mrs. Linde. Yes, a fair amount.

Helmer. Ah! well, it's very likely I may be able to find something for you

Nora (clapping her hands). What did I tell you? What did I tell you?

Helmer. You have just come at a fortunate moment, Mrs. Linde.

Mrs. Linde. How am I to thank you?

Helmer. There is no need. (Puts on his coat.) But today you must excuse me

Rank. Wait a minute; I will come with you. (Brings his fur coat from the hall and warms it at the fire.)

Nora. Don't be long away, Torvald dear.

Helmer. About an hour, not more.

Nora. Are you going too, Christine?

Mrs. Linde (putting on her cloak). Yes, I must go and look for a room.

Helmer. Oh, well then, we can walk down the street together.

Nora (helping her). What a pity it is we are so short of space here; I am afraid it is impossible for us

Mrs. Linde. Please don't think of it! Goodbye, Nora dear, and many thanks.

Nora. Goodbye for the present. Of course you will come back this evening. And you too, Dr. Rank. What do you say? If you are well enough? Oh, you must be! Wrap yourself up well. (They go to the door all talking together. Children's voices are heard on the staircase.)

Nora. There they are! There they are! (She runs to open the door. The NURSE comes in with the children.) Come in! Come in! (Stoops and kisses them.) Oh, you sweet blessings! Look at them, Christine! Aren't they darlings?

Rank. Don't let us stand here in the draught.

Helmer. Come along, Mrs. Linde; the place will only be bearable for a mother now!

(RANK, HELMER, and Mrs. LINDE go downstairs. The NURSE comes forward with the children; NORA shuts the hall door.)

Nora. How fresh and well you look! Such red cheeks like apples and roses. (The children all talk at once while she speaks to them.) Have you had great fun? That's splendid! What, you pulled both Emmy and Bob along on the sledge? both at once? that was good. You are a clever boy, Ivar. Let me take her for a little, Anne. My sweet little baby doll! (Takes the baby from the MAID and dances it up and down.) Yes, yes, mother will dance with Bob too. What! Have you been snowballing? I wish I had been there too! No, no, I will take their things off, Anne; please let me do it, it is such fun. Go in now, you look half frozen. There is some hot coffee for you on the stove.

(The NURSE goes into the room on the left. NORA takes off the children's things and throws them about, while they all talk to her at once.)

Nora. Really! Did a big dog run after you? But it didn't bite you? No, dogs don't bite nice little dolly children. You mustn't look at the parcels, Ivar. What are they? Ah, I daresay you would like to know. No, no, it's something nasty! Come, let us have a game! What shall we play at? Hide and Seek? Yes, we'll play Hide and Seek. Bob shall hide first. Must I hide? Very well, I'll hide first. (She and the children laugh and shout, and romp in and out of the room; at last NORA hides under the table, the children rush in and out for her, but do not see her; they hear her smothered laughter, run to the table, lift up the cloth and find her. Shouts of laughter. She crawls forward and pretends to frighten them. Fresh laughter. Meanwhile there has been a knock at the hall door, but none of them has noticed it. The door is half opened, and KROGSTAD appears, lie waits a little; the game goes on.)

Krogstad. Excuse me, Mrs. Helmer.

Nora (with a stifled cry, turns round and gets up on to her knees). Ah! what do you want?

Krogstad. Excuse me, the outer door was ajar; I suppose someone forgot to shut it.

Nora (rising). My husband is out, Mr. Krogstad.

Krogstad. I know that.

Nora. What do you want here, then?

Krogstad. A word with you.

Nora. With me? (To the children, gently.) Go in to nurse. What? No, the strange man won't do mother any harm. When he has gone we will have another game. (She takes the children into the room on the left, and shuts the door after them.) You want to speak to me?

Krogstad. Yes, I do.

Nora. Today? It is not the first of the month yet.

Krogstad. No, it is Christmas Eve, and it will depend on yourself what sort of a Christmas you will spend.

Nora. What do you mean? Today it is absolutely impossible for me

Krogstad. We won't talk about that until later on. This is something different. I presume you can give me a moment?

Nora. Yes, yes, I can, although

Krogstad. Good. I was in Olsen's Restaurant and saw your husband going down the street

Nora. Yes?

Krogstad. With a lady.

Nora. What then?

Krogstad. May I make so bold as to ask if it was a Mrs. Linde?

Nora. It was.

Krogstad. Just arrived in town?

Nora. Yes, today.

Krogstad. She is a great friend of yours, isn't she?

Nora. She is. But I don't see

Krogstad. I knew her too, once upon a time.

Nora. I am aware of that.

Krogstad. Are you? So you know all about it; I thought as much. Then I can ask you, without beating about the bush, is Mrs. Linde to have an appointment in the Bank?

Nora. What right have you to question me, Mr. Krogstad? You, one of my husband's subordinates! But since you ask, you shall know. Yes, Mrs. Linde is to have an appointment. And it was I who pleaded her cause, Mr. Krogstad, let me tell you that.

Krogstad. I was right in what I thought, then.

Nora (walking up and down the stage). Sometimes one has a tiny little bit of influence, I should hope. Because one is a woman, it does not necessarily follow that. When anyone is in a subordinate position, Mr. Krogstad, they should really be careful to avoid offending anyone who, who

Krogstad. Who has influence?

Nora. Exactly.

Krogstad (changing his tone). Mrs. Helmer, you will be so good as to use your influence on my behalf.

Nora. What? What do you mean?

Krogstad. You will be so kind as to see that I am allowed to keep my subordinate position in the Bank.

Nora. What do you mean by that? Who proposes to take your post away from you?

Krogstad. Oh, there is no necessity to keep up the pretence of ignorance. I can quite understand that your friend is not very anxious to expose herself to the chance of rubbing shoulders with me; and I quite understand, too, whom I have to thank for being turned off.

Nora. But I assure you

Krogstad. Very likely; but, to come to the point, the time has come when I should advise you to use your influence to prevent that.

Nora. But, Mr. Krogstad, I have no influence.

Krogstad. Haven't you? I thought you said yourself just now

Nora. Naturally I did not mean you to put that construction on it. I! What should make you think I have any influence of that kind with my husband?

Krogstad. Oh, I have known your husband from our student days. I don't suppose he is any more unassailable than other husbands.

Nora. If you speak slightingly of my husband, I shall turn you out of the house.

Krogstad. You are bold, Mrs. Helmer.

Nora. I am not afraid of you any longer. As soon as the New Year comes, I shall in a very short time be free of the whole thing.

Krogstad (controlling himself). Listen to me, Mrs. Helmer. If necessary, I am prepared to fight for my small post in the Bank as if I were fighting for my life.

Nora. So it seems.

Krogstad. It is not only for the sake of the money; indeed, that weighs least with me in the matter. There is another reason, well, I may as well tell you. My position is this. I daresay you know, like everybody else, that once, many years ago, I was guilty of an indiscretion.

Nora. I think I have heard something of the kind.

Krogstad. The matter never came into court; but every way seemed to be closed to me after that. So I took to the business that you know of. I had to do something; and, honestly, I don't think I've been one of the worst. But now I must cut myself free from all that. My sons are growing up; for their sake I must try and win back as much respect as I can in the town. This post in the Bank was like the first step up for me and now your husband is going to kick me downstairs again into the mud.

Nora. But you must believe me, Mr. Krogstad; it is not in my power to help you at all.

Krogstad. Then it is because you haven't the will; but I have means to compel you.

Nora. You don't mean that you will tell my husband that I owe you money?

Krogstad. Hm! suppose I were to tell him?

Nora. It would be perfectly infamous of you. (Sobbing.) To think of his learning my secret, which has been my joy and pride, in such an ugly, clumsy way, that he should learn it from you! And it would put me in a horribly disagreeable position

Krogstad. Only disagreeable?

Nora (impetuously). Well, do it, then! and it will be the worse for you. My husband will see for himself what a blackguard you are, and you certainly won't keep your post then.

Krogstad. I asked you if it was only a disagreeable scene at home that you were afraid of?

Nora. If my husband does get to know of it, of course he will at once pay you what is still owing, and we shall have nothing more to do with you.

Krogstad (coming a step nearer). Listen to me, Mrs. Helmer. Either you have a very bad memory or you know very little of business. I shall be obliged to remind you of a few details.

Nora. What do you mean?

Krogstad. When your husband was ill, you came to me to borrow two hundred and fifty pounds.

Nora. I didn't know anyone else to go to.

Krogstad. I promised to get you that amount

Nora. Yes, and you did so.

Krogstad. I promised to get you that amount, on certain conditions. Your mind was so taken up with your husband's illness, and you were so anxious to get the money for your journey, that you seem to have paid no attention to the conditions of our bargain. Therefore it will not be amiss if I remind you of them. Now, I promised to get the money on the security of a bond which I drew up.

Nora. Yes, and which I signed.

Krogstad. Good. But below your signature there were a few lines constituting your father a surety for the money; those lines your father should have signed.

Nora. Should? He did sign them.

Krogstad. I had left the date blank; that is to say, your father should himself have inserted the date on which he signed the paper. Do you remember that?

Nora. Yes, I think I remember

Krogstad. Then I gave you the bond to send by post to your father. Is that not so?

Nora. Yes.

Krogstad. And you naturally did so at once, because five or six days afterwards you brought me the bond with your father's signature. And then I gave you the money.

Nora. Well, haven't I been paying it off regularly?

Krogstad. Fairly so, yes. But, to come back to the matter in hand, that must have been a very trying time for you, Mrs. Helmer?

Nora. It was, indeed.

Krogstad. Your father was very ill, wasn't he?

Nora. He was very near his end.

Krogstad. And died soon afterwards?

Nora. Yes.

Krogstad. Tell me, Mrs. Helmer, can you by any chance remember what day your father died? on what day of the month, I mean.

Nora. Papa died on the 29th of September.

Krogstad. That is correct; I have ascertained it for myself. And, as that is so, there is a discrepancy (taking a paper from his pocket) which I cannot account for.

Nora. What discrepancy? I don't know

Krogstad. The discrepancy consists, Mrs. Helmer, in the fact that your father signed this bond three days after his death.

Nora. What do you mean? I don't understand

Krogstad. Your father died on the 29th of September. But, look here; your father has dated his signature the 2nd of October. It is a discrepancy, isn't it? (NORA is silent.) Can you explain it to me? (NORA is still silent.) It is a remarkable thing, too, that the words "2nd of October," as well as the year, are not written in your father's handwriting but in one that I think I know. Well, of course it can be explained; your father may have forgotten to date his signature, and someone else may have dated it haphazard before they knew of his death. There is no harm in that. It all depends on the signature of the name; and that is genuine, I suppose, Mrs. Helmer? It was your father himself who signed his name here?

Nora (after a short pause, throws her head up and looks defiantly at him). No, it was not. It was I that wrote papa's name.

Krogstad. Are you aware that is a dangerous confession?

Nora. In what way? You shall have your money soon.

Krogstad. Let me ask you a question; why did you not send the paper to your father?

Nora. It was impossible; papa was so ill. If I had asked him for his signature, I should have had to tell him what the money was to be used for; and when he was so ill himself I couldn't tell him that my husband's life was in danger, it was impossible.

Krogstad. It would have been better for you if you had given up your trip abroad.

Nora. No, that was impossible. That trip was to save my husband's life; I couldn't give that up.

Krogstad. But did it never occur to you that you were committing a fraud on me?

Nora. I couldn't take that into account; I didn't trouble myself about you at all. I couldn't bear you, because you put so many heartless difficulties in my way, although you knew what a dangerous condition my husband was in.

Krogstad. Mrs. Helmer, you evidently do not realise clearly what it is that you have been guilty of. But I can assure you that my one false step, which lost me all my reputation, was nothing more or nothing worse than what you have done.

Nora. You? Do you ask me to believe that you were brave enough to run a risk to save your wife's life?

Krogstad. The law cares nothing about motives.

Nora. Then it must be a very foolish law.

Krogstad. Foolish or not, it is the law by which you will be judged, if I produce this paper in court.

Nora. I don't believe it. Is a daughter not to be allowed to spare her dying father anxiety and care? Is a wife not to be allowed to save her husband's life? I don't know much about law; but I am certain that there must be laws permitting such things as that. Have you no knowledge of such laws, you who are a lawyer? You must be a very poor lawyer, Mr. Krogstad.

Krogstad. Maybe. But matters of business, such business as you and I have had together, do you think I don't understand that? Very well. Do as you please. But let me tell you this, if I lose my position a second time, you shall lose yours with me. (He bows, and goes out through the hall.)

Nora (appears buried in thought for a short time, then tosses her head). Nonsense! Trying to frighten me like that! I am not so silly as he thinks. (Begins to busy herself putting the children's things in order.) And yet? No, it's impossible! I did it for love's sake.

The Children (in the doorway on the left). Mother, the stranger man has gone out through the gate.

Nora. Yes, dears, I know. But, don't tell anyone about the stranger man. Do you hear? Not even papa.

Children. No, mother; but will you come and play again?

Nora. No, no, not now.

Children. But, mother, you promised us.

Nora. Yes, but I can't now. Run away in; I have such a lot to do. Run away in, my sweet little darlings. (She gets them into the room by degrees and shuts the door on them; then sits down on the sofa, takes up a piece of needlework and sews a few stitches, but soon stops.) No! (Throws down the work, gets up, goes to the hall door and calls out.) Helen! bring the Tree in. (Goes to the table on the left, opens a drawer, and stops again.) No, no! it is quite impossible!

Maid (coming in with the Tree). Where shall I put it, ma'am?

Nora. Here, in the middle of the floor.

Maid. Shall I get you anything else?

Nora. No, thank you. I have all I want. [Exit MAID.]

Nora (begins dressing the tree). A candle here-and flowers here. The horrible man! It's all nonsense, there's nothing wrong. The tree shall be splendid! I will do everything I can think of to please you, Torvald! I will sing for you, dance for you (HELMER comes in with some papers under his arm.) Oh! are you back already?

Helmer. Yes. Has anyone been here?

Nora. Here? No.

Helmer. That is strange. I saw Krogstad going out of the gate.

Nora. Did you? Oh yes, I forgot, Krogstad was here for a moment.

Helmer. Nora, I can see from your manner that he has been here begging you to say a good word for him.

Nora. Yes.

Helmer. And you were to appear to do it of your own accord; you were to conceal from me the fact of his having been here; didn't he beg that of you too?

Nora. Yes, Torvald, but -

Helmer. Nora, Nora, and you would be a party to that sort of thing? To have any talk with a man like that, and give him any sort of promise? And to tell me a lie into the bargain?

Nora. A lie?

Helmer. Didn't you tell me no one had been here? (Shakes his finger at her.) My little songbird must never do that again. A songbird must have a clean beak to chirp with, no false notes! (Puts his arm round her waist.) That is so, isn't it? Yes, I am sure it is. (Lets her go.) We will say no more about it. (Sits down by the stove.) How warm and snug it is here! (Turns over his papers.)

Nora (after a short pause, during which she busies herself with the Christmas Tree.) Torvald!

Helmer. Yes.

Nora. I am looking forward tremendously to the fancy-dress ball at the Stenborgs' the day after tomorrow.

Helmer. And I am tremendously curious to see what you are going to surprise me with.

Nora. It was very silly of me to want to do that.

Helmer. What do you mean?

Nora. I can't hit upon anything that will do; everything I think of seems so silly and insignificant.

Helmer. Does my little Nora acknowledge that at last?

Nora (standing behind his chair with her arms on the back of it). Are you very busy, Torvald?

Helmer. Well

Nora. What are all those papers?

Helmer. Bank business.

Nora. Already?

Helmer. I have got authority from the retiring manager to undertake the necessary changes in the staff and in the rearrangement of the work; and I must make use of the Christmas week for that, so as to have everything in order for the new year.

Nora. Then that was why this poor Krogstad

Helmer. Hm!

Nora (leans against the back of his chair and strokes his hair). If you hadn't been so busy I should have asked you a tremendously big favour, Torvald.

Helmer. What is that? Tell me.

Nora. There is no one has such good taste as you. And I do so want to look nice at the fancy-dress ball. Torvald, couldn't you take me in hand and decide what I shall go as, and what sort of a dress I shall wear?

Helmer. Aha! so my obstinate little woman is obliged to get someone to come to her rescue?

Nora. Yes, Torvald, I can't get along a bit without your help.

Helmer. Very well, I will think it over, we shall manage to hit upon something.

Nora. That is nice of you. (Goes to the Christmas Tree. A short pause.) How pretty the red flowers look. But, tell me, was it really something very bad that this Krogstad was guilty of?

Helmer. He forged someone's name. Have you any idea what that means?

Nora. Isn't it possible that he was driven to do it by necessity?

Helmer. Yes; or, as in so many cases, by imprudence. I am not so heartless as to condemn a man altogether because of a single false step of that kind.

Nora. No, you wouldn't, would you, Torvald?

Helmer. Many a man has been able to retrieve his character, if he has openly confessed his fault and taken his punishment.

Nora. Punishment?

Helmer. But Krogstad did nothing of that sort; he got himself out of it by a cunning trick, and that is why he has gone under altogether.

Nora. But do you think it would?

Helmer. Just think how a guilty man like that has to lie and play the hypocrite with every one, how he has to wear a mask in the presence of those near and dear to him, even before his own wife and children. And about the children, that is the most terrible part of it all, Nora.

Nora. How?

Helmer. Because such an atmosphere of lies infects and poisons the whole life of a home. Each breath the children take in such a house is full of the germs of evil.

Nora (coming nearer him). Are you sure of that?

Helmer. My dear, I have often seen it in the course of my life as a lawyer. Almost everyone who has gone to the bad early in life has had a deceitful mother.

Nora. Why do you only say mother?

Helmer. It seems most commonly to be the mother's influence, though naturally a bad father's would have the same result. Every lawyer is familiar with the fact. This Krogstad, now, has been persistently poisoning his own children with lies and dissimulation; that is why I say he has lost all moral character. (Holds out his hands to her.) That is why my sweet little Nora must promise me not to plead his cause. Give me your hand on it. Come, come, what is this? Give me your hand. There now, that's settled. I assure you it would be quite impossible for me to work with him; I literally feel physically ill when I am in the company of such people.

Nora (takes her hand out of his and goes to the opposite side of the Christmas Tree). How hot it is in here; and I have such a lot to do.

Helmer (getting up and putting his papers in order). Yes, and I must try and read through some of these before dinner; and I must think about your costume, too. And it is just possible I may have something ready in gold paper to hang up on the Tree. (Puts his hand on her head.) My precious little singing-bird! (He goes into his room and shuts the door after him.)

Nora (after a pause, whispers). No, no, it isn't true. It's impossible; it must be impossible.

(The NURSE opens the door on the left.)

Nurse. The little ones are begging so hard to be allowed to come in to mamma.

Nora. No, no, no! Don't let them come in to me! You stay with them, Anne.

Nurse. Very well, ma'am. (Shuts the door.)

Nora (pale with terror). Deprave my little children? Poison my home? (A short pause. Then she tosses her head.) It's not true. It can't possibly be true.

ACT II

(THE SAME SCENE. THE Christmas Tree is in the corner by the piano, stripped of its ornaments and with burnt-down candle-ends on its dishevelled branches. NORA'S cloak and hat are lying on the sofa. She is alone in the room, walking about uneasily. She stops by the sofa and takes up her cloak.)

Nora (drops her cloak). Someone is coming now! (Goes to the door and listens.) No, it is no one. Of course, no one will come today, Christmas Day, nor tomorrow either. But, perhaps (opens the door and looks out). No, nothing in the letterbox; it is quite empty. (Comes forward.) What rubbish! of course he can't be in earnest about it. Such a thing couldn't happen; it is impossible, I have three little children.

(Enter the NURSE from the room on the left, carrying a big cardboard box.)

Nurse. At last I have found the box with the fancy dress.

Nora. Thanks; put it on the table.

Nurse (doing so). But it is very much in want of mending.

Nora. I should like to tear it into a hundred thousand pieces.

Nurse. What an idea! It can easily be put in order, just a little patience.

Nora. Yes, I will go and get Mrs. Linde to come and help me with it.

Nurse. What, out again? In this horrible weather? You will catch cold, ma'am, and make yourself ill.

Nora. Well, worse than that might happen. How are the children?

Nurse. The poor little souls are playing with their Christmas presents, but -

Nora. Do they ask much for me?

Nurse. You see, they are so accustomed to have their mamma with them.

Nora. Yes, but, nurse, I shall not be able to be so much with them now as I was before.

Nurse. Oh well, young children easily get accustomed to anything.

Nora. Do you think so? Do you think they would forget their mother if she went away altogether?

Nurse. Good heavens! went away altogether?

Nora. Nurse, I want you to tell me something I have often wondered about, how could you have the heart to put your own child out among strangers?

Nurse. I was obliged to, if I wanted to be little Nora's nurse.

Nora. Yes, but how could you be willing to do it?

Nurse. What, when I was going to get such a good place by it? A poor girl who has got into trouble should be glad to. Besides, that wicked man didn't do a single thing for me.

Nora. But I suppose your daughter has quite forgotten you.

Nurse. No, indeed she hasn't. She wrote to me when she was confirmed, and when she was married.

Nora (putting her arms round her neck). Dear old Anne, you were a good mother to me when I was little.

Nurse. Little Nora, poor dear, had no other mother but me. Nora. And if my little ones had no other mother, I am sure you would. What nonsense I am talking! (Opens the box.) Go in to them. Now I must. You will see tomorrow how charming I shall look.

Nurse. I am sure there will be no one at the ball so charming as you, ma'am. (Goes into the room on the left.)

Nora (begins to unpack the box, but soon pushes it away from her). If only I dared go out. If only no one would come. If only I could be sure nothing would happen here in the meantime. Stuff and nonsense! No one will come. Only I mustn't think about it. I will brush my muff. What lovely, lovely gloves! Out of my thoughts, out of my thoughts! One, two, three, four, five, six (Screams.) Ah! there is someone coming. (Makes a movement towards the door, but stands irresolute.)

(Enter MRS. LINDE from the hall, where she has taken off her cloak and hat.)

Nora. Oh, it's you, Christine. There is no one else out there, is there? How good of you to come!

Mrs. Linde. I heard you were up asking for me.

Nora. Yes, I was passing by. As a matter of fact, it is something you could help me with. Let us sit down here on the sofa. Look here. Tomorrow evening there is to be a fancy-dress ball at the Stenborgs', who live above us; and Torvald wants me to go as a Neapolitan fisher-girl, and dance the Tarantella that I learned at Capri.

Mrs. Linde. I see; you are going to keep up the character.

Nora. Yes, Torvald wants me to. Look, here is the dress; Torvald had it made for me there, but now it is all so torn, and I haven't any idea

Mrs. Linde. We will easily put that right. It is only some of the trimming come unsewn here and there. Needle and thread? Now then, that's all we want.

Nora. It is nice of you.

Mrs. Linde (sewing). So you are going to be dressed up tomorrow Nora. I will tell you what, I shall come in for a moment and see you in your fine feathers. But I have completely forgotten to thank you for a delightful evening yesterday.

Nora (gets up, and crosses the stage). Well, I don't think yesterday was as pleasant as usual. You ought to have come to town a little earlier, Christine. Certainly Torvald does understand how to make a house dainty and attractive.

Mrs. Linde. And so do you, it seems to me; you are not your father's daughter for nothing. But tell me, is Doctor Rank always as depressed as he was yesterday?

Nora. No; yesterday it was very noticeable. I must tell you that he suffers from a very dangerous disease. He has consumption of the spine, poor creature. His father was a horrible man who committed all sorts of excesses; and that is why his son was sickly from childhood, do you understand?

Mrs. Linde (dropping her sewing). But, my dearest Nora, how do you know anything about such things?

Nora (walking about). Pooh! When you have three children, you get visits now and then from, from married women, who know something of medical matters, and they talk about one thing and another.

Mrs. Linde (goes on sewing. A short silence). Does Doctor Rank come here everyday?

Nora. Everyday regularly. He is Torvald's most intimate friend, and a great friend of mine too. He is just like one of the family.

Mrs. Linde. But tell me this, is he perfectly sincere? I mean, isn't he the kind of man that is very anxious to make himself agreeable?

Nora. Not in the least. What makes you think that?

Mrs. Linde. When you introduced him to me yesterday, he declared he had often heard my name mentioned in this house; but afterwards I noticed that your husband hadn't the slightest idea who I was. So how could Doctor Rank?

Nora. That is quite right, Christine. Torvald is so absurdly fond of me that he wants me absolutely to himself, as he says. At first he used to seem almost jealous if I mentioned any of the dear folk at home, so naturally I gave up doing so. But I often talk about such things with Doctor Rank, because he likes hearing about them.

Mrs. Linde. Listen to me, Nora. You are still very like a child in many things, and I am older than you in many ways and have a little more experience. Let me tell you this, you ought to make an end of it with Doctor Rank.

Nora. What ought I to make an end of?

Mrs. Linde. Of two things, I think. Yesterday you talked some nonsense about a rich admirer who was to leave you money

Nora. An admirer who doesn't exist, unfortunately! But what then?

Mrs. Linde. Is Doctor Rank a man of means?

Nora. Yes, he is.

Mrs. Linde. And has no one to provide for?

Nora. No, no one; but

Mrs. Linde. And comes here everyday?

Nora. Yes, I told you so.

Mrs. Linde. But how can this well-bred man be so tactless?

Nora. I don't understand you at all.

Mrs. Linde. Don't prevaricate, Nora. Do you suppose I don't guess who lent you the two hundred and fifty pounds?

Nora. Are you out of your senses? How can you think of such a thing! A friend of ours, who comes here everyday! Do you realise what a horribly painful position that would be?

Mrs. Linde. Then it really isn't he?

Nora. No, certainly not. It would never have entered into my head for a moment. Besides, he had no money to lend then; he came into his money afterwards.

Mrs. Linde. Well, I think that was lucky for you, my dear Nora.

Nora. No, it would never have come into my head to ask Doctor Rank. Although I am quite sure that if I had asked him

Mrs. Linde. But of course you won't.

Nora. Of course not. I have no reason to think it could possibly be necessary. But I am quite sure that if I told Doctor Rank

Mrs. Linde. Behind your husband's back?

Nora. I must make an end of it with the other one, and that will be behind his back too. I must make an end of it with him.

Mrs. Linde. Yes, that is what I told you yesterday, but -

Nora (walking up and down). A man can put a thing like that straight much easier than a woman

Mrs. Linde. One's husband, yes.

Nora. Nonsense! (Standing still.) When you pay off a debt you get your bond back, don't you?

Mrs. Linde. Yes, as a matter of course.

Nora. And can tear it into a hundred thousand pieces, and burn it up, the nasty dirty paper!

Mrs. Linde (looks hard at her, lays down her sewing and gets up slowly). Nora, you are concealing something from me.

Nora. Do I look as if I were?

Mrs. Linde. Something has happened to you since yesterday morning. Nora, what is it?

Nora (going nearer to her). Christine! (Listens.) Hush! there's Torvald come home. Do you mind going in to the children for the present? Torvald can't bear to see dressmaking going on. Let Anne help you.

Mrs. Linde (gathering some of the things together). Certainly but I am not going away from here until we have had it out with one another. (She goes into the room on the left, as HELMER comes in from the hall.)

Nora (going up to HELMER). I have wanted you so much, Torvald dear.

Helmer. Was that the dressmaker?

Nora. No, it was Christine; she is helping me to put my dress in order. You will see I shall look quite smart.

Helmer. Wasn't that a happy thought of mine, now?

Nora. Splendid! But don't you think it is nice of me, too, to do as you wish?

Helmer. Nice? because you do as your husband wishes? Well, well, you little rogue, I am sure you did not mean it in that way. But I am not going to disturb you; you will want to be trying on your dress, I expect.

Nora. I suppose you are going to work.

Helmer. Yes. (Shows her a bundle of papers.) Look at that. I have just been into the bank. (Turns to go into his room.)

Nora. Torvald.

Helmer. Yes.

Nora. If your little squirrel were to ask you for something very, very prettily?

Helmer. What then?

Nora. Would you do it?

Helmer. I should like to hear what it is, first.

Nora. Your squirrel would run about and do all her tricks if you would be nice, and do what she wants.

Helmer. Speak plainly.

Nora. Your skylark would chirp about in every room, with her song rising and falling

Helmer. Well, my skylark does that anyhow.

Nora. I would play the fairy and dance for you in the moonlight, Torvald.

Helmer. Nora, you surely don't mean that request you made to me this morning?

Nora (going near him). Yes, Torvald, I beg you so earnestly

Helmer. Have you really the courage to open up that question again?

Nora. Yes, dear, you must do as I ask; you must let Krogstad keep his post in the bank.

Helmer. My dear Nora, it is his post that I have arranged Mrs. Linde shall have.

Nora. Yes, you have been awfully kind about that; but you could just as well dismiss some other clerk instead of Krogstad.

Helmer. This is simply incredible obstinacy! Because you chose to give him a thoughtless promise that you would speak for him, I am expected to

Nora. That isn't the reason, Torvald. It is for your own sake. This fellow writes in the most scurrilous newspapers; you have told me so yourself. He can do you an unspeakable amount of harm. I am frightened to death of him

Helmer. Ah, I understand; it is recollections of the past that scare you.

Nora. What do you mean?

Helmer. Naturally you are thinking of your father.

Nora. Yes, yes, of course. Just recall to your mind what these malicious creatures wrote in the papers about papa, and how horribly they slandered him. I believe they would have procured his dismissal if the Department had not sent you over to inquire into it, and if you had not been so kindly disposed and helpful to him.

Helmer. My little Nora, there is an important difference between your father and me. Your father's reputation as a public official was not above suspicion. Mine is, and I hope it will continue to be so, as long as I hold my office.

Nora. You never can tell what mischief these men may contrive. We ought to be so well off, so snug and happy here in our peaceful home, and have no cares, you and I and the children, Torvald! That is why I beg you so earnestly

Helmer. And it is just by interceding for him that you make it impossible for me to keep him. It is already known at the Bank that I mean to dismiss Krogstad. Is it to get about now that the new manager has changed his mind at his wife's bidding

Nora. And what if it did?

Helmer. Of course! if only this obstinate little person can get her way! Do you suppose I am going to make myself ridiculous before my whole staff, to let people think that I am a man to be swayed by all sorts of outside influence? I should very soon feel the consequences of it, I can tell you! And besides, there is one thing that makes it quite impossible for me to have Krogstad in the Bank as long as I am manager.

Nora. Whatever is that?

Helmer. His moral failings I might perhaps have overlooked, if necessary

Nora. Yes, you could, couldn't you?

Helmer. And I hear he is a good worker, too. But I knew him when we were boys. It was one of those rash friendships that so often prove an incubus in afterlife. I may as well tell you plainly, we were once on very intimate terms with one another. But this tactless fellow lays no restraint on himself when other people are present. On the contrary, he thinks it gives him the right to adopt a familiar tone with me, and every minute it is "I say, Helmer, old fellow!" and that sort of thing. I assure you it is extremely painful for me. He would make my position in the Bank intolerable.

Nora. Torvald, I don't believe you mean that.

Helmer. Don't you? Why not?

Nora. Because it is such a narrow-minded way of looking at things.

Helmer. What are you saying? Narrow-minded? Do you think I am narrow-minded?

Nora. No, just the opposite, dear and it is exactly for that reason.

Helmer. It's the same thing. You say my point of view is narrow-minded, so I must be so too. Narrow-minded! Very well, I must put an end to this. (Goes to the hall door and calls.) Helen!

Nora. What are you going to do?

Helmer (looking among his papers). Settle it. (Enter MAID.) Look here; take this letter and go downstairs with it at once. Find a messenger and tell him to deliver it, and be quick. The address is on it, and here is the money.

Maid. Very well, sir. (Exit with the letter.)

Helmer (putting his papers together). Now then, little Miss Obstinate.

Nora (breathlessly). Torvald, what was that letter?

Helmer. Krogstad's dismissal.

Nora. Call her back, Torvald! There is still time. Oh Torvald, call her back! Do it for my sake, for your own sake, for the children's sake! Do you hear me, Torvald? Call her back! You don't know what that letter can bring upon us.

Helmer. It's too late.

Nora. Yes, it's too late.

Helmer. My dear Nora, I can forgive the anxiety you are in, although really it is an insult to me. It is, indeed. Isn't it an insult to think that I should be afraid of a starving quill-driver's vengeance? But I forgive you nevertheless, because it is such eloquent witness to your great love for me. (Takes her in his arms.) And that is as it should be, my own darling Nora. Come what will, you may be sure I shall have both courage and strength if they be needed. You will see I am man enough to take everything upon myself.

Nora (in a horror-stricken voice). What do you mean by that?

Helmer. Everything, I say

Nora (recovering herself). You will never have to do that.

Helmer. That's right. Well, we will share it, Nora, as man and wife should. That is how it shall be. (Caressing her.) Are you content now? There! There! not these frightened dove's eyes! The whole thing is only the wildest fancy! Now, you must go and play through the Tarantella and practise with your tambourine. I shall go into the inner office and shut the door, and I shall hear nothing; you can make as much noise as you please. (Turns back at the door.) And when Rank comes, tell him where he will find me. (Nods to her, takes his papers and goes into his room, and shuts the door after him.)

Nora (bewildered with anxiety, stands as if rooted to the spot, and whispers). He was capable of doing it. He will do it. He will do it in spite of everything. No, not that! Never, never! Anything rather than that! Oh, for some help, some way out of it! (The door-bell rings.) Doctor Rank! Anything rather than that anything, whatever it is! (She puts her hands over her face, pulls herself together, goes to the door and opens it. RANK is standing without, hanging up his coat. During the following dialogue it begins to grow dark.)

Nora. Good day, Doctor Rank. I knew your ring. But you mustn't go in to Torvald now; I think he is busy with something.

Rank. And you?

Nora (brings him in and shuts the door after him). Oh, you know very well I always have time for you.

Rank. Thank you. I shall make use of as much of it as I can.

Nora. What do you mean by that? As much of it as you can?

Rank. Well, does that alarm you?

Nora. It was such a strange way of putting it. Is anything likely to happen?

Rank. Nothing but what I have long been prepared for. But I certainly didn't expect it to happen so soon.

Nora (gripping him by the arm). What have you found out? Doctor Rank, you must tell me.

Rank (sitting down by the stove). It is all up with me. And it can't be helped.

Nora (with a sigh of relief). Is it about yourself?

Rank. Who else? It is no use lying to one's self. I am the most wretched of all my patients, Mrs. Helmer. Lately I have been taking stock of my internal economy. Bankrupt! Probably within a month I shall lie rotting in the churchyard.

Nora. What an ugly thing to say!

Rank. The thing itself is cursedly ugly, and the worst of it is that I shall have to face so much more that is ugly before that. I shall only make one more examination of myself; when I have done that, I shall know pretty certainly when it will be that the horrors of dissolution will begin. There is something I want to tell you. Helmer's refined nature gives him an unconquerable disgust at everything that is ugly; I won't have him in my sick-room.

Nora. Oh, but, Doctor Rank

Rank. I won't have him there. Not on any account. I bar my door to him. As soon as I am quite certain that the worst has come, I shall send you my card with a black cross on it, and then you will know that the loathsome end has begun.

Nora. You are quite absurd today. And I wanted you so much to be in a really good humour.

Rank. With death stalking beside me? To have to pay this penalty for another man's sin? Is there any justice in that? And in every single family, in one way or another, some such inexorable retribution is being exacted

Nora (putting her hands over her ears). Rubbish! Do talk of something cheerful.

Rank. Oh, it's a mere laughing matter, the whole thing. My poor innocent spine has to suffer for my father's youthful amusements.

Nora (sitting at the table on the left). I suppose you mean that he was too partial to asparagus and pate de foie gras, don't you?

Rank. Yes, and to truffles.

Nora. Truffles, yes. And oysters too, I suppose?

Rank. Oysters, of course, that goes without saying.

Nora. And heaps of port and champagne. It is sad that all these nice things should take their revenge on our bones.

Rank. Especially that they should revenge themselves on the unlucky bones of those who have not had the satisfaction of enjoying them.

Nora. Yes, that's the saddest part of it all.

Rank (with a searching look at her). Hm!

Nora (after a short pause). Why did you smile?

Rank. No, it was you that laughed.

Nora. No, it was you that smiled, Doctor Rank!

Rank (rising). You are a greater rascal than I thought.

Nora. I am in a silly mood today.

Rank. So it seems.

Nora (putting her hands on his shoulders). Dear, dear Doctor Rank, death mustn't take you away from Torvald and me.

Rank. It is a loss you would easily recover from. Those who are gone are soon forgotten.

Nora (looking at him anxiously). Do you believe that?

Rank. People form new ties, and then

Nora. Who will form new ties?

Rank. Both you and Helmer, when I am gone. You yourself are already on the high road to it, I think. What did that Mrs. Linde want here last night?

Nora. Oho! you don't mean to say you are jealous of poor Christine?

Rank. Yes, I am. She will be my successor in this house. When I am done for, this woman will

Nora. Hush! don't speak so loud. She is in that room.

Rank. Today again. There, you see.

Nora. She has only come to sew my dress for me. Bless my soul, how unreasonable you are! (Sits down on the sofa.) Be nice now, Doctor Rank, and tomorrow you will see how beautifully I shall dance, and you can imagine I am doing it all for you and for Torvald too, of course. (Takes various things out of the box.) Doctor Rank, come and sit down here, and I will show you something.

Rank (sitting down). What is it?

Nora. Just look at those!

Rank. Silk stockings.

Nora. Flesh-coloured. Aren't they lovely? It is so dark here now, but tomorrow. No, no, no! you must only look at the feet. Oh well, you may have leave to look at the legs too.

Rank. Hm! Nora. Why are you looking so critical? Don't you think they will fit me?

Rank. I have no means of forming an opinion about that.

Nora (looks at him for a moment). For shame! (Hits him lightly on the ear with the stockings.) That's to punish you. (Folds them up again.)

Rank. And what other nice things am I to be allowed to see?

Nora. Not a single thing more, for being so naughty. (She looks among the things, humming to herself.)

Rank (after a short silence). When I am sitting here, talking to you as intimately as this, I cannot imagine for a moment what would have become of me if I had never come into this house.

Nora (smiling). I believe you do feel thoroughly at home with us.

Rank (in a lower voice, looking straight in front of him). And to be obliged to leave it all

Nora. Nonsense, you are not going to leave it.

Rank (as before). And not be able to leave behind one the slightest token of one's gratitude, scarcely even a fleeting regret, nothing but an empty place which the first comer can fill as well as any other.

Nora. And if I asked you now for a? No!

Rank. For what?

Nora. For a big proof of your friendship

Rank. Yes, yes!

Nora. I mean a tremendously big favour

Rank. Would you really make me so happy for once?

Nora. Ah, but you don't know what it is yet.

Rank. No, but tell me.

Nora. I really can't, Doctor Rank. It is something out of all reason; it means advice, and help, and a favour

Rank. The bigger a thing it is the better. I can't conceive what it is you mean. Do tell me. Haven't I your confidence?

Nora. More than anyone else. I know you are my truest and best friend, and so I will tell you what it is. Well, Doctor Rank, it is something you must help me to prevent. You know how devotedly, how inexpressibly deeply Torvald loves me; he would never for a moment hesitate to give his life for me.

Rank (leaning towards her). Nora, do you think he is the only one?

Nora (with a slight start). The only one?

Rank. The only one who would gladly give his life for your sake.

Nora (sadly). Is that it?

Rank. I was determined you should know it before I went away, and there will never be a better opportunity than this. Now you know it, Nora. And now you know, too, that you can trust me as you would trust no one else.

Nora (rises, deliberately and quietly). Let me pass.

Rank (makes room for her to pass him, but sits still). Nora!

Nora (at the hall door). Helen, bring in the lamp. (Goes over to the stove.) Dear Doctor Rank, that was really horrid of you.

Rank. To have loved you as much as anyone else does? Was that horrid?

Nora. No, but to go and tell me so. There was really no need

Rank. What do you mean? Did you know? (MAID enters with lamp, puts it down on the table, and goes out.) Nora, Mrs. Helmer, tell me, had you any idea of this?

Nora. Oh, how do I know whether I had or whether I hadn't? I really can't tell you. To think you could be so clumsy, Doctor Rank! We were getting on so nicely.

Rank. Well, at all events you know now that you can command me, body and soul. So won't you speak out?

Nora (looking at him). After what happened?

Rank. I beg you to let me know what it is.

Nora. I can't tell you anything now.

Rank. Yes, yes. You mustn't punish me in that way. Let me have permission to do for you whatever a man may do.

Nora. You can do nothing for me now. Besides, I really don't need any help at all. You will find that the whole thing is merely fancy on my part. It really is so, of course it is! (Sits down in the rocking-chair, and looks at him with a smile.) You are a nice sort of man, Doctor Rank! don't you feel ashamed of yourself, now the lamp has come?

Rank. Not a bit. But perhaps I had better go, for ever?

Nora. No, indeed, you shall not. Of course you must come here just as before. You know very well Torvald can't do without you.

Rank. Yes, but you?

Nora. Oh, I am always tremendously pleased when you come.

Rank. It is just that, that put me on the wrong track. You are a riddle to me. I have often thought that you would almost as soon be in my company as in Helmer's.

Nora. Yes, you see there are some people one loves best, and others whom one would almost always rather have as companions.

Rank. Yes, there is something in that.

Nora. When I was at home, of course I loved papa best. But I always thought it tremendous fun if I could steal down into the maids' room, because they never moralised at all, and talked to each other about such entertaining things.

Rank. I see, it is their place I have taken.

Nora (jumping up and going to him). Oh, dear, nice Doctor Rank, I never meant that at all. But surely you can understand that being with Torvald is a little like being with papa (Enter MAID from the hall.)

Maid. If you please, ma'am. (Whispers and hands her a card.)

Nora (glancing at the card). Oh! (Puts it in her pocket.)

Rank. Is there anything wrong?

Nora. No, no, not in the least. It is only something, it is my new dress

Rank. What? Your dress is lying there.

Nora. Oh, yes, that one; but this is another. I ordered it. Torvald mustn't know about it

Rank. Oho! Then that was the great secret.

Nora. Of course. Just go in to him; he is sitting in the inner room. Keep him as long as

Rank. Make your mind easy; I won't let him escape.

(Goes into HELMER'S room.)

Nora (to the MAID). And he is standing waiting in the kitchen?

Maid. Yes; he came up the back stairs.

Nora. But didn't you tell him no one was in?

Maid. Yes, but it was no good.

Nora. He won't go away?

Maid. No; he says he won't until he has seen you, ma'am.

Nora. Well, let him come in but quietly. Helen, you mustn't say anything about it to anyone. It is a surprise for my husband.

Maid. Yes, ma'am, I quite understand. (Exit.)

Nora. This dreadful thing is going to happen! It will happen in spite of me! No, no, no, it can't happen, it shan't happen! (She bolts the door of HELMER'S room. The MAID opens the hall door for KROGSTAD and shuts it after him. He is wearing a fur coat, high boots and a fur cap.)

Nora (advancing towards him). Speak low, my husband is at home.

Krogstad. No matter about that.

Nora. What do you want of me?

Krogstad. An explanation of something.

Nora. Make haste then. What is it?

Krogstad. You know, I suppose, that I have got my dismissal.

Nora. I couldn't prevent it, Mr. Krogstad. I fought as hard as I could on your side, but it was no good.

Krogstad. Does your husband love you so little, then? He knows what I can expose you to, and yet he ventures

Nora. How can you suppose that he has any knowledge of the sort?

Krogstad. I didn't suppose so at all. It would not be the least like our dear Torvald Helmer to show so much courage

Nora. Mr. Krogstad, a little respect for my husband, please.

Krogstad. Certainly, all the respect he deserves. But since you have kept the matter so carefully to yourself, I make bold to suppose that you have a little clearer idea, than you had yesterday, of what it actually is that you have done?

Nora. More than you could ever teach me.

Krogstad. Yes, such a bad lawyer as I am.

Nora. What is it you want of me?

Krogstad. Only to see how you were, Mrs. Helmer. I have been thinking about you all day long. A mere cashier, a quill-driver, a, well, a man like me, even he has a little of what is called feeling, you know.

Nora. Show it, then; think of my little children.

Krogstad. Have you and your husband thought of mine? But never mind about that. I only wanted to tell you that you need not take this matter too seriously. In the first place there will be no accusation made on my part.

Nora. No, of course not; I was sure of that.

Krogstad. The whole thing can be arranged amicably; there is no reason why anyone should know anything about it. It will remain a secret between us three.

Nora. My husband must never get to know anything about it.

Krogstad. How will you be able to prevent it? Am I to understand that you can pay the balance that is owing?

Nora. No, not just at present.

Krogstad. Or perhaps that you have some expedient for raising the money soon?

Nora. No expedient that I mean to make use of.

Krogstad. Well, in any case, it would have been of no use to you now. If you stood there with ever so much money in your hand, I would never part with your bond.

Nora. Tell me what purpose you mean to put it to.

Krogstad. I shall only preserve it, keep it in my possession. No one who is not concerned in the matter shall have the slightest hint of it. So that if the thought of it has driven you to any desperate resolution

Nora. It has.

Krogstad. If you had it in your mind to run away from your home

Nora. I had.

Krogstad. Or even something worse

Nora. How could you know that?

Krogstad. Give up the idea.

Nora. How did you know I had thought of that?

Krogstad. Most of us think of that at first. I did, too but I hadn't the courage.

Nora (faintly). No more had I.

Krogstad (in a tone of relief). No, that's it, isn't it, you hadn't the courage either?

Nora. No, I haven't, I haven't.

Krogstad. Besides, it would have been a great piece of folly. Once the first storm at home is over. I have a letter for your husband in my pocket.

Nora. Telling him everything?

Krogstad. In as lenient a manner as I possibly could.

Nora (quickly). He mustn't get the letter. Tear it up. I will find some means of getting money.

Krogstad. Excuse me, Mrs. Helmer, but I think I told you just now

Nora. I am not speaking of what I owe you. Tell me what sum you are asking my husband for, and I will get the money.

Krogstad. I am not asking your husband for a penny.

Nora. What do you want, then?

Krogstad. I will tell you. I want to rehabilitate myself, Mrs. Helmer; I want to get on; and in that your husband must help me. For the last year and a half I have not had a hand in anything dishonourable, amid all that time I have been struggling in most restricted circumstances. I was content to work my way up step by step. Now I am turned out, and I am not going to be satisfied with merely being taken into favour again. I want to get on, I tell you. I want to get into the Bank again, in a higher position. Your husband must make a place for me

Nora. That he will never do!

Krogstad. He will; I know him; he dare not protest. And as soon as I am in there again with him, then you will see! Within a year I shall be the manager's right hand. It will be Nils Krogstad and not Torvald Helmer who manages the Bank.

Nora. That's a thing you will never see!

Krogstad. Do you mean that you will?

Nora. I have courage enough for it now.

Krogstad. Oh, you can't frighten me. A fine, spoilt lady like you

Nora. You will see, you will see.

Krogstad. Under the ice, perhaps? Down into the cold, coal-black water? And then, in the spring, to float up to the surface, all horrible and unrecognisable, with your hair fallen out

Nora. You can't frighten me.

Krogstad. Nor you me. People don't do such things, Mrs. Helmer. Besides, what use would it be? I should have him completely in my power all the same.

Nora. Afterwards? When I am no longer

Krogstad. Have you forgotten that it is I who have the keeping of your reputation? (NORA stands speechlessly looking at him.) Well, now, I have warned you. Do not do anything foolish. When Helmer has had my letter, I shall expect a message from him. And be sure you remember that it is your husband himself who has forced me into such ways as this again. I will never forgive him for that. Goodbye, Mrs. Helmer. (Exit through the hall.)

Nora (goes to the hall door, opens it slightly and listens.) He is going. He is not putting the letter in the box. Oh no, no! that's impossible! (Opens the door by degrees.) What is that? He is standing outside. He is not going downstairs. Is he hesitating? Can he? (A letter drops into the box; then KROGSTAD'S footsteps are heard, until they die away as he goes downstairs. NORA utters a stifled cry, and runs across the room to the table by the sofa. A short pause.)

Nora. In the letter-box. (Steals across to the hall door.) There it lies, Torvald, Torvald, there is no hope for us now!

(Mrs. LINDE comes in from the room on the left, carrying the dress.)

Mrs. Linde. There, I can't see anything more to mend now. Would you like to try it on?

Nora (in a hoarse whisper). Christine, come here.

Mrs. Linde (throwing the dress down on the sofa). What is the matter with you? You look so agitated!

Nora. Come here. Do you see that letter? There, look, you can see it through the glass in the letter-box.

Mrs. Linde. Yes, I see it.

Nora. That letter is from Krogstad.

Mrs. Linde. Nora, it was Krogstad who lent you the money!

Nora. Yes, and now Torvald will know all about it.

Mrs. Linde. Believe me, Nora, that's the best thing for both of you.

Nora. You don't know all. I forged a name.

Mrs. Linde. Good heavens!

Nora. I only want to say this to you, Christine, you must be my witness.

Mrs. Linde. Your witness? What do you mean? What am I to?

Nora. If I should go out of my mind and it might easily happen

Mrs. Linde. Nora!

Nora. Or if anything else should happen to me, anything, for instance, that might prevent my being here

Mrs. Linde. Nora! Nora! you are quite out of your mind.

Nora. And if it should happen that there were some one who wanted to take all the responsibility, all the blame, you understand

Mrs. Linde. Yes, yes but how can you suppose?

Nora. Then you must be my witness, that it is not true, Christine. I am not out of my mind at all; I am in my right senses now, and I tell you no one else has known anything about it; I, and I alone, did the whole thing. Remember that.

Mrs. Linde. I will, indeed. But I don't understand all this.

Nora. How should you understand it? A wonderful thing is going to happen!

Mrs. Linde. A wonderful thing?

Nora. Yes, a wonderful thing! But it is so terrible, Christine; it mustn't happen, not for all the world.

Mrs. Linde. I will go at once and see Krogstad.

Nora. Don't go to him; he will do you some harm.

Mrs. Linde. There was a time when he would gladly do anything for my sake.

Nora. He?

Mrs. Linde. Where does he live?

Nora. How should I know? Yes (feeling in her pocket), here is his card. But the letter, the letter!

Helmer (calls from his room, knocking at the door). Nora! Nora (cries out anxiously). Oh, what's that? What do you want?

Helmer. Don't be so frightened. We are not coming in; you have locked the door. Are you trying on your dress?

Nora. Yes, that's it. I look so nice, Torvald.

Mrs. Linde (who has read the card). I see he lives at the corner here.

Nora. Yes, but it's no use. It is hopeless. The letter is lying there in the box.

Mrs. Linde. And your husband keeps the key?

Nora. Yes, always.

Mrs. Linde. Krogstad must ask for his letter back unread, he must find some pretence

Nora. But it is just at this time that Torvald generally

Mrs. Linde. You must delay him. Go in to him in the meantime. I will come back as soon as I can. (She goes out hurriedly through the hall door.)

Nora (goes to HELMER'S door, opens it and peeps in). Torvald!

Helmer (from the inner room). Well? May I venture at last to come into my own room again? Come along, Rank, now you will see (Halting in the doorway.) But what is this?

Nora. What is what, dear?

Helmer. Rank led me to expect a splendid transformation.

Rank (in the doorway). I understood so, but evidently I was mistaken.

Nora. Yes, nobody is to have the chance of admiring me in my dress until tomorrow.

Helmer. But, my dear Nora, you look so worn out. Have you been practising too much?

Nora. No, I have not practised at all.

Helmer. But you will need to

Nora. Yes, indeed I shall, Torvald. But I can't get on a bit without you to help me; I have absolutely forgotten the whole thing.

Helmer. Oh, we will soon work it up again.

Nora. Yes, help me, Torvald. Promise that you will! I am so nervous about it, all the people. You must give yourself up to me entirely this evening. Not the tiniest bit of business, you mustn't even take a pen in your hand. Will you promise, Torvald dear?

Helmer. I promise. This evening I will be wholly and absolutely at your service, you helpless little mortal. Ah, by the way, first of all I will just (Goes towards the hall door.)

Nora. What are you going to do there?

Helmer. Only see if any letters have come.

Nora. No, no! don't do that, Torvald!

Helmer. Why not?

Nora. Torvald, please don't. There is nothing there.

Helmer. Well, let me look. (Turns to go to the letter-box. NORA, at the piano, plays the first bars of the Tarantella. HELMER stops in the doorway.) Aha!

Nora. I can't dance tomorrow if I don't practise with you.

Helmer (going up to her). Are you really so afraid of it, dear?

Nora. Yes, so dreadfully afraid of it. Let me practise at once; there is time now, before we go to dinner. Sit down and play for me, Torvald dear; criticise me, and correct me as you play.

Helmer. With great pleasure, if you wish me to. (Sits down at the piano.)

Nora (takes out of the box a tambourine and a long variegated shawl. She hastily drapes the shawl round her. Then she springs to the front of the stage and calls out). Now play for me! I am going to dance!

(HELMER plays and NORA dances. RANK stands by the piano behind HELMER, and looks on.)

Helmer (as he plays). Slower, slower!

Nora. I can't do it any other way.

Helmer. Not so violently, Nora!

Nora. This is the way.

Helmer (stops playing). No, no, that is not a bit right.

Nora (laughing and swinging the tambourine). Didn't I tell you so?

Rank. Let me play for her.

Helmer (getting up). Yes, do. I can correct her better then.

(RANK sits down at the piano and plays. NORA dances more and more wildly. HELMER has taken up a position beside the stove, and during her dance gives her frequent instructions. She does not seem to hear him; her hair comes down and falls over her shoulders; she pays no attention to it, but goes on dancing. Enter Mrs. LINDE.)

Mrs. Linde (standing as if spell-bound in the doorway). Oh!

Nora (as she dances). Such fun, Christine!

Helmer. My dear darling Nora, you are dancing as if your life depended on it.

Nora. So it does.

Helmer. Stop, Rank; this is sheer madness. Stop, I tell you! (RANK stops playing, and NORA suddenly stands still. HELMER goes up to her.) I could never have believed it. You have forgotten everything I taught you.

Nora (throwing away the tambourine). There, you see.

Helmer. You will want a lot of coaching.

Nora. Yes, you see how much I need it. You must coach me up to the last minute. Promise me that, Torvald!

Helmer. You can depend on me.

Nora. You must not think of anything but me, either today or tomorrow; you mustn't open a single letter, not even open the letter-box

Helmer. Ah, you are still afraid of that fellow

Nora. Yes, indeed I am.

Helmer. Nora, I can tell from your looks that there is a letter from him lying there.

Nora. I don't know; I think there is; but you must not read anything of that kind now. Nothing horrid must come between us until this is all over.

Rank (whispers to HELMER). You mustn't contradict her.

Helmer (taking her in his arms). The child shall have her way. But tomorrow night, after you have danced

Nora. Then you will be free. (The MAID appears in the doorway to the right.)

Maid. Dinner is served, ma'am.

Nora. We will have champagne, Helen.

Maid. Very good, ma'am. [Exit.

Helmer. Hullo! are we going to have a banquet?

Nora. Yes, a champagne banquet until the small hours. (Calls out.) And a few macaroons, Helen, lots, just for once!

Helmer. Come, come, don't be so wild and nervous. Be my own little skylark, as you used.

Nora. Yes, dear, I will. But go in now and you too, Doctor Rank. Christine, you must help me to do up my hair.

Rank (whispers to HELMER as they go out). I suppose there is nothing, she is not expecting anything?

Helmer. Far from it, my dear fellow; it is simply nothing more than this childish nervousness I was telling you of. (They go into the right-hand room.)

Nora. Well!

Mrs. Linde. Gone out of town.

Nora. I could tell from your face.

Mrs. Linde. He is coming home tomorrow evening. I wrote a note for him.

Nora. You should have let it alone; you must prevent nothing. After all, it is splendid to be waiting for a wonderful thing to happen.

Mrs. Linde. What is it that you are waiting for?

Nora. Oh, you wouldn't understand. Go in to them, I will come in a moment. (Mrs. LINDE goes into the dining-room. NORA stands still for a little while, as if to compose herself. Then she looks at her watch.) Five o'clock. Seven hours until midnight; and then four-and-twenty hours until the next midnight. Then the Tarantella will be over. Twenty-four and seven? Thirty-one hours to live.

Helmer (from the doorway on the right). Where's my little skylark?

Nora (going to him with her arms outstretched). Here she is!

ACT III

(THE SAME SCENE. The table has been placed in the middle of the stage, with chairs around it. A lamp is burning on the table. The door into the hall stands open. Dance music is heard in the room above. Mrs. LINDE is sitting at the table idly turning over the leaves of a book; she tries to read, but does not seem able to collect her thoughts. Every now and then she listens intently for a sound at the outer door.)

Mrs. Linde (looking at her watch). Not yet and the time is nearly up. If only he does not. (Listens again.) Ah, there he is. (Goes into the hall and opens the outer door carefully. Light footsteps are heard on the stairs. She whispers.) Come in. There is no one here.

Krogstad (in the doorway). I found a note from you at home. What does this mean?

Mrs. Linde. It is absolutely necessary that I should have a talk with you.

Krogstad. Really? And is it absolutely necessary that it should be here?

Mrs. Linde. It is impossible where I live; there is no private entrance to my rooms. Come in; we are quite alone. The maid is asleep, and the Helmers are at the dance upstairs.

Krogstad (coming into the room). Are the Helmers really at a dance tonight?

Mrs. Linde. Yes, why not?

Krogstad. Certainly, why not?

Mrs. Linde. Now, Nils, let us have a talk.

Krogstad. Can we two have anything to talk about?

Mrs. Linde. We have a great deal to talk about.

Krogstad. I shouldn't have thought so.

Mrs. Linde. No, you have never properly understood me.

Krogstad. Was there anything else to understand except what was obvious to all the world, a heartless woman jilts a man when a more lucrative chance turns up?

Mrs. Linde. Do you believe I am as absolutely heartless as all that? And do you believe that I did it with a light heart?

Krogstad. Didn't you?

Mrs. Linde. Nils, did you really think that?

Krogstad. If it were as you say, why did you write to me as you did at the time?

Mrs. Linde. I could do nothing else. As I had to break with you, it was my duty also to put an end to all that you felt for me.

Krogstad (wringing his hands). So that was it. And all this, only for the sake of money!

Mrs. Linde. You must not forget that I had a helpless mother and two little brothers. We couldn't wait for you, Nils; your prospects seemed hopeless then.

Krogstad. That may be so, but you had no right to throw me over for anyone else's sake.

Mrs. Linde. Indeed I don't know. Many a time did I ask myself if I had the right to do it.

Krogstad (more gently). When I lost you, it was as if all the solid ground went from under my feet. Look at me now, I am a shipwrecked man clinging to a bit of wreckage.

Mrs. Linde. But help may be near.

Krogstad. It was near; but then you came and stood in my way.

Mrs. Linde. Unintentionally, Nils. It was only today that I learned it was your place I was going to take in the Bank.

Krogstad. I believe you, if you say so. But now that you know it, are you not going to give it up to me?

Mrs. Linde. No, because that would not benefit you in the least.

Krogstad. Oh, benefit, benefit, I would have done it whether or no.

Mrs. Linde. I have learned to act prudently. Life, and hard, bitter necessity have taught me that.

Krogstad. And life has taught me not to believe in fine speeches.

Mrs. Linde. Then life has taught you something very reasonable. But deeds you must believe in?

Krogstad. What do you mean by that?

Mrs. Linde. You said you were like a shipwrecked man clinging to some wreckage.

Krogstad. I had good reason to say so.

Mrs. Linde. Well, I am like a shipwrecked woman clinging to some wreckage, no one to mourn for, no one to care for.

Krogstad. It was your own choice.

Mrs. Linde. There was no other choice then.

Krogstad. Well, what now?

Mrs. Linde. Nils, how would it be if we two shipwrecked people could join forces?

Krogstad. What are you saying?

Mrs. Linde. Two on the same piece of wreckage would stand a better chance than each on their own.

Krogstad. Christine I...

Mrs. Linde. What do you suppose brought me to town?

Krogstad. Do you mean that you gave me a thought?

Mrs. Linde. I could not endure life without work. All my life, as long as I can remember, I have worked, and it has been my greatest and only pleasure. But now I am quite alone in the world, my life is so dreadfully empty and I feel so forsaken. There is not the least pleasure in working for one's self. Nils, give me someone and something to work for.

Krogstad. I don't trust that. It is nothing but a woman's overstrained sense of generosity that prompts you to make such an offer of yourself.

Mrs. Linde. Have you ever noticed anything of the sort in me?

Krogstad. Could you really do it? Tell me, do you know all about my past life?

Mrs. Linde. Yes.

Krogstad. And do you know what they think of me here?

Mrs. Linde. You seemed to me to imply that with me you might have been quite another man.

Krogstad. I am certain of it.

Mrs. Linde. Is it too late now?

Krogstad. Christine, are you saying this deliberately? Yes, I am sure you are. I see it in your face. Have you really the courage, then?

Mrs. Linde. I want to be a mother to someone, and your children need a mother. We two need each other. Nils, I have faith in your real character, I can dare anything together with you.

Krogstad (grasps her hands). Thanks, thanks, Christine! Now I shall find a way to clear myself in the eyes of the world. Ah, but I forgot

Mrs. Linde (listening). Hush! The Tarantella! Go, go!

Krogstad. Why? What is it?

Mrs. Linde. Do you hear them up there? When that is over, we may expect them back.

Krogstad. Yes, yes, I will go. But it is all no use. Of course you are not aware what steps I have taken in the matter of the Helmers.

Mrs. Linde. Yes, I know all about that.

Krogstad. And in spite of that have you the courage to?

Mrs. Linde. I understand very well to what lengths a man like you might be driven by despair.

Krogstad. If I could only undo what I have done!

Mrs. Linde. You cannot. Your letter is lying in the letter-box now.

Krogstad. Are you sure of that?

Mrs. Linde. Quite sure, but -

Krogstad (with a searching look at her). Is that what it all means? that you want to save your friend at any cost? Tell me frankly. Is that it?

Mrs. Linde. Nils, a woman who has once sold herself for another's sake, doesn't do it a second time.

Krogstad. I will ask for my letter back.

Mrs. Linde. No, no.

Krogstad. Yes, of course I will. I will wait here until Helmer comes; I will tell him he must give me my letter back, that it only concerns my dismissal, that he is not to read it

Mrs. Linde. No, Nils, you must not recall your letter.

Krogstad. But, tell me, wasn't it for that very purpose that you asked me to meet you here?

Mrs. Linde. In my first moment of fright, it was. But twenty-four hours have elapsed since then, and in that time I have witnessed incredible things in this house. Helmer must know all about it. This unhappy secret must be disclosed; they must have a complete understanding between them, which is impossible with all this concealment and falsehood going on.

Krogstad. Very well, if you will take the responsibility. But there is one thing I can do in any case, and I shall do it at once.

Mrs. Linde (listening). You must be quick and go! The dance is over; we are not safe a moment longer.

Krogstad. I will wait for you below.

Mrs. Linde. Yes, do. You must see me back to my door...

Krogstad. I have never had such an amazing piece of good fortune in my life! (Goes out through the outer door. The door between the room and the hall remains open.)

Mrs. Linde (tidying up the room and laying her hat and cloak ready). What a difference! what a difference! Someone to work for and live for, a home to bring comfort into. That I will do, indeed. I wish they would be quick and come (Listens.) Ah, there they are now. I must put on my things. (Takes up her hat and cloak. HELMER'S and NORA'S voices are heard outside; a key is turned, and HELMER brings NORA almost by force into the hall. She is in an Italian costume with a large black shawl around her; he is in evening dress, and a black domino which is flying open.)

Nora (hanging back in the doorway, and struggling with him). No, no, no! don't take me in. I want to go upstairs again; I don't want to leave so early.

Helmer. But, my dearest Nora

Nora. Please, Torvald dear, please, please, only an hour more.

Helmer. Not a single minute, my sweet Nora. You know that was our agreement. Come along into the room; you are catching cold standing there. (He brings her gently into the room, in spite of her resistance.)

Mrs. Linde. Good evening.

Nora. Christine!

Helmer. You here, so late, Mrs. Linde?

Mrs. Linde. Yes, you must excuse me; I was so anxious to see Nora in her dress.

Nora. Have you been sitting here waiting for me?

Mrs. Linde. Yes, unfortunately I came too late, you had already gone upstairs; and I thought I couldn't go away again without having seen you.

Helmer (taking off NORA'S shawl). Yes, take a good look at her. I think she is worth looking at. Isn't she charming, Mrs. Linde?

Mrs. Linde. Yes, indeed she is.

Helmer. Doesn't she look remarkably pretty? Everyone thought so at the dance. But she is terribly self-willed, this sweet little person. What are we to do with her? You will hardly believe that I had almost to bring her away by force.

Nora. Torvald, you will repent not having let me stay, even if it were only for half an hour.

Helmer. Listen to her, Mrs. Linde! She had danced her Tarantella, and it had been a tremendous success, as it deserved, although possibly the performance was a trifle too realistic, a little more so, I mean, than was strictly compatible with the limitations of art. But never mind about that! The chief thing is, she had made a success, she had made a tremendous success. Do you think I was going to let her remain there after that, and spoil the effect? No, indeed! I took my charming little Capri maiden, my capricious little Capri maiden, I should say, on my arm; took one quick turn round the room; a curtsey on either side, and, as they say in novels, the beautiful apparition disappeared. An exit ought always to be effective, Mrs. Linde; but that is what I cannot make Nora understand. Pooh! this room is hot. (Throws his domino on a chair, and opens the door of his room.) Hullo! it's all dark in here. Oh, of course, excuse me. (He goes in, and lights some candles.)

Nora (in a hurried and breathless whisper). Well?

Mrs. Linde (in a low voice). I have had a talk with him.

Nora. Yes, and

Mrs. Linde. Nora, you must tell your husband all about it.

Nora (in an expressionless voice). I knew it.

Mrs. Linde. You have nothing to be afraid of as far as Krogstad is concerned; but you must tell him.

Nora. I won't tell him.

Mrs. Linde. Then the letter will.

Nora. Thank you, Christine. Now I know what I must do. Hush!

Helmer (coming in again). Well, Mrs. Linde, have you admired her?

Mrs. Linde. Yes, and now I will say goodnight.

Helmer. What, already? Is this yours, this knitting?

Mrs. Linde (taking it). Yes, thank you, I had very nearly forgotten it.

Helmer. So you knit?

Mrs. Linde. Of course.

Helmer. Do you know, you ought to embroider.

Mrs. Linde. Really? Why?

Helmer. Yes, it's far more becoming. Let me show you. You hold the embroidery thus in your left hand, and use the needle with the right, like this, with a long, easy sweep. Do you see?

Mrs. Linde. Yes, perhaps

Helmer. But in the case of knitting that can never be anything but ungraceful; look here, the arms close together, the knitting-needles going up and down, it has a sort of Chinese effect. That was really excellent champagne they gave us.

Mrs. Linde. Well, goodnight, Nora, and don't be self-willed any more.

Helmer. That's right, Mrs. Linde.

Mrs. Linde. Goodnight, Mr. Helmer.

Helmer (accompanying her to the door). Goodnight, goodnight. I hope you will get home all right. I should be very happy to but you haven't any great distance to go. Goodnight, goodnight. (She goes out; he shuts the door after her, and comes in again.) Ah! at last we have got rid of her. She is a frightful bore, that woman.

Nora. Aren't you very tired, Torvald?

Helmer. No, not in the least.

Nora. Nor sleepy?

Helmer. Not a bit. On the contrary, I feel extraordinarily lively. And you? you really look both tired and sleepy.

Nora. Yes, I am very tired. I want to go to sleep at once.

Helmer. There, you see it was quite right of me not to let you stay there any longer.

Nora. Everything you do is quite right, Torvald.

Helmer (kissing her on the forehead). Now my little skylark is speaking reasonably. Did you notice what good spirits Rank was in this evening?

Nora. Really? Was he? I didn't speak to him at all.

Helmer. And I very little, but I have not for a long time seen him in such good form. (Looks for a while at her and then goes nearer to her.) It is delightful to be at home by ourselves again, to be all alone with you, you fascinating, charming little darling!

Nora. Don't look at me like that, Torvald.

Helmer. Why shouldn't I look at my dearest treasure? at all the beauty that is mine, all my very own?

Nora (going to the other side of the table). You mustn't say things like that to me tonight.

Helmer (following her). You have still got the Tarantella in your blood, I see. And it makes you more captivating than ever. Listen, the guests are beginning to go now. (In a lower voice.) Nora, soon the whole house will be quiet.

Nora. Yes, I hope so.

Helmer. Yes, my own darling Nora. Do you know, when I am out at a party with you like this, why I speak so little to you, keep away from you, and only send a stolen glance in your direction now and then? do you know why I do that? It is because I make believe to myself that we are secretly in love, and you are my secretly promised bride, and that no one suspects there is anything between us.

Nora. Yes, yes, I know very well your thoughts are with me all the time.

Helmer. And when we are leaving, and I am putting the shawl over your beautiful young shoulders, on your lovely neck, then I imagine that you are my young bride and that we have just come from the wedding, and I am bringing you for the first time into our home, to be alone with you for the first time, quite alone with my shy little darling! All this evening I have longed for nothing but you. When I watched the seductive figures of the Tarantella, my blood was on fire; I could endure it no longer, and that was why I brought you down so early

Nora. Go away, Torvald! You must let me go. I won't

Helmer. What's that? You're joking, my little Nora! You won't, you won't? Am I not your husband? (A knock is heard at the outer door.)

Nora (starting). Did you hear?

Helmer (going into the hall). Who is it?

Rank (outside). It is I. May I come in for a moment?

Helmer (in a fretful whisper). Oh, what does he want now? (Aloud.) Wait a minute! (Unlocks the door.) Come, that's kind of you not to pass by our door.

Rank. I thought I heard your voice, and felt as if I should like to look in. (With a swift glance round.) Ah, yes! these dear familiar rooms. You are very happy and cosy in here, you two.

Helmer. It seems to me that you looked after yourself pretty well upstairs too.

Rank. Excellently. Why shouldn't I? Why shouldn't one enjoy everything in this world? at any rate as much as one can, and as long as one can. The wine was capital

Helmer. Especially the champagne.

Rank. So you noticed that too? It is almost incredible how much I managed to put away!

Nora. Torvald drank a great deal of champagne tonight too.

Rank. Did he?

Nora. Yes, and he is always in such good spirits afterwards.

Rank. Well, why should one not enjoy a merry evening after a well-spent day?

Helmer. Well spent? I am afraid I can't take credit for that.

Rank (clapping him on the back). But I can, you know!

Nora. Doctor Rank, you must have been occupied with some scientific investigation today.

Rank. Exactly.

Helmer. Just listen! little Nora talking about scientific investigations!

Nora. And may I congratulate you on the result?

Rank. Indeed you may.

Nora. Was it favourable, then?

Rank. The best possible, for both doctor and patient, certainty.

Nora (quickly and searchingly). Certainty?

Rank. Absolute certainty. So wasn't I entitled to make a merry evening of it after that?

Nora. Yes, you certainly were, Doctor Rank. Helmer. I think so too, so long as you don't have to pay for it in the morning.

Rank. Oh well, one can't have anything in this life without paying for it.

Nora. Doctor Rank, are you fond of fancy-dress balls?

Rank. Yes, if there is a fine lot of pretty costumes.

Nora. Tell me, what shall we two wear at the next?

Helmer. Little featherbrain! are you thinking of the next already?

Rank. We two? Yes, I can tell you. You shall go as a good fairy

Helmer. Yes, but what do you suggest as an appropriate costume for that?

Rank. Let your wife go dressed just as she is in everyday life.

Helmer. That was really very prettily turned. But can't you tell us what you will be?

Rank. Yes, my dear friend, I have quite made up my mind about that.

Helmer. Well?

Rank. At the next fancy-dress ball I shall be invisible.

Helmer. That's a good joke!

Rank. There is a big black hat, have you never heard of hats that make you invisible? If you put one on, no one can see you.

Helmer (suppressing a smile). Yes, you are quite right.

Rank. But I am clean forgetting what I came for. Helmer, give me a cigar, one of the dark Havanas.

Helmer. With the greatest pleasure. (Offers him his case.)

Rank (takes a cigar and cuts off the end). Thanks.

Nora (striking a match). Let me give you a light.

Rank. Thank you. (She holds the match for him to light his cigar.) And now goodbye!

Helmer. Goodbye, goodbye, dear old man!

Nora. Sleep well, Doctor Rank.

Rank. Thank you for that wish.

Nora. Wish me the same.

Rank. You? Well, if you want me to sleep well! And thanks for the light. (He nods to them both and goes out.)

Helmer (in a subdued voice). He has drunk more than he ought.

Nora (absently). Maybe. (HELMER takes a bunch of keys out of his pocket and goes into the hall.) Torvald! what are you going to do there?

Helmer. Emptying the letter-box; it is quite full; there will be no room to put the newspaper in tomorrow morning.

Nora. Are you going to work tonight?

Helmer. You know quite well I'm not. What is this? Someone has been at the lock.

Nora. At the lock?

Helmer. Yes, someone has. What can it mean? I should never have thought the maid. Here is a broken hairpin. Nora, it is one of yours.

Nora (quickly). Then it must have been the children

Helmer. Then you must get them out of those ways. There, at last I have got it open. (Takes out the contents of the letter-box, and calls to the kitchen.) Helen! Helen, put out the light over the front door. (Goes back into the room and shuts the door into the hall. He holds out his hand full of letters.) Look at that, look what a heap of them there are. (Turning them over.) What on earth is that?

Nora (at the window). The letter, No! Torvald, no!

Helmer. Two cards of Rank's.

Nora. Of Doctor Rank's?

Helmer (looking at them). Doctor Rank. They were on the top. He must have put them in when he went out.

Nora. Is there anything written on them?

Helmer. There is a black cross over the name. Look there, what an uncomfortable idea! It looks as if he were announcing his own death.

Nora. It is just what he is doing.

Helmer. What? Do you know anything about it? Has he said anything to you?

Nora. Yes. He told me that when the cards came it would be his leave-taking from us. He means to shut himself up and die.

Helmer. My poor old friend! Certainly I knew we should not have him very long with us. But so soon! And so he hides himself away like a wounded animal.

Nora. If it has to happen, it is best it should be without a word, don't you think so, Torvald?

Helmer (walking up and down). He had so grown into our lives. I can't think of him as having gone out of them. He, with his sufferings and his loneliness, was like a cloudy background to our sunlit happiness. Well, perhaps it is best so. For him, anyway. (Standing still.) And perhaps for us too, Nora. We two are thrown quite upon each other now. (Puts his arms round her.) My darling wife, I don't feel as if I could hold you tight enough. Do you know, Nora, I have often wished that you might be threatened by some great danger, so that I might risk my life's blood, and everything, for your sake.

Nora (disengages herself, and says firmly and decidedly). Now you must read your letters, Torvald.

Helmer. No, no; not tonight. I want to be with you, my darling wife.

Nora. With the thought of your friend's death

Helmer. You are right, it has affected us both. Something ugly has come between us, the thought of the horrors of death. We must try and rid our minds of that. Until then, we will each go to our own room.

Nora (hanging on his neck). Goodnight, Torvald, Goodnight!

Helmer (kissing her on the forehead). Goodnight, my little singing-bird. Sleep sound, Nora. Now I will read my letters through. (He takes his letters and goes into his room, shutting the door after him.)

Nora (gropes distractedly about, seizes HELMER'S domino, throws it round her, while she says in quick, hoarse, spasmodic whispers). Never to see him again. Never! Never! (Puts her shawl over her head.) Never to see my children again either, never again. Never! Never! Ah! the icy, black water, the unfathomable depths. If only it were over! He has got it now, now he is reading it. Goodbye, Torvald and my children! (She is about to rush out through the hall, when HELMER opens his door hurriedly and stands with an open letter in his hand.)

Helmer. Nora!

Nora. Ah!

Helmer. What is this? Do you know what is in this letter?

Nora. Yes, I know. Let me go! Let me get out!

Helmer (holding her back). Where are you going?

Nora (trying to get free). You shan't save me, Torvald!

Helmer (reeling). True? Is this true, that I read here? Horrible! No, no, it is impossible that it can be true.

Nora. It is true. I have loved you above everything else in the world.

Helmer. Oh, don't let us have any silly excuses.

Nora (taking a step towards him). Torvald!

Helmer. Miserable creature, what have you done?

Nora. Let me go. You shall not suffer for my sake. You shall not take it upon yourself.

Helmer. No tragic airs, please. (Locks the hall door.) Here you shall stay and give me an explanation. Do you understand what you have done? Answer me! Do you understand what you have done?

Nora (looks steadily at him and says with a growing look of coldness in her face). Yes, now I am beginning to understand thoroughly.

Helmer (walking about the room). What a horrible awakening! All these eight years, she who was my joy and pride; a hypocrite, a liar, worse, worse, a criminal! The unutterable ugliness of it all! For shame! For shame! (NORA is silent and looks steadily at him. He stops in front of her.) I ought to have suspected that something of the sort would happen. I ought to have foreseen it. All your father's want of principle, be silent! all your father's want of principle has come out in you. No religion, no morality, no sense of duty. How I am punished for having winked at what he did! I did it for your sake, and this is how you repay me.

Nora. Yes, that's just it.

Helmer. Now you have destroyed all my happiness. You have ruined all my future. It is horrible to think of! I am in the power of an unscrupulous man; he can do what he likes with me, ask anything he likes of me, give me any orders he pleases, I dare not refuse. And I must sink to such miserable depths because of a thoughtless woman!

Nora. When I am out of the way, you will be free.

Helmer. No fine speeches, please. Your father had always plenty of those ready, too. What good would it be to me if you were out of the way, as you say? Not the slightest. He can make the affair known everywhere; and if he does, I may be falsely suspected of having been a party to your criminal action. Very likely people will think I was behind it all, that it was I who prompted you! And I have to thank you for all this, you whom I have cherished during the whole of our married life. Do you understand now what it is you have done for me?

Nora (coldly and quietly). Yes.

Helmer. It is so incredible that I can't take it in. But we must come to some understanding. Take off that shawl. Take it off, I tell you. I must try and appease him some way or another. The matter must be hushed up at any cost. And as for you and me, it must appear as if everything between us were just as before but naturally only in the eyes of the world. You will still remain in my house, that is a matter of course. But I shall not allow you to bring up the children; I dare not trust them to you. To think that I should be obliged to say so to one whom I have loved so dearly, and whom I still. No, that is all over. From this moment happiness is not the question; all that concerns us is to save the remains, the fragments, the appearance

(A ring is heard at the front-door bell.)

Helmer (with a start). What is that? So late! Can the worst? Can he? Hide yourself, Nora. Say you are ill.

(NORA stands motionless. HELMER goes and unlocks the hall door.)

Maid (half-dressed, comes to the door). A letter for the mistress.

Helmer. Give it to me. (Takes the letter, and shuts the door.) Yes, it is from him. You shall not have it; I will read it myself.

Nora. Yes, read it.

Helmer (standing by the lamp). I scarcely have the courage to do it. It may mean ruin for both of us. No, I must know. (Tears open the letter, runs his eye over a few lines, looks at a paper enclosed, and gives a shout of joy.) Nora! (She looks at him questioningly.) Nora! No, I must read it once again. Yes, it is true! I am saved! Nora, I am saved!

Nora. And I?

Helmer. You too, of course; we are both saved, both you and I. Look, he sends you your bond back. He says he regrets and repents, that a happy change in his life, never mind what he says! We are saved, Nora! No one can do anything to you. Oh, Nora, Nora! no, first I must destroy these hateful things. Let me see. (Takes a look at the bond.) No, no, I won't look at it. The whole thing shall be nothing but a bad dream to me. (Tears up the bond and both letters, throws them all into the stove, and watches them burn.) There, now it doesn't exist any longer. He says that since Christmas Eve you. These must have been three dreadful days for you, Nora.

Nora. I have fought a hard fight these three days.

Helmer. And suffered agonies, and seen no way out but. No, we won't call any of the horrors to mind. We will only shout with joy, and keep saying, "It's all over! It's all over!" Listen to me, Nora. You don't seem to realise that it is all over. What is this? such a cold, set face! My poor little Nora, I quite understand; you don't feel as if you could believe that I have forgiven you. But it is true, Nora, I swear it; I have forgiven you everything. I know that what you did, you did out of love for me.

Nora. That is true.

Helmer. You have loved me as a wife ought to love her husband. Only you had not sufficient knowledge to judge of the means you used. But do you suppose you are any the less dear to me, because you don't understand how to act on your own responsibility? No, no; only lean on me; I will advise you and direct you. I should not be a man if this womanly helplessness did not just give you a double attractiveness in my eyes. You must not think anymore about the hard things I said in my first moment of consternation, when I thought everything was going to overwhelm me. I have forgiven you, Nora; I swear to you I have forgiven you.

Nora. Thank you for your forgiveness. (She goes out through the door to the right.)

Helmer. No, don't go. (Looks in.) What are you doing in there?

Nora (from within). Taking off my fancy dress.

Helmer (standing at the open door). Yes, do. Try and calm yourself, and make your mind easy again, my frightened little singing-bird. Be at rest, and feel secure; I have broad wings to shelter you under. (Walks up and down by the door.) How warm and cosy our home is, Nora. Here is shelter for you; here I will protect you like a hunted dove that I have saved from a hawk's claws; I will bring peace to your poor beating heart. It will come, little by little, Nora, believe me. Tomorrow morning you will look upon it all quite differently; soon everything will be just as it was before. Very soon you won't need me to assure you that I have forgiven you; you will yourself feel the certainty that I have done so. Can you suppose I should ever think of such a thing as repudiating you, or even reproaching you? You have no idea what a true man's heart is like, Nora. There is something so indescribably sweet and satisfying, to a man, in the knowledge that he has forgiven his wife, forgiven her freely, and with all his heart. It seems as if that had made her, as it were, doubly his own; he has given her a new life, so to speak; and she has in a way become both wife and child to him. So you shall be for me after this, my little scared, helpless darling. Have no anxiety about anything, Nora; only be frank and open with me, and I will serve as will and conscience both to you. What is this? Not gone to bed? Have you changed your things?

Nora (in everyday dress). Yes, Torvald, I have changed my things now.

Helmer. But what for? so late as this.

Nora. I shall not sleep tonight.

Helmer. But, my dear Nora

Nora (looking at her watch). It is not so very late. Sit down here, Torvald. You and I have much to say to one another. (She sits down at one side of the table.)

Helmer. Nora, what is this? this cold, set face?

Nora. Sit down. It will take some time; I have a lot to talk over with you.

Helmer (sits down at the opposite side of the table). You alarm me, Nora! and I don't understand you.

Nora. No, that is just it. You don't understand me, and I have never understood you either before tonight. No, you mustn't interrupt me. You must simply listen to what I say. Torvald, this is a settling of accounts.

Helmer. What do you mean by that?

Nora (after a short silence). Isn't there one thing that strikes you as strange in our sitting here like this?

Helmer. What is that?

Nora. We have been married now eight years. Does it not occur to you that this is the first time we two, you and I, husband and wife, have had a serious conversation?

Helmer. What do you mean by serious?

Nora. In all these eight years, longer than that, from the very beginning of our acquaintance, we have never exchanged a word on any serious subject.

Helmer. Was it likely that I would be continually and forever telling you about worries that you could not help me to bear?

Nora. I am not speaking about business matters. I say that we have never sat down in earnest together to try and get at the bottom of anything.

Helmer. But, dearest Nora, would it have been any good to you?

Nora. That is just it; you have never understood me. I have been greatly wronged, Torvald, first by papa and then by you.

Helmer. What! By us two, by us two, who have loved you better than anyone else in the world?

Nora (shaking her head). You have never loved me. You have only thought it pleasant to be in love with me.

Helmer. Nora, what do I hear you saying?

Nora. It is perfectly true, Torvald. When I was at home with papa, he told me his opinion about everything, and so I had the same opinions; and if I differed from him I concealed the fact, because he would not have liked it. He called me his doll-child, and he played with me just as I used to play with my dolls. And when I came to live with you

Helmer. What sort of an expression is that to use about our marriage?

Nora (undisturbed). I mean that I was simply transferred from papa's hands into yours. You arranged everything according to your own taste, and so I got the same tastes as your else I pretended to, I am really not quite sure which, I think sometimes the one and sometimes the other. When I look back on it, it seems to me as if I had been living here like a poor woman, just from hand to mouth. I have existed merely to perform tricks for you, Torvald. But you would have it so. You and papa have committed a great sin against me. It is your fault that I have made nothing of my life.

Helmer. How unreasonable and how ungrateful you are, Nora! Have you not been happy here?

Nora. No, I have never been happy. I thought I was, but it has never really been so.

Helmer. Not, not happy!

Nora. No, only merry. And you have always been so kind to me. But our home has been nothing but a playroom. I have been your doll-wife, just as at home I was papa's doll-child; and here the children have been my dolls. I thought it great fun when you played with me, just as they thought it great fun when I played with them. That is what our marriage has been, Torvald.

Helmer. There is some truth in what you say, exaggerated and strained as your view of it is. But for the future it shall be different. Playtime shall be over, and lesson-time shall begin.

Nora. Whose lessons? Mine, or the children's?

Helmer. Both yours and the children's, my darling Nora.

Nora. Alas, Torvald, you are not the man to educate me into being a proper wife for you.

Helmer. And you can say that!

Nora. And I, how am I fitted to bring up the children?

Helmer. Nora!

Nora. Didn't you say so yourself a little while ago, that you dare not trust me to bring them up?

Helmer. In a moment of anger! Why do you pay any heed to that?

Nora. Indeed, you were perfectly right. I am not fit for the task. There is another task I must undertake first. I must try and educate myself, you are not the man to help me in that. I must do that for myself. And that is why I am going to leave you now.

Helmer (springing up). What do you say?

Nora. I must stand quite alone, if I am to understand myself and everything about me. It is for that reason that I cannot remain with you any longer.

Helmer. Nora, Nora!

Nora. I am going away from here now, at once. I am sure Christine will take me in for the night

Helmer. You are out of your mind! I won't allow it! I forbid you!

Nora. It is no use forbidding me anything any longer. I will take with me what belongs to myself. I will take nothing from you, either now or later.

Helmer. What sort of madness is this!

Nora. Tomorrow I shall go home, I mean, to my old home. It will be easiest for me to find something to do there.

Helmer. You blind, foolish woman!

Nora. I must try and get some sense, Torvald.

Helmer. To desert your home, your husband and your children! And you don't consider what people will say!

Nora. I cannot consider that at all. I only know that it is necessary for me.

Helmer. It's shocking. This is how you would neglect your most sacred duties.

Nora. What do you consider my most sacred duties?

Helmer. Do I need to tell you that? Are they not your duties to your husband and your children?

Nora. I have other duties just as sacred.

Helmer. That you have not. What duties could those be?

Nora. Duties to myself.

Helmer. Before all else, you are a wife and a mother.

Nora. I don't believe that any longer. I believe that before all else I am a reasonable human being, just as you are or, at all events, that I must try and become one. I know quite well, Torvald, that most people would think you right, and that views of that kind are to be found in books; but I can no longer content myself with what most people say, or with what is found in books. I must think over things for myself and get to understand them.

Helmer. Can you not understand your place in your own home? Have you not a reliable guide in such matters as that? have you no religion?

Nora. I am afraid, Torvald, I do not exactly know what religion is.

Helmer. What are you saying?

Nora. I know nothing but what the clergyman said, when I went to be confirmed. He told us that religion was this, and that, and the other. When I am away from all this, and am alone, I will look into that matter too. I will see if what the clergyman said is true, or at all events if it is true for me.

Helmer. This is unheard of in a girl of your age! But if religion cannot lead you aright, let me try and awaken your conscience. I suppose you have some moral sense? Or, answer me, am I to think you have none?

Nora. I assure you, Torvald, that is not an easy question to answer. I really don't know. The thing perplexes me altogether. I only know that you and I look at it in quite a different light. I am learning, too, that the law is quite another thing from what I supposed; but I find it impossible to convince myself that the law is right. According to it a woman has no right to spare her old dying father, or to save her husband's life. I can't believe that.

Helmer. You talk like a child. You don't understand the conditions of the world in which you live.

Nora. No, I don't. But now I am going to try. I am going to see if I can make out who is right, the world or I.

Helmer. You are ill, Nora; you are delirious; I almost think you are out of your mind.

Nora. I have never felt my mind so clear and certain as tonight.

Helmer. And is it with a clear and certain mind that you forsake your husband and your children?

Nora. Yes, it is.

Helmer. Then there is only one possible explanation.

Nora. What is that?

Helmer. You do not love me anymore.

Nora. No, that is just it.

Helmer. Nora! and you can say that?

Nora. It gives me great pain, Torvald, for you have always been so kind to me, but I cannot help it. I do not love you any more.

Helmer (regaining his composure). Is that a clear and certain conviction too?

Nora. Yes, absolutely clear and certain. That is the reason why I will not stay here any longer.

Helmer. And can you tell me what I have done to forfeit your love?

Nora. Yes, indeed I can. It was tonight, when the wonderful thing did not happen; then I saw you were not the man I had thought you were.

Helmer. Explain yourself better. I don't understand you.

Nora. I have waited so patiently for eight years; for, goodness knows, I knew very well that wonderful things don't happen every day. Then this horrible misfortune came upon me; and then I felt quite certain that the wonderful thing was going to happen at last. When Krogstad's letter was lying out there, never for a moment did I imagine that you would consent to accept this man's conditions. I was so absolutely certain that you would say to him: Publish the thing to the whole world. And when that was done

Helmer. Yes, what then? when I had exposed my wife to shame and disgrace?

Nora. When that was done, I was so absolutely certain, you would come forward and take everything upon yourself, and say: I am the guilty one.

Helmer. Nora!

Nora. You mean that I would never have accepted such a sacrifice on your part? No, of course not. But what would my assurances have been worth against yours? That was the wonderful thing which I hoped for and feared; and it was to prevent that, that I wanted to kill myself.

Helmer. I would gladly work night and day for you, Nora, bear sorrow and want for your sake. But no man would sacrifice his honour for the one he loves.

Nora. It is a thing hundreds of thousands of women have done.

Helmer. Oh, you think and talk like a heedless child.

Nora. Maybe. But you neither think nor talk like the man I could bind myself to. As soon as your fear was over and it was not fear for what threatened me, but for what might happen to you, when the whole thing was past, as far as you were concerned it was exactly as if nothing at all had happened. Exactly as before, I was your little skylark, your doll, which you would in future treat with doubly gentle care, because it was so brittle and fragile. (Getting up.) Torvald, it was then it dawned upon me that for eight years I had been living here with a strange man, and had borne him three children. Oh, I can't bear to think of it! I could tear myself into little bits!

Helmer (sadly). I see, I see. An abyss has opened between us, there is no denying it. But, Nora, would it not be possible to fill it up?

Nora. As I am now, I am no wife for you.

Helmer. I have it in me to become a different man.

Nora. Perhaps, if your doll is taken away from you.

Helmer. But to part! to part from you! No, no, Nora, I can't understand that idea.

Nora (going out to the right). That makes it all the more certain that it must be done. (She comes back with her cloak and hat and a small bag which she puts on a chair by the table.)

Helmer. Nora, Nora, not now! Wait until tomorrow.

Nora (putting on her cloak). I cannot spend the night in a strange man's room.

Helmer. But can't we live here like brother and sister?

Nora (putting on her hat). You know very well that would not last long. (Puts the shawl round her.) Goodbye, Torvald. I won't see the little ones. I know they are in better hands than mine. As I am now, I can be of no use to them.

Helmer. But some day, Nora, some day?

Nora. How can I tell? I have no idea what is going to become of me.

Helmer. But you are my wife, whatever becomes of you.

Nora. Listen, Torvald. I have heard that when a wife deserts her husband's house, as I am doing now, he is legally freed from all obligations towards her. In any case, I set you free from all your obligations. You are not to feel yourself bound in the slightest way, any more than I shall. There must be perfect freedom on both sides. See, here is your ring back. Give me mine.

Helmer. That too?

Nora. That too.

Helmer. Here it is.

Nora. That's right. Now it is all over. I have put the keys here. The maids know all about everything in the house, better than I do. Tomorrow, after I have left her, Christine will come here and pack up my own things that I brought with me from home. I will have them sent after me.

Helmer. All over! All over! Nora, shall you never think of me again?

Nora. I know I shall often think of you, the children, and this house.

Helmer. May I write to you, Nora?

Nora. No, never. You must not do that.

Helmer. But at least let me send you

Nora. Nothing, nothing

Helmer. Let me help you if you are in want.

Nora. No. I can receive nothing from a stranger.

Helmer. Nora, can I never be anything more than a stranger to you?

Nora (taking her bag). Ah, Torvald, the most wonderful thing of all would have to happen.

Helmer. Tell me what that would be!

Nora. Both you and I would have to be so changed that. Oh, Torvald, I don't believe any longer in wonderful things happening.

Helmer. But I will believe in it. Tell me! So changed that?

Nora. That our life together would be a real wedlock. Goodbye. (She goes out through the hall.)

Helmer (sinks down on a chair at the door and buries his face in his hands). Nora! Nora! (Looks round, and rises.) Empty. She is gone. (A hope flashes across his mind.) The most wonderful thing of all?

(The sound of a door shutting is heard from below.)

Henrik Ibsen - An Enemy Of The People, A Play In Five Acts

Index Of Contents

DRAMATIS PERSONAE
Dr. Thomas Stockmann, Medical Officer of the Municipal Baths.
Mrs. Stockmann, his wife.
Petra (their daughter) a teacher.
Ejlif & Morten (their sons, aged 13 and 10 respectively).
Peter Stockmann (the Doctor's elder brother),

Mayor of the Town and Chief Constable, Chairman of the Baths' Committee, etc.
Morten Kiil, a tanner (Mrs. Stockmann's adoptive father).
Hovstad, editor of the "People's Messenger."
Billing, sub-editor.
Captain Horster.
Aslaksen, a printer.
Men of various conditions and occupations, a few women, and a troop of schoolboys, the audience at a public meeting.
The action takes place in a coastal town in southern Norway,

AN ENEMY OF THE PEOPLE

ACT I

(SCENE. DR. STOCKMANN'S sitting-room. It is evening. The room is plainly but neatly appointed and furnished. In the right-hand wall are two doors; the farther leads out to the hall, the nearer to the doctor's study. In the left-hand wall, opposite the door leading to the hall, is a door leading to the other rooms occupied by the family. In the middle of the same wall stands the stove, and, further forward, a couch with a looking-glass hanging over it and an oval table in front of it. On the table, a lighted lamp, with a lampshade. At the back of the room, an open door leads to the dining-room. BILLING is seen sitting at the dining table, on which a lamp is burning. He has a napkin tucked under his chin, and MRS. STOCKMANN is standing by the table handing him a large plate-full of roast beef. The other places at the table are empty, and the table somewhat in disorder, evidently a meal having recently been finished.)

Mrs. Stockmann. You see, if you come an hour late, Mr. Billing, you have to put up with cold meat.

Billing (as he eats). It is uncommonly good, thank you, remarkably good.

Mrs. Stockmann. My husband makes such a point of having his meals punctually, you know.

Billing. That doesn't affect me a bit. Indeed, I almost think I enjoy a meal all the better when I can sit down and eat all by myself, and undisturbed.

Mrs. Stockmann. Oh well, as long as you are enjoying it. (Turns to the hall door, listening.) I expect that is Mr. Hovstad coming too.

Billing. Very likely.

(PETER STOCKMANN comes in. He wears an overcoat and his official hat, and carries a stick.)

Peter Stockmann. Good evening, Katherine.

Mrs. Stockmann (coming forward into the sitting-room). Ah, good evening, is it you? How good of you to come up and see us!

Peter Stockmann. I happened to be passing, and so (looks into the dining-room). But you have company with you, I see.

Mrs. Stockmann (a little embarrassed). Oh, no, it was quite by chance he came in. (Hurriedly.) Won't you come in and have something, too?

Peter Stockmann. I! No, thank you. Good gracious, hot meat at night! Not with my digestion.

Mrs. Stockmann. Oh, but just once in a way

Peter Stockmann. No, no, my dear lady; I stick to my tea and bread and butter. It is much more wholesome in the long run and a little more economical, too.

Mrs. Stockmann (smiling). Now you mustn't think that Thomas and I are spendthrifts.

Peter Stockmann. Not you, my dear; I would never think that of you. (Points to the Doctor's study.) Is he not at home?

Mrs. Stockmann. No, he went out for a little turn after supper, he and the boys.

Peter Stockmann. I doubt if that is a wise thing to do. (Listens.) I fancy I hear him coming now.

Mrs. Stockmann. No, I don't think it is he. (A knock is heard at the door.) Come in! (HOVSTAD comes in from the hall.) Oh, it is you, Mr. Hovstad!

Hovstad. Yes, I hope you will forgive me, but I was delayed at the printers. Good evening, Mr. Mayor.

Peter Stockmann (bowing a little distantly). Good evening. You have come on business, no doubt.

Hovstad. Partly. It's about an article for the paper.

Peter Stockmann. So I imagined. I hear my brother has become a prolific contributor to the "People's Messenger."

Hovstad. Yes, he is good enough to write in the "People's Messenger" when he has any home truths to tell.

Mrs. Stockmann (to HOVSTAD). But won't you? (Points to the dining-room.)

Peter Stockmann. Quite so, quite so. I don't blame him in the least, as a writer, for addressing himself to the quarters where he will find the readiest sympathy. And, besides that, I personally have no reason to bear any ill will to your paper, Mr. Hovstad.

Hovstad. I quite agree with you.

Peter Stockmann. Taking one thing with another, there is an excellent spirit of toleration in the town, an admirable municipal spirit. And it all springs from the fact of our having a great common interest to unite us, an interest that is in an equally high degree the concern of every right-minded citizen.

Hovstad. The Baths, yes.

Peter Stockmann. Exactly, our fine, new, handsome Baths. Mark my words, Mr. Hovstad the Baths will become the focus of our municipal life! Not a doubt of it!

Mrs. Stockmann. That is just what Thomas says.

Peter Stockmann. Think how extraordinarily the place has developed within the last year or two! Money has been flowing in, and there is some life and some business doing in the town. Houses and landed property are rising in value every day.

Hovstad. And unemployment is diminishing,

Peter Stockmann. Yes, that is another thing. The burden on the poor rates has been lightened, to the great relief of the propertied classes; and that relief will be even greater if only we get a really good summer this year, and lots of visitors, plenty of invalids, who will make the Baths talked about.

Hovstad. And there is a good prospect of that, I hear.

Peter Stockmann. It looks very promising. Inquiries about apartments and that sort of thing are reaching us, every day.

Hovstad. Well, the doctor's article will come in very suitably.

Peter Stockmann. Has he been writing something just lately?

Hovstad. This is something he wrote in the winter; a recommendation of the Baths, an account of the excellent sanitary conditions here. But I held the article over, temporarily.

Peter Stockmann. Ah, some little difficulty about it, I suppose?

Hovstad. No, not at all; I thought it would be better to wait until the spring, because it is just at this time that people begin to think seriously about their summer quarters.

Peter Stockmann. Quite right; you were perfectly right, Mr. Hovstad.

Hovstad. Yes, Thomas is really indefatigable when it is a question of the Baths.

Peter Stockmann. Well remember, he is the Medical Officer to the Baths.

Hovstad. Yes, and what is more, they owe their existence to him.

Peter Stockmann. To him? Indeed! It is true I have heard from time to time that some people are of that opinion. At the same time I must say I imagined that I took a modest part in the enterprise.

Mrs. Stockmann. Yes, that is what Thomas is always saying.

Hovstad. But who denies it, Mr. Stockmann? You set the thing going and made a practical concern of it; we all know that. I only meant that the idea of it came first from the doctor.

Peter Stockmann. Oh, ideas yes! My brother has had plenty of them in his time unfortunately. But when it is a question of putting an idea into practical shape, you have to apply to a man of different mettle. Mr. Hovstad. And I certainly should have thought that in this house at least...

Mrs. Stockmann. My dear Peter

Hovstad. How can you think that?

Mrs. Stockmann. Won't you go in and have something, Mr. Hovstad? My husband is sure to be back directly.

Hovstad. Thank you, perhaps just a morsel. (Goes into the dining-room.)

Peter Stockmann (lowering his voice a little). It is a curious thing that these farmers' sons never seem to lose their want of tact.

Mrs. Stockmann. Surely it is not worth bothering about! Cannot you and Thomas share the credit as brothers?

Peter Stockmann. I should have thought so; but apparently some people are not satisfied with a share.

Mrs. Stockmann. What nonsense! You and Thomas get on so capitally together. (Listens.) There he is at last, I think. (Goes out and opens the door leading to the hall.)

Dr. Stockmann (laughing and talking outside). Look here, here is another guest for you, Katherine. Isn't that jolly! Come in, Captain Horster; hang your coat up on this peg. Ah, you don't wear an overcoat. Just think, Katherine; I met him in the street and could hardly persuade him to come up! (CAPTAIN HORSTER comes into the room and greets MRS. STOCKMANN. He is followed by DR. STOCKMANN.) Come along in, boys. They are ravenously hungry again, you know. Come along, Captain Horster; you must have a slice of beef. (Pushes HORSTER into the dining-room. EJLIF and MORTEN go in after them.)

Mrs. Stockmann. But, Thomas, don't you see?

Dr. Stockmann (turning in the doorway). Oh, is it you, Peter? (Shakes hands with him.) Now that is very delightful.

Peter Stockmann. Unfortunately I must go in a moment

Dr. Stockmann. Rubbish! There is some toddy just coming in. You haven't forgotten the toddy, Katherine?

Mrs. Stockmann. Of course not; the water is boiling now. (Goes into the dining-room.)

Peter Stockmann. Toddy too!

Dr. Stockmann. Yes, sit down and we will have it comfortably.

Peter Stockmann. Thanks, I never care about an evening's drinking.

Dr. Stockmann. But this isn't an evening's drinking.

Peter Stockmann. It seems to me. (Looks towards the dining-room.) It is extraordinary how they can put away all that food.

Dr. Stockmann (rubbing his hands). Yes, isn't it splendid to see young people eat? They have always got an appetite, you know! That's as it should be. Lots of food, to build up their strength! They are the people who are going to stir up the fermenting forces of the future, Peter.

Peter Stockmann. May I ask what they will find here to "stir up," as you put it?

Dr. Stockmann. Ah, you must ask the young people that when the times comes. We shan't be able to see it, of course. That stands to reason, two old fogies, like us.

Peter Stockmann. Really, really! I must say that is an extremely odd expression to

Dr. Stockmann. Oh, you mustn't take me too literally, Peter. I am so heartily happy and contented, you know. I think it is such an extraordinary piece of good fortune to be in the middle of all this growing, germinating life. It is a splendid time to live in! It is as if a whole new world were being created around one.

Peter Stockmann. Do you really think so?

Dr. Stockmann. Ah, naturally you can't appreciate it as keenly as I. You have lived all your life in these surroundings, and your impressions have been blunted. But I, who have been buried all these years in my little corner up north, almost without ever seeing a stranger who might bring new ideas with him, well, in my case it has just the same effect as if I had been transported into the middle of a crowded city.

Peter Stockmann. Oh, a city!

Dr. Stockmann. I know, I know; it is all cramped enough here, compared with many other places. But there is life here, there is promise, there are innumerable things to work for and fight for; and that is the main thing. (Calls.) Katherine, hasn't the postman been here?

Mrs. Stockmann (from the dining-room). No.

Dr. Stockmann. And then to be comfortably off, Peter! That is something one learns to value, when one has been on the brink of starvation, as we have.

Peter Stockmann. Oh, surely

Dr. Stockmann. Indeed I can assure you we have often been very hard put to it, up there. And now to be able to live like a lord! Today, for instance, we had roast beef for dinner and, what is more, for supper too. Won't you come and have a little bit? Or let me show it you, at any rate? Come here

Peter Stockmann. No, no, not for worlds!

Dr. Stockmann. Well, but just come here then. Do you see, we have got a table-cover?

Peter Stockmann. Yes, I noticed it.

Dr. Stockmann. And we have got a lamp-shade too. Do you see? All out of Katherine's savings! It makes the room so cosy. Don't you think so? Just stand here for a moment, no, no, not there, just here, that's it! Look now, when you get the light on it altogether. I really think it looks very nice, doesn't it?

Peter Stockmann. Oh, if you can afford luxuries of this kind

Dr. Stockmann. Yes, I can afford it now. Katherine tells me I earn almost as much as we spend.

Peter Stockmann. Almost, yes!

Dr. Stockmann. But a scientific man must live in a little bit of style. I am quite sure an ordinary civil servant spends more in a year than I do.

Peter Stockmann. I daresay. A civil servant, a man in a well-paid position...

Dr. Stockmann. Well, any ordinary merchant, then! A man in that position spends two or three times as much as

Peter Stockmann. It just depends on circumstances.

Dr. Stockmann. At all events I assure you I don't waste money unprofitably. But I can't find it in my heart to deny myself the pleasure of entertaining my friends. I need that sort of thing, you know. I have lived for so long shut out of it all, that it is a necessity of life to me to mix with young, eager, ambitious men, men of liberal and active minds; and that describes every one of those fellows who are enjoying their supper in there. I wish you knew more of Hovstad.

Peter Stockmann. By the way, Hovstad was telling me he was going to print another article of yours.

Dr. Stockmann. An article of mine?

Peter Stockmann. Yes, about the Baths. An article you wrote in the winter.

Dr. Stockmann. Oh, that one! No, I don't intend that to appear just for the present.

Peter Stockmann. Why not? It seems to me that this would be the most opportune moment.

Dr. Stockmann. Yes, very likely under normal conditions. (Crosses the room.)

Peter Stockmann (following him with his eyes). Is there anything abnormal about the present conditions?

Dr. Stockmann (standing still). To tell you the truth, Peter, I can't say just at this moment, at all events not tonight. There may be much that is very abnormal about the present conditions and it is possible there may be nothing abnormal about them at all. It is quite possible it may be merely my imagination.

Peter Stockmann. I must say it all sounds most mysterious. Is there something going on that I am to be kept in ignorance of? I should have imagined that I, as Chairman of the governing body of the Baths

Dr. Stockmann. And I should have imagined that I..... Oh, come, don't let us fly out at one another, Peter.

Peter Stockmann. Heaven forbid! I am not in the habit of flying out at people, as you call it. But I am entitled to request most emphatically that all arrangements shall be made in a businesslike manner, through the proper channels, and shall be dealt with by the legally constituted authorities. I can allow no going behind our backs by any roundabout means.

Dr. Stockmann. Have I ever at any time tried to go behind your backs?

Peter Stockmann. You have an ingrained tendency to take your own way, at all events; and, that is almost equally inadmissible in a well ordered community, The individual ought undoubtedly to acquiesce in subordinating himself to the community or, to speak more accurately, to the authorities who have the care of the community's welfare.

Dr. Stockmann. Very likely. But what the deuce has all this got to do with me?

Peter Stockmann. That is exactly what you never appear to be willing to learn, my dear Thomas. But, mark my words, some day you will have to suffer for it, sooner or later. Now I have told you. Good-bye.

Dr. Stockmann. Have you taken leave of your senses? You are on the wrong scent altogether.

Peter Stockmann. I am not usually that. You must excuse me now if I (calls into the dining-room). Good night, Katherine. Good night, gentlemen. (Goes out.)

Mrs. Stockmann (coming from the dining-room). Has he gone?

Dr. Stockmann. Yes, and in such a bad temper.

Mrs. Stockmann. But, dear Thomas, what have you been doing to him again?

Dr. Stockmann. Nothing at all. And, anyhow, he can't oblige me to make my report before the proper time.

Mrs. Stockmann. What have you got to make a report to him about?

Dr. Stockmann. Hm! Leave that to me, Katherine. It is an extraordinary thing that the postman doesn't come.

(HOVSTAD, BILLING and HORSTER have got up from the table and come into the sitting-room. EJLIF and MORTEN come in after them.)

Billing (stretching himself). Ah! one feels a new man after a meal like that.

Hovstad. The mayor wasn't in a very sweet temper tonight, then.

Dr. Stockmann. It is his stomach; he has wretched digestion.

Hovstad. I rather think it was us two of the "People's Messenger" that he couldn't digest.

Mrs. Stockmann. I thought you came out of it pretty well with him.

Hovstad. Oh yes; but it isn't anything more than a sort of truce.

Billing. That is just what it is! That word sums up the situation.

Dr. Stockmann. We must remember that Peter is a lonely man, poor chap. He has no home comforts of any kind; nothing but everlasting business. And all that infernal weak tea wash that he pours into himself! Now then, my boys, bring chairs up to the table. Aren't we going to have that toddy, Katherine?

Mrs. Stockmann (going into the dining-room). I am just getting it.

Dr. Stockmann. Sit down here on the couch beside me, Captain Horster. We so seldom see you. Please sit down, my friends. (They sit down at the table. MRS. STOCKMANN brings a tray, with a spirit-lamp, glasses, bottles, etc., upon it.)

Mrs. Stockmann. There you are! This is arrack, and this is rum, and this one is the brandy. Now every one must help themselves.

Dr. Stockmann (taking a glass). We will. (They all mix themselves some toddy.) And let us have the cigars. Ejlif, you know where the box is. And you, Morten, can fetch my pipe. (The two boys go into the room on the right.) I have a suspicion that Ejlif pockets a cigar now and then! but I take no notice of it. (Calls out.) And my smoking-cap too, Morten. Katherine, you can tell him where I left it. Ah, he has got it. (The boys bring the various things.) Now, my friends. I stick to my pipe, you know. This one has seen plenty of bad weather with me up north. (Touches glasses with them.) Your good health! Ah, it is good to be sitting snug and warm here.

Mrs. Stockmann (who sits knitting). Do you sail soon, Captain Horster?

Horster. I expect to be ready to sail next week.

Mrs. Stockmann. I suppose you are going to America?

Horster. Yes, that is the plan.

Mrs. Stockmann. Then you won't be able to take part in the coming election?

Horster. Is there going to be an election?

Billing. Didn't you know?

Horster. No, I don't mix myself up with those things.

Billing. But do you not take an interest in public affairs?

Horster. No, I don't know anything about politics.

Billing. All the same, one ought to vote, at any rate.

Horster. Even if one doesn't know anything about what is going on?

Billing. Doesn't know! What do you mean by that? A community is like a ship; everyone ought to be prepared to take the helm.

Horster. Maybe that is all very well on shore; but on board ship it wouldn't work.

Hovstad. It is astonishing how little most sailors care about what goes on on shore.

Billing. Very extraordinary.

Dr. Stockmann. Sailors are like birds of passage; they feel equally at home in any latitude. And that is only an additional reason for our being all the more keen, Hovstad. Is there to be anything of public interest in tomorrow's "Messenger"?

Hovstad. Nothing about municipal affairs. But the day after tomorrow I was thinking of printing your article

Dr. Stockmann. Ah, devil take it, my article! Look here, that must wait a bit.

Hovstad. Really? We had just got convenient space for it, and I thought it was just the opportune moment

Dr. Stockmann. Yes, yes, very likely you are right; but it must wait all the same. I will explain to you later. (PETRA comes in from the hall, in hat and cloak and with a bundle of exercise books under her arm.)

Petra. Good evening.

Dr. Stockmann. Good evening, Petra; come along.

(Mutual greetings; PETRA takes off her things and puts them down on a chair by the door.)

Petra. And you have all been sitting here enjoying yourselves, while I have been out slaving!

Dr. Stockmann. Well, come and enjoy yourself too!

Billing. May I mix a glass for you?

Petra (coming to the table). Thanks, I would rather do it; you always mix it too strong. But I forgot, father, I have a letter for you. (Goes to the chair where she has laid her things.)

Dr. Stockmann. A letter? From whom?

Petra (looking in her coat pocket). The postman gave it to me just as I was going out.

Dr. Stockmann (getting up and going to her). And you only give it to me now!

Petra. I really had not time to run up again. There it is!

Dr. Stockmann (seizing the letter). Let's see, let's see, child! (Looks at the address.) Yes, that's all right!

Mrs. Stockmann. Is it the one you have been expecting go anxiously, Thomas?

Dr. Stockmann. Yes, it is. I must go to my room now and... Where shall I get a light, Katherine? Is there no lamp in my room again?

Mrs. Stockmann. Yes, your lamp is already lit on your desk.

Dr. Stockmann. Good, good. Excuse me for a moment, (Goes into his study.)

Petra. What do you suppose it is, mother?

Mrs. Stockmann. I don't know; for the last day or two he has always been asking if the postman has not been.

Billing. Probably some country patient.

Petra. Poor old dad! he will overwork himself soon. (Mixes a glass for herself.) There, that will taste good!

Hovstad. Have you been teaching in the evening school again today?

Petra (sipping from her glass). Two hours.

Billing. And four hours of school in the morning?

Petra. Five hours.

Mrs. Stockmann. And you have still got exercises to correct, I see.

Petra. A whole heap, yes.

Horster. You are pretty full up with work too, it seems to me.

Petra. Yes but that is good. One is so delightfully tired after it.

Billing. Do you like that?

Petra. Yes, because one sleeps so well then.

Morten. You must be dreadfully wicked, Petra.

Petra. Wicked?

Morten. Yes, because you work so much. Mr. Rorlund says work is a punishment for our sins.

Ejlif. Pooh, what a duffer, you are, to believe a thing like that!

Mrs. Stockmann. Come, come, Ejlif!

Billing (laughing). That's capital!

Hovstad. Don't you want to work as hard as that, Morten?

Morten. No, indeed I don't.

Hovstad. What do you want to be, then?

Morten. I should like best to be a Viking,

Ejlif. You would have to be a pagan then.

Morten. Well, I could become a pagan, couldn't I?

Billing. I agree with you, Morten! My sentiments, exactly.

Mrs. Stockmann (signalling to him). I am sure that is not true, Mr. Billing.

Billing. Yes, I swear it is! I am a pagan, and I am proud of it. Believe me, before long we shall all be pagans.

Morten. And then shall be allowed to do anything we like?

Billing. Well, you'll see, Morten.

Mrs. Stockmann. You must go to your room now, boys; I am sure you have some lessons to learn for tomorrow.

Ejlif. I should like so much to stay a little longer

Mrs. Stockmann. No, no; away you go, both of you, (The boys say good night and go into the room on the left.)

Hovstad. Do you really think it can do the boys any harm to hear such things?

Mrs. Stockmann. I don't know; but I don't like it.

Petra. But you know, mother, I think you really are wrong about it.

Mrs. Stockmann. Maybe, but I don't like it, not in our own home.

Petra. There is so much falsehood both at home and at school. At home one must not speak, and at school we have to stand and tell lies to the children.

Horster. Tell lies?

Petra. Yes, don't you suppose we have to teach them all sorts of things that we don't believe?

Billing. That is perfectly true.

Petra. If only I had the means, I would start a school of my own; and it would be conducted on very different lines.

Billing. Oh, bother the means!

Horster. Well if you are thinking of that, Miss Stockmann, I shall be delighted to provide you with a schoolroom. The great big old house my father left me is standing almost empty; there is an immense dining-room downstairs

Petra (laughing). Thank you very much; but I am afraid nothing will come of it.

Hovstad. No, Miss Petra is much more likely to take to journalism, I expect. By the way, have you had time to do anything with that English story you promised to translate for us?

Petra. No, not yet, but you shall have it in good time.

(DR. STOCKMANN comes in from his room with an open letter in his hand.)

Dr. Stockmann (waving the letter). Well, now the town will have something new to talk about, I can tell you!

Billing. Something new?

Mrs. Stockmann. What is this?

Dr. Stockmann. A great discovery, Katherine.

Hovstad. Really?

Mrs. Stockmann. A discovery of yours?

Dr. Stockmann. A discovery of mine. (Walks up and down.) Just let them come saying, as usual, that it is all fancy and a crazy man's imagination! But they will be careful what they say this time, I can tell you!

Petra. But, father, tell us what it is.

Dr. Stockmann. Yes, yes, only give me time, and you shall know all about it. If only I had Peter here now! It just shows how we men can go about forming our judgments, when in reality we are as blind as any moles

Hovstad. What are you driving at, Doctor?

Dr. Stockmann (standing still by the table). Isn't it the universal opinion that our town is a healthy spot?

Hovstad. Certainly.

Dr. Stockmann. Quite an unusually healthy spot, in fact, a place that deserves to be recommended in the warmest possible manner either for invalids or for people who are well

Mrs. Stockmann. Yes, but my dear Thomas

Dr. Stockmann. And we have been recommending it and praising it, I have written and written, both in the "Messenger" and in pamphlets...

Hovstad. Well, what then?

Dr. Stockmann. And the Baths, we have called them the "main artery of the town's life-blood," the "nerve-centre of our town," and the devil knows what else

Billing. "The town's pulsating heart" was the expression I once used on an important occasion.

Dr. Stockmann. Quite so. Well, do you know what they really are, these great, splendid, much praised Baths, that have cost so much money, do you know what they are?

Hovstad. No, what are they?

Mrs. Stockmann. Yes, what are they?

Dr. Stockmann. The whole place is a pest-house!

Petra. The Baths, father?

Mrs. Stockmann (at the same time), Our Baths?

Hovstad. But, Doctor

Billing. Absolutely incredible!

Dr. Stockmann. The whole Bath establishment is a whited, poisoned sepulchre, I tell you, the gravest possible danger to the public health! All the nastiness up at Molledal, all that stinking filth, is infecting the water in the conduit-pipes leading to the reservoir; and the same cursed, filthy poison oozes out on the shore too

Horster. Where the bathing-place is?

Dr. Stockmann. Just there.

Hovstad. How do you come to be so certain of all this, Doctor?

Dr. Stockmann. I have investigated the matter most conscientiously. For a long time past I have suspected something of the kind. Last year we had some very strange cases of illness among the visitors, typhoid cases, and cases of gastric fever

Mrs. Stockmann. Yes, that is quite true.

Dr. Stockmann. At the time, we supposed the visitors had been infected before they came; but later on, in the winter, I began to have a different opinion; and so I set myself to examine the water, as well as I could.

Mrs. Stockmann. Then that is what you have been so busy with?

Dr. Stockmann. Indeed I have been busy, Katherine. But here I had none of the necessary scientific apparatus; so I sent samples, both of the drinking-water and of the sea-water, up to the University, to have an accurate analysis made by a chemist.

Hovstad. And have you got that?

Dr. Stockmann (showing him the letter). Here it is! It proves the presence of decomposing organic matter in the water, it is full of infusoria. The water is absolutely dangerous to use, either internally or externally.

Mrs. Stockmann. What a mercy you discovered it in time.

Dr. Stockmann. You may well say so.

Hovstad. And what do you propose to do now, Doctor?

Dr. Stockmann. To see the matter put right, naturally.

Hovstad. Can that be done?

Dr. Stockmann. It must be done. Otherwise the Baths will be absolutely useless and wasted. But we need not anticipate that; I have a very clear idea what we shall have to do.

Mrs. Stockmann. But why have you kept this all so secret, dear?

Dr. Stockmann. Do you suppose I was going to run about the town gossiping about it, before I had absolute proof? No, thank you. I am not such a fool.

Petra. Still, you might have told us

Dr. Stockmann. Not a living soul. But tomorrow you may run around to the old Badger

Mrs. Stockmann. Oh, Thomas! Thomas!

Dr. Stockmann. Well, to your grandfather, then. The old boy will have something to be astonished at! I know he thinks I am cracked and there are lots of other people who think so too, I have noticed. But now these good folks shall see, they shall just see! (Walks about, rubbing his hands.) There will be a nice upset in the town, Katherine; you can't imagine what it will be. All the conduit-pipes will have to be relaid.

Hovstad (getting up). All the conduit-pipes?

Dr. Stockmann. Yes, of course. The intake is too low down; it will have to be lifted to a position much higher up.

Petra. Then you were right after all.

Dr. Stockmann. Ah, you remember, Petra, I wrote opposing the plans before the work was begun. But at that time no one would listen to me. Well, I am going to let them have it now. Of course I have prepared a report for the Baths Committee; I have had it ready for a week, and was only waiting for this to come. (Shows the letter.) Now it shall go off at once. (Goes into his room and comes back with some papers.) Look at that! Four closely written sheets! and the letter shall go with them. Give me a bit of paper, Katherine, something to wrap them up in. That will do! Now give it to-to-(stamps his foot) what the deuce is her name? give it to the maid, and tell her to take it at once to the Mayor.

(Mrs. Stockmann takes the packet and goes out through the dining-room.)

Petra. What do you think Uncle Peter will say, father?

Dr. Stockmann. What is there for him to say? I should think he would be very glad that such an important truth has been brought to light.

Hovstad. Will you let me print a short note about your discovery in the "Messenger?"

Dr. Stockmann. I shall be very much obliged if you will.

Hovstad. It is very desirable that the public should be informed of it without delay.

Dr. Stockmann. Certainly.

Mrs. Stockmann (coming back). She has just gone with it.

Billing. Upon my soul, Doctor, you are going to be the foremost man in the town!

Dr. Stockmann (walking about happily). Nonsense! As a matter of fact I have done nothing more than my duty. I have only made a lucky find, that's all. Still, all the same...

Billing. Hovstad, don't you think the town ought to give Dr. Stockmann some sort of testimonial?

Hovstad. I will suggest it, anyway.

Billing. And I will speak to Aslaksen about it.

Dr. Stockmann. No, my good friends, don't let us have any of that nonsense. I won't hear anything of the kind. And if the Baths Committee should think of voting me an increase of salary, I will not accept it. Do you hear, Katherine? I won't accept it.

Mrs. Stockmann. You are quite right, Thomas.

Petra (lifting her glass). Your health, father!

Hovstad and Billing. Your health, Doctor! Good health!

Horster (touches glasses with DR. STOCKMANN). I hope it will bring you nothing but good luck.

Dr. Stockmann. Thank you, thank you, my dear fellows! I feel tremendously happy! It is a splendid thing for a man to be able to feel that he has done a service to his native town and to his fellow-citizens. Hurrah, Katherine! (He puts his arms round her and whirls her round and round, while she protests with laughing cries. They all laugh, clap their hands, and cheer the DOCTOR. The boys put their heads in at the door to see what is going on.)

ACT II

(SCENE, The same. The door into the dining room is shut. It is morning. MRS. STOCKMANN, with a sealed letter in her hand, comes in from the dining room, goes to the door of the DOCTOR'S study, and peeps in.)

Mrs. Stockmann. Are you in, Thomas?

Dr. Stockmann (from within his room). Yes, I have just come in. (Comes into the room.) What is it?

Mrs. Stockmann. A letter from your brother.

Dr. Stockmann. Aha, let us see! (Opens the letter and reads:) "I return herewith the manuscript you sent me" (reads on in a low murmur) H'm!

Mrs. Stockmann. What does he say?

Dr. Stockmann (putting the papers in his pocket). Oh, he only writes that he will come up here himself about midday.

Mrs. Stockmann. Well, try and remember to be at home this time.

Dr. Stockmann. That will be all right; I have got through all my morning visits.

Mrs. Stockmann. I am extremely curious to know how he takes it.

Dr. Stockmann. You will see he won't like it's having been I, and not he, that made the discovery.

Mrs. Stockmann. Aren't you a little nervous about that?

Dr. Stockmann. Oh, he really will be pleased enough, you know. But, at the same time, Peter is so confoundedly afraid of anyone's doing any service to the town except himself.

Mrs. Stockmann. I will tell you what, Thomas, you should be good natured, and share the credit of this with him. Couldn't you make out that it was he who set you on the scent of this discovery?

Dr. Stockmann. I am quite willing. If only I can get the thing set right. I

(MORTEN KIIL puts his head in through the door leading from the hall, looks around in an enquiring manner, and chuckles.)

Morten Kiil (slyly). Is it, is it true?

Mrs. Stockmann (going to the door). Father! is it you?

Dr. Stockmann. Ah, Mr. Kiil, good morning, good morning!

Mrs. Stockmann. But come along in.

Morten Kiil. If it is true, I will; if not, I am off.

Dr. Stockmann. If what is true?

Morten Kiil. This tale about the water supply, is it true?

Dr. Stockmann. Certainly it is true, but how did you come to hear it?

Morten Kid (coming in). Petra ran in on her way to the school

Dr. Stockmann. Did she?

Morten Kiil. Yes; and she declares that, I thought she was only making a fool of me, but it isn't like Petra to do that.

Dr. Stockmann. Of course not. How could you imagine such a thing!

Morten Kiil. Oh well, it is better never to trust anybody; you may find you have been made a fool of before you know where you are. But it is really true, all the same?

Dr. Stockmann. You can depend upon it that it is true. Won't you sit down? (Settles him on the couch.) Isn't it a real bit of luck for the town

Morten Kiil (suppressing his laughter). A bit of luck for the town?

Dr. Stockmann. Yes, that I made the discovery in good time.

Morten Kiil (as before). Yes, yes, Yes! But I should never have thought you the sort of man to pull your own brother's leg like this!

Dr. Stockmann. Pull his leg!

Mrs. Stockmann. Really, father dear

Morten Kiil (resting his hands and his chin on the handle of his stick and winking slyly at the DOCTOR). Let me see, what was the story? Some kind of beast that had got into the water-pipes, wasn't it?

Dr. Stockmann. Infusoria, yes.

Morten Kiil. And a lot of these beasts had got in, according to Petra, a tremendous lot.

Dr. Stockmann. Certainly; hundreds of thousands of them, probably.

Morten Kiil. But no one can see them, isn't that so?

Dr. Stockmann. Yes; you can't see them,

Morten Kiil (with a quiet chuckle). Damn, it's the finest story I have ever heard!

Dr. Stockmann. What do you mean?

Morten Kiil. But you will never get the Mayor to believe a thing like that.

Dr. Stockmann. We shall see.

Morten Kiil. Do you think he will be fool enough to?

Dr. Stockmann. I hope the whole town will be fools enough.

Morten Kiil. The whole town! Well, it wouldn't be a bad thing. It would just serve them right, and teach them a lesson. They think themselves so much cleverer than we old fellows. They hounded me out of the council; they did, I tell you they hounded me out. Now they shall pay for it. You pull their legs too, Thomas!

Dr. Stockmann. Really, I

Morten Kiil. You pull their legs! (Gets up.) If you can work it so that the Mayor and his friends all swallow the same bait, I will give ten pounds to a charity,like a shot!

Dr. Stockmann. That is very kind of you.

Morten Kiil. Yes, I haven't got much money to throw away, I can tell you; but, if you can work this, I will give five pounds to a charity at Christmas.

(HOVSTAD comes in by the hall door.)

Hovstad. Good morning! (Stops.) Oh, I beg your pardon

Dr. Stockmann. Not at all; come in.

Morten Kiil (with another chuckle). Oho! is he in this too?

Hovstad. What do you mean?

Dr. Stockmann. Certainly he is.

Morten Kiil. I might have known it! It must get into the papers. You know how to do it, Thomas! Set your wits to work. Now I must go.

Dr. Stockmann. Won't you stay a little while?

Morten Kiil. No, I must be off now. You keep up this game for all it is worth; you won't repent it, I'm damned if you will!

(He goes out; MRS. STOCKMANN follows him into the hall.)

Dr. Stockmann (laughing). Just imagine, the old chap doesn't believe a word of all this about the water supply.

Hovstad. Oh that was it, then?

Dr. Stockmann. Yes, that was what we were talking about. Perhaps it is the same thing that brings you here?

Hovstad. Yes, it is, Can you spare me a few minutes, Doctor?

Dr. Stockmann. As long as you like, my dear fellow.

Hovstad. Have you heard from the Mayor yet?

Dr. Stockmann. Not yet. He is coming here later.

Hovstad. I have given the matter a great deal of thought since last night.

Dr. Stockmann. Well?

Hovstad. From your point of view, as a doctor and a man of science, this affair of the water supply is an isolated matter. I mean, you do not realise that it involves a great many other things.

Dr. Stockmann. How, do you mean? Let us sit down, my dear fellow. No, sit here on the couch. (HOVSTAD Sits down on the couch, DR. STOCKMANN On a chair on the other side of the table.) Now then. You mean that?

Hovstad. You said yesterday that the pollution of the water was due to impurities in the soil.

Dr. Stockmann. Yes, unquestionably it is due to that poisonous morass up at Molledal.

Hovstad. Begging your pardon, Doctor, I fancy it is due to quite another morass altogether.

Dr. Stockmann. What morass?

Hovstad. The morass that the whole life of our town is built on and is rotting in.

Dr. Stockmann. What the deuce are you driving at, Hovstad?

Hovstad. The whole of the town's interests have, little by little, got into the hands of a pack of officials.

Dr. Stockmann. Oh, come! they are not all officials.

Hovstad. No, but those that are not officials are at any rate the officials' friends and adherents; it is the wealthy folk, the old families in the town, that have got us entirely in their hands.

Dr. Stockmann. Yes, but after all they are men of ability and knowledge.

Hovstad. Did they show any ability or knowledge when they laid the conduit pipes where they are now?

Dr. Stockmann. No, of course that was a great piece of stupidity on their part. But that is going to be set right now.

Hovstad. Do you think that will be all such plain sailing?

Dr. Stockmann. Plain sailing or no, it has got to be done, anyway.

Hovstad. Yes, provided the press takes up the question.

Dr. Stockmann. I don't think that will be necessary, my dear fellow, I am certain my brother

Hovstad. Excuse me, doctor; I feel bound to tell you I am inclined to take the matter up.

Dr. Stockmann. In the paper?

Hovstad. Yes. When I took over the "People's Messenger" my idea was to break up this ring of self-opinionated old fossils who had got hold of all the influence.

Dr. Stockmann. But you know you told me yourself what the result had been; you nearly ruined your paper.

Hovstad. Yes, at the time we were obliged to climb down a peg or two, it is quite true because there was a danger of the whole project of the Baths coming to nothing if they failed us. But now the scheme has been carried through, and we can dispense with these grand gentlemen.

Dr. Stockmann. Dispense with them, yes; but, we owe them a great debt of gratitude.

Hovstad. That shall be recognised ungrudgingly, But a journalist of my democratic tendencies cannot let such an opportunity as this slip. The bubble of official infallibility must be pricked. This superstition must be destroyed, like any other.

Dr. Stockmann. I am whole-heartedly with you in that, Mr. Hovstad; if it is a superstition, away with it!

Hovstad. I should be very reluctant to bring the Mayor into it, because he is your brother. But I am sure you will agree with me that truth should be the first consideration.

Dr. Stockmann. That goes without saying. (With sudden emphasis.) Yes, but - but

Hovstad. You must not misjudge me. I am neither more self-interested nor more ambitious than most men.

Dr. Stockmann. My dear fellow, who suggests anything of the kind?

Hovstad. I am of humble origin, as you know; and that has given me opportunities of knowing what is the most crying need in the humbler ranks of life. It is that they should be allowed some part in the direction of public affairs, Doctor. That is what will develop their faculties and intelligence and self respect

Dr. Stockmann. I quite appreciate that.

Hovstad. Yes, and in my opinion a journalist incurs a heavy responsibility if he neglects a favourable opportunity of emancipating the masses, the humble and oppressed. I know well enough that in exalted circles I shall be called an agitator, and all that sort of thing; but they may call what they like. If only my conscience doesn't reproach me, then

Dr. Stockmann. Quite right! Quite right, Mr. Hovstad. But all the same, devil take it! (A knock is heard at the door.) Come in!

(ASLAKSEN appears at the door. He is poorly but decently dressed, in black, with a slightly crumpled white neckcloth; he wears gloves and has a felt hat in his hand.)

Aslaksen (bowing). Excuse my taking the liberty, Doctor

Dr. Stockmann (getting up). Ah, it is you, Aslaksen!

Aslaksen. Yes, Doctor.

Hovstad (standing up). Is it me you want, Aslaksen?

Aslaksen. No; I didn't know I should find you here. No, it was the Doctor I

Dr. Stockmann. I am quite at your service. What is it?

Aslaksen. Is what I heard from Mr. Billing true, sir, that you mean to improve our water supply?

Dr. Stockmann. Yes, for the Baths.

Aslaksen. Quite so, I understand. Well, I have come to say that I will back that up by every means in my power.

Hovstad (to the DOCTOR). You see!

Dr. Stockmann. I shall be very grateful to you, but

Aslaksen. Because it may be no bad thing to have us small tradesmen at your back. We form, as it were, a compact majority in the town, if we choose. And it is always a good thing to have the majority with you, Doctor.

Dr. Stockmann. That is undeniably true; but I confess I don't see why such unusual precautions should be necessary in this case. It seems to me that such a plain, straightforward thing.

Aslaksen. Oh, it may be very desirable, all the same. I know our local authorities so well; officials are not generally very ready to act on proposals that come from other people. That is why I think it would not be at all amiss if we made a little demonstration.

Hovstad. That's right.

Dr. Stockmann. Demonstration, did you say? What on earth are you going to make a demonstration about?

Aslaksen. We shall proceed with the greatest moderation, Doctor. Moderation is always my aim; it is the greatest virtue in a citizen, at least, I think so.

Dr. Stockmann. It is well known to be a characteristic of yours, Mr. Aslaksen.

Aslaksen. Yes, I think I may pride myself on that. And this matter of the water supply is of the greatest importance to us small tradesmen. The Baths promise to be a regular gold-mine for the town. We shall all make our living out of them, especially those of us who are householders. That is why we will back up the project as strongly as possible. And as I am at present Chairman of the Householders' Association.

Dr. Stockmann. Yes?

Aslaksen. And, what is more, local secretary of the Temperance Society, you know, sir, I suppose, that I am a worker in the temperance cause?

Dr. Stockmann. Of course, of course.

Aslaksen. Well, you can understand that I come into contact with a great many people. And as I have the reputation of a temperate and law-abiding citizen, like yourself, Doctor, I have a certain influence in the town, a little bit of power, if I may be allowed to say so.

Dr. Stockmann. I know that quite well, Mr. Aslaksen.

Aslaksen. So you see it would be an easy matter for me to set on foot some testimonial, if necessary.

Dr. Stockmann. A testimonial?

Aslaksen. Yes, some kind of an address of thanks from the townsmen for your share in a matter of such importance to the community. I need scarcely say that it would have to be drawn up with the greatest regard to moderation, so as not to offend the authorities who, after all, have the reins in their hands. If we pay strict attention to that, no one can take it amiss, I should think!

Hovstad. Well, and even supposing they didn't like it

Aslaksen. No, no, no; there must be no discourtesy to the authorities, Mr. Hovstad. It is no use falling foul of those upon whom our welfare so closely depends. I have done that in my time, and no good ever comes of it. But no one can take exception to a reasonable and frank expression of a citizen's views.

Dr. Stockmann (shaking him by the hand). I can't tell you, dear Mr. Aslaksen, how extremely pleased I am to find such hearty support among my fellow-citizens. I am delighted, delighted! Now, you will take a small glass of sherry, eh?

Aslaksen. No, thank you; I never drink alcohol of that kind.

Dr. Stockmann. Well, what do you say to a glass of beer, then?

Aslaksen. Nor that either, thank you, Doctor. I never drink anything as early as this. I am going into town now to talk this over with one or two householders, and prepare the ground.

Dr. Stockmann. It is tremendously kind of you, Mr. Aslaksen; but I really cannot understand the necessity for all these precautions. It seems to me that the thing should go of itself.

Aslaksen. The authorities are somewhat slow to move, Doctor. Far be it from me to seem to blame them

Hovstad. We are going to stir them up in the paper tomorrow, Aslaksen.

Aslaksen. But not violently, I trust, Mr. Hovstad. Proceed with moderation, or you will do nothing with them. You may take my advice; I have gathered my experience in the school of life. Well, I must say goodbye, Doctor. You know now that we small tradesmen are at your back at all events, like a solid wall. You have the compact majority on your side Doctor.

Dr. Stockmann. I am very much obliged, dear Mr. Aslaksen, (Shakes hands with him.) Goodbye, goodbye.

Aslaksen. Are you going my way, towards the printing-office. Mr. Hovstad?

Hovstad, I will come later; I have something to settle up first.

Aslaksen. Very well. (Bows and goes out; STOCKMANN follows him into the hall.)

Hovstad (as STOCKMANN comes in again). Well, what do you think of that, Doctor? Don't you think it is high time we stirred a little life into all this slackness and vacillation and cowardice?

Dr. Stockmann. Are you referring to Aslaksen?

Hovstad, Yes, I am. He is one of those who are floundering in a bog, decent enough fellow though he may be, otherwise. And most of the people here are in just the same case, see-sawing and edging first to one side and then to the other, so overcome with caution and scruple that they never dare to take any decided step.

Dr. Stockmann, Yes, but Aslaksen seemed to me so thoroughly well-intentioned.

Hovstad. There is one thing I esteem higher than that; and that is for a man to be self-reliant and sure of himself.

Dr. Stockmann. I think you are perfectly right there.

Hovstad. That is why I want to seize this opportunity, and try if I cannot manage to put a little virility into these well-intentioned people for once. The idol of Authority must be shattered in this town. This gross and inexcusable blunder about the water supply must be brought home to the mind of every municipal voter.

Dr. Stockmann. Very well; if you are of opinion that it is for the good of the community, so be it. But not until I have had a talk with my brother.

Hovstad. Anyway, I will get a leading article ready; and if the Mayor refuses to take the matter up

Dr. Stockmann. How can you suppose such a thing possible!

Hovstad. It is conceivable. And in that case

Dr. Stockmann. In that case I promise you. Look here, in that case you may print my report, every word of it.

Hovstad. May I? Have I your word for it?

Dr. Stockmann (giving him the MS.). Here it is; take it with you. It can do no harm for you to read it through, and you can give it me back later on.

Hovstad. Good, good! That is what I will do. And now goodbye, Doctor.

Dr. Stockmann. Goodbye, goodbye. You will see everything will run quite smoothly, Mr. Hovstad, quite smoothly.

Hovstad. Hm! we shall see. (Bows and goes out.)

Dr. Stockmann (opens the dining-room door and looks in). Katherine! Oh, you are back, Petra?

Petra (coming in). Yes, I have just come from the school.

Mrs. Stockmann (coming in). Has he not been here yet?

Dr. Stockmann. Peter? No, but I have had a long talk with Hovstad. He is quite excited about my discovery, I find it has a much wider bearing than I at first imagined. And he has put his paper at my disposal if necessity should arise.

Mrs. Stockmann. Do you think it will?

Dr. Stockmann. Not for a moment. But at all events it makes me feel proud to know that I have the liberal-minded independent press on my side. Yes, and just imagine, I have had a visit from the Chairman of the Householders' Association!

Mrs. Stockmann. Oh! What did he want?

Dr. Stockmann. To offer me his support too. They will support me in a body if it should be necessary. Katherine, do you know what I have got behind me?

Mrs. Stockmann. Behind you? No, what have you got behind you?

Dr. Stockmann. The compact majority.

Mrs. Stockmann. Really? Is that a good thing for you Thomas?

Dr. Stockmann. I should think it was a good thing. (Walks up and down rubbing his hands.) By Jove, it's a fine thing to feel this bond of brotherhood between oneself and one's fellow citizens!

Petra. And to be able to do so much that is good and useful, father!

Dr. Stockmann. And for one's own native town into the bargain, my child!

Mrs. Stockmann. That was a ring at the bell.

Dr. Stockmann. It must be he, then. (A knock is heard at the door.) Come in!

Peter Stockmann (comes in from the hall). Good morning.

Dr. Stockmann. Glad to see you, Peter!

Mrs. Stockmann. Good morning, Peter, How are you?

Peter Stockmann. So so, thank you. (To DR. STOCKMANN.) I received from you yesterday, after office hours, a report dealing with the condition of the water at the Baths.

Dr. Stockmann. Yes. Have you read it?

Peter Stockmann. Yes, I have,

Dr. Stockmann. And what have you to say to it?

Peter Stockmann (with a sidelong glance). Hm!

Mrs. Stockmann. Come along, Petra. (She and PETRA go into the room on the left.)

Peter Stockmann (after a pause). Was it necessary to make all these investigations behind my back?

Dr. Stockmann. Yes, because until I was absolutely certain about it

Peter Stockmann. Then you mean that you are absolutely certain now?

Dr. Stockmann. Surely you are convinced of that.

Peter Stockmann. Is it your intention to bring this document before the Baths Committee as a sort of official communication?

Dr. Stockmann. Certainly. Something must be done in the matter and that quickly.

Peter Stockmann. As usual, you employ violent expressions in your report. You say, amongst other things, that what we offer visitors in our Baths is a permanent supply of poison.

Dr. Stockmann. Well, can you describe it any other way, Peter? Just think, water that is poisonous, whether you drink it or bathe in it! And this we offer to the poor sick folk who come to us trustfully and pay us at an exorbitant rate to be made well again!

Peter Stockmann. And your reasoning leads you to this conclusion, that we must build a sewer to draw off the alleged impurities from Molledal and must relay the water conduits.

Dr. Stockmann. Yes. Do you see any other way out of it? I don't.

Peter Stockmann. I made a pretext this morning to go and see the town engineer, and, as if only half seriously, broached the subject of these proposals as a thing we might perhaps have to take under consideration some time later on.

Dr. Stockmann. Some time later on!

Peter Stockmann. He smiled at what he considered to be my extravagance, naturally. Have you taken the trouble to consider what your proposed alterations would cost? According to the information I obtained, the expenses would probably mount up to fifteen or twenty thousand pounds.

Dr. Stockmann. Would it cost so much?

Peter Stockmann. Yes; and the worst part of it would be that the work would take at least two years.

Dr. Stockmann. Two years? Two whole years?

Peter Stockmann. At least. And what are we to do with the Baths in the meantime? Close them? Indeed we should be obliged to. And do you suppose anyone would come near the place after it had got out that the water was dangerous?

Dr. Stockmann. Yes but, Peter, that is what it is.

Peter Stockmann. And all this at this juncture, just as the Baths are beginning to be known. There are other towns in the neighbourhood with qualifications to attract visitors for bathing purposes. Don't you suppose they would immediately strain every nerve to divert the entire stream of strangers to themselves? Unquestionably they would; and then where should we be? We should probably have to abandon the whole thing, which has cost us so much money-and then you would have ruined your native town.

Dr. Stockmann. I should have ruined!

Peter Stockmann. It is simply and solely through the Baths that the town has before it any future worth mentioning. You know that just as well as I.

Dr. Stockmann. But what do you think ought to be done, then?

Peter Stockmann. Your report has not convinced me that the condition of the water at the Baths is as bad as you represent it to be.

Dr. Stockmann. I tell you it is even worse! or at all events it will be in summer, when the warm weather comes.

Peter Stockmann. As I said, I believe you exaggerate the matter considerably. A capable physician ought to know what measures to take, he ought to be capable of preventing injurious influences or of remedying them if they become obviously persistent.

Dr. Stockmann. Well? What more?

Peter Stockmann. The water supply for the Baths is now an established fact, and in consequence must be treated as such. But probably the Committee, at its discretion, will not be disinclined to consider the question of how far it might be possible to introduce certain improvements consistently with a reasonable expenditure.

Dr. Stockmann. And do you suppose that I will have anything to do with such a piece of trickery as that?

Peter Stockmann. Trickery!!

Dr. Stockmann. Yes, it would be a trick, a fraud, a lie, a downright crime towards the public, towards the whole community!

Peter Stockmann. I have not, as I remarked before, been able to convince myself that there is actually any imminent danger.

Dr. Stockmann. You have! It is impossible that you should not be convinced. I know I have represented the facts absolutely truthfully and fairly. And you know it very well, Peter, only you won't acknowledge it. It was owing to your action that both the Baths and the water conduits were built where they are; and that is what you won't acknowledge, that damnable blunder of yours. Pooh! do you suppose I don't see through you?

Peter Stockmann. And even if that were true? If I perhaps guard my reputation somewhat anxiously, it is in the interests of the town. Without moral authority I am powerless to direct public affairs as seems, to my judgment, to be best for the common good. And on that account, and for various other reasons too, it appears to me to be a matter of importance that your report should not be delivered to the Committee. In the interests of the public, you must withhold it. Then, later on, I will raise the question and we will do our best, privately; but, nothing of this unfortunate affair not a single word of it must come to the ears of the public.

Dr. Stockmann. I am afraid you will not be able to prevent that now, my dear Peter.

Peter Stockmann. It must and shall be prevented.

Dr. Stockmann. It is no use, I tell you. There are too many people that know about it.

Peter Stockmann. That know about it? Who? Surely you don't mean those fellows on the "People's Messenger"?

Dr. Stockmann. Yes, they know. The liberal-minded independent press is going to see that you do your duty.

Peter Stockmann (after a short pause). You are an extraordinarily independent man, Thomas. Have you given no thought to the consequences this may have for yourself?

Dr. Stockmann. Consequences? for me?

Peter Stockmann. For you and yours, yes.

Dr. Stockmann. What the deuce do you mean?

Peter Stockmann. I believe I have always behaved in a brotherly way to you, haven't I always been ready to oblige or to help you?

Dr. Stockmann. Yes, you have, and I am grateful to you for it.

Peter Stockmann. There is no need. Indeed, to some extent I was forced to do so, for my own sake. I always hoped that, if I helped to improve your financial position, I should be able to keep some check on you.

Dr. Stockmann. What! Then it was only for your own sake!

Peter Stockmann. Up to a certain point, yes. It is painful for a man in an official position to have his nearest relative compromising himself time after time.

Dr. Stockmann. And do you consider that I do that?

Peter Stockmann. Yes, unfortunately, you do, without even being aware of it. You have a restless, pugnacious, rebellious disposition. And then there is that disastrous propensity of yours to want to write about every sort of possible and impossible thing. The moment an idea comes into your head, you must needs go and write a newspaper article or a whole pamphlet about it.

Dr. Stockmann. Well, but is it not the duty of a citizen to let the public share in any new ideas he may have?

Peter Stockmann. Oh, the public doesn't require any new ideas. The public is best served by the good, old established ideas it already has.

Dr. Stockmann. And that is your honest opinion?

Peter Stockmann. Yes, and for once I must talk frankly to you. Hitherto I have tried to avoid doing so, because I know how irritable you are; but now I must tell you the truth, Thomas. You have no conception what an amount of harm you do yourself by your impetuosity. You complain of the authorities, you even complain of the government, you are always pulling them to pieces; you insist that you have been neglected and persecuted. But what else can such a cantankerous man as you expect?

Dr. Stockmann. What next! Cantankerous, am I?

Peter Stockmann. Yes, Thomas, you are an extremely cantankerous man to work with, I know that to my cost. You disregard everything that you ought to have consideration for. You seem completely to forget that it is me you have to thank for your appointment here as medical officer to the Baths.

Dr. Stockmann. I was entitled to it as a matter of course! I and nobody else! I was the first person to see that the town could be made into a flourishing watering-place, and I was the only one who saw it at that time. I had to fight single-handed in support of the idea for many years; and I wrote and wrote

Peter Stockmann. Undoubtedly. But things were not ripe for the scheme then, though, of course, you could not judge of that in your out-of-the-way corner up north. But as soon as the opportune moment came I, and the others, took the matter into our hands.

Dr. Stockmann. Yes, and made this mess of all my beautiful plan. It is pretty obvious now what clever fellows you were!

Peter Stockmann. To my mind the whole thing only seems to mean that you are seeking another outlet for your combativeness. You want to pick a quarrel with your superiors, an old habit of yours. You cannot put up with any authority over you. You look askance at anyone who occupies a superior official position; you regard him as a personal enemy, and then any stick is good enough to beat him with. But now I have called your attention to the fact that the town's interests are at stake and, incidentally, my own too. And therefore, I must tell you, Thomas, that you will find me inexorable with regard to what I am about to require you to do.

Dr. Stockmann. And what is that?

Peter Stockmann. As you have been so indiscreet as to speak of this delicate matter to outsiders, despite the fact that you ought to have treated it as entirely official and confidential, it is obviously impossible to hush it up now. All sorts of rumours will get about directly, and everybody who has a grudge against us will take care to embellish these rumours. So it will be necessary for you to refute them publicly.

Dr. Stockmann. I! How? I don't understand.

Peter Stockmann. What we shall expect is that, after making further investigations, you will come to the conclusion that the matter is not by any means as dangerous or as critical as you imagined in the first instance.

Dr. Stockmann. Oho! so that is what you expect!

Peter Stockmann. And, what is more, we shall expect you to make public profession of your confidence in the Committee and in their readiness to consider fully and conscientiously what steps may be necessary to remedy any possible defects.

Dr. Stockmann. But you will never be able to do that by patching and tinkering at it, never! Take my word for it, Peter; I mean what I say, as deliberately and emphatically as possible.

Peter Stockmann. As an officer under the Committee, you have no right to any individual opinion.

Dr. Stockmann (amazed). No right?

Peter Stockmann. In your official capacity, no. As a private person, it is quite another matter. But as a subordinate member of the staff of the Baths, you have no right to express any opinion which runs contrary to that of your superiors.

Dr. Stockmann. This is too much! I, a doctor, a man of science, have no right to!

Peter Stockmann. The matter in hand is not simply a scientific one. It is a complicated matter, and has its economic as well as its technical side.

Dr. Stockmann. I don't care what it is! I intend to be free to express my opinion on any subject under the sun.

Peter Stockmann. As you please but not on any subject concerning the Baths. That we forbid.

Dr. Stockmann (shouting). You forbid! You! A pack of

Peter Stockmann. I forbid it, I, your chief; and if I forbid it, you have to obey.

Dr. Stockmann (controlling himself). Peter, if you were not my brother

Petra (throwing open the door). Father, you shan't stand this!

Mrs. Stockmann (coming in after her). Petra, Petra!

Peter Stockmann. Oh, so you have been eavesdropping.

Mrs. Stockmann. You were talking so loud, we couldn't help it!

Petra. Yes, I was listening.

Peter Stockmann. Well, after all, I am very glad

Dr. Stockmann (going up to him). You were saying something about forbidding and obeying?

Peter Stockmann. You obliged me to take that tone with you.

Dr. Stockmann. And so I am to give myself the lie, publicly?

Peter Stockmann. We consider it absolutely necessary that you should make some such public statement as I have asked for.

Dr. Stockmann. And if I do not obey?

Peter Stockmann. Then we shall publish a statement ourselves to reassure the public.

Dr. Stockmann. Very well; but in that case I shall use my pen against you. I stick to what I have said; I will show that I am right and that you are wrong. And what will you do then?

Peter Stockmann. Then I shall not be able to prevent your being dismissed.

Dr. Stockmann. What?

Petra. Father, dismissed!

Mrs. Stockmann. Dismissed!

Peter Stockmann. Dismissed from the staff of the Baths. I shall be obliged to propose that you shall immediately be given notice, and shall not be allowed any further participation in the Baths' affairs.

Dr. Stockmann. You would dare to do that!

Peter Stockmann. It is you that are playing the daring game.

Petra. Uncle, that is a shameful way to treat a man like father!

Mrs. Stockmann. Do hold your tongue, Petra!

Peter Stockmann (looking at PETRA). Oh, so we volunteer our opinions already, do we? Of course. (To MRS. STOCKMANN.) Katherine, I imagine you are the most sensible person in this house. Use any influence you may have over your husband, and make him see what this will entail for his family as well as

Dr. Stockmann. My family is my own concern and nobody else's!

Peter Stockmann. - for his own family, as I was saying, as well as for the town he lives in.

Dr. Stockmann. It is I who have the real good of the town at heart! I want to lay bare the defects that sooner or later must come to the light of day. I will show whether I love my native town.

Peter Stockmann. You, who in your blind obstinacy want to cut off the most important source of the town's welfare?

Dr. Stockmann. The source is poisoned, man! Are you mad? We are making our living by retailing filth and corruption! The whole of our flourishing municipal life derives its sustenance from a lie!

Peter Stockmann. All imagination or something even worse. The man who can throw out such offensive insinuations about his native town must be an enemy to our community.

Dr. Stockmann (going up to him). Do you dare to!

Mrs. Stockmann (throwing herself between them). Thomas!

Petra (catching her father by the arm). Don't lose your temper, father!

Peter Stockmann. I will not expose myself to violence. Now you have had a warning; so reflect on what you owe to yourself and your family. Goodbye. (Goes out.)

Dr. Stockmann (walking up and down). Am I to put up with such treatment as this? In my own house, Katherine! What do you think of that!

Mrs. Stockmann. Indeed it is both shameful and absurd, Thomas

Petra. If only I could give uncle a piece of my mind

Dr. Stockmann. It is my own fault. I ought to have flown out at him long ago! shown my teeth! bitten! To hear him call me an enemy to our community! Me! I shall not take that lying down, upon my soul!

Mrs. Stockmann. But, dear Thomas, your brother has power on his side.

Dr. Stockmann. Yes, but I have right on mine, I tell you.

Mrs. Stockmann. Oh yes, right, right. What is the use of having right on your side if you have not got might?

Petra. Oh, mother! how can you say such a thing!

Dr. Stockmann. Do you imagine that in a free country it is no use having right on your side? You are absurd, Katherine. Besides, haven't I got the liberal-minded, independent press to lead the way, and the compact majority behind me? That is might enough, I should think!

Mrs. Stockmann. But, good heavens, Thomas, you don't mean to?

Dr. Stockmann. Don't mean to what?

Mrs. Stockmann. To set yourself up in opposition to your brother.

Dr. Stockmann. In God's name, what else do you suppose I should do but take my stand on right and truth?

Petra. Yes, I was just going to say that.

Mrs. Stockmann. But it won't do you any earthly good. If they won't do it, they won't.

Dr. Stockmann. Oho, Katherine! Just give me time, and you will see how I will carry the war into their camp.

Mrs. Stockmann. Yes, you carry the war into their camp, and you get your dismissal, that is what you will do.

Dr. Stockmann. In any case I shall have done my duty towards the public, towards the community, I, who am called its enemy!

Mrs. Stockmann. But towards your family, Thomas? Towards your own home! Do you think that is doing your duty towards those you have to provide for?

Petra. Ah, don't think always first of us, mother.

Mrs. Stockmann. Oh, it is easy for you to talk; you are able to shift for yourself, if need be. But remember the boys, Thomas; and think a little of yourself too, and of me

Dr. Stockmann. I think you are out of your senses, Katherine! If I were to be such a miserable coward as to go on my knees to Peter and his damned crew, do you suppose I should ever know an hour's peace of mind all my life afterwards?

Mrs. Stockmann. I don't know anything about that; but God preserve us from the peace of mind we shall have, all the same, if you go on defying him! You will find yourself again without the means of subsistence, with no income to count upon. I should think we had had enough of that in the old days. Remember that, Thomas; think what that means.

Dr. Stockmann (collecting himself with a struggle and clenching his fists). And this is what this slavery can bring upon a free, honourable man! Isn't it horrible, Katherine?

Mrs. Stockmann. Yes, it is sinful to treat you so, it is perfectly true. But, good heavens, one has to put up with so much injustice in this world. There are the boys, Thomas! Look at them! What is to become of them? Oh, no, no, you can never have the heart. (EJLIF and MORTEN have come in, while she was speaking, with their school books in their hands.)

Dr. Stockmann. The boys, I (Recovers himself suddenly.) No, even if the whole world goes to pieces, I will never bow my neck to this yokel (Goes towards his room.)

Mrs. Stockmann (following him). Thomas, what are you going to do!

Dr. Stockmann (at his door). I mean to have the right to look my sons in the face when they are grown men. (Goes into his room.)

Mrs. Stockmann (bursting into tears). God help us all!

Petra. Father is splendid! He will not give in.

(The boys look on in amazement; PETRA signs to them not to speak.)

ACT III

(SCENE. The editorial office of the "People's Messenger." The entrance door is on the left-hand side of the back wall; on the right-hand side is another door with glass panels through which the printing room can be seen. Another door in the right-hand wall. In the middle of the room is a large table covered with papers, newspapers and books. In the foreground on the left a window, before which stands a desk and a high stool. There are a couple of easy chairs by the table, and other chairs standing along the wall. The room is dingy and uncomfortable; the furniture is old, the chairs stained and torn. In the printing room the compositors are seen at work, and a printer is working a handpress. HOVSTAD is sitting at the desk, writing. BILLING comes in from the right with DR. STOCKMANN'S manuscript in his hand.)

Billing. Well, I must say!

Hovstad (still writing). Have you read it through?

Billing (laying the MS. on the desk). Yes, indeed I have.

Hovstad. Don't you think the Doctor hits them pretty hard?

Billing. Hard? Bless my soul, he's crushing! Every word falls like, how shall I put it? like the blow of a sledgehammer.

Hovstad. Yes, but they are not the people to throw up the sponge at the first blow.

Billing. That is true; and for that reason we must strike blow upon blow until the whole of this aristocracy tumbles to pieces. As I sat in there reading this, I almost seemed to see a revolution in being.

Hovstad (turning round). Hush! Speak so that Aslaksen cannot hear you.

Billing (lowering his voice). Aslaksen is a chicken-hearted chap, a coward; there is nothing of the man in him. But this time you will insist on your own way, won't you? You will put the Doctor's article in?

Hovstad. Yes, and if the Mayor doesn't like it

Billing. That will be the devil of a nuisance.

Hovstad. Well, fortunately we can turn the situation to good account, whatever happens. If the Mayor will not fall in with the Doctor's project, he will have all the small tradesmen down on him, the whole of the Householders' Association and the rest of them. And if he does fall in with it, he will fall out with the whole crowd of large shareholders in the Baths, who up to now have been his most valuable supporters

Billing. Yes, because they will certainly have to fork out a pretty penny

Hovstad. Yes, you may be sure they will. And in this way the ring will be broken up, you see, and then in every issue of the paper we will enlighten the public on the Mayor's incapability on one point and another, and make it clear that all the positions of trust in the town, the whole control of municipal affairs, ought to be put in the hands of the Liberals.

Billing. That is perfectly true! I see it coming, I see it coming; we are on the threshold of a revolution!

(A knock is heard at the door.)

Hovstad. Hush! (Calls out.) Come in! (DR. STOCKMANN comes in by the street door. HOVSTAD goes to meet him.) Ah, it is you, Doctor! Well?

Dr. Stockmann. You may set to work and print it, Mr. Hovstad!

Hovstad. Has it come to that, then?

Billing. Hurrah!

Dr. Stockmann. Yes, print away. Undoubtedly it has come to that. Now they must take what they get. There is going to be a fight in the town, Mr. Billing!

Billing. War to the knife, I hope! We will get our knives to their throats, Doctor!

Dr. Stockmann. This article is only a beginning. I have already got four or five more sketched out in my head. Where is Aslaksen?

Billing (calls into the printing-room). Aslaksen, just come here for a minute!

Hovstad. Four or five more articles, did you say? On the same subject?

Dr. Stockmann. No, far from it, my dear fellow. No, they are about quite another matter. But they all spring from the question of the water supply and the drainage. One thing leads to another, you know. It is like beginning to pull down an old house, exactly.

Billing. Upon my soul, it's true; you find you are not done till you have pulled all the old rubbish down.

Aslaksen (coming in). Pulled down? You are not thinking of pulling down the Baths surely, Doctor?

Hovstad. Far from it, don't be afraid.

Dr. Stockmann. No, we meant something quite different. Well, what do you think of my article, Mr. Hovstad?

Hovstad. I think it is simply a masterpiece.

Dr. Stockmann. Do you really think so? Well, I am very pleased, very pleased.

Hovstad. It is so clear and intelligible. One need have no special knowledge to understand the bearing of it. You will have every enlightened man on your side.

Aslaksen. And every prudent man too, I hope?

Billing. The prudent and the imprudent, almost the whole town.

Aslaksen. In that case we may venture to print it.

Dr. Stockmann. I should think so!

Hovstad. We will put it in tomorrow morning.

Dr. Stockmann. Of course, you must not lose a single day. What I wanted to ask you, Mr. Aslaksen, was if you would supervise the printing of it yourself.

Aslaksen. With pleasure.

Dr. Stockmann. Take care of it as if it were a treasure! No misprints, every word is important. I will look in again a little later; perhaps you will be able to let me see a proof. I can't tell you how eager I am to see it in print, and see it burst upon the public

Billing. Burst upon them, yes, like a flash of lightning!

Dr. Stockmann. - and to have it submitted to the judgment of my intelligent fellow townsmen. You cannot imagine what I have gone through today. I have been threatened first with one thing and then with another; they have tried to rob me of my most elementary rights as a man

Billing. What! Your rights as a man!

Dr. Stockmann. - they have tried to degrade me, to make a coward of me, to force me to put personal interests before my most sacred convictions.

Billing. That is too much, I'm damned if it isn't.

Hovstad. Oh, you mustn't be surprised at anything from that quarter.

Dr. Stockmann. Well, they will get the worst of it with me; they may assure themselves of that. I shall consider the "People's Messenger" my sheet-anchor now, and every single day I will bombard them with one article after another, like bombshells

Aslaksen. Yes, but

Billing. Hurrah! it is war, it is war!

Dr. Stockmann. I shall smite them to the ground, I shall crush them, I shall break down all their defenses, before the eyes of the honest public! That is what I shall do!

Aslaksen, Yes, but in moderation, Doctor, proceed with moderation.

Billing. Not a bit of it, not a bit of it! Don't spare the dynamite!

Dr. Stockmann. Because it is not merely a question of water-supply and drains now, you know. No, it is the whole of our social life that we have got to purify and disinfect

Billing. Spoken like a deliverer!

Dr. Stockmann. All the incapables must be turned out, you understand, and that in every walk of life! Endless vistas have opened themselves to my mind's eye today. I cannot see it all quite clearly yet, but I shall in time. Young and vigorous standard-bearers, those are what we need and must seek, my friends; we must have new men in command at all our outposts.

Billing. Hear hear!

Dr. Stockmann. We only need to stand by one another, and it will all be perfectly easy. The revolution will be launched like a ship that runs smoothly off the stocks. Don't you think so?

Hovstad. For my part I think we have now a prospect of getting the municipal authority into the hands where it should lie.

Aslaksen. And if only we proceed with moderation, I cannot imagine that there will be any risk.

Dr. Stockmann. Who the devil cares whether there is any risk or not! What I am doing, I am doing in the name of truth and for the sake of my conscience.

Hovstad. You are a man who deserves to be supported, Doctor.

Aslaksen. Yes, there is no denying that the Doctor is a true friend to the town, a real friend to the community, that he is.

Billing. Take my word for it, Aslaksen, Dr. Stockmann is a friend of the people.

Aslaksen. I fancy the Householders' Association will make use of that expression before long.

Dr. Stockmann (affected, grasps their hands). Thank you, thank you, my dear staunch friends. It is very refreshing to me to hear you say that; my brother called me something quite different. By Jove, he shall have it back, with interest! But now I must be off to see a poor devil, I will come back, as I said. Keep a very careful eye on the manuscript, Aslaksen, and don't for worlds leave out any of my notes of exclamation! Rather put one or two more in! Capital, capital! Well, good-bye for the present, goodbye, goodbye! (They show him to the door, and bow him out.)

Hovstad. He may prove an invaluably useful man to us.

Aslaksen. Yes, so long as he confines himself to this matter of the Baths. But if he goes farther afield, I don't think it would be advisable to follow him.

Hovstad. Hm! that all depends

Billing. You are so infernally timid, Aslaksen!

Aslaksen. Timid? Yes, when it is a question of the local authorities, I am timid, Mr. Billing; it is a lesson I have learned in the school of experience, let me tell you. But try me in higher politics, in matters that concern the government itself, and then see if I am timid.

Billing. No, you aren't, I admit. But this is simply contradicting yourself.

Aslaksen. I am a man with a conscience, and that is the whole matter. If you attack the government, you don't do the community any harm, anyway; those fellows pay no attention to attacks, you see they go on just as they are, in spite of them. But local authorities are different; they can be turned out, and then perhaps you may get an ignorant lot into office who may do irreparable harm to the householders and everybody else.

Hovstad. But what of the education of citizens by self government, don't you attach any importance to that?

Aslaksen. When a man has interests of his own to protect, he cannot think of everything, Mr. Hovstad.

Hovstad. Then I hope I shall never have interests of my own to protect!

Billing. Hear, hear!

Aslaksen (with a smile). Hm! (Points to the desk.) Mr. Sheriff Stensgaard was your predecessor at that editorial desk.

Billing (spitting). Bah! That turncoat.

Hovstad. I am not a weathercock and never will be.

Aslaksen. A politician should never be too certain of anything, Mr. Hovstad. And as for you, Mr. Billing, I should think it is time for you to be taking in a reef or two in your sails, seeing that you are applying for the post of secretary to the Bench.

Billing. I!

Hovstad. Are you, Billing?

Billing. Well, yes, but you must clearly understand I am only doing it to annoy the bigwigs.

Aslaksen. Anyhow, it is no business of mine. But if I am to be accused of timidity and of inconsistency in my principles, this is what I want to point out: my political past is an open book. I have never changed, except perhaps to become a little more moderate, you see. My heart is still with the people; but I don't deny that my reason has a certain bias towards the authorities, the local ones, I mean. (Goes into the printing room.)

Billing. Oughtn't we to try and get rid of him, Hovstad?

Hovstad. Do you know anyone else who will advance the money for our paper and printing bill?

Billing. It is an infernal nuisance that we don't possess some capital to trade on.

Hovstad (sitting down at his desk). Yes, if we only had that, then

Billing. Suppose you were to apply to Dr. Stockmann?

Hovstad (turning over some papers). What is the use? He has got nothing.

Billing. No, but he has got a warm man in the background, old Morten Kiil "the Badger," as they call him.

Hovstad (writing). Are you so sure he has got anything?

Billing. Good Lord, of course he has! And some of it must come to the Stockmanns. Most probably he will do something for the children, at all events.

Hovstad (turning half round). Are you counting on that?

Billing. Counting on it? Of course I am not counting on anything.

Hovstad. That is right. And I should not count on the secretaryship to the Bench either, if I were you; for I can assure you, you won't get it.

Billing. Do you think I am not quite aware of that? My object is precisely not to get it. A slight of that kind stimulates a man's fighting power, it is like getting a supply of fresh bile, and I am sure one needs that badly enough in a hole-and-corner place like this, where it is so seldom anything happens to stir one up.

Hovstad (writing). Quite so, quite so.

Billing. Ah, I shall be heard of yet! Now I shall go and write the appeal to the Householders' Association. (Goes into the room on the right.)

Hovstad (sitting al his desk, biting his penholder, says slowly). Hm! that's it, is it. (A knock is heard.) Come in! (PETRA comes in by the outer door. HOVSTAD gets up.) What, you! here?

Petra. Yes, you must forgive me

Hovstad (pulling a chair forward). Won't you sit down?

Petra. No, thank you; I must go again in a moment.

Hovstad. Have you come with a message from your father, by any chance?

Petra. No, I have come on my own account. (Takes a book out of her coat pocket.) Here is the English story.

Hovstad. Why have you brought it back?

Petra. Because I am not going to translate it.

Hovstad. But you promised me faithfully.

Petra. Yes, but then I had not read it, I don't suppose you have read it either?

Hovstad. No, you know quite well I don't understand English; but

Petra. Quite so. That is why I wanted to tell you that you must find something else. (Lays the book on the table.) You can't use this for the "People's Messenger."

Hovstad. Why not?

Petra. Because it conflicts with all your opinions.

Hovstad. Oh, for that matter

Petra. You don't understand me. The burden of this story is that there is a supernatural power that looks after the so-called good people in this world and makes everything happen for the best in their case, while all the so-called bad people are punished.

Hovstad. Well, but that is all right. That is just what our readers want.

Petra. And are you going to be the one to give it to them? For myself, I do not believe a word of it. You know quite well that things do not happen so in reality.

Hovstad. You are perfectly right; but an editor cannot always act as he would prefer. He is often obliged to bow to the wishes of the public in unimportant matters. Politics are the most important thing in life, for a newspaper, anyway; and if I want to carry my public with me on the path that leads to liberty and progress, I must not frighten them away. If they find a moral tale of this sort in the serial at the bottom of the page, they will be all the more ready to read what is printed above it; they feel more secure, as it were.

Petra. For shame! You would never go and set a snare like that for your readers; you are not a spider!

Hovstad (smiling). Thank you for having such a good opinion of me. No; as a matter of fact that is Billing's idea and not mine.

Petra. Billing's!

Hovstad. Yes; anyway, he propounded that theory here one day. And it is Billing who is so anxious to have that story in the paper; I don't know anything about the book.

Petra. But how can Billing, with his emancipated views

Hovstad. Oh, Billing is a many-sided man. He is applying for the post of secretary to the Bench, too, I hear.

Petra. I don't believe it, Mr. Hovstad. How could he possibly bring himself to do such a thing?

Hovstad. Ah, you must ask him that.

Petra. I should never have thought it of him.

Hovstad (looking more closely at her). No? Does it really surprise you so much?

Petra. Yes. Or perhaps not altogether. Really, I don't quite know

Hovstad. We journalists are not much worth, Miss Stockmann.

Petra. Do you really mean that?

Hovstad. I think so sometimes.

Petra. Yes, in the ordinary affairs of everyday life, perhaps; I can understand that. But now, when you have taken a weighty matter in hand

Hovstad. This matter of your father's, you mean?

Petra. Exactly. It seems to me that now you must feel you are a man worth more than most.

Hovstad. Yes, today I do feel something of that sort.

Petra. Of course you do, don't you? It is a splendid vocation you have chosen, to smooth the way for the march of unappreciated truths, and new and courageous lines of thought. If it were nothing more than because you stand fearlessly in the open and take up the cause of an injured man

Hovstad. Especially when that injured man is, ahem! I don't rightly know how to

Petra. When that man is so upright and so honest, you mean?

Hovstad (more gently). Especially when he is your father I meant.

Petra (suddenly checked). That?

Hovstad. Yes, Petra, Miss Petra.

Petra. Is it that, that is first and foremost with you? Not the matter itself? Not the truth? not my father's big generous heart?

Hovstad. Certainly, of course, that too.

Petra. No, thank you; you have betrayed yourself, Mr. Hovstad, and now I shall never trust you again in anything.

Hovstad. Can you really take it so amiss in me that it is mostly for your sake?

Petra. What I am angry with you for, is for not having been honest with my father. You talked to him as if the truth and the good of the community were what lay nearest to your heart. You have made fools of both my father and me. You are not the man you made yourself out to be. And that I shall never forgive you - never!

Hovstad. You ought not to speak so bitterly, Miss Petra, least of all now.

Petra. Why not now, especially?

Hovstad. Because your father cannot do without my help.

Petra (looking him up and down). Are you that sort of man too? For shame!

Hovstad. No, no, I am not. This came upon me so unexpectedly, you must believe that.

Petra. I know what to believe. Goodbye.

Aslaksen (coming from the printing room, hurriedly and with an air of mystery). Damnation, Hovstad! (Sees PETRA.) Oh, this is awkward

Petra. There is the book; you must give it to some one else. (Goes towards the door.)

Hovstad (following her). But, Miss Stockmann

Petra. Goodbye. (Goes out.)

Aslaksen. I say, Mr. Hovstad

Hovstad. Well well! what is it?

Aslaksen. The Mayor is outside in the printing room.

Hovstad. The Mayor, did you say?

Aslaksen. Yes he wants to speak to you. He came in by the back door, didn't want to be seen, you understand.

Hovstad. What can he want? Wait a bit, I will go myself. (Goes to the door of the printing room, opens it, bows and invites PETER STOCKMANN in.) Just see, Aslaksen, that no one

Aslaksen. Quite so. (Goes into the printing-room.)

Peter Stockmann. You did not expect to see me here, Mr. Hovstad?

Hovstad. No, I confess I did not.

Peter Stockmann (looking round). You are very snug in here, very nice indeed.

Hovstad. Oh

Peter Stockmann. And here I come, without any notice, to take up your time!

Hovstad. By all means, Mr. Mayor. I am at your service. But let me relieve you of your (takes STOCKMANN's hat and stick and puts them on a chair). Won't you sit down?

Peter Stockmann (sitting down by the table). Thank you. (HOVSTAD sits down.) I have had an extremely annoying experience to-day, Mr. Hovstad.

Hovstad. Really? Ah well, I expect with all the various business you have to attend to

Peter Stockmann. The Medical Officer of the Baths is responsible for what happened today.

Hovstad. Indeed? The Doctor?

Peter Stockmann. He has addressed a kind of report to the Baths Committee on the subject of certain supposed defects in the Baths.

Hovstad. Has he indeed?

Peter Stockmann. Yes, has he not told you? I thought he said

Hovstad. Ah, yes, it is true he did mention something about

Aslaksen (coming from the printing-room). I ought to have that copy.

Hovstad (angrily). Ahem! there it is on the desk.

Aslaksen (taking it). Right.

Peter Stockmann. But look there, that is the thing I was speaking of!

Aslaksen. Yes, that is the Doctor's article, Mr. Mayor.

Hovstad. Oh, is THAT what you were speaking about?

Peter Stockmann. Yes, that is it. What do you think of it?

Hovstad. Oh, I am only a layman and I have only taken a very cursory glance at it.

Peter Stockmann. But you are going to print it?

Hovstad. I cannot very well refuse a distinguished man.

Aslaksen. I have nothing to do with editing the paper, Mr. Mayor

Peter Stockmann. I understand.

Aslaksen. I merely print what is put into my hands.

Peter Stockmann. Quite so.

Aslaksen. And so I must (moves off towards the printing-room).

Peter Stockmann. No, but wait a moment, Mr. Aslaksen. You will allow me, Mr. Hovstad?

Hovstad. If you please, Mr. Mayor.

Peter Stockmann. You are a discreet and thoughtful man, Mr. Aslaksen.

Aslaksen. I am delighted to hear you think so, sir.

Peter Stockmann. And a man of very considerable influence.

Aslaksen. Chiefly among the small tradesmen, sir.

Peter Stockmann. The small tax-payers are the majority here as everywhere else.

Aslaksen. That is true.

Peter Stockmann. And I have no doubt you know the general trend of opinion among them, don't you?

Aslaksen. Yes I think I may say I do, Mr. Mayor.

Peter Stockmann. Yes. Well, since there is such a praiseworthy spirit of self-sacrifice among the less wealthy citizens of our town

Aslaksen. What?

Hovstad. Self-sacrifice?

Peter Stockmann. It is pleasing evidence of a public-spirited feeling, extremely pleasing evidence. I might almost say I hardly expected it. But you have a closer knowledge of public opinion than I.

Aslaksen. But, Mr. Mayor

Peter Stockmann. And indeed it is no small sacrifice that the town is going to make.

Hovstad. The town?

Aslaksen. But I don't understand. Is it the Baths?

Peter Stockmann. At a provisional estimate, the alterations that the Medical Officer asserts to be desirable will cost somewhere about twenty thousand pounds.

Aslaksen. That is a lot of money, but

Peter Stockmann. Of course it will be necessary to raise a municipal loan.

Hovstad (getting up). Surely you never mean that the town must pay?

Aslaksen. Do you mean that it must come out of the municipal funds? out of the ill-filled pockets of the small tradesmen?

Peter Stockmann. Well, my dear Mr. Aslaksen, where else is the money to come from?

Aslaksen. The gentlemen who own the Baths ought to provide that.

Peter Stockmann. The proprietors of the Baths are not in a position to incur any further expense.

Aslaksen. Is that absolutely certain, Mr. Mayor?

Peter Stockmann. I have satisfied myself that it is so. If the town wants these very extensive alterations, it will have to pay for them.

Aslaksen. But, damn it all, I beg your pardon, this is quite another matter, Mr. Hovstad!

Hovstad. It is, indeed.

Peter Stockmann. The most fatal part of it is that we shall be obliged to shut the Baths for a couple of years.

Hovstad. Shut them? Shut them altogether?

Aslaksen. For two years?

Peter Stockmann. Yes, the work will take as long as that, at least.

Aslaksen. I'm damned if we will stand that, Mr. Mayor! What are we householders to live upon in the meantime?

Peter Stockmann. Unfortunately, that is an extremely difficult question to answer, Mr. Aslaksen. But what would you have us do? Do you suppose we shall have a single visitor in the town, if we go about proclaiming that our water is polluted, that we are living over a plague spot, that the entire town

Aslaksen. And the whole thing is merely imagination?

Peter Stockmann. With the best will in the world, I have not been able to come to any other conclusion.

Aslaksen. Well then I must say it is absolutely unjustifiable of Dr. Stockmann, I beg your pardon, Mr. Mayor.

Peter Stockmann. What you say is lamentably true, Mr. Aslaksen. My brother has unfortunately always been a headstrong man.

Aslaksen. After this, do you mean to give him your support, Mr. Hovstad?

Hovstad. Can you suppose for a moment that I?

Peter Stockmann. I have drawn up a short resume of the situation as it appears from a reasonable man's point of view. In it I have indicated how certain possible defects might suitably be remedied without outrunning the resources of the Baths Committee.

Hovstad. Have you got it with you, Mr. Mayor?

Peter Stockmann (fumbling in his pocket). Yes, I brought it with me in case you should

Aslaksen. Good Lord, there he is!

Peter Stockmann. Who? My brother?

Hovstad. Where? Where?

Aslaksen. He has just gone through the printing room.

Peter Stockmann. How unlucky! I don't want to meet him here, and I had still several things to speak to you about.

Hovstad (pointing to the door on the right). Go in there for the present.

Peter Stockmann. But?

Hovstad. You will only find Billing in there.

Aslaksen. Quick, quick, Mr. Mayor, he is just coming.

Peter Stockmann. Yes, very well; but see that you get rid of him quickly. (Goes out through the door on the right, which ASLAKSEN opens for him and shuts after him.)

Hovstad. Pretend to be doing something, Aslaksen. (Sits down and writes. ASLAKSEN begins foraging among a heap of newspapers that are lying on a chair.)

Dr. Stockmann (coming in from the printing room). Here I am again. (Puts down his hat and stick.)

Hovstad (writing). Already, Doctor? Hurry up with what we were speaking about, Aslaksen. We are very pressed for time today.

Dr. Stockmann (to ASLAKSEN). No proof for me to see yet, I hear.

Aslaksen (without turning round). You couldn't expect it yet, Doctor.

Dr. Stockmann. No, no; but I am impatient, as you can understand. I shall not know a moment's peace of mind until I see it in print.

Hovstad. Hm! It will take a good while yet, won't it, Aslaksen?

Aslaksen. Yes, I am almost afraid it will.

Dr. Stockmann. All right, my dear friends; I will come back. I do not mind coming back twice if necessary. A matter of such great importance, the welfare of the town at stake, it is no time to shirk trouble, (is just going, but stops and comes back.) Look here, there is one thing more I want to speak to you about.

Hovstad. Excuse me, but could it not wait till some other time?

Dr. Stockmann. I can tell you in half a dozen words. It is only this. When my article is read tomorrow and it is realised that I have been quietly working the whole winter for the welfare of the town

Hovstad. Yes but, Doctor

Dr. Stockmann. I know what you are going to say. You don't see how on earth it was any more than my duty, my obvious duty as a citizen. Of course it wasn't; I know that as well as you. But my fellow citizens, you know! Good Lord, think of all the good souls who think so highly of me!

Aslaksen. Yes, our townsfolk have had a very high opinion of you so far, Doctor.

Dr. Stockmann. Yes, and that is just why I am afraid they. Well, this is the point; when this reaches them, especially the poorer classes, and sounds in their ears like a summons to take the town's affairs into their own hands for the future...

Hovstad (getting up). Ahem I Doctor, I won't conceal from you the fact

Dr. Stockmann. Ah I - I knew there was something in the wind! But I won't hear a word of it. If anything of that sort is being set on foot

Hovstad. Of what sort?

Dr. Stockmann. Well, whatever it is, whether it is a demonstration in my honour, or a banquet, or a subscription list for some presentation to me, whatever it is, you most promise me solemnly and faithfully to put a stop to it. You too, Mr. Aslaksen; do you understand?

Hovstad. You must forgive me, Doctor, but sooner or later we must tell you the plain truth

(He is interrupted by the entrance Of MRS. STOCKMANN, who comes in from the street door.)

Mrs. Stockmann (seeing her husband). Just as I thought!

Hovstad (going towards her). You too, Mrs. Stockmann?

Dr. Stockmann. What on earth do you want here, Katherine?

Mrs. Stockmann. I should think you know very well what I want.

Hovstad, Won't you sit down? Or perhaps

Mrs. Stockmann. No, thank you; don't trouble. And you must not be offended at my coming to fetch my husband; I am the mother of three children, you know.

Dr. Stockmann. Nonsense! we know all about that.

Mrs. Stockmann. Well, one would not give you credit for much thought for your wife and children today; if you had had that, you would not have gone and dragged us all into misfortune.

Dr. Stockmann. Are you out of your senses, Katherine! Because a man has a wife and children, is he not to be allowed to proclaim the truth, is he not to be allowed to be an actively useful citizen, is he not to be allowed to do a service to his native town!

Mrs. Stockmann. Yes, Thomas, in reason.

Aslaksen. Just what I say. Moderation in everything.

Mrs. Stockmann. And that is why you wrong us, Mr. Hovstad, in enticing my husband away from his home and making a dupe of him in all this.

Hovstad. I certainly am making a dupe of no one

Dr. Stockmann. Making a dupe of me! Do you suppose I should allow myself to be duped!

Mrs. Stockmann. It is just what you do. I know quite well you have more brains than anyone in the town, but you are extremely easily duped, Thomas. (To Hovstad.) Please do realise that he loses his post at the Baths if you print what he has written.

Aslaksen. What!

Hovstad. Look here, Doctor!

Dr. Stockmann (laughing). Ha-ha! just let them try! No, no, they will take good care not to. I have got the compact majority behind me, let me tell you!

Mrs. Stockmann. Yes, that is just the worst of it, your having any such horrid thing behind you.

Dr. Stockmann. Rubbish, Katherine! Go home and look after your house and leave me to look after the community. How can you be so afraid, when I am so confident and happy? (Walks up and down, rubbing his hands.) Truth and the People will win the fight, you may be certain! I see the whole of the broad-minded middle class marching like a victorious army! (Stops beside a chair.) What the deuce is that lying there?

Aslaksen Good Lord!

Hovstad. Ahem!

Dr. Stockmann. Here we have the topmost pinnacle of authority! (Takes the Mayor's official hat carefully between his finger-tips and holds it up in the air.)

Mrs. Stockmann. The Mayor's hat!

Dr. Stockmann. And here is the staff of office too. How in the name of all that's wonderful?

Hovstad. Well, you see

Dr. Stockmann. Oh, I understand. He has been here trying to talk you over. Ha-ha! he made rather a mistake there! And as soon as he caught sight of me in the printing room. (Bursts out laughing.) Did he run away, Mr. Aslaksen?

Aslaksen (hurriedly). Yes, he ran away, Doctor.

Dr. Stockmann. Ran away without his stick or his. Fiddlesticks! Peter doesn't run away and leave his belongings behind him. But what the deuce have you done with him? Ah! in there, of course. Now you shall see, Katherine!

Mrs. Stockmann. Thomas, please don't!

Aslaksen. Don't be rash, Doctor.

(DR. STOCKMANN has put on the Mayor's hat and taken his stick in his hand. He goes up to the door, opens it, and stands with his hand to his hat at the salute. PETER STOCKMANN comes in, red with anger. BILLING follows him.)

Peter Stockmann. What does this tomfoolery mean?

Dr. Stockmann. Be respectful, my good Peter. I am the chief authority in the town now. (Walks up and down.)

Mrs. Stockmann (almost in tears). Really, Thomas!

Peter Stockmann (following him about). Give me my hat and stick.

Dr. Stockmann (in the same tone as before). If you are chief constable, let me tell you that I am the Mayor, I am the master of the whole town, please understand!

Peter Stockmann. Take off my hat, I tell you. Remember it is part of an official uniform.

Dr. Stockmann. Pooh! Do you think the newly awakened lionhearted people are going to be frightened by an official hat? There is going to be a revolution in the town tomorrow, let me tell you. You thought you could turn me out; but now I shall turn you out, turn you out of all your various offices. Do you think I cannot? Listen to me. I have triumphant social forces behind me. Hovstad and Billing will thunder in the "People's Messenger," and Aslaksen will take the field at the head of the whole Householders' Association

Aslaksen. That I won't, Doctor.

Dr. Stockmann. Of course you will

Peter Stockmann. Ah! may I ask then if Mr. Hovstad intends to join this agitation?

Hovstad. No, Mr. Mayor.

Aslaksen. No, Mr. Hovstad is not such a fool as to go and ruin his paper and himself for the sake of an imaginary grievance.

Dr. Stockmann (looking round him). What does this mean?

Hovstad. You have represented your case in a false light, Doctor, and therefore I am unable to give you my support.

Billing. And after what the Mayor was so kind as to tell me just now, I

Dr. Stockmann. A false light! Leave that part of it to me. Only print my article; I am quite capable of defending it.

Hovstad. I am not going to print it. I cannot and will not and dare not print it.

Dr. Stockmann. You dare not? What nonsense! you are the editor; and an editor controls his paper, I suppose!

Aslaksen. No, it is the subscribers, Doctor.

Peter Stockmann. Fortunately, yes.

Aslaksen. It is public opinion, the enlightened public, householders and people of that kind; they control the newspapers.

Dr. Stockmann (composedly). And I have all these influences against me?

Aslaksen. Yes, you have. It would mean the absolute ruin of the community if your article were to appear.

Dr. Stockmann. Indeed.

Peter Stockmann. My hat and stick, if you please. (DR. STOCKMANN takes off the hat and lays it on the table with the stick. PETER STOCKMANN takes them up.) Your authority as mayor has come to an untimely end.

Dr. Stockmann. We have not got to the end yet. (To HOVSTAD.) Then it is quite impossible for you to print my article in the "People's Messenger"?

Hovstad. Quite impossible, out of regard for your family as well.

Mrs. Stockmann. You need not concern yourself about his family, thank you, Mr. Hovstad.

Peter Stockmann (taking a paper from his pocket). It will be sufficient, for the guidance of the public, if this appears. It is an official statement. May I trouble you?

Hovstad (taking the paper). Certainly; I will see that it is printed.

Dr. Stockmann. But not mine. Do you imagine that you can silence me and stifle the truth! You will not find it so easy as you suppose. Mr. Aslaksen, kindly take my manuscript at once and print it as a pamphlet at my expense. I will have four hundred copies, no, five or six hundred.

Aslaksen. If you offered me its weight in gold, I could not lend my press for any such purpose, Doctor. It would be flying in the face of public opinion. You will not get it printed anywhere in the town.

Dr. Stockmann. Then give it me back.

Hovstad (giving him the MS.). Here it is.

Dr. Stockmann (taking his hat and stick). It shall be made public all the same. I will read it out at a mass meeting of the townspeople. All my fellow-citizens shall hear the voice of truth!

Peter Stockmann. You will not find any public body in the town that will give you the use of their hall for such a purpose.

Aslaksen. Not a single one, I am certain.

Billing. No, I'm damned if you will find one.

Mrs. Stockmann. But this is too shameful! Why should every one turn against you like that?

Dr. Stockmann (angrily). I will tell you why. It is because all the men in this town are old women like you; they all think of nothing but their families, and never of the community.

Mrs. Stockmann (putting her arm into his). Then I will show them that an old woman can be a man for once. I am going to stand by you, Thomas!

Dr. Stockmann. Bravely said, Katherine! It shall be made public, as I am a living soul! If I can't hire a hall, I shall hire a drum, and parade the town with it and read it at every street-corner.

Peter Stockmann. You are surely not such an errant fool as that!

Dr. Stockmann. Yes, I am.

Aslaksen. You won't find a single man in the whole town to go with you.

Billing. No, I'm damned if you will.

Mrs. Stockmann. Don't give in, Thomas. I will tell the boys to go with you.

Dr. Stockmann. That is a splendid idea!

Mrs. Stockmann. Morten will be delighted; and Ejlif will do whatever he does.

Dr. Stockmann. Yes, and Petra! and you too, Katherine!

Mrs. Stockmann. No, I won't do that; but I will stand at the window and watch you, that's what I will do.

Dr. Stockmann (puts his arms round her and kisses her). Thank you, my dear! Now you and I are going to try a fall, my fine gentlemen! I am going to see whether a pack of cowards can succeed in gagging a patriot who wants to purify society! (He and his wife go out by the street door.)

Peter Stockmann (shaking his head seriously). Now he has sent her out of her senses, too.

ACT IV

(SCENE. A big old-fashioned room in CAPTAIN HORSTER'S house. At the back folding-doors, which are standing open, lead to an ante-room. Three windows in the left-hand wall. In the middle of the opposite wall a platform has been erected. On this is a small table with two candles, a water-bottle and glass, and a bell. The room is lit by lamps placed between the windows. In the foreground on the left there is a table with candles and a chair. To the right is a door and some chairs standing near it. The room is nearly filled with a crowd of townspeople of all sorts, a few women and schoolboys being amongst them. People are still streaming in from the back, and the room is soon filled.)

1st Citizen (meeting another). Hullo, Lamstad! You here too?

2nd Citizen. I go to every public meeting, I do.

3rd Citizen. Brought your whistle too, I expect!

2nd Citizen. I should think so. Haven't you?

3rd Citizen. Rather! And old Evensen said he was going to bring a cow-horn, he did.

2nd Citizen. Good old Evensen! (Laughter among the crowd.)

4th Citizen (coming up to them). I say, tell me what is going on here tonight?

2nd Citizen. Dr. Stockmann is going to deliver an address attacking the Mayor.

4th Citizen. But the Mayor is his brother.

1st Citizen. That doesn't matter; Dr. Stockmann's not the chap to be afraid.

Peter Stockmann. For various reasons, which you will easily understand, I must beg to be excused. But fortunately we have amongst us a man who I think will be acceptable to you all. I refer to the President of the Householders' Association, Mr. Aslaksen.

Several voices. Yes, Aslaksen! Bravo Aslaksen!

(DR. STOCKMANN takes up his MS. and walks up and down the platform.)

Aslaksen. Since my fellow-citizens choose to entrust me with this duty, I cannot refuse.

(Loud applause. ASLAKSEN mounts the platform.)

Billing (writing), "Mr. Aslaksen was elected with enthusiasm."

Aslaksen. And now, as I am in this position, I should like to say a few brief words. I am a quiet and peaceable man, who believes in discreet moderation, and, and in moderate discretion. All my friends can bear witness to that.

Several Voices. That's right! That's right, Aslaksen!

Aslaksen. I have learned in the school of life and experience that moderation is the most valuable virtue a citizen can possess

Peter Stockmann. Hear, hear!

Aslaksen. And moreover, that discretion and moderation are what enable a man to be of most service to the community. I would therefore suggest to our esteemed fellow-citizen, who has called this meeting, that he should strive to keep strictly within the bounds of moderation.

A Man by the door. Three cheers for the Moderation Society!

A Voice. Shame!

Several Voices. Sh!-Sh!

Aslaksen. No interruptions, gentlemen, please! Does anyone wish to make any remarks?

Peter Stockmann. Mr. Chairman.

Aslaksen. The Mayor will address the meeting.

Peter Stockmann. In consideration of the close relationship in which, as you all know, I stand to the present Medical Officer of the Baths, I should have preferred not to speak this evening. But my official position with regard to the Baths and my solicitude for the vital interests of the town compel me to bring forward a motion. I venture to presume that there is not a single one of our citizens present who considers it desirable that unreliable and exaggerated accounts of the sanitary condition of the Baths and the town should be spread abroad.

Several Voices. No, no! Certainly not! We protest against it!

Peter Stockmann. Therefore, I should like to propose that the meeting should not permit the Medical Officer either to read or to comment on his proposed lecture.

Dr. Stockmann (impatiently). Not permit! What the devil!

Mrs. Stockmann (coughing). Ahem!-ahem!

Dr. Stockmann (collecting himself). Very well, Go ahead!

Peter Stockmann. In my communication to the "People's Messenger," I have put the essential facts before the public in such a way that every fair-minded citizen can easily form his own opinion. From it you will see that the main result of the Medical Officer's proposals, apart from their constituting a vote of censure on the leading men of the town, would be to saddle the ratepayers with an unnecessary expenditure of at least some thousands of pounds.

(Sounds of disapproval among the audience, and some cat-calls.)

Aslaksen (ringing his bell). Silence, please, gentlemen! I beg to support the Mayor's motion. I quite agree with him that there is something behind this agitation started by the Doctor. He talks about the Baths; but it is a revolution he is aiming at, he wants to get the administration of the town put into new hands. No one doubts the honesty of the Doctor's intentions, no one will suggest that there can be any two opinions as to that, I myself am a believer in self-government for the people, provided it does not fall too heavily on the ratepayers. But that would be the case here; and that is why I will see Dr. Stockmann damned, I beg your pardon, before I go with him in the matter. You can pay too dearly for a thing sometimes; that is my opinion.

(Loud applause on all sides.)

Hovstad. I, too, feel called upon to explain my position. Dr. Stockmann's agitation appeared to be gaining a certain amount of sympathy at first, so I supported it as impartially as I could. But presently we had reason to suspect that we had allowed ourselves to be misled by misrepresentation of the state of affairs

Dr. Stockmann. Misrepresentation!

Hovstad. Well, let us say a not entirely trustworthy representation. The Mayor's statement has proved that. I hope no one here has any doubt as to my liberal principles; the attitude of the "People's Messenger" towards important political questions is well known to everyone. But the advice of experienced and thoughtful men has convinced me that in purely local matters a newspaper ought to proceed with a certain caution.

Aslaksen. I entirely agree with the speaker.

Hovstad. And, in the matter before us, it is now an undoubted fact that Dr. Stockmann has public opinion against him. Now, what is an editor's first and most obvious duty, gentlemen? Is it not to work in harmony with his readers? Has he not received a sort of tacit mandate to work persistently and assiduously for the welfare of those whose opinions he represents? Or is it possible I am mistaken in that?

Voices from the crowd. No, no! You are quite right!

Hovstad. It has cost me a severe struggle to break with a man in whose house I have been lately a frequent guest, a man who till today has been able to pride himself on the undivided goodwill of his fellow-citizens, a man whose only, or at all events whose essential, failing is that he is swayed by his heart rather than his head.

A few scattered voices. That is true! Bravo, Stockmann!

Hovstad. But my duty to the community obliged me to break with him. And there is another consideration that impels me to oppose him, and, as far as possible, to arrest him on the perilous course he has adopted; that is, consideration for his family

Dr. Stockmann. Please stick to the water-supply and drainage!

Hovstad. - consideration, I repeat, for his wife and his children for whom he has made no provision.

Morten. Is that us, mother?

Mrs. Stockmann. Hush!

Aslaksen. I will now put the Mayor's proposition to the vote.

Dr. Stockmann. There is no necessity! Tonight I have no intention of dealing with all that filth down at the Baths. No; I have something quite different to say to you.

Peter Stockmann (aside). What is coming now?

A Drunken Man (by the entrance door). I am a ratepayer! And therefore, I have a right to speak too! And my entire, firm, inconceivable opinion is

A number of voices. Be quiet, at the back there!

Others. He is drunk! Turn him out! (They turn him out.)

Dr. Stockmann. Am I allowed to speak?

Aslaksen (ringing his bell). Dr. Stockmann will address the meeting.

Dr. Stockmann. I should like to have seen anyone, a few days ago, dare to attempt to silence me as has been done tonight! I would have defended my sacred rights as a man, like a lion! But now it is all one to me; I have something of even weightier importance to say to you. (The crowd presses nearer to him, MORTEN Kiil conspicuous among them.)

Dr. Stockmann (continuing). I have thought and pondered a great deal, these last few days, pondered over such a variety of things that in the end my head seemed too full to hold them

Peter Stockmann (with a cough). Ahem!

Dr. Stockmann. - but I got them clear in my mind at last, and then I saw the whole situation lucidly. And that is why I am standing here to-night. I have a great revelation to make to you, my fellow-citizens! I will impart to you a discovery of a far wider scope than the trifling matter that our water supply is poisoned and our medicinal Baths are standing on pestiferous soil.

A number of voices (shouting). Don't talk about the Baths! We won't hear you! None of that!

Dr. Stockmann. I have already told you that what I want to speak about is the great discovery I have made lately, the discovery that all the sources of our moral life are poisoned and that the whole fabric of our civic community is founded on the pestiferous soil of falsehood.

Voices of disconcerted Citizens. What is that he says?

Peter Stockmann. Such an insinuation!

Aslaksen (with his hand on his bell). I call upon the speaker to moderate his language.

Dr. Stockmann. I have always loved my native town as a man only can love the home of his youthful days. I was not old when I went away from here; and exile, longing and memories cast as it were an additional halo over both the town and its inhabitants. (Some clapping and applause.) And there I stayed, for many years, in a horrible hole far away up north. When I came into contact with some of the people that lived scattered about among the rocks, I often thought it would of been more service to the poor half-starved creatures if a veterinary doctor had been sent up there, instead of a man like me. (Murmurs among the crowd.)

Billing (laying down his pen). I'm damned if I have ever heard!

Hovstad. It is an insult to a respectable population!

Dr. Stockmann. Wait a bit! I do not think anyone will charge me with having forgotten my native town up there. I was like one of the cider-ducks brooding on its nest, and what I hatched was the plans for these Baths. (Applause and protests.) And then when fate at last decreed for me the great happiness of coming home again, I assure you, gentlemen, I thought I had nothing more in the world to wish for. Or rather, there was one thing I wished for, eagerly, untiringly, ardently, and that was to be able to be of service to my native town and the good of the community.

Peter Stockmann (looking at the ceiling). You chose a strange way of doing it, ahem!

Dr. Stockmann. And so, with my eyes blinded to the real facts, I revelled in happiness. But yesterday morning, no, to be precise, it was yesterday afternoon, the eyes of my mind were opened wide, and the first thing I realised was the colossal stupidity of the authorities. (Uproar, shouts and laughter, MRS. STOCKMANN coughs persistently.)

Peter Stockmann. Mr. Chairman!

Aslaksen (ringing his bell). By virtue of my authority!

Dr. Stockmann. It is a petty thing to catch me up on a word, Mr. Aslaksen. What I mean is only that I got scent of the unbelievable piggishness our leading men had been responsible for down at the Baths. I can't stand leading men at any price! I have had enough of such people in my time. They are like billy-goats on a young plantation; they do mischief everywhere. They stand in a free man's way, whichever way he turns, and what I should like best would be to see them exterminated like any other vermin. (Uproar.)

Peter Stockmann. Mr. Chairman, can we allow such expressions to pass?

Aslaksen (with his hand on his bell). Doctor !

Dr. Stockmann. I cannot understand how it is that I have only now acquired a clear conception of what these gentry are, when I had almost daily before my eyes in this town such an excellent specimen of them, my brother Peter, slow-witted and hide-bound in prejudice. (Laughter, uproar and hisses. MRS. STOCKMANN Sits coughing assiduously. ASLAKSEN rings his bell violently.)

The Drunken Man (who has got in again). Is it me he is talking about? My name's Petersen, all right, but devil take me if I

Angry Voices. Turn out that drunken man! Turn him out. (He is turned out again.)

Peter Stockmann. Who was that person?

1st Citizen. I don't know who he is, Mr. Mayor.

2nd Citizen. He doesn't belong here.

3rd Citizen. I expect he is a navvy from over at (the rest is inaudible).

Aslaksen. He had obviously had too much beer. Proceed, Doctor; but please strive to be moderate in your language.

Dr. Stockmann. Very well, gentlemen, I will say no more about our leading men. And if anyone imagines, from what I have just said, that my object is to attack these people this evening, he is wrong, absolutely wide of the mark. For I cherish the comforting conviction that these parasites, all these venerable relics of a dying school of thought, are most admirably paving the way for their own extinction; they need no doctor's help to hasten their end. Nor is it folk of that kind who constitute the most pressing danger to the community. It is not they who are most instrumental in poisoning the sources of our moral life and infecting the ground on which we stand. It is not they who are the most dangerous enemies of truth and freedom amongst us.

Shouts from all sides. Who then? Who is it? Name! Name!

Dr. Stockmann. You may depend upon it, I shall name them! That is precisely the great discovery I made yesterday. (Raises his voice.) The most dangerous enemy of truth and freedom amongst us is the compact majority yes, the damned compact Liberal majority, that is it! Now you know! (Tremendous uproar. Most of the crowd are shouting, stamping and hissing. Some of the older men among them exchange stolen glances and seem to be enjoying themselves. MRS. STOCKMANN gets up, looking anxious. EJLIF and MORTEN advance threateningly upon some schoolboys who are playing pranks. ASLAKSEN rings his bell and begs for silence. HOVSTAD and BILLING both talk at once, but are inaudible. At last quiet is restored.)

Aslaksen. As Chairman, I call upon the speaker to withdraw the ill-considered expressions he has just used.

Dr. Stockmann. Never, Mr. Aslaksen! It is the majority in our community that denies me my freedom and seeks to prevent my speaking the truth.

Hovstad. The majority always has right on its side.

Billing. And truth too, by God!

Dr. Stockmann. The majority never has right on its side. Never, I say! That is one of these social lies against which an independent, intelligent man must wage war. Who is it that constitute the majority of the population in a country? Is it the clever folk, or the stupid? I don't imagine you will dispute the fact that at present the stupid people are in an absolutely overwhelming majority all the world over. But, good Lord! you can never pretend that it is right that the stupid folk should govern the clever ones I (Uproar and cries.) Oh, yes, you can shout me down, I know! But you cannot answer me. The majority has might on its side, unfortunately; but right it has not. I am in the right, I and a few other scattered individuals. The minority is always in the right. (Renewed uproar.)

Hovstad. Aha! so Dr. Stockmann has become an aristocrat since the day before yesterday!

Dr. Stockmann. I have already said that I don't intend to waste a word on the puny, narrow-chested, short-winded crew whom we are leaving astern. Pulsating life no longer concerns itself with them. I am thinking of the few, the scattered few amongst us, who have absorbed new and vigorous truths. Such men stand, as it were, at the outposts, so far ahead that the compact majority has not yet been able to come up with them; and there they are fighting for truths that are too newly-born into the world of consciousness to have any considerable number of people on their side as yet.

Hovstad. So the Doctor is a revolutionary now!

Dr. Stockmann. Good heavens, of course I am, Mr. Hovstad! I propose to raise a revolution against the lie that the majority has the monopoly of the truth. What sort of truths are they that the majority usually supports? They are truths that are of such advanced age that they are beginning to break up. And if a truth is as old as that, it is also in a fair way to become a lie, gentlemen. (Laughter and mocking cries.) Yes, believe me or not, as you like; but truths are by no means as long-lived at Methuselah, as some folk imagine. A normally constituted truth lives, let us say, as a rule seventeen or eighteen, or at most twenty years, seldom longer. But truths as aged as that are always worn frightfully thin, and nevertheless it is only then that the majority recognises them and recommends them to the community as wholesome moral nourishment. There is no great nutritive value in that sort of fare, I can assure you; and, as a doctor, I ought to know. These "majority truths" are like last year's cured meat, like rancid, tainted ham; and they are the origin of the moral scurvy that is rampant in our communities.

Aslaksen. It appears to me that the speaker is wandering a long way from his subject.

Peter Stockmann. I quite agree with the Chairman.

Dr. Stockmann. Have you gone clean out of your senses, Peter? I am sticking as closely to my subject as I can; for my subject is precisely this, that it is the masses, the majority, this infernal compact majority, that poisons the sources of our moral life and infects the ground we stand on.

Hovstad. And all this because the great, broadminded majority of the people is prudent enough to show deference only to well-ascertained and well-approved truths?

Dr. Stockmann. Ah, my good Mr. Hovstad, don't talk nonsense about well-ascertained truths! The truths of which the masses now approve are the very truths that the fighters at the outposts held to in the days of our grandfathers. We fighters at the outposts nowadays no longer approve of them; and I do not believe there is any other well-ascertained truth except this, that no community can live a healthy life if it is nourished only on such old marrowless truths.

Hovstad. But, instead of standing there using vague generalities, it would be interesting if you would tell us what these old marrowless truths are, that we are nourished on.

(Applause from many quarters.)

Dr. Stockmann. Oh, I could give you a whole string of such abominations; but to begin with I will confine myself to one well-approved truth, which at bottom is a foul lie, but upon which nevertheless Mr. Hovstad and the "People's Messenger" and all the "Messenger's" supporters are nourished.

Hovstad. And that is?

Dr. Stockmann. That is, the doctrine you have inherited from your forefathers and proclaim thoughtlessly far and wide, the doctrine that the public, the crowd, the masses, are the essential part of the population, that they constitute the People, that the common folk, the ignorant and incomplete element in the community, have the same right to pronounce judgment and to, approve, to direct and to govern, as the isolated, intellectually superior personalities in it.

Billing. Well, damn me if ever I

Hovstad (at the same time, shouting out). Fellow-citizens, take good note of that!

A number of voices (angrily). Oho! we are not the People! Only the superior folk are to govern, are they!

A Workman. Turn the fellow out for talking such rubbish!

Another. Out with him!

Another (calling out). Blow your horn, Evensen!

(A horn is blown loudly, amidst hisses and an angry uproar.)

Dr. Stockmann (when the noise has somewhat abated). Be reasonable! Can't you stand hearing the voice of truth for once? I don't in the least expect you to agree with me all at once; but I must say I did expect Mr. Hovstad to admit I was right, when he had recovered his composure a little. He claims to be a freethinker

Voices (in murmurs of astonishment). Freethinker, did he say? Is Hovstad a freethinker?

Hovstad (shouting). Prove it, Dr. Stockmann! When have I said so in print?

Dr. Stockmann (reflecting). No, confound it, you are right! you have never had the courage to. Well, I won't put you in a hole, Mr. Hovstad. Let us say it is I that am the freethinker, then. I am going to prove to you, scientifically, that the "People's Messenger" leads you by the nose in a shameful manner when it tells you that you, that the common people, the crowd, the masses, are the real essence of the People. That is only a newspaper lie, I tell you! The common people are nothing more than the raw material of which a People is made. (Groans, laughter and uproar.) Well, isn't that the case? Isn't there an enormous difference between a well-bred and an ill-bred strain of animals? Take, for instance, a common barn-door hen. What sort of eating do you get from a shrivelled up old scrag of a fowl like that? Not much, do you! And what sort of eggs does it lay? A fairly good crow or a raven can lay pretty nearly as good an egg. But take a well-bred Spanish or Japanese hen, or a good pheasant or a turkey, then you will see the difference. Or take the case of dogs, with whom we humans are on such intimate terms. Think first of an ordinary common cur, I mean one of the horrible, coarse-haired, low-bred curs that do nothing but run about the streets and befoul the walls of the houses. Compare one of these curs with a poodle whose sires for many generations have been bred in a gentleman's house, where they have had the best of food and had the opportunity of hearing soft voices and music. Do you not think that the poodle's brain is developed to quite a different degree from that of the cur? Of course it is. It is puppies of well-bred poodles like that, that showmen train to do incredibly clever tricks, things that a common cur could never learn to do even if it stood on its head. (Uproar and mocking cries.)

A Citizen (calls out). Are you going to make out we are dogs, now?

Another Citizen. We are not animals, Doctor!

Dr. Stockmann. Yes but, bless my soul, we are, my friend! It is true we are the finest animals anyone could wish for; but, even among us, exceptionally fine animals are rare. There is a tremendous difference between poodle-men and cur-men. And the amusing part of it is, that Mr. Hovstad quite agrees with me as long as it is a question of four-footed animals

Hovstad. Yes, it is true enough as far as they are concerned.

Dr. Stockmann. Very well. But as soon as I extend the principle and apply it to two-legged animals, Mr. Hovstad stops short. He no longer dares to think independently, or to pursue his ideas to their logical conclusion; so, he turns the whole theory upside down and proclaims in the "People's Messenger" that it is the barn-door hens and street curs that are the finest specimens in the menagerie. But that is always the way, as long as a man retains the traces of common origin and has not worked his way up to intellectual distinction.

Hovstad. I lay no claim to any sort of distinction, I am the son of humble country-folk, and I am proud that the stock I come from is rooted deep among the common people he insults.

Voices. Bravo, Hovstad! Bravo! Bravo!

Dr. Stockmann. The kind of common people I mean are not only to be found low down in the social scale; they crawl and swarm all around us, even in the highest social positions. You have only to look at your own fine, distinguished Mayor! My brother Peter is every bit as plebeian as anyone that walks in two shoes (laughter and hisses)

Peter Stockmann. I protest against personal allusions of this kind.

Dr. Stockmann (imperturbably). and that, not because he is like myself, descended from some old rascal of a pirate from Pomerania or thereabouts, because that is who we are descended from

Peter Stockmann. An absurd legend. I deny it!

Dr. Stockmann. but because he thinks what his superiors think, and holds the same opinions as they, People who do that are, intellectually speaking, common people; and, that is why my magnificent brother Peter is in reality so very far from any distinction and consequently also so far from being liberal-minded.

Peter Stockmann. Mr. Chairman!

Hovstad. So it is only the distinguished men that are liberal-minded in this country? We are learning something quite new! (Laughter.)

Dr. Stockmann. Yes, that is part of my new discovery too. And another part of it is that broad-mindedness is almost precisely the same thing as morality. That is why I maintain that it is absolutely inexcusable in the "People's Messenger" to proclaim, day in and day out, the false doctrine that it is the masses, the crowd, the compact majority, that have the monopoly of broad-mindedness and morality, and that vice and corruption and every kind of intellectual depravity are the result of culture, just as all the filth that is draining into our Baths is the result of the tanneries up at Molledal! (Uproar and interruptions. DR. STOCKMANN is undisturbed, and goes on, carried away by his ardour, with a smile.) And yet this same "People's Messenger" can go on preaching that the masses ought to be elevated to higher conditions of life! But, bless my soul, if the "Messenger's" teaching is to be depended upon, this very raising up the masses would mean nothing more or less than setting them straightway upon the paths of depravity! Happily the theory that culture demoralises is only an old falsehood that our forefathers believed in and we have inherited. No, it is ignorance, poverty, ugly conditions of life, that do the devil's work! In a house which does not get aired and swept every day, my wife Katherine maintains that the floor ought to be scrubbed as well, but that is a debatable question, in such a house, let me tell you, people will lose within two or three years the power of thinking or acting in a moral manner. Lack of oxygen weakens the conscience. And there must be a plentiful lack of oxygen in very many houses in this town, I should think, judging from the fact that the whole compact majority can be unconscientious enough to wish to build the town's prosperity on a quagmire of falsehood and deceit.

Aslaksen. We cannot allow such a grave accusation to be flung at a citizen community.

A Citizen. I move that the Chairman direct the speaker to sit down.

Voices (angrily). Hear, hear! Quite right! Make him sit down!

Dr. Stockmann (losing his self-control). Then I will go and shout the truth at every street corner! I will write it in other towns' newspapers! The whole country shall know what is going on here!

Hovstad. It almost seems as if Dr. Stockmann's intention were to ruin the town.

Dr. Stockmann. Yes, my native town is so dear to me that I would rather ruin it than see it flourishing upon a lie.

Aslaksen. This is really serious. (Uproar and cat-calls MRS. STOCKMANN coughs, but to no purpose; her husband does not listen to her any longer.)

Hovstad (shouting above the din). A man must be a public enemy to wish to ruin a whole community!

Dr. Stockmann (with growing fervor). What does the destruction of a community matter, if it lives on lies? It ought to be razed to the ground. I tell you, All who live by lies ought to be exterminated like vermin! You will end by infecting the whole country; you will bring about such a state of things that the whole country will deserve to be ruined. And if things come to that pass, I shall say from the bottom of my heart: Let the whole country perish, let all these people be exterminated!

Voices from the crowd. That is talking like an out-and-out enemy of the people!

Billing. There sounded the voice of the people, by all that's holy!

The whole crowd (shouting). Yes, yes! He is an enemy of the people! He hates his country! He hates his own people!

Aslaksen. Both as a citizen and as an individual, I am profoundly disturbed by what we have had to listen to. Dr. Stockmann has shown himself in a light I should never have dreamed of. I am unhappily obliged to subscribe to the opinion which I have just heard my estimable fellow-citizens utter; and I propose that we should give expression to that opinion in a resolution. I propose a resolution as follows: "This meeting declares that it considers Dr. Thomas Stockmann, Medical Officer of the Baths, to be an enemy of the people." (A storm of cheers and applause. A number of men surround the DOCTOR and hiss him. MRS. STOCKMANN and PETRA have got up from their seats. MORTEN and EJLIF are fighting the other schoolboys for hissing; some of their elders separate them.)

Dr. Stockmann (to the men who are hissing him). Oh, you fools! I tell you that

Aslaksen (ringing his bell). We cannot hear you now, Doctor. A formal vote is about to be taken; but, out of regard for personal feelings, it shall be by ballot and not verbal. Have you any clean paper, Mr. Billing?

Billing. I have both blue and white here.

Aslaksen (going to him). That will do nicely; we shall get on more quickly that way. Cut it up into small strips, yes, that's it. (To the meeting.) Blue means no; white means yes. I will come round myself and collect votes. (PETER STOCKMANN leaves the hall. ASLAKSEN and one or two others go round the room with the slips of paper in their hats.)

1st Citizen (to HOVSTAD). I say, what has come to the Doctor? What are we to think of it?

Hovstad. Oh, you know how headstrong he is.

2nd Citizen (to BILLING). Billing, you go to their house, have you ever noticed if the fellow drinks?

Billing. Well I'm hanged if I know what to say. There are always spirits on the table when you go.

3rd Citizen. I rather think he goes quite off his head sometimes.

1st Citizen. I wonder if there is any madness in his family?

Billing. I shouldn't wonder if there were.

4th Citizen. No, it is nothing more than sheer malice; he wants to get even with somebody for something or other.

Billing. Well certainly he suggested a rise in his salary on one occasion lately, and did not get it.

The Citizens (together). Ah! then it is easy to understand how it is!

The Drunken Man (who has got among the audience again). I want a blue one, I do! And I want a white one too!

Voices. It's that drunken chap again! Turn him out!

Morten Kiil. (going up to DR. STOCKMANN). Well, Stockmann, do you see what these monkey tricks of yours lead to?

Dr. Stockmann. I have done my duty.

Morten Kiil. What was that you said about the tanneries at Molledal?

Dr. Stockmann. You heard well enough. I said they were the source of all the filth.

Morten Kiil. My tannery too?

Dr. Stockmann. Unfortunately your tannery is by far the worst.

Morten Kiil. Are you going to put that in the papers?

Dr. Stockmann. I shall conceal nothing.

Morten Kiil. That may cost you dearly, Stockmann. (Goes out.)

A Stout Man (going UP to CAPTAIN HORSTER, Without taking any notice of the ladies). Well, Captain, so you lend your house to enemies of the people?

Horster. I imagine I can do what I like with my own possessions, Mr. Vik.

The Stout Man. Then you can have no objection to my doing the same with mine.

Horster. What do you mean, sir?

The Stout Man. You shall hear from me in the morning. (Turns his back on him and moves off.)

Petra. Was that not your owner, Captain Horster?

Horster. Yes, that was Mr. Vik the shipowner.

Aslaksen (with the voting-papers in his hands, gets up on to the platform and rings his bell). Gentlemen, allow me to announce the result. By the votes of every one here except one person

A Young Man. That is the drunk chap!

Aslaksen. By the votes of everyone here except a tipsy man, this meeting of citizens declares Dr. Thomas Stockmann to be an enemy of the people. (Shouts and applause.) Three cheers for our ancient and honourable citizen community! (Renewed applause.) Three cheers for our able and energetic Mayor, who has so loyally suppressed the promptings of family feeling! (Cheers.) The meeting is dissolved. (Gets down.)

Billing. Three cheers for the Chairman!

The whole crowd. Three cheers for Aslaksen! Hurrah!

Dr. Stockmann. My hat and coat, Petra! Captain, have you room on your ship for passengers to the New World?

Horster. For you and yours we will make room, Doctor.

Dr. Stockmann (as PETRA helps him into his coat), Good. Come, Katherine! Come, boys!

Mrs. Stockmann (in an undertone). Thomas, dear, let us go out by the back way.

Dr. Stockmann. No back ways for me, Katherine, (Raising his voice.) You will hear more of this enemy of the people, before he shakes the dust off his shoes upon you! I am not so forgiving as a certain Person; I do not say: "I forgive you, for ye know not what ye do."

Aslaksen (shouting). That is a blasphemous comparison, Dr. Stockmann!

Billing. It is, by God! It's dreadful for an earnest man to listen to.

A Coarse Voice. Threatens us now, does he!

Other Voices (excitedly). Let's go and break his windows! Duck him in the fjord!

Another Voice. Blow your horn, Evensen! Pip, pip!

(Horn-blowing, hisses, and wild cries. DR. STOCKMANN goes out through the hall with his family, HORSTER elbowing a way for them.)

The Whole Crowd (howling after them as they go). Enemy of the People! Enemy of the People!

Billing (as he puts his papers together). Well, I'm damned if I go and drink toddy with the Stockmanns tonight!

(The crowd press towards the exit. The uproar continues outside; shouts of "Enemy of the People!" are heard from without.)

ACT V

(SCENE. DR. STOCKMANN'S study. Bookcases and cabinets containing specimens, line the walls. At the back is a door leading to the hall; in the foreground on the left, a door leading to the sitting-room. In the righthand wall are two windows, of which all the panes are broken. The DOCTOR'S desk, littered with books and papers, stands in the middle of the room, which is in disorder. It is morning. DR. STOCKMANN in dressing-gown, slippers and a smoking-cap, is bending down and raking with an umbrella under one of the cabinets. After a little while he rakes out a stone.)

Dr. Stockmann (calling through the open sitting-room door). Katherine, I have found another one.

Mrs. Stockmann (from the sitting-room). Oh, you will find a lot more yet, I expect.

Dr. Stockmann (adding the stone to a heap of others on the table). I shall treasure these stones as relics. Ejlif and Morten shall look at them everyday, and when they are grown up they shall inherit them as heirlooms. (Rakes about under a bookcase.) Hasn't, what the deuce is her name? the girl, you know, hasn't she been to fetch the glazier yet?

Mrs. Stockmann (coming in). Yes, but he said he didn't know if he would be able to come today.

Dr. Stockmann. You will see he won't dare to come.

Mrs. Stockmann. Well, that is just what Randine thought, that he didn't dare to, on account of the neighbours. (Calls into the sitting-room.) What is it you want, Randine? Give it to me. (Goes in, and comes out again directly.) Here is a letter for you, Thomas.

Dr. Stockmann. Let me see it. (Opens and reads it.) Ah! of course.

Mrs. Stockmann. Who is it from?

Dr. Stockmann. From the landlord. Notice to quit.

Mrs. Stockmann. Is it possible? Such a nice man

Dr. Stockmann (looking at the letter). Does not dare do otherwise, he says. Doesn't like doing it, but dare not do otherwise, -on account of his fellow-citizens, out of regard for public opinion. Is in a dependent position, dares not offend certain influential men.

Mrs. Stockmann. There, you see, Thomas!

Dr. Stockmann. Yes, yes, I see well enough; the whole lot of them in the town are cowards; not a man among them dares do anything for fear of the others. (Throws the letter on to the table.) But it doesn't matter to us, Katherine. We are going to sail away to the New World, and

Mrs. Stockmann. But, Thomas, are you sure we are well advised to take this step?

Dr. Stockmann. Are you suggesting that I should stay here, where they have pilloried me as an enemy of the people, branded me, broken my windows! And just look here, Katherine, they have torn a great rent in my black trousers too!

Mrs. Stockmann. Oh, dear! and they are the best pair you have got!

Dr. Stockmann. You should never wear your best trousers when you go out to fight for freedom and truth. It is not that I care so much about the trousers, you know; you can always sew them up again for me. But that the common herd should dare to make this attack on me, as if they were my equals that is what I cannot, for the life of me, swallow!

Mrs. Stockmann. There is no doubt they have behaved very ill toward you, Thomas; but is that sufficient reason for our leaving our native country for good and all?

Dr. Stockmann. If we went to another town, do you suppose we should not find the common people just as insolent as they are here? Depend upon it, there is not much to choose between them. Oh, well, let the curs snap, that is not the worst part of it. The worst is that, from one end of this country to the other, every man is the slave of his Party. Although, as far as that goes, I daresay it is not much better in the free West either; the compact majority, and liberal public opinion, and all that infernal old bag of tricks are probably rampant there too. But there things are done on a larger scale, you see. They may kill you, but they won't put you to death by slow torture. They don't squeeze a free man's soul in a vice, as they do here. And, if need be, one can live in solitude. (Walks up and down.) If only I knew where there was a virgin forest or a small South Sea island for sale, cheap

Mrs. Stockmann. But think of the boys, Thomas!

Dr. Stockmann (standing still). What a strange woman you are, Katherine! Would you prefer to have the boys grow up in a society like this? You saw for yourself last night that half the population are out of their minds; and if the other half have not lost their senses, it is because they are mere brutes, with no sense to lose.

Mrs. Stockmann. But, Thomas dear, the imprudent things you said had something to do with it, you know.

Dr. Stockmann. Well, isn't what I said perfectly true? Don't they turn every idea topsy-turvy? Don't they make a regular hotchpotch of right and wrong? Don't they say that the things I know are true, are lies? The craziest part of it all is the fact of these "liberals," men of full age, going about in crowds imagining that they are the broad-minded party! Did you ever hear anything like it, Katherine!

Mrs. Stockmann. Yes, yes, it's mad enough of them, certainly; but (PETRA comes in from the silting-room). Back from school already?

Petra. Yes. I have been given notice of dismissal.

Mrs. Stockmann. Dismissal?

Dr. Stockmann. You too?

Petra. Mrs. Busk gave me my notice; so I thought it was best to go at once.

Dr. Stockmann. You were perfectly right, too!

Mrs. Stockmann. Who would have thought Mrs. Busk was a woman like that!

Petra. Mrs. Busk isn't a bit like that, mother; I saw quite plainly how it hurt her to do it. But she didn't dare do otherwise, she said; and so I got my notice.

Dr. Stockmann (laughing and rubbing his hands). She didn't dare do otherwise, either! It's delicious!

Mrs. Stockmann. Well, after the dreadful scenes last night

Petra. It was not only that. Just listen to this, father!

Dr. Stockmann. Well?

Petra. Mrs. Busk showed me no less than three letters she received this morning

Dr. Stockmann. Anonymous, I suppose?

Petra. Yes.

Dr. Stockmann. Yes, because they didn't dare to risk signing their names, Katherine!

Petra. And two of them were to the effect that a man, who has been our guest here, was declaring last night at the Club that my views on various subjects are extremely emancipated

Dr. Stockmann. You did not deny that, I hope?

Petra. No, you know I wouldn't. Mrs. Busk's own views are tolerably emancipated, when we are alone together; but now that this report about me is being spread, she dare not keep me on any longer.

Mrs. Stockmann. And someone who had been a guest of ours! That shows you the return you get for your hospitality, Thomas!

Dr. Stockmann. We won't live in such a disgusting hole any longer. Pack up as quickly as you can, Katherine; the sooner we can get away, the better.

Mrs. Stockmann. Be quiet, I think I hear someone in the hall. See who it is, Petra.

Petra (opening the door). Oh, it's you, Captain Horster! Do come in.

Horster (coming in). Good morning. I thought I would just come in and see how you were.

Dr. Stockmann (shaking his hand). Thanks, that is really kind of you.

Mrs. Stockmann. And thank you, too, for helping us through the crowd, Captain Horster.

Petra. How did you manage to get home again?

Horster. Oh, somehow or other. I am fairly strong, and there is more sound than fury about these folk.

Dr. Stockmann. Yes, isn't their swinish cowardice astonishing? Look here, I will show you something! There are all the stones they have thrown through my windows. Just look at them! I'm hanged if there are more than two decently large bits of hard stone in the whole heap; the rest are nothing but gravel, wretched little things. And yet they stood out there bawling and swearing that they would do me some violence; but as for doing anything, you don't see much of that in this town.

Horster. Just as well for you this time, doctor!

Dr. Stockmann. True enough. But it makes one angry all the same; because if some day it should be a question of a national fight in real earnest, you will see that public opinion will be in favour of taking to one's heels, and the compact majority will turn tail like a flock of sheep, Captain Horster. That is what is so mournful to think of; it gives me so much concern, that. No, devil take it, it is ridiculous to care about it! They have called me an enemy of the people, so an enemy of the people let me be!

Mrs. Stockmann. You will never be that, Thomas.

Dr. Stockmann. Don't swear to that, Katherine. To be called an ugly name may have the same effect as a pin-scratch in the lung. And that hateful name, I can't get quit of it. It is sticking here in the pit of my stomach, eating into me like a corrosive acid. And no magnesia will remove it.

Petra. Bah! you should only laugh at them, father,

Horster. They will change their minds some day, Doctor.

Mrs. Stockmann. Yes, Thomas, as sure as you are standing here.

Dr. Stockmann. Perhaps, when it is too late. Much good may it do them! They may wallow in their filth then and rue the day when they drove a patriot into exile. When do you sail, Captain Horster?

Horster. Hm! that was just what I had come to speak about

Dr. Stockmann. Why, has anything gone wrong with the ship?

Horster. No; but what has happened is that I am not to sail in it.

Petra. Do you mean that you have been dismissed from your command?

Horster (smiling). Yes, that's just it.

Petra. You too.

Mrs. Stockmann. There, you see, Thomas!

Dr. Stockmann. And that for the truth's sake! Oh, if I had thought such a thing possible

Horster. You mustn't take it to heart; I shall be sure to find a job with some ship-owner or other, elsewhere.

Dr. Stockmann. And that is this man Vik, a wealthy man, independent of everyone and everything! Shame on him!

Horster. He is quite an excellent fellow otherwise; he told me himself he would willingly have kept me on, if only he had dared

Dr. Stockmann. But he didn't dare? No, of course not.

Horster. It is not such an easy matter, he said, for a party man

Dr. Stockmann. The worthy man spoke the truth. A party is like a sausage machine; it mashes up all sorts of heads together into the same mincemeat, fatheads and blockheads, all in one mash!

Mrs. Stockmann. Come, come, Thomas dear!

Petra (to HORSTER). If only you had not come home with us, things might not have come to this pass.

Horster. I do not regret it.

Petra (holding out her hand to him). Thank you for that!

Horster (to DR. STOCKMANN). And so what I came to say was that if you are determined to go away, I have thought of another plan

Dr. Stockmann. That's splendid! if only we can get away at once.

Mrs. Stockmann. Hush! wasn't that some one knocking?

Petra. That is uncle, surely.

Dr. Stockmann. Aha! (Calls out.) Come in!

Mrs. Stockmann. Dear Thomas, promise me definitely. (PETER STOCKMANN comes in from the hall.)

Peter Stockmann. Oh, you are engaged. In that case, I will

Dr. Stockmann. No, no, come in.

Peter Stockmann. But I wanted to speak to you alone.

Mrs. Stockmann. We will go into the sitting-room in the meanwhile.

Horster. And I will look in again later.

Dr. Stockmann. No, go in there with them, Captain Horster; I want to hear more about.

Horster. Very well, I will wait, then. (He follows MRS. STOCKMANN and PETRA into the sitting-room.)

Dr. Stockmann. I daresay you find it rather draughty here today. Put your hat on.

Peter Stockmann. Thank you, if I may. (Does so.) I think I caught cold last night; I stood and shivered

Dr. Stockmann. Really? I found it warm enough.

Peter Stockmann. I regret that it was not in my power to prevent those excesses last night.

Dr. Stockmann. Have you anything in particular to say to me besides that?

Peter Stockmann (taking a big letter from his pocket). I have this document for you, from the Baths Committee.

Dr. Stockmann. My dismissal?

Peter Stockmann. Yes, dating from today. (Lays the letter on the table.) It gives us pain to do it; but, to speak frankly, we dared not do otherwise on account of public opinion.

Dr. Stockmann (smiling). Dared not? I seem to have heard that word before, today.

Peter Stockmann. I must beg you to understand your position clearly. For the future you must not count on any practice whatever in the town.

Dr. Stockmann. Devil take the practice! But why are you so sure of that?

Peter Stockmann. The Householders' Association is circulating a list from house to house. All right-minded citizens are being called upon to give up employing you; and I can assure you that not a single head of a family will risk refusing his signature. They simply dare not.

Dr. Stockmann. No, no; I don't doubt it. But what then?

Peter Stockmann. If I might advise you, it would be best to leave the place for a little while

Dr. Stockmann. Yes, the propriety of leaving the place has occurred to me.

Peter Stockmann. Good. And then, when you have had six months to think things over, if, after mature consideration, you can persuade yourself to write a few words of regret, acknowledging your error

Dr. Stockmann. I might have my appointment restored to me, do you mean?

Peter Stockmann. Perhaps. It is not at all impossible.

Dr. Stockmann. But what about public opinion, then? Surely you would not dare to do it on account of public feeling...

Peter Stockmann. Public opinion is an extremely mutable thing. And, to be quite candid with you, it is a matter of great importance to us to have some admission of that sort from you in writing.

Dr. Stockmann. Oh, that's what you are after, is it! I will just trouble you to remember what I said to you lately about foxy tricks of that sort!

Peter Stockmann. Your position was quite different then. At that time you had reason to suppose you had the whole town at your back

Dr. Stockmann. Yes, and now I feel I have the whole town ON my back (flaring up). I would not do it if I had the devil and his dam on my back! Never, never, I tell you!

Peter Stockmann. A man with a family has no right to behave as you do. You have no right to do it, Thomas.

Dr. Stockmann. I have no right! There is only one single thing in the world a free man has no right to do. Do you know what that is?

Peter Stockmann. No.

Dr. Stockmann. Of course you don't, but I will tell you. A free man has no right to soil himself with filth; he has no right to behave in a way that would justify his spitting in his own face.

Peter Stockmann. This sort of thing sounds extremely plausible, of course; and if there were no other explanation for your obstinacy. But as it happens that there is.

Dr. Stockmann. What do you mean?

Peter Stockmann. You understand, very well what I mean. But, as your brother and as a man of discretion, I advise you not to build too much upon expectations and prospects that may so very easily fail you.

Dr. Stockmann. What in the world is all this about?

Peter Stockmann. Do you really ask me to believe that you are ignorant of the terms of Mr. Kiil's will?

Dr. Stockmann. I know that the small amount he possesses is to go to an institution for indigent old workpeople. How does that concern me?

Peter Stockmann. In the first place, it is by no means a small amount that is in question. Mr. Kiil is a fairly wealthy man.

Dr. Stockmann. I had no notion of that!

Peter Stockmann. Hm! hadn't you really? Then I suppose you had no notion, either, that a considerable portion of his wealth will come to your children, you and your wife having a life-rent of the capital. Has he never told you so?

Dr. Stockmann. Never, on my honour! Quite the reverse; he has consistently done nothing but fume at being so unconscionably heavily taxed. But are you perfectly certain of this, Peter?

Peter Stockmann. I have it from an absolutely reliable source.

Dr. Stockmann. Then, thank God, Katherine is provided for and the children too! I must tell her this at once (calls out) Katherine, Katherine!

Peter Stockmann (restraining him). Hush, don't say a word yet!

Mrs. Stockmann (opening the door). What is the matter?

Dr. Stockmann. Oh, nothing, nothing; you can go back. (She shuts the door. DR. STOCKMANN walks up and down in his excitement.) Provided for! Just think of it, we are all provided for! And for life! What a blessed feeling it is to know one is provided for!

Peter Stockmann. Yes, but that is just exactly what you are not. Mr. Kiil can alter his will any day he likes.

Dr. Stockmann. But he won't do that, my dear Peter. The "Badger" is much too delighted at my attack on you and your wise friends.

Peter Stockmann (starts and looks intently at him). Ali, that throws a light on various things.

Dr. Stockmann. What things?

Peter Stockmann. I see that the whole thing was a combined manoeuvre on your part and his. These violent, reckless attacks that you have made against the leading men of the town, under the pretence that it was in the name of truth

Dr. Stockmann. What about them?

Peter Stockmann. I see that they were nothing else than the stipulated price for that vindictive old man's will.

Dr. Stockmann (almost speechless). Peter, you are the most disgusting plebeian I have ever met in all my life.

Peter Stockmann. All is over between us. Your dismissal is irrevocable, we have a weapon against you now. (Goes out.)

Dr. Stockmann. For shame! For shame! (Calls out.) Katherine, you must have the floor scrubbed after him! Let - what's her name, devil take it, the girl who has always got soot on her nose

Mrs. Stockmann. (in the sitting-room). Hush, Thomas, be quiet!

Petra (coming to the door). Father, grandfather is here, asking if he may speak to you alone.

Dr. Stockmann. Certainly he may. (Going to the door.) Come in, Mr. Kiil. (MORTEN KIIL comes in. DR. STOCKMANN shuts the door after him.) What can I do for you? Won't you sit down?

Morten Kiil. I won't sit. (Looks around.) You look very comfortable here today, Thomas.

Dr. Stockmann. Yes, don't we!

Morten Kiil. Very comfortable, plenty of fresh air. I should think you have got enough to-day of that oxygen you were talking about yesterday. Your conscience must be in splendid order to-day, I should think.

Dr. Stockmann. It is.

Morten Kiil. So I should think. (Taps his chest.) Do you know what I have got here?

Dr. Stockmann. A good conscience, too, I hope.

Morten Kiil. Bah! No, it is something better than that. (He takes a thick pocket-book from his breast-pocket, opens it, and displays a packet of papers.)

Dr. Stockmann (looking at him in astonishment). Shares in the Baths?

Morten Kiil. They were not difficult to get today.

Dr. Stockmann. And you have been buying?

Morten Kiil. As many as I could pay for.

Dr. Stockmann. But, my dear Mr. Kiil, consider the state of the Baths' affairs!

Morten Kiil. If you behave like a reasonable man, you can soon set the Baths on their feet again.

Dr. Stockmann. Well, you can see for yourself that I have done all I can, but. They are all mad in this town!

Morten Kiil. You said yesterday that the worst of this pollution came from my tannery. If that is true, then my grandfather and my father before me, and I myself, for many years past, have been poisoning the town like three destroying angels. Do you think I am going to sit quiet under that reproach?

Dr. Stockmann. Unfortunately I am afraid you will have to.

Morten Kiil. No, thank you. I am jealous of my name and reputation. They call me "the Badger," I am told. A badger is a kind of pig, I believe; but I am not going to give them the right to call me that. I mean to live and die a clean man.

Dr. Stockmann. And how are you going to set about it?

Morten Kiil. You shall cleanse me, Thomas.

Dr. Stockmann. I!

Morten Kiil. Do you know what money I have bought these shares with? No, of course you can't know but I will tell you. It is the money that Katherine and Petra and the boys will have when I am gone. Because I have been able to save a little bit after all, you know.

Dr. Stockmann (flaring up). And you have gone and taken Katherine's money for this!

Morten Kiil. Yes, the whole of the money is invested in the Baths now. And now I just want to see whether you are quite stark, staring mad, Thomas! If you still make out that these animals and other nasty things of that sort come from my tannery, it will be exactly as if you were to flay broad strips of skin from Katherine's body, and Petra's, and the boys'; and no decent man would do that, unless he were mad.

Dr. Stockmann (walking up and down). Yes, but I am mad; I am mad!

Morten Kiil. You cannot be so absurdly mad as all that, when it is a question of your wife and children.

Dr. Stockmann (standing still in front of him). Why couldn't you consult me about it, before you went and bought all that trash?

Morten Kiil. What is done cannot be undone.

Dr. Stockmann (walks about uneasily). If only I were not so certain about it! But I am absolutely convinced that I am right.

Morten Kiil (weighing the pocket-book in his hand). If you stick to your mad idea, this won't be worth much, you know. (Puts the pocket-book in his pocket.)

Dr. Stockmann. But, hang it all! It might be possible for science to discover some prophylactic, I should think, or some antidote of some kind

Morten Kiil. To kill these animals, do you mean?

Dr. Stockmann. Yes, or to make them innocuous.

Morten Kiil. Couldn't you try some rat's-bane?

Dr. Stockmann. Don't talk nonsense! They all say it is only imagination, you know. Well, let it go at that! Let them have their own way about it! Haven't the ignorant, narrow-minded curs reviled me as an enemy of the people? and haven't they been ready to tear the clothes off my back too?

Morten Kiil. And broken all your windows to pieces!

Dr. Stockmann. And then there is my duty to my family. I must talk it over with Katherine; she is great on those things.

Morten Kiil. That is right; be guided by a reasonable woman's advice.

Dr. Stockmann (advancing towards him). To think you could do such a preposterous thing! Risking Katherine's money in this way, and putting me in such a horribly painful dilemma! When I look at you, I think I see the devil himself.

Morten Kiil. Then I had better go. But I must have an answer from you before two o'clock, yes or no. If it is no, the shares go to a charity, and that this very day.

Dr. Stockmann. And what does Katherine get?

Morten Kiil. Not a halfpenny. (The door leading to the hall opens, and HOVSTAD and ASLAKSEN make their appearance.) Look at those two!

Dr. Stockmann (staring at them). What the devil! have YOU actually the face to come into my house?

Hovstad. Certainly.

Aslaksen. We have something to say to you, you see.

Morten Kiil (in a whisper). Yes or no, before two o'clock.

Aslaksen (glancing at HOVSTAD). Aha! (MORTEN KIIL goes out.)

Dr. Stockmann. Well, what do you want with me? Be brief.

Hovstad. I can quite understand that you are annoyed with us for our attitude at the meeting yesterday.

Dr. Stockmann. Attitude, do you call it? Yes, it was a charming attitude! I call it weak, womanish, damnably shameful!

Hovstad. Call it what you like, we could not do otherwise.

Dr. Stockmann. You DARED not do otherwise, isn't that it?

Hovstad. Well, if you like to put it that way.

Aslaksen. But why did you not let us have word of it beforehand? just a hint to Mr. Hovstad or to me?

Dr. Stockmann. A hint? Of what?

Aslaksen. Of what was behind it all.

Dr. Stockmann. I don't understand you in the least

Aslaksen (with a confidential nod). Oh yes, you do, Dr. Stockmann.

Hovstad. It is no good making a mystery of it any longer.

Dr. Stockmann (looking first at one of them and then at the other). What the devil do you both mean?

Aslaksen. May I ask if your father-in-law is not going round the town buying up all the shares in the Baths?

Dr. Stockmann. Yes, he has been buying Baths shares today; but

Aslaksen. It would have been more prudent to get someone else to do it, someone less nearly related to you.

Hovstad. And you should not have let your name appear in the affair. There was no need for anyone to know that the attack on the Baths came from you. You ought to have consulted me, Dr. Stockmann.

Dr. Stockmann (looks in front of him; then a light seems to dawn on him and he says in amazement.) Are such things conceivable? Are such things possible?

Aslaksen (with a smile). Evidently they are. But it is better to use a little finesse, you know.

Hovstad. And it is much better to have several persons in a thing of that sort; because the responsibility of each individual is lessened, when there are others with him.

Dr. Stockmann (composedly). Come to the point, gentlemen. What do you want?

Aslaksen. Perhaps Mr. Hovstad had better

Hovstad. No, you tell him, Aslaksen.

Aslaksen. Well, the fact is that, now we know the bearings of the whole affair, we think we might venture to put the "People's Messenger" at your disposal.

Dr. Stockmann. Do you dare do that now? What about public opinion? Are you not afraid of a storm breaking upon our heads?

Hovstad. We will try to weather it.

Aslaksen. And you must be ready to go off quickly on a new tack, Doctor. As soon as your invective has done its work

Dr. Stockmann. Do you mean, as soon as my father-in-law and I have got hold of the shares at a low figure?

Hovstad. Your reasons for wishing to get the control of the Baths are mainly scientific, I take it.

Dr. Stockmann. Of course; it was for scientific reasons that I persuaded the old "Badger" to stand in with me in the matter. So we will tinker at the conduit-pipes a little, and dig up a little bit of the shore, and it shan't cost the town a sixpence. That will be all right, eh?

Hovstad. I think so, if you have the "People's Messenger" behind you.

Aslaksen. The Press is a power in a free community. Doctor.

Dr. Stockmann. Quite so. And so is public opinion. And you, Mr. Aslaksen, I suppose you will be answerable for the Householders' Association?

Aslaksen. Yes, and for the Temperance Society. You may rely on that.

Dr. Stockmann. But, gentlemen, I really am ashamed to ask the question, but, what return do you?

Hovstad. We should prefer to help you without any return whatever, believe me. But the "People's Messenger" is in rather a shaky condition; it doesn't go really well; and I should be very unwilling to suspend the paper now, when there is so much work to do here in the political way.

Dr. Stockmann. Quite so; that would be a great trial to such a friend of the people as you are. (Flares up.) But I am an enemy of the people, remember! (Walks about the room.) Where have I put my stick? Where the devil is my stick?

Hovstad. What's that?

Aslaksen. Surely you never mean

Dr. Stockmann (standing still.) And suppose I don't give you a single penny of all I get out of it? Money is not very easy to get out of us rich folk, please to remember!

Hovstad. And you please to remember that this affair of the shares can be represented in two ways!

Dr. Stockmann. Yes, and you are just the man to do it. If I don't come to the rescue of the "People's Messenger," you will certainly take an evil view of the affair; you will hunt me down, I can well imagine, pursue me, try to throttle me as a dog does a hare.

Hovstad. It is a natural law; every animal must fight for its own livelihood.

Aslaksen. And get its food where it can, you know.

Dr. Stockmann (walking about the room). Then you go and look for yours in the gutter; because I am going to show you which is the strongest animal of us three! (Finds an umbrella and brandishes it above his head.) Ah, now!

Hovstad. You are surely not going to use violence!

Aslaksen. Take care what you are doing with that umbrella.

Dr. Stockmann. Out of the window with you, Mr. Hovstad!

Hovstad (edging to the door). Are you quite mad!

Dr. Stockmann. Out of the window, Mr. Aslaksen! Jump, I tell you! You will have to do it, sooner or later.

Aslaksen (running round the writing-table). Moderation, Doctor, I am a delicate man, I can stand so little (calls out) help, help!

(MRS. STOCKMANN, PETRA and HORSTER come in from the sitting-room.)

Mrs. Stockmann. Good gracious, Thomas! What is happening?

Dr. Stockmann (brandishing the umbrella). Jump out, I tell you! Out into the gutter!

Hovstad. An assault on an unoffending man! I call you to witness, Captain Horster. (Hurries out through the hall.)

Aslaksen (irresolutely). If only I knew the way about here. (Steals out through the sitting-room.)

Mrs. Stockmann (holding her husband back). Control yourself, Thomas!

Dr. Stockmann (throwing down the umbrella). Upon my soul, they have escaped after all.

Mrs. Stockmann. What did they want you to do?

Dr. Stockmann. I will tell you later on; I have something else to think about now. (Goes to the table and writes something on a calling-card.) Look there, Katherine; what is written there?

Mrs. Stockmann. Three big Noes; what does that mean.

Dr. Stockmann. I will tell you that too, later on. (Holds out the card to PETRA.) There, Petra; tell sooty-face to run over to the "Badger's" with that, as quick as she can. Hurry up! (PETRA takes the card and goes out to the hall.)

Dr. Stockmann. Well, I think I have had a visit from every one of the devil's messengers to-day! But now I am going to sharpen my pen till they can feel its point; I shall dip it in venom and gall; I shall hurl my inkpot at their heads!

Mrs. Stockmann. Yes, but we are going away, you know, Thomas.

(PETRA comes back.)

Dr. Stockmann. Well?

Petra. She has gone with it.

Dr. Stockmann. Good. Going away, did you say? No, I'll be hanged if we are going away! We are going to stay where we are, Katherine!

Petra. Stay here?

Mrs. Stockmann. Here, in the town?

Dr. Stockmann. Yes, here. This is the field of battle, this is where the fight will be. This is where I shall triumph! As soon as I have had my trousers sewn up I shall go out and look for another house. We must have a roof over our heads for the winter.

Horster. That you shall have in my house.

Dr. Stockmann. Can I?

Horsier. Yes, quite well. I have plenty of room, and I am almost never at home.

Mrs. Stockmann. How good of you, Captain Horster!

Petra. Thank you!

Dr. Stockmann (grasping his hand). Thank you, thank you! That is one trouble over! Now I can set to work in earnest at once. There is an endless amount of things to look through here, Katherine! Luckily I shall have all my time at my disposal; because I have been dismissed from the Baths, you know.

Mrs. Stockmann (with a sigh). Oh yes, I expected that.

Dr. Stockmann. And they want to take my practice away from me too. Let them! I have got the poor people to fall back upon, anyway, those that don't pay anything; and, after all, they need me most, too. But, by Jove, they will have to listen to me; I shall preach to them in season and out of season, as it says somewhere.

Mrs. Stockmann. But, dear Thomas, I should have thought events had showed you what use it is to preach.

Dr. Stockmann. You are really ridiculous, Katherine. Do you want me to let myself be beaten off the field by public opinion and the compact majority and all that devilry? No, thank you! And what I want to do is so simple and clear and straightforward. I only want to drum into the heads of these curs the fact that the liberals are the most insidious enemies of freedom, that party programmes strangle every young and vigorous truth, that considerations of expediency turn morality and justice upside down and that they will end by making life here unbearable. Don't you think, Captain Horster, that I ought to be able to make people understand that?

Horster. Very likely; I don't know much about such things myself.

Dr. Stockmann. Well, look here, I will explain! It is the party leaders that must be exterminated. A party leader is like a wolf, you see, like a voracious wolf. He requires a certain number of smaller victims to prey upon every year, if he is to live. Just look at Hovstad and Aslaksen! How many smaller victims have they not put an end to, or at any rate maimed and mangled until they are fit for nothing except to be householders or subscribers to the "People's Messenger"! (Sits down on the edge of the table.) Come here, Katherine, look how beautifully the sun shines to-day! And this lovely spring air I am drinking in!

Mrs. Stockmann. Yes, if only we could live on sunshine and spring air, Thomas.

Dr. Stockmann. Oh, you will have to pinch and save a bit, then we shall get along. That gives me very little concern. What is much worse is, that I know of no one who is liberal-minded and high-minded enough to venture to take up my work after me.

Petra. Don't think about that, father; you have plenty of time before you. Hello, here are the boys already!

(EJLIF and MORTEN come in from the sitting-room.)

Mrs. Stockmann. Have you got a holiday?

Morten. No; but we were fighting with the other boys between lessons

Ejlif. That isn't true; it was the other boys were fighting with us.

Morten. Well, and then Mr. Rorlund said we had better stay at home for a day or two.

Dr. Stockmann (snapping his fingers and getting up from the table). I have it! I have it, by Jove! You shall never set foot in the school again!

The Boys. No more school!

Mrs. Stockmann. But, Thomas

Dr. Stockmann. Never, I say. I will educate you myself; that is to say, you shan't learn a blessed thing

Morten. Hooray!

Dr. Stockmann. - but I will make liberal-minded and high-minded men of you. You must help me with that, Petra.

Petra, Yes, father, you may be sure I will.

Dr. Stockmann. And my school shall be in the room where they insulted me and called me an enemy of the people. But we are too few as we are; I must have at least twelve boys to begin with.

Mrs. Stockmann. You will certainly never get them in this town.

Dr. Stockmann. We shall. (To the boys.) Don't you know any street urchins, regular ragamuffins?

Morten. Yes, father, I know lots!

Dr. Stockmann. That's capital! Bring me some specimens of them. I am going to experiment with curs, just for once; there may be some exceptional heads among them.

Morten. And what are we going to do, when you have made liberal-minded and high-minded men of us?

Dr. Stockmann. Then you shall drive all the wolves out of the country, my boys!

(EJLIF looks rather doubtful about it; MORTEN jumps about crying "Hurrah!")

Mrs. Stockmann. Let us hope it won't be the wolves that will drive you out of the country, Thomas.

Dr. Stockmann. Are you out of your mind, Katherine? Drive me out! Now, when I am the strongest man in the town!

Mrs. Stockmann. The strongest, now?

Dr. Stockmann. Yes, and I will go so far as to say that now I am the strongest man in the whole world.

Morten. I say!

Dr. Stockmann (lowering his voice). Hush! You mustn't say anything about it yet; but I have made a great discovery.

Mrs. Stockmann. Another one?

Dr. Stockmann. Yes. (Gathers them round him, and says confidentially:) It is this, let me tell you, that the strongest man in the world is he who stands most alone.

Mrs. Stockmann (smiling and shaking her head). Oh, Thomas, Thomas!

Petra (encouragingly, as she grasps her father's hands). Father!

Henrik Ibsen - Cataline

Index Of Contents

Cataline

Author's Preface

The drama Catiline, with which I entered upon my literary career, was written during the winter of 1848-49, that is in my twenty-first year.

I was at the time in Grimstad, under the necessity of earning with my hands the wherewithal of life and the means for instruction preparatory to my taking the entrance examinations to the university. The age was one of great stress. The February revolution, the uprisings in Hungary and elsewhere, the Slesvig war, all this had a great effect upon and hastened my development, however immature it may have remained for some time after. I wrote ringing poems of encouragement to the Magyars, urging them for the sake of liberty and humanity to hold out in the righteous struggle against the "tyrants"; I wrote a long series of sonnets to King Oscar, containing particularly, as far as I can remember, an appeal to set aside all petty considerations and to march forthwith at the head of his army to the aid of our brothers on the outermost borders of Slesvig. In as much as I now, in contrast to those times, doubt that my winged appeals would in any material degree have helped the cause of the Magyars or the Scandinavians, I consider it fortunate that they remained within the more private sphere of the manuscript. I could not, however, on more formal occasions keep from expressing myself in the impassioned spirit of my poetic effusions, which meanwhile brought me nothing from friends or non-friends but a questionable reward; the former greeted me as peculiarly fitted for the unintentionally droll, and the latter thought it in the highest degree strange that a young person in my subordinate position could undertake to inquire into affairs concerning which not even they themselves dared to entertain an opinion. I owe it to truth to add that my conduct at various times did not justify any great hope that society might count on an increase in me of civic virtue, inasmuch as I also, with epigrams and caricatures, fell out with many who had deserved better of me and whose friendship I in reality prized. Altogether, while a great struggle raged on the outside, I found myself on a war-footing with the little society where I lived cramped by conditions and circumstances of life.

Such was the situation when amid the preparations for my examinations I read through Sallust's Catiline together with Cicero's Catilinarian orations. I swallowed these documents, and a few months later my drama was complete. As will be seen from my book, I did not share at that time the conception of the two ancient Roman writers respecting the character and conduct of Catiline, and I am even now prone to believe that there must after all have been something great and consequential in a man whom Cicero, the assiduous counsel of the majority, did not find it expedient to engage until affairs had taken such a turn that there was no longer any danger involved in the attack. It should also be remembered that there are few individuals in history whose renown has been more completely in the hands of enemies than that of Catiline.

My drama was written during the hours of the night. The leisure hours for my study I practically had to steal from my employer, a good and respectable man, occupied however heart and soul with his business, and from those stolen study hours I again stole moments for writing verse. There was consequently scarcely anything else to resort to but the night. I believe this is the unconscious reason that almost the entire action of the piece transpires at night.

Naturally a fact so incomprehensible to my associates as that I busied myself with the writing of plays had to be kept secret; but a twenty-year old poet can hardly continue thus without anybody being privy to it, and I confided therefore to two friends of my own age what I was secretly engaged upon.

The three of us pinned great expectations on Catiline when it had been completed. First and foremost it was now to be copied in order to be submitted under an assumed name to the theater in Christiania, and furthermore it was of course to be published. One of my faithful and trusting friends undertook to prepare a handsome and legible copy of my uncorrected draft, a task which he performed with such a degree of conscientiousness that he did not omit even a single one of the innumerable dashes which I in the heat of composition had liberally interspersed throughout wherever the exact phrase did not for the moment occur to me. The second of my friends, whose name I here mention since he is no longer among the living, Ole C. Schulerud, at that time a student, later a lawyer, went to Christiania with the transcript. I still remember one of his letters in which he informed me that Catiline had now been submitted to the theater; that it would soon be given a performance, about that there could naturally be no doubt inasmuch as the management consisted of very discriminating men; and that there could be as little doubt that the booksellers of the town would one and all gladly pay a round fee for the first edition, the main point being, he thought, only to discover the one who would make the highest bid.

After a long and tense period of waiting there began to appear in the meantime a few difficulties. My friend had the piece returned from the management with a particularly polite but equally peremptory rejection. He now took the manuscript from bookseller to bookseller; but all to a man expressed themselves to the same effect as the theatrical management. The highest bidder demanded so and so much to publish the piece without any fee.

All this, however, was far from lessening my friend's belief in victory. He wrote to the contrary that it was best even so; I should come forward myself as the publisher of my drama; the necessary funds he would advance me; the profits we should divide in consideration of his undertaking the business end of the deal, except the proof-reading, which he regarded as superfluous in view of the handsome and legible manuscript the printers had to follow. In a later letter he declared that, considering these promising prospects for the future, he contemplated abandoning his studies in order to consecrate himself completely to the publishing of my works; two or three plays a year, he thought, I should with ease be able to write, and according to a calculation of probabilities he had made he had discovered that with our surplus we should at no distant time be able to undertake the journey so often agreed upon or discussed, through Europe and the Orient.

My journey was for the time being limited to Christiania. I arrived there in the beginning of the spring of 1850 and just previous to my arrival Catiline had appeared in the bookstalls. The drama created a stir and awakened considerable interest among the students, but the critics dwelt largely on the faulty verses and thought the book in other respects immature. A more appreciative judgment was uttered from but one single quarter, but this expression came from a man whose appreciation has always been dear to me and weighty and whom I herewith offer my renewed gratitude. Not very many copies of the limited edition were sold; my friend had a good share of them in his custody, and I remember that one evening when our domestic arrangements heaped up for us insurmountable difficulties, this pile of printed matter was fortunately disposed of as waste paper to a huckster. During the days immediately following we lacked none of the prime necessities of life.

During my sojourn at home last summer and particularly since my return here there loomed up before me more clearly and more sharply than ever before the kaleidoscopic scenes of my literary life. Among other things I also brought out Catiline. The contents of the book as regards details I had almost forgotten; but by reading it through anew I found that it nevertheless contained a great deal which I could still acknowledge, particularly if it be remembered that it is my first undertaking. Much, around which my later writings center, the contradiction between ability and desire, between will and possibility, the intermingled tragedy and comedy in humanity and in the individual, appeared already here in vague foreshadowings, and I conceived therefore the plan of preparing a new edition, a kind of jubilee-edition, a plan to which my publisher with his usual readiness gave his approval.

But it was naturally not enough simply to reprint without further ado the old original edition, for this is, as already pointed out, nothing but a copy of my imperfect and uncorrected concept or of the very first rough draft. In the rereading of it I remembered clearly what I originally had had in mind, and I saw moreover that the form practically nowhere gave a satisfactory rendering of what I had wished.

I determined therefore to revise this drama of my youth in a way in which I believe even at that time I should have been able to do it had the time been at my disposal and the circumstances more favorable for me. The ideas, the conceptions, and the development of the whole, I have not on the other hand altered. The book has remained the original; only now it appears in a complete form.

With this in mind I pray that my friends in Scandinavia and elsewhere will receive it; I pray that they will receive it as a greeting from me at the close of a period which to me has been full of changes and rich in contradictions. Much of what I twenty-five years ago dreamed has been realized, even though not in the manner nor as soon as I then hoped. Yet I believe now that it was best for me thus; I do not wish that any of that which lies between should have been untried, and if I look back upon what I have lived through I do so with thanks for everything and thanks to all.

HENRIK IBSEN.

Dresden, February, 1875.

DRAMATIS PERSON

LUCIUS CATILINE - A noble Roman.

AURELIA - His wife.

FURIA - A vestal.

CURIUS - A youth related to Catiline.

MANLIUS - An old warrior.

LENTULUS - Young and noble Roman.

GABINIUS - Young and noble Roman.

STATILIUS - Young and noble Roman.

COEPARIUS - Young and noble Roman.

CETHEGUS - Young and noble Roman.

AMBIORIX - Ambassador of the Allobroges.

OLLOVICO - Ambassador of the Allobroges

An old MAN.

PRIESTESSES and SERVANTS in the Temple of Vesta.

GLADIATORS and WARRIORS.

ESCORT of the Allobroges.

Sulla's GHOST.

SETTING The first and second acts are laid in and near Rome, the third act in Etruria.

FIRST ACT

[The Flaminian Way outside of Rome. Off the road a wooded hillside. In the background loom the walls and the heights of the city. It is evening.] [CATILINE stands on the hill among the bushes, leaning against a tree.]

CATILINE. I must! I must! A voice deep in my soul Urges me on, and I will heed its call.

Courage I have and strength for something better, Something far nobler than this present life, a series of unbridled dissipations!

No, no; they do not satisfy the yearning soul.

CATILINE. I rave and rave, long only to forget. 'Tis past now, all is past! Life has no aim.

CATILINE. [After a pause.]

And what became of all my youthful dreams?

Like flitting summer clouds they disappeared, Left naught behind but sorrow and remorse; Each daring hope in turn fate robbed me of. [He strikes his forehead.]

CATILINE. Despise yourself! Catiline, scorn yourself! You feel exalted powers in your soul; and yet what is the goal of all your struggle?

The surfeiting of sensual desires.

CATILINE. [More calmly.]

But there are times, such as the present hour, When secret longings kindle in my breast.

Ah, when I gaze on yonder city, Rome, The proud, the rich, and when I see that ruin And wretchedness to which it now is sunk Loom up before me like the flaming sun, then loudly calls a voice within my soul: Up, Catiline; awake and be a man!

CATILINE. [Abruptly.] Ah, these are but delusions of the night, Mere dreaming phantoms born of solitude.

At the slightest sound from grim reality, they flee into the silent depths within. [The ambassadors of the Allobroges, AMBIORIX and OLLOVICO, with their Escort, come down the highway without noticing CATILINE.]

AMBIORIX. Behold our journey's end! The walls of Rome!

To heaven aspires the lofty Capitol.

OLLOVICO. So that is Rome? Italy's overlord, Germany's soon, and Gaul's as well, perchance.

AMBIORIX. Ah, yes, alas; so it may prove betimes; The sovereign power of Rome is merciless; It crushes all it conquers, down to earth.

Now shall we see what lot we may expect: If here be help against the wrongs at home, And peace and justice for our native land.

OLLOVICO. It will be granted us.

AMBIORIX. So let us hope; For we know nothing yet with certainty.

OLLOVICO. You fear somewhat, it seems?

AMBIORIX. And with good reason.

Jealous was ever Rome of her great power.

And bear in mind, this proud and haughty realm Is not by chieftains ruled, as is our land.

At home the wise man or the warrior reigns, the first in wisdom and in war the foremost; Him choose we as the leader of our people, As arbiter and ruler of our tribe. But here

CATILINE. [Calls down to them.] Here might and selfishness hold sway; intrigue and craft are here the keys to power.

OLLOVICO. Woe to us, brethren, woe! He spies upon us.

AMBIORIX. [To CATILINE.] Is such the practice of the high-born Roman? A woman's trick we hold it in our nation.

CATILINE. [comes down on the road.] Ah, have no fear; spying is not my business; By chance it was I heard your conversation. Come you from Allobrogia far away?

Justice you think to find in Rome? Ah, never! Turn home again! Here tyranny holds sway, And rank injustice lords it more than ever.

Republic to be sure it is in name; And yet all men are slaves who cringe and cower, Vassals involved in debt, who must acclaim A venal senate, ruled by greed and power.

Gone is the social consciousness of old, The magnanimity of former ages; security and life are favors sold, Which must be bargained for with hire and wages.

Not righteousness, but power here holds sway; The noble man is lost among the gilded AMBIORIX. But say, who then are you to tear away The pillars of the hope on which we builded?

CATILINE. A man who burns in freedom's holy zeal; An enemy of all unrighteous power; Friend of the helpless trodden under heel, eager to hurl the mighty from their tower.

AMBIORIX. The noble race of Rome? Ah, Roman, speak. Since we are strangers here you would deceive us?

Is Rome no more the guardian of the weak, The dread of tyrants, ready to relieve us?

CATILINE. [Points towards the city and speaks.] Behold the mighty Capitol that towers On yonder heights in haughty majesty.

See, in the glow of evening how it lowers, Tinged with the last rays of the western sky. So too Rome's evening glow is fast declining, Her freedom now is thraldom, dark as night. Yet in her sky a sun will soon be shining, Before which darkness quick will take its flight. [He goes.] - [A colonnade in Rome.] [LENTULUS, STATILIUS, COEPARIUS, and CETHEGUS enter, in eager conversation.]

COEPARIUS. Yes, you are right; things go from bad to worse; And what the end will be I do not know.

CETHEGUS. Bah! I am not concerned about the end. The fleeting moment I enjoy; each cup Of pleasure as it comes I empty, letting all else go on to ruin as it will.

LENTULUS. Happy is he who can. I am not blessed With your indifference, that can outface The day when nothing shall be left us more, Nothing with which to pay the final score.

STATILIUS. And not the faintest glimpse of better things! Yet it is true: a mode of life like ours

CETHEGUS. Enough of that!

LENTULUS. Today because of debt The last of my inheritance was seized.

CETHEGUS. Enough of sorrow and complaint! Come, friends! We'll drown them in a merry drinking bout!

COEPARIUS. Yes, let us drink. Come, come, my merry comrades!

LENTULUS. A moment, friends; I see old Manlius yonder, seeking us out, I think, as is his wont.

MANLIUS. [Enters impetuously.] Confound the shabby dogs, the paltry scoundrels! Justice and fairness they no longer know!

LENTULUS. Come, what has happened? Wherefore so embittered?

STATILIUS. Have usurers been plaguing you as well?

MANLIUS. Something quite different. As you all know, I served with honor among Sulla's troops; A bit of meadow land was my reward.

And when the war was at an end, I lived Thereon; it furnished me my daily bread.

Now is it taken from me! Laws decree State property shall to the state revert For equal distribution. Theft, I say, it is rank robbery and nothing else! Their greed is all they seek to satisfy.

COEPARIUS. Thus with our rights they sport to please themselves. The mighty always dare do what they will.

CETHEGUS. [Gaily.] Hard luck for Manlius! Yet, a worse mishap Has come to me, as I shall now relate.

Listen, you know my pretty mistress, Livia, the little wretch has broken faith with me, Just now when I had squandered for her sake The slender wealth that still remained to me.

STATILIUS. Extravagance, the cause of your undoing.

CETHEGUS. Well, as you please; but I will not forego My own desires; these, while the day is fair, To their full measure I will satisfy.

MANLIUS. And I who fought so bravely for the glory And might which now the vaunting tyrants boast! I shall! If but the brave old band were here, My comrades of the battlefield! But no; The greater part of them, alas, is dead; The rest live scattering in many lands. Oh, what are you, the younger blood, to them? You bend and cringe before authority; You dare not break the chains that bind you fast; You suffer patiently this life of bondage!

LENTULUS. By all the Gods, although indeed he taunts us, Yet, Romans, is there truth in what he says.

CETHEGUS. Oh, well, what of it? He is right, we grant, But where shall we begin? Ay, there's the rub.

LENTULUS. Yes, it is true. Too long have we endured This great oppression. Now, now is the time To break the bonds asunder that injustice And vain ambition have about us forged.

STATILIUS. Ah, Lentulus, I understand. Yet hold; For such a thing we need a mighty leader, with pluck and vision. Where can he be found?

LENTULUS. I know a man who has the power to lead us.

MANLIUS. Ah, you mean Catiline?

LENTULUS. The very man.

CETHEGUS. Yes, Catiline perchance is just the man.

MANLIUS. I know him well. I was his father's friend; Many a battle side by side we fought. Often his young son went with him to war. Even his early years were wild and headstrong; Yet he gave open proof of rare endowments. His mind was noble, dauntless was his courage.

LENTULUS. We'll find him, as I think, most prompt and willing. I met him late this evening much depressed; He meditates in secret some bold plan; some desperate scheme he long has had in mind.

STATILIUS. No doubt; the consulate he long has sought.

LENTULUS. His efforts are in vain; his enemies Have madly raged against him in the senate; He was himself among them; full of wrath He left the council brooding on revenge.

STATILIUS. Then will he surely welcome our proposal.

LENTULUS. I hope so. Yet must we in secret weigh Our enterprise. The time is opportune. [They go.] - [In the Temple of Vesta in Rome. On an altar in the background burns a lamp with the sacred fire.] [CATILINE, followed by CURIUS, comes stealing in between the pillars.]

CURIUS. What, Catiline, you mean to bring me here? In Vesta's temple!

CATILINE. [Laughing.] Well, yes; so you see!

CURIUS. Ye gods, what folly! On this very day Has Cicero denounced you in the council; And yet you dare,

CATILINE. Oh, let that be forgotten!

CURIUS. You are in danger, and forget it thus by rushing blindly into some new peril.

CATILINE. [Gaily.] Well, change is my delight. I never knew Ere now a vestal's love, forbidden fruit; wherefore I came to try my fortune here.

CURIUS. What, here, you say? Impossible! A jest!

CATILINE. A jest? Why, yes, as all my loving is. and yet I was in earnest when I spoke. During the recent games I chanced to see the priestesses in long and pompous train.

By accident I cast my roving eye on one of them, and with a hasty glance She met my gaze. It pierced me to the soul. Ah, the expression in those midnight eyes I never saw before in any woman.

CURIUS. Yes, yes, I know. But speak, what followed then?

CATILINE. A way into the temple I have found, and more than once I've seen and spoken to her.

Oh, what a difference between this woman and my Aurelia!

CURIUS. And you love them both At once? No, that I cannot understand.

CATILINE. Yes, strange, indeed; I scarcely understand myself. And yet I love them both, as you have said. But oh, how vastly different is this love! The one is kind: Aurelia often lulls With soothing words my soul to peace and rest; but Furia. Come, away; some one approaches. [They hide themselves among the pillars.]

FURIA. [Enters from the opposite side.] Oh, hated walls, witnesses of my anguish!
Home of the torment I must suffer still! My hopes and cherished aspirations languish Within my bosom, now with feverish chill Pervaded, now with all the heat of passion, More hot and burning than yon vestal fire.

FURIA. Ah, what a fate! And what was my transgression That chained me to this temple-prison dire, that robbed my life of every youthful pleasure, in life's warm spring each innocent delight?

FURIA. Yet tears I shall not shed in undue measure; Hatred and vengeance shall my heart excite.

CATILINE. [Comes forward.] Not even for me, my Furia, do you cherish Another feeling, one more mild than this?

FURIA. Ye gods! you, reckless man, you here again? Do you not fear to come?

CATILINE. I know no fear. 'Twas always my delight to mock at danger.

FURIA. Oh, splendid! Such is also my delight; this peaceful temple here I hate the more, Because I live in everlasting calm, And danger never lurks within its walls.

FURIA. Oh, this monotonous, inactive life, A life faint as the flicker of the lamp! How cramped a field it is for all my sum Of fervid longings and far-reaching plans!
Oh, to be crushed between these narrow walls; life here grows stagnant; every hope is quenched; The day creeps slowly on in drowsiness, and not one single thought is turned to deeds.

CATILINE. O Furia, strange, in truth, is your complaint! It seems an echo out of my own soul, as if with flaming script you sought to paint My every longing towards a worthy goal.

Rancour and hate in my soul likewise flourish; My heart, as yours, hate tempers into steel; I too was robbed of hopes I used to nourish; An aim in life I now no longer feel.

CATILINE. In silence still I mask my grief, my want; And none can guess what smoulders in my breast. They scoff and sneer at me, these paltry things; they can not grasp how high my bosom beats For right and freedom, all the noble thoughts that ever stirred within a Roman mind.

FURIA. I knew it! Ah, your soul, and yours alone, Is born for me, thus clearly speaks a voice That never fails and never plays me false. Then come! Oh, come and let us heed the call.

CATILINE. What do you mean, my sweet enthusiast?

FURIA. Come, let us leave this place, flee far away, And seek a new and better fatherland. Here is the spirit's lofty pride repressed; Here baseness smothers each auspicious spark Ere it can break into a burning flame. Come, let us fly; lo, to the free-born mind The world's wide compass is a fatherland!

CATILINE. Oh, irresistibly you lure me on

FURIA. Come, let us use the present moment then! High o'er the hills, beyond the sea's expanse, far, far from Rome we first will stay our journey. Thousands of friends will follow you outright; In foreign lands we shall a home design; There shall we rule; 'twill there be brought to light That no hearts ever beat as yours and mine.

CATILINE. Oh, wonderful! But flee? Why must we flee? Here too our love for freedom can be nourished; Here also is a field for thought and action, As vast as any that your soul desires.

FURIA. Here, do you say? Here, in this paltry Rome, Where naught exists but thraldom and oppression?

Ah, Lucius, are you likewise one of those Who can Rome's past recall without confession Of shame? Who ruled here then? Who rule to-day? Then an heroic race and now a rabble, The slaves of other slaves

CATILINE. Mock me you may; yet know, to save Rome's freedom from this babble, To see yet once again her vanished splendor, Gladly I should, like Curtius, throw myself Into the abyss

FURIA. I trust you, you alone; Your eyes glow bright; I know you speak the truth.
Yet go; the priestesses will soon appear; Their wont it is to meet here at this hour.

CATILINE. I go; but only to return again. A magic power binds me to your side; so proud a woman have I never seen.

FURIA. [With a wild smile.] Then pledge me this; and swear that you will keep Whatever you may promise. Will you, Lucius?

CATILINE. I will do aught my Furia may require; Command me, tell me what am I to promise.

FURIA. Then listen. Though I dwell a captive here, I know there lives a man somewhere in Rome Whom I have sworn deep enmity to death. And hatred even beyond the gloomy grave.

CATILINE. And then?

FURIA. Then swear, my enemy shall be Your enemy till death. Will you, my Lucius?

CATILINE. I swear it here by all the mighty gods! I swear it by my father's honored name And by my mother's memory! But, Furia, what troubles you? Your eyes are wildly flaming, and white as marble, deathlike, are your cheeks.

FURIA. I do not know myself. A fiery stream Flows through my veins. Swear to the end your oath!

CATILINE. Oh, mighty powers, pour out upon this head Your boundless fury, let your lightning wrath Annihilate me, if I break my oath; Aye, like a demon I shall follow him!

FURIA. Enough! I trust you. Ah, my heart is eased. In your hand now indeed rests my revenge.

CATILINE. It shall be carried out. But tell me this, who is your foe? And what was his transgression?

FURIA. Close by the Tiber, far from the city's tumult, My cradle stood; it was a quiet home! A sister much beloved lived with me there, A chosen vestal from her childhood days. Then came a coward to our distant valley; he saw the fair, young priestess of the future

CATILINE. [Surprised.] A priestess? Tell me! Speak!

FURIA. He ravished her. She sought a grave beneath the Tiber's stream.

CATILINE. [Uneasy.] You know him?

FURIA. I have never seen the man. When first I heard the tidings, all was past.
His name is all I know.

CATILINE. Then speak it out!

FURIA. Now is it famed. His name is Catiline.

CATILINE. [Taken aback.] What do you say? Oh, horrors! Furia, speak!

FURIA. Calm yourself! What perturbs you? You grow pale. My Lucius, is this man perhaps your friend?

CATILINE. My friend? Ah, Furia, no; no longer now. For I have cursed, and sworn eternal hate against myself.

FURIA. You, you are Catiline?

CATILINE. Yes, I am he.

FURIA. My Sylvia you disgraced?

Nemesis then indeed has heard my prayer; vengeance you have invoked on your own head! Woe on you, man of violence! Woe!

CATILINE. How blank The stare is in your eye. Like Sylvia's shade You seem to me in this dim candle light. [He rushes out; the lamp with the sacred fire goes out.]

FURIA. [After a pause.] Yes, now I understand it. From my eyes The veil is fallen, in the dark I see. Hatred it was that settled in my breast, When first I spied him in the market-place. A strange emotion; like a crimson flame! Ah, he shall know what such a hate as mine, Constantly brewing, never satisfied, Can fashion out in ruin and revenge!

A VESTAL. [Enters.] Go, Furia, go; your watch is at an end; Therefore I came. Yet, sacred goddess, here woe unto you! The vestal fire is dead!

FURIA. [Bewildered.] Dead, did you say? So bright it never burned; 'Twill never, never die!

THE VESTAL. Great heavens, what is this?

FURIA. The fires of hate are not thus lightly quenched! Behold, love bursts forth of a sudden, dies within the hour; but hate

THE VESTAL. By all the gods, this is sheer madness! [Calls out.] Come! Oh, help! Come, help! [VESTALS and temple SERVANTS rush in.]

SOME. What is amiss?

OTHERS. The vestal fire is dead!

FURIA. But hate burns on; revenge still blazes high!

THE VESTALS. Away with her to trial and punishment! [They carry her out between them.]

CURIUS. [Comes forward.] To prison now they take her. Thence to death. No, no, by all the gods, this shall not be! Must she, most glorious of womankind, Thus perish in disgrace, entombed alive? Oh, never have I felt so strangely moved. Is this then love? Yes, love it is indeed. Then shall I set her free! But Catiline? With hate and vengeance will she follow him.

Has he maligners not enough already?

Dare I still others to their number add?

He was to me as were an elder brother; And gratitude now bids me that I shield him. But what of love? Ah, what does it command?

And should he quake, the fearless Catiline, Before the intrigues of a woman? No; then to the rescue work this very hour!

Wait, Furia; I shall drag you from your grave To life again, though at the risk of death! [He goes away quickly.] - [A room in CATILINE's house.]

CATILINE. [Enters impetuous and uneasy.] "Nemesis then indeed has heard my prayer, Vengeance you have invoked on your own head!"

Such were the words from the enchantress' lips.

Remarkable! Perchance it was a sign, a warning of what time will bring to me.

CATILINE. Now therefore I have pledged myself on oath The blood avenger of my own misdeed.

Ah, Furia, still I seem to see your eye, wildly aflame like that of death's own goddess!

Your words still echo hollow in my ears; the oath I shall remember all my life. [During the following AURELIA enters and approaches him unnoticed.]

CATILINE. Yet, it is folly now to go on brooding Upon this nonsense; it is nothing else.

Far better things there are to think upon; A greater work awaits my energies.

The restless age is urgent with its plea; Toward this I must direct my thought in season; Of hope and doubt I am a stormy sea

AURELIA. [Seizes his hand.] And may not your Aurelia know the reason?

May she not know what moves within your breast, What stirs therein and rages with such madness?

May she not cheer and soothe your soul to rest, And banish from your brow its cloud of sadness?

CATILINE. [Tenderly.] O, my Aurelia, O, how kind and tender. Yet why should I embitter all your life? Why should I share with you my many sorrows? For my sake you have borne enough of anguish.

Henceforth upon my own head I shall bear What ill-designing fate allotted me, The curse that lies in such a soul as mine, Full of great spiritual energies, Of fervent longings for a life of deeds, Yet dwarfed in all its work by sordid cares. Must you, too, sharing in my wretched life, Bitter with blasted hopes, then with me perish?

AURELIA. To comfort is the role of every wife, Though dreams of greatness she may never cherish.

When the man, struggling for his lofty dream, Reaps nothing but adversity and sorrow, her words to him then sweet and tender seem, And give him strength sufficient for the morrow; And then he sees that even the quiet life Has pleasures which the most tumultuous lacks.

CATILINE. Yes, you are right; I know it all too well. And yet I cannot tear myself away. A ceaseless yearning surges in my breast, which only life's great tumult now can quiet.

AURELIA. Though your Aurelia be not all to you, though she can never still your restless soul, your heart yet open to a gentle word, A word of comfort from your loving wife.

Though she may never slake your fiery thirst, Nor follow in their flight your noble thoughts. Know this, that she can share your every sorrow, Has strength and fortitude to ease your burden.

CATILINE. Then listen, dear Aurelia; you shall hear What has of late depressed so deep my spirits.

You know, I long have sought the consulate. Without avail. You know the whole affair. How to increase the votes for my election, I have expended

AURELIA. Catiline, no more; You torture me

CATILINE. Do you too blame my course? What better means therefor had I to choose? In vain I lavished all that I possessed; My one reward was mockery and shame.

Now in the senate has my adversary, The crafty Cicero, trampled me to earth. His speech was a portrayal of my life, So glaring that I, even I, must gasp.

In every look I read dismay and fear; With loathing people speak of Catiline; To races yet unborn my name will be A symbol of a low and dreadful union Of sensuality and wretchedness, Of scorn and ridicule for what is noble. And there will be no deed to purge this name And crush to earth the lies that have been told! Each will believe whatever rumor tells

AURELIA. But I, dear husband, trust no such reports. Let the whole world condemn you if it will; And let it heap disgrace upon your head; I know you hide within your inmost soul a seed that still can blossom and bear fruit. Only it cannot burst forth here in Rome; Poisonous weeds would quickly prove the stronger.
Let us forsake this degradation's home; what binds you here? Why should we dwell here longer?

CATILINE. I should forsake the field, and go away? I should my greatest dreams in life surrender?

The drowning man still clutches firm and fast The broken spars, though hope is frail and slender; And should the wreck be swallowed in the deep, And the last hope of rescue fail forever, still clings he to the lone remaining spar, And sinks with it in one last vain endeavor.

AURELIA. But should a kindly seacoast smile on him, With groves all green along the rolling billows, Hope then awakens in his heart again. He struggles inward, toward the silvery willows.

There reigns a quiet peace; 'tis beautiful; There roll the waves, in silence, without number; His heated brow sweet evening breezes cool, As weary-limbed he rests himself in slumber; Each sorrow-laden cloud they drive away; A restful calm his weary mind assuages. There he finds shelter and prolongs his stay And soon forgets the sorry by-gone ages.

The distant echo of the world's unrest Alone can reach his dwelling unfrequented.
It does not break the calm within his breast; it makes his soul more happy and contented; It calls to mind the by-gone time of strife, Its shattered hopes and its unbridled pleasures; He finds twice beautiful this quiet life and would not change it for the greatest treasures.

CATILINE. You speak the truth; and in this very hour From strife and tumult I could go with you. But can you name me some such quiet spot, Where we can live in shelter and in peace?

AURELIA. [Joyful.] You will go, Catiline? What happiness, oh, richer than my bosom can contain! Let it be so, then! Come! This very night We'll go away

CATILINE. But whither shall we go? Name me the spot where I may dare to rest My head in homely peace!

AURELIA. How can you ask? Have you forgot our villa in the country, Wherein I passed my childhood days, where since, Enraptured during love's first happy dawn, We two spent many a blithesome summer day?

Where was the grass indeed so green as there? Where else the groves so shady and sweet-smelling? The snow-white villa from its wooded lair Peeps forth and bids us there to make our dwelling.

There let us flee and dedicate our life To rural duties and to sweet contentment; you will find comfort in a loving wife, And through her kisses banish all resentment. [Smiling.] And when with all the flowers of the land You come to me, your sovereign, in my bowers, Then shall I crown you with the laurel band, And cry, All hail to you, my king of flowers! But why do you grow pale? Wildly you press My hand, and strangely now your eyes are glowing

CATILINE. Aurelia, alas, past is your happiness; there we can never, never think of going. There we can never go!

AURELIA. You frighten me! Yet, surely, you are jesting, Catiline?

CATILINE. I jest! Would only that it were a jest!

Each word you speak, like the avenging dart Of Nemesis, pierces my heavy heart, Which fate will never grant a moment's rest.

AURELIA. O gods! speak, speak! What do you mean?

CATILINE. See here! Here is your villa, here your future joys! [He draws out a purse filled with gold and throws it on the table.]

AURELIA. Oh, you have sold?

CATILINE. Yes, all I sold today. And to what end? In order to corrupt

AURELIA. O Catiline, no more! Let us not think On this affair; sorrow is all it brings.

CATILINE. Your quiet-patience wounds me tenfold more Than would a cry of anguish from your lips! [An old SOLDIER enters and approaches CATILINE.]

THE SOLDIER. Forgive me, master, that thus unannounced I enter your abode at this late hour. Ah, be not wroth—

CATILINE. What is your errand here?

THE SOLDIER. My errand here is but a humble prayer, Which you will hear. I am a needy man, One who has sacrificed his strength for Rome. Now I am feeble, can no longer serve; Unused my weapons rust away at home. The hope of my old age was in a son, Who labored hard and was my one support. Alas, in prison now he's held for debt. And not a ray of hope. Oh, help me, master! [Kneeling.] If but a penny! I have gone on foot From house to house; each door is long since closed.

I know not what to do

CATILINE. The paltry knaves! A picture this is of the many's want. Thus they reward the old brave company. No longer gratitude is found in Rome!

Time was I might have wished in righteous wrath To punish them with sword and crimson flames; But tender words have just been spoken here; My soul is moved; I do not wish to punish; to ease misfortune likewise is a deed. Take this, old warrior; clear with this your debt. [He hands him the purse with the gold.]

THE SOLDIER. [Rising.] O gracious lord, dare I believe your words?

CATILINE. Yes; but be quick, old man; go free your son. [The SOLDIER goes hurriedly out.]

CATILINE. A better use, not so, Aurelia dear? Than bribery and purchasing of votes? Noble it is to crush the tyrant's might; Yet quiet solace too has its reward.

AURELIA. [Throws herself in his arms.] Oh, rich and noble is your spirit still.
Yes, now I know my Catiline again. - [An underground tomb with a freshly walled-in passage high on the rear wall.

A lamp burns faintly.] [FURIA, in long black robes, is standing in the tomb as if listening.]

FURIA. A hollow sound. 'Tis thunder rolls above. I hear its rumble even in the tomb. Yet is the tomb itself so still, so still!

Am I forever damned to drowsy rest? Never again am I to wander forth By winding paths, as ever was my wish?

FURIA. [After a pause.]

A strange, strange life it was; as strange a fate.

Meteor-like all came and disappeared.

He met me. A mysterious magic force, An inner harmony, together drew us.

I was his Nemesis; and he my victim; yet punishment soon followed the avenger.

FURIA. [Another pause.]

Now daylight rules the earth. Am I perchance To slip, unknowing, from the realm of light? 'Tis well, if so it be, if this delay Within the tomb be nothing but a flight Upon the wings of lightning into Hades, If I be nearing even now the Styx!

There roll the leaden billows on the shore; There silently old Charon plies his boat.

Soon am I there! Then shall I seat myself Beside the ferry, question every spirit, Each fleeting shadow from the land of life, As light of foot he nears the river of death, shall ask each one in turn how Catiline fares now among the mortals of the earth, shall ask each one how he has kept his oath.

I shall illumine with blue sulphur light Each spectral countenance and hollow eye, To ascertain if it be Catiline.

And when he comes, then shall I follow him; together we shall make the journey hence, Together enter Pluto's silent hall.

I too a shadow shall his shade pursue; where Catiline is, must Furia also be!

FURIA. [After a pause, more faintly.] The air is growing close and clammy here, and every breath in turn more difficult. Thus am I drawing near the gloomy swamps, Where creep the rivers of the underworld.

FURIA. [She listens; a dull noise is heard.] A muffled sound? 'Tis like the stroke of oars.

It is the ferryman of shades who comes To take me hence. No, here, here will I wait! [The stones in the freshly walled-in passage are broken asunder.

CURIUS comes into view on the outside; he beckons to her.]

FURIA. Ah, greetings, Charon! Are you ready now To lead me hence, a guest among the spirits?

Here will I wait!

CURIUS. [Whispering.] I come to set you free!

Second Act

[A room in CATILINE's house with a colonnade in the rear; a lamp lights up the room.] [CATILINE paces the floor back and forth; LENTULUS and CETHEGUS are with him.]

CATILINE. No, no! I say, you do not understand Yourselves what you demand of me. Should I Turn traitor and incite a civil war, besmear my hand with Roman blood? No, no! I'll never do it! Let the entire state Condemn me if

LENTULUS. You will not, Catiline?

CATILINE. No.

LENTULUS. Tell me, have you nothing to avenge?

No insult? No one here you fain would strike?

CATILINE. Let him who will avenge; I shall not stir. Yet silent scorn is likewise a revenge; and that alone shall be enough.

CETHEGUS. Aha, our visit was, I see, inopportune. Yet doubtless will the morrow bring you back To other thoughts.

CATILINE. But why the morrow?

CETHEGUS. There are mysterious rumors in the air.

A vestal recently was led to death

CATILINE. [Surprised.] A vestal, say you? Ah, what do you mean?

LENTULUS. Why, yes, a vestal. Many people murmur

CATILINE. What do they murmur?

CETHEGUS. That in this dark affair You are not altogether innocent.

CATILINE. This they believe of me?

LENTULUS. Such is the rumor; Of course, to us, to all your good old friends, Such talk is trifling and of no account; the world, however, judges more severely.

CATILINE. [Deep in thought.] And is she dead?

CETHEGUS. Undoubtedly she is. An hour's confinement in the convict tomb Is quite enough

LENTULUS. That is not our affair. It was not therefore that we spoke of her.
But hear me, Catiline! Bethink yourself.

You sought the consulate; and all your welfare Hung on that single fragile thread of hope. Now is it sundered; everything is lost.

CATILINE. [Still deep in thought.] "Vengeance you have invoked on your own head!"

CETHEGUS. Shake off these useless thoughts; they profit naught; Act like a man; still can this fight be won; A bold resolve now; you have friends enough; Speak but the word, and we shall follow you. You are not tempted? Answer!

CATILINE. No, I say! And why are you so eager to conspire? Be honest! Are you driven by thirst for freedom? Is it in order to renew Rome's splendor that you would ruin all?

LENTULUS. Indeed, 'tis not; Yet surely is the hope of personal greatness Sufficient motive for our enterprise!

CETHEGUS. And means enough to taste the joys of life Are not, in truth, to be so lightly scorned.

That is my motive; I am not ambitious.

CATILINE. I knew it. Only mean and paltry motives, The hope of private vantage, urge you on.

No, no, my friends; I aimed at nobler things!

True, I have sought with bribes and promises To seize ere now the consulate, and yet My plan was greater and comprised much more Than means like these would point to. Civic freedom, The welfare of the state, these were my aims.

Men have misjudged, appearances belied me; My fate has willed it so. It must so be!

CETHEGUS. True; but the thought of all your many friends Whom you can save from ruin and disgrace?

You know, we shall ere long be driven to take The beggars' staff because of our wild living.

CATILINE. Then stop in season; that is my resolve.

LENTULUS. What, Catiline, now you intend to change Your mode of life? Ha, ha! you surely jest?

CATILINE. I am in earnest, by the mighty gods!

CETHEGUS. Then there is nothing we can do with him.

Come, Lentulus, the others we'll inform What answer he has given. We shall find The merry company with Bibulus.

CATILINE. With Bibulus? How many a merry night We have caroused at Bibulus' table!

Now is the tempest of my wild life ended; Ere dawns the day I shall have left the city.

LENTULUS. What is all this?

CETHEGUS. You mean to go away?

CATILINE. This very night my wife and I together Shall bid farewell to Rome forevermore.

In quiet Gaul we two shall found a home; the land I cultivate shall nourish us.

CETHEGUS. You will forsake the city, Catiline?

CATILINE. I will; I must! Disgrace here weighs me down.

Courage I have to bear my poverty, But in each Roman face to read disdain And frank contempt! No, no; that is too much!

In Gaul I'll live in quiet solitude; There shall I soon forget my former self, Dull all my longings for the greater things, And as the vaguest dream recall the past.

LENTULUS. Then fare you well; may fortune follow you!

CETHEGUS. Remember us with kindness, Catiline, As we shall you remember! To our brothers We will relate this new and strange resolve.

CATILINE. Then give them all a brother's hearty greeting! [LENTULUS and CETHEGUS leave.] [AURELIA has entered from the side, hut-stops frightened at the sight of those who are leaving; when they are gone she approaches CATILINE.]

AURELIA. [Gently reprimanding.] Again these stormy comrades in your house?
O Catiline!

CATILINE. This was their final visit.

I bade them all farewell. Now every bond Forevermore is broken that bound me fast And fettered me to Rome.

AURELIA. I've gathered up Our bit of property. Not much perhaps; yet, Catiline, enough for our contentment.

CATILINE. [Engrossed in thought.]

More than enough for me who squandered all.

AURELIA. Oh, brood no more on things we can not change; forget what

CATILINE. Happy he who could forget, who could the memory tear from out his soul, The many hopes, the goal of all desires.

Ah, time is needed ere I reach that state; But I shall struggle

AURELIA. I shall help you strive; You shall be comforted for all your loss. Yet we must leave as soon as possible. Here life calls to you with a tempter's voice. Is it not so, we go this very night?

CATILINE. Yes, yes, we leave this very night, Aurelia!

AURELIA. The little money left I've gathered up; And for the journey it will be enough.

CATILINE. Good! I shall sell my sword and buy a spade. What value henceforth is a sword to me?

AURELIA. You clear the land, and I shall till the soil.

Around our home will grow in floral splendor A hedge of roses, sweet forget-me-nots, The silent tokens of a chastened soul, When as some youthful comrade you can greet Each memory recurrent of the past.

CATILINE. That time, Aurelia? Ah, beloved, I fear that hour lies in a distant future's keeping.

CATILINE. [In a milder tone.] But go, dear wife, and, while you may, repose.
Soon after midnight we shall start our journey.

The city then is lapped in deepest slumber, And none shall guess our hidden destination.

The first glow in the morning sky shall find us far, far away; there in the laurel grove We'll rest ourselves upon the velvet grass.

AURELIA. A new life opens up before us both, richer in happiness than this that's ended.

Now will I go. An hour's quiet rest Will give me strength. Good-night, my Catiline! [She embraces him and goes out.]

CATILINE. [Gazes after her.]

Now is she gone! And I, what a relief!

Now can I cast away this wearisome Hypocrisy, this show of cheerfulness, Which least of all is found within my heart.

She is my better spirit. She would grieve Were she to sense my doubt. I must dissemble.

Yet shall I consecrate this silent hour To contemplation of my wasted life. This lamp, ah, it disturbs my very thoughts. Dark it must be here, dark as is my soul! [He puts out the light; the moon shines through the pillars in the rear.]

CATILINE. Too light, yes, still too light! And yet, no matter; the pallid moonlight here does well befit The twilight and the gloom that shroud my soul, have ever shrouded all my earthly ways.

CATILINE. Hm, Catiline, then is this day your last; Tomorrow morning you will be no longer The Catiline you hitherto have been.

Distant in barren Gaul my life shall run Its course, unknown as is a forest stream. Now am I wakened from those many visions Of power, of greatness, of a life of deeds; they vanished like the dew; in my dark soul They struggled long and died, unseen of men.

CATILINE. Ah, it is not this dull and drowsy life, Far from all mundane tumult, that affrights me.

If only for a moment I could shine, And blaze in splendor like a shooting star, if only by a glorious deed I could Immortalize the name of Catiline With everlasting glory and renown, then gladly should I, in the hour of triumph, Forsake all things, flee to a foreign strand; I'd plunge the dagger in my exiled heart, Die free and happy; for I should have lived!

CATILINE. But oh, to die without first having lived. Can that be possible? Shall I so die? [With uplifted hands.]

CATILINE. A hint, oh angry powers, that it is My fate to disappear from life forgotten, Without a trace!

FURIA. [Outside behind the pillars.] It is not, Catiline!

CATILINE. [Taken aback.] Who speaks? What warning voice is this I hear? A spirit voice from out the underworld!

FURIA. [Comes forward in the moonlight.] I am your shadow.

CATILINE. [Terrified.] What, the vestal's ghost!

FURIA. Deep must your soul have sunk if you recoil From me!

CATILINE. Speak! Have you risen from the grave With hatred and with vengeance to pursue me?

FURIA. Pursue you, did you say? I am your shadow. I must be with you wheresoe'er you go. [She comes nearer.]

CATILINE. She lives! O gods, then it is she, no other, No disembodied ghost.

FURIA. Or ghost or not, it matters little; I must follow you.

CATILINE. With mortal hate!

FURIA. Hate ceases in the grave, As love and all the passions do that flourish Within an earthly soul. One thing alone in life and death remains unchangeable.

CATILINE. And what? Say forth!

FURIA. Your fate, my Catiline!

CATILINE. Only the gods of wisdom know my fate, no human being.

FURIA. Yet I know your fate.

I am your shadow; strange, mysterious ties bind us together.

CATILINE. Bonds of hatred.

FURIA. No! Rose ever spirit from the dankest grave For hate and vengeance? Listen, Catiline! The rivers of the underworld have quenched Each earthly flame that raged within my breast. As you behold me here, I am no longer The stormy Furia, wild and passionate, whom once you loved

CATILINE. You do not hate me then?

FURIA. Ah, now no more. When in the tomb I stood, and faltered on the path that separates This life from death, at any moment ready To greet the underworld, lo, seized me then An eerie shuddering; I know not what; I felt in me a mystic transformation; away flowed hate, revenge, my very soul; Each memory vanished and each earthly longing; only the name of "Catiline" remains Written in fiery letters on my heart.

CATILINE. Ah, wonderful! No matter who you are, a human form, a shadow from the dead, there lies withal a dreadful fascination In your dark eyes, in every word you speak.

FURIA. Your mind is strong as mine; yet you give up, Disheartened and irresolute, each hope Of triumph and dominion. You forsake The battlefield, where all your inmost plans Could grow and blossom forth into achievement.

CATILINE. I must! Inexorable fate decrees it!

FURIA. Your fate? Why were you given a hero's strength, if not to struggle with what you call fate?

CATILINE. Oh, I have fought enough! Was not my life A constant battle? What are my rewards? Disgrace and scorn!

FURIA. Ah, you are fallen low! You struggle towards a high and daring goal, Are eager to attain it; yet you fear Each trifling hindrance.

CATILINE. Fear is not the reason.

The goal I sought is unattainable; the whole was but a fleeting dream of youth.

FURIA. Now you deceive yourself, my Catiline!

You hover still about that single project; your soul is noble, worthy of a ruler, and you have friends. Ah, wherefore hesitate?

CATILINE. [Meditating.] I shall? What do you mean? With civil blood?

FURIA. Are you a man, yet lack a woman's courage? Have you forgot that nimble dame of Rome, Who sought the throne straight over a father's corpse? I feel myself a Tullia now; but you? Scorn and despise yourself, O Catiline!

CATILINE. Must I despise myself because my soul No longer harbors selfish aspirations?

FURIA. You stand here at a cross-road in your life; Yonder a dull, inactive course awaits you, a half-way something, neither sleep nor death; before you, on the other hand, you see A sovereign's throne. Then choose, my Catiline!

CATILINE. You tempt me and allure me to destruction.

FURIA. Cast but the die, and in your hand is placed Forevermore the welfare of proud Rome.

Glory and might your silent fate conceals, And yet you falter, dare not lift a hand!
You journey yonder to the forests, where Each longing that you cherished will be quenched. Ah, tell me, Catiline, is there no trace Of thirst for glory left within your heart? And must this princely soul, for triumphs born, Vanish unknown in yonder nameless desert? Hence, then! But know that thus you lose forever What here you could by daring deeds attain.

CATILINE. Go on, go on!

FURIA. With trembling and with fear The future generations will recall Your fate. Your life was all a daring game; yet in the lustre of atonement it would shine, Known to all men, if with a mighty hand You fought your way straight through this surging throng, if the dark night of thraldom through your rule Gave way before a new-born day of freedom, if at some time you

CATILINE. Hold! Ah, you have touched The string that quivers deepest in my soul.
Your every word sounds like a ringing echo Of what my heart has whispered day and night.

FURIA. Now, Catiline, I know you once again!

CATILINE. I shall not go! You have recalled to life My youthful zeal, my manhood's full-grown longings. Yes, I shall be a light to fallen Rome, daze them with fear like some erratic star!

You haughty wretches, you shall soon discover You have not humbled me, though for a time I weakened in the heat of battle!

FURIA. Listen! Whatever be the will of fate, whatever the mighty gods decree, we must obey.

Just so! My hate is gone; fate thus decreed, And so it had to be! Give me your hand In solemn compact! Ah, you hesitate?

You will not?

CATILINE. Will? I gaze upon your eyes: They flash, like lightning in the gloom of night.

Now did you smile! Just so I've often pictured Nemesis

FURIA. What? Herself you wish to see, then look within. Have you forgot your oath?

CATILINE. No, I remember; yet you seem to me a Nemesis

FURIA. I am an image born from your own soul.

CATILINE. [Meditating.] What is all this you say? I sense but vaguely what I fail to grasp; I glimpse mysterious, strangely clouded visions, but can not understand. I grope in darkness!

FURIA. It must be dark here. Darkness is our realm; in darkness is our rule. Give me your hand In solemn pledge!

CATILINE. [Wildly.] O lovely Nemesis, my shadow, image of my very soul, here is my hand in everlasting compact. [He seizes her hand violently; she looks at him with a stern smile.]

FURIA. Now we can never part!

CATILINE. Ah, like a stream Of fire your touch went coursing through my veins! 'Tis blood no more that flows, but fiery flames; my breast now cabins and confines my heart; My sight grows dull. Soon shall a flaming sea Illumine with its light the Roman state! [He draws his sword and brandishes it.]

CATILINE. My sword! My sword! Do you see how it flashes?

Soon will it redden in their tepid blood! What change is this in me? My brow burns hot; A multitude of visions flit before me. Vengeance it is, triumph for all those dreams Of greatness, regal power, and lasting fame.

My watch-word shall be: livid flames and death!

The capitol! Now first I am myself! [He rushes out; FURIA follows him.] - [The inside of a dimly illumined tavern.] [STATILIUS, GABINIUS, COEPARIUS, and other young ROMANS enter.]

STATILIUS. Here, comrades, we can while away the night; Here we are safe; no one will overhear us.

GABINIUS. Ah, yes; now let us drink, carouse, enjoy!

Who knows how long it will be granted us?

STATILIUS. No, let us first await whatever tidings Lentulus and Cethegus have for us.

GABINIUS. Bah, let them bring whatever news they will!

Meanwhile the wine is here; come, let us taste.

Quick, brothers, quick, let's have a merry song! [SERVANTS bring in wine and glasses.]

THE ASSEMBLED FRIENDS. (Sing.) -
Bacchus, all praise to thee!
Joyful we raise to thee Brimful the beaker!
Hail to thee, hail!
Wine, red and glowing, Merrily flowing,
Drink of the wine-god, This be our song.
Gracious and friendly Smiles father Liber;
Drunkenness waits us; Clear is the wine.
Come, do not tarry!
Wine will make merry, Joyful and airy, Body and soul.
Thou above all the Glittering bubbles,
Sparkling Falernian, Glorious drink!
Courage and power, These are your dower.
Gladsome the gift you Bring to the soul.
Bacchus, all praise to thee!
Joyful we raise to thee Brimful the beaker!
Hail to thee, hail!
Wine, red and glowing, Merrily flowing,
Drink of the wine-god, This be our song. –

[LENTULUS and CETHEGUS enter.]

LENTULUS. Cease all your song and merriment!

STATILIUS. What now? Is Catiline not in your company?

GABINIUS. Surely he was quite willing?

COEPARIUS. Come, say forth! What was his answer?

CETHEGUS. Ah, quite otherwise Than we expected was his answer.

GABINIUS. Well?

LENTULUS. Well, all of our proposals he declined; he would not even hearken to our counsels.

STATILIUS. Is this the truth?

COEPARIUS. And wherefore would he not?

LENTULUS. In short, he will not. He forsakes his friends, abandons us, and leaves the city.

STATILIUS. What? He leaves, you say?

CETHEGUS. 'Tis true; he goes away This very night. Yet, blamed he can not be; His ground was valid

LENTULUS. Fear was his excuse! In danger he forsakes us faithlessly.

GABINIUS. That is the friendship of our Catiline!

COEPARIUS. Never was Catiline faithless or afraid!

LENTULUS. And yet he leaves us now.

STATILIUS. Our hopes go with him. Where's now the man to take the leadership?

COEPARIUS. He'll not be found; our plan we must forego.

LENTULUS. Not yet, not yet, my friends! First you shall hear What I will say. Now what have we resolved?

That we should win at last by force of arms What an unrighteous destiny denied.
Tyrants oppress us; yet we wish to rule. We suffer want; yet wealth is our desire.

MANY VOICES. Yes, wealth and power! Wealth and power we want!

LENTULUS. Yes, yes; we chose a comrade as our chief, On whom there was no doubt we could rely. Our trust he fails and turns his back to danger.

Ah, brothers, be not daunted. He shall learn We can succeed without him. What we need Is some one man, fearless and resolute, To take the lead

SOME. Well, name us such a man!

LENTULUS. And should I name him, and should he comeforth, will you then straightway choose him as your leader?

SOME. Yes, we will choose him!

OTHERS. Yes, we will, we will!

STATILIUS. Then name him, friend!

LENTULUS. Suppose it were myself?

GABINIUS. Yourself?

COEPARIUS. You, Lentulus!

SEVERAL. [In doubt.] You wish to lead us?

LENTULUS. I do.

CETHEGUS. But can you? Such a task requires the strength and courage of a Catiline.

LENTULUS. I do not lack the courage, nor the strength.

Each to his task! Or will you now turn back, Now when the moment seems most opportune? 'Tis now or never! All things prophesy Success for us

STATILIUS. Good; we will follow you!

OTHERS. We'll follow you!

GABINIUS. Well, now that Catiline Forsakes our cause, you are no doubt the man To lead us in our enterprise.

LENTULUS. Then hear What plan of action I have outlined. First CATILINE enters hastily.]

CATILINE. Here, comrades, here I am!

ALL. Catiline!

LENTULUS. He? Oh, damned

CATILINE. Speak out, what do you ask of me? Yet stay; I know already what it is.
I'll lead you on. Say, will you follow me?

ALL (EXCEPT LENTULUS). Yes, Catiline, we follow if you lead!

STATILIUS. They have deceived us

GABINIUS. - and belied your name!

COEPARIUS. They said you did intend to leave the city and wash your hands completely of our cause.

CATILINE. Yes, so I did. Yet now no more; henceforth Only for this great purpose do I live.

LENTULUS. What is this mighty purpose you proclaim?

CATILINE. My purpose here is higher than you think. Perhaps than any thinks. Ah, hear me, friends!

First will I win to us each citizen Who prizes liberty and values most the public honor and his country's weal.

The spirit of ancient Rome is yet alive; the last faint spark is not yet wholly dead.

Now into brilliant flames it shall be fanned, More glorious than ever flames before!

Alas, too long the stifling gloom of thraldom, Dark as the night, lay blanketed on Rome.

Behold, this realm though proud and powerful it seems totters upon the edge of doom.

Therefore the stoutest hand must seize the helm.

Rome must be cleansed, cleansed to the very roots; The sluggish we must waken from their slumber, and crush to earth the power of these wretches Who sow their poison in the mind and stifle The slightest promise of a better life.

Look you, 'tis civic freedom I would further, the civic spirit that in former times Was regnant here. Friends, I shall conjure back the golden age, when Romans gladly gave their lives to guard the honor of the nation, and all their riches for the public weal!

LENTULUS. Ah, Catiline, you rave! Nothing of this Had we in mind.

GABINIUS. What will it profit us To conjure up again those ancient days with all their dull simplicity?

SOME. No, no! Might we demand

OTHERS. - and means enough to live A gay and carefree life!

MANY VOICES. That is our aim!

COEPARIUS. Is it for others' happiness and freedom we stake our lives upon a throw of dice?

THE WHOLE GROUP. We want the spoils of victory!

CATILINE. Paltry race! Are you the offspring of those ancient fathers? To heap dishonor on your country's name, in such a way you would preserve its lustre!

LENTULUS. And you dare taunt us, you who long since were a terrifying token

CATILINE. True, I was; I was a terror to the good; and yet, so paltry as you are was never I.

LENTULUS. Restrain your tongue; we brook no ridicule.

MANY. No, no, we will not

CATILINE. [Calmly.] So? You timid brood, you dare to think of doing something, you?

LENTULUS. Ah, down with him!

MANY VOICES. Yes, down with Catiline! [They draw their daggers and rush in on him;

CATILINE calmly removes the cloak from his breast and regards them with a cold, scornful smile; they lower their daggers.]

CATILINE. Thrust! Thrust! You dare not? Oh, my friends, my friends, I should respect you, if you plunged your daggers In this uncovered bosom, as you threaten. Is there no spark of courage in your souls?

SOME. He means our weal!

OTHERS. His taunts we have deserved.

CATILINE. You have, indeed. Yet, see, the hour is come when you can wash away the blot of shame. All that is of the past we will forget; a new existence is in store for us.

CATILINE. [With bitterness.] Fool that I am! To stake success on you! Burns any zeal within this craven mob?

CATILINE. [Carried away.] Time was my dreams were glorious; great visions Rushed through my mind or swept before my gaze.

I dreamed that, winged like Icarus of old, I flew aloft beneath the vault of heaven; I dreamed the gods endued my hands with strength Of giants, offered me the lightning flash.

And this hand seized the lightning in its flight And hurled it at the city far beneath.

And when the crimson flames lapped all, and rose As Rome fell crumbling in a heap of ruins, then called I with a loud and mighty voice, And conjured Cato's comrades from the grave; thousands of spirits heard my call and came, took life again - raised Rome from out her ashes. [He breaks off.]

CATILINE. These were but dreams! Gods do not conjure up The by-gone past into the light of day, and parted spirits never leave the grave.

CATILINE. [Wildly.] Is now this hand unable to restore The ancient Rome, our Rome it shall destroy.

Where marble colonnades now towering stand, Pillars of smoke through crackling flames shall whirl; Then shall the Capitol crumble from its heights, And palaces and temples sink to ruin!

CATILINE. Swear, comrades, that you dedicate your lives To this great purpose! I shall take the lead. Say, will you follow me?

STATILIUS. We'll follow you! [Several seem to be in doubt, and speak in whispers to one another.

CATILINE regards them with a scornful smile.]

LENTULUS. [In an undertone.] 'Tis best we follow him. In sunken ruins We're likeliest to realize our goal.

ALL. [Shouting.] Yes, Catiline; we'll all, all follow you!

CATILINE. Swear to me by the gods of our great sires that you will heed my every nod!

THE WHOLE GROUP. [With uplifted hands.] Yes, yes; We swear in all things blindly to obey!

CATILINE. Then singly steal your way, by different paths, into my house. Weapons you there will find.

I shall come later; you shall then discover what plan of action I propose. Now go! [They all go out.]

LENTULUS. [Detains CATILINE.] A word! Know you the Allobrogian tribes Have to the Senate sent ambassadors With grievances and charges?

CATILINE. Yes, I know. They came today into the city.

LENTULUS. Good. What if we should attune them to our plans? With them all Gaul will rise up in revolt; And stir up strife against our enemies.

CATILINE. [Reluctant.] Ah, we should seek barbarian allies?

LENTULUS. But such a league is a necessity.

With our own strength alone the fight is lost; Help from without

CATILINE. [With a bitter smile.] Ah, Rome is fallen low!

Her walls no longer harbor men with strength Enough to overthrow a tottering ruin! [They go out.] - [A garden to the rear of CATILINE's house, which is visible through the trees.

To the left a side-building.] [CURIUS, CETHEGUS, and OTHER CONSPIRATORS enter cautiously from the right in whispered conversation.]

CURIUS. But is it really true what you relate?

CETHEGUS. Yes, every word is true. A moment since It was decided.

CURIUS. He takes charge of all?

CETHEGUS. Of everything. Just speak with him yourself. [All, except CURIUS, enter the house.]

CURIUS. An eerie night! How all my thoughts are tossed About in circles! Did I dream perchance?

Ah, real or fancied, now I am awake, whichever way I turn I see her form. [CATILINE enters from the right.]

CATILINE. [Goes toward him.] You here, my Curius? I have missed you much. My visit with the vestal took a turn quite unexpected

CURIUS. [Confused.] So? Yes, you are right!

CATILINE. I shall no longer think of this affair. It was a visit fraught with fate for me.

CATILINE. [Meditating.] The furies, we are told, return at times From the dark underworld to follow us Through life forever. Ah, if it were so!

CURIUS. [Uneasy.] What? Have you seen her?

CATILINE. She was here tonight. Yet let this be forgotten. Curius, listen, a weighty undertaking is on foot

CURIUS. I know it all. Cethegus told me here

CATILINE. Who knows what issue for this work the gods Have set? Perchance it is my destiny To perish now, crushed by malignant forces, and never reach my goal. Well, be it so!

But you, dear Curius, you whom I have loved since childhood, you shall not be drawn within This fateful maelstrom. Promise me, remain within the city if I elsewhere choose to open my attack, which is quite likely; Nor aid us till success has crowned our work.

CURIUS. [Moved.] Oh, what a friend and father! All this care!

CATILINE. You promise this? Then here we say farewell; Wait but a moment; I shall soon return. [He goes into the house.]

CURIUS. [Gazing after him.] He loves me still. Of naught is he distrustful. [LENTULUS and OTHER CONSPIRATORS enter from the right.]

LENTULUS. Ah, Curius, did not Catiline just now Pass through the garden?

CURIUS. Yes, he is within. [They go into the house.]

CURIUS. [Paces about uneasy.] How shall I curb this longing in my soul? There is a restless turmoil in my blood. Ah, Furia, what a strange, mysterious woman!
Where are you? When shall I see your face again?

CURIUS. Where has she fled? Ah, shadow-like she slipped away, when I had freed her from the grave.

And those mysterious, prophetic words, and more, her eyes, gleaming at once and dimmed!

What if it were but madness? Has the grave With all its terror darkened?

FURIA. [Behind him among the trees.] No, pale youth!

CURIUS. [With a cry.] My Furia! You?

FURIA. [Comes nearer.] Here dwells Catiline. Where he is, there must Furia also be.

CURIUS. Oh, come with me, beloved. I shall lead You into safety. Think if some one saw you!

FURIA. The dead need have no fear. Have you forgotten. You took my corpse and brought it from the grave?

CURIUS. Again those terrifying words! Oh, hear me; come to your senses, come with me away! [He tries to seize her hand.]

FURIA. [Thrusts him wildly back.] You reckless fool, do you not shrink with fear Before this child of death, but risen up A fleeting moment from the underworld?

CURIUS. Before you now I fear. And yet this fear, This strange, mysterious dread, is my delight.

FURIA. What would you me? In vain is all your pleading. I'm of the grave, and yonder is my home; with dawn's approach I must again be speeding back to the vale of shadows whence I come.

You doubt me, do not think that I have sat Among the pallid shades in Pluto's hall?
I tell you, I was even now below, beyond the river and the gloomy marshes.

CURIUS. Then lead me there!

FURIA. You?

CURIUS. I shall gladly follow, Though you should lead me through the jaws of death!

FURIA. It cannot be! On earth we two must part; yonder the dead and living dare not meet.

FURIA. Why do you rob me of my fleeting moments? I've but the hours of night in which to work; My task is of the night; I am its herald.

But where is Catiline?

CURIUS. Ah, him you seek?

FURIA. Yes, him I seek.

CURIUS. Then him you still pursue?

FURIA. Why rose I from the spirit underworld tonight, if not because of Catiline?

CURIUS. Alas, this fury that has seized your soul! Yet you are lovely even in your madness. Oh, Furia, think no more of Catiline!

Come, flee with me! Command me, I shall serve you! [He prostrates himself before her.]

CURIUS. A prostrate slave I here entreat of you one single look. Oh, hear me, Furia, hear me!

I love but you! A sweet and lethal fire Consumes my soul, and you, ah, you alone can ease my suffering.

FURIA. [Looks towards the house.] Yonder there's a light and many men. What now is going on within the house of Catiline?

CURIUS. [Jumps up.] Again This name! Around him hover all your thoughts. Oh, I could hate him!

FURIA. Has he then resolved to launch at last the daring enterprise he long has cherished?

CURIUS. Then you know?

FURIA. Yes, all.

CURIUS. Ah, then you doubtless know, too, he himself Is foremost in this daring enterprise? Yet, I adjure you, beg you, think no more Of Catiline!

FURIA. Answer me this alone; 'Tis all I ask of you. Do you go with him?

CURIUS. He is to me a tender father

FURIA. [Smiling.] He? My Catiline?

CURIUS. Ah!

FURIA. He, round whom my thoughts Course without rest?

CURIUS. My brain is in a tumult, I hate this man! Oh, I could murder him!

FURIA. Did you not lately swear you were prepared to do my bidding?

CURIUS. Ask me what you will; in everything I serve you and obey! I only beg, forget this Catiline.

FURIA. I shall forget him first when he has stepped into his grave.

CURIUS. [Draws back.] Ah, you demand that I?

FURIA. You need not use the steel; you can betray his enterprise

CURIUS. Murder and treachery At once! Remember, Furia, he is still My foster-father and

FURIA. My aim in life!

Ah, timid fool, so you dare speak of love, who lack the fortitude to strike him down That stands across your path? Away from me! [She turns her back on him.]

CURIUS. [Holding her back.] No; do not leave me! I am in all things willing!

A shudder chills me as I look on you; And yet I cannot break this net asunder Wherein you trapped my soul.

FURIA. Then you are willing?

CURIUS. Why do you mock me with such questioning?

If I am willing? Have I any will?

Your gaze is like the serpent's when 'tis fixed With magic power upon the bird, that circles Wildly about in terror-stricken awe, Drawn ever nearer to the dreadful fangs.

FURIA. Then to your task!

CURIUS. And when I've sacrificed my friendship to my love for you, what then?

FURIA. I shall forget that Catiline existed.

Then will my task be ended. Ask no more!

CURIUS. For this reward I should?

FURIA. You hesitate? Is then your hope so faint that you forget What gifts a grateful woman can bestow, When first the time?

CURIUS. By all the powers of night, I'll not delay! He only stands between us.
Then let him perish! Quenched is every spark Of feeling for him; every bond is sundered! Who are you, lovely vision of the night?

Near you I'm turned to marble, burned to ashes. My longing chills me, terror fires the soul; My love is blended hate and sorcery.

Who am I now? I know myself no more; One thing I know; I am not he I was, Ere you I saw. I'll plunge into the deep To follow you! Doomed, doomed is Catiline!

I'll to the Capitol. This very night The senate is assembled. Then farewell!

A written note betrays his enterprise. [He goes out hastily.]

FURIA. [To herself.] The heavens grow dark; soon will the lightning play.
The end is fast approaching, Catiline; with measured steps you journey to your grave! [The Allobrogian ambassadors, AMBIORIX and OLLOVICO, come out of the house without noticing FURIA, who stands half concealed in the shade between the trees.]

AMBIORIX. So then it is decided! Venturesome It was to enter into such a compact.

OLLOVICO. True; Yet their refusal of each righteous claim Opens no other way to liberty.

The prize of victory, should our friends succeed, outweighs indeed the perils of the conflict That now awaits us.

AMBIORIX. Brother, so it is!

OLLOVICO. Emancipation from the rule of Rome, freedom long lost is surely worth a struggle.

AMBIORIX. Now we must hasten homeward with all speed, Kindling through Gaul the flames of insurrection.

It will be easy to persuade the tribes To 'rise up in revolt; they'll follow us And join the partisans of Catiline.

OLLOVICO. Hard will the fight be; mighty still is Rome.

AMBIORIX. It must be risked. Come, Ollovico, come!

FURIA. [Calls warningly to them.] Woe unto you!

AMBIORIX. [Startled.] By all the gods!

OLLOVICO. [Terrified.] Ah, hear! A voice cries warning to us in the dark!

FURIA. Woe to your people!

OLLOVICO. Yonder stands she, brother, the pale and ill-foreboding shadow. See!

FURIA. Woe unto all who follow Catiline!

AMBIORIX. Home, home! Away! We'll break all promises!

OLLOVICO. A voice has warned us, and we shall obey. [They go out hurriedly to the right.] [CATILINE comes out of the house in the background.]

CATILINE. Ah, desperate hope to think of crushing Rome with such a host of cowards and poltroons!

What spurs them on? With frankness they confess their only motive is their want and greed.

Is it then worth the trouble for such aims To shed men's blood? And what have I to win? What can I gain?

FURIA. [Invisible among the trees.] Revenge, my Catiline!

CATILINE. [Startled.] Who speaks! Who wakes the spirit of revenge From slumber? Came this voice then from the deep Within my soul? Revenge? Yes, that's the word, my watch-word and my battle-cry. Revenge!

Revenge for all the hopes and all the dreams Which ever a vindictive fate destroyed!

Revenge for all my years of wasted life! [The CONSPIRATORS come armed out of the house.]

LENTULUS. Still rest the shades of darkness on the city. Now is it time to break away.

SEVERAL. [Whispering.] Away! [AURELIA comes out of the side-building without noticing the CONSPIRATORS.]

AURELIA. Beloved, are you here?

CATILINE. [With a cry.] Aurelia!

AURELIA. Say, have you been waiting for me? [She becomes aware of the Conspirators and rushes to him.]

AURELIA. Gracious gods!

CATILINE. [Thrusts her aside.] Woman, away from me!

AURELIA. Speak, Catiline! These many men in arms? And you as well? Oh, you will go

CATILINE. [Wildly.] Yes, by the spirits of night, a merry journey! See this flashing sword! It thirsts for blood! I go to quench its thirst.

AURELIA. My hope, my dream! Ah, blissful was my dream!

Thus am I wakened from my dreaming

CATILINE. Silence! Stay here, or follow! But my heart is cold To tears and lamentations. Friends, behold How bright the full moon in the west declines!

When next that full moon in its orient shines, An avalanche of fire shall sweep the state And all its golden glory terminate.

A thousand years from now, when it shall light Mere crumbling ruins in the desert night, one pillar in the dust of yonder dome shall tell the weary wanderer: Here stood Rome! [He rushes out to the right; all follow him.]

Third Act

[CATILINE's camp in a wooded field in Etruria. To the right is seen CATILINE's tent and close by it an old oak tree. A camp fire is burning outside the tent; similar fires are to be seen among the trees in the background. It is night. At intervals the moon breaks through the clouds.] [STATILIUS lies stretched out asleep by the camp fire. MANLIUS paces back and forth in front of the tent.] MANLIUS. Such is the way of young and buoyant souls.

They slumber on as peaceful and secure As though embosomed in their mothers' arms, Instead of in a forest wilderness.

They rest as though they dream some merry game Were held in store for them when they awake, Instead of battle, the last one, perchance, That will be theirs to fight.

STATILIUS. [Awakes and rises.] Still standing guard? You must be weary? I'll relieve you now.

MANLIUS. Go rest yourself instead. Youth needs his sleep; His untamed passions tax his native strength. 'Tis otherwise when once the hair turns gray, when in our veins the blood flows lazily, and age weighs heavily upon our shoulders.

STATILIUS. Yes, you are right. Thus I too shall in time, An old and hardened warrior

MANLIUS. Are you sure The fates decreed you such a destiny?

STATILIUS. And pray, why not? Why all these apprehensions? Has some misfortune chanced?

MANLIUS. You think no doubt That we have naught to fear, foolhardy youth?

STATILIUS. Our troops are strongly reinforced

MANLIUS. Indeed, with fugitive slaves and gladiators

STATILIUS. Well, grant that they are; together they may prove No little aid, and all the tribes of Gaul will send us help

MANLIUS. Which has not yet arrived.

STATILIUS. You doubt that the Allobroges will keep Their promised word?

MANLIUS. I know these people well From days gone by. However, let that pass.
The day that dawns will doubtless bring to light What destinies the gods have set for us.

MANLIUS. But go the rounds, my friend, and ascertain If all the guards perform their proper tasks.

For we must fend against a night attack; We know not where the enemy makes his stand. [STATILIUS goes into the forest.]

MANLIUS. [Alone by the camp fire.]

The clouds begin to gather thick and fast; It is a dark and storm-presaging night; a misty fog hangs heavy on my breast, As though foreboding mishap to us all.
Where is it now, that easy carefree spirit With which in former times I went to war?

Ah, can it be the weight of years alone That now I feel? Strange, strange, indeed, last night Even the young seemed sorely out of heart.

MANLIUS. [After a pause.] The gods shall know revenge was not the aim for which I joined and followed Catiline.

My wrath flared up within me for a space When first I felt I had been wronged, insulted; the old blood is not yet entirely cold; Now and again it courses warmly through my veins.

But the humiliation is forgotten. I followed Catiline for his own sake; And I shall watch o'er him with zealous care.

Here stands he all alone amidst these hosts Of paltry knaves and dissolute companions.

They cannot comprehend him, he in turn is far too proud to wish to fathom them. [He throws some branches on the fire and remains standing in silence.

CATILINE comes out of the tent.]

CATILINE. [To himself.] Midnight approaches. Everything is hushed; only to my poor eyes sleep fails to come.

Cold is the night wind; 'twill refresh my soul And give me strength anew. I sorely need it! [He becomes aware of MANLIUS.]

CATILINE. 'Tis you, old Manlius? And do you stand guard alone on such a night?

MANLIUS. Oft have I stood Guard over you in childhood's early days. Say, do you not recall?

CATILINE. Those days are gone; With them, my peace; wherever now I go, I'm haunted by a multitude of visions.

All things find shelter in my bosom, Manlius; save peace alone. That, that is far away.

MANLIUS. Cast off these gloomy thoughts and take your rest!

Remember that the morrow may require Your utmost strength for our deliverance.

CATILINE. I cannot rest. If I but close my eyes One fleeting moment in forgetful slumber, I'm tossed about in strange, fantastic dreams.

Here on my couch I lay now, half asleep, When these same visions reappeared again, More strange than ever, more mysterious And puzzling. Ah, if I could only know What this forebodes! But no

MANLIUS. Confide your dream To me. Perhaps I can expound its meaning.

CATILINE. [After a pause.] If I slept or if I waked, scarcely can I say; Visions fast pursued each other in a mad array.

Soon a deepening twilight settles over everything; And a night swoops down upon me on her wide-spread wing, Terrible and dark, unpierced, save by the lightning's flare; I am in a grave-like dungeon, filled with clammy air.

Lofty is the ceiling and with thunderclouds o'ercast; Multitudes of shadow forms go racing wildly past, Whirl around in roaring eddies, as the ocean wave Draws the raging storm and breaks against a rocky cave.

Yet amid this frenzied tumult children often come, Decked in flowers, singing of a half-forgotten home.

Soon the darkness round them changes to a vivid glare, dimly in the center I descry a lonely pair; Ah, two women, stern the one and gloomy as the night, and the other gentle, like the evening in its flight.

How familiar to my eyes the two lone figures seemed!

With her smiling countenance the one upon me beamed; Like the zigzag lightning flashed the other's piercing eye; Terror seized my soul, yet on I gazed in ecstasy.

Proudly upright stands the one, the other leans in weariness on the solitary table, where they play a game of chess.

Pawns they barter, or they move them now from place to place; then the game is lost and won, she fades away in space, she who radiantly smiled, ah, she who lost the game; instantly the bands of children vanish whence they came.

Tumult rises; darkness deepens; but from out the night Two eyes fix upon me, in a victor's gloating right; Then my brain reels; I see nothing but those baleful eyes.

But what else I dreamed of in that frenzied slumber lies Far within me hidden, buried deep beyond recall.

Could I but remember. Gone forever is it all.

MANLIUS. Remarkable, indeed, my Catiline, Is this your dream.

CATILINE. [Meditating.] If I could but remember. But no; my memory fails me

MANLIUS. Brood no longer Upon these thoughts. For what are dreams, indeed, But pale chimeras only, darkling visions, On nothing founded, and by naught explained?

CATILINE. Yes, you are right; I will no longer brood; already I am calm. But go your way; You need some rest. The meanwhile I shall walk In privacy and meditate my plans. [MANLIUS goes into the forest.]

CATILINE. [Paces for some time back and forth by the camp fire, which is about to go out; then he stops and speaks thoughtfully.] If I could only. Ah, it is unmanly To brood and be distressed by thoughts like these.

And yet, here in the stillness of the night, This lonely solitude, again I see Rising before me life-like all I dreamed. [A SHADOW, attired like an old warrior in armor and toga, stems to rise from the earth among the trees a short distance from him.]

CATILINE. [Recoils before THE SHADOW.] Great powers of heaven!

THE SHADOW. Greetings, Catiline!

CATILINE. What will you have? Who are you, pallid shade?

THE SHADOW. One moment! It is here my right to question, and you shall answer. Do you no longer know This voice from ages long since passed away?

CATILINE. Methinks I do; yet certain I am not.

But speak, whom seek you at this midnight hour?

THE SHADOW. 'Tis you I seek. Know that this hour alone Is granted me as respite here on earth.

CATILINE. By all the gods! Who are you? Speak!

THE SHADOW. Be calm! Hither I come to call you to account. Why do you envy me the peace of death?

Why do you drive me from my earthly dwelling?

Why do you mar my rest with memories, That I must seek you, whisper menaces, To guard the honor I so dearly bought?

CATILINE. Alas! this voice! Somehow I seem to know

THE SHADOW. What is there left of my imperial power?

A shadow like myself; yes, scarcely that.

Both sank into the grave and came to naught. 'Twas dearly bought; dear, dear was it attained.

For it I sacrificed all peace in life, and waived all claims to peace beyond the grave.

And now you come and want to wrest from me with daring hands what little I have left.

Are there not paths enough to noble deeds?

Why must you choose the one that I have chosen?

I gave up everything in life to power; My name, so dreamed I, should forever stand, Not beaming like a star with friendly lustre, no, like a flash against the midnight sky!

I did not covet fame, the goal of hundreds, For magnanimity and noble deeds; Nor admiration; far too many share That fate already: so will many more Until the end of time. Of blood and horror I wished to build me my renown and fame.

With silent dread, as on some meteor That now appears in mystery and is gone Again, men should gaze back upon my life, And look askance on me, whom no one ever, Before or since then, dared to emulate.

Yes, thus I dreamed and dreamed, and was deceived.

Why did I not surmise, when you stood near me, The secret thoughts then growing in your soul.

Yet, Catiline, beware; know that I see Beyond the veil that hides from you the future.

Written among the stars, I read your fate!

CATILINE. You read my fate? Expound it then to me!

THE SHADOW. No, first beyond death's gloomy gate Shall fade away the mists that hide The gruesome and the nobly great, Borne ever on by time and tide.

This from thy book of fate alone A liberated soul may tell thee:

Perish thou shalt by deed thine own, And yet a stranger's hand shall fell thee. [THE SHADOW glides away as in a mist.]

CATILINE. [After a pause.] Ah, he has vanished. Was it but a dream?

No, no; even here he stood; the moonbeams played Upon his sallow visage. Yes, I knew him!

It was the man of blood, the old dictator, Who sallied from his grave to frighten me.

He feared lest he should lose the victor's crown, not the reward of honor, but the terror Whereby his memory lives. Are bloodless shades Spurred onward also by the thought of glory? [Paces to and fro uneasily.]

CATILINE. All things storm in upon me. Now Aurelia in gentle admonition speaks, and now In me re echoes Furia's warning cry.

Nay, more than that; out of the grave appear The pallid shadows of a by-gone age.

They threaten me. I should now stop and pause?

I should turn back? No. I shall venture on Unfaltering; the victory soon is mine! [CURIUS comes through the forest in great agitation.]

CURIUS. O Catiline!

CATILINE. [Surprised.] What, you, you here, my friend!

CURIUS. I had to

CATILINE. Wherefore staid you not in town?

CURIUS. Fear prompted me; I had to seek you here.

CATILINE. You rush for my sake blindly into danger.

You thoughtless lad! Yet, come into my arms! [Moves to embrace him.]

CURIUS. [Draws back.]

No! Do not touch me! Do not even come near me!

CATILINE. What ails you, my dear Curius?

CURIUS. Up! Break camp!

Flee, if you can, even this very hour!

On every highway come the enemy troops; Your camp is being surrounded.

CATILINE. Calm yourself; You rave. Speak, has the journey shaken you?

CURIUS. Oh no; but save yourself while there is time!

You are betrayed [Prostrates himself before him.]

CATILINE. [Starts back.] Betrayed! What are you saying?

CURIUS. Betrayed by one in friendly guise!

CATILINE. You err; These stormy friends are loyal even as you.

CURIUS. Then woe to you for all their loyalty!

CATILINE. Compose yourself! It is your love for me, Your interest in my safety, that has wakened Imaginary dangers in your mind.

CURIUS. Oh, do you know these words do murder me?

But flee! I do entreat you earnestly

CATILINE. Be calm and speak your mind. Why should I flee?

The enemy knows not where I make my stand.

CURIUS. Indeed he does, he knows your every plan!

CATILINE. What, are you mad? He knows? Impossible!

CURIUS. Oh, were it so! But use the hour remaining; Still you may save yourself perhaps in flight!

CATILINE. Betrayed? No, ten times no; impossible!

CURIUS. [Seizes his dagger and holds it out to him.]

Catiline, plunge this dagger in my bosom; straight through the heart! 'Twas I betrayed your plans!

CATILINE. You? What madness!

CURIUS. Yes, it was in madness!

Ask not the reason; scarce I know myself; I say, I have revealed your every counsel.

CATILINE. [In bitter grief.] Now have you killed my faith in sacred friendship!

CURIUS. Oh, send the dagger home, and torture me No longer with forbearance!

CATILINE. [Kindly.] Live, my Curius! Arise! You erred; but I forgive you all.

CURIUS. [Overcome.] O Catiline, my heart is crushed with grief! But hasten; flee! There is no time to tarry.

Soon will the Roman troops invade your camp; They're under way; on every side they come.

CATILINE. Our comrades in the city?

CURIUS. They are captured; Some were imprisoned, most of them were killed!

CATILINE. [To himself.] What fate, what fate!

CURIUS. [Again holds out the dagger to him.] Then plunge it in my heart!

CATILINE. [Looks at him calmly.] No, you were but a tool. You acted well

CURIUS. Oh, let me die and expiate my sin!

CATILINE. I have forgiven you.

CATILINE. [As he goes.] But one thing now is there to choose!

CURIUS. [Jumps up.] Yes, flight!

CATILINE. Heroic death! [He goes away through the forest.]

CURIUS. 'Tis all in vain! Ruin awaits him here.

This mildness is a tenfold punishment!

I'll follow him; one thing I shall be granted: To perish fighting by the hero's side! [He rushes out. LENTULUS and TWO GLADIATORS come stealing among the trees.]

LENTULUS. [Softly.] Some one was speaking

ONE OF THE GLADIATORS. Aye, but now all's quiet.

THE OTHER GLADIATOR. Perchance it was the sentinel relieved Of duty.

LENTULUS. That may be. This is the place; Here shall you wait. Are both your weapons sharp, Ground for their purpose?

THE FIRST GLADIATOR. Bright as is the lightning!

THE SECOND GLADIATOR. Mine, too, cuts well. In the last Roman games Two gladiators died beneath this sword.

LENTULUS. Then stand you ready in this thicket here.

And when a man, whom I shall designate, Goes toward the tent, then shall you rush out quick And strike him from behind.

THE FIRST GLADIATOR. It shall be done! [Both GLADIATORS conceal themselves; LENTULUS goes spying around.]

LENTULUS. [To himself.]

It is a daring game I here attempt; yet must it be performed this very night, If done at all. If Catiline should fall, No one can lead them on except myself; I'll purchase them with golden promises, And march without delay upon the city, Where still the senate, struck with panic fear, Neglects to arm itself against the danger. [He goes in among the trees.]

THE FIRST GLADIATOR. [Softly to the other.] Who is this stranger we must fall upon?

THE SECOND GLADIATOR. What matters it to us who he may be?

Lentulus pays our hire; the blame is his:

He must himself defend the act we do.

LENTULUS. [Returns quickly.] Stand ready now; the man we wait is coming! [LENTULUS and the GLADIATORS lie in wait among the bushes.] [Soon after, CATILINE comes through the forest and goes toward the tent.]

LENTULUS. [Whispering.] Out! Fall upon him! Strike him from behind! [All three rush on CATILINE.]

CATILINE. [Draws his sword and defends himself.] Ah, scoundrels, do you dare to?

LENTULUS. [To the GLADIATORS.] Cut him down!

CATILINE. [Recognizes him.] You, Lentulus, would murder Catiline?

THE FIRST GLADIATOR. [Terrified.] He it is!

THE SECOND GLADIATOR. [Draws back.] Catiline! I'll never use The sword on him. Come flee! [Both GLADIATORS make their escape.]

LENTULUS. Then die by mine! [They fight; CATILINE strikes the sword from the hand of Lentulus; the latter tries to escape, but CATILINE holds him fast.]

CATILINE. Murderer! Traitor!

LENTULUS. [Entreating.] Mercy, Catiline!

CATILINE. I spell your plans upon your countenance.

You wished to murder me, and put yourself Into the chieftain's place. Was it not so?

LENTULUS. Yes, Catiline, it was even so!

CATILINE. [Looks at him with repressed scorn.] What then? If 'tis the power you want, so let it be!

LENTULUS. Explain, what do you mean?

CATILINE. I shall resign; And you may lead the army

LENTULUS. [Surprised.] You resign?

CATILINE. I shall. But be prepared for all events; Know this, our undertaking is revealed: The senate is informed of every plan; Its troops hem us about

LENTULUS. What do you say?

CATILINE. Now shall I call a council of our friends; Do you come too, announce your leadership; I shall resign.

LENTULUS. [Detains him.] One moment, Catiline!

CATILINE. Your time is precious; ere the dawn of day You may expect an onslaught

LENTULUS. [Anxiously.] Hear me, friend!

Surely you jest? It is impossible

CATILINE. Our project, I have told you, is betrayed. Show now your firmness and sagacity!

LENTULUS. Betrayed? Then woe to us!

CATILINE. [Smiles scornfully.] You paltry coward! You tremble now; yet you would murder me; you think a man like you is called to rule?

LENTULUS. Forgive me, Catiline!

CATILINE. Make your escape By hurried flight, if still it can be done.

LENTULUS. Ah, you permit me then?

CATILINE. And did you think It was my purpose to forsake this post In such an hour as this? You little know me.

LENTULUS. O, Catiline!

CATILINE. [Coldly.] Waste not your moments here! Seek your own safety; I know how to die. [He turns away from him.]

LENTULUS. [To himself.] I thank you for these tidings, Catiline; I shall make use of them to serve my end. 'Twill stand me in good stead now that I know This region well; I'll seek the hostile army And guide it hitherward by secret paths, To your destruction and to my salvation. The serpent that you trample in the dust So arrogantly still retains its sting! [He goes.]

CATILINE. [After a pause.] This is the trust I built my hopes upon!

Thus one by one they leave me. Oh ye gods!

Treason and cowardice alone stir up The sullen currents of their slavish souls.

Oh, what a fool am I with all my hopes!

I would destroy yon viper's nest, that Rome, which is long since a heap of sunken ruins. [The sound of arms is heard approaching; he listens.]

CATILINE. They come, they come! Still are there valiant men among them. Ah, the joyous clang of steel!

The merry clash of shields against each other!

Anew the fire kindles in my breast; The reckoning is near, the mighty hour that settles every doubt. I hail the day! [MANLIUS, STATILIUS, GABINIUS, and many OTHER CONSPIRATORS come through the forest.]

MANLIUS. Here, Catiline, come your friends and comrades true; In camp I spread the alarm, as you commanded

CATILINE. And have you told them?

MANLIUS. Yes, they know our plight.

STATILIUS. We know it well, and we shall follow you with sword in hand to fight for life and death.

CATILINE. I thank you all, my comrades brave in arms!

But do not think, my friends, that life or death is ours to choose; our only choice is this:

Death in heroic battle with the foe, or death by torture when like savage beasts we shall be hounded down relentlessly.

Ah, which do you prefer? To risk in flight A wretched life prolonged in misery, Or like your proud and worthy sires of old to perish nobly on the battlefield?

GABINIUS. We choose to fight and die!

MANY VOICES. Lead us to death!

CATILINE. Then let us be off! Through death we shall achieve the glorious life of immortality.

Our fall, our name, through distant generations Shall be proclaimed with lofty pride

FURIA. [Calls out behind him among the trees.] O terror!

SOME VOICES. Behold, a woman!

CATILINE. [Startled.] Furia! You, you here? What brought you here?

FURIA. Ah, I must lead you on to your great goal.

CATILINE. Where is my goal, then? Speak!

FURIA. Each mortal seeks his goal in his own way.

And you seek yours through ever hopeless strife; the struggle yields defeat and certain death.

CATILINE. Yet also honor and immortal fame!

Go, woman! Great and noble is this hour!

My heart is closed against your raucous cries. [AURELIA appears in the door of the tent.]

AURELIA. My Catiline! [She stops, terrified at the sight of the throng.]

CATILINE. [Painfully.] Aurelia, oh, Aurelia!

AURELIA. What is the trouble? All this stir in camp. What is on foot here?

CATILINE. You I could forget! What will your fate be now?

FURIA. [Whispers scornfully, unnoticed by AURELIA.] Ah, Catiline, Already wavering in your high resolve? Is this your death defiance?

CATILINE. [Flaring up.] No, by the gods!

AURELIA. [Comes nearer.] Oh, speak, beloved! Keep me in doubt no longer

FURIA. [In an undertone behind him.] Flee with your wife, the while your comrades die!

MANLIUS. Tarry no longer; lead us out to battle

CATILINE. Oh, what a choice! And yet, here is no choice; I must go on, I dare not stop midway. [Calls out.] Then follow me to battle on the plain!

AURELIA. [Throws herself in his arms.] Catiline, do not leave me, take me with you!

CATILINE. No, stay, Aurelia!

FURIA. [As before.] Take her, Catiline! Worthy your death will be, as was your life, When you are vanquished in a woman's arms!

CATILINE. [Thrusts AURELIA aside.] Away, you who would rob me of my fame!
Death shall o'ertake me in the midst of men. I have a life to atone, a name to clear

FURIA. Just so; just so, my gallant Catiline!

CATILINE. All things I will uproot from out my soul that bind me to my life of empty dreams!

All that is of the past shall henceforth be As if 'twere not

AURELIA. Oh, cast me not away!

By all the love I bear you, Catiline, I beg you, I adjure, let us not part!

CATILINE. My heart is dead, my sight is blind to love.

From life's great mockery I turn my eyes; And gaze but on the dim, yet mighty star Of fame that is to be!

AURELIA. O gods of mercy! [She leans faint against the tree outside the tent.]

CATILINE. [To the Warriors.] And now away!

MANLIUS. The din of arms I hear!

SEVERAL VOICES. They come, they come.

CATILINE. Good! We will heed their warning. Long was our night of shame; our dawn is near. To battle in the crimson sky of morning!

By Roman sword, with Roman fortitude, The last of Romans perish in their blood! [They rush out through the forest; a great alarm, rent with battle-cries, is heard from within the camp.]

FURIA. He is gone forever. My great task in life is done. Cold and rigid we shall find him in the morning sun.

AURELIA. [Aside.] In his passion-glutted bosom then should love no longer dwell?
Was it nothing but a dream? His angry words I heard full well.

FURIA. Hark, the weapons clash; already at the brink of death he stands; Soon a noiseless shadow he will hasten toward the spirit lands.

AURELIA. [Startled.] Who are you, prophetic voice, that yonder comes to me, like the night-owl's cry of warning from some far-off tree!

Are you from the clammy underworld of spirits come Hence to lead my Catiline into your gloomy home?

FURIA. Home is ay the journey's goal, and all his wanderings lay Through the reeking swamps of life

AURELIA. But only for a day. Free and noble was his heart, his spirit strong and true, Till around it serpent-like a poisoned seedling grew.

FURIA. So the plane-tree, too, keeps fresh and green its leafy dress, till its trunk is smothered in a clinging vine's caress.

AURELIA. Now did you betray your source. For time and time again echoed from the lips of Catiline this one refrain.

You the serpent are, who poisoned all my joy in life, steeled his heart against my kindness through your deadly strife.

From those waking night-dreams well I know your infamy, like a threat I see you stand between my love and me.

With my husband at my side I cherished in my breast longings for a tranquil life, a home of peace and rest.

Ah, a garden-bed I planted in his weary heart; As its fairest ornament our love I hedged apart.

Flower and all have you uprooted with malignant hand; In the dust it lies where thriving it did lately stand.

FURIA. Foolish weakling; you would guide the steps of Catiline?

Do you not perceive his heart was never wholly thine?

Think you that in such a soil your flower can survive?

In the sunny springtime only violets can thrive, While the henbane grows in strength beneath a clouded grey; And his soul was long ago a clouded autumn day.

All is lost to you. Soon dies the spark within his breast; As a victim of revenge he shall go to his rest.

AURELIA. [With increasing vehemence.] Thus he shall not perish; no, by all the gods of day!

To his weary heart my tears will somehow force a way.

If I find him pale and gory on the battlefield, I shall throw my arms about him and his bosom shield, Breathe upon his speechless lips the love within my soul, Ease the pain within him and his suffering mind console.

Herald of revenge, your victim from you I shall wrest, Bind him to the land of sunshine, to a home of rest; If his eyes be dimmed already, stilled his beating heart, Linked together arm in arm we shall this life depart.

Grant me, gods of mercy, in return for what I gave, By the side of him I love, the stillness of the grave. [She goes.]

FURIA. [Gazes after her.] Seek him, deluded soul; I have no fear; I hold the victory safe within my hands.

FURIA. The roar of battle grows; its rumble blends with death-cries and the crash of broken shields.

Is he perchance now dying? Still alive?

Oh, blessed is this hour! The sinking moon Secludes herself in massive thunderclouds.

One moment more it will be night anew Ere comes the day; and with the coming day All will be over. In the dark he dies, As in the dark he lived. O blessed hour! [She listens.]

FURIA. Now sweeps the wind by, like an autumn gust, And lapses slowly in the far-off distance.

The ponderous armies slowly sweep the plain.

Like angry ocean billows on they roll, Unyielding, trampling down the fallen dead.

Out yonder I hear whines and moans and sighs, the final lullaby, wherewith they lull Themselves to rest and all their pallid brothers.

Now speaks the night-owl forth to welcome them Into the kingdom of the gloomy shadows.

FURIA. [After a pause.] How still it is. Now is he mine at last, aye, mine alone, and mine forevermore.

Now we can journey toward the river Lethe and far beyond where never dawns the day.

Yet first I'll seek his bleeding body yonder, And freely glut my eyes upon those features, Hated and yet so fair, ere they be marred By rising sunshine and by watchful vultures. [She starts to go, but is suddenly startled at something.]

FURIA. What is that gliding o'er the meadow yonder?

Is it the misty vapors of the moor That form a picture in the morning chill?

Now it draws near. The shade of Catiline!

His spectre! I can see his misty eye, His broken shield, his sword bereft of blade.

Ah, he is surely dead; one thing alone, remarkable, his wound I do not see. [CATILINE comes through the forest, pale and weary, with drooping head and troubled countenance.]

CATILINE. [To himself.] "Perish thou shalt by deed thine own, and yet a stranger's hand shall fell thee."

Such was his prophecy. Now am I fallen, though struck by no one. Who will solve the riddle?

FURIA. I greet you after battle, Catiline!

CATILINE. Ah, who are you?

FURIA. I am a shadow's shadow.

CATILINE. You, Furia, you it is! You welcome me?

FURIA. Welcome at last into our common home!

Now we can go, two shades, to Charon's bark.

Yet first, accept the wreath of victory. [She picks some flowers, which she weaves into a wreath during the following.]

CATILINE. What make you there?

FURIA. Your brow I shall adorn.

But wherefore come you hither all alone?

A chieftain's ghost ten thousand dead should follow.

Then where are all your comrades, Catiline?

CATILINE. They slumber, Furia!

FURIA. Ah, they slumber still?

CATILINE. They slumber still, and they will slumber long.

They slumber all. Steal softly through the forest, Peer out across the plain, disturb them not!

There will you find them in extended ranks.

They fell asleep lulled by the clang of steel; They fell asleep, and wakened not, as I did, When in the distant hills the echoes died.

A shadow now you called me. True, I am a shadow of myself. But do not think Their slumber yonder is so undisturbed and void of dreams. Oh, do not think so!

FURIA. Speak! What may your comrades dream?

CATILINE. Ah, you shall hear. I led the battle with despairing heart, And sought my death beneath the play of swords.

To right and left I saw my comrades fall; Statilius first, then one by one the rest; m y Curius fell trying to shield my breast; All perished there beneath Rome's flaming sword, the sword that me alone passed by untouched.

Yes, Catiline was spared by the sword of Rome.

Half-stunned I stood there with my broken shield, Aware of nothing as the waves of battle Swept o'er me. I recovered first my senses When all grew still again, and I looked up And saw the struggle seething far behind me!

How long I stood there? Only this I know, I stood alone among my fallen comrades.

But there was life within those misty eyes; The corners of their mouths betrayed a smile; And they addressed their smile and gaze to me, Who stood alone erect among the dead, who had for ages fought for them and Rome, who stood there lonely and disgraced, untouched By Roman sword. Then perished Catiline.

FURIA. False have you read your fallen comrades' dreams; False have you judged the reason of your fall.

Their smiles and glances were but invitations To sleep with them

CATILINE. Yes, if I only could!

FURIA. Have courage, spectre of a former hero; Your hour of rest is near. Come, bend your head; I shall adorn you with the victor's crown. [She offers the wreath to him.]

CATILINE. Bah, what is that? A poppy-wreath!

FURIA. [With wild glee.] Well, yes; Are not such poppies pretty? They will glow around your forehead like a fringe of blood.

CATILINE. No, cast the wreath away! I hate this crimson.

FURIA. [Laughs aloud.] Ah, you prefer the pale and feeble shades?

Good! I shall bring the garland of green rushes that Sylvia carried in her dripping locks, The day she came afloat upon the Tiber?

CATILINE. Alas, what visions!

FURIA. Shall I bring you rather The thorny brambles from the market-place, With crimson-spots, the stain of civic blood, That flowed at your behest, my Catiline?

CATILINE. Enough!

FURIA. Or would you like a crown of leaves From the old winter oak near mother's home, That withered when a young dishonored woman With piercing cries distraught leaped in the river?

CATILINE. Pour out at once your measures of revenge Upon my head

FURIA. I am your very eye, your very memory, your very doom.

CATILINE. But wherefore now?

FURIA. His goal at length attained, The traveller spent looks back from whence he came.

CATILINE. Have I then reached my goal? Is this the goal?

I am no longer living, nor yet buried.

Where lies the goal?

FURIA. In sight, if you but will.

CATILINE. A will I have no longer; my will perished When all the things I willed once, came to naught.

CATILINE. [Waves his arms.] Away, away from me, ye sallow shades!

What claim you here of me, ye men and women?

I cannot give you! Oh, this multitude!

FURIA. To earth your spirit still is closely bound!

These thousand-threaded nets asunder tear!

Come, let me press this wreath upon your locks, 'Tis gifted with a strong and soothing virtue; It kills the memory, lulls the soul to rest!

CATILINE. [Huskily.] It kills the memory? Dare I trust your word?

Then press your poison-wreath upon my forehead.

FURIA. [Puts the wreath on his head.]

Now it is yours! Thus decked you shall appear Before the prince of darkness, Catiline!

CATILINE. Away! away! I yearn to go below; I long to pass into the spirit lands.

Let us together go! What holds me here?

What stays my steps? Behind me here I feel Upon the morning sky a misty star; it holds me in the land of living men; It draws me as the moon attracts the sea.

FURIA. Away! Away!

CATILINE. It beckons and it twinkles.

I cannot follow you until this light Is quenched entirely, or by clouds obscured, I see it clearly now; 'tis not a star; It is a human heart, throbbing and warm; It binds me here; it fascinates and draws me As draws the evening star the eye of children.

FURIA. Then stop this beating heart!

CATILINE. What do you mean?

FURIA. The dagger in your belt. A single thrust, the star will vanish and the heart will die That stand between us like an enemy.

CATILINE. Ah, I should? Sharp and shining is the dagger

CATILINE. [With a cry.] Aurelia! O Aurelia, where, where are you?

Were you but here! No, no, I will not see you!

And yet methinks all would be well again, And peace would come, if I could lay my head Upon your bosom and repent, repent!

FURIA. And what would you repent?

CATILINE. Oh, everything! That I have been, that I have ever lived.

FURIA. 'Tis now too late, too late! Whence now you stand No path leads back again. Go try it, fool!

Now am I going home. Place you your head Upon her breast and see if there you find The blessed peace your weary soul desires.

FURIA. [With increasing wildness.] Soon will the thousand dead rise up again; Dishonored women will their numbers join; And all, aye, they will all demand of you The life, the blood, the honor you destroyed.

In terror you will flee into the night, will roam about the earth on every strand, Like old Actean, hounded by his dogs, a shadow hounded by a thousand shades!

CATILINE. I see it, Furia. Here I have no peace. I am an exile in the world of light!

I'll go with you into the spirit realms; the bond that binds me I will tear asunder.

FURIA. Why grope you with the dagger?

CATILINE. She shall die. [The lightning strikes and the thunder rolls.]

FURIA. The mighty powers rejoice at your resolve! See, Catiline, see, yonder comes your wife. [AURELIA comes through the forest in an anxious search.]

AURELIA. Where shall I find him? Where, where can he be! I've searched in vain among the dead [Discovers him.]

AURELIA. Great heavens, my Catiline! [She rushes toward him.]

CATILINE. [Bewildered.] Speak not that name again!

AURELIA. You are alive? [Is about to throw herself in his arms.]

CATILINE. [Thrusting her aside.] Away! I'm not alive.

AURELIA. Oh, hear me, dearest!

CATILINE. No, I will not hear! I hate you. I see through your cunning wiles.
You wish to chain me to a living death.

Cease staring at me! Ah, your eyes torment me. They pierce like daggers through my very soul!

Ah, yes, the dagger! Die! Come, close your eyes [He draws the dagger and seizes her by the hand.]

AURELIA. Keep guard, oh gracious gods, o'er him and me!

CATILINE. Quick, close your eyes; close them, I say; in them I see the starlight and the morning sky.

Now shall I quench the heavenly star of dawn! [The thunder rolls again.]

CATILINE. Your heart; your blood! Now speak the gods of life Their last farewell to you and Catiline! [He lifts the dagger toward her bosom; she escapes into the tent; he pursues her.]

FURIA. [Listens.] She stretches out her hand imploringly.

She pleads with him for life. He hears her not.

He strikes her down! She reels in her own blood! [CATILINE comes slowly out of the tent with the dagger in his hand.]

CATILINE. Now am I free. Soon I shall cease to be.

Now sinks my soul in vague oblivion.

My eyes are growing dim, my hearing faint, As if through rushing waters. Ah, do you know What I have slain with this my little dagger?

Not her alone, but all the hearts on earth, all living things, all things that grow and bloom; the starlight have I dimmed, the crescent moon, The flaming sun. Ah, see, it fails to rise; 'Twill never rise again; the sun is dead.

Now is the whole wide realm of earth transformed Into a huge and clammy sepulchre, Its vault of leaden grey; beneath this vault Stand you and I, bereft of light and darkness, Of death and life, two restless exiled shadows.

FURIA. Now stand we, Catiline, before our goal!

CATILINE. No, one step more before I reach my goal.

Relieve me of my burden! Do you not see, I bend beneath the corpse of Catiline?

A dagger through the corpse of Catiline! [He shows her the dagger.]

CATILINE. Come, Furia, set me free! Come, take this dagger; on it the star of morning I impaled; take it and plunge it straightway through the corpse; Then it will loose its hold, and I am free.

FURIA. [Takes the dagger.] Your will be done, whom I have loved in hate!

Shake off your dust and come with me to rest. [She buries the dagger deep in his heart; he sinks down at the foot of the tree.]

CATILINE. [After a moment comes to consciousness again, passes his hand across his forehead, and speaks faintly.] Now, mysterious voice, your prophecy I understand!

I shall perish by my own, yet by a stranger's hand.

Nemesis has wrought her end. Shroud me, gloom of night!

Raise your billows, murky Styx, roll on in all your might!

Ferry me across in safety; speed the vessel on Toward the silent prince's realm, the land of shadows wan.

Two roads there are running yonder; I shall journey dumb Toward the left

AURELIA. [From the tent, pale and faltering, her bosom bloody.] no, toward the right! Oh, toward Elysium!

CATILINE. [Startled.] How this bright and lurid picture fills my soul with dread!
She herself it is! Aurelia, speak, are you not dead?

AURELIA. [Kneels before him.] No, I live that I may still your agonizing cry, live that I may lean my bosom on your breast and die.

CATILINE. Oh, you live!

AURELIA. I did but swoon; though my two eyes grew blurred, dimly yet I followed you and heard your every word.

And my love a spouse's strength again unto me gave; breast to breast, my Catiline, we go into the grave!

CATILINE. Oh, how gladly would I go! Yet all in vain you sigh.

We must part. Revenge compels me with a hollow cry.

You can hasten, free and blithesome, forth to peace and light; I must cross the river Lethe down into the night. [The day dawns in the background.]

AURELIA. [Points toward the increasing light.] No, the terrors and the gloom of death love scatters far.

See, the storm-clouds vanish; faintly gleams the morning star.

AURELIA. [With uplifted arms.] Light is victor! Grand and full of freshness dawns the day!

Follow me, then! Death already speeds me on his way. [She sinks down over him.]

CATILINE. [Presses her to himself and speaks with his last strength.] Oh, how sweet! Now I remember my forgotten dream, how the darkness was dispersed before a radiant beam, How the song of children ushered in the new-born day.

Ah, my eye grows dim, my strength is fading fast away; but my mind is clearer now than ever it has been:

All the wanderings of my life loom plainly up within.

Yes, my life a tempest was beneath the lightning blaze; but my death is like the morning's rosy-tinted haze. [Bends over her.]

CATILINE. You have driven the gloom away; peace dwells within my breast.

I shall seek with you the dwelling place of light and rest!

CATILINE. [He tears the dagger quickly out of his breast and speaks with dying voice.] The gods of dawn are smiling in atonement from above; All the powers of darkness you have conquered with your love! [During the last scene FURIA has withdrawn farther and farther into the background and disappears at last among the trees.

CATILINE's head sinks down on AURELIA's breast; they die.]

THE END.

Henrik Ibsen - The Feast At Solhoug

Index Of Contents

PREFACE

I wrote The Feast at Solhoug in Bergen in the summer of 1855, that is to say, about twenty-eight years ago.

The play was acted for the first time on January 2, 1856, also at Bergen, as a gala performance on the anniversary of the foundation of the Norwegian Stage.

As I was then stage-manager of the Bergen Theatre, it was I myself who conducted the rehearsals of my play. It received an excellent, a remarkably sympathetic interpretation. Acted with pleasure and enthusiasm, it was received in the same spirit. The "Bergen emotionalism," which is said to have decided the result of the latest elections in those parts, ran high that evening in the crowded theatre. The performance ended with repeated calls for the author and for the actors. Later in the evening I was serenaded by the orchestra, accompanied by a great part of the audience. I almost think that I went so far as to make some kind of speech from my window; certain I am that I felt extremely happy.

A couple of months later, The Feast of Solhoug was played in Christiania. There also it was received by the public with much approbation, and the day after the first performance Bjornson wrote a friendly, youthfully ardent article on it in the Morgenblad. It was not a notice or criticism proper, but rather a free, fanciful improvisation on the play and the performance.

On this, however, followed the real criticism, written by the real critics.

How did a man in the Christiania of those days by which I mean the years between 1850 and 1860, or thereabouts become a real literary, and in particular dramatic, critic?

As a rule, the process was as follows: After some preparatory exercises in the columns of the Samfundsblad, and after the play, the future critic betook himself to Johan Dahl's bookshop and ordered from Copenhagen a copy of J. L. Heiberg's Prose Works, among which was to be found, so he had heard it said, an essay entitled On the Vaudeville. This essay was in due course read, ruminated on, and possibly to a certain extent understood. From Heiberg's writings the young man, moreover, learned of a controversy which that author had carried on in his day with Professor Oehlenschlager and with the Soro poet, Hauch. And he was simultaneously made aware that J. L. Baggesen (the author of Letters from the Dead) had at a still earlier period made a similar attack on the great author who wrote both Axel and Valborg and Hakon Jarl.

A quantity of other information useful to a critic was to be extracted from these writings. From them one learned, for instance, that taste obliged a good critic to be scandalised by a hiatus. Did the young critical Jeronimuses of Christiania encounter such a monstrosity in any new verse, they were as certain as their prototype in Holberg to shout their "Hoity-toity! the world will not last till Easter!"

The origin of another peculiar characteristic of the criticism then prevalent in the Norwegian capital was long a puzzle to me. Every time a new author published a book or had a little play acted, our critics were in the habit of flying into an ungovernable passion and behaving as if the publication of the book or the performance of the play were a mortal insult to themselves and the newspapers in which they wrote. As already remarked, I puzzled long over this peculiarity. At last I got to the bottom of the matter. Whilst reading the Danish Monthly Journal of Literature I was struck by the fact that old State-Councillor Molbech was invariably seized with a fit of rage when a young author published a book or had a play acted in Copenhagen.

Thus, or in a manner closely resembling this, had the tribunal qualified itself, which now, in the daily press, summoned The Feast at Solhoug to the bar of criticism in Christiania. It was principally composed of young men who, as regards criticism, lived upon loans from various quarters. Their critical thought had long ago been thought and expressed by others; their opinions had long ere now been formulated elsewhere. Their aesthetic principles were borrowed; their critical method was borrowed; the polemical tactics they employed were borrowed in every particular, great and small. Their very frame of mind was borrowed. Borrowing, borrowing, here, there, and everywhere! The single original thing about them was that they invariably made a wrong and unseasonable application of their borrowings.

It can surprise no one that this body, the members of which, as critics, supported themselves by borrowing, should have presupposed similar action on my part, as author. Two, possibly more than two, of the newspapers promptly discovered that I had borrowed this, that, and the other thing form Henrik Hertz's play, Svend Dyring's House.

This is a baseless and indefensible critical assertion. It is evidently to be ascribed to the fact that the metre of the ancient ballads is employed in both plays. But my tone is quite different from Hertz's; the language of my play has a different ring; a light summer breeze plays over the rhythm of my verse: over that or Hertz's brood the storms of autumn.

Nor, as regards the characters, the action, and the contents of the plays generally, is there any other or any greater resemblance between them than that which is a natural consequence of the derivation of the subjects of both from the narrow circle of ideas in which the ancient ballads move.

It might be maintained with quite as much, or even more, reason that Hertz in his Svend Dyring's House had borrowed, and that to no inconsiderable extent, from Heinrich von Kleist's Kathchen von Heilbronn, a play written at the beginning of this century. Kathchen's relation to Count Wetterstrahl is in all essentials the same as Tagnhild's to the knight, Stig Hvide. Like Ragnhild, Kathchen is compelled by a mysterious, inexplicable power to follow the man she loves wherever he goes, to steal secretly after him, to lay herself down to sleep near him, to come back to him, as by some innate compulsion, however often she may be driven away. And other instances of supernatural interference are to be met with both in Kleist's and in Hertz's play.

But does anyone doubt that it would be possible, with a little good or a little ill-will, to discover among still older dramatic literature a play from which it could be maintained that Kleist had borrowed here and there in his Kathchen von Heilbronn? I, for my part, do not doubt it. But such suggestions of indebtedness are futile. What makes a work of art the spiritual property of its creator is the fact that he has imprinted on it the stamp of his own personality. Therefore I hold that, in spite of the above-mentioned points of resemblance, Svend Dyring's House is as incontestably and entirely an original work by Henrick Hertz as Katchen von Heilbronn is an original work by Heinrich von Kleist.

I advance the same claim on my own behalf as regards The Feast at Solhoug, and I trust that, for the future, each of the three namesakes* will be permitted to keep, in its entirety, what rightfully belongs to him.

In writing The Feast of Solhoug in connection with Svend Dyring's House, George Brandes expresses the opinion, not that the former play is founded upon any idea borrowed from the latter, but that it has been written under an influence exercised by the older author upon the younger. Brandes invariably criticises my work in such a friendly spirit that I have all reason to be obliged to him for this suggestion, as for so much else.

Nevertheless I must maintain that he, too, is in this instance mistaken. I have never specially admired Henrik Hertz as a dramatist. Hence it is impossible for me to believe that he should, unknown to myself, have been able to exercise any influence on by dramatic production.

As regards this point and the matter in general, I might confine myself to referring those interested to the writings of Dr. Valfrid Vasenius, lecturer on Aesthetics at the University of Helsingfors. In the thesis which gained him his degree of Doctor of Philosophy, Henrik Ibsen's Dramatic Poetry in its First stage (1879), and also in Henrik Ibsen: The Portrait of a Skald (Jos. Seligman & Co., Stockholm, 1882), Valsenious states and supports his views on the subject of the play at present in question, supplementing them in the latter work by what I told him, very briefly, when we were together at Munich three years ago.

But, to prevent all misconception, I will now myself give a short account of the origin of The Feast at Solhoug.

I began this Preface with the statement that The Feast at Solhoug was written in the summer 1855.

In 1854 I had written Lady Inger of Ostrat. This was a task which had obliged me to devote much attention to the literature and history of Norway during the Middle Ages, especially the latter part of that period. I did my utmost to familiarise myself with the manners and customs, with the emotions, thought, and language of the men of those days.

The period, however, is not one over which the student is tempted to linger, nor does it present much material suitable for dramatic treatment.

Consequently I soon deserted it for the Saga period. But the Sagas of the Kings, and in general the more strictly historical traditions of that far-off age, did not attract me greatly; at that time I was unable to put the quarrels between kings and chieftains, parties and clans, to any dramatic purpose. This was to happen later.

In the Icelandic "family" Sagas, on the other hand, I found in abundance what I required in the shape of human garb for the moods, conceptions, and thoughts which at that time occupied me, or were, at least, more or less distinctly present in my mind. With these Old Norse contributions to the personal history of our Saga period I had had no previous acquaintance; I had hardly so much as heard them named. But now N. M. Petersen's excellent translation, excellent, at least, as far as the style is concerned, fell into my hands. In the pages of these family chronicles, with their variety of scenes and of relations between man and man, between woman and woman, in short, between human being and human being, there met me a personal, eventful, really living life; and as the result of my intercourse with all these distinctly individual men and women, there presented themselves to my mind's eye the first rough, indistinct outlines of The Vikings at Helgeland.

How far the details of that drama then took shape, I am no longer able to say. But I remember perfectly that the two figures of which I first caught sight were the two women who in course of time became Hiordis and Dagny. There was to be a great banquet in the play, with passion-rousing, fateful quarrels during its course. Of other characters and passions, and situations produced by these, I meant to include whatever seemed to me most typical of the life which the Sagas reveal. In short, it was my intention to reproduce dramatically exactly what the Saga of the Volsungs gives in epic form.

I made no complete, connected plan at that time; but it was evident to me that such a drama was to be my first undertaking.

Various obstacles intervened. Most of them were of a personal nature, and these were probably the most decisive; but it undoubtedly had its significance that I happened just at this time to make a careful study of Landstad's collection of Norwegian ballads, published two years previously. My mood of the moment was more in harmony with the literary romanticism of the Middle Ages than with the deeds of the Sagas, with poetical than with prose composition, with the word-melody of the ballad than with the characterisation of the Saga.

Thus it happened that the fermenting, formless design for the tragedy, The Vikings at Helgeland, transformed itself temporarily into the lyric drama, The Feast at Solhoug.

The two female characters, the foster sisters Hiordis and Dagny, of the projected tragedy, became the sisters Margit and Signe of the completed lyric drama. The derivation of the latter pair from the two women of the Saga at once becomes apparent when attention is drawn to it. The relationship is unmistakable. The tragic hero, so far only vaguely outlined, Sigurd, the far-travelled Viking, the welcome guest at the courts of kings, became the knight and minstrel, Gudmund Alfson, who has likewise been long absent in foreign lands, and has lived in the king's household. His attitude towards the two sisters was changed, to bring it into accordance with the change in time and circumstances; but the position of both sisters to him remained practically the same as that in the projected and afterwards completed tragedy. The fateful banquet, the presentation of which had seemed to me of the first importance in my original plan, became in the drama the scene upon which its personages made their appearance; it became the background against which the action stood out, and communicated to the picture as a whole the general tone at which I aimed. The ending of the play was, undoubtedly, softened and subdued into harmony with its character as drama, not tragedy; but orthodox aestheticians may still, perhaps, find it indisputable whether, in this ending, a touch of pure tragedy has not been left behind, to testify to the origin of the drama.

Upon this subject, however, I shall not enter at present. My object has simply been to maintain and prove that the play under consideration, like all my other dramatic works, is an inevitable outcome of the tenor of my life at a certain period. It had its origin within, and was not the result of any outward impression or influence.

This, and no other, is the true account of the genesis of The Feast at Solhoug.

Henrik Ibsen. Rome, April, 1883.

*Heinrich von Kleist, Henrik Hertz, Henrik Ibsen.

THE FEAST AT SOLHOUG

CHARACTERS

BENGT GAUTESON, Master of Solhoug.

MARGIT, his wife.

SIGNE, her sister.

GUDMUND ALFSON, their kinsman.

KNUT GESLING, the King's sheriff.

ERIK OF HEGGE, his friend.

A HOUSE-CARL.

ANOTHER HOUSE-CARL.

THE KING'S ENVOY.

AN OLD MAN.

A MAIDEN.

GUESTS, both MEN and LADIES.

MEN of KNUT GESLING'S TRAIN.

SERVING-MEN and MAIDENS at SOLHOUG.

The action passes at Solhoug in the Fourteenth Century.

PLAY IN THREE ACTS

ACT FIRST

A stately room, with doors in the back and to both sides. In front   on the right, a bay window with small round panes, set in lead,   and near the window a table, on which is a quantity of feminine   ornaments. Along the left wall, a longer table with silver   goblets and drinking-horns. The door in the back leads out to a passage-way,* through which can be seen a spacious   fiord-landscape.

BENGT GAUTESON, MARGIT, KNUT GESLING and ERIK OF HEGGE are seated   around the table on the left. In the background are KNUT's   followers, some seated, some standing; one or two flagons of   ale are handed round among them. Far off are heard church   bells, ringing to Mass.

*This no doubt means a sort of arcaded veranda running along the outer wall of the house.

ERIK. [Rising at the table.] In one word, now, what answer have you to make to my wooing on Knut Gesling's behalf?

BENGT. [Glancing uneasily towards his wife.] Well, I, to me it seems [As she remains silent.] H'm, Margit, let us first hear your thought in the matter.

MARGIT. [Rising.] Sir Knut Gesling, I have long known all that Erik of Hegge has told of you. I know full well that you come of a lordly house; you are rich in gold and gear, and you stand in high favour with our royal master.

BENGT. [To KNUT.] In high favour, so say I too.

MARGIT. And doubtless my sister could choose her no doughtier mate

BENGT. None doughtier; that is what I say too.

MARGIT. If so be that you can win her to think kindly of you.

BENGT. [Anxiously, and half aside.] Nay, nay, my dear wife

KNUT. [Springing up.] Stands it so, Dame Margit! You think that your sister

BENGT. [Seeking to calm him.] Nay, nay, Knut Gesling! Have patience, now. You must understand us aright.

MARGIT. There is naught in my words to wound you. My sister knows you only by the songs that are made about you and these songs sound but ill in gentle ears.

No peaceful home is your father's house. With your lawless, reckless crew, Day out, day in, must you hold carouse. God help her who mates with you. God help the maiden you lure or buy With gold and with forests green. Soon will her sore heart long to lie Still in the grave, I ween.

ERIK. Aye, aye, true enough, Knut Gesling lives not overpeaceably. But there will soon come a change in that, when he gets him a wife in his hall.

KNUT. And this I would have you mark, Dame Margit: it may be a week since, I was at a feast at Hegge, at Erik's bidding, whom here you see. I vowed a vow that Signe, your fair sister, should be my wife, and that before the year was out. Never shall it be said of Knut Gesling that he brake any vow. You can see, then, that you must e'en choose me for your sister's husband, be it with your will or against it.

MARGIT. Ere that may be, I must tell you plain, You must rid yourself of your ravening train. You must scour no longer with yell and shout O'er the country-side in a galloping rout; You must still the shudder that spreads around When Knut Gesling is to a bride-ale bound. Courteous must your mien be when a-feasting you ride; Let your battle-axe hang at home at the chimney-side. It ever sits loose in your hand, well you know, When the mead has gone round and your brain is aglow. From no man his rightful gear shall you wrest, You shall harm no harmless maiden; You shall send no man the shameless hest That when his path crosses yours, he were best Come with his grave-clothes laden. And if you will so bear you till the year be past, You may win my sister for your bride at last.

KNUT. [With suppressed rage.] You know how to order your words cunningly, Dame Margit. Truly, you should have been a priest, and not your husbands wife.

BENGT. Oh, for that matter, I too could

KNUT. [Paying no heed to him.] But I would have you take note that had a sword-bearing man spoken to me in such wise

BENGT. Nay, but listen, Knut Gesling, you must understand us!

KNUT. [As before.] Well, briefly, he should have learnt that the axe sits loose in my hand, as you said but now.

BENGT. [Softly.] There we have it! Margit, Margit, this will never end well.

MARGIT. [To KNUT.] You asked for a forthright answer, and that I have given you.

KNUT. Well, well; I will not reckon too closely with you, Dame Margit. You have more wit than all the rest of us together. Here is my hand; it may be there was somewhat of reason in the keen-edged words you spoke to me.

MARGIT. This I like well; now are you already on the right way to amendment. Yet one word more, to-day we hold a feast at Solhoug.

KNUT. A feast?

BENGT. Yes, Knut Gesling: you must know that it is our wedding day; this day three years ago made me Dame Margit's husband.

MARGIT.

[Impatiently, interrupting.] As I said, we hold a feast to-day. When Mass is over, and your other business done, I would have you ride hither again, and join in the banquet. Then you can learn to know my sister.

KNUT. So be it, Dame Margit; I thank you. Yet 'twas not to go to Mass that I rode hither this morning. Your kinsman, Gudmund Alfson, was the cause of my coming.

MARGIT. [Starts.] He! My kinsman? Where would you seek him?

KNUT. His homestead lies behind the headland, on the other side of the fiord.

MARGIT. But he himself is far away.

ERIK. Be not so sure; he may be nearer than you think.

KNUT. [Whispers.] Hold your peace!

MARGIT. Nearer? What mean you?

KNUT. Have you not heard, then, that Gudmund Alfson has come back to Norway? He came with the Chancellor Audun of Hegranes, who was sent to France to bring home our new Queen.

MARGIT. True enough, but in these very days the King holds his wedding- feast in full state at Bergen, and there is Gudmund Alfson a guest.

BENGT. And there could we too have been guests had my wife so willed it.

ERIK. [Aside to KNUT.] Then Dame Margit knows not that?

KNUT. [Aside.] So it would seem; but keep your counsel. [Aloud.] Well, well, Dame Margit, I must go my way none the less, and see what may betide. At nightfall I will be here again.

MARGIT. And then you must show whether you have power to bridle your unruly spirit.

BENGT. Aye, mark you that.

MARGIT. You must lay no hand on your axe, hear you, Knut Gesling?

BENGT. Neither on your axe, nor on your knife, nor on any other weapon whatsoever.

MARGIT. For then can you never hope to be one of our kindred.

BENGT. Nay, that is our firm resolve.

KNUT. [To MARGIT.] Have no fear.

BENGT. And what we have firmly resolved stands fast.

KNUT. That I like well, Sir Bengt Gauteson. I, too, say the same; and I have pledged myself at the feast-board to wed your kinswoman. You may be sure that my pledge, too, will stand fast. God's peace till to-night!

[He and ERIK, with their men, go out at the back. [BENGT accompanies them to the door. The sound of the bells has in the meantime ceased.

BENGT. [Returning.] Methought he seemed to threaten us as he departed.

MARGIT. [Absently.] Aye, so it seemed.

BENGT. Knut Gesling is an ill man to fall out with. And when I bethink me, we gave him over many hard words. But come, let us not brood over that. To-day we must be merry, Margit! as I trow we have both good reason to be.

MARGIT. [With a weary smile.] Aye, surely, surely.

BENGT. Tis true I was no mere stripling when I courted you. But well I wot I was the richest man for many and many a mile. You were a fair maiden, and nobly born; but your dowry would have tempted no wooer.

MARGIT. [To herself.] Yet was I then so rich.

BENGT. What said you, my wife?

MARGIT. Oh, nothing, nothing. [Crosses to the right.] I will deck me with pearls and rings. Is not to-night a time of rejoicing for me?

BENGT. I am fain to hear you say it. Let me see that you deck you in your best attire, that our guests may say: Happy she who mated with Bengt Gauteson. But now must I to the larder; there are many things to-day that must not be over-looked.

[He goes out to the left.

MARGIT. [Sinks down on a chair by the table on the right.] 'Twas well he departed. While here he remains Meseems the blood freezes within my veins; Meseems that a crushing mighty and cold My heart in its clutches doth still enfold. [With tears she cannot repress.

He is my husband! I am his wife! How long, how long lasts a woman's life? Sixty years, mayhap, God pity me Who am not yet full twenty-three! [More calmly after a short silence.

Hard, so long in a gilded cage to pine; Hard a hopeless prisoner's lot and mine.   [Absently fingering the ornaments on the table, and beginning to put them on.

With rings, and with jewels, and all of my best By his order myself I am decking. But oh, if to-day were my burial-feast, 'Twere little that I'd be recking. [Breaking off.

But if thus I brood I must needs despair; I know a song that can lighten care. [She sings.

The Hill-King to the sea did ride;
Oh, sad are my days and dreary
To woo a maiden to be his bride.
I am waiting for thee, I am weary.

The Hill-King rode to Sir Hakon's hold;
Oh, sad are my days and dreary
Little Kirsten sat combing her locks of gold.
I am waiting for thee, I am weary.

The Hill-King wedded the maiden fair;
Oh, sad are my days and dreary
A silvern girdle she ever must wear.
I am waiting for thee, I am weary.

The Hill-King wedded the lily-wand,
Oh, sad are my days and dreary
With fifteen gold rings on either hand.
I am waiting for thee, I am weary.

Three summers passed, and there passed full five;
Oh, sad are my days and dreary
In the hill little Kirsten was buried alive.
I am waiting for thee, I am weary.

Five summers passed, and there passed full nine;
Oh, sad are my days and dreary
Little Kirsten ne'er saw the glad sunshine.
I am waiting for thee, I am weary.

In the dale there are flowers and the birds' blithe song;
Oh, sad are my days and dreary
In the hill there is gold and the night is long.
I am waiting for thee, I am weary.

[She rises and crosses the room.

How oft in the gloaming would Gudmund sing This song in my father's hall. There was somewhat in it, some strange, sad thing That took my heart in thrall; Though I scarce understood, I could ne'er forget. And the words and the thoughts they haunt me yet.   [Stops horror-struck.

Rings of red gold! And a belt beside! 'Twas with gold the Hill-King wedded his bride!   [In despair; sinks down on a bench beside the table on the left.

Woe! Woe! I myself am the Hill-King's wife! And there cometh none to free me from the prison of my life.

[SIGNE, radiant with gladness, comes running in from the back.

SIGNE. [Calling.] Margit, Margit, he is coming!

MARGIT. [Starting up.] Coming? Who is coming?

SIGNE. Gudmund, our kinsman!

MARGIT. Gudmund Alfson! Here! How can you think?

SIGNE. Oh, I am sure of it.

MARGIT. [Crosses to the right.] Gudmund Alfson is at the wedding-feast in the King's hall; you know that as well as I.

SIGNE. Maybe; but none the less I am sure it was he.

MARGIT. Have you seen him?

SIGNE. Oh, no, no; but I must tell you

MARGIT. Yes, haste you, tell on!

SIGNE. 'Twas early morn, and the church bells rang, To Mass I was fain to ride; The birds in the willows twittered and sang, In the birch-groves far and wide. All earth was glad in the clear, sweet day; And from church it had well-nigh stayed me; For still, as I rode down the shady way, Each rosebud beguiled and delayed me. Silently into the church I stole; The priest at the altar was bending; He chanted and read, and with awe in their soul, The folk to God's word were attending. Then a voice rang out o'er the fiord so blue; And the carven angels, the whole church through, Turned round, methought, to listen thereto.

MARGIT. O Signe, say on! Tell me all, tell me all!

SIGNE. 'Twas as though a strange, irresistible call Summoned me forth from the worshipping flock, Over hill and dale, over mead and rock. 'Mid the silver birches I listening trod, Moving as though in a dream; Behind me stood empty the house of God; Priest and people were lured by the magic 'twould seem, Of the tones that still through the air did stream. No sound they made; they were quiet as death; To hearken the song-birds held their breath, The lark dropped earthward, the cuckoo was still, As the voice re-echoed from hill to hill.

MARGIT. Go on.

SIGNE. They crossed themselves, women and men; [Pressing her hands to her breast]. But strange thoughts arose within me then; For the heavenly song familiar grew: Gudmund oft sang it to me and you. Ofttimes has Gudmund carolled it, And all he e'er sang in my heart is writ.

MARGIT. And you think that it may be?

SIGNE. I know it is he! I know it? I know it! You soon shall see! [Laughing]. From far-off lands, at the last, in the end, Each song-bird homeward his flight doth bend! I am so happy though why I scarce know! Margit, what say you? I'll quickly go And take down his harp, that has hung so long In there on the wall that 'tis rusted quite; Its golden strings I will polish bright, And tune them to ring and to sing with his song.

MARGIT. [Absently.] Do as you will

SIGNE. [Reproachfully.] Nay, this in not right. [Embracing her]. But when Gudmund comes will your heart grow light. Light, as when I was a child, again.

MARGIT. So much has changed, ah, so much! since then

SIGNE. Margit, you shall be happy and gay! Have you not serving-maids many, and thralls? Costly robes hang in rows on your chamber walls; How rich you are, none can say. By day you can ride in the forest deep, Chasing the hart and the hind; By night in a lordly bower you can sleep, On pillows of silk reclined.

MARGIT. [Looking toward the window.] And he comes to Solhoug! He, as a guest!

SIGNE. What say you?

MARGIT. [Turning.] Naught. Deck you out in your best. That fortune which seemeth to you so bright May await yourself.

SIGNE. Margit, say what you mean!

MARGIT. [Stroking her hair.] I mean, nay, no more! 'Twill shortly be seen; I mean, should a wooer ride hither to-night?

SIGNE. A wooer? For whom?

MARGIT. For you.

SIGNE. [Laughing.] For me? That he'd ta'en the wrong road full soon he would see.

MARGIT. What would you say if a valiant knight Begged for your hand?

SIGNE. That my heart was too light To think upon suitors or choose a mate.

MARGIT. But if he were mighty, and rich, and great?

SIGNE. O, were he a king, did his palace hold Stores of rich garments and ruddy gold, 'Twould ne'er set my heart desiring. With you I am rich enough here, meseeems, With summer and sun and the murmuring streams, And the birds in the branches quiring. Dear sister mine, here shall my dwelling be; And to give any wooer my hand in fee, For that I am too busy, and my heart too full of glee!

[SIGNE runs out to the left, singing.

MARGIT. [After a pause.] Gudmund Alfson coming hither! Hither to Solhoug? No, no, it cannot be. Signe heard him singing, she said! When I have heard the pine-trees moaning in the forest afar, when I have heard the waterfall thunder and the birds pipe their lure in the tree-tops, it has many a time seemed to me as though, through it all, the sound of Gudmund's songs came blended. And yet he was far from here. Signe has deceived herself. Gudmund cannot be coming.

[BENGT enters hastily from the back.

BENGT. [Entering, calls loudly.] An unlooked-for guest my wife!

MARGIT. What guest?

BENGT. Your kinsman, Gudmund Alfson! [Calls through the doorway on the right.] Let the best guest-room be prepared and that forthwith!

MARGIT. Is he, then, already here?

BENGT. [Looking out through the passage-way.] Nay, not yet; but he cannot be far off. [Calls again to the right.] The carved oak bed, with the dragon-heads! [Advances to MARGIT.] His shield-bearer brings a message of greeting from him; and he himself is close behind.

MARGIT. His shield-bearer! Comes he hither with a shield-bearer!

BENGT. Aye, by my faith he does. He has a shield-bearer and six armed men in his train. What would you? Gudmund Alfson is a far other man than he was when he set forth to seek his fortune. But I must ride forth to seek him. [Calls out.] The gilded saddle on my horse! And forget not the bridle with the serpents' heads! [Looks out to the back.] Ha, there he is already at the gate! Well, then, my staff, my silver-headed staff! Such a lordly knight. Heaven save us! we must receive him with honour, with all seemly honour!

[Goes hastily out to the back.

MARGIT. [Brooding] Alone he departed, a penniless swain; With esquires and henchmen now comes he again. What would he? Comes he, forsooth, to see My bitter and gnawing misery? Would he try how long, in my lot accurst, I can writhe and moan, ere my heart-strings burst. Thinks he that? Ah, let him only try! Full little joy shall he reap thereby.   [She beckons through the doorway on the right. Three handmaidens enter.

List, little maids, what I say to you: Find me my silken mantle blue. Go with me into my bower anon: My richest of velvets and furs do on. Two of you shall deck me in scarlet and vair, The third shall wind pearl-strings into my hair. All my jewels and gauds bear away with ye! [The handmaids go out to the left, taking the ornaments with them.

Since Margit the Hill-King's bride must be, Well! don we the queenly livery!

[She goes out to the left. [BENGT ushers in GUDMUND ALFSON, through the pent-house   passage at the back.

BENGT. And now once more welcome under Solhoug's roof, my wife's kinsman.

GUDMUND. I thank you. And how goes it with her? She thrives well in every way, I make no doubt?

BENGT. Aye, you may be sure she does. There is nothing she lacks. She has five handmaidens, no less, at her beck and call; a courser stands ready saddled in the stall when she lists to ride abroad. In one word, she has all that a noble lady can desire to make her happy in her lot.

GUDMUND. And Margit, is she then happy?

BENGT. God and all men would think that she must be; but, strange to say

GUDMUND. What mean you?

BENGT. Well, believe it or not as you list, but it seems to me that Margit was merrier of heart in the days of her poverty, than since she became the lady of Solhoug.

GUDMUND. [To himself.] I knew it; so it must be.

BENGT. What say you, kinsman?

GUDMUND. I say that I wonder greatly at what you tell me of your wife.

BENGT. Aye, you may be sure I wonder at it too. On the faith and troth of an honest gentleman, 'tis beyond me to guess what more she can desire. I am about her all day long; and no one can say of me that I rule her harshly. All the cares of household and husbandry I have taken on myself; yet notwithstanding. Well, well, you were ever a merry heart; I doubt not you will bring sunshine with you. Hush! here comes Dame Margit! Let her not see that I

[MARGIT enters from the left, richly dressed.

GUDMUND. [Going to meet her.] Margit, my dear Margit!

MARGIT. [Stops, and looks at him without recognition.] Your pardon, Sir Knight; but? [As though she only now recognized him.] Surely, if I mistake not, 'tis Gudmund Alfson.

[Holding out her hand to him.

GUDMUND. [Without taking it.] And you did not at once know me again?

BENGT. [Laughing.] Why, Margit, of what are you thinking? I told you but a moment agone that your kinsman

MARGIT. [Crossing to the table on the right.] Twelve years is a long time, Gudmund. The freshest plant may wither ten times over in that space.

GUDMUND. 'Tis seven years since last we met.

MARGIT. Surely it must be more than that.

GUDMUND. [Looking at her.] I could almost think so. But 'tis as I say.

MARGIT. How strange! I must have been but a child then; and it seems to me a whole eternity since I was a child. [Throws herself down on a chair.] Well, sit you down, my kinsman! Rest you, for to-night you shall dance, and rejoice us with your singing. [With a forced smile.] Doubtless you know we are merry here to-day, we are holding a feast.

GUDMUND. 'Twas told me as I entered your homestead.

BENGT. Aye, 'tis three years to-day since I became

MARGIT. [Interrupting.] My kinsman has already heard it. [To GUDMUND.] Will you not lay aside your cloak?

GUDMUND. I thank you, Dame Margit; but it seems to me cold here, colder than I had foreseen.

BENGT. For my part, I am warm enough; but then I have a hundred things to do and to take order for. [To MARGIT.] Let not the time seem long to our guest while I am absent. You can talk together of the old days.

[Going. MARGIT.

[Hesitating.] Are you going? Will you not rather?

BENGT. [Laughing, to GUDMUND, as he comes forward again.] See you well, Sir Bengt of Solhoug is the man to make the women fain of him. How short so e'er the space, my wife cannot abide to be without me. [To MARGIT, caressing her.] Content you; I shall soon be with you again.

[He goes out to the back.

MARGIT. [To herself.] Oh, torture, to have to endure it all.

[A short silence.

GUDMUND. How goes it, I pray, with your sister dear?

MARGIT. Right well, I thank you.

GUDMUND. They said she was here With you.

MARGIT. She has been here ever since we [Breaks off.

She came, now three years since, to Solhoug with me. [After a pause]. Ere long she'll be here, her friend to greet.

GUDMUND. Well I mind me of Signe's nature sweet. No guile she dreamed of, no evil knew. When I call to remembrance her eyes so blue I must think of the angels in heaven. But of years there have passed no fewer than seven; In that time much may have altered. Oh, say If she, too, has changed so while I've been away?

MARGIT. She too? Is it, pray, in the halls of kings That you learn such courtly ways, Sir Knight? To remind me thus of the change time brings

GUDMUND. Nay, Margit, my meaning you read aright! You were kind to me, both, in those far-away years. Your eyes, when we parted were wet with tears. We swore like brother and sister still To hold together in good hap or ill. 'Mid the other maids like a sun you shone, Far, far and wide was your beauty known. You are no less fair than you were, I wot; But Solhoug's mistress, I see, has forgot The penniless kinsman. So hard is your mind That ever of old was gentle and kind.

MARGIT. [Choking back her tears.] Aye, of old!

GUDMUND. [Looks compassionately at her, is silent for a little, then says in a subdued voice.

Shall we do as your husband said? Pass the time with talk of the dear old days?

MARGIT. [Vehemently.] No, no, not of them! Their memory's dead. My mind unwillingly backward strays. Tell rather of what your life has been, Of what in the wide world you've done and seen. Adventures you've lacked not, well I ween. In all the warmth and the space out yonder, That heart and mind should be light, what wonder?

GUDMUND. In the King's high hall I found not the joy That I knew by my own poor hearth as a boy.

MARGIT. [Without looking at him.] While I, as at Solhoug each day flits past, Thank Heaven that here has my lot been cast.

GUDMUND. 'Tis well if for this you can thankful be

MARGIT. [Vehemently.] Why not? For am I not honoured and free? Must not all folk here obey my hest? Rule I not all things as seemeth me best? Here I am first, with no second beside me; And that, as you know, from of old satisfied me. Did you think you would find me weary and sad? Nay, my mind is at peace and my heart is glad. You might, then, have spared your journey here To Solhoug; 'twill profit you little, I fear.

GUDMUND. What, mean you, Dame Margit?

MARGIT. [Rising.] I understand all. I know why you come to my lonely hall.

GUDMUND. And you welcome me not, though you know why I came? [Bowing and about to go. God's peace and farewell, then, my noble dame!

MARGIT. To have stayed in the royal hall, indeed, Sir Knight, had better become your fame.

GUDMUND. [Stops.] In the royal hall? Do you scoff at my need?

MARGIT. Your need? You are ill to content, my friend; Where, I would know, do you think to end? You can dress you in velvet and cramoisie, You stand by the throne, and have lands in fee

GUDMUND. Do you deem, then, that fortune is kind to me? You said but now that full well you knew What brought me to Solhoug

MARGIT. I told you true!

GUDMUND. Then you know what of late has befallen me; You have heard the tale of my outlawry?

MARGIT. [Terror-struck.] An outlaw! You, Gudmund!

GUDMUND. I am indeed. But I swear, by the Holy Christ I swear, Had I known the thoughts of your heart, I ne'er Had bent me to Solhoug in my need. I thought that you still were gentle-hearted, As you ever were wont to be ere we parted: But I truckle not to you; the wood is wide, My hand and my bow shall fend for me there; I will drink of the mountain brook, and hide My head in the beast's lair.

[On the point of going.

MARGIT. [Holding him back.] Outlawed! Nay, stay! I swear to you That naught of your outlawry I knew.

GUDMUND. It is as I tell you. My life's at stake; And to live are all men fain. Three nights like a dog 'neath the sky I've lain, My couch on the hillside forced to make, With for pillow the boulder grey. Though too proud to knock at the door of the stranger, And pray him for aid in the hour of danger, Yet strong was my hope as I held on my way: I thought: When to Solhoug you come at last Then all your pains will be done and past. You have sure friends there, whatever betide. But hope like a wayside flower shrivels up; Though your husband met me with flagon and cup, And his doors flung open wide, Within, your dwelling seems chill and bare; Dark is the hall; my friends are not there. 'Tis well; I will back to my hills from your halls.

MARGIT. [Beseechingly.] Oh, hear me!

GUDMUND. My soul is not base as a thrall's. Now life to me seems a thing of nought; Truly I hold it scarce worth a thought. You have killed all that I hold most dear; Of my fairest hopes I follow the bier. Farewell, then, Dame Margit!

MARGIT. Nay, Gudmund, hear! By all that is holy!

GUDMUND. Live on as before Live on in honour and joyance. Never shall Gudmund darken your door, Never shall cause you 'noyance.

MARGIT. Enough, enough. Your bitterness You presently shall rue. Had I known you outlawed, shelterless, Hunted the country through. Trust me, the day that brought you here Would have seemed the fairest of many a year; And a feast I had counted it indeed When you turned to Solhoug for refuge in need.

GUDMUND. What say you? How shall I read your mind?

MARGIT. [Holding out her hand to him.]

Read this: that at Solhoug dwell kinsfolk kind.

GUDMUND. But you said of late?

MARGIT. To that pay no heed, Or hear me, and understand indeed. For me is life but a long, black night, Nor sun, nor star for me shines bright. I have sold my youth and my liberty, And none from my bargain can set me free. My heart's content I have bartered for gold, With gilded chains I have fettered myself; Trust me, it is but comfort cold To the sorrowful soul, the pride of pelf. How blithe was my childhood, how free from care! Our house was lowly and scant our store; But treasures of hope in my breast I bore.

GUDMUND. [Whose eyes have been fixed upon her.] E'en then you were growing to beauty rare.

MARGIT. Mayhap; but the praises showered on me Caused the wreck of my happiness, that I now see. To far-off lands away you sailed; But deep in my heart was graven each song You had ever sung; and their glamour was strong; With a mist of dreams my brow they veiled. In them all the joys you had dwelt upon That can find a home in the beating breast; You had sung so oft of the lordly life 'Mid knights and ladies. And lo! anon Came wooers a many from east and from west; And so I became Bengt Gauteson's wife.

GUDMUND. Oh, Margit!

MARGIT. The days that passed were but few Ere with tears my folly I 'gan to rue. To think, my kinsman and friend, on thee Was all the comfort left to me. How empty now seemed Solhoug's hall, How hateful and drear its great rooms all! Hither came many a knight and dame, Came many a skald to sing my fame. But never a one who could fathom aright My spirit and all its yearning, I shivered, as though in the Hill-King's might; Yet my head throbbed, my blood was burning.

GUDMUND. But your husband?

MARGIT. He never to me was dear. 'Twas his gold was my undoing. When he spoke to me, aye, or e'en drew near, My spirit writhed with ruing. [Clasping her hands]. And thus have I lived for three long years. A life of sorrow, of unstanched tears! Your coming was rumoured. You know full well What pride deep down in my heart doth dwell. I hid my anguish, I veiled my woe, For you were the last that the truth must know.

GUDMUND. [Moved.] 'Twas therefore, then, that you turned away

MARGIT. [Not looking at him.] I thought you came at my woe to jeer.

GUDMUND. Margit, how could you think?

MARGIT. Nay, nay, There was reason enough for such a fear. But thanks be to Heaven that fear is gone; And now no longer I stand alone; My spirit now is as light and free As a child's at play 'neath the greenwood tree. [With a sudden start of fear]. Ah, where are my wits fled! How could I forget? Ye saints, I need sorely your succor yet! An outlaw, you said?

GUDMUND. [Smiling.] Nay, now I'm at home; Hither the King's men scarce dare come.

MARGIT. Your fall has been sudden. I pray you, tell How you lost the King's favour.

GUDMUND. 'Twas thus it befell. You know how I journeyed to France of late, When the Chancellor, Audun of Hegranes, Fared thither from Bergen, in royal state, To lead home the King's bride, the fair Princess, With her squires, and maidens, and ducats bright. Sir Audun's a fair and stately knight, The Princess shone with a beauty rare. Her eyes seemed full of a burning prayer. They would oft talk alone and in whispers, the two. Of what? That nobody guessed or knew. There came a night when I leant at ease Against the galley's railing; My thought flew onward to Norway's leas, With the milk-white seagulls sailing. Two voices whispered behind my back; I turned, it was he and she; I knew them well, though the night was black, But they, they saw not me. She gazed upon him with sorrowful eyes And whispered: "Ah, if to southern skies We could turn the vessel's prow, And we were alone in the bark, we twain, My heart, methinks, would find peace again, Nor would fever burn my brow." Sir Audun answers; and straight she replies, In words so fierce, so bold; Like glittering stars I can see her eyes; She begged him [Breaking off]. My blood ran cold.

MARGIT. She begged?

GUDMUND. I arose, and they vanished apace; All was silent, fore and aft: [Producing a small phial]. But this I found by their resting place.

MARGIT. And that?

GUDMUND. [Lowering his voice.] Holds a secret draught. A drop of this in your enemy's cup And his life will sicken and wither up. No leechcraft helps 'gainst the deadly thing.

MARGIT. And that?

GUDMUND. That draught was meant for the King.

MARGIT. Great God!

GUDMUND. [Putting up the phial again.] That I found it was well for them all. In three days more was our voyage ended; Then I fled, by my faithful men attended. For I knew right well, in the royal hall, That Audun subtly would work my fall, Accusing me

MARGIT. Aye, but at Solhoug he Cannot harm you. All as of old will be.

GUDMUND. All? Nay, Margit, you then were free.

MARGIT. You mean?

GUDMUND. I? Nay, I meant naught. My brain Is wildered; but ah, I am blithe and fain To be, as of old, with you sisters twain. But tell me, Signe?

MARGIT. [Points smiling towards the door on the left.] She comes anon. To greet her kinsman she needs must don Her trinkets, a task that takes time, 'tis plain.

GUDMUND. I must see, I must see if she knows me again.

[He goes out to the left.

MARGIT. [Following him with her eyes.] How fair and manlike he is! [With a sigh.] There is little likeness 'twixt him and [Begins putting things in order on the table, but presently stops.] "You then were free," he said. Yes, then! [A short pause.] 'Twas a strange tale, that of the Princess who - She held another dear, and then - Aye, those women of far-off lands. I have heard it before they are not weak as we are; they do not fear to pass from thought to deed. [Takes up a goblet which stands on the table.] 'Twas in this beaker that Gudmund and I, when he went away, drank to his happy return. 'Tis well-nigh the only heirloom I brought with me to Solhoug. [Putting the goblet away in a cupboard.] How soft is this summer day; and how light it is in here! So sweetly has the sun not shone for three long years.

[SIGNE, and after her GUDMUND, enters from the left.

SIGNE. [Runs laughing up to MARGIT.] Ha, ha, ha! He will not believe that 'tis I!

MARGIT. [Smiling to GUDMUND.] You see: while in far-off lands you strayed, She, too, has altered, the little maid.

GUDMUND. Aye truly! But that she should be. Why, 'Tis a marvel in very deed.   [Takes both SIGNE's hands and looks at her]. Yet, when I look in these eyes so blue, The innocent child-mind I still can read. Yes, Signe, I know that 'tis you! I needs must laugh when I think how oft I have thought of you perched on my shoulder aloft As you used to ride. You were then a child; Now you are a nixie, spell-weaving, wild.

SIGNE. [Threatening with her finger.] Beware! If the nixie's ire you awaken, Soon in her nets you will find yourself taken.

GUDMUND. [To himself.] I am snared already, it seems to me.

SIGNE. But, Gudmund, wait, you have still to see How I've shielded your harp from the dust and the rust. [As she goes out to the left]. You shall teach me all of your songs! You must!

GUDMUND. [Softly, as he follows her with his eyes.] She has flushed to the loveliest rose of May, That was yet but a bud in the morning's ray.

SIGNE. [Returning with the harp.] Behold!

GUDMUND. [Taking it.] My harp! As bright as of yore! [Striking one or two chords]. Still the old chords ring sweet and clear. On the wall, untouched, thou shalt hang no more.

MARGIT. [Looking out at the back.] Our guests are coming.

SIGNE. [While GUDMUND preludes his song.] Hush, hush! Oh, hear!

GUDMUND. [Sings.] I roamed through the uplands so heavy of cheer; The little birds quavered in bush and in brere; The little birds quavered, around and above: Wouldst know of the sowing and growing of love?

It grows like the oak tree through slow-rolling years; 'Tis nourished by dreams, and by songs, and by tears; But swiftly 'tis sown; ere a moment speeds by, Deep, deep in the heart love is rooted for aye.

[As he strikes the concluding chords, he goes towards the back where he lays down his harp].

SIGNE. [Thoughtfully, repeats to herself.] But swiftly 'tis sown; ere a moment speeds by, Deep, deep in the heart love is rooted for aye.

MARGIT. [Absently.] Did you speak to me? I heard not clearly?

SIGNE. I? No, no. I only meant [She again becomes absorbed in dreams.]

MARGIT. [Half aloud; looking straight before her.] It grows like the oak tree through slow-rolling years; 'Tis nourished by dreams, and by songs and by tears.

SIGNE. [Returning to herself.] You said that?

MARGIT. [Drawing her hand over her brow.] Nay, 'twas nothing. Come, we must go meet our guests.

[BENGT enters with many GUESTS, both men and women, through the passageway.

GUESTS. With song and harping enter we
The feast-hall opened wide;
Peace to our hostess kind and free,
All happiness to her betide.
O'er Solhoug's roof for ever may
Bright as to-day
The heavens abide.

ACT SECOND

A birch grove adjoining the house, one corner of which is seen to   the left. At the back, a footpath leads up the hillside. To the right of the footpath a river comes tumbling down a ravine and loses itself among boulders and stones. It is a light   summer evening. The door leading to the house stands open; the windows are lighted up. Music is heard from within.

THE GUESTS. [Singing in the Feast Hall.]

Set bow to fiddle! To sound of strings We'll dance till night shall furl her wings,   Through the long hours glad and golden! Like blood-red blossom the maiden glows. Come, bold young wooer and hold the rose In a soft embrace enfolden.

[KNUT GESLING and ERIK OF HEGGE enter from the house. Sounds of music, dancing and merriment are heard from within during what follows.

ERIK. If only you come not to repent it, Knut.

KNUT. That is my affair.

ERIK. Well, say what you will, 'tis a daring move. You are the King's Sheriff. Commands go forth to you that you shall seize the person of Gudmund Alfson, wherever you may find him. And now, when you have him in your grasp, you proffer him your friendship, and let him go freely, whithersoever he will.

KNUT. I know what I am doing. I sought him in his own dwelling, but there he was not to be found. If, now, I went about to seize him here, think you that Dame Margit would be minded to give me Signe to wife?

ERIK. [With deliberation.] No, by fair means it might scarcely be, but

KNUT. And by foul means I am loth to proceed. Moreover, Gudmund is my friend from bygone days; and he can be helpful to me. [With decision.] Therefore it shall be as I have said. This evening no one at Solhoug shall know that Gudmund Alfson is an outlaw; to-morrow he must look to himself.

ERIK. Aye, but the King's decree?

KNUT. Oh, the King's decree! You know as well as I that the King's decree is but little heeded here in the uplands. Were the King's decree to be enforced, many a stout fellow among us would have to pay dear both for bride-rape and for man-slaying. Come this way, I would fain know where Signe?

[They go out to the right. [GUDMUND and SIGNE come down the footpath at the back.

SIGNE. Oh, speak! Say on! For sweeter far Such words than sweetest music are.

GUDMUND. Signe, my flower, my lily fair!

SIGNE. [In subdued, but happy wonderment.] I am dear to him - I! Gudmund. As none other I swear.

SIGNE. And is it I that can bind your will! And is it I that your heart can fill! Oh, dare I believe you?

GUDMUND. Indeed you may. List to me, Signe! The years sped away, But faithful was I in my thoughts to you, My fairest flowers, ye sisters two. My own heart I could not clearly read. When I left, my Signe was but a child, A fairy elf, like the creatures wild Who play, while we sleep, in wood and mead. But in Solhoug's hall to-day, right loud My heart spake, and right clearly; It told me that Margit's a lady proud, Whilst you're the sweet maiden I love most dearly.

SIGNE. [Who has only half listened to his words.] I mind me, we sat in the hearth's red glow, One winter evening, 'tis long ago. And you sang to me of the maiden fair Whom the neckan had lured to his watery lair. There she forgot both father and mother, There she forgot both sister and brother; Heaven and earth and her Christian speech, And her God, she forgot them all and each. But close by the strand a stripling stood And he was heartsore and heavy of mood. He struck from his harpstrings notes of woe, That wide o'er the waters rang loud, rang low. The spell-bound maid in the tarn so deep, His strains awoke from her heavy sleep, The neckan must grant her release from his rule, She rose through the lilies afloat on the pool. Then looked she to heaven while on green earth she trod, And wakened once more to her faith and her God.

GUDMUND. Signe, my fairest of flowers!

SIGNE. It seems That I, too, have lived in a world of dreams. But the strange deep words you to-night have spoken, Of the power of love, have my slumber broken. The heavens seemed never so blue to me, Never the world so fair; I can understand, as I roam with thee, The song of the birds in air.

GUDMUND. So mighty is love, it stirs in the breast Thought and longings and happy unrest. But come, let us both to your sister go.

SIGNE. Would you tell her?

GUDMUND. Everything she must know.

SIGNE. Then go you alone; I feel that my cheek Would be hot with blushes to hear you speak.

GUDMUND. So be it, I go.

SIGNE. And here will I bide; [Listening towards the right]. Or better, down by the riverside, I hear Knut Gesling, with maidens and men.

GUDMUND. There will you stay?

SIGNE. Till you come again [She goes out to the right. GUDMUND goes into the house.   MARGIT enters from behind the house on the left].

MARGIT. In the hall there is gladness and revelry; The dancers foot it with jest and glee. The air weighed hot on my brow and breast; For Gudmund, he was not there. [She draws a deep breath.

Out here 'tis better: here's quiet and rest. How sweet is the cool night air! [A brooding silence.

The horrible thought! Oh, why should it be That wherever I go it follows me? The phial, doth a secret contain; A drop of this in my enemy's cup, And his life would sicken and wither up; The leech's skill would be tried in vain. [Again a silence.

Were I sure that Gudmund, held me dear. Then little I'd care for

[GUDMUND enters from the house].

GUDMUND. You, Margit, here? And alone? I have sought you everywhere.

MARGIT. 'Tis cool here. I sickened of heat and glare. See you how yonder the white mists glide Softly over the marshes wide? Here it is neither dark nor light, But midway between them [To herself]. as in my breast. [Looking at him]. Is't not so, when you wander on such a night You hear, though but half to yourself confessed, A stirring of secret life through the hush, In tree and in leaf, in flower and in rush? [With a sudden change of tone. Can you guess what I wish?

GUDMUND. Well?

MARGIT. That I could be The nixie that haunts yonder upland lea. How cunningly I should weave my spell! Trust me!

GUDMUND. Margit, what ails you? Tell!

MARGIT. [Paying no heed to him.] How I should quaver my magic lay! Quaver and croon it both night and day! [With growing vehemence.

How I would lure the knight so bold Through the greenwood glades to my mountain hold. There were the world and its woes forgot In the burning joys of our blissful lot.

GUDMUND. Margit! Margit!

MARGIT. [Ever more wildly.] At midnight's hour Sweet were our sleep in my lonely bower; And if death should come with the dawn, I trow 'Twere sweet to die so; what thinkest thou?

GUDMUND. You are sick!

MARGIT. [Bursting into laughter.] Ha, ha! Let me laugh! 'Tis good To laugh when the heart is in laughing mood!

GUDMUND. I see that you still have the same wild soul As of old

MARGIT. [With sudden seriousness.] Nay, let not that vex your mind, 'Tis only at midnight it mocks control; By day I am timid as any hind. How tame I have grown, you yourself must say, When you think on the women in lands far away. Of that fair Princess ah, she was wild! Beside her lamblike am I and mild. She did not helplessly yearn and brood, She would have acted; and that

GUDMUND. 'Tis good You remind me; Straightway I'll cast away What to me is valueless after this day [Takes out the phial].

MARGIT. The phial! You meant?

GUDMUND. I thought it might be At need a friend that should set me free Should the King's men chance to lay hands on me. But from to-night it has lost its worth; Now will I fight all the kings of earth, Gather my kinsfolk and friends to the strife, And battle right stoutly for freedom and life.

[Is about to throw the phial against a rock].

MARGIT. [Seizing his arm.] Nay, hold! Let me have it

GUDMUND. First tell me why?

MARGIT. I'd fain fling it down to the neckan hard by, Who so often has made my dull hours fleet With his harping and songs, so strange and sweet. Give it me! [Takes the phial from his hand]. There!

[Feigns to throw it into the river.

GUDMUND. [Goes to the right, and looks down into the ravine.] Have you thrown it away?

MARGIT. [Concealing the phial.] Aye, surely! You saw [Whispers as she goes towards the house]. Now God help and spare me! [Aloud]. Gudmund!

GUDMUND. [Approaching.] What would you?

MARGIT. Teach me, I pray, How to interpret the ancient lay They sing of the church in the valley there: A gentle knight and a lady fair, They loved each other well. That very day on her bier she lay He on his sword-point fell. They buried her by the northward spire, And him by the south kirk wall; And theretofore grew neither bush nor briar In the hallowed ground at all. But next spring from their coffins twain Two lilies fair upgrew. And by and by, o'er the roof-tree high, They twined and they bloomed the whole year through. How read you the riddle?

GUDMUND. [Looks searchingly at her.] I scarce can say.

MARGIT. You may doubtless read it in many a way; But its truest meaning, methinks, is clear: The church can never sever two that hold each other dear.

GUDMUND. [To himself.] Ye saints, if she should? Lest worse befall, 'Tis time indeed I told her all! [Aloud]. Do you wish for my happiness, Margit, tell!

MARGIT. [In joyful agitation.] Wish for it! I!

GUDMUND. Then, wot you well, The joy of my life now rests with you

MARGIT. [With an outburst.] Gudmund!

GUDMUND. Listen! 'tis the time you knew

[He stops suddenly]. [Voices and laughter are heard by the river bank. SIGNE and   other GIRLS enter from the right, accompanied by KNUT, ERIK, and several YOUNGER MEN.

KNUT. [Still at a distance.] Gudmund Alfson! Wait; I must speak a word with you.

[He stops, talking to ERIK. The other GUESTS in the meantime enter the house.

MARGIT. [To herself.] The joy of his life! What else can he mean but! [Half aloud.] Signe, my dear, dear sister!

[She puts her arm round SIGNE's waist, and they go towards the back talking to each other.

GUDMUND. [Softly as he follows them with his eyes.] Aye, so it were wisest. Both Signe and I must away from Solhoug. Knut Gesling has shown himself my friend; he will help me.

KNUT. [Softly, to ERIK.] Yes, yes, I say, Gudmund is her kinsman; he can best plead my cause.

ERIK. Well, as you will.

[He goes into the house.

KNUT. [Approaching.] Listen, Gudmund

GUDMUND. [Smiling.] Come you to tell me that you dare no longer let me go free.

KNUT. Dare! Be at your ease as to that. Knut Gesling dares whatever he will. No, 'tis another matter. You know that here in the district, I am held to be a wild, unruly companion

GUDMUND. Aye, and if rumour lies not

KNUT. Why no, much that it reports may be true enough. But now, I must tell you [They go, conversing, up towards the back].

SIGNE. [To MARGIT, as they come forward beside the house.] I understand you not. You speak as though an unlooked-for happiness had befallen you. What is in your mind?

MARGIT. Signe, you are still a child; you know not what it means to have ever in your heart the dread of [Suddenly breaking off.] Think, Signe, what it must be to wither and die without ever having lived.

SIGNE. [Looks at her in astonishment, and shakes her head.] Nay, but, Margit?

MARGIT. Aye, aye, you do not understand, but none the less

[They go up again, talking to each other. GUDMUND and KNUT come down on the other side.

GUDMUND. Well, if so it be, if this wild life no longer contents you, then I will give you the best counsel that ever friend gave to friend: take to wife an honourable maiden.

KNUT. Say you so? And if I now told you that 'tis even that I have in mind?

GUDMUND. Good luck and happiness to you then, Knut Gesling! And now you must know that I too

KNUT. You? Are you, too, so purposed?

GUDMUND. Aye truly. But the King's wrath, I am a banished man

KNUT. Nay, to that you need give but little thought. As yet there is no one here, save Dame Margit, that knows aught of the matter; and so long as I am your friend, you have one in whom you can trust securely. Now I must tell you

[He proceeds in a whisper as they go up again].

SIGNE. [As she and MARGIT again advance.] But tell me then Margit!

MARGIT. More I dare not tell you.

SIGNE. Then will I be more open-hearted than you. But first answer me one question. [Bashfully, with hesitation.] Is there no one who has told you anything concerning me?

MARGIT. Concerning you? Nay, what should that be?

SIGNE. [As before, looking downwards.] You said to me this morning: if a wooer came riding hither?

MARGIT. That is true. [To herself.] Knut Gesling, has he already? [Eagerly to SIGNE.] Well? What then?

SIGNE. [Softly, but with exultation.] The wooer has come! He has come, Margit! I knew not then whom you meant; but now!

MARGIT. And what have you answered him?

SIGNE. Oh, how should I know? [Flinging her arms round her sister's neck.] But the world seems to me so rich and beautiful since the moment when he told me that he held me dear.

MARGIT. Why, Signe, Signe, I cannot understand that you should so quickly! You scarce knew him before to-day.

SIGNE. Oh, 'tis but little I yet know of love; but this I know that what the song says is true: Full swiftly 'tis sown; ere a moment speeds by, Deep, deep in the heart love is rooted for aye

MARGIT. So be it; and since so it is, I need no longer hold aught concealed from you. Ah [She stops suddenly, as she sees KNUT and GUDMUND approaching].

KNUT. [In a tone of satisfaction.] Ha, this is as I would have it, Gudmund. Here is my hand!

MARGIT. [To herself.] What is this?

GUDMUND. [To KNUT.] And here is mine!

[They shake hands].

KNUT. But now we must each of us name who it is

GUDMUND. Good. Here at Solhoug, among so many fair women, I have found her whom

KNUT. I too. And I will bear her home this very night, if it be needful.

MARGIT. [Who has approached unobserved.] All saints in heaven!

GUDMUND. [Nods to KNUT.] The same is my intent.

SIGNE. [Who has also been listening.] Gudmund!

GUDMUND AND KNUT. [Whispering to each other, as they both point at Signe.] There she is!

GUDMUND. [Starting.] Aye, mine.

KNUT. [Likewise.] No, mine!

MARGIT. [Softly, half bewildered.] Signe!

GUDMUND. [As before, to KNUT.] What mean you by that?

KNUT. I mean that 'tis Signe whom I

GUDMUND. Signe! Signe is my betrothed in the sight of God.

MARGIT. [With a cry.] It was she! No, no!

GUDMUND. [To himself, as he catches sight of her.] Margit! She has heard everything.

KNUT. Ho, ho! So this is how it stands? Nay, Dame Margit, 'tis needless to put on such an air of wonder; now I understand everything.

MARGIT. [To SIGNE.] But not a moment ago you said? [Suddenly grasping the situation.] 'Twas Gudmund you meant!

SIGNE. [Astonished.] Yes, did you not know it! But what ails you, Margit?

MARGIT. [In an almost toneless voice.] Nay, nothing, nothing.

KNUT. [To MARGIT.] And this morning, when you made me give my word that I would stir no strife here to-night, you already knew that Gudmund Alfson was coming. Ha, ha, think not that you can hoodwink Knut Gesling! Signe has become dear to me. Even this morning 'twas but my hasty vow that drove me to seek her hand; but now

SIGNE. [To MARGIT.] He? Was this the wooer that was in your mind?

MARGIT. Hush, hush!

KNUT. [Firmly and harshly.] Dame Margit, you are her elder sister; you shall give me an answer.

MARGIT. [Battling with herself.] Signe has already made her choice; I have naught to answer.

KNUT. Good; then I have nothing more to do at Solhoug. But after midnight, mark you this, the day is at an end; then you may chance to see me again, and then Fortune must decide whether it be Gudmund or I that shall bear Signe away from this house.

GUDMUND. Aye, try if you dare; it shall cost you a bloody sconce.

SIGNE. [In terror.] Gudmund! By all the saints!

KNUT. Gently, gently, Gudmund Alfson! Ere sunrise you shall be in my power. And she, your lady-love [Goes up to the door, beckons and calls in a low voice.] Erik! Erik! come hither! we must away to our kinsfolk. [Threateningly, while ERIK shows himself in the doorway.] Woe upon you all when I come again!

[He and ERIK go off to the left at the back].

SIGNE. [Softly to GUDMUND.] Oh, tell me, what does all this mean?

GUDMUND. [Whispering.] We must both leave Solhoug this very night.

SIGNE. God shield me, you would!

GUDMUND. Say nought of it! No word to any one, not even to your sister.

MARGIT. [To herself.] She, it is she! She of whom he had scarce thought before to-night. Had I been free, I know well whom he had chosen. Aye, free!

[BENGT and GUESTS, both Men and Women enter from the house.

YOUNG MEN AND MAIDENS. Out here, out here be the feast arrayed, While the birds are asleep in the greenwood shade, How sweet to sport in the flowery glade 'Neath the birches.

Out here, out here, shall be mirth and jest, No sigh on the lips and no care in the breast, When the fiddle is tuned at the dancers' 'hest, 'Neath the birches.

BENGT. That is well, that is well! So I fain would see it! I am merry, and my wife likewise; and therefore I pray ye all to be merry along with us.

ONE OF THE GUESTS. Aye, now let us have a stave-match.*

*A contest in impromptu verse-making.

MANY. [Shout.] Yes, yes, a stave-match!

ANOTHER GUEST. Nay, let that be; it leads but to strife at the feast. [Lowering his voice.] Bear in mind that Knut Gesling is with us to-night.

SEVERAL. [Whispering among themselves.] Aye, aye, that is true. Remember the last time, how he. Best beware.

AN OLD MAN. But you, Dame Margit, I know your kind had ever wealth of tales in store; and you yourself, even as a child, knew many a fair legend.

MARGIT. Alas! I have forgot them all. But ask Gudmund Alfson, my kinsman; he knows a tale that is merry enough.

GUDMUND. [In a low voice, imploringly.] Margit!

MARGIT. Why, what a pitiful countenance you put on! Be merry, Gudmund! Be merry! Aye, aye, it comes easy to you, well I wot. [Laughing, to the GUESTS.] He has seen the huldra to-night. She would fain have tempted him; but Gudmund is a faithful swain. [Turns again to GUDMUND.] Aye, but the tale is not finished yet. When you bear away your lady-love, over hill and through forest, be sure you turn not round; be sure you never look back, the huldra sits laughing behind every bush; and when all is done [In a low voice, coming close up to him.] you will go no further than she will let you.

[She crosses to the right].

SIGNE. Oh, God! Oh, God!

BENGT. [Going around among the GUESTS in high contentment.] Ha, ha, ha! Dame Margit knows how to set the mirth afoot! When she takes it in hand, she does it much better than I.

GUDMUND. [To himself.] She threatens! I must tear the last hope out of her breast; else will peace never come to her mind. [Turns to the GUESTS.] I mind me of a little song. If it please you to hear it

SEVERAL OF THE GUESTS. Thanks, thanks, Gudmund Alfson!

[They close around him some sitting, others standing. MARGIT leans against a tree in front on the right. SIGNE stands on the left, near the house.

GUDMUND. I rode into the wildwood,
I sailed across the sea,
But 'twas at home I wooed and won
A maiden fair and free.

It was the Queen of Elfland,
She waxed full wroth and grim:
Never, she swore, shall that maiden fair
Ride to the church with him.

Hear me, thou Queen of Elfland,
Vain, vain are threat and spell;
For naught can sunder two true hearts
That love each other well!

AN OLD MAN. That is a right fair song. See how the young swains cast their glances thitherward! [Pointing towards the GIRLS.] Aye, aye, doubtless each has his own.

BENGT. [Making eyes at MARGIT.] Yes, I have mine, that is sure enough. Ha, ha, ha!

MARGIT. [To herself, quivering.] To have to suffer all this shame and scorn! No, no; now to essay the last remedy.

BENGT. What ails you? Meseems you look so pale.

MARGIT. 'Twill soon pass over. [Turns to the GUESTS.] Did I say e'en now that I had forgotten all my tales? I bethink me now that I remember one.

BENGT. Good, good, my wife! Come, let us hear it.

YOUNG GIRLS. [Urgently.] Yes, tell it us, tell it us, Dame Margit!

MARGIT. I almost fear that 'twill little please you; but that must be as it may.

GUDMUND. [To himself.] Saints in heaven, surely she would not!

MARGIT. It was a fair and noble maid, She dwelt in her father's hall; Both linen and silk did she broider and braid, Yet found in it solace small. For she sat there alone in cheerless state, Empty were hall and bower; In the pride of her heart, she was fain to mate With a chieftain of pelf and power. But now 'twas the Hill King, he rode from the north, With his henchmen and his gold; On the third day at night he in triumph fared forth, Bearing her to his mountain hold. Full many a summer she dwelt in the hill; Out of beakers of gold she could drink at her will. Oh, fair are the flowers of the valley, I trow, But only in dreams can she gather them now!

'Twas a youth, right gentle and bold to boot, Struck his harp with such magic might That it rang to the mountain's inmost root, Where she languished in the night. The sound in her soul waked a wondrous mood. Wide open the mountain-gates seemed to stand; The peace of God lay over the land, And she saw how it all was fair and good. There happened what never had happened before; She had wakened to life as his harp-strings thrilled; And her eyes were opened to all the store Of treasure wherewith the good earth is filled. For mark this well: it hath ever been found That those who in caverns deep lie bound Are lightly freed by the harp's glad sound. He saw her prisoned, he heard her wail. But he cast unheeding his harp aside, Hoisted straightway his silken sail, And sped away o'er the waters wide To stranger strands with his new-found bride. [With ever-increasing passion].

So fair was thy touch on the golden strings That my breast heaves high and my spirit sings! I must out, I must out to the sweet green leas! I die in the Hill-King's fastnesses! He mocks at my woe as he clasps his bride And sails away o'er the waters wide.   [Shrieks]. With me all is over; my hill-prison barred; Unsunned is the day, and the night all unstarred.

[She totters and, fainting, seeks to support herself against the trunk of a tree].

SIGNE. [Weeping, has rushed up to her, and takes her in her arms.] Margit! My sister!

GUDMUND. [At the same time, supporting her.] Help! help! she is dying!

[BENGT and the GUESTS flock round them with cries of alarm.

ACT THIRD

The hall at Solhoug as before, but now in disorder after the feast. It is night still, but with a glimmer of approaching dawn in the room and over the landscape without.

BENGT stands outside in the passage-way, with a beaker of ale in his hand. A party of GUESTS are in the act of leaving the house. In the room a MAID-SERVANT is restoring order.

BENGT. [Calls to the departing GUESTS.] God speed you, then, and bring you back ere long to Solhoug. Methinks you, like the rest, might have stayed and slept till morning. Well, well! Yet hold, I'll e'en go with you to the gate. I must drink your healths once more.

[He goes out].

GUESTS. [Sing in the distance.]

Farewell, and God's blessing on one and all
Beneath this roof abiding! The road must be faced.
To the fiddler we call: Tune up! Our cares deriding,
With dance and with song We'll shorten the way so weary and long.
Right merrily off we go.

[The song dies away in the distance]

[MARGIT enters the hall by the door on the right].

MAID. God save us, my lady, have you left your bed?

MARGIT. I am well. Go you and sleep. Stay, tell me, are the guests all gone?

MAID. No, not all; some wait till later in the day; ere now they are sleeping sound.

MARGIT. And Gudmund Alfson?

MAID. He, too, is doubtless asleep. [Points to the right.] 'Tis some time since he went to his chamber, yonder, across the passage.

MARGIT. Good; you may go.

[The MAID goes out to the left].

[MARGIT walks slowly across the hall, seats herself by the table on the right, and gazes out at the open window].

MARGIT. To-morrow, then, Gudmund will ride away Out into the world so great and wide. Alone with my husband here I must stay; And well do I know what will then betide. Like the broken branch and the trampled flower I shall suffer and fade from hour to hour. [Short pause; she leans back in her chair.

I once heard a tale of a child blind from birth, Whose childhood was full of joy and mirth; For the mother, with spells of magic might, Wove for the dark eyes a world of light. And the child looked forth with wonder and glee Upon the valley and hill, upon land and sea. Then suddenly the witchcraft failed. The child once more was in darkness pent; Good-bye to games and merriment; With longing vain the red cheeks paled. And its wail of woe, as it pined away, Was ceaseless, and sadder than words can say. Oh! like the child's my eyes were sealed, To the light and the life of summer blind [She springs up]. But now! And I in this cage confined! No, now is the worth of my youth revealed! Three years of life I on him have spent. My husband but were I longer content This hapless, hopeless weird to dree, Meek as a dove I needs must be. I am wearied to death of petty brawls; The stirring life of the great world calls. I will follow Gudmund with shield and bow, I will share his joys, I will soothe his woe, Watch o'er him both by night and day. All that behold shall envy the life Of the valiant knight and Margit his wife. His wife!   [Wrings her hands]. Oh God, what is this I say! Forgive me, forgive me, and oh! let me feel The peace that hath power both to soothe and to heal. [Walks back and forward, brooding silently.

Signe, my sister? How hateful 'twere To steal her glad young life from her! But who can tell? In very sooth She may love him but with the light love of youth. [Again silence; she takes out the little phial, looks long at it and says under her breath:

This phial, were I its powers to try. My husband would sleep for ever and aye!   [Horror-struck]. No, no! To the river's depths with it straight! [In the act of throwing it out of the window, stops]. And yet I could, 'tis not yet too late. [With an expression of mingled horror and rapture, whispers.

With what a magic resistless might Sin masters us in our own despite! Doubly alluring methinks is the goal I must reach through blood, with the wreck of my soul.

[BENGT, with the empty beaker in his hand, comes in from the passageway; his face is red; he staggers slightly.

BENGT. [Flinging the beaker upon the table on the left.] My faith, this has been a feast that will be the talk of the country. [Sees MARGIT.] Eh, are you there? You are well again. Good, good.

MARGIT. [Who in the meantime has concealed the phial.] Is the door barred?

BENGT. [Seating himself at the table on the left.] I have seen to everything. I went with the last guests as far as the gates. But what became of Knut Gesling to-night? Give me mead, Margit! I am thirsty Fill this cup.

[MARGIT fetches a flagon of the mead from a cupboard, and, and fills the goblet which is on the table before him.

MARGIT. [Crossing to the right with the flagon.] You asked about Knut Gesling.

BENGT. That I did. The boaster, the braggart! I have not forgot his threats of yester-morning.

MARGIT. He used worse words when he left to-night.

BENGT. He did? So much the better. I will strike him dead.

MARGIT. [Smiling contemptuously.] H'm

BENGT. I will kill him, I say! I fear not to face ten such fellows as he. In the store-house hangs my grandfather's axe; its shaft is inlaid with silver; with that axe in my hands, I tell you! [Thumps the table and drinks.] To-morrow I shall arm myself, go forth with all my men, and slay Knut Gesling. [Empties the beaker].

MARGIT. [To herself.] Oh, to have to live with him!

[Is in the act of leaving the room].

BENGT. Margit, come here! Fill my cup again. [She approaches; he tries to draw her down on his knee.] Ha, ha, ha! You are right fair, Margit! I love thee well!

MARGIT. [Freeing herself.] Let me go!

[Crosses, with the goblet in her hand, to the left.

BENGT. You are not in the humour to-night. Ha, ha, ha! That means no great matter, I know.

MARGIT. [Softly, as she fills the goblet.] Oh, that this might be the last beaker I should fill for you. [She leaves the goblet on the table and is making her way out to the left.

BENGT. Hark to me, Margit. For one thing you may thank Heaven, and that is, that I made you my wife before Gudmund Alfson came back.

MARGIT. Why so?

BENGT. Why, say you? Am not I ten times the richer man? And certain I am that he would have sought you for his wife, had you not been the mistress of Solhoug.

MARGIT. [Drawing nearer and glancing at the goblet.] Say you so?

BENGT. I could take my oath upon it. Bengt Gauteson has two sharp eyes in his head. But he may still have Signe.

MARGIT. And you think he will?

BENGT. Take her? Aye, since he cannot have you. But had you been free, then. Ha, ha, ha! Gudmund is like the rest. He envies me my wife. That is why I set such store by you, Margit. Here with the goblet again. And let it be full to the brim!

MARGIT. [Goes unwillingly across to the right.] You shall have it straightway.

BENGT. Knut Gesling is a suitor for Signe, too, but him I am resolved to slay. Gudmund is an honourable man; he shall have her. Think, Margit, what good days we shall have with them for neighbours. We will go a-visiting each other, and then will we sit the live-long day, each with his wife on his knee, drinking and talking of this and that.

MARGIT. [Whose mental struggle is visibly becoming more severe, involuntarily takes out the phial as she says:] No doubt no doubt!

BENGT. Ha, ha, ha! it may be that at first Gudmund will look askance at me when I take you in my arms; but that, I doubt not, he will soon get over.

MARGIT. This is more than woman can bear! [Pours the contents of the phial into the goblet, goes to the window and throws out the phial, then says, without looking at him.] Your beaker is full.

BENGT. Then bring it hither!

MARGIT. [Battling in an agony of indecision, at last says.] I pray you drink no more to-night!

BENGT. [Leans back in his chair and laughs.] Oho! You are impatient for my coming? Get you in; I will follow you soon.

MARGIT. [Suddenly decided.] Your beaker is full. [Points.] There it is.

[She goes quickly out to the left].

BENGT. [Rising.] I like her well. It repents me not a whit that I took her to wife, though of heritage she owned no more than yonder goblet and the brooches of her wedding gown.

[He goes to the table at the window and takes the goblet].
[A HOUSE-CARL enters hurriedly and with scared looks, from the back.

HOUSE-CARL. [Calls.] Sir Bengt, Sir Bengt! haste forth with all the speed you can! Knut Gesling with an armed train is drawing near the house.

BENGT. [Putting down the goblet.] Knut Gesling? Who brings the tidings?

HOUSE-CARL. Some of your guests espied him on the road beneath, and hastened back to warn you.

BENGT. E'en so. Then will I! Fetch me my grandfather's battle-axe!

[He and the HOUSE-CARL go out at the back].
[Soon after, GUDMUND and SIGNE enter quietly and cautiously by the door at the back.

SIGNE. [In muffled tones.] It must then, be so!

GUDMUND. [Also softly.] Necessity's might Constrains us.

SIGNE. Oh! thus under cover of night To steal from the valley where I was born?   [Dries her eyes.

Yet shalt thou hear no plaint forlorn. 'Tis for thy sake my home I flee; Wert thou not outlawed, Gudmund dear, I'd stay with my sister.

GUDMUND. Only to be Ta'en by Knut Gesling, with bow and spear, Swung on the croup of his battle-horse, And made his wife by force.

SIGNE. Quick, let us flee. But whither go?

GUDMUND. Down by the fiord a friend I know; He'll find us a ship. O'er the salt sea foam We'll sail away south to Denmark's bowers. There waits you there a happy home; Right joyously will fleet the hours; The fairest of flowers they bloom in the shade Of the beech-tree glade.

SIGNE. [Bursts into tears.] Farewell, my poor sister! Like my mother tender Thou hast guarded the ways my feet have trod, Hast guided my footsteps, aye praying to God, The Almighty, to be my defender. Gudmund, here is a goblet filled with mead; Let us drink to her; let us wish that ere long Her soul may again be calm and strong, And that God may be good to her need.

[She takes the goblet into her hands].

GUDMUND. Aye, let us drain it, naming her name! [Starts]. Stop! [Takes the goblet from her]. For meseems it is the same

SIGNE. 'Tis Margit's beaker.

GUDMUND. [Examining it carefully.] By Heaven, 'tis so! I mind me still of the red wine's glow As she drank from it on the day we parted To our meeting again in health and glad-hearted. To herself that draught betided woe. No, Signe, ne'er drink wine or mead From that goblet. [Pours its contents out at the window]. We must away with all speed.

[Tumult and calls without, at the back].

SIGNE. List, Gudmund! Voices and trampling feet!

GUDMUND. Knut Gesling's voice!

SIGNE. O save us, Lord!

GUDMUND. [Places himself in front of her.] Nay, nay, fear nothing, Signe sweet, I am here, and my good sword.

[MARGIT comes in in haste from the left].

MARGIT. [Listening to the noise.] What means this? Is my husband?

GUDMUND AND SIGNE. Margit!

MARGIT. [Catches sight of them.] Gudmund! And Signe! Are you here?

SIGNE. [Going towards her.] Margit, dear sister!

MARGIT. [Appalled, having seen the goblet which GUDMUND still holds in his hand.] The goblet! Who has drunk from it?

GUDMUND. [Confused.] Drunk? I and Signe, we meant

MARGIT. [Screams.] O God, have mercy! Help! Help! They will die!

GUDMUND. [Setting down the goblet.] Margit!

SIGNE. What ails you, sister?

MARGIT. [Towards the back.] Help, help! Will no one help?

[A HOUSE-CARL rushes in from the passage-way].

HOUSE-CARL. [Calls in a terrified voice.] Lady Margit! Your husband!

MARGIT. He, has he, too, drunk!

GUDMUND. [To himself.] Ah! now I understand

HOUSE-CARL. Knut Gesling has slain him.

SIGNE. Slain!

GUDMUND. [Drawing his sword.] Not yet, I hope. [Whispers to MARGIT.] Fear not. No one has drunk from your goblet.

MARGIT. Then thanks be to God, who has saved us all!

[She sinks down on a chair to the left. Gudmund hastens towards the door at the back].

ANOTHER HOUSE-CARL. [Enters, stopping him.] You come too late. Sir Bengt is dead.

GUDMUND. Too late, then, too late.

HOUSE-CARL. The guests and your men have prevailed against the murderous crew. Knut Gesling and his men are prisoners. Here they come.

[GUDMUND's men, and a number of GUESTS and HOUSE-CARLS,lead in KNUT GESLING, ERIK OF HEGGE, and several of KNUT's men, bound].

KNUT. [Who is pale, says in a low voice.] Man-slayer, Gudmund. What say you to that?

GUDMUND. Knut, Knut, what have you done?

ERIK. 'Twas a mischance, of that I can take my oath.

KNUT. He ran at me swinging his axe; I meant but to defend myself, and struck the death-blow unawares.

ERIK. Many here saw all that befell.

KNUT. Lady Margit, crave what fine you will. I am ready to pay it.

MARGIT. I crave naught. God will judge us all. Yet stay, one thing I require. Forgo your evil design upon my sister.

KNUT. Never again shall I essay to redeem my baleful pledge. From this day onward I am a better man. Yet would I fain escape dishonourable punishment for my deed. [To GUDMUND.] Should you be restored to favour and place again, say a good word for me to the King!

GUDMUND. I? Ere the sun sets, I must have left the country.

[Astonishment amongst the GUESTS. ERIK in whispers, explains the situation].

MARGIT. [To GUDMUND.] You go? And Signe with you?

SIGNE. [Beseechingly.] Margit!

MARGIT. Good fortune follow you both!

SIGNE. [Flinging her arms round MARGIT's neck.] Dear sister!

GUDMUND. Margit, I thank you. And now farewell. [Listening.] Hush! I hear the tramp of hoofs in the court-yard.

SIGNE. [Apprehensively.] Strangers have arrived.

[A HOUSE-CARL appears in the doorway at the back].

HOUSE-CARL. The King's men are without. They seek Gudmund Alfson.

SIGNE. Oh God!

MARGIT. [In great alarm.] The King's men!

GUDMUND. All is at an end, then. Oh Signe, to lose you now, could there be a harder fate?

KNUT. Nay, Gudmund; sell your life dearly, man! Unbind us; we are ready to fight for you, one and all.

ERIK. [Looks out.] 'Twould be in vain; they are too many for us.

SIGNE. Here they come. Oh Gudmund, Gudmund!

[The KING's MESSENGER enters from the back, with his escort].

MESSENGER. In the King's name I seek you, Gudmund Alfson, and bring you his behests.

GUDMUND. Be it so. Yet am I guiltless; I swear it by all that is holy!

MESSENGER. We know it.

GUDMUND. What say you?

[Agitation amongst those present].

MESSENGER. I am ordered to bid you as a guest to the King's house. His friendship is yours as it was before, and along with it he bestows on you rich fiefs.

GUDMUND. Signe!

SIGNE. Gudmund!

GUDMUND. But tell me?

MESSENGER. Your enemy, the Chancellor Audun Hugleikson, has fallen.

GUDMUND. The Chancellor!

GUESTS. [To each other, in half-whisper.] Fallen!

MESSENGER. Three days ago he was beheaded at Bergen. [Lowering his voice.] His offence was against Norway's Queen.

MARGIT. [Placing herself between GUDMUND and SIGNE.] Thus punishment treads on the heels of crime! Protecting angels, loving and bright, Have looked down in mercy on me to-night, And come to my rescue while yet it was time. Now know I that life's most precious treasure Is nor worldly wealth nor earthly pleasure, I have felt the remorse, the terror I know, Of those who wantonly peril their soul, To St. Sunniva's cloister forthwith I go. [Before GUDMUND and SIGNE can speak]. Nay: think not to move me or control. [Places SIGNE's hand in GUDMUND's]. Take her then Gudmund, and make her your bride. Your union is holy; God's on your side.

[Waving farewell, she goes towards the doorway on the left. GUDMUND and SIGNE follow her, she stops them with a motion of her hand, goes out, and shuts the door behind her. At this moment the sun rises and sheds its light in the hall].

GUDMUND. Signe, my wife! See, the morning glow! 'Tis the morning of our young love. Rejoice!

SIGNE. All my fairest of dreams and of memories I owe To the strains of thy harp and the sound of thy voice. My noble minstrel, to joy or sadness Tune thou that harp as seems thee best; There are chords, believe me, within my breast To answer to thine, or of woe or of gladness.

CHORUS OF MEN AND WOMEN. Over the earth keeps watch the eye of light, Guardeth lovingly the good man's ways, Sheddeth round him its consoling rays; Praise be to the Lord in heaven's height!

Henrik Ibsen - Lady Inger

Index Of Contents

CHARACTERS.

LADY INGER OTTISDAUGHTER ROMER, widow of High Steward Nils Gyldenlove.
ELINA GYLDENLOVE, her daughter.
NILS LYKKE, Danish knight and councilor.

OLAF SKAKTAVL, an outlawed Norwegian noble.
NILS STENSSON.
JENS BIELKE, Swedish commander.
BIORN, major-domo at Ostrat.
FINN, a servant.
EINAR HUK, bailiff at Ostrat.
Servants, peasants, and Swedish men-at-arms.

The action takes place at Ostrat Manor, on the Trondhiem Fiord, the year 1528.

ACT FIRST.

(A room at Ostrat. Through an open door in the back, the Banquet Hall is seen in faint moonlight, which shines fitfully through a deep bow-window in the opposite wall. To the right, an entrance- door; further forward, a curtained window. On the left, a door leading to the inner rooms; further forward a large, open fireplace, which casts a glow over the room. It is a stormy evening.)

(BIORN and FINN are sitting by the fireplace. The latter is occupied in polishing a helmet. Several pieces of armour lie near them, along with a sword and shield.)

FINN (after a pause). Who was Knut* Alfson?

* Pronounce *Knoot*.

BIORN. My Lady says he was the last of Norway's knighthood.

FINN. And the Danes killed him at Oslo-fiord?

BIORN. Ask any child of five, if you know not that.

FINN. So Knut Alfson was the last of our knighthood? And now he's dead and gone! (Holds up the helmet.) Well then, hang thou scoured and bright in the Banquet Hall; for what art thou now but an empty nut-shell? The kernel, the worms have eaten that many a winter agone. What say you, Biorn, may not one call Norway's land an empty nut- shell, even like the helmet here; bright without, worm-eaten within?

BIORN. Hold your peace, and mind your work! Is the helmet ready?

FINN. It shines like silver in the moonlight.

BIORN. Then put it by. See here; scrape the rust off the sword.

FINN (turning the sword over and examining it). Is it worth while?

BIORN. What mean you?

FINN. The edge is gone.

BIORN. What's that to you? Give it me. Here, take the shield.

FINN (as before). There's no grip to it!

BIORN (mutters). If once I got a grip on you

(FINN hums to himself for a while.)

BIORN. What now?

FINN. An empty helmet, an edgeless sword, a shield without a grip, there's the whole glory for you. I see not that any can blame Lady Inger for leaving such weapons to hang scoured and polished on the walls, instead of rusting them in Danish blood.

BIORN. Folly! Is there not peace in the land?

FINN. Peace? Ay, when the peasant has shot away his last arrow, and the wolf has reft the last lamb from the fold, then is there peace between them. But 'tis a strange friendship. Well well; let that pass. It is fitting, as I said, that the harness hang bright in the hall; for you know the old saw: "Call none a man but the knightly man." Now there is no knight left in our land; and where no man is, there must women order things; therefore

BIORN. Therefore, therefore I order you to hold your foul prate! (Rises.) It grows late. Go hang helm and harness in the hall again.

FINN (in a low voice). Nay, best let it be till tomorrow.

BIORN. What, do you fear the dark?

FINN. Not by day. And if so be I fear it at even, I am not the only one. Ah, you look; I tell you in the housefolk's room there is talk of many things. (Lower.) They say that night by night a tall figure, clad in black, walks the Banquet Hall.

BIORN. Old wives' tales!

FINN. Ah, but they all swear 'tis true.

BIORN. That I well believe.

FINN. The strangest of all is that Lady Inger thinks the same

BIORN (starting). Lady Inger? What does she think?

FINN. What Lady Inger thinks no one can tell. But sure it is that she has no rest in her. See you not how day by day she grows thinner and paler? (Looks keenly at him.) They say she never sleeps and that it is because of the dark figure

(While he is speaking, ELINA GYLDENLOVE has appeared in the half-open door on the left. She stops and listens, unobserved.)

BIORN. And you believe such follies?

FINN. Well, half and half. There be folk, too, that read things another way. But that is pure malice, for sure. Hearken, Biorn, know you the song that is going round the country?

BIORN. A song?

FINN. Ay, 'tis on all folks' lips. 'Tis a shameful scurril thing, for sure; yet it goes prettily. Just listen (sings in a low voice):

 Dame Inger sitteth in Ostrat fair,
 She wraps her in costly furs
 She decks her in velvet and ermine and vair,
 Red gold are the beads that she twines in her hair
 But small peace in that soul of hers.
 Dame Inger hath sold her to Denmark's lord.
 She bringeth her folk 'neath the stranger's yoke
 In guerdon whereof

(BIORN enraged, seizes him by the throat. ELINA GYLDENLOVE withdraws without having been seen.)

BIORN. And I will send you guerdonless to the foul fiend, if you prate of Lady Inger but one unseemly word more.

FINN (breaking from his grasp). Why did I make the song?

(The blast of a horn is heard from the right.)

BIORN. Hush, what is that?

FINN. A horn. So we are to have guests to-night.

BIORN (at the window). They are opening the gate. I hear the clatter of hoofs in the courtyard. It must be a knight.

FINN. A knight? A knight can it scarce be.

BIORN. Why not?

FINN. You said it yourself: the last of our knighthood is dead and gone. (Goes out to the right.)

BIORN. The accursed knave, with his prying and peering! What avails all my striving to hide and hush things? They whisper of her even now; ere long will all men be clamouring for

ELINA (comes in again through the door on the left; looks round her, and says with suppressed emotion). Are you alone, Biorn?

BIORN. Is it you, Mistress Elina?

ELINA. Come, Biorn, tell me one of your stories; I know you have more to tell than those that

BIORN. A story? Now, so late in the evening?

ELINA. If you count from the time when it grew dark at Ostrat, it is late indeed.

BIORN. What ails you? Has aught crossed you? You seem so restless.

ELINA. May be so.

BIORN. There is something the matter. I have hardly known you this half year past.

ELINA. Bethink you: this half year past my dearest sister Lucia has been sleeping in the vault below.

BIORN. That is not all, Mistress Elina, it is not that alone that makes you now thoughtful and white and silent, now restless and ill at ease, as you are to-night.

ELINA. You think so? And wherefore not? Was she not gentle and pure and fair as a summer night? Biorn, I tell you, Lucia was dear to me as my life. Have you forgotten how many a time, as children, we sat on your knee in the winter evenings? You sang songs to us, and told us tales

BIORN. Ay, then your were blithe and gay.

ELINA. Ah, then, Biorn! Then I lived a glorious life in the fable-land of my own imaginings. Can it be that the sea-strand was naked then as now? If it were so, I did not know it. It was there I loved to go, weaving all my fair romances; my heroes came from afar and sailed again across the sea; I lived in their midst, and set forth with them when they sailed away. (Sinks on a chair.) Now I feel so faint and weary; I can live no longer in my tales. They are only tales. (Rises hastily.) Biorn, do you know what has made me sick? A truth; a hateful, hateful truth, that gnaws me day and night.

BIORN. What mean you?

ELINA. Do you remember how sometimes you would give us good counsel and wise saws? Sister Lucia followed them; but I, ah, well-a-day!

BIORN (consoling her). Well, well!

ELINA. I know it, I was proud and self-centred! In all our games, I would still be the Queen, because I was the tallest, the fairest, the wisest! I know it!

BIORN. That is true.

ELINA. Once you took me by the hand and looked earnestly at me, and said: "Be not proud of your fairness, or your wisdom; but be proud as the mountain eagle as often as you think: I am Inger Gyldenlove's daughter!"

BIORN. And was it not matter enough for pride?

ELINA. You told me so often enough, Biorn! Oh, you told me so many tales in those days. (Presses his hand.) Thanks for them all! Now, tell me one more; it might make me light of heart again, as of old.

BIORN. You are a child no longer.

ELINA. Nay, indeed! But let me dream that I am. Come, tell on!

(Throws herself into a chair. BIORN sits in the chimney-corner.)

BIORN. Once upon a time there was a high-born knight

ELINA (who has been listening restlessly in the direction of the hall, seizes his arm and breaks out in a vehement whisper). Hush! No need to shout so loud; I can hear well!

BIORN (more softly). Once upon a time there was a high-born knight, of whom there went the strange report

(ELINA half-rises and listens in anxious suspense in the direction of the hall.)

BIORN. Mistress Elina, what ails you?

ELINA (sits down again). Me? Nothing. Go on.

BIORN. Well, as I was saying, when he did but look straight in a woman's eyes, never could she forget it after; her thoughts must follow him wherever he went, and she must waste away with sorrow.

ELINA. I have heard that tale And, moreover, 'tis no tale you are telling, for the knight you speak of is Nils Lykke, who sits even now in the Council of Denmark

BIORN. May be so.

ELINA. Well, let it pass, go on!

BIORN. Now it happened once

ELINA (rises suddenly). Hush; be still!

BIORN. What now? What is the matter?

ELINA. It is there! Yes, by the cross of Christ it is there!

BIORN (rises). What is there? Where?

ELINA. It is she, in the hall. (Goes hastily towards the hall.)

BIORN (following). How can you think? Mistress Elina, go to your chamber!

ELINA. Hush; stand still! Do not move; do not let her see you! Wait, the moon is coming out. Can you not see the black-robed figure?

BIORN. By all the holy!

ELINA. Do you see, she turns Knut Alfson's picture to the wall. Ha-ha; be sure it looks her too straight in the eyes!

BIORN. Mistress Elina, hear me!

ELINA (going back towards the fireplace). Now I know what I know!

BIORN (to himself). Then it is true!

ELINA. Who was it, Biorn? Who was it?

BIORN. You saw as plainly as I.

ELINA. Well? Whom did I see?

BIORN. You saw your mother.

ELINA (half to herself). Night after night I have heard her steps in there. I have heard her whispering and moaning like a soul in pain. And what says the song Ah, now I know! Now I know that

BIORN. Hush!

(LADY INGER GYLDENLOVE enters rapidly from the hall, without noticing the others; she goes to the window, draws the curtain, and gazes out as if watching for some one on the high road; after a while, she turns and goes slowly back into the hall.)

ELINA (softly, following her with her eyes). White as a corpse!

(An uproar of many voices is heard outside the door on the right.)

BIORN. What can this be?

ELINA. Go out and see what is amiss.

(EINAR HUK, the bailiff, appears in the ante-room, with a crowd of Retainers and Peasants.)

EINAR HUK (in the doorway). Straight in to her! And see you lose not heart!

BIORN. What do you seek?

EINAR HUK. Lady Inger herself.

BIORN. Lady Inger? So late?

EINAR HUK. Late, but time enough, I wot.

THE PEASANTS. Yes, yes; she must hear us now!

(The whole rabble crowds into the room. At the same moment, LADY INGER appears in the doorway of the hall. A sudden silence.)

LADY INGER. What would you with me?

EINAR HUK. We sought you, noble lady, to

LADY INGER. Well, speak out!

EINAR HUK. Why, we are not ashamed of our errand. In one word, we come to pray you for weapons and leave

LADY INGER. Weapons and leave? And for what?

EINAR HUK. There has come a rumour from Sweden that the people of the Dales have risen against King Gustav

LADY INGER. The people of the Dales?

EINAR HUK. Ay, so the tidings run, and they seem sure enough.

LADY INGER. Well, if it were so, what have you to do with the Dale-folk's rising?

THE PEASANTS. We will join them! We will help! We will free ourselves!

LADY INGER (aside). Can the time be come?

EINAR HUK. From all our borderlands the peasants are pouring across to the Dales. Even outlaws that have wandered for years in the mountains are venturing down to the homesteads again, and drawing men together, and whetting their rusty swords.

LADY INGER (after a pause). Tell me, men, have you thought well of this? Have you counted the cost, if King Gustav's men should win?

BIORN (softly and imploringly to LADY INGER). Count the cost to the Danes if King Gustav's men should lose.

LADY INGER (evasively). That reckoning is not for me to make. (Turns to the people). You know that King Gustav is sure of help from Denmark. King Frederick is his friend, and will never leave him in the lurch

EINAR HUK. But if the people were now to rise all over Norway's land? if we all rose as one man, nobles and peasants together? ay, Lady Inger Gyldenlove, the time we have waited for is surely come. We have but to rise now to drive the strangers from the land.

THE PEASANTS. Ay, out with the Danish sheriffs! Out with the foreign masters! Out with the Councillors' lackeys!

LADY INGER (aside). Ah, there is metal in them; and yet, yet!

BIORN (to himself). She is of two minds. (To ELINA.) What say you now, Mistress Elina, have you not sinned in misjudging your mother?

ELINA. Biorn, if my eyes have deceived me, I could tear them out of my head!

EINAR HUK. See you not, my noble lady, King Gustav must be dealt with first. Once his power is gone, the Danes cannot long hold this land

LADY INGER. And then?

EINAR HUK. Then we shall be free. We shall have no more foreign masters, and can choose ourselves a king, as the Swedes have done before us.

LADY INGER (with animation). A king for ourselves. Are you thinking of the Sture stock?

EINAR HUK. King Christiern and others after him have swept bare our ancient houses. The best of our nobles are outlaws on the hill- paths, if so be they still live; nevertheless, it might still be possible to find one or other shoot of the old stems

LADY INGER (hastily). Enough, Einar Huk, enough! (To herself.) Ah, my dearest hope! (Turns to the Peasants and Retainers.) I have warned you, now, as well as I can. I have told you how great is the risk you run. But if you are fixed in your purpose, it were folly of me to forbid what I have no power to prevent.

EINAR HUK. Then we have your leave to?

LADY INGER. You have your own firm will; take counsel with that. If it be as you say, that you are daily harassed and oppressed I know but little of these matters, and would not know more. What can I, a lonely woman? Even if you were to plunder the Banquet Hall and there's many a good weapon on the walls, you are the masters at Ostrat to-night. You must do as seems good to you. Good-night!

(Loud cries of joy from the multitude. Candles are lighted; the retainers bring weapons of different kinds from the hall.)

BIORN (seizes LADY INGER'S hand as she is going). Thanks, my noble and high-souled mistress! I, that have known you from childhood up, I have never doubted you.

LADY INGER. Hush, Biorn. It is a dangerous game that I have ventured this night. The others stake only their lives; but I, trust me, a thousandfold more!

BIORN. How mean you? Do you fear for your power and your favour with?

LADY INGER. My power? O God in Heaven!

A RETAINER (comes from the hall with a large sword). See, here's a real good wolf's-tooth to flay the blood-suckers' lackeys with!

EINAR HUK. 'Tis too good for such as you. Look, here is the shaft of Sten Sture's lance; hang the breastplate upon it, and we shall have the noblest standard heart can desire.

FINN (comes from the door on the left, with a letter in his hand, and goes towards LADY INGER). I have sought you through all the house.

LADY INGER. What do you want?

FINN (hands her the letter). A messenger is come from Trondhiem with a letter for you.

LADY INGER. Let me see! (opening the letter). From Trondhiem? What can it be? (Runs through the letter.) Help, Christ! From him! and here in Norway

(Reads on with strong emotion, while the men go on bringing out arms from the hall.)

LADY INGER (to herself). He is coming here. He is coming to- night! Ay, then 'tis with our wits we must fight, not with the sword.

EINAR HUK. Enough, enough, good fellows; we are well armed now, and can set forth on our way.

LADY INGER (with a sudden change of tone). No man shall leave my house to-night!

EINAR HUK. But the wind is fair, noble lady; we can sail up the fiord, and

LADY INGER. It shall be as I have said.

EINAR HUK. Are we to wait till to-morrow, then?

LADY INGER. Till to-morrow, and longer still. No armed man shall go forth from Ostrat yet awhile.

(Signs of displeasure from the crowd.)

SOME OF THE PEASANTS. We will go all the same, Lady Inger!

THE CRY SPREADS. Yes, yes; we will go!

LADY INGER (advancing a step towards them). Who dares to move? (A silence. After a moment's pause, she adds:) I have thought for you. What do you common folk know of the country's needs? How dare you judge of such things? You must even bear your oppressions and burdens yet awhile. Why murmur at that, when you see that we, your leaders, are as ill bested as you? Take all the weapons back to the hall. You shall know my further will hereafter. Go!

(The Retainers take back the arms, and the whole crowd then withdraws by the door on the right.)

ELINA (softly to BIORN). Do you still think I have sinned in misjudging, the Lady of Ostrat?

LADY INGER (beckons to BIORN, and says). Have a guest chamber ready.

BIORN. It is well, Lady Inger!

LADY INGER. And let the gate stand open to all that knock.

BIORN. But?

LADY INGER. The gate open!

BIORN. The gate open. (Goes out to the right.)

LADY INGER (to ELINA, who has already reached the door on the left). Stay here! Elina, my child, I have something to say to you alone.

ELINA. I hear you.

LADY INGER. Elina you think evil of your mother.

ELINA. I think, to my sorrow, what your deeds have forced me to think.

LADY INGER. You answer out of the bitterness of your heart.

ELINA. Who has filled my heart with bitterness? From my childhood I have been wont to look up to you as a great and high-souled woman. It was in your likeness I pictured the women we read of in the chronicles and the Book of Heroes. I thought the Lord God himself had set his seal on your brow, and marked you out as the leader of the helpless and the oppressed. Knights and nobles sang your praise in the feast-hall, and the peasants, far and near, called you the country's pillar and its hope. All thought that through you the good times were to come again! All thought that through you a new day was to dawn over the land! The night is still here; and I no longer know if I dare look for any morning to come through you.

LADY INGER. It is easy to see whence you have learnt such venomous words. You have let yourself give ear to what the thoughtless rabble mutters and murmurs about things it can little judge of.

ELINA. "Truth is in the people's mouth," was your word when they praised you in speech and song.

LADY INGER. May be so. But if indeed I had chosen to sit here idle, though it was my part to act, do you not think that such a choice were burden enough for me, without your adding to its weight?

ELINA. The weight I add to your burden bears on me as heavily as on you. Lightly and freely I drew the breath of life, so long as I had you to believe in. For my pride is my life; and well had it become me, if you had remained what once you were.

LADY INGER. And what proves to you I have not? Elina, how can you know so surely that you are not doing your mother wrong?

ELINA (vehemently). Oh, that I were!

LADY INGER. Peace! You have no right to call your mother to account With a single word I could ; but it would be an ill word for you to hear; you must await what time shall bring; may be that

ELINA (turns to go). Sleep well, my mother!

LADY INGER (hesitates). Nay, stay with me; I have still somewhat. Come nearer; you must hear me, Elina!

(Sits down by the table in front of the window.)

ELINA. I am listening.

LADY INGER. For as silent as you are, I know well that you often long to be gone from here. Ostrat is too lonely and lifeless for you.

ELINA. Do you wonder at that, my mother?

LADY INGER. It rests with you whether all this shall henceforth be changed.

ELINA. How so?

LADY INGER. Listen. I look for a guest to-night.

ELINA (comes nearer). A guest?

LADY INGER. A stranger, who must remain a stranger to all. None must know whence he comes or whither he goes.

ELINA (throws herself, with a cry of joy, at her mother's feet and seizes her hands). My mother! My mother! Forgive me, if you can, all the wrong I have done you!

LADY INGER. What do you mean? Elina, I do not understand you.

ELINA. Then they were all deceived! You are still true at heart!

LADY INGER. Rise, rise and tell me

ELINA. Do you think I do not know who the stranger is?

LADY INGER. You know? And yet?

ELINA. Do you think the gates of Ostrat shut so close that never a whisper of evil tidings can slip through? Do you think I do not know that the heir of many a noble line wanders outlawed, without rest or shelter, while Danish masters lord it in the home of their fathers?

LADY INGER. And what then?

ELINA. I know well that many a high-born knight is hunted through the woods like a hungry wolf. No hearth has he to rest by, no bread to eat

LADY INGER (coldly). Enough! Now I understand you.

ELINA (continuing). And that is why the gates of Ostrat must stand open by night! That is why he must remain a stranger to all, this guest of whom none must know whence he comes or whither he goes! You are setting at naught the harsh decree that forbids you to harbour or succor the exiles

LADY INGER. Enough, I say! (After a short silence, adds with an effort:) You mistake, Elina, it is no outlaw that I look for

ELINA (rises). Then I have understood you ill indeed.

LADY INGER. Listen to me, my child; but think as you listen; if indeed you can tame that wild spirit of yours.

ELINA. I am tame, till you have spoken.

LADY INGER. Then hear what I have to say, I have sought, so far as lay in my power, to keep you in ignorance of all our griefs and miseries. What could it avail to fill your young heart with wrath and care? It is not weeping and wailing of women that can free us from our evil lot; we need the courage and strength of men.

ELINA. Who has told you that, when courage and strength are indeed needed, I shall be found wanting?

LADY INGER. Hush, child; I might take you at your word.

ELINA. How mean you, my mother?

LADY INGER. I might call on you for both; I might; but let me say my say out first. Know then that the time seems now to be drawing nigh, towards which the Danish Council have been working for many a year, the time for them to strike a final blow at our rights and our freedom. Therefore must we now

ELINA (eagerly). Throw off the yoke, my mother?

LADY INGER. No; we must gain breathing-time. The Council is now sitting in Copenhagen, considering how best to aim the blow. Most of them are said to hold that there can be no end to dissensions till Norway and Denmark are one; for if we should still have our rights as a free land when the time comes to choose the next king, it is most like that the feud will break out openly. Now the Danish Councillors would hinder this

ELINA. Ay, they would hinder it! But are we to endure such things? Are we to look on quietly while?

LADY INGER. No, we will not endure it. But to take up arms, to begin open warfare, what would come of that, so long as we are not united? And were we ever less united in this land than we are even now? No, if aught is to be done, it must be done secretly and in silence. Even as I said, we must have time to draw breath. In the South, a good part of the nobles are for the Dane; but here in the North they are still in doubt. Therefore King Frederick has sent hither one of his most trusted councillors, to assure himself with his own eyes how we stand affected.

ELINA (anxiously). Well, and then?

LADY INGER. He is the guest I look for to-night.

ELINA. He comes here? And to-night?

LADY INGER. He reached Trondhiem yesterday by a trading ship. Word has just been brought that he is coming to visit me; he may be here within the hour.

ELINA. Have you not thought, my mother, how it will endanger your fame thus to receive the Danish envoy? Do not the people already regard you with distrustful eyes? How can you hope that, when the time comes, they will let you rule and guide them, if it be known

LADY INGER. Fear not. All this I have fully weighed; but there is no danger. His errand in Norway is a secret; he has come unknown to Trondhiem, and unknown shall he be our guest at Ostrat.

ELINA. And the name of this Danish lord?

LADY INGER. It sounds well, Elina; Denmark has scarce a nobler name.

ELINA. But what do you propose then? I cannot yet grasp your meaning.

LADY INGER. You will soon understand. Since we cannot trample on the serpent, we must bind him.

ELINA. Take heed that he burst not your bonds.

LADY INGER. It rests with you to tighten them as you will.

ELINA. With me?

LADY INGER. I have long seen that Ostrat is as a cage to you. The young falcon chafes behind the iron bars.

ELINA. My wings are clipped. Even if you set me free it would avail me little.

LADY INGER. Your wings are not clipped, except by your own will.

ELINA. Will? My will is in your hands. Be what you once were, and I too

LADY INGER. Enough, enough. Hear what remains It would scarce break your heart to leave Ostrat?

ELINA. Maybe not, my mother!

LADY INGER. You told me once, that you lived your happiest life in tales and histories. What if that life were to be yours once more?

ELINA. What mean you?

LADY INGER. Elina, if a mighty noble were now to come and lead you to his castle, where you should find damsels and pages, silken robes and lofty halls awaiting you?

ELINA. A noble, you say?

LADY INGER. A noble.

ELINA (more softly). And the Danish envoy comes here to-night?

LADY INGER. To-night.

ELINA. If so be, then I fear to read the meaning of your words.

LADY INGER. There is nought to fear if you misread them not. Be sure it is far from my thought to put force upon you. You shall choose for yourself in this matter, and follow your own counsel.

ELINA (comes a step nearer). Have you heard the story of the mother that drove across the hills by night with her little children by her in the sledge? The wolves were on her track; it was life or death with her; and one by one she cast out her little ones, to gain time and save herself.

LADY INGER. Nursery tales! A mother would tear the heart from her breast, before she would cast her child to the wolves!

ELINA. Were I not my mother's daughter, I would say you were right. But you are like that mother; one by one you have cast out your daughters to the wolves. The eldest went first. Five years ago Merete went forth from Ostrat; now she dwells in Bergen and is Vinzents Lunge's wife. But think you she is happy as the Danish noble's lady? Vinzents Lunge is mighty, well-nigh as a king; Merete has damsels and pages, silken robes and lofty halls; but the day has no sunshine for her, and the night no rest; for she has never loved him. He came hither and he wooed her; for she was the greatest heiress in Norway, and he needed to gain a footing in the land. I know it; I know it well! Merete bowed to your will; she went with the stranger lord. But what has it cost her? More tears than a mother should wish to answer for at the day of reckoning.

LADY INGER. I know my reckoning, and I fear it not.

ELINA. Your reckoning ends not here. Where is Lucia, your second child?

LADY INGER. Ask God, who took her.

ELINA. It is you I ask; it is you that must answer for her young life. She was glad as a bird in spring when she sailed from Ostrat to be Merete's guest. A year passed, and she stood in this room once more; but her cheeks were white, and death had gnawed deep into her breast. Ah, you wonder at me, my mother! You thought that the ugly secret was buried with her; but she told me all. A courtly knight had won her heart. He would have wedded her. You knew that her honour was at stake; yet your will never bent and your child had to die. You see, I know all!

LADY INGER. All? Then she told you his name?

ELINA. His name? No; his name she did not tell me. His name was a torturing horror to her; she never uttered it.

LADY INGER (relieved, to herself). Ah, then you do not know all Elina, it is true that the whole of this matter was well known to me. But there is one thing about it you seem not to have noted. The lord whom Lucia met in Bergen was a Dane

ELINA. That too I know.

LADY INGER. And his love was a lie. With guile and soft speeches he had ensnared her.

ELINA. I know it; but nevertheless she loved him; and had you had a mother's heart, your daughter's honour had been more to you than all.

LADY INGER. Not more than her happiness. Do you think that, with Merete's lot before my eyes, I could sacrifice my second child to a man that loved her not?

ELINA. Cunning words may befool many, but they befool not me Think not I know nothing of all that is passing in our land. I understand your counsels but too well. I know well that our Danish lords have no true friend in you. It may be that you hate them; but your fear them too. When you gave Merete to Vinzents Lunge the Danes held the mastery on all sides throughout our land. Three years later, when you forbade Lucia to wed the man she had given her life to, though he had deceived her, things were far different then. The King's Danish governors had shamefully misused the common people, and you thought it not wise to link yourself still more closely to the foreign tyrants. And what have you done to avenge her that had to die so young? You have done nothing. Well then, I will act in your stead; I will avenge all the shame they have brought upon our people and our house.

LADY INGER. You? What will you do?

ELINA. I shall go my way, even as you go yours. What I shall do I myself know not; but I feel within me the strength to dare all for our righteous cause.

LADY INGER. Then you have a hard fight before you. I once promised as you do now and my hair has grown grey under the burden of that promise.

ELINA. Good-night! Your guest will soon be here, and at that meeting I should be out of place. It may be there is yet time for you ; well, God strengthen you and guide your way! Forget not that the eyes of many thousands are fixed upon you. Think on Merete, weeping late and early over her wasted life. Think on Lucia, sleeping in her black coffin. And one thing more. Forget not that in the game you play this night, your stake is your last child.

(Goes out to the left.)

LADY INGER (looks after her awhile). My last child? You know not how true was that word But the stake is not my child only. God help me, I am playing to-night for the whole of Norway's land. Ah, is not that some one riding through the gateway? (Listens at the window.) No; not yet. Only the wind; it blows cold as the grave Has God a right to do this? To make me a woman and then to lay a man's duty upon my shoulders? For I have the welfare of the country in my hands. It is in my power to make them rise as one man. They look to me for the signal; and if I give it not now it may never be given. To delay? To sacrifice the many for the sake of one? Were it not better if I could ? No, no, no, I will not! I cannot! (Steals a glance towards the Banquet Hall, but turns away again as if in dread, and whispers:) I can see them in there now. Pale spectres, dead ancestors, fallen kinsfolk. Ah, those eyes that pierce me from every corner! (Makes a backward gesture with her hand, and cries:) Sten Sture! Knut Alfson! Olaf Skaktavl! Back, back! I cannot do this!

(A STRANGER, strongly built, and with grizzled hair and beard, has entered from the Banquet Hall. He is dressed in a torn lambskin tunic; his weapons are rusty.)

THE STRANGER (stops in the doorway, and says in a low voice). Hail to you, Inger Gyldenlove!

LADY INGER (turns with a scream). Ah, Christ in heaven save me!

(Falls back into a chair. The STRANGER stands gazing at her, motionless, leaning on his sword.)

Act Second

(The room at Ostrat, as in the first Act.)

(LADY INGER GYLDENLOVE is seated at the table on the right, by the window. OLAF SKAKTAVL is standing a little way from her. Their faces show that they have been engaged in an animated discussion.)

OLAF SKAKTAVL. For the last time, Inger Gyldenlove, you are not to be moved from your purpose?

LADY INGER. I can do nought else. And my counsel to you is: do as I do. If it be heaven's will that Norway perish utterly, perish it must, for all we may do to save it.

OLAF SKAKTAVL. And think you I can content myself with words like these? Shall I sit and look quietly on, now that the hour is come? Do you forget the reckoning I have to pay? They have robbed me of my lands, and parcelled them out among themselves. My son, my only child, the last of my race, they have slaughtered like a dog. Myself they have outlawed and forced to lurk by forest and fell these twenty years. Once and again have folk whispered of my death; but this I believe, that they shall not lay me beneath the earth before I have seen my vengeance.

LADY INGER. Then is there a long life before you. What would you do?

OLAF SKAKTAVL. Do? How should I know what I will do? It has never been my part to plot and plan. That is where you must help me. You have the wit for that. I have but my sword and my two arms.

LADY INGER. Your sword is rusted, Olaf Skaktavl! All the swords in Norway are rusted.

OLAF SKAKTAVL. That is doubtless why some folk fight only with their tongues. Inger Gyldenlove, great is the change in you. Time was when the heart of a man beat in your breast.

LADY INGER. Put me not in mind of what was.

OLAF SKAKTAVL. 'Tis for that alone I am here. You shall hear me, even if

LADY INGER. Be it so then; but be brief; for, I must say it, this is no place of safety for you.

OLAF SKAKTAVL. Ostrat is no place of safety for an outlaw? That I have long known. But you forget that an outlaw is unsafe wheresoever he may wander.

LADY INGER. Speak then; I will not hinder you.

OLAF SKAKTAVL. It is nigh on thirty years now since first I saw you. It was at Akershus in the house of Knut Alfson and his wife. You were scarce more than a child then; yet you were bold as the soaring falcon, and wild and headstrong too at times. Many were the wooers around you. I too held you dear, dear as no woman before or since. But you cared for nothing, thought of nothing, save your country's evil case and its great need.

LADY INGER. I counted but fifteen summers then, remember that. And was it not as though a frenzy had seized us all in those days?

OLAF SKAKTAVL. Call it what you will; but one thing I know, even the old and sober men among us doubted not that it was written in the counsels of the Lord that you were she who should break our thraldom and win us all our rights again. And more: you yourself then thought as we did.

LADY INGER. It was a sinful thought, Olaf Skaktavl. It was my proud heart, and not the Lord's call, that spoke in me.

OLAF SKAKTAVL. You could have been the chosen one had you but willed it. You came of the noblest blood in Norway; power and riches were at your feet; and you had an ear for the cries of anguish then! Do you remember that afternoon when Henrik Krummedike and the Danish fleet anchored off Akershus? The captains of the fleet offered terms of settlement, and, trusting to the safe-conduct, Knut Alfson rowed on board. Three hours later, we bore him through the castle gate

LADY INGER. A corpse; a corpse!

OLAF SKAKTAVL. The best heart in Norway burst, when Krummedike's hirelings struck him down. Methinks I still can see the long procession that passed into the banquet-hall, heavily, two by two. There he lay on his bier, white as a spring cloud, with the axe- cleft in his brow. I may safely say that the boldest men in Norway were gathered there that night. Lady Margrete stood by her dead husband's head, and we swore as one man to venture lands and life to avenge this last misdeed and all that had gone before. Inger Gyldenlove, who was it that burst through the circle of men? A maiden, then almost a child, with fire in her eyes and her voice half choked with tears. What was it she swore? Shall I repeat your words?

LADY INGER. And how did the others keep their promise? I speak not of you, Olaf Skaktavl, but of your friends, all our Norwegian nobles? Not one of them, in all these years, has had the courage to be a man; and yet they lay it to my charge that I am a woman.

OLAF SKAKTAVL. I know what you would say. Why have they bent to the yoke, and not defied the tyrants to the last? 'Tis but too true; there is base metal enough in our noble houses nowadays. But had they held together, who knows what might have been? And you could have held them together, for before you all had bowed.

LADY INGER. My answer were easy enough, but it would scarce content you. So let us leave speaking of what cannot be changed. Tell me rather what has brought you to Ostrat. Do you need harbour? Well, I will try to hide you. If you would have aught else, speak out; you shall find me ready

OLAF SKAKTAVL. For twenty years have I been homeless. In the mountains of Jaemteland my hair has grown grey. My dwelling has been with wolves and bears. You see, Lady Inger, I need you not; but both nobles and people stand in sore need of you.

LADY INGER. The old burden.

OLAF SKAKTAVL. Ay, it sounds but ill in your ears, I know; yet hear it you must for all that. In brief, then: I come from Sweden: troubles are at hand: the Dales are ready to rise.

LADY INGER. I know it.

OLAF SKAKTAVL. Peter Kanzler is with us, secretly, you understand.

LADY INGER (starting). Peter Kanzler?

OLAF SKAKTAVL. It is he that has sent me to Ostrat.

LADY INGER (rises). Peter Kanzler, say you?

OLAF SKAKTAVL. He himself; but mayhap you no longer know him?

LADY INGER (half to herself). Only too well! But tell me, I pray you, what message do you bring?

OLAF SKAKTAVL. When the rumour of the rising reached the border mountains, where I then was, I set off at once into Sweden. 'Twas not hard to guess that Peter Kanzler had a finger in the game. I sought him out and offered to stand by him; he knew me of old, as you know, and knew that he could trust me; so he has sent me hither.

LADY INGER (impatiently). Yes yes, he sent you hither to?

OLAF SKAKTAVL (with secrecy). Lady Inger, a stranger comes to Ostrat to-night.

LADY INGER (surprised). What? Know you that?

OLAF SKAKTAVL. Assuredly I know it. I know all. 'Twas to meet him that Peter Kanzler sent me hither.

LADY INGER. To meet him? Impossible, Olaf Skaktavl, impossible!

OLAF SKAKTAVL. 'Tis as I tell you. If he be not already come, he will soon

LADY INGER. Yes, I know; but

OLAF SKAKTAVL. Then you know of his coming?

LADY INGER. Ay, surely. He sent me a message. That was why they opened to you as soon as you knocked.

OLAF SKAKTAVL (listens). Hush! some one is riding along the road. (Goes to the window.) They are opening the gate.

LADY INGER (looks out). It is a knight and his attendant. They are dismounting in the courtyard.

OLAF SKAKTAVL. Then it is he. His name?

LADY INGER. You know not his name?

OLAF SKAKTAVL. Peter Kanzler refused to tell it me. He would only say that I should find him at Ostrat the third evening after Martinmas

LADY INGER. Ay; even to-night.

OLAF SKAKTAVL. He was to bring letters with him, and from them, and from you, I was to learn who he is.

LADY INGER. Then let me lead you to your chamber. You have need of rest and refreshment. You shall soon have speech with the stranger.

OLAF SKAKTAVL. Well, be it as you will. (Both go out to the left.)

(After a short pause, FINN enters cautiously through the door on the right, looks round the room, and peeps into the Banquet Hall; he then goes back to the door, and makes a sign to some one outside. Immediately after, enter COUNCILLOR NILS LYKKE and the Swedish Commander, JENS BIELKE.)

NILS LYKKE (softly). No one?

FINN (in the same tone). No one, master!

NILS LYKKE. And we may depend on you in all things?

FINN. The commandant in Trondhiem has ever given me a name for trustiness.

NILS LYKKE. It is well; he has said as much to me. First of all, then, has there come any stranger to Ostrat to-night, before us?

FINN. Ay; a stranger came an hour since.

NILS LYKKE (softly, to JENS BIELKE). He is here. (Turns again to FINN.) Would you know him again? Have you seen him?

FINN. Nay, none have seen him, that I know, but the gatekeeper. He was brought at once to Lady Inger, and she

NILS LYKKE. Well? What of her? He is not gone again already?

FINN. No; but it seems she keeps him hidden in one of her own rooms; for

NILS LYKKE. It is well.

JENS BIELKE (whispers). Then the first thing is to put a guard on the gate; then we are sure of him.

NILS LYKKE (with a smile). Hm! (To FINN.) Tell me, is there any way of leaving the castle but by the gate? Gape not at me so! I mean, can one escape from Ostrat unseen, while the castle gate is shut?

FINN. Nay, that I know not. 'Tis true they talk of secret ways in the vaults beneath; but no one knows them save Lady Inger and mayhap Mistress Elina.

JENS BIELKE. The devil!

NILS LYKKE. It is well. You may go.

FINN. And should you need me in aught again, you have but to open the second door on the right in the Banquet Hall, and I shall presently be at hand.

NILS LYKKE. Good. (Points to the entrance-door. FINN goes out.)

JENS BIELKE. Now, by my soul, dear friend and brother, this campaign is like to end but scurvily for both of us.

NILS LYKKE (with a smile). Oh, not for me, I hope.

JENS BIELKE. Not? First of all, there is small honour to be got in hunting an overgrown whelp like this Nils Sture. Are we to think him mad or in his sober senses after the pranks he has played? First he breeds bad blood among the peasants; promises them help and all their hearts can desire; and then, when it comes to the pinch, off he runs to hide behind a petticoat! Moreover, to tell the truth, I repent that I followed your counsel and went not my own way.

NILS LYKKE (aside). Your repentance comes somewhat late, my brother.

JENS BIELKE. Look you, I have never loved digging at a badger's earth. I look for quite other sport. Here have I ridden all the way from the Jaemteland with my horsemen, and have got me a warrant from the Trondhiem commandant to search for the rebel wheresoever I please. All his tracks point towards Ostrat

NILS LYKKE. He is here! He is here, I tell you!

JENS BIELKE. If that were so, should we not have found the gate barred and well guarded? Would that we had; then could I have found use for my men-at-arms

NILS LYKKE. But instead, the gate is opened for us in hospitality. Mark now, if Inger Gyldenlove's fame belie her not, I warrant she will not let her guests lack for either meat or drink.

JENS BIELKE. Ay, to turn us aside from our errand! And what wild whim was that of yours to persuade me to leave my horsemen a good mile from the castle? Had we come in force

NILS LYKKE. She had made us none the less welcome for that. But mark well that then our coming had made a stir. The peasants round about had held it for an outrage against Lady Inger; she had risen high in their favour once more and with that, look you, we were ill served.

JENS BIELKE. May be so. But what am I to do now? Count Sture is in Ostrat, you say. Ay, but how does that profit me? Be sure Lady Inger Gyldenlove has as many hiding-places as the fox, and more than one outlet to them. We two can go snuffing about here alone as long as we please. I would the devil had the whole affair!

NILS LYKKE. Well, then, my friend, if you like not the turn your errand has taken, you have but to leave the field to me.

JENS BIELKE. To you? What will you do?

NILS LYKKE. Caution and cunning may here do more than could be achieved by force of arms. And to say truth, Captain Jens Bielke, something of the sort has been in my mind ever since we met in Trondhiem yesterday.

JENS BIELKE. Was that why you persuaded me to leave the men at arms?

NILS LYKKE. Both your purpose at Ostrat and mine could best be served without them; and so

JENS BIELKE. The foul fiend seize you, I had almost said! And me to boot! Might I not have known that there is guile in all your dealings?

NILS LYKKE. Be sure I shall need all my guile here, if I am to face my foe with even weapons. And let me tell you 'tis of the utmost moment to me that I acquit me of my mission secretly and well. You must know that when I set forth I was scarce in favour with my lord the King. He held me in suspicion; though I dare swear I have served him as well as any man could, in more than one ticklish charge.

JENS BIELKE. That you may safely boast. God and all men know you for the craftiest devil in all the three kingdoms.

NILS LYKKE. You flatter! But after all, 'tis not much to say. Now this present errand I hold for the crowning proof of my policy; for here I have to outwit a woman

JENS BIELKE. Ha-ha-ha! In that art you have long since given crowning proofs of your skill, dear brother. Think you we in Sweden know not the song

Fair maidens a-many they sigh and they pine; "Ah God, that Nils Lykke were mine, mine, mine!"

NILS LYKKE. Alas, it is women of twenty and thereabouts that ditty speaks of. Lady Inger Gyldenlove is nigh on fifty, and wily to boot beyond all women. It will be no light matter to overcome her. But it must be done, at any cost. If I succeed in winning certain advantages over her that the King has long desired, I can reckon on the embassy to France next spring. You know that I spent three years at the University in Paris? My whole soul is bent on coming thither again, most of all if I can appear in lofty place, a king's ambassador. Well, then, is it agreed? do you leave Lady Inger to me? Remember, when you were last at Court in Copenhagen, I made way for you with more than one fair lady

JENS BIELKE. Nay, truly now, that generosity cost you little; one and all of them were at your beck and call. But let that pass; now that I have begun amiss in this matter, I had as lief that you should take it on your shoulders. One thing, though, you must promise, if the young Count Sture be in Ostrat, you will deliver him into my hands, dead or alive!

NILS LYKKE. You shall have him all alive. I, at any rate, mean not to kill him. But now you must ride back and join your people. Keep guard on the road. Should I mark aught that mislikes me, you shall know it forthwith.

JENS BIELKE. Good, good. But how am I to get out?

NILS LYKKE. The fellow that brought us in will show the way. But go quietly.

JENS BIELKE. Of course, of course. Well, good fortune to you!

NILS LYKKE. Fortune has never failed me in a war with women. Haste you now!

(JENS BIELKE goes out to the right.)

NILS LYKKE (stands still for a while; then walks about the room, looking round him; at last he says softly). So I am at Ostrat at last, the ancient seat that a child, two years ago, told me so much of. Lucia. Ay, two years ago she was still a child. And now, now she is dead. (Hums with a half-smile.) "Blossoms plucked are blossoms withered " (Looks round him again.)

Ostrat. 'Tis as though I had seen it all before; as though I were at home here. In there is the Banquet Hall. And underneath is, the grave-vault. It must be there that Lucia lies.

(In a lower voice, half seriously, half with forced gaiety.)

Were I timorous, I might well find myself fancying that when I set foot within Ostrat gate she turned about in her coffin; as I walked across the courtyard she lifted the lid; and when I named her name but now, 'twas as though a voice summoned her forth from the grave-vault. Maybe she is even now groping her way up the stairs. The face-cloth blinds her, but she gropes on and on in spite of it. Now she has reached the Banquet Hall; she stands watching me from behind the door!

(Turns his head backwards over one shoulder, nods, and says aloud:)

Come nearer, Lucia! Talk to me a little! Your mother keeps me waiting. 'Tis tedious waiting and you have helped me to while away many a tedious hour

(Passes his hand over his forehead, and takes one or two turns up and down.)

Ah, there! Right, right; there is the the deep curtained window. It is there that Inger Gyldenlove is wont to stand gazing out over the road, as though looking for one that never comes. In there (looks towards the door on the left) somewhere in there is Sister Elina's chamber. Elina? Ay, Elina is her name. Can it be that she is so rare a being, so wise and so brave as Lucia drew her? Fair, too, they say. But for a wedded wife? I should not have written so plainly

(Lost in thought, he is on the point of sitting down by the table, but stands up again.)

How will Lady Inger receive me? She will scarce burn the castle over our heads, or slip me through a trap-door. A stab from behind? No, not that way either

(Listens towards the hall.)

Aha!

(LADY INGER GYLDENLOVE enters from the hall.)

LADY INGER (coldly). My greeting to you, Sir Councillor

NILS LYKKE (bows deeply). Ah, the Lady of Ostrat!

LADY INGER. And thanks that you have forewarned me of your visit.

NILS LYKKE. I could do no less. I had reason to think that my coming might surprise you

LADY INGER. In truth, Sir Councillor, you thought right there. Nils Lykke was certainly the last guest I looked to see at Ostrat.

NILS LYKKE. And still less, mayhap, did you think to see him come as a friend?

LADY INGER. As a friend? You add insult to all the shame and sorrow you have heaped upon my house? After bringing my child to the grave, you still dare

NILS LYKKE. With your leave, Lady Inger Gyldenlove, on that matter we should scarce agree; for you count as nothing what I lost by that same unhappy chance. I purposed nought but in honour. I was tired of my unbridled life; my thirtieth year was already past; I longed to mate me with a good and gentle wife. Add to all this the hope of becoming your son-in-law

LADY INGER. Beware, Sir Councillor! I have done all in my power to hide my child's unhappy fate. But because it is out of sight, think not it is out of mind. It may yet happen

NILS LYKKE. You threaten me, Lady Inger? I have offered you my hand in amity; you refuse to take it. Henceforth, then, it is to be open war between us?

LADY INGER. Was there ever aught else?

NILS LYKKE. Not on your side, mayhap. I have never been your enemy, though as a subject of the King of Denmark I lacked not good cause.

LADY INGER. I understand you. I have not been pliant enough. It has not proved so easy as some of you hoped to lure me over into your camp. Yet methinks you have nought to complain of. My daughter Merete's husband is your countryman, further I cannot go. My position is no easy one, Nils Lykke!

NILS LYKKE. That I can well believe. Both nobles and people here in Norway think they have an ancient claim on you, a claim, 'tis said, you have but half fulfilled.

LADY INGER. Your pardon, Sir Councillor, I account for my doings to none but God and myself. If it please you, then, let me understand what brings you hither.

NILS LYKKE. Gladly, Lady Inger! The purport of my mission to this country can scarce be unknown to you?

LADY INGER. I know the mission that report assigns you. Our King would fain know how the Norwegian nobles stand affected towards him.

NILS LYKKE. Assuredly.

LADY INGER. Then that is why you visit Ostrat?

NILS LYKKE. In part. But it is far from my purpose to demand any profession of loyalty from you

LADY INGER. What then?

NILS LYKKE. Hearken to me, Lady Inger! You said yourself but now that your position is no easy one. You stand half way between two hostile camps, neither of which dares trust you fully. Your own interest must needs bind you to us. On the other hand, you are bound to the disaffected by the bond of nationality, and who knows? mayhap by some secret tie as well.

LADY INGER (aside). A secret tie! Christ, does he?

NILS LYKKE (notices her emotion, but makes no sign and continues without change of manner). You cannot but see that such a position must ere long become impossible. Suppose, now, it lay in my power to free you from these embarrassments which

LADY INGER. In your power, you say?

NILS LYKKE. First of all, Lady Inger, I would beg you to lay no stress on any careless words I may have used concerning that which lies between us two. Think not that I have forgotten for a moment the wrong I have done you. Suppose, now, I had long purposed to make atonement, as far as might be, where I had sinned. Suppose that were my reason for undertaking this mission.

LADY INGER. Speak your meaning more clearly, Sir Councillor; I cannot follow you.

NILS LYKKE. I can scarce be mistaken in thinking that you, as well as I, know of the threatened troubles in Sweden. You know, or at least you can guess, that this rising is of far wider aim than is commonly supposed, and you understand therefore that our King cannot look on quietly and let things take their course. Am I not right?

LADY INGER. Go on.

NILS LYKKE (searchingly, after a short pause). There is one possible chance that might endanger Gustav Vasa's throne

LADY INGER (aside). Whither is he tending?

NILS LYKKE. the chance, namely, that there should exist in Sweden a man entitled by his birth to claim election to the kingship.

LADY INGER (evasively). The Swedish nobles have been even as bloodily hewn down as our own, Sir Councillor. Where would you seek for?

NILS LYKKE (with a smile). Seek? The man is found already

LADY INGER (starts violently). Ah! He is found?

NILS LYKKE. And he is too closely akin to you, Lady Inger, to be far from your thoughts at this moment. (Looks at her.) The last Count Sture left a son

LADY INGER (with a cry). Holy Saviour, how know you?

NILS LYKKE (surprised). Be calm, Madam, and let me finish. This young man has lived quietly till now with his mother, Sten Sture's widow.

LADY INGER (breathes more freely). With? Ah, yes, true, true!

NILS LYKKE. But now he has come forward openly. He has shown himself in the Dales as leader of the peasants; their numbers are growing day by day; and, as perhaps you know, they are finding friends among the peasants on this side of the border-hills.

LADY INGER (who has in the meantime regained her composure). Sir Councillor, you speak of all these things as though they must of necessity be known to me. What ground have I given you to believe so? I know, and wish to know, nothing. All my care is to live quietly within my own domain; I give no helping hand to the rebels; but neither must you count on me if it be your purpose to put them down.

NILS LYKKE (in a low voice). Would you still be inactive, if it were my purpose to stand by them?

LADY INGER. How am I to understand you?

NILS LYKKE. Have you not seen whither I have been aiming all this time? Well, I will tell you all, honestly and straightforwardly. Know, then, that the King and his Council see clearly that we can have no sure footing in Norway so long as the nobles and the people continue, as now, to think themselves wronged and oppressed. We understand to the full that willing allies are better than sullen subjects; and we have therefore no heartier wish than to loosen the bonds that hamper us, in effect, quite as straitly as you. But you will scarce deny that the temper of Norway towards us makes such a step too dangerous, so long as we have no sure support behind us.

LADY INGER. And this support?

NILS LYKKE. Should naturally come from Sweden. But, mark well, not so long as Gustav Vasa holds the helm; his reckoning with Denmark is not settled yet, and mayhap never will be. But a new king of Sweden, who had the people with him, and who owed his throne to the help of Denmark Well, you begin to understand me? Then we could safely say to you Norwegians: "Take back your old ancestral rights; choose you a ruler after your own mind; be our friends in need, as we will be in yours!" Mark you well, Lady Inger, herein is our generosity less than it may seem; for you must see that, far from weakening, 'twill rather strengthen us. And now I have opened my heart to you so fully, do you too cast away all mistrust. And therefore (confidently) the knight from Sweden, who came hither an hour before me

LADY INGER. Then you already know of his coming?

NILS LYKKE. Most certainly. It is him I seek.

LADY INGER (to herself). Strange! It must be as Olaf Skaktavl said. (To NILS LYKKE.) I pray you wait here, Sir Councillor! I go to bring him to you.

(Goes out through the Banquet Hall.)

NILS LYKKE (looks after her a while in exultant astonishment). She is bringing him! Ay, truly, she is bringing him! The battle is half won. I little thought it would go so smoothly She is deep in the counsels of the rebels; she started in terror when I named Sten Sture's son And now? Hm! Since Lady Inger has been simple enough to walk into the snare, Nils Sture will not make many difficulties. A hot-blooded boy, thoughtless and rash With my promise of help he will set forth at once, unhappily Jens Bielke will snap him up by the way and the whole rising will be nipped in the bud. And then? Then one step more in our own behalf. It is spread abroad that the young Count Sture has been at Ostrat, that a Danish envoy has had audience of Lady Inger, that thereupon the young Count Nils has been snapped up by King Gustav's men-at-arms a mile from the castle Let Inger Gyldenlove's name among the people stand never so high, it will scarce recover from such a blow. (Starts up in sudden uneasiness.) By all the devils! What if she has scented mischief! It may be he is slipping through our fingers even now (Listens toward the hall, and says with relief.) Ah, there is no fear. Here they come.

(LADY INGER GYLDENLOVE enters from the hall along with OLAF SKAKTAVL.)

LADY INGER (to NILS LYKKE). Here is the man you seek.

NILS LYKKE (aside). In the name of hell, what means this?

LADY INGER. I have told this knight your name and all that you have imparted to me

NILS LYKKE (irresolutely). Ay? Have you so? Well

LADY INGER And I will not hide from you that his faith in your help is none of the strongest.

NILS LYKKE. Is it not?

LADY INGER. Can you marvel at that? You know, surely, both the cause he fights for and his bitter fate

NILS LYKKE. This man's? Ah, yes, truly

OLAF SKAKTAVL (to NILS LYKKE). But seeing 'tis Peter Kanzler himself that has appointed us this meeting

NILS LYKKE. Peter Kanzler? (Recovers himself quickly.) Ay, right, I have a mission from Peter Kanzler

OLAF SKAKTAVL. He must know best whom he can trust. So why should I trouble my head with thinking how

NILS LYKKE. Ay, you are right, noble Sir; that were folly indeed.

OLAF SKAKTAVL. Rather let us come straight to the matter.

NILS LYKKE. Straight to the point; no beating about the bush 'tis ever my fashion.

OLAF SKAKTAVL. Then will you tell me your mission here?

NILS LYKKE. Methinks you can partly guess my errand

OLAF SKAKTAVL. Peter Kanzler said something of papers that

NILS LYKKE. Papers? Ay, true, the papers!

OLAF SKAKTAVL. Doubtless you have them with you?

NILS LYKKE. Of course; safely bestowed; so safely that I cannot at once (Appears to search the inner pockets of his doublet; says to himself:) Who the devil is he? What pretext shall I make? I may be on the brink of great discoveries (Notices that the Servants are laying the table and lighting the lamps in the Banquet Hall, and says to OLAF SKAKTAVL:) Ah, I see Lady Inger has taken order for the evening meal. We could perhaps better talk of our affairs at table.

OLAF SKAKTAVL. Good; as you will.

NILS LYKKE (aside). Time gained, all gained! (To LADY INGER with a show of great friendliness.) And meanwhile we might learn what part Lady Inger Gyldenlove purposes to take in our design?

LADY INGER. I? None.

NILS LYKKE AND OLAF SKAKTAVL. None!

LADY INGER. Can ye marvel, noble Sirs, that I venture not on a game, wherein all is staked on one cast? And that, too, when none of my allies dare trust me fully.

NILS LYKKE. That reproach touches not me. I trust you blindly; I pray you be assured of that.

OLAF SKAKTAVL. Who should believe in you, if not your countrymen?

LADY INGER. Truly, this confidence rejoices me.

(Goes to a cupboard in the back wall and fills two goblets with wine.)

NILS LYKKE (aside). Curse her, will she slip out of the noose?

LADY INGER (hands a goblet to each). And since so it is, I offer you a cup of welcome to Ostrat. Drink, noble knights! Pledge me to the last drop! (Looks from one to the other after they have drunk, and says gravely:) But now I must tell you, one goblet held a welcome for my friend; the other, death for my enemy.

NILS LYKKE (throws down the goblet). Ah, I am poisoned!

OLAF SKAKTAVL (at the same time, clutches his sword). Death and hell, have you murdered me?

LADY INGER (to OLAF SKAKTAVL, pointing to NILS LYKKE.) You see the Danes' trust in Inger Gyldenlove (To NILS LYKKE, pointing to OLAF SKAKTAVL.) and likewise my countrymen's faith in me! (To both of them.) And I am to place myself in your power? Gently, noble Sirs, gently! The Lady of Ostrat is not yet in her dotage.

(ELINA GYLDENLOVE enters by the door on the left.)

ELINA. I heard voices! What is amiss?

LADY INGER (to NILS LYKKE). My daughter Elina.

NILS LYKKE (softly). Elina! I had not pictured her thus.

(ELINA catches sight of NILS LYKKE, and stands still, as in surprise, gazing at him.)

LADY INGER (touches her arm). My child, this knight is

ELINA (motions her mother back with her hand, still looking intently at him, and says:) There is no need! I see who he is. He is Nils Lykke.

NILS LYKKE (aside, to LADY INGER). How? Does she know me? Can Lucia have? Can she know?

LADY INGER. Hush! She knows nothing.

ELINA (to herself). I knew it; even so must Nils Lykke appear.

NILS LYKKE (approaches her). Yes, Elina Gyldenlove, you have guessed rightly. And as it seems that, in some sense, you know me, and moreover, as I am your mother's guest, you will not deny me the flower-spray you wear in your bosom. So long as it is fresh and fragrant I shall have in it an image of yourself.

ELINA (proudly, but still gazing at him). Pardon me, Sir Knight, it was plucked in my own chamber, and there can grow no flower for you.

NILS LYKKE (loosening a spray of flowers that he wears in the front of his doublet). At least you will not disdain this humble gift. 'Twas a farewell token from a courtly lady when I set forth from Trondhiem this morning. But mark me, noble maiden, were I to offer you a gift that were fully worthy of you, it could be naught less than a princely crown.

ELINA (who has taken the flowers passively). And were it the royal crown of Denmark you held forth to me, before I shared it with you, I would crush it to pieces between my hands, and cast the fragments at your feet!

(Throws down the flowers at his feet, and goes into the Banquet Hall.)

OLAF SKAKTAVL (mutters to himself). Bold, as Inger Ottisdaughter by Knut Alfson's bier!

LADY INGER (softly, after looking alternately at ELINA and NILS LYKKE). The wolf can be tamed. Now to forge the fetters.

NILS LYKKE (picks up the flowers and gazes in rapture after ELINA). God's holy blood, but she is proud and fair

Act Third

(The Banquet Hall. A high bow-window in the background; a smaller window in front on the left. Several doors on each side. The roof is supported by massive wooden pillars, on which, as well as on the walls, are hung all sorts of weapons. Pictures of saints, knights, and ladies hang in long rows. Pendent from the roof a large many-branched lamp, alight. In front, on the right, an ancient carven high-seat. In the middle of the hall, a table with the remnants of the evening meal.)

(ELINA GYLDENLOVE enters from the left, slowly and in deep thought. Her expression shows that she is going over again in her mind the scene with NILS LYKKE. At last she repeats the motion with which she flung away the flowers, and says in a low voice:)

ELINA. And then he gathered up the fragments of the crown of Denmark, no, 'twas the flowers and: "God's holy blood, but she is proud and fair!" Had he whispered the words in the remotest corner, long leagues from Ostrat, still had I heard them! How I hate him! How I have always hated him, this Nils Lykke! There lives not another man like him, 'tis said. He plays with women and treads them under his feet. And it was to him my mother thought to offer me! How I hate him! They say Nils Lykke is unlike all other men. It is not true! There is nothing strange in him. There are many, many like him! When Biorn used to tell me his tales, all the princes looked as Nils Lykke looks. When I sat lonely here in the hall and dreamed my histories, and my knights came and went, they were one and all even as he. How strange and how good it is to hate! Never have I known how sweet it can be till to-night. Ah, not to live a thousand years would I sell the moments I have lived since I saw him! "God's holy blood, but she is proud "

(Goes slowly towards the background, opens the window and looks out. NILS LYKKE comes in by the first door on the right.)

NILS LYKKE (to himself). "Sleep well at Ostrat, Sir Knight," said Inger Gyldenlove as she left me. Sleep well? Ay, it is easily said, but Out there, sky and sea in tumult; below, in the grave-vault, a young girl on her bier; the fate of two kingdoms in my hand; and in my breast a withered flower that a woman has flung at my feet. Truly, I fear me sleep will be slow of coming.

(Notices ELINA, who has left the window, and is going out on the left.)

There she is. Her haughty eyes seem veiled with thought. Ah, if I but dared (aloud). Mistress Elina!

ELINA (stops at the door). What will you? Why do you pursue me?

NILS LYKKE. You err; I pursue you not. I am myself pursued.

ELINA. You?

NILS LYKKE. By a multitude of thoughts. Therefore 'tis with sleep as with you: it flees me.

ELINA. Go to the window, and there you will find pastime; a storm-tossed sea

NILS LYKKE (smiles). A storm-tossed sea? That I may find in you as well.

ELINA. In me?

NILS LYKKE. Ay, of that our first meeting has assured me.

ELINA. And that offends you?

NILS LYKKE. Nay, in nowise; yet I could wish to see you of milder mood.

ELINA (proudly). Think you that you will ever have your wish?

NILS LYKKE. I am sure of it. I have a welcome word to say to you.

ELINA. What is it?

NILS LYKKE. Farewell.

ELINA (comes a step nearer him). Farewell? You are leaving Ostrat so soon?

NILS LYKKE. This very night.

ELINA (seems to hesitate for a moment; then says coldly:) Then take my greeting, Sir Knight! (Bows and is about to go.)

NILS LYKKE. Elina Gyldenlove, I have no right to keep you here; but 'twill be unlike your nobleness if you refuse to hear what I have to say to you.

ELINA. I hear you, Sir Knight.

NILS LYKKE. I know you hate me.

ELINA. You are keen-sighted, I perceive.

NILS LYKKE. But I know, too, that I have fully merited your hate. Unseemly and insolent were the words I wrote of you in my letter to Lady Inger.

ELINA. It may be; I have not read them.

NILS LYKKE. But at least their purport is not unknown to you; I know your mother has not left you in ignorance of the matter; at the least she has told you how I praised the lot of the man who; surely you know the hope I nursed

ELINA. Sir Knight, if it is of that you would speak

NILS LYKKE. I speak of it only to excuse what I have done; for no other reason, I swear to you. If my fame has reached you, as I have too much cause of fear, before I myself set foot in Ostrat, you must needs know enough of my life not to wonder that in such things I should go to work something boldly. I have met many women, Elina Gyldenlove; but not one have I found unyielding. Such lessons, look you, teach a man to be secure. He loses the habit of roundabout ways

ELINA. May be so. I know not of what metal those women can have been. For the rest, you err in thinking 'twas your letter to my mother that aroused my soul's hatred and bitterness against you. It is of older date.

NILS LYKKE (uneasily). Of older date? What mean you?

ELINA. 'Tis as you guessed: your fame has gone before you to Ostrat, even as over all the land. Nils Lykke's name is never spoken save with the name of some woman whom he has beguiled and cast off. Some speak it in wrath, others with laughter and wanton jeering at those weak-souled creatures. But through the wrath and the laughter and the jeers rings the song they have made of you, masterful and insolent as an enemy's song of triumph. 'Tis all this that has begotten my hate for you. Your were ever in my thoughts, and I longed to meet you face to face, that you might learn that there are women on whom your soft speeches are lost, if you should think to use them.

NILS LYKKE. You judge me unjustly, if you judge from what rumour has told of me. Even if there be truth in all you have heard, you know not the causes that have made me what I am. As a boy of seventeen I began my course of pleasure. I have lived full fifteen years since then. Light women granted me all that I would, even before the wish had shaped itself into a prayer; and what I offered them they seized with eager hands. You are the first woman that has flung back a gift of mine with scorn at my feet.

Think not I reproach you. Rather I honour you for it, as never before have I honoured woman. But for this I reproach my fate and the thought is a gnawing pain to me that I did not meet you sooner

Elina Gyldenlove! Your mother has told me of you. While far from Ostrat life ran its restless course, you went your lonely way in silence, living in your dreams and histories. Therefore you will understand what I have to tell you. Know, then, that once I too lived even such a life as yours. Methought that when I stepped forth into the great world, a noble and stately woman would come to meet me, and would beckon me to her and point me the path towards a lofty goal. I was deceived, Elina Gyldenlove! Women came to meet me; but she was not among them. Ere yet I had come to full manhood, I had learnt to despise them all.

Was it my fault? Why were not the others even as you? I know the fate of your fatherland lies heavy on your soul, and you know the part I have in these affairs 'Tis said of me that I am false as the sea-foam. Mayhap I am; but if I be, it is women who have made me so. Had I sooner found what I sought, had I met a woman proud and noble and high-souled even as you, then had my path been different indeed. At this moment, maybe, I had been standing at your side as the champion of all that suffer wrong in Norway's land. For this I believe: a woman is the mightiest power in the world, and in her hand it lies to guide a man whither God Almighty would have him go.

ELINA (to herself). Can it be as he says? Nay nay; there is falsehood in his eyes and deceit on his lips. And yet no song is sweeter than his words.

NILS LYKKE (coming closer, speaks low and more intimately). How often, when you have been sitting here at Ostrat, alone with your changeful thoughts, have you felt your bosom stifling; how often have the roof and walls seemed to shrink together till they crushed your very soul. Then have your longings taken wing with you; then have you yearned to fly far from here, you knew not whither. How often have you not wandered alone by the fiord; far out a ship has sailed by in fair array, with knights and ladies on her deck with song and music of stringed instruments; a faint, far-off rumour of great events has reached your ears; and you have felt a longing in your breast, an unconquerable craving to know all that lies beyond the sea. But you have not understood what ailed you. At times you have thought it was the fate of your fatherland that filled you with all these restless broodings. You deceived yourself; a maiden so young as you has other food for musing

Elina Gyldenlove! Have you never had visions of an unknown power, a strong mysterious might, that binds together the destinies of mortals? When you dreamed of knightly jousts and joyous festivals, saw you never in your dreams a knight, who stood in the midst of the gayest rout, with a smile on his lips and with bitterness in his heart, a knight that had once dreamed a dream as fair as yours, of a woman noble and stately, for whom he went ever seeking, and in vain?

ELINA. Who are you, that have power to clothe my most secret thought in words? How can you tell me what I have borne in my inmost soul and knew it not myself? How know you?

NILS LYKKE. All that I have told you, I have read in your eyes.

ELINA. Never has any man spoken to me as you have. I have understood you but dimly; and yet all, all seems changed since (To herself.) Now I understand why they said that Nils Lykke was unlike all other.

NILS LYKKE. There is one thing in the world that might drive a man to madness, but to think of it; and that is the thought of what might have been if things had fallen out in this way or that. Had I met you on my path while the tree of my life was yet green and budding, at this hour, mayhap, you had been But forgive me, noble lady! Our speech of these past few moments has made me forget how we stand one to another. 'Twas as though a secret voice had told me from the first that to you I could speak openly, without flattery or dissimulation.

ELINA. That can you.

NILS LYKKE. 'Tis well; and it may be that this openness has already in part reconciled us. Ay, my hope is yet bolder. The time may yet come when you will think of the stranger knight without hate or bitterness in your soul. Nay, mistake me not! I mean not now but some time, in the days to come. And that this may be the less hard for you and as I have begun once for all to speak to you plainly and openly let me tell you

ELINA. Sir Knight!

NILS LYKKE (smiling). Ah, I see the thought of my letter still affrights you. Fear nought on that score. I would from my heart it were unwritten, for I know 'twill concern you little enough, so I may even say it right out, for I love you not, and shall never come to you. Fear nothing, therefore, as I said before; I shall in no wise seek to But what ails you?

ELINA. Me? Nothing, nothing. Tell me but one thing. Why do you still wear those flowers? What would you with them?

NILS LYKKE. These? Are they not a gage of battle you have thrown down to the wicked Nils Lykke on behalf of all womankind? What could I do but take it up? You asked what I would with them. (Softly.) When I stand again amidst the fair ladies of Denmark, when the music of the strings is hushed and there is silence in the hall, then will I bring forth these flowers and tell a tale of a young maiden sitting alone in a gloomy black-beamed hall, far to the north in Norway (Breaks off and bows respectfully.) But I fear I keep the noble daughter of the house too long. We shall meet no more; for before day-break I shall be gone. So now I bid you farewell.

ELINA. Fare you well, Sir Knight!

(A short silence.)

NILS LYKKE. Again you are deep in thought, Elina Gyldenlove! Is it the fate of your fatherland that weighs upon you still?

ELINA (shakes her head, absently gazing straight in front of her). My fatherland? I think not of my fatherland.

NILS LYKKE. Then 'tis the strife and misery of the time that cause you dread.

ELINA. The time? I have forgotten time. You go to Denmark? Said you not so?

NILS LYKKE. I go to Denmark.

ELINA. Can I see towards Denmark from this hall?

NILS LYKKE (points to the window on the left). Ay, from this window. Denmark lies there, to the south.

ELINA. And is it far from here? More than a hundred miles?

NILS LYKKE. Much more. The sea lies between you and Denmark.

ELINA (to herself). The sea? Thought has seagull's wings. The sea cannot stay it.

(Goes out to the left.)

NILS LYKKE (looks after her awhile; then says:) If I could but spare two days now, or even one, I would have her in my power, even as the others. And yet is there rare stuff in this maiden. She is proud. Might I not after all? No; rather humble her

(Paces the room.)

Verily, I believe she has set my blood on fire. Who would have thought it possible after all these years? Enough of this! I must get out of the tangle I am entwined in here.

(Sits in a chair on the right.)

What is the meaning of it? Both Olaf Skaktavl and Inger Gyldenlove seem blind to the mistrust 'twill waken, when 'tis rumoured that I am in their league. Or can Lady Inger have seen through my purpose? Can she have seen that all my promises were but designed to lure Nils Sture forth from his hiding-place?

(Springs up.)

Damnation! Is it I that have been fooled? 'Tis like enough that Count Sture is not at Ostrat at all? It may be the rumour of his flight was but a feint. He may be safe and sound among his friends in Sweden, while I

(Walks restlessly up and down.)

And to think I was so sure of success! If I should effect nothing? If Lady Inger should penetrate my designs and publish my discomfiture To be a laughing-stock both here and in Denmark! To have sought to lure Lady Inger into a trap, and given her cause the help it most needed, strengthened her in the people's favour! Ah, I could well-nigh sell myself to the Evil One, would he but help me to lay hands on Count Sture.

(The window in the background is pushed open. NILS STENSSON is seen outside.)

NILS LYKKE (clutches at his sword). What now?

NILS STENSSON (jumps down on to the floor). Ah; here I am at last then!

NILS LYKKE (aside). What means this?

NILS STENSSON. God's peace, master!

NILS LYKKE. Thanks, good Sir! Methinks yo have chosen a strange mode of entrance.

NILS STENSSON. Ay, what the devil was I to do? The gate was shut. Folk must sleep in this house like bears at Yuletide.

NILS LYKKE. God be thanked! Know you not that a good conscience is the best pillow?

NILS STENSSON. Ay, it must be even so; for all my rattling and thundering, I

NILS LYKKE. You won not in?

NILS STENSSON. You have hit it. So I said to myself: As you are bidden to be in Ostrat to-night, if you have to go through fire and water, you may surely make free to creep through a window.

NILS LYKKE (aside). Ah, if it should be! (Moves a step or two nearer.) Was it, then, of the last necessity that you should reach Ostrat to-night?

NILS STENSSON. Was it? Ay, faith but it was. I love not to keep folk waiting, I can tell you.

NILS LYKKE. Aha, then Lady Inger Gyldenlove looks for your coming?

NILS STENSSON. Lady Inger Gyldenlove? Nay, that I can scarce say for certain; (with a sly smile) but there might be some one else

NILS LYKKE (smiles in answer). Ah, so there might be some one else?

NILS STENSSON. Tell me, are you of the house?

NILS LYKKE. I? Well, in so far that I am Lady Inger's guest this evening.

NILS STENSSON. A guest? Is not to-night the third night after Martinmas?

NILS LYKKE. The third night after? Ay, right enough. Would you seek the lady of the house at once? I think she is not yet gone to rest. But might you not sit down and rest awhile, dear young Sir? See, here is yet a flagon of wine remaining, and doubtless you will find some food. Come, fall to; you will do wisely to refresh your strength.

NILS STENSSON. You are right, Sir; 'twere not amiss. (Sits down by the table and eats and drinks.) Both roast meat and sweet cakes! Why, you live like lords here! When one has slept, as I have, on the naked ground, and lived on bread and water for four or five days

NILS LYKKE (looks at him with a smile). Ay, such a life must be hard for one that is wont to sit at the high-table in noble halls

NILS STENSSON. Noble halls?

NILS LYKKE. But now can you take your rest at Ostrat, as long as it likes you.

NILS STENSSON (pleased). Ay? Can I truly? Then I am not to begone again so soon?

NILS LYKKE. Nay, that I know not. Sure you yourself can best say that.

NILS STENSSON (softly). Oh, the devil! (Stretches himself in the chair.) Well, you see 'tis not yet certain. I, for my part, were nothing loath to stay quiet here awhile; but

NILS LYKKE. But you are not in all points your own master? There be other duties and other circumstances?

NILS STENSSON. Ay, that is just the rub. Were I to choose, I would rest me at Ostrat at least the winter through; I have seldom led aught but a soldier's life (Interrupts himself suddenly, fills a goblet, and drinks.) Your health, Sir!

NILS LYKKE. A soldier's life? Hm!

NILS STENSSON. Nay, what I would have said is this: I have been eager to see Lady Inger Gyldenlove, whose fame has spread so wide. She must be a queenly woman, is't not so? The one thing I like not in her, is that she shrinks so cursedly from open action.

NILS LYKKE. From open action?

NILS STENSSON. Ay ay, you understand me; I mean she is so loath to take a hand in driving the foreign rulers out of the land.

NILS LYKKE. Ay, you are right. But if you do your best now, you will doubtless work her to your will.

NILS STENSSON. I? God knows it would but little serve if I

NILS LYKKE. Yet 'tis strange you should seek her here if you have so little hope.

NILS STENSSON. What mean you? Tell me, know you Lady Inger?

NILS LYKKE. Surely; I am her guest, and

NILS STENSSON. Ay, but it does not at all follow that you know her. I too am her guest, yet have I never seen so much as her shadow.

NILS LYKKE. Yet did you speak of her

NILS STENSSON. As all folk speak. Why should I not? And besides, I have often enough heard from Peter Kanzler

(Stops in confusion, and begins eating again.)

NILS LYKKE. You would have said?

NILS STENSSON (eating). I? Nay, 'tis all one.

(NILS LYKKE laughs.)

NILS STENSSON. Why laugh you, Sir?

NILS LYKKE. 'Tis nought, Sir!

NILS STENSSON (drinks). A pretty vintage ye have in this house.

NILS LYKKE (approaches him confidentially). Listen, were it not time now to throw off the mask?

NILS STENSSON (smiling). The mask? Why, do as seems best to you.

NILS LYKKE. Then off with all disguise. You are known, Count Sture!

NILS STENSSON (with a laugh). Count Sture? Do you too take me for Count Sture? (Rises from the table.) You mistake, Sir; I am not Count Sture.

NILS LYKKE. You are not? Then who are you?

NILS STENSSON. My name is Nils Stensson.

NILS LYKKE (looks at him with a smile). Hm! Nils Stensson? But you are not Sten Sture's son Nils? The name chimes at least.

NILS STENSSON. True enough; but God knows what right I have to bear it. My father I never knew; my mother was a poor peasant woman, that was robbed and murdered in one of the old feuds. Peter Kanzler chanced to be on the spot; he took me into his care, brought me up, and taught me the trade of arms. As you know, King Gustav has been hunting him this many a year; and I have followed him faithfully, wherever he went.

NILS LYKKE. Peter Kanzler has taught you more than the trade of arms, meseems Well, well; then you are not Nils Sture. But at least you come from Sweden. Peter Kanzler has sent you here to find a stranger, who

NILS STENSSON (nods cunningly). Who is found already.

NILS LYKKE (somewhat uncertain). And whom you do not know?

NILS STENSSON. As little as you know me; for I swear to you by God himself: I am not Count Sture!

NILS LYKKE. In sober earnest, Sir?

NILS STENSSON. As truly as I live! Wherefore should I deny it, if I were?

NILS LYKKE. Then where is Count Sture?

NILS STENSSON (in a low voice). Ay, that is just the secret.

NILS LYKKE (whispers). Which is known to you, is it not?

NILS STENSSON (nods). And which I have to tell to you.

NILS LYKKE. To me? Well then, where is he?

(NILS STENSSON points upwards.)

NILS LYKKE. Up there? Lady Inger holds him hidden in the loft- room?

NILS STENSSON. Nay, nay; you mistake me. (Looks round cautiously.) Nils Sture is in Heaven!

NILS LYKKE. Dead? And where?

NILS STENSSON. In his mother's castle, three weeks since.

NILS LYKKE. Ah, you are deceiving me! 'Tis but five or six days since he crossed the frontier into Norway.

NILS STENSSON. Oh, that was I.

NILS LYKKE. But just before that the Count had appeared in the Dales. The people were restless already, and on his coming they broke out openly and would have chosen him for king.

NILS STENSSON. Ha-ha-ha; that was me too!

NILS LYKKE. You?

NILS STENSSON. I will tell you how it came about. One day Peter Kanzler called me to him and gave me to know that great things were preparing. He bade me set out for Norway and go to Ostrat, where I must be on a certain fixed day

NILS LYKKE (nods). The third night after Martinmas.

NILS STENSSON. I was to meet a stranger there

NILS LYKKE. Ay, right; I am he.

NILS STENSSON. He was to tell me what more I had to do. Moreover, I was to let him know that the Count was dead of a sudden, but that as yet 'twas known to no one save to his mother the Countess, together with Peter Kanzler and a few old servants of the Stures.

NILS LYKKE. I understand. The Count was the peasants' rallying- point. Were the tidings of his death to spread, they would fall asunder, and the whole project would come to nought.

NILS STENSSON. Ay, maybe so; I know little of such matters.

NILS LYKKE. But how came you to give yourself out for the Count?

NILS STENSSON. How came I to? Nay, what know I? Many's the mad prank I've hit on in my day. And yet 'twas not I hit on it neither; wherever I appeared in the Dales, the people crowded round me and greeted me as Count Sture. Deny it as I pleased, 'twas wasted breath. The Count had been there two years before, they said and the veriest child knew me again. Well, be it so, thought I; never again will you be a Count in this life; why not try what 'tis like for once?

NILS LYKKE. Well, and what did you more?

NILS STENSSON. I? I ate and drank and took my ease. Pity 'twas that I must away again so soon. But when I set forth across the frontier, ha-ha-ha, I promised them I would soon be back with three or four thousand men, I know not how many I said and then we would lay on in earnest.

NILS LYKKE. And you did not bethink you that you were acting rashly?

NILS STENSSON. Ay, afterwards; but then, to be sure, 'twas too late.

NILS LYKKE. It grieves me for you, my young friend; but you will soon come to feel the effects of your folly. Let me tell you that you are pursued. A troop of Swedish men-at-arms is out after you.

NILS STENSSON. After me? Ha-ha-ha. Nay, that is rare! And when they come and think they have Count Sture in their clutches, ha-ha-ha!

NILS LYKKE (gravely). Then farewell to your life.

NILS STENSSON. My? But I am not Count Sture.

NILS LYKKE. You have called the people to arms. You have given seditious promises, and raised troubles in the land.

NILS STENSSON. Ay, but 'twas only in jest!

NILS LYKKE. King Gustav will scarce look on the matter in that light.

NILS STENSSON. Truly, there is something in what you say. To think I could be such a madman Well well, I'm not a dead man yet! You will protect me; and besides the men-at-arms can scarce be at my heels.

NILS LYKKE. But what else have you to tell me?

NILS STENSSON. I? Nothing. When once I have given you the packet

NILS LYKKE (unguardedly). The packet?

NILS STENSSON. Ay, sure you know

NILS LYKKE. Ah, right, right; the papers from Peter Kanzler

NILS STENSSON. See, here they all are.

(Takes out a packet from inside his doublet, and hands it to NILS LYKKE.)

NILS LYKKE (aside). Letters and papers for Olaf Skaktavl. (To NILS STENSSON.) The packet is open, I see. 'Tis like you know what it contains?

NILS STENSSON. No, good sir; I am ill at reading writing; and for reason good.

NILS LYKKE. I understand; you have given most care to the trade of arms. (Sits down by the table on the right, and runs through the papers.) Aha! Here is light enough and to spare on what is brewing. This small letter tied with a silken thread (Examines the address.) This too for Olaf Skaktavl. (Opens the letter, and glances through its contents.) From Peter Kanzler. I thought as much. (Reads under his breath.) "I am hard bested, for; ay, sure enough; here it stands, "Young Count Sture has been gathered to his fathers, even at the time fixed for the revolt to break forth" - "but all may yet be made good" What now? (Reads on in astonishment.) "You must know, then, Olaf Skaktavl, that the young man who brings you this letter is a son of" Heaven and earth, can it be so? Ay, by Christ's blood, even so 'tis written! (Glances at NILS STENSSON.) Can he be? Ah, if it were so! (Reads on.) "I have nurtured him since he was a year old; but up to this day I have ever refused to give him back, trusting to have in him a sure hostage for Inger Gyldenlove's faithfulness to us and to our friends. Yet in that respect he has been of but little service to us. You may marvel that I told you not this secret when you were with me here of late; therefore will I confess freely that I feared you might seize upon him, even as I had done. But now, when you have seen Lady Inger, and have doubtless assured yourself how loath she is to have a hand in our undertaking, you will see that 'tis wisest to give her back her own as soon as may be. Well might it come to pass that in her joy and security and thankfulness" - "that is now our last hope."

(Sits for awhile as though struck dumb with surprise; then exclaims in a low voice:)

Aha, what a letter! Gold would not buy it!

NILS STENSSON. 'Tis plain I have brought you weighty tidings. Ay, ay, Peter Kanzler has many irons in the fire, folk say.

NILS LYKKE (to himself). What to do with all this? A thousand paths are open to me Suppose I? No, 'twere to risk too much. But if, ah, if I? I will venture it.

(Tears the letter across, crumples up the pieces, and hides them inside his doublet; puts back the other papers into the packet, which he sticks inside his belt; rises and says:)

A word, my friend!

NILS STENSSON. Well, your looks say that the game goes bravely.

NILS LYKKE. Ay, by my soul it does. You have given me a hand of nought but court cards, queens and knaves and

NILS STENSSON. But what of me, that have brought all these good tidings? Have I nought more to do?

NILS LYKKE. You? Ay, that have you. You belong to the game. You are a king and king of trumps too.

NILS STENSSON. I a king? Oh, now I understand; you are thinking of my exaltation

NILS LYKKE. Your exaltation?

NILS STENSSON. Ay; that which you foretold me, if King Gustav's men got me in their clutches

(Makes a motion to indicate hanging.)

NILS LYKKE. True enough; but let that trouble you no more. It now lies with yourself alone whether within a month you shall have the hempen noose or a chain of gold about your neck.

NILS STENSSON. A chain of gold? And it lies with me?

(NILS LYKKE nods.)

NILS STENSSON. Why then, the devil take musing! Do you tell me what I am to do.

NILS LYKKE. I will. But first you must swear me a solemn oath that no living creature in the wide world shall know what I am to tell you.

NILS STENSSON. Is that all? You shall have ten oaths if you will.

NILS LYKKE. Not so lightly, young Sir! It is no jesting matter.

NILS STENSSON. Well well; I am grave enough.

NILS LYKKE. In the Dales you called yourself a Count's son; is't not so?

NILS STENSSON. Nay, begin you now on that again? Have I not made free confession

NILS LYKKE. You mistake me. What you said in the Dales was the truth.

NILS STENSSON. The truth? What mean you by that? Tell me but!

NILS LYKKE. First your oath! The holiest, the most inviolable you can swear.

NILS STENSSON. That you shall have. Yonder on the wall hangs the picture of the Holy Virgin

NILS LYKKE. The Holy Virgin has grown impotent of late. Know you not what the monk of Wittenberg maintains?

NILS STENSSON. Fie! how can you heed the monk of Wittenberg? Peter Kanzler says he is a heretic.

NILS LYKKE. Nay, let us not wrangle concerning him. Here can I show you a saint will serve full well to make oath to. (Points to a picture hanging on one of the panels.) Come hither, swear that you will be silent till I myself release your tongue silent, as you hope for Heaven's salvation for yourself and for the man whose picture hangs there.

NILS STENSSON (approaching the picture). I swear it, so help me God's holy word! (Falls back a step in amazement.) But, Christ save me!

NILS LYKKE. What now?

NILS STENSSON. The picture! Sure 'tis myself!

NILS LYKKE. 'Tis old Sten Sture, even as he lived and moved in his youthful years.

NILS STENSSON. Sten Sture! And the likeness? And said you not I spoke the truth, when I called myself a Count's son? Was't not so?

NILS LYKKE. So it was.

NILS STENSSON. Ah, I have it, I have it! I am

NILS LYKKE. You are Sten Sture's son, good Sir.

NILS STENSSON (with the quiet of amazement). I Sten Sture's son!

NILS LYKKE. On the mother's side too your blood is noble. Peter Kanzler spoke not the truth, if he said that a poor peasant woman was your mother.

NILS STENSSON. Oh strange, oh marvellous! But can I believe?

NILS LYKKE. You may believe all I tell you. But remember, all this will be merely your ruin, if you should forget what you swore to me by your father's salvation.

NILS STENSSON. Forget it? Nay, that you may be sure I never shall. But you to whom I have given my word, tell me, who are you?

NILS LYKKE. My name is Nils Lykke.

NILS STENSSON (surprised). Nils Lykke? Surely not the Danish Councillor?

NILS LYKKE. Even so.

NILS STENSSON. And it was you? 'Tis strange. How come you?

NILS LYKKE. To be receiving missives from Peter Kanzler? You marvel at that?

NILS STENSSON. I cannot deny it. He has ever named you as our bitterest foe

NILS LYKKE. And therefore you mistrust me?

NILS STENSSON. Nay, not wholly that; but well, the devil take musing!

NILS LYKKE. Well said. Go but your own way, and you are as sure of the halter as you are of a Count's title and a chain of gold if you trust to me.

NILS STENSSON. That will I. My hand upon it, dear Sir! Do you but help me with good counsel as long as there is need; when counsel gives place to blows I shall look to myself.

NILS LYKKE. It is well. Come with me now into yonder chamber, and I will tell you how all these matters stand, and what you have still to do.

(Goes out to the right.)

NILS STENSSON (with a glance at the picture). I Sten Sture's son! Oh, marvellous as a dream!

(Goes out after NILS LYKKE.)

Act Fourth

(The Banquet Hall, as before, but without the supper-table.)

(BIORN, the major-domo, enters carrying a lighted branch-candlestick, and lighting in LADY INGER and OLAF SKAKTAVL by the second door, on the left. LADY INGER has a bundle of papers in her hand.)

LADY INGER (to BIORN). And you are sure my daughter spoke with the knight, here in the hall?

BIORN (putting down the branch-candlestick on the table on the left). Sure as may be. I met her even as she stepped into the passage.

LADY INGER. And she seemed greatly moved? Said you not so?

BIORN. She looked all pale and disturbed. I asked if she were sick; she answered not, but said: "Go to mother and tell her the knight sets forth ere daybreak; if she have letters or messages for him, beg her not to delay him needlessly." And then she added somewhat that I heard not rightly.

LADY INGER. Did you not hear it at all?

BIORN. It sounded to me as though she said: "I almost fear he has already stayed too long at Ostrat."

LADY INGER. And the knight? Where is he?

BIORN. In his chamber belike, in the gate-wing.

LADY INGER. It is well. What I have to send by him is ready. Go to him and say I await him here in the hall.

(BIORN goes out to the right.)

OLAF SKAKTAVL. Know you, Lady Inger, 'tis true that in such things I am blind as a mole; yet seems it to me as though, hm!

LADY INGER. Well?

OLAF SKAKTAVL. As though Nils Lykke loved your daughter.

LADY INGER. Then it seems you are not so blind after all; I am the more deceived if you be not right. Marked you not at supper how eagerly he listened to the least word I let fall concerning Elina?

OLAF SKAKTAVL. He forgot both food and drink.

LADY INGER. And our secret business as well.

OLAF SKAKTAVL. Ay, and what is more, the papers from Peter Kanzler.

LADY INGER. And from all this you conclude?

OLAF SKAKTAVL. From all this I chiefly conclude that, as you know Nils Lykke and the name he bears, especially as concerns women

LADY INGER. I should be right glad to know him outside my gates?

OLAF SKAKTAVL. Ay; and that as soon as may be.

LADY INGER (smiling). Nay, the case is just the contrary, Olaf Skaktavl!

OLAF SKAKTAVL. How mean you?

LADY INGER. If things be as we both think, Nils Lykke must in nowise depart from Ostrat yet awhile.

OLAF SKAKTAVL (looks at her with disapproval). Are you beginning on crooked courses again, Lady Inger? What scheme have you now in your mind? Something that may increase your own power at the cost of our

LADY INGER. Oh this blindness, that makes you all unjust to me! I see well you think I purpose to make Nils Lykke my daughter's husband. Were such a thought in my mind, why had I refused to take part in what is afoot in Sweden, when Nils Lykke and all the Danish crew seem willing to support it?

OLAF SKAKTAVL. Then if it be not your wish to win him and bind him to you, what would you with him?

LADY INGER. I will tell you in few words. In a letter to me, Nils Lykke has spoken of the high fortune it were to be allied to our house; and I do not say but, for a moment, I let myself think of the matter.

OLAF SKAKTAVL. Ay, see you!

LADY INGER. To wed Nils Lykke to one of my house were doubtless a great step toward reconciling many jarring forces in our land.

OLAF SKAKTAVL. Meseems your daughter Merete's marriage with Vinzents Lunge might have taught you the cost of such a step as this. Scarce had my lord gained a firm footing in our midst, when he began to make free with both our goods and our rights

LADY INGER. I know it even too well, Olaf Skaktavl! But times there be when my thoughts are manifold and strange. I cannot impart them fully either to you or to any one else. Often I know not what were best for me. And yet, a second time to choose a Danish lord for a son-in-law, nought but the uttermost need could drive me to that resource; and heaven be praised, things have not yet come to that!

OLAF SKAKTAVL. I am no wiser than before, Lady Inger; why would you keep Nils Lykke at Ostrat?

LADY INGER (softly). Because I owe him an undying hate. Nils Lykke has done me deadlier wrong than any other man. I cannot tell you wherein it lies; but I shall never rest till I am avenged on him. See you not now? Say that Nils Lykke were to love my daughter, as meseems were like enough. I will persuade him to remain here; he shall learn to know Elina well. She is both fair and wise. Ah if he should one day come before me, with hot love in his heart, to beg for her hand! Then to chase him away like a hound; to drive him off with jibes and scorn; to make it known over all the land that Nils Lykke had come a-wooing to Ostrat in vain! I tell you I would give ten years of my life but to see that day!

OLAF SKAKTAVL. In faith and truth, Inger Gyldenlove, is this your purpose towards him?

LADY INGER. This and nought else, as sure as God lives! Trust me, Olaf Skaktavl, I mean honestly by my countrymen; but I am in no way my own master. Things there be that must be kept hidden, or 'twere my death-blow. But let me once be safe on that side, and you shall see if I have forgotten the oath I swore by Knut Alfson's corpse.

OLAF SKAKTAVL (shakes her by the hand). Thanks for those words! I am loath indeed to think evil of you. Yet, touching your design towards this knight, methinks 'tis a dangerous game you would play. What if you had misreckoned? What if your daughter? 'Tis said no woman can stand against this subtle devil.

LADY INGER. My daughter? Think you that she? Nay, have no fear of that; I know Elina better. All she has heard of his renown has but made her hate him the more. You saw with your own eyes

OLAF SKAKTAVL. Ay, but a woman's mind is shifting ground to build on. 'Twere best you looked well before you.

LADY INGER. That will I, be sure; I will watch them narrowly. But even were he to succeed in luring her into his toils, I have but to whisper two words in her ear, and

OLAF SKAKTAVL. What then?

LADY INGER. She will shrink from him as though he were sent by the foul Tempter himself. Hist, Olaf Skaktavl! Here he comes. Now be cautious.

(NILS LYKKE enters by the foremost door on the right.)

NILS LYKKE (approaches LADY INGER courteously). My noble hostess has summoned me.

LADY INGER. I have learned through my daughter that you are minded to leave us to-night.

NILS LYKKE. Even so, to my sorrow; since my business at Ostrat is over.

OLAF SKAKTAVL. Not before I have the papers.

NILS LYKKE. True, true. I had well-nigh forgotten the weightiest part of my errand. 'Twas the fault of our noble hostess. With such pleasant skill did she keep her guests in talk at the table

LADY INGER. That you no longer remembered what had brought you hither? I rejoice to hear it; For that was my design. Methought that if my guest, Nils Lykke, were to feel at ease in Ostrat, he must forget

NILS LYKKE. What, lady?

LADY INGER. First of all his errand and then all that had gone before it.

NILS LYKKE (to OLAF SKAKTAVL, while he takes out the packet and hands it to him). The papers from Peter Kanzler. You will find them a full account of our partizans in Sweden.

OLAF SKAKTAVL. It is well.

(Sits down by the table on the left, where he opens the packet and examines its contents.)

NILS LYKKE. And now, Lady Inger Gyldenlove, I know not that aught remains to keep me here.

LADY INGER. Were it things of state alone that had brought us together, you might be right. But I should be loath to think so.

NILS LYKKE. You would say?

LADY INGER. I would say that 'twas not alone as a Danish Councillor or as the ally of Peter Kanzler that Nils Lykke came to be my guest. Do I err in fancying that somewhat you may have heard down in Denmark may have made you desirous of closer acquaintance with the Lady of Ostrat.

NILS LYKKE. Far be it from me to deny

OLAF SKAKTAVL (turning over the papers). Strange. No letter.

NILS LYKKE. Lady Inger Gyldenlove's fame is all too widely spread that I should not long have been eager to see her face to face.

LADY INGER. So I thought. But what, then, is an hour's jesting talk at the supper-table? Let us try to sweep away all that has separated us till now; it may well happen that the Nils Lykke I know may wipe out the grudge I bore the one I knew not. Prolong your stay here but a few days, Sir Councillor! I dare not persuade Olaf Skaktavl thereto, since his secret charge in Sweden calls him hence. But as for you, doubtless your sagacity has placed all things beforehand in such train, that your presence can scarce be needed. Trust me, your time shall not pass tediously with us; at least you will find me and my daughter heartily desirous to do all we may to pleasure you.

NILS LYKKE. I doubt neither your goodwill toward me nor your daughter's; of that I have had full proof. And you will doubtless allow that the necessity which calls for my presence elsewhere must be more vital, since, despite your kindness, I must declare my longer stay at Ostrat impossible.

LADY INGER. Is it even so! Know you, Sir Councillor, were I evilly disposed, I might fancy you had come to Ostrat to try a fall with me, and that, having lost, you like not to linger on the battlefield among the witnesses of your defeat.

NILS LYKKE (smiling). There might be some show of reason for such a reading of the case; but sure it is that as yet I hold not the battle lost.

LADY INGER. Be that as it may, it might at any rate be retrieved, if you would tarry some days with us. You see yourself, I am still doubting and wavering at the parting of the ways, persuading my redoubtable assailant not to quit the field. Well, to speak plainly, the thing is this: your alliance with the disaffected in Sweden still seems to me somewhat, ay, what shall I call it? somewhat miraculous, Sir Councillor! I tell you this frankly, dear Sir! The thought that has moved the King's Council to this secret step is in truth most politic; but it is strangely at variance with the deeds of certain of your countrymen in bygone years. Be not offended, then, if my trust in your fair promises needs to be somewhat strengthened ere I can place my whole welfare in your hands.

NILS LYKKE. A longer stay at Ostrat would scarce help towards that end; since I purpose not to make any further effort to shake your resolution.

LADY INGER. Then must I pity you from my heart. Ay, Sir Councillor, 'tis true I stand here an unfriended widow; yet may you trust my word when I prophesy that this visit to Ostrat will strew your future path with thorns.

NILS LYKKE (with a smile). Is that your prophecy, Lady Inger?

LADY INGER. Truly it is! What can one say dear Sir? 'Tis a calumnious age. Many a scurril knave will make scornful rhymes concerning you. Ere half a year is out, you will be all men's fable; people will stop and gaze after you on the high roads; 'twill be: "Look, look; there rides Sir Nils Lykke, that fared north to Ostrat to trap Inger Gyldenlove, and was caught in his own nets."Nay nay, why so impatient, Sir Knight! 'Tis not that I think so; I do but forecast the thought of the malicious and evil-minded; and of them, alas! there are many. Ay, 'tis shame; but so it is, you will reap nought but mockery, mockery, because a woman was craftier than you. "Like a cunning fox," men will say, "he crept into Ostrat; like a beaten hound he slunk away."And one thing more: think you not that Peter Kanzler and his friends will forswear your alliance, when 'tis known that I venture not to fight under a standard borne by you?

NILS LYKKE. You speak wisely, lady! And so, to save myself from mockery and further, to avoid breaking with all our dear friends in Sweden, I must needs

LADY INGER (hastily). prolong your stay at Ostrat?

OLAF SKAKTAVL (who has been listening). He is in the trap!

NILS LYKKE. No, my noble lady; I must needs bring you to terms within this hour.

LADY INGER. But what if you should fail?

NILS LYKKE. I shall not fail.

LADY INGER. You lack not confidence, it seems.

NILS LYKKE. What shall we wager that you make not common cause with myself and Peter Kanzler?

LADY INGER. Ostrat Castle against your knee-buckles.

NILS LYKKE (points to himself and cries:) Olaf Skaktavl here stands the master of Ostrat!

LADY INGER. Sir Councillor!

NILS LYKKE (to LADY INGER). I accept not the wager; for in a moment you will gladly give Ostrat Castle, and more to boot, to be freed from the snare wherein not I but you are tangled.

LADY INGER. Your jest, Sir, grows a vastly merry one.

NILS LYKKE. 'Twill be merrier yet at least for me. You boast that you have overreached me. You threaten to heap on me all men's scorn and mockery. Ah, beware that you stir not up my vengefulness; For with two words I can bring you to your knees at my feet.

LADY INGER. Ha-ha ! (Stops suddenly, as if struck by a foreboding.) And the two words, Nils Lykke? the two words?

NILS LYKKE. The secret of Sten Sture's son and yours.

LADY INGER (with a shriek). Oh, Jesus Christ!

OLAF SKAKTAVL. Inger Gyldenlove's son! What say you?

LADY INGER (half kneeling to NILS LYKKE). Mercy! oh be merciful!

NILS LYKKE (raises her up). Collect yourself, and let us talk calmly.

LADY INGER (in a low voice, as though bewildered). Did you hear it, Olaf Skaktavl? or was it but a dream? Heard you what he said?

NILS LYKKE. It was no dream, Lady Inger!

LADY INGER. And you know it! You, you! Where is he then? Where have you got him? What would you do with him? (Screams.) Do not kill him, Nils Lykke! Give him back to me! Do not kill my child!

OLAF SKAKTAVL. Ah, I begin to understand

LADY INGER. And this fearthis torturing dread! Through all these years it has been ever with me and then all fails at last, and I must bear this agony! Oh Lord my God, is it right of thee? Was it for this thou gavest him to me? (Controls herself and says with forced composure:) Nils Lykke, tell me one thing. Where have you got him? Where is he?

NILS LYKKE. With his foster-father.

LADY INGER. Still with his foster-father. Oh, that merciless man! For ever to deny my prayers. But it must not go on thus! Help me, Olaf Skaktavl!

OLAF SKAKTAVL. I?

NILS LYKKE. There will be no need, if only you

LADY INGER. Hearken, Sir Councillor! What you know you shall know thoroughly. And you too, my old and faithful friend! Listen then. To-night you bade me call to mind that fatal day when Knut Alfson was slain at Oslo. You bade me remember the promise I made as I stood by his corpse amid the bravest men in Norway. I was scarce full-grown then; but I felt God's strength in me, and methought, as many have thought since, that the Lord himself had set his mark on me and chosen me to fight in the forefront for my country's cause.

Was it vanity? Or was it a calling from on high? That I have never clearly known. But woe to him that has a great mission laid upon him.

For seven years I fear not to say that I kept my promise faithfully. I stood by my countrymen in all their miseries. All my playmates were now wives and mothers. I alone could give ear to no wooer, not to one. That you know best, Olaf Skaktavl!

Then I saw Sten Sture for the first time. Fairer man had never met my sight.

NILS LYKKE. Ah, now it grows clear to me! Sten Sture was then in Norway on a secret errand. We Danes were not to know that he wished your friends well.

LADY INGER. Disguised as a mean serving-man he lived a whole winter under one roof with me. That winter I thought less and less of the country's weal . So fair a man had I never seen, and I had lived well-nigh five-and-twenty years. Next autumn Sten Sture came once more; and when he departed again he took with him, in all secrecy, a little child. "Twas not folk's evil tongues I feared; but our cause would have suffered had it got about the Sten Sture stood so near to me. The child was given to Peter Kanzler to rear. I waited for better times, that were soon to come. They never came. Sten Sture took a wife two years later in Sweden, and, dying, left a widow

OLAF SKAKTAVL. And with her a lawful heir to his name and rights.

LADY INGER. Time after time I wrote to Peter Kanzler and besought him to give me back my child. But he was ever deaf to my prayers. "Cast in your lot with us once for all," he said, "and I send your son back to Norway; not before." But 'twas even that I dared not do. We of the disaffected party were then ill regarded by many timorous folk. If these had got tidings of how things stood, oh, I know it! to cripple the mother they had gladly meted to the child the fate that would have been King Christiern's had he not saved himself by flight. But besides that, the Danes were active. They spared neither threats nor promises to force me to join them.

OLAF SKAKTAVL. 'Twas but reason. The eyes of all men were fixed on you as the vane that should show them how to shape their course.

LADY INGER. Then came Herlof Hyttefad's revolt. Do you remember that time, Olaf Skaktavl? Was it not as though the whole land was filled with the sunlight of a new spring. Mighty voices summoned me to come forth; yet I dared not. I stood doubting, far from the strife, in my lonely castle. At times it seemed as though the Lord God himself were calling me; but then would come the killing dread again to paralyse my will. "Who will win?" that was the question that was ever ringing in my ears. 'Twas but a short spring that had come to Norway. Herlof Hyttefad, and many more with him, were broken on the wheel during the months that followed. None could call me to account; yet there lacked not covert threats from Denmark. What if they knew the secret? At last methought they must know; I knew not how else to understand their words.

'Twas even in that time of agony that Gyldenlove the High Steward, came hither and sought me in marriage. Let any mother that has feared for her child think herself in my place! and homeless in the hearts of my countrymen.

Then came the quiet years. There was now no whisper of revolt. Our masters might grind us down even as heavily as they listed. There were times when I loathed myself. What had I to do? Nought but to endure terror and scorn and bring forth daughters into the world. My daughters! God forgive me if I have had no mother's heart towards them. My wifely duties were as serfdom to me; how then could I love my daughters? Oh, how different with my son! He was the child of my very soul. He was the one thing that brought to mind the time when I was a woman and nought but a woman and him they had taken from me! He was growing up among strangers, who might sow in him the seed of destruction! Olaf Skaktavl had I wandered like you on the lonely hills, hunted and forsaken, in winter and storm, if I had but held my child in my arms, trust me, I had not sorrowed and wept so sore as I have sorrowed and wept for him from his birth even to this hour.

OLAF SKAKTAVL. There is my hand. I have judged you too hardly, Lady Inger! Command me even as before; I will obey. Ay, by all the saints, I know what it is to sorrow for a child.

LADY INGER. Yours was slain by bloody men. But what is death to the restless terror of all these long years?

NILS LYKKE. Mark, then, 'tis in your power to end this terror. You have but to reconcile the opposing parties, and neither will think of seizing on your child as a pledge of your faith.

LADY INGER (to herself). This is the vengeance of Heaven. (Looks at him.) In one word, what do you demand?

NILS LYKKE. I demand first that you shall call the people of the northern districts to arms, in support of the disaffected in Sweden.

LADY INGER. And next?

NILS LYKKE. that you do your best to advance young Count Sture's ancestral claim to the throne of Sweden.

LADY INGER. His? You demand that I?

OLAF SKAKTAVL (softly). It is the wish of many Swedes, and 'twould serve our turn too.

NILS LYKKE. You hesitate, lady? You tremble for your son's safety. What better can you wish than to see his half-brother on the throne?

LADY INGER (in thought). True, true

NILS LYKKE (looks at her sharply). Unless there be other plans afoot

LADY INGER. What mean you?

NILS LYKKE. Inger Gyldenlove might have a mind to be a, a kings mother.

LADY INGER. No, no! Give me back my child, and let who will have the crowns. But know you so surely that Count Sture is willing?

NILS LYKKE. Of that he will himself assure you.

LADY INGER. Himself?

NILS LYKKE. Even now.

OLAF SKAKTAVL. How now?

LADY INGER. What say you?

NILS LYKKE. In one word, Count Sture is in Ostrat.

OLAF SKAKTAVL. Here?

NILS LYKKE (to LADY INGER). You have doubtless been told that another rode through the gate along with me? The Count was my attendant.

LADY INGER (softly). I am in his power. I have no longer any choice. (Looks at him and says:) 'Tis well, Sir Councillor, I will assure you of my support.

NILS LYKKE. In writing?

LADY INGER. As you will.

(Goes to the table on the left, sits down, and takes writing materials from the drawer.)

NILS LYKKE (aside, standing by the table on the right). At last, then, I win!

LADY INGER (after a moment's thought, turns suddenly in her chair to OLAF SKAKTAVL and whispers). Olaf Skaktavl I am certain of it now, Nils Lykke is a traitor!

OLAF SKAKTAVL (softly). What? You think?

LADY INGER. He has treachery in his heart

(Lays the paper before her and dips the pen in the ink.)

OLAF SKAKTAVL. And yet you would give him a written promise that may be your ruin?

LADY INGER. Hush; leave me to act. Nay, wait and listen first

(Talks with him in a whisper.)

NILS LYKKE (softly, watching them). Ah, take counsel together as much as ye list! All danger is over now. With her written consent in my pocket, I can denounce her when I please. A secret message to Jens Bielke this very night. I tell him but the truth that the young Count Sture is not at Ostrat. And then to-morrow, when the road is open to Trondhiem with my young friend, and thence by ship to Copenhagen with him as my prisoner. Once we have him safe in the castle-tower, we can dictate to Lady Inger what terms we will. And I? Methinks after this the King will scarce place the French mission in other hands than mine.

LADY INGER (still whispering to OLAF SKAKTAVL). Well, you understand me?

OLAF SKAKTAVL. Ay, fully. Let us risk it.

(Goes out by the back, to the right. NILS STENSSON comes in by the first door on the right, unseen by LADY INGER, who has begun to write.)

NILS STENSSON (in a low voice). Sir Knight, Sir Knight!

NILS LYKKE (moves towards him). Rash boy! What would you here? Said I not you were to wait within until I called you?

NILS STENSSON. How could I? Now you have told me that Inger Gyldenlove is my mother, I thirst more than ever to see her face to face Oh, it is she! How proud and lofty she seems! Even thus did I ever picture her. Fear not, dear Sir, I shall do nought rashly. Since I have learnt this secret, I feel, as it were, older and wiser. I will no longer be wild and heedless; I will be even as other well-born youths. Tell me, knows she that I am here? Surely you have prepared her?

NILS LYKKE. Ay, sure enough; but

NILS STENSSON. Well?

NILS LYKKE. She will not own you for her son.

NILS STENSSON. Will not own me? But she is my mother. Oh, if there be no other way (takes out a ring which he wears on a cord round his neck) show her this ring. I have worn it since my earliest childhood; she must surely know its history.

NILS LYKKE. Hide the ring, man! Hide it, I say! You mistake me. Lady Inger doubts not at all that you are her child; but, ay, look about you; look at all this wealth; look at these mighty ancestors and kinsmen whose pictures deck the walls both high and low; look lastly at herself, the haughty dame, used to bear sway as the first noblewoman in the kingdom. Think you it can be to her mind to take a poor ignorant youth by the hand before all men's eyes and say: Behold my son!

NILS STENSSON. Ay, you are right, I am poor and ignorant. I have nought to offer her in return for what I crave. Oh, never have I felt my poverty weigh on me till this hour! But tell me, what think you I should do to win her love? Tell me, dear Sir; sure you must know.

NILS LYKKE. You must win your father's kingdom. But until that may be, look well that you wound not her ears by hinting at kinship or the like. She will bear her as though she believed you to be the real Count Sture, until you have made yourself worthy to be called her son.

NILS STENSSON. Oh, but tell me!

NILS LYKKE. Hush; hush!

LADY INGER (rises and hands him a paper). Sir Knight, here is my promise.

NILS LYKKE. I thank you.

LADY INGER (notices NILS STENSSON). Ah, this young man is?

NILS LYKKE. Ay, Lady Inger, he is Count Sture.

LADY INGER (aside, looks at him stealthily). Feature for feature; ay, by God, it is Sten Sture's son! (Approaches him and says with cold courtesy.) I bid you welcome under my roof, Count! It rests with you whether or not we shall bless this meeting a year hence.

NILS STENSSON. With me? Oh, do but tell me what I must do! Trust me, I have courage and good-will enough

NILS LYKKE (listens uneasily). What is this noise and uproar, Lady Inger? There are people pressing hitherward. What does this mean?

LADY INGER (in a loud voice). 'Tis the spirits awaking!

(OLAF SKAKTAVL, EINAR HUK, BIORN, FINN, and a number of Peasants and Retainers come in from the back, on the right.)

THE PEASANTS AND RETAINERS. Hail to Lady Inger Gyldenlove!

LADY INGER (to OLAF SKAKTAVL). Have you told them what is in hand?

OLAF SKAKTAVL. I have told them all they need to know.

LADY INGER (to the Crowd). Ay, now, my faithful house-folk and peasants, now must ye arm you as best you can and will. What I forbade you to-night you have now my fullest leave to do. And here I present to you the young Count Sture, the coming ruler of Sweden and Norway too, if God will it so.

THE WHOLE CROWD. Hail to him! Hail to Count Sture!

(General excitement. The Peasants and Retainers choose out weapons and put on breastplates and helmets, amid great noise.)

NILS LYKKE (softly and uneasily). The spirits awaking, she said? I but feigned to conjure up the devil of revolt, 'twere a cursed spite if he got the upper hand of us.

LADY INGER (to NILS STENSSON). Here I give you the first earnest of our service, thirty mounted men, to follow you as bodyguard. Trust me, ere you reach the frontier many hundreds will have ranged themselves under my banner and yours. Go, then, and God be with you!

NILS STENSSON. Thanks, Inger Gyldenlove! Thanks and be sure that you shall never have cause to shame you for, for Count Sture! If you see me again I shall have won my father's kingdom.

NILS LYKKE (to himself). Ay, if she see you again!

OLAF SKAKTAVL. The horses wait, good fellows! Are ye ready?

THE PEASANTS. Ay, ay, ay!

NILS LYKKE (uneasily, to LADY INGER). What? You mean not to-night, even now?

LADY INGER. This very moment, Sir Knight!

NILS LYKKE. Nay, nay, impossible!

LADY INGER. I have said it.

NILS LYKKE (softly, to NILS STENSSON). Obey her not!

NILS STENSSON. How can I otherwise? I will; I must!

NILS LYKKE (with authority). And me!

NILS STENSSON. I shall keep my word; be sure of that. The secret shall not pass my lips till you yourself release me. But she is my mother!

NILS LYKKE (aside). And Jens Bielke in wait on the road! Damnation! He will snatch the prize out of my fingers (To LADY INGER.) Wait till to-morrow!

LADY INGER (to NILS STENSSON). Count Sture, do you obey me or not?

NILS STENSSON. To horse! (Goes up towards the background).

NILS LYKKE (aside). Unhappy boy! He knows not what he does. (To LADY INGER.) Well, since so it must be, farewell!

(Bows hastily, and begins to move away.)

LADY INGER (detains him). Nay, stay! Not so, Sir Knight, not so!

NILS LYKKE. What mean you?

LADY INGER (in a low voice). Nils Lykke, you are a traitor! Hush! Let no one see there is dissension in the camp of the leaders. You have won Peter Kanzler's trust by some devilish cunning that as yet I see not through. You have forced me to rebellious acts, not to help our cause, but to further your own plots, whatever they may be. I can draw back no more. But think not therefore that you have conquered! I shall contrive to make you harmless

NILS LYKKE (lays his hand involuntarily on his sword). Lady Inger!

LADY INGER. Be calm, Sir Councillor! Your life is safe. But you come not outside the gates of Ostrat before victory is ours.

NILS LYKKE. Death and destruction!

LADY INGER. It boots not to resist. You come not from this place. So rest you quiet; 'tis your wisest course.

NILS LYKKE (to himself). Ah, I am overreached. She has been craftier than I. (A thought strikes him.) But if I yet?

LADY INGER (to OLAF SKAKTAVL). Ride with Count Sture's troops to the frontier; then without pause to Peter Kanzler, and bring me back my child. Now has he no longer any plea for keeping from me what is my own. (Adds, as OLAF SKAKTAVL is going:) Wait; a token. He that wears Sten Sture's ring is my son.

OLAF SKAKTAVL. By all the saints, you shall have him!

LADY INGER. Thanks, thanks, my faithful friend!

NILS LYKKE (to FINN, whom he has beckoned to him unobserved, and with whom he has been whispering). Good, now manage to slip out. Let none see you. The Swedes are in ambush two miles hence. Tell the commander that Count Sture is dead. The young man you see there must not be touched. Tell the commander so. Tell him the boy's life is worth thousands to me.

FINN. It shall be done.

LADY INGER (who has meanwhile been watching NILS LYKKE). And now go, all of you; go with God! (Points to NILS LYKKE.) This noble knight cannot find it in his heart to leave his friends at Ostrat so hastily. He will abide here with me till the tidings of your victory arrive.

NILS LYKKE (to himself). Devil!

NILS STENSSON (seizes his hand). Trust me, you shall not have long to wait!

NILS LYKKE. It is well; it is well! (Aside.) All may yet be saved. If only my message reach Jens Bielke in time

LADY INGER (to EINAR HUK, the bailiff, pointing to FINN). And let that man be placed under close guard in the castle dungeon.

FINN. Me?

THE BAILIFF AND THE SERVANTS. Finn!

NILS LYKKE (aside). My last anchor gone!

LADY INGER (imperatively). To the dungeon with him!

(EINAR HUK, BIORN, and a couple of the house-servants lead FINN out to the left.)

ALL THE REST (except NILS LYKKE, rushing out to the right). Away! To horse, to horse! Hail to Lady Inger Gyldenlove!

LADY INGER (passes close to NILS LYKKE as she follows the others). Who wins?

NILS LYKKE (remains alone). Who? Ay, woe to you; your victory will cost you dear. I wash my hands of it. 'Tis not I that am murdering him. But my prey is escaping me none the less; and the revolt will grow and spread! Ah, 'tis a foolhardy, a frantic game I have been playing here! (Listens at the window.) There they go clattering out through the gateway. Now 'tis closed after them and I am left here a prisoner. No way of escape! Within half-an-hour the Swedes will be upon him. 'Twill be life or death. But if they should take him alive after all? Were I but free, I could overtake the Swedes ere they reach the frontier, and make them deliver him up. (Goes towards the window in the background and looks out.) Damnation! Guards outside on every hand. Can there be no way out of this? (Comes quickly forward again; suddenly stops and listens.) What is that? Music and singing. It seems to come from Elina's chamber. Ay, it is she that is singing. Then she is still awake (A thought seems to strike him.) Elina! Ah, if that could be! If it could butAnd why should I not? Am I not still myself? Says not the song:

Fair maidens a-many they sigh and they pine; "Ah God, that Nils Lykke were mine, mine, mine."

And she? Elina Gyldenlove shall set me free!

(Goes quickly but stealthily towards the first door on the left.)

NOTES.

[1] King Christian II. of Denmark (the perpetrator of the massacre at Stockholm known as the Blood-Bath) fled to Holland in 1523, five years before the date assigned to this play, in order to escape death or imprisonment at the hands of his rebellious nobles, who summoned his uncle, Frederick I., to the throne. Returning to Denmark in 1532, Christian was thrown into prison, where he spent the last twenty-seven years of his life.

Act Fifth

(The Banquet Hall. It is still night. The hall is but dimly lighted by a branch-candlestick on the table, in front, on the right.)

(LADY INGER is sitting by the table, deep in thought.)

LADY INGER (after a pause). They call me keen-witted beyond all others in the land. I believe they are right. The keenest- witted No one knows how I became so. For more than twenty years I have fought to save my child. That is the key to the riddle. Ay, that sharpens the wits!

My wits? Where have they flown to-night? What has become of my forethought? There is a ringing and rushing in my ears. I see shapes before me, so life-like that methinks I could lay hold on them.

(Springs up.)

Lord Jesus, what is this? Am I no longer mistress of my reason? Is it to come to that?

(Presses her clasped hands over her head; sits down again, and says more calmly:)

Nay, 'tis nought. It will pass. There is no fear; it will pass. How peaceful it is in the hall to-night! No threatening looks from forefathers or kinsfolk. No need to turn their faces to the wall.

(Rises again.)

Ay, 'twas well that I took heart at last. We shall conquer; and then I am at the end of my longings. I shall have my child again.

(Takes up the light as if to go, but stops and says musingly:)

At the end? The end? To get him back? Is that all? is there nought further?

(Sets the light down on the table.)

That heedless word that Nils Lykke threw forth at random How could he see my unborn thought?

(More softly.)

A king's mother? A king's mother, he saidWhy not? Have not my forefathers ruled as kings, even though they bore not the kingly name? Has not my son as good a title as the other to the rights of the house of Sture? In the sight of God he has, if so be there is justice in Heaven.

And in an hour of terror I have signed away his rights. I have recklessly squandered them, as a ransom for his freedom. If they could be recovered? Would Heaven be angered, if I? Would it call down fresh troubles on my head if I were to? Who knows; who knows! It may be safest to refrain. (Takes up the light again.) I shall have my child again. That must suffice me. I will try to rest. All these desperate thoughts, I will sleep them away.

(Goes towards the back, but stops in the middle of the hall, and says broodingly:)

A king's mother!

(Goes slowly out at the back, to the left.)

(After a short pause, NILS LYKKE and ELINA GYLDENLOVE enter noiselessly by the first door on the left. NILS LYKKE has a small lantern in his hand.)

NILS LYKKE. (throws the light from his lantern around, so as to search the room). All is still. I must begone.

ELINA. Oh, let me look but once more into your eyes, before you leave me.

NILS LYKKE (embraces her). Elina!

ELINA (after a short pause). Will you come nevermore to Ostrat?

NILS LYKKE. How can you doubt that I will come? Are you not henceforth my betrothed? But will you be true to me, Elina? Will you not forget me ere we meet again?

ELINA. Do you ask if I will be true? Have I any will left then? Have I power to be untrue to you, even if I would? you came by night; you knocked upon my door; and I opened to you. You spoke to me. What was it you said? You gazed in my eyes. What was the mystic might that turned my brain and lured me, as it were, within a magic net? (Hides her face on his shoulder.) Oh, look not on me, Nils Lykke! You must not look upon me after this True, say you ? Do you not own me? I am yours; I must be yours, to all eternity.

NILS LYKKE. Now, by my knightly honour, ere the year be past, you shall sit as my wife in the hall of my fathers.

ELINA. No vows, Nils Lykke! No oaths to me.

NILS LYKKE. What mean you? Why do you shake your head so mournfully?

ELINA. Because I know that the same soft words wherewith you turned my brain, you have whispered to so many a one before. Nay, nay, be not angry, my beloved! In nought do I reproach you, as I did while yet I knew you not. Now I understand how high above all others is your goal. How can love be aught to you but a pastime, or woman but a toy?

NILS LYKKE. Elina, hear me!

ELINA. As I grew up, your name was ever in my ears. I hated the name, for meseemed that all women were dishonoured by your life. And yet, how strange! when I built up in my dreams the life that should be mine, you were ever my hero, though I knew it not. Now I understand it all, now know I what it was I felt. It was a foreboding, a mysterious longing for you, you only one, for you that were one day to come and glorify my life.

NILS LYKKE (aside, putting down the lantern on the table). How is it with me? This dizzy fascination If this it be to love, then have I never known it till this hour. Is there not yet time ? Oh horror, Lucia!

(Sinks into a chair.)

ELINA. What ails you? So heavy a sigh

NILS LYKKE. O, 'tis nought, nought! Elina, now will I confess all to you. I have have beguiled many with both words and glances; I have said to many a one what I whispered to you this night. But trust me

ELINA. Hush! No more of that. My love is no exchange for that you give me. No, no; I love you because your every glance commands it like a king's decree.

(Lies down at his feet.)

Oh, let me once more stamp that kingly message deep into my soul, though well I know it stands imprinted there for all time and eternity.

Dear God, how little I have known myself! 'Twas but to-night I said to my mother: "My pride is my life." And what is my pride? Is it to know that my countrymen are free, or that my house is held in honour throughout the lands? Oh, no, no! My love is my pride. The little dog is proud when he may sit by his master's feet and eat bread-crumbs from his hand. Even so am I proud, so long as I may sit at your feet, while your looks and your words nourish me with the bread of life. See, therefore, I say to you, even as I said but now to my mother: "My love is my life;" for therein lies all my pride, now and evermore.

NILS LYKKE (raises her up on his lap). Nay, nay, not at my feet, but at my side is your place, should fate set me never so high. Ay, Elina, you have led me into a better path; and if it be granted me some day to atone by a deed of fame for the sins of my reckless youth, the honour shall be yours as well as mine.

ELINA. Ah, you speak as though I were still the Elina that but this evening flung down the flowers at your feet. I have read in my books of the many-coloured life in far-off lands. To the winding of horns the knight rides forth into the greenwood, with his falcon on his wrist. Even so do you go your way through life; your name rings out before you whithersoever you fare. All that I desire of your glory, is to rest like the falcon on your arm. I too was blind as he to light and life, till you loosed the hood from my eyes and set me soaring high over the leafy tree-tops; But, trust me, bold as my flight may be, yet shall I ever turn back to my cage.

NILS LYKKE (rises). Then I bid defiance to the past! See now; take this ring, and be mine before God and men, mine, ay, though it should trouble the dreams of the dead.

ELINA. You make me afraid. What is it that?

NILS LYKKE. It is nought. Come, let me place the ring on your finger. Even so, now are you my betrothed!

ELINA. I Nils Lykke's bride! It seems but a dream, all that has befallen this night. Oh, but so fair a dream! My breast is so light. No longer is there bitterness and hatred in my soul. I will atone to all whom I have wronged. I have been unloving to my mother. To-morrow will I go to her; she must forgive me my offence.

NILS LYKKE. And give her consent to our bond.

ELINA. That will she. Oh, I am sure she will. My mother is kind; all the world is kind; I can feel hatred no more for any living soul save one.

NILS LYKKE. Save one?

ELINA. Ah, it is a mournful history. I had a sister

NILS LYKKE. Lucia?

ELINA. Have you known Lucia?

NILS LYKKE. No, no; I have but heard her name.

ELINA. She too gave her heart to a knight. He betrayed her; and now she is in Heaven.

NILS LYKKE. And you?

ELINA. I hate him.

NILS LYKKE. Hate him not! If there be mercy in your heart, forgive him his sin. Trust me, he bears his punishment in his own breast.

ELINA. Him I will never forgive! I cannot, even if I would; for I have sworn so dear an oath (Listening.) Hush! Can you hear?

NILS LYKKE. What? Where?

ELINA. Without; far off. The noise of many horsemen on the high-road.

NILS LYKKE. Ah, it is they! And I had forgotten! They are coming hither. Then is the danger great; I must begone!

ELINA. But whither? Oh, Nils Lykke, what are you hiding?

NILS LYKKE. To-morrow, Elina; for as God lives, I will return then. Quickly now, where is the secret passage you told me of?

ELINA. Through the grave-vault. See, here is the trap-door.

NILS LYKKE. The grave-vault! (To himself.) No matter, he must be saved!

ELINA (by the window). The horsemen have reached the gate

(Hands him the lantern.)

NILS LYKKE. Well, now I go

(Begins to descend.)

ELINA. Go forward along the passage till you reach the coffin with the death's-head and the black cross; it is Lucia's

NILS LYKKE (climbs back hastily and shuts the trap-door to). Lucia's! Pah!

ELINA. What said you?

NILS LYKKE. Nay, nought. It was the scent of the grave that made me dizzy.

ELINA. Hark; they are hammering at the gate!

NILS LYKKE (lets the lantern fall). Ah! too late!

(BIORN enters hurriedly from the right, carrying a light.)

ELINA (goes towards him). What is amiss, Biorn? What is it?

BIORN. An ambuscade! Count Sture

ELINA. Count Sture? What of him?

NILS LYKKE. Have they killed him?

BIORN (to ELINA). Where is your mother?

TWO HOUSE-SERVANTS (rushing in from the right). Lady Inger! Lady Inger!

(LADY INGER GYLDENLOVE enters by the first door on the left, with a branch-candlestick, lighted, in her hand, and says quickly:)

LADY INGER. I know all. Down with you to the courtyard! Keep the gate open for our friends, but closed against all others!

(Puts down the candlestick on the table to the left. BIORN and the two House-Servants go out again to the right.)

LADY INGER (to NILS LYKKE). So that was the trap, Sir Councillor!

NILS LYKKE. Inger Gyldenlove, trust me!

LADY INGER. An ambuscade that was to snap him up, as soon as you had got the promise that should destroy me!

NILS LYKKE (takes out the paper and tears it to pieces). There is your promise. I keep nothing that can bear witness against you.

LADY INGER. What will you do?

NILS LYKKE. From this hour I am your champion. If I have sinned against you, by Heaven I will strive to repair my crime. But now I must out, if I have to hew my way through the gate! Elina, tell your mother all! And you, Lady Inger, let our reckoning be forgotten! Be generous and silent! Trust me, ere the day dawns you shall owe me a life's gratitude.

(Goes out quickly to the right.)

LADY INGER (looks after him with exultation). It is well! I understand him!

(Turns to ELINA.)

Nils Lykke? Well?

ELINA. He knocked upon my door, and set this ring upon my finger.

LADY INGER. And he loves you with all his heart?

ELINA. My mother, you are so strange. Oh, ay, I know, it is my unloving ways that have angered you.

LADY INGER. Not so, dear Elina! You are an obedient child. You have opened your door to him; you have hearkened to his soft words. I know full well what it must have cost you for I know your hatred

ELINA. But, my mother

LADY INGER. Hush! We have played into each other's hands. What wiles did you use, my subtle daughter? I saw the love shine out of his eyes. Hold him fast now! Draw the net closer and closer about him, and then Ah, Elina, if we could but rend his perjured heart within his breast!

ELINA. Woe is me, what is it you say?

LADY INGER. Let not your courage fail you. Hearken to me. I know a word that will keep you firm. Know then (Listening.) They are fighting outside the gate. Courage! Now comes the pinch! (Turns again to ELINA.) Know then, Nils Lykke was the man that brought your sister to her grave.

ELINA (with a shriek). Lucia!

LADY INGER. He it was, as truly as there is an Avenger above us!

ELINA. Then Heaven be with me!

LADY INGER (appalled). Elina?!

ELINA. I am his bride in the sight of God.

LADY INGER. Unhappy child, what have you done?

ELINA (in a toneless voice). Made shipwreck of my soul. Good-night, my mother!

(She goes out to the left.)

LADY INGER. Ha-ha-ha! It goes down-hill now with Inger Gyldenlove's house. There went the last of my daughters. Why could I not keep silence? Had she known nought, it may be she had been happy, after a kind.

It was to be so. It is written up there in the stars that I am to break off one green branch after another, till the trunk stand leafless at last.

'Tis well, 'tis well! I am to have my son again. Of the others, of my daughters, I will not think.

My reckoning? To face my reckoning? It falls not due till the last great day of wrath. That comes not yet awhile.

NILS STENSSON (calling from outside on the right). Ho, shut the gate!

LADY INGER. Count Sture's voice!

NILS STENSSON (rushes in, unarmed, and with his clothes torn, and shouts with a desperate laugh). Well met again, Inger Gyldenlove!

LADY INGER. What have you lost?

NILS STENSSON. My kingdom and my life!

LADY INGER. And the peasants? My servants? where are they?

NILS STENSSON. You will find the carcasses along the highway. Who has the rest, I know not.

OLAF SKAKTAVL (outside on the right). Count Sture! Where are you?

NILS STENSSON. Here, here!

(OLAF SKAKTAVL comes in with his right hand wrapped in a cloth).

LADY INGER. Alas Olaf Skaktavl, you too!

OLAF SKAKTAVL. It was impossible to break through.

LADY INGER. You are wounded, I see!

OLAF SKAKTAVL. A finger the less; that is all.

NILS STENSSON. Where are the Swedes?

OLAF SKAKTAVL. At our heels. They are breaking open the gate

NILS STENSSON. Oh, Jesus! No, no! I cannot, I will not die.

OLAF SKAKTAVL. A hiding-place, Lady Inger! Is there no corner where we can hide him?

LADY INGER. But if they search the castle?

NILS STENSSON. Ay, ay; they will find me! And then to be dragged to prison, or strung up! Oh no, Inger Gyldenlove, I know full well, you will never suffer that to be!

OLAF SKAKTAVL (listening). There burst the lock.

LADY INGER (at the window). Many men rush in at the gateway.

NILS STENSSON. And to lose my life now! Now, when my true life was but beginning! Now, when I have so lately learnt that I have aught to live for. No, no, no! Think not I am a coward. Might I but have time to show

LADY INGER. I hear them now in the hall below.

(Firmly to OLAF SKAKTAVL.)

He must be saved, cost what it will!

NILS STENSSON (seizes her hand). Oh, I knew it; you are noble and good!

OLAF SKAKTAVL. But how? Since we cannot hide him

NILS STENSSON. Ah, I have it! I have it! The secret!

LADY INGER. The secret?

NILS STENSSON. Even so; yours and mine!

LADY INGER. Christ in Heaven, you know it?

NILS STENSSON. From first to last. And now when 'tis life or death Where is Nils Lykke?

LADY INGER. Fled.

NILS STENSSON. Fled? Then God help me; for he only can unseal my lips. But what is a promise against a life! When the Swedish captain comes

LADY INGER. What then? What will you do?

NILS STENSSON. Purchase life and freedom; tell him all.

LADY INGER. Oh no, no; be merciful!

NILS STENSSON. Nought else can save me. When I have told him what I know

LADY INGER (looks at him with suppressed excitement). You will be safe?

NILS STENSSON. Ay, safe! Nils Lykke will speak for me. You see, 'tis the last resource.

LADY INGER (composedly, with emphasis). The last resource? Right, right, the last resource stands open to all. (Points to the left.) See, meanwhile you can hide in there.

NILS STENSSON (softly). Trust me, you will never repent of this.

LADY INGER (half to herself). God grant that you speak the truth!

(NILS STENSSON goes out hastily by the furthest door on the left. OLAF SKAKTAVL is following; but LADY INGER detains him.)

LADY INGER. Did you understand his meaning?

OLAF SKAKTAVL. The dastard! He would betray your secret. He would sacrifice your son to save himself.

LADY INGER. When life is at stake, he said, we must try the last resource. It is well, Olaf Skaktavl, let it be as he has said!

OLAF SKAKTAVL. What mean you?

LADY INGER. Life for life! One of them must perish.

OLAF SKAKTAVL. Ah, you would?

LADY INGER. If we close not the lips of him that is within ere he come to speech with the Swedish captain, then is my son lost to me. But if he be swept from my path, when the time comes I can claim all his rights for my own child. Then shall you see that Inger Ottisdaughter has metal in her yet. And be assured you shall not have long to wait for the vengeance you have thirsted after for twenty years. Hark! They are coming up the stairs! Olaf Skaktavl, it lies with you whether to-morrow I shall be a childless woman, or

OLAF SKAKTAVL. So be it! I have one sound hand left yet. (Gives her his hand.) Inger Gyldenlove, your name shall not die out through me.

(Follows NILS STENSSON into the inner room.)

LADY INGER (pale and trembling). But dare I?

(A noise is heard in the room; she rushes with a scream towards the door.)

No, no, it must not be!

(A heavy fall is heard within; she covers her ears with her hands and hurries back across the hall with a wild look. After a pause she takes her hands cautiously away, listens again and says softly:)

Now it is over. All is still within Thou sawest it, God, I repented me! But Olaf Skaktavl was too swift of hand.

(OLAF SKAKTAVL comes silently into the hall.)

LADY INGER (after a pause, without looking at him). Is it done?

OLAF SKAKTAVL. You need fear him no more; he will betray no one.

LADY INGER (as before). Then he is dumb?

OLAF SKAKTAVL. Six inches of steel in his breast. I felled him with my left hand.

LADY INGER. Ay, the right was too good for such work.

OLAF SKAKTAVL. That is your affair; the thought was yours. And now to Sweden! Peace be with you meanwhile! When next we meet at Ostrat, I shall bring another with me.

(Goes out by the furthest door on the right.)

LADY INGER. Blood on my hands. Then it was to come to that! He begins to be dear-bought now.

(BIORN comes in, with a number of Swedish men-at-arms, by the first door on the right.)

ONE OF THE MEN-AT-ARMS. Pardon me, if you are the lady of the house

LADY INGER. Is it Count Sture you seek?

THE MAN-AT-ARMS. The same.

LADY INGER. Then you are on the right scent. The Count has sought refuge with me.

THE MAN-AT-ARMS. Refuge? Pardon, my noble lady, you have no power to harbour him; for

LADY INGER. That the Count himself has doubtless understood; and therefore he has, -ay, look for yourselves therefore he has taken his own life.

THE MAN-AT-ARMS. His own life!

LADY INGER. Look for yourselves. You will find the corpse within there. And since he already stands before another judge, it is my prayer that he may be borne hence with all the honour that beseems his noble birth. Biorn, you know my own coffin has stood ready this many a year in the secret chamber. (To the Men- at-Arms.) I pray that in it you will bear Count Sture's body to Sweden.

THE MAN-AT-ARMS. It shall be as you command. (To one of the others.) Haste with these tidings to Jens Bielke. He holds the road with the rest of the troop. We others must in and

(One of the Men-at-Arms goes out to the right; the others go with BIORN into the room on the left.)

LADY INGER (moves about for a time in uneasy silence). If Count Sture had not said farewell to the world so hurriedly, within a month he had hung on a gallows, or had sat for all his days in a dungeon. Had he been better served with such a lot?

Or else he had bought his life by betraying my child into the hands of my foes. Is it I, then, that have slain him? Does not even the wolf defend her cubs? Who dare condemn me for striking my claws into him that would have reft me of my flesh and blood? It had to be. No mother but would have done even as I.

But 'tis no time for idle musings now. I must to work.

(Sits down by the table on the left.)

I will write to all my friends throughout the land. They rise as one man to support the great cause. A new king, regent first, and then king

(Begins to write, but falls into thought, and says softly:)

Whom will they choose in the dead man's place? A king's mother? 'Tis a fair word. It has but one blemish, the hateful likeness to another word. King's mother and king's murderer.King's mother, one that takes a king's life. King's mother, one that gives a king life.

(She rises.)

Well, then; I will make good what I have taken. My son shall be king!

(She sits down again and begins writing, but pushes the paper away again, and leans back in her chair.)

There is no comfort in a house where lies a corpse. 'Tis therefore I feel so strangely. (Turns her head to one side as if speaking to some one.) Not therefore? Why else should it be?

(Broodingly.)

Is there such a great gulf, then, between openly striking down a foe and slaying one thus? Knut Alfson had cleft many a brain with his sword; yet was his own as peaceful as a child's. Why then do I ever see this (makes a motion as though striking with a knife) this stab in the heart and the gush of red blood after?

(Rings, and goes on speaking while shifting about her papers.)

Hereafter I will have none of these ugly sights. I will work both day and night. And in a month, in a month my son will be here

BIORN (entering). Did you strike the bell, my lady?

LADY INGER (writing). Bring more lights. See to it in future that there are many lights in the room

(BIORN goes out again to the left.)

LADY INGER (after a pause, rises impetuously). No, no, no; I cannot guide the pen to-night! My head is burning and throbbing

(Startled, listens.)

What is that? Ah, they are screwing the lid on the coffin in there.

When I was a child they told me the story of Sir Age, who rose up and walked with his coffin on his back. If he in there were one night to think of coming with the coffin on his back, to thank me for the loan? (Laughs quietly.) Hm, what have we grown people to do with childish fancies? (Vehemently.) But such stories are hurtful none the less! They give uneasy dreams. When my son is king, they shall be forbidden.

(Goes up and down once or twice; then opens the window.) How long is it, commonly, ere a body begins to rot? All the rooms must be aired. 'Tis not wholesome here till that be done.

(BIORN comes in with two lighted branch-candlesticks, which he places on the tables.)

LADY INGER (who has begun on the papers again). It is well. See you forget not what I have said. Many lights on the table! What are they about now in there?

BIORN. They are busy screwing down the coffin-lid.

LADY INGER (writing). Are they screwing it down tight?

BIORN. As tight as need be.

LADY INGER. Ay, ay who can tell how tight it needs to be? Do you see that 'tis well done. (Goes up to him with her hand full of papers, and says mysteriously:) Biorn, you are an old man; but one counsel I will give you. Be on your guard against all men, both those that are dead and those that are still to die. Now go in, go in and see to it that they screw the lid down tightly.

BIORN (softly, shaking his head). I cannot make her out.

(Goes back again into the room on the left.)

LADY INGER (begins to seal a letter, but throws it down half-closed; walks up and down awhile, and then says vehemently:)

Were I a coward I had never done it, never to all eternity!

Were I a coward, I had shrieked to myself: Refrain, ere yet thy soul is utterly lost!

(Her eye falls on Sten Sture's picture; she turns to avoid seeing it, and says softly:)

He is laughing down at me as though he were alive! Pah!

(Turns the picture to the wall without looking at it.)

Wherefore did you laugh? Was it because I did evil to your son? But the other, is not he your son too? And he is mine as well; mark that!

(Glances stealthily along the row of pictures.)

So wild as they are to-night, I have never seen them yet. Their eyes follow me wherever I may go. (Stamps on the floor.) I will not have it! (Begins to turn all the pictures to the wall.) Ay, if it were the Holy Virgin herself - Thinkest thou now is the time? Why didst thou never hear my prayers, my burning prayers, that I might get back my child? Why? Because the monk of Wittenberg is right. There is no mediator between God and man!

(She draws her breath heavily and continues in ever-increasing distraction.)

It is well that I know what to think in such things. There was no one to see what was done in there. There is none to bear witness against me.

(Suddenly stretches out her hands and whispers:)

My son! My beloved child! Come to me! Here I am! Hush! I will tell you something: They hate me up there, beyond the stars, because I bore you into the world. It was meant that I should bear the Lord God's standard over all the land. But I went my own way. It is therefore I have had to suffer so much and so long.

BIORN (comes from the room on the left). My lady, I have to tell you Christ save me, what is this?

LADY INGER (has climbed up into the high-seat by the right-hand wall). Hush! Hush! I am the King's mother. They have chosen my son king. The struggle was hard ere it came to this, for 'twas with the Almighty One himself I had to strive.

NILS LYKKE (comes in breathless from the right). He is saved! I have Jens Bielke's promise. Lady Inger, know that

LADY INGER. Peace, I say! look how the people swarm.

(A funeral hymn is heard from the room within.)

There comes the procession. What a throng! All bow themselves before the King's mother. Ay, ay; has she not fought for her son, even till her hands grew red withal? Where are my daughters? I see them not.

NILS LYKKE. God's blood! what has befallen here?

LADY INGER. My daughters, my fair daughters! I have none any more. I had one left, and her I lost even as she was mounting her bridal bed. (Whispers.) Lucia's corpse lay in it. There was no room for two.

NILS LYKKE. Ah, it has come to this! The Lord's vengeance is upon me.

LADY INGER. Can you see him? Look, look! It is the King. It is Inger Gyldenlove's son! I know him by the crown and by Sten Sture's ring that he wears round his neck. Hark, what a joyful sound! He is coming! Soon will he be in my arms! Ha-ha! who conquers, God or I.

(The Men-at-Arms come out with the coffin.)

LADY INGER (clutches at her head and shrieks). The corpse! (Whispers.) Pah! It is a hideous dream.

(Sinks back into the high-seat.)

JENS BIELKE (who has come in from the right, stops and cries in astonishment). Dead! Then after all

ONE OF THE MEN-AT-ARMS. It was himself

JENS BIELKE (with a look at NILS LYKKE). He himself?

NILS LYKKE. Hush!

LADY INGER (faintly, coming to herself). Ay, right; now I remember it all.

JENS BIELKE (to the Men-at-Arms). Set down the corpse. It is not Count Sture.

ONE OF THE MEN-AT-ARMS. Your pardon, Captain; this ring that he wore round his neck

NILS LYKKE (seizes his arm). Be still!

LADY INGER (starts up). The ring? The ring?

(Rushes up and snatches the ring from him.)

Sten Sture's ring! (With a shriek.) Oh, Jesus Christ, my son!

(Throws herself down on the coffin.)

THE MEN-AT-ARMS. Her son?

JENS BIELKE (at the same time). Inger Gyldenlove's son?

NILS LYKKE. So it is.

JENS BIELKE. But why did you not tell me?

BIORN (trying to raise her up). Help! help! My lady, what ails you?

LADY INGER (in a faint voice, half raising herself). What ails me? I lack but another coffin, and a grave beside my child.

(Sinks again, senseless on the coffin. NILS LYKKE goes hastily out to the right. General consternation among the rest.)

THE END.

Henrik Ibsen - The Vikings Of Hegeland

Index Of Contents

THE VIKINGS OF HELGELAND. PLAY IN FOUR ACTS.

CHARACTERS.

ORNULF OF THE FIORDS, an Icelandic Chieftain.
SIGURD THE STRONG, a Sea-King.
GUNNAR HEADMAN,[1] a rich yeoman of Helgeland.
DAGNY, Ornulf's daughter.
HIORDIS, his foster-daughter.
KARE THE PEASANT, a Helgeland-man.
EGIL, Gunnar's son, four years old.
ORNULF'S SIX OLDER SONS.
ORNULF'S AND SIGURD'S MEN.
Guests, house-carls, serving-maids, outlaws, etc.

The action takes place in the time of Erik Blood-axe (about A.D. 933) at, and in the neighbourhood of, Gunnar's house on the island of Helgeland, in the north of Norway.

ACT FIRST.

(A rocky coast, running precipitously down to the sea at the back. To the left, a boat-house; to the right, rocks and pine-woods. The masts of two war-ships can be seen down in the cove. Far out to the right, the ocean, dotted with reefs and rocky islands; the sea is running high; it is a stormy snow-grey winter day.)

(SIGURD comes up from the ships; he is clad in a white tunic with a silver belt, a blue cloak, cross-gartered hose, untanned shoes, and a steel cap; at his side hangs a short sword. ORNULF comes in sight immediately afterwards, up among the rocks, clad in a dark lamb-skin tunic with a breastplate and greaves, woollen stockings, and untanned shoes; over his shoulders he has a cloak of brown frieze, with the hood drawn over his steel cap, so that his face is partly hidden. He is very tall, and massively built, with a long white beard, but somewhat bowed by age; his weapons are a round shield, sword, and spear.)

SIGURD (enters first, looks around, sees the boat-shed, goes quickly up to it, and tries to burst open the door.)

ORNULF (appears among the rocks, starts on seeing SIGURD, seems to recognise him, descends and cries:) Give place, Viking!

SIGURD (turns, lays his hand on his sword, and answers:) 'Twere the first time if I did!

ORNULF. Thou shalt and must! I have need of the shelter for my stiff-frozen men.

SIGURD. Then must outlaws be highly prized in Helgeland!

ORNULF. Dearly shalt thou aby that word!

SIGURD. Now will it go ill with thee, old man!

(ORNULF rushes upon him; SIGURD defends himself.) (DAGNY and some of SIGURD'S men come up from the strand; Ornulf's six sons appear on the rocks to the right.)

DAGNY (who is a little in front, clad in a red kirtle, blue cloak, and fur hood, calls down to the ships:) Up, all Sigurd's men! My husband is fighting with a stranger!

ORNULF'S SONS. Help for Ornulf! (They descend.)

SIGURD (to his men). Hold! I can master him alone!

ORNULF (to his sons). Let me fight in peace! (Rushes in upon SIGURD.) I will see thy blood!

SIGURD. First see thine own! (Wounds him in the arm so that his spear falls.)

ORNULF.

 A stout stroke, Viking!
Swift the sword thou swingest,
keen thy blows and biting;
Sigurd's self, the Stalwart,
stood before thee shame-struck.

SIGURD (smiling). Then were his shame his glory!

ORNULF'S SONS (with a cry of wonder). Sigurd himself! Sigurd the Strong!

ORNULF. But sharper was thy stroke that night thou didst bear away Dagny, my daughter. (Casts his hood back.)

SIGURD AND HIS MEN. Ornulf of the Fiords!

DAGNY (glad, yet uneasy). My father and my brothers!

SIGURD. Stand thou behind me.

ORNULF. Nay, no need. (Approaching SIGURD.) I knew thy face as soon as I was ware of thee, and therefore I stirred the strife; I was fain to prove the fame that tells of thee as the stoutest man of his hands in Norway. Henceforth let peace be between us.

SIGURD. Best if so it could be.

ORNULF. Here is my hand. Thou art a warrior indeed; stouter strokes than these has old Ornulf never given or taken.

SIGURD (seizes his outstretched hand). Let them be the last strokes given and taken between us two; and do thou thyself adjudge the matter between us. Art thou willing?

ORNULF. That am I, and straightway shall the quarrel be healed. (To the others.) Be the matter, then, known to all. Five winters ago came Sigurd and Gunnar Headman as vikings to Iceland; they lay in harbour close under my homestead. Then Gunnar, by force and craft, carried away my foster-daughter, Hiordis; but thou, Sigurd, didst take Dagny, my own child, and sailed with her over the sea. For that thou art now doomed to pay three hundred pieces of silver, and thereby shall thy misdeed be atoned.

SIGURD. Fair is thy judgment, Ornulf; the three hundred pieces will I pay, and add thereto a silken cloak fringed with gold. It is a gift from King AEthelstan of England, and better has no Icelander yet borne.

DAGNY. So be it, my brave husband; and my father, I thank thee. Now at last is my mind at ease.

(She presses her father's and brothers' hands, and talks low to them.)

ORNULF. Then thus stands the treaty between us; and from this day shall Dagny be to the full as honourably regarded as though she had been lawfully betrothed to thee, with the good will of her kin.

SIGURD. And in me canst thou trust, as in one of thine own blood.

ORNULF. That doubt I not; and see! I will forthwith prove thy friendship.

SIGURD. Ready shalt thou find me; say, what dost thou crave?

ORNULF. Thy help in rede and deed. I have sailed hither to Helgeland to seek out Gunnar Headman and draw him to reckoning for the carrying away of Hiordis.

SIGURD (surprised). Gunnar!

DAGNY (in the same tone). And Hiordis, where are they?

ORNULF. In Gunnar's homestead, I ween.

SIGURD. And it is?

ORNULF. Not many bow-shots hence; did ye not know?

SIGURD (with suppressed emotion). No, truly. Small tidings have I had of Gunnar since we sailed from Iceland together. I have wandered far and wide and served many outland kings, while Gunnar sat at home. Hither we drive at day-dawn before the storm; I knew, indeed, that Gunnar's homestead lay here in the north, but

DAGNY (to ORNULF). So that errand has brought thee hither?

ORNULF. That and no other. (To SIGURD.) Our meeting is the work of the Mighty Ones above; they willed it so. Had I wished to find thee, little knew I where to seek.

SIGURD (thoughtfully). True, true! But concerning Gunnar, tell me, Ornulf, art thou minded to go sharply to work, with all thy might, be it for good or ill?

ORNULF. That must I. Listen, Sigurd, for thus it stands: Last summer I rode to the Council where many honourable men were met. When the Council-days were over, I sat in the hall and drank with the men of my hundred, and the talk fell upon the carrying-away of the women; scornful words they gave me, because I had let that wrong rest unavenged. Then, in my wrath, I swore to sail to Norway, seek out Gunnar, and crave reckoning or revenge, and never again to set foot in Iceland till my claim was made good.

SIGURD. Ay, ay, since so it stands, I see well that if need be the matter must be pressed home.

ORNULF. It must; but I shall not crave over much, and Gunnar has the fame of an honourable man. Glad am I, too, that I set about this quest; the time lay heavy on me in Iceland; out upon the blue waters had I grown old and grey, and I longed to fare forth once again before I; well well, Bergthora, my good wife, was dead these many years; my eldest sons sailed on viking-ventures summer by summer; and since Thorolf was growing up

DAGNY (gladly). Thorolf is with thee? Where is he?

ORNULF. On board the ship. (Points towards the background, to the right.) Scarce shalt thou know the boy again, so stout and strong and fair has he grown. He will be a mighty warrior, Sigurd; one day he will equal thee.

DAGNY (smiling). I see it is now as ever; Thorolf stands nearest thy heart.

ORNULF. He is the youngest, and like his mother; therefore it is.

SIGURD. But tell me, thy errand to Gunnar, thinkest thou to-day?

ORNULF. Rather to-day than to-morrow. Fair amends will content me; if Gunnar says me nay, then must he take what comes.

(KARE THE PEASANT enters hastily from the right; he is clad in a grey frieze cloak and low-brimmed felt hat; he carries in his hand a broken fence-rail.)

KARE. Well met, Vikings!

ORNULF. Vikings are seldom well met.

KARE. If ye be honourable men, ye will grant me refuge among you; Gunnar Headman's house-carls are hunting me to slay me.

ORNULF. Gunnar's?

SIGURD. Then has thou done him some wrong!

KARE. I have done myself right. Our cattle fed together upon an island, hard by the coast; Gunnar's men carried off my best oxen, and one of them flouted me for a thrall. Then bare I arms against him and slew him.

ORNULF. That was a lawful deed.

KARE. But this morning his men came in wrath against me. By good hap I heard of their coming, and fled; but my foemen are on my tracks, and short shrift can I look for at their hands.

SIGURD. Ill can I believe thee, peasant! In bygone days I knew Gunnar as I know myself, and this I wot, that never did he wrong a peaceful man.

KARE. Gunnar has no part in this wrong-doing; he is in the south-land; nay, it is Hiordis his wife

DAGNY. Hiordis!

ORNULF (to himself). Ay, ay, 'tis like her!

KARE. I offered Gunnar amends for the thrall, and he was willing; but then came Hiordis, and egged her husband on with scornful words, and hindered the peace. Since then has Gunnar gone to the south, and to-day

SIGURD (looking out to the left). Here come wayfarers northward. Is it not?

KARE. It is Gunnar himself!

ORNULF. Be of good heart; methinks I can make peace between you.

(GUNNAR HEADMAN, with several men, enters from the left. He is in a brown tunic, cross-gartered hose, a blue mantle, and a broad hat; he has no weapon but a small axe.)

GUNNAR (stops in surprise and uncertainty on seeing the knot of men). Ornulf of the Fiords! Yes, it is!

ORNULF. Thou seest aright.

GUNNAR (approaching). Then peace and welcome to thee in my land, if thou come in peace.

ORNULF. If thy will be as mine, there shall be no strife between us.

SIGURD (standing forward). Well met, Gunnar!

GUNNAR (gladly). Sigurd, foster-brother! (Shakes his hand.) Now truly, since thou art here, I know that Ornulf comes in peace. (To ORNULF.) Give me thy hand, greybeard! Thy errand here in the north is lightly guessed: it has to do with Hiordis, thy foster-daughter.

ORNULF. As thou sayest; great wrong was done me when thou didst bear her away from Iceland without my will.

GUNNAR. Thy claim is just; what youth has marred, the man must mend. Long have I looked for thee, Ornulf, for this cause; and if amends content thee, we shall soon be at one.

SIGURD. So deem I too. Ornulf will not press thee hard.

GUNNAR (warmly). Nay, Ornulf, didst thou crave her full worth, all my goods would not suffice.

ORNULF. I shall go by law and usage, be sure of that. But now another matter. (Pointing to KARE.) Seest thou yonder man?

GUNNAR. Kare! (To ORNULF.) Thou knowest, then, that there is a strife between us?

ORNULF. Thy men have stolen his cattle, and theft must be atoned.

GUNNAR. Murder no less; he has slain my thrall.

KARE. Because he flouted me.

GUNNAR. I have offered thee terms of peace.

KARE. But that had Hiordis no mind to, and this morning, whilst thou wert gone, she fell upon me and hunts me now to my death.

GUNNAR (angrily). Is it true what thou sayest? Has she?

KARE. True, every word.

ORNULF. Therefore the peasant besought me to stand by him, and that will I do.

GUNNAR (after a moment's thought). Honourably hast thou dealt with me, Ornulf; therefore is it fit that I should yield to thy will. Hear then, Kare: I am willing to let the slaying of the thrall and the wrongs done toward thee quit each other.

KARE (gives GUNNAR his hand). It is a good offer; I am content.

ORNULF. And he shall have peace for thee and thine?

GUNNAR. Peace shall he have, here and overall.

SIGURD (pointing to the right). See yonder!

GUNNAR (disturbed). It is Hiordis!

ORNULF. With armed men!

KARE. She is seeking me!

(HIORDIS enters, with a troop of house-carls. She is clad in black, wearing a kirtle, cloak, and hood; the men are armed with swords and axes; she herself carries a light spear.)

HIORDIS (stops on entering). A meeting of many, meseems.

DAGNY (rushes to meet her). Peace and joy to thee, Hiordis!

HIORDIS (coldly). Thanks. It was told me that thou wast not far off. (Comes forward, looking sharply at those assembled.) Gunnar, and Kare, my foeman, Ornulf and his sons and (As she catches sight of SIGURD, she starts almost imperceptibly, is silent a moment, but collects herself and says:) Many I see here who are known to me but little I know who is best minded towards me.

ORNULF. We are all well-minded towards thee.

HIORDIS. If so be, thou wilt not deny to give Kare into my husband's hands.

ORNULF. There is no need.

GUNNAR. There is peace and friendship between us.

HIORDIS (with suppressed scorn). Friendship? Well well, I know thou art a wise man, Gunnar! Kare has met mighty friends, and well I woth thou deem'st it safest

GUNNAR. Thy taunts avail not! (With dignity.) Kare is at peace with us!

HIORDIS (restraining herself). Well and good; if thou hast sworn him peace, the vow must be held.

GUNNAR (forcibly, but without anger). It must and it shall.

ORNULF (to HIORDIS). Another pact had been well-nigh made ere thy coming.

HIORDIS (sharply). Between thee and Gunnar.

ORNULF (nods). It had to do with thee.

HIORDIS. Well can I guess what it had to do with; but this I tell thee, foster-father, never shall it be said that Gunnar let himself be cowed because thou camest in arms to the isle. Hadst thou come alone, a single wayfarer, to our hall, the quarrel had more easily been healed.

GUNNAR. Ornulf and his sons come in peace.

HIORDIS. Mayhap; but otherwise will it sound in the mouths of men; and thou thyself, Gunnar, didst show scant trust in the peace yesterday, in sending our son Egil to the southland so soon as it was known that Ornulf's warship lay in the fiord.

SIGURD (to GUNNAR). Didst thou send thy sons to the south?

HIORDIS. Ay, that he might be in safety should Ornulf fall upon us.

ORNULF. Scoff not at that, Hiordis; what Gunnar has done may prove wise in the end, if so be thou hinderest the pact.

HIORDIS. Life must take its chance; come what will, I had liever die than save my life by a shameful pact.

DAGNY. Sigurd makes atonement, and will not be deemed the lesser man for that.

HIORDIS. Sigurd best knows what his own honour can bear.

SIGURD. On that score shall I never need reminding.

HIORDIS. Sigurd has done famous deeds, but the boldest deed of all was Gunnar's, when he slew the white bear that guarded my bower.

GUNNAR (with an embarrassed glance at SIGURD). Nay nay, no more of that!

ORNULF. In truth it was the boldest deed that e'er was seen in Iceland; and therefore

SIGURD. The more easily can Gunnar yield, and not be deemed a coward.

HIORDIS. If amends are to be made, amends shall also be craved. Bethink thee, Gunnar, of thy vow!

GUNNAR. That vow was ill bethought; wilt thou hold me to it?

HIORDIS. That will I, if we two are to dwell under one roof after this day. Know then, Ornulf, that if atonement is to be made for the carrying away of thy foster-daughter, thou, too, must atone for the slaying of Jokul my father, and the seizure of his goods and gear.

ORNULF. Jokul was slain in fair fight;[1] thy kinsmen did me a worse wrong when they sent thee to Iceland and entrapped me into adopting[2] thee, unwitting who thou wast.

[1] "I aerling holmgang." The established form of duel in the viking times was to land the combatants on one of the rocky islets or "holms" that stud the Norwegian coast, and there let them fight it out. Hence "holmgang"=duel. [2] "At knaessette"=to knee-set a child, to take it on one's knee, an irrevocable form of adoption.

HIORDIS. Honour, and now wrong, befell thee in adopting Jokul's daughter.

ORNULF. Nought but strife hast thou brought me, that I know.

HIORDIS. Sterner strife may be at hand, if

ORNULF. I came not hither to bandy words with women! Gunnar, hear my last word: art willing to make atonement?

HIORDIS (to GUNNAR). Think of thy vow!

GUNNAR (to ORNULF). Thou hearest, I have sworn a vow, and that must I

ORNULF (irritated). Enough, enough! Never shall it be said that I made atonement for slaying in fair fight.

HIORDIS (forcibly). Then we bid defiance to thee and thine.

ORNULF (in rising wrath). And who has the right to crave atonement for Jokul? Where are his kinsmen? There is none alive! Where is his lawful avenger?

HIORDIS. That is Gunnar, on my behalf.

ORNULF. Gunnar! Ay, hadst thou been betrothed to him with thy foster-father's good-will, or had he made atonement for carrying thee away, then were he thy father's lawful avenger; but

DAGNY (apprehensive and imploring). Father, father!

SIGURD (quickly). Do not speak it!

ORNULF (raising his voice). Nay, loudly shall it be spoken! A woman wedded by force has no lawful husband!

GUNNAR (vehemently). Ornulf!

HIORDIS (in a wild outburst). Flouted and shamed! (In a quivering voice.) This, this shalt thou come to rue!

ORNULF (continuing). A woman wedded by force is lawfully no more than a leman! Wilt thou regain thine honour, then must thou

HIORDIS (controlling herself). Nay, Ornulf, I know better what is fitting. If I am to be held as Gunnar's leman, well and good, then must he win me honour by his deeds by deeds so mighty that my shame shall be shame no more! And thou, Ornulf, beware! Here our ways part, and from this day I shall make war upon thee and thine whensoever and wheresoever it may be; thou shalt know no safety, thou, or any whom thou (Looking fiercely at KARE.) Kare! Ornulf has stood thy friend, forsooth, and there is peace between us; but I counsel thee not to seek thy home yet awhile; the man thou slewest has many avengers, and it well might befall See, I have shown thee the danger; thou must e'en take what follows. Come, Gunnar, we must gird ourselves for the fight. A famous deed didst thou achieve in Iceland, but greater deeds must here be done, if thou wouldst not have thy, thy leman shrink with shame from thee and from herself!

GUNNAR. Curb thyself, Hiordis; it is unseemly to bear thee thus.

DAGNY (imploringly). Stay, foster-sister, stay; I will appease my father.

HIORDIS (without listening to her). Homewards, homewards! Who could have foretold me that I should wear out my life as a worthless leman? But if I am to bear this life of shame, ay, even a single day longer, then must my husband do such a deed, such a deed as shall make his name more famous than all other names of men.

(Goes out to the right.)

GUNNAR (softly). Sigurd, this thou must promise me, that we shall have speech together ere thou leave the land.

(Goes out with his men to the right.) (The storm has meanwhile ceased; the mid-day sun is now visible, like a red disc, low upon the rim of the sea.)

ORNULF (threateningly). Dearly shalt thou aby this day's work, foster-daughter!

DAGNY. Father, father! Surely thou wilt not harm her!

ORNULF. Let me be! Now, Sigurd, now can no amends avail between Gunnar and me.

SIGURD. What thinkest thou to do?

ORNULF. That I know not; but far and wide shall the tale be told how Ornulf of the Fiords came to Gunnar's hall.

SIGURD (with quiet determination). That may be; but this I tell thee, Ornulf, that thou shalt never bear arms against him so long as I am alive.

ORNULF. So, so! And what if it be my will to?

SIGURD. It shall not be, let thy will be never so strong.

ORNULF (angrily). Go then; join thou with my foes; I can match the twain of you!

SIGURD. Hear me out, Ornulf; the day shall never dawn that shall see thee and me at strife. There is honourable peace between us, Dagny is dearer to me than weapons or gold, and never shall I forget that thou art her nearest kinsman.

ORNULF. There I know thee again, brave Sigurd!

SIGURD. But Gunnar is my foster-brother; faith and friendship have we sworn each other. Both in war and peace have we faced fortune together, and of all men he is dearest to me. Stout though he be, he loves not war; but as for me, ye know, all of you, that I shrink not from strife; yet here I stand forth, Ornulf, and pray for peace on Gunnar's behalf. Let me have my will!

ORNULF. I cannot; I should be a scoff to all brave men, were I to fare empty-handed back to Iceland.

SIGURD. Empty-handed shalt thou not fare. Here in the cove my two long-ships are lying, with all the wealth I have won in my viking- ventures. There are many costly gifts from outland kings, good weapons by the chestful, and other priceless chattels. Take thou one of the ships; choose which thou wilt, and it shall be thine with all it contains be that the atonement for Hiordis, and let Gunnar be at peace.

ORNULF. Brave Sigurd, wilt thou do this for Gunnar?

SIGURD. For a faithful friend, no man can do too much.

ORNULF. Give half thy goods and gear!

SIGURD (urgently). Take the whole, take both my ships, take all that is mine, and let me fare with thee to Iceland as the poorest man in thy train. What I give, I can win once more; but if thou and Gunnar come to strife, I shall never see a glad day again. Now Ornulf, thy answer?

ORNULF (reflecting). Two good long-ships, weapons and other chattels, too much gear can no man have; but (vehemently) no, no! Hiordis has threatened me; I will not! It were shameful for me to take thy goods!

SIGURD. Yet listen

ORNULF. No, I say! I must fight my own battle, be my fortune what it may.

KARE (approaching). Right friendly is Sigurd's rede, but if thou wilt indeed fight thine own battle with all thy might, I can counsel thee better. Dream not of atonement so long as Hiordis has aught to say; but revenge can be thine if thou wilt hearken to me.

ORNULF. Revenge? What dost thou counsel?

SIGURD. Evil, I can well see.

DAGNY (to ORNULF). Oh, do not hear him!

KARE. Hiordis has declared me an outlaw; with cunning will she seek to take my life; do thou swear to see me scatheless, and this night will I burn Gunnar's hall and all within it. Is that to thy mind?

SIGURD. Dastard!

ORNULF (quietly). To my mind? Knowest thou, Kare, what were more to my mind? (In a voice of thunder.) To hew off thy nose and ears, thou vile thrall. Little dost thou know old Ornulf if thou thinkest to have his help in such a deed of shame!

KARE (who has shrunk backwards). If thou fall not upon Gunnar he will surely fall upon thee.

ORNULF. Have I not weapons, and strength to wield them?

SIGURD (to KARE). And now away with thee! Thy presence is a shame to honourable men!

KARE (going off). Well well, I must shield myself as best I can. But this I tell you: if ye think to deal gently with Hiordis, ye will come to rue it; I know her and I know where to strike her sorest!

(Goes down towards the shore.)

DAGNY. He is plotting revenge. Sigurd, it must be hindered!

ORNULF (with annoyance). Nay, let him do as he will; she is worth no better!

DAGNY. That meanest thou not; bethink thee she is thy foster-child.

ORNULF. Woe worth the day when I took her under my roof! Jokul's words are coming true.

SIGURD. Jokul's?

ORNULF. Ay, her father's. When I gave him his death-wound he fell back upon the sword, and fixed his eyes on on me and sang:

> Jokul's kin for Jokul's slayer
> many a woe shall still be weaving;
> Jokul's hoard whoe'er shall harry
> heartily shall rue his rashness.

When he had sung that, he was silent a while, and laughed; and thereupon he died.

SIGURD. Why should'st thou heed his words?

ORNULF. Who knows? The story goes, and many believe it, that Jokul gave his children a wolf's heart to eat, that they might be fierce and fell; and Hiordis has surely had her share, that one can well see. (Breaks off, on looking out towards the right.) Gunnar! Are we two to meet again!

GUNNAR (enters). Ay, Ornulf, think of me what thou wilt, but I cannot part from thee as thy foe.

ORNULF. What is thy purpose?

GUNNAR. To hold out the hand of fellowship to thee ere thou depart. Hear me all of you: go with me to my homestead, and be my guests as long as ye will. We lack not meat or drink or sleeping-room, and there shall be no talk of our quarrel either to-day or to-morrow.

SIGURD. But Hiordis?

GUNNAR. Yields to my will; she changed her thought on the homeward way, and deemed, as I did, that we would soon be at one if ye would but be our guests.

DAGNY. Yes, yes; let it be so.

SIGURD (doubtfully). But I know not whether

DAGNY. Gunnar is thy foster-brother; little I know thee if thou say him nay.

GUNNAR (to SIGURD). Thou hast been my friend where'er we fared; thou wilt not stand against me now.

DAGNY. And to depart from the land, leaving Hiordis with hate in her heart, no, no, that must we not!

GUNNAR. I have done Ornulf a great wrong; until it is made good, I cannot be at peace with myself.

SIGURD (vehemently). All else will I do for thee, Gunnar, but not stay here! (Mastering himself.) I am in King AEthelstan's service, and I must be with him in England ere the winter is out.

DAGNY. But that thou canst be, nevertheless.

GUNNAR. No man can know what lot awaits him; mayhap this is our last meeting, Sigurd, and thou wilt repent that thou didst not stand by me to the end.

DAGNY. And long will it be ere thou see me glad again, if thou set sail to-day.

SIGURD (determined). Well, be it so! It shall be as ye will, although But no more of that; here is my hand; I will stay to feast with thee and Hiordis.

GUNNAR (shakes his hand). Thanks, Sigurd, I never doubted thee. And thou, Ornulf, dost thou say likewise?

ORNULF (unappeased). I shall think upon it. Bitterly has Hiordis wounded me; I will not answer to-day.

GUNNAR. It is well, old warrior; Sigurd and Dagny will know how to soothe thy brow. Now must I prepare the feast; peace be with you the while, and well met in my hall! (Goes out by the right.)

SIGURD (to himself). Hiordis has changed her thought, said he? Little he knows her; I rather deem that she is plotting (interrupting himself and turning to his men.) Come, follow me all to the ships; good gifts will I choose for Gunnar and his household.

DAGNY. Gifts of the best we have. And thou, father, thou shalt have no peace for me until thou yield thee. (She goes with SIGURD and his men down towards the shore at the back.)

ORNULF. Yield me? Ay, if there were no women-folk in Gunnar's house, then Oh, if I but knew how to pierce her armour! Thorolf, thou here!

THOROLF (who has entered hastily). As thou seest. Is it true that thou hast met with Gunnar?

ORNULF. Yes.

THOROLF. And art at enmity with him?

ORNULF. Hm, at least with Hiordis.

THOROLF. Then be of good cheer; soon shalt thou be avenged!

ORNULF. Avenged? Who shall avenge me?

THOROLF. Listen: as I stood on board the ship, there came a man running, with a staff in his hand, and called to me: "If thou be of Ornulf's shipfolk, then greet him from Kare the Peasant, and say that now am I avenging the twain of us." Thereupon he took a boat and rowed away, saying as he passed: "Twenty outlaws are at haven in the fiord; with them I fare southward, and ere eventide shall Hiordis be childless."

ORNULF. He said that! Ha, now I understand; Gunnar has sent his son away; Kare is at feud with him

THOROLF. And now he is rowing southward to slay the boy!

ORNULF (with sudden resolution). Up all! That booty will we fight for!

THOROLF. What wilt thou do?

ORNULF. Ask me not; it shall be I, and not Kare, that will take revenge!

THOROLF. I will go with thee!

ORNULF. Nay, do thou follow with Sigurd and thy sister to Gunnar's hall.

THOROLF. Sigurd? Is he in the isle?

ORNULF. There may'st thou see his warships; we are at one, do thou go with him.

THOROLF. Among thy foes?

ORNULF. Go thou to the feast. Now shall Hiordis learn to know old Ornulf! But hark thee, Thorolf, to no one must thou speak of what I purpose; dost hear? to no one!

THOROLF. I promise.

ORNULF (takes his hand and looks at him affectionately). Farewell then, my fair boy; bear thee in courtly wise at the feast-house, that I may have honour of thee. Beware of idle babbling; but what thou sayest, let it be keen as a sword. Be friendly to those that deal with thee in friendly wise; but if thou be taunted, hold not thy peace. Drink not more than thou canst bear; but put not the horn aside when it is offered thee in measure, lest thou be deemed womanish.

THOROLF. Nay, be at ease.

ORNULF. Then away to the feast at Gunnar's hall. I too will come to the feast, and that in the guise they least think of. (Blithely to the rest.) Come, my wolf-cubs; be your fangs keen; now shall ye have blood to drink.

(He goes off with his elder sons to the right, at the back.) (SIGURD and DAGNY come up from the ships, richly dressed for the banquet. They are followed by two men, carrying a chest, who lay it down and return as they came.)

THOROLF (looking out after his father). Now fare they all forth to fight, and I must stay behind; it is hard to be the youngest of the house. Dagny! all hail and greetings to thee, sister mine!

DAGNY. Thorolf! All good powers! thou art a man, grown!

THOROLF. That may I well be, forsooth, in five years

DAGNY. Ay, true, true.

SIGURD (giving his his hand). In thee will Ornulf find a stout carl, or I mistake me.

THOROLF. Would he but prove me!

DAGNY (smiling). He spares thee more than thou hast a mind to? Thou wast ever well-nigh too dear to him.

SIGURD. Whither has he gone?

THOROLF. Down to his ships; he will return ere long.

SIGURD. I await my men; they are mooring my ships and bringing ashore wares.

THOROLF. There must I lend a hand!

(Goes down towards the shore.)

SIGURD (after a moment's reflection). Dagny, my wife, we are alone; I have that to tell thee which must no longer be hidden.

DAGNY (surprised). What meanest thou?

SIGURD. There may be danger in this faring to Gunnar's hall.

DAGNY. Danger? Thinkest thou that Gunnar?

SIGURD. Nay, Gunnar is brave and true, yet better had it been that I had sailed from the isle without crossing his threshold.

DAGNY. Thou makest me fear! Sigurd, what is amiss?

SIGURD. First answer me this: the golden ring that I gave thee, where hast thou it?

DAGNY (showing it). Here, on my arm; thou badest me wear it.

SIGURD. Cast it to the bottom of the sea, so deep that none may ever set eyes on it again; else may it be the bane of many men.

DAGNY. The ring!

SIGURD (in a low voice). That evening when we carried away thy father's daughters, dost remember it?

DAGNY. Do I remember it!

SIGURD. It is of that I would speak.

DAGNY (in suspense). What is it? Say on!

SIGURD. Thou knowest there had been a feast; thou didst seek thy chamber betimes; but Hiordis still sat among the men in the feast-hall. The horn went busily round, and many a great vow was sworn. I swore to bear away a fair maid with me from Iceland; Gunnar swore the same as I, and passed the cup to Hiordis. She grasped it and stood up, and vowed this vow, that no warrior should have her to wife, save he who should go to her bower, slay the white bear that stood bound at the door, and carry her away in his arms.

DAGNY. Yes, yes; all this I know!

SIGURD. All men deemed that it might not be, for the bear was the fiercest of beasts; none but Hiordis might come near it, and it had the strength of twenty men.

DAGNY. But Gunnar slew it, and by that deed won fame throughout all lands.

SIGURD (in a low voice). He won the fame but I did the deed!

DAGNY (with a cry). Thou!

SIGURD. When the men left the feast-hall, Gunnar prayed me to come with him alone to our sleeping-place. Then said he: "Hiordis is dearer to me than all women; without her I cannot live." I answered him: "Then go to her bower; thou knowest the vow she hath sworn." But he said: "Life is dear to him that loves; if I should assail the bear, the end were doubtful, and I am loath to lose my life, for then should I lose Hiordis too." Long did we talk, and the end was that Gunnar made ready his ship, while I drew my sword, donned Gunnar's harness, and went to the bower.

DAGNY (with pride and joy). And thou, thou didst slay the bear!

SIGURD. I slew him. In the bower it was dark as under a raven's wing; Hiordis deemed it was Gunnar that sat by her, she was heated with the mead, she drew a ring from her arm and gave it to me, it is that thou wearest now.

DAGNY (hesitating). And thou didst pass the night with Hiordis in her bower?

SIGURD. My sword lay drawn between us. (A short pause.) Ere the dawn, I bore Hiordis to Gunnar's ship; she dreamed not or our wiles, and he sailed away with her. Then went I to thy sleeping-place and found thee there among thy women; what followed, thou knowest; I sailed from Iceland with a fair maid, as I had sworn, and from that day hast thou stood faithfully at my side whithersoever I might wander.

DAGNY (much moved). My brave husband! And that great deed was thine! Oh, I should have known it; none but thou would have dared! Hiordis, that proud and stately woman, couldst thou have won, yet didst choose me! Now wouldst thou be tenfold dearer to me, wert thou not already dearer than all the world.

SIGURD. Dagny, my sweet wife, now thou knowest all that is needful. I could not but warn thee; for that ring, Hiordis must never set eyes on it! Wouldst thou do my will, then cast it from thee into the depths of the sea.

DAGNY. Nay, Sigurd, it is too dear to me; is it not thy gift? But be thou at ease, I shall hide it from every eye, and never shall I breathe a word of what thou hast told me.

(THOROLF comes up from the ships, with SIGURD'S men.)

THOROLF. All is ready for the feast.

DAGNY. Come then, Sigurd, my brave, my noble warrior!

SIGURD. Beware, Dagny, beware! It rests with thee now whether this meeting shall end peacefully or in bloodshed. (Cheerfully to the others.) Away then, to the feast in Gunnar's hall!

(Goes out with DAGNY to the right; the others follow.)

Act Second

(The feast-room in GUNNAR'S house. The entrance-door is in the back; smaller doors in the side-walls. In front, on the left, the greater high-seat; opposite it on the right, the lesser. In the middle of the floor, a wood fire is burning on a built-up hearth. In the background, on both sides of the door, are daises for the women of the household. From each of the high-seats, a long table, with benches, stretches backwards, parallel with the wall. It is dark outside; the fire lights the room.)

(HIORDIS and DAGNY enter from the right.)

DAGNY. Nay, Hiordis, I cannot understand thee. Thou hast shown me all the house; I know not what thing thou lackest, and all thou hast is fair and goodly; then why bemoan thy lot?

HIORDIS. Cage an eagle and it will bite at the wires, be they of iron or of gold.

DAGNY. In one thing at least thou art richer than I; thou hast Egil, thy little son.

HIORDIS. Better no child, than one born in shame.

DAGNY. In shame?

HIORDIS. Dost thou forgot thy father's saying? Egil is the son of a leman; that was his word.

DAGNY. A word spoken in wrath, why wilt thou heed it?

HIORDIS. Nay, nay, Ornulf was right; Egil is weak; one can see he is no freeborn child.

DAGNY. Hiordis, how canst thou?

HIORDIS (unheeding). Thus is shame sucked into the blood, like the venom of a snake-bite. Of another mettle are the freeborn sons of mighty men. I have heard of a queen that took her son and sewed his kirtle fast to his flesh, yet he never blinked an eye. (With a look of cruelty.) Dagny, that will I try with Egil!

DAGNY (horrified). Hiordis, Hiordis!

HIORDIS (laughing). Ha-ha-ha! Dost thou think I meant my words? (Changing her tone.) But, believe me or not as thou wilt, there are times when such deeds seem to lure me; it must run in the blood, for I am of the race of the Jotuns,[1] they say. Come, sit thou here, Dagny. Far hast thou wandered in these five long years; tell me, thou hast ofttimes been a guest in the halls of kings?

[1] The giants or Titans of Scandinavian mythology.

DAGNY. Many a time and chiefly with AEthelstan of England.

HIORDIS. And everywhere thou hast been held in honour, and hast sat in the highest seats at the board?

DAGNY. Doubtless. As Sigurd's wife

HIORDIS. Ay, ay, a famous man is Sigurd though Gunnar stands above him.

DAGNY. Gunnar?

HIORDIS. One deed did Gunnar do that Sigurd shrank from. But let that be! Tell me, when thou didst go a-viking with Sigurd, when thou didst hear the sword-blades sing in the fierce war-game, when the blood streamed red on the deck, came there not over thee an untameable longing to plunge into the strife? Didst thou not don harness and take up arms?

DAGNY. Never! How canst thou think it? I, a woman!

HIORDIS. A woman, a woman, who knows what a woman may do! But one thing thou canst tell me, Dagny, for that thou surely knowest: when a man clasps to his breast the woman he loves, is it true that her blood burns, that her bosom throbs, that she swoons in a shuddering ecstasy?

DAGNY (blushing). Hiordis, how canst thou!

HIORDIS. Come, tell me!

DAGNY. Surely thou thyself hast known it.

HIORDIS. Ay once, and only once; it was that night when Gunnar sat with me in my bower; he crushed me in his arms till his byrnie burst, and then, then!

DAGNY (exclaiming). What! Sigurd!

HIORDIS. Sigurd? What of Sigurd? I spoke of Gunnar that night when he bore me away

DAGNY (collecting herself). Yes, yes, I remember I know well

HIORDIS. That was the only time; never, never again! I deemed I was bewitched; for that Gunnar could clasp a woman (Stops and looks at DAGNY.) What ails thee? Methinks thou turnest pale and red!

DARNY. Nay, nay!

HIORDIS (without noticing her). The merry viking-raid should have been my lot; it had been better for me, and mayhap for all of us. That were life, full and rich life! Dost thou not wonder, Dagny, to find me here alive? Art not afraid to be alone with me in the hall? Deem'st thou not that I must have died in all these years, and that it is my ghost that stands at thy side?

DAGNY (painfully affected). Come, let us go, to the others.

HIORDIS (seizing her by the arm). No, stay! Seems it not strange to thee, Dagny, that any woman can yet live after five such nights?

DAGNY. Five nights?

HIORDIS. Here in the north each night is a whole winter long. (Quickly and with an altered expression.) Yet the place is fair enough, doubt it not! Thou shalt see sights here such as thou hast not seen in the halls of the English king. We shall be together as sisters whilst thou bidest with me; we shall go down to the sea when the storm begins once more; thou shalt see the billows rushing upon the land like wild, white-maned horses and then the whales far out in the offing! They dash one against another like steel-clad knights! Ha, what joy to be a witching-wife and ride on the whale's back to speed before the skiff, and wake the storm, and lure men to the deeps with lovely songs of sorcery!

DAGNY. Fie, Hiordis, how canst thou talk so!

HIORDIS. Canst thou sing sorceries, Dagny?

DAGNY (with horror). I!

HIORDIS. I trow thou canst; how else didst thou lure Sigurd to thee?

DAGNY. Thou speakest shameful things; let me go!

HIORDIS (holding her back). Because I jest! Nay, hear me to the end! Think, Dagny, what it is to sit by the window in the eventide and hear the kelpie[1] wailing in the boat-house; to sit waiting and listening for the dead men's ride to Valhal; for their way lies past us here in the north. They are the brave men that fell in fight, the strong women that did not drag out their lives tamely, like thee and me; they sweep through the storm-night on their black horses, with jangling bells! (Embraces DAGNY, and presses her wildly in her arms.) Ha, Dagny! think of riding the last ride on so rare a steed!

[1] "Draugen," a vague and horrible sea-monster.

DAGNY (struggling to escape). Hiordis, Hiordis! Let me go! I will not hear thee!

HIORDIS (laughing). Weak art thou of heart, and easily affrighted.

(GUNNAR enters from the back, with SIGURD and THOROLF.)

GUNNAR. Now, truly, are all things to my very mind! I have found thee again, Sigurd, my brave brother, as kind and true as of old. I have Ornulf's son under my roof, and the old man himself follows speedily after; is it not so?

THOROLF. So he promised.

GUNNAR. Then all I lack is that Egil should be here.

THOROLF. 'Tis plain thou lovest the boy, thou namest him so oft.

GUNNAR. Truly I love him; he is my only child; and he is like to grow up fair and kindly.

HIORDIS. But no warrior.

GUNNAR. Nay, that thou must not say.

SIGURD. I marvel thou didst send him from thee

GUNNAR. Would that I had not! (Half aside.) But thou knowest, Sigurd, he who loves overmuch, takes not always the manliest part. (Aloud.) I had few men in my house, and none could be sure of his life when it was known that Ornulf lay in the cove with a ship of war.

HIORDIS. One thing I know that ought first to be made safe, life afterwards.

THOROLF. And that is?

HIORDIS. Honour and fame among men.

GUNNAR. Hiordis!

SIGURD. It shall not be said of Gunnar that he has risked his honour by doing this.

GUNNAR (sternly). None shall make strife between me and Ornulf's kinsfolk!

HIORDIS (smiling). Hm; tell me, Sigurd, can thy ship sail with any wind?

SIGURD. Ay, when it is cunningly steered.

HIORDIS. Good! I too will steer my ship cunningly, and make my way whither I will.

(Retires towards the back.)

DAGNY (whispers, uneasily). Sigurd, let us hence, this very night!

SIGURD. It is too late now; it was thou that

DAGNY. Then I held Hiordis dear; but now; I have heard her speak words I shudder to think of.

(SIGURD'S men, with other guests, men and women, house-carls and handmaidens, enter from the back.)

GUNNAR (after a short pause for the exchange of greetings and so forth). Now to the board! My chief guest, Ornulf of the Fiords, comes later; so Thorolf promises.

HIORDIS (to the house-folk). Pass ale and mead around, that hearts may wax merry and tongues may be loosened.

(GUNNAR leads SIGURD to the high-seat on the right. DAGNY seats herself on SIGURD'S right, HIORDIS opposite him at the other side of the same table. THOROLF is in like manner ushered to a place at the other table, and thus sits opposite GUNNAR, who occupies the greater high-seat. The others take their seats further back.)

HIORDIS (after a pause in which they drink with each other and converse quietly across the tables). It seldom chances that so many brave men are seated together, as I see to-night in our hall. It were fitting, then, that we should essay the old pastime: Let each man name his chief exploit, that all may judge which is the mightiest.

GUNNAR. That is an ill custom at a drinking-feast; it will oft breed strife.

HIORDIS. Little did I deem that Gunnar was afraid.

SIGURD. That no one deems; but it were long ere we came to an end, were we all to tell of our exploits, so many as we be. Do thou rather tell us, Gunnar, of thy journey to Biarmeland; 'tis no small exploit to fare so far to the north, and gladly would we hear of it.

HIORDIS. The journey to Biarmeland is chapman's work, and little worth to be named among warriors. Nay, do thou begin, Sigurd, if thou would'st not have me deem that thou shrinkest from hearing my husband's praise! Say on; name that one of thy deeds which thou dost prize the highest.

SIGURD. Well, since thou will have it so, so must it be. Let it be told, then, that I lay a-viking among the Orkneys; there came foemen against us, but we swept them from their ships, and I fought alone against eight men.

HIORDIS. Good was that deed; but wast thou fully armed?

SIGURD. Fully armed, with axe, spear, and sword.

HIORDIS. Still the deed was good. Now must thou, my husband, name that which thou deemest the greatest among thy exploits.

GUNNAR (unwillingly). I slew two berserkers who had seized a merchant-ship; and thereupon I sent the captive chapmen home, giving them there ship freely, without ransom. The King of England deemed well of that deed; he said that I had done hounourably, and gave me thanks and good gifts.

HIORDIS. Nay truly, Gunnar, a better deed than that couldst thou name.

GUNNAR (vehemently). I will boast of no other deed! Since last I fared from Iceland I have lived at peace and traded in merchandise. No more word on this matter!

HIORDIS. If thou thyself wilt hide thy renown, thy wife shall speak.

GUNNAR. Peace, Hiordis, I command thee!

HIORDIS. Sigurd fought with eight men, being fully armed; Gunnar came to my bower in the black night, slew the bear that had twenty men's strength, and yet had but a short sword in his hand.

GUNNAR (violently agitated). Woman, not a word more!

DAGNY (softly). Sigurd, wilt thou bear?

SIGURD (likewise). Be still!

HIORDIS (to the company). And now, ye brave men, which is the mightier, Sigurd or Gunnar?

GUNNAR. Silence!

HIORDIS (loudly). Speak out; I have the right to crave your judgement.

AN OLD MAN (among the guests). If the truth be told, then is Gunnar's deed greater than all other deeds of men; Gunnar is the mightiest warrior, and Sigurd is second to him.

GUNNAR (with a glance across the table). Ah, Sigurd, Sigurd, didst thou but know!

DAGNY (softly). This is too much, even for a friend!

SIGURD. Peace, wife! (Aloud, to the others.) Ay truly, Gunnar is the most honourable of all men; so would I esteem him to my dying day, even had he never done that deed; for that I hold more lightly than ye.

HIORDIS. There speaks thy envy, Sigurd Viking!

SIGURD (smiling). Mightily art thou mistaken. (Kindly, to GUNNAR, drinking to him across the table.) Hail, noble Gunnar; our friendship shall stand fast, whosoever may seek to break it.

HIORDIS. No one, that I wot of, has such a thought.

SIGURD. Say not that; I could almost find it in me to think that thou hadst bidden us hither to stir up strife.

HIORDIS. That is like thee, Sigurd; now art thou wroth that thou may'st not be held the mightiest man at the feast-board.

SIGURD. I have ever esteemed Gunnar more highly than myself.

HIORDIS. Well, well, second to Gunnar is still a good place, and (with a side-glance at THOROLF) had Ornulf been here, he could have had the third seat.

THOROLF. Then would Jokul, thy father, find a low place indeed; for he fell before Ornulf.

(The following dispute is carried on, by both parties, with rising and yet repressed irritation.)

HIORDIS. That shalt thou never say! Ornulf is a skald, and men whisper that he has praised himself for greater deeds than he has done.

THOROLF. Then woe to him who whispers so loudly that it comes to my ear!

HIORDIS (with a smile of provocation). Wouldst thou avenge it?

THOROLF. Ay, so that my vengeance should be told of far and wide.

HIORDIS. Then here I pledge a cup to this, that thou may'st first have a beard on thy chin.

THOROLF. Even a beardless lad is too good to wrangle with women.

HIORDIS. But too weak to fight with men; therefore thy father let thee lie by the hearth at home in Iceland, whilst thy brothers went a-viking.

THOROLF. It had been well had he kept as good an eye on thee; for then hadst thou not left Iceland a dishonoured woman.

GUNNAR AND SIGURD. Thorolf!

DAGNY (simultaneously). Brother!

HIORDIS (softly, and quivering with rage). Ha! Wait, wait!

THOROLF (gives GUNNAR his hand). Be not wroth, Gunnar; evil words came to my tongue; but thy wife egged me!

DAGNY (softly and imploringly). Foster-sister, by any love thou hast ever borne me, stir not up strife!

HIORDIS (laughing). Jests must pass at the feast-board if the merriment is to thrive.

GUNNAR (who has been talking softly to THOROLF). Thou art a brave lad! (Hands him a sword which hangs beside the high-seat.) Here, Thorolf, here is a good gift for thee. Wield it well, and let us be friends.

HIORDIS. Beware how thou givest away thy weapons, Gunnar; for men may say thou dost part with things thou canst not use!

THOROLF (who has meanwhile examined the sword). Thanks for the gift, Gunnar; it shall never be drawn in an unworthy cause.

HIORDIS. If thou wilt keep that promise, then do thou never lend the sword to thy brothers.

GUNNAR. Hiordis!

HIORDIS (continuing). Neither let it hang on thy father's wall; for there it would hang with base men's weapons.

THOROLF. True enough, Hiordis, for there thy father's axe and shield have hung this many a year.

HIORDIS (mastering herself). That Ornulf slew my father, that deed is ever on thy tongue; but if report speak true, it was scarce so honourable a deed as thou deemest.

THOROLF. Of what report dost thou speak?

HIORDIS. I dare not name it, for it would make thee wroth.

THOROLF. Then hold thy peace, I ask no better.

(Turns from her.)

HIORDIS. Nay, why should I not tell it? Is it true, Thorolf, that for three nights thy father sat in woman's weed, doing sorceries with the witch of Smalserhorn, ere he dared face Jokul in fight.

(All rise; violent excitement among the guests.)

GUNNAR, SIGURD, AND DAGNY. Hiordis!

THOROLF (bitterly exasperated). So base a lie has no man spoken of Ornulf of the Fiords! Thou thyself hast made it, for no one less venomous than thou could dream of such a thing. The blackest crime a man can do hast thou laid at my father's door. (Throwing the sword away.) There, Gunnar, take thy gift again; I can take nought from the house wherein my father is reviled.

GUNNAR. Thorolf, hear me!

THOROLF. Let me go! But beware both thou and Hiordis; for my father has now in his power one whom ye hold dearest of all!

HIORDIS (starting). Thy father has!

GUNNAR (with a cry). What sayst thou!

SIGURD (vehemently). Where is Ornulf?

THOROLF (with mocking laughter). Gone southward, with my brothers.

GUNNAR. Southward!

HIORDIS (shrieking). Gunnar! Ornulf has slain Egil, our son.

GUNNAR. Slain! Egil slain! Then woe to Ornulf and all his race! Thorolf, speak out; is this true?

SIGURD. Gunnar, Gunnar, hear me!

GUNNAR. Speak out, if thou care for thy life!

THOROLF. Thou canst not fright me! Wait till my father comes; he shall plant a mark of shame over against Gunnar's house! And meanwhile, Hiordis, do thou cheer thee with these words I heard to-day: "Ere eventide shall Gunnar and his wife be childless."

(Goes out by the back.)

GUNNAR (in the deepest pain). Slain, slain! My little Egil slain!

HIORDIS (wildly). And thou, dost thou let him go? Let Egil, thy child, lie unavenged! Then wert thou the dastard of dastards!

GUNNAR (as if beside himself). A sword, an axe! It is the last message he shall bring!

(Seizes an axe from the bystanders and rushes out.)

SIGURD (about to follow). Gunnar, hold thy hand!

HIORDIS (holding him back). Stay, stay! The men will part them; I know Gunnar!

(A cry from the crowd, which has flocked together at the main door.)

SIGURD AND DAGNY. What is it?

A VOICE AMONG THE CROWD. Thorolf has fallen.

SIGURD. Thorolf! Ha, let me go!

DAGNY. My brother! Oh, my brother!

(SIGURD is on the point of rushing out. At the same moment, the crowd parts, GUNNAR enters, and throws down the axe at the door.)

GUNNAR. Now it is done. Egil is avenged!

SIGURD. Well for thee if thy hand has not been too hasty.

GUNNAR. Mayhap, mayhap; but Egil, Egil, my sweet boy!

HIORDIS. Now must we arm us, and seek help among our friends; for Thorolf has many avengers.

GUNNAR (gloomily). He will be his own worst avenger; he will haunt me night and day.

HIORDIS. Thorolf got his reward. Kinsmen must suffer for kinsmen's deeds.

GUNNAR. True, true; but this I know, my mind was lighter ere this befell.

HIORDIS. This first night (1) is ever the worst; Ornulf has sought his revenge by shameful wiles; he would not come against us in open strife; he feigned to be peacefully-minded; and then he falls upon our defenceless child! Ha, I saw more clearly than ye; well I deemed that Ornulf was evil-minded and false; I had good cause to egg thee on against him and all his faithless tribe!

[1] Literally the "blood-night."

GUNNAR (fiercely). That hadst thou! My vengeance is poor beside Ornulf's crime. He has lost Thorolf, but he has six sons left and I have none, none!

A HOUSE-CARL (enters hastily from the back). Ornulf of the Fiords is at hand!

GUNNAR. Ornulf!

HIORDIS AND SEVERAL MEN. To arms! to arms!

DAGNY (simultaneously). My father!

SIGURD (as if seized by a foreboding). Ornulf! Ah, Gunnar, Gunnar!

GUNNAR (draws his sword). Up all my men! Vengeance for Egil's death!

(ORNULF enters, with EGIL in his arms.)

GUNNAR (with a shriek). Egil!

ORNULF. Here I bring thee little Egil.

ALL (one to another). Egil! Egil alive!

GUNNAR (letting his sword fall). Woe is me! what have I done?

DAGNY. Oh, Thorolf, my brother!

SIGURD. I knew it! I knew it!

ORNULF (setting EGIL down). There, Gunnar, hast thou thy pretty boy again.

EGIL. Father! Old Ornulf would not do me ill, as thou saidst when I went away.

ORNULF (to HIORDIS). Now have I atoned for thy father; now surely there may be peace between us.

HIORDIS (with repressed emotion). Mayhap!

GUNNAR (as if waking up). Is it a ghastly dream that maddens me! Thou, thou bringest Egil home!

ORNULF. As thou seest; but in truth he has been near his death.

GUNNAR. That I know.

ORNULF. And hast no more joy in his return?

GUNNAR. Had he come sooner, I had been glad indeed. But tell me all that has befallen!

ORNULF. That is soon done. Kare the Peasant was plotting evil against you; with other caitiffs he fared southward after Egil.

GUNNAR. Kare! (To himself.) Ha, now I understand Thorolf's words!

ORNULF. His purpose came to my ears; I needs must thwart so black a deed. I would not give atonement for Jokul, and, had things so befallen, I had willingly slain thee, Gunnar, in single combat, yet I could not but protect thy child. With my sons, I hasted after Kare.

SIGURD (softly). An accursed deed has here been done.

ORNULF. When I came up with him, Egil's guards lay bound; thy son was already in thy foemen's hand, and they would not long have spared him. Hot was the fight! Seldom have I given and taken keener strokes; Kare and two men fled inland; the rest sleep safely, and will be hard to waken.

GUNNAR (in eager suspense). But thou, thou, Ornulf?

ORNULF (gloomily). Six sons followed me into the fight.

GUNNAR (breathlessly). But homewards?

ORNULF. None.

GUNNAR (appalled). None! (Softly.) And Thorolf, Thorolf!

(Deep emotion among the bystanders. HIORDIS shows signs of a violent mental struggle; DAGNY weeps silently by the high-seat on the right. SIGURD stands beside her, painfully agitated.)

ORNULF (after a short pause). It is hard for a many-branching pine to be stripped in a single storm. But men die and men live; I will drink to my sons' memory. (One of SIGURD'S men hands him a horn.) Hail to you where now ye ride, my bold sons! Close upon your heels shall the copper-gates not clang, for ye come to the hall with a great following. (Drinks, and hands back the horn.) And now home to Iceland! Ornulf has fought his last fight; the old tree has but one green branch left, and it must be shielded warily. Where is Thorolf?

EGIL (to his father). Ay, show me Thorolf! Ornulf told me he would carve me a ship with many, many warriors on board.

ORNULF. I praise all good wights that Thorolf came not with us; for if he too, nay, strong though I be, that had been too heavy for me to bear. But why comes he not? He was ever the first to meet his father; for both of us it seemed we could not live without each other a single day.

GUNNAR. Ornulf, Ornulf!

ORNULF (with growing uneasiness). Ye stand all silent, I mark it now. What ails you? Where is Thorolf?

DAGNY. Sigurd, Sigurd, this will be the direst blow to him!

GUNNAR (struggling with himself). Old man! No and yet, it cannot be hid

ORNULF (vehemently). My son! Where is he!

GUNNAR. Thorolf is slain!

ORNULF. Slain! Thorolf? Thorolf? Ha, thou liest!

GUNNAR. I would give my warmest heart-blood to know him alive!

HIORDIS (to ORNULF). Thorolf was himself to blame for what befell; with dark sayings he gave us to wit that thou hadst fallen upon Egil and slain him; we had parted half in wrath, and thou hast ere now brought death among my kindred. And moreover, Thorolf bore himself at the feast like a wanton boy; he brooked not our jesting, and spoke many evil things. Not till then did Gunnar wax wroth; not till then did he raise his hand upon thy son; and well I wot that he had good and lawful ground for that deed.

ORNULF (calmly). Well may we see that thou art a woman, for thou usest many words. To what end? If Thorolf is slain, then is his saga over.

EGIL. If Thorolf is slain, I shall have no warriors.

ORNULF. Nay, Egil, we have lost our warriors, but thou and I. (To HIORDIS.) Thy father sang:

> Jokul's kin for Jokul's slayer
> many a woe shall still be weaving.

Well has thou wrought that his words should come true. (Pauses a moment, then turns to one of the men.) Where got he his death-wound?

THE MAN. Right across his brow.

ORNULF (pleased). Hm; that is an honourable spot; he did not turn his back. But fell he sideways, or in towards Gunnar's feet?

THE MAN. Half sideways and half towards Gunnar.

ORNULF. That bodes but half vengeance; well well, we shall see!

GUNNAR (approaching). Ornulf, I know well that all my goods were naught against thy loss; but crave of me what thou wilt

ORNULF (sternly interrupting him). Give me Thorolf's body, and let me go! Where lies he?

(GUNNAR points silently to the back.)

ORNULF (takes a step or two, but turns and says in a voice of thunder to SIGURD, DAGNY, and others who are preparing to follow him, sorrowing). Stay! Think ye Ornulf will be followed by a train of mourners, like a whimpering woman? Stay, I say! I can bear my Thorolf alone. (With calm strength.) Sonless I go; but none shall say that he saw me bowed. (He goes slowly out.)

HIORDIS (with forced laughter). Ay, let him go as he will; we shall scarce need many men to face him should he come with strife again! Now, Dagny, I wot it is the last time thy father shall sail from Iceland on such a quest!

SIGURD (indignant). Oh, shame!

DAGNY (likewise). And thou canst scoff at him, -scoff at him, after all that has befallen?

HIORDIS. A deed once done, 'tis wise to praise it. This morning I swore hate and vengeance against Ornulf; the slaying of Jokul I might have forgotten, all, save that he cast shame upon my lot. He called me a leman; if it be so, it shames me not; for Gunnar is mightier now than thy father; he is greater and more famous than Sigurd, thine own husband!

DAGNY (in wild indignation). There thou errest, Hiordis and even now shall all men know that thou dwellest under a weakling's roof!

SIGURD (vehemently). Dagny, beware!

GUNNAR. A weakling!

DAGNY. It shall no longer be hidden; I held my peace till thou didst scoff at my father and my dead brothers; I held my peace while Ornulf was here, lest he should learn that Thorolf fell by a dastard's hand. But now, praise Gunnar nevermore for that deed in Iceland; for Gunnar is a weakling! The sword that lay drawn between thee and the bear-slayer hangs at my husband's side and the ring thou didst take from thy arm thou gavest to Sigurd. (Takes it off and holds if aloft.) Behold it!

HIORDIS (wildly). Sigurd!

THE CROWD. Sigurd! Sigurd did the deed!

HIORDIS (quivering with agitation). He! he! Gunnar, is this true?

GUNNAR (with lofty calm). It is all true save only that I am a weakling; I am neither a weakling nor a coward.

SIGURD (moved). That art thou not, Gunnar! That hast thou never been! (To the rest.) Away, my men! Away from here!

DAGNY (at the door, to HIORDIS). Who is now the mightiest man at the board, my husband or thine?

HIORDIS (to herself). Now have I but one thing left to do but one deed to brood upon: Sigurd or I must die!

Act Third

(The hall in GUNNAR'S house. It is day.)

(HIORDIS sits on the bench in front of the smaller high-seat busy weaving a bow-string; on the table lie a bow and some arrows.)

HIORDIS (pulling at the bow-string). It is tough and strong; (with a glance at the arrows) the shaft is both keen and well-weighted (lets her hands fall in her lap) but where is the hand that! (Vehemently.) Befooled, befooled by him, by Sigurd! I must hate him more than others, that can I well mark; but ere many days have passed I will (Meditating.) Ay, but the arm, the arm that shall do the deed?

(GUNNAR enters, silent and thoughtful, from the back.)

HIORDIS (after a short pause). How goes it with thee, my husband?

GUNNAR. Ill, Hiordis; I cannot away with that deed of yesterday; it lies heavy on my heart.

HIORDIS. Do as I do; get thee some work to busy thee.

GUNNAR. Doubtless I must.

(A pause; GUNNAR paces up and down the hall, notices what HIORDIS is doing, and approaches her.)

GUNNAR. What dost thou there?

HIORDIS (without looking up). I am weaving a bow-string; canst thou not see?

GUNNAR. A bow-string of thine own hair?

HIORDIS (smiling). Great deeds are born with every hour in these times; yesterday thou didst slay my foster-brother, and I have woven this since day-break.

GUNNAR. Hiordis, Hiordis!

HIORDIS (looking up). What is amiss?

GUNNAR. Where wast thou last night?

HIORDIS. Last night?

GUNNAR. Thou wast not in the sleeping-room.

HIORDIS. Know'st thou that?

GUNNAR. I could not sleep; I tossed in restless dreams of that, that which befell Thorolf. I dreamt that he came No matter; I awakened. Then meseemed I heard a strange, fair song through all the house; I arose; I stole hither to the door; here I saw thee sitting by the log-fire, it burned blue and red, fixing arrow-heads, and singing sorceries over them.

HIORDIS. The work was not wasted; for strong is the breast that must be pierced this day.

GUNNAR. I understand thee well; thou wouldst have Sigurd slain.

HIORDIS. Hm, mayhap.

GUNNAR. Thou shalt never have thy will. I shall keep peace with Sigurd, howe'er thou goad me.

HIORDIS (smiling). Dost think so?

SIGURD. I know it!

HIORDIS (hands him the bow-string). Tell me, Gunnar, canst loose this knot?

GUNNAR (tries it). Nay it is too cunningly and firmly woven.

HIORDIS (rising). The Norns[1] weave yet more cunningly; their web is still harder to unravel.

[1] The "Nornir" were the Fates of northern mythology.

GUNNAR. Dark are the ways of the Mighty Ones; neither thou nor I know aught of them.

HIORDIS. Yet one thing I know surely: that to both of us must Sigurd's life be baleful.

(A pause; GUNNAR stands lost in thought.)

HIORDIS (who has been silently watching him). Of what thinkest thou?

GUNNAR. Of a dream I had of late. Methought I had done the deed thou cravest; Sigurd lay slain on the earth; thou didst stand beside him, and thy face was wondrous pale. Then said I: "Art thou glad, now that I have done thy will?" But thou didst laugh and answer: "Blither were I didst thou, Gunnar, lie there in Sigurd's stead."

HIORDIS (with forced laughter). Ill must thou know me if such a senseless dream can make thee hold thy hand.

GUNNAR. Hm! Tell me, Hiordis, what thinkest thou of this hall?

HIORDIS. To speak truly, Gunnar, it sometimes seems to me to be straitened.

GUNNAR. Ay, ay, so I have thought; we are one too many.

HIORDIS. Two, mayhap.

GUNNAR (who has not heard her last words). But that shall be remedied.

HIORDIS (looks at him interrogatively). Remedied? Then thou art minded to?

GUNNAR. To fit out my warships and put to sea; I will win back the honour I have lost because thou wast dearer to me than all beside.

HIORDIS (thoughtfully). Thou wilt put to sea? Ay, so it may be best for us both.

GUNNAR. Even from the day we sailed from Iceland, I saw that it would go ill with us. Thy soul is strong and proud; there are times when I well nigh fear thee; yet, it is strange, chiefly for that do I hold thee so dear. Dread enwraps thee like a spell; methinks thou could'st lure me to the blackest deeds, and all would seem good to me that thou didst crave. (Shaking his head reflectively.) Unfathomable is the Norn's rede; Sigurd should have been thy husband.

HIORDIS (vehemently). Sigurd!

GUNNAR. Yes, Sigurd. Vengefulness and hatred blind thee, else would'st thou prize him better. Had I been like Sigurd, I could have made life bright for thee.

HIORDIS (with strong but suppressed emotion). That, that deemest thou Sigurd could have done?

GUNNAR. He is strong of soul, and proud as thou to boot.

HIORDIS (violently). If that be so (Collecting herself.) No matter, no matter! (With a wild outburst.) Gunnar, take Sigurd's life!

GUNNAR. Never!

HIORDIS. By fraud and falsehood thou mad'st me thy wife, that shall be forgotten! Five joyless years have I spent in this house, all shall be forgotten from the day when Sigurd lives no more!

GUNNAR. From my hand he need fear no harm. (Shrinks back involuntarily.) Hiordis, Hiordis, tempt me not!

HIORDIS. Then must I find another avenger; Sigurd shall not live long to flout at me and thee! (Clenching her hands in convulsive rage.) With her, that simpleton, with her mayhap he is even now sitting alone, dallying, and laughing at us; speaking of the bitter wrong that was done me when in thy stead he bore me away; telling how he laughed over his guile as he stood in my dark bower, and I knew him not!

GUNNAR. Nay, nay, he does not so!

HIORDIS (firmly). Sigurd and Dagny must die! I cannot breathe till they are gone! (Comes close up to him, with sparkling eyes, and speaks passionately, but in a whisper.) Would'st thou help me with that, Gunnar, then should I live in love with thee; then should I clasp thee in such warm and wild embraces as thou hast never dreamt of!

GUNNAR (wavering). Hiordis! Would'st thou

HIORDIS. Do the deed, Gunnar, and the heavy days shall be past. I will no longer quit the hall when thou comest, no longer speak harsh things and quench thy smile when thou art glad. I will clothe me in furs and costly silken robes. When thou goest to war, I will ride by thy side. At the feast I will sit by thee and fill thy horn, and drink to thee and sing fair songs to make glad thy heart!

GUNNAR (almost overcome). Is it true? Thou wouldst!

HIORDIS. More than that, trust me, ten times more! Give me revenge! Revenge on Sigurd and Dagny, and I will (Stops as she sees the door open.) Dagny, comest thou here!

DAGNY (from the back). Haste thee, Gunnar! Call thy men to arms!

GUNNAR. To arms! Against whom?

DAGNY. Kare the Peasant is coming, and many outlaws with him; he means thee no good; Sigurd has barred his way for the time; but who can tell

GUNNAR (moved). Sigurd has done this for me!

DAGNY. Sigurd is ever thy faithful friend.

GUNNAR. And we, Hiordis, we, who thought to! It is as I say, there is a spell in all thy speech; no deed but seemeth fair to me, when thou dost name it.

DAGNY (astonished). What meanest thou?

GUNNAR. Nothing, nothing! Thanks for thy tidings, Dagny; I go to gather my men together. (Turns towards the door, but stops and comes forward again.) Tell me, how goes it with Ornulf?

DAGNY (bowing her head). Ask me not. Yesterday he bore Thorolf's body to the ships; now he is raising a grave-mound on the shore; there shall his son be laid.

(GUNNAR says nothing and goes out by the back.)

DAGNY. Until evening there is no danger. (Coming nearer.) Hiordis, I have another errand in thy house; it is to thee I come.

HIORDIS. To me? After all that befell yesterday?

DAGNY. Just because of that. Hiordis, foster-sister, do not hate me; forget the words that sorrow and evil spirits placed in my mouth; forgive me all the wrong I have done thee; for, trust me, I am tenfold more hapless than thou!

HIORDIS. Hapless thou! Sigurd's wife!

DAGNY. It was my doing, all that befell, the stirring up of strife, and Thorolf's death, and all the scorn that fell upon Gunnar and thee. Mine is all the guilt! Woe upon me! I have lived so happily; but after this day I shall never know joy again.

HIORDIS (as if seized by a sudden thought). But before, in these five long years, all that time hast thou been happy?

DAGNY. Canst thou doubt it?

HIORDIS. Hm; yesterday I doubted it not; but

DAGNY. What meanest thou?

HIORDIS. Nay, 'tis nought; let us speak of other matters.

DAGNY. No truly. Hiordis, tell me!

HIORDIS. It will profit thee little; but since thou wilt have it so (With a malignant expression.) Canst thou remember once, over in Iceland, we had followed with Ornulf thy father to the Council, and we sat with our playmates in the Council Hall, as is the manner of women. Then came two strangers into the hall.

DAGNY. Sigurd and Gunnar.

HIORDIS. They greeted us in courteous fashion, and sat on the bench beside us; and there passed between us much merry talk. There were some who must needs know why these two vikings came thither, and if they were not minded to take them wives there in the island. Then said Sigurd: "It will be hard for me to find the woman that shall be to my mind." Ornulf laughed, and said there was no lack of high-born and well-dowered women in Iceland; but Sigurd answered: "The warrior needs a high-souled wife. She whom I choose must not rest content with a humble lot; no honour must seem to high for her to strive for; she must go with me gladly a-viking; war-weed must she wear; she must egg me on to strife, and never wink her eyes where sword-blades lighten; for if she be faint-hearted, scant honour will befall me." Is it not true, so Sigurd spake?

DAGNY (hesitatingly). True, he did, but

HIORDIS. Such was she to be, the woman who could make life fair to him; and then (with a scornful smile) then he chose thee!

DAGNY (starting, as in pain). Ha, thou wouldst say that?

HIORDIS. Doubtless thou has proved thyself proud and high-souled; hast claimed honour of all, that Sigurd might be honoured in thee, is it not so?

DAGNY. Nay, Hiordis, but

HIORDIS. Thou hast egged him on to great deeds, followed him in war- weed, and joyed to be where the strife raged hottest, hast thou not?

DAGNY (deeply moved). No, no!

HIORDIS. Hast thou, then, been faint of heart, so that Sigurd has been put to shame?

DAGNY (overpowered). Hiordis, Hiordis!

HIORDIS (smiling scornfully). Yet thy lot has been a happy one all these years; think'st thou that Sigurd can say the same?

DAGNY. Torture me not. Woe is me! thou hast made me see myself too clearly.

HIORDIS. A jesting word, and at once thou art in tears! Think no more of it. Look what I have done to-day. (Takes some arrows from the table.) Are they not keen and biting, feel! I know well how to sharpen arrows, do I not?

DAGNY. And to use them too; thou strikest surely, Hiordis! All that thou hast said to me, I have never thought of before. (More vehemently.) But that Sigurd! That for all these years I should have made his life heavy and unhonoured; no, no, it cannot be true!

HIORDIS. Nay now, comfort thee, Dagny; indeed it is not true. Were Sigurd of the same mind as in former days, it might be true enough; for then was his whole soul bent on being the foremost man in the land; now he is content with a lowlier lot.

DAGNY. No, Hiordis; Sigurd is high-minded now as ever; I see it well, I am not the right mate for him. He has hidden it from me; but it shall be so no longer.

HIORDIS. What wilt thou do?

DAGNY. I will no longer hang like a clog upon his feet; I will be a hindrance to him no longer.

HIORDIS. Then thou wilt?

DAGNY. Peace; some one comes!

(A House-carl enters from the back.)

THE CARL. Sigurd Viking is coming to the hall.

HIORDIS. Sigurd! Then call Gunnar hither.

THE CARL. Gunnar has ridden forth to gather his neighbours together; for Kare the Peasant would

HIORDIS. Good, good, I know it; go! (The Carl goes. To DAGNY, who is also going.) Whither wilt thou?

DAGNY. I will not meet Sigurd. Too well I feel that we must part; but to meet him now, no, no, I cannot!

(Goes out to the left.)

HIORDIS (looks after her in silence for a moment). And it was she I would have (completes her thought by a glance at the bow-string). That would have been a poor revenge; nay, I have cut deeper now! Hm; it is hard to die, but sometimes it is harder still to live!

(SIGURD enters from the back.)

HIORDIS. Doubtless thou seekest Gunnar; be seated, he will be here even now.

(Is going.)

SIGURD. Nay, stay; it is thee I seek, rather than him.

HIORDIS. Me?

SIGURD. And 'tis well I find thee alone.

HIORDIS. If thou comest to mock me, it would sure be no hindrance to thee though the hall were full of men and women.

SIGURD. Ay, ay, well I know what thoughts thou hast of me.

HIORDIS (bitterly). I do thee wrong mayhap! Nay, nay, Sigurd, thou hast been as a poison to all my days. Bethink thee who it was that wrought that shameful guile; who it was that lay by my side in the bower, feigning love with the laugh of cunning in his heart; who it was that flung me forth to Gunnar, since for him I was good enough, forsooth, and then sailed away with the woman he held dear!

SIGURD. Man's will can do this and that; but fate rules in the deeds that shape our lives, so has it gone with us twain.

HIORDIS. True enough; evil Norns hold sway over the world; but their might is little if they find not helpers in our own heart. Happy is he who has strength to battle with the Norn and it is that I now in hand.

SIGURD. What mean'st thou?

HIORDIS. I will essay a trial of strength against those, those who are over me. But let us not talk more of this; I have much to do to-day. (She seats herself at the table.)

SIGURD (after a pause). Thou makest good weapons for Gunnar.

HIORDIS (with a quiet smile). Not for Gunnar, but against thee.

SIGURD. Most like it is the same thing.

HIORDIS. Ay, most like it is; for if I be a match for the Norn, then sooner or later shalt thou and Gunnar (breaks off, leans backwards against the table, and says with an altered ring in her voice:) Hm; knowest thou what I sometimes dream? I have often made it my pastime to limn pleasant pictures in my mind; I sit and close my eyes and think: Now comes Sigurd the Strong to the isle; he will burn us in our house, me and my husband. All Gunnar's men have fallen; only he and I are left; they set light to the roof from without: "A bow-shot," cries Gunnar, "one bow-shot may save us;" then the bow-string breaks "Hiordis, cut a tress of thy hair and make a bow-string of it, our life is at stake." But then I laugh "Let it burn, let it burn to me, life is not worth a handful of hair!"

SIGURD. There is a strange might in all thy speech. (Approaches her.)

HIORDIS (looks coldly at him). Wouldst sit beside me?

SIGURD. Thou deemest my heart is bitter towards thee. Hiordis, this is the last time we shall have speech together; there is something that gnaws me like a sore sickness, and thus I cannot part from thee; thou must know me better.

HIORDIS. What wouldst thou?

SIGURD. Tell thee a saga.

HIORDIS. Is it sad?

SIGURD. Sad, as life itself.

HIORDIS (bitterly). What knowest thou of the sadness of life?

SIGURD. Judge when my saga is over.

HIORDIS. Then tell it me; I shall work the while.

(He sits on a low stool to her right.)

SIGURD. Once upon a time there were two young vikings, who set forth from Norway to win wealth and honour; they had sworn each other friendship; and held truly together, how far soever thy might fare.

HIORDIS. And the two young vikings hight Sigurd and Gunnar?

SIGURD. Ay, we may call them so. At last they came to Iceland; and there dwelt an old chieftain, who had come forth from Norway in King Harald's days. He had two fair women in his house; but one, his foster-daughter, was the noblest, for she was wise and strong of soul; and the vikings spoke of her between themselves, and never had they seen a fairer woman, so deemed they both.

HIORDIS (in suspense). Both? Wilt thou mock me?

SIGURD. Gunnar thought of her night and day, and that did Sigurd no less; but both held their peace, and no man could say from her bearing whether Gunnar found favour in her eyes; but that Sigurd misliked her, that was easy to discern.

HIORDIS (breathlessly). Go on, go on!

SIGURD. Yet ever the more must Sigurd dream of her; but of that wist no man. Now it befell one evening that there was a drinking-feast; and then swore that proud woman that no man should possess her save he who wrought a mighty deed, which she named. High beat Sigurd's heart for joy; for he felt within him the strength to do that deed; but Gunnar took him apart and told him of his love; Sigurd said naught of his, but went to the

HIORDIS (vehemently). Sigurd, Sigurd! (Controlling herself.) And this saga, is it true?

SIGURD. True it is. One of us had to yield; Gunnar was my friend; I could do aught else. So thou becamest Gunnar's wife, and I wedded another woman.

HIORDIS. And came to love her!

SIGURD. I learned to prize her; but one woman only has Sigurd loved, and that is she who frowned upon him from the first day they met. Here ends my saga; and now let us part. Farewell, Gunnar's wife; never shall we meet again.

HIORDIS (springing up). Stay, stay! Woe to us both; Sigurd, what hast thou done?

SIGURD (starting). I, done? What ails thee?

HIORDIS. And all this dost thou tell me now! But no, it cannot be true!

SIGURD. These are my last words to thee, and every word is true. I would not thou shouldst think hardly of me, therefore I needs must speak.

HIORDIS (involuntarily clasps her hands together and gazes at him in voiceless astonishment). Loved, loved me thou! (Vehemently, coming close up to him.) I will not believe thee! (Looks hard at him.) Yes, it is true, and baleful for us both!

(Hides her face in her hands, and turns away from him.)

SIGURD (terror-stricken). Hiordis!

HIORDIS (softly, struggling with tears and laughter). Nay, heed me not! This was all I meant, that (Lays her hand on his arm.) Sigurd, thou hast not told thy saga to the end; that proud woman thou didst tell of, she returned thy love!

SIGURD (starts backwards). Thou?

HIORDIS (with composure). Yes, Sigurd, I have loved thee, at last I understand it. Thou sayest I was ungentle and short of speech towards thee; what wouldst thou have a woman do? I could not offer thee my love, for then had I been little worthy of thee. I deemed thee ever the noblest man of men; and then to know thee another's husband 'twas that caused me the bitter pain, that myself I could not understand!

SIGURD (much moved). A baleful web has the Norn woven around us twain.

HIORDIS. The blame is thine own; bravely and firmly it becomes a man to act. When I set that hard proof for him who should win me, my thought was of thee; yet could'st thou!

SIGURD. I knew Gunnar's soul-sickness; I alone could heal it; was there aught for me to choose? And yet, had I known what I now know, I scarce dare answer for myself; for great is the might of love.

HIORDIS (with animation). But now, Sigurd! A baleful hap has held us apart all these years; now the knot is loosed; the days to come shall make good the past to us.

SIGURD (shaking his head). It cannot be; we must part again.

HIORDIS. Nay, we must not. I love thee, that may I now say unashamed; for my love is no mere dalliance, like a weak woman's; were I a man by all the Mighty Ones, I could still love thee, even as now I do! Up then, Sigurd! Happiness is worth a daring deed; we are both free if we but will it, and then the game is won.

SIGURD. Free? What meanest thou?

HIORDIS. What is Dagny to thee? What can she be to thee? No more than I count Gunnar in my secret heart. What matters it though two worthless lives be wrecked?

SIGURD. Hiordis, Hiordis!

HIORDIS. Let Gunnar stay where he is; let Dagny fare with her father to Iceland; I will follow thee in harness of steel, withersoever thou wendest. (SIGURD makes a movement.) Not as thy wife will I follow thee; for I have belonged to another, and the woman lives that has lain by thy side. No, Sigurd, not as they wife, but like those mighty women, like Hilde's sisters,[1] will I follow thee, and fire thee to strife and to manly deeds, so that thy name shall be heard over every land. In the sword-game will I stand by thy side; I will fare forth among thy warriors on the stormy viking-raids; and when the death-song is sung, it shall tell of Sigurd and Hiordis in one!

[1] The Valkyries.

SIGURD. Once was that my fairest dream; now, it is too late. Gunnar and Dagny stand between us, and that by right. I crushed my love for Gunnar's sake; how great soever my suffering, I cannot undo my deed. And Dagny, full of faith and trust she left her home and kindred; never must she dream that I longed for Hiordis as often as she took me to her breast.

HIORDIS. And for such a cause wilt thou lay a burden on thy life! To what end hast thou strength and might, and therewith all noble gifts of the mind? And deemest thou it can now beseem me to dwell beneath Gunnar's roof? Nay, Sigurd, trust me, there are many tasks awaiting such a man as thou. Erik is king of Norway, do thou rise against him! Many goodly warriors will join thee and swear thee fealty; with unconquerable might will we press onward, and fight and toil unresting until thou art seated on the throne of Harfager!

SIGURD. Hiordis, Hiordis, so have I dreamt in my wild youth; let it be forgotten, tempt me not!

HIORDIS (impressively). It is the Norn's will that we two shall hold together; it cannot be altered. Plainly now I see my task in life: to make thee famous over all the world. Thou hast stood before me every day, every hour of my life; I sought to tear thee out of my mind, but I lacked the might; now it is needless, now that I know thou lovest me.

SIGURD (with forced coldness). If that be so, then know, I have loved thee; it is past now; I have forgot those days.

HIORDIS. Sigurd, in that thou liest! So much at least am I worth, that if thou hast loved me once, thou canst never forget it.

SIGURD (vehemently). I must; and now I will.

HIORDIS. So be it; but thou canst not. Thou wilt seek to hinder me, but in vain; ere evening falls, Gunnar and Dagny shall know all.

SIGURD. Ha, that wilt thou never do!

HIORDIS. That will I do!

SIGURD. Then must I know thee ill; high-souled have I ever deemed thee.

HIORDIS. Evil days breed evil thoughts; too great has been thy trust in me. I will, I must, go forth by thy side, forth to face life and strife; Gunnar's roof-tree is too low for me.

SIGURD (with emphasis). But honour between man and man hast thou highly prized. There lack not grounds for strife between me and Gunnar; say, now, that he fell by my hand, wouldst thou still make all known and follow me?

HIORDIS (starting). Wherefore askest thou?

SIGURD. Answer me first: what wouldst thou do, were I to thy husband his bane.

HIORDIS (looks hard at him). Then must I keep silence and never rest until I had seen thee slain.

SIGURD (with a smile). It is well, Hiordis, I knew it.

HIORDIS (hastily). But it can never come to pass!

SIGURD. It must come to pass; thou thyself hast cast the die for Gunnar's life and mine.

(GUNNAR, with some House-carls, enters from the back.)

GUNNAR (gloomily, to HIORDIS). See now; the seed thou hast sown is shooting bravely!

SIGURD (approaching). What is amiss with thee?

GUNNAR. Sigurd, is it thou? What is amiss? Nought but what I might well have foreseen. As soon as Dagny, thy wife, had brought tidings of Kare the Peasant, I took horse and rode to my neighbours to crave help against him.

HIORDIS (eagerly). Well?

GUNNAR. I was answered awry where'er I came: my dealings with Kare had been little to my honour, it was said; hm, other things were said to boot, that I will not utter. I am spurned at by all; I am thought to have done a dastard deed; men hold it a shame to make common cause with me.

SIGURD. It shall not long be held a shame; ere evening comes, thou shalt have men enough to face Kare.

GUNNAR. Sigurd!

HIORDIS (in a low voice, triumphantly). Ha, I knew it well!

SIGURD (with forced resolution). But then is there an end to the peace between us; for hearken to my words, Gunnar, thou hast slain Thorolf, my wife's kinsman, and therefore do I challenge thee to single combat to-morrow at break of day.

(HIORDIS, in violent inward emotion, makes a stride towards SIGURD, but collects herself and remains standing motionless during the following.)

GUNNAR (in extreme astonishment). To single combat! Me! Thou art jesting, Sigurd!

SIGURD. Thou art lawfully challenged to single combat; 'twill be a game for life or death; one of us must fall!

GUNNAR (bitterly). Ha, I understand it well. When I came, thou didst talk with Hiordis alone; she has goaded thee afresh!

SIGURD. May hap. (Half towards HIORDIS.) A high-souled woman must ever guard her husband's honour. (To the men in the background.) And do ye, house-carls, now go to Gunnar's neighbours, and say to them that to-morrow he is to ply sword-strokes with me; none dare call that man a dastard who bears arms against Sigurd Viking!

(The House-carls go out by the back.)

GUNNAR (goes quickly up to SIGURD and presses his hands, in strong emotion). Sigurd, my brave brother, now I understand thee! Thou venturest thy life for my honour, as of old for my happiness!

SIGURD. Thank thy wife; she has the largest part in what I do. To-morrow at break of day

GUNNAR. I will meet thee. (Tenderly.) Foster-brother, wilt thou have a good blade of me? It is a gift of price.

SIGURD. I thank thee; but let it hang. Who knows if next evening I may have any use for it.

GUNNAR (shakes his hand). Farewell, Sigurd!

SIGURD. Again farewell, and fortune befriend thee this night!

(They part. GUNNAR goes out to the right. SIGURD casts a glance at HIORDIS, and goes out by the back.)

HIORDIS (after a pause, softly and thoughtfully). To-morrow they fight! Which will fall? (After a moment's silence, she bursts forth as if seized by a strong resolution.) Let fall who will, Sigurd and I shall still be together!

Act Fourth

(By the coast. It is evening; the moon breaks forth now and again, from among dark and ragged storm-clouds. At the back, a black grave-mound, newly heaped up.)

(ORNULF sits on a stone, in front on the right, his head bare, his elbows resting on his knees, and his face buried in his hands. His men are digging at the mound; some give light with pine-knot torches. After a short pause, SIGURD and DAGNY enter from the boat-house, where a wood fire is burning.)

DAGNY (in a low voice). There sits he still. (Holding SIGURD back.) Nay, speak not to him!

SIGURD. Thou say'st well; it is too soon; best leave him!

DAGNY (goes over to the right, and gazes at her father in quiet sorrow). So strong was he yesterday when he bore Thorolf's body on his back; strong was he as he helped to heap the grave-mound; but when they were all laid to rest, and earth and stones piled over them, then the sorrow seized him; then seemed it of a sudden as though his fire were quenched. (Dries her tears.) Tell me, Sigurd, when thinkest thou to fare homeward to Iceland?

SIGURD. So soon as the storm abates, and my quarrel with Gunnar is ended.

DAGNY. And then wilt thou buy land and build thee a homestead, and go a-viking no more?

SIGURD. Yes, yes, that have I promised.

DAGNY. And I may believe without doubt that Hiordis spoke falsely when she said that I was unworthy to be thy wife?

SIGURD. Yes yes, Dagny, trust thou to my word.

DAGNY. Then am I glad again, and will try to forget all the evil that here has been wrought. In the long winter evenings we will talk together of Gunnar and Hiordis, and

SIGURD. Nay, Dagny, wouldst thou have things go well with us, do thou never speak Hiordis' name when we sit together in Iceland.

DAGNY (mildly upbraiding him). Unjust is thy hatred towards her. Sigurd, Sigurd, it is unlike thee.

ONE OF THE MEN (approaching). There now, the mound is finished.

ORNULF (as if awaking). The mound? Is it, ay, ay

SIGURD. Now speak to him, Dagny.

DAGNY (approaching). Father, it is cold out here; a storm is gathering to-night.

ORNULF. Hm; heed it not; the mound is close-heaped and crannyless; they lie warm in there.

DAGNY. Ay, but thou

ORNULF. I? I am not cold.

DAGNY. Nought hast thou eaten today; wilt thou not go in? The supper-board stands ready.

ORNULF. Let the supper-board stand; I have no hunger.

DAGNY. But to sit here so still, trust me, thou wilt take hurt of it; thou art ever wont to be stirring.

ORNULF. True, true; there is somewhat that crushes my breast; I cannot draw breath.

(He hides his face in his hands. A pause. DAGNY seats herself beside him.)

DAGNY. To-morrow wilt thou make ready thy ship and set forth for Iceland?

ORNULF (without looking up). What should I do there? Nay, I will to my sons.

DAGNY (with pain). Father!

ORNULF (raises his head). Go in and let me sit here; when the storm has played with me for a night or two, the game will be over, I ween.

SIGURD. Thou canst not think to deal thus with thyself.

ORNULF. Dost marvel that I fain would rest? My day's work is done; I have laid my sons in their grave. (Vehemently.) Go from me! Go, go!

(He hides his face.)

SIGURD (softly, to DAGNY, who rises). Let him sit yet a while.

DAGNY. Nay, I have one rede yet untried; I know him. (To Ornulf.) Thy day's work done, say'st thou? Nay, that it is not. Thou hast laid thy sons in the grave; but art thou not a skald? It is meet that thou should'st sing their memory.

ORNULF (shaking his head). Sing? Nay, nay; yesterday I could sing; I am too old to-day.

DAGNY. But needs must thou; honourable men were thy sons, one and all; a song must be made of them, and that can none of our kin but thou.

ORNULF (looks inquiringly at SIGURD). To sing? What thinkest thou, Sigurd?

SIGURD. Meseems it is but meet; thou must e'en do as she says.

DAGNY. Thy neighbours in Iceland will deem it ill done when the grave-ale is drunk over Ornulf's children, and there is no song to sing with it. Thou hast ever time enough to follow thy sons.

ORNULF. Well well, I will try it; and thou, Dagny, give heed, that afterwards thou may'st carve the song on staves.

(The men approach with the torches, forming a group around him; he is silent for a time, reflecting; then he says:)

Bragi's[1] gift is bitter
when the heart is broken;
sorrow-laden singer,
singing, suffers sorely.
Natheless, since the Skald-god
gave me skill in song-craft,
in a lay loud-ringing
be my loss lamented!

(Rises.)

Ruthless Norn[2] and wrathful
wrecked my life and ravaged,
wiled away my welfare,
wasted Ornulf's treasure.
Sons had Ornulf seven,
by the great gods granted;
lonely now and life-sick
goes the greybeard, sonless.
Seven sons so stately,
bred among the sword-blades,
made a mighty bulwark
round the snow-locked sea-king.
Levelled lies the bulwark,
dead my swordsmen seven;
gone the greybeard's gladness,
desolate his dwelling.
Thorolf, thou my last-born!
Of the bold the boldest!
Soon were spent my sorrow
so but thou wert left me!
Fair thou wast as springtide,
fond towards thy father,
waxing straight and stalwart
to so wight a warrior.
Dark and drear his death-wound
leaves my life's lone evening;
grief hath gripped my bosom
as 'twixt hurtling targes.
Nought the Norn denied me
of her rueful riches,

showering woes unstinted
over Ornulf's world-way.
Weak are now my weapons.
But, were god-might given me,
then, oh Norn, I swear it,
scarce should'st thou go scatheless!
Dire were then my vengeance;
then had dawned thy doomsday,
Norn, that now hast left me
nought but yonder grave-mound.
Nought, I said? Nay, truly,
somewhat still is Ornulf's,
since of Suttung's[3] mead-horn
he betimes drank deeply.

   (With rising enthusiasm.)

Though she stripped me sonless,
one great gift she gave me
songcraft's mighty secret,
skill to sing my sorrows.
On my lips she laid it,
goodly gift of songcraft;
loud, then, let my lay sound,
e'en where they are lying!
Hail, my stout sons seven!
Hail, as homeward ride ye!
Songcraft's glorious god-gift
stauncheth woe and wailing.

[1] Bragi, the god of poetry and eloquence.

[2] See note, p. 175 [The "Nornir" were the Fates of northern mythology.]

[3] Suttung was a giant who kept guard over the magic mead of poetical inspiration.

(He draws a deep breath, throws back the hair from his brow, and says calmly:)

So, so; now is Ornulf sound and strong again. (To the men.) Follow me to the supper-board, lads; we have had a heavy day's work!

(Goes with the men into the boat-house.)

DAGNY. Praised be the Mighty Ones on high that gave me so good a rede. (To SIGURD.) Wilt thou not go in?

SIGURD. Nay, I list not to. Tell me, are all things ready for to-morrow?

DAGNY. They are; a silk-sewn shroud lies on the bench; but I know full surely that thou wilt hold thee against Gunnar, so I have not wept over it.

SIGURD. Grant all good powers, that thou may'st never weep for my sake. (He stops and looks out.)

DAGNY. What art thou listening to?

SIGURD. Hear'st thou nought there?

(Points towards the left.)

DAGNY. Ay, there goes a fearsome storm over the sea!

SIGURD (going up a little towards the background). Hm, there will fall hard hailstones in that storm. (Shouts.) Who comes?

KARE THE PEASANT (without on the left). Folk thou wot'st of, Sigurd Viking!

(KARE THE PEASANT, with a band of armed men, enters from the left.)

SIGURD. Whither would ye?

KARE. To Gunnar's hall.

SIGURD. As foemen?

KARE. Ay, trust me for that! Thou didst hinder me before; but now I ween thou wilt scarce do the like.

SIGURD. Maybe not.

KARE. I have heard of thy challenge to Gunnar; but if things go to my mind, weak will be his weapons when the time comes for your meeting.

SIGURD. 'Tis venturesome work thou goest about; take heed for thyself, Peasant!

KARE (with defiant laughter). Leave that to me; if thou wilt tackle thy ship to-night, we will give thee light for the task! Come, all my men; here goes the way.

(They go off to the right, at the back.)

DAGNY. Sigurd, Sigurd, this misdeed must thou hinder.

SIGURD (goes quickly to the door of the hut, and calls in). Up from the board, Ornulf; take vengeance on Kare the Peasant.

ORNULF (comes out, with the rest). Kare the Peasant, where is he?

SIGURD. He is making for Gunnar's hall to burn it over their heads.

ORNULF. Ha-ha, let him do as he will; so shall I be avenged on Gunnar and Hiordis, and afterwards I can deal with Kare.

SIGURD. Ay, that rede avails not; wouldst thou strike at Kare, thou must seek him out to-night; for when his misdeed is done, he will take to the mountains. I have challenged Gunnar to single combat; him thou hast safely enough, unless I myself but no matter. To-night he must be shielded from his foes; it would ill befit thee to let such a dastard as Kare rob thee of thy revenge.

ORNULF. Thou say'st truly. To-night will I shield the slayer of Thorolf; but to-morrow he must die.

SIGURD. He or I, doubt not of that!

ORNULF. Come then, to take vengeance for Ornulf's sons.

(He goes out with his men by the back, to the right.)

SIGURD. Dagny, do thou follow them; I must bide here; for the rumour of the combat is already abroad, and I may not meet Gunnar ere the time comes. But thou, do thou keep rein on thy father; he must go honourably to work; in Gunnar's hall there are many women; no harm must befall Hiordis or the rest.

DAGNY. Yes, I will follow them. Thou hast a kind thought even for Hiordis; I thank thee.

SIGURD. Go, go, Dagny!

DAGNY. I go; but be thou at ease as to Hiordis; she has gilded armour in her bower, and will know how to shield herself.

SIGURD. That deem I too; but go thou nevertheless; guide thy father's course; watch over all and over Gunnar's wife!

DAGNY. Trust to me. Farewell, till we meet again.

(She follows the others.)

SIGURD. 'Tis the first time, foster-brother, that I stand weaponless whilst thou art in danger. (Listens.) I hear shouts and sword-strokes; they are already at the hall. (Goes towards the right, but stops and recoils in astonishment.) Hiordis! Comes she hither!

(HIORDIS enters, clad in a short scarlet kirtle, with gilded armour: helmet, hauberk, arm-plates, and greaves. Her hair is flying loose; at her back hangs a quiver, and at her belt a small shield. She has in her hand the bow strung with her hair.)

HIORDIS (hastily looking behind her, as though in dread of something pursuing her, goes close up to SIGURD, seizes him by the arm, and whispers:) Sigurd, Sigurd, canst thou see it?

SIGURD. What? Where ?

HIORDIS. The wolf there, close behind me; it does not move; it glares at me with its two red eyes. It is my wraith,[1], Sigurd! Three times has it appeared to me; that bodes that I shall surely die to-night!

[1] The word "wraith" is here used in an obviously inexact sense; but the wraith seemed to be the nearest equivalent in English mythology to the Scandinavian "fylgie," an attendant spirit, often regarded as a sort of emanation from the person it accompanied, and sometimes (as in this case) typifying that person's moral attributes.

SIGURD. Hiordis, Hiordis!

HIORDIS. It has sunk into the earth! Yes, yes, now it has warned me.

SIGURD. Thou art sick; come, go in with me.

HIORDIS. Nay, here will I bide; I have but little time left.

SIGURD. What has befallen thee?

HIORDIS. What has befallen? That know I not; but true was it what thou said'st to-day, that Gunnar and Dagny stand between us; we must away from them and from life: then can we be together!

SIGURD. We? Ha, thou meanest!

HIORDIS (with dignity). I have been homeless in this world from that day thou didst take another to wife. That was ill done of thee! All good gifts may a man give his faithful friend all, save the woman he loves; for if he do that, he rends the Norn's secret web, and two lives are wrecked. An unerring voice within me tells me I came into the world that my strong soul might cheer and sustain thee through heavy days, and that thou wast born to the end I might find in one man all that seemed to me great and noble; for this I know Sigurd had we two held together, thou hadst become more famous than all others, and I happier.

SIGURD. It avails not now to mourn. Thinkest thou it is a merry life that awaits me? To be by Dagny's side day be day, and feign a love my heart shrinks from? Yet so it must be; it cannot be altered.

HIORDIS (in a growing frenzy). It shall be altered! We must out of this life, both of us! Seest thou this bow-string? With it can I surely hit my mark; for I have crooned fair sorceries over it! (Places an arrow in the bow, which is strung.) Hark! hearest thou that rushing in the air? It is the dead men's ride to Nalhal: I have bewitched them hither; we two will join them in their ride!

SIGURD (shrinking back). Hiordis, Hiordis, I fear thee!

HIORDIS (not heeding him). Our fate no power can alter now! Oh, 'tis better so than if thou hadst wedded me here in this life, if I had sat in thy homestead weaving linen and wool for thee and bearing thee children, pah!

SIGURD. Hold, hold! Thy sorcery has been too strong for thee; thou art soul-sick, Hiordis! (Horror-struck.) Ha, see, see! Gunnar's hall, it is burning!

HIORDIS. Let it burn, let it burn! The cloud-hall up yonder is loftier than Gunnar's rafter-roof!

SIGURD. But Egil, thy son, they are slaying him!

HIORDIS. Let him die, my shame dies with him!

SIGURD. And Gunnar, they are taking thy husband's life!

HIORDIS. What care I! A better husband shall I follow home this night! Ay, Sigurd, so must it be; here on this earth is no happiness for me. The White God is coming northward; him will I not meet; the old gods are strong no longer; they sleep, they sit half shadow-high; with them will we strive! Out of this life, Sigurd; I will enthrone thee king in heaven, and I will sit at thy side. (The storm bursts wildly.) Hark, hark, here comes our company! Canst see the black steeds galloping? one is for me and one for thee. (Draws the arrow to her ear and shoots.) Away, then, on thy last ride home!

SIGURD. Well aimed, Hiordis!

(He falls.)

HIORDIS (jubilant, rushes up to him). Sigurd, my brother, now art thou mine at last!

SIGURD. Now less than ever. Here our ways part; for I am a Christian man.

HIORDIS (appalled). Thou! Ha, no, no!

SIGURD. The White God is mine; King AEthelstan taught me to know him; it is to him I go.

HIORDIS (in despair). And I! (Drops her bow.) Woe! woe!

SIGURD. Heavy has my life been from the hour I tore thee out of my own heart and gave thee to Gunnar. Thanks, Hiordis; now am I so light and free.

(Dies.)

HIORDIS (quietly). Dead! Then truly have I brought my soul to wreck!

(The storm increases; she breaks forth wildly.) They come! I have bewitched them hither! No, no! I will not go with you! I will not ride without Sigurd! It avails not, they see me; they laugh and beckon to me; they spur their horses! (Rushes out to the edge of the cliff at the back.) They are upon me; and no shelter no hiding-place! Ay, mayhap at the bottom of the sea!

(She casts herself over.)

(ORNULF, DAGNY, GUNNAR, with EGIL, followed by SIGURD'S and ORNULF'S men, gradually enter from the right.)

ORNULF (turning towards the grave-mound). Now may ye sleep in peace; for ye lie not unavenged.

DAGNY (entering). Father, father, I die of fear, all that bloody strife, and the storm; hark, hark!

GUNNAR (carrying EGIL). Peace, and shelter for my child!

ORNULF. Gunnar!

GUNNAR. Ay, Ornulf, my homestead is burnt and my men are slain; I am in thy power; do with me what thou wilt!

ORNULF. That Sigurd must look to. But in, under roof! It is not safe out here.

DAGNY. Ay, in, in! (Goes towards the boat-house, catches sight of SIGURD'S body, and shrieks.) Sigurd, my husband! They have slain him! (Throwing herself upon him.)

ORNULF (rushes up). Sigurd!

GUNNAR (sets EGIL down). Sigurd dead!

DAGNY (looks despairingly at the men, who surround the body). No, no, it is not so; he must be alive! (Catches sight of the bow.) Ha, what is that? (Rises.)

ORNULF. Daughter, it is as first thou sadist, Sigurd is slain.

GUNNAR (as if seized by a sudden thought). And Hiordis! Has Hiordis been here?

DAGNY (softly and with self-control). I know not; but this I know, that her bow has been here.

GUNNAR. Ay, I thought as much!

DAGNY. Hush, hush! (To herself.) So bitterly did she hate him!

GUNNAR (aside). She has slain him, the night before the combat; then she loved me after all.

(A thrill of dread runs through the whole group; ASGARDSREIEN, the ride of the fallen heroes to Valhal, hurtles through the air.)

EGIL (in terror). Father! See, see!

GUNNAR. What is it?

EGIL. Up there, all the black horses!

GUNNAR. It is the clouds that

ORNULF. Nay, it is the dead men's home-faring.

EGIL (with a shriek). Mother is with them!

DAGNY. All good spirits!

GUNNAR. Child, what say'st thou?

EGIL. There, in front, on the black horse! Father, father!

(EGIL clings in terror to his father; a short pause; the storm passes over, the clouds part, the moon shines peacefully on the scene.)

GUNNAR (in quiet sorrow). Now is Hiordis surely dead!

ORNULF. So it must be, Gunnar; and my vengeance was rather against her than thee. Dear has this meeting been to both of us; there is my hand; be there peace between us!

GUNNAR. Thanks, Ornulf! And now aboard; I sail with thee to Iceland.

ORNULF. Ay, to Iceland! Long will it be ere our forth-faring is forgotten.

> Weapon wielding warrior's meeting,
>
> woeful by the northern seaboard,
>
> still shall live in song and saga
>
> while our stem endure in Iceland.

THE END.

Henrik Ibsen - Pillars Of Society

Index Of Contents

Dramatis Personae

Karsten Bernick, a shipbuilder.
Mrs. Bernick, his wife.
Olaf, their son, thirteen years old.
Martha Bernick, Karsten Bernick's sister.
Johan Tonnesen, Mrs. Bernick's younger brother.
Lona Hessel, Mrs. Bernick's elder half-sister.
Hilmar Tonnesen, Mrs. Bernick's cousin.
Dina Dorf, a young girl living with the Bernicks.
Rorlund, a schoolmaster.
Rummel, a merchant.
Vigeland and Sandstad, tradesman
Krap, Bernick's confidential clerk.
Aune, foreman of Bernick's shipbuilding yard.
Mrs.Rummel.
Hilda Rummel, her daughter.
Mrs.Holt.
Netta Holt, her daughter.
Mrs.Lynge.

Townsfolk and visitors, foreign sailors, steamboat passengers, etc., etc.

(The action takes place at the Bernicks' house in one of the smaller coast towns in Norway)

Act I.

(SCENE. A spacious garden-room in the BERNICKS' house. In the foreground on the left is a door leading to BERNICK'S business room; farther back in the same wall, a similar door. In the middle of the opposite wall is a large entrance-door, which leads to the street. The wall in the background is almost wholly composed of plate-glass; a door in it opens upon a broad flight of steps which lead down to the garden; a sun-awning is stretched over the steps. Below the steps a part of the garden is visible, bordered by a fence with a small gate in it. On the other side of the fence runs a street, the opposite side of which is occupied by small wooden houses painted in bright colours. It is summer, and the sun is shining warmly. People are seen, every now and then, passing along the street and stopping to talk to one another; others going in and out of a shop at the corner, etc.

In the room a gathering of ladies is seated round a table. MRS. BERNICK is presiding; on her left side are MRS. HOLT and her daughter NETTA, and next to them MRS. RUMMEL and HILDA RUMMEL. On MRS. BERNICK'S right are MRS. LYNGE, MARTHA BERNICK and DINA DORF. All the ladies are busy working. On the table lie great piles of linen garments and other articles of clothing, some half finished, and some merely cut out. Farther back, at a small table on which two pots of flowers and a glass of sugared water are standing, RORLUND is sitting, reading aloud from a book with gilt edges, but only loud enough for the spectators to catch a word now and then. Out in the garden OLAF BERNICK is running about and shooting at a target with a toy crossbow.

After a moment AUNE comes in quietly through the door on the right. There is a slight interruption in the reading. MRS. BERNICK nods to him and points to the door on the left. AUNE goes quietly across, knocks softly at the door of BERNICK'S room, and after a moment's pause, knocks again. KRAP comes out of the room, with his hat in his hand and some papers under his arm.)

KRAP
Oh, it was you knocking?

AUNE
Mr. Bernick sent for me.

KRAP
He did but he cannot see you. He has deputed me to tell you.

AUNE
Deputed you? All the same, I would much rather

KRAP
deputed me to tell you what he wanted to say to you. You must give up these Saturday lectures of yours to the men.

AUNE
Indeed? I supposed I might use my own time

KRAP
You must not use your own time in making the men useless in working hours. Last Saturday you were talking to them of the harm that would be done to the workmen by our new machines and the new working methods at the yard. What makes you do that?

AUNE
I do it for the good of the community.

KRAP
That's curious, because Mr. Bernick says it is disorganising the community.

AUNE
My community is not Mr. Bernick's, Mr. Krap! As President of the Industrial Association, I must

KRAP
You are, first and foremost, President of Mr. Bernick's shipbuilding yard; and, before everything else, you have to do your duty to the community known as the firm of Bernick & Co.; that is what every one of us lives for. Well, now you know what Mr. Bernick had to say to you.

AUNE
Mr. Bernick would not have put it that way, Mr. Krap! But I know well enough whom I have to thank for this. It is that damned American boat. Those fellows expect to get work done here the way they are accustomed to it over there, and that.

KRAP
Yes, yes, but I can't go into all these details. You know now what Mr. Bernick means, and that is sufficient. Be so good as to go back to the yard; probably you are needed there. I shall be down myself in a little while. Excuse me, ladies! (Bows to the ladies and goes out through the garden and down the street. AUNE goes

quietly out to the right. RORLUND, who has continued his reading during the foregoing conversation, which has been carried on in low tones, has now come to the end of the book, and shuts it with a bang.)

RORLUND
There, my dear ladies, that is the end of it.

MRS. RUMMEL
What an instructive tale!

MRS. HOLT
And such a good moral!

MRS. BERNICK
A book like that really gives one something to think about.

RORLUND
Quite so; it presents a salutary contrast to what, unfortunately, meets our eyes every day in the newspapers and magazines. Look at the gilded and painted exterior displayed by any large community, and think what it really conceals! emptiness and rottenness, if I may say so; no foundation of morality beneath it. In a word, these large communities of ours now-a-days are whited sepulchres.

MRS. HOLT
How true! How true!

MRS. RUMMEL
And for an example of it, we need look no farther than at the crew of the American ship that is lying here just now.

RORLUND
Oh, I would rather not speak of such offscourings of humanity as that. But even in higher circles what is the case there? A spirit of doubt and unrest on all sides; minds never at peace, and instability characterising all their behaviour. Look how completely family life is undermined over there! Look at their shameless love of casting doubt on even the most serious truths!

DINA (without looking up from her work)
But are there not many big things done there too?

RORLUND
Big things done? I do not understand.

MRS. HOLT (in amazement)
Good gracious, Dina!

MRS. RUMMEL (in the same breath)
Dina, how can you?

RORLUND
I think it would scarcely be a good thing for us if such "big things" became the rule here. No, indeed, we ought to be only too thankful that things are as they are in this country. It is true enough that tares grow up amongst our wheat here too, alas; but we do our best conscientiously to weed them out as well as we are able. The important thing is to keep society pure, ladies to ward off all the hazardous experiments that a restless age seeks to force upon us.

MRS.HOLT
And there are more than enough of them in the wind, unhappily.

MRS.RUMMEL
Yes, you know last year we only by a hair's breadth escaped the project of having a railway here.

MRS.BERNICK
Ah, my husband prevented that.

RORLUND

Providence, Mrs. Bernick. You may be certain that your husband was the instrument of a higher Power when he refused to have anything to do with the scheme.

MRS.BERNICK

And yet they said such horrible things about him in the newspapers! But we have quite forgotten to thank you, Mr. Rorlund. It is really more than friendly of you to sacrifice so much of your time to us.

RORLUND

Not at all. This is holiday time, and

MRS.BERNICK

Yes, but it is a sacrifice all the same, Mr. Rorlund.

RORLUND (drawing his chair nearer)

Don't speak of it, my dear lady. Are you not all of you making some sacrifice in a good cause? and that willingly and gladly? These poor fallen creatures for whose rescue we are working may be compared to soldiers wounded on the field of battle; you, ladies, are the kind-hearted sisters of mercy who prepare the lint for these stricken ones, lay the bandages softly on their wounds, heal them and cure them.

MRS.BERNICK

It must be a wonderful gift to be able to see everything in such a beautiful light.

RORLUND

A good deal of it is inborn in one but it can be to a great extent acquired, too. All that is needful is to see things in the light of a serious mission in life. (To MARTHA:) What do you say, Miss Bernick? Have you not felt as if you were standing on firmer ground since you gave yourself up to your school work?

MARTHA

I really do not know what to say. There are times, when I am in the schoolroom down there, that I wish I were far away out on the stormy seas.

RORLUND

That is merely temptation, dear Miss Bernick. You ought to shut the doors of your mind upon such disturbing guests as that. By the "stormy seas" for of course you do not intend me to take your words literally, you mean the restless tide of the great outer world, where so many are shipwrecked. Do you really set such store on the life you hear rushing by outside? Only look out into the street. There they go, walking about in the heat of the sun, perspiring and tumbling about over their little affairs. No, we undoubtedly have the best of it, who are able to sit here in the cool and turn our backs on the quarter from which disturbance comes.

MARTHA

Yes,I have no doubt you are perfectly right.

RORLUND

And in a house like this,in a good and pure home, where family life shows in its fairest colours, where peace and harmony rule (To MRS. BERNICK:) What are you listening to, Mrs. Bernick?

MRS.BERNICK (who has turned towards the door of BERNICK'S room)

They are talking very loud in there.

RORLUND

Is there anything particular going on?

MRS.BERNICK

I don't know. I can hear that there is somebody with my husband.

(HILMAR TONNESEN, smoking a cigar, appears in the doorway on the right, but stops short at the sight of the company of ladies.)

HILMAR

Oh, excuse me (Turns to go back.)

MRS.BERNICK

No, Hilmar, come along in; you are not disturbing us. Do you want something?

HILMAR
No, I only wanted to look in here. Good morning, ladies. (To MRS. BERNICK:) Well, what is the result?

MRS.BERNICK
Of what?

HILMAR
Karsten has summoned a meeting, you know.

MRS.BERNICK
Has he? What about?

HILMAR
Oh, it is this railway nonsense over again.

MRS.RUMMEL
Is it possible?

MRS.BERNICK
Poor Karsten, is he to have more annoyance over that?

RORLUND
But how do you explain that, Mr. Tonnesen? You know that last year Mr. Bernick made it perfectly clear that he would not have a railway here.

HILMAR
Yes, that is what I thought, too; but I met Krap, his confidential clerk, and he told me that the railway project had been taken up again, and that Mr. Bernick was in consultation with three of our local capitalists.

MRS.RUMMEL
Ah, I was right in thinking I heard my husband's voice.

HILMAR
Of course Mr. Rummel is in it, and so are Sandstad and Michael Vigeland,"Saint Michael", as they call him.

RORLUND
Ahem!

HILMAR
I beg your pardon, Mr. Rorlund?

MRS.BERNICK
Just when everything was so nice and peaceful.

HILMAR
Well, as far as I am concerned, I have not the slightest objection to their beginning their squabbling again. It will be a little diversion, any way.

RORLUND
I think we can dispense with that sort of diversion.

HILMAR
It depends how you are constituted. Certain natures feel the lust of battle now and then. But unfortunately life in a country town does not offer much in that way, and it isn't given to every one to (turns the leaves of the book RORLUND has been reading). "Woman as the Handmaid of Society." What sort of drivel is this?

MRS.BERNICK
My dear Hilmar, you must not say that. You certainly have not read the book.

HILMAR
No, and I have no intention of reading it, either.

MRS.BERNICK
Surely you are not feeling quite well today.

HILMAR
No, I am not.

MRS.BERNICK
Perhaps you did not sleep well last night?

HILMAR
No, I slept very badly. I went for a walk yesterday evening for my health's sake; and I finished up at the club and read a book about a Polar expedition. There is something bracing in following the adventures of men who are battling with the elements.

MRS.RUMMEL
But it does not appear to have done you much good, Mr. Tonnesen.

HILMAR
No, it certainly did not. I lay all night tossing about, only half asleep, and dreamt that I was being chased by a hideous walrus.

OLAF (who meanwhile has come up the steps from the garden)
Have you been chased by a walrus, uncle?

HILMAR
I dreamt it, you duffer! Do you mean to say you are still playing about with that ridiculous bow? Why don't you get hold of a real gun?

OLAF
I should like to, but

HILMAR
There is some sense in a thing like that; it is always an excitement every time you fire it off.

OLAF
And then I could shoot bears, uncle. But daddy won't let me.

MRS.BERNICK
You really mustn't put such ideas into his head, Hilmar.

HILMAR
Hm! It's a nice breed we are educating up now-a-days, isn't it! We talk a great deal about manly sports, goodness knows but we only play with the question, all the same; there is never any serious inclination for the bracing discipline that lies in facing danger manfully. Don't stand pointing your crossbow at me, blockhead, it might go off!

OLAF
No, uncle, there is no arrow in it.

HILMAR
You don't know that there isn't, there may be, all the same. Take it away, I tell you ! Why on earth have you never gone over to America on one of your father's ships? You might have seen a buffalo hunt then, or a fight with Red Indians.

MRS.BERNICK
Oh, Hilmar!

OLAF
I should like that awfully, uncle; and then perhaps I might meet Uncle Johan and Aunt Lona.

HILMAR
Hm! Rubbish.

MRS.BERNICK
You can go down into the garden again now, Olaf.

OLAF

Mother, may I go out into the street too?

MRS.BERNICK

Yes, but not too far, mind.

(OLAF runs down into the garden and out through the gate in the fence.)

RORLUND

You ought not to put such fancies into the child's head, Mr. Tonnesen.

HILMAR

No, of course he is destined to be a miserable stay-at-home, like so many others.

RORLUND

But why do you not take a trip over there yourself?

HILMAR

I? With my wretched health? Of course I get no consideration on that account. But putting that out of the question, you forget that one has certain obligations to perform towards the community of which one forms a part. There must be some one here to hold aloft the banner of the Ideal. Ugh, there he is shouting again !

THE LADIES

Who is shouting?

HILMAR

I am sure I don't know. They are raising their voices so loud in there that it gets on my nerves.

MRS.BERNICK

I expect it is my husband, Mr. Tonnesen. But you must remember he is so accustomed to addressing large audiences.

RORLUND

I should not call the others low-voiced, either.

HILMAR

Good Lord, no! not on any question that touches their pockets. Everything here ends in these petty material considerations. Ugh!

MRS.BERNICK

Anyway, that is a better state of things than it used to be when everything ended in mere frivolity.

MRS.LYNGE

Things really used to be as bad as that here?

MRS.RUMMEL

Indeed they were, Mrs. Lynge. You may think yourself lucky that you did not live here then.

MRS.HOLT

Yes, times have changed, and no mistake, when I look back to the days when I was a girl.

MRS. RUMMEL

Oh, you need not look back more than fourteen or fifteen years. God forgive us, what a life we led! There used to be a Dancing Society and a Musical Society

MRS.BERNICK

And the Dramatic Club. I remember it very well.

MRS.RUMMEL

Yes, that was where your play was performed, Mr. Tonnesen.

HILMAR (from the back of the room)

What, what?

RORLUND
A play by Mr. Tonnesen?

MRS.RUMMEL
Yes, it was long before you came here, Mr. Rorlund. And it was only performed once.

MRS.LYNGE
Was that not the play in which you told me you took the part of a young man's sweetheart, Mrs. Rummel?

MRS.RUMMEL (glancing towards RORLUND)
I? I really cannot remember, Mrs.Lynge. But I remember well all the riotous gaiety that used to go on.

MRS.HOLT
Yes, there were houses I could name in which two large dinner-parties were given in one week.

MRS.LYNGE
And surely I have heard that a touring theatrical company came here, too?

MRS.RUMMEL
Yes, that was the worst thing of the lot.

MRS.HOLT (uneasily)
Ahem!

MRS.RUMMEL
Did you say a theatrical company? No, I don't remember that at all.

MRS.LYNGE
Oh yes, and I have been told they played all sorts of mad pranks. What is really the truth of those stories?

MRS.RUMMEL
There is practically no truth in them, Mrs. Lynge.

MRS.HOLT
Dina, my love, will you give me that linen?

MRS.BERNICK (at the same time)
Dina, dear, will you go and ask Katrine to bring us our coffee?

MARTHA
I will go with you, Dina. (DINA and MARTHA go out by the farther door on, the left.)

MRS. BERNICK (getting up)
Will you excuse me for a few minutes? I think we will have our coffee outside. (She goes out to the verandah and sets to work to lay a table. RORLUND stands in the doorway talking to her. HILMAR sits outside, smoking.)

MRS. RUMMEL (in a low voice)
My goodness, Mrs. Lynge, how you frightened me!

MRS.LYNGE
I?

MRS.HOLT
Yes, but you know it was you that began it, Mrs. Rummel.

MRS.RUMMEL
I? How can you say such a thing, Mrs. Holt? Not a syllable passed my lips!

MRS.LYNGE
But what does it all mean?

MRS.RUMMEL
What made you begin to talk about? Think, did you not see that Dina was in the room?

MRS.LYNGE
Dina? Good gracious, is there anything wrong with?

MRS.HOLT
And in this house, too! Did you not know it was Mrs. Bernick's brother?

MRS.LYNGE
What about him? I know nothing about it at all; I am quite new to the place, you know.

MRS.RUMMEL
Have you not heard that? Ahem! (To her daughter) Hilda, dear, you can go for a little stroll in the garden?

MRS.HOLT
You go too, Netta. And be very kind to poor Dina when she comes back. (HILDA and NETTA go out into the garden.)

MRS.LYNGE
Well, what about Mrs. Bernick's brother?

MRS.RUMMEL
Don't you know the dreadful scandal about him?

MRS.LYNGE
A dreadful scandal about Mr. Tonnesen?

MRS.RUMMEL
Good Heavens, no. Mr. Tonnesen is her cousin, of course, Mrs. Lynge. I am speaking of her brother

MRS.HOLT
The wicked Mr. Tonnesen

MRS.RUMMEL
His name was Johan. He ran away to America.

MRS.HOLT
Had to run away, you must understand.

MRS.LYNGE
Then it is he the scandal is about?

MRS.RUMMEL
Yes; there was something, how shall I put it? there was something of some kind between him and Dina's mother. I remember it all as if it were yesterday. Johan Tonnesen was in old Mrs. Bernick's office then; Karsten Bernick had just come back from Paris, he had not yet become engaged

MRS.LYNGE
Yes, but what was the scandal?

MRS.RUMMEL
Well, you must know that Moller's company were acting in the town that winter

MRS.HOLT
And Dorf, the actor, and his wife were in the company. All the young men in the town were infatuated with her.

MRS.RUMMEL
Yes, goodness knows how they could think her pretty. Well, Dorf came home late one evening

MRS.HOLT
Quite unexpectedly.

MRS.RUMMEL
And found his - No, really it isn't a thing one can talk about.

MRS.HOLT

After all, Mrs. Rummel, he didn't find anything, because the door was locked on the inside.

MRS.RUMMEL

Yes, that is just what I was going to say, he found the door locked. And just think of it, the man that was in the house had to jump out of the window.

MRS.HOLT

Right down from an attic window.

MRS.LYNGE

And that was Mrs. Bernick's brother?

MRS.RUMMEL

Yes, it was he.

MRS.LYNGE

And that was why he ran away to America?

MRS.HOLT

Yes, he had to run away, you may be sure.

MRS.RUMMEL

Because something was discovered afterwards that was nearly as bad; just think, he had been making free with the cash-box...

MRS.HOLT

But, you know, no one was certain of that, Mrs. Rummel; perhaps there was no truth in the rumour.

MRS.RUMMEL

Well, I must say! Wasn't it known all over the town? Did not old Mrs. Bernick nearly go bankrupt as the result of it? However, God forbid I should be the one to spread such reports.

MRS.HOLT

Well, anyway, Mrs. Dorf didn't get the money, because she

MRS.LYNGE

Yes, what happened to Dina's parents afterwards?

MRS.RUMMEL

Well, Dorf deserted both his wife and his child. But madam was impudent enough to stay here a whole year. Of course she had not the face to appear at the theatre any more, but she kept herself by taking in washing and sewing

MRS.HOLT

And then she tried to set up a dancing school.

MRS.RUMMEL

Naturally that was no good. What parents would trust their children to such a woman? But it did not last very long. The fine madam was not accustomed to work; she got something wrong with her lungs and died of it.

MRS.LYNGE

What a horrible scandal!

MRS.RUMMEL

Yes, you can imagine how hard it was upon the Bernicks. It is the dark spot among the sunshine of their good fortune, as Rummel once put it. So never speak about it in this house, Mrs. Lynge.

MRS.HOLT

And for heaven's sake never mention the stepsister, either!

MRS.LYNGE

Oh, so Mrs. Bernick has a step-sister, too?

MRS.RUMMEL

Had, luckily for the relationship between them is all over now. She was an extraordinary person too! Would you believe it, she cut her hair short, and used to go about in men's boots in bad weather!

MRS.HOLT

And when her step-brother, the black sheep, had gone away, and the whole town naturally was talking about him, what do you think she did? She went out to America to him!

MR.RUMMEL

Yes, but remember the scandal she caused before she went, Mrs. Holt.

MRS.HOLT

Hush, don't speak of it.

MRS.LYNGE

My goodness, did she create a scandal too?

MRS.RUMMEL

I think you ought to hear it, Mrs. Lynge. Mr. Bernick had just got engaged to Betty Tonnesen, and the two of them went arm in arm into her aunt's room to tell her the news

MRS.HOLT

The Tonnesens' parents were dead, you know

MRS.RUMMEL

When, suddenly, up got Lona Hessel from her chair and gave our refined and well-bred Karsten Bernick such a box on the ear that his head swam.

MRS.LYNGE

Well, I am sure I never

MRS.HOLT

It is absolutely true.

MRS.RUMMEL

And then she packed her box and went away to America.

MRS.LYNGE

I suppose she had had her eye on him for herself.

MRS.RUMMEL

Of course she had. She imagined that he and she would make a match of it when he came back from Paris.

MRS.HOLT

The idea of her thinking such a thing! Karsten Bernick, a man of the world and the pink of courtesy, a perfect gentleman, the darling of all the ladies...

MRS.RUMMEL

And, with it all, such an excellent young man, Mrs. Holt, so moral.

MRS.LYNGE

But what has this Miss Hessel made of herself in America?

MRS.RUMMEL

Well, you see, over that (as my husband once put it) has been drawn a veil which one should hesitate to lift.

MRS.LYNGE

What do you mean?

MRS.RUMMEL

She no longer has any connection with the family, as you may suppose; but this much the whole town knows, that she has sung for money in drinking saloons over there

MRS.HOLT
And has given lectures in public

MRS.RUMMEL
And has published some mad kind of book.

MRS.LYNGE
You don't say so! Mrs.Rummel: Yes, it is true enough that Lona Hessel is one of the spots on the sun of the Bernick family's good fortune. Well, now you know the whole story, Mrs. Lynge. I am sure I would never have spoken about it except to put you on your guard.

MRS.LYNGE
Oh, you may be sure I shall be most careful. But that poor child Dina Dorf! I am truly sorry for her.

MRS.RUMMEL
Well, really it was a stroke of good luck for her. Think what it would have meant if she had been brought up by such parents! Of course we did our best for her, every one of us, and gave her all the good advice we could. Eventually Miss Bernick got her taken into this house.

MRS.HOLT
But she has always been a difficult child to deal with. It is only natural with all the bad examples she had had before her. A girl of that sort is not like one of our own; one must be lenient with her.

MRS.RUMMEL
Hush, here she comes. (In a louder voice.) Yes, Dina is really a clever girl. Oh, is that you, Dina? We are just putting away the things.

MRS.HOLT
How delicious your coffee smells, my dear Dina. A nice cup of coffee like that

MRS.BERNICK (calling in from the verandah)
Will you come out here? (Meanwhile MARTHA and DINA have helped the Maid to bring out the coffee. All the ladies seat themselves on the verandah, and talk with a great show of kindness to DINA. In a few moments DINA comes back into the room and looks for her sewing.)

Mrs. Bernick (from the coffee table)
Dina, won't you?

DINA
No, thank you. (Sits down to her sewing. MRS. BERNICK and RORLUND exchange a few words; a moment afterwards he comes back into the room, makes a pretext for going up to the table, and begins speaking to DINA in low tones.)

RORLUND
Dina.

DINA
Yes?

RORLUND
Why don't you want to sit with the others?

DINA
When I came in with the coffee, I could see from the strange lady's face that they had been talking about me.

RORLUND
But did you not see as well how agreeable she was to you out there?

DINA
That is just what I will not stand

RORLUND
You are very self-willed, Dina.

DINA
Yes.

RORLUND
But why?

DINA
Because it is my nature.

RORLUND
Could you not try to alter your nature?

DINA
No.

RORLUND
Why not?

DINA (looking at him)
Because I am one of the "poor fallen creatures", you know.

RORLUND
For shame, Dina.

DINA
So was my mother.

RORLUND
Who has spoken to you about such things?

DINA
No one; they never do. Why don't they? They all handle me in such a gingerly fashion, as if they thought I should go to pieces if they. Oh, how I hate all this kind-heartedness.

RORLUND
My dear Dina, I can quite understand that you feel repressed here, but

DINA
Yes; if only I could get right away from here. I could make my own way quite well, if only I did not live amongst people who are so, so

RORLUND
So what?

DINA
So proper and so moral.

RORLUND
Oh but, Dina, you don't mean that.

DINA
You know quite well in what sense I mean it. Hilda and Netta come here every day, to be exhibited to me as good examples. I can never be so beautifully behaved as they; I don't want to be. If only I were right away from it all, I should grow to be worth something.

RORLUND
But you are worth a great deal, Dina dear.

DINA
What good does that do me here?

RORLUND
Get right away, you say? Do you mean it seriously?

DINA

I would not stay here a day longer, if it were not for you.

RORLUND

Tell me, Dina, why is it that you are fond of being with me?

DINA

Because you teach me so much that is beautiful.

RORLUND

Beautiful? Do you call the little I can teach you, beautiful?

DINA

Yes. Or perhaps, to be accurate, it is not that you teach me anything; but when I listen to you talking I see beautiful visions.

RORLUND

What do you mean exactly when you call a thing beautiful?

DINA

I have never thought it out.

RORLUND

Think it out now, then. What do you understand by a beautiful thing?

DINA

A beautiful thing is something that is great and far off.

RORLUND

Hm! Dina, I am so deeply concerned about you, my dear.

DINA

Only that?

RORLUND

You know perfectly well that you are dearer to me than I can say.

DINA

If I were Hilda or Netta, you would not be afraid to let people see it.

RORLUND

Ah, Dina, you can have no idea of the number of things I am forced to take into consideration. When it is a man's lot to be a moral pillar of the community he lives in, he cannot be too circumspect. If only I could be certain that people would interpret my motives properly. But no matter for that; you must, and shall be, helped to raise yourself. Dina, is it a bargain between us that when I come, when circumstances allow me to come to you and say: "Here is my hand," you will take it and be my wife? Will you promise me that, Dina?

DINA

Yes.

RORLUND

Thank you, thank you! Because for my part, too, oh, Dina, I love you so dearly. Hush! Some one is coming. Dina, for my sake, go out to the others.(She goes out to the coffee table. At the same moment RUMMEL, SANDSTAD and VIGELAND come out of BERNICK'S room, followed by Bernick, who has a bundle of papers in his hand.)

BERNICK

Well, then, the matter is settled.

VIGELAND

Yes, I hope to goodness it is.

RUMMEL

It is settled, Bernick. A Norseman's word stands as firm as the rocks on Dovrefjeld, you know!

BERNICK
And no one must falter, no one give way, no matter what opposition we meet with.

RUMMEL
We will stand or fall together, Bernick.

HILMAR (coming in from the verandah)
Fall? If I may ask, isn't it the railway scheme that is going to fall?

BERNICK
No, on the contrary, it is going to proceed

RUMMEL
Full steam, Mr. Tonnesen.

HILMAR (coming nearer)
Really?

RORLUND
How is that?

Mrs. Bernick (at the verandah door)
Karsten, dear, what is it that?

BERNICK
My dear Betty, how can it interest you? (To the three men.) We must get out lists of subscribers, and the sooner the better. Obviously our four names must head the list. The positions we occupy in the community makes it our duty to make ourselves as prominent as possible in the affair.

SANDSTAD
Obviously, Mr. Bernick.

RUMMEL
The thing shall go through, Bernick; I swear it shall!

BERNICK
Oh, I have not the least anticipation of failure. We must see that we work, each one among the circle of his own acquaintances; and if we can point to the fact that the scheme is exciting a lively interest in all ranks of society, then it stands to reason that our Municipal Corporation will have to contribute its share.

MRS.BERNICK
Karsten, you really must come out here and tell us

BERNICK
My dear Betty, it is an affair that does not concern ladies at all.

HILMAR
Then you are really going to support this railway scheme after all?

BERNICK
Yes, naturally.

RORLUND
But last year, Mr. Bernick

BERNICK
Last year it was quite another thing. At that time it was a question of a line along the coast

VIGELAND
Which would have been quite superfluous, Mr. Rorlund; because, of course, we have our steamboat service

SANDSTAD
And would have been quite unreasonably costly

RUMMEL

Yes, and would have absolutely ruined certain important interests in the town.

BERNICK

The main point was that it would not have been to the advantage of the community as a whole. That is why I opposed it, with the result that the inland line was resolved upon.

HILMAR

Yes, but surely that will not touch the towns about here.

BERNICK

It will eventually touch our town, my dear Hilmar, because we are going to build a branch line here.

HILMAR

Aha, a new scheme, then?

RUMMEL

Yes, isn't it a capital scheme? What?

RORLUND

Hm!

VIGELAND

There is no denying that it looks as though Providence had just planned the configuration of the country to suit a branch line.

RORLUND

Do you really mean it, Mr. Vigeland?

BERNICK

Yes, I must confess it seems to me as if it had been the hand of Providence that caused me to take a journey on business this spring, in the course of which I happened to traverse a valley through which I had never been before. It came across my mind like a flash of lightning that this was where we could carry a branch line down to our town. I got an engineer to survey the neighbourhood, and have here the provisional calculations and estimate; so there is nothing to hinder us.

Mrs.Bernick (who is still with the other ladies at the verandah door): But, my dear Karsten, to think that you should have kept it all a secret from us!

BERNICK

Ah, my dear Betty, I knew you would not have been able to grasp the exact situation. Besides, I have not mentioned it to a living soul until today. But now the decisive moment has come, and we must work openly and with all our might. Yes, even if I have to risk all I have for its sake, I mean to push the matter through.

RUMMEL

And we will back you up, Bernick; you may rely upon that.

RORLUND

Do you really promise us so much, then, from this undertaking, gentlemen?

BERNICK

Yes, undoubtedly. Think what a lever it will be to raise the status of our whole community. Just think of the immense tracts of forest-land that it will make accessible; think of all the rich deposits of minerals we shall be able to work; think of the river with one waterfall above another! Think of the possibilities that open out in the way of manufactories!

RORLUND

And are you not afraid that an easier intercourse with the depravity of the outer world?

BERNICK

No, you may make your mind quite easy on that score, Mr. Rorlund. Our little hive of industry rests now-a-days, God be thanked, on such a sound moral basis; we have all of us helped to drain it, if I may use the expression; and that we will continue to do, each in his degree. You, Mr. Rorlund, will continue your richly blessed activity in our schools and our homes. We, the practical men of business, will be the support of the community by extending its welfare within as wide a radius as possible; and our women, yes, come nearer ladies, you will like to hear it, our women, I say, our wives and daughters, you, ladies will work on undisturbed in the service of charity, and moreover will be a help and a comfort to your nearest and dearest, as my dear Betty and Martha are to me and Olaf.(Looks around him.) Where is Olaf today?

MRS. BERNICK
Oh, in the holidays it is impossible to keep him at home.

BERNICK
I have no doubt he is down at the shore again. You will see he will end by coming to some harm there.

HILMAR
Bah! A little sport with the forces of nature

MRS.RUMMEL
Your family affection is beautiful, Mr. Bernick!

BERNICK
Well, the family is the kernel of society. A good home, honoured and trusty friends, a little snug family circle where no disturbing elements can cast their shadow (KRAP comes in from the right, bringing letters and papers.)

KRAP
The foreign mail, Mr. Bernick and a telegram from New York.

BERNICK (taking the telegram)
Ah, from the owners of the "Indian Girl".

RUMMEL
Is the mail in? Oh, then you must excuse me.

VIGELAND
And me too.

SANDSTAD
Good day, Mr. Bernick.

BERNICK
Good day, good day, gentlemen. And remember, we have a meeting this afternoon at five o'clock.

THE THREE MEN
Yes, quite so, of course. (They go out to the right.)

BERNICK (who has read the telegram)
This is thoroughly American! Absolutely shocking!

MRS.BERNICK
Good gracious, Karsten, what is it?

BERNICK
Look at this, Krap! Read it!

KRAP *(reading)*
"Do the least repairs possible. Send over 'Indian Girl' as soon as she is ready to sail; good time of year; at a pinch her cargo will keep her afloat." Well, I must say

RORLUND
You see the state of things in these vaunted great communities!

BERNICK
You are quite right; not a moment's consideration for human life, when it is a question of making a profit. (To KRAP:) Can the "Indian Girl" go to sea in four or five days?

KRAP
Yes, if Mr. Vigeland will agree to our stopping work on the "Palm Tree" meanwhile.

BERNICK
Hm, he won't. Well, be so good as to look through the letters. And look here, did you see Olaf down at the quay?

KRAP
No, Mr. Bernick. (Goes into BERNICK'S room.)

BERNICK (looking at the telegram again)
These gentlemen think nothing of risking eight men's lives

HILMAR
Well, it is a sailor's calling to brave the elements; it must be a fine tonic to the nerves to be like that, with only a thin plank between one and the abyss

BERNICK
I should like to see the ship-owner amongst us who would condescend to such a thing! There is not one that would do it, not a single one! (Sees OLAF coming up to the house.) Ah, thank Heaven, here he is, safe and sound. (OLAF, with a fishing-line in his hand, comes running up the garden and in through the verandah.)

OLAF
Uncle Hilmar, I have been down and seen the steamer.

BERNICK
Have you been down to the quay again?

OLAF
No, I have only been out in a boat. But just think, Uncle Hilmar, a whole circus company has come on shore, with horses and animals; and there were such lots of passengers.

MRS.RUMMEL
No, are we really to have a circus?

RORLUND
We? I certainly have no desire to see it.

MRS.RUMMEL
No, of course I don't mean we, but

DINA
I should like to see a circus very much.

OLAF
So should I.

HILMAR
You are a duffer. Is that anything to see? Mere tricks. No, it would be something quite different to see the Gaucho careering over the Pampas on his snorting mustang. But,Heaven help us, in these wretched little towns of ours.

OLAF (pulling at MARTHA'S dress)
Look, Aunt Martha! Look, there they come!

MRS.HOLT
Good Lord, yes, here they come.

MRS.LYNGE
Ugh, what horrid people!

(A number of passengers and a whole crowd of townsfolk, are seen coming up the street.)

MRS.RUMMEL
They are a set of mountebanks, certainly. Just look at that woman in the grey dress, Mrs. Holt, the one with a knapsack over her shoulder.

MRS.HOLT
Yes, look, she has slung it on the handle of her parasol. The manager's wife, I expect.

MRS.RUMMEL
And there is the manager himself, no doubt. He looks a regular pirate. Don't look at him, Hilda!

MRS.HOLT
Nor you, Netta!

OLAF
Mother, the manager is bowing to us.

BERNICK
What?

MRS. BERNICK
What are you saying, child?

MRS. RUMMEL
Yes, and good Heavens the woman is bowing to us too.

BERNICK
That is a little too cool

MARTHA (exclaims involuntarily)
Ah!

MRS.BERNICK
What is it, Martha?

MARTHA
Nothing, nothing. I thought for a moment

OLAF (shrieking with delight)
Look, look, there are the rest of them, with the horses and animals! And there are the Americans, too! All the sailors from the "Indian Girl"! (The strains of "Yankee Doodle," played on a clarinet and a drum, are heard.)

HILMAR *(stopping his ears)*
Ugh, ugh, ugh!

RORLUND
I think we ought to withdraw ourselves from sight a little, ladies; we have nothing to do with such goings on. Let us go to our work again.

MRS.BERNICK
Do you think we had better draw the curtains?

RORLUND
Yes, that was exactly what I meant.

(The ladies resume their places at the work-table; RORLUND shuts the verandah door, and draws the curtains over it and over the windows, so that the room becomes half dark.)

OLAF (peeping out through the curtains)
Mother, the manager's wife is standing by the fountain now, washing her face.

MRS.BERNICK
What? In the middle of the marketplace?

MRS.RUMMEL
And in broad daylight, too!

HILMAR
Well, I must say if I were travelling across a desert waste and found myself beside a well, I am sure I should not stop to think whether. Ugh, that frightful clarinet!

RORLUND
It is really high time the police interfered.

BERNICK
Oh no; we must not be too hard on foreigners. Of course these folk have none of the deep-seated instincts of decency which restrain us within proper bounds. Suppose they do behave outrageously, what does it concern us? Fortunately this spirit of disorder, that flies in the face of all that is customary and right, is absolutely a stranger to our community, if I may say so. What is this! (LONA HESSEL walks briskly in from the door on the right.)

THE LADIES (in low, frightened tones)
The circus woman! The manager's wife!

MRS.BERNICK
Heavens, what does this mean?

MARTHA (jumping up)
Ah!

LONA
How do you do, Betty dear! How do you do, Martha! How do you do, brother-in-law!

MRS.BERNICK (with a cry)
Lona!

BERNICK (stumbling backwards)
As sure as I am alive!

MRS.HOLT
Mercy on us!

MRS.RUMMEL
It cannot possibly be!

HILMAR
Well! Ugh!

MRS.BERNICK
Lona! Is it really?

LONA
Really me? Yes, indeed it is; you may fall on my neck if you like.

HILMAR
Ugh, ugh!

MRS.BERNICK
And coming back here as?

MRS.BERNICK
And actually mean to appear in?

LONA
Appear? Appear in what?

BERNICK
Well, I mean, in the circus

LONA
Ha, ha, ha! Are you mad, brother-in-law? Do you think I belong to the circus troupe? No,certainly I have turned my hand to a good many things and made a fool of myself in a good many ways

MRS.RUMMEL
Hm!

LONA
But I have never tried circus riding.

BERNICK
Then you are not?

MRS.BERNICK
Thank Heaven!

LONA
No, we travelled like other respectable folk, second-class, certainly, but we are accustomed to that.

MRS.BERNICK
We, did you say?

BERNICK (taking a step for-ward)
Whom do you mean by "we"?

LONA
I and the child, of course.

THE LADIES (with a cry)
The child!

HILMAR
What?

RORLUND
I really must say!

MRS.BERNICK
But what do you mean, Lona?

LONA
I mean John, of course; I have no other child, as far as I know, but John, or Johan as you used to call him.

MRS.BERNICK
Johan

MRS.RUMMEL (in an undertone to MRS. LYNGE)
The scapegrace brother!

BERNICK (hesitatingly)
Is Johan with you?

LONA
Of course he is; I certainly would not come without him. Why do you look so tragical? And why are you sitting here in the gloom, sewing white things? There has not been a death in the family, has there?

RORLUND
Madam,you find yourself in the Society for Fallen Women.

LONA (half to herself)
What? Can these nice, quiet-looking ladies possibly be?

MRS.RUMMEL
Well, really!

LONA

Oh, I understand! But, bless my soul, that is surely Mrs. Rummel? And Mrs. Holt sitting there too! Well, we three have not grown younger since the last time we met. But listen now, good people; let the Fallen Women wait for a day, they will be none the worse for that. A joyful occasion like this

RORLUND

A home-coming is not always a joyful occasion.

LONA

Indeed? How do you read your Bible, Mr. Parson?

RORLUND

I am not a parson.

LONA

Oh, you will grow into one, then. But, faugh! this moral linen of yours smells tainted, just like a winding-sheet. I am accustomed to the air of the prairies, let me tell you.

BERNICK (wiping his forehead)
Yes, it certainly is rather close in here.

LONA

Wait a moment; we will resurrect ourselves from this vault. (Pulls the curtains to one side) We must have broad daylight in here when the boy comes. Ah, you will see a boy then that has washed himself.

HILMAR

Ugh!

LONA (opening the verandah door and window)
I should say, when he has washed himself, up at the hotel, for on the boat he got piggishly dirty.

HILMAR

Ugh, ugh!

LONA

Ugh? Why, surely isn't that? (Points at HILDAR and asks the others): Is he still loafing about here saying "Ugh"?

HILMAR

I do not loaf; it is the state of my health that keeps me here.

RORLUND

Ahem! Ladies, I do not think

LONA (who has noticed OLAF)
Is he yours, Betty? Give me a paw, my boy! Or are you afraid of your ugly old aunt?

RORLUND (putting his book under his arm)
Ladies, I do not think any of us is in the mood for any more work today. I suppose we are to meet again tomorrow?

LONA (while the others are getting up and taking their leave)
Yes, let us. I shall be on the spot.

RORLUND

You? Pardon me, Miss Hessel, but what do you propose to do in our Society?

LONA

I will let some fresh air into it, Mr. Parson.

Act II

SCENE. The same room. MRS. BERNICK is sitting alone at the work-table, sewing. BERNICK comes in from the right, wearing his hat and gloves and carrying a stick.)

MRS. BERNICK
Home already, Karsten?

BERNICK
Yes, I have made an appointment with a man.

MRS. BERNICK *(with a sigh)*
Oh yes, I suppose Johan is coming up here again.

BERNICK
With a man, I said. (Lays down his hat.) What has become of all the ladies today?

MRS. BERNICK
Mrs. Rummel and Hilda hadn't time to come.

BERNICK
Oh ! did they send any excuse?

MRS. BERNICK
Yes, they had so much to do at home.

BERNICK
Naturally. And of course the others are not coming either?

MRS. BERNICK
No, something has prevented them today, too.

BERNICK
I could have told you that, beforehand. Where is Olaf?

MRS. BERNICK
I let him go out a little with Dina.

BERNICK
Hm, she is a giddy little baggage. Did you see how she at once started making a fuss of Johan yesterday?

MRS. BERNICK
But, my dear Karsten, you know Dina knows nothing whatever of

BERNICK
No, but in any case Johan ought to have had sufficient tact not to pay her any attention. I saw quite well, from his face, what Vigeland thought of it.

MRS. BERNICK *(laying her sewing down on her lap)*
Karsten, can you imagine what his objective is in coming here?

BERNICK
Well, I know he has a farm over there, and I fancy he is not doing particularly well with it; she called attention yesterday to the fact that they were obliged to travel second class

MRS. BERNICK
Yes, I am afraid it must be something of that sort. But to think of her coming with him! She! After the deadly insult she offered you!

BERNICK
Oh, don't think about that ancient history.

MRS. BERNICK
How can I help thinking of it just now? After all, he is my brother still, it is not on his account that I am distressed, but because of all the unpleasantness it would mean for you. Karsten, I am so dreadfully afraid!

BERNICK
Afraid of what?

MRS. BERNICK
Isn't it possible that they may send him to prison for stealing that money from your mother?

BERNICK
What rubbish! Who can prove that the money was stolen?

MRS. BERNICK
The whole town knows it, unfortunately; and you know you said yourself.

BERNICK
I said nothing. The town knows nothing whatever about the affair; the whole thing was no more than idle rumour.

MRS. BERNICK
How magnanimous you are, Karsten!

BERNICK
Do not let us have any more of these reminiscences, please! You don't know how you torture me by raking all that up. (Walks up and down; then flings his stick away from him.) And to think of their coming home now just now, when it is particularly necessary for me that I should stand well in every respect with the town and with the Press. Our newspaper men will be sending paragraphs to the papers in the other towns about here. Whether I receive them well, or whether I receive them ill, it will all be discussed and talked over. They will rake up all those old stories as you do. In a community like ours (Throws his gloves down on the table.) And I have not a soul here to whom I can talk about it and to whom I can go for support.

MRS. BERNICK
No one at all, Karsten?

BERNICK
No, who is there? And to have them on my shoulders just at this moment! Without a doubt they will create a scandal in some way or another, she, in particular. It is simply a calamity to be connected with such folk in any way!

MRS. BERNICK
Well, I can't help their

BERNICK
What can't you help? Their being your relations? No, that is quite true.

MRS. BERNICK
And I did not ask them to come home.

BERNICK
That's it, go on! "I did not ask them to come home; I did not write to them; I did not drag them home by the hair of their heads!" Oh, I know the whole rigmarole by heart.

MRS. BERNICK (bursting into tears)
You need not be so unkind

BERNICK
Yes, that's right, begin to cry, so that our neighbours may have that to gossip about too. Do stop being so foolish, Betty. Go and sit outside; some one may come in here. I don't suppose you want people to see the lady of the house with red eyes? It would be a nice thing, wouldn't it, if the story got out about that. There, I hear some one in the passage. (A knock is heard at the door.) Come in! (MRS. BERNICK takes her sewing and goes out down the garden steps. AUNE comes in from the right.)

AUNE
Good morning, Mr. Bernick.

BERNICK
Good morning. Well, I suppose you can guess what I want you for?

AUNE

Mr. Krap told me yesterday that you were not pleased with

BERNICK

I am displeased with the whole management of the yard, Aune. The work does not get on as quickly as it ought. The "Palm Tree" ought to have been under sail long ago. Mr. Vigeland comes here every day to complain about it; he is a difficult man to have with one as part owner.

AUNE

The "Palm Tree" can go to sea the day after tomorrow.

BERNICK

At last. But what about the American ship, the "Indian Girl," which has been laid up here for five weeks and

AUNE

The American ship? I understood that, before everything else, we were to work our hardest to get your own ship ready.

BERNICK

I gave you no reason to think so. You ought to have pushed on as fast as possible with the work on the American ship also; but you have not.

AUNE

Her bottom is completely rotten, Mr. Bernick; the more we patch it, the worse it gets.

BERNICK

That is not the reason. Krap has told me the whole truth. You do not understand how to work the new machines I have provided or rather, you will not try to work them.

AUNE

Mr. Bernick, I am well on in the fifties; and ever since I was a boy I have been accustomed to the old way of working

BERNICK

We cannot work that way now-a-days. You must not imagine, Aune, that it is for the sake of making profit; I do not need that, fortunately; but I owe consideration to the community I live in, and to the business I am at the head of. I must take the lead in progress, or there would never be any.

AUNE

I welcome progress too, Mr. Bernick.

BERNICK

Yes, for your own limited circle, for the working class. Oh, I know what a busy agitator you are; you make speeches, you stir people up; but when some concrete instance of progress presents itself as now, in the case of our machines, you do not want to have anything to do with it; you are afraid.

AUNE

Yes, I really am afraid, Mr. Bernick. I am afraid for the number of men who will have the bread taken out of their mouths by these machines. You are very fond, sir, of talking about the consideration we owe to the community; it seems to me, however, that the community has its duties too. Why should science and capital venture to introduce these new discoveries into labour, before the community has had time to educate a generation up to using them?

BERNICK

You read and think too much, Aune; it does you no good, and that is what makes you dissatisfied with your lot.

AUNE

It is not, Mr. Bernick; but I cannot bear to see one good workman dismissed after another, to starve because of these machines.

BERNICK

Hm! When the art of printing was discovered, many a quill-driver was reduced to starvation.

AUNE

Would you have admired the art so greatly if you had been a quill-driver in those days, sir?

BERNICK

I did not send for you to argue with you. I sent for you to tell you that the "Indian Girl" must be ready to put to sea the day after tomorrow.

AUNE

But, Mr. Bernick

BERNICK

The day after tomorrow, do you hear? at the same time as our own ship, not an hour later. I have good reasons for hurrying on the work. Have you seen today's paper? Well, then you know the pranks these American sailors have been up to again. The rascally pack are turning the whole town upside down. Not a night passes without some brawling in the taverns or the streets not to speak of other abominations.

AUNE

Yes, they certainly are a bad lot.

BERNICK

And who is it that has to bear the blame for all this disorder? It is I! Yes, it is I who have to suffer for it. These newspaper fellows are making all sorts of covert insinuations because we are devoting all our energies to the "Palm Tree." I, whose task in life it is to influence my fellow-citizens by the force of example, have to endure this sort of thing cast in my face. I am not going to stand that. I have no fancy for having my good name smirched in that way.

AUNE

Your name stands high enough to endure that and a great deal more, sir.

BERNICK

Not just now. At this particular moment I have need of all the respect and goodwill my fellow-citizens can give me. I have a big undertaking on, the stocks, as you probably have heard; but, if it should happen that evil-disposed persons succeeded in shaking the absolute confidence I enjoy, it might land me in the greatest difficulties. That is why I want, at any price, to avoid these shameful innuendoes in the papers, and that is why I name the day after tomorrow as the limit of the time I can give you.

AUNE

Mr. Bernick, you might just as well name this afternoon as the limit.

BERNICK

You mean that I am asking an impossibility?

AUNE

Yes, with the hands we have now at the yard.

BERNICK

Very good; then we must look about elsewhere.

AUNE

Do you really mean, sir, to discharge still more of your old workmen?

BERNICK

No, I am not thinking of that.

AUNE

Because I think it would cause bad blood against you both among the townsfolk and in the papers, if you did that.

BERNICK

Very probably; therefore, we will not do it. But, if the "Indian Girl" is not ready to sail the day after tomorrow, I shall discharge you.

AUNE (with a start)

Me! (He laughs.) You are joking, Mr. Bernick.

BERNICK

I should not be so sure of that, if I were you.

AUNE

Do you mean that you can contemplate discharging me? Me, whose father and grandfather worked in your yard all their lives, as I have done myself?

BERNICK

Who is it that is forcing me to do it?

AUNE

You are asking what is impossible, Mr. Bernick.

BERNICK

Oh, where there's a will there's a way. Yes or no; give me a decisive answer, or consider yourself discharged on the spot.

AUNE (coming a step nearer to him)

Mr. Bernick, have you ever realised what discharging an old workman means? You think he can look about for another job? Oh, yes, he can do that; but does that dispose of the matter? You should just be there once, in the house of a workman who has been discharged, the evening he comes home bringing all his tools with him.

BERNICK

Do you think I am discharging you with a light heart? Have I not always been a good master to you?

AUNE

So much the worse, Mr. Bernick. Just for that very reason those at home will not blame you; they will say nothing to me, because they dare not; but they will look at me when I am not noticing, and think that I must have deserved it. You see, sir, that is, that is what I cannot bear. I am a mere nobody, I know; but I have always been accustomed to stand first in my own home. My humble home is a little community too, Mr. Bernick, a little community which I have been able to support and maintain because my wife has believed in me and because my children have believed in me. And now it is all to fall to pieces.

BERNICK

Still, if there is nothing else for it, the lesser must go down before the greater; the individual must be sacrificed to the general welfare. I can give you no other answer; and that, and no other, is the way of the world. You are an obstinate man, Aune! You are opposing me, not because you cannot do otherwise, but because you will not exhibit 'the superiority of machinery over manual labour'.

AUNE

And you will not be moved, Mr. Bernick, because you know that if you drive me away you will at all events have given the newspapers proof of your good will.

BERNICK

And suppose that were so? I have told you what it means for me, either bringing the Press down on my back, or making them well-disposed to me at a moment when I am working for an objective which will mean the advancement of the general welfare. Well, then, can I do otherwise than as I am doing? The question, let me tell you, turns upon this, whether your home is to be supported, as you put it, or whether hundreds of new homes are to be prevented from existing, hundreds of homes that will never be built, never have a fire lighted on their hearth, unless I succeed in carrying through the scheme I am working for now. That is the reason why I have given you your choice.

AUNE

Well, if that is the way things stand, I have nothing more to say.

BERNICK

Hm, my dear Aune, I am extremely grieved to think that we are to part.

AUNE

We are not going to part, Mr. Bernick.

BERNICK

How is that?

AUNE
Even a common man like myself has something he is bound to maintain.

BERNICK
Quite so, quite so, then I presume you think you may promise?

AUNE
The "Indian Girl" shall be ready to sail the day after tomorrow. (Bows and goes out to the right.)

BERNICK
Ah, I have got the better of that obstinate fellow! I take it as a good omen. (HILMAR comes in through the garden door, smoking a cigar.)

HILMAR (as he comes up the steps to the verandah)
Good morning, Betty! Good morning, Karsten!

MRS. BERNICK
Good morning.

HILMAR
Ah, I see you have been crying, so I suppose you know all about it too?

MRS. BERNICK
Know all about what?

HILMAR
That the scandal is in full swing. Ugh!

BERNICK
What do you mean?

HILMAR (coming into the room)
Why, that our two friends from America are displaying themselves about the streets in the company of Dina Dorf.

MRS. BERNICK (coming in after him)
Hilmar, is it possible?

HILMAR
Yes, unfortunately, it is quite true. Lona was even so wanting in tact as to call after me, but of course I appeared not to have heard her.

BERNICK
And no doubt all this has not been unnoticed.

HILMAR
You may well say that. People stood still and looked at them. It spread like wildfire through the town, just like a prairie fire out West. In every house people were at the windows waiting for the procession to pass, cheek by jowl behind the curtains, ugh! Oh, you must excuse me, Betty, for saying "ugh" this has got on my nerves. If it is going on, I shall be forced to think about getting right away from here.

MRS. BERNICK
But you should have spoken to him and represented to him that

HILMAR
In the open street? No, excuse me, I could not do that. To think that the fellow should dare to show himself in the town at all! Well, we shall see if the Press doesn't put a stopper on him; yes, forgive me, Betty, but

BERNICK
The Press, do you say? Have you heard a hint of anything of the sort?

HILMAR
There are such things flying about. When I left here yesterday evening I looked in at the club, because I did not feel well. I saw at once, from the sudden silence that fell when I went in, that our American couple had

been the subject of conversation. Then that impudent newspaper fellow, Hammer, came in and congratulated me at the top of his voice on the return of my rich cousin.

BERNICK
Rich?

HILMAR
Those were his words. Naturally I looked him up and down in the manner he deserved, and gave him to understand that I knew nothing about Johan Tonnesen's being rich. "Really," he said, "that is very remarkable. People usually get on in America when they have something to start with, and I believe your cousin did not go over there quite empty-handed."

BERNICK
Hm, now will you oblige me by

MRS. BERNICK (distressed)
There, you see, Karsten!

HILMAR
Anyhow, I have spent a sleepless night because of them. And here he is, walking about the streets as if nothing were the matter. Why couldn't he disappear for good and all? It really is insufferable how hard some people are to kill.

MRS. BERNICK
My dear Hilmar, what are you saying P

HILMAR
Oh, nothing. But here this fellow escapes with a whole skin from railway accidents and fights with California grizzlies and Blackfoot Indians, has not even been scalped. Ugh, here they come!

BERNICK (looking down the street)
Olaf is with them too!

HILMAR
Of course! They want to remind everybody that they belong to the best family in the town. Look there! look at the crowd of loafers that have come out of the chemist's to stare at them and make remarks. My nerves really won't stand it; how a man is to be expected to keep the banner of the Ideal flying under such circumstances, I

BERNICK
They are coming here. Listen, Betty; it is my particular wish that you should receive them in the friendliest possible way.

MRS. BERNICK
Oh, may I, Karsten.

BERNICK
Certainly, certainly and you too, Hilmar. It is to be hoped they will not stay here very long; and when we are quite by ourselves, no allusions to the past; we must not hurt their feelings in any way.

MRS. BERNICK
How magnanimous you are, Karsten!

BERNICK
Oh, don't speak of that.

MRS. BERNICK
But you must let me thank you; and you must forgive me for being so hasty. I am sure you had every reason to

BERNICK
Don't talk about it, please.

HILMAR
Ugh!

(JOHAN TONNESEN and DINA come up through the garden, followed by LONA and OLAF.)

LONA
Good morning, dear people!

JOHAN
We have been out having a look round the old place, Karsten.

BERNICK
So I hear. Greatly altered, is it not?

LONA
Mr. Bernick's great and good works everywhere. We have been up into the Recreation Ground you have presented to the town.

BERNICK
Have you been there?

LONA
"The gift of Karsten Bernick," as it says over the gateway. You seem to be responsible for the whole place here.

JOHAN
Splendid ships you have got, too. I met my old schoolfellow, the captain of the "Palm Tree."

LONA
And you have built a new school-house too; and I hear that the town has to thank you for both the gas supply and the water supply.

BERNICK
Well, one ought to work for the good of the community one lives in.

LONA
That is an excellent sentiment, brother-in-law, but it is a pleasure, all the same, to see how people appreciate you. I am not vain, I hope; but I could not resist reminding one or two of the people we talked to that we were relations of yours.

HILMAR
Ugh!

LONA
Do you say "ugh" to that?

HILMAR
No, I said "ahem."

LONA
Oh, poor chap, you may say that if you like. But are you all by yourselves today?

BERNICK
Yes, we are by ourselves today.

LONA
Ah, yes, we met a couple of members of your Morality Society up at the market; they made out they were very busy. You and I have never had an opportunity for a good talk yet. Yesterday you had your three pioneers here, as well as the parson.

HILMAR
The schoolmaster.

LONA
I call him the parson. But now tell me what you think of my work during these fifteen years? Hasn't he grown a fine fellow? Who would recognise the madcap that ran away from home?

HILMAR
Hm!

JOHAN
Now, Lona, don't brag too much about me.

LONA
Well, I can tell you I am precious proud of him. Goodness knows it is about the only thing I have done in my life; but it does give me a sort of right to exist. When I think, Johan, how we two began over there with nothing but our four bare fists.

HILMAR
Hands.

LONA
I say fists; and they were dirty fists.

HILMAR
Ugh!

LONA
And empty, too.

HILMAR
Empty? Well, I must say

LONA
What must you say?

BERNICK
Ahem!

HILMAR
I must say, ugh! (Goes out through the garden.)

LONA
What is the matter with the man?

BERNICK
Oh, do not take any notice of him; his nerves are rather upset just now. Would you not like to take a look at the garden? You have not been down there yet, and I have got an hour to spare.

LONA
With pleasure. I can tell you my thoughts have been with you in this garden many and many a time.

MRS. BERNICK
We have made a great many alterations there too, as you will see. (BERNICK, MRS. BERNICK, and LONA go down to the garden, where they are visible every now and then during the following scene.)

OLAF (coming to the verandah door)
Uncle Hilmar, do you know what uncle Johan asked me? He asked me if I would go to America with him.

HILMAR
You, you duffer, who are tied to your mother's apron strings!

OLAF
Ah, but I won't be that any longer. You will see, when I grow big.

HILMAR
Oh, fiddlesticks! You have no really serious bent towards the strength of character necessary to.

(They go down to the garden. DINA meanwhile has taken off her hat and is standing at the door on the right, shaking the dust off her dress.)

JOHAN *(to DINA)*

The walk has made you pretty warm.

DINA

Yes, it was a splendid walk. I have never had such a splendid walk before.

JOHAN

Do you not often go for a walk in the morning?

DINA

Oh, yes, but only with Olaf.

JOHAN

I see. Would you rather go down into the garden than stay here?

DINA

No, I would rather stay here.

JOHAN.

So would I. Then shall we consider it a bargain that we are to go for a walk like this together every morning?

DINA

No, Mr. Tonnesen, you mustn't do that.

JOHAN

What mustn't I do? You promised, you know.

DINA

Yes, but on second thought, you mustn't go out with me.

JOHAN

But why not?

DINA

Of course, you are a stranger, you cannot understand; but I must tell you

JOHAN

Well?

DINA

No, I would rather not talk about it.

JOHAN

Oh, but you must; you can talk to me about whatever you like.

DINA

Well, I must tell you that I am not like the other young girls here. There is something, something or other about me. That is why you mustn't.

JOHAN

But I do not understand anything about it. You have not done anything wrong?

DINA

No, not I, but, no, I am not going to talk any more about it now. You will hear about it from the others, sure enough.

JOHAN

Hm!

DINA

But there is something else I want very much to ask you.

JOHAN

What is that?

DINA

I suppose it is easy to make a position for oneself over in America?

JOHAN

No, it is not always easy; at first you often have to rough it and work very hard.

DINA

I should be quite ready to do that.

JOHAN

You?

DINA

I can work now; I am strong and healthy; and Aunt Martha taught me a lot.

JOHAN

Well, hang it, come back with us!

DINA

Ah, now you are only making fun of me; you said that to Olaf too. But what I wanted to know is if people are so very, so very moral over there?

JOHAN

Moral?

DINA

Yes; I mean are they as, as proper and as well-behaved as they are here?

JOHAN

Well, at all events they are not so bad as people here make out. You need not be afraid on that score.

DINA

You don't understand me. What I want to hear is just that they are not so proper and so moral.

JOHAN

Not? What would you wish them to be, then?

DINA

I would wish them to be natural.

JOHAN

Well, I believe that is just what they are.

DINA

Because in that case I should get on if I went there.

JOHAN

You would, for certain! and that is why you must come back with us.

DINA

No, I don't want to go with you; I must go alone. Oh, I would make something of my life; I would get on

Bernick (speaking to LONA and his wife at the foot of the garden steps): Wait a moment I will fetch it, Betty dear; you might so easily catch cold. (Comes into the room and looks for his wife's shawl.)

MRS. BERNICK (from outside)

You must come out too, Johan; we are going down to the grotto.

BERNICK

No, I want Johan to stay here. Look here, Dina; you take my wife's shawl and go with them. Johan is going to stay here with me, Betty dear. I want to hear how he is getting on over there.

MRS. BERNICK

Very well, then you will follow us; you know where you will find us. (MRS. BERNICK, LONA and DINA go out through the garden, to the left. BERNICK looks after them for a moment, then goes to the farther door on the left and locks it, after which he goes up to JOHAN, grasps both his hands, and shakes them warmly.)

BERNICK
Johan, now that we are alone, you must let me thank you.

JOHAN
Oh, nonsense!

BERNICK
My home and all the happiness that it means to me, my position here as a citizen, all these I owe to you.

JOHAN
Well, I am glad of it, Karsten; some good came of that mad story after all, then.

BERNICK (grasping his hands again)
But still you must let me thank you! Not one in ten thousand would have done what you did for me.

JOHAN
Rubbish! Weren't we, both of us, young and thoughtless? One of us had to take the blame, you know.

BERNICK
But surely the guilty one was the proper one to do that?

JOHAN
Stop! At the moment the innocent one happened to be the proper one to do it. Remember, I had no ties, I was an orphan; it was a lucky chance to get free from the drudgery of the office. You, on the other hand, had your old mother still alive; and, besides that, you had just become secretly engaged to Betty, who was devoted to you. What would have happened between you and her if it had come to her ears?

BERNICK
That is true enough, but still

JOHAN
And wasn't it just for Betty's sake that you broke off your acquaintance with Mrs. Dorf? Why, it was merely in order to put an end to the whole thing that you were up there with her that evening.

BERNICK
Yes, that unfortunate evening when that drunken creature came home! Yes, Johan, it was for Betty's sake; but, all the same, it was splendid of you to let all the appearances go against you, and to go away.

JOHAN
Put your scruples to rest, my dear Karsten. We agreed that it should be so; you had to be saved, and you were my friend. I can tell you, I was uncommonly proud of that friendship. Here was I, drudging away like a miserable stick-in-the-mud, when you came back from your grand tour abroad, a great swell who had been to London and to Paris; and you chose me for your chum, although I was four years younger than you, it is true it was because you were courting Betty, I understand that now but I was proud of it! Who would not have been? Who would not willingly have sacrificed himself for you? especially as it only meant a month's talk in the town, and enabled me to get away into the wide world.

BERNICK
Ah, my dear Johan, I must be candid and tell you that the story is not so completely forgotten yet.

JOHAN
Isn't it? Well, what does that matter to me, once I am back over there on my farm again?

BERNICK
Then you mean to go back?

JOHAN
Of course.

BERNICK
But not immediately, I hope?

JOHAN

As soon as possible. It was only to humour Lona that I came over with her, you know.

BERNICK

Really? How so?

JOHAN

Well, you see, Lona is no longer young, and lately she began to be obsessed with home-sickness; but she never would admit it. (Smiles.) How could she venture to risk leaving such a flighty fellow as me alone, who before I was nineteen had been mixed up in...

BERNICK

Well, what then?

JOHAN

Well, Karsten, now I am coming to a confession that I am ashamed to make.

BERNICK

You surely haven't confided the truth to her?

JOHAN

Yes. It was wrong of me, but I could not do otherwise. You can have no conception what Lona has been to me. You never could put up with her; but she has been like a mother to me. The first year we were out there, when things went so badly with us, you have no idea how she worked! And when I was ill for a long time, and could earn nothing and could not prevent her, she took to singing ballads in taverns, and gave lectures that people laughed at; and then she wrote a book that she has both laughed and cried over since then, all to keep the life in me. Could I look on when in the winter she, who had toiled and drudged for me, began to pine away? No, Karsten, I couldn't. And so I said, "You go home for a trip, Lona; don't be afraid for me, I am not so flighty as you think." And so the end of it was that she had to know.

BERNICK

And how did she take it?

JOHAN

Well, she thought, as was true, that as I knew I was innocent nothing need prevent me from taking a trip over here with her. But make your mind easy; Lona will let nothing out, and I shall keep my mouth shut as I did before.

BERNICK

Yes, yes I rely on that.

JOHAN

Here is my hand on it. And now we will say no more about that old story; luckily it is the only mad prank either of us has been guilty of, I am sure. I want thoroughly to enjoy the few days I shall stay here. You cannot think what a delightful walk we had this morning. Who would have believed that that little imp, who used to run about here and play angels' parts on the stage! But tell me, my dear fellow, what became of her parents afterwards?

BERNICK

Oh, my boy, I can tell you no more than I wrote to you immediately after you went away. I suppose you got my two letters?

JOHAN

Yes, yes, I have them both. So that drunken fellow deserted her?

BERNICK

And drank himself to death afterwards.

JOHAN

And she died soon afterwards, too?

BERNICK

She was proud; she betrayed nothing, and would accept nothing.

JOHAN

Well, at all events you did the right thing by taking Dina into your house.

BERNICK

I suppose so. As a matter of fact it was Martha that brought that about.

JOHAN

So it was Martha? By the way, where is she today?

BERNICK

She? Oh, when she hasn't her school to look after, she has her sick people to see to.

JOHAN

So it was Martha who interested herself in her.

BERNICK

Yes, you know Martha has always had a certain liking for teaching; so she took a post in the boarding-school. It was very ridiculous of her.

JOHAN

I thought she looked very worn yesterday; I should be afraid her health was not good enough for it.

BERNICK

Oh, as far as her health goes, it is all right enough. But it is unpleasant for me; it looks as though I, her brother, were not willing to support her.

JOHAN

Support her? I thought she had means enough of her own.

BERNICK

Not a penny. Surely you remember how badly off our mother was when you went away? She carried things on for a time with my assistance, but naturally I could not put up with that state of affairs permanently. I made her take me into the firm, but even then things did not go well. So I had to take over the whole business myself, and when we made up our balance-sheet, it became evident that there was practically nothing left as my mother's share. And when mother died soon afterwards, of course Martha was left penniless.

JOHAN

Poor Martha!

BERNICK

Poor! Why? You surely do not suppose I let her want for anything? No, I venture to say I am a good brother. Of course she has a home here with us; her salary as a teacher is more than enough for her to dress on; what more could she want?

JOHAN

Hm, that is not our idea of things in America.

BERNICK

No, I dare say not, in such a revolutionary state of society as you find there. But in our small circle, in which, thank God, depravity has not gained a footing, up to now at all events, women are content to occupy a seemly, as well as modest, position. Moreover, it is Martha's own fault; I mean, she might have been provided for long ago, if she had wished.

JOHAN

You mean she might have married?

BERNICK

Yes, and married very well, too. She has had several good offers curiously enough, when you think that she is a poor girl, no longer young, and, besides, quite an insignificant person.

JOHAN

Insignificant?

BERNICK

Oh, I am not blaming her for that. I most certainly would not wish her otherwise. I can tell you it is always a good thing to have a steady-going person like that in a big house like this, some one you can rely on in any contingency.

JOHAN

Yes, but what does she?

BERNICK

She? How? Oh well, of course she has plenty to interest herself in; she has Betty and Olaf and me. People should not think first of themselves, women least of all. We have all got some community, great or small, to work for. That is my principle, at all events. (Points to KRAP, who has come in from the right.) Ah, here is an example of it, ready to hand. Do you suppose that it is my own affairs that are absorbing me just now? By no means. (Eagerly to KRAP.) Well?

KRAP (in an undertone, showing him a bundle of papers)
Here are all the sale contracts, completed.

BERNICK

Capital! Splendid! Well, Johan, you must really excuse me for the present. (In a low voice, grasping his hand.) Thanks, Johan, thanks! And rest assured that anything I can do for you. Well, of course you understand. Come along, Krap. (They go into BERNICK'S room.)

JOHAN (looking after them for a moment)
Hm! (Turns to go down to the garden. At the same moment MARTHA comes in from the right, with a little basket over her arm.) Martha!

MARTHA

Ah, Johan, is it you?

JOHAN

Out so early?

MARTHA

Yes. Wait a moment; the others are just coming. (Moves towards the door on the left.)

JOHAN

Martha, are you always in such a hurry?

MARTHA

I?

JOHAN

Yesterday you seemed to avoid me, so that I never managed to have a word with you, we two old playfellows.

MARTHA

Ah, Johan; that is many, many years ago.

JOHAN

Good Lord, why, it is only fifteen years ago, no more and no less. Do you think I have changed so much?

MARTHA

You? Oh yes, you have changed too, although

JOHAN

What do you mean?

MARTHA

Oh, nothing.

JOHAN

You do not seem to be very glad to see me again.

MARTHA

I have waited so long, Johan, too long.

JOHAN

Waited? For me to come?

MARTHA

Yes.

Johan. And why did you think I would come?

MARTHA

To atone for the wrong you had done.

JOHAN

I?

MARTHA

Have you forgotten that it was through you that a woman died in need and in shame? Have you forgotten that it was through you that the best years of a young girl's life were embittered?

JOHAN

And you can say such things to me? Martha, has your brother never?

MARTHA

Never what?

JOHAN

Has he never, oh, of course, I mean has he never so much as said a word in my defence?

MARTHA

Ah, Johan, you know Karsten's high principles.

JOHAN

Hm! Oh, of course; I know my old friend Karsten's high principles! But really this is. Well, well. I was having a talk with him just now. He seems to me to have altered considerably.

MARTHA

How can you say that? I am sure Karsten has always been an excellent man.

JOHAN

Yes, that was not exactly what I meant but never mind. Hm! Now I understand the light you have seen me in; it was the return of the prodigal that you were waiting for.

MARTHA

Johan, I will tell you what light I have seen you in. (Points down to the garden.) Do you see that girl playing on the grass down there with Olaf? That is Dina. Do you remember that incoherent letter you wrote me when you went away? You asked me to believe in you. I have believed in you, Johan. All the horrible things that were rumoured about you after you had gone must have been done through being led astray from thoughtlessness, without premeditation.

JOHAN

What do you mean?

MARTHA

Oh! you understand me well enough not a word more of that. But of course you had to go away and begin afresh, a new life. Your duties here which you never remembered to undertake, or never were able to undertake, I have undertaken for you. I tell you this, so that you shall not have that also to reproach yourself with. I have been a mother to that much-wronged child; I have brought her up as well as I was able.

JOHAN

And have wasted your whole life for that reason.

MARTHA
It has not been wasted. But you have come late, Johan.

JOHAN
Martha, if only I could tell you. Well, at all events let me thank you for your loyal friendship.

MARTHA (with a sad smile)
Hm. Well, we have had it out now, Johan. Hush, some one is coming. Goodbye, I can't stay now. (Goes out through the farther door on the left. LONA comes in from the garden, followed by MRS. BERNICK.)

MRS. BERNICK
But good gracious, Lona, what are you thinking of?

LONA
Let me be, I tell you! I must and will speak to him.

MRS. BERNICK
But it would be a scandal of the worst sort! Ah, Johan, still here?

LONA
Out with you, my boy; don't stay here in doors; go down into the garden and have a chat with Dina.

JOHAN
I was just thinking of doing so.

MRS. BERNICK
But

LONA
Look here, Johan, have you had a good look at Dina?

JOHAN
I should think so!

LONA
Well, look at her to some purpose, my boy. That would be somebody for you!

MRS. BERNICK
But, Lona!

JOHAN
Somebody for me?

LONA
Yes, to look at, I mean. Be off with you!

JOHAN
Oh, I don't need any pressing. (Goes down into the garden.)

MRS. BERNICK
Lona, you astound me! You cannot possibly be serious about it?

LONA
Indeed I am. Isn't she sweet and healthy and honest? She is exactly the wife for Johan. She is just what he needs over there; it will be a change from an old step-sister.

MRS. BERNICK
Dina? Dina Dorf? But think

LONA
I think first and foremost of the boy's happiness. Because, help him I must; he has not much idea of that sort of thing; he has never had much of an eye for girls or women.

MRS. BERNICK

He? Johan? Indeed I think we have had only too sad proofs that

LONA

Oh, devil take all those stupid stories! Where is Karsten? I mean to speak to him.

MRS. BERNICK

Lona, you must not do it, I tell you.

LONA

I am going to. If the boy takes a fancy to her, and she to him, then they shall make a match of it. Karsten is such a clever man, he must find some way to bring it about.

MRS. BERNICK

And do you think these American indecencies will be permitted here?

LONA

Bosh, Betty!

MRS. BERNICK

Do you think a man like Karsten, with his strictly moral way of thinking

LONA

Pooh! he is not so terribly moral.

MRS. BERNICK

What have you the audacity to say?

LONA

I have the audacity to say that Karsten is not any more particularly moral than anybody else.

MRS. BERNICK

So you still hate him as deeply as that! But what are you doing here, if you have never been able to forget that? I cannot understand how you, dare look him in the face after the shameful insult you put upon him in the old days.

LONA

Yes, Betty, that time I did forget myself badly.

MRS. BERNICK

And to think how magnanimously he has forgiven you, he, who had never done any wrong! It was not his fault that you encouraged yourself with hopes. But since then you have always hated me too. (Bursts into tears.) You have always begrudged me my good fortune. And now you come here to heap all this on my head, to let the whole town know what sort of a family I have brought Karsten into. Yes, it is me that it all falls upon, and that is what you want. Oh, it is abominable of you! (Goes out by the door on the left, in tears.)

LONA *(looking after her)*

Poor Betty! (BERNICK comes in from his room. He stops at the door to speak to KRAP.)

BERNICK

Yes, that is excellent, Krap, capital! Send twenty pounds to the fund for dinners to the poor. (Turns round.) Lona! (Comes forward.) Are you alone? Is Betty not coming in?

LONA

No. Would you like me to call her?

BERNICK

No, no, not at all. Oh, Lona, you don't know how anxious I have been to speak openly to you after having begged for your forgiveness.

LONA

Look here, Karsten, do not let us be sentimental; it doesn't suit us.

BERNICK

You must listen to me, Lona. I know only too well how much appearances are against me, as you have learnt all about that affair with Dina's mother. But I swear to you that it was only a temporary infatuation; I was really, truly and honestly, in love with you once.

LONA

Why do you think I have come home?

BERNICK

Whatever you have in your mind, I entreat, you to do nothing until I have exculpated myself. I can do that, Lona; at all events I can excuse myself.

LONA

Now you are frightened. You once were in love with me, you say. Yes, you told me that often enough in your letters; and perhaps it was true, too, in a way, as long as you were living out in the great, free world which gave you the courage to think freely and greatly. Perhaps you found in me a little more character and strength of will and independence than in most of the folk at home here. And then we kept it secret between us; nobody could make fun of your bad taste.

BERNICK

Lona, how can you think?

LONA

But when you came back, when you heard the gibes that were made at me on all sides, when you noticed how people laughed at what they called my absurdities...

BERNICK

You were regardless of people's opinion at that time.

LONA

Chiefly to annoy the petticoated and trousered prudes that one met at every turn in the town. And then, when you met that seductive young actress

BERNICK

It was a boyish escapade, nothing more; I swear to you that there was no truth in a tenth part of the rumours and gossip that went about.

LONA

Maybe. But then, when Betty came home, a pretty young girl, idolised by every one, and it became known that she would inherit all her aunt's money and that I would have nothing!

BERNICK

That is just the point, Lona; and now you shall have the truth without any beating about the bush. I did not love Betty then; I did not break off my engagement with you because of any new attachment. It was entirely for the sake of the money. I needed it; I had to make sure of it.

LONA

And you have the face to tell me that?

BERNICK

Yes, I have. Listen, Lona.

LONA

And yet you wrote to me that an unconquerable passion for Betty had overcome you, invoked my magnanimity, begged me, for Betty's sake, to hold my tongue about all that had been between us.

BERNICK

I had to, I tell you.

LONA

Now, by Heaven, I don't regret that I forgot myself as I did that time

BERNICK

Let me tell you the plain truth of how things stood with me then. My mother, as you remember, was at the head of the business, but she was absolutely without any business ability whatever. I was hurriedly summoned home from Paris; times were critical, and they relied on me to set things straight. What did I find? I found, and you must keep this a profound secret, a house on the brink of ruin. Yes, as good as on the brink of ruin, this old respected house which had seen three generations of us. What else could I, the son, the only son, do than look about for some means of saving it?

LONA
And so you saved the house of Bernick at the cost of a woman.

BERNICK
You know quite well that Betty was in love with me.

LONA
But what about me?

BERNICK
Believe me, Lona, you would never have been happy with me.

LONA
Was it out of consideration for my happiness that you sacrificed me?

BERNICK
Do you suppose I acted as I did from selfish motives? If I had stood alone then, I would have begun all over again with cheerful courage. But you do not understand how the life of a man of business, with his tremendous responsibilities, is bound up with that of the business which falls to his inheritance. Do you realise that the prosperity or the ruin of hundreds, of thousands, depends on him? Can you not take into consideration the fact that the whole community in which both you and I were born would have been affected to the most dangerous extent if the house of Bernick had gone to smash?

LON
Then is it for the sake of the community that you have maintained your position these fifteen years upon a lie?

BERNICK
Upon a lie?

LONA
What does Betty know of all this...that underlies her union with you?

BERNICK
Do you suppose that I would hurt her feelings to no purpose by disclosing the truth?

LONA
To no purpose, you say? Well, well. You are a man of business; you ought to understand what is to the purpose. But listen to me, Karsten, I am going to speak the plain truth now. Tell me, are you really happy?

BERNICK
In my family life, do you mean?

LONA
Yes.

BERNICK
I am, Lona. You have not been a self-sacrificing friend to me in vain. I can honestly say that I have grown happier every year. Betty is good and willing; and if I were to tell you how, in the course of years, she has learned to model her character on the lines of my own

LONA
Hm!

BERNICK
At first, of course, she had a whole lot of romantic notions about love; she could not reconcile herself to the idea that, little by little, it must change into a quiet comradeship.

LONA

But now she is quite reconciled to that?

BERNICK

Absolutely. As you can imagine, daily intercourse with me has had no small share in developing her character. Every one, in their degree, has to learn to lower their own pretensions, if they are to live worthily of the community to which they belong. And Betty, in her turn, has gradually learned to understand this; and that is why our home is now a model to our fellow citizens.

LONA

But your fellow citizens know nothing about the lie?

BERNICK

The lie?

LONA

Yes, the lie you have persisted in for these fifteen years.

BERNICK

Do you mean to say that you call that?

LONA

I call it a lie, a threefold lie: first of all, there is the lie towards me; then, the lie towards Betty; and then, the lie towards Johan.

BERNICK

Betty has never asked me to speak.

LONA

Because she has known nothing.

BERNICK

And you will not demand it, out of consideration for her.

LONA

Oh, no, I shall manage to put up with their gibes well enough; I have broad shoulders.

BERNICK

And Johan will not demand it either; he has promised me that.

LONA

But you yourself, Karsten? Do you feel within yourself no impulse urging you to shake yourself free of this lie?

BERNICK

Do you suppose that of my own free will I would sacrifice my family happiness and my position in the world?

LONA

What right have you to the position you hold?

BERNICK

Every day during these fifteen years I have earned some little right to it, by my conduct, and by what I have achieved by my work.

LONA

True, you have achieved a great deal by your work, for yourself as well as for others. You are the richest and most influential man in the town; nobody in it dares do otherwise than defer to your will, because you are looked upon as a man without spot or blemish; your home is regarded as a model home, and your conduct as a model of conduct. But all this grandeur, and you with it, is founded on a treacherous morass. A moment may come and a word may be spoken, when you and all your grandeur will be engulfed in the morass, if you do not save yourself in time.

BERNICK

Lona, what is your object in coming here?

LONA

I want to help you to get firm ground under your feet, Karsten.

BERNICK

Revenge! you want to revenge yourself! I suspected it. But you won't succeed! There is only one person here that can speak with authority, and he will be silent.

LONA

You mean Johan?

BERNICK

Yes, Johan. If any one else accuses me, I shall deny everything. If any one tries to crush me, I shall fight for my life. But you will never succeed in that, let me tell you! The one who could strike me down will say nothing and is going away.

(RUMMEL and VIGELAND come in from the right.)

RUMMEL

Good morning, my dear Bernick, good morning. You must come up with us to the Commercial Association. There is a meeting about the railway scheme, you know.

BERNICK

I cannot. It is impossible just now.

VIGELAND

You really must, Mr. Bernick.

RUMMEL

Bernick, you must. There is an opposition to us on foot. Hammer, and the rest of those who believe in a line along the coast, are declaring that private interests are at the back of the new proposals.

BERNICK

Well then, explain to them

VIGELAND

Our explanations have no effect, Mr. Bernick.

RUMMEL

No, no, you must come yourself. Naturally, no one would dare to suspect you of such duplicity.

LONA

I should think not.

BERNICK

I cannot, I tell you; I am not well. Or, at all events, wait, let me pull myself together. (RORLUND comes in from the right.)

RORLUND

Excuse me, Mr. Bernick, but I am terribly upset.

BERNICK

Why, what is the matter with you?

Rorlund. I must put a question to you, Mr. Bernick. Is it with your consent that the young girl who has found a shelter under your roof shows herself in the open street in the company of a person who

LONA

What person, Mr. Parson?

RORLUND

With the person from whom, of all others in the world, she ought to be kept farthest apart!

LONA

Ha! ha!

RORLUND
Is it with your consent, Mr. Bernick?

Bernick (looking for his hat and gloves). I know nothing about it. You must excuse me; I am in a great hurry. I am due at the Commercial Association.

(HILMAR comes up from the garden and goes over to the farther door on the left.)

HILMAR
Betty, Betty, I want to speak to you.

MRS. BERNICK (coming to the door)
What is it?

HILMAR
You ought to go down into the garden and put a stop to the flirtation that is going on between a certain person and Dina Dorf! It has quite got on my nerves to listen to them.

LONA
Indeed! And what has the certain person been saying?

HILMAR
Oh, only that he wishes she would go off to America with him. Ugh!

RORLUND
Is it possible?

MRS. BERNICK
What do you say?

LONA
But that would be perfectly splendid!

BERNICK
Impossible! You cannot have heard right.

HILMAR
Ask him yourself, then. Here comes the pair of them. Only, leave me out of it, please.

BERNICK (to RUMMEL and VIGELAND)
I will follow you, in a moment. (RUMMEL and VIGELAND go out to the right. JOHAN and DINA come up from the garden.)

JOHAN
Hurrah, Lona, she is going with us!

MRS. BERNICK
But, Johan, are you out of your senses?

RORLUND
Can I believe my ears! Such an atrocious scandal! By what arts of seduction have you?

JOHAN
Come, come, sir, what are you saying?

RORLUND
Answer me, Dina; do you mean to do this, entirely of your own free will?

DINA
I must get away from here.

RORLUND
But with him! with him!

DINA

Can you tell me of any one else here who would have the courage to take me with him?

RORLUND

Very well, then, you shall learn who he is.

JOHAN

Do not speak!

BERNICK

Not a word more!

RORLUND

If I did not, I should be unworthy to serve a community of whose morals I have been appointed a guardian, and should be acting most unjustifiably towards this young girl, in whose upbringing I have taken a material part, and who is to me

JOHAN

Take care what you are doing!

RORLUND

She shall know! Dina, this is the man who was the cause of all your mother's misery and shame.

BERNICK

Mr. Rorlund?

DINA

He! (TO JOHAN.) Is this true?

JOHAN

Karsten, you answer.

BERNICK

Not a word more! Do not let us say another word about it today.

DINA

Then it is true.

RORLUND

Yes, it is true. And more than that, this fellow, whom you were going to trust, did not run away from home empty-handed; ask him about old Mrs. Bernick's cash-box.... Mr. Bernick can bear witness to that!

LONA

Liar

BERNICK

Ah!

MRS. BERNICK

My God! my God!

JOHAN (rushing at RORLUND with uplifted arm)

And you dare to

LONA (restraining him)

Do not strike him, Johan!

RORLUND

That is right, assault me! But the truth will out; and it is the truth, Mr. Bernick has admitted it and the whole town knows it. Now, Dina, you know him. (A short silence.)

JOHAN (softly, grasping BERNICK by the arm)

Karsten, Karsten, what have you done?

MRS. BERNICK (in tears)
Oh, Karsten, to think that I should have mixed you up in all this disgrace!

Sandstad (coming in hurriedly from the right, and calling out, with his hand still on the door-handle): You positively must come now, Mr. Bernick. The fate of the whole railway is hanging by a thread.

BERNICK (abstractedly)
What is it? What have I to

LONA (earnestly and with emphasis)
You have to go and be a pillar of society, brother-in-law.

SANDSTAD
Yes, come along; we need the full weight of your moral excellence on our side.

JOHAN (aside, to BERNICK)
Karsten, we will have a talk about this tomorrow. (Goes out through the garden. BERNICK, looking half dazed, goes out to the right with SANDSTAD.)

Act III

(SCENE. The same room. BERNICK, with a cane in his hand and evidently in a great rage, comes out of the farther room on the left, leaving the door half-open behind him.)

BERNICK (speaking to his wife, who is in the other room)
There! I have given it him in earnest now; I don't think he will forget that thrashing! What do you say? And I say that you are an injudicious mother! You make excuses for him, and countenance any sort of rascality on his part. Not rascality? What do you call it, then? Slipping out of the house at night, going out in a fishing boat, staying away till well on in the day, and giving me such a horrible fright when I have so much to worry me! And then the young scamp has the audacity to threaten that he will run away! Just let him try it! You? No, very likely; you don't trouble yourself much about what happens to him. I really believe that if he were to get killed! Oh, really? Well, I have work to leave behind me in the world; I have no fancy for being left childless. Now, do not raise objections, Betty; it shall be as I say, he is confined to the house. (Listens.) Hush; do not let any one notice anything. (KRAP comes in from the right.)

KRAP
Can you spare me a moment, Mr. Bernick?

BERNICK (throwing away the cane)
Certainly, certainly. Have you come from the yard?

KRAP
Yes. Ahem!

BERNICK
Well? Nothing wrong with the "Palm Tree," I hope?

KRAP
The "Palm Tree " can sail tomorrow, but

BERNICK
It is the "Indian Girl," then? I had a suspicion that that obstinate fellow

KRAP
The "Indian Girl" can sail tomorrow, too; but I am sure she will not get very far.

BERNICK
What do you mean?

KRAP
Excuse me, sir; that door is standing ajar, and I think there is some one in the other room

BERNICK *(shutting the door)*
There, then! But what is this that no one else must hear?

KRAP
Just this, that I believe Aune intends to let the "Indian Girl" go to the bottom with every mother's son on board.

BERNICK
Good God! what makes you think that?

KRAP
I cannot account for it any other way, sir.

BERNICK
Well, tell me as briefly as you can

KRAP
I will. You know yourself how slowly the work has gone on in the yard since we got the new machines and the new inexperienced hands?

BERNICK
Yes, yes.

KRAP
But this morning, when I went down there, I noticed that the repairs to the American boat had made extraordinary progress; the great hole in the bottom, the rotten patch, you know

BERNICK
Yes, yes, what about it?

KRAP
Was completely repaired, to all appearance at any rate, covered up, looked as good as new. I heard that Aune himself had been working at it by lantern light the whole night.

BERNICK
Yes, yes, well?

KRAP
I turned it over in my head for a bit; the hands were away at their breakfast, so I found an opportunity to have a look around the boat, both outside and in, without anyone seeing me. I had a job to get down to the bottom through the cargo, but I learned the truth. There is something very suspicious going on, Mr. Bernick.

BERNICK
I cannot believe it, Krap. I cannot and will not believe such a thing of Aune.

KRAP
I am very sorry but it is the simple truth. Something very suspicious is going on. No new timbers put in, as far as I could see, only stopped up and tinkered at, and covered over with sailcloth and tarpaulins and that sort of thing, an absolute fraud. The "Indian Girl" will never get to New York; she will go to the bottom like a cracked pot.

BERNICK
This is most horrible! But what can be his object, do you suppose?

KRAP
Probably he wants to bring the machines into discredit, wants to take his revenge, wants to force you to take the old hands on again.

BERNICK
And to do this he is willing to sacrifice the lives of all on board.

KRAP
He said the other day that there were no men on board the "Indian Girl" only wild beasts.

BERNICK

Yes, but, apart from that, has he no regard for the great loss of capital it would mean?

KRAP

Aune does not look upon capital with a very friendly eye, Mr. Bernick.

BERNICK

That is perfectly true; he is an agitator and a fomenter of discontent; but such an unscrupulous thing as this. Look here, Krap; you must look into the matter once more. Not a word of it to any one. The blame will fall on our yard if any one hears anything of it.

KRAP

Of course, but

BERNICK

When the hands are away at their dinner you must manage to get down there again; I must have absolute certainty about it.

KRAP

You shall, sir; but, excuse me, what do you propose to do?

BERNICK

Report the affair, naturally. We cannot, of course, let ourselves become accomplices in such a crime. I could not have such a thing on my conscience. Moreover, it will make a good impression, both on the press and on the public in general, if it is seen that I set all personal interests aside and let justice take its course.

KRAP

Quite true, Mr. Bernick.

BERNICK

But first of all I must be absolutely certain. And meanwhile, do not breathe a word of it.

KRAP

Not a word, sir. And you shall have your certainty. (Goes out through the garden and down the street.)

BERNICK (half aloud)

Shocking! But no, it is impossible! Inconceivable!

(As he turns to go into his room, HILMAR comes in from the right.)

HILMAR

Good morning, Karsten. Let me congratulate you on your triumph at the Commercial Association yesterday.

BERNICK

Thank you.

HILMAR

It was a brilliant triumph, I hear; the triumph of intelligent public spirit over selfishness and prejudice, something like a raid of French troops on the Kabyles. It is astonishing that after that unpleasant scene here, you could

BERNICK

Yes, yes, quite so.

HILMAR

But the decisive battle has not been fought yet.

BERNICK

In the matter of the railway, do you mean?

HILMAR

Yes; I suppose you know the trouble that Hammer is brewing?

BERNICK (anxiously)
No, what is that?

HILMAR
Oh, he is greatly taken up with the rumour that is going around, and is preparing to dish up an article about it.

BERNICK
What rumour?

HILMAR
About the extensive purchase of property along the branch line, of course.

BERNICK
What? Is there such a rumour as that going about?

HILMAR
It is all over the town. I heard it at the club when I looked in there. They say that one of our lawyers has quietly bought up, on commission, all the forest land, all the mining land, all the waterfalls

BERNICK
Don't they say whom it was for?

HILMAR
At the club they thought it must be for some company, not connected with this town, that has got a hint of the scheme you have in hand, and has made haste to buy before the price of these properties went up. Isn't it villainous? ugh!

BERNICK
Villainous?

HILMAR
Yes, to have strangers putting their fingers into our pie and one of our own local lawyers lending himself to such a thing! And now it will be outsiders that will get all the profits!

BERNICK
But, after all, it is only an idle rumour.

HILMAR
Meanwhile people are believing it, and tomorrow or the next day, I have no doubt Hammer will nail it to the counter as a fact. There is a general sense of exasperation in the town already. I heard several people say that if the rumour were confirmed they would take their names off the subscription lists.

BERNICK
Impossible!

HILMAR
Is it? Why do you suppose these mercenary-minded creatures were so willing to go into the undertaking with you? Don't you suppose they have scented profit for themselves

BERNICK
It is impossible, I am sure; there is so much public spirit in our little community

HILMAR
In our community? Of course you are a confirmed optimist, and so you judge others by yourself. But I, who am a tolerably experienced observer! There isn't a single soul in the place, excepting ourselves, of course, not a single soul in the place who holds up the banner of the Ideal. (Goes towards the verandah.) Ugh, I can see them there

BERNICK
See whom?

HILMAR
Our two friends from America. (Looks out to the right.) And who is that they are walking with? As I am alive, if it is not the captain of the "Indian Girl." Ugh!

BERNICK
What can they want with him?

Hilmar. Oh, he is just the right company for them. He looks as if he had been a slave-dealer or a pirate; and who knows what the other two may have been doing all these years.

BERNICK
Let me tell you that it is grossly unjust to think such things about them.

HILMAR
Yes, you are an optimist. But here they are, bearing down upon us again; so I will get away while there is time. (Goes towards the door on the left. LONA comes in from the right.)

LONA
Oh, Hilmar, am I driving you away?

HILMAR
Not at all; I am in rather a hurry; I want to have a word with Betty. (Goes into the farthest room on the left.)

BERNICK (after a moment's silence)
Well, Lona?

LONA
Yes?

BERNICK
What do you think of me today?

LONA
The same as I did yesterday. A lie more or less

BERNICK
I must enlighten you about it. Where has Johan gone?

LONA
He is coming; he had to see a man first.

BERNICK
After what you heard yesterday, you will understand that my whole life will be ruined if the truth comes to light.

LONA
I can understand that.

BERNICK
Of course, it stands to reason that I was not guilty of the crime there was so much talk about here.

LONA
That stands to reason. But who was the thief?

BERNICK
There was no thief. There was no money stolen, not a penny.

LONA
How is that?

BERNICK
Not a penny, I tell you.

LONA
But those rumours? How did that shameful rumour get about that Johan

BERNICK

Lona, I think I can speak to you as I could to no one else. I will conceal nothing from you. I was partly to blame for spreading the rumour.

LONA

You? You could act in that way towards a man who for your sake!

BERNICK

Do not condemn me without bearing in mind how things stood at that time. I told you about it yesterday. I came home and found my mother involved in a mesh of injudicious undertakings; we had all manner of bad luck, it seemed as if misfortunes were raining upon us, and our house was on the verge of ruin. I was half reckless and half in despair. Lona, I believe it was mainly to deaden my thoughts that I let myself drift into that entanglement that ended in Johan's going away.

LONA

Hm

BERNICK

You can well imagine how every kind of rumour was set on foot after you and he had gone. People began to say that it was not his first piece of folly, that Dorf had received a large sum of money to hold his tongue and go away; other people said that she had received it. At the same time it was obvious that our house was finding it difficult to meet its obligations. What was more natural than that scandal-mongers should find some connection between these two rumours? And as the woman remained here, living in poverty, people declared that he had taken the money with him to America; and every time rumour mentioned the sum, it grew larger.

LONA

And you, Karsten?

BERNICK

I grasped at the rumour like a drowning man at a straw.

LONA

You helped to spread it?

BERNICK

I did not contradict it. Our creditors had begun to be pressing, and I had the task of keeping them quiet. The result was the dissipating of any suspicion as to the stability of the firm; people said that we had been hit by a temporary piece of ill-luck, that all that was necessary was that they should not press us, only give us time and every creditor would be paid in full.

LONA

And every creditor was paid in full?

BERNICK

Yes, Lona, that rumour saved our house and made me the man I now am.

LONA

That is to say, a lie has made you the man you now are.

BERNICK

Whom did it injure at the time? It was Johan's intention never to come back.

LONA

You ask whom it injured. Look into your own heart, and tell me if it has not injured you.

BERNICK

Look into any man's heart you please, and you will always find, in every one, at least one black spot which he has to keep concealed.

LONA

And you call yourselves pillars of society!

BERNICK

Society has none better.

LONA

And of what consequence is it whether such a society be propped up or not? What does it all consist of? Show and lies and nothing else. Here are you, the first man in the town, living in grandeur and luxury, powerful and respected, you, who have branded an innocent man as a criminal.

BERNICK

Do you suppose I am not deeply conscious of the wrong I have done him? And do you suppose I am not ready to make amends to him for it?

LONA

How? By speaking out?

BERNICK

Would you have the heart to insist on that?

LONA

What else can make amends for such a wrong?

BERNICK

I am rich, Lona; Johan can demand any sum he pleases.

LONA

Yes, offer him money, and you will hear what he will say.

BERNICK

Do you know what he intends to do?

LONA

No; since yesterday he has been dumb. He looks as if this had made a grown man of him all at once.

BERNICK

I must talk to him.

LONA

Here he comes. (JOHAN comes in from the right.)

BERNICK (going towards hint)

Johan!

JOHAN (motioning him away)

Listen to me first. Yesterday morning I gave you my word that I would hold my tongue.

BERNICK

You did.

JOHAN

But then I did not know

BERNICK

Johan, only let me say a word or two to explain the circumstances

JOHAN

It is unnecessary; I understand the circumstances perfectly. The firm was in a dangerous position at the time; I had gone off, and you had my defenceless name and reputation at your mercy. Well, I do not blame you so very much for what you did; we were young and thoughtless in those days. But now I have need of the truth, and now you must speak.

BERNICK

And just now I have need of all my reputation for morality, and therefore I cannot speak.

JOHAN

I don't take much account of the false reports you spread about me; it is the other thing that you must take the blame of. I shall make Dina my wife, and here, here in your town, I mean to settle down and live with her.

LONA
Is that what you mean to do?

BERNICK
With Dina? Dina as your wife? in this town?

JOHAN
Yes, here and nowhere else. I mean to stay here to defy all these liars and slanderers. But before I can win her, you must exonerate me.

BERNICK
Have you considered that, if I confess to the one thing, it will inevitably mean making myself responsible for the other as well? You will say that I can show by our books that nothing dishonest happened? But I cannot; our books were not so accurately kept in those days. And even if I could, what good would it do? Should I not in any case be pointed at as the man who had once saved himself by an untruth, and for fifteen years had allowed that untruth and all its consequences to stand without having raised a finger to demolish it? You do not know our community very much, or you would realise that it would ruin me utterly.

JOHAN
I can only tell you that I mean to make Mrs. Dorf's daughter my wife, and live with her in this town.

BERNICK (wiping the perspiration from his forehead)
Listen to me, Johan and you too, Lona. The circumstances I am in just now are quite exceptional. I am situated in such a way that if you aim this blow at me you will not only destroy me, but will also destroy a great future, rich in blessings, that lies before the community which, after all, was the home of your childhood.

JOHAN
And if I do not aim this blow at you, I shall be destroying all my future happiness with my own hand.

LONA
Go on, Karsten.

BERNICK
I will tell you, then. It is mixed up with the railway project, and the whole thing is not quite so simple as you think. I suppose you have heard that last year there was some talk of a railway line along the coast? Many influential people backed up the idea, people in the town and the suburbs, and especially the press; but I managed to get the proposal quashed, on the ground that it would have injured our steamboat trade along the coast.

LONA
Have you any interest in the steamboat trade?

BERNICK
Yes. But no one ventured to suspect me on that account; my honoured name fully protected me from that. For the matter of that, I could have stood the loss; but the place could not have stood it. So the inland line was decided upon. As soon as that was done, I assured myself, without saying anything about it, that a branch line could be laid to the town.

LONA
Why did you say nothing about it, Karsten?

BERNICK
Have you heard the rumours of extensive buying up of forest lands, mines and waterfalls?

JOHAN
Yes, apparently it is some company from another part of the country.

BERNICK
As these properties are situated at present, they are as good as valueless to their owners, who are scattered about the neighbourhood; they have therefore been sold comparatively cheap. If the purchaser had waited till the branch line began to be talked of, the proprietors would have asked exorbitant prices.

LONA
Well, what then?

BERNICK

Now I am going to tell you something that can be construed in different ways, a thing to which, in our community, a man could only confess provided he had an untarnished and honoured name to take his stand upon.

LONA

Well?

BERNICK

It is I that have bought up the whole of them.

LONA

You?

JOHAN

On your own account?

BERNICK

On my own account. If the branch line becomes an accomplished fact, I am a millionaire; if it does not, I am ruined.

LONA

It is a big risk, Karsten.

BERNICK

I have risked my whole fortune on it.

LONA

I am not thinking of your fortune; but if it comes to light that

Bernick. Yes, that is the critical part of it. With the unblemished and honoured name I have hitherto borne, I can take the whole thing upon my shoulders, carry it through, and say to my fellow-citizens: "See, I have taken this risk for the good of the community."

LONA

Of the community?

BERNICK

Yes; and not a soul will doubt my motives.

LONA

Then some of those concerned in it have acted more openly, without any secret motives or considerations.

BERNICK

Who?

LONA

Why, of course, Rummel and Sandstad and Vigeland.

BERNICK

To get them on my side I was obliged to let them into the secret.

LONA

And they?

BERNICK

They have stipulated for a fifth part of the profits as their share.

LONA

Oh, these pillars of society.

BERNICK

And isn't it society itself that forces us to use these underhanded means? What would have happened if I had not acted secretly? Everybody would have wanted to have a hand in the undertaking; the whole thing would have been divided up, mismanaged and bungled. There is not a single man in the town except myself who is capable of directing so big an affair as this will be. In this country, almost without exception, it is only foreigners who have settled here who have the aptitude for big business schemes. That is the reason why my conscience acquits me in the matter. It is only in my hands that these properties can become a real blessing to the many who have to make their daily bread.

LONA
I believe you are right there, Karsten.

JOHAN
But I have no concern with the many, and my life's happiness is at stake.

BERNICK
The welfare of your native place is also at stake. If things come out which cast reflections on my earlier conduct, then all my opponents will fall upon me with united vigour. A youthful folly is never allowed to be forgotten in our community. They would go through the whole of my previous life, bring up a thousand little incidents in it, interpret and explain them in the light of what has been revealed; they would crush me under the weight of rumours and slanders. I should be obliged to abandon the railway scheme; and, if I take my hand off that, it will come to nothing, and I shall be ruined and my life as a citizen will be over.

LONA
Johan, after what we have just heard, you must go away from here and hold your tongue.

BERNICK
Yes, yes, Johan, you must!

JOHAN
Yes, I will go away, and I will hold my tongue; but I shall come back, and then I shall speak.

BERNICK
Stay over there, Johan; hold your tongue, and I am willing to share with you

JOHAN
Keep your money, but give me back my name and reputation.

BERNICK
And sacrifice my own!

JOHAN
You and your community must get out of that the best way you can. I must and shall win Dina for my wife. And therefore, I am going to sail tomorrow in the "Indian Girl"

BERNICK
In the "Indian Girl"?

JOHAN
Yes. The captain has promised to take me. I shall go over to America, as I say; I shall sell my farm, and set my affairs in order. In two months I shall be back.

BERNICK
And then you will speak?

JOHAN
Then the guilty man must take his guilt on himself.

BERNICK
Have you forgotten that, if I do that, I must also take on myself guilt that is not mine?

JOHAN
Who is it that for the last fifteen years has benefited by that shameful rumour?

BERNICK
You will drive me to desperation! Well, if you speak, I shall deny everything! I shall say it is a plot against me, that you have come here to blackmail me!

LONA
For shame, Karsten!

BERNICK
I am a desperate man, I tell you, and I shall fight for my life. I shall deny everything, everything!

JOHAN
I have your two letters. I found them in my box among my other papers. This morning I read them again; they are plain enough.

BERNICK
And will you make them public?

JOHAN
If it becomes necessary.

BERNICK
And you will be back here in two months?

JOHAN
I hope so. The wind is fair. In three weeks I shall be in New York if the "Indian Girl" does not go to the bottom.

BERNICK (with a start)
Go to the bottom? Why should the "Indian Girl" go to the bottom?

JOHAN
Quite so, why should she?

BERNICK (scarcely audibly)
Go to the bottom?

JOHAN
Well, Karsten, now you know what is before you. You must find your own way out. Good-bye! You can say good-bye to Betty for me, although she has not treated me like a sister. But I must see Martha. She shall tell Dina; she shall promise me (Goes out through the farther door on the left.)

BERNICK (to himself)
The "Indian Girl"? (Quickly.) Lona, you must prevent that!

LONA
You see for yourself, Karsten, I have no influence over him any longer. (Follows JOHAN into the other room.)

BERNICK (a prey to uneasy thoughts)
Go to the bottom?

(AUNE comes in from the right.)

AUNE
Excuse me, sir, but if it is convenient

BERNICK (turning round angrily)
What do you want?

AUNE
To know if I may ask you a question, sir.

BERNICK
Be quick about it, then. What is it?

AUNE
I wanted to ask if I am to consider it as certain, absolutely certain, that I should be dismissed from the yard if the "Indian Girl" were not ready to sail tomorrow?

BERNICK
What do you mean? The ship is ready to sail?

AUNE
Yes, it is. But suppose it were not, should I be discharged?

BERNICK
What is the use of asking such idle questions?

AUNE
Only that I should like to know, sir. Will you answer me that? should I be discharged?

BERNICK
Am I in the habit of keeping my word or not?

AUNE
Then tomorrow I should have lost the position I hold in my house and among those near and dear to me, lost my influence over men of my own class, lost all opportunity of doing anything for the cause of the poorer and needier members of the community?

BERNICK
Aune, we have discussed all that before.

AUNE
Quite so, then the "Indian Girl" will sail.

(A short silence.)

BERNICK
Look here, it is impossible for me to have my eyes everywhere, I cannot be answerable for everything. You can give me your assurance, I suppose, that the repairs have been satisfactorily carried out?

AUNE
You gave me very short grace, Mr. Bernick.

BERNICK
But I understand you to warrant the repairs?

AUNE
The weather is fine, and it is summer.

(Another pause.)

BERNICK
Have you anything else to say to me?

AUNE
I think not, sir.

BERNICK
Then the "Indian Girl" will sail...

AUNE
Tomorrow?

BERNICK
Yes.

AUNE
Very good. (Bows and goes out. BERNICK stands for a moment irresolute; then walks quickly towards the door, as if to call AUNE back; but stops, hesitatingly, with his hand on the door-handle. At that moment the door is opened from without, and KRAP comes in.)

KRAP *(in a low voice)*
Aha, he has been here. Has he confessed?

BERNICK
Hm; have you discovered anything?

KRAP
What need of that, sir? Could you not see the evil conscience looking out of the man's eyes?

BERNICK
Nonsense, such things don't show. Have you discovered anything, I want to know?

KRAP
I could not manage it; I was too late. They had already begun hauling the ship out of the dock. But their very haste in doing that plainly shows that

BERNICK
It shows nothing. Has the inspection taken place, then?

KRAP
Of course; but

BERNICK
There, you see! And of course they found nothing to complain of?

KRAP
Mr. Bernick, you know very well how much this inspection means, especially in a yard that has such a good name as ours has.

BERNICK
No matter, it takes all responsibility off us.

KRAP
But, sir, could you really not tell from Aune's manner that?

BERNICK
Aune has completely reassured me, let me tell you.

KRAP
And let me tell you, sir, that I am morally certain that

BERNICK
What does this mean, Krap? I see plainly enough that you want to get your knife into this man; but if you want to attack him, you must find some other occasion. You know how important it is to me or, I should say, to the owners that the "Indian Girl" should sail to-morrow.

KRAP
Very well, so be it; but if ever we hear of that ship again, hm!

(VIGELAND comes in from the right.)

VIGELAND
I wish you a very good morning, Mr. Bernick. Have you a moment to spare?

BERNICK
At your service, Mr. Vigeland.

VIGELAND
I only want to know if you are also of opinion that the "Palm Tree" should sail tomorrow?

BERNICK
Certainly; I thought that was quite settled.

VIGELAND
Well, the captain came to me just now and told me that storm signals have been hoisted.

BERNICK
Oh! Are we to expect a storm?

VIGELAND
A stiff breeze, at all events; but not a contrary wind, just the opposite.

BERNICK
Hm, well, what do you say?

VIGELAND
I say, as I said to the captain, that the "Palm Tree" is in the hands of Providence. Besides, they are only going across the North Sea at first; and in England, freights are running tolerably high just now, so that

BERNICK
Yes, it would probably mean a loss for us if we waited.

VIGELAND
Besides, she is a stout ship, and fully insured as well. It is more risky, now, for the "Indian Girl"

BERNICK
What do you mean?

VIGELAND
She sails tomorrow, too.

BERNICK
Yes, the owners have been in such a hurry, and, besides

VIGELAND
Well, if that old hulk can venture out, and with such a crew, into the bargain, it would be a disgrace to us if we

BERNICK
Quite so. I presume you have the ship's papers with you.

VIGELAND
Yes, here they are.

BERNICK
Good; then will you go in with Mr. Krap?

KRAP
Will you come in here, sir, and we will dispose of them at once.

VIGELAND
Thank you. And the issue we leave in the hands of the Almighty, Mr. Bernick. (Goes with KRAP into BERNICK'S room. RORLUND comes up from the garden.)

RORLUND
At home at this time of day, Mr. Bernick?

BERNICK (lost in thought)
As you see.

RORLUND
It was really on your wife's account I came. I thought she might be in need of a word of comfort.

BERNICK
Very likely she is. But I want to have a little talk with you, too.

RORLUND
With the greatest of pleasure, Mr. Bernick. But what is the matter with you? You look quite pale and upset.

BERNICK

Really? Do I? Well, what else could you expect, a man so loaded with responsibilities as I am? There is all my own big business, and now the planning of this railway. But tell me something, Mr. Rorlund, let me put a question to you.

RORLUND

With pleasure, Mr. Bernick.

BERNICK

It is about a thought that has occurred to me. Suppose a man is face to face with an undertaking which will concern the welfare of thousands, and suppose it should be necessary to make a sacrifice of one?

RORLUND

What do you mean?

BERNICK

For example, suppose a man were thinking of starting a large factory. He knows for certain, because all his experience has taught him so, that sooner or later a toll of human life will be exacted in the working of that factory.

RORLUND

Yes, that is only too probable.

BERNICK

Or, say a man embarks on a mining enterprise. He takes into his service fathers of families and young men in the first flush of their youth. Is it not quite safe to predict that all of them will not come out of it alive?

RORLUND

Yes, unhappily that is quite true.

BERNICK

Well, a man in that position will know beforehand that the undertaking he proposes to start must undoubtedly, at some time or other, mean a loss of human life. But the undertaking itself is for the public good; for every man's life that it costs, it will undoubtedly promote the welfare of many hundreds.

RORLUND

Ah, you are thinking of the railway of all the dangerous excavating and blasting, and that sort of thing

BERNICK

Yes, quite so, I am thinking of the railway. And, besides, the coming of the railway will mean the starting of factories and mines. But do not think, nevertheless

RORLUND

My dear Mr. Bernick, you are almost over-conscientious. What I think is that, if you place the affair in the hands of Providence

BERNICK

Yes, exactly; Providence

RORLUND

You are blameless in the matter. Go on and build your railway hopefully.

BERNICK

Yes, but now I will put a special instance to you. Suppose a charge of blasting-powder had to be exploded in a dangerous place, and that unless it were exploded the line could not be constructed? Suppose the engineer knew that it would cost the life of the workman who lit the fuse, but that it had to be lit, and that it was the engineer's duty to send a workman to do it?

RORLUND

Hm

BERNICK

I know what you will say. It would be a splendid thing if the engineer took the match himself and went and lit the fuse. But that is out of the question, so he must sacrifice a workman.

RORLUND

That is a thing no engineer here would ever do.

BERNICK

No engineer in the bigger countries would think twice about doing it.

RORLUND

In the bigger countries? No, I can quite believe it. In those depraved and unprincipled communities.

BERNICK

Oh, there is a good deal to be said for those communities.

RORLUND

Can you say that? you, who yourself

BERNICK

In the bigger communities a man finds space to carry out a valuable project, finds the courage to make some sacrifice in a great cause; but here, a man is cramped by all kinds of petty considerations and scruples.

RORLUND

Is human life a petty consideration?

BERNICK

When that human life threatens the welfare of thousands.

RORLUND

But you are suggesting cases that are quite inconceivable, Mr. Bernick! I do not understand you at all today. And you quote the bigger countries, well, what do they think of human life there? They look upon it simply as part of the capital they have to use. But we look at things from a somewhat different moral standpoint, I should hope. Look at our respected shipping industry! Can you name a single one of our ship-owners who would sacrifice a human life for the sake of paltry gain? And then think of those scoundrels in the bigger countries, who for the sake of profit send out freights in one unseaworthy ship after another

BERNICK

I am not talking of unseaworthy ships!

RORLUND

But I am, Mr. Bernick.

BERNICK

Yes, but to what purpose? They have nothing to do with the question. Oh, these small, timid considerations! If a General from this country were to take his men under fire and some of them were shot, I suppose he would have sleepless nights after it! It is not so in other countries. You should bear what that fellow in there says

RORLUND

He? Who? The American?

BERNICK

Yes. You should hear how in America

RORLUND

He, in there? And you did not tell me? I shall at once

BERNICK

It is no use; you won't be able to do anything with him.

RORLUND

We shall see. Ah, here he comes. (JOHAN comes in from the other room.)

JOHAN (talking back through the open door)

Yes, yes, Dina, as you please; but I do not mean to give you up, all the same. I shall come back, and then everything will come right between us.

RORLUND

Excuse me, but what did you mean by that? What is it you propose to do?

JOHAN

I propose that that young girl, before whom you blackened my character yesterday, shall become my wife.

RORLUND

Your wife? And can you really suppose that?

JOHAN

I mean to marry her.

RORLUND

Well, then you shall know the truth. (Goes to the half-open door.) Mrs. Bernick, will you be so kind as to come and be a witness and you too, Miss Martha. And let Dina come. (Sees LONA at the door.) Ah, you here too?

LONA

Shall I come too?

RORLUND

As many as you please, the more the better.

BERNICK

What are you going to do? (LONA, MRS. BERNICK, MARTHA, DINA and HILMAR come in from the other room.)

MRS. BERNICK

Mr. Rorlund, I have tried my hardest, but I cannot prevent him...

RORLUND

I shall prevent him, Mrs. Bernick. Dina, you are a thoughtless girl, but I do not blame you so greatly. You have too long lacked the necessary moral support that should have sustained you. I blame myself for not having afforded you that support.

DINA

You mustn't speak now!

MRS. BERNICK

What is it?

RORLUND

It is now that I must speak, Dina, although your conduct yesterday and today has made it ten times more difficult for me. But all other considerations must give way to the necessity for saving you. You remember that I gave you my word; you remember what you promised you would answer when I judged that the right time had come. Now I dare not hesitate any longer, and therefore- -. (Turns to JOHAN.) This young girl, whom you are persecuting, is my betrothed.

MRS. BERNICK

What?

BERNICK

Dina!

JOHAN

She? Your?

MARTHA

No, no, Dina!

LONA

It is a lie!

JOHAN

Dina, is this man speaking the truth?

DINA (after a short pause)
Yes.

RORLUND
I hope this has rendered all your arts of seduction powerless. The step I have determined to take for Dina's good, I now wish openly proclaimed to every one. I cherish the certain hope that it will not be misinterpreted. And now, Mrs. Bernick, I think it will be best for us to take her away from here, and try to bring back peace and tranquillity to her mind.

MRS. BERNICK
Yes, come with me. Oh, Dina, what a lucky girl you are! (Takes DINA Out to the left; RORLUND follows them.)

MARTHA
Good-bye, Johan! (Goes out.)

HILMAR (at the verandah door)
Hm, I really must say...

LONA (who has followed DINA with her eyes, to JOHAN)
Don't be downhearted, my boy! I shall stay here and keep my eye on the parson. (Goes out to the right.)

BERNICK
Johan, you won't sail in the "Indian Girl" now?

JOHAN
Indeed I shall.

BERNICK
But you won't come back?

JOHAN
I am coming back.

BERNICK
After this? What have you to do here after this?

JOHAN
Revenge myself on you all; crush as many of you as I can. (Goes out to the right. VIGELAND and KRAP come in from BERNICK'S room.)

VIGELAND
There, now the papers are in order, Mr. Bernick.

BERNICK
Good, good.

KRAP (in a low voice)
And I suppose it is settled that the "Indian Girl" is to sail tomorrow?

BERNICK
Yes. (Goes into his room. VIGELAND and KRAP go out to the right. HILMAR is just going after them, when OLAF puts his head carefully out of the door on the left.)

OLAF
Uncle! Uncle Hilmar!

HILMAR
Ugh, is it you? Why don't you stay upstairs? You know you are confined to the house.

OLAF (coming a step or two nearer)
Hush! Uncle Hilmar, have you heard the news?

HILMAR
Yes, I have heard that you got a thrashing today.

OLAF (looking threateningly towards his father's room)

He shan't thrash me any more. But have you heard that Uncle Johan is going to sail tomorrow with the Americans?

HILMAR

What has that got to do with you? You had better run upstairs again.

OLAF

Perhaps I shall be going for a buffalo hunt, too, one of these days, uncle.

HILMAR

Rubbish! A coward like you

OLAF

Yes, just you wait! You will learn something tomorrow!

HILMAR

Duffer! (Goes out through the garden. OLAF runs into the room again and shuts the door, as he sees KRAP coming in from the right.)

Krap (going to the door of BERNICK'S room and opening it slightly): Excuse my bothering you again, Mr. Bernick; but there is a tremendous storm blowing up. (Waits a moment, but there is no answer.) Is the "Indian Girl" to sail, for all that? (After a short pause, the following answer is heard.)

BERNICK (from his room)

The "Indian Girl" is to sail, for all that.

(KRAP Shuts the door and goes out again to the right.)

Act IV

(SCENE. The same room. The work-table has been taken away. It is a stormy evening and already dusk. Darkness sets in as the following scene is in progress. A man-servant is lighting the chandelier; two maids bring in pots of flowers, lamps and candles, which they place on tables and stands along the walls. RUMMEL, in dress clothes, with gloves and a white tie, is standing in the room giving instructions to the servants.)

RUMMEL

Only every other candle, Jacob. It must not look as if it were arranged for the occasion, it has to come as a surprise, you know. And all these flowers? Oh, well, let them be; it will probably look as if they stood there everyday. (BERNICK comes out of his room.)

BERNICK (stopping at the door)

What does this mean?

RUMMEL

Oh dear, is it you? (To the servants.) Yes, you might leave us for the present. (The servants go out.)

BERNICK

But, Rummel, what is the meaning of this?

RUMMEL

It means that the proudest moment of your life has come. A procession of his fellow citizens is coming to do honour to the first man of the town.

BERNICK

What!

RUMMEL

In procession, with banners and a band! We ought to have had torches too; but we did not like to risk that in this stormy weather. There will be illuminations, and that always sounds well in the newspapers.

BERNICK

Listen, Rummel I won't have anything to do with this.

RUMMEL

But it is too late now; they will be here in half-an- hour.

BERNICK

But why did you not tell me about this before?

RUMMEL

Just because I was afraid you would raise objections to it. But I consulted your wife; she allowed me to take charge of the arrangements, while she looks after the refreshments.

BERNICK (listening)

What is that noise? Are they coming already? I fancy I hear singing.

RUMMEL (going to the verandah door)

Singing? Oh, that is only the Americans. The "Indian Girl" is being towed out.

BERNICK

Towed out? Oh, yes. No, Rummel, I cannot this evening; I am not well.

RUMMEL

You certainly do look bad. But you must pull yourself together; devil take it, you must! Sandstad and Vigeland and I all attach the greatest importance to carrying this thing through. We have got to crush our opponents under the weight of as complete an expression of public opinion as possible. Rumours are getting about the town; our announcement about the purchase of the property cannot be withheld any longer. It is imperative that this very evening, after songs and speeches, amidst the clink of glasses, in a word, in an ebullient atmosphere of festivity, you should inform them of the risk you have incurred for the good of the community. In such an ebullient atmosphere of festivity as I just now described it, you can do an astonishing lot with the people here. But you must have that atmosphere, or the thing won't go.

BERNICK

Yes, yes.

RUMMEL

And especially when so delicate and ticklish a point has to be negotiated. Well, thank goodness, you have a name that will be a tower of strength, Bernick. But listen now; we must make our arrangements, to some extent. Mr. Hilmar Tonnesen has written an ode to you. It begins very charmingly with the words: "Raise the Ideal's banner high!" And Mr. Rorlund has undertaken the task of making the speech of the evening. Of course you must reply to that.

BERNICK

I cannot tonight, Rummel. Couldn't you?

RUMMEL

It is impossible, however willing I might be; because, as you can imagine, his speech will be especially addressed to you. Of course it is possible he may say a word or two about the rest of us; I have spoken to Vigeland and Sandstad about it. Our idea is that, in replying, you should propose the toast of "Prosperity to our Community"; Sandstad will say a few words on the subject of harmonious relations between the different strata of society; then Vigeland will express the hope that this new undertaking may not disturb the sound moral basis upon which our community stands; and I propose, in a few suitable words, to refer to the ladies, whose work for the community, though more inconspicuous, is far from being without its importance. But you are not listening to me.

BERNICK

Yes, indeed I am. But, tell me, do you think there is a very heavy sea running outside?

RUMMEL

Why, are you nervous about the "Palm Tree"? She is fully insured, you know.

BERNICK

Yes, she is insured; but

RUMMEL

And in good repair and that is the main thing.

BERNICK

Hm. Supposing anything does happen to a ship, it doesn't follow that human life will be in danger, does it? The ship and the cargo may be lost and one might lose one's boxes and papers

RUMMEL

Good Lord, boxes and papers are not of much consequence.

BERNICK

Not of much consequence! No, no; I only meant. Hush, I hear voices again.

RUMMEL

It is on board the "Palm Tree."

(VIGELAND comes in from the right.)

VIGELAND

Yes, they are just towing the "Palm Tree" out. Good evening, Mr. Bernick.

BERNICK

And you, as a seafaring man, are still of opinion that

VIGELAND

I put my trust in Providence, Mr. Bernick. Moreover, I have been on board myself and distributed a few small tracts which I hope may carry a blessing with them.

(SANDSTAD and KRAP come in from the right.)

SANDSTAD (to some one at the door)

Well, if that gets through all right, anything will. (Comes in.) Ah, good evening, good evening!

BERNICK

Is anything the matter, Krap?

KRAP

I say nothing, Mr. Bernick.

SANDSTAD

The entire crew of the "Indian Girl" are drunk; I will stake my reputation on it that they won't come out of it alive. (LONA comes in from the right.)

LONA

Ah, now I can say his good-byes for him.

BERNICK

Is he on board already?

LONA

He will be directly, at any rate. We parted outside the hotel.

BERNICK

And he persists in his intention?

LONA

As firm as a rock.

RUMMEL (who is fumbling at the window)

Confound these new-fangled contrivances; I cannot get the curtains drawn.

LONA

Do you want them drawn? I thought, on the contrary

RUMMEL

Yes, drawn at first, Miss Hessel. You know what is in the wind, I suppose?

LONA

Yes. Let me help you. (Takes hold of the cords.) I will draw down the curtains on my brother-in-law, though I would much rather draw them up.

RUMMEL

You can do that too, later on. When the garden is filled with a surging crowd, then the curtains shall be drawn back, and they will be able to look in upon a surprised and happy family. Citizens' lives should be such that they can live in glass houses! (BERNICK opens his mouth, as though he were going to say something; but he turns hurriedly away and goes into his room.)

RUMMEL

Come along, let us have a final consultation. Come in, too, Mr. Krap; you must assist us with information on one or two points of detail. (All the men go into BERNICK'S room. LONA has drawn the curtains over the windows, and is just going to do the same over the open glass door, when OLAF jumps down from the room above on to the garden steps; he has a wrap over his shoulders and a bundle in his hand.)

LONA

Bless me, child, how you frightened me!

OLAF (hiding his bundle)

Hush, aunt!

LONA

Did you jump out of the window? Where are you going?

OLAF

Hush! don't say anything. I want to go to Uncle Johan, only on to the quay, you know, only to say goodbye to him. Good- night, aunt! (Runs out through the garden.)

LONA

No, stop! Olaf, Olaf!

(JOHAN, dressed for his journey, with a bag over his shoulder, comes warily in by the door on the right.)

JOHAN

Lona!

LONA *(turning round)*

What! Back again?

JOHAN

I have still a few minutes. I must see her once more; we cannot part like this. (The farther door on the left opens, and MARTHA and DINA, both with cloaks on, and the latter carrying a small travelling bag in her hand, come in.)

DINA

Let me go to him! Let me go to him!

MARTHA

Yes, you shall go to him, Dina!

DINA

There he is!

JOHAN

Dina!

DINA

Take me with you! Johan: What!

LONA
You mean it?

DINA
Yes, take me with you. The other has written to me that he means to announce to everyone this evening.

JOHAN
Dina, you do not love him?

DINA
I have never loved the man! I would rather drown myself in the fjord than be engaged to him! Oh, how he humiliated me yesterday with his condescending manner! How clear he made it that he felt he was lifting up a poor despised creature to his own level! I do not mean to be despised any longer. I mean to go away. May I go with you?

JOHAN
Yes, yes, a thousand times, yes!

DINA
I will not be a burden to you long. Only help me to get over there; help me to go the right way about things at first.

JOHAN
Hurrah, it is all right after all, Dina!

LONA (pointing to BERNICK'S door)
Hush! gently, gently!

JOHAN
Dina, I shall look after you.

DINA
I am not going to let you do that. I mean to look after myself; over there, I am sure I can do that. Only let me get away from here. Oh, these women! you don't know, they have written to me today, too, exhorting me to realise my good fortune, impressing on me how magnanimous he has been. Tomorrow, and every day afterwards, they would be watching me to see if I were making myself worthy of it all. I am sick and tired of all this goodness!

JOHAN
Tell me, Dina, is that the only reason you are coming away? Am I nothing to you?

DINA
Yes, Johan, you are more to me than any one else in the world.

JOHAN
Oh, Dina!

DINA
Every one here tells me I ought to hate and detest you, that it is my duty; but I cannot see that it is my duty, and shall never be able to.

LONA
No more you shall, my dear!

MARTHA
No, indeed you shall not; and that is why you shall go with him as his wife.

JOHAN
Yes, yes!

LONA
What? Give me a kiss, Martha. I never expected that from you!

MARTHA

No, I dare say not; I would not have expected it myself. But I was bound to break out some time! Ah, what we suffer under the tyranny of habit and custom! Make a stand against that, Dina. Be his wife. Let me see you defy all this convention.

JOHAN

What is your answer, Dina?

DINA

Yes, I will be your wife.

JOHAN

Dina!

DINA

But first of all I want to work, to make something of myself, as you have done. I am not going to be merely a thing that is taken.

LONA

Quite right, that is the way.

JOHAN

Very well; I shall wait and hope

LONA

And win, my boy! But now you must get on board!

JOHAN

Yes, on board! Ah, Lona, my dear sister, just one word with you. Look here (He takes her into the background and talks hurriedly to her.)

MARTHA

Dina, you lucky girl, let me look at you, and kiss you once more, for the last time.

DINA

Not for the last time; no, my darling aunt, we shall meet again.

MARTHA

Never! Promise me, Dina, never to come back! (Grasps her hands and looks at her.) Now go to your happiness, my dear child, across the sea. How often, in my schoolroom, I have yearned to be over there! It must be beautiful; the skies are loftier than here, a freer air plays about your head

DINA

Oh, Aunt Martha, some day you will follow us.

MARTHA

I? Never, never. I have my little vocation here, and now I really believe I can live to the full the life that I ought.

DINA

I cannot imagine being parted from you.

MARTHA

Ah, one can part from much, Dina. (Kisses her.) But I hope you may never experience that, my sweet child. Promise me to make him happy.

DINA

I will promise nothing; I hate promises; things must happen as they will.

MARTHA

Yes, yes, that is true; only remain what you are, true and faithful to yourself.

DINA

I will, aunt.

Lona (putting into her pocket some papers that JOHAN has given her): Splendid, splendid, my dear boy. But now you must be off.

JOHAN
Yes, we have no time to waste now. Goodbye, Lona, and thank you for all your love. Goodbye, Martha, and thank you, too, for your loyal friendship.

MARTHA
Goodbye, Johan! Goodbye, Dina! And may you be happy all your lives! (She and LONA hurry them to the door at the back. JOHAN and DINA go quickly down the steps and through the garden. LONA shuts the door and draws the curtains over it.)

LONA
Now we are alone, Martha. You have lost her and I him.

MARTHA
You, lost him?

LONA
Oh, I had already half lost him over there. The boy was longing to stand on his own feet; that was why I pretended to be suffering from homesickness.

MARTHA
So that was it? Ah, then I understand why you came. But he will want you back, Lona.

LONA
An old step-sister, what use will he have for her now? Men break many very dear ties to win their happiness.

MARTHA
That sometimes is so.

LONA
But we two will stick together, Martha.

MARTHA
Can I be anything to you?

LONA
Who more so? We two foster-sisters, haven't we both lost our children? Now we are alone.

MARTHA
Yes, alone. And therefore, you ought to know this too, I loved him more than anything in the world.

LONA
Martha! (Grasps her by the arm.) Is that true?

MARTHA
All my existence lies in those words. I have loved him and waited for him. Every summer I waited for him to come. And then he came but he had no eyes for me.

LONA
You loved him! And it was you yourself that put his happiness into his hands.

MARTHA
Ought I not to be the one to put his happiness into his hands, since I loved him? Yes, I have loved him. All my life has been for him, ever since he went away. What reason had I to hope, you mean? Oh, I think I had some reason, all the same. But when he came back, then it seemed as if everything had been wiped out of his memory. He had no eyes for me.

LONA
It was Dina that overshadowed you, Martha?

MARTHA
And it is a good thing she did. At the time he went away, we were of the same age; but when I saw him again,

oh, that dreadful moment! I realised that now I was ten years older than he. He had gone out into the bright sparkling sunshine, and breathed in youth and health with every breath; and here I sat meanwhile, spinning and spinning

LONA
Spinning the thread of his happiness, Martha.

MARTHA
Yes, it was a golden thread I spun. No bitterness! We have been two good sisters to him, haven't we, Lona?

LONA (throwing her arms round her)
Martha!

(BERNICK comes in from his room.)

BERNICK (to the other men, who are in his room)
Yes, yes, arrange it any way you please. When the time comes, I shall be able to. (Shuts the door.) Ah, you are here. Look here, Martha- -I think you had better change your dress; and tell Betty to do the same. I don't want anything elaborate, of course, something homely, but neat. But you must make haste.

LONA
And a bright, cheerful face, Martha; your eyes must look happy.

BERNICK
Olaf is to come downstairs too; I will have him beside me.

LONA
Hm! Olaf.

MARTHA
I will give Betty your message. (Goes out by the farther door on the left.)

LONA
Well, the great and solemn moment is at hand.

BERNICK (walking uneasily up and down)
Yes, it is.

LONA
At such a moment I should think a man would feel proud and happy.

BERNICK (looking at her)
Hm!

LONA
I hear the whole town is to be illuminated.

BERNICK
Yes, they have some idea of that sort.

LONA
All the different clubs will assemble with their banners, your name will blaze out in letters of fire, tonight the telegraph will flash the news to every part of the country: "In the bosom of his happy family, Mr. Bernick received the homage of his fellow citizens, as one of the pillars of society."

BERNICK
That is so; and they will begin to cheer outside, and the crowd will shout in front of my house until I shall be obliged to go out and bow to them and thank them.

LONA
Obliged to?

Bernick. Do you suppose I shall feel happy at that moment?

LONA
No, I don't suppose you will feel so very happy.

BERNICK
Lona, you despise me.

LONA
Not yet.

BERNICK
And you have no right to; no right to despise me! Lona, you can have no idea how utterly alone I stand in this cramped and stunted community, where I have had, year after year, to stifle my ambition for a fuller life. My work may seem many-sided, but what have I really accomplished? Odds and ends, scraps. They would not stand anything else here. If I were to go a step in advance of the opinions and views that are current at the moment, I should lose all my influence. Do you know what we are, we who are looked upon as pillars of society? We are nothing more, nor less, than the tools of society.

LONA
Why have you only begun to realise that now?

BERNICK
Because I have been thinking a great deal lately, since you came back, and this evening I have thought more seriously than ever before. Oh, Lona, why did not I really know you then, in the old days, I mean?

LONA
And if you had?

BERNICK
I should never have let you go; and, if I had had you, I should not be in the position I am in tonight.

LONA
And do you never consider what she might have been to you, she whom you chose in my place?

BERNICK
I know, at all events, that she has been nothing to me of what I needed.

LONA
Because you have never shared your interests with her; because you have never allowed her full and frank exchange of thoughts with you; because you have allowed her to be borne under by self-reproach for the shame you cast upon one who was dear to her.

BERNICK
Yes, yes; it all comes from lying and deceit.

LONA
Then why not break with all this lying and deceit?

BERNICK
Now? It is too late now, Lona.

LONA
Karsten, tell me, what gratification does all this show and deception bring you?

BERNICK
It brings me none. I must disappear someday, and all this community of bunglers with me. But a generation is growing up that will follow us; it is my son that I work for, I am providing a career for him. There will come a time when truth will enter into the life of the community, and on that foundation he shall build up a happier existence than his father.

LONA
With a lie at the bottom of it all? Consider what sort of an inheritance it is that you are leaving to your son.

BERNICK (in tones of suppressed despair)
It is a thousand times worse than you think. But surely some day the curse must be lifted; and yet,

nevertheless. (Vehemently.) How could I bring all this upon my own head! Still, it is done now; I must go on with it now. You shall not succeed in crushing me! (HILMAR comes in hurriedly and agitatedly from the right, with an open letter in his hand.)

HILMAR

But this is, Betty, Betty.

BERNICK

What is the matter? Are they coming already?

HILMAR

No, no, but I must speak to some one immediately. (Goes out through the farther door on the left.)

LONA

Karsten, you talk about our having come here to crush you. So let me tell you what sort of stuff this prodigal son, whom your moral community shuns as if he had the plague, is made of. He can do without any of you for he is away now.

BERNICK

But he said he meant to come back

LONA

Johan will never come back. He is gone for good, and Dina with him.

BERNICK

Never come back? and Dina with him?

LONA

Yes, to be his wife. That is how these two strike your virtuous community in the face, just as I did once but never mind that.

BERNICK

Gone, and she too, in the "Indian Girl"

LONA

No; he would not trust so precious a freight to that rascally crew. Johan and Dina are on the "Palm Tree."

BERNICK

Ah! Then it is all in vain (Goes hurriedly to the door of his room, opens it and calls in.) Krap, stop the "Indian Girl" she must not sail tonight!

KRAP (from within)

The "Indian Girl" is already standing out to sea, Mr. Bernick.

BERNICK (shutting the door and speaking faintly)

Too late, and all to no purpose

LONA

What do you mean?

BERNICK

Nothing, nothing. Leave me alone!

LONA

Hm! look here, Karsten. Johan was good enough to say that he entrusted to me the good name and reputation that he once lent to you, and also the good name that you stole from him while he was away. Johan will hold his tongue; and I can act just as I please in the matter. See, I have two letters in my hand.

BERNICK

You have got them! And you mean now, this very evening, perhaps when the procession comes

LONA

I did not come back here to betray you, but to stir your conscience so that you should speak of your own free will. I did not succeed in doing that so you must remain as you are, with your life founded upon a lie. Look, I am tearing your two letters in pieces. Take the wretched things, there you are. Now there is no evidence against you, Karsten. You are safe now; be happy, too, if you can.

BERNICK (much moved)
Lona, why did you not do that sooner! Now it is too late; life no longer seems good to me; I cannot live on after today.

LONA
What has happened?

BERNICK
Do not ask me. But I must live on, nevertheless! I will live for Olaf's sake. He shall make amends for everything, expiate everything.

LONA
Karsten! (HILMAR comes hurriedly back.)

HILMAR
I cannot find anyone; they are all out, even Betty!

BERNICK
What is the matter with you?

HILMAR
I daren't tell you.

BERNICK
What is it? You must tell me!

HILMAR
Very well, Olaf has run away, on board the "Indian Girl."

BERNICK *(stumbling back)*
Olaf, on board the "Indian Girl"! No, no!

LONA
Yes, he is! Now I understand, I saw him jump out of the window.

Bernick (calls in through the door of his room in a despairing voice): Krap, stop the "Indian Girl" at any cost!

KRAP
It is impossible, sir. How can you suppose?

BERNICK
We must stop her; Olaf is on board!

KRAP
What!

RUMMEL (coming out of BERNICK'S room)
Olaf, run away? Impossible!

SANDSTAD (following him)
He will be sent back with the pilot, Mr. Bernick.

HILMAR
No, no; he has written to me. (Shows the letter.) He says he means to hide among the cargo till they are in the open sea.

BERNICK
I shall never see him again!

RUMMEL
What nonsense! a good strong ship, newly repaired...

VIGELAND (who has followed the others out of BERNICK'S room)
And in your own yard, Mr. Bernick!

BERNICK
I shall never see him again, I tell you. I have lost him, Lona; and I see it now, he never was really mine. (Listens.) What is that?

RUMMEL
Music. The procession must be coming.

Bernick. I cannot take any part in it, I will not.

RUMMEL
What are you thinking of! That is impossible.

SANDSTAD
Impossible, Mr. Bernick; think what you have at stake.

BERNICK
What does it all matter to me now? What have I to work for now?

RUMMEL
Can you ask? You have us and the community.

VIGELAND
Quite true.

SANDSTAD
And surely, Mr. Bernick, you have not forgotten that we.(MARTHA comes in through the farther door to the left. Music is heard in the distance, down the street.)

MARTHA
The procession is just coming, but Betty is not in the house. I don't understand where she

BERNICK
Not in the house! There, you see, Lona, no support to me, either in gladness or in sorrow.

RUMMEL
Draw back the curtains! Come and help me, Mr. Krap and you, Mr. Sandstad. It is a thousand pities that the family should not be united just now; it is quite contrary to the program. (They draw back all the curtains. The whole street is seen to be illuminated. Opposite the house is a large transparency, bearing the words: "Long live Karsten Bernick, Pillar of our Society")

BERNICK *(shrinking back)*
Take all that away! I don't want to see it! Put it out, put it out!

RUMMEL
Excuse me, Mr. Bernick, but are you not well?

MARTHA
What is the matter with him, Lona?

LONA
Hush! (Whispers to her.)

BERNICK
Take away those mocking words, I tell you! Can't you see that all these lights are grinning at us?

RUMMEL
Well, really, I must confess

BERNICK
Oh, how could you understand! But I, I! It is all like candles in a dead-room!

RUMMEL
Well, let me tell you that you are taking the thing a great deal too seriously.

SANDSTAD
The boy will enjoy a trip across the Atlantic, and then you will have him back.

VIGELAND
Only put your trust in the Almighty, Mr. Bernick.

RUMMEL
And in the vessel, Bernick; it is not likely to sink, I know.

KRAP
Hm

RUMMEL
Now if it were one of those floating coffins that one hears are sent out by men in the bigger countries

BERNICK
I am sure my hair must be turning grey

(MRS. BERNICK comes in from the garden, with a shawl thrown over her head.)

MRS. BERNICK
Karsten, Karsten, do you know?

BERNICK
Yes. I know; but you, you, who see nothing that is going on, you, who have no mother's eyes for your son!

MRS. BERNICK
Listen to me, do!

BERNICK
Why did you not look after him? Now I have lost him. Give him back to me, if you can.

MRS. BERNICK
I can! I have got him.

BERNICK
You have got him!

THE MEN
Ah!

HILMAR
Yes, I thought so.

MARTHA
You have got him back, Karsten.

LONA
Yes, make him your own, now.

BERNICK
You have got him! Is that true? Where is he?

MRS. BERNICK
I shall not tell you, till you have forgiven him.

BERNICK
Forgiven! But how did you know?

MRS. BERNICK

Do you not think a mother sees? I was in mortal fear of your getting to know anything about it. Some words he let fall yesterday and then his room was empty, and his knapsack and clothes missing...

BERNICK

Yes, yes?

MRS. BERNICK

I ran, and got hold of Aune; we went out in his boat; the American ship was on the point of sailing. Thank God, we were in time, got on board, searched the hold, found him! Oh, Karsten, you must not punish him!

BERNICK

Betty!

MRS. BERNICK

Nor Aune, either!

BERNICK

Aune? What do you know about him? Is the "Indian Girl" under sail again?

MRS. BERNICK

No, that is just it.

BERNICK

Speak, speak!

MRS. BERNICK

Aune was just as agitated as I was; the search took us some time; it had grown dark, and the pilot made objections; and so Aune took upon himself, in your name

BERNICK

Well?

MRS. BERNICK

To stop the ship's sailing till tomorrow.

KRAP

Hm

BERNICK

Oh, how glad I am!

MRS. BERNICK

You are not angry?

BERNICK

I cannot tell you how glad I am, Betty

RUMMEL

You really take things far too seriously.

HILMAR

Oh yes, as soon as it is a question of a little struggle with the elements, ugh!

KRAP *(going to the window)*

The procession is just coming through your garden gate, Mr. Bernick.

BERNICK

Yes, they can come now.

RUMMEL

The whole garden is full of people.

SANDSTAD
The whole street is crammed.

RUMMEL
The whole town is afoot, Bernick. It really is a moment that makes one proud.

VIGELAND
Let us take it in a humble spirit, Mr. Rummel.

RUMMEL
All the banners are out! What a procession! Here comes the committee with Mr. Rorlund at their head.

BERNICK
Yes, let them come in!

RUMMEL
But, Bernick, in your present agitated frame of mind

BERNICK
Well, what?

RUMMEL
I am quite willing to speak instead of you, if you like.

BERNICK
No, thank you; I will speak for myself tonight.

RUMMEL
But are you sure you know what to say?

BERNICK
Yes, make your mind easy, Rummel. I know now what to say. (The music grows louder. The verandah door is opened. RORLUND comes in, at the head of the Committee, escorted by a couple of hired waiters, who carry a covered basket. They are followed by townspeople of all classes, as many as can get into the room. An apparently endless crowd of people, waving banners and flags, are visible in the garden and the street.)

RORLUND
Mr. Bernick! I see, from the surprise depicted upon your face, that it is as unexpected guests that we are intruding upon your happyfamily circle and your peaceful fireside, where we find you surrounded by honoured and energetic fellow citizens and friends. But it is our hearts that have bidden us come to offer you our homage, not for the first time, it is true, but for the first time on such a comprehensive scale. We have on many occasions given you our thanks for the broad moral foundation upon which you have, so to speak, reared the edifice of our community. On this occasion we offer our homage especially to the clear-sighted, indefatigable, unselfish, nay, self-sacrificing citizen who has taken the initiative in an undertaking which, we are assured on all sides, will give a powerful impetus to the temporal prosperity and welfare of our community.

VOICES
Bravo, bravo!

RORLUND
You, sir, have for many years been a shining example in our midst. This is not the place for me to speak of your family life, which has been a model to us all; still less to enlarge upon your unblemished personal character. Such topics belong to the stillness of a man's own chamber, not to a festal occasion such as this! I am here to speak of your public life as a citizen, as it lies open to all men's eyes. Well-equipped vessels sail away from your shipyard and carry our flag far and wide over the seas. A numerous and happy band of workmen look up to you as to a father. By calling new branches of industry into

existence, you have laid the foundations of the welfare of hundreds of families. In a word, you are, in the fullest sense of the term, the mainstay of our community.

VOICES
Hear, hear! Bravo!

RORLUND

And, sir, it is just that disinterestedness, which colours all your conduct, that is so beneficial to our community, more so than words can express, and especially at the present moment. You are now on the point of procuring for us what I have no hesitation in calling bluntly by its prosaic name, a railway!

VOICES

Bravo, bravo!

RORLUND

But it would seem as though the undertaking were beset by certain difficulties, the outcome of narrow and selfish considerations.

VOICES

Hear, hear!

RORLUND

For the fact has come to light that certain individuals, who do not belong to our community, have stolen a march upon the hard- working citizens of this place, and have laid hands on certain sources of profit which by rights should have fallen to the share of our town.

VOICES

That's right! Hear, hear!

RORLUND

This regrettable fact has naturally come to your knowledge also, Mr. Bernick. But it has not had the slightest effect in deterring you from proceeding steadily with your project, well knowing that a patriotic man should not solely take local interests into consideration.

VOICES

Oh! No, no! Yes, yes!

RORLUND

It is to such a man, to the patriot citizen, whose character we all should emulate that we bring our homage this evening. May your undertaking grow to be a real and lasting source of good fortune to this community! It is true enough that a railway may be the means of our exposing ourselves to the incursion of pernicious influences from without; but it gives us also the means of quickly expelling them from within. For even we, at the present time, cannot boast of being entirely free from the danger of such outside influences; but as we have, on this very evening, if rumour is to be believed, fortunately got rid of certain elements of that nature, sooner than was to be expected

VOICES

Order, order!

RORLUND: I regard the occurrence as a happy omen for our undertaking. My alluding to such a thing at such a moment only emphasises the fact that the house in which we are now standing is one where the claims of morality are esteemed even above ties of family.

VOICES

Hear, hear! Bravo!

BERNICK (at the same moment)
Allow me

RORLUND

I have only a few more words to say, Mr. Bernick. What you have done for your native place we all know has not been done with any underlying idea of its bringing tangible profit to yourself. But, nevertheless, you must not refuse to accept a slight token of grateful appreciation at the hands of your fellow-citizens, least of all at this important moment when, according to the assurances of practical men, we are standing on the threshold of a new era.

VOICES

Bravo! Hear, hear!

(RORLUND aigns to the servants, who bring forward the basket. During the following speech, members of the Committee take out and present the various objects mentioned.)

RORLUND
And so, Mr. Bernick, we have the pleasure of presenting you with this silver coffee-service. Let it grace your board when in the future, as so often in the past, we have the happiness of being assembled under your hospitable roof. You, too, gentlemen, who have so generously seconded the leader of our community, we ask to accept a small souvenir. This silver goblet is for you, Mr. Rummel. Many a time have you, amidst the clink of glasses, defended the interests of your fellow-citizens in well-chosen words; may you often find similar worthy opportunities to raise and empty this goblet in some patriotic toast! To you, Mr. Sandstad, I present this album containing photographs of your fellow-citizens. Your well-known and conspicuous liberality has put you in the pleasant position of being able to number your friends amongst all classes of society. And to you, Mr. Vigeland, I have to offer this book of Family Devotions, printed on vellum and handsomely bound, to grace your study table. The mellowing influence of time has led you to take an earnest view of life; your zeal in carrying out your daily duties has, for a long period of years, been purified and enobled by thoughts of higher and holier things. (Turns to the crowd.) And now, friends, three cheers for Mr. Bernick and his fellow-workers! Three cheers for the Pillars of our Society!

THE WHOLE CROWD
Bernick! Pillars of Society! Hurrah-hurrah-hurrah!

LONA
I congratulate you, brother-in-law.

(An expectant hush follows.)

BERNICK (speaking seriously and slowly)
Fellow citizens, your spokesman said just now that tonight we are standing on the threshold of a new era. I hope that will prove to be the case. But before that can come to pass, we must lay fast hold of truth, truth which, till tonight, has been altogether and in all circumstances a stranger to this community of ours. (Astonishment among the audience.) To that end, I must begin by deprecating the praises with which you, Mr. Rorlund, according to custom on such occasions, have overwhelmed me. I do not deserve them; because, until today, my actions have by no means been disinterested. Even though I may not always have aimed at pecuniary profit, I at all events recognise now that a craving for power, influence and position has been the moving spirit of most of my actions.

RUMMEL (half aloud)
What next!

BERNICK
Standing before my fellow citizens, I do not reproach myself for that; because I still think I am entitled to a place in the front rank of our capable men of affairs.

VOICES
Yes, yes, yes!

BERNICK
But what I charge myself with is that I have so often been weak enough to resort to deceitfulness, because I knew and feared the tendency of the community to espy unclean motives behind everything a prominent man here undertakes. And now I am coming to a point which will illustrate that.

RUMMEL (uneasily)
Hm-hm!

BERNICK
There have been rumours of extensive purchases of property outside the town. These purchases have been made by me, by me alone, and by no one else. (Murmurs are heard: "What does he say? He? Bernick?") The properties are, for the time being, in my hands. Naturally I have confided in my fellow-workers, Mr. Rummel, Mr. Vigeland and Mr. Sandstad, and we are all agreed that

RUMMEL
It is not true! Prove it, prove it!

VIGELAND

We are not all agreed about anything!

SANDSTAD

Well, really I must say!

BERNICK

That is quite true, we are not yet agreed upon the matter I was going to mention. But I confidently hope that these three gentlemen will agree with me when I announce to you that I have tonight come to the decision that these properties shall be exploited as a company of which the shares shall be offered for public subscription; any one that wishes can take shares.

VOICES

Hurrah! Three cheers for Bernick!

RUMMEL (in a low voice, to BERNICK)

This is the basest treachery!

SANDSTAD (also in an undertone)

So you have been fooling us!

VIGELAND

Well, then, devil take! Good Lord, what am I saying? (Cheers are heard without.)

BERNICK

Silence, gentlemen. I have no right to this homage you offer me; because the decision I have just come to does not represent what was my first intention. My intention was to keep the whole thing for myself; and, even now, I am of opinion that these properties would be worked to best advantage if they remained in one man's hands. But you are at liberty to choose. If you wish it, I am willing to administer them to the best of my abilities.

VOICES

Yes, yes, yes!

BERNICK

But, first of all, my fellow townsmen must know me thoroughly. And let each man seek to know himself thoroughly, too; and so let it really come to pass that tonight we begin a new era. The old era with its affectation, its hypocrisy and its emptiness, its pretence of virtue and its miserable fear of public opinion, shall be for us like a museum, open for purposes of instruction; and to that museum we will present, shall we not, gentlemen? the coffee service, and the goblet, and the album, and the Family Devotions printed on vellum, and handsomely bound.

RUMMEL

Oh, of course.

VIGELAND (muttering)

If you have taken everything else, then

SANDSTAD

By all means.

BERNICK

And now for the principal reckoning I have to make with the community. Mr. Rorlund said that certain pernicious elements had left us this evening. I can add what you do not yet know. The man referred to did not go away alone; with him, to become his wife, went

LONA (loudly)

Dina Dorf!

RORLUND

What?

MRS. BERNICK

What? (Great commotion.)

RORLUND
Fled? Run away with him! Impossible!

BERNICK
To become his wife, Mr. Rorlund. And I will add more. (In a low voice, to his wife.) Betty, be strong to bear what is coming. (Aloud.) This is what I have to say : hats off to that man, for he has nobly taken another's guilt upon his shoulders. My friends, I want to have done with falsehood; it has very nearly poisoned every fibre of my being. You shall know all. Fifteen years ago, I was the guilty man.

MRS. BERNICK (softly and tremblingly)
Karsten!

MARTHA (similarly)
Ah, Johan!

LONA
Now at last you have found yourself!

(Speechless consternation among the audience.)

BERNICK
Yes, friends, I was the guilty one, and he went away. The vile and lying rumours that were spread abroad afterwards, it is beyond human power to refute now; but I have no right to complain of that. For fifteen years I have climbed up the ladder of success by the help of those rumours; whether now they are to cast me down again, or not, each of you must decide in his own mind.

RORLUND
What a thunderbolt! Our leading citizen! (In a low voice, to BETTY.) How sorry I am for you, Mrs. Bernick!

HILMAR
What a confession! Well, I must say!

BERNICK
But come to no decision tonight. I entreat every one to go home, to collect his thoughts, to look into his own heart. When once more you can think calmly, then it will be seen whether I have lost or won by speaking out. Goodbye! I have still much, very much, to repent of; but that concerns my own conscience only. Good night! Take away all these signs of rejoicing. We must all feel that they are out of place here.

RORLUND
That they certainly are. (In an undertone to MRS. BERNICK.) Run away! So then she was completely unworthy of me. (Louder, to the Committee.) Yes, gentlemen, after this I think we had better disperse as quietly as possible.

HILMAR
How, after this, any one is to manage to hold the Ideal's banner high, Ugh!

(Meantime the news has been whispered from mouth to mouth. The crowd gradually disperses from the garden. RUMMEL, SANDSTAD and VIGELAND go out, arguing eagerly but in a low voice. HILMAR slinks away to the right. When silence is restored, there only remain in the room BERNICK, MRS. BERNICK, MARTHA, LONA and KRAP.)

BERNICK
Betty, can you forgive me?

MRS. BERNICK (looking at him with a smile)
Do you know, Karsten, that you have opened out for me the happiest prospect I have had for many a year?

BERNICK
How?

MRS. BERNICK
For many years, I have felt that once you were mine and that I had lost you. Now I know that you never have been mine yet; but I shall win you.

BERNICK (folding her in his arms)
Oh, Betty, you have won me. It was through Lona that I first learned really to know you. But now let Olaf come to me.

MRS. BERNICK
Yes, you shall have him now. Mr. Krap! (Talks softly to KRAP in the background. He goes out by the garden door. During what follows, the illuminations and lights in the houses are gradually extinguished.)

BERNICK (in a low voice)
Thank you, Lona, you have saved what was best in me, and for me.

LONA
Do you suppose I wanted to do anything else?

BERNICK
Yes, was that so or not? I cannot quite make you out.

LONA
Hm

BERNICK
Then it was not hatred? Not revenge? Why did you come back, then?

LONA
Old friendship does not rust.

BERNICK
Lona!

LONA
When Johan told me about the lie, I swore to myself that the hero of my youth should stand free and true.

BERNICK
What a wretch I am! and how little I have deserved it of you!

Lona. Oh, if we women always looked for what we deserve, Karsten! (AUNE comes in with OLAF from the garden.)

BERNICK (going to meet them)
Olaf!

OLAF
Father, I promise I will never do it again

BERNICK
Never run away?

OLAF
Yes, yes, I promise you, father.

BERNICK
And I promise you, you shall never have reason to. For the future you shall be allowed to grow up, not as the heir to my life's work, but as one who has his own life's work before him.

OLAF
And shall I be allowed to be what I like, when I grow up?

BERNICK
Yes.

Olaf. Oh, thank you! Then I won't be a pillar of society.

BERNICK
No? Why not?

OLAF

No, I think it must be so dull.

BERNICK

You shall be yourself, Olaf; the rest may take care of itself. And you, Aune...

AUNE

I know, Mr. Bernick; I am dismissed.

BERNICK

We remain together, Aune; and forgive me.

AUNE

What? The ship has not sailed tonight.

BERNICK

Nor will it sail tomorrow, either. I gave you too short grace. It must be looked to more thoroughly.

AUNE

It shall, Mr. Bernick and with the new machines!

BERNICK

By all means but thoroughly and conscientiously. There are many among us who need thorough and conscientious repairs, Aune. Well, good night.

AUNE

Good-night, sir and thank you, thank you. (Goes out.)

MRS. BERNICK

Now they are all gone.

BERNICK

And we are alone. My name is not shining in letters of fire any longer; all the lights in the windows are out.

LONA

Would you wish them lit again?

BERNICK

Not for anything in the world. Where have I been! You would be

horrified if you knew. I feel now as if I had come back to my right senses, after being poisoned. But I feel this that I can be young and healthy again. Oh, come nearer, come closer round me. Come, Betty! Come, Olaf, my boy! And you, Martha, it seems to me as if I had never seen you all these years.

LONA

No, I can believe that. Your community is a community of bachelor souls; you do not see women.

BERNICK

That is quite true; and for that very reason this is a bargain, Lona, you must not leave Betty and me.

MRS. BERNICK

No, Lona, you must not.

LONA

No, how could I have the heart to go away and leave you young people who are just setting up housekeeping? Am I not your foster-mother? You and I, Martha, the two old aunts. What are you looking at?

MARTHA

Look how the sky is clearing, and how light it is over the sea. The "Palm Tree" is going to be lucky.

LONA

It carries its good luck on board.

BERNICK

And we, we have a long earnest day of work ahead of us; I most of all. But let it come; only keep close round me you true, loyal women. I have learned this too, in these last few days; it is you women that are the pillars of society.

LONA

You have learned a poor sort of wisdom, then, brother-in-law. (Lays her hand firmly upon his shoulder.) No, my friend; the spirit of truth and the spirit of freedom, they are the pillars of society.

Henrik Ibsen - Ghosts

Index Of Contents

GHOSTS, A FAMILY-DRAMA IN THREE ACTS. (1881)

CHARACTERS.

MRS. HELEN ALVING, widow of Captain Alving, late Chamberlain to the King.

OSWALD ALVING, her son, a painter.

PASTOR MANDERS.

JACOB ENGSTRAND, a carpenter.

REGINA ENGSTRAND, Mrs. Alving's maid.

The action takes place at Mrs. Alving's country house, beside one of the large fjords in Western Norway.

ACT FIRST.

[A spacious garden-room, with one door to the left, and two doors to the right. In the middle of the room a round table, with chairs about it. On the table lie books, periodicals, and newspapers. In the foreground to the left a window, and by it a small sofa, with a worktable in front of it. In the background, the room is continued into a somewhat narrower conservatory, the walls of which are formed by large panes of glass. In the right-hand wall of the conservatory is a door leading down into the garden. Through the glass wall a gloomy fjord landscape is faintly visible, veiled by steady rain.]

[ENGSTRAND, the carpenter, stands by the garden door. His left leg is somewhat bent; he has a clump of wood under the sole of his boot. REGINA, with an empty garden syringe in her hand, hinders him from advancing.]

REGINA. [In a low voice.] What do you want? Stop where you are. You're positively dripping.

ENGSTRAND. It's the Lord's own rain, my girl.

REGINA. It's the devil's rain, I say.

ENGSTRAND. Lord, how you talk, Regina. [Limps a step or two forward into the room.] It's just this as I wanted to say

REGINA. Don't clatter so with that foot of yours, I tell you! The young master's asleep upstairs.

ENGSTRAND. Asleep? In the middle of the day?

REGINA. It's no business of yours.

ENGSTRAND. I was out on the loose last night

REGINA. I can quite believe that.

ENGSTRAND. Yes, we're weak vessels, we poor mortals, my girl

REGINA. So it seems.

ENGSTRAND. - and temptations are manifold in this world, you see. But all the same, I was hard at work, God knows, at half-past five this morning.

REGINA. Very well; only be off now. I won't stop here and have rendezvous's with you.

ENGSTRAND. What do you say you won't have?

REGINA. I won't have any one find you here; so just you go about your business.

ENGSTRAND. [Advances a step or two.] Blest if I go before I've had a talk with you. This afternoon I shall have finished my work at the school house, and then I shall take to-night's boat and be off home to the town.

REGINA. [Mutters.] Pleasant journey to you!

ENGSTRAND. Thank you, my child. To-morrow the Orphanage is to be opened, and then there'll be fine doings, no doubt, and plenty of intoxicating drink going, you know. And nobody shall say of Jacob Engstrand that he can't keep out of temptation's way.

REGINA. Oh!

ENGSTRAND. You see, there's to be heaps of grand folks here to-morrow. Pastor Manders is expected from town, too.

REGINA. He's coming to-day.

ENGSTRAND. There, you see! And I should be cursedly sorry if he found out anything against me, don't you understand?

REGINA. Oho! is that your game?

ENGSTRAND. Is what my game?

REGINA. [Looking hard at him.] What are you going to fool Pastor Manders into doing, this time?

ENGSTRAND. Sh! sh! Are you crazy? Do I want to fool Pastor Manders? Oh no! Pastor Manders has been far too good a friend to me for that. But I just wanted to say, you know that I mean to be off home again to-night.

REGINA. The sooner the better, say I.

ENGSTRAND. Yes, but I want you with me, Regina.

REGINA. [Open-mouthed.] You want me? What are you talking about?

ENGSTRAND. I want you to come home with me, I say.

REGINA. [Scornfully.] Never in this world shall you get me home with you.

ENGSTRAND. Oh, we'll see about that.

REGINA. Yes, you may be sure we'll see about it! Me, that have been brought up by a lady like Mrs Alving! Me, that am treated almost as a daughter here! Is it me you want to go home with you? to a house like yours? For shame!

ENGSTRAND. What the devil do you mean? Do you set yourself up against your father, you hussy?

REGINA. [Mutters without looking at him.] You've sail often enough I was no concern of yours.

ENGSTRAND. Pooh! Why should you bother about that -

REGINA. Haven't you many a time sworn at me and called me a -? Fi donc!

ENGSTRAND. Curse me, now, if ever I used such an ugly word.

REGINA. Oh, I remember very well what word you used.

ENGSTRAND. Well, but that was only when I was a bit on, don't you know? Temptations are manifold in this world, Regina.

REGINA. Ugh!

ENGSTRAND. And besides, it was when your mother was that aggravating, I had to find something to twit her with, my child. She was always setting up for a fine lady. [Mimics.] "Let me go, Engstrand; let me be. Remember I was three years in Chamberlain Alving's family at Rosenvold." [Laughs.] Mercy on us! She could never forget that the Captain was made a Chamberlain while she was in service here.

REGINA. Poor mother! you very soon tormented her into her grave.

ENGSTRAND. [With a twist of his shoulders.] Oh, of course! I'm to have the blame for everything.

REGINA. [Turns away; half aloud.] Ugh! And that leg too!

ENGSTRAND. What do you say, my child?

REGINA. Pied de mouton.

ENGSTRAND. Is that English, eh?

REGINA. Yes.

ENGSTRAND. Ay, ay; you've picked up some learning out here; and that may come in useful now, Regina.

REGINA. [After a short silence.] What do you want with me in town?

ENGSTRAND. Can you ask what a father wants with his only child? A'n't I a lonely, forlorn widower?

REGINA. Oh, don't try on any nonsense like that with me! Why do you want me?

ENGSTRAND. Well, let me tell you, I've been thinking of setting up in a new line of business.

REGINA. [Contemptuously.] You've tried that often enough, and much good you've done with it.

ENGSTRAND. Yes, but this time you shall see, Regina! Devil take me -

REGINA. [Stamps.] Stop your swearing!

ENGSTRAND. Hush, hush; you're right enough there, my girl. What I wanted to say was just this, I've laid by a very tidy pile from this Orphanage job.

REGINA. Have you? That's a good thing for you.

ENGSTRAND. What can a man spend his ha'pence on here in this country hole?

REGINA. Well, what then?

ENGSTRAND. Why, you see, I thought of putting the money into some paying speculation. I thought of a sort of a sailor's tavern

REGINA. Pah!

ENGSTRAND. A regular high-class affair, of course; not any sort of pig-sty for common sailors. No! damn it! it would be for captains and mates, and, and, regular swells, you know.

REGINA. And I was to?

ENGSTRAND. You were to help, to be sure. Only for the look of the thing, you understand. Devil a bit of hard work shall you have, my girl. You shall do exactly what you like.

REGINA. Oh, indeed!

ENGSTRAND. But there must be a petticoat in the house; that's as clear as daylight. For I want to have it a bit lively like in the evenings, with singing and dancing, and so on. You must remember they're weary wanderers on the ocean of life. [Nearer.] Now don't be a fool and stand in your own light, Regina. What's to become of you out here? Your mistress has given you a lot of learning; but what good is that to you? You're to look after the children at the new Orphanage, I hear. Is that the sort of thing for you, eh? Are you so dead set on wearing your life out for a pack of dirty brats?

REGINA. No; if things go as I want them to. Well there's no saying, there's no saying.

ENGSTRAND. What do you mean by "there's no saying"?

REGINA. Never you mind. How much money have you saved?

ENGSTRAND. What with one thing and another, a matter of seven or eight hundred crowns. [A "krone" is equal to one shilling and three-halfpence.]

REGINA. That's not so bad.

ENGSTRAND. It's enough to make a start with, my girl.

REGINA. Aren't you thinking of giving me any?

ENGSTRAND. No, I'm blest if I am!

REGINA. Not even of sending me a scrap of stuff for a new dress?

ENGSTRAND. Come to town with me, my lass, and you'll soon get dresses enough.

REGINA. Pooh! I can do that on my own account, if I want to.

ENGSTRAND. No, a father's guiding hand is what you want, Regina. Now, I've got my eye on a capital house in Little Harbour Street. They don't want much ready-money; and it could be a sort of a Sailors' Home, you know.

REGINA. But I will not live with you! I have nothing whatever to do with you. Be off!

ENGSTRAND. You wouldn't stop long with me, my girl. No such luck! If you knew how to play your cards, such a fine figure of a girl as you've grown in the last year or two

REGINA. Well?

ENGSTRAND. You'd soon get hold of some mate or maybe even a captain

REGINA. I won't marry any one of that sort. Sailors have no savoir vivre.

ENGSTRAND. What's that they haven't got?

REGINA. I know what sailors are, I tell you. They're not the sort of people to marry.

ENGSTRAND. Then never mind about marrying them. You can make it pay all the same. [More confidentially.] He, the Englishman, the man with the yacht, he came down with three hundred dollars, he did; and she wasn't a bit handsomer than you.

REGINA. [Making for him.] Out you go!

ENGSTRAND. [Falling back.] Come, come! You're not going to hit me, I hope.

REGINA. Yes, if you begin talking about mother I shall hit you. Get away with you, I say! [Drives him back towards the garden door.] And don't slam the doors. Young Mr. Alving

ENGSTRAND. He's asleep; I know. You're mightily taken up about young Mr. Alving [More softly.] Oho! you don't mean to say it's him as?

REGINA. Be off this minute! You're crazy, I tell you! No, not that way. There comes Pastor Manders. Down the kitchen stairs with you.

ENGSTRAND. [Towards the right.] Yes, yes, I'm going. But just you talk to him as is coming there. He's the man to tell you what a child owes its father. For I am your father all the same, you know. I can prove it from the church register.

[He goes out through the second door to the right, which REGINA has opened, and closes again after him. REGINA glances hastily at herself in the mirror, dusts herself with her pocket handkerchief; and settles her necktie; then she busies herself with the flowers.]

[PASTOR MANDERS, wearing an overcoat, carrying an umbrella, and with a small travelling-bag on a strap over his shoulder, comes through the garden door into the conservatory.]

MANDERS. Good-morning, Miss Engstrand.

REGINA. [Turning round, surprised and pleased.] No, really! Good morning, Pastor Manders. Is the steamer in already?

MANDERS. It is just in. [Enters the sitting-room.] Terrible weather we have been having lately.

REGINA. [Follows him.] It's such blessed weather for the country, sir.

MANDERS. No doubt; you are quite right. We townspeople give too little thought to that. [He begins to take off his overcoat.]

REGINA. Oh, mayn't I help you? There! Why, how wet it is! I'll just hang it up in the hall. And your umbrella, too. I'll open it and let it dry.

[She goes out with the things through the second door on the right. PASTOR MANDERS takes off his travelling bag and lays it and his hat on a chair. Meanwhile REGINA comes in again.]

MANDERS. Ah, it's a comfort to get safe under cover. I hope everything is going on well here?

REGINA. Yes, thank you, sir.

MANDERS. You have your hands full, I suppose, in preparation for to-morrow?

REGINA. Yes, there's plenty to do, of course.

MANDERS. And Mrs. Alving is at home, I trust?

REGINA. Oh dear, yes. She's just upstairs, looking after the young master's chocolate.

MANDERS. Yes, by-the-bye. I heard down at the pier that Oswald had arrived.

REGINA. Yes, he came the day before yesterday. We didn't expect him before to-day.

MANDERS. Quite strong and well, I hope?

REGINA. Yes, thank you, quite; but dreadfully tired with the journey. He has made one rush right through from Paris, the whole way in one train, I believe. He's sleeping a little now, I think; so perhaps we'd better talk a little quietly.

MANDERS. Sh! as quietly as you please.

REGINA. [Arranging an arm-chair beside the table.] Now, do sit down, Pastor Manders, and make yourself comfortable. [He sits down; she places a footstool under his feet.] There! Are you comfortable now, sir?

MANDERS. Thanks, thanks, extremely so. [Looks at her.] Do you know, Miss Engstrand, I positively believe you have grown since I last saw you.

REGINA. Do you think so, Sir? Mrs. Alving says I've filled out too.

MANDERS. Filled out? Well, perhaps a little; just enough.

[Short pause.]

REGINA. Shall I tell Mrs. Alving you are here?

MANDERS. Thanks, thanks, there is no hurry, my dear child. By-the-bye, Regina, my good girl, tell me: how is your father getting on out here?

REGINA. Oh, thank you, sir, he's getting on well enough.

MANDERS. He called upon me last time he was in town.

REGINA. Did he, indeed? He's always so glad of a chance of talking to you, sir.

MANDERS. And you often look in upon him at his work, I daresay?

REGINA. I? Oh, of course, when I have time, I -

MANDERS. Your father is not a man of strong character, Miss Engstrand. He stands terribly in need of a guiding hand.

REGINA. Oh, yes; I daresay he does.

MANDERS. He requires some one near him whom he cares for, and whose judgment he respects. He frankly admitted as much when he last came to see me.

REGINA. Yes, he mentioned something of the sort to me. But I don't know whether Mrs. Alving can spare me; especially now that we've got the new Orphanage to attend to. And then I should be so sorry to leave Mrs. Alving; she has always been so kind to me.

MANDERS. But a daughter's duty, my good girl. Of course, we should first have to get your mistress's consent.

REGINA. But I don't know whether it would be quite proper for me, at my age, to keep house for a single man.

MANDERS. What! My dear Miss Engstrand! When the man is your own father!

REGINA. Yes, that may be; but all the same. Now, if it were in a thoroughly nice house, and with a real gentleman

MANDERS. Why, my dear Regina

REGINA. - one I could love and respect, and be a daughter to

MANDERS. Yes, but my dear, good child

REGINA. Then I should be glad to go to town. It's very lonely out here; you know yourself, sir, what it is to be alone in the world. And I can assure you I'm both quick and willing. Don't you know of any such place for me, sir?

MANDERS. I? No, certainly not.

REGINA. But, dear, dear Sir, do remember me if

MANDERS. [Rising.] Yes, yes, certainly, Miss Engstrand.

REGINA. For if I

MANDERS. Will you be so good as to tell your mistress I am here?

REGINA. I will, at once, sir. [She goes out to the left.]

MANDERS. [Paces the room two or three times, stands a moment in the background with his hands behind his back, and looks out over the garden. Then he returns to the table, takes up a book, and looks at the title-page; starts, and looks at several books.] Ha, indeed!

[MRS. ALVING enters by the door on the left; she is followed by REGINA, who immediately goes out by the first door on the right.]

MRS. ALVING. [Holds out her hand.] Welcome, my dear Pastor.

MANDERS. How do you do, Mrs. Alving? Here I am as I promised.

MRS. ALVING. Always punctual to the minute.

MANDERS. You may believe it was not so easy for me to get away. With all the Boards and Committees I belong to

MRS. ALVING. That makes it all the kinder of you to come so early. Now we can get through our business before dinner. But where is your portmanteau?

MANDERS. [Quickly.] I left it down at the inn. I shall sleep there to-night.

MRS. ALVING. [Suppressing a smile.] Are you really not to be persuaded, even now, to pass the night under my roof?

MANDERS. No, no, Mrs. Alving; many thanks. I shall stay at the inn, as usual. It is so conveniently near the landing-stage.

MRS. ALVING. Well, you must have your own way. But I really should have thought we two old people

MANDERS. Now you are making fun of me. Ah, you're naturally in great spirits to-day, what with to-morrow's festival and Oswald's return.

MRS. ALVING. Yes; you can think what a delight it is to me! It's more than two years since he was home last. And now he has promised to stay with me all the winter.

MANDERS. Has he really? That is very nice and dutiful of him. For I can well believe that life in Rome and Paris has very different attractions from any we can offer here.

MRS. ALVING. Ah, but here he has his mother, you see. My own darling boy, he hasn't forgotten his old mother!

MANDERS. It would be grievous indeed, if absence and absorption in art and that sort of thing were to blunt his natural feelings.

MRS. ALVING. Yes, you may well say so. But there's nothing of that sort to fear with him. I'm quite curious to see whether you know him again. He'll be down presently; he's upstairs just now, resting a little on the sofa. But do sit down, my dear Pastor.

MANDERS. Thank you. Are you quite at liberty?

MRS. ALVING. Certainly. [She sits by the table.]

MANDERS. Very well. Then let me show you [He goes to the chair where his travelling-bag lies, takes out a packet of papers, sits down on the opposite side of the table, and tries to find a clear space for the papers.] Now, to begin with, here is [Breaking off.] Tell me, Mrs. Alving, how do these books come to be here?

MRS. ALVING. These books? They are books I am reading.

MANDERS. Do you read this sort of literature?

MRS. ALVING. Certainly I do.

MANDERS. Do you feel better or happier for such reading?

MRS. ALVING. I feel, so to speak, more secure.

MANDERS. That is strange. How do you mean?

MRS. ALVING. Well, I seem to find explanation and confirmation of all sorts of things I myself have been thinking. For that is the wonderful part of it, Pastor Manders there is really nothing new in these books, nothing but what most people think and believe. Only most people either don't formulate it to themselves, or else keep quiet about it.

MANDERS. Great heavens! Do you really believe that most people?

MRS. ALVING. I do, indeed.

MANDERS. But surely not in this country? Not here among us?

MRS. ALVING. Yes, certainly; here as elsewhere.

MANDERS. Well, I really must say!

MRS. ALVING. For the rest, what do you object to in these books?

MANDERS. Object to in them? You surely do not suppose that I have nothing better to do than to study such publications as these?

MRS. ALVING. That is to say, you know nothing of what you are condemning?

MANDERS. I have read enough about these writings to disapprove of them.

MRS. ALVING. Yes; but your own judgment

MANDERS. My dear Mrs. Alving, there are many occasions in life when one must rely upon others. Things are so ordered in this world; and it is well that they are. Otherwise, what would become of society?

MRS. ALVING. Well, well, I daresay you're right there.

MANDERS. Besides, I of course do not deny that there may be much that is attractive in such books. Nor can I blame you for wishing to keep up with the intellectual movements that are said to be going on in the great world-where you have let your son pass so much of his life. But

MRS. ALVING. But?

MANDERS. [Lowering his voice.] But one should not talk about it, Mrs. Alving. One is certainly not bound to account to everybody for what one reads and thinks within one's own four walls.

MRS. ALVING. Of course not; I quite agree with you.

MANDERS. Only think, now, how you are bound to consider the interests of this Orphanage, which you decided on founding at a time when, if I understand you rightly, you thought very differently on spiritual matters.

MRS. ALVING. Oh, yes; I quite admit that. But it was about the Orphanage

MANDERS. It was about the Orphanage we were to speak; yes. All I say is: prudence, my dear lady! And now let us get to business. [Opens the packet, and takes out a number of papers.] Do you see these?

MRS. ALVING. The documents?

MANDERS. All, and in perfect order. I can tell you it was hard work to get them in time. I had to put on strong pressure. The authorities are almost morbidly scrupulous when there is any decisive step to be taken. But here they are at last. [Looks through the bundle.] See! here is the formal deed of gift of the parcel of ground known as Solvik in the Manor of Rosenvold, with all the newly constructed buildings, schoolrooms, master's house, and chapel. And here is the legal fiat for the endowment and for the Bye-laws of the Institution. Will you look at them? [Reads.] "Bye-laws for the Children's Home to be known as 'Captain Alving's Foundation.'"

MRS. ALVING. (Looks long at the paper.) So there it is.

MANDERS. I have chosen the designation "Captain" rather than "Chamberlain." "Captain" looks less pretentious.

MRS. ALVING. Oh, yes; just as you think best.

MANDERS. And here you have the Bank Account of the capital lying at interest to cover the current expenses of the Orphanage.

MRS. ALVING. Thank you; but please keep it, it will be more convenient.

MANDERS. With pleasure. I think we will leave the money in the Bank for the present. The interest is certainly not what we could wish, four per cent. and six months' notice of withdrawal. If a good mortgage could be found later on, of course it must be a first mortgage and an unimpeachable security, then we could consider the matter.

MRS. ALVING. Certainly, my dear Pastor Manders. You are the best judge in these things.

MANDERS. I will keep my eyes open at any rate. But now there is one thing more which I have several times been intending to ask you.

MRS. ALVING. And what is that?

MANDERS. Shall the Orphanage buildings be insured or not?

MRS. ALVING. Of course they must be insured.

MANDERS. Well, wait a moment, Mrs. Alving. Let us look into the matter a little more closely.

MRS. ALVING. I have everything insured; buildings and movables and stock and crops.

MANDERS. Of course you have, on your own estate. And so have I, of course. But here, you see, it is quite another matter. The Orphanage is to be consecrated, as it were, to a higher purpose.

MRS. ALVING. Yes, but that's no reason

MANDERS. For my own part, I should certainly not see the smallest impropriety in guarding against all contingencies

MRS. ALVING. No, I should think not.

MANDERS. But what is the general feeling in the neighbourhood? You, of course, know better than I.

MRS. ALVING. Well the general feeling

MANDERS. Is there any considerable number of people, really responsible people, who might be scandalised?

MRS. ALVING. What do you mean by "really responsible people"?

MANDERS. Well, I mean people in such independent and influential positions that one cannot help attaching some weight to their opinions.

MRS. ALVING. There are several people of that sort here, who would very likely be shocked if

MANDERS. There, you see! In town we have many such people. Think of all my colleague's adherents! People would be only too ready to interpret our action as a sign that neither you nor I had the right faith in a Higher Providence.

MRS. ALVING. But for your own part, my dear Pastor, you can at least tell yourself that

MANDERS. Yes, I know, I know; my conscience would be quite easy, that is true enough. But nevertheless we should not escape grave misinterpretation; and that might very likely react unfavourably upon the Orphanage.

MRS. ALVING. Well, in that case

MANDERS. Nor can I entirely lose sight of the difficult, I may even say painful, position in which I might perhaps be placed. In the leading circles of the town, people take a lively interest in this Orphanage. It is, of course, founded partly for the benefit of the town, as well; and it is to be hoped it will, to a considerable extent, result in lightening our Poor Rates. Now, as I have been your adviser, and have had the business arrangements in my hands, I cannot but fear that I may have to bear the brunt of fanaticism

MRS. ALVING. Oh, you mustn't run the risk of that.

MANDERS. To say nothing of the attacks that would assuredly be made upon me in certain papers and periodicals, which

MRS. ALVING. Enough, my dear Pastor Manders. That consideration is quite decisive.

MANDERS. Then you do not wish the Orphanage to be insured?

MRS. ALVING. No. We will let it alone.

MANDERS. [Leaning hack in his chair.] But if, now, a disaster were to happen? One can never tell. Should you be able to make good the damage?

MRS. ALVING. No; I tell you plainly I should do nothing of the kind.

MANDERS. Then I must tell you, Mrs. Alving, we are taking no small responsibility upon ourselves.

MRS. ALVING. Do you think we can do otherwise?

MANDERS. No, that is just the point; we really cannot do otherwise. We ought not to expose ourselves to misinterpretation; and we have no right whatever to give offence to the weaker brethren.

MRS. ALVING. You, as a clergyman, certainly should not.

MANDERS. I really think, too, we may trust that such an institution has fortune on its side; in fact, that it stands under a special providence.

MRS. ALVING. Let us hope so, Pastor Manders.

MANDERS. Then we will let it take its chance?

MRS. ALVING. Yes, certainly.

MANDERS. Very well. So be it. [Makes a note.] Then, no insurance.

MRS. ALVING. It's odd that you should just happen to mention the matter to-day

MANDERS. I have often thought of asking you about it

MRS. ALVING. - for we very nearly had a fire down there yesterday.

MANDERS. You don't say so!

MRS. ALVING. Oh, it was a trifling matter. A heap of shavings had caught fire in the carpenter's workshop.

MANDERS. Where Engstrand works?

MRS. ALVING. Yes. They say he's often very careless with matches.

MANDERS. He has so much on his mind, that man, so many things to fight against. Thank God, he is now striving to lead a decent life, I hear.

MRS. ALVING. Indeed! Who says so?

MANDERS. He himself assures me of it. And he is certainly a capital workman.

MRS. ALVING. Oh, yes; so long as he's sober

MANDERS. Ah, that melancholy weakness! But, a is often driven to it by his injured leg, lie says,' Last time he was in town I was really touched by him. He came and thanked me so warmly for having got him work here, so that he might be near Regina.

MRS. ALVING. He doesn't see much of her.

MANDERS. Oh, yes; he has a talk with her every day. He told me so himself.

MRS. ALVING. Well, it may be so.

MANDERS. He feels so acutely that he needs some one to keep a firm hold on him when temptation comes. That is what I cannot help liking about Jacob Engstrand: he comes to you so helplessly, accusing himself and confessing his own weakness. The last time he was talking to me. Believe me, Mrs. Alving, supposing it were a real necessity for him to have Regina home again

MRS. ALVING. [Rising hastily.] Regina!

MANDERS. - you must not set yourself against it.

MRS. ALVING. Indeed I shall set myself against it. And besides, Regina is to have a position in the Orphanage.

MANDERS. But, after all, remember he is her father

MRS. ALVING. Oh, I know very well what sort of a father he has been to her. No! She shall never go to him with my goodwill.

MANDERS. [Rising.] My dear lady, don't take the matter so warmly. You sadly misjudge poor Engstrand. You seem to be quite terrified

MRS. ALVING. [More quietly.] It makes no difference. I have taken Regina into my house, and there she shall stay. [Listens.] Hush, my dear Mr. Manders; say no more about it. [Her face lights up with gladness.] Listen! there is Oswald coming downstairs. Now we'll think of no one but him.

[OSWALD ALVING, in a light overcoat, hat in hand, and smoking a large meerschaum, enters by the door on the left; he stops in the doorway.]

OSWALD. Oh, I beg your pardon; I thought you were in the study. [Comes forward.] Good-morning, Pastor Manders.

MANDERS. [Staring.] Ah! How strange!

MRS. ALVING. Well now, what do you think of him, Mr. Manders?

MANDERS. I-I-can it really be?

OSWALD. Yes, it's really the Prodigal Son, sir.

MANDERS. [Protesting.] My dear young friend

OSWALD. Well, then, the Lost Sheep Found.

MRS. ALVING. Oswald is thinking of the time when you were so much opposed to his becoming a painter.

MANDERS. To our human eyes many a step seems dubious, which afterwards proves [Wrings his hand.] But first of all, welcome, welcome home! Do not think, my dear Oswald, I suppose I may call you by your Christian name?

OSWALD. What else should you call me?

MANDERS. Very good. What I wanted to say was this, my dear Oswald you must not think that I utterly condemn the artist's calling. I have no doubt there are many who can keep their inner self unharmed in that profession, as in any other.

OSWALD. Let us hope so.

MRS. ALVING. [Beaming with delight.] I know one who has kept both his inner and his outer self unharmed. Just look at him, Mr. Manders.

OSWALD. [Moves restlessly about the room.] Yes, yes, my dear mother; let's say no more about it.

MANDERS. Why, certainly, that is undeniable. And you have begun to make a name for yourself already. The newspapers have often spoken of you, most favourably. Just lately, by-the-bye, I fancy I haven't seen your name quite so often.

OSWALD. [Up in the conservatory.] I haven't been able to paint so much lately.

MRS. ALVING. Even a painter needs a little rest now and then.

MANDERS. No doubt, no doubt. And meanwhile he can be preparing himself and mustering his forces for some great work.

OSWALD. Yes. Mother, will dinner soon be ready?

MRS. ALVING. In less than half an hour. He has a capital appetite, thank God.

MANDERS. And a taste for tobacco, too.

OSWALD. I found my father's pipe in my room

MANDERS. Aha, then that accounts for it!

MRS. ALVING. For what?

MANDERS. When Oswald appeared there, in the doorway, with the pipe in his mouth, I could have sworn I saw his father, large as life.

OSWALD. No, really?

MRS. ALVING. Oh, how can you say so? Oswald takes after me.

MANDERS. Yes, but there is an expression about the corners of the mouth, something about the lips, that reminds one exactly of Alving: at any rate, now that he is smoking.

MRS. ALVING. Not in the least. Oswald has rather a clerical curve about his mouth, I think.

MANDERS. Yes, yes; some of my colleagues have much the same expression.

MRS. ALVING. But put your pipe away, my dear boy; I won't have smoking in here.

OSWALD. [Does so.] By all means. I only wanted to try it; for I once smoked it when I was a child.

MRS. ALVING. You?

OSWALD. Yes. I was quite small at the time. I recollect I came up to father's room one evening when he was in great spirits.

MRS. ALVING. Oh, you can't recollect anything of those times.

OSWALD. Yes, I recollect it distinctly. He took me on his knee, and gave me the pipe. "Smoke, boy," he said; "smoke away, boy!" And I smoked as hard as I could, until I felt I was growing quite pale, and the perspiration stood in great drops on my forehead. Then he burst out laughing heartily

MANDERS. That was most extraordinary.

MRS. ALVING. My dear friend, it's only something Oswald has dreamt.

OSWALD. No, mother, I assure you I didn't dream it. For, don't you remember this? you came and carried me out into the nursery. Then I was sick, and I saw that you were crying. Did father often play such practical jokes?

MANDERS. In his youth he overflowed with the joy of life

OSWALD. And yet he managed to do so much in the world; so much that was good and useful; although he died so early.

MANDERS. Yes, you have inherited the name of an energetic and admirable man, my dear Oswald Alving. No doubt it will be an incentive to you

OSWALD. It ought to, indeed.

MANDERS. It was good of you to come home for the ceremony in his honour.

OSWALD. I could do no less for my father.

MRS. ALVING. And I am to keep him so long! That is the best of all.

MANDERS. You are going to pass the winter at home, I hear.

OSWALD. My stay is indefinite, sir. But, ah! it is good to be at home!

MRS. ALVING. [Beaming.] Yes, isn't it, dear?

MANDERS. [Looking sympathetically at him.] You went out into the world early, my dear Oswald.

OSWALD. I did. I sometimes wonder whether it wasn't too early.

MRS. ALVING. Oh, not at all. A healthy lad is all the better for it; especially when he's an only child. He oughtn't to hang on at home with his mother and father, and get spoilt.

MANDERS. That is a very disputable point, Mrs. Alving. A child's proper place is, and must be, the home of his fathers.

OSWALD. There I quite agree with you, Pastor Manders.

MANDERS. Only look at your own son, there is no reason why we should not say it in his presence, what has the consequence been for him? He is six or seven and twenty, and has never had the opportunity of learning what a well-ordered home really is.

OSWALD. I beg your pardon, Pastor; there you're quite mistaken.

MANDERS. Indeed? I thought you had lived almost exclusively in artistic circles.

OSWALD. So I have.

MANDERS. And chiefly among the younger artists?

OSWALD. Yes, certainly.

MANDERS. But I thought few of those young fellows could afford to set up house and support a family.

OSWALD. There are many who cannot afford to marry, sir.

MANDERS. Yes, that is just what I say.

OSWALD. But they may have a home for all that. And several of them have, as a matter of fact; and very pleasant, well-ordered homes they are, too.

[MRS. ALVING follows with breathless interest; nods, but says nothing.]

MANDERS. But I'm not talking of bachelors' quarters. By a "home" I understand the home of a family, where a man lives with his wife and children.

OSWALD. Yes; or with his children and his children's mother.

MANDERS. [Starts; clasps his hands.] But, good heavens

OSWALD. Well?

MANDERS. Lives with his children's mother!

OSWALD. Yes. Would you have him turn his children's mother out of doors?

MANDERS. Then it is illicit relations you are talking of! Irregular marriages, as people call them!

OSWALD. I have never noticed anything particularly irregular about the life these people lead.

MANDERS. But how is it possible that a, a young man or young woman with any decency of feeling can endure to live in that way? in the eyes of all the world!

OSWALD. What are they to do? A poor young artist, a poor girl, marriage costs a great deal. What are they to do?

MANDERS. What are they to do? Let me tell you, Mr. Alving, what they ought to do. They ought to exercise self-restraint from the first; that is what they ought to do.

OSWALD. That doctrine will scarcely go down with warm-blooded young people who love each other.

MRS. ALVING. No, scarcely!

MANDERS. [Continuing.] How can the authorities tolerate such things! Allow them to go on in the light of day! [Confronting MRS. ALVING.] Had I not cause to be deeply concerned about your son? In circles where open immorality prevails, and has even a sort of recognised position!

OSWALD. Let me tell you, sir, that I have been in the habit of spending nearly all my Sundays in one or two such irregular homes

MANDERS. Sunday of all days!

OSWALD. Isn't that the day to enjoy one's self? Well, never have I heard an offensive word, and still less have I witnessed anything that could be called immoral. No; do you know when and where I have come across immorality in artistic circles?

MANDERS. No, thank heaven, I don't!

OSWALD. Well, then, allow me to inform you. I have met with it when one or other of our pattern husbands and fathers has come to Paris to have a look round on his own account, and has done the artists the honour of visiting their humble haunts. They knew what was what. These gentlemen could tell us all about places and things we had never dreamt of.

MANDERS. What! Do you mean to say that respectable men from home here would?

OSWALD. Have you never heard these respectable men, when they got home again, talking about the way in which immorality runs rampant abroad?

MANDERS. Yes, no doubt

MRS. ALVING. I have too.

OSWALD. Well, you may take their word for it. They know what they are talking about! [Presses has hands to his head.] Oh! that that great, free, glorious life out there should be defiled in such a way!

MRS. ALVING. You mustn't get excited, Oswald. It's not good for you.

OSWALD. Yes; you're quite right, mother. It's bad for me, I know. You see, I'm wretchedly worn out. I shall go for a little turn before dinner. Excuse me, Pastor: I know you can't take my point of view; but I couldn't help speaking out. [He goes out by the second door to the right.]

MRS. ALVING. My poor boy!

MANDERS. You may well say so. Then this is what he has come to!

[MRS. ALVING looks at him silently.]

MANDERS. [Walking up and down.] He called himself the Prodigal Son. Alas! alas!

[MRS. ALVING continues looking at him.]

MANDERS. And what do you say to all this?

MRS. ALVING. I say that Oswald was right in every word.

MANDERS. [Stands still.] Right? Right! In such principles?

MRS. ALVING. Here, in my loneliness, I have come to the same way of thinking, Pastor Manders. But I have never dared to say anything. Well! now my boy shall speak for me.

MANDERS. You are greatly to be pitied, Mrs. Alving. But now I must speak seriously to you. And now it is no longer your business manager and adviser, your own and your husband's early friend, who stands before you. It is the priest, the priest who stood before you in the moment of your life when you had gone farthest astray.

MRS. ALVING. And what has the priest to say to me?

MANDERS. I will first stir up your memory a little. The moment is well chosen. To-morrow will be the tenth anniversary of your husband's death. To-morrow the memorial in his honour will be unveiled. To-morrow I shall have to speak to the whole assembled multitude. But to-day I will speak to you alone.

MRS. ALVING. Very well, Pastor Manders. Speak.

MANDERS. Do you remember that after less than a year of married life you stood on the verge of an abyss? That you forsook your house and home? That you fled from your husband? Yes, Mrs. Alving fled, fled, and refused to return to him, however much he begged and prayed you?

MRS. ALVING. Have you forgotten how infinitely miserable I was in that first year?

MANDERS. It is the very mark of the spirit of rebellion to crave for happiness in this life. What right have we human beings to happiness? We have simply to do our duty, Mrs. Alving! And your duty was to hold firmly to the man you had once chosen, and to whom you were bound by the holiest ties.

MRS. ALVING. You know very well what sort of life Alving was leading, what excesses he was guilty of.

MANDERS. I know very well what rumours there were about him; and I am the last to approve the life he led in his young days, if report did not wrong him. But a wife is not appointed to be her husband's judge. It was your duty to bear with humility the cross which a Higher Power had, in its wisdom, laid upon you. But instead of that you rebelliously throw away the cross, desert the backslider whom you should have supported, go and risk your good name and reputation, and nearly succeed in ruining other people's reputation into the bargain.

MRS. ALVING. Other people's? One other person's, you mean.

MANDERS. It was incredibly reckless of you to seek refuge with me.

MRS. ALVING. With our clergyman? With our intimate friend?

MANDERS. Just on that account. Yes, you may thank God that I possessed the necessary firmness; that I succeeded in dissuading you from your wild designs; and that it was vouchsafed me to lead you back to the path of duty, and home to your lawful husband.

MRS. ALVING. Yes, Pastor Manders, that was certainly your work.

MANDERS. I was but a poor instrument in a Higher Hand. And what a blessing has it not proved to you, all the days of your life, that I induced you to resume the yoke of duty and obedience! Did not everything happen as I foretold? Did not Alving turn his back on his errors, as a man should? Did he not live with you from that time, lovingly and blamelessly, all his days? Did he not become a benefactor to the whole district? And did he not help you to rise to his own level, so that you, little by little, became his assistant in all his undertakings? And a capital assistant, too, oh, I know, Mrs. Alving, that praise is due to you. But now I come to the next great error in your life.

MRS. ALVING. What do you mean?

MANDERS. Just as you once disowned a wife's duty, so you have since disowned a mother's.

MRS. ALVING. Ah -!

MANDERS. You have been all your life under the dominion of a pestilent spirit of self-will. The whole bias of your mind has been towards insubordination and lawlessness. You have never known how to endure any bond. Everything that has weighed upon you in life you have cast away without care or conscience, like a burden you were free to throw off at will. It did not please you to be a wife any longer, and you left your husband. You found it troublesome to be a mother, and you sent your child forth among strangers.

MRS. ALVING. Yes, that is true. I did so.

MANDERS. And thus you have become a stranger to him.

MRS. ALVING. No! no! I am not.

MANDERS. Yes, you are; you must be. And in what state of mind has he returned to you? Bethink yourself well, Mrs. Alving. You sinned greatly against your husband; that you recognise by raising yonder memorial to him. Recognise now, also, how you have sinned against your son, there may yet be time to lead him back from the paths of error. Turn back yourself, and save what may yet be saved in him. For [With uplifted forefinger] verily, Mrs. Alving, you are a guilt-laden mother! This I have thought it my duty to say to you.

[Silence.]

MRS. ALVING. [Slowly and with self-control.] You have now spoken out, Pastor Manders; and to-morrow you are to speak publicly in memory of my husband. I shall not speak to-morrow. But now I will speak frankly to you, as you have spoken to me.

MANDERS. To be sure; you will plead excuses for your conduct

MRS. ALVING. No. I will only tell you a story.

MANDERS. Well?

MRS. ALVING. All that you have just said about my husband and me, and our life after you had brought me back to the path of duty, as you called it, about all that you know nothing from personal observation. From that moment you, who had been our intimate friend, never set foot in our house gain.

MANDERS. You and your husband left the town immediately after.

MRS. ALVING. Yes; and in my husband's lifetime you never came to see us. It was business that forced you to visit me when you undertook the affairs of the Orphanage.

MANDERS. [Softly and hesitatingly.] Helen, if that is meant as a reproach, I would beg you to bear in mind

MRS. ALVING. - the regard you owed to your position, yes; and that I was a runaway wife. One can never be too cautious with such unprincipled creatures.

MANDERS. My dear Mrs. Alving, you know that is an absurd exaggeration

MRS. ALVING. Well well, suppose it is. My point is that your judgment as to my married life is founded upon nothing but common knowledge and report.

MANDERS. I admit that. What then?

MRS. ALVING. Well, then, Pastor Manders I will tell you the truth. I have sworn to myself that one day you should know it, you alone!

MANDERS. What is the truth, then?

MRS. ALVING. The truth is that my husband died just as dissolute as he had lived all his days.

MANDERS. [Feeling after a chair.] What do you say?

MRS. ALVING. After nineteen years of marriage, as dissolute, in his desires at any rate, as he was before you married us.

MANDERS. And those-those wild oats, those irregularities, those excesses, if you like, you call "a dissolute life"?

MRS. ALVING. Our doctor used the expression.

MANDERS. I do not understand you.

MRS. ALVING. You need not.

MANDERS. It almost makes me dizzy. Your whole married life, the seeming union of all these years, was nothing more than a hidden abyss!

MRS. ALVING. Neither more nor less. Now you know it.

MANDERS. This is, this is inconceivable to me. I cannot grasp it! I cannot realise it! But how was it possible to? How could such a state of things be kept secret?

MRS. ALVING. That has been my ceaseless struggle, day after day. After Oswald's birth, I thought Alving seemed to be a little better. But it did not last long. And then I had to struggle twice as hard, fighting as though for life or death, so that nobody should know what sort of man my child's father was. And you know what power Alving had of winning people's hearts. Nobody seemed able to believe anything but good of him. He was one of those people whose life does not bite upon their reputation. But at last, Mr. Manders, for you must know the whole story, the most repulsive thing of all happened.

MANDERS. More repulsive than what you have told me?

MRS. ALVING. I had gone on bearing with him, although I knew very well the secrets of his life out of doors. But when he brought the scandal within our own walls

MANDERS. Impossible! Here!

MRS. ALVING. Yes; here in our own home. It was there [Pointing towards the first door on the right], in the dining-room, that I first came to know of it. I was busy with something in there, and the door was standing ajar. I heard our housemaid come up from the garden, with water for those flowers.

MANDERS. Well?

MRS. ALVING. Soon after, I heard Alving come in too. I heard him say something softly to her. And then I heard [With a short laugh] oh! it still sounds in my ears, so hateful and yet so ludicrous, I heard my own servant-maid whisper, "Let me go, Mr. Alving! Let me be!"

MANDERS. What unseemly levity on his part'! But it cannot have been more than levity, Mrs. Alving; believe me, it cannot.

MRS. ALVING. I soon knew what to believe. Mr. Alving had his way with the girl; and that connection had consequences, Mr. Manders.

MANDERS. [As though petrified.] Such things in this house, in this house!

MRS. ALVING. I had borne a great deal in this house. To keep him at home in the evenings, and at night, I had to make myself his boon companion in his secret orgies up in his room. There I have had to sit alone with him, to clink glasses and drink with him, and to listen to his ribald, silly talk. I have had to fight with him to get him dragged to bed

MANDERS. [Moved.] And you were able to bear all this!

MRS. ALVING. I had to bear it for my little boy's sake. But when the last insult was added; when my own servant-maid; then I swore to myself: This shall come to an end! And so I took the reins into my own hand, the whole control, over him and everything else. For now I had a weapon against him, you see; he dared not oppose me. It was then I sent Oswald away from home. He was nearly seven years old, and was beginning to observe and ask questions, as children do. That I could not bear. It seemed to me the child must be poisoned by merely breathing the air of this polluted home. That was why I sent him away. And now you can see, too, why he was never allowed to set foot inside his home so long as his father lived. No one knows what that cost me.

MANDERS. You have indeed had a life of trial.

MRS. ALVING. I could never have borne it if I had not had my work. For I may truly say that I have worked! All the additions to the estate, all the improvements, all the labour-saving appliances, that Alving was so much praised for having introduced, do you suppose he had energy for anything of the sort? he, who lay all day on the sofa, reading an old Court Guide! No; but I may tell you this too: when he had his better intervals, it was I who urged him on; it was I who had to drag the whole load when he relapsed into his evil ways, or sank into querulous wretchedness.

MANDERS. And it is to this man that you raise a memorial?

MRS. ALVING. There you see the power of an evil conscience.

MANDERS. Evil? What do you mean?

MRS. ALVING. It always seemed to me impossible but that the truth must come out and be believed. So the Orphanage was to deaden all rumours and set every doubt at rest.

MANDERS. In that you have certainly not missed your aim, Mrs. Alving.

MRS. ALVING. And besides, I had one other reason. I was determined that Oswald, my own boy, should inherit nothing whatever from his father.

MANDERS. Then it is Alving's fortune that?

MRS. ALVING. Yes. The sums I have spent upon the Orphanage, year by year, make up the amount, I have reckoned it up precisely, the amount which made Lieutenant Alving "a good match" in his day.

MANDERS. I don't understand

MRS. ALVING. It was my purchase-money. I do not choose that that money should pass into Oswald's hands. My son shall have everything from me, everything.

[OSWALD ALVING enters through the second door to the right; he has taken of his hat and overcoat in the hall.]

MRS. ALVING. [Going towards him.] Are you back again already? My dear, dear boy!

OSWALD. Yes. What can a fellow do out of doors in this eternal rain? But I hear dinner is ready. That's capital!

REGINA. [With a parcel, from the dining-room.] A parcel has come for you, Mrs. Alving. [Hands it to her.]

MRS. ALVING. [With a glance at MR. MANDERS.] No doubt copies of the ode for to-morrow's ceremony.

MANDERS. H'm

REGINA. And dinner is ready.

MRS. ALVING. Very well. We will come directly. I will just [Begins to open the parcel.]

REGINA. [To OSWALD.] Would Mr. Alving like red or white wine?

OSWALD. Both, if you please.

REGINA. Bien. Very well, sir. [She goes into the dining-room.]

OSWALD. I may as well help to uncork it. [He also goes into the dining room, the door of which swings half open behind him.]

MRS. ALVING. [Who has opened the parcel.] Yes, I thought so. Here is the Ceremonial Ode, Pastor Manders.

MANDERS. [With folded hands.] With what countenance I am to deliver my discourse to-morrow!

MRS. ALVING. Oh, you will get through it somehow.

MANDERS. [Softly, so as not to be heard in the dining-room.] Yes; it would not do to provoke scandal.

MRS. ALVING. [Under her breath, but firmly.] No. But then this long, hateful comedy will be ended. From the day after to-morrow, I shall act in every way as though he who is dead had never lived in this house. There shall be no one here but my boy and his mother.

[From the dining-room comes the noise of a chair overturned, and at the same moment is heard:]

REGINA. [Sharply, but in a whisper.] Oswald! take care! are you mad? Let me go!

MRS. ALVING. [Starts in terror.] Ah!

[She stares wildly towards the half-open door. OSWALD is heard laughing and humming. A bottle is uncorked.]

MANDERS. [Agitated.] What can be the matter? What is it, Mrs. Alving?

MRS. ALVING. [Hoarsely.] Ghosts! The couple from the conservatory risen again!

MANDERS. Is it possible! Regina? Is she?

MRS. ALVING. Yes. Come. Not a word!

[She seizes PASTOR MANDERS by the arm, and walks unsteadily towards the dining-room.]

ACT SECOND.

[The same room. The mist still lies heavy over the landscape.]

[MANDERS and MRS. ALVING enter from the dining-room.]

MRS. ALVING. [Still in the doorway.] Velbekomme [Note: A phrase equivalent to the German Prosit die Mahlzeit. May good digestion wait on appetite.], Mr. Manders. [Turns back towards the dining-room.] Aren't you coming too, Oswald?

OSWALD. [From within.] No, thank you. I think I shall go out a little.

MRS. ALVING. Yes, do. The weather seems a little brighter now. [She shuts the dining-room door, goes to the hall door, and calls:] Regina!

REGINA. [Outside.] Yes, Mrs. Alving?

MRS. ALVING. Go down to the laundry, and help with the garlands.

REGINA. Yes, Mrs. Alving.

[MRS. ALVING assures herself that REGINA goes; then shuts the door.]

MANDERS. I suppose he cannot overhear us in there?

MRS. ALVING. Not when the door is shut. Besides, he's just going out.

MANDERS. I am still quite upset. I don't know how I could swallow a morsel of dinner.

MRS. ALVING. [Controlling her nervousness, walks up and down.] Nor I. But what is to be done now?

MANDERS. Yes; what is to be done? I am really quite at a loss. I am so utterly without experience in matters of this sort.

MRS. ALVING. I feel sure that, so far, no mischief has been done.

MANDERS. No; heaven forbid! But it is an unseemly state of things, nevertheless.

MRS. ALVING. It is only an idle fancy on Oswald's part; you may be sure of that.

MANDERS. Well, as I say, I am not accustomed to affairs of the kind. But I should certainly think

MRS. ALVING. Out of the house she must go, and that immediately. That is as clear as daylight

MANDERS. Yes, of course she must.

MRS. ALVING. But where to? It would not be right to

MANDERS. Where to? Home to her father, of course.

MRS. ALVING. To whom did you say?

MANDERS. To her. But then, Engstrand is not? Good God, Mrs. Alving, it's impossible! You must be mistaken after all.

MRS. ALVING. Unfortunately there is no possibility of mistake. Johanna confessed everything to me; and Alving could not deny it. So there was nothing to be done but to get the matter hushed up.

MANDERS. No, you could do nothing else.

MRS. ALVING. The girl left our service at once, and got a good sum of money to hold her tongue for the time. The rest she managed for herself when she got to town. She renewed her old acquaintance with Engstrand, no doubt let him see that she had money in her purse, and told him some tale about a foreigner who put in here with a yacht that summer. So she and Engstrand got married in hot haste. Why, you married them yourself.

MANDERS. But then how to account for? I recollect distinctly Engstrand coming to give notice of the marriage. He was quite overwhelmed with contrition, and bitterly reproached himself for the misbehaviour he and his sweetheart had been guilty of.

MRS. ALVING. Yes; of course he had to take the blame upon himself.

MANDERS. But such a piece of duplicity on his part! And towards me too! I never could have believed it of Jacob Engstrand. I shall not fail to take him seriously to task; he may be sure of that. And then the immorality of such a connection! For money! How much did the girl receive?

MRS. ALVING. Three hundred dollars.

MANDERS. Just think of it, for a miserable three hundred dollars, to go and marry a fallen woman!

MRS. ALVING. Then what have you to say of me? I went and married a fallen man.

MANDERS. Why, good heavens! what are you talking about! A fallen man!

MRS. ALVING. Do you think Alving was any purer when I went with him to the altar than Johanna was when Engstrand married her?

MANDERS. Well, but there is a world of difference between the two cases

MRS. ALVING. Not so much difference after all except in the price:- a miserable three hundred dollars and a whole fortune.

MANDERS. How can you compare such absolutely dissimilar cases? You had taken counsel with your own heart and with your natural advisers.

MRS. ALVING. [Without looking at him.] I thought you understood where what you call my heart had strayed to at the time.

MANDERS. [Distantly.] Had I understood anything of the kind, I should not have been a daily guest in your husband's house.

MRS. ALVING. At any rate, the fact remains that with myself I took no counsel whatever.

MANDERS. Well then, with your nearest relatives, as your duty bade you, with your mother and your two aunts.

MRS. ALVING. Yes, that is true. Those three cast up the account for me. Oh, it's marvellous how clearly they made out that it would be downright madness to refuse such an offer. If mother could only see me now, and know what all that grandeur has come to!

MANDERS. Nobody can be held responsible for the result. This, at least, remains clear: your marriage was in full accordance with law and order.

MRS. ALVING. [At the window.] Oh, that perpetual law and order! I often think that is what does all the mischief in this world of ours.

MANDERS. Mrs. Alving, that is a sinful way of talking.

MRS. ALVING. Well, I can't help it; I must have done with all this constraint and insincerity. I can endure it no longer. I must work my way out to freedom.

MANDERS. What do you mean by that?

MRS. ALVING. [Drumming on the window frame.] I ought never to have concealed the facts of Alving's life. But at that time I dared not do anything else-I was afraid, partly on my own account. I was such a coward.

MANDERS. A coward?

MRS. ALVING. If people had come to know anything, they would have said "Poor man! with a runaway wife, no wonder he kicks over the traces."

MANDERS. Such remarks might have been made with a certain show of right.

MRS. ALVING. [Looking steadily at him.] If I were what I ought to be, I should go to Oswald and say, "Listen, my boy: your father led a vicious life"

MANDERS. Merciful heavens!

MRS. ALVING. - and then I should tell him all I have told you, every word of it.

MANDERS. You shock me unspeakably, Mrs. Alving.

MRS. ALVING. Yes; I know that. I know that very well. I myself am shocked at the idea. [Goes away from the window.] I am such a coward.

MANDERS. You call it "cowardice" to do your plain duty? Have you forgotten that a son ought to love and honour his father and mother?

MRS. ALVING. Do not let us talk in such general terms. Let us ask: Ought Oswald to love and honour Chamberlain Alving?

MANDERS. Is there no voice in your mother's heart that forbids you to destroy your son's ideals?

MRS. ALVING. But what about the truth?

MANDERS. But what about the ideals?

MRS. ALVING. Oh, ideals, ideals! If only I were not such a coward!

MANDERS. Do not despise ideals, Mrs. Alving; they will avenge themselves cruelly. Take Oswald's case: he, unfortunately, seems to have few enough ideals as it is; but I can see that his father stands before him as an ideal.

MRS. ALVING. Yes, that is true.

MANDERS. And this habit of mind you have yourself implanted and fostered by your letters.

MRS. ALVING. Yes; in my superstitious awe for duty and the proprieties, I lied to my boy, year after year. Oh, what a coward, what a coward I have been!

MANDERS. You have established a happy illusion in your son's heart, Mrs. Alving; and assuredly you ought not to undervalue it.

MRS. ALVING. H'm; who knows whether it is so happy after all? But, at any rate, I will not have any tampering wide Regina. He shall not go and wreck the poor girl's life.

MANDERS. No; good God, that would be terrible!

MRS. ALVING. If I knew he was in earnest, and that it would be for his happiness

MANDERS. What? What then?

MRS. ALVING. But it couldn't be; for unfortunately Regina is not the right sort of woman.

MANDERS. Well, what then? What do you mean?

MRS. ALVING. If I weren't such a pitiful coward, I should say to him, "Marry her, or make what arrangement you please, only let us have nothing underhand about it."

MANDERS. Merciful heavens, would you let them marry! Anything so dreadful, ! so unheard of

MRS. ALVING. Do you really mean "unheard of"? Frankly, Pastor Manders, do you suppose that throughout the country there are not plenty of married couples as closely akin as they?

MANDERS. I don't in the least understand you.

MRS. ALVING. Oh yes, indeed you do.

MANDERS. Ah, you are thinking of the possibility that Alas! yes, family life is certainly not always so pure as it ought to be. But in such a case as you point to, one can never know, at least with any certainty. Here, on the other hand that you, a mother, can think of letting your son

MRS. ALVING. But I cannot, I wouldn't for anything in the world; that is precisely what I am saying.

MANDERS. No, because you are a "coward," as you put it. But if you were not a "coward," then? Good God! a connection so shocking!

MRS. ALVING. So far as that goes, they say we are all sprung from connections of that sort. And who is it that arranged the world so, Pastor Manders?

MANDERS. Questions of that kind I must decline to discuss with you, Mrs. Alving; you are far from being in the right frame of mind for them. But that you dare to call your scruples "cowardly"!

MRS. ALVING. Let me tell you what I mean. I am timid and faint-hearted because of the ghosts that hang about me, and that I can never quite shake off.

MANDERS. What do you say hangs about you?

MRS. ALVING. Ghosts! When I heard Regina and Oswald in there, it was as though ghosts rose up before me. But I almost think we are all of us ghosts, Pastor Manders. It is not only what we have inherited from our father and mother that "walks" in us. It is all sorts of dead ideas, and lifeless old beliefs, and so forth. They have no vitality, but they cling to us all the same, and we cannot shake them off. Whenever I take up a newspaper, I seem to see ghosts gliding between the lines. There must be ghosts all the country over, as thick as the sands of the sea. And then we are, one and all, so pitifully afraid of the light.

MANDERS. Aha, here we have the fruits of your reading. And pretty fruits they are, upon my word! Oh, those horrible, revolutionary, free-thinking books!

MRS. ALVING. You are mistaken, my dear Pastor. It was you yourself who set me thinking; and I thank you for it with all my heart.

MANDERS. I!

MRS. ALVING. Yes, when you forced me under the yoke of what you called duty and obligation; when you lauded as right and proper what my whole soul rebelled against as something loathsome. It was then that I began to look into the seams of your doctrines. I wanted only to pick at a single knot; but when I had got that undone, the whole thing ravelled out. And then I understood that it was all machine-sewn.

MANDERS. [Softly, with emotion.] And was that the upshot of my life's hardest battle?

MRS. ALVING. Call it rather your most pitiful defeat.

MANDERS. It was my greatest victory, Helen, the victory over myself.

MRS. ALVING. It was a crime against us both.

MANDERS. When you went astray, and came to me crying, "Here I am; take me!" I commanded you, saying, "Woman, go home to your lawful husband." Was that a crime?

MRS. ALVING. Yes, I think so.

MANDERS. We two do not understand each other.

MRS. ALVING. Not now, at any rate.

MANDERS. Never, never in my most secret thoughts have I regarded you otherwise than as another's wife.

MRS. ALVING. Oh, indeed?

MANDERS. Helen!

MRS. ALVING. People so easily forget their past selves.

MANDERS. I do not. I am what I always was.

MRS. ALVING. [Changing the subject.] Well well well; don't let us talk of old times any longer. You are now over head and ears in Boards and Committees, and I am fighting my battle with ghosts, both within me and without.

MANDERS. Those without I shall help you to lay. After all the terrible things I have heard from you today, I cannot in conscience permit an unprotected girl to remain in your house.

MRS. ALVING. Don't you think the best plan would be to get her provided for? I mean, by a good marriage.

MANDERS. No doubt. I think it would be desirable for her in every respect. Regina is now at the age when...Of course I don't know much about these things, but

MRS. ALVING. Regina matured very early.

MANDERS. Yes, I thought so. I have an impression that she was remarkably well developed, physically, when I prepared her for confirmation. But in the meantime, she ought to be at home, under her father's eye. Ah! but Engstrand is not. That he, that he could so hide the truth from me! [A knock at the door into the hall.]

MRS. ALVING. Who can this be? Come in!

ENGSTRAND. [In his Sunday clothes, in the doorway.] I humbly beg your pardon, but

MANDERS. Aha! H'm

MRS. ALVING. Is that you, Engstrand?

ENGSTRAND. - there was none of the servants about, so I took the great liberty of just knocking.

MRS. ALVING. Oh, very well. Come in. Do you want to speak to me?

ENGSTRAND. [Comes in.] No, I'm obliged to you, ma'am; it was with his Reverence I wanted to have a word or two.

MANDERS. [Walking up and down the room.] Ah, indeed! You want to speak to me, do you?

ENGSTRAND. Yes, I'd like so terribly much to

MANDERS. [Stops in front of him.] Well; may I ask what you want?

ENGSTRAND. Well, it was just this, your Reverence: we've been paid off down yonder, my grateful thanks to you, ma'am, and now everything's finished, I've been thinking it would be but right and proper if we, that have been working so honestly together all this time well, I was thinking we ought to end up with a little prayer-meeting to-night.

MANDERS. A prayer-meeting? Down at the Orphanage?

ENGSTRAND. Oh, if your Reverence doesn't think it proper

MANDERS. Oh yes, I do; but, h'm

ENGSTRAND. I've been in the habit of offering up a little prayer in the evenings, myself

MRS. ALVING. Have you?

ENGSTRAND. Yes, every now and then just a little edification, in a manner of speaking. But I'm a poor, common man, and have little enough gift, God help me! and so I thought, as the Reverend Mr. Manders happened to be here, I'd

MANDERS. Well, you see, Engstrand, I have a question to put to you first. Are you in the right frame of mind for such a meeting! Do you feel your conscience clear and at ease?

ENGSTRAND. Oh, God help us, your Reverence! we'd better not talk about conscience.

MANDERS. Yes, that is just what we must talk about. What have you to answer?

ENGSTRAND. Why, a man's conscience, it can be bad enough now and then.

MANDERS. Ah, you admit that. Then perhaps you will make a clean breast of it, and tell me the real truth about Regina?

MRS. ALVING. [Quickly.] Mr. Manders!

MANDERS. [Reassuringly.] Please allow me

ENGSTRAND. About Regina! Lord, what a turn you gave me! [Looks at MRS. ALVING.] There's nothing wrong about Regina, is there?

MANDERS. We will hope not. But I mean, what is the truth about you and Regina? You pass for her father, eh!

ENGSTRAND. [Uncertain.] Well, h'm, your Reverence knows all about me and poor Johanna.

MANDERS. Come now, no more prevarication! Your wife told Mrs. Alving the whole story before quitting her service.

ENGSTRAND. Well, then, may! Now, did she really?

MANDERS. You see we know you now, Engstrand.

ENGSTRAND. And she swore and took her Bible oath

MANDERS. Did she take her Bible oath?

ENGSTRAND. No; she only swore; but she did it that solemn-like.

MANDERS. And you have hidden the truth from me all these years? Hidden it from me, who have trusted you without reserve, in everything.

ENGSTRAND. Well, I can't deny it.

MANDERS. Have I deserved this of you, Engstrand? Have I not always been ready to help you in word and deed, so far as it lay in my power? Answer me. Have I not?

ENGSTRAND. It would have been a poor look-out for me many a time but for the Reverend Mr. Manders.

MANDERS. And this is how you reward me! You cause me to enter falsehoods in the Church Register, and you withhold from me, year after year, the explanations you owed alike to me and to the truth. Your conduct has been wholly inexcusable, Engstrand; and from this time forward I have done with you!

ENGSTRAND. [With a sigh.] Yes! I suppose there's no help for it.

MANDERS. How can you possibly justify yourself?

ENGSTRAND. Who could ever have thought she'd have gone and made bad worse by talking about it? Will your Reverence just fancy yourself in the same trouble as poor Johanna

MANDERS. I!

ENGSTRAND. Lord bless you, I don't mean just exactly the same. But I mean, if your Reverence had anything to be ashamed of in the eyes of the world, as the saying goes. We menfolk oughtn't to judge a poor woman too hardly, your Reverence.

MANDERS. I am not doing so. It is you I am reproaching.

ENGSTRAND. Might I make so bold as to ask your Reverence a bit of a question?

MANDERS. Yes, if you want to.

ENGSTRAND. Isn't it right and proper for a man to raise up the fallen?

MANDERS. Most certainly it is.

ENGSTRAND. And isn't a man bound to keep his sacred word?

MANDERS. Why, of course he is; but

ENGSTRAND. When Johanna had got into trouble through that Englishman or it might have been an American or a Russian, as they call them, well, you see, she came down into the town. Poor thing, she'd sent me about my business once or twice before: for she couldn't bear the sight of anything as wasn't handsome; and I'd got this damaged leg of mine. Your Reverence recollects how I ventured up into a dancing saloon, where seafaring men was carrying on with drink and devilry, as the saying goes. And then, when I was for giving them a bit of an admonition to lead a new life

MRS. ALVING. [At the window.] H'm

MANDERS. I know all about that, Engstrand; the ruffians threw you downstairs. You have told me of the affair already. Your infirmity is an honour to you.

ENGSTRAND. I'm not puffed up about it, your Reverence. But what I wanted to say was, that when she cane and confessed all to me, with weeping and gnashing of teeth, I can tell your Reverence I was sore at heart to hear it.

MANDERS. Were you indeed, Engstrand? Well, go on.

ENGSTRAND. So I says to her, "The American, he's sailing about on the boundless sea. And as for you, Johanna," says I, "you've committed a grievous sin, and you're a fallen creature. But Jacob Engstrand," says I, "he's got two good legs to stand upon, he has" You see, your Reverence, I was speaking figurative-like.

MANDERS. I understand quite well. Go on.

ENGSTRAND. Well, that was how I raised her up and made an honest woman of her, so as folks shouldn't get to know how as she'd gone astray with foreigners.

MANDERS. In all that you acted very well. Only I cannot approve of your stooping to take money

ENGSTRAND. Money? I? Not a farthing!

MANDERS. [Inquiringly to MRS. ALVING.] But

ENGSTRAND. Oh, wait a minute! now I recollect. Johanna did have a trifle of money. But I would have nothing to do with that. "No," says I, "that's mammon; that's the wages of sin. This dirty gold, or notes, or whatever it was, we'll just flint, that back in the American's face," says I. But he was off and away, over the stormy sea, your Reverence.

MANDERS. Was he really, my good fellow?

ENGSTRAND. He was indeed, sir. So Johanna and I, we agreed that the money should go to the child's education; and so it did, and I can account for every blessed farthing of it.

MANDERS. Why, this alters the case considerably.

ENGSTRAND. That's just how it stands, your Reverence. And I make so bold as to say as I've been an honest father to Regina, so far as my poor strength went; for I'm but a weak vessel, worse luck!

MANDERS. Well, well, my good fellow

ENGSTRAND. All the same, I bear myself witness as I've brought up the child, and lived kindly with poor Johanna, and ruled over my own house, as the Scripture has it. But it couldn't never enter my head to go to your Reverence and puff myself up and boast because even the likes of me had done some good in the world. No, sir; when anything of that sort happens to Jacob Engstrand, he holds his tongue about it. It don't happen so terrible often, I daresay. And when I do come to see your Reverence, I find a mortal deal that's wicked and weak to talk about. For I said it before, and I says it again, a man's conscience isn't always as clean as it might be.

MANDERS. Give me your hand, Jacob Engstrand.

ENGSTRAND. Oh, Lord! your Reverence

MANDERS. Come, no nonsense [wrings his hand]. There we are!

ENGSTRAND. And if I might humbly beg your Reverence's pardon

MANDERS. You? On the contrary, it is I who ought to beg your pardon

ENGSTRAND. Lord, no, Sir!

MANDERS. Yes, assuredly. And I do it with all my heart. Forgive me for misunderstanding you. I only wish I could give you some proof of my hearty regret, and of my good-will towards you

ENGSTRAND. Would your Reverence do it?

MANDERS. With the greatest pleasure.

ENGSTRAND. Well then, here's the very chance. With the bit of money I've saved here, I was thinking I might set up a Sailors' Home down in the town.

MRS. ALVING. You?

ENGSTRAND. Yes; it might be a sort of Orphanage, too, in a manner of speaking. There's such a many temptations for seafaring folk ashore. But in this Home of mine, a man might feel like as he was under a father's eye, I was thinking.

MANDERS. What do you say to this, Mrs. Alving?

ENGSTRAND. It isn't much as I've got to start with, Lord help me! But if I could only find a helping hand, why

MANDERS. Yes, yes; we will look into the matter more closely. I entirely approve of your plan. But now, go before me and make everything ready, and get the candles lighted, so as to give the place an air of festivity. And then we will pass an edifying hour together, my good fellow; for now I quite believe you are in the right frame of mind.

ENGSTRAND. Yes, I trust I am. And so I'll say good-bye, ma'am, and thank you kindly; and take good care of Regina for me [Wipes a tear from his eye] poor Johanna's child. Well, it's a queer thing, now; but it's just like as if she'd growd into the very apple of my eye. It is, indeed. [He bows and goes out through the hall.]

MANDERS. Well, what do you say of that man now, Mrs. Alving? That was a very different account of matters, was it not?

MRS. ALVING. Yes, it certainly was.

MANDERS. It only shows how excessively careful one ought to be in judging one's fellow creatures. But what a heartfelt joy it is to ascertain that one has been mistaken! Don't you think so?

MRS. ALVING. I think you are, and will always be, a great baby, Manders.

MANDERS. I?

MRS. ALVING. [Laying her two hands upon his shoulders.] And I say that I have half a mind to put my arms round your neck, and kiss you.

MANDERS. [Stepping hastily back.] No, no! God bless me! What an idea!

MRS. ALVING. [With a smile.] Oh, you needn't be afraid of me.

MANDERS. [By the table.] You have sometimes such an exaggerated way of expressing yourself. Now, let me just collect all the documents, and put them in my bag. [He does so.] There, that's all right. And now, good-bye for the present. Keep your eyes open when Oswald comes back. I shall look in again later. [He takes his hat and goes out through the hall door.]

MRS. ALVING. [Sighs, looks for a moment out of the window, sets the room in order a little, and is about to go into the dining-room, but stops at the door with a half-suppressed cry.] Oswald, are you still at table?

OSWALD. [In the dining room.] I'm only finishing my cigar.

MRS. ALVING. I thought you had gone for a little walk.

OSWALD. In such weather as this?

[A glass clinks. MRS. ALVING leaves the door open, and sits down with her knitting on the sofa by the window.]

OSWALD. Wasn't that Pastor Manders that went out just now?

MRS. ALVING. Yes; he went down to the Orphanage.

OSWALD. H'm. [The glass and decanter clink again.]

MRS. ALVING. [With a troubled glance.] Dear Oswald, you should take care of that liqueur. It is strong.

OSWALD. It keeps out the damp.

MRS. ALVING. Wouldn't you rather come in here, to me?

OSWALD. I mayn't smoke in there.

MRS. ALVING. You know quite well you may smoke cigars.

OSWALD. Oh, all right then; I'll come in. Just a tiny drop more first. There! [He comes into the room with his cigar, and shuts the door after him. A short silence.] Where has the pastor gone to?

MRS. ALVING. I have just told you; he went down to the Orphanage.

OSWALD. Oh, yes; so you did.

MRS. ALVING. You shouldn't sit so long at table, Oswald.

OSWALD. [Holding his cigar behind him.] But I find it so pleasant, mother. [Strokes and caresses her.] Just think what it is for me to come home and sit at mother's own table, in mother's room, and eat mother's delicious dishes.

MRS. ALVING. My dear, dear boy!

OSWALD. [Somewhat impatiently, walks about and smokes.] And what else can I do with myself here? I can't set to work at anything.

MRS. ALVING. Why can't you?

OSWALD. In such weather as this? Without a single ray of sunshine the whole day? [Walks up the room.] Oh, not to be able to work!

MRS. ALVING. Perhaps it was not quite wise of you to come home?

OSWALD. Oh, yes, mother; I had to.

MRS. ALVING. You know I would ten times rather forgo the joy of having you here, than let you

OSWALD. [Stops beside the table.] Now just tell me, mother: does it really make you so very happy to have me home again?

MRS. ALVING. Does it make me happy!

OSWALD. [Crumpling up a newspaper.] I should have thought it must be pretty much the same to you whether I was in existence or not.

MRS. ALVING. Have you the heart to say that to your mother, Oswald?

OSWALD. But you've got on very well without me all this time.

MRS. ALVING. Yes; I have got on without you. That is true.

[A silence. Twilight slowly begins to fall. OSWALD paces to and fro across the room. He has laid his cigar down.]

OSWALD. [Stops beside MRS. ALVING.] Mother, may I sit on the sofa beside you?

MRS. ALVING. [Makes room for him.] Yes, do, my dear boy.

OSWALD. [Sits down.] There is something I must tell you, mother.

MRS. ALVING. [Anxiously.] Well?

OSWALD. [Looks fixedly before him.] For I can't go on hiding it any longer.

MRS. ALVING. Hiding what? What is it?

OSWALD. [As before.] I could never bring myself to write to you about it; and since I've come home

MRS. ALVING. [Seizes him by the arm.] Oswald, what is the matter?

OSWALD. Both yesterday and to-day I have tried to put the thoughts away from me, to cast them off; but it's no use.

MRS. ALVING. [Rising.] Now you must tell me everything, Oswald!

OSWALD. [Draws her down to the sofa again.] Sit still; and then I will try to tell you. I complained of fatigue after my journey

MRS. ALVING. Well? What then?

OSWALD. But it isn't that that is the matter with me; not any ordinary fatigue

MRS. ALVING. [Tries to jump up.] You are not ill, Oswald?

OSWALD. [Draws her down again.] Sit still, mother. Do take it quietly. I'm not downright ill, either; not what is commonly called "ill." [Clasps his hands above his head.] Mother, my mind is broken down, ruined, I shall never be able to work again! [With his hands before his face, he buries his head in her lap, and breaks into bitter sobbing.]

MRS. ALVING. [White and trembling.] Oswald! Look at me! No, no; it's not true.

OSWALD. [Looks up with despair in his eyes.] Never to be able to work again! Never! never! A living death! Mother, can you imagine anything so horrible?

MRS. ALVING. My poor boy! How has this horrible thing come upon you?

OSWALD. [Sitting upright again.] That's just what I cannot possibly grasp or understand. I have never led a dissipated life never, in any respect. You mustn't believe that of me, mother! I've never done that.

MRS. ALVING. I am sure you haven't, Oswald.

OSWALD. And yet this has come upon me just the same, this awful misfortune!

MRS. ALVING. Oh, but it will pass over, my dear, blessed boy. It's nothing but over-work. Trust me, I am right.

OSWALD. [Sadly.] I thought so too, at first; but it isn't so.

MRS. ALVING. Tell me everything, from beginning to end.

OSWALD. Yes, I will.

MRS. ALVING. When did you first notice it?

OSWALD. It was directly after I had been home last time, and had got back to Paris again. I began to feel the most violent pains in my head, chiefly in the back of my head, they seemed to come. It was as though a tight iron ring was being screwed round my neck and upwards.

MRS. ALVING. Well, and then?

OSWALD. At first I thought it was nothing but the ordinary headache I had been so plagued with while I was growing up

MRS. ALVING. Yes, yes

OSWALD. But it wasn't that. I soon found that out. I couldn't work any more. I wanted to begin upon a big new picture, but my powers seemed to fail me; all my strength was crippled; I could form no definite images; everything swam before me, whirling round and round. Oh, it was an awful state! At last I sent for a doctor and from him I learned the truth.

MRS. ALVING. How do you mean?

OSWALD. He was one of the first doctors in Paris. I told him my symptoms; and then he set to work asking me a string of questions which I thought had nothing to do with the matter. I couldn't imagine what the man was after

MRS. ALVING. Well?

OSWALD. At last he said: "There has been something worm-eaten in you from your birth." He used that very word "vermoulu".

MRS. ALVING. [Breathlessly.] What did he mean by that?

OSWALD. I didn't understand either, and begged him to explain himself more clearly. And then the old cynic said [Clenching his fist] Oh!

MRS. ALVING. What did he say?

OSWALD. He said, "The sins of the fathers are visited upon the children."

MRS. ALVING. [Rising slowly.] The sins of the fathers!

OSWALD. I very nearly struck him in the face

MRS. ALVING. [Walks away across the room.] The sins of the fathers

OSWALD. [Smiles sadly.] Yes; what do you think of that? Of course I assured him that such a thing was out of the question. But do you think he gave in? No, he stuck to it; and it was only when I produced your letters and translated the passages relating to father

MRS. ALVING. But then?

OSWALD. Then of course he had to admit that he was on the wrong track; and so I learned the truth, the incomprehensible truth! I ought not to have taken part with my comrades in that lighthearted, glorious life of theirs. It had been too much for my strength. So I had brought it upon myself!

MRS. ALVING. Oswald! No, no; do not believe it!

OSWALD. No other explanation was possible, he said. That's the awful part of it. Incurably ruined for life, by my own heedlessness! All that I meant to have done in the world, I never dare think of it again, I'm not able to think of it. Oh! if I could only live over again, and undo all I have done! [He buries his face in the sofa.]

MRS. ALVING. [Wrings her hands and walks, in silent struggle, backwards and forwards.]

OSWALD. [After a while, looks up and remains resting upon his elbow.] If it had only been something inherited, something one wasn't responsible for! But this! To have thrown away so shamefully, thoughtlessly, recklessly, one's own happiness, one's own health, everything in the world, one's future, one's very life!

MRS. ALVING. No, no, my dear, darling boy; this is impossible! [Bends over him.] Things are not so desperate as you think.

OSWALD. Oh, you don't know [Springs up.] And then, mother, to cause you all this sorrow! Many a time I have almost wished and hoped that at bottom you didn't care so very much about me.

MRS. ALVING. I, Oswald? My only boy! You are all I have in the world! The only thing I care about!

OSWALD. [Seizes both her hands and kisses them.] Yes, yes, I see it. When I'm at home, I see it, of course; and that's almost the hardest part for me. But now you know the whole story and now we won't talk any more about it to-day. I daren't think of it for long together. [Goes up the room.] Get me something to drink, mother.

MRS. ALVING. To drink? What do you want to drink now?

OSWALD. Oh, anything you like. You have some cold punch in the house.

MRS. ALVING. Yes, but my dear Oswald

OSWALD. Don't refuse me, mother. Do be kind, now! I must have something to wash down all these gnawing thoughts. [Goes into the conservatory.] And then it's so dark here! [MRS. ALVING pulls a bell-rope on the right.] And this ceaseless rain! It may go on week after week, for months together. Never to get a glimpse of the sun! I can't recollect ever having seen the sun shine all the times I've been at home.

MRS. ALVING. Oswald, you are thinking of going away from me.

OSWALD. H'm [Drawing a heavy breath.] I'm not thinking of anything. I cannot think of anything! [In a low voice.] I let thinking alone.

REGINA. [From the dining-room.] Did you ring, ma'am?

MRS. ALVING. Yes; let us have the lamp in.

REGINA. Yes, ma'am. It's ready lighted. [Goes out.]

MRS. ALVING. [Goes across to OSWALD.] Oswald, be frank with me.

OSWALD. Well, so I am, mother. [Goes to the table.] I think I have told you enough.

[REGINA brings the lamp and sets it upon the table.]

MRS. ALVING. Regina, you may bring us a small bottle of champagne.

REGINA. Very well, ma'am. [Goes out.]

OSWALD. [Puts his arm round MRS. ALVING's neck.] That's just what I wanted. I knew mother wouldn't let her boy go thirsty.

MRS. ALVING. My own, poor, darling Oswald; how could I deny you anything now?

OSWALD. [Eagerly.] Is that true, mother? Do you mean it?

MRS. ALVING. How? What?

OSWALD. That you couldn't deny me anything.

MRS. ALVING. My dear Oswald

OSWALD. Hush!

REGINA. [Brings a tray with a half-bottle of champagne and two glasses, which she sets on the table.] Shall I open it?

OSWALD. No, thanks. I will do it myself.

[REGINA goes out again.]

MRS. ALVING. [Sits down by the table.] What was it you meant, that I musn't deny you?

OSWALD. [Busy opening the bottle.] First let us have a glass or two.

[The cork pops; he pours wine into one glass, and is about to pour it into the other.]

MRS. ALVING. [Holding her hand over it.] Thanks; not for me.

OSWALD. Oh! won't you? Then I will!

[He empties the glass, fells, and empties it again; then he sits down by the table.]

MRS. ALVING. [In expectancy.] Well?

OSWALD. [Without looking at her.] Tell me, I thought you and Pastor Manders seemed so odd, so quiet, at dinner to-day.

MRS. ALVING. Did you notice it?

OSWALD. Yes. H'm [After a short silence.] Tell me: what do you think of Regina?

MRS. ALVING. What do I think?

OSWALD. Yes; isn't she splendid?

MRS. ALVING. My dear Oswald, you don't know her as I do

OSWALD. Well?

MRS. ALVING. Regina, unfortunately, was allowed to stay at home too long. I ought to have taken her earlier into my house.

OSWALD. Yes, but isn't she splendid to look at, mother? [He fills his glass.]

MRS. ALVING. Regina has many serious faults

OSWALD. Oh, what does that matter? [He drinks again.]

MRS. ALVING. But I am fond of her, nevertheless, and I am responsible for her. I wouldn't for all the world have any harm happen to her.

OSWALD. [Springs up.] Mother, Regina is my only salvation!

MRS. ALVING. [Rising.] What do you mean by that?

OSWALD. I cannot go on bearing all this anguish of soul alone.

MRS. ALVING. Have you not your mother to share it with you?

OSWALD. Yes; that's what I thought; and so I came home to you. But that will not do. I see it won't do. I cannot endure my life here.

MRS. ALVING. Oswald!

OSWALD. I must live differently, mother. That is why I must leave you. I will not have you looking on at it.

MRS. ALVING. My unhappy boy! But, Oswald, while you are so ill as this

OSWALD. If it were only the illness, I should stay with you, mother, you may be sure; for you are the best friend I have in the world.

MRS. ALVING. Yes, indeed I am, Oswald; am I not?

OSWALD. [Wanders restlessly about.] But it's all the torment, the gnawing remorse and then, the great, killing dread. Oh, that awful dread!

MRS. ALVING. [Walking after him.] Dread? What dread? What do you mean?

OSWALD. Oh, you mustn't ask me any more. I don't know. I can't describe it.

MRS. ALVING. [Goes over to the right and pulls the bell.]

OSWALD. What is it you want?

MRS. ALVING. I want my boy to be happy, that is what I want. He sha'n't go on brooding over things [To REGINA, who appears at the door:] More champagne - a large bottle. [REGINA goes.]

OSWALD. Mother!

MRS. ALVING. Do you think we don't know how to live here at home?

OSWALD. Isn't she splendid to look at? How beautifully she's built! And so thoroughly healthy!

MRS. ALVING. [Sits by the table.] Sit down, Oswald; let us talk quietly together.

OSWALD. [Sits.] I daresay you don't know, mother, that I owe Regina some reparation.

MRS. ALVING. You!

OSWALD. For a bit of thoughtlessness, or whatever you like to call it, very innocent, at any rate. When I was home last time

MRS. ALVING. Well?

OSWALD. She used often to ask me about Paris, and I used to tell her one thing and another. Then I recollect I happened to say to her one day, "Shouldn't you like to go there yourself?"

MRS. ALVING. Well?

OSWALD. I saw her face flush, and then she said, "Yes, I should like it of all things." "Ah, well," I replied, "it might perhaps be managed" or something like that.

MRS. ALVING. And then?

OSWALD. Of course I had forgotten all about it; but the day before yesterday I happened to ask her whether she was glad I was to stay at home so long

MRS. ALVING. Yes?

OSWALD. And then she gave me such a strange look, and asked, "But what's to become of my trip to Paris?"

MRS. ALVING. Her trip!

OSWALD. And so it came out that she had taken the thing seriously; that she had been thinking of me the whole time, and had set to work to learn French

MRS. ALVING. So that was why!

OSWALD. Mother, when I saw that fresh, lovely, splendid girl standing there before me, till then I had hardly noticed her but when she stood there as though with open arms ready to receive me

MRS. ALVING. Oswald!

OSWALD. - then it flashed upon me that in her lay my salvation; for I saw that she was full of the joy of life.

MRS. ALVING. [Starts.] The joy of life? Can there be salvation in that?

REGINA. [From the dining room, with a bottle of champagne.] I'm sorry to have been so long, but I had to go to the cellar. [Places the bottle on the table.]

OSWALD. And now bring another glass.

REGINA. [Looks at him in surprise.] There is Mrs. Alving's glass, Mr. Alving.

OSWALD. Yes, but bring one for yourself, Regina. [REGINA starts and gives a lightning-like side glance at MRS. ALVING.] Why do you wait?

REGINA. [Softly and hesitatingly.] Is it Mrs. Alving's wish?

MRS. ALVING. Bring the glass, Regina.

[REGINA goes out into the dining-room.]

OSWALD. [Follows her with his eyes.] Have you noticed how she walks? so firmly and lightly!

MRS. ALVING. This can never be, Oswald!

OSWALD. It's a settled thing. Can't you see that? It's no use saying anything against it.

[REGINA enters with an empty glass, which she keeps in her hand.]

OSWALD. Sit down, Regina.

[REGINA looks inquiringly at MRS. ALVING.]

MRS. ALVING. Sit down. [REGINA sits on a chair by the dining room door, still holding the empty glass in her hand.] Oswald, what were you saying about the joy of life?

OSWALD. Ah, the joy of life, mother, that's a thing you don't know much about in these parts. I have never felt it here.

MRS. ALVING. Not when you are with me?

OSWALD. Not when I'm at home. But you don't understand that.

MRS. ALVING. Yes, yes; I think I almost understand it now.

OSWALD. And then, too, the joy of work! At bottom, it's the same thing. But that, too, you know nothing about.

MRS. ALVING. Perhaps you are right. Tell me more about it, Oswald.

OSWALD. I only mean that here people are brought up to believe that work is a curse and a punishment for sin, and that life is something miserable, something; it would be best to have done with, the sooner the better.

MRS. ALVING. "A vale of tears," yes; and we certainly do our best to make it one.

OSWALD. But in the great world people won't hear of such things. There, nobody really believes such doctrines any longer. There, you feel it a positive bliss and ecstasy merely to draw the breath of life. Mother, have you noticed that everything I have painted has turned upon the joy of life? always, always upon the joy of life? light and sunshine and glorious air-and faces radiant with happiness. That is why I'm afraid of remaining at home with you.

MRS. ALVING. Afraid? What are you afraid of here, with me?

OSWALD. I'm afraid lest all my instincts should be warped into ugliness.

MRS. ALVING. [Looks steadily at him.] Do you think that is what would happen?

OSWALD. I know it. You may live the same life here as there, and yet it won't be the same life.

MRS. ALVING. [Who has been listening eagerly, rises, her eyes big with thought, and says:] Now I see the sequence of things.

OSWALD. What is it you see?

MRS. ALVING. I see it now for the first time. And now I can speak.

OSWALD. [Rising.] Mother, I don't understand you.

REGINA. [Who has also risen.] Perhaps I ought to go?

MRS. ALVING. No. Stay here. Now I can speak. Now, my boy, you shall know the whole truth. And then you can choose. Oswald! Regina!

OSWALD. Hush! The Pastor

MANDERS. [Enters by the hall door.] There! We have had a most edifying time down there.

OSWALD. So have we.

MANDERS. We must stand by Engstrand and his Sailors' Home. Regina must go to him and help him

REGINA. No thank you, sir.

MANDERS. [Noticing her for the first tine.] What? You here? And with a glass in your hand!

REGINA. [Hastily putting the glass down.] Pardon!

OSWALD. Regina is going with me, Mr. Manders.

MANDERS. Going! With you!

OSWALD. Yes; as my wife, if she wishes it.

MANDERS. But, merciful God!

REGINA. I can't help it, sir.

OSWALD. Or she'll stay here, if I stay.

REGINA. [Involuntarily.] Here!

MANDERS. I am thunderstruck at your conduct, Mrs. Alving.

MRS. ALVING. They will do neither one thing nor the other; for now I can speak out plainly.

MANDERS. You surely will not do that! No, no, no!

MRS. ALVING. Yes, I can speak and I will. And no ideals shall suffer after all.

OSWALD. Mother, what is it you are hiding from me?

REGINA. [Listening.] Oh, ma'am, listen! Don't you hear shouts outside. [She goes into the conservatory and looks out.]

OSWALD. [At the window on the left.] What's going on? Where does that light come from?

REGINA. [Cries out.] The Orphanage is on fire!

MRS. ALVING. [Rushing to the window.] On fire!

MANDERS. On fire! Impossible! I've just come from there.

OSWALD. Where's my hat? Oh, never mind it, Father's Orphanage! [He rushes out through the garden door.]

MRS. ALVING. My shawl, Regina! The whole place is in a blaze!

MANDERS. Terrible! Mrs. Alving, it is a judgment upon this abode of lawlessness.

MRS. ALVING. Yes, of course. Come, Regina. [She and REGINA hasten out through the hall.]

MANDERS. [Clasps his hands together.] And we left it uninsured! [He goes out the same way.]

ACT THIRD.

[The room as before. All the doors stand open. The lamp is still burning on the table. It is dark out of doors; there is only a faint glow from the conflagration in the background to the left.]

[MRS. ALVING, with a shawl over her head, stands in the conservatory, looking out. REGINA, also with a shawl on, stands a little behind her.]

MRS. ALVING. The whole thing burnt! burnt to the ground!

REGINA. The basement is still burning.

MRS. ALVING. How is it Oswald doesn't come home? There's nothing to be saved.

REGINA. Should you like me to take down his hat to him?

MRS. ALVING. Has he not even got his hat on?

REGINA. [Pointing to the hall.] No; there it hangs.

MRS. ALVING. Let it be. He must come up now. I shall go and look for him myself. [She goes out through the garden door.]

MANDERS. [Comes in from the hall.] Is not Mrs. Alving here?

REGINA. She has just gone down the garden.

MANDERS. This is the most terrible night I ever went through.

REGINA. Yes; isn't it a dreadful misfortune, sir?

MANDERS. Oh, don't talk about it! I can hardly bear to think of it.

REGINA. How can it have happened?

MANDERS. Don't ask me, Miss Engstrand! How should I know? Do you, too? Is it not enough that your father?

REGINA. What about him?

MANDERS. Oh, he has driven me distracted

ENGSTRAND. [Enters through the hall.] Your Reverence

MANDERS. [Turns round in terror.] Are you after me here, too?

ENGSTRAND. Yes, strike me dead, but I must ! Oh, Lord! what am I saying? But this is a terrible ugly business, your Reverence.

MANDERS. [Walks to and fro.] Alas! alas!

REGINA. What's the matter?

ENGSTRAND. Why, it all came of this here prayer-meeting, you see. [Softly.] The bird's limed, my girl. [Aloud.] And to think it should be my doing that such a thing should be his Reverence's doing!

MANDERS. But I assure you, Engstrand

ENGSTRAND. There wasn't another soul except your Reverence as ever laid a finger on the candles down there.

MANDERS. [Stops.] So you declare. But I certainly cannot recollect that I ever had a candle in my hand.

ENGSTRAND. And I saw as clear as daylight how your Reverence took the candle and snuffed it with your fingers, and threw away the snuff among the shavings.

MANDERS. And you stood and looked on?

ENGSTRAND. Yes; I saw it as plain as a pike-staff, I did.

MANDERS. It's quite beyond my comprehension. Besides, it has never been my habit to snuff candles with my fingers.

ENGSTRAND. And terrible risky it looked, too, that it did! But is there such a deal of harm done after all, your Reverence?

MANDERS. [Walks restlessly to and fro.] Oh, don't ask me!

ENGSTRAND. [Walks with him.] And your Reverence hadn't insured it, neither?

MANDERS. [Continuing to walk up and down.] No, no, no; I have told you so.

ENGSTRAND. [Following him.] Not insured! And then to go straight away down and set light to the whole thing! Lord, Lord, what a misfortune!

MANDERS. [Wipes the sweat from his forehead.] Ay, you may well say that, Engstrand.

ENGSTRAND. And to think that such a thing should happen to a benevolent Institution, that was to have been a blessing both to town and country, as the saying goes! The newspapers won't be for handling your Reverence very gently, I expect.

MANDERS. No; that is just what I am thinking of. That is almost the worst of the whole matter. All the malignant attacks and imputations! Oh, it makes me shudder to think of it!

MRS. ALVING. [Comes in from the garden.] He is not to be persuaded to leave the fire.

MANDERS. Ah, there you are, Mrs. Alving.

MRS. ALVING. So you have escaped your Inaugural Address, Pastor Manders.

MANDERS. Oh, I should so gladly

MRS. ALVING. [In an undertone.] It is all for the best. That Orphanage would have done no one any good.

MANDERS. Do you think not?

MRS. ALVING. Do you think it would?

MANDERS. It is a terrible misfortune, all the same.

MRS. ALVING. Let us speak of it plainly, as a matter of business. Are you waiting for Mr. Manders, Engstrand?

ENGSTRAND. [At the hall door.] That's just what I'm a-doing of, ma'am.

MRS. ALVING. Then sit down meanwhile.

ENGSTRAND. Thank you, ma'am; I'd as soon stand.

MRS. ALVING. [To MANDERS.] I suppose you are going by the steamer?

MANDERS. Yes; it starts in an hour.

MRS. ALVING. Then be so good as to take all the papers with you. I won't hear another word about this affair. I have other things to think of

MANDERS. Mrs. Alving

MRS. ALVING. Later on I shall send you a Power of Attorney to settle everything as you please.

MANDERS. That I will very readily undertake. The original destination of the endowment must now be completely changed, alas!

MRS. ALVING. Of course it must.

MANDERS. I think, first of all, I shall arrange that the Solvik property shall pass to the parish. The land is by no means without value. It can always be turned to account for some purpose or other. And the interest of the money in the Bank I could, perhaps, best apply for the benefit of some undertaking of acknowledged value to the town.

MRS. ALVING. Do just as you please. The whole matter is now completely indifferent to me.

ENGSTRAND. Give a thought to my Sailors' Home, your Reverence.

MANDERS. Upon my word, that is not a bad suggestion. That must be considered.

ENGSTRAND. Oh, devil take considering, Lord forgive me!

MANDERS. [With a sigh.] And unfortunately I cannot tell how long I shall be able to retain control of these things, whether public opinion may not compel me to retire. It entirely depends upon the result of the official inquiry into the fire

MRS. ALVING. What are you talking about?

MANDERS. And the result can by no means be foretold.

ENGSTRAND. [Comes close to him.] Ay, but it can though. For here stands old Jacob Engstrand.

MANDERS. Well well, but?

ENGSTRAND. [More softly.] And Jacob Engstrand isn't the man to desert a noble benefactor in the hour of need, as the saying goes.

MANDERS. Yes, but my good fellow, how?

ENGSTRAND. Jacob Engstrand may be likened to a sort of a guardian angel, he may, your Reverence.

MANDERS. No, no; I really cannot accept that.

ENGSTRAND. Oh, that'll be the way of it, all the same. I know a man as has taken others' sins upon himself before now, I do.

MANDERS. Jacob! [Wrings his hand.] Yours is a rare nature. Well, you shall be helped with your Sailors' Home. That you may rely upon. [ENGSTRAND tries to thank him, but cannot for emotion.]

MANDERS. [Hangs his travelling-bag over his shoulder.] And now let us set out. We two will go together.

ENGSTRAND. [At the dining-room door, softly to REGINA.] You come along too, my lass. You shall live as snug as the yolk in an egg.

REGINA. [Tosses her head.] Merci! [She goes out into the hall and fetches MANDERS' overcoat.]

MANDERS. Good-bye, Mrs. Alving! and may the spirit of Law and Order descend upon this house, and that quickly.

MRS. ALVING. Good-bye, Pastor Manders. [She goes up towards the conservatory, as she sees OSWALD coming in through the garden door.]

ENGSTRAND. [While he and REGINA help MANGERS to get his coat on.] Good-bye, my child. And if any trouble should come to you, you know where Jacob Engstrand is to be found. [Softly.] Little Harbour Street, h'm! [To MRS. ALVING and OSWALD.] And the refuge for wandering mariners shall be called "Chamberlain Alving's Home," that it shall! And if so be as I'm spared to carry on that house in my own way, I make so bold as to promise that it shall be worthy of the Chamberlain's memory.

MANDERS. [In the doorway.] H'm, h'm! Come along, my dear Enstrand. Good-bye! Good-bye! [He and ENGSTRAND go out through the hall.]

OSWALD. [Goes towards the table.] What house was he talking about?

MRS. ALVING. Oh, a kind of Home that he and Pastor Manders want to set up.

OSWALD. It will burn down like the other.

MRS. ALVING. What makes you think so?

OSWALD. Everything will burn. All that recalls father's memory is doomed. Here am I, too, burning down. [REGINA starts and looks at him.]

MRS. ALVING. Oswald! You oughtn't to have remained so long down there, my poor boy.

OSWALD. [Sits down by the table.] I almost think you are right.

MRS. ALVING. Let me dry your face, Oswald; you are quite wet. [She dries his face with her pocket-handkerchief.]

OSWALD. [Stares indifferently in front of him.] Thanks, mother.

MRS. ALVING. Are you not tired, Oswald? Should you like to sleep?

OSWALD. [Nervously.] No, no not to sleep! I never sleep. I only pretend to. [Sadly.] That will come soon enough.

MRS. ALVING. [Looking sorrowfully at him.] Yes, you really are ill, my blessed boy.

REGINA. [Eagerly.] Is Mr. Alving ill?

OSWALD. [Impatiently.] Oh, do shut all the doors! This killing dread

MRS. ALVING. Close the doors, Regina.

[REGINA shuts them and remains standing by the hall door. MRS. ALVING takes her shawl off: REGINA does the same. MRS. ALVING draws a chair across to OSWALD'S, and sits by him.]

MRS. ALVING. There now! I am going to sit beside you

OSWALD. Yes, do. And Regina shall stay here too. Regina shall be with me always. You will come to the rescue, Regina, won't you?

REGINA. I don't understand

MRS. ALVING. To the rescue?

OSWALD. Yes, when the need comes.

MRS. ALVING. Oswald, have you not your mother to come to the rescue?

OSWALD. You? [Smiles.] No, mother; that rescue you will never bring me. [Laughs sadly.] You! ha ha! [Looks earnestly at her.] Though, after all, who ought to do it if not you? [Impetuously.] Why can't you say "thou" to me, Regina? [Note: "Sige du" = Fr. tutoyer] Why do'n't you call me "Oswald"?

REGINA. [Softly.] I don't think Mrs. Alving would like it.

MRS. ALVING. You shall have leave to, presently. And meanwhile sit over here beside us.

[REGINA seats herself demurely and hesitatingly at the other side of the table.]

MRS. ALVING. And now, my poor suffering boy, I am going to take the burden off your mind

OSWALD. You, mother?

MRS. ALVING. - all the gnawing remorse and self-reproach you speak of.

OSWALD. And you think you can do that?

MRS. ALVING. Yes, now I can, Oswald. A little while ago you spoke of the joy of life; and at that word a new light burst for me over my life and everything connected with it.

OSWALD. [Shakes his head.] I don't understand you.

MRS. ALVING. You ought to have known your father when he was a young lieutenant. He was brimming over with the joy of life!

OSWALD. Yes, I know he was.

MRS. ALVING. It was like a breezy day only to look at him. And what exuberant strength and vitality there was in him!

OSWALD. Well?

MRS. ALVING. Well then, child of joy as he was, for he was like a child in those days, he had to live at home here in a half-grown town, which had no joys to offer him only dissipations. He had no object in life only an official position. He had no work into which he could throw himself heart and soul; he had only business. He had not a single comrade that could realise what the joy of life meant only loungers and boon-companions

OSWALD. Mother!

MRS. ALVING. So the inevitable happened.

OSWALD. The inevitable?

MRS. ALVING. You told me yourself, this evening, what would become of you if you stayed at home.

OSWALD. Do you mean to say that father?

MRS. ALVING. Your poor father found no outlet for the overpowering joy of life that was in him. And I brought no brightness into his home.

OSWALD. Not even you?

MRS. ALVING. They had taught me a great deal about duties and so forth, which I went on obstinately believing in. Everything was marked out into duties, into my duties, and his duties, and I am afraid I made his home intolerable for your poor father, Oswald.

OSWALD. Why have you never spoken of this in writing to me?

MRS. ALVING. I have never before seen it in such a light that I could speak of it to you, his son.

OSWALD. In what light did you see it, then?

MRS. ALVING. [Slowly.] I saw only this one thing: that your father was a broken-down man before you were born.

OSWALD. [Softly.] Ah! [He rises and walks away to the window.]

MRS. ALVING. And then; day after day, I dwelt on the one thought that by rights Regina should be at home in this house, just like my own boy.

OSWALD. [Turning round quickly.] Regina!

REGINA. [Springs up and asks, with bated breath.] I?

MRS. ALVING. Yes, now you know it, both of you.

OSWALD. Regina!

REGINA. [To herself.] So mother was that kind of woman.

MRS. ALVING. Your mother had many good qualities, Regina.

REGINA. Yes, but she was one of that sort, all the same. Oh, I've often suspected it; but - And now, if you please, ma'am, may I be allowed to go away at once?

MRS. ALVING. Do you really wish it, Regina?

REGINA. Yes, indeed I do.

MRS. ALVING. Of course you can do as you like; but

OSWALD. [Goes towards REGINA.] Go away now? Your place is here.

REGINA. Merci, Mr. Alving! or now, I suppose, I may say Oswald. But I can tell you this wasn't at all what I expected.

MRS. ALVING. Regina, I have not been frank with you

REGINA. No, that you haven't indeed. If I'd known that Oswald was an invalid, why - And now, too, that it can never come to anything serious between us I really can't stop out here in the country and wear myself out nursing sick people.

OSWALD. Not even one who is so near to you?

REGINA. No, that I can't. A poor girl must make the best of her young days, or she'll be left out in the cold before she knows where she is. And I, too, have the joy of life in me, Mrs. Alving!

MRS. ALVING. Unfortunately, you leave. But don't throw yourself away, Regina.

REGINA. Oh, what must be, must be. If Oswald takes after his father, I take after my mother, I daresay. May I ask, ma'am, if Pastor Manders knows all this about me?

MRS. ALVING. Pastor Manders knows all about it.

REGINA. [Busied in putting on her shawl.] Well then, I'd better make haste and get away by this steamer. The Pastor is such a nice man to deal with; and I certainly think I've as much right to a little of that money as he has, that brute of a carpenter.

MRS. ALVING. You are heartily welcome to it, Regina.

REGINA. [Looks hard at her.] I think you might have brought me up as a gentleman's daughter, ma'am; it would have suited me better. [Tosses her head.] But pooh, what does it matter! [With a bitter side glance at the corked bottle.] I may come to drink champagne with gentlefolks yet.

MRS. ALVING. And if you ever need a home, Regina, come to me.

REGINA. No, thank you, ma'am. Pastor Manders will look after me, I know. And if the worst comes to the worst, I know of one house where I've every right to a place.

MRS. ALVING. Where is that?

REGINA. "Chamberlain Alving's Home."

MRS. ALVING. Regina, now I see it, you are going to your ruin.

REGINA. Oh, stuff! Good-bye. [She nods and goes out through the hall.]

OSWALD. [Stands at the window and looks out.] Is she gone?

MRS. ALVING. Yes.

OSWALD. [Murmuring aside to himself.] I think it was a mistake, this.

MRS. ALVING. [Goes up behind him and lays her hands on his shoulders.] Oswald, my dear boy, has it shaken you very much?

OSWALD. [Turns his face towards her.] All that about father, do you mean?

MRS. ALVING. Yes, about your unhappy father. I am so afraid it may have been too much for you.

OSWALD. Why should you fancy that? Of course it came upon me as a great surprise; but it can make no real difference to me.

MRS. ALVING. [Draws her hands away.] No difference! That your father was so infinitely unhappy!

OSWALD. Of course I can pity him, as I would anybody else; but

MRS. ALVING. Nothing more! Your own father!

OSWALD. [Impatiently.]Oh, "father," - "father"! I never knew anything of father. I remember nothing about him, except that he once made me sick.

MRS. ALVING. This is terrible to think of! Ought not a son to love his father, whatever happens?

OSWALD. When a son has nothing to thank his father for? has never known him? Do you really cling to that old superstition? you who are so enlightened in other ways?

MRS. ALVING. Can it be only a superstition?

OSWALD. Yes; surely you can see that, mother. It's one of those notions that are current in the world, and so

MRS. ALVING. [Deeply moved.] Ghosts!

OSWALD. [Crossing the room.] Yes; you may call them ghosts.

MRS. ALVING. [Wildly.] Oswald, then you don't love me, either!

OSWALD. You I know, at any rate

MRS. ALVING. Yes, you know me; but is that all!

OSWALD. And, of course, I know how fond you are of me, and I can't but be grateful to you. And then you can be so useful to me, now that I am ill.

MRS. ALVING. Yes, cannot I, Oswald? Oh, I could almost bless the illness that has driven you home to me. For I see very plainly that you are not mine: I have to win you.

OSWALD. [Impatiently.] Yes yes yes; all these are just so many phrases. You must remember that I am a sick man, mother. I can't be much taken up with other people; I have enough to do thinking about myself.

MRS. ALVING. [In a low voice.] I shall be patient and easily satisfied.

OSWALD. And cheerful too, mother!

MRS. ALVING. Yes, my dear boy, you are quite right. [Goes towards him.] Have I relieved you of all remorse and self-reproach now?

OSWALD. Yes, you have. But now who will relieve me of the dread?

MRS. ALVING. The dread?

OSWALD. [Walks across the room.] Regina could have been got to do it.

MRS. ALVING. I don't understand you. What is this about dread and Regina?

OSWALD. Is it very late, mother?

MRS. ALVING. It is early morning. [She looks out through the conservatory.] The day is dawning over the mountains. And the weather is clearing, Oswald. In a little while you shall see the sun.

OSWALD. I'm glad of that. Oh, I may still have much to rejoice in and live for

MRS. ALVING. I should think so, indeed!

OSWALD. Even if I can't work

MRS. ALVING. Oh, you'll soon be able to work again, my dear boy, now that you haven't got all those gnawing and depressing thoughts to brood over any longer.

OSWALD. Yes, I'm glad you were able to rid me of all those fancies. And when I've got over this one thing more [Sits on the sofa.] Now we will have a little talk, mother

MRS. ALVING. Yes, let us. [She pushes an arm-chair towards the sofa, and sits down close to him.]

OSWALD. And meantime the sun will be rising. And then you will know all. And then I shall not feel this dread any longer.

MRS. ALVING. What is it that I am to know?

OSWALD. [Not listening to her.] Mother, did you not say a little while ago, that there was nothing in the world you would not do for me, if I asked you?

MRS. ALVING. Yes, indeed I said so!

OSWALD. And you'll stick to it, mother?

MRS. ALVING. You may rely on that, my dear and only boy! I have nothing in the world to live for but you alone.

OSWALD. Very well, then; now you shall hear Mother, you have a strong, steadfast mind, I know. Now you're to sit quite still when you hear it.

MRS. ALVING. What dreadful thing can it be ?

OSWALD. You're not to scream out. Do you hear? Do you promise me that? We will sit and talk about it quietly. Do you promise me, mother?

MRS. ALVING. Yes, yes; I promise. Only speak!

OSWALD. Well, you must know that all this fatigue and my inability to think of work all that is not the illness itself

MRS. ALVING. Then what is the illness itself?

OSWALD. The disease I have as my birthright [He points to his forehead and adds very softly] is seated here.

MRS. ALVING. [Almost voiceless.] Oswald! No, no!

OSWALD. Don't scream. I can't bear it. Yes, mother, it is seated here waiting. And it may break out any day at any moment.

MRS. ALVING. Oh, what horror!

OSWALD. Now, quiet, quiet. That is how it stands with me

MRS. ALVING. [Springs up.] It's not true, Oswald! It's impossible! It cannot be so!

OSWALD. I have had one attack down there already. It was soon over. But when I came to know the state I had been in, then the dread descended upon me, raging and ravening; and so I set off home to you as fast as I could.

MRS. ALVING. Then this is the dread!

OSWALD. Yes, it's so indescribably loathsome, you know. Oh, if it had only been an ordinary mortal disease! For I'm not so afraid of death, though I should like to live as long as I can.

MRS. ALVING. Yes, yes, Oswald, you must!

OSWALD. But this is so unutterably loathsome. To become a little baby again! To hive to be fed! To have to - Oh, it's not to be spoken of!

MRS. ALVING. The child has his mother to nurse him.

OSWALD. [Springs up.] No, never that! That is just what I will not have. I can't endure to think that perhaps I should lie in that state for many years and get old and grey. And in the meantime you might die and leave me. [Sits in MRS. ALVING'S chair.] For the doctor said it wouldn't necessarily prove fatal at once. He called it a sort of softening of the brain or something like that. [Smiles sadly.] I think that expression sounds so nice. It always sets me thinking of cherry-coloured velvet, something soft and delicate to stroke.

MRS. ALVING. [Shrieks.] Oswald!

OSWALD. [Springs up and paces the room.] And now you have taken Regina from me. If I could only have had her! She would have come to the rescue, I know.

MRS. ALVING. [Goes to him.] What do you mean by that, my darling boy? Is there any help in the world that I would not give you?

OSWALD. When I got over my attack in Paris, the doctor told me that when it comes again, and it will come, there will be no more hope.

MRS. ALVING. He was heartless enough to

OSWALD. I demanded it of him. I told him I had preparations to make [He smiles cunningly.] And so I had. [He takes a little box from his inner breast pocket and opens it.] Mother, do you see this?

MRS. ALVING. What is it?

OSWALD. Morphia.

MRS. ALVING. [Looks at him horror-struck.] Oswald, my boy!

OSWALD. I've scraped together twelve pilules

MRS. ALVING. [Snatches at it.] Give me the box, Oswald.

OSWALD. Not yet, mother. [He hides the box again in his pocket.]

MRS. ALVING. I shall never survive this!

OSWALD. It must be survived. Now if I'd had Regina here, I should have told her how things stood with me and begged her to come to the rescue at the last. She would have done it. I know she would.

MRS. ALVING. Never!

OSWALD. When the horror had come upon me, and she saw me lying there helpless, like a little new-born baby, impotent, lost, hopeless, past all saving

MRS. ALVING. Never in all the world would Regina have done this!

OSWALD. Regina would have done it. Regina was so splendidly light-hearted. And she would soon have wearied of nursing an invalid like me.

MRS. ALVING. Then heaven be praised that Regina is not here.

OSWALD. Well then, it is you that must come to the rescue, mother.

MRS. ALVING. [Shrieks aloud.] I!

OSWALD. Who should do it if not you?

MRS. ALVING. I! your mother!

OSWALD. For that very reason.

MRS. ALVING. I, who gave you life!

OSWALD. I never asked you for life. And what sort of a life have you given me? I will not have it! You shall take it back again!

MRS. ALVING. Help! Help! [She runs out into the hall.]

OSWALD. [Going after her.] Do not leave me! Where are you going?

MRS. ALVING. [In the hall.] To fetch the doctor, Oswald! Let me pass!

OSWALD. [Also outside.] You shall not go out. And no one shall come in. [The locking of a door is heard.]

MRS. ALVING. [Comes in again.] Oswald! Oswald, my child!

OSWALD. [Follows her.] Have you a mother's heart for me and yet can see me suffer from this unutterable dread?

MRS. ALVING. [After a moment's silence, commands herself, and says:] Here is my hand upon it.

OSWALD. Will you?

MRS. ALVING. If it should ever be necessary. But it will never be necessary. No, no; it is impossible.

OSWALD. Well, let us hope so. And let us live together as long as we can. Thank you, mother. [He seats himself in the arm-chair which MRS. ALVING has moved to the sofa. Day is breaking. The lamp is still burning on the table.]

MRS. ALVING. [Drawing near cautiously.] Do you feel calm now?

OSWALD. Yes.

MRS. ALVING. [Bending over him.] It has been a dreadful fancy of yours, Oswald, nothing but a fancy. All this excitement has been too much for you. But now you shall have along rest; at home with your mother, my own blessëd boy. Everything you point to you shall have, just as when you were a little child. There now. The crisis is over. You see how easily it passed! Oh, I was sure it would. And do you see, Oswald, what a lovely day we are going to have? Brilliant sunshine! Now you can really see your home. [She goes to the table and puts out the lamp. Sunrise. The glacier and the snow-peaks in the background glow in the morning light.]

OSWALD. [Sits in the arm-chair with his back towards the landscape, without moving. Suddenly he says:] Mother, give me the sun.

MRS. ALVING. [By the table, starts and looks at him.] What do you say?

OSWALD. [Repeats, in a dull, toneless voice.] The sun. The sun.

MRS. ALVING. [Goes to him.] Oswald, what is the matter with you?

OSWALD. [Seems to shrink together to the chair; all his muscles relax; his face is expressionless, his eyes have a glassy stare.]

MRS. ALVING. [Quivering with terror.] What is this? [Shrieks.] Oswald! what is the matter with you? [Falls on her knees beside him and shakes him.] Oswald! Oswald! look at me! Don't you know me?

OSWALD. [Tonelessly as before.] The sun. The sun.

MRS. ALVING. [Springs up in despair, entwines her hands in her hair and shrieks.] I cannot bear it! [Whispers, as though petrified]; I cannot bear it! Never! [Suddenly.] Where has he got them? [Fumbles hastily in his breast.] Here! [Shrinks back a few steps and screams:] No! No; no! Yes! No; no!

[She stands a few steps away from him with her hands twisted in her hair, and stares at him in speechless horror.]

OSWALD. [Sits motionless as before and says.] The sun. The sun.

THE END

Henrik Ibsen - Rommersholm

Index Of Contents

Dramatis Personae

John Rosmer, of Rosmersholm, an ex-clergyman.
Rebecca West, one of his household, originally engaged as companion to the late Mrs. Rosmer.
Kroll, headmaster of the local grammar school, Rosmer's brother- in-law.
Ulrik Brendel.
Peter Mortensgaard.
Mrs. Helseth, Rosmer's housekeeper.

(The action takes place at Rosmersholm, an old manor-house in the neighbourhood of a small town on a fjord in western Norway.)

ACT I

(SCENE. The sitting-room at Rosmersholm; a spacious room, comfortably furnished in old-fashioned style. In the foreground, against the right-hand wall, is a stove decorated with sprigs of fresh birch and wild flowers. Farther back, a door. In the back wall folding doors leading into the entrance hall. In the left- hand wall a window, in front of which is a stand filled with flowers and plants. Near the stove stand a table, a couch and an easy-chair. The walls are hung round with portraits, dating from various periods, of clergymen, military officers and other officials in uniform. The window is open, and so are the doors into the lobby and the outer door. Through the latter is seen an avenue of old trees leading to a courtyard. It is a summer evening, after sunset. REBECCA WEST is sitting by the window crocheting a large white woollen shawl, which is nearly completed. From time to time she peeps out of window through the flowers. MRS. HELSETH comes in from the right.)

MRS HELSETH
Hadn't I better begin and lay the table for supper, miss?

REBECCA
Yes, do. Mr. Rosmer ought to be in directly.

MRS HELSETH
Isn't there a draught where you are sitting, miss?

REBECCA
There is a little. Will you shut up, please? (Mrs HELSETH goes to the hall door and shuts it. Then she goes to the window, to shut it, and looks out.)

MRS HELSETH
Isn't that Mr. Rosmer coming there?

REBECCA
Where? (Gets up.) Yes, it is he. (Stands behind the window-curtain.) Stand on one side. Don't let him catch sight of us.

MRS HELSETH *(stepping back)*
Look, miss, he is beginning to use the mill path again.

REBECCA
He came by the mill path the day before yesterday too. (Peeps out between the curtain and the window-frame). Now we shall see whether

MRS HELSETH
Is he going over the wooden bridge?

REBECCA
That is just what I want to see. (After a moment.) No. He has turned aside. He is coming the other way round to-day too. (Comes away from the window.) It is a long way round.

MRS HELSETH
Yes, of course. One can well understand his shrinking from going over that bridge. The spot where such a thing has happened is

REBECCA *(folding up her work)*
They cling to their dead a long time at Rosmersholm.

MRS HELSETH
If you ask me, miss, I should say it is the dead that cling to Rosmersholm a long time.

REBECCA *(looking at her)*
The dead?

MRS HELSETH
Yes, one might almost say that they don't seem to be able to tear themselves away from those they have left behind.

REBECCA
What puts that idea into your head?

MRS HELSETH
Well, otherwise I know the White Horses would not be seen here.

REBECCA
Tell me, Mrs Helseth, what is this superstition about the White Horses?

MRS HELSETH
Oh, it is not worth talking about. I am sure you don't believe in such things, either.

REBECCA
Do you believe in them?

MRS HELSETH (goes to the window and shuts it)
Oh, I am not going to give you a chance of laughing at me, miss. (Looks out.) See, is that not Mr. Rosmer out on the mill path again?

REBECCA (looking out)
That man out there? (Goes to the window.) Why, that is Mr. Kroll, of course!

MRS HELSETH
So it is, to be sure.

REBECCA
That is delightful, because he is certain to be coming here.

MRS HELSETH
He actually comes straight over the wooden bridge, he does for all that she was his own sister. Well, I will go in and get the supper laid, miss. (Goes out to the right. REBECCA stands still for a moment, then waves her hand out of the window, nodding and smiling. Darkness is beginning to fall.)

REBECCA (going to the door on the right and calling through it). Mrs Helseth, I am sure you won't mind preparing something extra nice for supper? You know what dishes Mr. Kroll is especially fond of.

MRS HELSETH
Certainly, miss. I will.

Rebecca (opening the door into the lobby)
At last, Mr. Kroll! I am so glad to see you!

KROLL (coming into the lobby and putting down his stick)
Thank you. Are you sure I am not disturbing you?

REBECCA
You? How can you say such a thing?

KROLL (coming into the room)
You are always so kind. (Looks round the room.) Is John up in his room?

REBECCA
No, he has gone out for a walk. He is later than usual of coming in, but he is sure to be back directly. (Points to the sofa.) Do sit down and wait for him.

KROLL (putting down his hat)
Thank you. (Sits down and looks about him.) How charmingly pretty you have made the old room look! Flowers everywhere!

REBECCA
Mr. Rosmer is so fond of having fresh flowers about him.

KROLL
And so are you, I should say.

REBECCA
Yes, I am. I think their scent has such a delicious effect on one and till lately we had to deny ourselves that pleasure, you know.

KROLL *(nodding slowly)*
Poor Beata could not stand the scent of them.

REBECCA
Nor their colours either. They made her feel dazed.

KROLL
Yes, I remember. (Continues in a more cheerful tone of voice). Well, and how are things going here?

REBECCA
Oh, everything goes on in the same quiet, placid way. One day is exactly like another. And how are things with you? Is your wife?

KROLL
Oh, my dear Miss West, don't let us talk about my affairs. In a family there is always something or other going awry, especially in such times as we live in now.

REBECCA *(after a short pause, sitting down in an easy-chair near the sofa)*
Why have you never once been near us during the whole of your holidays?

KROLL
Oh, it doesn't do to be importunate, you know.

REBECCA
If you only knew how we have missed you.

KROLL
And, besides, I have been away, you know.

REBECCA
Yes, for a fortnight or so. I suppose you have been going the round of the public meetings?

KROLL *(nods)*
Yes, what do you say to that? Would you ever have thought I would become a political agitator in my old age, eh?

REBECCA *(smilingly)*
You have always been a little bit of an agitator, Mr. Kroll.

KROLL
Oh, yes; just for my own amusement. But for the future it is going to be in real earnest. Do you ever read the Radical newspapers?

REBECCA
Yes, I won't deny that!

KROLL
My dear Miss West, there is no objection to that, not as far as you are concerned.

REBECCA
No, that is just what I think. I must follow the course of events, keep up with what is happening.

KROLL
Well, under any circumstances, I should never expect you, as a woman, to side actively with either party in the

civic dispute, indeed one might more properly call it the civil war, that is raging here. I dare say you have read, then, the abuse these "nature's gentlemen" are pleased to shower upon me, and the scandalous coarseness they consider they are entitled to make use of?

REBECCA
Yes, but I think you have held your own pretty forcibly.

KROLL
That I have, though I say it. I have tasted blood now, and I will make them realise that I am not the sort of man to take it lying down. (Checks himself.) No, no, do not let us get upon that sad and distressing topic this evening.

REBECCA
No, my dear Mr. Kroll, certainly not.

KROLL
Tell me, instead, how you find you get on at Rosmersholm, now that you are alone here, I mean, since our poor Beata

REBECCA
Oh, thanks, I get on very well here. Her death has made a great gap in the house in many ways, of course and one misses her and grieves for her, naturally. But in other respects

KROLL
Do you think you will remain here? Permanently, I mean?

REBECCA
Dear Mr. Kroll, I really never think about it at all. The fact is that I have become so thoroughly domesticated here that I almost feel as if I belonged to the place too.

KROLL
You? I should think you did!

REBECCA
And as long as Mr. Rosmer finds I can be any comfort or any use to him, I will gladly remain here, undoubtedly.

KROLL (looking at her, with some emotion)
You know, there is something splendid about a woman's sacrificing the whole of her youth for others.

REBECCA
What else have I had to live for?

KROLL
At first when you came here there was your perpetual worry with that unreasonable cripple of a foster-father of yours

REBECCA
You mustn't think that Dr. West was as unreasonable as that when we lived in Finmark. It was the trying journeys by sea that broke him up. But it is quite true that after we had moved here there were one or two hard years before his sufferings were over.

KROLL
Were not the years that followed even harder for you?

REBECCA
No; how can you say such a thing! I, who was so genuinely fond of Beata! And she, poor soul was so sadly in need of care and sympathetic companionship.

KROLL
You deserve to be thanked and rewarded for the forbearance with which you speak of her.

REBECCA (moving a little nearer to him)
Dear Mr. Kroll, you say that so kindly and so sincerely that I feel sure you really bear me no ill-will.

KROLL

Ill-will? What do you mean?

REBECCA

Well, it would not be so very surprising if it were rather painful for you to see me, a stranger, doing just as I like here at Rosmersholm.

KROLL

How in the world could you think!

REBECCA

Then it is not so? (Holds out her hand to, him.) Thank you, Mr. Kroll; thank you for that.

KROLL

But what on earth could make you take such an idea into your head?

REBECCA

I began to be afraid it might be so, as you have so seldom been out here to see us lately.

KROLL

I can assure you, you have been on the wrong scent entirely, Miss West. And, in any case, the situation of affairs is unchanged in any essential point; because during the last sad years of poor Beata's life it was you and you alone, even then, that looked after everything here.

REBECCA

But it was more like a kind of regency in the wife's name.

KROLL

Whatever it was, I. I will tell you what, Miss West; as far as I am concerned I should have nothing whatever to say against it if you. But it doesn't do to say such things.

REBECCA

What things?

KROLL

Well, if it so happened that you were to step into the empty place

REBECCA

I have the place I want, already, Mr. Kroll.

KROLL

Yes, as far as material benefits go; but not

REBECCA (interrupting him, in a serious voice)
For shame, Mr. Kroll! How can you sit there and jest about such things!

KROLL

Oh, well, I dare say our good John Rosmer thinks he has had more than enough of married life. But, all the same

REBECCA

Really, you almost make me feel inclined to laugh at you.

KROLL

All the same, tell me, Miss West, if I may be allowed the question, how old are you?

REBECCA

I am ashamed to say I was twenty-nine on my last birthday, Mr. Kroll. I am nearly thirty.

KROLL

Quite so. And Rosmer, how old is he? Let me see. He is five years younger than me, so he must be just about forty-three. It seems to me it would be very suitable.

REBECCA
No doubt, no doubt. It would be remarkably suitable. Will you stop and have supper with us?

KROLL
Thank you. I had meant to pay you a good long visit, because there is a matter I want to talk over with our excellent friend. Well, then, Miss West, to prevent your taking foolish ideas into your head again, I will come out here again from time to time, as in the old days.

REBECCA
Yes, please do. (Holds out her hand to, him.) Thank you, thank you! You are really uncommonly good-natured.

KROLL (with a little grumble)
Am I? I can tell you that is more than they say at home. (ROSMER comes in by the door on the right.)

REBECCA
Mr. Rosmer, do you see who is sitting here?

ROSMER
Mrs Helseth told me. (KROLL gets up.) I am so glad to see you here again, my dear fellow. (Puts his hands on KROLL'S shoulders and looks him in the face.) Dear old friend! I knew that one day we should be on our old footing again.

KROLL
My dear fellow, have you that insane idea in your head too, that any thing could come between us?

REBECCA (to ROSMER)
Isn't it delightful to think it was all our imagination!

ROSMER
Is that really true, Kroll? But why have you kept so obstinately away from us?

KROLL (seriously, and in, a subdued voice)
Because I did not want to come here like a living reminder of the unhappy time that is past and of her who met her death in the mill-race.

ROSMER
It was a very kind thought on your part. You are always so considerate. But it was altogether unnecessary to keep away from us on that account. Come along, let us sit down on the sofa. (They sit down.) I can assure you it is not in the least painful for me to think about Beata. We talk about her every day. She seems to us to have a part in the house still.

KROLL
Does she really?

REBECCA (lighting the lamp)
Yes, it is really quite true.

ROSMER
She really does. We both think so affectionately of her. And both Rebecca, both Miss West and I know in our hearts that we did all that lay in our power for the poor afflicted creature. We have nothing to reproach ourselves with. That is why I feel there is something sweet and peaceful in the way we can think of Beata now.

KROLL
You dear good people! In future I am coming out to see you every day.

REBECCA (sitting down in an arm-chair)
Yes, let us see that you keep your word.

ROSMER (with a slight hesitation)
I assure you, my dear fellow, my dearest wish would be that our intimacy should never suffer in any way. You know, you have seemed to be my natural adviser as long as we have known one another, even from my student days.

KROLL

I know, and I am very proud of the privilege. Is there by any chance anything in particular just now?

ROSMER

There are a great many things that I want very much to talk over with you frankly, things that lie very near my heart.

REBECCA

I feel that is so, too, Mr. Rosmer. It seems to me it would be such a good thing if you two old friends

KROLL

Well, I can assure you I have even more to talk over with you because I have become an active politician, as I dare say you know.

ROSMER

Yes, I know you have. How did that come about?

KROLL

I had to, you see, whether I liked it or not. It became impossible for me to remain an idle spectator any longer. Now that the Radicals have become so distressingly powerful, it was high time. And that is also why I have induced our little circle of friends in the town to bind themselves more definitely together. It was high time, I can tell you!

REBECCA *(with a slight smile)*

As a matter of fact, isn't it really rather late now?

KROLL

There is no denying it would have been more fortunate if we had succeeded in checking the stream at an earlier point. But who could really foresee what was coming? I am sure I could not. (Gets up and walks up and down.) Anyway, my eyes are completely opened now; for the spirit of revolt has spread even into my school.

ROSMER

Into the school? Surely not into your school?

KROLL

Indeed it has. Into my own school. What do you think of this? I have got wind of the fact that the boys in the top class or rather, a part of the boys in it have formed themselves into a secret society and have been taking in Mortensgaard's paper!

REBECCA

Ah, the "Searchlight".

KROLL

Yes, don't you think that is a nice sort of intellectual pabulum for future public servants? But the saddest part of it is that it is all the most promising boys in the class that have conspired together and hatched this plot against me. It is only the duffers and dunces that have held aloof from it.

REBECCA

Do you take it so much to heart, Mr. Kroll?

KROLL

Do I take it to heart, to find myself so hampered and thwarted in my life's work? (Speaking more gently.) I might find it in my heart to say that I could even take that for what it is worth; but I have not told you the worst of it yet. (Looks round the room.) I suppose nobody is likely to be listening at the doors?

REBECCA

Oh, certainly not.

KROLL

Then let me tell you that the revolt and dissension has spread into my own home, into my own peaceful home, and has disturbed the peace of my family life.

ROSMER *(getting up)*

Do you mean it? In your own home?

REBECCA *(going up to Kroll)*
Dear Mr. Kroll, what has happened?

KROLL
Would you believe it that my own children. To make a long story short, my boy Laurits is the moving spirit of the conspiracy at the school. And Hilda has embroidered a red portfolio to keep the numbers of the "Searchlight" in.

ROSMER
I should never have dreamed of such a thing; in your family, in your own house!

KROLL
No, who would ever have dreamed of such a thing? In my house, where obedience and order have always ruled, where hitherto there has never been anything but one unanimous will

REBECCA
How does your wife take it?

KROLL
Ah, that is the most incredible part of the whole thing. She, who all her days, in great things and small, has concurred in my opinions and approved of all my views, has actually not refrained from throwing her weight on the children's side on many points. And now she considers I am to blame for what has happened. She says I try to coerce the young people too much. Just as if it were not necessary to. Well, those are the sort of dissensions I have going on at home. But naturally I talk as little about it as possible; it is better to be silent about such things. *(Walks across the floor.)* Oh, yes. Oh, yes. *(Stands by the window, with his hands behind his back, and looks out.)*

REBECCA *(goes up to ROSMER, and speaks in low, hurried tones, unheard by KROLL)*
Do it!

ROSMER *(in the same tone)*
Not to-night.

REBECCA *(as before)*
Yes, this night of all others. *(Goes away from him and adjusts the lamp.)*

KROLL *(coming back)*
Yes, my dear John, so now you know the sort of spirit of the age that has cast its shadow both over my home life and my official work. Ought I not to oppose this appalling, destructive, disorganising tendency with all the weapons I can lay my hands upon? Of course it is certainly my duty and that both with my pen and my tongue.

ROSMER
But have you any hope that you can produce any effect in that way?

KROLL
At all events I mean to take my share in the fight as a citizen. And I consider that it is the duty of every patriotic man, every man who is concerned about what is right, to do the same. And, I may as well tell you, that is really the reason why I have come here to see you to-night.

ROSMER
My dear fellow, what do you mean? What can I?

KROLL
You are going to help your old friends, and do as we are doing, take your share in it to the best of your ability.

REBECCA
But, Mr. Kroll, you know how little taste Mr. Rosmer has for that sort of thing.

KROLL
Then he has got to overcome that distaste now. You do not keep abreast of the times, John. You sit here and bury yourself in your historical researches. Goodness knows, I have the greatest respect for family pedigrees and all that they imply. But this is not the time for such occupations, unhappily. You have no conception of the state of affairs that is going on all over the country. Every single idea is turned upside down, or very nearly so. It will be a hard fight to get all the errors straightened out again.

ROSMER

I can quite believe it. But that sort of a fight is not in my line at all.

REBECCA

Besides, I rather fancy that Mr. Rosmer has come to look at the affairs of life with wider opened eyes than before.

KROLL *(with a start)*
Wider opened eyes?

REBECCA

Yes, or with an opener mind, with less prejudice.

KROLL

What do you mean by that? John, surely you could never be so weak as to allow yourself to be deluded by the accidental circumstance that the demagogues have scored a temporary success!

ROSMER

My dear fellow, you know very well that I am no judge of politics; but it certainly seems to me that of late years individual thought has become somewhat more independent.

KROLL

Quite so, but do you consider that as a matter of course to be a good thing? In any case you are vastly mistaken, my friend. Just inquire a little into the opinions that are current amongst the Radicals, both out here in the country and in town. You will find them to be nothing else than the words of wisdom that appear in the "Searchlight".

REBECCA

Yes, Mortensgaard has a great deal of influence over the people about here.

KROLL

Yes, just think of it, a man with as dirty a record as his! A fellow that was turned out of his place as a schoolmaster because of his immoral conduct! This is the sort of man that poses as a leader of the people! And successfully, too! actually successfully! I hear that he means to enlarge his paper now. I know, on reliable authority, that he is looking for a competent assistant.

REBECCA

It seems to me surprising that you and your friends do not start an opposition paper.

KROLL

That is exactly what we intend to do. This very day we have bought the "County News." There was no difficulty about the financial side of the matter; but (Turns towards ROSMER) Now we have come to the real purport of my visit. It is the Management of it, the editorial management, that is the difficulty, you see. Look here, Rosmer, don't you feel called upon to undertake it, for the sake of the good cause?

ROSMER *(in a tone of consternation)*
I!

REBECCA

How can you think of such a thing!

KROLL

I can quite understand your having a horror of public meetings and being unwilling to expose yourself to the mercies of the rabble that frequents them. But an editor's work, which is carried on in much greater privacy, or rather

ROSMER

No, no, my dear fellow, you must not ask that of me.

KROLL

It would give me the greatest pleasure to have a try at work of that sort myself, only it would be quite out of the question for me; I am already saddled with such an endless number of duties. You, on the other hand, who are no longer hampered by any official duties, might. Of course the rest of us would give you all the help in our power.

ROSMER

I cannot do it, Kroll. I am not fitted for it.

KROLL

Not fitted for it? That was just what you said when your father got you your living.

ROSMER

I was quite right; and that was why I resigned it, too.

KROLL

Well, if you only make as good an editor as you did a parson, we shall be quite satisfied.

ROSMER

My dear Kroll, once for all, I cannot do it.

KROLL

Well, then, I suppose you will give us the use of your name, at all events?

ROSMER

My name?

KROLL

Yes, the mere fact of John Rosmer's name being connected with it will be a great advantage to the paper. We others are looked upon as pronounced partisans. I myself even have the reputation of being a wicked fanatic, I am told. Therefore we cannot count upon our own names to give us any particular help in making the paper known to the misguided masses. But you, on the contrary, have always held aloof from this kind of fighting. Your gentle and upright disposition, your polished mind, your unimpeachable honour, are known to and appreciated by every one about here. And then there is the deference and respect that your former position as a clergyman ensures for you, and, besides that, there is the veneration in which your family, name is held!

ROSMER

Oh, my family name.

KROLL (pointing to the portraits)

Rosmers of Rosmersholm, clergymen, soldiers, men who have filled high places in the state, men of scrupulous honour, every one of them, a family that has been rooted here, the most influential in the place, for nearly two centuries. (Lays his hand on ROSMER'S shoulder.) John, you owe it to yourself and to the traditions of your race to join us in defence of all that has hitherto been held sacred in our community. (Turning to REBECCA.) What do you say, Miss West?

REBECCA (with a quiet little laugh)

My dear Mr. Kroll, it all sounds so absurdly ludicrous to me.

KROLL

What! Ludicrous?

REBECCA

Yes, because it is time you were told plainly

ROSMER (hurriedly)

No, no, don't! Not now!

KROLL (looking from one to the other)

But, my dear friends, what on earth? (Breaks off, as Mrs HELSETH comes in, by the door on the right.) Ahem!

MRS HELSETH

There is a man at the kitchen door, sir. He says he wants to see you.

ROSMER (in a relieved voice)

Is there? Well, ask him to come in.

MRS HELSETH

Shall I show him in here, sir?

ROSMER
Certainly.

MRS HELSETH
But he doesn't look the sort of man one ought to allow in here.

REBECCA
What does he look like, Mrs Helseth?

MRS HELSETH
Oh, he is not much to look at, Miss.

ROSMER
Did he not give you his name?

MRS HELSETH
Yes, I think he said it was Hekman, or something like that.

ROSMER
I do not know any one of that name.

MRS HELSETH
And he said his Christian name was Ulrik.

ROSMER (with a start of surprise)
Ulrik Hetman! Was that it?

MRS HELSETH
Yes, sir, it was Hetman.

KROLL
I am certain I have heard that name before.

REBECCA
Surely it was the name that strange creature used to write under

ROSMER (to Kroll)
It is Ulrik Brendel's pseudonym, you know.

KROLL
That scamp Ulrik Brendel. You are quite right.

REBECCA
So he is alive still.

ROSMER
I thought he was travelling with a theatrical company.

KROLL
The last I heard of him was that he was in the workhouse.

ROSMER
Ask him to come in, Mrs Helseth.

MRS HELSETH
Yes, sir. (Goes out.)

KROLL
Do you really mean to allow this fellow into your house?

ROSMER
Oh, well, you know he was my tutor once.

KROLL
I know that what he did was to stuff your head with revolutionary ideas, and that in consequence your father turned him out of the house with a horsewhip.

ROSMER (a little bitterly)
Yes, my father was always the commanding officer, even at home.

KROLL
Be grateful to his memory for that, my dear John. Ah! (Mrs HELSETH shows ULRIK BRENDEL in at the door, then goes out and shuts the door after her. BRENDEL is a good-looking man with grey hair and beard; somewhat emaciated, but active and alert; he is dressed like a common tramp, in a threadbare frock coat, shoes with holes in them, and no visible linen at his neck or wrists. He wears a pair of old black gloves, carries a dirty soft hat under his arm, and has a walking-stick in his hand. He looks puzzled at first, then goes quickly up to KROLL and holds out his hand to him.)

BRENDEL
Good-evening, John!

KROLL
Excuse me

BRENDEL
Did you ever expect to see me again? And inside these hated walls, too?

KROLL
Excuse me. (Points to ROSMER.) Over there.

BRENDEL (turning round)
Quite right. There he is. John, my boy, my favourite pupil!

ROSMER (shaking hands with him)
My old tutor!

BRENDEL
In spite of certain recollections, I could not pass by Rosmersholm without paying you a flying visit.

ROSMER
You are very welcome here now. Be sure of that.

BRENDEL
And this charming lady? (Bows to Rebecca.) Your wife, of course.

ROSMER
Miss West.

BRENDEL
A near relation, I presume. And our stranger friend here? A colleague, I can see.

ROSMER
Mr. Kroll, master of the grammar school here.

BRENDEL
Kroll? Kroll? Wait a moment. Did you take the Philology course in your student days?

KROLL
Certainly I did.

BRENDEL
By Jove, I used to know you, then

KROLL
Excuse me

BRENDEL

Were you not

KROLL

Excuse me

BRENDEL

One of those champions of all the virtues that got me turned out of the Debating Society?

KROLL

Very possibly. But I disclaim any other acquaintance with you.

BRENDEL

All right, all right! Nach Belieben, Mr. Kroll. I dare say I shall get over it. Ulrik Brendel will still be himself in spite of it.

REBECCA

Are you on your way to the town, Mr. Brendel?

BRENDEL

You have hit the nail on the head, ma'am. At certain intervals I am obliged to do something for my living. I do not do it willingly, but, enfin, when needs must

ROSMER

My dear Mr. Brendel, will you not let me be of assistance to you? In some way or another, I mean

BRENDEL

Ah, what a proposal to come from you! Could you wish to soil the tie that binds us together? Never, John, never!

ROSMER

But what do you propose to do in the town, then? I assure you, you won't find it so easy

BRENDEL

Leave that to me, my boy. The die is cast. The unworthy individual who stands before you is started on an extensive campaign, more extensive than all his former excursions put together. (To KROLL.) May I venture to ask you, Professor, unter uns, are there in your esteemed town any fairly decent, respectable and spacious assembly-rooms?

KROLL

The most spacious is the hall belonging to the Working Men's Association.

BRENDEL

May I ask, sir, if you have any special influence with that no doubt most useful Association?

KROLL

I have nothing whatever to do with it.

REBECCA (to BRENDEL)

You ought to apply to Peter Mortensgaard.

BRENDEL

Pardon, madame, what sort of an idiot is he?

ROSMER

Why do you make up your mind he is an idiot?

BRENDEL

Do you suppose I can't tell, from the sound of the name, that it belongs to a plebeian?

KROLL

I did not expect that answer.

BRENDEL

But I will conquer my prejudices. There is nothing else for it. When a man stands at a turning-point in his life, as I do. That is settled. I shall, put myself into communication with this person, commence direct negotiations.

ROSMER

Are you in earnest when you say you are standing at a turning-point in your life?

BRENDEL

Does my own boy not know that wherever Ulrik Brendel stands he is always in earnest about it? Look here, I mean to become a new man now, to emerge from the cloak of reserve in which I have hitherto shrouded myself.

ROSMER

In what way?

BRENDEL

I mean to take an active part in life, to step forward, to look higher. The atmosphere we breathe is heavy with storms. I want now to offer my mite upon the altar of emancipation.

KROLL

You too?

BRENDEL (to them all)

Has your public here any intimate acquaintance with my scattered writings?

KROLL

No, I must candidly confess that

REBECCA

I have read several of them. My foster-father had them.

BRENDEL

My dear lady, then you have wasted your, time. They are simply trash, allow me to tell you.

REBECCA

Really?

BRENDEL

Those you have read, yes. My really important works no man or woman knows anything about. No one, except myself.

REBECCA

How is that?

BRENDEL

Because they are not yet written.

ROSMER

But, my dear Mr. Brendel

BRENDEL

You know, my dear John, that I am a bit of a sybarite, a gourmet. I have always been so. I have a taste for solitary enjoyment, because in that way my enjoyment is twice, ten times, as keen. It is, like this. When I have been wrapped in a haze of golden dreams that have descended on me, when new, intoxicating, momentous thoughts have had their birth in my mind, and I have been fanned by the beat of their wings as they bore me aloft at such moments I have transformed them into poetry, into visions, into pictures. In general outlines, that is to say.

ROSMER

Quite so.

BRENDEL

You cannot imagine the luxury of enjoyment I have experienced! The mysterious rapture of creation! in, general outlines, as I said. Applause, gratitude, eulogies, crowns of laurel! all these I have culled with full hands trembling with joy. In my secret ecstasies I have steeped myself in a happiness so, intoxicating

KROLL
Ahem!

ROSMER
But you have never written anything of it down?

BRENDEL
Not a word. The thought of the dull clerk's work that it would mean has always moved me to a nauseating sense of disgust. Besides, why should I profane my own ideals when I could enjoy them, in all their purity, by myself? But now they shall be sacrificed. Honestly, I feel as a mother must do when she entrusts her young daughter to the arms of a husband. But I am going to, sacrifice them nevertheless, sacrifice them on the altar of emancipation. A series of carefully thought-out lectures, to be delivered all over the country!

REBECCA (impetuously)
That is splendid of you, Mr. Brendel! You are giving up the most precious thing you possess.

ROSMER
The only thing.

REBECCA (looking meaningly at ROSMER)
I wonder how many there are who would do as much, who dare do it?

ROSMER (returning her look)
Who knows?

BRENDEL
My audience is moved. That refreshes my heart and strengthens my will and now I shall proceed upon my task forthwith. There is one other point, though. (To KROLL.) Can you inform me, sir, whether there is an Abstainers' Society in the town? A Total Abstainers' Society? I feel sure there must be.

KROLL
There is one, at your service. I am the president.

BRENDEL
I could tell that as soon as I saw you! Well, it is not at all impossible that I may come to you and become a member for a week.

KROLL
Excuse me, we do not accept weekly members.

BRENDEL
A la bonne heure, my good sir. Ulrik Brendel has never been in the habit of forcing himself upon societies of that kind. (Turns to go But I must not prolong my stay in this house, rich as it is in memories. I must go into the town and find some suitable lodging. I shall find a decent hotel of some kind there, I hope?

REBECCA
Will you not have something hot to drink before you go?

BRENDEL
Of what nature, dear lady?

REBECCA
A cup of tea, or

BRENDEL
A thousand thanks to the most generous of hostesses! but I do not like trespassing on private hospitality. (Waves his hand.) Good-bye to you all! (Goes to the door, but turns back.) Oh, by the way, John, Mr. Rosmer, will you do your former tutor a service for old friendship's sake?

ROSMER
With the greatest of pleasure.

BRENDEL
Good. Well, then, lend me, just for a day or two, a starched shirt.

ROSMER
Nothing more than that!

BRENDEL
Because, you see, I am travelling on foot, on this occasion. My trunk is being sent after me.

ROSMER
Quite so. But, in that case, isn't there anything else?

BRENDEL
Well, I will tell you what, perhaps you have an old, worn-out summer coat that you could spare?

ROSMER
Certainly I have.

BRENDEL
And if there happened to be a pair of presentable shoes that would go with the coat

ROSMER
I am sure we can manage that, too. As soon as you let us know your address, we will send the things to you.

BRENDEL
Please don't think of it! No one must be put to any inconvenience on my account! I will take the trifles with me.

ROSMER
Very well. Will you come upstairs with me, then?

REBECCA
Let me go. Mrs Helseth and I will see about it.

BRENDEL
I could never think of allowing this charming lady

REBECCA
Nonsense! Come along, Mr. Brendel. (She goes out by the door on the right.)

ROSMER (holding BRENDEL back)
Tell me, is there no other way I can be of service to you?

BRENDEL
I am sure I do not know of any. Yes, perdition seize it! now that I come to think of it, John, do you happen to have seven or eight shillings on you?

ROSMER
I will see. (Opens his purse.) I have two half-sovereigns here.

BRENDEL
Oh, well, never mind. I may as well take them. I can always get change in town. Thanks, in the meantime. Remember that it was two half-sovereigns I had. Good-night, my own dear boy! Good-night to you, sir! (Goes out by the door on the right, where ROSMER takes leave of him and shuts the door after him.)

KROLL
Good heavens, and that is the Ulrik Brendel of whom people once thought that he would do great things!

ROSMER
At all events he has had the courage to live his life in his own way. I do not think that is such a small thing, after all.

KROLL
What? A life like his? I almost believe he would have the power, even now, to disturb all your ideas.

ROSMER

No, indeed. I have come to a clear understanding with myself now, upon all points.

KROLL

I wish I could believe it, my dear Rosmer. You are so dreadfully susceptible to impressions from without.

ROSMER

Let us sit down. I want to have a talk with you.

KROLL

By all means. (They sit down on the couch.)

ROSMER *(after a short pause)*

Don't you think everything here looks very pleasant and comfortable?

KROLL

Yes, it looks very pleasant and comfortable now and peaceful. You have made yourself a real home, Rosmer. And I have lost mine.

ROSMER

My dear fellow, do not say that. There may seem to be a rift just now, but it will heal again.

KROLL

Never, never. The sting will always remain. Things can never be as they were before.

ROSMER

I want to ask you something, Kroll. You and I have been the closest of friends now for so many years, does it seem to you conceivable that anything could destroy our friendship?

KROLL

I cannot imagine anything that could cause a breach between us. What has put that into your head?

ROSMER

Well, your attaching such tremendous importance to similarity of opinions and views.

KROLL

Certainly I do; but then we two hold pretty similar opinions at all events on the most essential points.

ROSMER *(gently)*

No. Not any longer.

KROLL *(trying to jump up from his seat)*

What is this?

ROSMER *(restraining him)*

No, you must sit still. Please, Kroll.

KROLL

What does it all mean? I do not understand you. Tell me, straight out!

ROSMER

A new summer has blossomed in my heart, my eyes have regained the clearness of youth. And, accordingly, I am now standing where

KROLL

Where? Where are you standing?

ROSMER

Where your children are standing.

KROLL

You? You! The thing is impossible! Where do you say you are standing?

ROSMER

On the same side as Laurits and Hilda.

KROLL *(letting his head drop)*

An apostate. John Rosmer an apostate.

ROSMER

What you are calling apostasy ought to have made me feel sincerely happy and fortunate; but for all that I have suffered keenly, because I knew quite well it would cause you bitter sorrow.

KROLL

Rosmer, Rosmer, I shall never get over this. (Looks at him sadly.) To think that you, too, could bring yourself to sympathise with and join in the work of disorder and ruin that is playing havoc with our unhappy country.

ROSMER

It is the work of emancipation that I sympathise with.

KROLL

Oh yes, I know all about that. That is what it is called, by both those who are leading the people astray and by their misguided victims. But, be sure of this, you need expect no emancipation to be the result of the spirit that relies on the poisoning of the whole of our social life.

ROSMER

I do not give my allegiance to the spirit that is directing this, nor to any of those who are leading the fight. I want to try to bring men of all shades of opinion together, as many as I can reach, and bind them as closely together as I can. I want to live for and devote all the strength that is in me to one end only, to create a real public opinion in the country.

KROLL

So you do not consider that we have sufficient public opinion! I, for my part, consider that the whole lot of us are on the high road to be dragged down into the mire where otherwise only the common people would be wallowing.

ROSMER

It is just for that reason that I have made up my mind as to what should be the real task of public opinion.

KROLL

What task?

ROSMER

The task of making all our fellow-countrymen into men of nobility.

KROLL

All our fellow-countrymen!

ROSMER

As many as possible, at all events.

KROLL

By what means?

ROSMER

By emancipating their ideas and purifying their aspirations, it seems to me.

KROLL

You are a dreamer, Rosmer. Are you going to emancipate them? Are you going to purify them?

ROSMER

No, my dear fellow, I can only try to awake the desire for it in them. The doing of it rests with themselves.

KROLL

And do you think they are capable of it?

ROSMER

Yes.

KROLL

Of their own power?

ROSMER

Yes, of their own power. There is no other that can do it.

KROLL (getting up)

Is that speaking as befits a clergyman?

ROSMER

I am a clergyman no longer.

KROLL

Yes, but what of the faith you were brought up in?

ROSMER

I have it no longer.

KROLL

You have it no longer?

ROSMER (getting up)

I have given it up. I had to give it up, Kroll.

KROLL (controlling his emotion)

I see. Yes, yes. The one thing implies the other. Was that the reason, then, why you left the service of the Church?

ROSMER

Yes. When my mind was clearly made up, when I felt the certainty that it Was not merely a transitory temptation, but that it was something that I would neither have the power nor the desire to dismiss from my mind then I took that step.

KROLL

So it has been fermenting in your mind as long as that. And we, your friends, have never been allowed to know anything of it. Rosmer, Rosmer, how could you hide the sorrowful truth from us!

ROSMER

Because I considered it was a matter that only concerned myself; and therefore I did not wish to cause you and my other friends any unnecessary pain. I thought I should be able to live my life here as I have done hitherto peacefully and happily. I wanted to read, and absorb myself in all the works that so far had been sealed books to me, to familiarise myself thoroughly with the great world of truth and freedom that has been disclosed to me now.

KROLL

An apostate. Every word you say bears witness to that. But, for all that, why have you made this confession of your secret apostasy? Or why just at the present moment?

ROSMER

You yourself have compelled me to it, Kroll.

KROLL

I? I have compelled you?

ROSMER

When I heard of your violent behaviour at public meetings, when I read the reports of all the vehement speeches you made there of all your bitter attacks upon those that were on the other side, your scornful censure of your opponents, oh, Kroll, to think that you, you could be the man to do that! then my eyes were opened to my imperative duty. Mankind is suffering from the strife that is going on now, and we ought to bring peace and happiness and a spirit of reconciliation into their souls. That is why I step forward now and confess myself openly for what I am, and, besides, I want to put my powers to the test, as well as others. Could not you, from your side, go with me in that, Kroll?

KROLL
Never, as long as I live, will I make any alliance with the forces of disorder in the community.

ROSMER
Well, let us at least fight with honourable weapons, since it seems we must fight.

KROLL
I can have nothing more to do with any one who does not think with me on matters of vital importance, and I owe such a man no consideration.

ROSMER
Does that apply even to me?

KROLL
You yourself have broken with me, Rosmer.

ROSMER
But does this really mean a breach between us?

KROLL
Between us! It is a breach with all those who have hitherto stood shoulder to shoulder with you. And now you must take the consequences.

(REBECCA comes in from the room on the right and opens the door wide.)

REBECCA
Well, that is done! We have started him off on the road to his great sacrifice, and now we can go in to supper. Will you come in, Mr. Kroll?

KROLL (taking his hat)
Good-night, Miss West. This is no longer any place for me.

REBECCA (excitedly)
What do you mean? (Shuts the door and comes nearer to the two men.) Have you told him?

ROSMER
He knows now.

KROLL
We shall not let you slip out of our hands, Rosmer. We shall compel you to come back to us again.

ROSMER
I shall never find myself there any more.

KROLL
We shall see. You are not the man to endure standing alone.

ROSMER
I am not so entirely alone, even now. There are two of us to bear the solitude together here.

KROLL
Ah! (A suspicion appears to cross his mind.) That too! Beata's words!

ROSMER
Beata's?

KROLL (dismissing the thought from his mind)
No, no, that was odious of me. Forgive me.

ROSMER
What? What do you mean?

KROLL
Think no more about it. I am ashamed of it. Forgive me and good-bye. (Goes out by the door to the hall.)

ROSMER (following him)
Kroll! We cannot end everything between us like this. I will come and see you to-morrow.

KROLL (turning round in the hall)
You shall not set your foot in my house. (Takes his stick and goes.)

ROSMER stands for a while at the open door; then shuts it and comes back into the room.)

ROSMER
That does not matter, Rebecca. We shall be able to go through with it, for all that, we two trusty friends, you and I.

REBECCA
What do you suppose he meant just now when he said he was ashamed of himself?

ROSMER
My dear girl, don't bother your head about that. He didn't even believe what he meant, himself. But I will go and see him tomorrow. Goodnight!

REBECCA
Are you going up so early to-night after this?

ROSMER
As early to-night as I usually do. I feel such a sense of relief now that it is over. You see, my dear Rebecca, I am perfectly calm, so you take it calmly, too. Good-night.

REBECCA
Good-night, dear friend and sleep well! (ROSMER goes out by the door to the lobby; then his footsteps are heard as he goes upstairs. REBECCA goes to the wall and rings a bell, which is answered by Mrs HELSETH.)
You can clear the table again, Mrs Helseth. Mr. Rosmer does not want anything, and Mr. Kroll has gone home.

MRS HELSETH
Gone home? What was wrong with him, miss?

REBECCA (taking up her crochet-work)
He prophesied that there was a heavy storm brewing

MRS HELSETH
That is very strange, miss, because there isn't a scrap of cloud in the sky.

REBECCA
Let us hope he doesn't meet the White Horse. Because I am afraid it will not be long before we hear something of the family ghost.

MRS HELSETH
God forgive you, miss, don't talk of such a dreadful thing!

REBECCA
Oh, come, come!

MRS HELSETH (lowering her voice)
Do you really think, miss, that some one here is to go soon?

REBECCA
Not a bit of it. But there are so many sorts of white horses in this world, Mrs Helseth. Well, good-night. I shall go to my room now.

MRS HELSETH
Good-night, miss. (Rebecca takes her work and goes out to the right. Mrs HELSETH shakes her head, as she turns down the lamp, and mutters to herself): Lord, Lord! how queer Miss West does talk sometimes!

ACT II

(SCENE. ROSMER'S study. The door into it is in the left-hand wall. At the back of the room is a doorway with a curtain drawn back from it, leading to his bedroom. On the right, a window, in front of which is a writing-table strewn with books and papers. Bookshelves and cupboards on the walls. Homely furniture. On the left, an old-fashioned sofa with a table in front of it. ROSMER, wearing a smoking-jacket, is sitting at the writing-table on a high-backed chair. He is cutting and turning over the leaves of a magazine, and dipping into it here and there. A knock is heard at the door on the left.)

ROSMER (without turning round)
Come in.

(REBECCA comes in, wearing a morning wrapper.)

REBECCA
Good morning.

ROSMER (still turning over the leaves of his book)
Good morning, dear. Do you want anything?

REBECCA
Only to ask if you have slept well?

ROSMER
I went to sleep feeling so secure and happy. I did not even dream. (Turns round.) And you?

REBECCA
Thanks, I got to sleep in the early morning.

ROSMER
I do not think I have felt so light-hearted for a long time as I do to-day. I am so glad that I had the opportunity to say what I did.

REBECCA
Yes, you should not have been silent so long, John.

ROSMER
I cannot understand how I came to be such a coward.

REBECCA
I am sure it was not really from cowardice.

ROSMER
Yes, indeed. I can see that at bottom there was some cowardice about it.

REBECCA
So much the braver of you to face it as you did. (Sits down beside him on a chair by the writing-table.) But now I want to confess something that I have done, something that you must not be vexed with me about.

ROSMER
Vexed? My dear girl, how can you think?

REBECCA
Yes, because I dare say it was a little presumptuous of me, but

ROSMER
Well, let me hear what it was.

REBECCA
Last night, when that Ulrick Brendel was going, I wrote him a line or two to take to Mortensgaard.

ROSMER *(a little doubtfully)*
But, my dear Rebecca. What did you write, then?

REBECCA
I wrote that he would be doing you a service if he would interest himself a little in that unfortunate man, and help him in any way he could.

ROSMER
My dear, you should not have done that. You have only done Brendel harm by doing so. And besides, Mortensgaard is a man I particularly wish to have nothing to do with. You know I have been at loggerheads once with him already.

REBECCA
But do you not think that now it might be a very good thing if you got on to good terms with him again?

ROSMER
I? With Mortensgaard? For what reason, do you mean?

REBECCA
Well, because you cannot feel altogether secure now, since this has come between you and your friends.

ROSMER *(looking at her and shaking his head)*
Is it possible that you think either Kroll or any of the others would take a revenge on me, that they could be capable of

REBECCA
In their first heat of indignation dear. No one can be certain of that. I think, after the way Mr. Kroll took it

ROSMER
Oh, you ought to know him better than that. Kroll is an honourable man, through and through. I will go into town this afternoon, and have a talk with him. I will have a talk with them all. Oh, you will see how smoothly everything will go. (Mrs HELSETH comes in by the door on the left.)

REBECCA *(getting up)*
What is it, Mrs Helseth?

MRS HELSETH
Mr. Kroll is downstairs in the hall, miss.

ROSMER *(getting up quickly)*
Kroll!

REBECCA
Mr. Kroll! What a surprise!

MRS HELSETH
He asks if he may come up and speak to Mr. Rosmer.

ROSMER *(to REBECCA)*
What did I say! (To Mrs HELSETH). Of course he may. (Goes to the door and calls down the stairs.) Come up, my dear fellow! I am delighted to see you! (He stands holding the door open. Mrs HELSETH goes out. REBECCA draws the curtain over the doorway at the back, and then begins to tidy the room. KROLL comes in with his hat in his hand.)

ROSMER *(quietly, and with some emotion)*
I knew quite well it would not be the last time

KROLL
To-day I see the matter in quite a different light from yesterday.

ROSMER
Of course you do, Kroll! Of course you do! You have been thinking things over

KROLL

You misunderstand me altogether. (Puts his hat down on the table.) It is important that I should speak to you alone.

ROSMER

Why may not Miss West?

REBECCA

No, no, Mr. Rosmer. I will go.

KROLL (looking meaningly at her)

And I see I ought to apologise to you, Miss West, for coming here so early in the morning. I see I have taken you by surprise, before you have had time to

REBECCA (with a start)

Why so? Do you find anything out of place in the fact of my wearing a morning wrapper at home here?

KROLL

By no means! Besides, I have no knowledge of what customs may have grown up at Rosmersholm.

ROSMER

Kroll, you are not the least like yourself to-day.

REBECCA

I will wish you good morning, Mr. Kroll. (Goes out to the left.)

KROLL

If. you will allow me (Sits down on the couch.)

ROSMER

Yes, my dear fellow, let us make ourselves comfortable and have a confidential talk. (Sits down on a chair facing KROLL.)

KROLL

I have not been able to close an eye since yesterday. I lay all night, thinking and thinking.

ROSMER

And what have you got to say to-day?

KROLL

It will take me some time, Rosmer. Let me begin with a sort of introduction. I can give you some news of Ulrick Brendel.

ROSMER

Has he been to see you?

KROLL

No. He took up his quarters in a low-class tavern, in the lowest kind of company, of course; drank, and stood drinks to others, as long as he had any money left; and then began to abuse the whole lot of them as a contemptible rabble and, indeed, as far as that goes he was quite right. But the result was, that he got a thrashing and was thrown out into the gutter.

ROSMER

I see he is altogether incorrigible.

KROLL

He had pawned the coat you gave him, too, but that is going to be redeemed for him. Can you guess by whom?

ROSMER

By yourself, perhaps?

KROLL

No. By our noble friend Mr. Mortensgaard.

ROSMER

Is that so?

KROLL

I am informed that Mr. Brendel's first visit was paid to the "idiot" and "plebeian".

ROSMER

Well, it was very lucky for him

KROLL

Indeed it was. (Leans over the table, towards ROSMER.) Now I am coming to a matter of which, for the sake of our old, our former, friendship, it is my duty to warn you.

ROSMER

My dear fellow, what is that?

KROLL

It is this; that certain games are going on behind your back in this house.

ROSMER

How can you think that? Is it Rebec-is it Miss West you are alluding to?

KROLL

Precisely. And I can quite understand it on her part; she has been accustomed, for such a long time now, to do as she likes here. But nevertheless

ROSMER

My dear Kroll, you are absolutely mistaken. She and I have no secrets from one another about anything whatever.

KROLL

Then has she confessed to you that she has been corresponding with the editor of the "Searchlight"?

ROSMER

Oh, you mean the couple of lines she wrote to him on Ulrik Brendel's behalf?

KROLL

You have found that out, then? And do you approve of her being on terms of this sort with that scurrilous hack, who almost every week tries to pillory me for my attitude in my school and out of it?

ROSMER

My dear fellow, I don't suppose that side of the question has ever occurred to her. And in any case, of course she has entire freedom of action, just as I have myself.

KROLL

Indeed? Well, I suppose that is quite in accordance with the new turn your views have taken because I suppose Miss West looks at things from the same standpoint as you?

ROSMER

She does. We two have worked our way forward in complete companionship.

KROLL (looking at him and shaking his head slowly)

Oh, you blind, deluded man!

ROSMER

I? What makes you say that?

KROLL

Because I dare not, I WILL not think the worst. No, no, let me finish what I want to say. Am I to believe that you really prize my friendship, Rosmer? And my respect, too? Do you?

ROSMER

Surely I need not answer that question.

KROLL

Well, but there are other things that require answering, that require full explanation on your part. Will you submit to it if I hold a sort of inquiry?

ROSMER

An inquiry?

KROLL

Yes, if I ask you questions about one or two things that it may be painful for you to recall to mind. For instance, the matter of your apostasy well, your emancipation, if you choose to call it so, is bound up with so much else for which, for your own sake, you ought to account to me.

ROSMER

My dear fellow, ask me about anything you please. I have nothing to conceal.

KROLL

Well, then, tell me this, what do you yourself believe was the real reason of Beata's making away with herself?

ROSMER

Can you have any doubt? Or perhaps I should rather say, need one look for reasons for what an unhappy sick woman, who is unaccountable for her actions, may do?

KROLL

Are you certain that Beata was so entirely unaccountable for her actions? The doctors, at all events, did not consider that so absolutely certain.

ROSMER

If the doctors had ever seen her in the state in which I have so often seen her, both night and day, they would have had no doubt about it.

KROLL

I did not doubt it either, at the time.

ROSMER

Of course not. It was impossible to doubt it, unfortunately. You remember what I told you of her ungovernable, wild fits of passion, which she expected me to reciprocate. She terrified me! And think how she tortured herself with baseless self-reproaches in the last years of her life!

KROLL

Yes, when she knew that she would always be childless.

ROSMER

Well, think what it meant, to be perpetually in the clutches of such agony of mind over a thing that she was not in the slightest degree responsible for! Are you going to suggest that she was accountable for her actions?

KROLL

Hm! Do you remember whether at that time you had, in the house any books dealing with the purport of marriage, according to the advanced views of to-day?

ROSMER

I remember Miss West's lending me a work of the kind. She inherited Dr. West's library, you know. But, my dear Kroll, you surely do not suppose that we were so imprudent as to let the poor sick creature get wind of any such ideas? I can solemnly swear that we were in no way to blame. It was the overwrought nerves of her own brain that were responsible for these frantic aberrations.

KROLL

There is one thing, at any rate, that I can tell you now, and that is that your poor tortured and overwrought Beata put an end to her own life in order that yours might be happy and that you might be free to live as you pleased.

ROSMER (starting half up from his chair)
What do you mean by that?

KROLL

You must listen to me quietly, Rosmer because now I can speak of it. During the last year of her life she came twice to see me, to tell me what she suffered from her fears and her despair.

ROSMER

On that point?

KROLL

No. The first time she came she declared that you were on the high road to apostasy, that you were going to desert the faith that your father had taught you.

ROSMER (eagerly)

What you say is impossible, Kroll! absolutely impossible! You must be wrong about that.

KROLL

Why?

ROSMER

Because as long as Beata lived I was still doubting and fighting with myself. And I fought out that fight alone and in the completest secrecy. I do not imagine that even Rebecca

KROLL

Rebecca?

ROSMER

Oh, well, Miss West. I call her Rebecca for the sake of convenience.

KROLL

So I have observed.

ROSMER

That is why it is so incomprehensible to me that Beata should have had any suspicion of it. Why did she never speak to me about it? for she never did, by a single word.

KROLL

Poor soul, she begged and implored me to speak to you.

ROSMER

Then why did you never do so?

KROLL

Do you think I had a moment's doubt, at that time, that her mind was unhinged? Such an accusation as that, against a man like you! Well, she came to see me again, about a month later. She seemed calmer then; but, as she was going away, she said: "They may expect to see the White Horse soon at Rosmersholm."

ROSMER

Yes, I know, the White Horse. She often used to talk about that.

KROLL

And then, when I tried to distract her from such unhappy thoughts, she only answered: "I have not much time left; for John must marry Rebecca immediately now."

ROSMER (almost speechless)

What are you saying! I marry!

KROLL

That was on a Thursday afternoon. On the Saturday evening she threw herself from the footbridge into the millrace.

ROSMER

And you never warned us!

KROLL

Well, you know yourself how constantly she used to say that she was sure she would die before long.

ROSMER

Yes, I know. But, all the same, you ought to have warned us!

KROLL

I did think of doing so. But then it was too late.

ROSMER

But since then, why have you not? Why have you kept all this to yourself?

KROLL

What good would it have done for me to come here and add to your pain and distress? Of course I thought the whole thing was merely wild, empty fancy, until yesterday evening.

ROSMER

Then you do not think so any longer?

KROLL

Did not Beata see clearly enough, when she saw that you were going to fall away from your childhood's faith?

ROSMER (staring in front of him)

Yes, I cannot understand that. It is the most incomprehensible thing in the world to me.

KROLL

Incomprehensible or not, the thing is true. And now I ask you, Rosmer, how much truth is there in her other accusation? the last one, I mean.

ROSMER

Accusation? Was that an accusation, then?

KROLL

Perhaps you did not notice how it was worded. She said she meant to stand out of the way. Why? Well?

ROSMER

In order that I might marry Rebecca, apparently.

KROLL

That was not quite how it was worded. Beata expressed herself differently. She said "I have not much time left; for John must marry Rebecca IMMEDIATELY now."

ROSMER (looks at him for a moment; then gets up)

Now I understand you, Kroll.

KROLL

And if you do? What answer have you to make?

ROSMER (in an even voice, controlling himself)

To such an unheard of? The only fitting answer would be to point to the door.

KROLL (getting up)

Very good.

ROSMER (standing face to face with him)

Listen to me. For considerably more than a year to be precise, since Beata's death, Rebecca West and I have lived here alone at Rosmersholm. All that time you have known of the charge Beata made against us; but I have never for one moment seen you appear the least scandalised at our living together here.

KROLL

I never knew, till yesterday evening, that it was a case of an apostate man and an "emancipated" woman living together.

ROSMER

Ah! So then you do not believe in any purity of life among apostates or emancipated folk? You do not believe that they may have the instinct of morality ingrained in their natures?

KROLL

I have no particular confidence in the kind of morality that is not rooted in the Church's faith.

ROSMER

And you mean that to apply to Rebecca and myself? to my relations with Rebecca?

KROLL

I cannot make any departure, in favour of you two, from my opinion that there is certainly no very wide gulf between free thinking and, ahem!

ROSMER

And what?

KROLL

And free love, since you force me to say it.

ROSMER *(gently)*

And you are not ashamed to say that to me! you, who have known me ever since I was a boy.

KROLL

It is just for that reason. I know how easily you allow yourself to be influenced by those you associate with. And as for your Rebecca, well, your Miss West, then, to tell the truth, we know very little about her. To cut the matter short, Rosmer, I am not going to give you up. And you, on your part, ought to try and save yourself in time.

ROSMER

Save myself? How? (Mrs HELSETH looks in through the door on the left.) What do you want?

MRS HELSETH

I wanted to ask Miss West to come down, sir.

ROSMER

Miss West is not up here.

MRS HELSETH

Indeed, sir? (Looks round the room.) That is very strange. (Goes out.)

ROSMER

You were saying?

KROLL

Listen to me. As to what may have gone on here in secret while Beata was alive, and as to what may be still going on here, I have no wish to inquire more closely. You were, of course, extremely unhappy in your marriage and to some extent that may be urged in your excuse

ROSMER

Oh, how little you really know me!

KROLL

Do not interrupt me. What I want to say is this. If you definitely must continue living with Miss West, it is absolutely necessary that you should conceal the revolution of opinion, I mean the distressing apostasy, that she has beguiled you into. Let me speak! Let me speak! I say that, if you are determined to go on with this folly, for heaven's sake hold any variety of ideas or opinions or beliefs you like but keep your opinions to yourself. It is a purely personal matter, and there is not the slightest necessity to go proclaiming it all over the countryside.

ROSMER

It is a necessity for me to abandon a false and equivocal position.

KROLL

But you have a duty towards the traditions of your family, Rosmer! Remember that! From time immemorial Rosmersholm has been a stronghold of discipline and order, of respect and esteem for all that the best people in our community have upheld and sanctioned. The whole neighbourhood has taken its tone from

Rosmersholm. If the report gets about that you yourself have broken with what I may call the Rosmer family tradition, it will evoke an irreparable state of unrest.

ROSMER
My dear Kroll, I cannot see the matter in that light. It seems to me that it is my imperative duty to bring a little light and happiness into the place where the race of Rosmers has spread darkness and oppression for all these long years.

KROLL *(looking severely at him)*
Yes, that would be a worthy action for the man with whom the race will disappear. Let such things alone, my friend. It is no suitable task for you. You were meant to lead the peaceful life of a student.

ROSMER
Yes, that may be so. But nevertheless I want to try and play my humble part in the struggles of life.

KROLL
The struggles of life! Do you know what that will mean for you? It will mean war to the death with all your friends.

ROSMER *(quietly)*
I do not imagine they are all such fanatics as you.

KROLL
You are a simple-minded creature, Rosmer, an inexperienced creature. You have no suspicion of the violence of the storm that will burst upon you. (Mrs HELSETH slightly opens the door on the left.)

MRS HELSETH
Miss West wishes me to ask you, sir

ROSMER
What is it?

MRS HELSETH
There is some one downstairs that wishes to speak to you for a minute, sir.

ROSMER
Is it the gentleman that was here yesterday afternoon, by any chance?

MRS HELSETH
No, it is that Mr. Mortensgaard.

ROSMER
Mortensgaard?

KROLL
Aha! So matters have got as far as that already, have they!

ROSMER
What does he want with me? Why did you not send him away?

MRS HELSETH
Miss West told me to ask you if he might come up.

ROSMER
Tell him I am engaged, and

KROLL *(to Mrs HELSETH)*
No; show him up, please. (Mrs HELSETH goes out. KROLL takes up his hat.) I quit the field temporarily. But we have not fought the decisive action yet.

ROSMER
As truly as I stand here, Kroll, I have absolutely nothing to do with Mortensgaard.

KROLL

I do not believe you any longer on any point. Under no circumstances shall I have any faith in you after this. It is war to the knife now. We shall try if we cannot make you powerless to do any harm.

ROSMER

Oh, Kroll, how you have sunk! How low you have sunk!

KROLL

I? And a man like you has the face to say so? Remember Beata!

ROSMER

Are you harking back to that again!

KROLL

No. You must solve the riddle of the millrace as your conscience will allow you, if you have any conscience still left. (PETER MORTENSGAARD comes in softly and quietly, by the door on the left. He is a short, slightly built man with sparse reddish hair and beard. KROLL gives him a look of hatred.) The "Searchlight" too, I see. Lighted at Rosmersholm! (Buttons up his coat.) That leaves me no doubt as to the course I should steer.

MORTENSGAARD (*quietly*)

The "Searchlight" will always be ready burning to light Mr. Kroll home.

KROLL

Yes, you have shown me your goodwill for a long time. To be sure there is a Commandment that forbids us to bear false witness against our neighbour

MORTENSGAARD

Mr. Kroll has no need to instruct me in the Commandments.

KROLL

Not even in the sixth?

ROSMER

Kroll!

MORTENSGAARD

If I needed such instruction, Mr. Rosmer is the most suitable person to give it me.

KROLL (*with scarcely concealed scorn*)

Mr. Rosmer? Oh yes, the Reverend Mr. Rosmer is undoubtedly the most suitable man for that! I hope you will enjoy yourselves, gentlemen. (Goes out and slams the door after him.)

ROSMER (*stands looking at the door, and says to himself*)

Yes, yes, it had to be so. (Turns round.) Will you tell me, Mr. Mortensgaard, what has brought you out here to see me?

MORTENSGAARD

It was really Miss West I wanted to see. I thought I ought to thank her for the kind letter I received from her yesterday.

ROSMER

I know she has written to you. Have you had a talk with her?

MORTENSGAARD

Yes, a little. (Smiles slightly.) I hear that there has been a change of views in certain respects at Rosmersholm.

ROSMER

My views have changed to a very considerable extent; I might almost say entirely.

MORTENSGAARD

That is what Miss West said. And that was why she thought I ought to come up and have a little chat with you about this.

ROSMER
About what, Mr. Mortensgaard?

MORTENSGAARD
May I have your permission to announce in the "Searchlight" that you have altered your opinions, and are going to devote yourself to the cause of free thought and progress?

ROSMER
By all means. I will go so far as to ask you to make the announcement.

MORTENSGAARD
Then it shall appear to-morrow. It will be a great and weighty piece of news that the Reverend Mr. Rosmer of Rosmersholm has made up his mind to join the forces of light in that direction too.

ROSMER
I do not quite understand you.

MORTENSGAARD
What I mean is that it implies the gain of strong moral support for our party every time we win over an earnest, Christian-minded adherent.

ROSMER *(with some astonishment)*
Then you don't know? Did Miss West not tell you that as well?

MORTENSGAARD
What, Mr. Rosmer? Miss West was in a considerable hurry. She told me to come up, and that I would hear the rest of it from yourself.

ROSMER
Very well, then; let me tell you that I have cut myself free entirely on every side. I have now, no connection of any kind with the tenets of the Church. For the future such matters have not the smallest signification for me.

MORTENSGAARD *(looking at him in perplexity)*
Well, if the moon had fallen down from the sky, I could not be more! To think that I should ever hear you yourself renounce!

ROSMER
Yes, I stand now where you have stood for a long time. You can announce that in the "Searchlight" to-morrow too.

MORTENSGAARD
That, too? No, my dear Mr. Rosmer, you must excuse me but it is not worth touching on that side of the matter.

ROSMER
Not touch on it?

MORTENSGAARD
Not at first, I think.

ROSMER
But I do not understand

MORTENSGAARD
Well, it is like this, Mr. Rosmer. You are not as familiar with all the circumstances of the case as I am, I expect. But if you, too, have joined the forces of freedom and if you, as Miss West says you do, mean to take part in the movement. I conclude you do so with the desire to be as useful to the movement as you possibly can, in practice as well as, in theory.

ROSMER
Yes, that is my most sincere wish.

MORTENSGAARD

Very well. But I must impress on you, Mr. Rosmer, that if you come forward openly with this news about your defection from the Church, you will tie your own hands immediately.

ROSMER

Do you think so?

MORTENSGAARD

Yes, you may be certain that there is not much that you would be able to do hereabouts. And besides, Mr. Rosmer, we have quite enough freethinkers already indeed, I was going to say we have too many of those gentry. What the party needs is a Christian element, something that every one must respect. That is what we want badly. And for that reason it is most advisable that you should hold your tongue about any matters that do not concern the public. That is my opinion.

ROSMER

I see. Then you would not risk having anything to do with me if I were to confess my apostasy openly?

MORTENSGAARD (shaking his head)

I should not like to, Mr. Rosmer. Lately I have made it a rule never to support anybody or anything that is opposed to the interests of the Church.

ROSMER

Have you, then, entered the fold of the Church again lately? Mortensgaard. That is another matter altogether.

ROSMER

Oh, that is how it is. Yes, I understand you now.

MORTENSGAARD

Mr. Rosmer, you ought to remember that I, of all people, have not absolute freedom of action.

ROSMER

What hampers you?

MORTENSGAARD

What hampers me is that I am a marked man.

ROSMER

Ah, of course.

MORTENSGAARD

A marked man, Mr. Rosmer. And you, of all people, ought to remember that because you were responsible, more than any one else, for my being branded.

ROSMER

If I had stood then where I stand now, I should have handled the affair more judiciously.

MORTENSGAARD

I think so too. But it is too late now; you have branded me, once for all, branded me for life. I do not suppose you can fully realise what such a thing means. But it is possible that you may soon feel the smart of it yourself now, Mr. Rosmer.

ROSMER

I?

MORTENSGAARD

Yes. You surely do not suppose that Mr. Kroll and his gang will be inclined to forgive a rupture such as yours? And the "County News" is going to be pretty bloodthirsty, I hear. It may very well come to pass that you will be a marked man, too.

ROSMER

On personal grounds, Mr. Mortensgaard, I feel myself to be invulnerable. My conduct does not offer any point of attack.

MORTENSGAARD (*with a quiet smile*)
That is saying a good deal, Mr. Rosmer.

ROSMER
Perhaps it is. But I have the right to say as much.

MORTENSGAARD
Even if you were inclined to overhaul your conduct as thoroughly as you once overhauled mine?

ROSMER
You say that very strangely. What are you driving at? is it anything definite?

MORTENSGAARD
Yes, there is one definite thing, no more than a single one. But it might be quite awkward enough if malicious opponents got a hint of it.

ROSMER
Will you have the kindness to tell me what on earth it is?

MORTENSGAARD
Can you not guess, Mr. Rosmer?

ROSMER
No, not for a moment.

MORTENSGAARD
All right. I must come out with it, then. I have in my possession a remarkable letter, that was written here at Rosmersholm.

ROSMER
Miss West's letter, you mean? Is it so remarkable?

MORTENSGAARD
No, that letter is not remarkable. But I received a letter from this house on another occasion.

ROSMER
From Miss West?

MORTENSGAARD
No, Mr. Rosmer.

ROSMER
Well, from whom, then? From whom?

MORTENSGAARD
From your late wife.

ROSMER
From my wife? You had a letter from my wife?

MORTENSGAARD
Yes, I did.

ROSMER
When?

MORTENSGAARD
It was during the poor lady's last days. It must be about a year and a half ago now. And that is the letter that is so remarkable.

ROSMER
Surely you know that my wife's mind was affected at that time?

MORTENSGAARD

I know there were a great many people who thought so. But, in my opinion, no one would have imagined anything of the kind from the letter. When I say the letter is a remarkable one, I mean remarkable in quite another way.

ROSMER

And what in the world did my poor wife find to write to you about?

MORTENSGAARD

I have the letter at home. It begins more or less to the effect that she is living in perpetual terror and dread, because of the fact that there are so many evilly disposed people about her whose only desire is to do you harm and mischief.

ROSMER

Me?

MORTENSGAARD

Yes, so she says. And then follows the most remarkable part of it all. Shall I tell you, Mr. Rosmer?

ROSMER

Of course! Tell me everything, without any reserve.

MORTENSGAARD

The poor lady begs and entreats me to be magnanimous. She says that she knows it was you, who got me dismissed from my post as schoolmaster, and implores me most earnestly not to revenge myself upon you.

ROSMER

What way did she think you could revenge yourself, then?

MORTENSGAARD

The letter goes on to say that if I should hear that anything sinful was going on at Rosmersholm, I was not to believe a word of it; that it would be only the work of wicked folk who were spreading the rumours on purpose to do you harm.

ROSMER

Does the letter say that?

MORTENSGAARD

You may read it at your convenience, Mr. Rosmer.

ROSMER

But I cannot understand? What did she imagine there could be any wicked rumours about?

MORTENSGAARD

In the first place, that you had broken away from the faith of your childhood. Mrs Rosmer denied that absolutely at that time. And, in the next place, ahem !

ROSMER

In the next place?

MORTENSGAARD

Well, in the next place she writes, though rather confusedly, that she has no knowledge of any sinful relations existing at Rosmersholm; that she has never been wronged in any way; and that if any rumours of that sort should get about, she entreats me not to allude to them in the "Searchlight".

ROSMER

Does she mention any names?

MORTENSGAARD

No.

ROSMER

Who brought you the letter?

MORTENSGAARD
I promised not to tell that. It was brought to me one evening after dark.

ROSMER
If you had made inquiries at the time, you would have learnt that my poor unhappy wife was not fully accountable for her actions.

MORTENSGAARD
I did make inquiries, Mr. Rosmer; but I must say I did not get exactly that impression.

ROSMER
Not? But why have you chosen this moment to enlighten me as to the existence of this old crazy letter?

MORTENSGAARD
With the object of advising you to be extremely cautious, Mr. Rosmer.

ROSMER
As to my way of life, do you mean?

MORTENSGAARD
Yes. You must remember that for the future you will not be unassailable.

ROSMER
So you persist in thinking that I have something to conceal here?

MORTENSGAARD
I do not see any reason why a man of emancipated ideas should refrain from living his life as fully as possible. Only, as I have already said, you should be cautious in future. If rumours should get about of anything that offends people's prejudices, you may be quite certain that the whole cause of freedom of thought will suffer for it. Good-bye, Mr. Rosmer.

ROSMER
Good-bye.

MORTENSGAARD
I shall go straight to the printing-office now and have the great piece of news inserted in the "Searchlight".

ROSMER
Put it all in.

MORTENSGAARD
I will put in as much as there is any need for the public to know. (Bows, and goes out. ROSMER stands at the door, while MORTENSGAARD goes downstairs. The front door is heard shutting.)

ROSMER (still standing in the doorway, calls softly)
Rebecca! Reb-ahem! (Calls loudly.) Mrs Helseth, is Miss West downstairs?

MRS HELSETH (from below)
No, sir, she is not here.

(The curtain at the end of the room is drawn back, disclosing REBECCA standing in the doorway.)

REBECCA
John!

ROSMER (turning round)
What! Were you in there, in my bedroom! My dear, what were you doing there?

REBECCA (going up to him)
I have been listening.

ROSMER
Rebecca! Could you do a thing like that?

REBECCA

Indeed I could. It was so horrid the way he said that about my morning wrapper.

ROSMER

Ah, so you were in there too when Kroll?

REBECCA

Yes. I wanted to know what was at the bottom of his mind.

ROSMER

You know I would have told you.

REBECCA

I scarcely think you would have told me everything, certainly not in his own words.

ROSMER

Did you hear everything, then?

REBECCA

Most of it, I think. I had to go down for a moment when Mortensgaard came.

ROSMER

And then came up again?

REBECCA

Do not take it ill of me, dear friend.

ROSMER

Do anything that you think right and proper. You have full freedom of action. But what do you say to it all, Rebecca? Ah, I do not think I have ever stood so much in need of you as I do to-day.

REBECCA

Surely both you and I have been prepared for what would happen some day.

ROSMER

No, no, not for this.

REBECCA

Not for this?

ROSMER

It is true that I used to think that sooner or later our beautiful pure friendship would come to be attacked by calumny and suspicion, not on Kroll's part, for I never would have believed such a thing of him but on the part of the coarse-minded and ignoble-eyed crowd. Yes, indeed; I had good reason enough for so jealously drawing a veil of concealment over our compact. It was a dangerous secret.

REBECCA

Why should we pay any heed to what all these other people think? You and I know that we have nothing to reproach ourselves with.

ROSMER

I? Nothing to reproach myself with? It is true enough that I thought so until to-day. But now, now, Rebecca

REBECCA

Yes? Now?

ROSMER

How am I to account to myself for Beata's horrible accusation?

REBECCA *(impetuously)*

Oh, don't talk about Beata! Don't think about Beata any more! She is dead, and you seemed at last to have been able to get away from the thought of her.

ROSMER

Since I have learnt of this, it seems just as if she had come to life again in some uncanny fashion.

REBECCA

Oh no, you must not say that, John! You must not!

ROSMER

I tell you it is so. We must try and get to the bottom of it. How can she have strayed into such a woeful misunderstanding of me?

REBECCA

Surely you too are not beginning to doubt that she was very nearly insane?

ROSMER

Well, I cannot deny it is just of that fact that I feel I cannot be so altogether certain any longer. And besides if it were so

REBECCA

If it were so? What then?

ROSMER

What I mean is, where are we to look for the actual cause of her sick woman's fancies turning into insanity?

REBECCA

What good can it possibly do for you to indulge in such speculations!

ROSMER

I cannot do otherwise, Rebecca. I cannot let this doubt go on gnawing at my heart, however unwilling I may be to face it.

REBECCA

But it may become a real danger to you to be perpetually dwelling on this one lugubrious topic.

ROSMER (walking about restlessly and absorbed in the idea)

I must have betrayed myself in some way or other. She must have noticed how happy I began to feel from the day you came to us.

REBECCA

Yes; but dear, even if that were so

ROSMER

You may be sure she did not fail to notice that we read the same books; that we sought one another's company, and discussed every new topic together. But I cannot understand it because I was always so careful to spare her. When I look back, it seems to me that I did everything I could to keep her apart from our lives. Or did I not, Rebecca?

REBECCA

Yes, yes, undoubtedly you did.

ROSMER

And so did you, too. And notwithstanding that! Oh, it is horrible to think of! To think that here she was with her affection all distorted by illness, never saying a word, watching us, noticing everything and, and misconstruing everything.

REBECCA (wringing her hands)

Oh, I never ought to have come to Rosmersholm.

ROSMER

Just think what she must have suffered in silence! Think of all the horrible things her poor diseased brain must have led her to believe about us and store up in her mind about us! Did she never speak to you of anything that could give you any kind of clue?

REBECCA (as if startled)

To me! Do you suppose I should have remained here a day longer, if she had?

ROSMER

No, no, that is obvious. What a fight she must have fought and fought alone, Rebecca! In despair, and all alone. And then, in the end, the poignant misery of her victory, which was also her accusation of us, in the mill-race! (Throws himself into a chair, rests his elbows on the table, and hides his face in his hands.)

REBECCA (coming quietly up behind him)

Listen to me, John. If it were in your power to call Beata back, to you, to Rosmersholm, would you do it?

ROSMER

How can I tell what I would do or what I would not do! I have no thoughts for anything but the one thing which is irrevocable.

REBECCA

You ought to be beginning to live now, John. You were beginning. You had freed yourself completely on all sides. You were feeling so happy and so light hearted

ROSMER

I know, that is true enough. And then comes this overwhelming blow.

REBECCA (standing behind him, with her arms on the back of his chair)

How beautiful it was when we used to sit there downstairs in the dusk and helped each other to plan our lives out afresh. You wanted to catch hold of actual life, the actual life of the day, as you used to say. You wanted to pass from house to house like a guest who brought emancipation with him, to win over men's thoughts and wills to your own, to fashion noble men all around you, in a wider and wider circle, noble men!

ROSMER

Noble men and happy men.

REBECCA

Yes, happy men.

ROSMER

Because it is happiness that gives the soul nobility, Rebecca.

REBECCA

Do you not think suffering too? The deepest suffering?

ROSMER

Yes, if one can win through it, conquer it, conquer it completely.

REBECCA

That is what you must do.

ROSMER (shaking his head sadly)

I shall never conquer this completely. There will always be a doubt confronting me, a question. I shall never again be able to lose myself in the enjoyment of what makes life so wonderfully beautiful.

REBECCA (speaking over the back of his chair, softly)

What do you mean, John?

ROSMER (looking up at her)

Calm and happy innocence.

REBECCA (taking a step backwards)

Of course. Innocence. (A short silence.)

ROSMER (resting his head on his hands with his elbows on the table, and looking straight in front of him)

How ingeniously, how systematically, she must have put one thing together with another! First of all she begins to have a suspicion as to my orthodoxy. How on earth did she get that idea in her mind? Any way, she did; and the idea grew into a certainty. And then, then, of course, it was easy for her to think everything else possible. (Sits up in his chair and, runs his hands through his hair.) The wild fancies I am haunted with! I shall never get quit of them. I am certain of that, certain. They will always be starting up before me to remind me of the dead.

REBECCA

Like the White Horse of Rosmersholm.

ROSMER

Yes, like that. Rushing at me out of the dark, out of the silence.

REBECCA

And, because of this morbid fancy of yours, you are going to give up the hold you had just gained upon real life?

ROSMER

You are right, it seems hard, hard, Rebecca. But I have no power of choice in the matter. How do you think I could ever get the mastery over it?

REBECCA *(standing behind his chair)*

By making new ties for yourself.

ROSMER *(starts, and looks up)*

New ties?

REBECCA

Yes, new ties with the outside world. Live, work, do something! Do not sit here musing and brooding over insoluble conundrums.

ROSMER *(getting up)*

New ties! (Walks across the room, turns at the door and comes back again.) A question occurs to my mind. Has it not occurred to you too, Rebecca?

REBECCA *(catching her breath)*

Let me hear what it is.

ROSMER

What do you suppose will become of the tie between us, after to-day?

REBECCA

I think surely our friendship can endure, come what may.

ROSMER

Yes, but that is not exactly what I meant. I was thinking of what brought us together from the first, what links us so closely to one another, our common belief in the possibility of a man and a woman living together in chastity.

REBECCA

Yes, yes, what of it?

ROSMER

What I mean is, does not such a tie as that, such a tie as ours, seem to belong properly to a life lived in quiet, happy peacefulness?

REBECCA

Well?

ROSMER

But now I see stretching before me a life of strife and unrest and violent emotions. For I mean to live my life, Rebecca! I am not going to let myself be beaten to the ground by the dread of what may happen. I am not going to have my course of life prescribed for me, either by any living soul or by another.

REBECCA

No, no, do not! Be a free man in everything, John!

ROSMER

Do you understand what is in my Mind, then? Do you not know? Do you not see how I could best win my freedom from all these harrowing memories from the whole sad past?

REBECCA
Tell me!

ROSMER
By setting up, in opposition to them, a new and living reality.

REBECCA *(feeling for the back of the chair)*
A living? What do you mean?

ROSMER *(coming closer to her)*
Rebecca, suppose I asked you now, will you be my second wife?

REBECCA *(is speechless for a moment, then gives a cry of joy). Your wife! Yours! I!*

ROSMER
Yes, let us try what that will do. We two shall be one. There must no longer be any empty place left by the dead in this house.

REBECCA
I, in Beata's place?

ROSMER
And then that chapter of my life will be closed, completely closed, never to be reopened.

Rebecca (in a low, trembling voice)
Do you think so, John?

ROSMER
It must be so! It must! I cannot, I will not go through life with a dead body on my back. Help me to throw it off, Rebecca; and then let us stifle all memories in our sense of freedom, in joy, in passion. You shall be to me the only wife I have ever had.

REBECCA *(controlling herself)*
Never speak of this, again. I will never be your wife.

ROSMER
What! Never? Do you think, then, that you could not learn to love me? Is not our friendship already tinged with love?

REBECCA *(stopping her ears, as if in fear)*
Don't speak like that, John! Don't say such things!

ROSMER *(catching her by the arm)*
It is true! There is a growing possibility in the tie that is between us. I can see that you feel that, as well as I, do you not, Rebecca?

REBECCA *(controlling herself completely)*
Listen. Let me tell you this, if you persist in this, I shall leave Rosmersholm.

ROSMER
Leave Rosmersholm! You! You cannot do that. It is impossible.

REBECCA
It is still more impossible for me to become your wife. Never, as long as I live, can I be that.

ROSMER *(looks at her in surprise)*
You say "can" and you say it so strangely. Why can you not?

REBECCA *(taking both his hands in hers)*
Dear friend, for your own sake, as well as for mine, do not ask me why. (Lets go of his hands.) So, John. (Goes towards the door on the left.)

ROSMER
For the future the world will hold only one question for me, why?

REBECCA *(turns and looks at him)*
In that case everything is at an end.

ROSMER
Between you and me?

REBECCA
Yes.

ROSMER
Things can never be at an end between us two. You shall never leave Rosmersholm.

REBECCA *(with her hand on the door-handle)*
No, I dare say I shall not. But, all the same, if you question me again, it will mean the end of everything.

ROSMER
The end of everything, all the same? How?

REBECCA
Because then I shall go the way Beata went. Now you know, John.

ROSMER
Rebecca!

REBECCA *(stops at the door and nods: slowly)*
Now you know. (Goes out.)

ROSMER *(stares in bewilderment at the shut door, and says to himself): What can it mean?*

ACT III

(SCENE - The sitting-room at Rosmersholm. The window and the hall- door are open. The morning sun is seen shining outside. REBECCA, dressed as in ACT I., is standing by the window, watering and arranging the flowers. Her work is lying on the armchair. Mrs HELSETH is going round the room with a feather brush, dusting the furniture.)

Rebecca (after a short pause)
I wonder why Mr. Rosmer is so late in coming down to-day?

MRS HELSETH
Oh, he is often as late as this, miss. He is sure to be down directly.

REBECCA
Have you seen anything of him?

MRS HELSETH
No, miss, except that as I took his coffee into his study he went into his bedroom to finish dressing.

REBECCA
The reason I ask is that he was not very well yesterday.

MRS HELSETH
No, he did not look well. It made me wonder whether something had gone amiss between him and his brother-in-law.

REBECCA
What do you suppose could go amiss between them?

MRS HELSETH
I can't say, miss. Perhaps it was that fellow Mortensgaard set them at loggerheads.

REBECCA
It is quite possible. Do you know anything of this Peter Mortensgaard?

MRS HELSETH
Not I! How could you think so, miss, a man like that!

REBECCA
Because of that horrid paper he edits, you mean?

MRS HELSETH
Not only because of that, miss. I suppose you have heard that a certain married woman, whose husband had deserted her, had a child by him?

REBECCA
I have heard it; but of course that was long before I came here.

MRS HELSETH
Bless me, yes, he was quite a young man then. But she might have had more sense than he had. He wanted to marry her, too, but that could not be done; and so he had to pay heavily for it. But since then, my word! Mortensgaard has risen in the world. There are lots of people who run after him now.

REBECCA
I believe most of the poor people turn to him first when they are in any trouble.

MRS HELSETH
Oh, not only the poor people, miss

REBECCA (glancing at her unobserved)
Indeed?

MRS HELSETH (standing at the sofa, dusting vigorously)
People you would least expect, sometimes, miss.

REBECCA (arranging the flowers)
Yes, but that is only an idea of yours, Mrs Helseth. You cannot know that for certain.

MRS HELSETH
You think I don't know anything about that for certain, do you, miss? Indeed I do. Because, if I must let out the secret at last, I carried a letter to Mortensgaard myself once.

REBECCA (turns round)
No, did you!

MRS HELSETH
Yes, that I did. And that letter, let me tell you, was written here at Rosmersholm.

REBECCA
Really, Mrs Helseth?

MRS HELSETH
I give you my word it was, miss. And it was written on good note-paper and sealed with beautiful red sealing-wax.

REBECCA
And you were entrusted with the delivery of it? Dear Mrs Helseth, it is not very difficult to guess whom it was from.

MRS HELSETH
Who, then?

REBECCA
Naturally, it was something that poor Mrs Rosmer in her invalid state

MRS HELSETH

Well, you have mentioned her name, miss, not I.

REBECCA

But what was in the letter? No, of course, you cannot know that.

MRS HELSETH

Hm! it is just possible I may know, all the same.

REBECCA

Did she tell you what she was writing about, then?

MRS HELSETH

No, she did not do that. But when Mortensgaard had read it, he set to work and cross-questioned me, so that I got a very good idea of what was in it.

REBECCA

What do you think was in it, then? Oh, dear, good Mrs Helseth, do tell me!

MRS HELSETH

Certainly not, miss. Not for worlds.

REBECCA

Oh, you can tell me. You and I are such friends, you know.

MRS HELSETH

Heaven forbid I should tell you anything about that, miss. I shall not tell you anything, except that it was some dreadful idea that they had gone and put into my poor sick mistress's head.

REBECCA

Who had put it into her head?

MRS HELSETH

Wicked people, miss. Wicked people.

REBECCA

Wicked?

MRS HELSETH

Yes, I say it again, very wicked people, they must have been.

REBECCA

And what do you think it could be?

MRS HELSETH

Oh, I know what I think but, please Heaven, I'll keep my mouth shut. At the same time, there is a certain lady in the town, hm!

REBECCA

I can see you mean Mrs Kroll.

MRS HELSETH

Yes, she is a queer one, she is. She has always been very much on the high horse with me. And she has never looked with any friendly eye on you, either, miss.

REBECCA

Do you think Mrs Rosmer was quite in her right mind when she wrote that letter to Mortensgaard?

MRS HELSETH

It is so difficult to tell, miss. I certainly don't think she was quite out of her mind.

REBECCA

But you know she seemed to go quite distracted when she learnt that she would never be able to have a child. That was when her madness first showed itself.

MRS HELSETH
Yes, that had a terrible effect on her, poor lady.

REBECCA *(taking up her work, and sitting down on a chair by the window)*
But, in other respects, do you not think that was really a good thing for Mr. Rosmer, Mrs Helseth?

MRS HELSETH
What, miss?

REBECCA
That there were no children?

MRS HELSETH
Hm! I really do not know what to say to that.

REBECCA
Believe me, it was best for him. Mr. Rosmer was never meant to be surrounded by crying children.

MRS HELSETH
Little children do not cry at Rosmersholm, Miss West.

REBECCA *(looking at her)*
Not cry?

MRS HELSETH
No. In this house, little children have never been known to cry, as long as any one can remember.

REBECCA
That is very strange.

MRS HELSETH
Yes, isn't it, miss? But it runs in the family. And there is another thing that is just as strange; when they grow up they never laugh, never laugh, all their lives.

REBECCA
But that would be extraordinary

MRS HELSETH
Have you ever once heard or seen Mr. Rosmer laugh, miss?

REBECCA
No, now that I think of it, I almost believe you are right. But I fancy most of the folk hereabouts laugh very little.

MRS HELSETH
That is quite true. People say it began at Rosmersholm, and I expect it spread like a sort of infection.

REBECCA
You are a sagacious woman, Mrs Helseth!

MRS HELSETH
Oh, you mustn't sit there and make game of me, miss. (Listens.) Hush, hush, Mr. Rosmer is coming down. He doesn't like to see brooms about. (Goes out by the door on the right. ROSMER, with his stick and hat in his hand, comes in from the lobby.)

ROSMER
Good-morning, Rebecca.

REBECCA
Good-morning, dear. (She goes on working for a little while in silence.) Are you going out?

ROSMER
Yes.

REBECCA

It is such a lovely day.

ROSMER

You did not come up to see me this morning.

REBECCA

No, I didn't. Not to-day.

ROSMER

Don't you mean to do so in future, either? Rebecca. I cannot say yet, dear.

ROSMER

Has anything come for me?

REBECCA

The "County News" has come.

ROSMER

The "County News"!

REBECCA

There it is, on the table.

ROSMER (*putting down his hat and stick*)

Is there anything?

REBECCA

Yes.

ROSMER

And you did not send it up to me

REBECCA

You will read it quite soon enough.

ROSMER

Well, let us see. (Takes up the paper and stands by the table reading it.) What! "cannot pronounce too emphatic a warning against unprincipled deserters." (Looks at her.) They call me a deserter, Rebecca.

REBECCA

They mention no names at all.

ROSMER

It comes to the same thing. (Goes on reading.) "Secret traitors to the good cause." - "Judas-like creatures, who shamelessly confess their apostasy as soon as they think the most opportune and most profitable moment has arrived." - "A reckless outrage on the fair fame of honoured ancestors" - "in the expectation that those who are enjoying a brief spell of authority will not disappoint them of a suitable reward." (Lays the paper down on the table.) And they write that of me, these men who have known me so long and so intimately, write a thing that they do not even believe themselves! They know there is not a single word of truth in it and yet they write it.

REBECCA

There is more of it yet.

ROSMER (*taking up the paper again*)

"Make some allowance for inexperience and want of judgment" - "a pernicious influence which, very possibly, has extended even to matters which for the present we will refrain from publicly discussing or condemning." (Looks at her.) What does that mean?

REBECCA

That is a hit at me, obviously.

ROSMER *(laying down the paper)*
Rebecca, this is the conduct of dishonourable men.

REBECCA
Yes, it seems to me they have no right to talk about Mortensgaard.

ROSMER *(walking up and down the room)*
They must be saved from this sort of thing. All the good that is in men is destroyed, if it is allowed to go on. But it shall not be so! How happy, how happy I should feel if I could succeed in bringing a little light into all this murky ugliness.

REBECCA *(getting up)*
I am sure of it. There is something great, something splendid, for you to live for!

ROSMER
Just think of it, if I could wake them to a real knowledge of themselves, bring them to be angry with and ashamed of themselves, induce them to be at one with each other in toleration, in love, Rebecca!

REBECCA
Yes! Give yourself up entirely to that task, and you will see that you will succeed.

ROSMER
I think it might be done. What happiness it would be to live one's life, then! No more hateful strife, only emulation; every eye fixed on the same goal; every man's will, every man's thoughts moving forward-upward, each in its own inevitable path Happiness for all and through the efforts of all! (Looks out of the window as he speaks, then gives a start and says gloomily:) Ah! not through me.

REBECCA
Not, not through you?

ROSMER
Nor for me, either.

REBECCA
Oh, John, have no such doubts.

ROSMER
Happiness, dear Rebecca, means first and foremost the calm, joyous sense of innocence.

REBECCA *(staring in front of her)*
Ah, innocence

ROSMER
You need fear nothing on that score. But I

REBECCA
You least of all men!

ROSMER *(pointing out of the window)*
The mill-race.

REBECCA
Oh, John! (Mrs HELSETH looks in in through the door on the left.)

MRS HELSETH
Miss West!

REBECCA
Presently, presently. Not now.

MRS HELSETH
Just a word, miss! (REBECCA goes to the door. Mrs HELSETH tells her something, and they whisper together for a moment; then Mrs HELSETH nods and goes away.)

ROSMER *(uneasily)*
Was it anything for me?

REBECCA
No, only something about the housekeeping. You ought to go out into the open air now, John dear. You should go for a good long walk.

ROSMER *(taking up his hat)*
Yes, come along; we will go together.

REBECCA
No, dear, I can't just now. You must go by yourself. But shake off all these gloomy thoughts, promise me that!

ROSMER
I shall never be able to shake them quite off, I am afraid.

REBECCA
Oh, but how can you let such groundless fancies take such a hold on you!

ROSMER
Unfortunately they are not so groundless as you think, dear. I have lain, thinking them over, all night. Perhaps Beata saw things truly after all.

REBECCA
In what way do you mean?

ROSMER
Saw things truly when she believed I loved you, Rebecca.

REBECCA
Truly in THAT respect?

ROSMER *(laying his hat down on the table)*
This is the question I have been wrestling with, whether we two have deluded ourselves the whole time, when we have been calling the tie between us merely friendship.

REBECCA
Do you mean, then, that the right name for it would have been?

ROSMER
Love. Yes, dear, that is what I mean. Even while Beata was alive, it was you that I gave all my thoughts to. It was you alone I yearned for. It was with you that I experienced peaceful, joyful, passionless happiness. When we consider it rightly, Rebecca, our life together began like the sweet, mysterious love of two children for one another, free from desire or any thought of anything more. Did you not feel it in that way too? Tell me.

REBECCA *(struggling with herself)*
Oh, I do not know what to answer.

ROSMER
And it was this life of intimacy, with one another and for one another, that we took to be friendship. No, dear, the tie between us has been a spiritual marriage, perhaps from the very first day. That is why I am guilty. I had no right to it, no right to it for Beata's sake.

REBECCA
No right to a happy life? Do you believe that, John?

ROSMER
She looked at the relations between us through the eyes of HER love, judged them after the nature of HER love. And it was only natural. She could not have judged them otherwise than she did.

REBECCA
But how can you so accuse yourself for Beata's delusions?

ROSMER

It was for love of me, in her own way that, she threw herself into the mill-race. That fact is certain, Rebecca. I can never get beyond that.

REBECCA

Oh, do not think of anything else but the great, splendid task that you are going to devote your life to!

ROSMER (shaking his head)

It can never be carried through. Not by me. Not after what I know now.

REBECCA

Why not by you?

ROSMER

Because no cause can ever triumph which has its beginnings in guilt.

REBECCA (impetuously)

Oh, these are nothing but prejudices you have inherited, these doubts, these fears, these scruples! You have a legend here that your dead return to haunt you in the form of white horses. This seems to me to be something of that sort.

ROSMER

Be that as it may, what difference does it make if I cannot shake it off? Believe me, Rebecca, it is as I say, any cause which is to win a lasting victory must be championed by a man who is joyous and innocent.

REBECCA

But is joy so absolutely indispensable to you, John?

ROSMER

Joy? Yes, indeed it is.

REBECCA

To you, who never laugh?

ROSMER

Yes, in spite of that. Believe me, I have a great capacity for joy.

REBECCA

Now you really must go out, dear, for a long walk, a really long one, do you hear? There is your hat, and there is your stick.

ROSMER (taking them from her)

Thank you. And you won't come too?

REBECCA

No, no, I can't come now.

ROSMER

Very well. You are none the less always with me now. (Goes out by the entrance hall. After a moment REBECCA peeps out from behind the door which he has left open. Then she goes to the door on the right, which she opens.)

REBECCA (in a whisper)

Now, Mrs Helseth. You can let him come in now. (Crosses to the window. A moment later, KROLL comes in from the right. He bows to her silently and formally and keeps his hat in his hand.)

KROLL

Has he gone, then?

REBECCA

Yes.

KROLL

Does he generally stay out long?

REBECCA

Yes. But to-day he is in a very uncertain mood so, if you do not want to meet him

KROLL

Certainly not. It is you I wish to speak to, and quite alone.

REBECCA

Then we had better make the best of our time. Please sit down. (She sits down in an easy-chair by the window. KROLL takes a chair beside her.)

KROLL

Miss West, you can scarcely have any idea how deeply pained and unhappy I am over this revolution that has taken place in John Rosmer's ideas.

REBECCA

We were prepared for that being so, at first.

KROLL

Only at first?

ROSMER

Mr. Rosmer hoped confidently that sooner or later you would take your place beside him.

KROLL

I?

REBECCA

You and all his other friends.

KROLL

That should convince you how feeble his judgment is on any matter concerning his fellow-creatures and the affairs of real life.

REBECCA

In any case, now that he feels the absolute necessity of cutting himself free on all sides

KROLL

Yes; but, let me tell you, that is exactly what I do not believe.

REBECCA

What do you believe, then?

KROLL

I believe it is you that are at the bottom of the whole thing.

REBECCA

Your wife put that into your head, Mr. Kroll.

KROLL

It does not matter who put it into my head. The point is this, that I feel grave doubts, exceedingly grave doubts, when I recall and think over the whole of your behaviour since you came here.

REBECCA *(looking at him)*

I have a notion that there was a time when you had an exceedingly strong BELIEF in me, dear Mr. Kroll, I might almost say, a warm belief.

KROLL *(in a subdued voice)*

I believe you could bewitch any one if you set yourself to do it.

REBECCA

And you say I set myself to do it!

KROLL

Yes, you did. I am no longer such a simpleton as to suppose that sentiment entered into your little game at all.

You simply wanted to secure yourself admission to Rosmersholm, to establish yourself here. That was what I was to help you to. I see it now.

REBECCA
Then you have completely forgotten that it was Beata that begged and entreated me to come and live here.

KROLL
Yes, because you had bewitched her too. Are you going to pretend that friendship is the name for what she came to feel towards you? It was idolatry, adoration. It degenerated into a, what shall I call, it? a sort of desperate passion. Yes, that is just the word for it.

REBECCA
Have the goodness to remember the condition your sister was in. As far as I am concerned I do not think I can be said to be particularly emotional in any way.

KROLL
No, you certainly are not. But that makes you all the more dangerous to those whom you wish to get into your power. It comes easy to you to act with deliberation and careful calculation, just because you have a cold heart.

REBECCA
Cold? Are you so sure of that?

KROLL
I am certain of it now. Otherwise you could not have pursued your object here so unswervingly, year after year. Yes, yes, you have gained what you wanted. You have got him and everything else here into your power. But, to carry out your schemes, you have not scrupled to make him unhappy.

REBECCA
That is not true. It is not I; it is you yourself that have made him unhappy.

KROLL
I!

REBECCA
Yes, by leading him to imagine that he was responsible for the terrible end that overtook Beata.

KROLL
Did that affect him so deeply, then?

REBECCA
Of course. A man of such gentle disposition as he

KROLL
I imagined that one of your so-called "emancipated" men would know how to overcome any scruples. But there it is! Oh, yes, as a matter of fact it turned out just as I expected. The descendant of the men who are looking at us from these walls need not think he can break loose from what has been handed down as an inviolable inheritance from generation to generation.

REBECCA (looking thoughtfully in front of her)
John Rosmer's nature is deeply rooted in his ancestors. That is certainly very true.

KROLL
Yes, and you ought to have taken that into consideration, if you had had any sympathy for him. But I dare say you were incapable of that sort of consideration. Your starting-point is so very widely-removed from his, you see.

REBECCA
What do you mean by my starting-point?

KROLL
I mean the starting-point of origin, of parentage, Miss West.

REBECCA
I see. Yes, it is quite true that my origin is very humble. But nevertheless

KROLL
I am not alluding to rank or position. I am thinking of the moral aspect of your origin.

REBECCA
Of my origin? In what respect?

KROLL
In respect of your birth generally.

REBECCA
What are you saying!

KROLL
I am only saying it because it explains the whole of your conduct.

REBECCA
I do not understand. Be so good as to tell me exactly what you mean.

KROLL
I really thought you did not need telling. Otherwise it would seem a very strange thing that you let yourself be adopted by Dr. West.

REBECCA *(getting up)*
Oh, that is it! Now I understand.

KROLL
And took his name. Your mother's name was Gamvik.

REBECCA *(crossing the room)*
My father's name was Gamvik, Mr. Kroll.

KROLL
Your mother's occupation must, of course, have brought her continually into contact with the district physician.

REBECCA
You are quite right.

KROLL
And then he takes you to live with him, immediately upon your mother's death. He treats you harshly, and yet you stay with him. You know that he will not leave you a single penny, as a matter of fact you only got a box of books, and yet you endure living with him, put up with his behaviour, and nurse him to the end.

REBECCA *(comes to the table and looks at him scornfully)*
And my doing all that makes it clear to you that there was something immoral, something criminal about my birth!

KROLL
What you did for him, I attributed to an unconscious filial instinct. And, as far as the rest of it goes, I consider that the whole of your conduct has been the outcome of your origin.

REBECCA *(hotly)*
But there is not a single word of truth in what you say! And I can prove it! Dr. West had not come to Finmark when I was born.

KROLL
Excuse me, Miss West. He went there a year before you were born. I have ascertained that.

REBECCA
You are mistaken, I tell you! You are absolutely mistaken!

KROLL

You said here, the day before yesterday, that you were twenty-nine, going on for thirty.

REBECCA

Really? Did I say that?

KROLL

Yes, you did. And from that I can calculate

REBECCA

Stop! That will not help you to calculate. For, I may as well tell you at once, I am a year older than I give myself out to be.

KROLL (smiling incredulously)

Really? That is something new. How is that?

REBECCA

When I had passed my twenty-fifth birthday, I thought I was getting altogether too old for an unmarried girl, so I resolved to tell a lie and take a year off my age.

KROLL

You, an emancipated woman, cherishing prejudices as to the marriageable age!

REBECCA

I know it was a silly thing to do and ridiculous, too. But every one has some prejudice or another that they cannot get quite rid of. We are like that.

KROLL

Maybe. But my calculation may be quite correct, all the same; because Dr. West was up in Finmark for a flying visit the year before he was appointed.

REBECCA (impetuously)

That is not true

KROLL

Isn't it?

REBECCA

No. My mother never mentioned it.

KROLL

Didn't she, really!

REBECCA

No, never. Nor Dr. West, either. Never a word of it.

KROLL

Might that not be because they both had good reason to jump over a year? Just as you have done yourself, Miss West? Perhaps it is a family failing.

REBECCA (walking about, wringing her hands)

It is impossible. It is only something you want to make me believe. Nothing in the world will make me believe it. It cannot be true! Nothing in the world

KROLL (getting up)

But, my dear Miss West, why in Heaven's name do you take it in this way? You quite alarm me! What am I to believe and think?

REBECCA

Nothing. Neither believe nor think anything.

KROLL

Then you really must give me some explanation of your taking this matter, this possibility, so much to heart.

REBECCA (controlling herself)
It is quite obvious, I should think, Mr. Kroll. I have no desire for people here to think me an illegitimate child.

KROLL
Quite so. Well, well, let us be content with your explanation, for the present. But you see that is another point on which you have cherished a certain prejudice.

REBECCA
Yes, that is quite true.

KROLL
And it seems to me that very much the same applies to most of this "emancipation" of yours, as you call it. Your reading has introduced you to a hotch-potch of new ideas and opinions; you have made a certain acquaintance with researches that are going on in various directions, researches that seem to you to upset a good many ideas that people have hitherto considered incontrovertible and unassailable. But all this has never gone any further than knowledge in your case, Miss West, a mere matter of the intellect. It has not got into your blood.

REBECCA (thoughtfully)
Perhaps you are right.

KROLL
Yes, only test yourself, and you will see! And if it is true in your case, it is easy to recognise how true it must be in John Rosmer's. Of course it is madness, pure and simple. He will be running headlong to his ruin if he persists in coming openly forward and proclaiming himself an apostate! Just think of it, he, with his shy disposition! Think of HIM disowned, hounded out of the circle to which he has always belonged, exposed to the uncompromising attacks of all the best people in the place. Nothing would ever make him the man to endure that.

REBECCA
He MUST endure it! It is too late now for him to draw back.

KROLL
Not a bit too late, not by any means too late. What has happened can be hushed up, or at any rate can be explained away as a purely temporary, though regrettable, aberration. But there is one step that it is absolutely essential he should take.

REBECCA
And that is?

KROLL
You must get him to legalise his position, Miss West.

REBECCA
The position in which he stands to me?

KROLL
Yes. You must see that you get him to do that.

REBECCA
Then you can't rid yourself of the conviction that the relations between us need "legalising," as you say?

KROLL
I do not wish to go any more precisely into the question. But I certainly have observed that the conditions under which it always seems easiest for people to abandon all their so-called prejudices are when, ahem!

REBECCA
When it is a question of the relations between a man and a woman, I suppose you mean?

KROLL
Yes, to speak candidly, that is what I mean.

REBECCA (walks across the room and looks out of the window)
I was on the point of saying that I wish you had been right, Mr. Kroll.

KROLL

What do you mean by that? You say it so strangely!

REBECCA

Oh, nothing! Do not let us talk any more about it. Ah, there he is!

KROLL

Already! I will go, then.

REBECCA *(turning to him)*

No, stay here, and you will hear something.

KROLL

Not now. I do not think I could bear to see him.

REBECCA

I beg you to stay. Please do, or you will regret it later. It is the last time I shall ever ask you to do anything.

KROLL *(looks at her in surprise, and lays his hat down)*

Very well, Miss West. It shall be as you wish. (A short pause. Then ROSMER comes in from the hall.)

ROSMER *(stops at the door, as he sees KROLL)*

What! you here?

REBECCA

He wanted to avoid meeting you, John.

KROLL *(involuntarily)*

"John?"

REBECCA

Yes, Mr. Kroll. John and I call each other by our Christian names. That is a natural consequence of the relations between us.

KROLL

Was that what I was to hear if I stayed?

REBECCA

Yes, that and something else.

ROSMER *(coming into the room)*

What is the object of your visit here to-day?

KROLL

I wanted to make one more effort to stop you, and win you back.

ROSMER *(pointing to the newspaper)*

After that?

KROLL

I did not write it.

ROSMER

Did you take any steps to prevent its appearing?

KROLL

That would have been acting unjustifiably towards the cause I serve. And, besides that, I had no power to prevent it.

REBECCA *(tears the newspaper into pieces, which she crumples up and throws into the back of the stove)*

There! Now it is out of sight; let it be out of mind too. Because there will be no more of that sort of thing, John.

KROLL

Indeed, I wish you could ensure that.

REBECCA

Come, and let us sit down, dear, all three of us. Then I will tell you all about it.

ROSMER *(sitting down involuntarily)*

What has come over you, Rebecca? You are so unnaturally calm. What is it?

REBECCA

The calmness of determination. (Sits down.) Please sit down too, Mr. Kroll. (He takes a seat on the couch.)

ROSMER

Determination, you say. Determination to do what?

REBECCA

I want to give you back what you need in order to live your life. You shall have your happy innocence back, dear friend.

ROSMER

But what do you mean?

REBECCA

I will just tell you what happened. That is all that is necessary.

ROSMER

Well?

REBECCA

When I came down here from Finmark with Dr. West, it seemed to me that a new, great, wide world was opened to me. Dr. West had given me an erratic sort of education, -had taught me all the odds and ends that I knew about life then. (Has an evident struggle with herself, and speaks in barely audible tones.) And then

KROLL

And then?

ROSMER

But, Rebecca, I know all this.

REBECCA *(collecting herself)*

Yes, that is true enough. You know it only too well.

KROLL *(looking fixedly at her)*

Perhaps it would be better if I left you.

REBECCA

No, stay where you are, dear Mr. Kroll. (To ROSMER.) Well, this was how it was. I wanted to play my part in the new day that was dawning, to have a share in all the new ideas. Mr. Kroll told me one day that Ulrik Brendel had had a great influence over you once, when you were a boy. I thought it might be possible for me to resume that influence here.

ROSMER

Did you come here with a covert design?

REBECCA

What I wanted was that we two should go forward together on the road towards freedom, always forward, and further forward! But there was that gloomy, insurmountable barrier between you and a full, complete emancipation.

ROSMER

What barrier do you mean?

REBECCA

I mean, John, that you could never have attained freedom except in the full glory of the sunshine. And, instead of that, here you were, ailing and languishing in the gloom of such a marriage as yours.

ROSMER

You have never spoken to me of my marriage in that way, before to-day.

REBECCA

No, I did not dare, for fear of frightening you.

KROLL *(nodding to ROSMER)*

You hear that!

REBECCA *(resuming)*

But I saw quite well where your salvation lay, your only salvation. And so I acted.

ROSMER

How do you mean, you acted?

KROLL

Do you mean that?

REBECCA

Yes, John. (Gets up.) No, do not get up. Nor you either, Mr. Kroll. But we must let in. the daylight now. It was not you, John. You are innocent. It was I that lured, that ended by luring, Beata into the tortuous path

ROSMER *(springing up)*

Rebecca!

KROLL *(getting up)*

Into the tortuous path!

REBECCA

Into the path that, led to the mill-race. Now you know it, both of you.

ROSMER *(as if stunned)*

But I do not understand. What is she standing there saying? I do not understand a word

KROLL

Yes, yes. I begin to understand.

ROSMER

But what did you do? What did you find to tell her? Because there was nothing, absolutely nothing!

REBECCA

She got to know that you were determined to emancipate yourself from all your old prejudices.

ROSMER

Yes, but at that time I had come to no decision.

REBECCA

I knew that you soon would come to one.

KROLL *(nodding to ROSMER)*

Aha!

ROSMER

Well, and what more? I want to know everything now.

REBECCA

Some time afterwards, I begged and implored her to let me leave Rosmersholm.

ROSMER

Why did you want to leave here then?

REBECCA

I did not want to. I wanted to remain where I was. But I told her that it would be best for us all if I went away in time. I let her infer that if I remained here any longer I could not tell what, what might happen.

ROSMER

That is what you said and did, then?

REBECCA

Yes, John.

ROSMER

That is what you referred to when you said that you "acted"?

REBECCA *(in a broken voice)*

Yes, that was it.

ROSMER *(after a pause)*

Have you confessed everything now, Rebecca?

REBECCA

Yes.

KROLL

Not everything.

REBECCA *(looking at him in terror)*

What else can there be?

KROLL

Did you not eventually lead Beata to believe that it was necessary, not merely that it should be best but that it was necessary, both for your own sake and for John's, that you should go away somewhere else as soon as possible? Well?

REBECCA *(speaking low and indistinctly)*

Perhaps I did say something of the sort.

ROSMER *(sinking into a chair by the window)*

And she, poor sick creature, believed in this tissue of lies and deceit! Believed in it so completely, so absolutely! (Looks up at REBECCA.) And she never came to me about it, never said a word! Ah, Rebecca, I see it in your face, YOU dissuaded her from doing so.

REBECCA

You know she had taken it into her head that she, a childless wife, had no right to be here. And so she persuaded herself that her duty to you was to give place to another.

ROSMER

And you, you did nothing to rid her mind of such an idea?

REBECCA

No.

KROLL

Perhaps you encouraged her in the idea? Answer! Did you not do so?

REBECCA

That was how she understood me, I believe.

ROSMER

Yes, yes, and she bowed to your will in everything. And so she gave place. (Springs up.) How could you, how could you go on with this terrible tragedy!

REBECCA

I thought there were two lives here to choose between, John.

KROLL *(severely and with authority)*

You had no right to make any such choice.

REBECCA *(impetuously)*

Surely you do not think I acted with cold and calculating composure! I am a different woman now, when I am telling you this, from what I was then. And I believe two different kinds of will can exist at the same time in one person. I wanted Beata away, in one way or the other; but I never thought it would happen, all the same. At every step I ventured and risked, I seemed to hear a voice in me crying: "No further! Not a step further!" And yet, at the same time, I COULD not stop. I HAD to venture a little bit further, just one step. And then another, and always another, and at last it happened. That is how such things go of themselves. *(A short silence.)*

ROSMER *(to REBECCA)*

And how do you think it will go with YOU in the future? after this?

REBECCA

Things must go with me as they can. It is of very little consequence.

KROLL

Not a word suggestive of remorse! Perhaps you feel none?

REBECCA *(dismissing his remark coldly)*

Excuse me, Mr. Kroll, that is a matter that is no concern of any one else's. That is an account I must settle with myself.

KROLL *(to ROSMER)*

And this is the woman you have been living under the same roof with, in relations of the completest confidence. *(Looks up at the portraits on the walls.)* If only those that are gone could look down now!

ROSMER

Are you going into the town?

KROLL *(taking up his hat)*

Yes. The sooner the better.

ROSMER *(taking his hat also)*

Then I will go with you.

KROLL

You will! Ah, I thought we had not quite lost you.

ROSMER

Come, then, Kroll. Come! *(They both go out into the hall without looking at REBECCA. After a minute REBECCA goes cautiously to the window and peeps out between the flowers.)*

REBECCA *(speaking to herself, half aloud)*

Not over the bridge to-day either. He is going round. Never over the millrace, never. *(Comes away from the window.)* As I thought! *(She goes over to the bell, and rings it. Soon afterwards Mrs HELSETH comes in from the right.)*

MRS HELSETH

What is it, miss?

REBECCA

Mrs Helseth, will you be so good as to fetch my travelling trunk down from the loft?

MRS HELSETH

Your trunk?

REBECCA

Yes, the brown hair-trunk, you know.

MRS HELSETH

Certainly, miss. But, bless my soul, are you going away on a journey, miss?

REBECCA

Yes, I am going away on a journey, Mrs Helseth.

MRS HELSETH
And immediately!

REBECCA
As soon as I have packed.

MRS HELSETH
I never heard of such a thing! But you are coming back again soon, I suppose, miss?

REBECCA
I am never coming back again.

MRS HELSETH
Never! But, my goodness, what is to become of us at Rosmersholm if Miss West is not here any longer? Just as everything was making poor Mr. Rosmer so happy and comfortable!

REBECCA
Yes, but to-day I have had a fright, Mrs Helseth.

MRS HELSETH
A fright! Good heavens-how?

REBECCA
I fancy I have had a glimpse of the White Horse.

MRS HELSETH
Of the White Horse! In broad daylight!

REBECCA
Ah! they are out both early and late, the White Horses of Rosmersholm. (Crosses the room.) Well, we were speaking of my trunk, Mrs Helseth.

MRS HELSETH
Yes, miss. Your trunk.

(They both go out to the right.)

ACT IV

(SCENE. The same room in the late evening. The lamp, with a shade on it, is burning on the table. REBECCA is standing by the table, packing some small articles in a travelling-bag. Her cloak, hat, and the white crochetted shawl are hanging on the back of the couch. Mrs HELSETH comes in from the right.)

MRS HELSETH *(speaking in low tones and with a reserved manner). Yes, all your things have been taken down, miss. They are in the kitchen passage.*

REBECCA
Thank you. You have ordered the carriage?

MRS HELSETH
Yes, miss. The coachman wants to know what time he shall bring it round.

REBECCA
I think at about eleven o'clock. The boat goes at midnight.

Mrs Helseth (with a little hesitation)
But what about Mr. Rosmer? Suppose he is not back by that time?

REBECCA
I shall start, all the same. If I should not see him, you can tell him I will write to him, a long letter, say that.

MRS HELSETH

Yes, I dare say it will be all right to write. But, poor dear, I really think that you ought to try and have a talk with him once more.

REBECCA

Perhaps I ought, or perhaps not, after all.

MRS HELSETH

Dear, dear! I never thought I should, live to see such a thing as this!

REBECCA

What did you think, then, Mrs Helseth?

MRS HELSETH

To tell the truth, miss, I thought Mr. Rosmer was an honester man than that.

REBECCA

Honester?

MRS HELSETH

Yes, miss, that is the truth.

REBECCA

But, my dear Mrs Helseth, what do you mean by that?

MRS HELSETH

I mean what is true and right, miss. He should not get out of it in this way, that he shouldn't.

REBECCA (looking at her)

Now look here, Mrs Helseth. Tell me, honestly and frankly, why you think I am going away.

MRS HELSETH

Good Lord, miss, because it is necessary, I suppose. Well, well! Still, I certainly do not think Mr. Rosmer has behaved well. There was some excuse in Mortensgaard's case, because the woman's husband was still alive; so that it was impossible for them to marry, however much they wished it. But Mr. Rosmer, he could, ahem!

REBECCA (with a faint smile)

Is it possible that you could think such things about me and Mr. Rosmer?

MRS HELSETH

Not for a moment, until to-day, I mean.

REBECCA

But why to-day?

MRS HELSETH

Well, after all the horrible things they tell me one may see in the papers about Mr. Rosmer

REBECCA

Ah!

MRS HELSETH

What I mean is this, if a man can go over to Mortensgaard's religion, you may believe him capable of anything. And that's the truth.

REBECCA

Yes, very likely. But about me? What have you got to say about me?

MRS HELSETH

Well, I am sure, miss, I do not think you are so greatly to be blamed. It is not always so easy for a lone woman to resist, I dare say. We are all human after all, Miss West.

REBECCA

That is very true, Mrs Helseth. We are all human, after all. What are you listening to?

MRS HELSETH *(in a low voice)*
Good Lord! I believe that is him coming now.

REBECCA *(with a start)*
In spite of everything, then! (Speaks with determination.) Very well. So be it. (ROSMER comes in from the hall. He sees the luggage, and turns to REBECCA.)

ROSMER
What does this mean?

REBECCA
I am going away.

ROSMER
At once?

REBECCA
Yes. (To Mrs HELSETH.) Eleven o'clock, then.

MRS HELSETH
Very well, miss. (Goes out to the right.)

ROSMER *(after a short pause)*
Where are you going, Rebecca?

REBECCA
I am taking the boat for the north.

ROSMER
North? What are you going there for?

REBECCA
It is where I came from.

ROSMER
But you have no more ties there now.

REBECCA
I have none here, either.

ROSMER
What do you propose to do?

REBECCA
I do not know. I only want to make an end of it.

ROSMER
Make an end of what?

REBECCA
Rosmersholm has broken me.

ROSMER *(more attentively)*
What is that?

REBECCA
Broken me utterly. I had a will of my own, and some courage, when I came here. Now I am crushed under the law of strangers. I do not think I shall have the courage to begin anything else in the world after this.

ROSMER
Why not? What do you mean by being crushed under a law?

REBECCA
Dear friend, do not let us talk about that now. Tell me what passed between you and Mr. Kroll.

ROSMER
We have made our peace.

REBECCA
Quite so. So it came to that.

ROSMER
He got together all our old circle of friends at his house. They convinced me that the work of ennobling men's souls was not in my line at all. Besides, it is such a hopeless task, any way. I shall let it alone.

REBECCA
Well, perhaps it is better so.

ROSMER
Do you say THAT now? Is that what your opinion is now?

REBECCA
I have come to that opinion in the last day or two.

ROSMER
You are lying, Rebecca.

REBECCA
Lying?

ROSMER
Yes, lying. You have never believed in me. You have never believed me to be the man to lead the cause to victory.

REBECCA
I have believed that we two together would be equal to it.

ROSMER
That is not true. You have believed that you could accomplish something big in life yourself, that you could use me to further your plans, that I might be useful to you in the pursuit of your object. That is what you have believed.

REBECCA
Listen to me, John

ROSMER (sitting down wearily on the couch)
Oh, let me be! I see the whole thing clearly now. I have been like a glove in your hands.

REBECCA
Listen to me, John. Let us talk this thing over. It will be for the last time. (Sits down in a chair by the couch.) I had intended to write to you about it all when I had gone back north. But it is much better that you should hear it at once.

ROSMER
Have you something more to tell, then?

REBECCA
The most important part of it all.

ROSMER
What do you mean?

REBECCA
Something that you have never suspected. Something that puts all the rest in its true light.

ROSMER (shaking his head)
I do not understand, at all.

REBECCA

It is quite true that at one time I did play my cards so as to secure admission to Rosmersholm. My idea was that I should succeed in doing well for myself here, either in one way or in another, you understand.

ROSMER

Well, you succeeded in carrying your scheme through, too.

REBECCA

I believe I could have carried anything through at that time. For then I still had the courage of a free will. I had no one else to consider, nothing to turn me from my path. But then began what has broken down my will and filled the whole of my life with dread and wretchedness.

ROSMER

What began? Speak so that I can understand you.

REBECCA

There came over me, a wild, uncontrollable passion. Oh, John!

ROSMER

Passion? You! For what?

REBECCA

For you.

ROSMER (getting up)

What does this mean!

REBECCA (preventing him)

Sit still, dear. I will tell you more about it.

ROSMER

And you mean to say, that you have loved me, in that way!

REBECCA

I thought I might call it loving you, then. I thought it was love. But it was not. It was what I have said, a wild, uncontrollable passion.

ROSMER (speaking with difficulty)

Rebecca, is it really you, you who are sitting here telling me this?

REBECCA

Yes, indeed it is, John.

ROSMER

Then it was as the outcome of this and under the influence of this, that you "acted," as you called it.

REBECCA

It swept over me like a storm over the sea, like one of the storms we have in winter in the north. They catch you up and rush you along with them, you know, until their fury is expended. There is no withstanding them.

ROSMER

So it swept poor unhappy Beata into the mill-race.

REBECCA

Yes, it was like a fight for life between Beata and me at that time.

ROSMER

You proved the strongest of us all at Rosmersholm, stronger than both Beata and me put together.

REBECCA

I knew you well enough to know that I could not get at you in any way until you were set free, both in actual circumstances and in your soul.

ROSMER

But I do not understand you, Rebecca. You, you yourself and your whole conduct are an insoluble riddle to me. I am free now, both in my soul and my circumstances. You are absolutely in touch with the goal you set before yourself from the beginning. And nevertheless

REBECCA

I have never stood farther from my goal than I do now.

ROSMER

And nevertheless, I say, when yesterday I asked you, urged you, to become my wife, you cried out that it never could be.

REBECCA

I cried out in despair, John.

ROSMER

Why?

REBECCA

Because Rosmersholm has unnerved me. All the courage has been sapped out of my will here, crushed out! The time has gone for me to dare risk anything whatever. I have lost all power of action, John.

ROSMER

Tell me how that has come about.

REBECCA

It has come about through my living with you.

ROSMER

But how? How?

REBECCA

When I was alone with you here and you had really found yourself

ROSMER

Yes, yes?

REBECCA

For you never really found yourself as long as Beata was alive

ROSMER

Alas, you are right in that.

REBECCA

When it came about that I was living together with you here, in peace and solitude, when you exchanged all your thoughts with me unreservedly, your every mood, however tender or intimate, then the great change happened in me. Little by little, you understand. Almost imperceptibly but overwhelmingly in the end, till it reached the uttermost depths of my soul.

ROSMER

What does this mean, Rebecca?

REBECCA

All the other feeling, all that horrible passion that had drowned my better self, left me entirely. All the violent emotions that had been roused in me were quelled and silenced. A peace stole over my soul, a quiet like that of one of our mountain peaks up under the midnight sun.

ROSMER

Tell me more of it, all that you can.

REBECCA

There is not much more to tell. Only that this was how love grew up in my heart, a great, self-denying love, content with such a union of hearts as there has been between us two.

ROSMER

Oh, if only I had had the slightest suspicion of all this!

REBECCA

It is best as it is. Yesterday, when you asked me if I would be your wife, I gave a cry of joy

ROSMER

Yes, it was that, Rebecca, was it not! I thought that was what it meant.

REBECCA

For a moment, yes-I forgot myself for a moment. It was my dauntless will of the old days that was struggling to be free again. But now it has no more strength, it has lost it for ever.

ROSMER

How do you explain what has taken place in you?

REBECCA

It is the Rosmer attitude towards life, or your attitude towards life, at any rate that has infected my will.

ROSMER

Infected?

REBECCA

Yes, and made it sickly, bound it captive under laws that formerly had no meaning for me. You, my life together with you, have ennobled my soul

ROSMER

Ah, if I dared believe that to be true!

REBECCA

You may believe it confidently. The Rosmer attitude towards life ennobles. But-(shakes her head) but, but

ROSMER

But? Well?

REBECCA

But it kills joy, you know.

ROSMER

Do you say that, Rebecca?

REBECCA

For me, at all events.

ROSMER

Yes, but are you so sure of that? If I asked you again now? Implored you?

REBECCA

Oh, my dear, never go back to that again! It is impossible. Yes, impossible, because I must tell you this, John. I have a past behind me.

ROSMER

Something more than you have told me?

REBECCA

Yes, something more and something different.

ROSMER *(with a faint smile)*

It is very strange, Rebecca, but, do you know, the idea of such a thing has occurred to me more than once.

REBECCA

It has? And yet, notwithstanding that, you?

ROSMER
I never believed in it. I only played with the idea, nothing more.

REBECCA
If you wish, I will tell you all about it at once.

ROSMER (*stopping her*)
No, no! I do not want to hear a word about it. Whatever it is, it shall be forgotten, as far as I am concerned.

REBECCA
But I cannot forget it.

ROSMER
Oh, Rebecca!

REBECCA
Yes, dear, that is just the dreadful part of it, that now, when all the happiness of life is freely and fully offered to me, all I can feel is that I am barred out from it by my past.

ROSMER
Your past is dead, Rebecca. It has no longer any hold on you, has nothing to do with you, as you are now.

REBECCA
Ah, my dear, those are mere words, you know. What about innocence, then? Where am I to get that from?

ROSMER (*gloomily*)
Ah, yes, innocence.

REBECCA
Yes, innocence, which is at the root of all joy and happiness. That was the teaching, you know, that you wanted to see realised by all the men you were going to raise up to nobility and happiness.

ROSMER
Ah, do not remind me of that. It was nothing but a half-dreamt dream, Rebecca, a rash suggestion that I have no longer any faith in. Human nature cannot be ennobled by outside influences, believe me.

REBECCA (*gently*)
Not by a tranquil love, do you think?

ROSMER (*thoughtfully*)
Yes, that would be a splendid thing- almost the most glorious thing in life, I think if it were so. (Moves restlessly.) But how am I ever to clear up the question? how am I to get to the bottom of it?

REBECCA
Do you not believe in me, John?

ROSMER
Ah, Rebecca, how can I believe you entirely, you whose life here has been nothing but continual concealment and secrecy! And now you have this new tale to tell. If it is cloaking some design of yours, tell me so openly. Perhaps there is something or other that you hope to gain by that means? I will gladly do anything that I can for you.

REBECCA (*wringing her hands*)
Oh, this killing doubt! John, John!

ROSMER
Yes, I know, dear, it is horrible but I cannot help it. I shall never be able to free myself from it, never be able to feel certain that your love for me is genuine and pure.

REBECCA
But is there nothing in your own heart that bears witness to the transformation that has taken place in me and taken place through your influence, and yours alone!

ROSMER

Ah, my dear, I do not believe any longer in my power to transform people. I have no belief in myself left at all. I do not believe either in myself or in you.

REBECCA (looking darkly at him)

How are you going to live out your life, then?

ROSMER

That is just what I do not know and cannot imagine. I do not believe I can live it out. And, moreover, I do not know anything in the world that would be worth living for.

REBECCA

Life carries a perpetual rebirth with it. Let us hold fast to it, dear. We shall be finished with it quite soon enough.

ROSMER (getting up restlessly)

Then give me my faith back again! my faith in you, Rebecca, my faith in your love! Give me a proof of it! I must have some proof!

REBECCA

Proof? How can I give you a proof!

ROSMER

You must! (Crosses the room.) I cannot bear this desolate, horrible loneliness, this, this. (A knock is heard at the hall door.)

REBECCA (getting up from her chair)

Did you hear that?

(The door opens, and ULRIK BRENDEL comes in. Except that he wears a white shirt, a black coat and, a good pair of high boots, he is dressed as in the first act. He looks troubled.)

ROSMER

Ah, it is you, Mr. Brendel!

BRENDEL

John, my boy, I have come to say good-bye to you!

ROSMER

Where are you going, so late as this?

BRENDEL

Downhill.

ROSMER

How?

BRENDEL

I am on my way home, my beloved pupil. I am homesick for the great Nothingness.

ROSMER

Something has happened to you, Mr. Brendel! What is it?

BRENDEL

Ah, you notice the transformation, then? Well, it is evident enough. The last time I entered your doors I stood before you a man of substance, slapping a well-filled pocket.

ROSMER

Really? I don't quite understand

BRENDEL

And now, as you see me to-night, I am a deposed monarch standing over the ashes of my burnt-out palace.

ROSMER

If there is any way I can help you

BRENDEL

You have preserved your childlike heart, John, can you let me have a loan?

ROSMER

Yes, most willingly!

BRENDEL

Can you spare me an ideal or two?

ROSMER

What do you say?

BRENDEL

One or two cast-off ideals? You will be doing a good deed. I am cleaned out, my dear boy, absolutely and entirely.

REBECCA

Did you not succeed in giving your lecture?

BRENDEL

No, fair lady. What do you think? just as I was standing ready to pour out the contents of my horn in plenty, I made the painful discovery that I was bankrupt.

REBECCA

But what of all your unwritten works, then?

BRENDEL

For five and twenty years I have been like a miser sitting on his locked money-chest. And then to-day, when I opened it to take out my treasure, there was nothing there! The mills of time had ground it into dust. There was not a blessed thing left of the whole lot.

ROSMER

But are you certain of that?

BRENDEL

There is no room for doubt, my dear boy. The President has convinced me of that.

ROSMER

The President?

BRENDEL

Oh, well. His Excellency, then. Ganz nach Belieben.

ROSMER

But whom do you mean?

BRENDEL

Peter Mortensgaard, of course.

ROSMER

What!

BRENDEL *(mysteriously)*

Hush, hush, hush! Peter Mortensgaard is Lord and Chieftain of the Future. I have never stood in a more august presence. Peter Mortensgaard has the power of omnipotence in him. He can do whatever he wants.

ROSMER

Oh, come, don't you believe that!

BRENDEL

It is true, my boy because Peter Mortensgaard never wants to do more than he can. Peter Mortensgaard is capable of living his life without ideals. And that, believe me, is precisely the great secret of success in life. It sums up all the wisdom of the world. Basta!

ROSMER *(in a low voice)*
Now I see that you are going away from here poorer than you came.

BRENDEL
Bien! Then take an example from your old tutor. Erase from your mind everything that he imprinted there. Do not build your castle upon the shifting sand. And look well ahead, and be sure of your ground, before you build upon the charming creature who is sweetening your life here.

REBECCA
Do you mean me?

BRENDEL
Yes, most attractive mermaid!

REBECCA
Why am I not fit to build upon?

BRENDEL *(taking a step nearer to her)*
I understood that my former pupil had a cause which it was his life's work to lead to victory.

REBECCA
And if he has?

BRENDEL
He is certain of victory but, be it distinctly understood, on one unalterable condition.

REBECCA
What is that?

BRENDEL *(taking her gently by the wrist)*
That the woman who loves him shall gladly go out into the kitchen and chop off her dainty, pink and white little finger, here, just at the middle joint. Furthermore, that the aforesaid loving woman shall, also gladly, clip off her incomparably moulded left ear. (Lets her go, and turns to ROSMER.) Good-bye, John the Victorious!

ROSMER
Must you go now, in this dark night?

BRENDEL
The dark night is best. Peace be with you! (He goes out. Silence in the room for a short time.)

REBECCA *(breathing heavily)*
How close and sultry it is in here! (Goes to the window, opens it and stands by it.)

ROSMER *(sitting down on a chair by the stove)*
There is nothing else for it after all, Rebecca, I can see that. You must go away.

REBECCA
Yes, I do not see that I have any choice.

ROSMER
Let us make use of our last hour together. Come over here and sit beside me.

REBECCA *(goes and sits down on the couch)*
What do you want, John?

ROSMER
In the first place I want to tell you that you need have no anxiety about your future.

REBECCA *(with a smile)*
Hm! My future!

ROSMER

I have foreseen all contingencies long ago. Whatever may happen, you are provided for.

REBECCA

Have you even done that for me, dear?

ROSMER

You might have known that I should.

REBECCA

It is many a long day since I thought about anything of the kind.

ROSMER

Yes, of course. Naturally, you thought things could never be otherwise between us than as they were.

REBECCA

Yes, that was what I thought.

ROSMER

So did I. But if anything were to happen to me now

REBECCA

Oh, John, you will live longer than I shall.

ROSMER

I can dispose of my miserable existence as I please, you know.

REBECCA

What do you mean? You surely are never thinking of!

ROSMER

Do you think it would be so surprising? After the pitiful, lamentable defeat I have suffered? I, who was to have made it my life's work to lead my cause to victory! And here I am, a deserter before the fight has even really begun!

REBECCA

Take up the fight again, John! Only try and you will see that you will conquer. You will ennoble hundreds, thousands, of souls. Only try!

ROSMER

I, Rebecca, who no longer believe even in my having a mission in life?

REBECCA

But your mission has stood the test. You have at all events ennobled one of your fellow-creatures for the rest of her life, I mean myself.

ROSMER

Yes, if I dared believe you about that.

REBECCA *(wringing her hands)*

But, John, do you know of nothing, nothing that would make you believe that?

ROSMER *(starts, as if with fear)*

Don't venture on that subject! No further, Rebecca! Not a single word more!

REBECCA

Indeed, that is just the subject we must venture upon. Do you know of anything that would stifle your doubts? For I know of nothing in the world.

ROSMER

It is best for you not to know. Best for us both.

REBECCA
No, no, no, I have no patience with that sort of thing! If you know of anything that would acquit me in your eyes, I claim it as my right that you should name it.

ROSMER *(as if impelled against his will)*
Well, let us see. You say that you have great love in your heart; that your soul has been ennobled through me. Is that so? Have you counted the cost? Shall we try and balance our accounts? Tell me.

REBECCA
I am quite ready.

ROSMER
Then when shall it be?

REBECCA
Whenever you like. The sooner the better.

ROSMER
Then let me see, Rebecca, whether you, for my sake-this very night. (Breaks off.) Oh, no, no!

REBECCA
Yes, John! Yes, yes! Say it, and you shall see.

ROSMER
Have you the courage, are you willing, gladly, as Ulrik Brendel said, for my sake, to-night, gladly, to go the same way that Beata went!

REBECCA *(gets up slowly from the couch, and says almost inaudibly): John!*

ROSMER
Yes, dear, that is the question I shall never be able to rid my thoughts of, when you have gone away. Every hour of the day I shall come back to it. Ah, I seem to see you bodily before me, standing out on the foot-bridge-right out in the middle. Now you lean out over the railing! You grow dizzy as you feel drawn down towards the mill-race! No, you recoil. You dare not do what she dared.

REBECCA
But if I had the courage? and willingly and gladly? What then?

ROSMER
Then I would believe in you. Then I should get back my faith in my mission in life, my faith in my power to ennoble my fellow men, my faith in mankind's power to be ennobled.

Rebecca (takes up her shawl slowly, throws it over her head. and says, controlling herself): You shall have your faith back.

ROSMER
Have you the courage and the strength of will for that, Rebecca?

REBECCA
Of that you must judge in the morning, or later, when they take up my body.

Rosmer (burying his head in his hands)
There is a horrible temptation in this!

REBECCA
Because I should not like to be left lying there any longer than need be. You must take care that they find me.

ROSMER *(springing up)*
But all this is madness, you know. Go away, or stay! I will believe you on your bare word this time too.

REBECCA
Those are mere words, John. No more cowardice or evasion! How can you believe me on my bare word after today?

ROSMER

But I do not want to see your defeat, Rebecca.

REBECCA

There will be no defeat.

ROSMER

There will. You will never have the heart to go Beata's way.

REBECCA

Do you believe that?

ROSMER

Never. You are not like Beata. You are not under the influence of a distorted view of life.

REBECCA

But I am under the influence of the Rosmersholm view of Life now. Whatever my offences are it is right that I should expiate them.

ROSMER *(looking at her fixedly)*

Have you come to that decision?

REBECCA

Yes.

ROSMER

Very well. Then I too am under the influence of our unfettered view of life, Rebecca. There is no one that can judge us. And therefore we must be our own judges.

REBECCA *(misunderstanding his meaning)*

That too. That too. My leaving you will save the best that is in you.

ROSMER

Ah, there is nothing left to save in me.

REBECCA

There is. But I, after this I should only be like some sea-sprite hanging on to the barque you are striving to sail forward in, and, hampering its progress. I must go overboard. Do you think I could go through the world bearing the burden of a spoiled life, brooding for ever over the happiness which I have forfeited by my past? I must throw up the game, John.

ROSMER

If you go, then I go with you.

REBECCA *(looks at him with an almost imperceptible smile, and says more gently): Yes, come with me, dear, and be witness*

ROSMER

I go with you, I said.

REBECCA

As far as the bridge, yes. You never dare go out on to it, you know.

ROSMER

Have you noticed that?

REBECCA *(in sad and broken tones)*

Yes. That was what made my love hopeless.

ROSMER

Rebecca, now I lay my hand on your head. (Does as he says.) And I take you for my true and lawful wife.

REBECCA *(taking both his hands in hers, and bowing her head on to his breast)*

Thank you, John. (Lets him go.) And now I am going gladly.

ROSMER

Man and wife should go together.

REBECCA

Only as far as the bridge, John.

ROSMER

And out on to it, too. As far as you go, so far I go with you. I dare do it now.

REBECCA

Are you absolutely certain that way is the best for you?

ROSMER

I know it is the only way.

REBECCA

But suppose you are only deceiving yourself? Suppose it were only a delusion, one of these White Horses of Rosmersholm?

ROSMER

It may be so. We can never escape from them, we of my race.

REBECCA

Then stay, John!

ROSMER

The man shall cleave to his wife, as the wife to her husband.

REBECCA

Yes, but first tell me this, is it you that go with me, or I that go with you?

ROSMER

We shall never get to the bottom of that.

REBECCA

Yet I should dearly like to know.

ROSMER

We two go with each other, Rebecca. I with you, and you with me.

REBECCA

I almost believe that is true.

ROSMER

For now we two are one.

REBECCA

Yes. We are one now. Come! We can go gladly now. (They go out, hand in hand, through the hall, and are seen to turn to the left. The door stands open after them. The room is empty for a little while. Then Mrs HELSETH opens the door on the right.)

MRS HELSETH

The carriage, miss, is (Looks round the room.) Not here? Out together at this time of night? Well, well, I must say! Hm! (Goes out into the hall, looks round and comes in again.) Not sitting on the bench, ah, well! (Goes to the window and looks out.) Good heavens! What is that white thing! As I am a living soul, they are both out on the foot-bridge! God forgive the sinful creatures if they are not in each other's arms! (Gives a wild scream.) Ah! they are over, both of them! Over into the mill-race! Help! help! (Her knees tremble, she holds on shakily to the back of a chair and can scarcely get her words out.) No. No help here. The dead woman has taken them.

Henrik Ibsen - Lady From The Sea

Index Of Contents

DRAMATIS PERSONAE

Doctor Wangel.
Ellida Wangel, his second wife.
Bolette,
Hilde (not yet grown up), his daughters by his first wife.
Arnholm (second master at a college).
Lyngstrand.
Ballested.
A Stranger.
Young People of the Town.
Tourists.
Visitors.

(The action takes place in small fjord town, Northern Norway.)

ACT I

(SCENE. DOCTOR WANGEL'S house, with a large verandah garden in front of and around the house. Under the verandah a flagstaff. In the garden an arbour, with table and chairs. Hedge, with small gate at the back. Beyond, a road along the seashore. An avenue of trees along the road. Between the trees are seen the fjord, high mountain ranges and peaks. A warm and brilliantly clear summer morning.

BALLESTED, middle-aged, wearing an old velvet jacket, and a broad-brimmed artist's hat, stands under the flagstaff, arranging the ropes. The flag is lying on the ground. A little way from him is an easel, with an outspread canvas. By the easel on a camp-stool, brushes, a palette, and box of colours.

BOLETTE WANGEL comes from the room opening on the verandah. She carries a large vase with flowers, which she puts down on the table.)

Bolette. Well, Ballested, does it work smoothly?

Ballested. Certainly, Miss Bolette, that's easy enough. May I ask, do you expect any visitors today?

Bolette. Yes, we're expecting Mr. Arnholm this morning. He got to town in the night.

Ballested. Arnholm? Wait a minute, wasn't Arnholm the man who was tutor here several years ago?

Bolette. Yes, it is he.

Ballested. Oh, really! Is he coming into these parts again?

Bolette. That's why we want to have the flag up.

Ballested. Well, that's reasonable enough.

(BOLETTE goes into the room again. A little after LYNGSTRAND enters from the road and stands still, interested by the easel and painting gear. He is a slender youth, poorly but carefully dressed, and looks delicate.)

Lyngstrand (on the other side of the hedge). Good-morning.

Ballested (turning round). Hallo! Good-morning. (Hoists up flag). That's it! Up goes the balloon. (Fastens the ropes, and then busies himself about the easel.) Good-morning, my dear sir. I really don't think I've the pleasure of Lyngstrand. I'm sure you're a painter.

Ballested. Of course I am. Why shouldn't I be?

Lyngstrand. Yes, I can see you are. May I take the liberty of coming in a moment?

Ballested. Would you like to come in and see?

Lyngstrand. I should like to immensely.

Ballested. Oh! there's nothing much to see yet. But come in. Come a little closer.

Lyngstrand. Many thanks. (Comes in through the garden gate.)

Ballested (painting). It's the fjord there between the islands I'm working at.

Lyngstrand. So I see.

Ballested. But the figure is still wanting. There's not a model to be got in this town.

Lyngstrand. Is there to be a figure, too?

Ballested. Yes. Here by the rocks in the foreground a mermaid is to lie, half-dead.

Lyngstrand. Why is she to be half-dead?

Ballested. She has wandered hither from the sea, and can't find her way out again. And so, you see, she lies there dying in the brackish water.

Lyngstrand. Ah, I see.

Ballested. The mistress of this house put it into my head to do something of the kind.

Lyngstrand. What shall you call the picture when it's finished?

Ballested. I think of calling it "The Mermaid's End."

Lyngstrand. That's capital! You're sure to make something fine of it.

Ballested (looking at him). In the profession too, perhaps?

Lyngstrand. Do you mean a painter?

Ballested. Yes.

Lyngstrand. No, I'm not that; but I'm going to be a sculptor. My name is Hans Lyngstrand.

Ballested. So you're to be a sculptor? Yes, yes; the art of sculpture is a nice, pretty art in its way. I fancy I've seen you in the street once or twice. Have you been staying here long?

Lyngstrand. No; I've only been here a fortnight. But I shall try to stop till the end of the summer.

Ballested. For the bathing?

Lyngstrand. Yes; I wanted to see if I could get a little stronger.

Ballested. Not delicate, surely?

Lyngstrand. Yes, perhaps I am a little delicate; but it's nothing dangerous. Just a little tightness on the chest.

Ballested. Tush! a bagatelle! You should consult a good doctor.

Lyngstrand. Yes, I thought of speaking to Doctor Wangel one of these times.

Ballested. You should. (Looks out to the left.) There's another steamer, crowded with passengers. It's really marvellous how travelling has increased here of late years.

Lyngstrand. Yes, there's a good deal of traffic here, I think.

Ballested. And lots of summer visitors come here too. I often hear our good town will lose its individuality with all these foreign goings on.

Lyngstrand. Were you born in the town?

Ballested. No; but I have accla - acclimatised myself. I feel united to the place by the bonds of time and habit.

Lyngstrand. Then you've lived here a long time?

Ballested. Well, about seventeen or eighteen years. I came here with Skive's Dramatic Company. But then we got into difficulties, and so the company broke up and dispersed in all directions.

Lyngstrand. But you yourself remained here?

Ballested. I remained, and I've done very well. I was then working chiefly as decorative artist, don't you know.

(BOLETTE comes out with a rocking-chair, which she places on the verandah.)

Bolette (speaking into the room). Hilde, see if you can find the embroidered footstool for father.

Lyngstrand (going up to the verandah, bows). Good-morning, Miss Wangel.

Bolette (by the balustrade). What! Is it you, Mr. Lyngstrand? Good-morning. Excuse me one moment, I'm only (Goes into room.)

Ballested. Do you know the family?

Lyngstrand. Not well. I've only met the young ladies now and again in company; and I had a chat with Mrs. Wangel the last time we had music up at the "View." She said I might come and see them.

Ballested. Now, do you know, you ought to cultivate their acquaintance.

Lyngstrand. Yes; I'd been thinking of paying a visit. Just a sort of call. If only I could find some excuse

Ballested. Excuse! Nonsense! (Looking out to the left.) Damn it! (Gathering his things.) The steamer's by the pier already. I must get off to the hotel. Perhaps some of the new arrivals may want me. For I'm a hairdresser, too, don't you know.

Lyngstrand. You are certainly very many-sided, sir.

Ballested. In small towns one has to try to acclam - acclimatise Oneself in various branches. If you should require anything in the hair line, a little pomatum or such like, you've only to ask for Dancing-master Ballested.

Lyngstrand. Dancing master!

Ballested. President of the "Wind Band Society," by your leave. We've a concert on this evening up at the "View." Goodbye, goodbye!

(He goes out with his painting gear through the garden gate.

HILDE comes out with the footstool. BOLETTE brings more flowers. LYNGSTRAND bows to HILDE from the garden below.)

Hilde (by the balustrade, not returning his bow). Bolette said you had ventured in today.

Lyngstrand. Yes; I took the liberty of coming in for a moment.

Hilde. Have you been out for a morning walk?

Lyngstrand. Oh, no! nothing came of the walk this morning.

Hilde. Have you been bathing, then?

Lyngstrand. Yes; I've been in the water a little while. I saw your mother down there. She was going into her bathing-machine.

Hilde. Who was?

Lyngstrand. Your mother.

Hilde. Oh! I see. (She puts the stool in front of the rocking- chair.)

Bolette (interrupting). Didn't you see anything of father's boat out on the fjord?

Lyngstrand. Yes; I thought I saw a sailing-boat that was steering inland.

Bolette. I'm sure that was father. He's been to visit patients on the islands. (She is arranging things on the table.)

Lyngstrand (taking a step up the stairs to the verandah). Why, how everything's decorated here with flowers!

Bolette. Yes; doesn't it look nice?

Lyngstrand. It looks lovely! It looks as if it were some festival day in the house.

Hilde. That's exactly what it is.

Lyngstrand. I might have guessed it! I'm sure it's your father's birthday.

Bolette (warningly to HILDE). Hm, hm!

Hilde (taking no notice of her). No, mother's.

Lyngstrand. Oh! Your mother's!

Bolette (in low voice, angrily). Really, Hilde!

Hilde (the same). Let me be! (To LYNGSTRAND.) I suppose you're going home to breakfast now?

Lyngstrand (going down steps). Yes, I suppose I must go and get something to eat.

Hilde. I'm sure you find the living very good at the hotel!

Lyngstrand. I'm not staying at the hotel now. It was too expensive for me.

Hilde. Where are you staying, then?

Lyngstrand. I'm staying up at Mrs. Jensen's.

Hilde. What Mrs. Jensen's?

Lyngstrand. The midwife.

Hilde. Excuse me, Mr. Lyngstrand, but I really have other matters to attend to-

Lyngstrand. Oh! I'm sure I ought not to have said that.

Hilde. Said what?

Lyngstrand. What I said.

Hilde (looking contemptuously at him). I don't understand you in the least.

Lyngstrand. No, no. But I must say goodbye for the present.

Bolette (comes forward to the steps). Good-bye, good-bye, Mr. Lyngstrand. You must excuse us now. But another day, when you've plenty of time, and inclination, you really must come in and see father and the rest of us.

Lyngstrand. Yes; thanks, very much. I shall be delighted. (Bows, and goes out through the garden gate. As he goes along the road he bows again towards the verandah.)

Hilde (in low voice). Adieu, Monsieur! Please remember me to Mother Jensen.

Bolette (in a low voice, shaking her arm). Hilde! You naughty child! Are you quite crazy? He might have heard you.

Hilde. Pshaw! Do you think I care about that?

Bolette (looking out to the right). Here's father!

(WANGEL, in travelling dress and carrying a small bag, comes from the footpath.)

Wangel. See! I'm back again, little girls! (He enters through the garden gate.)

Bolette (going towards him at the bottom of the garden). Oh! It is delightful that you've come!

Hilde (also going up to him). Now have you got off for the whole day, father?

Wangel. Oh! no. I must go down to the office for a little while presently. I say, do you know if Arnholm has come?

Bolette. Yes; he arrived in the night. We sent to the hotel to enquire.

Wangel. Then you've not seen him yet?

Bolette. No; but he's sure to come here this morning.

Wangel. Yes; he's sure to do that.

Hilde (pulling him). Father, now you must look round.

Wangel (looking towards the verandah). Yes, I see well enough, child. It's quite festive.

Bolette. Now, don't you think we've arranged it nicely?

Wangel. I must say you have. Are, are we alone at home now?

Hilde. Yes; she's gone to

Bolette (interrupting quickly). Mother has gone to bathe.

Wangel (looks lovingly at BOLETTE, and pats her head. Then he says, hesitating). Look here, little ones. Do you want to keep this up all day? And the flag hoisted, too?

Hilde. Surely you understand that, father!

Wangel. Hm! Yes; but you see

Bolette (looks at him and nods). Surely you can understand we've been doing all this in honour of Mr. Arnholm. When such a good friend comes to see you for the first time

Hilde (smiling, and shaking him). Think! he who used to be Bolette's tutor, father!

Wangel (with a half-smile). You're a pair of sly minxes. Well, good heavens, after all, it's but natural we should remember her who is no more with us. Here, Hilde (Gives her his bag), take that down to the office. No, children. I don't like this, the way, I mean. This habit of every year, well, what can one say? I suppose it can't be managed any other way.

Hilde (about to go out of garden, and, with the bag, stops short, turns, and points out). Look at that gentleman coming up here. I'm sure it's your tutor.

Bolette (looks in that direction). He? (Laughs.) That is good! Do you think that middle-aged fellow is Arnholm?

Wangel. Wait a moment, child. Why, by Jove, I do believe it is he. Yes, it certainly is.

Bolette (staring at him in quiet amazement). Yes; I almost think

(ARNHOLM, in elegant morning dress, with gold spectacles, and a thin cane, comes along the road. He looks overworked. He looks in at the garden, bows in friendly fashion, and enters by the garden gate.)

Wangel (going to meet him). Welcome, dear Arnholm! Heartily welcome back to your old quarters again!

Arnholm. Thanks, thanks, Doctor Wangel. A thousand thanks. (They shake hands and walk up the garden together.) And there are the children! (Holds out his hands and looks at them.) I should hardly have known these two again.

Wangel. No, I believe you.

Arnholm. And yet perhaps Bolette, yes, I should have known Bolette again.

Wangel. Hardly, I think. Why, it is eight, nine years since you saw her. Ah, yes! Many a thing has changed here meanwhile.

Arnholm (looking round). I really don't see it; except that the trees have grown remarkably, and that you've set up that arbour.

Wangel. Oh! No, outwardly.

Arnholm (smiling). And then, of course, you've two grown-up daughters here now.

Wangel. Grown up! Well, there's only one grown up.

Hilde (aside). Just listen to father!

Wangel. But now let's sit down up there on the verandah. It's cooler than here. Won't you?

Arnholm. Thanks, thanks, dear doctor.

(They go up. WANGEL motions him to the rocking-chair.)

Wangel. That's right! Now make yourself comfortable, and rest, for you seem rather tired after your journey.

Arnholm. Oh, that's nothing. Here, amid these surroundings-

Bolette (to WANGEL). Hadn't we better have some soda and syrup in the sitting-room? It's sure to be too hot out here soon.

Wangel. Yes, girls. Let's have some soda and syrup, and perhaps a drop of Cognac, too.

Bolette. Cognac, too!

Wangel. Just a little, in case anyone should like some.

Bolette. All right. Hilde, go down to the office with the bag.

(BOLETTE goes into the room, and closes the door after her.

HILDE takes the bag, and goes through the garden to the back of the house.)

Arnholm (who has followed BOLETTE with his eyes). What a splendid. They are both splendid girls, who've grown up here for you.

Wangel (sitting down). Yes; you think so, too?

Arnholm. Why, it's simply amazing, how Bolette! and Hilde, too! But now, you yourself, dear doctor. Do you think of staying here all your life?

Wangel. Yes; I suppose so. Why, I've been born and bred here, so to say. I lived here so very happily with her who left us so early, she whom you knew when you were here before, Arnholm.

Arnholm. Yes, yes!

Wangel. And now I live here so happily with her who has taken her place. Ah! On the whole, fate has been very good to me.

Arnholm. You have no children by your second marriage? Wangel. We had a little boy, two, two and a half years ago. But he didn't stay long. He died when he was four, five months old.

Arnholm. Isn't your wife at home today?

Wangel. Oh, yes. She's sure to be here soon. She's down there bathing. She does so every blessed day no matter what the weather.

Arnholm. Is she ill, then?

Wangel. Not exactly ill, although she has been extremely nervous for the last few years, that is to say, she is now and then. I can't make out what really ails her. But to plunge into the sea is her joy and delight.

Arnholm. Yes; I remember that of old.

Wangel (with an almost imperceptible smile). To be sure! You knew Ellida when you were teacher out there at Skjoldviken.

Arnholm. Certainly. She used often to visit at the Parsonage. But I mostly met her when I went to the lighthouse to see her father.

Wangel. Those times out there, you may believe me, have set deep marks upon her. The people in the town here can't understand her at all. They call her the "Lady from the Sea."

Arnholm. Do they?

Wangel. Yes. And so now, you see, speak to her of the old days, dear Arnholm, it will do her good.

Arnholm (looks at him in doubt). Have you any reason for thinking so?

Wangel. Assuredly I have.

Ellida (her voice is heard outside the garden). Are you there, Wangel?

Wangel (rising). Yes, dear.

(Mrs. ELLIDA WANGEL, in a large, light wrap, and with wet hair hanging loose over her shoulders, comes from between the trees of the arbour. ARNHOLM rises.)

Wangel (smiling, and holding out his hands to her). Ah! So now we have our Mermaid!

Ellida (goes quickly up the verandah, and seizes his hands). Thank God that I see you again! When did you come?

Wangel. Just now; a little while since. (Pointing to ARNHOLM.) But won't you greet an old acquaintance?

Ellida (holding out her hand to ARNHOLM). So here you are! Welcome! And forgive me for not being at home

Arnholm. Don't mention it, don't stand on any ceremony.

Wangel. Was the water nice and fresh today?

Ellida. Fresh! Oh! The water here never is fresh. It is so tepid and lifeless. Ugh! The water in the fjord here is sick.

Arnholm. Sick?

Ellida. Yes, sick. And I believe it makes one sick, too.

Wangel (smiling). You're giving our bathing resort a good name!

Arnholm. I should rather believe, Mrs. Wangel, that you have a peculiar relation to the sea, and to all that belongs to it.

Ellida. Perhaps; I almost think so myself. But do you see how festively the girls have arranged everything in your honour?

Wangel (embarrassed). Hm! (Looks at his watch.) Well, I suppose I must be quick and

Arnholm. Is it really for me?

Ellida. Yes. You may be sure we don't decorate like this every day. Ugh! How suffocatingly hot it is under this roof. (Goes down into the garden.) Come over here. Here at least there is a little air. (Sits down in arbour.)

Arnholm (going thither). I think the air quite fresh here.

Ellida. Yes, you, who are used to the stifling air of the town! It's terrible there in the summer, I hear.

Wangel (who has also gone into the garden). Hm, dear Ellida, you must just entertain our friend alone for a little while.

Ellida. Are you busy?

Wangel. Yes, I must go down to the office. And then I must change. But I won't be long.

Arnholm (sitting down in arbour). Now, don't hurry, dear doctor. Your wife and I will manage to kill the time.

Wangel (nodding). Oh, yes! I'm sure you will. Well, goodbye for the present. (He goes out through the garden.)

Ellida (after a short pause). Don't you think it's pleasant sitting out here?

Arnholm. I think I've a pleasant seat now.

Ellida. They call this my arbour, because I had it fitted up, or rather Wangel did, for me.

Arnholm. And you usually sit here?

Ellida. Yes, I pass most of the day here.

Arnholm. With the girls, I suppose?

Ellida. No, the girls usually sit on the verandah.

Arnholm. And Wangel himself?

Ellida. Oh! Wangel goes to and fro, now he comes to me, and then he goes to his children.

Arnholm. And is it you who wish this?

Ellida. I think all parties feel most comfortable in this way. You know we can talk across to one another if we happen to find there is anything to say.

Arnholm (after thinking awhile). When I last crossed your path out at Skjoldviken, I mean, Hm! That is long ago now.

Ellida. It's quite ten years since you were there with us.

Arnholm. Yes, about that. But when I think of you out there in the lighthouse! The heathen, as the old clergyman called you, because your father had named you, as he said, after an old ship, and hadn't given you a name fit for a Christian.

Ellida. Well, what then?

Arnholm. The last thing I should then have believed was that I should see you again down here as the wife of Wangel.

Ellida. No; at that time Wangel wasn't, at that time the girls' first mother was still living. Their real mother, so

Arnholm. Of course, of course! But even if that had not been, even if he had been free, still, I could never have believed this would come about.

Ellida. Nor I. Never on earth then.

Arnholm. Wangel is such a good fellow. So honourable. So thoroughly good and kind to all men.

Ellida (warmly and heartily). Yes, he is indeed.

Arnholm. But he must be so absolutely different from you, I fancy.

Ellida. You are right there. So he is.

Arnholm. Well, but how did it happen? How did it come about?

Ellida. Ah! dear Arnholm, you mustn't ask me about that. I couldn't explain it to you, and even if I could, you would never be able to understand, in the least.

Arnholm. Hm! (In lower tone.) Have you ever confided anything about me to your husband? Of course, I meant about the useless step, I allowed myself to be moved to.

Ellida. No. You may be sure of that. I've not said a word to him about, about what you speak of.

Arnholm. I am glad. I felt rather awkward at the thought that

Ellida. There was no need. I have only told him what is true, that I liked you very much, and that you were the truest and best friend I had out there.

Arnholm. Thanks for that. But tell me, why did you never write to me after I had gone away?

Ellida. I thought that perhaps it would pain you to hear from one who, who could not respond as you desired. It seemed like re- opening a painful subject.

Arnholm. Hm. Yes, yes, perhaps you were right.

Ellida. But why didn't you write?

Arnholm (looks at her and smiles, half reproachfully). I make the first advance? Perhaps expose myself to the suspicion of wanting to begin all over again? After such a repulse as I had had?

Ellida. Oh no! I understand very well. Have you never since thought of forming any other tie?

Arnholm. Never! I have been faithful to my first memories.

Ellida (half jestingly). Nonsense! Let the sad old memories alone. You'd better think of becoming a happy husband, I should say.

Arnholm. I should have to be quick about it, then, Mrs. Wangel. Remember, I'm already, I'm ashamed to say, I'm past thirty-seven.

Ellida. Well, all the more reason for being quick. (She is silent for a moment, and then says, earnestly, in a low voice.) But listen, dear Arnholm; now I am going to tell you something that I could not have told you then, to save my life.

Arnholm. What is it?

Ellida. When you took the, the useless step you were just speaking of I could not answer you otherwise than I did.

Arnholm. I know that you had nothing but friendship to give me; I know that well enough.

Ellida. But you did not know that all my mind and soul were then given elsewhere.

Arnholm. At that time!

Ellida. Yes.

Arnholm. But it is impossible. You are mistaken about the time. I hardly think you knew Wangel then.

Ellida. It is not Wangel of whom I speak.

Arnholm. Not Wangel? But at that time, out there at Skjoldviken. I can't remember a single person whom I can imagine the possibility of your caring for.

Ellida. No, no, I quite believe that; for it was all such bewildering madness, all of it.

Arnholm. But tell me more of this.

Ellida. Oh! it's enough if you know I was bound then; and you know it now.

Arnholm. And if you had not been bound?

Ellida. Well?

Arnholm. Would your answer to my letter have been different?

Ellida. How can I tell? When Wangel came the answer was different.

Arnholm. What is your object, then, in telling me that you were bound?

Ellida (getting up, as if in fear and unrest). Because I must have someone in whom to confide. No, no; sit still.

Arnholm. Then your husband knows nothing about this?

Ellida. I confessed to him from the first that my thoughts had once been elsewhere. He never asked to know more, and we have never touched upon it since. Besides, at bottom it was simply madness. And then it was over directly, that is to a certain extent.

Arnholm (rising). Only to a certain extent? Not quite?

Ellida. Yes, yes, it is! Oh, good heavens! Dear Arnholm, it is not what you think. It is something so absolutely incomprehensible, I don't know how I could tell it you. You would only think I was ill, or quite mad.

Arnholm. My dearest lady! Now you really must tell me all about it.

Ellida. Well, then, I'll try to. How will you, as a sensible man, explain to yourself that (Looks round, and breaks off.) Wait a moment. Here's a visitor.

(LYNGSTRAND comes along the road, and enters the garden. He has a flower in his button-hole, and carries a large, handsome bouquet done up in paper and silk ribbons. He stands somewhat hesitatingly and undecidedly by the verandah.)

Ellida (from the arbour). Have you come to see the girls, Mr. Lyngstrand?

Lyngstrand (turning round). Ah, madam, are you there? (Bows, and comes nearer.) No, it's not that. It's not the young ladies. It's you yourself, Mrs. Wangel. You know you gave me permission to come and see you-

Ellida. Of course I did. You are always welcome here.

Lyngstrand. Thanks; and as it falls out so luckily that it's a festival here today

Ellida. Oh! Do you know about that?

Lyngstrand. Rather! And so I should like to take the liberty of presenting this to Mrs. Wangel. (Bows, and offers her the bouquet.)

Ellida (smiling). But, my dear Mr. Lyngstrand, oughtn't you to give these lovely flowers to Mr. Arnholm himself? For you know it's really he-

Lyngstrand (looking uncertainly at both of them). Excuse me, but I don't know this gentleman. It's only. I've only come about the birthday, Mrs. Wangel.

Ellida. Birthday? You've made a mistake, Mr. Lyngstrand. There's no birthday here today.

Lyngstrand (smiling slyly). Oh! I know all about that! But I didn't think it was to be kept so dark.

Ellida. What do you know?

Lyngstrand. That it is Madam's birthday.

Ellida. Mine?

Arnholm (looks questioningly at her). Today? Surely not.

Ellida (to LYNGSTRAND). Whatever made you think that?

Lyngstrand. It was Miss Hilde who let it out. I just looked in here a little while ago, and I asked the young ladies why they were decorating the place like this, with flowers and flags.

Ellida. Well?

Lyngstrand. And so Miss Hilde said, "Why, today is mother's birthday."

Ellida. Mother's! I see.

Arnholm. Aha! (He and ELLIDA exchange a meaning look.) Well, now that the young man knows about it

Ellida (to LYNGSTRAND). Well, now that you know

Lyngstrand (offering her the bouquet again). May I take the liberty of congratulating you?

Ellida (taking the flowers). My best thanks. Won't you sit down a moment, Mr. Lyngstrand? (ELLIDA, ARNHOLM, and LYNGSTRAND sit down in the arbour.) This birthday business was to have been kept secret, Mr. Arnholm.

Arnholm. So I see. It wasn't for us uninitiated folk!

Ellida (putting down the bouquet). Just so. Not for the uninitiated.

Lyngstrand. 'Pon my word, I won't tell a living soul about it.

Ellida. Oh, it wasn't meant like that. But how are you getting on? I think you look better than you did.

Lyngstrand. Oh! I think I'm getting on famously. And by next year, if I can go south

Ellida. And you are going south, the girls tell me.

Lyngstrand. Yes, for I've a benefactor and friend at Bergen, who looks after me, and has promised to help me next year.

Ellida. How did you get such a friend?

Lyngstrand. Well, it all happened so very luckily. I once went to sea in one of his ships.

Ellida. Did you? So you wanted to go to sea?

Lyngstrand. No, not at all. But when mother died, father wouldn't have me knocking about at home any longer, and so he sent me to sea. Then we were wrecked in the English Channel on our way home; and that was very fortunate for me.

Arnholm. What do you mean?

Lyngstrand. Yes, for it was in the shipwreck that I got this little weakness of my chest. I was so long in the ice-cold water before they picked me up; and so I had to give up the sea. Yes, that was very fortunate.

Arnholm. Indeed! Do you think so?

Lyngstrand. Yes, for the weakness isn't dangerous; and now I can be a sculptor, as I so dearly want to be. Just think; to model in that delicious clay, that yields so caressingly to your fingers!

Ellida. And what are you going to model? Is it to be mermen and mermaids? Or is it to be old Vikings?

Lyngstrand. No, not that. As soon as I can set about it, I am going to try if I can produce a great work, a group, as they call it.

Ellida. Yes; but what's the group to be?

Lyngstrand. Oh! something I've experienced myself.

Arnholm. Yes, yes; always stick to that.

Ellida. But what's it to be?

Lyngstrand. Well, I thought it should be the young wife of a sailor, who lies sleeping in strange unrest, and she is dreaming. I fancy I shall do it so that you will see she is dreaming.

Arnholm. Is there anything else?

Lyngstrand. Yes, there's to be another figure, a sort of apparition, as they say. It's her husband, to whom she has been faithless while he was away, and he is drowned at sea.

Arnholm. What?

Ellida. Drowned?

Lyngstrand. Yes, he was drowned on a sea voyage. But that's the wonderful part of it, he comes home all the same. It is night-time. And he is standing by her bed looking at her. He is to stand there dripping wet, like one drawn from the sea.

Ellida (leaning back in her chair). What an extraordinary idea! (Shutting her eyes.) Oh! I can see it so clearly, living before me!

Arnholm. But how on earth, Mr., Mr., I thought you said it was to be something you had experienced.

Lyngstrand. Yes. I did experience that, that is to say, to a certain extent.

Arnholm. You saw a dead man?

Lyngstrand. Well, I don't mean I've actually seen this, experienced it in the flesh. But still

Ellida (quickly, intently). Oh! tell me all you can about it! I must understand about all this.

Arnholm (smiling). Yes, that'll be quite in your line. Something that has to do with sea fancies.

Ellida. What was it, Mr. Lyngstrand?

Lyngstrand. Well, it was like this. At the time when we were to sail home in the brig from a town they called Halifax, we had to leave the boatswain behind in the hospital. So we had to engage an American instead. This new boatswain-

Ellida. The American?

Lyngstrand. Yes, one day he got the captain to lend him a lot of old newspapers and he was always reading them. For he wanted to teach himself Norwegian, he said.

Ellida. Well, and then?

Lyngstrand. It was one evening in rough weather. All hands were on deck except the boatswain and myself. For he had sprained his foot and couldn't walk, and I was feeling rather low, and was lying in my berth. Well, he was sitting there in the forecastle, reading one of those old papers again.

Ellida. Well, well!

Lyngstrand. But just as he was sitting there quietly reading, I heard him utter a sort of yell. And when I looked at him, I saw his face was as white as chalk. And then he began to crush and crumple the paper, and to tear it into a thousand shreds. But he did it so quietly, quietly.

Ellida. Didn't he say anything? Didn't he speak?

Lyngstrand. Not directly; but a little after he said to himself, as it were: "Married to another man. While I was away."

Ellida (closes her eyes, and says, half to herself). He said that?

Lyngstrand. Yes. And think he said it in perfect Norwegian. That man must have learnt foreign languages very easily

Ellida. And what then? What else happened?

Lyngstrand. Well, now the remarkable part is coming that I shall never forget as long as I live. For he added, and that quite quietly, too: "But she is mine, and mine she shall remain. And she shall follow me, if I should come home and fetch her, as a drowned man from the dark sea."

Ellida (pouring herself out a glass of water. Her hand trembles). Ah! How close it is here today.

Lyngstrand. And he said this with such strength of will that I thought he must be the man to do it.

Ellida. Don't you know anything about what became of the man?

Lyngstrand. Oh! madam, he's certainly not living now.

Ellida (quickly). Why do you think that?

Lyngstrand. Why? Because we were shipwrecked afterwards in the Channel. I had got into the longboat with the captain and five others. The mate got into the stern-boat; and the American was in that too, and another man.

Ellida. And nothing has been heard of them since?

Lyngstrand. Not a word. The friend who looks after me said so quite recently in a letter. But it's just because of this I was so anxious to make it into a work of art. I see the faithless sailor-wife so life-like before me, and the avenger who is drowned, and who nevertheless comes home from the sea. I can see them both so distinctly.

Ellida. I, too. (Rises.) Come; let us go in or, rather, go down to Wangel. I think it is so suffocatingly hot. (She goes out of the arbour.)

Lyngstrand (who has also risen). I, for my part, must ask you to excuse me. This was only to be a short visit because of the birthday.

Ellida. As you wish. (Holds out her hand to him.) Goodbye, and thank you for the flowers.

(LYNGSTRAND bows, and goes off through the garden gate.)

Arnholm (rises, and goes up to ELLIDA). I see well enough that this has gone to your heart, Mrs. Wangel.

Ellida. Yes; you may well say so. Although

Arnholm. But still, after all, it's no more than you were bound to expect.

Ellida (looks at him surprised). Expect!

Arnholm. Well, so it seems to me.

Ellida. Expect that anyone should come back again! come to life again like that!

Arnholm. But what on earth! is it that mad sculptor's sea story, then?

Ellida. Oh, dear Arnholm, perhaps it isn't so mad after all!

Arnholm. Is it that nonsense about the dead man that has moved you so? And I who thought that

Ellida. What did you think?

Arnholm. I naturally thought that was only a make-believe of yours. And that you were sitting here grieving because you had found out a family feast was being kept secret; because your husband and his children live a life of remembrances in which you have no part.

Ellida. Oh! no, no! That may be as it may. I have no right to claim my husband wholly and solely for myself.

Arnholm. I should say you had.

Ellida. Yes. Yet, all the same, I have not. That is it. Why, I, too, live in something from which they are shut out.

Arnholm. You! (In lower tone.) Do you mean? you, you do not really love your husband!

Ellida. Oh! yes, yes! I have learnt to love him with all my heart! And that's why it is so terrible, so inexplicable, so absolutely inconceivable!

Arnholm. Now you must and shall confide all your troubles to me. Will you, Mrs. Wangel?

Ellida. I cannot, dear friend. Not now, in any case. Later, perhaps.

(BOLETTE comes out into the verandah, and goes down into the garden.)

Bolette. Father's coming up from the office. Hadn't we better all of us go into the sitting-room?

Ellida. Yes, let us.

(WANGEL, in other clothes, comes with HILDE from behind the house.)

Wangel. Now, then, here I am at your service. And now we shall enjoy a good glass of something cool.

Ellida. Wait a moment. (She goes into the arbour and fetches the bouquet.)

Hilde. I say! All those lovely flowers! Where did you get them?

Ellida. From the sculptor, Lyngstrand, my dear Hilde.

Hilde (starts). From Lyngstrand?

Bolette (uneasily). Has Lyngstrand been here again?

Ellida (with a half-smile). Yes. He came here with these. Because of the birthday, you understand.

Bolette (looks at HILDE). Oh!

Hilde (mutters). The idiot!

Wangel (in painful confusion to ELLIDA). Hm! yes, well you see-I must tell you, my dear, good, beloved Ellida

Ellida (interrupting). Come, girls! Let us go and put my flowers in the water together with the others. (Goes up to the verandah.)

Bolette (to HILDE). Oh! After all she is good at heart.

Hilde (in a low tone with angry look). Fiddlesticks! She only does it to take in father.

Wangel (on the verandah, presses ELLIDA'S hand). Thanks-thanks! My heartfelt thanks for that, dear Ellida.

Ellida (arranging the flowers). Nonsense! Should not I, too, be in it, and take part in, in mother's birthday?

Arnholm. Hm!

(He goes up to WANGEL, and ELLIDA, BOLETTE, and HILDE remain in the garden below.)

Act II

(SCENE. At the "View," a shrub-covered hill behind the town. A little in the background, a beacon and a vane. Great stones arranged as seats around the beacon, and in the foreground. Farther back the outer fjord is seen, with islands and outstanding headlands. The open sea is not visible. It is a summer's evening, and twilight. A golden-red shimmer is in the airand over the mountain-tops in the far distance. A quartette is faintly heard singing below in the background. Young townsfolk, ladies and gentlemen, come up in pairs, from the right, and, talking familiarly, pass out beyond the beacon. A little after, BALLESTED enters, as guide to a party of foreign tourists with their ladies. He is laden with shawls and travelling bags.)

Ballested (pointing upwards with a stick). Sehen Sie, meine Herrschaften, dort, out there, liegt eine andere mountain, That wollen wir also besteigen, and so herunter. (He goes on with the conversation in French, and leads the party off to the left. HILDE comes quickly along the uphill path, stands still, and looks back. Soon after BOLETTE comes up the same way.)

Bolette. But, dear, why should we run away from Lyngstrand?

Hilde. Because I can't bear going uphill so slowly. Look, look at him crawling up!

Bolette. Ah! But you know how delicate he is.

Hilde. Do you think it's very dangerous?

Bolette. I certainly do.

Hilde. He went to consult father this afternoon. I should like to know what father thinks about him.

Bolette. Father told me it was a thickening of the lungs, or something of the sort. He won't live to be old, father says.

Hilde. No! Did he say it? Fancy, that's exactly what I thought.

Bolette. For heaven's sake don't show it!

Hilde. How can you imagine such a thing? (In an undertone.) Look, here comes Hans crawling up. Don't you think you can see by the look of him that he's called Hans?

Bolette (whispering). Now do behave! You'd better!

(LYNGSTRAND comes in from the right, a parasol in his hand.)

Lyngstrand. I must beg the young ladies to excuse me for not getting along as quickly as they did.

Hilde. Have you got a parasol too, now?

Lyngstrand. It's your mother's. She said I was to use it as a stick. I hadn't mine with me.

Bolette. Are they down there still, father and the others?

Lyngstrand. Yes; your father looked in at the restaurant for a moment, and the others are sitting out there listening to the music. But they were coming up here presently, your mother said.

Hilde (stands looking at him). I suppose you're thoroughly tired out now?

Lyngstrand. Yes; I almost think I'm a little tired now. I really believe I shall have to sit down a moment. (He sits on one of the stones in the foreground.)

Hilde (standing in front of him). Do you know there's to be dancing down there on the parade?

Lyngstrand. Yes; I heard there was some talk about it.

Hilde. I suppose you think dancing's great fun?

Bolette (who begins gathering small flowers among the heather). Oh, Hilde! Now do let Mr. Lyngstrand get his breath.

Lyngstrand (to HILDE). Yes, Miss Hilde; I should very much like to dance, if only I could.

Hilde. Oh, I see! Haven't you ever learnt?

Lyngstrand. No, I've not. But it wasn't that I meant. I meant I couldn't because of my chest.

Hilde. Because of that weakness you said you suffered from?

Lyngstrand. Yes; because of that.

Hilde. Aren't you very sorry you've that weakness?

Lyngstrand. Oh, no! I can't say I am (smiling), for I think it's because of it that everyone is so good, and friendly, and kind to me.

Hilde. Yes. And then, besides, it's not dangerous.

Lyngstrand. No; it's not at all dangerous. So I gathered from what your father said to me.

Hilde. And then it will pass away as soon as ever you begin travelling.

Lyngstrand. Of course it will pass away.

Bolette (with flowers). Look here, Mr. Lyngstrand, you are to put this in your button-hole.

Lyngstrand. Oh! A thousand thanks, Miss Wangel. It's really too good of you.

Hilde (looking down the path). There they are, coming along the road.

Bolette (also looking down). If only they know where to turn off. No; now they're going wrong.

Lyngstrand (rising). I'll run down to the turning and call out to them.

Hilde. You'll have to call out pretty loud.

Bolette. No; it's not worth while. You'll only tire yourself again.

Lyngstrand. Oh, it's so easy going downhill. (Goes off to the right.)

Hilde. Down-hill, yes. (Looking after him.) Why, he's actually jumping! And he never remembers he'll have to come up again.

Bolette. Poor fellow!

Hilde. If Lyngstrand were to propose, would you accept him?

Bolette. Are you quite mad?

Hilde. Of course, I mean if he weren't troubled with that "weakness." And if he weren't to die so soon, would you have him then?

Bolette. I think you'd better have him yourself!

Hilde. No, that I wouldn't! Why, he hasn't a farthing. He hasn't enough even to keep himself.

Bolette. Then why are you always going about with him?

Hilde. Oh, I only do that because of the weakness.

Bolette. I've never noticed that you in the least pity him for it!

Hilde. No, I don't. But I think it so interesting.

Bolette. What is?

Hilde. To look at him and make him tell you it isn't dangerous; and that he's going abroad, and is to be an artist. He really believes it all, and is so thoroughly happy about it. And yet nothing will ever come of it; nothing whatever. For he won't live long enough. I feel that's so fascinating to think of.

Bolette. Fascinating!

Hilde. Yes, I think it's most fascinating. I take that liberty.

Bolette. Hilde, you really are a dreadful child!

Hilde. That's just what I want to be, out of spite. (Looking down.) At last! I shouldn't think Arnholm liked coming up-hill. (Turns round.) By the way, do you know what I noticed about Arnholm at dinner?

Bolette. Well?

Hilde. Just think, his hair's beginning to come off, right on the top of his head.

Bolette. Nonsense! I'm sure that's not true.

Hilde. It is! And then he has wrinkles round both his eyes. Good gracious, Bolette, how could you be so much in love with him when he used to read with you?

Bolette (smiling). Yes. Can you believe it? I remember I once shed bitter tears because he thought Bolette was an ugly name.

Hilde. Only to think! (Looking down.) No! I say, do just look down here! There's the "Mermaid" walking along and chatting with him. Not with father. I wonder if those two aren't making eyes at one another.

Bolette. You ought to be ashamed of yourself! How can you stand there and say such a thing of her? Now, when everything was beginning to be so pleasant between us.

Hilde. Of course, just try and persuade yourself of that, my child! Oh, no! It will never be pleasant between us and her. For she doesn't belong to us at all. And we don't belong to her either. Goodness knows what father dragged her into the house for! I shouldn't wonder if some fine day she went mad under our very eyes.

Bolette. Mad! How can you think such a thing?

Hilde. Oh! it wouldn't be so extraordinary. Her mother went mad, too. She died mad, I know that.

Bolette. Yes, heaven only knows what you don't poke your nose into. But now don't go chattering about this. Do be good, for father's sake. Do you hear, Hilde?

(WANGEL, ELLIDA, ARNHOLM and LYNGSTRAND come up from the right.)

Ellida (pointing to the background). Out there it lies.

Arnholm. Quite right. It must be in that direction.

Ellida. Out there is the sea.

Bolette (to ARNHOLM). Don't you think it is delightful up here?

Arnholm. It's magnificent, I think. Glorious view!

Wangel. I suppose you never used to come up here?

Arnholm. No, never. In my time I think it was hardly accessible; there wasn't any path even.

Wangel. And no grounds. All this has been done during the last few years.

Bolette. And there, at the "Pilot's Mount," it's even grander than here.

Wangel. Shall we go there, Ellida?

Ellida (sitting down on one of the stones). Thanks, not I; but you others can. I'll sit here meanwhile.

Wangel. Then I'll stay with you. The girls can show Arnholm about.

Bolette. Would you like to go with us, Mr. Arnholm?

Arnholm. I should like to, very much. Does a path lead up there too?

Bolette. Oh yes. There's a nice broad path.

Hilde. The path is so broad that two people can walk along it comfortably, arm in arm.

Arnholm (jestingly). Is that really so, little Missie? (To BOLETTE.) Shall we two see if she is right?

Bolette (suppressing a smile). Very well, let's go. (They go out to the left, arm in arm.)

Hilde (to LYNGSTRAND). Shall we go too?

Lyngstrand. Arm in arm?

Hilde. Oh, why not? For aught I care!

Lyngstrand (taking her arm, laughing contentedly). This is a jolly lark.

Hilde. Lark?

Lyngstrand. Yes; because it looks exactly as if we were engaged.

Hilde. I'm sure you've never walked out arm in arm with a lady before, Mr. Lyngstrand. (They go off.)

Wangel (who is standing beside the beacon). Dear Ellida, now we have a moment to ourselves.

Ellida. Yes; come and sit down here, by me.

Wangel (sitting down). It is so free and quiet. Now we can have a little talk together.

Ellida. What about?

Wangel. About yourself, and then about us both. Ellida, I see very well that it can't go on like this.

Ellida. What do you propose instead?

Wangel. Perfect confidence, dear. A true life together as before.

Ellida. Oh, if that could be! But it is so absolutely impossible!

Wangel. I think I understand you, from certain things you have let fall now and again.

Ellida (passionately). Oh, you do not! Don't say you understand!

Wangel. Yes. Yours is an honest nature, Ellida, yours is a faithful mind.

Ellida. It is.

Wangel. Any position in which you could feel safe and happy must be a completely true and real one.

Ellida (looking eagerly at him). Well, and then?

Wangel. You are not suited to be a man's second wife.

Ellida. What makes you think that?

Wangel. It has often flashed across me like a foreboding. Today it was clear to me. The children's memorial feast, you saw in me a kind of accomplice. Well, yes; a man's memories, after all, cannot be wiped out, not so mine, anyhow. It isn't in me.

Ellida. I know that. Oh! I know that so well.

Wangel. But you are mistaken all the same. To you it is almost as if the children's mother were still living as if she were still here invisible amongst us. You think my heart is equally divided between you and her. It is this thought that shocks you. You see something immoral in our relation, and that is why you no longer can or will live with me as my wife.

Ellida (rising). Have you seen all that, Wangel seen into all this?

Wangel. Yes; today I have at last seen to the very heart of it, to its utmost depths.

Ellida. To its very heart, you say? Oh, do not think that!

Wangel (rising). I see very well that there is more than this, dear Ellida.

Ellida (anxiously). You know there is more?

Wangel. Yes. You cannot bear your surroundings here. The mountains crush you, and weigh upon your heart. Nothing is open enough for you here. The heavens above you are not spacious enough. The air is not strong and bracing enough.

Ellida. You are right. Night and day, winter and summer, it weighs upon me, this irresistible home-sickness for the sea.

Wangel. I know it well, dear Ellida (laying his hands upon her head). And that is why the poor sick child shall go home to her own again.

Ellida. What do you mean?

Wangel. Something quite simple. We are going away.

Ellida. Going away?

Wangel. Yes. Somewhere by the open sea, a place where you can find a true home, after your own heart.

Ellida. Oh, dear, do not think of that! That is quite impossible. You can live happily nowhere on earth but here!

Wangel. That must be as it may. And, besides, do you think I can live happily here without you?

Ellida. But I am here. And I will stay here. You have me.

Wangel. Have I, Ellida?

Ellida. Oh! don't speak of all this. Why, here you have all that you love and strive for. All your life's work lies here.

Wangel. That must be as it may, I tell you. We are going away from here, are going somewhere, out there. That is quite settled now, dear Ellida.

Ellida. What do you think we should gain by that?

Wangel. You would regain your health and peace of mind.

Ellida. Hardly. And then you, yourself! Think of yourself, too! What of you?

Wangel. I would win you back again, my dearest.

Ellida. But you cannot do that! No, no, you can't do that, Wangel! That is the terrible part of it, heart-breaking to think of.

Wangel. That remains to be proved. If you are harbouring such thoughts, truly there is no other salvation for you than to go hence. And the sooner the better. Now this is irrevocably settled, do you hear?

Ellida. No! Then in heaven's name I had better tell you everything straight out. Everything just as it is.

Wangel. Yes, yes! Do.

Ellida. For you shall not ruin your happiness for my sake, especially as it can't help us in any way.

Wangel. I have your word now that you will tell me everything just as it is.

Ellida. I'll tell you everything as well as I can, and as far as I understand it. Come here and sit by me. (They sit down on the stones.)

Wangel. Well, Ellida, so

Ellida. That day when you came out there and asked me if I would be yours, you spoke so frankly and honestly to me about your first marriage. It had been so happy, you said.

Wangel. And so it was.

Ellida. Yes, yes! I am sure of that, dear! It is not for that I am referring to it now. I only want to remind you that I, on my side, was frank with you. I told you quite openly that once in my life I had cared for another. That there had been a, a kind of engagement between us.

Wangel. A kind of

Ellida. Yes, something of the sort. Well, it only lasted such a very short time. He went away; and after that I put an end to it. I told you all that.

Wangel. Why rake up all this now? It really didn't concern me; nor have I once asked you who he was!

Ellida. No, you have not. You are always so thoughtful for me.

Wangel (smiling). Oh, in this case I could guess the name well enough for myself.

Ellida. The name?

Wangel. Out in Skjoldviken and thereabouts there weren't many to choose from; or, rather, there was only a single one.

Ellida. You believe it was Arnholm!

Wangel. Well, wasn't it?

Ellida. No!

Wangel. Not he? Then I don't in the least understand.

Ellida. Can you remember that late in the autumn a large American ship once put into Skjoldviken for repairs?

Wangel. Yes, I remember it very well. It was on board that ship that the captain was found one morning in his cabin - murdered. I myself went out to make the post-mortem.

Ellida. Yes, it was you.

Wangel. It was the second mate who had murdered him.

Ellida. No one can say that. For it was never proved.

Wangel. There was enough against him anyhow, or why should he have drowned himself as he did?

Ellida. He did not drown himself. He sailed in a ship to the north.

Wangel (startled). How do you know?

Ellida (with an effort). Well, Wangel, it was this second mate to whom I was betrothed.

Wangel (springing up). What! Is it possible!

Ellida. Yes, it is so. It was to him!

Wangel. But how on earth, Ellida! How did you come to betroth yourself to such a man? To an absolute stranger! What is his name?

Ellida. At that time he called himself Friman. Later, in his letters he signed himself Alfred Johnston.

Wangel. And where did he come from?

Ellida. From Finmark, he said. For the rest, he was born in Finland, had come to Norway there as a child with his father, I think.

Wangel. A Finlander, then?

Ellida. Yes, so he called himself.

Wangel. What else do you know about him?

Ellida. Only that he went to sea very young. And that he had been on long voyages.

Wangel. Nothing more?

Ellida. No. We never spoke of such things.

Wangel. Of what did you speak, then?

Ellida. We spoke mostly about the sea.

Wangel. Ah! About the sea

Ellida. About storms and calm. Of dark nights at sea. And of the sea in the glittering sunshiny days we spoke also. But we spoke most of the whales, and the dolphins, and the seals who lie out there on the rocks in the midday sun. And then we spoke of the gulls, and the eagles, and all the other sea birds. I think isn't it wonderful? when we talked of such things it seemed to me as if both the sea beasts and sea birds were one with him.

Wangel. And with you?

Ellida. Yes; I almost thought I belonged to them all, too.

Wangel. Well, well! And so it was that you betrothed yourself to him?

Ellida. Yes. He said I must.

Wangel. You must? Had you no will of your own, then?

Ellida. Not when he was near. Ah! afterwards I thought it all so inexplicable.

Wangel. Were you often together?

Ellida. No; not very often. One day he came out to our place, and looked over the lighthouse. After that I got to know him, and we met now and again. But then that happened about the captain, and so he had to go away.

Wangel. Yes, yes. Tell me more about that.

Ellida. It was just daybreak when I had a note from him. He said in it I was to go out to him at the Bratthammer. You know the headland there between the lighthouse and Skjoldviken?

Wangel. I know, I know!

Ellida. I was to go out there at once, he wrote, because he wanted to speak to me.

Wangel. And you went?

Ellida. Yes. I could not do otherwise. Well, then he told me he had stabbed the captain in the night.

Wangel. He said that himself! Actually said so!

Ellida. Yes. But he had only acted rightly and justly, he said.

Wangel. Rightly and justly! Why did he stab him then?

Ellida. He wouldn't speak out about that. He said it was not fit for me to hear.

Wangel. And you believed his naked, bare word?

Ellida. Yes. It never occurred to me to do otherwise. Well, anyhow, he had to go away. But now, when he was to bid me farewell. No; you never could imagine what he thought of

Wangel. Well? Tell me.

Ellida. He took from his pocket a key-ring and drew a ring that he always wore from his finger, and he took a small ring I had. These two he put on the key-ring. And then he said we should wed ourselves to the sea.

Wangel. Wed?

Ellida. Yes, so he said. And with that he threw the key-ring, and our rings, with all his might, as far as he could into the deep.

Wangel. And you, Ellida, you did all this?

Ellida. Yes, only think, it then seemed to me as if it must be so. But, thank God I, he went away.

Wangel. And when he was gone?

Ellida. Oh! You can surely understand that I soon came to my senses again, that I saw how absolutely mad and meaningless it had all been.

Wangel. But you spoke just now of letters. So you have heard from him since?

Ellida. Yes, I have heard from him. First I had a few short lines from Archangel. He only wrote he was going to America. And then he told me where to send an answer.

Wangel. And did you?

Ellida. At once. I wrote him, of course, that all must be at an end between us; and that he must no longer think of me, just as I should no longer think of him.

Wangel. But did he write again?

Ellida. Yes, he wrote again.

Wangel. And what was his answer to your communication?

Ellida. He took no notice of it. It was exactly as if I had never broken with him. He wrote quite composedly and calmly that I must wait for him. When he could have me he would let me know, and then I was to go to him at once.

Wangel. So he would not release you?

Ellida. No. Then I wrote again, almost word for word as I had before; or perhaps more firmly.

Wangel. And he gave in?

Ellida. Oh, no! Don't think that! He wrote quietly, as before not a word of my having broken with him. Then I knew it was useless, and so I never wrote to him again.

Wangel. And you never heard from him?

Ellida. Oh, yes! I have had three letters since then. Once he wrote to me from California, and a second time from China. The last letter I had from him was from Australia. He wrote he was going to the gold-mines; but since then he has made no sign.

Wangel. This man has had a strange power over you, Ellida.

Ellida. Yes, yes! The terrible man!

Wangel. But you mustn't think of that any more. Never again, never! Promise me that, my dear, beloved Ellida. Now we must try another treatment for you. Fresher air than here within the fjords. The salt, fresh air of the sea! Dear, what say you to that?

Ellida. Oh! don't speak of it! Don't think of it! There is no help in this for me. I feel that so well. I can't shake it off not even there.

Wangel. What, dear? What do you really mean?

Ellida. I mean the horror of it, this incomprehensible power over the mind.

Wangel. But you have shaken it off, long since, when you broke with him. Why, all this is long past now.

Ellida (springing up). No; that it is not, it is not!

Wangel. Not past?

Ellida. No, Wangel, it is not past; and I fear it never will be never, in all our life.

Wangel (in a pained voice). Do you mean to say that in your innermost heart you have never been able to forget this strange man?

Ellida. I had forgotten him; but then it was as if he had suddenly come back again.

Wangel. How long ago is that?

Ellida. It's about three years ago, now, or a little longer. It was just when I expected the child.

Wangel. Ah! at that time? Yes, Ellida, now I begin to understand many things.

Ellida. You are mistaken, dear. What has come to me? Oh! I believe nothing on earth will ever make it clear.

Wangel (looking sadly at her). Only to think that all these three years you have cared for another man. Cared for another. Not for me but for another!

Ellida. Oh! you are so utterly mistaken! I care for no one but you.

Wangel (in a subdued voice). Why, then, in all this time have you not lived with me as my wife?

Ellida. Because of the horror that comes from the strange man.

Wangel. The horror?

Ellida. Yes, the horror. A horror so terrible, such as only the sea could hold. For now you shall hear, Wangel.

(The young townsfolk come back, bow, and pass out to the right. Together with them come ARNHOLM, BOLETTE, HILDE, and LYNGSTRAND.)

Bolette (as she passes by). Well, are you still walking about up here?

Ellida. Yes, it is so cool and pleasant up here on the heights.

Arnholm. We, for our part, are going down for a dance.

Wangel. All right. We'll soon come down, we also.

Hilde. Goodbye, for the present!

Ellida. Mr. Lyngstrand, will you wait one moment? (LYNGSTRAND Stops. ARNHOLM, BOLETTE and HILDE go out. To LYNGSTRAND.) Are you going to dance too?

Lyngstrand. No, Mrs. Wangel. I don't think I dare.

Ellida. No, you should be careful, you know, your chest. You're not quite well yet, you see.

Lyngstrand. Not quite.

Ellida (with some hesitation). How long may it be now since you went on that voyage?

Lyngstrand. That time when I contracted this weakness?

Ellida. Yes, that voyage you told me about this morning?

Lyngstrand. Oh! it's about, wait a moment, yes, it's a good three years now.

Ellida. Three years, then.

Lyngstrand. Perhaps a little more. We left America in February, and we were wrecked in March. It was the equinoctial gales we came in for.

Ellida (looking at WANGEL). So it was at that time

Wangel. But, dear Ellida

Ellida. Well, don't let me detain you, Mr. Lyngstrand. Now go down, but don't dance.

Lyngstrand. No, I'll only look on. (He goes out.)

Ellida. Johnston was on board too, I am quite certain of it.

Wangel. What makes you think so?

Ellida (without answering). He learnt on board that I had married another while he was away. And so that very hour this came over me.

Wangel. The horror?

Ellida. Yes, all of a sudden I see him alive right in front of me; or, rather a little in profile. He never looks at me, only he is there.

Wangel. How do you think he looks?

Ellida. Exactly as when I saw him last.

Wangel. Ten years ago?

Ellida. Yes; out there at Bratthammeren. Most distinctly of all I see his breastpin, with a large bluish-white pearl in it. The pearl is like a dead fish's eye, and it seems to glare at me.

Wangel. Good God! You are more ill than I thought. More ill than you yourself know, Ellida.

Ellida. Yes, yes! Help me if you can, for I feel how it is drawing closer and more close.

Wangel. And you have gone about in this state three whole years, bearing for yourself this secret suffering, without confiding in me.

Ellida. But I could not; not till it became necessary for your own sake. If I had confided in you I should also have had to confide to you the unutterable.

Wangel. Unutterable?

Ellida. No, no, no! Do not ask. Only one thing, nothing more. Wangel, when shall we understand that mystery of the boy's eyes?

Wangel. My dear love, Ellida, I assure you it was only your own fancy. The child had exactly the same eyes as other normal children have.

Ellida. No, he had not. And you could not see it! The child's eyes changed colour with the sea. When the fjord lay bathed in sunshine, so were his eyes. And so in storm. Oh, I saw it, if you did not!

Wangel (humouring her). Maybe. But even if it were true, what then?

Ellida (in lower voice, and coming nearer). I have seen such eyes before.

Wangel. Well? Where?

Ellida. Out at Bratthammeren, ten years ago.

Wangel (stepping back). What does it mean?

Ellida (whispers, trembling). The child had the strange man's eyes.

Wangel (cries out reluctantly). Ellida!

Ellida (clasps her hands despairingly about her head). Now you understand why I would not, why I dared not, live with you as your wife. (She turns suddenly and rushes off over the heights.)

Wangel (hurrying after her and calling). Ellida, Ellida! My poor unhappy Ellida!

Act III

(SCENE. A more remote part of DOCTOR WANGEL'S garden. It is boggy and overshadowed by large old trees. To the right is seen the margin of a dank pond. A low, open fence separates the garden from the footpath, and the fjord in the background. Beyond is the range of mountains, with its peaks. It is afternoon, almost evening. BOLETTE sits on a stone seat, and on the seat lie some books and a work-basket. HILDE and LYNGSTRAND, both with fishing-tackle, walk along the bank of the pond.)

Hilde (making a sign to LYNGSTRAND). I can see a large one.

Lyngstrand (looking). Where?

Hilde (pointing). Can't you see? He's down there. Good gracious! There's another! (Looks through the trees.) Out there. Now he's coming to frighten him away!

Bolette (looking up). Who's coming?

Hilde. Your tutor, Miss!

Bolette. Mine?

Hilde. Yes. Goodness knows he never was mine.

(ARNHOLM enters from between the trees.)

Arnholm. Are there fish in the pond now?

Hilde. There are some very ancient carp.

Arnholm. No! Are the old carp still alive?

Hilde. Yes; they're pretty tough. But now we're going to try and get rid of some of them.

Arnholm. You'd better try out there at the fjord.

Lyngstrand. No; the pond is—well, so to say, more mysterious.

Hilde. Yes; it's fascinating here. Have you been in the sea?

Arnholm. Yes; I've come straight from the baths.

Hilde. I suppose you kept in the enclosure?

Arnholm. Yes; I'm not much of a swimmer.

Hilde. Can you swim on your back?

Arnholm. No.

Hilde. I can. (To LYNGSTRAND.) Let's try out there on the other side. (They go off along the pond.)

Arnholm (coming closer to BOLETTE). Are you sitting all alone here, Bolette?

Bolette. Yes; I generally do.

Arnholm. Isn't your mother down here in the garden?

Bolette. No, she's sure to be out with father.

Arnholm. How is she this afternoon?

Bolette. I don't quite know. I forgot to ask.

Arnholm. What books have you there?

Bolette. The one's something about botany. And the other's a geography.

Arnholm. Do you care about such things?

Bolette. Yes, if only I had time for it. But, first of all, I've to look after the housekeeping.

Arnholm. Doesn't your mother help you, your stepmother, doesn't she help with that?

Bolette. No, that's my business. Why, I saw to that during the two years father was alone. And so it has been since.

Arnholm. But you're as fond as ever of reading.

Bolette. Yes, I read all the useful books I can get hold of. One wants to know something about the world. For here we live so completely outside of all that's going on or almost.

Arnholm. Now don't say that, dear Bolette.

Bolette. Yes! I think we live very much as the carp down there in the pond. They have the fjord so near them, where the shoals of wild fishes pass in and out. But the poor, tame house-fishes know nothing, and they can take no part in that.

Arnholm. I don't think it would fare very well with them if they could get out there.

Bolette. Oh! it would be much the same, I expect.

Arnholm. Moreover, you can't say that one is so completely out of the world here, not in the summer anyhow. Why, nowadays this is quite a rendezvous for the busy world, almost a terminus for the time being.

Bolette. Ah, yes! you who yourself are only here for the time being it is easy for you to make fun of us.

Arnholm. I make fun? How can you think that?

Bolette. Well, all that about this being a rendezvous, and a terminus for the busy world, that's something you've heard the townsfolk here saying. Yes, they're in the habit of saying that sort of thing.

Arnholm. Well, frankly, I've noticed that, too.

Bolette. But really there's not an atom of truth in it. Not for us who always live here. What good is it to us that the great strange world comes hither for a time on its way North to see the midnight sun? We ourselves have no part in that; we see nothing of the midnight sun! No! We've got to be good, and live our lives here in our carp pond.

Arnholm (sitting down by her). Now tell me, dear Bolette, isn't there something or other, something definite you are longing for?

Bolette. Perhaps.

Arnholm. What is it, really? What is it you are longing for?

Bolette. Chiefly to get away.

Arnholm. That above all, then?

Bolette. Yes; and then to learn more. To really know something about everything.

Arnholm. When I used to teach you, your father often said he would let you go to college.

Bolette. Yes, poor father! He says so many things. But when it comes to the point he - there's no real stamina in father.

Arnholm. No, unfortunately you're right there. He has not exactly stamina. But have you ever spoken to him about it, spoken really earnestly and seriously?

Bolette. No, I've not quite done that.

Arnholm. But really you ought to. Before it is too late, Bolette, why don't you?

Bolette. Oh! I suppose it's because there's no real stamina in me either. I certainly take after father in that.

Arnholm. Hm, don't you think you're unjust to yourself there?

Bolette. No, unfortunately. Besides, father has so little time for thinking of me and my future, and not much desire to either. He prefers to put such things away from him whenever he can. He is so completely taken up with Ellida.

Arnholm. With whom? What?

Bolette. I mean that he and my stepmother (breaks off). Father and mother suffice one another, as you see.

Arnholm. Well, so much the better if you were to get away from here.

Bolette. Yes; but I don't think I've a right to; not to forsake father.

Arnholm. But, dear Bolette, you'll have to do that sometime, anyhow. So it seems to me the sooner the better.

Bolette. I suppose there is nothing else for it. After all, I must think of myself, too. I must try and get occupation of some sort. When once father's gone, I have no one to hold to. But, poor father! I dread leaving him.

Arnholm. Dread?

Bolette. Yes, for father's sake.

Arnholm. But, good heavens! Your stepmother? She is left to him.

Bolette. That's true. But she's not in the least fit to do all that mother did so well. There is so much she doesn't see, or that she won't see, or that she doesn't care about. I don't know which it is.

Arnholm. Um, I think I understand what you mean.

Bolette. Poor father! He is weak in some things. Perhaps you've noticed that yourself? He hasn't enough occupation, either, to fill up his time. And then she is so thoroughly incapable of helping him; however, that's to some extent his own fault.

Arnholm. In what way?

Bolette. Oh! father always likes to see happy faces about him. There must be sunshine and joy in the house, he says. And so I'm afraid he often gives her medicine which will do her little good in the long run.

Arnholm. Do you really think that?

Bolette. Yes; I can't get rid of the thought. She is so odd at times. (Passionately.) But isn't it unjust that I should have to stay at home here? Really it's not of any earthly use to father. Besides, I have a duty towards myself, too, I think.

Arnholm. Do you know what, Bolette? We two must talk these matters over more carefully.

Bolette. Oh! That won't be much use. I suppose I was created to stay here in the carp pond.

Arnholm. Not a bit of it. It depends entirely upon yourself.

Bolette (quickly). Do you think so?

Arnholm. Yes, believe me, it lies wholly and solely in your own hands.

Bolette. If only that were true! Will you perhaps put in a good word for me with father?

Arnholm. Certainly. But first of all I must speak frankly and freely with you yourself, dear.

Bolette (looks out to the left). Hush! don't let them notice anything. We'll speak of this later.

(ELLIDA enters from the left. She has no hat on, but a large shawl is thrown over her head and shoulders.)

Ellida (with restless animation). How pleasant it is here! How delightful it is here!

Arnholm (rising). Have you been for a walk?

Ellida. Yes, a long, long lovely walk up there with Wangel. And now we're going for a sail.

Bolette. Won't you sit down?

Ellida. No, thanks; I won't sit down.

Bolette (making room on seat). Here's a pleasant seat.

Ellida (walking about). No, no, no! I'll not sit down, not sit down!

Arnholm. I'm sure your walk has done you good. You look quite refreshed.

Ellida. Oh, I feel so thoroughly well, I feel so unspeakably happy. So safe, so safe! (Looking out to the left.) What great steamer is that coming along there?

Bolette (rising, and also looking out). It must be the large English ship.

Arnholm. It's passing the buoy. Does it usually stop here?

Bolette. Only for half an hour. It goes farther up the fjord.

Ellida. And then sails away again tomorrow, away over the great open sea, right over the sea. Only think! to be with them. If one could. If only one could!

Arnholm. Have you never been any long sea voyage, Mrs. Wangel?

Ellida. Never; only those little trips in the fjord here.

Bolette (with a sigh). Ah, no! I suppose we must put up with the dry land.

Arnholm. Well, after all, that really is our home.

Ellida. No; I don't think it is.

Arnholm. Not the land?

Ellida. No; I don't believe so. I think that if only men had from the beginning accustomed themselves to live on the sea, or in the sea perhaps, we should be more perfect than we are both better and happier.

Arnholm. You really think that?

Ellida. Yes. I should like to know if we should not. I've often spoken to Wangel about it.

Arnholm. Well, and he?

Ellida. He thinks it might be so.

Arnholm (jestingly). Well, perhaps! But it can't be helped. We've once for all entered upon the wrong path, and have become land beasts instead of sea beasts. Anyhow, I suppose it's too late to make good the mistake now.

Ellida. Yes, you've spoken a sad truth. And I think men instinctively feel something of this themselves. And they bear it about with them as a secret regret and sorrow. Believe me, herein lies the deepest cause for the sadness of men. Yes, believe me, in this.

Arnholm. But, my dearest Mrs. Wangel, I have not observed that men are so extremely sad. It seems to me, on the contrary, that most of them take life easily and pleasantly and with a great, quiet, unconscious joy.

Ellida. Oh! no, it is not so. The joy is, I suppose, something like our joy at the long pleasant summer days, it has the presentiment of the dark days coming. And it is this presentiment that casts its shadows over the joy of men, just as the driving clouds cast their shadow over the fjords. It lies there so bright and blue and of a sudden.

Arnholm. You shouldn't give way to such sad thoughts. Just now you were so glad and so bright.

Ellida. Yes, yes, so I was. Oh, this, this is so stupid of me. (Looking about her uneasily.) If only Wangel would come! He promised me so faithfully he would. And yet he does not come. Dear Mr. Arnholm, won't you try and find him for me?

Arnholm. Gladly!

Ellida. Tell him he must come here directly now. For now I can't see him.

Arnholm. Not see him?

Ellida. Oh! you don't understand. When he is not by me I often can't remember how he looks. And then it is as if I had quite lost him. That is so terribly painful. But do go, please. (She paces round the pond.)

Bolette (to ARNHOLM). I will go with you, you don't know the way.

Arnholm. Nonsense, I shall be all right.

Bolette (aside). No, no, no. I am anxious. I'm afraid he is on board the steamer.

Arnholm. Afraid?

Bolette. Yes. He usually goes to see if there are any acquaintances of his. And there's a restaurant on board.

Arnholm. Ah! Come then.

(He and BOLETTE go off. ELLIDA stands still awhile, staring down at the pond. Now and again she speaks to herself in a low voice, and breaks off. Along the footpath beyond the garden fence a STRANGER in travelling dress comes from the left. His hair and beard are bushy and red. He has a Scotch cap on, and a travelling bag with strap across his shoulders.)

The Stranger (goes slowly along by the fence and peeps into the garden. When he catches sight of ELLIDA he stands still, looks at her fixedly and searchingly, and speaks in a low voice). Good- evening, Ellida!

Ellida (turns round with a cry). Oh dear! have you come at last!

The Stranger. Yes, at last.

Ellida (looking at him astonished and frightened). Who are you? Do you seek anyone here?

The Stranger. You surely know that well enough, Ellida.

Ellida (starting). What is this! How do you address me? Whom are you looking for?

The Stranger. Well, I suppose I'm looking for you.

Ellida (shuddering). Oh! (She stares at him, totters back, uttering a half-suffocating cry.) The eyes! the eyes!

The Stranger. Are you beginning to recognise me at last? I knew you at once, Ellida.

Ellida. The eyes! Don't look at me like that! I shall cry for help!

The Stranger. Hush, hush! Do not fear. I shan't hurt you.

Ellida (covering her eyes with her hands). Do not look at me like that, I say!

The Stranger (leaning with his arms on the garden fence). I came with the English steamer.

Ellida (stealing a frightened look at him). What do you want with me?

The Stranger. I promised you to come as soon as I could

Ellida. Go, go away! Never, never come here again! I wrote to you that everything must be over between us, everything! Oh! you know that!

The Stranger (imperturbably, and not answering her). I would gladly have come to you sooner; but I could not. Now, at last I am able to, and I am here, Ellida.

Ellida. What is it you want with me? What do you mean? Why have you come here?

The Stranger. Surely you know I've come to fetch you.

Ellida (recoils in terror). To fetch me! Is that what you mean?

The Stranger. Of course.

Ellida. But surely you know that I am married?

The Stranger. Yes, I know.

Ellida. And yet and yet you have come to, to fetch me!

The Stranger. Certainly I have.

Ellida (seizing her head with both her hands). Oh! this misery, this horror! This horror!

The Stranger. Perhaps you don't want to come?

Ellida (bewildered). Don't look at me like that.

The Stranger. I was asking you if you didn't want to come.

Ellida. No, no, no! Never in all eternity! I will not, I tell you. I neither can nor will. (In lower tone.) I dare not.

The Stranger (climbs over the fence, and comes into the garden). Well, Ellida, let me tell you one thing before I go.

Ellida (wishes to fly, but cannot. She stands as one paralysed with terror, and leans for support against the trunk of a tree by the pond). Don't touch me! Don't come near me! No nearer! Don't touch me, I say!

The Stranger (cautiously coming a few steps nearer). You need not be so afraid of me, Ellida.

Ellida (covering her eyes with her hands). Don't look at me like that.

The Stranger. Do not be afraid, not afraid.

(WANGEL comes through the garden, from the left.)

Wangel (still half-way between the trees). Well, you've had to wait for me a long while.

Ellida (rushes towards him, clings fast to his arm, and cries out). Oh! Wangel! Save me! You save me, if you can!

Wangel. Ellida! What in heaven's name!

Ellida. Save me, Wangel! Don't you see him there? Why, he is standing there!

Wangel (looking thither). That man? (Coming nearer.) May I ask you who you are, and what you have come into this garden for?

The Stranger (motions with a nod towards ELLIDA). I want to talk to her.

Wangel. Oh! indeed. So I suppose it was you. (To ELLIDA.) I hear a stranger has been to the house and asked for you?

The Stranger. Yes, it was I.

Wangel. And what do you want with my wife? (Turning round.) Do you know him, Ellida?

Ellida (in a low voice and wringing her hands). Do I know him! Yes, yes, yes!

Wangel (quickly). Well!

Ellida. Why, it is he, Wangel! he himself! He who you know!

Wangel. What! What is it you say? (Turning.) Are you the Johnston who once...

The Stranger. You may call me Johnston for aught I care! However, that's not my name,

Wangel. It is not?

The Stranger. It is no longer. No!

Wangel. And what may you want with my wife? For I suppose you know the lighthouse-keeper's daughter has been married this long time, and whom she married, you of course also know.

The Stranger. I've known it over three years.

Ellida (eagerly). How did you come to know it?

The Stranger. I was on my way home to you, Ellida. I came across an old newspaper. It was a paper from these parts, and in it there was that about the marriage.

Ellida (looking straight in front of her). The marriage! So it was that!

The Stranger. It seemed so wonderful to me. For the rings, why that, too, was a marriage, Ellida.

Ellida (covering her face with her hands). Oh! Wangel. How dare you?

The Stranger. Have you forgotten that?

Ellida (feeling his look, suddenly cries out). Don't stand there and look at me like that!

Wangel (goes up to him). You must deal with me, and not with her. In short, now that you know the circumstances, what is it you really want here? Why do you seek my wife?

The Stranger. I promised Ellida to come to her as soon as I could.

Wangel. Ellida, again!

The Stranger. And Ellida promised faithfully she would wait for me until I came.

Wangel. I notice you call my wife by her first name. This kind of familiarity is not customary with us here.

The Stranger. I know that perfectly. But as she first, and above all, belongs to me

Wangel. To you, still

Ellida (draws back behind WANGEL). Oh! he will never release me!

Wangel. To you? You say she belongs to you?

The Stranger. Has she told you anything about the two rings, my ring and Ellida's?

Wangel. Certainly. And what then? She put an end to that long ago. You have had her letters, so you know this yourself.

The Stranger. Both Ellida and I agreed that what we did should have all the strength and authority of a real and full marriage.

Ellida. But you hear, I will not! Never on earth do I wish to know anything more of you. Do not look at me like that. I will not, I tell you!

Wangel. You must be mad to think you can come here, and base any claim upon such childish nonsense.

The Stranger. That's true. A claim, in your sense, I certainly have not.

Wangel. What do you mean to do, then? You surely do not imagine you can take her from me by force, against her own will?

The Stranger. No. What would be the good of that? If Ellida wishes to be with me she must come freely.

Ellida (starts, crying out). Freely!

Wangel. And you actually believe that

Ellida (to herself). Freely!

Wangel. You must have taken leave of your senses! Go your ways. We have nothing more to do with you.

The Stranger (looking at his watch). It is almost time for me to go on board again. (Coming nearer.) Yes, yes, Ellida, now I have done my duty. (Coming still nearer.) I have kept the word I gave you.

Ellida (beseechingly drawing away). Oh! don't touch me!

The Stranger. And so now you must think it over till tomorrow night

Wangel. There is nothing to think over here. See that you get away.

The Stranger (still to ELLIDA). Now I'm going with the steamer up the fjord. Tomorrow night I will come again, and then I shall look for you here. You must wait for me here in the garden, for I prefer settling the matter with you alone; you understand?

Ellida (in low, trembling tone). Do you hear that, Wangel?

Wangel. Only keep calm. We shall know how to prevent this visit.

The Stranger. Goodbye for the present, Ellida. So tomorrow night

Ellida (imploringly). Oh! no, no! Do not come tomorrow night! Never come here again!

The Stranger. And should you then have a mind to follow me over the seas

Ellida. Oh, don't look at me like that!

The Stranger. I only mean that you must then be ready to set out.

Wangel. Go up to the house, Ellida.

Ellida. I cannot! Oh, help me! Save me, Wangel!

The Stranger. For you must remember that if you do not go with me tomorrow, all is at an end.

Ellida (looks tremblingly at him). Then all is at an end? Forever?

The Stranger (nodding). Nothing can change it then, Ellida. I shall never again come to this land. You will never see me again, nor hear from me either. Then I shall be as one dead and gone from you forever.

Ellida (breathing with difficulty). Oh!

The Stranger. So think carefully what you do. Goodbye! (He goes to the fence and climbs over it, stands still, and says.) Yes, Ellida; be ready for the journey tomorrow night. For then I shall come and fetch you. (He goes slowly and calmly down the footpath to the right.)

Ellida (looking after him for a time). Freely, he said; think he said that I must go with him freely!

Wangel. Only keep calm. Why, he's gone now, and you'll never see him again.

Ellida. Oh! how can you say that? He's coming again tomorrow night!

Wangel. Let him come. He shall not meet you again in any case.

Ellida (shaking her head). Ah, Wangel! Do not believe you can prevent him.

Wangel. I can, dearest; only trust me.

Ellida (pondering, and not listening to him). Now when he's been here tomorrow night and then when he has gone over seas in the steamer

Wangel. Yes; what then?

Ellida. I should like to know if he will never, never come back again.

Wangel. No, dear Ellida. You may be quite sure of that. What should he do here after this? Now that he has learnt from your own lips that you will have nothing more to do with him. With that the whole thing is over.

Ellida (to herself). Tomorrow, then, or never!

Wangel. And should it ever occur to him to come here again

Ellida. Well?

Wangel. Why, then, it is in our power to make him harmless.

Ellida. Oh! do not think that!

Wangel. It is in our power, I tell you. If you can get rid of him in no other way, he must expiate the murder of the captain.

Ellida (passionately). No, no, no! Never that! We know nothing about the murder of the captain! Nothing whatever!

Wangel. Know nothing? Why, he himself confessed it to you!

Ellida. No, nothing of that. If you say anything of it I shall deny it. He shall not be imprisoned. He belongs out there, to the open sea. He belongs out there!

Wangel (looks at her and says slowly). Ah! Ellida, Ellida!

Ellida (clinging passionately to him). Oh! dear, faithful one, save me from this man!

Wangel (disengaging himself gently). Come, come with me! (LYNGSTRAND and HILDE, both with fishing tackle, come in from the right, along the pond.)

Lyngstrand (going quickly up to ELLIDA). Now, Mrs. Wangel, you must hear something wonderful.

Wangel. What is it?

Lyngstrand. Fancy! We've seen the American!

Wangel. The American?

Hilde. Yes, I saw him, too.

Lyngstrand. He was going round the back of the garden, and thence on board the great English steamer.

Wangel. How do you know the man?

Lyngstrand. Why, I went to sea with him once. I felt so certain he'd been drowned and now he's very much alive!

Wangel. Do you know anything more about him?

Lyngstrand. No. But I'm sure he's come to revenge himself upon his faithless sailor-wife.

Wangel. What do you mean?

Hilde. Lyngstrand's going to use him for a work of art.

Wangel. I don't understand one word.

Ellida. You shall hear afterwards.

(ARNHOLM and BOLETTE come from the left along the footpath outside the garden.)

Bolette (to those in the garden). Do come and see! The great English steamer's just going up the fjord.

(A large steamer glides slowly past in the distance.)

Lyngstrand (to HILDE behind the garden fence). Tonight he's sure to come to her.

Hilde (nods). To the faithless sailor-wife, yes.

Lyngstrand. Fancy, at midnight!

Hilde. That must be so fascinating.

Ellida (looking after the ship). Tomorrow, then!

Wangel. And then never again.

Ellida (in a low, imploring tone). Oh! Wangel, save me from myself!

Wangel (looks anxiously at her). Ellida, I feel there is something behind this

Ellida. There is the temptation!

Wangel. Temptation?

Ellida. The man is like the sea!

(She goes slowly and thoughtfully through the garden, and out to the left. WANGEL walks uneasily by her side, watching her closely.)

Act IV

(SCENE. DOCTOR WANGEL'S garden-room. Doors right and left. In the background, between the windows, an open glass door leading out on to the verandah. Below this, a portion of the garden is visible. A sofa and table down left. To the right a piano, and farther back a large flower-stand. In the middle of the room a round table, with chairs. On the table is a rose-tree in bloom, and other plants around it. Morning.

In the room, by the table, BOLETTE is sitting on the sofa, busy with some embroidery. LYNGSTRAND is seated on a chair at the upper end of the table. In the garden below BALLESTED sits painting. HILDE stands by watching him.)

Lyngstrand (with his arms on the table, sits silent awhile, looking at BOLETTE'S work). It must be awfully difficult to do a border like that, Miss Wangel?

Bolette. Oh, no! It's not very difficult, if only you take care to count right.

Lyngstrand. To count? Must you count, too?

Bolette. Yes, the stiches. See!

Lyngstrand. So you do! Just fancy! Why, it's almost a kind of art. Can you design, too?

Bolette. Oh, yes! When I've a copy.

Lyngstrand. Not unless?

Bolette. No.

Lyngstrand. Well, then, after all, it's not a real art?

Bolette. No; it is rather only a sort of handicraft.

Lyngstrand. But still, I think that perhaps you could learn art.

Bolette. If I haven't any talent?

Lyngstrand. Yes; if you could always be with a real true artist

Bolette. Do you think, then, I could learn it from him?

Lyngstrand. Not exactly learn in the ordinary sense; but I think it would grow upon you little by little by a kind of miracle as it were, Miss Wangel.

Bolette. That would be wonderful.

Lyngstrand (after a pause). Have you ever thought about, I mean, have you ever thought deeply and earnestly about marriage, Miss Wangel?

Bolette (looking quickly at him). About, no!

Lyngstrand. I have.

Bolette. Really? Have you?

Lyngstrand. Oh yes! I often think about things of that sort, especially about marriage; and, besides, I've read several books about it. I think marriage must be counted a sort of miracle that a woman should gradually change until she is like her husband.

Bolette. You mean has like interests?

Lyngstrand. Yes, that's it.

Bolette. Well, but his abilities, his talents, and his skill?

Lyngstrand. Hm, well, I should like to know if all that too

Bolette. Then, perhaps, you also believe that everything a man has read for himself, and thought out for himself, that this, too, can grow upon his wife?

Lyngstrand. Yes, I think it can. Little by little; as by a sort of miracle. But, of course, I know such things can only happen in a marriage that is faithful, and loving, and really happy.

Bolette. Has it never occurred to you that a man, too, might, perhaps, be thus drawn over to his wife? Grow like her, I mean.

Lyngstrand. A man? No, I never thought of that.

Bolette. But why not one as well as the other?

Lyngstrand. No; for a man has a calling that he lives for; and that's what makes a man so strong and firm, Miss Wangel. He has a calling in life.

Bolette. Has every man?

Lyngstrand. Oh no! I am thinking more especially of artists.

Bolette. Do you think it right of an artist to get married?

Lyngstrand. Yes, I think so. If he can find one he can heartily love, I

Bolette. Still, I think he should rather live for his art alone.

Lyngstrand. Of course he must; but he can do that just as well, even if he marries.

Bolette. But how about her?

Lyngstrand. Her? Who?

Bolette. She whom he marries. What is she to live for?

Lyngstrand. She, too, is to live for his art. It seems to me a woman must feel so thoroughly happy in that.

Bolette. Hm, I don't exactly know

Lyngstrand. Yes, Miss Wangel, you may be sure of that. It is not merely all the honour and respect she enjoys through him; for that seems almost the least important to me. But it is this; that she can help him to create, that she can lighten his work for him, be about him and see to his comfort, and tend him well, and make his life thoroughly pleasant. I should think that must be perfectly delightful to a woman.

Bolette. Ah! You don't yourself know how selfish you are!

Lyngstrand. I, selfish! Good heavens! Oh, if only you knew me a little better than you do! (Bending closer to her.) Miss Wangel, when once I am gone and that will be very soon now

Bolette (looks pityingly at him). Oh, don't think of anything so sad!

Lyngstrand. But, really, I don't think it is so very sad.

Bolette. What do you mean?

Lyngstrand. Well, you know that I set out in a month. First from here, and then, of course, I'm going south.

Bolette. Oh, I see! Of course.

Lyngstrand. Will you think of me sometimes, then, Miss Wangel?

Bolette. Yes, gladly.

Lyngstrand (pleased). No, promise!

Bolette. I promise.

Lyngstrand. By all that is sacred, Miss Bolette?

Bolette. By all that is sacred. (In a changed manner.) Oh, but what can come of it all? Nothing on earth can come of it!

Lyngstrand. How can you say that! It would be so delightful for me to know you were at home here thinking of me!

Bolette. Well, and what else?

Lyngstrand. I don't exactly know of anything else.

Bolette. Nor I either. There are so many things in the way. Everything stands in the way, I think.

Lyngstrand. Oh, another miracle might come about. Some happy dispensation of fortune, or something of the sort; for I really believe I shall be lucky now.

Bolette (eagerly). Really? You do believe that?

Lyngstrand. Yes, I believe it thoroughly. And so, after a few years, when I come home again as a celebrated sculptor, and well off, and in perfect health!

Bolette. Yes, yes! Of course, we will hope so.

Lyngstrand. You may be perfectly certain about it. Only think faithfully and kindly of me when I am down there in the south; and now I have your word that you will.

Bolette. You have (shaking her head). But, all the same, nothing will surely come of it.

Lyngstrand. Oh! yes, Miss Bolette. At least this will come of it. I shall get on so much more easily and quickly with my art work.

Bolette. Do you believe that, too?

Lyngstrand. I have an inner conviction of it. And I fancy it will be so cheering for you too here in this out-of-the-way place-to know within yourself that you are, so to say, helping me to create.

Bolette (looking at him). Well; but you on your side?

Lyngstrand. I?

Bolette (looking out into the garden). Hush! Let us speak of something else. Here's Mr. Arnholm.

(ARNHOLM is seen in the garden below. He stops and talks to HILDE and BALLESTED.)

Lyngstrand. Are you fond of your old teacher, Miss Bolette?

Bolette. Fond of him?

Lyngstrand. Yes; I mean do you care for him?

Bolette. Yes, indeed I do, for he is a true friend and adviser, too and then he is always so ready to help when he can.

Lyngstrand. Isn't it extraordinary that he hasn't married!

Bolette. Do you think it is extraordinary?

Lyngstrand. Yes, for you say he's well-to-do.

Bolette. He is certainly said to be so. But probably it wasn't so easy to find anyone who'd have him.

Lyngstrand. Why?

Bolette. Oh! He's been the teacher of nearly all the young girls that he knows. He says that himself.

Lyngstrand. But what does that matter?

Bolette. Why, good heavens! One doesn't marry a man who's been your teacher!

Lyngstrand. Don't you think a young girl might love her teacher?

Bolette. Not after she's really grown up.

Lyngstrand. No, fancy that!

Bolette (cautioning him). Sh! sh!

(Meanwhile BALLESTED has been gathering together his things, and carries them out from the garden to the right. HILDE helps him. ARNHOLM goes up the verandah, and comes into the room.)

Arnholm. Good-morning, my dear Bolette. Good-morning, Mr., Mr., hm (He looks displeased, and nods coldly to LYNGSTRAND, who rises.)

Bolette (rising up and going up to ARNHOLM). Good-morning, Mr. Arnholm.

Arnholm. Everything all right here today?

Bolette. Yes, thanks, quite.

Arnholm. Has your stepmother gone to bathe again today?

Bolette. No. She is upstairs in her room.

Arnholm. Not very bright?

Bolette. I don't know, for she has locked herself in.

Arnholm. Hm, has she?

Lyngstrand. I suppose Mrs. Wangel was very much frightened about that American yesterday?

Arnholm. What do you know about that?

Lyngstrand. I told Mrs. Wangel that I had seen him in the flesh behind the garden.

Arnholm. Oh! I see.

Bolette (to ARNHOLM). No doubt you and father sat up very late last night, talking?

Arnholm. Yes, rather late. We were talking over serious matters.

Bolette. Did you put in a word for me, and my affairs, too?

Arnholm. No, dear Bolette, I couldn't manage it. He was so completely taken up with something else.

Bolette (sighs). Ah! yes; he always is.

Arnholm (looks at her meaningly). But later on today we'll talk more fully about the matter. Where's your father now? Not at home?

Bolette. Yes, he is. He must be down in the office. I'll fetch him.

Arnholm. No, thanks. Don't do that. I'd rather go down to him.

Bolette (listening). Wait one moment, Mr. Arnholm; I believe that's father on the stairs. Yes, I suppose he's been up to look after her.

(WANGEL comes in from the door on the left.)

Wangel (shaking ARNHOLM'S hand). What, dear friend, are you here already? It was good of you to come so early, for I should like to talk a little further with you.

Bolette (to LYNGSTRAND). Hadn't we better go down to Hilde in the garden?

Lyngstrand. I shall be delighted, Miss Wangel.

(He and BOLETTE go down into the garden, and pass out between the trees in the background.)

Arnholm (following them with his eyes, turns to WANGEL). Do you know anything about that young man?

Wangel. No, nothing at all.

Arnholm. But do you think it right he should knock about so much with the girls?

Wangel. Does he? I really hadn't noticed it.

Arnholm. You ought to see to it, I think.

Wangel. Yes, I suppose you're right. But, good Lord! What's a man to do? The girls are so accustomed to look after themselves now. They won't listen to me, nor to Ellida.

Arnholm. Not to her either?

Wangel. No; and besides I really cannot expect Ellida to trouble about such things. She's not fit for that (breaking off). But it wasn't that which we were to talk of. Now tell me, have you thought the matter over, thought over all I told you of?

Arnholm. I have thought of nothing else ever since we parted last night.

Wangel. And what do you think should be done?

Arnholm. Dear Wangel, I think you, as a doctor, must know that better than I.

Wangel. Oh! if you only knew how difficult it is for a doctor to judge rightly about a patient who is so dear to him! Besides, this is no ordinary illness. No ordinary doctor and no ordinary medicines can help her.

Arnholm. How is she today?

Wangel. I was upstairs with her just now, and then she seemed to me quite calm; but behind all her moods something lies hidden which it is impossible for me to fathom; and then she is so changeable, so capricious, she varies so suddenly.

Arnholm. No doubt that is the result of her morbid state of mind.

Wangel. Not altogether. When you go down to the bedrock, it was born in her. Ellida belongs to the sea-folk. That is the matter.

Arnholm. What do you really mean, my dear doctor?

Wangel. Haven't you noticed that the people from out there by the open sea are, in a way, a people apart? It is almost as if they themselves lived the life of the sea. There is the rush of waves, and ebb and flow too, both in their thoughts and in their feelings, and so they can never bear transplanting. Oh! I ought to have remembered that. It was a sin against Ellida to take her away from there, and bring her here.

Arnholm. You have come to that opinion?

Wangel. Yes, more and more. But I ought to have told myself this beforehand. Oh! I knew it well enough at bottom! But I put it from me. For, you see, I loved her so! Therefore, I thought of myself first of all. I was inexcusably selfish at that time!

Arnholm. Hm. I suppose every man is a little selfish under such circumstances. Moreover, I've never noticed that vice in you, Doctor Wangel.

Wangel (walks uneasily about the room). Oh, yes! And I have been since then, too. Why, I am so much, much older than she is. I ought to have been at once as a father to her and a guide. I ought to have done my best to develop and enlighten her mind. Unfortunately nothing ever came of that. You see, I hadn't stamina enough, for I preferred her just as she was. So things went worse and worse with her, and then I didn't know what to do. (In a lower voice.) That was why I wrote to you in my trouble, and asked you to come here.

Arnholm (looks at him in astonishment). What, was it for this you wrote?

Wangel. Yes; but don't let anyone notice anything.

Arnholm. How on earth, dear doctor, what good did you expect me to be? I don't understand it.

Wangel. No, naturally. For I was on an altogether false track. I thought Ellida's heart had at one time gone out to you, and that she still secretly cared for you a little, that perhaps it would do her good to see you again, and talk of her home and the old days.

Arnholm. So it was your wife you meant when you wrote that she expected me, and, and perhaps longed for me.

Wangel. Yes, who else?

Arnholm (hurriedly). No, no. You're right. But I didn't understand.

Wangel. Naturally, as I said, for I was on an absolutely wrong track.

Arnholm. And you call yourself selfish!

Wangel. Ah! but I had such a great sin to atone for. I felt I dared not neglect any means that might give the slightest relief to her mind.

Arnholm. How do you really explain the power this stranger exercises over her?

Wangel. Hm, dear friend, there may be sides to the matter that cannot be explained.

Arnholm. Do you mean anything inexplicable in itself, absolutely inexplicable?

Wangel. In any case not explicable as far as we know.

Arnholm. Do you believe there is something in it, then?

Wangel. I neither believe nor deny; I simply don't know. That's why I leave it alone.

Arnholm. Yes. But just one thing: her extraordinary, weird assertion about the child's eyes

Wangel (eagerly). I don't believe a word about the eyes. I will not believe such a thing. It must be purely fancy on her part, nothing else.

Arnholm. Did you notice the man's eyes when you saw him yesterday?

Wangel. Of course I did.

Arnholm. And you saw no sort of resemblance?

Wangel (evasively). Hm, good heavens! What shall I say? It wasn't quite light when I saw him; and, besides, Ellida had been saying so much about this resemblance, I really don't know if I was capable of observing quite impartially.

Arnholm. Well, well, may be. But that other matter? All this terror and unrest coming upon her at the very time, as it seems, this strange man was on his way home.

Wangel. That, oh! that's something she must have persuaded and dreamed herself into since it happened. She was not seized with this so suddenly, all at once, as she now maintains. But since she heard from young Lyngstrand that Johnston or Friman, or whatever his name is, was on his way hither, three years ago, in the month of March, she now evidently believes her unrest of mind came upon her at that very time.

Arnholm. It was not so, then?

Wangel. By no means. There were signs and symptoms of it before this time, though it did happen, by chance, that in that month of March, three years ago, she had a rather severe attack.

Arnholm. After all, then?

Wangel. Yes, but that is easily accounted for by the circumstances, the condition she happened to be in at the time.

Arnholm. So, symptom for symptom, then.

Wangel (wringing his hands). And not to be able to help her! Not to know how to counsel her! To see no way!

Arnholm. Now if you could make up your mind to leave this place, to go somewhere else, so that she could live amid surroundings that would seem more homelike to her?

Wangel. Ah, dear friend! Do you think I haven't offered her that, too? I suggested moving out to Skjoldviken, but she will not.

Arnholm. Not that either?

Wangel. No, for she doesn't think it would be any good; and perhaps she's right.

Arnholm. Hm. Do you say that?

Wangel. Moreover, when I think it all over carefully, I really don't know how I could manage it. I don't think I should be justified, for the sake of the girls, in going away to such a desolate place. After all, they must live where there is at least a prospect of their being provided for someday.

Arnholm. Provided for! Are you thinking about that already?

Wangel. Heaven knows, I must think of that too! But then, on the other hand, again, my poor sick Ellida! Oh, dear Arnholm! in many respects I seem to be standing between fire and water!

Arnholm. Perhaps you've no need to worry on Bolette's account. (Breaking off.) I should like to know where she, where they have gone. (Goes up to the open door and looks out.)

Wangel. Oh, I would so gladly make any sacrifice for all three of them, if only I knew what!

(ELLIDA enters from the door on the left.)

Ellida (quickly to WANGEL). Be sure you don't go out this morning.

Wangel. No, no! of course not. I will stay at home with you. (Pointing to ARNHOLM, who is coming towards them.) But won't you speak to our friend?

Ellida (turning). Oh, are you here, Mr. Arnholm? (Holding out her hand to him.) Good-morning.

Arnholm. Good-morning, Mrs. Wangel. So you've not been bathing as usual today?

Ellida. No, no, no! That is out of the question today. But won't you sit down a moment?

Arnholm. No, thanks, not now. (Looks at WANGEL.) I promised the girls to go down to them in the garden.

Ellida. Goodness knows if you'll find them there. I never know where they may be rambling.

Wangel. They're sure to be down by the pond.

Arnholm. Oh! I shall find them right enough. (Nods, and goes out across the verandah into the garden.)

Ellida. What time is it, Wangel?

Wangel (looking at his watch). A little past eleven.

Ellida. A little past. And at eleven o'clock, or half-past eleven tonight, the steamer is coming. If only that were over!

Wangel (going nearer to her). Dear Ellida, there is one thing I should like to ask you.

Ellida. What is it?

Wangel. The evening before last, up at the "View", you said that during the last three years you had so often seen him bodily before you.

Ellida. And so I have. You may believe that.

Wangel. But, how did you see him?

Ellida. How did I see him?

Wangel. I mean, how did he look when you thought you saw him?

Ellida. But, dear Wangel, why, you now know yourself how he looks.

Wangel. Did he look exactly like that in your imagination?

Ellida. He did.

Wangel. Exactly the same as you saw him in reality yesterday evening?

Ellida. Yes, exactly.

Wangel. Then how was it you did not at once recognise him?

Ellida. Did I not?

Wangel. No; you said yourself afterwards that at first you did not at all know who the strange man was.

Ellida (perplexed). I really believe you are right. Don't you think that strange, Wangel? Fancy my not knowing him at once!

Wangel. It was only the eyes, you said.

Ellida. Oh, yes! The eyes, the eyes.

Wangel. Well, but at the "View" you said that he always appeared to you exactly as he was when you parted out there ten years ago.

Ellida. Did I?

Wangel. Yes.

Ellida. Then, I suppose he did look much as he does now.

Wangel. No. On our way home, the day before yesterday, you gave quite another description of him. Ten years ago he had no beard, you said. His dress, too, was quite different. And that breast- pin with the pearl? That man yesterday wore nothing of the sort.

Ellida. No, he did not.

Wangel (looks searchingly at her). Now just think a little, dear Ellida. Or perhaps you can't quite remember how he looked when he stood by you at Bratthammer?

Ellida (thoughtfully closing her eyes for a moment). Not quite distinctly. No, today I can't. Is it not strange?

Wangel. Not so very strange after all. You have now been confronted by a new and real image, and that overshadows the old one, so that you can no longer see it.

Ellida. Do you believe that, Wangel?

Wangel. Yes. And it overshadows your sick imaginings, too. That is why it is good a reality has come.

Ellida. Good? Do you think it good?

Wangel. Yes. That it has come. It may restore you to health.

Ellida (sitting down on sofa). Wangel, come and sit down by me. I must tell you all my thoughts.

Wangel. Yes, do, dear Ellida.

(He sits down on a chair on the other side of the table.)

Ellida. It was really a great misfortune, for us both, that we two of all people should have come together.

Wangel (amazed). What are you saying?

Ellida. Oh, yes, it was. And it's so natural. It could bring nothing but unhappiness, after the way in which we came together.

Wangel. What was there in that way?

Ellida. Listen, Wangel; it's no use going on, lying to ourselves and to one another.

Wangel. Are we doing so? Lying, you say?

Ellida. Yes, we are; or, at least, we suppress the truth. For the truth, the pure and simple truth is, that you came out there and bought me.

Wangel. Bought, you say bought!

Ellida. Oh! I wasn't a bit better than you. I accepted the bargain. Sold myself to you!

Wangel (looks at her full of pain). Ellida, have you really the heart to call it that?

Ellida. But is there any other name for it? You could no longer bear the emptiness of your house. You were on the look-out for a new wife.

Wangel. And a new mother for the children, Ellida.

Ellida. That too, perhaps, by the way; although you didn't in the least know if I were fit for the position. Why, you had only seen me and spoken to me a few times. Then you wanted me, and so

Wangel. Yes, you may call it as you will.

Ellida. And I, on my side why, I was so helpless and bewildered, and so absolutely alone. Oh! it was so natural I should accept the bargain, when you came and proposed to provide for me all my life.

Wangel. Assuredly it did not seem to me a providing for you, dear Ellida. I asked you honestly if you would share with me and the children the little I could call my own.

Ellida. Yes, you did; but all the same, I should never have accepted! Never have accepted that at any price! Not sold myself! Better the meanest work, better the poorest life, after one's own choice.

Wangel (rising). Then have the five, six years that we have lived together been so utterly worthless to you?

Ellida. Oh! Don't think that, Wangel. I have been as well cared for here as human being could desire. But I did not enter your house freely. That is the thing.

Wangel (looking at her). Not freely!

Ellida. No. It was not freely that I went with you.

Wangel (in subdued tone). Ah! I remember your words of yesterday.

Ellida. It all lies in those words. They have enlightened me; and so I see it all now.

Wangel. What do you see?

Ellida. I see that the life we two live together is really no marriage.

Wangel (bitterly). You have spoken truly there. The life we now live is not a marriage.

Ellida. Nor was it formerly. Never, not from the very first (looks straight in front of her). The first that might have been a complete and real marriage.

Wangel. The first, what do you mean?

Ellida. Mine, with him.

Wangel (looks at her in astonishment). I do not in the least understand you.

Ellida. Ah! dear Wangel, let us not lie to one another, nor to ourselves.

Wangel. Well, what more?

Ellida. You see, we can never get away from that one thing, that a freely given promise is fully as binding as a marriage.

Wangel. But what on earth

Ellida (rising impetuously). Set me free, Wangel!

Wangel. Ellida! Ellida!

Ellida. Yes, yes! Oh! grant me that! Believe me, it will come to that all the same, after the way we two came together.

Wangel (conquering his pain). It has come to this, then?

Ellida. It has come to this. It could not be otherwise.

Wangel (looking gloomily at her). So I have not won you by our living together. Never, never possessed you quite.

Ellida. Ah! Wangel if only I could love you, how gladly I would as dearly as you deserve. But I feel it so well, that will never be.

Wangel. Divorce, then? It is a divorce, a complete, legal divorce that you want?

Ellida. Dear, you understand me so little! I care nothing for such formalities. Such outer things matter nothing, I think. What I want is that we should, of our own free will, release each other.

Wangel (bitterly, nods slowly). To cry off the bargain again, yes.

Ellida (quickly). Exactly. To cry off the bargain.

Wangel. And then, Ellida? Afterwards? Have you reflected what life would be to both of us? What life would be to both you and me?

Ellida. No matter. Things must turn out afterwards as they may. What I beg and implore of you, Wangel, is the most important. Only set me free! Give me back my complete freedom!

Wangel. Ellida, it is a fearful thing you ask of me. At least give me time to collect myself before I come to a decision. Let us talk it over more carefully. And you yourself take time to consider what you are doing.

Ellida. But we have no time to lose with such matters. I must have my freedom again today.

Wangel. Why today?

Ellida. Because he is coming tonight.

Wangel (starts). Coming! He! What has this stranger to do with it?

Ellida. I want to face him in perfect freedom.

Wangel. And what, what else do you intend to do?

Ellida. I will not hide behind the fact that I am the wife of another man; nor make the excuse that I have no choice, for then it would be no decision.

Wangel, You speak of a choice. Choice, Ellida! A choice in such a matter!

Ellida. Yes, I must be free to choose, to choose for either side. I must be able to let him go away alone, or to go with him.

Wangel. Do you know what you are saying? Go with him, give your whole life into his hands!

Ellida. Didn't I give my life into your hands, and without any ado?

Wangel. Maybe. But he! He! an absolute stranger! A man of whom you know so little!

Ellida. Ah! but after all I knew you even less; and yet I went with you.

Wangel. Then you knew to some extent what life lay before you. But now? Think! What do you know? You know absolutely nothing. Not even who or what he is.

Ellida (looking in front of her). That is true; but that is the terror.

Wangel. Yes, indeed, it is terrible!

Ellida. That is why I feel I must plunge into it.

Wangel (looking at her). Because it seems terrible?

Ellida. Yes; because of that.

Wangel (coming closer). Listen, Ellida. What do you really mean by terrible?

Ellida (reflectively). The terrible is that which repels and attracts.

Wangel. Attracts, you say?

Ellida. Attracts most of all, I think.

Wangel (slowly). You are one with the sea.

Ellida. That, too, is a terror.

Wangel. And that terror is in you. You both repel and attract.

Ellida. Do you think so, Wangel?

Wangel. After all, I have never really known you, never really. Now I am beginning to understand.

Ellida. And that is why you must set me free! Free me from every bond to you and yours. I am not what you took me for. Now you see it yourself. Now we can part as friends and freely.

Wangel (sadly). Perhaps it would be better for us both if we parted. And yet, I cannot! You are the terror to me, Ellida; the attraction is what is strongest in you.

Ellida. Do you say that?

Wangel. Let us try and live through this day wisely, in perfect quiet of mind. I dare not set you free, and release you today. I have no right to. No right for your own sake, Ellida. I exercise my right and my duty to protect you.

Ellida. Protect? What is there to protect me from? I am not threatened by any outward power. The terror lies deeper, Wangel. The terror is, the attraction in my own mind. And what can you do against that?

Wangel. I can strengthen and urge you to fight against it.

Ellida. Yes; if I wished to fight against it.

Wangel. Then you do not wish to?

Ellida. Oh! I don't know myself.

Wangel. Tonight all will be decided, dear Ellida

Ellida (bursting out). Yes, think! The decision so near, the decision for one's whole life!

Wangel. And then tomorrow, Ellida. Tomorrow! Perhaps my real future will have been ruined.

Wangel. Your real, Ellida. The whole, full life of freedom lost, lost for me, and perhaps for him also.

Wangel (in a lower tone, seizing her wrist). Ellida, do you love this stranger?

Ellida. Do I? Oh, how can I tell! I only know that to me he is a terror, and that

Wangel. And that

Ellida (tearing herself away). And that it is to him I think I belong.

Wangel (bowing his head). I begin to understand better.

Ellida. And what remedy have you for that? What advice to give me?

Wangel (looking sadly at her). Tomorrow he will be gone, then the misfortune will be averted from your head; and then I will consent to set you free. We will cry off the bargain tomorrow, Ellida.

Ellida. Ah, Wangel, tomorrow! That is too late.

Wangel (looking towards garden). The children, the children! Let us spare them, at least for the present.

(ARNHOLM, BOLETTE, HILDE, and LYNGSTRAND come into the garden. LYNGSTRAND says goodbye in the garden, and goes out. The rest come into the room.)

Arnholm. You must know we have been making plans.

Hilde. We're going out to the fjord tonight and

Bolette. No; you mustn't tell.

Wangel. We two, also, have been making plans.

Arnholm. Ah! really?

Wangel. Tomorrow Ellida is going away to Skjoldviken for a time.

Bolette. Going away?

Arnholm. Now, look here, that's very sensible, Mrs. Wangel.

Wangel. Ellida wants to go home again, home to the sea.

Hilde (springing towards ELLIDA). You are going away, away from us?

Ellida (frightened). Hilde! What is the matter?

Hilde (controlling herself). Oh, it's nothing. (In a low voice, turning from her.) Are only you going?

Bolette (anxiously). Father, I see it, you, too, are going to Skjoldviken!

Wangel. No, no! Perhaps I shall run out there every now and again.

Bolette. And come here to us?

Wangel. I will, Bolette. Every now and again!

Wangel. Dear child, it must be. (He crosses the room.)

Arnholm (whispers). We will talk it over later, Bolette. (He crosses to WANGEL. They speak in low tones up stage by the door.)

Ellida (aside to BOLETTE). What was the matter with Hilde? She looked quite scared.

Bolette. Have you never noticed what Hilde goes about here, day in, day out, hungering for?

Ellida. Hungering for?

Bolette. Ever since you came into the house?

Ellida. No, no. What is it?

Bolette. One loving word from you.

Ellida. Oh! If there should be something for me to do here!

(She clasps her hands together over her head, and looks fixedly in front of her, as if torn by contending thoughts and emotions. WANGEL and ARNHOLM come across the room whispering. BOLETTE goes to the side room, and looks in. Then she throws open the door.)

Bolette. Father, dear, the table is laid, if you

Wangel (with forced composure). Is it, child? That's well. Come, Arnholm! We'll go in and drink a farewell cup with the "Lady from the Sea." (They go out through the right.)

Act V

(SCENE. The distant part of DOCTOR WANGEL'S garden, and the carp pond. The summer night gradually darkens.

ARNHOLM, BOLETTE, LYNGSTRAND and HILDE are in a boat, punting along the shore to the left.)

Hilde. See! We can jump ashore easily here.

Arnholm. No, no; don't!

Lyngstrand. I can't jump, Miss Hilde.

Hilde. Can't you jump either, Arnholm?

Arnholm. I'd rather not try.

Bolette. Then let's land down there, by the bathing steps.

(They push off. At the same moment BALLESTED comes along the footpath, carrying music-books and a French horn. He bows to those in the boat, turns and speaks to them. The answers are heard farther and farther away.)

Ballested. What do you say? Yes, of course it's on account of the English steamer; for this is her last visit here this year. But if you want to enjoy the pleasures of melody, you mustn't wait too long. (Calling out.) What? (Shaking his head.) Can't hear what you say!

(ELLIDA, with a shawl over her head, enters, followed by DOCTOR WANGEL.)

Wangel. But, dear Ellida, I assure you there's plenty of time.

Ellida. No, no, there is not! He may come any moment.

Ballested (outside the fence). Hallo! Good-evening, doctor. Good- evening, Mrs. Wangel.

Wangel (noticing him). Oh! is it you? Is there to be music tonight?

Ballested. Yes; the Wind Band Society thought of making themselves heard. We've no dearth of festive occasions nowadays. Tonight it's in honour of the English ship.

Ellida. The English ship! Is she in sight already?

Ballested. Not yet. But you know she comes from between the islands. You can't see anything of her, and then she's alongside of you.

Ellida. Yes, that is so.

Wangel (half to ELLIDA). Tonight is the last voyage, then she will not come again.

Ballested. A sad thought, doctor, and that's why we're going to give them an ovation, as the saying is. Ah! Yes, ah! yes. The glad summertime will soon be over now. Soon all ways will be barred, as they say in the tragedy.

Ellida. All ways barred, yes!

Ballested. It's sad to think of. We have been the joyous children of summer for weeks and months now. It's hard to reconcile yourself to the dark days, just at first, I mean. For men can accli–a-acclimatise themselves, Mrs. Wangel. Ay, indeed they can. (Bows, and goes off to the left.)

Ellida (looking out at the fjord). Oh, this terrible suspense! This torturing last half-hour before the decision!

Wangel. You are determined, then, to speak to him yourself?

Ellida. I must speak to him myself; for it is freely that I must make my choice.

Wangel. You have no choice, Ellida. You have no right to choose, no right without my permission.

Ellida. You can never prevent the choice, neither you nor anyone. You can forbid me to go away with him, to follow him, in case I should choose to do that. You can keep me here by force against my will. That you can do. But that I should choose, choose from my very soul choose him, and not you, in case I would and did choose thus, this you cannot prevent.

Wangel. No; you are right. I cannot prevent that.

Ellida. And so I have nothing to help me to resist. Here, at home, there is no single thing that attracts me and binds me. I am so absolutely rootless in your house, Wangel. The children are not mine, their hearts, I mean never have been. When I go, if I do go, either with him tonight, or to Skjoldviken tomorrow, I haven't a key to give up, an order to give about anything whatsoever. I am absolutely rootless in your house, I have been absolutely outside everything from the very first.

Wangel. You yourself wished it.

Ellida. No, no, I did not. I neither wished nor did not wish it. I simply left things just as I found them the day I came here. It is you, and no one else, who wished it.

Wangel. I thought to do all for the best for you.

Ellida. Yes, Wangel, I know it so well! But there is retribution in that, a something that avenges itself. For now I find no binding power here-nothing to strengthen me, nothing to help me, nothing to draw me towards what should have been the strongest possession of us both.

Wangel. I see it, Ellida. And that is why from tomorrow you shall have back your freedom. Henceforth, you shall live your own life.

Ellida. And you call that my own life! No! My own true life lost its bearings when I agreed to live with you. (Clenches her hand in fear and unrest.) And now, tonight, in half an hour, he whom I forsook is coming, he to whom I should have cleaved forever, even as he has cleaved to me! Now he is coming to offer me, for the last and only time, the chance of living my life over again, of living my own true life, the life that terrifies and attracts and I can not forgo that, not freely.

Wangel. That is why it is necessary your husband, and your doctor, should take the power of acting from you, and act on your behalf.

Ellida. Yes, Wangel, I quite understand. Believe me, there are times when I think it would be peace and deliverance if with all my soul I could be bound to you and try to brave all that terrifies and attracts. But I cannot! No, no, I cannot do that!

Wangel. Come, Ellida, let us walk up and down together for awhile.

Ellida. I would gladly but I dare not. For he said I was to wait for him here.

Wangel. Come! There is time enough.

Ellida. Do you think so?

Wangel. Plenty of time, I tell you.

Ellida. Then let us go, for a little while.

(They pass out in the foreground. At the same time ARNHOLM and BOLETTE appear by the upper bank of the pond.)

Bolette (noticing the two as they go out). See there

Arnholm (in low voice). Hush! Let them go. Bolette. Can you understand what has been going on between them these last few days?

Arnholm. Have you noticed anything?

Bolette. Have I not!

Arnholm. Anything peculiar?

Bolette. Yes, one thing and another. Haven't you?

Arnholm. Well, I don't exactly know.

Bolette. Yes, you have; only you won't speak out about it.

Arnholm. I think it will do your stepmother good to go on this little journey.

Bolette. Do you think so?

Arnholm. I should say it would be well for all parties that she should get away every now and then.

Bolette. If she does go home to Skjoldviken tomorrow, she will never come back here again!

Arnholm. My dear Bolette, whatever makes you think that?

Bolette. I am quite convinced of it. Just you wait; you'll see that she'll not come back again; not anyhow as long as I and Hilde are in the house here.

Arnholm. Hilde, too?

Bolette. Well, it might perhaps be all right with Hilde. For she is scarcely more than a child. And I believe that at bottom she worships Ellida. But, you see, it's different with me, a stepmother who isn't so very much older than oneself!

Arnholm. Dear Bolette, perhaps it might, after all, not be so very long before you left.

Bolette (eagerly). Really! Have you spoken to father about it?

Arnholm. Yes, I have.

Bolette. Well, what does he say?

Arnholm. Hm! Well, your father's so thoroughly taken up with other matters just now

Bolette. Yes, yes! that's how I knew it would be.

Arnholm. But I got this much out of him. You mustn't reckon upon any help from him.

Bolette. No?

Arnholm. He explained his circumstances to me clearly; he thought that such a thing was absolutely out of the question, impossible for him.

Bolette (reproachfully). And you had the heart to come and mock me?

Arnholm. I've certainly not done that, dear Bolette. It depends wholly and solely upon yourself whether you go away or not.

Bolette. What depends upon me?

Arnholm. Whether you are to go out into the world, learn all you most care for, take part in all you are hungering after here at home, live your life under brighter conditions, Bolette.

Bolette (clasping her hands together). Good God! But it's impossible! If father neither can nor will and I have no one else on earth to whom I could turn, Arnholm. Couldn't you make up your mind to accept a little help from your old - from your former teacher?

Bolette. From you, Mr. Arnholm! Would you be willing to

Arnholm. Stand by you! Yes, with all my heart. Both with word and in deed. You may count upon it. Then you accept? Well? Do you agree?

Bolette. Do I agree! To get away, to see the world, to learn something thoroughly! All that seemed to be a great, beautiful impossibility!

Arnholm. All that may now become a reality to you, if only you yourself wish it.

Bolette. And to all this unspeakable happiness you will help me! Oh, no! Tell me, can I accept such an offer from a stranger?

Arnholm. You can from me, Bolette. From me you can accept anything.

Bolette (seizing his hands). Yes, I almost think I can! I don't know how it is, but (bursting out) Oh! I could both laugh and cry for joy, for happiness! Then I should know life really after all. I began to be so afraid life would pass me by.

Arnholm. You need not fear that, Bolette. But now you must tell me quite frankly, if there is anything, anything you are bound to here.

Bolette. Bound to? Nothing.

Arnholm. Nothing whatever?

Bolette. No, nothing at all. That is I am bound to father to some extent. And to Hilde, too. But

Arnholm. Well, you'll have to leave your father sooner or later. And some time Hilde also will go her own way in life. That is only a question of time. Nothing more. And so there is nothing else that binds you, Bolette? Not any kind of connection?

Bolette. Nothing whatever. As far as that goes, I could leave at any moment.

Arnholm. Well, if that is so, dear Bolette, you shall go away with me!

Bolette (clapping her hands). Oh God! What joy to think of it!

Arnholm. For I hope you trust me fully?

Bolette. Indeed, I do!

Arnholm. And you dare to trust yourself and your future fully and confidently into my hands, Bolette? Is that true? You will dare to do this?

Bolette. Of course; how could I not do so? Could you believe anything else? You, who have been my old teacher, my teacher in the old days, I mean.

Arnholm. Not because of that. I will not consider that side of the matter; but, well, so you are free, Bolette! There is nothing that binds you, and so I ask you, if you could, if you could bind yourself to me for life?

Bolette (steps back frightened). What are you saying?

Arnholm. For all your life, Bolette. Will you be my wife?

Bolette (half to herself). No, no, no! That is impossible, utterly impossible!

Arnholm. It is really so absolutely impossible for you to

Bolette. But, surely, you cannot mean what you are saying, Mr. Arnholm! (Looking at him.) Or, yet, was that what you meant when you offered to do so much for me?

Arnholm. You must listen to me one moment, Bolette. I suppose I have greatly surprised you!

Bolette. Oh! how could such a thing from you, how could it but, but surprise me!

Arnholm. Perhaps you are right. Of course, you didn't, you could not know it was for your sake I made this journey.

Bolette. Did you come here for, for my sake?

Arnholm. I did, Bolette. In the spring I received a letter from your father, and in it there was a passage that made me think, hm, that you held your former teacher in, in a little more than friendly remembrance.

Bolette. How could father write such a thing?

Arnholm. He did not mean it so. But I worked myself into the belief that here was a young girl longing for me to come again. No, you mustn't interrupt me, dear Bolette! And you see, when a man like myself, who is no longer quite young, has such a belief or fancy, it makes an overwhelming impression. There grew within me a living, a grateful affection for you; I thought I must come to you, see you again, and tell you I shared the feelings that I fancied you had for me.

Bolette. And now you know it is not so! that it was a mistake!

Arnholm. It can't be helped, Bolette. Your image, as I bear it within myself, will always be coloured and stamped with the impression that this mistake gave me. Perhaps you cannot understand this; but still it is so.

Bolette. I never thought such a thing possible.

Arnholm. But now you have seen that it is possible, what do you say now, Bolette? Couldn't you make up your mind to be, yes, to be my wife?

Bolette. Oh! it seems so utterly impossible, Mr. Arnholm. You, who have been my teacher! I can't imagine ever standing in any other relation towards you.

Arnholm. Well, well, if you think you really cannot. Then our old relations remain unchanged, dear Bolette.

Bolette. What do you mean?

Arnholm. Of course, to keep my promise all the same. I will take care you get out into the world and see something of it. Learn some things you really want to know; live safe and independent. Your future I shall provide for also, Bolette. For in me you will always have a good, faithful, trustworthy friend. Be sure of that.

Bolette. Good heavens! Mr. Arnholm, all that is so utterly impossible now.

Arnholm. Is that impossible too?

Bolette. Surely you can see that! After what you have just said to me, and after my answer. Oh! you yourself must see that it is impossible for me now to accept so very much from you. I can accept nothing from you, nothing after this.

Arnholm. So you would rather stay at home here, and let life pass you by?

Bolette. Oh! it is such dreadful misery to think of that.

Arnholm. Will you renounce knowing something of the outer world? Renounce bearing your part in all that you yourself say you are hungering for? To know there is so infinitely much, and yet never really to understand anything of it? Think carefully, Bolette.

Bolette. Yes, yes! You are right, Mr. Arnholm.

Arnholm. And then, when one day your father is no longer here, then perhaps to be left helpless and alone in the world; or live to give yourself to another man, whom you, perhaps, will also feel no affection for

Bolette. Oh, yes! I see how true all you say is. But stil, and yet perhaps,

Arnholm (quickly). Well?

Bolette (looking at him hesitatingly). Perhaps it might not be so impossible after all.

Arnholm. What, Bolette?

Bolette. Perhaps it might be possible to accept, what you proposed to me.

Arnholm. Do you mean that, after all, you might be willing to, that at all events you could give me the happiness of helping you as a steadfast friend?

Bolette. No, no, no! Never that, for that would be utterly impossible now. No, Mr. Arnholm, rather take me.

Arnholm. Bolette! You will?

Bolette. Yes, I believe I will.

Arnholm. And after all you will be my wife?

Bolette. Yes; if you still think that, that you will have me.

Arnholm. Think! (Seizing her hand.) Oh, thanks, thanks, Bolette. All else that you said, your former doubts, these do not frighten me. If I do not yet possess your whole heart, I shall know how to conquer it. Oh, Bolette, I will wait upon you hand and foot!

Bolette. And then I shall see something of the world? Shall live! You have promised me that?

Arnholm. And will keep my promise.

Bolette. And I may learn everything I want to?

Arnholm. I, myself, will be your teacher as formerly, Bolette. Do you remember the last school year?

Bolette (quietly and absently). To think, to know one's self free, and to get out into the strange world, and then, not to need to be anxious for the future, not to be harassed about one's stupid livelihood!

Arnholm. No, you will never need to waste a thought upon such matters. And that's a good thing, too, in its way, dear Bolette, isn't it? Eh?

Bolette. Indeed it is. That is certain.

Arnholm (putting his arms about her). Oh, you will see how comfortably and easily we shall settle down together! And how well and safely and trustfully we two shall get on with one another, Bolette.

Bolette. Yes. I also begin to, I believe really, it will answer. (Looks out to the right, and hurriedly frees herself.) Oh, don't say anything about this.

Arnholm. What is it, dear?

Bolette. Oh! it's that poor (pointing) see out there.

Arnholm. Is it your father?

Bolette. No. It's the young sculptor. He's down there with Hilde.

Arnholm. Oh, Lyngstrand! What's really the matter with him?

Bolette. Why, you know how weak and delicate he is.

Arnholm. Yes. Unless it's simply imaginary.

Bolette. No, it's real enough! He'll not last long. But perhaps that's best for him.

Arnholm. Dear, why should that be best?

Bolette. Because, because nothing would come of his art anyhow. Let's go before they come.

Arnholm. Gladly, my dear Bolette.

(HILDE and LYNGSTRAND appear by the pond.)

Hilde. Hi, hi! Won't your honours wait for us?

Arnholm. Bolette and I would rather go on a little in advance. (He and BOLETTE go out to the Left.)

Lyngstrand (laughs quietly). It's very delightful here now. Everybody goes about in pairs, always two and two together.

Hilde (looking after them). I could almost swear he's proposing to her.

Lyngstrand. Really? Have you noticed anything?

Hilde. Yes. It's not very difficult if you keep your eyes open.

Lyngstrand. But Miss Bolette won't have him. I'm certain of that.

Hilde. No. For she thinks he's got so dreadfully old-looking, and she thinks he'll soon get bald.

Lyngstrand. It's not only because of that. She'd not have him anyhow.

Hilde. How can you know?

Lyngstrand. Well, because there's someone else she's promised to think of.

Hilde. Only to think of?

Lyngstrand. While he is away, yes.

Hilde. Oh! then I suppose it's you she's to think of.

Lyngstrand. Perhaps it might be.

Hilde. She promised you that?

Lyngstrand. Yes, think, she promised me that! But mind you don't tell her you know.

Hilde. Oh! I'll be mum! I'm as secret as the grave.

Lyngstrand. I think it's awfully kind of her.

Hilde. And when you come home again, are you going to be engaged to her, and then marry her?

Lyngstrand. No, that wouldn't very well do. For I daren't think of such a thing during the first years. And when I shall be able to, she'll be rather too old for me, I fancy.

Hilde. And yet you wish her to think of you?

Lyngstrand. Yes; that's so useful to me. You see, I'm an artist. And she can very well do it, because she herself has no real calling. But all the same, it's kind of her.

Hilde. Do you think you'll be able to get on more quickly with your work if you know that Bolette is here thinking of you?

Lyngstrand. Yes, I fancy so. To know there is a spot on earth where a young, gentle, reserved woman is quietly dreaming about you, I fancy it must be so, so, well, I really don't exactly know what to call it.

Hilde. Perhaps you mean fascinating?

Lyngstrand. Fascinating! Oh, yes! Fascinating was what I meant, or something like it. (Looks at her for a moment.) You are so clever, Miss Hilde. Really you are very clever. When I come home again you'll be about the same age as your sister is now. Perhaps, too, you'll look like your sister looks now. And perhaps, too, you'll be of the same mind she is now. Then, perhaps, you'll be both yourself and your sister in one form, so to say.

Hilde. Would you like that?

Lyngstrand. I hardly know. Yes; I almost think I should. But now, for this summer, I would rather you were like yourself alone, and exactly as you are.

Hilde. Do you like me best as I am?

Lyngstrand. Yes, I like you immensely as you are.

Hilde. Hm. Tell me, you who are an artist, do you think I'm right always to wear bright-coloured summer dresses?

Lyngstrand. Yes; I think you're quite right!

Hilde. You think bright colours suit me, then?

Lyngstrand. They suit you charmingly, to my taste.

Hilde. But tell me, as an artist, how do you think I should look in black?

Lyngstrand. In black, Miss Hilde?

Hilde. Yes, all in black. Do you think I should look well?

Lyngstrand. Black's hardly suitable for the summer. However, you'd probably look remarkably well in black, especially with your appearance.

Hilde (looking straight in front of her). All in black, up to the throat; black frilling round that, black gloves, and a long black veil hanging down behind.

Lyngstrand. If you were dressed so, Miss Hilde, I should wish I were a painter, and I'd paint you as a young, beautiful, sorrowing widow!

Hilde. Or as a young, sorrowing, betrothed girl!

Lyngstrand. Yes, that would be better still. But you can't wish to be dressed like that?

Hilde. I hardly know; but I think it's fascinating.

Lyngstrand. Fascinating?

Hilde. Fascinating to think of, yes. (Suddenly pointing to the left.) Oh, just look there!

Lyngstrand (looking). The great English steamer; and right by the pier!

(WANGEL and ELLIDA come in past the pond.)

Wangel. No; I assure you, dear Ellida, you are mistaken. (Seeing the others.) What, are you two here? It's not in sight yet; is it, Mr. Lyngstrand?

Lyngstrand. The great English ship?

Wangel. Yes.

Lyngstrand (pointing). There she is already, doctor.

Ellida. I knew it.

Wangel. Come!

Lyngstrand. Come like a thief in the night, as one might say, so quietly and noiselessly.

Wangel. You must go to the pier with Hilde. Be quick! I'm sure she wants to hear the music.

Lyngstrand. Yes; we were just going there, doctor.

Wangel. Perhaps we'll follow you. We'll come directly.

Hilde (whispering to LYNGSTRAND). They're hunting in couples, too!

(HILDE and LYNGSTRAND go out through the garden. Music is heard in the distance out at the fiord during the following.)

Ellida. Come! He is here! Yes, yes, I feel it.

Wangel. You'd better go in, Ellida. Let me talk with him alone.

Ellida. Oh! that's impossible, impossible, I say. (With a cry.) Ah! do you see him, Wangel?

(The STRANGER enters from the left, and remains on the pathway outside the fence.)

The Stranger (bowing). Good-evening. You see I am here again, Ellida.

Ellida. Yes, yes. The time has come now.

The Stranger. And are you ready to start, or not?

Wangel. You can see for yourself that she is not.

The Stranger. I'm not asking about a travelling dress, or anything of that kind, nor about packed trunks. All that is needed for a journey I have with me on board. I've also secured a cabin for her. (To ELLIDA.) So I ask you if you are ready to go with me, to go with me freely?

Ellida. Oh! do not ask me! Do not tempt me!

(A ship's bell is heard in the distance.)

The Stranger. That is the first bell for going on board. Now you must say "Yes" or "No."

Ellida (wringing her hands). To decide, decide for one's whole life! Never to be able to undo it again!

The Stranger. Never. In half an hour it will be too late.

Ellida (looking shyly and searchingly at him). Why is it you hold to me so resolutely?

The Stranger. Don't you feel, as I do, that we two belong together?

Ellida. Do you mean because of the vow?

The Stranger. Vows bind no one, neither man nor woman. If I hold so steadfastly to you, it is because I cannot do otherwise.

Ellida (in a low, trembling voice). Why didn't you come before?

Wangel. Ellida!

Ellida (bursting out). Ah! All that attracts, and tempts, and lures into the unknown! All the strength of the sea concentrated in this one thing!

(The STRANGER climbs over the fence.)

Ellida (stepping back to WANGEL). What is it? What do you want?

The Stranger. I see it and I hear it in you, Ellida. After all, you will choose me in the end.

Wangel (going towards him). My wife has no choice here, I am here both to choose for her and to defend her. Yes, defend! If you do not go away from here, away from this land, and never come back again. Do you know to what you are exposing yourself?

Ellida. No, no, Wangel, not that!

The Stranger. What will you do to me?

Wangel. I will have you arrested as a criminal, at once, before you go on board; for I know all about the murder at Skjoldviken.

Ellida. Ah! Wangel, how can you?

The Stranger. I was prepared for that, and so (takes a revolver from his breast pocket) I provided myself with this.

Ellida (throwing herself in front of him). No, no; do not kill him! Better kill me!

The Stranger. Neither you nor him, don't fear that. This is for myself, for I will live and die a free man.

Ellida (with growing excitement). Wangel, let me tell you this, tell it you so that he may hear it. You can indeed keep me here! You have the means and the power to do it. And you intend to do it. But my mind, all my thoughts, all the longings and desires of my soul, these you cannot bind! These will rush and press out into the unknown that I was created for, and that you have kept from me!

Wangel (in quiet sorrow). I see it, Ellida. Step by step you are slipping from me. The craving for the boundless, the infinite, the unattainable will drive your soul into the darkness of night at last.

Ellida. Yes! I feel it hovering over me like black noiseless wings.

Wangel. It shall not come to that. No other deliverance is possible for you. I at least can see no other. And so, so I cry off our bargain at once. Now you can choose your own path in perfect, perfect freedom.

Ellida (stares at him a while as if stricken dumb). Is it true, true what you say? Do you mean that, mean it with all your heart?

Wangel. Yes, with all my sorrowing heart, I mean it.

Ellida. And can you do it? Can you let it be so?

Wangel. Yes, I can. Because I love you so dearly.

Ellida (in a low, trembling voice). And have I come so near, so close to you?

Wangel. The years and the living together have done that.

Ellida (clasping her hands together). And I, who so little understood this!

Wangel. Your thoughts went elsewhere. And now, now you are completely free of me and mine, and, and mine. Now your own true life may resume its real bent again, for now you can choose in freedom, and on your own responsibility, Ellida.

Ellida (clasps her head with her hands, and stares at WANGEL). In freedom, and on my own responsibility! Responsibility, too? That changes everything.

(The ship bell rings again.)

The Stranger. Do you hear, Ellida? It has rung now for the last time. Come.

Ellida (turns towards him, looks firmly at him, and speaks in a resolute voice). I shall never go with you after this!

The Stranger. You will not!

Ellida (clinging to WANGEL). I shall never go away from you after this.

The Stranger. So it is over?

Ellida. Yes. Over for all time.

The Stranger. I see. There is something here stronger than my will.

Ellida. Your will has not a shadow of power over me any longer. To me you are as one dead, who has come home from the sea, and who returns to it again. I no longer dread you. And I am no longer drawn to you.

The Stranger. Goodbye, Mrs. Wangel! (He swings himself over the fence.) Henceforth, you are nothing but a shipwreck in my life that I have tided over. (He goes out.)

Wangel (looks at her for a while). Ellida, your mind is like the sea, it has ebb and flow. Whence came the change?

Ellida. Ah! don't you understand that the change came, was bound to come when I could choose in freedom?

Wangel. And the unknown? It no longer lures you?

Ellida. Neither lures nor frightens me. I could have seen it, gone out into it, if only I myself had willed it. I could have chosen it. And that is why I could also renounce it.

Wangel. I begin to understand little by little. You think and conceive in pictures, in visible figures. Your longing and aching for the sea, your attraction towards this strange man, these were the expression of an awakening and growing desire for freedom; nothing else.

Ellida. I don't know about that. But you have been a good physician for me. You found, and you dared to use the right remedy, the only one that could help me.

Wangel. Yes, in utmost need and danger we doctors dare much. And now you are coming back to me again, Ellida?

Ellida. Yes, dear, faithful Wangel, now I am coming back to you again. Now I can. For now I come to you freely, and on my own responsibility.

Wangel (looks lovingly at her). Ellida! Ellida! To think that now we can live wholly for one another

Ellida. And with common memories. Yours, as well as mine.

Wangel. Yes, indeed, dear.

Ellida. And for our children, Wangel?

Wangel. You call them ours!

Ellida. They who are not mine yet, but whom I shall win.

Wangel. Ours! (Gladly and quickly kisses her hands.) I cannot speak my thanks for those words!

(HILDE, BALLESTED, LYNGSTRAND, ARNHOLM, and BOLETTE come into the garden. At the same time a number of young townspeople and visitors pass along the footpath.)

Hilde (aside to LYNGSTRAND). See! Why, she and father look exactly as if they were a betrothed couple!

Ballested (who has overheard). It is summertime, little Missie.

Arnholm (looking at WANGEL and ELLIDA). The English steamer is putting off.

Bolette (going to the fence). You can see her best from here.

Lyngstrand. The last voyage this year.

Ballested. Soon all the sea-highways will be closed, as the poet says. It is sad, Mrs. Wangel. And now we're to lose you also for a time. Tomorrow you're off to Skjoldviken, I hear.

Wangel. No; nothing will come of that. We two have changed our mind tonight.

Arnholm (looking from one to the other). Oh! really!

Bolette (coming forward). Father, is that true?

Hilde (going towards ELLIDA). Are you going to stay with us after all?

Ellida. Yes, dear Hilde, if you'll have me.

Hilde (struggling between tears and laughter). Fancy! Have you!

Arnholm (to ELLIDA). But this is quite a surprise!

Ellida (smiling earnestly). Well, you see, Mr. Arnholm. Do you remember we talked about it yesterday? When you have once become a land-creature you can no longer find your way back again to the sea, nor to the sea-life either.

Ballested. Why, that's exactly the case with my mermaid.

Ellida. Something like, yes.

Ballested. Only with this difference, that the mermaid dies of it, it, while human beings can acclam-acclimatise themselves. Yes yes. I assure you, Mrs. Wangel, they can ac-climatise themselves.

Ellida. In freedom they can, Mr. Ballested.

Wangel. And when they act on their own responsibility, dear Ellida.

Ellida (quickly holding out her hand to him). Exactly. (The great steamer glides noiselessly out beyond the fjord. The music is heard nearer land.)

THE END.

Henrik Ibsen - Little Eyolf

LITTLE EYOLF

CHARACTERS

ALFRED ALLMERS, landed proprietor and man of letters formerly a tutor.
MRS. RITA ALLMERS, his wife.
EYOLF, their child, nine years old.
MISS ASTA ALLMERS, Alfred's younger half-sister.
ENGINEER BORGHEIM.
THE RAT-WIFE.

The action takes place on ALLMERS'S property, bordering on the fjord, twelve or fourteen miles from Christiania.

ACT FIRST

[A pretty and richly-decorated garden-room, full of furniture, flowers, and plants. At the back, open glass doors, leading out to a verandah. An extensive view over the fiord. In the distance, wooded hillsides. A door in each of the side walls, the one on the right a folding door, placed far back. In front on the right, a sofa, with cushions and rugs. Beside the sofa, a small table, and chairs. In front, on the left, a larger table, with arm-chairs around it. On the table stands an open hand-bag. It is an early summer morning, with warm sunshine.]

[Mrs. RITA ALLMERS stands beside the table, facing towards the left, engaged in unpacking the bag. She is a handsome, rather tall, well-developed blonde, about thirty years of age, dressed in a light-coloured morning-gown.]

[Shortly after, Miss ASTA ALLMERS enters by the door on the right, wearing a light brown summer dress, with hat, jacket, and parasol. Under her arm she carries a locked portfolio of considerable size. She is slim, of middle height, with dark hair, and deep, earnest eyes. Twenty-five years old.]

ASTA. [As she enters.] Good-morning, my dear Rita.

RITA. [Turns her head, and nods to her.] What! is that you, Asta? Come all the way from town so early?

ASTA. [Takes of her things, and lays them on a chair beside the door.] Yes, such a restless feeling came over me. I felt I must come out to-day, and see how little Eyolf was getting on, and you too. [Lays the portfolio on the table beside the sofa.] So I took the steamer, and here I am.

RITA. [Smiling to her.] And I daresay you met one or other of your friends on board? Quite by chance, of course.

ASTA. [Quietly.] No, I did not meet a soul I knew. [Sees the bag.] Why, Rita, what have you got there?

RITA. [Still unpacking.] Alfred's travelling-bag. Don't you recognise it?

ASTA. [Joyfully, approaching her.] What! Has Alfred come home?

RITA. Yes, only think, he came quite unexpectedly by the late train last night.

ASTA. Oh, then that was what my feeling meant! It was that that drew me out here! And he hadn't written a line to let you know? Not even a post-card?

RITA. Not a single word.

ASTA. Did he not even telegraph?

RITA. Yes, an hour before he arrived quite curtly and coldly. [Laughs.] Don't you think that was like him, Asta?

ASTA. Yes; he goes so quietly about everything.

RITA. But that made it all the more delightful to have him again.

ASTA. Yes, I am sure it would.

RITA. A whole fortnight before I expected him!

ASTA. And is he quite well? Not in low spirits?

RITA. [Closes the bag with a snap, and smiles at her.] He looked quite transfigured as he stood in the doorway.

ASTA. And was he not the least bit tired either?

RITA. Oh, yes, he seemed to be tired enough, very tired, in fact. But, poor fellow, he had come on foot the greater part of the way.

ASTA. And then perhaps the high mountain air may have been rather too keen for him.

RITA. Oh, no; I don't think so at all. I haven't heard him cough once.

ASTA. Ah, there you see now! It was a good thing, after all, that the doctor talked him into taking this tour.

RITA. Yes, now that it is safely over. But I can tell you it has been a terrible time for me, Asta. I have never cared to talk about it and you so seldom came out to see me, too

ASTA. Yes, I daresay that wasn't very nice of me, but -

RITA. Well, well, well, of course you had your school to attend to in town. [Smiling.] And then our road-maker friend, of course he was away too.

ASTA. Oh, don't talk like that, Rita.

RITA. Very well, then; we will leave the road-maker out of the question. You can't think how I have been longing for Alfred! How empty the place seemed! How desolate! Ugh, it felt as if there had been a funeral in the house!

ASTA. Why, dear me, only six or seven weeks

RITA. Yes; but you must remember that Alfred has never been away from me before, never so much as twenty-four hours. Not once in all these ten years.

ASTA. No; but that is just why I really think it was high time he should have a little outing this year. He ought to have gone for a tramp in the mountains every summer, he really ought.

RITA. [Half smiling.] Oh yes, it's all very well fair you to talk. If I were as, as reasonable its you, I suppose I should have let him go before perhaps. But I positively could not, Asta! It seemed to me I should never get him back again. Surely you can understand that?

ASTA. No. But I daresay that is because I have no one to lose.

RITA. [With a teasing smile.] Really? No one at all?

ASTA. Not that *I* know of. [Changing the subject.] But tell me, Rita, where is Alfred? Is he still asleep?

RITA. Oh, not at all. He got up as early as ever to-day.

ASTA. Then he can't have been so very tired after all.

RITA. Yes, he was last night, when he arrived. But now he has had little Eyolf with him in his room for a whole hour and more.

ASTA. Poor little white-faced boy! Has he to be for ever at his lessons again?

RITA. [With a slight shrug.] Alfred will have it so, you know.

ASTA. Yes; but I think you ought to put down your foot about it, Rita.

RITA. [Somewhat impatiently.] Oh no; come now, I really cannot meddle with that. Alfred knows so much better about these things than I do. And what would you have Eyolf do? He can't run about and play, you see like other children.

ASTA. [With decision.] I will talk to Alfred about this.

RITA. Yes, do; I wish you would. Oh! here he is.

[ALFRED ALLMERS, dressed in light summer clothes, enters by the door on the left, leading EYOLF by the hand. He is a slim, lightly-built man of about thirty-six or thirty-seven, with gentle eyes, and thin brown hair and beard. His expression is serious and thoughtful. EYOLF wears a suit cut like a uniform, with gold braid and gilt military buttons. He is lame, and walks with a crutch under his left arm. His leg is shrunken. He is undersized, and looks delicate, but has beautiful intelligent eyes.]

ALLMERS. [Drops EYOLF's hand, goes up to ASTA with an expression of marked pleasure, and holds out both his hands to her.] Asta! My dearest Asta! To think of your coming! To think of my seeing you so soon!

ASTA. I felt I must. Welcome home again!

ALLMERS. [Shaking her hands.] Thank you for coming.

RITA. Doesn't he look well?

ASTA. [Gazes fixedly at him.] Splendid! Quite splendid! His eyes are so much brighter! And I suppose you have done a great deal of writing on your travels? [With an outburst of joy.] I shouldn't wonder if you had finished the whole book, Alfred?

ALLMERS. [Shrugging his shoulders.] The book? Oh, the book

ASTA. Yes, I was sure you would find it go so easily when once you got away.

ALLMERS. So I thought too. But, do you know, I didn't find it so at all. The truth is, I have not written a line of the book.

ASTA. Not a line?

RITA. Oho! I wondered when I found all the paper lying untouched in your bag.

ASTA. But, my dear Alfred, what have you been doing all this time?

ALLMERS. [Smiling.] Only thinking and thinking and thinking.

RITA. [Putting her arm round his neck.] And thinking a little, too, of those you had left at home?

ALLMERS. Yes, you may be sure of that. I have thought a great deal of you every single day.

RITA. [Taking her arm away.] Ah, that is all I care about.

ASTA. But you haven't even touched the book! And yet you can look so happy and contented! That is not what you generally do, I mean when your work is going badly.

ALLMERS. You are right there. You see, I have been such a fool hitherto. All the best that is in you goes into thinking. What you put on paper is worth very little.

ASTA. [Exclaiming.] Worth very little!

RITA. [Laughing.] What an absurd thing to say, Alfred.

EYOLF. [Looks confidingly up at him.] Oh yes, Papa, what you write is worth a great deal!

ALLMERS. [Smiling and stroking his hair.] Well, well, since you say so. But I can tell you, some one is coming after me who will do it better.

EYOLF. Who can that be? Oh, tell me!

ALLMERS. Only wait, you may be sure he will come, and let us hear of him.

EYOLF. And what will you do then?

ALLMERS. [Seriously.] Then I will go to the mountains again

RITA. Fie, Alfred! For shame!

ALLMERS. - up to the peaks and the great waste places.

EYOLF. Papa, don't you think I shall soon be well enough for you to take me with you?

ALLMERS. [With painful emotion.] Oh, yes, perhaps, my little boy.

EYOLF. It would be so splendid, you know, if I could climb the mountains, like you.

ASTA. [Changing the subject.] Why, how beautifully you are dressed to-day, Eyolf!

EYOLF. Yes, don't you think so, Auntie?

ASTA. Yes, indeed. Is it in honour of Papa that you have got your new clothes on?

EYOLF. Yes, I asked Mama to let me. I wanted so to let Papa see me in them.

ALLMERS. [In a low voice, to RITA.] You shouldn't have given him clothes like that.

RITA. [In a low voice.] Oh, he has teased me so long about them, he had set his heart on them. He gave me no peace.

EYOLF. And I forgot to tell you, Papa, Borgheim has bought me a new bow. And he has taught me how to shoot with it too.

ALLMERS. Ah, there now, that's just the sort of thing for you, Eyolf.

EYOLF. And next time he comes, I shall ask him to teach me to swim, too.

ALLMERS. To swim! Oh, what makes you want to learn swimming?

EYOLF. Well, you know, all the boys down at the beach can swim. I am the only one that can't.

ALLMERS. [With emotion, taking him in his arms.] You shall learn whatever you like, everything you really want to.

EYOLF. Then do you know what I want most of all, Papa?

ALLMERS. No; tell me.

EYOLF. I want most of all to be a soldier.

ALLMERS. Oh, little Eyolf, there are many, many other things that are better than that.

EYOLF. Ah, but when I grow big, then I shall have to be a soldier. You know that, don't you?

ALLMERS. [Clenching his hands together.] Well, well, well: we shall see

ASTA. [Seating herself at the table on the left.] Eyolf! Come here to me, and I will tell you something.

EYOLF. [Goes up to her.] What is it, Auntie?

ASTA. What do you think, Eyolf, I have seen the Rat-Wife.

EYOLF. What! Seen the Rat-Wife! Oh, you're only making a fool of me!

ASTA. No; it's quite true. I saw her yesterday.

EYOLF. Where did you see her?

ASTA. I saw her on the road, outside the town.

ALLMERS. I saw her, too, somewhere up in the country.

RITA. [Who is sitting on the sofa.] Perhaps it will be out turn to see her next, Eyolf.

EYOLF. Auntie, isn't it strange that she should be called the Rat-Wife?

ASTA. Oh, people just give her that name because she wanders round the country driving away all the rats.

ALLMERS. I have heard that her real name is Varg.

EYOLF. Varg! That means a wolf, doesn't it?

ALLMERS. [Patting him on the head.] So you know that, do you?

EYOLF. [Cautiously.] Then perhaps it may be true, after all, that she is a were-wolf at night. Do you believe that, Papa?

ALLMERS. Oh, no; I don't believe it. Now you ought to go and play a little in the garden.

EYOLF. Should I not take some books with me?

ALLMERS. No, no books after this. You had better go down to the beach to the other boys.

EYOLF. [Shyly.] No, Papa, I won't go down to the boys to-day.

ALLMERS. Why not?

EYOLF. Oh, because I have these clothes on.

ALLMERS. [Knitting his brows.] Do you mean that they make fun of, of your pretty clothes?

EYOLF. [Evasively.] No, they daren't for then I would thrash them.

ALLMERS. Aha! then why?

EYOLF. You see, they are so naughty, these boys. And then they say I can never be a soldier.

ALLMERS. [With suppressed indignation.] Why do they say that, do you think?

EYOLF. I suppose they are jealous of me. For you know, Papa, they are so poor, they have to go about barefoot.

ALLMERS. [Softly, with choking voice.] Oh, Rita, how it wrings my heart!

RITA. [Soothingly, rising.] There, there, there!

ALLMERS. [Threateningly.] But these rascals shall soon find out who is the master down at the beach!

ASTA. [Listening.] There is some one knocking.

EYOLF. Oh, I'm sure it's Borgheim!

RITA. Come in.

[The RAT-WIFE comes softly and noiselessly in by the door on the right. She is a thin little shrunken figure, old and grey-haired, with keen, piercing eyes, dressed in an old-fashioned flowered gown, with a black hood and cloak. She has in her hand a large red umbrella, and carries a black bag by a loop over her arm.]

EYOLF. [Softly, taking hold of ASTA's dress.] Auntie! That must surely be her!

THE RAT-WIFE. [Curtseying at the door.] I humbly beg pardon but are your worships troubled with any gnawing things in the house?

ALLMERS. Here? No, I don't think so.

THE RAT-WIFE. For it would be such a pleasure to me to rid your worships' house of them.

RITA. Yes, yes; we understand. But we have nothing of the sort here.

THE RAT-WIFE. That's very unlucky, that is; for I just happened to be on my rounds now, and goodness knows when I may be in these parts again. Oh, how tired I am!

ALLMERS. [Pointing to a chair.] Yes, you look tired.

THE RAT-WIFE. I know one ought never to get tired of doing good to the poor little things that are hated and persecuted so cruelly. But it takes your strength out of you, it does.

RITA. Won't you sit down and rest a little?

THE RAT-WIFE. I thank your ladyship with all my heart. [Seats herself on a chair between the door and the sofa.] I have been out all night at my work.

ALLMERS. Have you indeed?

THE RAT-WIFE. Yes, over on the islands. [With a chuckling laugh.] The people sent for me, I can assure you. They didn't like it a bit; but there was nothing else to be done. They had to put a good face on it, and bite the sour apple. [Looks at EYOLF, and nods.] The sour apple, little master, the sour apple.

EYOLF. [Involuntarily, a little timidly.] Why did they have to?

THE RAT-WIFE. What?

EYOLF. To bite it?

THE RAT-WIFE. Why, because they couldn't keep body and soul together on account of the rats and all the little rat-children, you see, young master.

RITA. Ugh! Poor people! Have they so many of them?

THE RAT-WIFE. Yes, it was all alive and swarming with them. [Laughs with quiet glee.] They came creepy-crawly up into the beds all night long. They plumped into the milk-cans, and they went pittering and pattering all over the floor, backwards and forwards, and up and down.

EYOLF. [Softly, to ASTA.] I shall never go there, Auntie.

THE RAT-WIFE. But then I came I, and another along with me. And we took them with us, every one, the sweet little creatures! We made an end of every one of them.

EYOLF. [With a shriek.] Papa, look! look!

RITA. Good Heavens, Eyolf!

ALLMERS. What's the matter?

EYOLF. [Pointing.] There's something wriggling in the bag!

RITA. [At the extreme left, shrieks.] Ugh! Send her away, Alfred.

THE RAT-WIFE. [Laughing.] Oh, dearest lady, you needn't be frightened of such a little mannikin.

ALLMERS. But what is the thing?

THE RAT-WIFE. Why, it's only little Mopsëman. [Loosening the string of the bag.] Come up out of the dark, my own little darling friend.

[A little dog with a broad black snout pokes its head out of the bag.]

THE RAT-WIFE. [Nodding and beckoning to EYOLF.] Come along, don't be afraid, my little wounded warrior! He won't bite. Come here! Come here!

EYOLF. [Clinging to ASTA.] No, I dare not.

THE RAT-WIFE. Don't you think he has a gentle, lovable countenance, my young master?

EYOLF. [Astonished, pointing.] That thing there?

THE RAT-WIFE. Yes, this thing here.

EYOLF. [Almost under his breath, staring fixedly at the dog.] I think he has the horriblest countenance I ever saw.

THE RAT-WIFE. [Closing the bag.] Oh, it will come, it will come, right enough.

EYOLF. [Involuntarily drawing nearer, at last goes right up to her, and strokes the bag.] But he is lovely, lovely all the same.

THE RAT-WIFE. [In a tone of caution.] But now he is so tired and weary, poor thing. He's utterly tired out, he is. [Looks at ALLMERS.] For it takes the strength out of you, that sort of game, I can tell you, sir.

ALLMERS. What sort of game do you mean?

THE RAT-WIFE. The luring game.

ALLMERS. Do you mean that it is the dog that lures the rats?

THE RAT-WIFE. [Nodding.] Mopsëman and I, we two do it together. And it goes so smoothly, for all you can see, at any rate. I just slip a string through his collar, and then I lead him three times round the house, and play on my Pan's-pipes. When they hear that, they have got to come up from the cellars, and down from the garrets, and out of flour boles, all the blessed little creatures.

EYOLF. And does he bite them to death then?

THE RAT-WIFE. Oh, not at all! No, we go down to the boat, he and I do and then they follow after us, both the big ones and the little ratikins.

EYOLF. [Eagerly.] And what then tell me!

THE RAT-WIFE. Then we push out from the land, and I scull with one oar, and play on my Pan's-pipes. And Mopsëman, he swims behind. [With glittering eyes.] And all the creepers and crawlers, they follow and follow us out into the deep, deep waters. Ay, for they have to.

EYOLF. Why do they have to?

THE RAT-WIFE. Just because they want not to, just because they are so deadly afraid of the water. That is why they have got to plunge into it.

EYOLF. Are they drowned, then?

THE RAT-WIFE. Every blessed one. [More softly.] And there it is all as still, and soft, and dark as their hearts can desire, the lovely little things. Down there they sleep a long, sweet sleep, with no one to hate them or persecute them any more. [Rises.] In the old days, I can tell you, I didn't need any Mopsëman. Then I did the luring myself, I alone.

EYOLF. And what did you lure then?

THE RAT-WIFE. Men. One most of all.

EYOLF. [With eagerness.] Oh, who was that one? Tell me!

THE RAT-WIFE. [Laughing.] It was my own sweetheart, it was, little heart-breaker!

EYOLF. And where is he now, then?

THE RAT-WIFE. [Harshly.] Down where all the rats are. [Resuming her milder tone.] But now I must be off and get to business again. Always on the move. [To RITA.] So your ladyship has no sort of use for me to-day? I could finish it all off while I am about it.

RITA. No, thank you; I don't think we require anything.

THE RAT-WIFE. Well, well, your sweet ladyship, you can never tell. If your ladyship should find that there is anything lure that keeps nibbling and gnawing, and creeping and crawling, then just see and get hold of me and Mopsëman. Good-bye, good-bye, a kind good-bye to you all. [She goes out by the door on the right.]

EYOLF. [Softly and triumphantly, to ASTA.] Only think, Auntie, now I have seen the Rat-Wife too!

[RITA goes out upon the verandah, and fans herself with her pocket-handkerchief. Shortly afterwards, EYOLF slips cautiously and unnoticed out to the right.]

ALLMERS. [Takes up the portfolio from the table by the sofa.] Is this your portfolio, Asta?

ASTA. Yes. I have some of the old letters in it.

ALLMERS. Ah, the family letters

ASTA. You know you asked me to arrange them for you while you were away.

ALLMERS. [Pats her on the head.] And you have actually found time to do that, dear?

ASTA. Oh, yes. I have done it partly out here and partly at my own rooms in town.

ALLMERS. Thanks, dear. Did you find anything particular in them?

ASTA. [Lightly.] Oh, you know you always find something or other in such old papers. [Speaking lower and seriously.] It is the letters to mother that are in this portfolio.

ALLMERS. Those, of course, you must keep yourself.

ASTA. [With an effort.] No; I am determined that you shall look through them, too, Alfred. Some time, later on in life. I haven't the key of the portfolio with me just now.

ALLMERS. It doesn't matter, my dear Asta, for I shall never read your mother's letters in any case.

ASTA. [Fixing her eyes on him.] Then some time or other, some quiet evening, I will tell you a little of what is in them.

ALLMERS. Yes, that will be much better. But do you keep your mother's letters, you haven't so many mementos of her.

[He hands ASTA the portfolio. She takes it, and lays it on the chair under her outdoor things. RITA comes into the room again.]

RITA. Ugh! I feel as if that horrible old woman had brought a sort of graveyard smell with her.

ALLMERS. Yes, she was rather horrible.

RITA. I felt almost sick while she was in the room.

ALLMERS. However, I can very well understand the sort of spellbound fascination that she talked about. The loneliness of the mountain-peaks and of the great waste places has something of the same magic about it.

ASTA. [Looks attentively at him.] What is it that has happened to you, Alfred?

ALLMERS. [Smiling.] To me?

ASTA. Yes, something has happened, something seems almost to have transformed you. Rita noticed it too.

RITA. Yes, I saw it the moment you came. A change for the better, I hope, Alfred?

ALLMERS. It ought to be for the better. And it must and shall come to good.

RITA. [With an outburst.] You have had some adventure on your journey! Don't deny it! I can see it in your face!

ALLMERS. [Shaking his head.] No adventure in the world, outwardly at least. But

RITA. [Eagerly.] But?

ALLMERS. It is true that within me there has been something of a revolution.

RITA. Oh Heavens!

ALLMERS. [Soothingly, patting her hand.] Only for the better, my dear Rita. You may be perfectly certain of that.

RITA. [Seats herself on the sofa.] You must tell us all about it, at once, tell us everything!

ALLMERS. [Turning to ASTA.] Yes, let us sit down, too, Asta. Then I will try to tell you as well as I can.

[He seats himself on the sofa at RITA's side. ASTA moves a chair forward, and places herself near him.]

RITA. [Looking at him expectantly.] Well?

ALLMERS. [Gazing straight before him.] When I look back over my life and my fortunes for the last ten or eleven years, it seems to me almost like a fairy-tale or a dream. Don't you think so too, Asta?

ASTA. Yes, in many ways I think so.

ALLMERS. [Continuing.] When I remember what we two used to be, Asta, we two poor orphan children

RITA. [Impatiently.] Oh, that is such an old, old story.

ALLMERS. [Not listening to her.] And now here I am in comfort and luxury. I have been able to follow my vocation. I have been able to work and study, just as I had always longed to. [Holds out his hand.] And all this great, this fabulous good fortune we owe to you, my dearest Rita.

RITA. [Half playfully, half angrily, slaps his hand.] Oh, I do wish you would stop talking like that.

ALLMERS. I speak of it only as a sort of introduction.

RITA. Then do skip the introduction!

ALLMERS. Rita, you must not think it was the doctor's advice that drove me up to the mountains.

ASTA. Was it not, Alfred?

RITA. What was it, then?

ALLMERS. It was this: I found there was no more peace for me, there in my study.

RITA. No peace! Why, who disturbed you?

ALLMERS. [Shaking his head.] No one from without. But I felt as though I were positively abusing or, say rather, wasting my best powers frittering away the time.

ASTA. [With wide eyes.] When you were writing at your book?

ALLMERS. [Nodding.] For I cannot think that my powers are confined to that alone. I must surely have it in me to do one or two other things as well.

RITA. Was that what you sat there brooding over?

ALLMERS. Yes, mainly that.

RITA. And so that is what has made you so discontented with yourself of late; and with the rest of us as well. For you know you were discontented, Alfred.

ALLMERS. [Gazing straight before him.] There I sat bent over my table, day after day, and often half the night too, writing and writing at the great thick book on "Human Responsibility." H'm!

ASTA. [Laying her hand upon his arm.] But, Alfred, that book is to be your life-work.

RITA. Yes, you have said so often enough.

ALLMERS. I thought so. Ever since I grew up, I have thought so. [With an affectionate expression in his eyes.] And it was you that enabled me to devote myself to it, my dear Rita

RITA. Oh, nonsense!

ALLMERS. [Smiling to her.] you, with your gold, and your green forests

RITA. [Half laughing, half vexed.] If you begin all that rubbish again, I shall beat you.

ASTA. [Looking sorrowfully at him.] But the book, Alfred?

ALLMERS. It began, as it were, to drift away from me. But I was more and more beset by the thought of the higher duties that laid their claims upon me.

RITA. [Beaming, seizes his hand.] Alfred!

ALLMERS. The thought of Eyolf, my dear Rita.

RITA. [Disappointed, drops his hand.] Ah, of Eyolf!

ALLMERS. Poor little Eyolf has taken deeper and deeper hold of me. After that unlucky fall from the table and especially since we have been assured that the injury is incurable

RITA. [Insistently.] But you take all the care you possibly can of him, Alfred!

ALLMERS. As a schoolmaster, yes; but not as a father. And it is a father that I want henceforth to be to Eyolf.

RITA. [Looking at him and shaking her head.] I don't think I quite understand you.

ALLMERS. I mean that I will try with all my might to make his misfortune as painless and easy to him as it can possibly be.

RITA. Oh, but, dear, thank Heaven, I don't think he feels it so deeply.

ASTA. [With emotion.] Yes, Rita, he does.

ALLMERS. Yes, you may be sure he feels it deeply.

RITA. [Impatiently.] But, Alfred, what more can you do for him?

ALLMERS. I will try to perfect all the rich possibilities that are dawning in his childish soul. I will foster all the germs of good in his nature, make them blossom and bear fruit. [With more and more warmth, rising.] And I will do more than that! I will help him to bring his desires into harmony with what lies attainable before him. That is just what at present they are not. All his longings are for things that must for ever remain unattainable to him. But I will create a conscious happiness in his mind. [He goes once or twice up and down the room. ASTA and RITA follow him with their eyes.]

RITA. You should take these things more quietly, Alfred!

ALLMERS. [Stops beside the table on the left, and looks at them.] Eyolf shall carry on my life-work, if he wants to. Or he shall choose one that is altogether his own. Perhaps that would be best. At all events, I shall let mine rest as it is.

RITA. [Rising.] But, Alfred dear, can you not work both for yourself and for Eyolf?

ALLMERS. No, I cannot. It is impossible! I cannot divide myself in this matter and therefore I efface myself. Eyolf shall be the complete man of our race. And it shall be my new life-work to make him the complete man.

ASTA. [Has risen and now goes up to him.] This must have cost you a terribly hard struggle, Alfred?

ALLMERS. Yes, it has. At home here, I should never have conquered myself, never brought myself to the point of renunciation. Never at home!

RITA. Then that was why you went away this summer?

ALLMERS. [With shining eyes.] Yes! I went up into the infinite solitudes. I saw the sunrise gleaming on the mountain peaks. I felt myself nearer the stars, I seemed almost to be in sympathy and communion with them. And then I found the strength for it.

ASTA. [Looking sadly at him.] But you will never write any more of your book on "Human Responsibility"?

ALLMERS. No, never, Asta. I tell you I cannot split up my life between two vocations. But I will act out my "human responsibility" in my own life.

RITA. [With a smile.] Do you think you can live up to such high resolves at home here?

ALLMERS. [Taking her hand.] With you to help me, I can. [Holds out the other hand.] And with you too, Asta.

RITA. [Drawing her hand away.] Ah, with both of us! So, after all, you can divide yourself.

ALLMERS. Why, my dearest Rita!

[RITA moves away from him and stands in the garden doorway. A light and rapid knock is heard at the door on the right. Engineer BORGHEIM enters quickly. He is a young man of a little over thirty. His expression is bright and cheerful, and he holds himself erect.]

BORGHEIM. Good morning, Mrs. Allmers. [Stops with an expression of pleasure on seeing ALLMERS.] Why, what's this? Home again already, Mr. Allmers?

ALLMERS. [Shaking hands with him.] Yes, I arrived list night.

RITA. [Gaily.] His leave was up, Mr. Borgheim.

ALLMERS. No, you know it wasn't, Rita

RITA. [Approaching.] Oh yes, but it was, though. His furlough had run out.

BORGHEIM. I see you hold your husband well in hand, Mrs. Allmers.

RITA. I hold to my rights. And besides, everything must have an end.

BORGHEIM. Oh, not everything, I hope. Good morning, Miss Allmers!

ASTA. [Holding aloof from him.] Good morning.

RITA. [Looking at BORGHEIM.] Not everything, you say?

BORGHEIM. Oh, I am firmly convinced that there are some things in the world that will never come to an end.

RITA. I suppose you are thinking of love and that sort of thing.

BORGHEIM. [Warmly.] I am thinking of all that is lovely!

RITA. And that never comes to an end. Yes, let us think of that, hope for that, all of us.

ALLMERS. [Coming up to them.] I suppose you will soon have finished your road-work out here?

BORGHEIM. I have finished it already, finished it yesterday. It has been a long business, but, thank Heaven, that has come to an end.

RITA. And you are beaming with joy over that?

BORGHEIM. Yes, I am indeed!

RITA. Well, I must say

BORGHEIM. What, Mrs. Allmers?

RITA. I don't think it is particularly nice of you, Mr. Borgheim.

BORGHEIM. Indeed! Why not?

RITA. Well, I suppose we sha'n't often see you in these parts after this.

BORGHEIM. No, that is true. I hadn't thought of that.

RITA. Oh well, I suppose you will be able to look in upon us now and then all the same.

BORGHEIM. No, unfortunately that will be out of my power for a very long time.

ALLMERS. Indeed! How so?

BORGHEIM. The fact is, I have got a big piece of new work that I must set about at once.

ALLMERS. Have you indeed? [Pressing his hand.] I am heartily glad to hear it.

RITA. I congratulate you, Mr. Borgheim!

BORGHEIM. Hush, hush, I really ought not to talk openly of it as yet! But I can't help coming out with it! It is a great piece of road-making, up in the north, with mountain ranges to cross, and the most tremendous difficulties to overcome! [With an outburst of gladness.] Oh, what a glorious world this is and what a joy it is to be a road-maker in it!

RITA. [Smiling, and looking teasingly at him.] Is it road-making business that has brought you out here to-day in such wild spirits?

BORGHEIM. No, not that alone. I am thinking of all the bright and hopeful prospects that are opening out before me.

RITA. Aha, then perhaps you have something still more exquisite in reserve!

BORGHEIM. [Glancing towards ASTA.] Who knows! When once happiness comes to us, it is apt to come like it spring flood. [Turns to ASTA.] Miss Allmers, would you not like to take a little walk with me? As we used to?

ASTA. [Quickly.] No, no, thank you. Not now. Not to-day.

BORGHEIM. Oh, do come! Only a little bit of a walk! I have so much I want to talk to you about before I go.

RITA. Something else, perhaps, that you must not talk openly about as yet?

BORGHEIM. H'm, that depends

RITA. But there is nothing to prevent your whispering, you know. [Half aside.] Asta, you must really go with him.

ASTA. But, my dear Rita

BORGHEIM. [Imploringly.] Miss Asta, remember it is to be a farewell walk, the last for many a day.

ASTA. [Takes her hat and parasol.] Very well, suppose we take a stroll in the garden, then.

BORGHEIM. Oh, thank you, thank you!

ALLMERS. And while you are there you can see what Eyolf is doing.

BORGHEIM. Ah, Eyolf, by the bye! Where is Eyolf to-day? I've got something for him.

ALLMERS. He is out playing somewhere.

BORGHEIM. Is he really! Then he has begun to play now? He used always to be sitting indoors over his books.

ALLMERS. There is to be an end of that now. I am going to make a regular open-air boy of him.

BORGHEIM. Ah, now, that's right! Out into the open air with him, poor little fellow! Good Lord, what can we possibly do better than play in this blessed world? For my part, I think all life is one long playtime! Come, Miss Asta!

[BORGHEIM and ASTA go out on the verandah and down through the garden.]

ALLMERS. [Stands looking after them.] Rita, do you think there is anything between those two?

RITA. I don't know what to say. I used to think there was. But Asta has grown so strange to me, so utterly incomprehensible of late.

ALLMERS. Indeed! Has she? While I have been away?

RITA. Yes, within the last week or two.

ALLMERS. And you think she doesn't care very much about him now?

RITA. Not, seriously; not utterly and entirely; not unreservedly, I am sure she doesn't. [Looks searchingly at him.] Would it displease you if she did?

ALLMERS. It would not exactly displease me. But it would certainly be a disquieting thought

RITA. Disquieting?

ALLMERS. Yes; you must remember that I am responsible for Asta for her life's happiness.

RITA. Oh, come responsible! Surely Asta has come to years of discretion? I should say she was capable of choosing for herself.

ALLMERS. Yes, we must hope so, Rita.

RITA. For my part, I don't think at all ill of Borgheim.

ALLMERS. No, dear, no more do I, quite the contrary. But all the same

RITA. [Continuing.] And I should be very glad indeed if he and Asta were to make a match of it.

ALLMERS. [Annoyed.] Oh, why should you be?

RITA. [With increasing excitement.] Why, for then she would have to go far, far away with him! And she could never come out here to us, as she does now.

ALLMERS. [Stares at her in astonishment.] What! Can you really wish Asta to go away?

RITA. Yes, yes, Alfred!

ALLMERS. Why in all the world?

RITA. [Throwing her arms passionately round his neck.] For then, at last, I should have you to myself alone! And yet, not even then! Not wholly to myself! [Bursts into convulsive weeping.] Oh, Alfred, Alfred, I cannot give you up!

ALLMERS. [Gently releasing himself.] My dearest Rita, do be reasonable!

RITA. I don't care a bit about being reasonable! I care only for you! Only for you in all the world! [Again throwing her arms round his neck.] For you, for you, for you!

ALLMERS. Let me go, let me go, you are strangling me!

RITA. [Letting him go.] How I wish I could! [Looking at him with flashing eyes.] Oh, if you knew how I have hated you!

ALLMERS. Hated me!

RITA. Yes, when you shut yourself up in your room and brooded over your work, till long, long into the night. [Plaintively.] So long, so late, Alfred. Oh, how I hated your work!

ALLMERS. But now I have done with that.

RITA. [With a cutting laugh.] Oh yes! Now you have given yourself up to something worse.

ALLMERS. [Shocked.] Worse! Do you call our child something worse?

RITA. [Vehemently.] Yes, I do. As he comes between you and me, I call him so. For the book, the book was not a living being, as the child is. [With increasing impetuosity.] But I won't endure it, Alfred! I will not endure it, I tell you so plainly!

ALLMERS. [Looks steadily at her, and says in a low voice.] I am often almost afraid of you, Rita.

RITA. [Gloomily.] I am often afraid of myself. And for that very reason you must not awake the evil in me.

ALLMERS. Why, good Heavens, do I do that?

RITA. Yes, you do, when you tear to shreds the holiest bonds between us.

ALLMERS. [Urgently.] Think what you're saying, Rita. It is your own child, our only child, that you are speaking of.

RITA. The child is only half mine. [With another outburst.] But you shall be mine alone! You shall be wholly mine! That I have a right to demand of you!

ALLMERS. [Shrugging his shoulders.] Oh, my dear Rita, it is of no use demanding anything. Everything must be freely given.

RITA. [Looks anxiously at him.] And that you cannot do henceforth?

ALLMERS. No, I cannot. I must divide myself between Eyolf and you.

RITA. But if Eyolf had never been born? What then?

ALLMERS. [Evasively.] Oh, that would be another matter. Then I should have only you to care for.

RITA. [Softly, her voice quivering.] Then I wish he had never been born.

ALLMERS. [Flashing out.] Rita! You don't know what you are saying!

RITA. [Trembling with emotion.] It was in pain unspeakable that I brought him into the world. But I bore it all with joy and rapture for your sake.

ALLMERS. [Warmly.] Oh yes, I know, I know.

RITA. [With decision.] But there it must end. I will live my life, together with you, wholly with you. I cannot go on being only Eyolf's mother, only his mother and nothing more. I will not, I tell you! I cannot! I will be all in all to you! To you, Alfred!

ALLMERS. But that is just what you are, Rita. Through our child

RITA. Oh, vapid, nauseous phrases, nothing else! No, Alfred, I am not to be put off like that. I was fitted to become the child's mother, but not to be a mother to him. You must take me as I am, Alfred.

ALLMERS. And yet you used to be so fond of Eyolf.

RITA. I was so sorry for him, because you troubled yourself so little about him. You kept him reading and grinding at books. You scarcely even saw him.

ALLMERS. [Nodding slowly.] No; I was blind. The time had not yet come for me.

RITA. [Looking in his face.] But now, I suppose, it has come?

ALLMERS. Yes, at, last. Now I see that the highest task I can have in the world is to be a true father to Eyolf.

RITA. And to me? what will you be to me?

ALLMERS. [Gently.] I will always go on caring for you, with calm, deep tenderness. [He tries to take her hands.]

RITA. [Evading him.] I don't care a bit for your calm, deep tenderness. I want you utterly and entirely and alone! Just as I had you in the first rich, beautiful days. [Vehemently and harshly.] Never, never will I consent to be put off with scraps and leavings, Alfred!

ALLMERS. [In a conciliatory tone.] I should have thought there was happiness in plenty for all three of us, Rita.

RITA. [Scornfully.] Then you are easy to please. [Seats herself at the table on the left.] Now listen to me.

ALLMERS. [Approaching.] Well, what is it?

RITA. [Looking up at him with a veiled glow in her eyes.] When I got your telegram yesterday evening

ALLMERS. Yes? What then?

RITA. - then I dressed myself in white

ALLMERS. Yes, I noticed you were in white when I arrived.

RITA. I had let down my hair

ALLMERS. Your sweet masses of hair

RITA. - so that it flowed down my neck and shoulders

ALLMERS. I saw it, I saw it. Oh, how lovely you were, Rita!

RITA. There were rose-tinted shades over both the lamps. And we were alone, we two, the only waking beings in the whole house. And there was champagne on the table.

ALLMERS. I did not drink any of it.

RITA. [Looking bitterly at him.] No, that is true. [Laughs harshly.] "There stood the champagne, but you tasted it not" as the poet says.

[She rises from the armchair, goes with an air of weariness over to the sofa, and seats herself, half reclining, upon it.]

ALLMERS. [Crosses the room and stands before her.] I was so taken up with serious thoughts. I had made up my mind to talk to you of our future, Rita and first and foremost of Eyolf.

RITA. [Smiling.] And so you did

ALLMERS. No, I had not time to, for you began to undress.

RITA. Yes, and meanwhile you talked about Eyolf. Don't you remember? You wanted to know all about little Eyolf's digestion.

ALLMERS. [Looking reproachfully at her.] Rita!

RITA. And then you got into your bed, and slept the sleep of the just.

ALLMERS. [Shaking his head.] Rita, Rita!

RITA. [Lying at full length and looking up at him.] Alfred?

ALLMERS. Yes?

RITA. "There stood your champagne, but you tasted it not."

ALLMERS. [Almost harshly.] No. I did not taste it.

[He goes away from her and stands in the garden doorway. RITA lies for some time motionless, with closed eyes.]

RITA. [Suddenly springing up.] But let me tell you one thing, Alfred.

ALLMERS. [Turning in the doorway.] Well?

RITA. You ought not to feel quite so secure as you do!

ALLMERS. Not secure?

RITA. No, you ought not to be so indifferent! Not certain of your property in me!

ALLMERS. [Drawing nearer.] What do you mean by that?

RITA. [With trembling lips.] Never in a single thought have I been untrue to you, Alfred! Never for an instant.

ALLMERS. No, Rita, I know that I, who know you so well.

RITA. [With sparkling eyes.] But if you disdain me!

ALLMERS. Disdain! I don't understand what you mean!

RITA. Oh, you don't know all that might rise up within me, if

ALLMERS. If?

RITA. If I should ever see that you did not care for me that you did not love me as you used to.

ALLMERS. But, my dearest Rita, years bring a certain change with them and that must one day occur even in us, as in everyone else.

RITA. Never in me! And I will not hear of any change in you either, I could not bear it, Alfred. I want to keep you to myself alone.

ALLMERS. [Looking at her with concern.] You have a terribly jealous nature

RITA. I can't make myself different from what I am. [Threateningly.] If you go and divide yourself between me and anyone else

ALLMERS. What then?

RITA. Then I will take my revenge on you, Alfred!

ALLMERS. How "take your revenge"?

RITA. I don't know how. Oh yes, I do know, well enough!

ALLMERS. Well?

RITA. I will go and throw myself away

ALLMERS. Throw yourself away, do you say?

RITA. Yes, that I will. I'll throw myself straight into the arms of the first man that comes in my way

ALLMERS. [Looking tenderly at her and shaking his head.] That you will never do, my loyal, proud, true-hearted Rita!

RITA. [Putting her arms round his neck.] Oh, you don't know what I might come to be if you, if you did not love me any more.

ALLMERS. Did not love you, Rita? How can you say such a thing!

RITA. [Half laughing, lets him go.] Why should I not spread my nets for that, that road-maker man that hangs about here?

ALLMERS. [Relieved.] Oh, thank goodness, you are only joking.

RITA. Not at all. He would do as well as any one else.

ALLMERS. Ah, but I suspect he is more or less taken up already.

RITA. So much the better! For then I should take him away from some one else; and that is just what Eyolf has done to me.

ALLMERS. Can you say that our little Eyolf has done that?

RITA. [Pointing with her forefinger.] There, you see! You see! The moment you mention Eyolf's name, you grow tender and your voice quivers! [Threateningly, clenching her hands.] Oh, you almost tempt we to wish

ALLMERS. [Looking at her anxiously.] What do I tempt you to wish, Rita?

RITA. [Vehemently, going away from him.] No, no, no, I won't tell you that! Never!

ALLMERS. [Drawing nearer to her.] Rita! I implore you, for my sake and for your own, do not let yourself he tempted into evil.

[BORGHEIM and ASTA come up from the garden. They both show signs of restrained emotion. They look serious and dejected. ASTA remains out on the verandah. BORGHEIM comes into the room.]

BORGHEIM. So that is over, Miss Allmers and I have had our last walk together.

RITA. [Looks at him with surprise.] Ah! And there is no longer journey to follow the walk?

BORGHEIM. Yes, for me.

RITA. For you alone?

BORGHEIM. Yes, for me alone.

RITA. [Glances darkly at ALLMERS.] Do you hear that? [Turns to BORGHEIM.] I'll wager it is some one with the evil eye that has played you this trick.

BORGHEIM. [Looks at her.] The evil eye?

RITA. [Nodding.] Yes, the evil eye.

BORGHEIM. Do you believe in the evil eye, Mrs. Allmers?

RITA. Yes. I have begun to believe in the evil eye. Especially in a child's evil eye.

ALLMERS. [Shocked, whispers.] Rita, how can you?

RITA. [Speaking low.] It is you that make me so wicked and hateful, Alfred.

[Confused cries and shrieks are heard in the distance, from the direction of the fiord.]

BORGHEIM. [Going to the glass door.] What noise is that?

ASTA. [In the doorway.] Look at all those people running down to the pier!

ALLMERS. What can it be? [Looks out for a moment.] No doubt it's those street urchins at some mischief again.

BORGHEIM. [Calls, leaning over the verandah railings.] I say, you boys down there! What's the matter?

[Several voices are heard answering indistinctly and confusedly.]

RITA. What do they say?

BORGHEIM. They say it's a child that's drowned.

ALLMERS. A child drowned?

ASTA. [Uneasily.] A little boy, they say.

ALLMERS. Oh, they can all swim, every one of them.

RITA. [Shrieks in terror.] Where is Eyolf?

ALLMERS. Keep quiet, quiet. Eyolf is down in the garden, playing.

ASTA. No, he wasn't in the garden.

RITA. [With upstretched arms.] Oh, if only it isn't he!

BORGHEIM. [Listens, and calls down.] Whose child is it, do you say?

[Indistinct voices are heard. BORGHEIM and ASTA utter a suppressed cry, and rush out through the garden.]

ALLMERS. [In an agony of dread.] It isn't Eyolf! It isn't Eyolf, Rita!

RITA. [On the verandah, listening.] Hush! Be quiet! Let me hear what they are saying!

[RITA rushes back with a piercing shriek, into the room.]

ALLMERS. [Following her.] What did they say?

RITA. [Sinking down beside the armchair on the left.] They said: "The crutch is floating!"

ALLMERS. [Almost paralysed.] No! No! No!

RITA. [Hoarsely.] Eyolf! Eyolf! Oh, but they must save him!

ALLMERS. [Half distracted.] They must, they must! So precious a life!

[He rushes down through the garden.]

Act Second

[A little narrow glen by the side of the fiord, on ALLMERS'S property. On the left, lofty old trees overarch the spot. Down the slope in the background a brook comes leaping, and loses itself among the stones on the margin of the wood. A path winds along by the brook-side. To the right there are only a few single trees, between which the fiord is visible. In front is seen the corner of a boat-shed with a boat drawn up. Under the old trees on the left stands a table with a bench and one or two chairs, all made of thin birch-staves. It is a heavy, damp day, with driving mist wreaths.]

[ALFRED ALLMERS, dressed as before, sits on the bench, leaning his arms on the table. His hat lies before him. He gazes absently and immovably out over the water.]

[Presently ASTA ALLMERS comes down the woodpath. She is carrying an open umbrella.]

ASTA. [Goes quietly and cautiously up to him.] You ought not to sit down here in this gloomy weather, Alfred.

ALLMERS. [Nods slowly without answering.]

ASTA. [Closing her umbrella.] I have been searching for you such a long time.

ALLMERS. [Without expression.] Thank you.

ASTA. [Moves a chair and seats herself close to him.] Have you been sitting here long? All the time?

ALLMERS. [Does not answer at first. Presently he says.] No, I cannot grasp it. It seems so utterly impossible.

ASTA. [Laying her hand compassionately on his arm.] Poor Alfred!

ALLMERS. [Gazing at her.] Is it really true then, Asta? Or have I gone mad? Or am I only dreaming? Oh, if it were only a dream! Just think, if I were to waken now!

ASTA. Oh, if I could only waken you!

ALLMERS. [Looking out over the water.] How pitiless the fiord looks to-day, lying so heavy and drowsy, leaden-grey, with splashes of yellow and reflecting the rain-clouds.

ASTA. [Imploringly.] Oh, Alfred, don't sit staring out over the fiord!

ALLMERS. [Not heeding her.] Over the surface, yes. But in the depths, there sweeps the rushing undertow

ASTA. [In terror.] Oh, for God's sake don't think of the depths!

ALLMERS. [Looking gently at her.] I suppose you think he is lying close outside here? But he is not, Asta. You must not think that. You must remember how fiercely the current sweeps gut here straight to the open sea.

ASTA. [Throws herself forward against the table, and, sobbing, buries her face in her hands.] Oh, God! Oh, God!

ALLMERS. [Heavily.] So you see, little Eyolf has passed so far, far away from us now.

ASTA. [Looks imploringly up at him.] Oh, Alfred, don't say such things!

ALLMERS. Why, you can reckon it out for yourself, you that are so clever. In eight-and-twenty hours, nine-and-twenty hours. Let me see! Let me see!

ASTA. [Shrieking and stopping her ears.] Alfred!

ALLMERS. [Clenching his hand firmly upon the table.] Can you conceive the meaning of a thing like this?

ASTA. [Looks at him.] Of what?

ALLMERS. Of this that has been done to Rita and me.

ASTA. The meaning of it?

ALLMERS. [Impatiently.] Yes, the meaning, I say. For, after all, there must be a meaning in it. Life, existence, destiny, cannot be so utterly meaningless.

ASTA. Oh, who can say anything with certainty about these things, my dear Alfred?

ALLMERS. [Laughs bitterly.] No, no; I believe you are right there. Perhaps the whole thing goes simply by haphazard, taking its own course, like a drifting wreck without a rudder. I daresay that is how it is. At least, it seems very like it.

ASTA. [Thoughtfully.] What if it only seems?

ALLMERS. [Vehemently.] Ah? Perhaps you can unravel the mystery for me? I certainly cannot. [More gently.] Here is Eyolf, just entering upon conscious life: full of such infinite possibilities, splendid possibilities perhaps: he would have filled my life with pride and gladness. And then a crazy old woman has only to come this way and show a cur in a bag

ASTA. But we don't in the least know how it really happened.

ALLMERS. Yes, we do. The boys saw her row out over the fiord. They saw Eyolf standing alone at the very end of the pier. They saw him gazing after her and then he seemed to turn giddy. [Quivering.] And that was how he fell over and disappeared.

ASTA. Yes, yes. But all the same

ALLMERS. She has drawn him down into the depths, that you may be sure of, dear.

ASTA. But, Alfred, why should she?

ALLMERS. Yes, that is just the question! Why should she? There is no retribution behind it all, no atonement, I mean. Eyolf never did her any harm. He never called names after her; he never threw stones at her dog. Why, he had never set eyes either on her or her dog till yesterday. So there is no retribution; the whole thing is utterly groundless and meaningless, Asta. And yet the order of the world requires it.

ASTA. Have you spoken to Rita of these things?

ALLMERS. [Shakes his head.] I feel as if I can talk better to you about them. [Drawing a deep breath.] And about everything else as well.

[ASTA takes serving-materials and a little paper parcel out of her pocket. ALLMERS sits looking on absently.]

ALLMERS. What leave you got there, Asta?

ASTA. [Taking his hat.] Some black crape.

ALLMERS. Oh, what is the use of that?

ASTA. Rita asked me to put it on. May I?

ALLMERS. Oh, yes; as far as I'm concerned [She sews the crape on his hat.]

ALLMERS. [Sitting and looking at her.] Where is Rita?

ASTA. She is walking about the garden a little, I think. Borgheim is with her.

ALLMERS. [Slightly surprised.] Indeed! Is Borgheim out here to-day again?

ASTA. Yes. He came out by the mid-day train.

ALLMERS. I didn't expect that.

ASTA. [Serving.] He was so fond of Eyolf.

ALLMERS. Borgheim is a faithful soul, Asta.

ASTA. [With quiet warmth.] Yes, faithful he is, indeed. That is certain.

ALLMERS. [Fixing his eyes upon her.] You are really fond of him?

ASTA. Yes, I am.

ALLMERS. And yet you cannot make up your mind to?

ASTA. [Interrupting.] Oh, my dear Alfred, don't talk of that!

ALLMERS. Yes, yes; tell me why you cannot?

ASTA. Oh, no! Please! You really must not ask me. You see, it's so painful for me. There now! The hat is done.

ALLMERS. Thank you.

ASTA. And now for the left arm.

ALLMERS. Am I to have crape on it too?

ASTA. Yes, that is the custom.

ALLMERS. Well, as you please.

[She moves close up to him and begins to sew.]

ASTA. Keep your arm still then I won't prick you.

ALLMERS. [With a half-smile.] This is like the old days.

ASTA. Yes, don't you think so?

ALLMERS. When you were a little girl you used to sit just like this, mending my clothes. The first thing you ever sewed for me that was black crape, too.

ASTA. Was it?

ALLMERS. Round my student's cap at the time of father's death.

ASTA. Could I sew then? Fancy, I have forgotten it.

ALLMERS. Oh, you were such a little thing then.

ASTA. Yes, I was little then.

ALLMERS. And then, two years afterwards, when we lost your mother, then again you sewed a big crape band on my sleeve.

ASTA. I thought it was the right thing to do.

ALLMERS. [Patting her hand.] Yes, yes, it was the right thing to do, Asta. And then when we were left alone in the world, we two. Are you done already?

ASTA. Yes. [Putting together her sewing-materials.] It was really a beautiful time for us, Alfred. We two alone.

ALLMERS. Yes, it was, though we had to toil so hard.

ASTA. You toiled.

ALLMERS. [With more life.] Oh, you toiled too, in your way, I can assure you [smiling] my dear, faithful, Eyolf.

ASTA. Oh, you mustn't remind me of that stupid nonsense about the name.

ALLMERS. Well, if you had been a boy, you would have been called Eyolf.

ASTA. Yes, if! But when you began to go to college. [Smiling involuntarily.] I wonder how you could be so childish.

ALLMERS. Was it I that was childish?

ASTA. Yes, indeed, I think it was, as I look back upon it all. You were ashamed of having no brother only a sister.

ALLMERS. No, no, it was you, dear, you were ashamed.

ASTA. Oh yes, I too, perhaps a little. And somehow or other I was sorry for you

ALLMERS. Yes, I believe you were. And then you hunted up some of my old boy's clothes-

ASTA. Your fine Sunday clothes, yes. Do you remember the blue blouse and knickerbockers?

ALLMERS. [His eyes dwelling upon her.] I remember so well how you looked when you used to wear them.

ASTA. Only when we were at home, alone, though.

ALLMERS. And how serious we were, dear, and how mightily pleased with ourselves. I always called you Eyolf.

ASTA. Oh, Alfred, I hope you have never told Rita this?

ALLMERS. Yes, I believe I did once tell her.

ASTA. Oh, Alfred, how could you do that?

ALLMERS. Well, you see, one tells one's wife everything, very nearly.

ASTA. Yes, I suppose one does.

ALLMERS. [As if awakening, clutches at his forehead and starts up.] Oh, how can I sit here and

ASTA. [Rising, looks sorrowfully at him.] What is the matter?

ALLMERS. He had almost passed away from me. He had passed quite away.

ASTA. Eyolf!

ALLMERS. Here I sat, living in these recollections and he had no part in them.

ASTA. Yes, Alfred, little Eyolf was behind it all.

ALLMERS. No, he was not. He slipped out of my memory, out of my thoughts. I did not see him for a moment as we sat here talking. I utterly forgot him all that time.

ASTA. But surely you must take some rest in your sorrow.

ALLMERS. No, no, no; that is just what I will not do! I must not, I have no right and no heart for it, either. [Going in great excitement towards the right.] All my thoughts must be out there, where he lies drifting in the depths!

ASTA. [Following him and holding him back.] Alfred, Alfred! Don't go to the fiord.

ALLMERS. I must go out to him! Let me go, Asta! I will take the boat.

ASTA. [In terror.] Don't go to the fiord, I say!

ALLMERS. [Yielding.] No, no, I will not. Only let me alone.

ASTA. [Leading him back to the table.] You must rest from your thoughts, Alfred. Come here and sit down.

ALLMERS. [Making as if to seat himself on the bench.] Well, well, as you please.

ASTA. No, I won't let you sit there.

ALLMERS. Yes, let me.

ASTA. No, don't. For then you will only sit looking out [Forces him down upon a chair, with his back to the right.] There now. Now that's right. [Seats herself upon the bench.] And now we can talk a little again.

ALLMERS. [Drawing a deep breath audibly.] It was good to deaden the sorrow and heartache for a moment.

ASTA. You insist do so, Alfred.

ALLMERS. But don't you think it is terribly weak and unfeeling of me, to be able to do so?

ASTA. Oh, no, I am sure it is impossible to keep circling for ever round one fixed thought.

ALLMERS. Yes, for me it is impossible. Before you came to me, here I sat, torturing myself unspeakably with this crushing, gnawing sorrow

ASTA. Yes?

ALLMERS. And would you believe it, Asta? H'm

ASTA. Well?

ALLMERS. In the midst of all the agony, I found myself speculating what we should have for dinner to-day.

ASTA. [Soothingly.] Well, well, if only it rests you to

ALLMERS. Yes, just fancy, dear, t seemed as if it did give me rest. [Holds out, his hand to her across the table.] How good it is, Asta, that I have you with me. I am so glad of that. Glad, glad, even in my sorrow.

ASTA. [Looking earnestly at him.] You ought most of all to be glad that you have Rita.

ALLMERS. Yes, of course I should. But Rita is no kin to me, it isn't like having a sister.

ASTA. [Eagerly.] Do you say that, Alfred?

ALLMERS. Yes, our family is a thing apart. [Half jestingly.] We have always had vowels for our initials. Don't you remember how often we used to speak of that? And all our relations, all equally poor. And we have all the same colour of eyes.

ASTA. Do you think I have?

ALLMERS. No, you take entirely after your mother. You are not in the least like the rest of us, not even like father. But all the same

ASTA. All the same?

ALLMERS. Well, I believe that living together has, as it were, stamped us in each other's image, mentally, I mean.

ASTA. [With warm emotion.] Oh, you must never say that, Alfred. It is only I that have taken my stamp from you; and it is to you that I owe everything, every good thing in the world.

ALLMERS. [Shaking his head.] You owe me nothing, Asta. On the contrary

ASTA. I owe you everything! You must never doubt that. No sacrifice has been too great for you

ALLMERS. [Interrupting.] Oh, nonsense, sacrifice! Don't talk of such a thing. I have only loved you, Asta, ever since you were a little child. [After a short pause.] And then it always seemed to me that I had so much injustice to make up to you for.

ASTA. [Astonished.] Injustice? You?

ALLMERS. Not precisely on my own account. But

ASTA. [Eagerly.] But?

ALLMERS. On father's.

ASTA. [Half rising from the bench.] On father's! [Sitting down again.] What do you mean by that, Alfred?

ALLMERS. Father was never really kind to you.

ASTA. [Vehemently.] Oh, don't say that!

ALLMERS. Yes, it is true. He did not love you, not as he ought to have.

ASTA. [Evasively.] No, perhaps not as he loved you. That was only natural.

ALLMERS. [Continuing.] And he was often hard to your mother, too, at least in the last years.

ASTA. [Softly.] Mother was so much, much younger than he, remember that.

ALLMERS. Do you think they were not quite suited to each other?

ASTA. Perhaps not.

ALLMERS. Yes, but still. Father, who in other ways was so gentle and warm-hearted, so kindly towards every one

ASTA. [Quietly.] Mother, too, was not always as she ought to have been.

ALLMERS. Your mother was not!

ASTA. Perhaps not always.

ALLMERS. Towards father, do you mean?

ASTA. Yes.

ALLMERS. I never noticed that.

ASTA. [Struggling with her tears, rises.] Oh, my dear Alfred, let them rest, those who are gone. [She goes towards the right.]

ALLMERS. [Rising.] Yes, let them rest. [Wringing his hands.] But those who are gone, it is they that won't let us rest, Asta. Neither day nor night.

ASTA. [Looks warmly at him.] Time will make it all seem easier, Alfred.

ALLMERS. [Looking helplessly at her.] Yes, don't you think it will? But how I am to get over these terrible first days [Hoarsely.] that is what I cannot imagine.

ASTA. [Imploringly, laying her hands on his shoulders.] Go up to Rita. Oh, please do

ALLMERS. [Vehemently, withdrawing from her.] No, no, no, don't talk to me of that! I cannot, I tell you. [More calmly.] Let me remain here, with you.

ASTA. Well, I will not leave you.

ALLMERS. [Seizing her hand and holding it fast.] Thank you for that! [Looks out for a time over the fiord.] Where is my little Eyolf now? [Smiling .sadly to her.] Can you tell me that my big, wise Eyolf? [Shaking his head.] No one in all the world can tell me that. I know only this one terrible thing, that he is gone from me.

ASTA. [Looking up to the left, and withdrawing her hand.] Here they are coming.

[MRS. ALLMERS and Engineer BORGHEIM come down by the wood-path, she leading the way. She wears a dark dress and a black veil over her head. He has an umbrella under his arm.]

ALLMERS. [Going to meet her.] How is it with you, Rita?

RITA. [Passing him.] Oh, don't ask.

ALLMERS. Why do you come here?

RITA. Only to look for you. What are you doing?

ALLMERS. Nothing. Asta came down to me.

RITA. Yes, but before Asta came? You have been away from me all the morning.

ALLMERS. I have been sitting here looking out over the water.

RITA. Ugh, how can you?

ALLMERS. [Impatiently.] I like best to be alone now.

RITA. [Moving restlessly about.] And then to sit still! To stay in one place!

ALLMERS. I have nothing in the world to move for.

RITA. I cannot bear to be anywhere long. Least of all here, with the fiord at my very feet.

ALLMERS. It is just the nearness of the fiord

RITA. [To BORGHEIM.] Don't you think he should come back with the rest of us?

BORGHEIM. [To ALLMERS.] I believe it would be better for you.

ALLMERS. No, no; let me stay where I am.

RITA. Then I will stay with you, Alfred.

ALLMERS. Very well; do so, then. You remain too, Asta.

ASTA. [Whispers to BORGHEIM.] Let us leave them alone!

BORGHEIM. [With a glance of comprehension.] Miss Allmers, shall we go a little further along the shore? For the very last time?

ASTA. [Taking her umbrella.] Yes, come. Let us go a little further.

[ASTA and BORGHEIM go out together behind the boat-shed. ALLMERS wanders about for a little. Then he seats himself on a stone under the trees on the left.]

RITA. [Comes up and stands before him, her hands folded and hanging down.] Can you think the thought, Alfred, that we have lost Eyolf?

ALLMERS. [Looking sadly at the ground.] We must accustom ourselves to think it.

RITA. I cannot. I cannot. And then that horrible sight that will haunt me all my life long.

ALLMERS. [Looking up.] What sight? What have you seen?

RITA. I have seen nothing myself. I have only heard it told. Oh!

ALLMERS. You may as well tell me at once.

RITA. I got Borgheim to go down with me to the pier

ALLMERS. What did you want there?

RITA. To question the boys as to how it happened.

ALLMERS. But we know that.

RITA. We got to know more.

ALLMERS. Well?

RITA. It is not true that he disappeared all at once.

ALLMERS. Do they say that now?

RITA. Yes. They say they saw him lying down on the bottom. Deep down in the clear water.

ALLMERS. [Grinding his teeth.] And they didn't save him!

RITA. I suppose they could not.

ALLMERS. They could swim, every one of them. Did they tell you how he was lying whilst they could see him?

RITA. Yes. They said he was lying on his back. And with great, open eyes.

ALLMERS. Open eyes. But quite still?

RITA. Yes, quite still. And then something came and swept him away. They called it the undertow.

ALLMERS. [Nodding slowly.] So that was the last they saw of him.

RITA. [Suffocated with tears.] Yes.

ALLMERS. [In a dull voice.] And never, never will any one see him again.

RITA. [Wailing.] I shall see him day and night, as he lay down there.

ALLMERS. With great, open eyes.

RITA. [Shuddering.] Yes, with great, open eyes. I see them! I see them now!

ALLMERS. [Rises slowly and looks with quiet menace at her.] Were they evil, those eyes, Rita?

RITA. [Turning pale.] Evil!

ALLMERS. [Going close up to her.] Were they evil eyes that stared up? Up from the depths?

RITA. [Shrinking from him.] Alfred!

ALLMERS. [Following her.] Answer me! Were they a child's evil eyes?

RITA. [Shrieks.] Alfred! Alfred!

ALLMERS. Now things have come about, just as you wished, Rita.

RITA. I! What did I wish?

ALLMERS. That Eyolf were not here.

RITA. Never for a moment have I wished that! That Eyolf should not stand between us, that was what I wished.

ALLMERS. Well, well, he does not stand between us any more.

RITA. [Softly, gazing straight before her.] Perhaps now more than ever. [With a sudden shudder.] Oh, that horrible sight!

ALLMERS. [Nods.] The child's evil eyes.

RITA. [In dread, recoiling from him.] Let me be, Alfred! I am afraid of you. I have never seen you like this before.

ALLMERS. [Looks harshly and coldly at her.] Sorrow makes us wicked and hateful.

RITA. [Terrified, and yet defiant.] That is what I feel, too.

[ALLMERS goes towards the right and looks out over the fiord. RITA seats herself at the table. A short pause.]

ALLMERS. [Turning his head towards her.] You never really and truly loved him, never!

RITA. [With cold self-control.] Eyolf would never let me take him really and truly to my heart.

ALLMERS. Because you did not want to.

RITA. Oh yes, I did. I did want to. But some one stood in the way, even from the first.

ALLMERS. [Turning right round.] Do you mean that I stood in the way?

RITA. Oh, no, not at first.

ALLMERS. [Coming nearer her.] Who, then?

RITA. His aunt.

ALLMERS. Asta?

RITA. Yes. Asta stood and barred the way for me.

ALLMERS. Can you say that, Rita?

RITA. Yes. Asta, she took him to her heart, from the moment that happened, that miserable fall.

ALLMERS. If she did so, she did it in love.

RITA. [Vehemently.] That is just it! I cannot endure to share anything with any one! Not in love.

ALLMERS. We two should have shared him between us in love.

RITA. [Looking scornfully at him.] We? Oh, the truth is you have never had any real love for him either.

ALLMERS. [Looks at her in astonishment.] I have not!

RITA. No, you have not. At first you were so utterly taken up by that book of yours about Responsibility.

ALLMERS. [Forcibly.] Yes, I was. But my very book I sacrificed for Eyolf's sake.

RITA. Not out of love for him.

ALLMERS. Why then, do you suppose?

RITA. Because you were consumed with mistrust of yourself. Because you had begun to doubt whether you had any great vocation to live for in the world.

ALLMERS. [Observing her closely.] Could you see that in me?

RITA. Oh, yes, little by little. And then you needed something new to fill up your life. It seems *I* was not enough for you any longer.

ALLMERS. That is the law of change, Rita.

RITA. And that was why you wanted to make a prodigy of poor little Eyolf.

ALLMERS. That was not what I wanted. I wanted to make a happy human being of him. That, and nothing more.

RITA. But not out of love for him. Look into yourself! [With a certain shyness of expression.] Search out all that lies under and behind your action.

ALLMERS. [Avoiding her eyes.] There is something you shrink from saying.

RITA. And you too.

ALLMERS. [Looks thoughtfully at her.] If it is as you say, then we two have never really possessed our own child.

RITA. No. Not in perfect love.

ALLMERS. And yet we are sorrowing so bitterly for him.

RITA. [With sarcasm.] Yes, isn't it curious that we should grieve like this over a little stranger boy?

ALLMERS. [With an outburst.] Oh, don't call him a stranger!

RITA. [Sadly shaking her head.] We never won the boy, Alfred. Not I, nor you either.

ALLMERS. [Wringing his hands.] And now it is too late! Too late!

RITA. And no consolation anywhere, in anything.

ALLMERS. [With sudden passion.] You are the guilty one in this!

RITA. [Rising.] I!

ALLMERS. Yes, you! It was your fault that he became what he was! It was your fault that he could not save himself when he fell into the water.

RITA. [With a gesture of repulsion.] Alfred, you shall not throw the blame upon me!

ALLMERS. [More and more beside himself.] Yes, yes, I do! It was you that left the helpless child unwatched upon the table.

RITA. He was lying so comfortably among the cushions, and sleeping so soundly. And you had promised to look after him.

ALLMERS. Yes, I had. [Lowering his voice.] But then you came, you, you, you, and lured me to you.

RITA. [Looking defiantly at him.] Oh, better own at once that you forgot the child and everything else.

ALLMERS. [In suppressed desperation.] Yes, that is true. [Lower.] I forgot the child in your arms!

RITA. [Exasperated.] Alfred! Alfred, this is intolerable of you!

ALLMERS. [In a low voice, clenching his fists before her face.] In that hour you condemned little Eyolf to death.

RITA. [Wildly.] You, too! You, too, if it is as you say!

ALLMERS. Oh yes, call me to account, too, if you will. We have sinned, both of us. And so, after all, there was retribution in Eyolf's death.

RITA. Retribution?

ALLMERS. [With more self-control.] Yes. Judgment upon you and me. Now, as we stand here, we have our deserts. While he lived, we let ourselves shrink away from him in secret, abject remorse. We could not bear to see it, the thing he had to drag with him

RITA. [Whispers.] The crutch.

ALLMERS. Yes, that. And now, what we now call sorrow and heartache is really the gnawing of conscience, Rita. Nothing else.

RITA. [Gazing helplessly at him.] I feel as if all this must end in despair in madness for both of us. For we can never, never make it good again.

ALLMERS. [Passing into a calmer mood.] I dreamed about Eyolf last night. I thought I saw him coming up from the pier. He could run like other boys. So nothing had happened to him, neither the one thing nor the other. And the torturing reality was nothing but a dream, I thought. Oh, how I thanked and blessed [Checking himself.] H'm!

RITA. [Looking at him.] Whom?

ALLMERS. [Evasively.] Whom?

RITA. Yes; whom did you thank and bless?

ALLMERS. [Putting aside the question.] I was only dreaming, you know

RITA. One whom you yourself do not believe in?

ALLMERS. That was how I felt, all the same. Of course, I was sleeping

RITA. [Reproachfully.] You should not have taught me to doubt, Alfred.

ALLMERS. Would it leave been right of me to let you go through life with your mind full of empty fictions?

RITA. It would have been better for me; for then I should have had something to take refuge in. Now I am utterly at sea.

ALLMERS. [Observing her closely.] If you had the choice now. If you could follow Eyolf to where he is?

RITA. Yes? What then?

ALLMERS. If you were fully assured that you would find him again, know him, understand him?

RITA. Yes, yes; what then?

ALLMERS. Would you, of your own free will, take the leap over to him? Of your own free will leave everything behind you? Renounce your whole earthly life? Would you, Rita?

RITA. [Softly.] Now, at once?

ALLMERS. Yes; to-day. This very hour. Answer me would you?

RITA. [Hesitating.] Oh, I don't know, Alfred. No! I think I should have to stay here with you, a little while.

ALLMERS. For my sake?

RITA. Yes. only for your sake.

ALLMERS. And afterwards? Would you then? Answer!

RITA. Oh, what can I answer? I could not go away from you. Never! Never!

ALLMERS. But suppose now *I* went to Eyolf? And you had the fullest assurance that you would meet both him and me there. Then would you come over to us?

RITA. I should want to so much! so much! But

ALLMERS. Well? I I?

RITA. [Moaning softly.] I could not, I feel it. No, no, I never could! Not for all the glory of heaven!

ALLMERS. Nor I.

RITA. No, you feel it so, too, don't you, Alfred! You could not either, could you?

ALLMERS. No. For it is here, in the life of earth, that we living beings are at home.

RITA. Yes, here lies the kind of happiness that we can understand.

ALLMERS. [Darkly.] Oh, happiness, happiness

RITA. You mean that happiness, that we can never find it again? [Looks inquiringly at him.] But if? [Vehemently.] No, no; I dare not say it! Nor even think it!

ALLMERS. Yes, say it, say it, Rita.

RITA. [Hesitatingly.] Could we not try to? Would it not be possible to forget him?

ALLMERS. Forget Eyolf?

RITA. Forget the anguish and remorse, I mean.

ALLMERS. Can you wish it?

RITA. Yes, if it were possible. [With an outburst.] For this, I cannot bear this for ever! Oh, can we not think of something that will bring its forgetfulness!

ALLMERS. [Shakes his head.] What could that be?

RITA. Could we not see what travelling would do, far away from here?

ALLMERS. From home? When you know you are never really well anywhere but here.

RITA. Well, then, let us have crowds of people about us! Keep open house! Plunge into something that can deaden and dull our thoughts!

ALLMERS. Such it life would be impossible for me. No, rather than that, I would try to take up my work again.

RITA. [Bitingly.] Your work, the work that has always stood like a dead wall between us!

ALLMERS. [Slowly, looking fixedly at her.] There must always be a dead wall between us two, from this time forth.

RITA. Why must there?

ALLMERS. Who knows but that a child's great, open eyes are watching us day and night.

RITA. [Softly, shuddering.] Alfred, how terrible to think of!

ALLMERS. Our love has been like a consuming fire. Now it must be quenched

RITA. [With a movement towards him.] Quenched!

ALLMERS. [Hardly.] It is quenched in one of us.

RITA. [As if petrified.] And you dare say that to me!

ALLMERS. [More gently.] It is dead, Rita. But in what I now feel for you, in our common guilt and need of atonement, I seem to foresee a sort of resurrection

RITA. [Vehemently.] I don't care a bit about any resurrection!

ALLMERS. Rita!

RITA. I am a warm-blooded being! I don't go drowsing about, with fishes' blood in my veins. [Wringing her hands.] And now to be imprisoned for life, in anguish and remorse! Imprisoned with one who is no longer mine, mine, mine!

ALLMERS. It must have ended so, sometime, Rita.

RITA. Must have ended so! The love that in the beginning rushed forth so eagerly to meet with love!

ALLMERS. My love did not rush forth to you in the beginning.

RITA. What did you feel for me, first of all?

ALLMERS. Dread.

RITA. That I can understand. How was it, then, that I won you after all?

ALLMERS. [In a low voice.] You were so entrancingly beautiful, Rita.

RITA. [Looks searchingly at him.] Then that was the only reason? Say it, Alfred! The only reason?

ALLMERS. [Conquering himself.] No, there was another as well.

RITA. [With an outburst.] I can guess what that was! It was "my gold, and my green forests," as you call it. Was it not so, Alfred?

ALLMERS. Yes.

RITA. [Looks at him with deep reproach.] How could you, how could you!

ALLMERS. I had Asta to think of.

RITA. [Angrily.] Yes, Asta! [Bitterly.] Then it was really Asta that brought us two together?

ALLMERS. She knew nothing about it. She has no suspicion of it, even to this day.

RITA. [Rejecting the plea.] It was Asta, nevertheless! [Smiling, with a sidelong glance of scorn.] Or, no, it was little Eyolf. Little Eyolf, my dear!

ALLMERS. Eyolf?

RITA. Yes, you used to call her Eyolf, did you not? I seem to remember your telling me so, once, in a moment of confidence. [Coming up to him.] Do you remember it, that entrancingly beautiful hour, Alfred?

ALLMERS. [Recoiling, as if in horror.] I remember nothing! I will not remember!

RITA. [Following him.] It was in that hour, when your other little Eyolf was crippled for life!

ALLMERS. [In a hollow voice, supporting himself against the table.] Retribution!

RITA. [Menacingly.] Yes, retribution!

[ASTA and BORGHEIM return by way of the boat-shed. She is carrying some water-lilies in her hand.]

RITA. [With self-control.] Well, Asta, have you and Mr. Borgheim talked things thoroughly over?

ASTA. Oh, yes, pretty well.

[She puts down her umbrella and lays the flowers upon a chair.]

BORGHEIM. Miss Allmers has been very silent during our walk.

RITA. Indeed, has she? Well, Alfred and I have talked things out thoroughly enough

ASTA. [Looking eagerly at both of them.] What is this?

RITA. Enough to last all our lifetime, I say. [Breaking off.] Come now, let us go up to the house, all four of us. We must have company about us in future. It will never do for Alfred and me to be alone.

ALLMERS. Yes, do you go ahead, you two. [Turning.] I must speak a word to you before we go, Asta.

RITA. [Looking at him.] Indeed? Well then, you come with me, Mr. Borgheim.

[RITA and BORGHEIM go up the wood-path.]

ASTA. [Anxiously.] Alfred, what is the matter?

ALLMERS. [Darkly.] Only that I cannot endure to be here any more.

ASTA. Here! With Rita, do you mean?

ALLMERS. Yes. Rita and I cannot go on living together.

ASTA. [Seizes his arm and shakes it.] Oh, Alfred, don't say anything so terrible!

ALLMERS. It is the truth. I am telling you. We are making each other wicked and hateful.

ASTA. [With painful emotion.] I had never, never dreamt of anything like this!

ALLMERS. I did not realise it either, till to-day.

ASTA. And now you want to! What is it you really want, Alfred?

ALLMERS. I want to get away from everything here, far, far away from it all.

ASTA. And to stand quite alone in the world?

ALLMERS. [Nods.] As I used to, before, yes.

ASTA. But you are not fitted for living alone!

ALLMERS. Oh, yes. I was so in the old days, at any rate.

ASTA. In the old days, yes; for then you had me with you.

ALLMERS. [Trying to take her hand.] Yes. And it is to you, Asta, that I now want to come home again.

ASTA. [Eluding him.] To me! No, no, Alfred! That is quite impossible.

ALLMERS. [Looks sadly at her.] Then Borgheim stands in the way after all?

ASTA. [Earnestly.] No, no; he does not! That is quite a mistake!

ALLMERS. Good. Then I will come to you, my dear, dear sister. I must come to you again, home to you, to be purified and ennobled after my life with

ASTA. [Shocked.] Alfred, you are doing Rita a great wrong!

ALLMERS. I have done her a great wrong. But not in this. Oh, think of it, Asta, think of our life together, yours and mine. Was it not like one long holy-day from first to last?

ASTA. Yes, it was, Alfred. But we can never live it over again.

ALLMERS. [Bitterly.] Do you mean that marriage has so irreparably ruined me?

ASTA. [Quietly.] No, that is not what I mean.

ALLMERS. Well, then we two will live our old life over again.

ASTA. [With decision.] We cannot, Alfred.

ALLMERS. Yes, we can. For the love of a brother and sister

ASTA. [Eagerly.] What of it?

ALLMERS. That is the only relation in life that is not subject to the law of change.

ASTA. [Softly and tremblingly.] But if that relation were not

ALLMERS. Not?

ASTA. - not our relation?

ALLMERS. [Stares at her in astonishment.] Not ours? Why, what can you mean by that?

ASTA. It is best I should tell you at once, Alfred.

ALLMERS. Yes, yes; tell me!

ASTA. The letters to mother. Those in my portfolio

ALLMERS. Well?

ASTA. You must read them, when I am gone.

ALLMERS. Why must I?

ASTA. [Struggling with herself.] For then you will see that

ALLMERS. Well?

ASTA. - that I have no right to bear your father's name.

ALLMERS. [Staggering backwards.] Asta! What is this you say!

ASTA. Read the letters. Then you will see and understand. And perhaps have some forgiveness, for mother, too.

ALLMERS. [Clutching at his forehead.] I cannot grasp this, I cannot realise the thought. You, Asta, you are not

ASTA. You are not my brother, Alfred.

ALLMERS. [Quickly, half defiantly, looking at her.] Well, but what difference does that really make in our relation? Practically none at all.

ASTA. [Shaking her head.] It makes all the difference, Alfred. Our relation is not that of brother and sister.

ALLMERS. No, no. But it is none the less sacred for that, it will always be equally sacred.

ASTA. Do not forget that it is subject to the law of change, as you said just now.

ALLMERS. [Looks inquiringly at her.] Do you mean that

ASTA. [Quietly, but with rearm emotion.] Not a word more my dear, dear Alfred. [Takes up the flowers from the chair.] Do you see these water-lilies?

ALLMERS. [Nodding slowly.] They are the sort that shoot up from the very depth.

ASTA. I pulled them in the tarn, where it flows out into the fiord. [Holds them out to him.] Will you take them, Alfred?

ALLMERS. [Taking them.] Thanks.

ASTA. [With tears in her eyes.] They are a last greeting to you, from, from little Eyolf.

ALLMERS. [Looking at her.] From Eyolf out yonder? Or from you?

ASTA. [Softly.] From both of us. [Taking up her umbrella.] Now come with me to Rita.

[She goes up the wood-path.]

ALLMERS. [Takes up his hat from the table, and whispers sadly.] Asta. Eyolf. Little Eyolf!

[He follows her up the path.]

Act Third

[An elevation, overgrown with shrubs, in ALLMERS'S garden. At the back a sheer cliff, with a railing along its edge, and with steps on the left leading downwards. An extensive view over the fiord, which lies deep below. A flagstaff with lines, but no flag, stands by the railing. In front, on the right, a summer-house, covered with creepers and wild vines. Outside it, a bench. It is a late summer evening, with clear sky. Deepening twilight.]

[ASTA is sitting on the bench, with her hands in her lap. She is wearing her outdoor dress and a hat, has her parasol at her side, and a little travelling-bag on a strap over her shoulder.]

[BORGHEIM comes up from the back on the left. He, too, has a travelling-bag over his shoulder. He is carrying a rolled-up flag.]

BORGHEIM. [Catching sight of ASTA.] Oh, so you are up here!

ASTA. Yes, I am taking my last look out over the fiord.

BORGHEIM. Then I am glad I happened to come up.

ASTA. Have you been searching for me?

BORGHEIM. Yes, I have. I wanted to say good-bye to you for the present. Not for good and all, I hope.

ASTA. [With a faint smile.] You are persevering.

BORGHEIM. A road-maker has got to be.

ASTA. Have you seen anything of Alfred? Or of Rita?

BORGHEIM. Yes, I saw them both.

ASTA. Together?

BORGHEIM. No, apart.

ASTA. What are you going to do with that flag?

BORGHEIM. Mrs. Allmers asked me to come up and hoist it.

ASTA. Hoist a flag just now?

BORGHEIM. Half-mast high. She wants it to fly both night and day, she says.

ASTA. [Sighing.] Poor Rita! And poor Alfred!

BORGHEIM. [Busied with the flag.] Have you the heart to leave them? I ask, because I see you are in travelling-dress.

ASTA. [In a low voice.] I must go.

BORGHEIM. Well, if you must, then

ASTA. And you are going, too, to-night?

BORGHEIM. I must, too. I am going by the train. Are you going that way?

ASTA. No. I shall take the steamer.

BORGHEIM. [Glancing at her.] We each take our own way, then?

ASTA. Yes.

[She sits and looks on while he hoists the flag half-mast high. When he has done he goes up to her.]

BORGHEIM. Miss Asta, you can't think how grieved I am about little Eyolf.

ASTA. [Looks up at him.] Yes, I am sure you feel it deeply.

BORGHEIM. And the feeling tortures me. For the fact is, grief is not much in my way.

ASTA. [Raising her eyes to the flag.] It will pass over in time, all of it. All our sorrow.

BORGHEIM. All? Do you believe that?

ASTA. Like a squall at sea. When once you have got far away from here, then

BORGHEIM. It will have to be very far away indeed.

ASTA. And then you have this great new road-work, too.

BORGHEIM. But no one to help me in it.

ASTA. Oh yes, surely you have.

BORGHEIM. [Shaking his head.] No one. No one to share the gladness with. For it is gladness that most needs sharing.

ASTA. Not the labour and trouble?

BORGHEIM. Pooh, that sort of thing one can always get through alone.

ASTA. But the gladness, that must be shared with some one, you think?

BORGHEIM. Yes; for if not, where would be the pleasure in being glad?

ASTA. Ah yes, perhaps there is something in that.

BORGHEIM. Oh, of course, for a certain time you can go on feeling glad in your own heart. But it won't do in the long run. No, it takes two to be glad.

ASTA. Always two? Never more? Never many?

BORGHEIM. Well, you see, then it becomes a quite different matter. Miss Asta, are you sure you can never make up your mind to share gladness and success and, and labour and trouble, with one, with one alone in all the world?

ASTA. I have tried it once.

BORGHEIM. Have you?

ASTA. Yes, all the time that my brother, that Alfred and I lived together.

BORGHEIM. Oh, with your brother, yes. But that is altogether different. That ought rather to be called peace than happiness, I should say.

ASTA. It was delightful, all the same.

BORGHEIM. There now, you see even that seemed to you delightful. But just think now, if he had not been your brother!

ASTA. [Makes a movement to rise, but remains sitting.] Then we should never have been together. For I was a child then and he wasn't much more.

BORGHEIM. [After a pause.] Was it so delightful that time?

ASTA. Oh yes, indeed it was.

BORGHEIM. Was there much that was really bright and happy in your life then?

ASTA. Oh yes, so much. You cannot think how much.

BORGHEIM. Tell me a little about it, Miss Asta.

ASTA. Oh, there are only trifles to tell.

BORGHEIM. Such as? Well?

ASTA. Such as the time when Alfred had passed his examination and had distinguished himself. And then, from time, to time, when he got a post in some school or other. Or when he would sit at home working at an article and would read it aloud to me. And then when it would appear in some magazine.

BORGHEIM. Yes, I can quite see that it must have been a peaceful, delightful life, a brother and sister sharing all their joys. [Shaking his head.] What I cannot understand is that your brother could ever give you up, Asta.

ASTA. [With suppressed emotion.] Alfred married, you know.

BORGHEIM. Was not that very hard for you?

ASTA. Yes, at first. It seemed as though I had utterly lost him all at once.

BORGHEIM. Well, luckily it was not so bad as that.

ASTA. No.

BORGHEIM. But, all the same how could he! Go and marry, I mean, when he could have kept you with him, alone!

ASTA. [Looking straight in front of her.] He was subject to the law of change, I suppose.

BORGHEIM. The law of change?

ASTA. So Alfred calls it.

BORGHEIM. Pooh, what a stupid law that must be! I don't believe a bit in that law.

ASTA. [Rising.] You may come to believe in it, in time.

BORGHEIM. Never in all my life! [Insistently.] But listen now, Miss Asta! Do be reasonable for once in a way, in this matter, I mean

ASTA. [Interrupting him.] Oh, no, no, don't let us begin upon that again!

BORGHEIM. [Continuing as before.] Yes, Asta, I can't possibly give you up so easily. Now your brother has everything as he wishes it. He can live his life quite contentedly without you. He doesn't require you at all. Then this, this, that at one blow has changed your whole position here

ASTA. [With a start.] What do you mean by that?

BORGHEIM. The loss of the child. What else should I mean?

ASTA. [Recovering her self-control.] Little Eyolf is gone, yes.

BORGHEIM. And what more does that leave you to do here? You have not the poor little boy to take care of now. You have no duties, no claims upon you of any sort.

ASTA. Oh, please, Mr. Borgheim, don't make it so hard for me.

BORGHEIM. I must; I should be mad if I did not try my uttermost. I shall be leaving town before very long, rind perhaps I shall have no opportunity of meeting you there. Perhaps I shall not see you again for a long, long time. And who knows what may happen in the meanwhile?

ASTA. [With a grave smile.] So you are afraid of the law of change, after all?

BORGHEIM. No, not in the least. [Laughing bitterly.] And there is nothing to be changed, either, not in you. I mean. For I can see you don't care much about me.

ASTA. You know very well that I do.

BORGHEIM. Perhaps, but not nearly enough. Not as I want you to. [More forcibly.] By Heaven, Asta, Miss Asta, I cannot tell you how strongly I feel that you are wrong in this! A little onward, perhaps, from to-day and to-morrow, all life's happiness may be awaiting us. And we must needs pass it by! Do you think we will not come to repent of it, Asta?

ASTA. [Quietly.] I don't know. I only know that they are not for us all these bright possibilities.

BORGHEIM. [Looks at her with self-control.] Then I must make my roads alone?

ASTA. [Warmly.] Oh, how I wish I could stand by you in it all! Help you in the labour, share the gladness with you

BORGHEIM. Would you, if you could?

ASTA. Yes, that I would.

BORGHEIM. But you cannot?

ASTA. [Looking down.] Would you be content to have only half of me?

BORGHEIM. No. You must be utterly and entirely mine.

ASTA. [Looks at him, and says quietly.] Then I cannot.

BORGHEIM. Good-bye then, Miss Asta.

[He is on the point of going. ALLMERS comes up from the left at the back. BORGHEIM stops.]

ALLMERS. [The moment he has reached the top of the steps, points, and says in a low voice.] Is Rita in there, in the summer-house?

BORGHEIM. No; there is no one here but Miss Asta.

[ALLMERS comes forward.]

ASTA. [Going towards him.] Shall I go down and look for her? Shall I get her to come up here?

ALLMERS. [With a negative gesture.] No, no, no, let it alone. [To BORGHEIM.] Is it you that have hoisted the flag?

BORGHEIM. Yes. Mrs. Allmers asked me to. That was what brought me up here.

ALLMERS. And you are going to start to-night?

BORGHEIM. Yes. To-night I go away in good earnest.

ALLMERS. [With a glance at ASTA.] And you have made sure of pleasant company, I daresay.

BORGHEIM. [Shaking his head.] I am going alone.

ALLMERS. [With surprise.] Alone!

BORGHEIM. Utterly alone.

ALLMERS. [Absently.] Indeed?

BORGHEIM. And I shall have to remain alone, too.

ALLMERS. There is something horrible in being alone. The thought of it runs like ice through my blood

ASTA. Oh, but, Alfred, you are not alone.

ALLMERS. There may be something horrible in that too, Asta.

ASTA. [Oppressed.] Oh, don't talk like that! Don't think like that!

ALLMERS. [Not listening to her.] But since you are not going with him? Since there is nothing to bind you? Why will you not remain out here with me and with Rita?

ASTA. [Uneasily.] No, no, I cannot. I must go back to town now.

ALLMERS. But only in to town, Asta. Do you hear!

ASTA. Yes.

ALLMERS. And you must promise me that you will soon come out again.

ASTA. [Quickly.] No, no, I dare not promise you that, for the present.

ALLMERS. Well as you will. We shall soon meet in town, then.

ASTA. [Imploringly.] But, Alfred, you must stay at home here with Rita now.

ALLMERS. [Without answering, turns to BORGHEIM.] You may find it a good thing, after all, that you have to take your journey alone.

BORGHEIM. [Annoyed.] Oh, how can you say such a thing?

ALLMERS. You see, you can never tell whom you might happen to meet afterwards, on the way.

ASTA. [Involuntarily.] Alfred!

ALLMERS. The right fellow-traveller, when it is too late, too late.

ASTA. [Softly, quivering.] Alfred! Alfred!

BORGHEIM. [Looking front one to the other.] What is the meaning of this? I don't understand

[RITA comes up from the left at the back.]

RITA. [Plaintively.] Oh, don't go away from me, all of you!

ASTA. [Going towards her.] You said you preferred to be alone.

RITA. Yes, but I dare not. It is getting so horribly dark. I seem to see great, open eyes fixed upon me!

ASTA. [Tenderly and sympathetically.] What if it were so, Rita? You ought not to be afraid of those eyes.

RITA. How can you say so! Not afraid!

ALLMERS. [Insistently.] Asta, I beg you, for Heaven's sake, remain here with Rita!

RITA. Yes! And with Alfred, too. Do! Do, Asta!

ASTA. [Struggling with herself.] Oh, I want to so much

RITA. Well, then, do it! For Alfred and I cannot go alone through the sorrow and heartache.

ALLMERS. [Darkly.] Say, rather, through the ranklings of remorse.

RITA. Oh, whatever you like to call it, we cannot bear it alone, we two. Oh, Asta, I beg and implore you! Stay here and help us! Take Eyolf's place for us

ASTA. [Shrinking.] Eyolf's

RITA. Yes, would you not have it so, Alfred?

ALLMERS. If she can and will.

RITA. You used to call her your little Eyolf. [Seizes her hand.] Henceforth you shall be our Eyolf, Asta! Eyolf, as you were before.

ALLMERS. [With concealed emotion.] Remain and share our life with us, Asta. With Rita. With me. With me, your brother!

ASTA. [With decision, snatches her hand away.] No. I cannot. [Turning.] Mr. Borgheim, what time does the steamer start?

BORGHEIM. Now, at once.

ASTA. Then I must go on board. Will you go with me?

BORGHEIM. [With a suppressed outburst of joy.] Will I? Yes, yes!

ASTA. Then come!

RITA. [Slowly.] Ah! That is how it is. Well, then, you cannot stay with us.

ASTA. [Throwing her arms round her neck.] Thanks for everything, Rita! (Goes up to ALLMERS and grasps his hand.) Alfred-good-bye! A thousand times, good-bye!

ALLMERS. [oftly and eagerly.] What is this, Asta? It seems as though you were taking flight.

ASTA. [In subdued anguish.] Yes, Alfred, I am taking flight.

ALLMERS. Flight, from me!

ASTA. [Whispering.] From you and from myself.

ALLMERS. [Shrinking back.] Ah!

[ASTA rushes down the steps at the back. BORGHEIM waves his hat and follows her. RITA leans against the entrance to the summer-house. ALLMERS goes, in strong inward emotion, up to the railing, and stands there gazing downwards. A pause.]

ALLMERS. [Turns, and says with hard-won composure.] There comes the steamer. Look, Rita.

RITA. I dare not look at it.

ALLMERS. You dare not?

RITA. No. For it has a red eye and a green one, too. Great, glowing eyes.

ALLMERS. Oh, those are only the lights, you know.

RITA. Henceforth they are eyes, for me. They stare and stare out of the darkness, and into the darkness.

ALLMERS. Now she is putting in to shore.

RITA. Where are they mooring her this evening, then?

ALLMERS. [Coming forward.] At the pier, as usual

RITA. [Drawing herself up.] How can they moor her there!

ALLMERS. They must.

RITA. But it was there that Eyolf! How can they moor her there!

ALLMERS. Yes, life is pitiless, Rita.

RITA. Men are heartless. They take no thought, whether for the living or for the dead.

ALLMERS. There you are right. Life goes its own way, just as if nothing in the world had happened.

RITA. [Gazing straight before her.] And nothing has happened, either. Not to others. Only to us two.

ALLMERS. [The pain re-awakening.] Yes, Rita, so it was to no purpose that you bore him in sorrow and anguish. For now he is gone again and has left no trace behind him.

RITA. Only the crutch was saved.

ALLMERS. [Angrily.] Be silent! Do not let me hear that word!

RITA. [Plaintively.] Oh, I cannot bear the thought that he is gone from us.

ALLMERS. [Coldly and bitterly.] You could very well do without him while he was with us. Half the day would often pass without your setting eyes on him.

RITA. Yes, for I knew that I could see him whenever I wanted to.

ALLMERS. Yes, that is how we have gone and squandered the short time we had with Little Eyolf.

RITA. [Listening, in dread.] Do you hear, Alfred! Now it is ringing again!

ALLMERS. [Looking over the fiord.] It is the steamer's bell that is ringing. She is just starting.

RITA. Oh, it's not that bell I mean. All day I have heard it ringing in my ears. Now it is ringing again!

ALLMERS. [Going up to her.] You are mistaken, Rita.

RITA. No, I hear it so plainly. It sounds like a knell. Slow. Slow. And always the same words.

ALLMERS. Words? What words?

RITA. [Nodding her head in the rhythm.] "The crútch is flóating. The crútch is flóating." Oh, surely you must hear it, too!

ALLMERS. [Shaking his head.] I hear nothing. And there is nothing to hear.

RITA. Oh, you may say what you will, I hear it so plainly.

ALLMERS. [Looking out over the railing.] Now they are on board, Rita. Now the steamer is on her way to the town.

RITA. Is it possible you do not hear it? "The crútch is flóating. The crútch is -"

ALLMERS. [Coming forward.] You shall not stand there listening to a sound that does not exist. I tell You, Asta and Borgheim are on board. They have started already. Asta is gone.

RITA. [Looks timidly at him.] Then I suppose you will soon be gone, too, Alfred?

ALLMERS. [Quickly.] What do you mean by that?

RITA. That you will follow your sister.

ALLMERS. Has Asta told you anything?

RITA. No. But you said yourself it was for Asta's sake that, that we came together.

ALLMERS. Yes, but you, you yourself, have bound me to you by our life together.

RITA. Oh, in your eyes I am not, I am not, entrancingly beautiful any more.

ALLMERS. The law of change may perhaps keep us together, none the less.

RITA. [Nodding slowly.] There is a change in me now, I feel the anguish of it.

ALLMERS. Anguish?

RITA. Yes, for change, too, is a sort of birth.

ALLMERS. It is or a resurrection. Transition to a higher life.

RITA. [Gazing sadly before her.] Yes, with the loss of all, all life's happiness.

ALLMERS. That loss is just the gain.

RITA. [Vehemently.] Oh, phrases! Good God, we are creatures of earth after all.

ALLMERS. But something akin to the sea and the heavens too, Rita.

RITA. You perhaps. Not I.

ALLMERS. Oh, yes, you too, more than you yourself suspect.

RITA. [Advancing a pace towards him.] Tell me, Alfred, could you think of taking up your work again?

ALLMERS. The work that you have hated so?

RITA. I am easier to please now. I am willing to share you with the book.

ALLMERS. Why?

RITA. Only to keep you here with me, to have you near me.

ALLMERS. Oh, it is so little I can do to help you, Rita.

RITA. But perhaps I could help you.

ALLMERS. With my book, do you mean?

RITA. No; but to live your life.

ALLMERS. [Shaking his head.] I seem to have no life to live.

RITA. Well then, to endure your life.

ALLMERS. [Darkly, looking away from her.] I think it would be best for both of us that we should part.

RITA. [Looking curiously at him.] Then where would you go? Perhaps to Asta, after all?

ALLMERS. No, never again to Asta.

RITA. Where then?

ALLMERS. Up into the solitudes.

RITA. Up among the mountains? Is that what you mean?

ALLMERS. Yes.

RITA. But all that is mere dreaming, Alfred! You could not live up there.

ALLMERS. And yet I feel myself drawn to them.

RITA. Why? Tell me!

ALLMERS. Sit down and I will tell you something.

RITA. Something that happened to you up there?

ALLMERS. Yes.

RITA. And that you never told Asta and me?

ALLMERS. Yes.

RITA. Oh, you are so silent about everything. You ought not to be.

ALLMERS. Sit down there and I will tell you about it.

RITA. Yes, yes, tell me!

[She sits on the bench beside the summer-house.]

ALLMERS. I was alone up there, in the heart of the great mountains. I came to a wide, dreary mountain lake; and that lake I had to cross. But I could not, for there was neither a boat nor any one there.

RITA. Well? And then?

ALLMERS. Then I went without any guidance into a side valley. I thought that by that way I could push on over the heights and between the peaks and then down again on the other side of the lake.

RITA. Oh, and you lost yourself, Alfred!

ALLMERS. Yes; I mistook the direction, for there was no path or track. And all day I went on and all the next night. And at last I thought I should never see the face of man again.

RITA. Not come home to us? Oh, then, I am sure your thoughts were with us here.

ALLMERS. No, they were not.

RITA. Not?

ALLMERS. No. It was so strange. Both you and Eyolf seemed to have drifted far, far away from me and Asta, too.

RITA. Then what did you think of?

ALLMERS. I did not think. I dragged myself along among the precipices and revelled in the peace and luxury of death.

RITA. [Springing up.] Oh, don't speak in that way of that horror!

ALLMERS. I did not feel it so. I had no fear. Here went death and I, it seemed to me, like two good fellow-travellers. It all seemed so natural, so simple, I thought. In my family, we don't live to be old

RITA. Oh, don't say such things, Alfred! You see you came safely out of it, after all.

ALLMERS. Yes; all of a sudden, I found myself where I wanted to be, on the other side of the lake.

RITA. It must have been a night of terror for you, Alfred. But now that it is over, you will not admit it to yourself.

ALLMERS. That night sealed my resolution. And it was then that I turned about and came straight homewards. To Eyolf.

RITA. [Softly.] Too late.

ALLMERS. Yes. And then when my fellow-traveller came and took him, then I felt the horror of it; of it all; of all that, in spite of everything, we dare not tear ourselves away from. So earthbound are we, both of us, Rita.

RITA. [With a gleam of joy.] Yes, you are, too, are you not! [Coming close to him.] Oh, let us live our life together as long as we can!

ALLMERS. [Shrugging his shoulders.] Live our life, yes! And have nothing to fill life with. An empty void on all sides, wherever I look.

RITA. [In fear.] Oh, sooner or later you will go away from me, Alfred! I feel it! I can see it in your face! You will go away from me.

ALLMERS. With my fellow-traveller, do you mean?

RITA. No, I mean worse than that. Of your own free will, you will leave me, for you think it's only here, with me, that you have nothing to live for. Is not that what is in your thoughts?

ALLMERS. [Looking steadfastly at her.] What if it were?

[A disturbance, and the noise of angry, quarrelling voices is heard from down below, in the distance. ALLMERS goes to the railing.]

RITA. What is that? [With an outburst.] Oh, you'll see, they have found him!

ALLMERS. He will never be found.

RITA. But what is it then?

ALLMERS. [Coming forward.] Only fighting, as usual.

RITA. Down on the beach?

ALLMERS. Yes. The whole village down there ought to be swept away. Now the men have come home drunk, as they always are. They are beating the children, do you hear the boys crying! The women are shrieking for help for them

RITA. Should we not get some one to go down and help them?

ALLMERS. [Harshly and angrily.] Help them, who did not help Eyolf! Let them go as they let Eyolf go.

RITA. Oh, you must not talk like that, Alfred! Nor think like that!

ALLMERS. I cannot think otherwise. All the old hovels ought to be torn down.

RITA. And then what is to become of all the poor people?

ALLMERS. They must go somewhere else.

RITA. And the children, too?

ALLMERS. Does it make much difference where they go to the dogs?

RITA. [Quietly and reproachfully.] You are forcing yourself into this harshness, Alfred.

ALLMERS. [Vehemently.] I have a right to be harsh now! It is my duty.

RITA. Your duty?

ALLMERS. My duty to Eyolf. He must not lie unavenged. Once for all, Rita, it is as I tell you! Think it over! Have the whole place down there razed to the ground when I am gone.

RITA. [Looks intently at him.] When you are gone?

ALLMERS. Yes. For that will at least give you something to fill your life with and something you must have.

RITA. [Firmly and decidedly.] There you are right, I must. But can you guess what I will set about when you are gone?

ALLMERS. Well, what?

RITA. [Slowly and with resolution.] As soon as you are gone from me, I will go down to the beach, and bring all the poor neglected children home with me. All the mischievous boys

ALLMERS. What will you do with them here?

RITA. I will take them to my heart.

ALLMERS. You!

RITA. Yes, I will. From the day you leave me, they shall all be here, all of them, as if they were mine.

ALLMERS. [Shocked.] In our little Eyolf's place!

RITA. Yes, in our little Eyolf's place. They shall live in Eyolf's rooms. They shall read his books. They shall play with his toys. They shall take it in turns to sit in his chair at table.

ALLMERS. But this is sheer madness in you! I do not know a creature in the world that is less fitted than you for anything of that sort.

RITA. Then I shall have to educate myself for it; to train myself; to discipline myself.

ALLMERS. If you are really in earnest about this, about all you say, then there must indeed be a change in you.

RITA. Yes, there is, Alfred and for that I have you to thank. You have made an empty place within me; and I must try to fill it up with something with something that is a little like love.

ALLMERS. [Stands for a moment lost in thought; then looks at her.] The truth is, we have not done much for the poor people down there.

RITA. We have done nothing for them.

ALLMERS. Scarcely even thought of them.

RITA. Never thought of them in sympathy.

ALLMERS. We, who had "the gold, and the green forests"

RITA. Our hands were closed to them. And our hearts too.

ALLMERS. [Nods.] Then it was perhaps natural enough, after all, that they should not risk their lives to save little Eyolf.

RITA. [Softly.] Think, Alfred! Are you so certain that, that we would have risked ours?

ALLMERS. [With an uneasy gesture of repulsion.] You must never doubt that.

RITA. Oh, we are children of earth.

ALLMERS. What do you really think you can do with all these neglected children?

RITA. I suppose I must try if I cannot lighten and, and ennoble their lot in life.

ALLMERS. If you can do that, then Eyolf was not born in vain.

RITA. Nor taken from us in vain, either.

ALLMERS. [Looking steadfastly at her.] Be quite clear about one thing, Rita, it is not love that is driving you to this.

RITA. No, it is not, at any rate, not yet.

ALLMERS. Well, then what is it?

RITA. [Half-evasively.] You have so often talked to Asta of human responsibility

ALLMERS. Of the book that you hated.

RITA. I hate that book still. But I used to sit and listen to what you told her. And now I will try to continue it in my own way.

ALLMERS. [Shaking his head.] It is not for the sake of that unfinished book

RITA. No, I have another reason as well.

ALLMERS. What is that?

RITA. [Softly, with a melancholy smile.] I want to make my peace with the great, open eyes, you see.

ALLMERS. [Struck, fixing his eyes upon her.] Perhaps, I could join you in that? And help you, Rita?

RITA. Would you?

ALLMERS. Yes, if I were only sure I could.

RITA. [Hesitatingly.] But then you would have to remain here.

ALLMERS. [Softly.] Let us try if it could not be so.

RITA. [Almost inaudibly.] Yes, let us, Alfred.

[Both are silent. Then ALLMERS goes up to the flagstaff and hoists the flag to the top. RITA stands beside the summer-house and looks at him in silence.]

ALLMERS. [Coming forward again.] We have a heavy day of work before us, Rita.

RITA. You will see that now and then a Sabbath peace will descend on us.

ALLMERS. [Quietly, with emotion.] Then, perhaps, we shall know that the spirits are with us.

RITA. [Whispering.] The spirits?

ALLMERS. [As before.] Yes, they will perhaps be around us, those whom we have lost.

RITA. [Nods slowly.] Our little Eyolf. And your big Eyolf, too.

ALLMERS. [Gazing straight before him.] Now and then, perhaps, we may still, on the way through life, have a little, passing glimpse of them.

RITA. When, shall we look for them, Alfred?

ALLMERS. [Fixing his eyes upon her.] Upwards.

RITA. [Nods in approval.] Yes, yes, upwards.

ALLMERS. Upwards towards the peaks. Towards the stars. And towards the great silence.

RITA. [Giving him her hand.] Thanks!

THE END.

John Gabriel Borkman, By Henrik Ibsen

John Gabriel Borkman

PERSONS.

JOHN GABRIEL BORKMAN, formerly Managing Director of a Bank.

MRS. GUNHILD BORKMAN, his wife.

ERHART BORKMAN, their son, a student.

MISS ELLA RENTHEIM, Mrs. Borkman's twin sister.

MRS. FANNY WILTON.

VILHELM FOLDAL, subordinate clerk in a Government office.

FRIDA FOLDAL, his daughter.

MRS. BORKMAN'S MAID.

The action passes one winter evening, at the Manorhouse of the Rentheim family, in the neighbourhood of Christiania.

ACT FIRST

MRS. BORKMAN's drawing-room, furnished with old-fashioned, faded splendour. At the back, an open sliding-door leads into a garden-room, with windows and a glass door. Through it a view over the garden; twilight with driving snow. On the right, a door leading from the hall. Further forward, a large old-fashioned iron stove, with the fire lighted. On the left, towards the back, a single smaller door. In front, on the same side, a window, covered with thick curtains. Between the window and the door a horsehair sofa, with a table in front of it covered with a cloth. On the table, a lighted lamp with a shade. Beside the stove a high-backed armchair.

MRS. GUNHILD BORKMAN sits on the sofa, crocheting. She is an elderly lady, of cold, distinguished appearance, with stiff carriage and immobile features. Her abundant hair is very grey. Delicate transparent hands. Dressed in a gown of heavy dark silk, which has originally been handsome, but is now somewhat worn and shabby. A woollen shawl over her shoulders.

She sits for a time erect and immovable at her crochet. Then the bells of a passing sledge are heard.

MRS. BORKMAN. [Listens; her eyes sparkle with gladness and she involuntarily whispers]. Erhart! At last!

[She rises and draws the curtain a little aside to look out. Appears disappointed, and sits down to her work again, on the sofa. Presently THE MAID enters from the hall with a visiting card on a small tray.

MRS. BORKMAN. [Quickly.] Has Mr. Erhart come after all?

THE MAID. No, ma'am. But there's a lady

MRS. BORKMAN. [Laying aside her crochet.] Oh, Mrs. Wilton, I suppose

THE MAID. [Approaching.] No, it's a strange lady

MRS. BORKMAN. [Taking the card.] Let me see [Reads it; rises hastily and looks intently at the girl.] Are you sure this is for me?

THE MAID. Yes, I understand it was for you, ma'am.

MRS. BORKMAN. Did she say she wanted to see Mrs. Borkman?

THE MAID. Yes, she did.

MRS. BORKMAN. [Shortly, resolutely.] Good. Then say I am at home.

[THE MAID opens the door for the strange lady and goes out. MISS ELLA RENTHEIM enters. She resembles her sister; but her face has rather a suffering than a hard expression. It still shows signs of great beauty, combined with strong character. She has a great deal of hair, which is drawn back from the forehead in natural ripples, and is snow-white. She is dressed in black velvet, with a hat and a fur-lined cloak of the same material.

[The two sisters stand silent for a time, and look searchingly at each other. Each is evidently waiting for the other to speak first.

ELLA RENTHEIM. [Who has remained near the door.] You are surprised to see me, Gunhild.

MRS. BORKMAN. [Standing erect and immovable between the sofa and the table, resting her finger-tips upon the cloth.] Have you not made a mistake? The bailiff lives in the side wing, you know.

ELLA RENTHEIM. It is not the bailiff I want to see to-day.

MRS. BORKMAN. Is it me you want, then?

ELLA RENTHEIM. Yes. I have a few words to say to you.

MRS. BORKMAN. [Coming forward into the middle of the room.] Well, then sit down.

ELLA RENTHEIM. Thank you. I can quite well stand for the present.

MRS. BORKMAN. Just as you please. But at least loosen your cloak.

ELLA RENTHEIM. [Unbuttoning her cloak.] Yes, it is very warm here.

MRS. BORKMAN. I am always cold.

ELLA RENTHEIM. [Stands looking at her for a time with her arms resting on the back of the armchair.] Well, Gunhild, it is nearly eight years now since we saw each other last.

MRS. BORKMAN. [Coldly.] Since last we spoke to each other at any rate.

ELLA RENTHEIM. True, since we spoke to each other. I daresay you have seen me now and again when I came on my yearly visit to the bailiff.

MRS. BORKMAN. Once or twice, I have.

ELLA RENTHEIM. I have caught one or two glimpses of you, too, there, at the window.

MRS. BORKMAN. You must have seen me through the curtains then. You have good eyes. [Harshly and cuttingly.] But the last time we spoke to each other it was here in this room

ELLA RENTHEIM. [Trying to stop her.] Yes, yes; I know, Gunhild!

MRS. BORKMAN. - the week before he, before he was let out.

ELLA RENTHEIM. [Moving towards the back.] O, don't speak about that.

MRS. BORKMAN. [Firmly, but in a low voice.] It was the week before he was set at liberty.

ELLA RENTHEIM. [Coming down.] Oh yes, yes, yes! I shall never forget that time! But it is too terrible to think of! Only to recall it for the moment, oh!

MRS. BORKMAN. [Gloomily.] And yet one's thoughts can never get away from it. [Vehemently; clenching her hands together.] No, I can't understand how such a thing, how anything so horrible can come upon one single family! And then that it should be our family! So old a family as ours! Think of its choosing us out!

ELLA RENTHEIM. Oh, Gunhild, there were many, many families besides ours that that blow fell upon.

MRS. BORKMAN. Oh yes; but those others don't trouble me very much. For in their case it was only a matter of a little money or some papers. But for us! For me! And then for Erhart! My little boy, as he then was! [In rising excitement.] The shame that fell upon us two innocent ones! The dishonour! The hateful, terrible dishonour! And then the utter ruin too!

ELLA RENTHEIM. [Cautiously.] Tell me, Gunhild, how does he bear it?

MRS. BORKMAN. Erhart, do you mean?

ELLA RENTHEIM. No, he himself. How does he bear it?

MRS. BORKMAN. [Scornfully.] Do you think I ever ask about that?

ELLA RENTHEIM. Ask? Surely you do not require to ask

MRS. BORKMAN. [Looks at her in surprise.] You don't suppose I ever have anything to do with him? That I ever meet him? That I see anything of him?

ELLA RENTHEIM. Not even that!

MRS. BORKMAN. [As before.] The man was in gaol, in gaol for five years! [Covers her face with her hands.] Oh, the crushing shame of it! [With increased vehemence.] And then to think of all that the name of John Gabriel Borkman used to mean! No, no, no, I can never see him again! Never!

ELLA RENTHEIM. [Looks at her for a while.] You have a hard heart, Gunhild.

MRS. BORKMAN. Towards him, yes.

ELLA RENTHEIM. After all, he is your husband.

MRS. BORKMAN. Did he not say in court that it was I who began his ruin? That I spent money so recklessly?

ELLA RENTHEIM. [Tentatively.] But is there not some truth in that?

MRS. BORKMAN. Why, it was he himself that made me do it! He insisted on our living in such an absurdly lavish style

ELLA RENTHEIM. Yes, I know. But that is just where you should have restrained him; and apparently you didn't.

MRS. BORKMAN. How was I to know that it was not his own money he gave me to squander? And that he himself used to squander, too, ten times more than I did!

ELLA RENTHEIM. [Quietly.] Well, I daresay his position forced him to do that, to some extent at any rate.

MRS. BORKMAN. [Scornfully.] Yes, it was always the same story, we were to "cut a figure." And he did "cut a figure" to some purpose! He used to drive about with a four-in-hand as if he were a king. And he had people bowing and scraping to him just as to a king. [With a laugh.] And they always called him by his Christian names, all the country over, as if he had been the king himself. "John Gabriel," "John Gabriel," "John Gabriel." Every one knew what a great man "John Gabriel" was!

ELLA RENTHEIM. [Warmly and emphatically.] He was a great man then.

MRS. BORKMAN. Yes, to all appearance. But he never breathed a single word to me as to his real position, never gave a hint as to where he got his means from.

ELLA RENTHEIM. No, no; and other people did not dream of it either.

MRS. BORKMAN. I don't care about the other people. But it was his duty to tell me the truth. And that he never did! He kept on lying to me, lying abominably

ELLA RENTHEIM. [Interrupting.] Surely not, Gunhild. He kept things back perhaps, but I am sure he did not lie.

MRS. BORKMAN. Well, well; call it what you please; it makes no difference. And then it all fell to pieces, the whole thing.

ELLA RENTHEIM. [To herself.] Yes, everything fell to pieces, for him, and for others.

MRS. BORKMAN. [Drawing herself up menacingly.] But I tell you this, Ella, I do not give in yet! I shall redeem myself yet, you may make up your mind to that!

ELLA RENTHEIM. [Eagerly.] Redeem yourself! What do you mean by that?

MRS. BORKMAN. Redeem my name, and honour, and fortune! Redeem my ruined life, that is what I mean! I have some one in reserve, let me tell you, one who will wash away every stain that he has left.

ELLA RENTHEIM. Gunhild! Gunhild!

MRS. BORKMAN. [With rising excitement.] There is an avenger living, I tell you! One who will make up to me for all his father's sins!

ELLA RENTHEIM. Erhart you mean.

MRS. BORKMAN. Yes, Erhart, my own boy! He will redeem the family, the house, the name. All that can be redeemed. And perhaps more besides.

ELLA RENTHEIM. And how do you think that is to be done?

MRS. BORKMAN. It must be done as best it can; I don't know how. But I know that it must and shall be done. [Looks searchingly at her.] Come now, Ella; isn't that really what you have had in mind too, ever since he was a child?

ELLA RENTHEIM. No, I can't exactly say that.

MRS. BORKMAN. No? Then why did you take charge of him when the storm broke upon, upon this house?

ELLA RENTHEIM. You could not look after him yourself at that time, Gunhild.

MRS. BORKMAN. No, no, I could not. And his father, he had a valid enough excuse, while he was there, in safe keeping

ELLA RENTHEIM. [Indignant.] Oh, how can you say such things! You!

MRS. BORKMAN. [With a venomous expression.] And how could you make up your mind to take charge of the child of a, a John Gabriel! Just as if he had been your own? To take the child away from me, home with you, and keep him there year after year, until the boy was nearly grown up. [Looking suspiciously at her.] What was your real reason, Ella? Why did you keep him with you?

ELLA RENTHEIM. I came to love him so dearly

MRS. BORKMAN. More than I, his mother?

ELLA RENTHEIM. [Evasively.] I don't know about that. And then, you know, Erhart was rather delicate as a child

MRS. BORKMAN. Erhart, delicate!

ELLA RENTHEIM. Yes, I thought so, at that time at any rate. And you know the air of the west coast is so much milder than here.

MRS. BORKMAN. [Smiling bitterly.] H'm, is it indeed? [Breaking off.] Yes, it is true you have done a great deal for Erhart. [With a change of tone.] Well, of course, you could afford it. [Smiling.] You were so lucky, Ella; you managed to save all your money.

ELLA RENTHEIM. [Hurt.] I did not manage anything about it, I assure you. I had no idea until long, long afterwards, that the securities belonging to me, that they had been left untouched.

MRS. BORKMAN. Well, well; I don't understand anything about these things! I only say you were lucky. [Looking inquiringly at her.] But when you, of your own accord, undertook to educate Erhart for me, what was your motive in that?

ELLA RENTHEIM. [Looking at her.] My motive?

MRS. BORKMAN. Yes, some motive you must have had. What did you want to do with him? To make of him, I mean?

ELLA RENTHEIM. [Slowly.] I wanted to smooth the way for Erhart to happiness in life.

MRS. BORKMAN. [Contemptuously.] Pooh, people situated as we are have something else than happiness to think of.

ELLA RENTHEIM. What, then?

MRS. BORKMAN. [Looking steadily and earnestly at her.] Erhart has in the first place to make so brilliant a position for himself, that no trace shall be left of the shadow his father has cast upon my name and my son's.

ELLA RENTHEIM. [Searchingly.] Tell me, Gunhild, is this what Erhart himself demands of his life?

MRS. BORKMAN. [Slightly taken aback.] Yes, I should hope so!

ELLA RENTHEIM. Is it not rather what you demand of him?

MRS. BORKMAN. [Curtly.] Erhart and I always make the same demands upon ourselves.

ELLA RENTHEIM. [Sadly and slowly.] You are so very certain of your boy, then, Gunhild?

MRS. BORKMAN. [With veiled triumph.] Yes, that I am, thank Heaven. You may be sure of that!

ELLA RENTHEIM. Then I should think in reality you must be happy after all; in spite of all the rest.

MRS. BORKMAN. So I am, so far as that goes. But then, every moment, all the rest comes rushing in upon me like a storm.

ELLA RENTHEIM. [With a change of tone.] Tell me, you may as well tell me at once, for that is really what I have come for

MRS. BORKMAN. What?

ELLA RENTHEIM. Something I felt I must talk to you about. Tell me, Erhart does not live out here with, with you others?

MRS. BORKMAN. [Harshly.] Erhart cannot live out here with me. He has to live in town

ELLA RENTHEIM. So he wrote to me.

MRS. BORKMAN. He must, for the sake of his studies. But he comes out to me for a little while every evening.

ELLA RENTHEIM. Well, may I see him then? May I speak to him at once?

MRS. BORKMAN. He has not come yet; but I expect him every moment.

ELLA RENTHEIM. Why, Gunhild, surely he must have come. I can hear his footsteps overhead.

MRS. BORKMAN. [With a rapid upward glance.] Up in the long gallery?

ELLA RENTHEIM. Yes. I have heard him walking up and down there ever since I came.

MRS. BORKMAN. [Looking away from her.] That is not Erhart, Ella.

ELLA RENTHEIM. [Surprised.] Not Erhart? [Divining.] Who is it then?

MRS. BORKMAN. It is he.

ELLA RENTHEIM. [Softly, with suppressed pain.] Borkman? John Gabriel Borkman?

MRS. BORKMAN. He walks up and down like that, backwards and forwards, from morning to night, day out and day in.

ELLA RENTHEIM. I have heard something of this

MRS. BORKMAN. I daresay. People find plenty to say about us, no doubt.

ELLA RENTHEIM. Erhart has spoken of it in his letters. He said that his father generally remained by himself, up there, and you alone down here.

MRS. BORKMAN. Yes; that is how it has been, Ella, ever since they let him out, and sent him home to me. All these long eight years.

ELLA RENTHEIM. I never believed it could really be so. It seemed impossible!

MRS. BORKMAN. [Nods.] It is so; and it can never be otherwise.

ELLA RENTHEIM. [Looking at her.] This must be a terrible life, Gunhild.

MRS. BORKMAN. Worse than terrible, almost unendurable.

ELLA RENTHEIM. Yes, it must be.

MRS. BORKMAN. Always to hear his footsteps up there, from early morning till far into the night. And everything sounds so clear in this house!

ELLA RENTHEIM. Yes, it is strange how clear the sound is.

MRS. BORKMAN. I often feel as if I had a sick wolf pacing his cage up there in the gallery, right over my head. [Listens and whispers.] Hark! Do you hear! Backwards and forwards, up and down, goes the wolf.

ELLA RENTHEIM. [Tentatively.] Is no change possible, Gunhild?

MRS. BORKMAN. [With a gesture of repulsion.] He has never made any movement towards a change.

ELLA RENTHEIM. Could you not make the first movement, then?

MRS. BORKMAN. [Indignantly.] I! After all the wrong he has done me! No thank you! Rather let the wolf go on prowling up there.

ELLA RENTHEIM. This room is too hot for me. You must let me take off my things after all.

MRS. BORKMAN. Yes, I asked you to.

[ELLA RENTHEIM takes off her hat and cloak and lays them on a chair beside the door leading to the hall.

ELLA RENTHEIM. Do you never happen to meet him, away from home?

MRS. BORKMAN. [With a bitter laugh.] In society, do you mean?

ELLA RENTHEIM. I mean, when he goes out walking. In the woods, or

MRS. BORKMAN. He never goes out.

ELLA RENTHEIM. Not even in the twilight?

MRS. BORKMAN. Never.

ELLA RENTHEIM. [With emotion.] He cannot bring himself to go out?

MRS. BORKMAN. I suppose not. He has his great cloak and his hat hanging in the cupboard, the cupboard in the hall, you know

ELLA RENTHEIM. [To herself.] The cupboard we used to hide in when we were little.

MRS. BORKMAN. [Nods.] And now and then, late in the evening, I can hear him come down as though to go out. But he always stops when he is halfway downstairs, and turns back, straight back to the gallery.

ELLA RENTHEIM. [Quietly.] Do none of his old friends ever come up to see him?

MRS. BORKMAN. He has no old friends.

ELLA RENTHEIM. He had so many, once.

MRS. BORKMAN. H'm! He took the best possible way to get rid of them. He was a dear friend to his friends, was John Gabriel.

ELLA RENTHEIM. Oh, yes, that is true, Gunhild.

MRS. BORKMAN. [Vehemently.] All the same, I call it mean, petty, base, contemptible of them, to think so much of the paltry losses they may have suffered through him. They were only money losses, nothing more.

ELLA RENTHEIM. [Not answering her.] So he lives up there quite alone. Absolutely by himself.

MRS. BORKMAN. Yes, practically so. They tell me an old clerk or copyist or something comes out to see him now and then.

ELLA RENTHEIM. Ah, indeed; no doubt it is a man called Foldal. I know they were friends as young men.

MRS. BORKMAN. Yes, I believe they were. But I know nothing about him. He was quite outside our circle, when we had a circle

ELLA RENTHEIM. So he comes out to see Borkman now?

MRS. BORKMAN. Yes, he condescends to. But of course he only comes when it is dark.

ELLA RENTHEIM. This Foldal he was one of those that suffered when the bank failed?

MRS. BORKMAN. [Carelessly.] Yes, I believe I heard he had lost some money. But no doubt it was something quite trifling.

ELLA RENTHEIM. [With slight emphasis.] It was all he possessed.

MRS. BORKMAN. [Smiling.] Oh, well; what he possessed must have been little enough, nothing to speak of.

ELLA RENTHEIM. And he did not speak of it, Foldal I mean, during the investigation.

MRS. BORKMAN. At all events, I can assure you Erhart has made ample amends for any little loss he may have suffered.

ELLA RENTHEIM. [With surprise.] Erhart! How can Erhart have done that?

MRS. BORKMAN. He has taken an interest in Foldal's youngest daughter. He has taught her things, and put her in the way of getting employment, and some day providing for herself. I am sure that is a great deal more than her father could ever have done for her.

ELLA RENTHEIM. Yes, I daresay her father can't afford to do much.

MRS. BORKMAN. And then Erhart has arranged for her to have lessons in music. She has made such progress already that she can come up to, to him in the gallery, and play to him.

ELLA RENTHEIM. So he is still fond of music?

MRS. BORKMAN. Oh yes, I suppose he is. Of course he has the piano you sent out here when he was expected back

ELLA RENTHEIM. And she plays to him on it?

MRS. BORKMAN. Yes, now and then, in the evenings. That is Erhart's doing, too.

ELLA RENTHEIM. Has the poor girl to come all the long way out here, and then back to town again?

MRS. BORKMAN. No, she doesn't need to. Erhart has arranged for her to stay with a lady who lives near us, a Mrs. Wilton

ELLA RENTHEIM. [With interest.] Mrs. Wilton?

MRS. BORKMAN. A very rich woman. You don't know her.

ELLA RENTHEIM. I have heard her name. Mrs. Fanny Wilton, is it not?

MRS. BORKMAN. Yes, quite right.

ELLA RENTHEIM. Erhart has mentioned her several times. Does she live out here now?

MRS. BORKMAN. Yes, she has taken a villa here; she moved out from town some time ago.

ELLA RENTHEIM. [With a slight hesitation.] They say she is divorced from her husband.

MRS. BORKMAN. Her husband has been dead for several years.

ELLA RENTHEIM. Yes, but they were divorced. He got a divorce.

MRS. BORKMAN. He deserted her, that is what he did. I am sure the fault wasn't hers.

ELLA RENTHEIM. Do you know her at all intimately, Gunhild?

MRS. BORKMAN. Oh yes, pretty well. She lives close by here; and she looks in every now and then.

ELLA RENTHEIM. And do you like her?

MRS. BORKMAN. She is unusually intelligent; remarkably clear in her judgments.

ELLA RENTHEIM. In her judgments of people, do you mean?

MRS. BORKMAN. Yes, principally of people. She has made quite a study of Erhart; looked deep into his character, into his soul. And the result is she idolises him, as she could not help doing.

ELLA RENTHEIM. [With a touch of finesse.] Then perhaps she knows Erhart still better than she knows you?

MRS. BORKMAN. Yes, Erhart saw a good deal of her in town, before she came out here.

ELLA RENTHEIM. [Without thinking.] And in spite of that she moved out of town?

MRS. BORKMAN. [Taken aback, looking keenly at her.] In spite of that! What do you mean?

ELLA RENTHEIM. [Evasively.] Oh, nothing particular.

MRS. BORKMAN. You said it strangely, you did mean something by it, Ella!

ELLA RENTHEIM. [Looking her straight in the eyes.] Yes, that is true, Gunhild! I did mean something by it.

MRS. BORKMAN. Well, then, say it right out.

ELLA RENTHEIM. First let me tell you, I think I too have a certain claim upon Erhart. Do you think I haven't?

MRS. BORKMAN. [Glancing round the room.] No doubt, after all the money you have spent upon him.

ELLA RENTHEIM. Oh, not on that account, Gunhild. But because I love him.

MRS. BORKMAN. [Smiling scornfully.] Love my son? Is it possible? You? In spite of everything?

ELLA RENTHEIM. Yes, it is possible, in spite of everything. And it is true. I love Erhart as much as I can love any one, now, at my time of life.

MRS. BORKMAN. Well, well, suppose you do: what then?

ELLA RENTHEIM. Why, then, I am troubled as soon as I see anything threatening him.

MRS. BORKMAN. Threatening Erhart! Why, what should threaten him? Or who?

ELLA RENTHEIM. You in the first place, in your way.

MRS. BORKMAN. [Vehemently.] I!

ELLA RENTHEIM. And then this Mrs. Wilton, too, I am afraid.

MRS. BORKMAN. [Looks at her for a moment in speechless surprise.] And you think such things of Erhart! Of my own boy! He, who has his great mission to fulfil!

ELLA RENTHEIM. [Lightly.] Oh, his mission!

MRS. BORKMAN. [Indignantly.] How dare you say that so scornfully?

ELLA RENTHEIM. Do you think a young man of Erhart's age, full of health and spirits, do you think he is going to sacrifice himself for, for such a thing as a "mission"?

MRS. BORKMAN. [Firmly and emphatically.] Erhart will! I know he will.

ELLA RENTHEIM. [Shaking her head.] You neither know it nor believe it, Gunhild.

MRS. BORKMAN. I don't believe it!

ELLA RENTHEIM. It is only a dream that you cherish. For if you hadn't that to cling to, you feel that you would utterly despair.

MRS. BORKMAN. Yes, indeed I should despair. [Vehemently.] And I daresay that is what you would like to see, Ella!

ELLA RENTHEIM. [With head erect.] Yes, I would rather see that than see you "redeem" yourself at Erhart's expense.

MRS. BORKMAN. [Threateningly.] You want to come between us? Between mother and son? You?

ELLA RENTHEIM. I want to free him from your power, your will, your despotism.

MRS. BORKMAN. [Triumphantly.] You are too late! You had him in your nets all these years until he was fifteen. But now I have won him again, you see!

ELLA RENTHEIM. Then I will win him back from you! [Hoarsely, half whispering.] We two have fought a life-and-death battle before, Gunhild, for a man's soul!

MRS. BORKMAN. [Looking at her in triumph.] Yes, and I won the victory.

ELLA RENTHEIM. [With a smile of scorn.] Do you still think that victory was worth the winning?

MRS. BORKMAN. [Darkly.] No; Heaven knows you are right there.

ELLA RENTHEIM. You need look for no victory worth the winning this time either.

MRS. BORKMAN. Not when I am fighting to preserve a mother's power over my son!

ELLA RENTHEIM. No; for it is only power over him that you want.

MRS. BORKMAN. And you?

ELLA RENTHEIM. [Warmly.] I want his affection, his soul, his whole heart!

MRS. BORKMAN. [With an outburst.] That you shall never have in this world!

ELLA RENTHEIM. [Looking at her.] You have seen to that?

MRS. BORKMAN. [Smiling.] Yes, I have taken that liberty. Could you not see that in his letters?

ELLA RENTHEIM. [Nods slowly.] Yes. I could see you, the whole of you, in his letters of late.

MRS. BORKMAN. [Gallingly.] I have made the best use of these eight years. I have had him under my own eye, you see.

ELLA RENTHEIM. [Controlling herself.] What have you said to Erhart about me? Is it the sort of thing you can tell me?

MRS. BORKMAN. Oh yes, I can tell you well enough.

ELLA RENTHEIM. Then please do.

MRS. BORKMAN. I have only told him the truth.

ELLA RENTHEIM. Well?

MRS. BORKMAN. I have impressed upon him, every day of his life, that he must never forget that it is you we have to thank for being able to live as we do, for being able to live at all.

ELLA RENTHEIM. Is that all?

MRS. BORKMAN. Oh, that is the sort of thing that rankles; I feel that in my own heart.

ELLA RENTHEIM. But that is very much what Erhart knew already.

MRS. BORKMAN. When he came home to me, he imagined that you did it all out of goodness of heart. [Looks malignly at her.] Now he does not believe that any longer, Ella.

ELLA RENTHEIM. Then what does he believe now?

MRS. BORKMAN. He believes what is the truth. I asked him how he accounted for the fact that Aunt Ella never came here to visit us

ELLA RENTHEIM. [Interrupting.] He knew my reasons already!

MRS. BORKMAN. He knows them better now. You had got him to believe that it was to spare me and, and him up there in gallery

ELLA RENTHEIM. And so it was.

MRS. BORKMAN. Erhart does not believe that for a moment, now.

ELLA RENTHEIM. What have you put in his head?

MRS. BORKMAN. He thinks, what is the truth, that you are ashamed of us, that you despise us. And do you pretend that you don't? Were you not once planning to take him quite away from me? Think, Ella; you cannot have forgotten.

ELLA RENTHEIM. [With a gesture of negation.] That was at the height of the scandal, when the case was before the courts. I have no such designs now.

MRS. BORKMAN. And it would not matter if you had. For in that case what would become of his mission? No, thank you. It is me that Erhart needs not you. And therefore he is as good as dead to you and you to him.

ELLA RENTHEIM. [Coldly, with resolution.] We shall see. For now I shall remain out here.

MRS. BORKMAN. [Stares at her.] Here? In this house?

ELLA RENTHEIM. Yes, here.

MRS. BORKMAN. Here with us? Remain all night?

ELLA RENTHEIM. I shall remain here all the rest of my days if need be.

MRS. BORKMAN. [Collecting herself.] Very well, Ella; the house is yours

ELLA RENTHEIM. Oh, nonsense

MRS. BORKMAN. Everything is yours. The chair I am sitting in is yours. The bed I lie and toss in at night belongs to you. The food we eat comes to us from you.

ELLA RENTHEIM. It can't be arranged otherwise, you know. Borkman can hold no property of his own; for some one would at once come and take it from him.

MRS. BORKMAN. Yes, I know. We must be content to live upon your pity and charity.

ELLA RENTHEIM. [Coldly.] I cannot prevent you from looking at it in that light, Gunhild.

MRS. BORKMAN. No, you cannot. When do you want us to move out?

ELLA RENTHEIM. [Looking at her.] Move out?

MRS. BORKMAN. [In great excitement.] Yes; you don't imagine that I will go on living under the same roof with you! I tell you, I would rather go to the workhouse or tramp the roads!

ELLA RENTHEIM. Good. Then let me take Erhart with me

MRS. BORKMAN. Erhart? My own son? My child?

ELLA RENTHEIM. Yes; for then I would go straight home again.

MRS. BORKMAN. [After reflecting a moment, firmly.] Erhart himself shall choose between us.

ELLA RENTHEIM. [Looking doubtfully and hesitatingly at her.] He choose? Dare you risk that, Gunhild?

MRS. BORKMAN. [With a hard laugh.] Dare I? Let my boy choose between his mother and you? Yes, indeed I dare!

ELLA RENTHEIM. [Listening.] Is there some one coming? I thought I heard

MRS. BORKMAN. Then it must be Erhart.

[There is a sharp knock at the door leading in from the hall, which is immediately opened. MRS. WILTON enters, in evening dress, and with outer wraps. She is followed by THE MAID, who has not had time to announce her, and looks bewildered. The door remains half open. MRS. WILTON is a strikingly handsome, well-developed woman in the thirties. Broad, red, smiling lips, sparkling eyes. Luxuriant dark hair.

MRS. WILTON. Good evening, my dearest Mrs. Borkman!

MRS. BORKMAN. [Rather drily.] Good evening, Mrs. Wilton. [To THE MAID, pointing toward the garden-room.] Take the lamp that is in there and light it.

[THE MAID takes the lamp and goes out with it.

MRS. WILTON. [Observing ELLA RENTHEIM.] Oh, I beg your pardon, you have a visitor.

MRS. BORKMAN. Only my sister, who has just arrived from

[ERHART BORKMAN flings the half-open door wide open and rushes in. He is a young man with bright cheerful eyes. He is well dressed; his moustache is beginning to grow.

ERHART. [Radiant with joy; on the threshold.] What is this! Is Aunt Ella here? [Rushing up to her and seizing her hands.] Aunt, aunt! Is it possible? Are you here?

ELLA RENTHEIM. [Throws her arms round his neck.] Erhart! My dear, dear boy! Why, how big you have grown! Oh, how good it is to see you again!

MRS. BORKMAN. [Sharply.] What does this mean, Erhart? Were you hiding out in the hallway?

MRS. WILTON. [Quickly.] Erhart, Mr. Borkman came in with me.

MRS. BORKMAN. [Looking hard at him.] Indeed, Erhart! You don't come to your mother first?

ERHART. I had just to look in at Mrs. Wilton's for a moment to call for little Frida.

MRS. BORKMAN. Is that Miss Foldal with you too?

MRS. WILTON. Yes, we have left her in the hall.

ERHART. [Addressing some one through the open door.] You can go right upstairs, Frida.

[Pause. ELLA RENTHEIM observes ERHART. He seems embarrassed and a little impatient; his face has assumed a nervous and colder expression.

[THE MAID brings the lighted lamp into the garden-room, goes out again and closes the door behind her.

MRS. BORKMAN. [With forced politeness.] Well, Mrs. Wilton, if you will give us the pleasure of your company this evening, won't you

MRS. WILTON. Many thanks, my dear lady, but I really can't. We have another invitation. We're going down to the Hinkels'.

MRS. BORKMAN. [Looking at her.] We? Whom do you mean by we?

MRS. WILTON. [Laughing.] Oh, I ought really to have said I. But I was commissioned by the ladies of the house to bring Mr. Borkman with me if I happened to see him.

MRS. BORKMAN. And you did happen to see him, it appears.

MRS. WILTON. Yes, fortunately. He was good enough to look in at my house to call for Frida.

MRS. BORKMAN. [Drily.] But, Erhart, I did not know that you knew that family, those Hinkels?

ERHART. [Irritated.] No, I don't exactly know them. [Adds rather impatiently.] You know better than anybody, mother, what people I know and don't know.

MRS. WILTON. Oh, it doesn't matter! They soon put you at your ease in that house! They are such cheerful, hospitable people, the house swarms with young ladies.

MRS. BORKMAN. [With emphasis.] If I know my son rightly, Mrs. Wilton, they are no fit company for him.

MRS. WILTON. Why, good gracious, dear lady, he is young, too, you know!

MRS. BORKMAN. Yes, fortunately he's young. He would need to be young.

ERHART. [Concealing his impatience.] Well, well, well, mother, it's quite clear I can't got to the Hinkels' this evening. Of course I shall remain here with you and Aunt Ella.

MRS. BORKMAN. I knew you would, my dear Erhart.

ELLA RENTHEIM. No, Erhart, you must not stop at home on my account

ERHART. Yes, indeed, my dear Aunt; I can't think of going. [Looking doubtfully at MRS. WILTON.] But how shall we manage? Can I get out of it? You have said "Yes" for me, haven't you?

MRS. WILTON. [Gaily.] What nonsense! Not get out of it! When I make my entrance into the festive halls, just imagine it! deserted and forlorn, then I must simply say "No" for you.

ERHART. [Hesitatingly.] Well, if you really think I can get out of it

MRS. WILTON. [Putting the matter lightly aside.] I am quite used to saying both yes and no, on my own account. And you can't possibly think of leaving your aunt the moment she has arrived! For shame, Monsieur Erhart! Would that be behaving like a good son?

MRS. BORKMAN. [Annoyed.] Son?

MRS. WILTON. Well, adopted son then, Mrs. Borkman.

MRS. BORKMAN. Yes, you may well add that.

MRS. WILTON. Oh, it seems to me we have often more cause to be grateful to a foster-mother than to our own mother.

MRS. BORKMAN. Has that been your experience?

MRS. WILTON. I knew very little of my own mother, I am sorry to say. But if I had had a good foster-mother, perhaps I shouldn't have been so, so naughty, as people say I am. [Turning towards ERHART.] Well, then we stop peaceably at home like a good boy, and drink tea with mamma and auntie! [To the ladies.] Good-bye, good-bye Mrs. Borkman! Good-bye Miss Rentheim.

[The ladies bow silently. She goes toward the door.

ERHART. [Following her.] Shan't I go a little bit of the way with you?

MRS. WILTON. [In the doorway, motioning him back.] You shan't go a step with me. I am quite accustomed to taking my walks alone. [Stops on the threshold, looks at him and nods.] But now beware, Mr. Borkman, I warn you!

ERHART. What am I to beware of?

MRS. WILTON. [Gaily.] Why, as I go down the road, deserted and forlorn, as I said before, I shall try if I can't cast a spell upon you.

ERHART. [Laughing.] Oh, indeed! Are you going to try that again?

MRS. WILTON. [Half seriously.] Yes, just you beware! As I go down the road, I will say in my own mind, right from the very centre of my will, I will say: "Mr. Erhart Borkman, take your hat at once!"

MRS. BORKMAN. And you think he will take it?

MRS. WILTON. [Laughing.] Good heavens, yes, he'll snatch up his hat instantly. And then I will say: "Now put on your overcoat, like a good boy, Erhart Borkman! And your goloshes! Be sure you don't forget the goloshes! And then follow me! Do as I bid you, as I bid you, as I bid you!"

ERHART. [With forced gaiety.] Oh, you may rely on that.

MRS. WILTON. [Raising her forefinger.] As I bid you! As I bid you! Good-night!

[She laughs and nods to the ladies, and closes the door behind her.

MRS. BORKMAN. Does she really play tricks of that sort?

ERHART. Oh, not at all. How can you think so! She only says it in fun. [Breaking off.] But don't let us talk about Mrs. Wilton. [He forces ELLA RENTHEIM to seat herself at the armchair beside the stove, then stands and looks at her.] To think of your having taken all this long journey, Aunt Ella! And in winter too!

ELLA RENTHEIM. I found I had to, Erhart.

ERHART. Indeed? Why so?

ELLA RENTHEIM. I had to come to town after all, to consult the doctors.

ERHART. Oh, I'm glad of that!

ELLA RENTHEIM. [Smiling.] Are you glad of that?

ERHART. I mean I am glad you made up your mind to it at last.

MRS. BORKMAN. [On the sofa, coldly.] Are you ill, Ella?

ELLA RENTHEIM. [Looking hardly at her.] You know quite well that I am ill.

MRS. BORKMAN. I knew you were not strong, and hadn't been for years.

ERHART. I told you before I left you that you ought to consult a doctor.

ELLA RENTHEIM. There is no one in my neighbourhood that I have any real confidence in. And, besides, I did not feel it so much at that time.

ERHART. Are you worse, then, Aunt?

ELLA RENTHEIM. Yes, my dear boy; I am worse now.

ERHART. But there's nothing dangerous?

ELLA RENTHEIM. Oh, that depends how you look at it.

ERHART. [Emphatically.] Well, then, I tell you what it is, Aunt Ella; you mustn't think of going home again for the present.

ELLA RENTHEIM. No, I am not thinking of it.

ERHART. You must remain in town; for here you can have your choice of all the best doctors.

ELLA RENTHEIM. That was what I thought when I left home.

ERHART. And then you must be sure and find a really nice place to live, quiet, comfortable rooms.

ELLA RENTHEIM. I went this morning to the old ones, where I used to stay before.

ERHART. Oh, well, you were comfortable enough there.

ELLA RENTHEIM. Yes, but I shall not be staying there after all.

ERHART. Indeed? Why not?

ELLA RENTHEIM. I changed my mind after coming out here.

ERHART. [Surprised.] Really? Changed you mind?

MRS. BORKMAN. [Crocheting; without looking up.] Your aunt will live here, in her own house, Erhart.

ERHART. [Looking from one to the other alternately.] Here, with us? Is this true, Aunt?

ELLA RENTHEIM. Yes, that is what I made up my mind to do.

MRS. BORKMAN. [As before.] Everything here belongs to your aunt, you know.

ELLA RENTHEIM. I intend to remain here, Erhart, just now, for the present. I shall set up a little establishment of my own, over in the bailiff's wing.

ERHART. Ah, that's a good idea. There are plenty of rooms there. [With sudden vivacity.] But, by-the-bye, Aunt, aren't you very tired after your journey?

ELLA RENTHEIM. Oh yes, rather tired.

ERHART. Well, then, I think you ought to go quite early to bed.

ELLA RENTHEIM. [Looks at him smilingly.] I mean to.

ERHART. [Eagerly.] And then we could have a good long talk to-morrow, or some other day, of course, about this and that, about things in general, you and mother and I. Wouldn't that be much the best plan, Aunt Ella?

MRS. BORKMAN. [With an outburst, rising from the sofa.] Erhart, I can see you are going to leave me!

ERHART. [Starts.] What do you mean by that?

MRS. BORKMAN. You are going down to, to the Hinkels'?

ERHART. [Involuntarily.] Oh, that! [Collecting himself.] Well, you wouldn't have me sit here and keep Aunt Ella up half the night? Remember, she's an invalid, mother.

MRS. BORKMAN. You are going to the Hinkels', Erhart!

ERHART. [Impatiently.] Well, really, mother, I don't think I can well get out of it. What do you say, Aunt?

ELLA RENTHEIM. I should like you to feel quite free, Erhart.

MRS. BORKMAN. [Goes up to her menacingly.] You want to take him away from me!

ELLA RENTHEIM. [Rising.] Yes, if only I could, Gunhild! [Music is heard from above.

ERHART. [Writhing as if in pain.] Oh, I can't endure this! [Looking round.] What have I done with my hat? [To ELLA RENTHEIM.] Do you know the air that she is playing up there?

ELLA RENTHEIM. No. What is it?

ERHART. It's the *Danse Macabre,* the Dance of Death! Don't you know the Dance of Death, Aunt?

ELLA RENTHEIM. [Smiling sadly.] Not yet, Erhart.

ERHART. [To MRS. BORKMAN.] Mother, I beg and implore you, let me go!

MRS. BORKMAN. [Looks hardly at him.] Away from your mother? So that is what you want to do?

ERHART. Of course I'll come out again, to-morrow perhaps.

MRS. BORKMAN. [With passionate emotion.] You want to go away from me! To be with those strange people! With, with, no, I will not even think of it!

ERHART. There are bright lights down there, and young, happy faces; and there's music there, mother!

MRS. BORKMAN. [Pointing upwards.] There is music here, too, Erhart.

ERHART. Yes, it's just that music that drives me out of the house.

ELLA RENTHEIM. Do you grudge your father a moment of self-forgetfulness?

ERHART. No, I don't. I'm very, very glad that he should have it, if only *I* don't have to listen.

MRS. BORKMAN. [Looking solemnly at him.] Be strong, Erhart! Be strong, my son! Do not forget that you have your great mission.

ERHART. Oh, mother, do spare me these phrases! I wasn't born to be a "missionary." Good-night, aunt dear! Good-night, mother. [He goes hastily out through the hall.

MRS. BORKMAN. [After a short silence.] It has not taken you long to recapture him, Ella, after all.

ELLA RENTHEIM. I wish I could believe it.

MRS. BORKMAN. But you shall see you won't be allowed to keep him long.

ELLA RENTHEIM. Allowed? By you, do you mean?

MRS. BORKMAN. By me or by her, the other one

ELLA RENTHEIM. Then rather she than you.

MRS. BORKMAN. [Nodding slowly.] That I understand. I say the same. Rather she than you.

ELLA RENTHEIM. Whatever should become of him in the end

MRS. BORKMAN. It wouldn't greatly matter, I should say.

ELLA RENTHEIM. [Taking her outdoor things upon her arm.] For the first time in our lives, we twin sisters are of one mind. Good-night, Gunhild.

[She goes out by the hall. The music sounds louder from above.

MRS. BORKMAN. [Stands still for a moment, starts, shrinks together, and whispers involuntarily.] The wolf is whining again, the sick wolf. [She stands still for a moment, then flings herself down on the floor, writhing in agony and whispering:] Erhart! Erhart! be true to me! Oh, come home and help your mother! For I can bear this life no longer!

Act Second

The great gallery on the first floor of the Rentheim House. The walls are covered with old tapestries, representing hunting-scenes, shepherds and shepherdesses, all in faded colours. A folding-door to the left, and further forward a piano. In the left-hand corner, at the back, a door, cut in the tapestry, and covered with tapestry, without any frame. Against the middle of the right wall, a large writing-table of carved oak, with many books and papers. Further forward on the same side, a sofa with a table and chairs in front of it. The furniture is all of a stiff Empire style. Lighted lamps on both tables.

JOHN GABRIEL BORKMAN stands with his hands behind his back, beside the piano, listening to FRIDA FOLDAL, who is playing the last bars of the "Danse Macabre."

BORKMAN is of middle height, a well-knit, powerfully-built man, well on in the sixties. His appearance is distinguished, his profile finely cut, his eyes piercing, his hair and beard curly and greyish-white. He is dressed in a slightly old-fashioned black coat, and wears a white necktie. FRIDA FOLDAL is a pretty, pale girl of fifteen, with a somewhat weary and overstrained expression. She is cheaply dressed in light colours.

BORKMAN. Can you guess where I first heard tones like these?

FRIDA. [Looking up at him.] No, Mr. Borkman.

BORKMAN. It was down in the mines.

FRIDA. [Not understanding.] Indeed? Down in the mines?

BORKMAN. I am a miner's son, you know. Or perhaps you did not know?

FRIDA. No, Mr. Borkman.

BORKMAN. A miner's son. And my father used sometimes to take me with him into the mines. The metal sings down there.

FRIDA. Really? Sings?

BORKMAN. [Nodding.] When it is loosened. The hammer-strokes that loosen it are the midnight bell clanging to set it free; and that is why the metal sings, in its own way, for gladness.

FRIDA. Why does it do that, Mr. Borkman?

BORKMAN. It wants to come up into the light of day and serve mankind. [He paces up and down the gallery, always with his hands behind his back.

FRIDA. [Sits waiting a little, then looks at her watch and rises.] I beg your pardon, Mr. Borkman; but I am afraid I must go.

BORKMAN. [Stopping before her.] Are you going already?

FRIDA. [Putting her music in its case.] I really must. [Visibly embarrassed.] I have an engagement this evening.

BORKMAN. For a party?

FRIDA. Yes.

BORKMAN. And you are to play before the company?

FRIDA. [Biting her lip.] No; at least I am only to play for dancing.

BORKMAN. Only for dancing?

FRIDA. Yes; there is to be a dance after supper.

BORKMAN. [Stands and looks at her.] Do you like playing dance music? At parties, I mean?

FRIDA. [Putting on her outdoor things.] Yes, when I can get an engagement. I can always earn a little in that way.

BORKMAN. [With interest.] Is that the principal thing in your mind as you sit playing for the dancers?

FRIDA. No; I'm generally thinking how hard it is that I mayn't join in the dance myself.

BORKMAN. [Nodding.] That is just what I wanted to know. [Moving restlessly about the room.] Yes, yes, yes. That you must not join in the dance, that is the hardest thing of all. [Stopping.] But there is one thing that should make up to you for that, Frida.

FRIDA. [Looking inquiringly at him.] What is that, Mr. Borkman?

BORKMAN. The knowledge that you have ten times more music in you than all the dancers together.

FRIDA. [Smiling evasively.] Oh, that's not at all so certain.

BORKMAN. [Holding up his fore-finger warningly.] You must never be so mad as to have doubts of yourself!

FRIDA. But since no one knows it

BORKMAN. So long as you know it yourself, that is enough. Where is it you are going to play this evening?

FRIDA. Over at the Hinkel's.

BORKMAN. [With a swift, keen glance at her.] Hinkel's, you say!

FRIDA. Yes.

BORKMAN. [With a cutting smile.] Does that man give parties? Can he get people to visit him?

FRIDA. Yes, they have a great many people about them, Mrs. Wilton says.

BORKMAN. [Vehemently.] But what sort of people? Can you tell me that?

FRIDA. [A little nervously.] No, I really don't know. Yes, by-the-bye, I know that young Mr. Borkman is to be there this evening.

BORKMAN. [Taken aback.] Erhart? My son?

FRIDA. Yes, he is going there.

BORKMAN. How do you know that?

FRIDA. He said so himself an hour ago.

BORKMAN. Is he out here to-day?

FRIDA. Yes, he has been at Mrs. Wilton's all the afternoon.

BORKMAN. [Inquiringly.] Do you know if he called here too? I mean, did he see any one downstairs?

FRIDA. Yes, he looked in to see Mrs. Borkman.

BORKMAN. [Bitterly.] Aha, I might have known it.

FRIDA. There was a strange lady calling upon her, I think.

BORKMAN. Indeed? Was there? Oh yes, I suppose people do come now and then to see Mrs. Borkman.

FRIDA. If I meet young Mr. Borkman this evening, shall I ask him to come up and see you too?

BORKMAN. [Harshly.] You shall do nothing of the sort! I won't have it on any account. The people who want to see me can come of their own accord.

FRIDA. Oh, very well; I shan't say anything then. Good-night, Mr. Borkman.

BORKMAN. [Pacing up and down and growling.] Good-night.

FRIDA. Do you mind if I run down by the winding stair? It's the shortest way.

BORKMAN. Oh, by all means; take whatever stair you please, so far as I am concerned. Good-night to you!

FRIDA. Good-night, Mr. Borkman.

[She goes out by the little tapestry door in the back on the left.

[BORKMAN, lost in thought, goes up to the piano, and is about to close it, but changes his mind. Looks round the great empty room, and sets to pacing up and down it from the corner at the back on the right, pacing backward and forward uneasily and incessantly. At last he goes up to the writing-table, listens in the direction of the folding door, hastily snatches up a hand-glass, looks at himself in it, and straightens his necktie.

[A knock at the folding door. BORKMAN hears it, looks rapidly towards the door, but says nothing.

[In a little there comes another knock, this time louder.

BORKMAN. [Standing beside the writing-table with his left hand resting upon it, and his right thrust in the breast of his coat.] Come in!

[VILHELM FOLDAL comes softly into the room. He is a bent and worn man with mild blue eyes and long, thin grey hair straggling down over his coat collar. He has a portfolio under his arm, a soft felt hat, and large horn spectacles, which he pushes up over his forehead.

BORKMAN. [Changes his attitude and looks at FOLDAL with a half disappointed, half pleased expression.] Oh, is it only you?

FOLDAL. Good evening, John Gabriel. Yes, you see it is me.

BORKMAN. [With a stern glance.] I must say you are rather a late visitor.

FOLDAL. Well, you know, it's a good bit of a way, especially when you have to trudge it on foot.

BORKMAN. But why do you always walk, Vilhelm? The tramway passes your door.

FOLDAL. It's better for you to walk and then you always save twopence. Well, has Frida been playing to you lately?

BORKMAN. She has just this moment gone. Did you not meet her outside?

FOLDAL. No, I have seen nothing of her for a long time; not since she went to live with this Mrs. Wilton.

BORKMAN. [Seating himself on the sofa and waving his hand toward a chair.] You may sit down, Vilhelm.

FOLDAL. [Seating himself on the edge of a chair.] Many thanks. [Looks mournfully at him.] You can't think how lonely I feel since Frida left home.

BORKMAN. Oh, come, you have plenty left.

FOLDAL. Yes, God knows I have, five of them. But Frida was the only one who at all understood me. [Shaking his head sadly.] The others don't understand me a bit.

BORKMAN. [Gloomily, gazing straight before him, and drumming on the table with his fingers.] No, that's just it. That is the curse we exceptional, chosen people have to bear. The common herd, the average man and woman, they do not understand us, Vilhelm.

FOLDAL. [With resignation.] If it were only the lack of understanding, with a little patience, one could manage to wait for that awhile yet. [His voice choked with tears.] But there is something still bitterer.

BORKMAN. [Vehemently.] There is nothing bitterer than that.

FOLDAL. Yes, there is, John Gabriel. I have gone through a domestic scene to-night, just before I started.

BORKMAN. Indeed? What about?

FOLDAL. [With an outburst.] My people at home, they despise me.

BORKMAN. [Indignantly.] Despise?

FOLDAL. [Wiping his eyes.] I have long known it; but to-day it came out unmistakably.

BORKMAN. [After a short silence.] You made an unwise choice, I fear, when you married.

FOLDAL. I had practically no choice in the matter. And, you see, one feels a need for companionship as one begins to get on in years. And so crushed as I then was, so utterly broken down

BORKMAN. [Jumping up in anger.] Is this meant for me? A reproach!

FOLDAL. [Alarmed.] No, no, for Heaven's sake, John Gabriel!

BORKMAN. Yes, you are thinking of the disaster to the bank, I can see you are.

FOLDAL. [Soothingly.] But I don't blame you for that! Heaven forbid!

BORKMAN. [Growling, resumes his seat.] Well, that is a good thing, at any rate.

FOLDAL. Besides, you mustn't think it is my wife that I complain of. It is true she has not much polish, poor thing; but she is a good sort of woman all the same. No, it's the children.

BORKMAN. I thought as much.

FOLDAL. For the children, well, they have more culture and therefore they expect more of life.

BORKMAN. [Looking at him sympathetically.] And so your children despise you, Vilhelm?

FOLDAL. [Shrugging his shoulders.] I haven't made much of a career, you see, there is no denying that.

BORKMAN. [Moving nearer to him, and laying his hand upon his arm.] Do they not know, then, that in your young days you wrote a tragedy?

FOLDAL. Yes, of course they know that. But it doesn't seem to make much impression on them.

BORKMAN. Then they don't understand these things. For your tragedy is good. I am firmly convinced of that.

FOLDAL. [Brightening up.] Yes, don't you think there are some good things in it, John Gabriel? Good God, if I could only manage to get it placed! [Opens his portfolio, and begins eagerly turning over the contents.] Look here! Just let me show you one or two alterations I have made.

BORKMAN. Have you it with you?

FOLDAL. Yes, I thought I would bring it. It's so long now since I have read it to you. And I thought perhaps it might amuse you to hear an act or two.

BORKMAN. [Rising, with a negative gesture.] No, no, we will keep that for another time.

FOLDAL. Well, well, as you please.

[BORKMAN paces up and down the room. FOLDAL puts the manuscript up again.

BORKMAN. [Stopping in front of him.] You are quite right in what you said just now, you have not made any career. But I promise you this, Vilhelm, that when once the hour of my restoration strikes

FOLDAL. [Making a movement to rise.] Oh, thanks, thanks!

BORKMAN. [Waving his hand.] No, please be seated. [With rising excitement.] When the hour of my restoration strikes, when they see that they cannot get on without me, when they come to me, here in the gallery, and crawl to my feet, and beseech me to take the reins of the bank again! The new bank, that they have founded and can't carry on [Placing himself beside the writing-table in the same attitude as before, and striking his breast.] Here I shall stand, and receive them! And it shall be known far and wide, all the country over, what conditions John Gabriel Borkman imposes before he will [Stopping suddenly and staring at FOLDAL.] You're looking so doubtfully at me! Perhaps you do not believe that they will come? That they must, must, must come to me some day? Do you not believe it?

FOLDAL. Yes, Heaven knows I do, John Gabriel.

BORKMAN. [Seating himself again on the sofa.] I firmly believe it. I am immovably convinced I know that they will come. If I had not been certain of that I would have put a bullet through my head long ago.

FOLDAL. [Anxiously.] Oh no, for Heaven's sake!

BORKMAN. [Exultantly.] But they will come! They will come sure enough! You shall see! I expect them any day, any moment. And you see, I hold myself in readiness to receive them.

FOLDAL. [With a sigh.] If only they would come quickly.

BORKMAN. [Restlessly.] Yes, time flies: the years slip away; life Ah, no, I dare not think of it! [Looking at him.] Do you know what I sometimes feel like?

FOLDAL. What?

BORKMAN. I feel like a Napoleon who has been maimed in his first battle.

FOLDAL. [Placing his hand upon his portfolio.] I have that feeling too.

BORKMAN. Oh, well, that is on a smaller scale, of course.

FOLDAL. [Quietly.] My little world of poetry is very precious to me, John Gabriel.

BORKMAN. [Vehemently.] Yes, but think of me, who could have created millions! All the mines I should have controlled! New veins innumerable! And the water-falls! And the quarries! And the trade routes, and the steamship-lines all the wide world over! I would have organised it all, I alone!

FOLDAL. Yes, I know, I know. There was nothing in the world you would have shrunk from.

BORKMAN. [Clenching his hands together.] And now I have to sit here, like a wounded eagle, and look on while others pass me in the race, and take everything away from me, piece by piece!

FOLDAL. That is my fate too.

BORKMAN. [Not noticing him.] Only to think of it; so near to the goal as I was! If I had only had another week to look about me! All the deposits would have been covered. All the securities I had dealt with so daringly should have been in their places again as before. Vast companies were within a hair's-breadth of being floated. Not a soul should have lost a half-penny.

FOLDAL. Yes, yes; you were on the very verge of success.

BORKMAN. [With suppressed fury.] And then treachery overtook me! Just at the critical moment! [Looking at him.] Do you know what I hold to be the most infamous crime a man can be guilty of?

FOLDAL. No, tell me.

BORKMAN. It is not murder. It is not robbery or house-breaking. It is not even perjury. For all these things people do to those they hate, or who are indifferent to them, and do not matter.

FOLDAL. What is the worst of all then, John Gabriel?

BORKMAN. [With emphasis.] The most infamous of crimes is a friend's betrayal of his friend's confidence.

FOLDAL. [Somewhat doubtfully.] Yes, but you know

BORKMAN. [Firing up.] What are you going to say? I see it in your face. But it is of no use. The people who had their securities in the bank should have got them all back again, every farthing. No; I tell you the most infamous crime a man can commit is to misuse a friend's letters; to publish to all the world what has been confided to him alone, in the closest secrecy, like a whisper in an empty, dark, double-locked room. The man who can do such things is infected and poisoned in every fibre with the morals of the higher rascality. And such a friend was mine and it was he who crushed me.

FOLDAL. I can guess whom you mean.

BORKMAN. There was not a nook or cranny of my life that I hesitated to lay open to him. And then, when the moment came, he turned against me the weapons I myself had placed in his hands.

FOLDAL. I have never been able to understand why he Of course, there were whispers of all sorts at the time.

BORKMAN. What were the whispers? Tell me. You see I know nothing. For I had to go straight into, into isolation. What did people whisper, Vilhelm?

FOLDAL. You were to have gone into the Cabinet, they said.

BORKMAN. I was offered a portfolio, but I refused it.

FOLDAL. Then it wasn't there you stood in his way?

BORKMAN. Oh, no; that was not the reason he betrayed me.

FOLDAL. Then I really can't understand

BORKMAN. I may as well tell you, Vilhelm

FOLDAL. Well?

BORKMAN. There was in fact, there was a woman in the case.

FOLDAL. A woman in the case? Well but, John Gabriel

BORKMAN. [Interrupting.] Well, well, let us say no more of these stupid old stories. After all, neither of us got into the Cabinet, neither he nor I.

FOLDAL. But he rose high in the world.

BORKMAN. And I fell into the abyss.

FOLDAL. Oh, it's a terrible tragedy

BORKMAN. [Nodding to him.] Almost as terrible as yours, I fancy, when I come to think of it.

FOLDAL. [Naively.] Yes, at least as terrible.

BORKMAN. [Laughing quietly.] But looked at from another point of view, it is really a sort of comedy as well.

FOLDAL. A comedy? The story of your life?

BORKMAN. Yes, it seems to be taking a turn in that direction. For let me tell you

FOLDAL. What?

BORKMAN. You say you did not meet Frida as you came in?

FOLDAL. No.

BORKMAN. At this moment, as we sit here, she is playing waltzes for the guests of the man who betrayed and ruined me.

FOLDAL. I hadn't the least idea of that.

BORKMAN. Yes, she took her music, and went straight from me to, to the great house.

FOLDAL. [Apologetically.] Well, you see, poor child

BORKMAN. And can you guess for whom she is playing among the rest?

FOLDAL. No.

BORKMAN. For my son.

FOLDAL. What?

BORKMAN. What do you think of that, Vilhelm? My son is down there in the whirl of the dance this evening. Am I not right in calling it a comedy?

FOLDAL. But in that case you may be sure he knows nothing about it.

BORKMAN. What does he know?

FOLDAL. You may be sure he doesn't know how he, that man

BORKMAN. Do not shrink from his name. I can quite well bear it now.

FOLDAL. I'm certain your son doesn't know the circumstances, John Gabriel.

BORKMAN. [Gloomily, sitting and beating the table.] Yes, he knows, as surely as I am sitting here.

FOLDAL. Then how can he possibly be a guest in that house?

BORKMAN. [Shaking his head.] My son probably does not see things with my eyes. I'll take my oath he is on my enemies' side! No doubt he thinks, as they do, that Hinkel only did his confounded duty when he went and betrayed me.

FOLDAL. But, my dear friend, who can have got him to see things in that light?

BORKMAN. Who? Do you forget who has brought him up? First his aunt, from the time he was six or seven years old; and now, of late years, his mother!

FOLDAL. I believe you are doing them an injustice.

BORKMAN. [Firing up.] I never do any one injustice! Both of them have gone and poisoned his mind against me, I tell you!

FOLDAL. [Soothingly.] Well, well, well, I suppose they have.

BORKMAN. [Indignantly.] Oh these women! They wreck and ruin life for us! Play the devil with our whole destiny, our triumphal progress.

FOLDAL. Not all of them!

BORKMAN. Indeed? Can you tell me of a single one that is good for anything?

FOLDAL. No, that is the trouble. The few that I know are good for nothing.

BORKMAN. [With a snort of scorn.] Well then, what is the good of it? What is the good of such women existing, if you never know them?

FOLDAL. [Warmly.] Yes, John Gabriel, there is good in it, I assure you. It is such a blessed, beneficial thought that here or there in the world, somewhere, far away, the true woman exists after all.

BORKMAN. [Moving impatiently on the sofa.] Oh, do spare me that poetical nonsense.

FOLDAL. [Looks at him, deeply wounded.] Do you call my holiest faith poetical nonsense?

BORKMAN. [Harshly.] Yes I do! That is what has always prevented you from getting on in the world. If you would get all that out of your head, I could still help you on in life, help you to rise.

FOLDAL. [Boiling inwardly.] Oh, you can't do that.

BORKMAN. I can when once I come into power again.

FOLDAL. That won't be for many a day.

BORKMAN. [Vehemently.] Perhaps you think that day will never come? Answer me!

FOLDAL. I don't know what to answer.

BORKMAN. [Rising, cold and dignified, and waving his hand towards the door.] Then I no longer have any use for you.

FOLDAL. [Starting up.] No use!

BORKMAN. Since you do not believe that the tide will turn for me

FOLDAL. How can I believe in the teeth of all reason? You would have to be legally rehabilitated

BORKMAN. Go on! go on!

FOLDAL. It's true I never passed my examination; but I have read enough law to know that

BORKMAN. [Quickly.] It is impossible, you mean?

FOLDAL. There is no precedent for such a thing.

BORKMAN. Exceptional men are above precedents.

FOLDAL. The law knows nothing of such distinctions.

BORKMAN. [Harshly and decisively.] You are no poet, Vilhelm.

FOLDAL. [Unconsciously folding his hands.] Do you say that in sober earnest?

BORKMAN. [Dismissing the subject, without answering.] We are only wasting each other's time. You had better not come here again.

FOLDAL. Then you really want me to leave you?

BORKMAN. [Without looking at him.] I have no longer any use for you.

FOLDAL. [Softly, taking his portfolio.] No, no, no; I daresay not.

BORKMAN. Here you have been lying to me all the time.

FOLDAL. [Shaking his head.] Never lying, John Gabriel.

BORKMAN. Have you not sat here feeding me with hope, and trust, and confidence, that was all a lie?

FOLDAL. It wasn't a lie so long as you believed in my vocation. So long as you believed in me, I believed in you.

BORKMAN. Then we have been all the time deceiving each other. And perhaps deceiving ourselves, both of us.

FOLDAL. But isn't that just the essence of friendship, John Gabriel?

BORKMAN. [Smiling bitterly.] Yes, you are right there. Friendship means deception. I have learnt that once before.

FOLDAL. [Looking at him.] I have no poetic vocation! And you could actually say it to me so bluntly.

BORKMAN. [In a gentler tone.] Well, you know, I don't pretend to know much about these matters.

FOLDAL. Perhaps you know more than you think.

BORKMAN. I?

FOLDAL. [Softly.] Yes, you. For I myself have had my doubts, now and then, I may tell you. The horrible doubt that I may have bungled my life for the sake of a delusion.

BORKMAN. If you have no faith in yourself, you are on the downward path indeed.

FOLDAL. That was why I found such comfort in coming here to lean upon your faith in me. [Taking his hat.] But now you have become a stranger to me.

BORKMAN. And you to me.

FOLDAL. Good night, John Gabriel.

BORKMAN. Good night, Vilhelm. [Foldal goes out to the left.

[BORKMAN stands for a moment gazing at the closed door; makes a movement as though to call FOLDAL back, but changes his mind, and begins to pace the floor with his hands behind his back. Then he stops at the table beside the sofa and puts out the lamp. The room becomes half dark. After a short pause, there comes a knock at the tapestry door.

BORKMAN. [At the table, starts, turns, and asks in a loud voice:] Who is that knocking? [No answer, another knock.

BORKMAN. [Without moving.] Who is it? Come in!

[ELLA RENTHEIM, with a lighted candle in her hand, appears in the doorway. She wears her black dress, as before, with her cloak thrown loosely round her shoulders.

BORKMAN. [Staring at her.] Who are you? What do you want with me?

ELLA RENTHEIM. [Closes the door and advances.] It is I, Borkman.

[She puts down the candle on the piano and remains standing beside it.

BORKMAN. [Stands as though thunderstruck, stares fixedly at her, and says in a half-whisper.] Is it, is it Ella? Is it Ella Rentheim?

ELLA RENTHEIM. Yes, it's "your" Ella, as you used to call me in the old days; many, many years ago.

BORKMAN. [As before.] Yes, it is you Ella, I can see you now.

ELLA RENTHEIM. Can you recognise me?

BORKMAN. Yes, now I begin to

ELLA RENTHEIM. The years have told on me, and brought winter with them, Borkman. Do you not think so?

BORKMAN. [In a forced voice.] You are a good deal changed, just at first glance.

ELLA RENTHEIM. There are no dark curls on my neck now, the curls you once loved to twist round your fingers.

BORKMAN. [Quickly.] True! I can see now, Ella, you have done your hair differently.

ELLA RENTHEIM. [With a sad smile.] Precisely; it is the way I do my hair that makes the difference.

BORKMAN. [Changing the subject.] I had no idea that you were in this part of the world.

ELLA RENTHEIM. I have only just arrived.

BORKMAN. Why have you come all this way now, in winter?

ELLA RENTHEIM. That you shall hear.

BORKMAN. Is it me you have come to see?

ELLA RENTHEIM. You among others. But if I am to tell you my errand, I must begin far back.

BORKMAN. You look tired.

ELLA RENTHEIM. Yes, I am tired.

BORKMAN. Won't you sit down? There on the sofa.

ELLA RENTHEIM. Yes, thank you; I need rest.

[She crosses to the right and seats herself in the furthest forward corner of the sofa. BORKMAN stands beside the table with his hands behind his back looking at her. A short silence.

ELLA RENTHEIM. It seems an endless time since we two met, Borkman, face to face.

BORKMAN. [Gloomily.] It is a long, long time. And terrible things have passed since then.

ELLA RENTHEIM. A whole lifetime has passed, a wasted lifetime.

BORKMAN. [Looking keenly at her.] Wasted!

ELLA RENTHEIM. Yes, I say wasted for both of us.

BORKMAN. [In a cold business tone.] I cannot regard my life as wasted yet.

ELLA RENTHEIM. And what about mine?

BORKMAN. There you have yourself to blame, Ella.

ELLA RENTHEIM. [With a start.] And you can say that?

BORKMAN. You could quite well have been happy without me.

ELLA RENTHEIM. Do you believe that?

BORKMAN. If you had made up your mind to.

ELLA RENTHEIM. [Bitterly.] Oh, yes, I know well enough there was some one else ready to marry me.

BORKMAN. But you rejected him.

ELLA RENTHEIM. Yes, I did.

BORKMAN. Time after time you rejected him. Year after year

ELLA RENTHEIM. [Scornfully.] Year after year I rejected happiness, I suppose you think?

BORKMAN. You might perfectly well have been happy with him. And then I should have been saved.

ELLA RENTHEIM. You?

BORKMAN. Yes, you would have saved me, Ella.

ELLA RENTHEIM. How do you mean?

BORKMAN. He thought I was at the bottom of your obstinacy, of your perpetual refusals. And then he took his revenge. It was so easy for him; he had all my frank, confiding letters in his keeping. He made his own use of them; and then it was all over with me, for the time, that is to say. So you see it is all your doing, Ella!

ELLA RENTHEIM. Oh indeed, Borkman. If we look into the matter, it appears that it is I who owe you reparation.

BORKMAN. It depends how you look at it. I know quite well all that you have done for us. You bought in this house, and the whole property, at the auction. You placed the house entirely at my disposal and your sister too. You took charge of Erhart, and cared for him in every way

ELLA RENTHEIM. As long as I was allowed to

BORKMAN. By your sister, you mean. I have never mixed myself up in these domestic affairs. As I was saying, I know all the sacrifices you have made for me and for your sister. But you were in a position to do so, Ella; and you must not forget that it was I who placed you in that position.

ELLA RENTHEIM. [Indignantly.] There you make a great mistake, Borkman! It was the love of my inmost heart for Erhart, and for you too, that made me do it!

BORKMAN. [Interrupting.] My dear Ella, do not let us get upon questions of sentiment and that sort of thing. I mean, of course, that if you acted generously, it was I that put it in your power to do so.

ELLA RENTHEIM. [Smiling.] H'm! In my power

BORKMAN. [Warmly.] Yes, put it in your power, I say! On the eve of the great decisive battle, when I could not afford to spare either kith or kin, when I had to grasp at, when I did grasp at the millions that were entrusted to me, then I spared all that was yours, every farthing, although I could have taken it, and made use of it, as I did of all the rest!

ELLA RENTHEIM. [Coldly and quietly.] That is quite true, Borkman.

BORKMAN. Yes it is. And that was why, when they came and took me, they found all your securities untouched in the strong-room of the bank.

ELLA RENTHEIM. [Looking at him.] I have often and often wondered what was your real reason for sparing all my property? That, and that alone.

BORKMAN. My reason?

ELLA RENTHEIM. Yes, your reason. Tell me.

BORKMAN. [Harshly and scornfully.] Perhaps you think it was that I might have something to fall back upon, if things went wrong?

ELLA RENTHEIM. Oh no, I am sure you did not think of that in those days.

BORKMAN. Never! I was so absolutely certain of victory.

ELLA RENTHEIM. Well then, why was it that?

BORKMAN. [Shrugging his shoulders.] Upon my soul, Ella, it is not so easy to remember one's motives of twenty years ago. I only know that when I used to grapple, silently and alone, with all the great projects I had in my mind, I had something like the feeling of a man who is starting on a balloon voyage. All through my sleepless nights I was inflating my giant balloon, and preparing to soar away into perilous, unknown regions.

ELLA RENTHEIM. [Smiling.] You, who never had the least doubt of victory?

BORKMAN. [Impatiently.] Men are made so, Ella. They both doubt and believe at the same time. [Looking straight before him.] And I suppose that was why I would not take you and yours with me in the balloon.

ELLA RENTHEIM. [Eagerly.] Why, I ask you? Tell me why!

BORKMAN. [Without looking at her.] One shrinks from risking what one holds dearest on such a voyage.

ELLA RENTHEIM. You had risked what was dearest to you on that voyage. Your whole future life

BORKMAN. Life is not always what one holds dearest.

ELLA RENTHEIM. [Breathlessly.] Was that how you felt at that time?

BORKMAN. I fancy it was.

ELLA RENTHEIM. I was the dearest thing in the world to you?

BORKMAN. I seem to remember something of the sort.

ELLA RENTHEIM. And yet years had passed since you had deserted me and married, married another!

BORKMAN. Deserted you, you say? You must know very well that it was higher motives, well then, other motives that compelled me. Without his support I could not have done anything.

ELLA RENTHEIM. [Controlling herself.] So you deserted me from higher motives.

BORKMAN. I could not get on without his help. And he made you the price of helping me.

ELLA RENTHEIM. And you paid the price. Paid it in full, without haggling.

BORKMAN. I had no choice. I had to conquer or fall.

ELLA RENTHEIM. [In a trembling voice, looking at him.] Can what you tell me be true, that I was then the dearest thing in the world to you?

BORKMAN. Both then and afterwards, long, long, after.

ELLA RENTHEIM. But you bartered me away none the less; drove a bargain with another man for your love. Sold my love for a, for a directorship.

BORKMAN. [Gloomily and bowed down.] I was driven by inexorable necessity, Ella.

ELLA RENTHEIM. [Rises from the sofa, quivering with passion.] Criminal!

BORKMAN. [Starts, but controls himself.] I have heard that word before.

ELLA RENTHEIM. Oh, don't imagine I'm thinking of anything you may have done against the law of the land! The use you made of all those vouchers and securities, or whatever you call them, do you think I care a straw about that! If I could have stood at your side when the crash came

BORKMAN. [Eagerly.] What then, Ella?

ELLA RENTHEIM. Trust me, I should have borne it all so gladly along with you. The shame, the ruin, I would have helped you to bear it all, all!

BORKMAN. Would you have had the will, the strength?

ELLA RENTHEIM. Both the will and the strength. For then I did not know of your great, your terrible crime.

BORKMAN. What crime? What are you speaking of?

ELLA RENTHEIM. I am speaking of that crime for which there is no forgiveness.

BORKMAN. [Staring at her.] You must be out of your mind.

ELLA RENTHEIM. [Approaching him.] You are a murderer! You have committed the one mortal sin!

BORKMAN. [Falling back towards the piano.] You are raving, Ella!

ELLA RENTHEIM. You have killed the love-life in me. [Still nearer him.] Do you understand what that means? The Bible speaks of a mysterious sin for which there is no forgiveness. I have never understood what it could be; but now I understand. The great, unpardonable sin is to murder the love-life in a human soul.

BORKMAN. And you say I have done that?

ELLA RENTHEIM. You have done that. I have never rightly understood until this evening what had really happened to me. That you deserted me and turned to Gunhild instead, I took that to be mere common fickleness on your part, and the result of heartless scheming on hers. I almost think I despised you a little, in spite of everything. But now I see it! You deserted the woman you loved! Me, me, me! What you held dearest in the world you were ready to barter away for gain. That is the double murder you have committed! The murder of your own soul and of mine!

BORKMAN. [With cold self-control.] How well I recognise your passionate, ungovernable spirit, Ella. No doubt it is natural enough that you should look at the thing in this light. Of course, you are a woman, and therefore it would seem that your own heart is the one thing you know or care about in this world.

ELLA RENTHEIM. Yes, yes it is.

BORKMAN. Your own heart is the only thing that exists for you.

ELLA RENTHEIM. The only thing! The only thing! You are right there.

BORKMAN. But you must remember that I am a man. As a woman, you were the dearest thing in the world to me. But if the worst comes to the worst, one woman can always take the place of another.

ELLA RENTHEIM. [Looks at him with a smile.] Was that your experience when you had made Gunhild your wife?

BORKMAN. No. But the great aims I had in life helped me to bear even that. I wanted to have at my command all the sources of power in this country. All the wealth that lay hidden in the soil, and the rocks, and the forests, and the sea, I wanted to gather it all into my hands to make myself master of it all, and so to promote the well-being of many, many thousands.

ELLA RENTHEIM. [Lost in recollection.] I know it. Think of all the evenings we spent in talking over your projects.

BORKMAN. Yes, I could talk to you, Ella.

ELLA RENTHEIM. I jested with your plans, and asked whether you wanted to awaken all the sleeping spirits of the mine.

BORKMAN. [Nodding.] I remember that phrase. [Slowly.] All the sleeping spirits of the mine.

ELLA RENTHEIM. But you did not take it as a jest. You said: "Yes, yes, Ella, that is just what I want to do."

BORKMAN. And so it was. If only I could get my foot in the stirrup And that depended on that one man. He could and would secure me the control of the bank if I on my side

ELLA RENTHEIM. Yes, just so! If you on your side would renounce the woman you loved and who loved you beyond words in return.

BORKMAN. I knew his consuming passion for you. I knew that on no other condition would he

ELLA RENTHEIM. And so you struck the bargain.

BORKMAN. [Vehemently.] Yes, I did, Ella! For the love of power is uncontrollable in me, you see! So I struck the bargain; I had to. And he helped me half-way up towards the beckoning heights that I was bent on reaching. And I mounted and mounted; year by year I mounted

ELLA RENTHEIM. And I was as though wiped out of your life.

BORKMAN. And after all he hurled me into the abyss again. On account of you, Ella.

ELLA RENTHEIM. [After a short thoughtful silence.] Borkman, does it not seem to you as if there had been a sort of curse on our whole relation?

BORKMAN. [Looking at her.] A curse?

ELLA RENTHEIM. Yes. Don't you think so?

BORKMAN. [Uneasily.] Yes. But why is it? [With an outburst.] Oh Ella, I begin to wonder which is in the right, you or I!

ELLA RENTHEIM. It is you who have sinned. You have done to death all the gladness of my life in me.

BORKMAN. [Anxiously.] Do not say that, Ella!

ELLA RENTHEIM. All a woman's gladness at any rate. From the day when your image began to dwindle in my mind, I have lived my life as though under an eclipse. During all these years it has grown harder and harder for me, and at last utterly impossible, to love any living creature. Human beings, animals, plants: I shrank from all, from all but one

BORKMAN. What one?

ELLA RENTHEIM. Erhart, of course.

BORKMAN. Erhart?

ELLA RENTHEIM. Erhart, your son, Borkman.

BORKMAN. Has he really been so close to your heart?

ELLA RENTHEIM. Why else should I have taken him to me, and kept him as long as ever I could? Why?

BORKMAN. I thought it was out of pity, like all the rest that you did.

ELLA RENTHEIM. [In strong inward emotion.] Pity! Ha, ha! I have never known pity, since you deserted me. I was incapable of feeling it. If a poor starved child came into my kitchen, shivering, and crying, and begging for a morsel of food, I let the servants look to it. I never felt any desire to take the child to myself, to warm it at my own hearth, to have the pleasure of seeing it eat and be satisfied. And yet I was not like that when I was young; that I remember clearly! It is you that have created an empty, barren desert within me and without me too!

BORKMAN. Except only for Erhart.

ELLA RENTHEIM. Yes, except for your son. But I am hardened to every other living thing. You have cheated me of a mother's joy and happiness in life and of a mother's sorrows and tears as well. And perhaps that is the heaviest part of the loss to me.

BORKMAN. Do you say that, Ella?

ELLA RENTHEIM. Who knows? It may be that a mother's sorrows and tears were what I needed most. [With still deeper emotion.] But at that time I could not resign myself to my loss; and that was why I took Erhart to me. I won him entirely. Won his whole, warm, trustful childish heart until Oh!

BORKMAN. Until what?

ELLA RENTHEIM. Until his mother, his mother in the flesh, I mean, took him from me again.

BORKMAN. He had to leave you in any case; he had to come to town.

ELLA RENTHEIM. [Wringing her hands.] Yes, but I cannot bear the solitude, the emptiness! I cannot bear the loss of your son's heart!

BORKMAN. [With an evil expression in his eyes.] H'm, I doubt whether you have lost it, Ella. Hearts are not so easily lost to a certain person, in the room below.

ELLA RENTHEIM. I have lost Erhart here, and she has won him back again. Or if not she, some one else. That is plain enough in the letters he writes me from time to time.

BORKMAN. Then it is to take him back with you that you have come here?

ELLA RENTHEIM. Yes, if only it were possible!

BORKMAN. It is possible enough, if you have set your heart upon it. For you have the first and strongest claims upon him.

ELLA RENTHEIM. Oh, claims, claims! What is the use of claims? If he is not mine of his own free will, he is not mine at all. And have him I must! I must have my boy's heart, whole and undivided, now!

BORKMAN. You must remember that Erhart is well into his twenties. You could scarcely reckon on keeping his heart very long undivided, as you express it.

ELLA RENTHEIM. [With a melancholy smile.] It would not need to be for so very long.

BORKMAN. Indeed? I should have thought that when you want a thing, you want it to the end of your days.

ELLA RENTHEIM. So I do. But that need not mean for very long.

BORKMAN. [Taken aback.] What do you mean by that?

ELLA RENTHEIM. I suppose you know I have been in bad health for many years past?

BORKMAN. Have you?

ELLA RENTHEIM. Do you not know that?

BORKMAN. No, I cannot say I did

ELLA RENTHEIM. [Looking at him in surprise.] Has Erhart not told you so?

BORKMAN. I really don't remember at the moment.

ELLA RENTHEIM. Perhaps he has not spoken of me at all?

BORKMAN. Oh, yes, I believe he has spoken of you. But the fact is, I so seldom see anything of him, scarcely ever. There is a certain person below that keeps him away from me. Keeps him away, you understand?

ELLA RENTHEIM. Are you quite sure of that, Borkman?

BORKMAN. Yes, absolutely sure. [Changing his tone.] And so you have been in bad health, Ella?

ELLA RENTHEIM. Yes, I have. And this autumn I grew so much worse that I had to come to town and take better medical advice.

BORKMAN. And you have seen the doctors already?

ELLA RENTHEIM. Yes, this morning.

BORKMAN. And what did they say to you?

ELLA RENTHEIM. They gave me full assurance of what I had long suspected.

BORKMAN. Well?

ELLA RENTHEIM. [Calmly and quietly.] My illness will never be cured, Borkman.

BORKMAN. Oh, you must not believe that, Ella.

ELLA RENTHEIM. It is a disease that there is no help or cure for. The doctors can do nothing with it. They must just let it take its course. They cannot possibly check it; at most, they can allay the suffering. And that is always something.

BORKMAN. Oh, but it will take a long time to run its course. I am sure it will.

ELLA RENTHEIM. I may perhaps last out the winter, they told me.

BORKMAN. [Without thinking.] Oh, well, the winter is long.

ELLA RENTHEIM. [Quietly.] Long enough for me, at any rate.

BORKMAN. [Eagerly, changing the subject.] But what in all the world can have brought on this illness? You, who have always lived such a healthy and regular life? What can have brought it on?

ELLA RENTHEIM. [Looking at him.] The doctors thought that perhaps at one time in my life I had had to go through some great stress of emotion.

BORKMAN. [Firing up.] Emotion! Aha, I understand! You mean that it is my fault?

ELLA RENTHEIM. [With increasing inward agitation.] It is too late to go into that matter now! But I must have my heart's own child again before I go! It is so unspeakably sad for me to think that I must go away from all that is called life, away from sun, and light, and air and not leave behind me one single human being who will think of me, who will remember me lovingly and mournfully as a son remembers and thinks of the mother he has lost.

BORKMAN. [After a short pause.] Take him, Ella, if you can win him.

ELLA RENTHEIM. [With animation.] Do you give your consent? Can you?

BORKMAN. [Gloomily.] Yes. And it is no great sacrifice either. For in any case he is not mine.

ELLA RENTHEIM. Thank you, thank you all the same for the sacrifice! But I have one thing more to beg of you, a great thing for me, Borkman.

BORKMAN. Well, what is it?

ELLA RENTHEIM. I daresay you will think it childish of me, you will not understand

BORKMAN. Go on, tell me what it is.

ELLA RENTHEIM. When I die, as I must soon, I shall have a fair amount to leave behind me.

BORKMAN. Yes, I suppose so.

ELLA RENTHEIM. And I intend to leave it all to Erhart.

BORKMAN. Well, you have really no one nearer to you than he.

ELLA RENTHEIM. [Warmly.] No, indeed, I have no one nearer me than he.

BORKMAN. No one of your own family. You are the last.

ELLA RENTHEIM. [Nodding slowly.] Yes, that is just it. When I die, the name of Rentheim dies with me. And that is such a torturing thought to me. To be wiped out of existence, even to your very name

BORKMAN. [Firing up.] Ah, I see what you are driving at!

ELLA RENTHEIM. [Passionately.] Do not let this be my forte. Let Erhart bear my name after me!

BORKMAN. I understand you well enough. You want to save my son from having to bear his father's name. That is your meaning.

ELLA RENTHEIM. No, no, not that! I myself would have borne it proudly and gladly along with you! But a mother who is at the point of death There is more binding force in a name than you think or believe, Borkman.

BORKMAN. [Coldly and proudly.] Well and good, Ella. I am man enough to bear my own name alone.

ELLA RENTHEIM. [Seizing and pressing his hand.] Thank you, thank you! Now there has been a full settlement between us! Yes, yes, let it be so! You have made all the atonement in your power. For when I have gone from the world, I shall leave Erhart Rentheim behind me!

[The tapestry door is thrown open. MRS. BORKMAN, with the large shawl over her head, stands in the doorway.

MRS. BORKMAN. [In violent agitation.] Never to his dying day shall Erhart be called by that name!

ELLA RENTHEIM. [Shrinking back.] Gunhild!

BORKMAN. [Harshly and threateningly.] I allow no one to come up to my room!

MRS. BORKMAN. [Advancing a step.] I do not ask your permission.

BORKMAN. [Going towards her.] What do you want with me?

MRS. BORKMAN. I will fight with all my might for you. I will protect you from the powers of evil.

ELLA RENTHEIM. The worst "powers of evil" are in yourself, Gunhild!

MRS. BORKMAN. [Harshly.] So be it then. [Menacingly, with upstretched arm.] But this I tell you, he shall bear his father's name! And bear it aloft in honour again! My son's heart shall be mine, mine and no other's.

[She goes out by the tapestry door and shuts it behind her.

ELLA RENTHEIM. [Shaken and shattered.] Borkman, Erhart's life will be wrecked in this storm. There must be an understanding between you and Gunhild. We must go down to her at once.

BORKMAN. [Looking at her.] We? I too, do you mean?

ELLA RENTHEIM. Both you and I.

BORKMAN. [Shaking his head.] She is hard, I tell you. Hard as the metal I once dreamed of hewing out of the rocks.

ELLA RENTHEIM. Then try it now!

[BORKMAN does not answer, but stands looking doubtfully at her.

Act Third

MRS. BORKMAN's drawing room. The lamp is still burning on the table beside the sofa in front. The garden-room at the back is quite dark.

MRS. BORKMAN, with the shawl still over her head, enters, in violent agitation, by the hall door, goes up to the window, draws the curtain a little aside, and looks out; then she seats herself beside the stove, but immediately springs up again, goes to the bell-pull and rings. Stands beside the sofa, and waits a moment. No one comes. Then she rings again, this time more violently.

THE MAID presently enters from the hall. She looks sleepy and out of temper, and appears to have dressed in great haste.

MRS. BORKMAN. [Impatiently.] What has become of you, Malena? I have rung for you twice!

THE MAID. Yes, ma'am, I heard you.

MRS. BORKMAN. And yet you didn't come?

THE MAID. [Sulkily.] I had to put some clothes on first, I suppose.

MRS. BORKMAN. Yes, you must dress yourself properly, and then you must run and fetch my son.

THE MAID. [Looking at her in astonishment.] You want me to fetch Mr. Erhart?

MRS. BORKMAN. Yes; tell him he must come home to me at once; I want to speak to him.

THE MAID. [Grumbling.] Then I'd better go to the bailiff's and call up the coachman.

MRS. BORKMAN. Why?

THE MAID. To get him to harness the sledge. The snow's dreadful to-night.

MRS. BORKMAN. Oh, that doesn't matter; only make haste and go. It's just round the corner.

THE MAID. Why, ma'am you can't call that just round the corner!

MRS. BORKMAN. Of course it is. Don't you know Mr. Hinkel's villa?

THE MAID. [With malice.] Oh, indeed! It's there Mr. Erhart is this evening?

MRS. BORKMAN. [Taken aback.] Why, where else should he be?

THE MAID. [With a slight smile.] Well, I only thought he might be where he usually is.

MRS. BORKMAN. Where do you mean?

THE MAID. At Mrs. Wilton's, as they call her.

MRS. BORKMAN. Mrs. Wilton's? My son isn't so often there.

THE MAID. [Half muttering.] I've heard say as he's there every day of his life.

MRS. BORKMAN. That's all nonsense, Malena. Go straight to Mr. Hinkel's and try to to get hold of him.

THE MAID. [With a toss of her head.] Oh, very well; I'm going.

[She is on the point of going out by the hall, but just at that moment the hall door is opened, and ELLA RENTHEIM and BORKMAN appear on the threshold.

MRS. BORKMAN. [Staggers a step backwards.] What does this mean?

THE MAID. [Terrified, instinctively folding her hands.] Lord save us!

MRS. BORKMAN. [Whispers to THE MAID.] Tell him he must come this instant.

THE MAID. [Softly.] Yes, ma'am.

[ELLA RENTHEIM and, after her, BORKMAN enter the room. THE MAID sidles behind them to the door, goes out, and closes it after her.

MRS. BORKMAN. [Having recovered her self-control, turns to ELLA.] What does he want down here in my room?

ELLA RENTHEIM. He wants to come to an understanding with you, Gunhild.

MRS. BORKMAN. He has never tried that before.

ELLA RENTHEIM. He is going to, this evening.

MRS. BORKMAN. The last time we stood face to face, it was in the Court, when I was summoned to give an account

BORKMAN. [Approaching.] And this evening it is *I* who will give an account of myself.

MRS. BORKMAN. [Looking at him.] You?

BORKMAN. Not of what I have done amiss. All the world knows that.

MRS. BORKMAN. [With a bitter sigh.] Yes, that is true; all the world knows that.

BORKMAN. But it does not know why I did it; why I had to do it. People do not understand that I had to, because I was myself, because I was John Gabriel Borkman, myself, and not another. And that is what I will try to explain to you.

MRS. BORKMAN. [Shaking her head.] It is of no use. Temptations and promptings acquit no one.

BORKMAN. They may acquit one in one's own eyes.

MRS. BORKMAN. [With a gesture of repulsion.] Oh, let all that alone! I have thought over that black business of yours enough and to spare.

BORKMAN. I too. During those five endless years in my cell, and elsewhere, I had time to think it over. And during the eight years up there in the gallery I have had still more ample time. I have re-tried the whole case by myself. Time after time I have re-tried it. I have been my own accuser, my own defender, and my own judge. I have been more impartial than any one else could be, that I venture to say. I have paced up and down the gallery there, turning every one of my actions upside down and inside out. I have examined them from all sides as unsparingly, as pitilessly, as any lawyer of them all. And the final judgment I have always come to is this: the one person I have sinned against is myself.

MRS. BORKMAN. And what about me? What about your son?

BORKMAN. You and he are included in what I mean when I say myself.

MRS. BORKMAN. And what about the hundreds of others, then, the people you are said to have ruined?

BORKMAN. [More vehemently.] I had power in my hands! And then I felt the irresistible vocation within me! The prisoned millions lay all over the country, deep in the bowels of the earth, calling aloud to me! They shrieked to me to free them! But no one else heard their cry, I alone had ears for it.

MRS. BORKMAN. Yes, to the branding of the name of Borkman.

BORKMAN. If the others had had the power, do you think they would not have acted exactly as I did?

MRS. BORKMAN. No one, no one but you would have done it!

BORKMAN. Perhaps not. But that would have been because they had not my brains. And if they had done it, it would not have been with my aims in view. The act would have been a different act. In short, I have acquitted myself.

ELLA RENTHEIM. [Softly and appealingly.] Oh, can you say that so confidently, Borkman?

BORKMAN. [Nodding.] Acquitted myself on that score. But then comes the great, crushing self-accusation.

MRS. BORKMAN. What is that?

BORKMAN. I have skulked up there and wasted eight precious years of my life! The very day I was set free, I should have gone forth into the world, out into the steel-hard, dreamless world of reality! I should have begun at the bottom and swung myself up to the heights anew, higher than ever before, in spite of all that lay between.

MRS. BORKMAN. Oh, it would have been the same thing over again; take my word for that.

BORKMAN. [Shakes his head, and looks at her with a sententious air.] It is true that nothing new happens; but what has happened does not repeat itself either. It is the eye that transforms the action. The eye, born anew, transforms the old action. [Breaking off.] But you do not understand this.

MRS. BORKMAN. [Curtly.] No, I do not understand it.

BORKMAN. Ah, that is just the curse, I have never found one single soul to understand me.

ELLA RENTHEIM. [Looking at him.] Never, Borkman?

BORKMAN. Except one, perhaps. Long, long ago. In the days when I did not think I needed understanding. Since then, at any rate, no one has understood me! There has been no one alive enough to my needs to be afoot and rouse me, to ring the morning bell for me, to call me up to manful work anew. And to impress upon me that I had done nothing inexpiable.

MRS. BORKMAN. [With a scornful laugh.] So, after all, you require to have that impressed on you from without?

BORKMAN. [With increasing indignation.] Yes, when the whole world hisses in chorus that I have sunk never to rise again, there come moments when I almost believe it myself. [Raising his head.] But then my inmost assurance rises again triumphant; and that acquits me.

MRS. BORKMAN. [Looking harshly at him.] Why have you never come and asked me for what you call understanding?

BORKMAN. What use would it have been to come to you?

MRS. BORKMAN. [With a gesture of repulsion.] You have never loved anything outside yourself; that is the secret of the whole matter.

BORKMAN. [Proudly.] I have loved power.

MRS. BORKMAN. Yes, power!

BORKMAN. The power to create human happiness in wide, wide circles around me!

MRS. BORKMAN. You had once the power to make me happy. Have you used it to that end?

BORKMAN. [Without looking at her.] Some one must generally go down in a shipwreck.

MRS. BORKMAN. And your own son! Have you used your power, have you lived and laboured, to make him happy?

BORKMAN. I do not know him.

MRS. BORKMAN. No, that is true. You do not even know him.

BORKMAN. [Harshly.] You, his mother, have taken care of that!

MRS. BORKMAN. [Looking at him with a lofty air.] Oh, you do not know what I have taken care of!

BORKMAN. You?

MRS. BORKMAN. Yes, I. I alone.

BORKMAN. Then tell me.

MRS. BORKMAN. I have taken care of your memory.

BORKMAN. [With a short dry laugh.] My memory? Oh, indeed! It sounds almost as if I were dead already.

MRS. BORKMAN. [With emphasis.] And so you are.

BORKMAN. [Slowly.] Yes, perhaps you are right. [Firing up.] But no, no! Not yet! I have been close to the verge of death. But now I have awakened. I have come to myself. A whole life lies before me yet. I can see it awaiting me, radiant and quickening. And you, you shall see it too.

MRS. BORKMAN. [Raising her hand.] Never dream of life again! Lie quiet where you are.

ELLA RENTHEIM. [Shocked.] Gunhild! Gunhild, how can you!

MRS. BORKMAN. [Not listening to her.] I will raise the monument over your grave.

BORKMAN. The pillar of shame, I suppose you mean?

MRS. BORKMAN. [With increasing excitement.] Oh, no, it shall be no pillar of metal or stone. And no one shall be suffered to carve any scornful legend on the monument I shall raise. There shall be, as it were, a quickset hedge of trees and bushes, close, close around your tomb. They shall hide away all the darkness that has been. The eyes of men and the thoughts of men shall no longer dwell on John Gabriel Borkman!

BORKMAN. [Hoarsely and cuttingly.] And this labour of love you will perform?

MRS. BORKMAN. Not by my own strength. I cannot think of that. But I have brought up one to help me, who shall live for this alone. His life shall be so pure and high and bright, that your burrowing in the dark shall be as though it had never been!

BORKMAN. [Darkly and threateningly.] If it is Erhart you mean, say so at once!

MRS. BORKMAN. [Looking him straight in the eyes.] Yes, it is Erhart; my son; he whom you are ready to renounce in atonement for your own acts.

BORKMAN. [With a look towards ELLA.] In atonement for my blackest sin.

MRS. BORKMAN. [Repelling the idea.] A sin towards a stranger only. Remember the sin towards me! [Looking triumphantly at them both.] But he will not obey you! When I cry out to him in my need, he will come to me! It is with me that he will remain! With me, and never with any one else. [Suddenly listens, and cries.] I hear him! He is here, he is here! Erhart!

[ERHART BORKMAN hastily tears open the hall door, and enters the room. He is wearing an overcoat and has his hat on.

ERHART. [Pale and anxious.] Mother! What in Heaven's name! [Seeing BORKMAN, who is standing beside the doorway leading into the garden-room, he starts and takes off his hat. After a moment's silence, he asks:] What do you want with me, mother? What has happened?

MRS. BORKMAN. [Stretching her arms towards him.] I want to see you, Erhart! I want to have you with me, always!

ERHART. [Stammering.] Have me? Always? What do you mean by that?

MRS. BORKMAN. I will have you, I say! There is some one who wants to take you away from me!

ERHART. [Recoiling a step.] Ah, so you know?

MRS. BORKMAN. Yes. Do you know it, too?

ERHART. [Surprised, looking at her.] Do *I* know it? Yes, of course.

MRS. BORKMAN. Aha, so you have planned it all out! Behind my back! Erhart! Erhart!

ERHART. [Quickly.] Mother, tell me what it is you know!

MRS. BORKMAN. I know everything. I know that your aunt has come here to take you from me.

ERHART. Aunt Ella!

ELLA RENTHEIM. Oh, listen to me a moment, Erhart!

MRS. BORKMAN. [Continuing.] She wants me to give you up to her. She wants to stand in your mother's place to you, Erhart! She wants you to be her son, and not mine, from this time forward. She wants you to inherit everything from her; to renounce your own name and take hers instead!

ERHART. Aunt Ella, is this true?

ELLA RENTHEIM. Yes, it is true.

ERHART. I knew nothing of this. Why do you want to have me with you again?

ELLA RENTHEIM. Because I feel that I am losing you here.

MRS. BORKMAN. [Hardly.] You are losing him to me, yes. And that is just as it should be.

ELLA RENTHEIM. [Looking beseechingly at him.] Erhart, I cannot afford to lose you. For, I must tell you I am a lonely, dying woman.

ERHART. Dying?

ELLA RENTHEIM. Yes, dying. Will you came and be with me to the end? Attach yourself wholly to me? Be to me, as though you were my own child?

MRS. BORKMAN. [Interrupting.] And forsake your mother, and perhaps your mission in life as well? Will you, Erhart?

ELLA RENTHEIM. I am condemned to death. Answer me, Erhart.

ERHART. [Warmly, with emotion.] Aunt Ella, you have been unspeakably good to me. With you I grew up in as perfect happiness as any boy can ever have known

MRS. BORKMAN. Erhart, Erhart!

ELLA RENTHEIM. Oh, how glad I am that you can still say that!

ERHART. But I cannot sacrifice myself to you now. It is not possible for me to devote myself wholly to taking a son's place towards you.

MRS. BORKMAN. [Triumphing.] Ah, I knew it! You shall not have him! You shall not have him, Ella!

ELLA RENTHEIM. [Sadly.] I see it. You have won him back.

MRS. BORKMAN. Yes, yes! Mine he is, and mine he shall remain! Erhart, say it is so, dear; we two have still a long way to go together, have we not?

ERHART. [Struggling with himself.] Mother, I may as well tell you plainly

MRS. BORKMAN. [Eagerly.] What?

ERHART. I am afraid it is only a very little way you and I can go together.

MRS. BORKMAN. [Stands as though thunderstruck.] What do yo mean by that?

ERHART. [Plucking up spirit.] Good heavens, mother, I am young, after all! I feel as if the close air of this room must stifle me in the end.

MRS. BORKMAN. Close air? Here with me?

ERHART. Yes, here with you, mother.

ELLA RENTHEIM. Then come with me, Erhart.

ERHART. Oh, Aunt Ella, it's not a whit better with you. It's different, but no better, no better for me. It smells of rose-leaves and lavender there too; it is as airless there as here.

MRS. BORKMAN. [Shaken, but having recovered her composure with an effort.] Airless in your mother's room, you say!

ERHART. [In growing impatience.] Yes, I don't know how else to express it. All this morbid watchfulness and, and idolisation, or whatever you like to call it I can't endure it any longer!

MRS. BORKMAN. [Looking at him with deep solemnity.] Have you forgotten what you have consecrated your life to, Erhart?

ERHART. [With an outburst.] Oh, say rather what you have consecrated my life to. You, you have been my will. You have never given me leave to have any of my own. But now I cannot bear this yoke any longer. I am young; remember that, mother. [With a polite, considerate glance towards BORKMAN.] I cannot consecrate my life to making atonement for another, whoever that other may be.

MRS. BORKMAN. [Seized with growing anxiety.] Who is it that has transformed you, Erhart?

ERHART. [Struck.] Who? Can you not conceive that it is I myself?

MRS. BORKMAN. No, no, no! You have come under some strange power. You are not in your mother's power any longer; nor in your, your foster-mother's either.

ERHART. [With laboured defiance.] I am in my own power, mother! And working my own will!

BORKMAN. [Advancing towards ERHART.] Then perhaps my hour has come at last.

ERHART. [Distantly and with measured politeness.] How so! How do you mean, sir?

MRS. BORKMAN. [Scornfully.] Yes, you may well ask that.

BORKMAN. [Continuing undisturbed.] Listen, Erhart, will you not cast in your lot with your father? It is not through any other man's life that a man who has fallen can be raised up again. These are only empty fables that have been told to you down here in the airless room. If you were to set yourself to live your life like all the saints together, it would be of no use whatever to me.

ERHART. [With measured respectfulness.] That is very true indeed.

BORKMAN. Yes, it is. And it would be of no use either if I should resign myself to wither away in abject penitence. I have tried to feed myself upon hopes and dreams, all through these years. But I am not the man to be content with that; and now I mean to have done with dreaming.

ERHART. [With a slight bow.] And what will, what will you do, sir?

BORKMAN. I will work out my own redemption, that is what I will do. I will begin at the bottom again. It is only through his present and his future that a man can atone for his past. Through work, indefatigable work, for all that, in my youth, seemed to give life its meaning and that now seems a thousand times greater than it did then. Erhart, will you join with me and help me in this new life?

MRS. BORKMAN. [Raising her hand warningly.] Do not do it, Erhart!

ELLA RENTHEIM. [Warmly.] Yes, yes do it! Oh, help him, Erhart!

MRS. BORKMAN. And you advise him to do that? You, the lonely dying woman.

ELLA RENTHEIM. I don't care about myself.

MRS. BORKMAN. No, so long as it is not I that take him from you.

ELLA RENTHEIM. Precisely so, Gunhild.

BORKMAN. Will you, Erhart?

ERHART. [Wrung with pain.] Father, I cannot now. It is utterly impossible!

BORKMAN. What do you want to do then?

ERHART. [With a sudden glow.] I am young! I want to live, for once in a way, as well as other people! I want to live my own life!

ELLA RENTHEIM. You cannot give up two or three little months to brighten the close of a poor waning life?

ERHART. I cannot, Aunt, however much I may wish to.

ELLA RENTHEIM. Not for the sake of one who loves you so dearly?

MRS. BORKMAN. [Looking sharply at him.] And your mother has no power over you either, any more?

ERHART. I will always love you, mother; but I cannot go on living for you alone. This is no life for me.

BORKMAN. Then come and join with me, after all! For life, life means work, Erhart. Come, we two will go forth into life and work together!

ERHART. [Passionately.] Yes, but I don't want to work now! For I am young! That's what I never realised before; but now the knowledge is tingling through every vein in my body. I will not work! I will only live, live, live!

MRS. BORKMAN. [With a cry of divination.] Erhart, what will you live for?

ERHART. [With sparkling eyes.] For happiness, mother!

MRS. BORKMAN. And where do you think you can find that?

ERHART. I have found it, already!

MRS. BORKMAN. [Shrieks.] Erhart! [ERHART goes quickly to the hall door and throws it open.]

ERHART. [Calls out.] Fanny, you can come in now!

[MRS. WILTON, in outdoor wraps, appears on the threshold.

MRS. BORKMAN. [With uplifted hands.] Mrs. Wilton!

MRS. WILTON. [Hesitating a little, with an enquiring glance at ERHART.] Do you want me to?

ERHART. Yes, now you can come in. I have told them everything.

[MRS. WILTON comes forward into the room. ERHART closes the door behind her. She bows formally to BORKMAN, who returns her bow in silence. A short pause.

MRS. WILTON. [In a subdued but firm voice.] So the word has been spoken and I suppose you all think I have brought a great calamity upon this house?

MRS. BORKMAN. [Slowly, looking hard at her.] You have crushed the last remnant of interest in life for me. [With an outburst.] But all of this, all this is utterly impossible!

MRS. WILTON. I can quite understand that it must appear impossible to you, Mrs. Borkman.

MRS. BORKMAN. Yes, you can surely see for yourself that it is impossible. Or what?

MRS. WILTON. I should rather say that it seems highly improbable. But it's so, none the less.

MRS. BORKMAN. [Turning.] Are you really in earnest about this, Erhart?

ERHART. This means happiness for me, mother, all the beauty and happiness of life. That is all I can say to you.

MRS. BORKMAN. [Clenching her hands together; to MRS. WILTON.] Oh, how you have cajoled and deluded my unhappy son!

MRS. WILTON. [Raising her head proudly.] I have done nothing of the sort.

MRS. BORKMAN. You have not, say you!

MRS. WILTON. No. I have neither cajoled nor deluded him. Erhart came to me of his own free will. And of my own free will I went out half-way to meet him.

MRS. BORKMAN. [Measuring her scornfully with her eye.] Yes, indeed! That I can easily believe.

MRS. WILTON. [With self-control.] Mrs. Borkman, there are forces in human life that you seem to know very little about.

MRS. BORKMAN. What forces, may I ask?

MRS. WILTON. The forces which ordain that two people shall join their lives together, indissolubly and fearlessly.

MRS. BORKMAN. [With a smile.] I thought you were already indissolubly bound to another.

MRS. WILTON. [Shortly.] That other has deserted me.

MRS. BORKMAN. But he is still living, they say.

MRS. WILTON. He is dead to me.

ERHART. [Insistently.] Yes, mother, he is dead to Fanny. And besides, this other makes no difference to me!

MRS. BORKMAN. [Looking sternly at him.] So you know all this, about the other.

ERHART. Yes, mother, I know quite well, all about it!

MRS. BORKMAN. And yet you can say that it makes no difference to you?

ERHART. [With defiant petulance.] I can only tell you that it is happiness I must have! I am young! I want to live, live, live!

MRS. BORKMAN. Yes, you are young, Erhart. Too young for this.

MRS. WILTON. [Firmly and earnestly.] You must not think, Mrs. Borkman, that I haven't said the same to him. I have laid my whole life before him. Again and again I have reminded him that I am seven years older than he

ERHART. [Interrupting.] Oh, nonsense, Fanny, I knew that all the time.

MRS. WILTON. But nothing, nothing was of any use.

MRS. BORKMAN. Indeed? Nothing? Then why did you not dismiss him without more ado? Close your door to him? You should have done that, and done it in time!

MRS. WILTON. [Looks at her, and says in a low voice.] I could not do that, Mrs. Borkman.

MRS. BORKMAN. Why could you not?

MRS. WILTON. Because for me too this meant happiness.

MRS. BORKMAN. [Scornfully.] H'm, happiness, happiness

MRS. WILTON. I have never before known happiness in life. And I cannot possibly drive happiness away from me, merely because it comes so late.

MRS. BORKMAN. And how long do you think this happiness will last?

ERHART. [Interrupting.] Whether it lasts or does not last, mother, it doesn't matter now!

MRS. BORKMAN. [In anger.] Blind boy that you are! Do you not see where all this is leading you?

ERHART. I don't want to look into the future. I don't want to look around me in any direction; I am only determined to live my own life at last!

MRS. BORKMAN. [With deep pain.] And you call this life, Erhart!

ERHART. Don't you see how lovely she is!

MRS. BORKMAN. [Wringing her hands.] And I have to bear this load of shame as well!

BORKMAN. [At the back, harshly and cuttingly.] Ho, you are used to bearing things of that sort, Gunhild!

ELLA RENTHEIM. [Imploringly.] Borkman!

ERHART. [Similarly.] Father!

MRS. BORKMAN. Day after day I shall have to see my own son linked to a, a

ERHART. [Interrupting her harshly.] You shall see nothing of the kind, mother! You may make your mind easy on that point. I shall not remain here.

MRS. WILTON. [Quickly and with decision.] We are going away, Mrs. Borkman.

MRS. BORKMAN. [Turning pale.] Are you going away, too? Together, no doubt?

MRS. WILTON. [Nodding.] Yes, I am going abroad, to the south. I am taking a young girl with me. And Erhart is going along with us.

MRS. BORKMAN. With you and a young girl?

MRS. WILTON. Yes. It is little Frida Foldal, whom I have had living with me. I want her to go abroad and get more instruction in music.

MRS. BORKMAN. So you are taking her with you?

MRS. WILTON. Yes; I can't well send her out into the world alone.

MRS. BORKMAN. [Suppressing a smile.] What do you say to this, Erhart?

ERHART. [With some embarrassment, shrugging his shoulders.] Well, mother, since Fanny will have it so

MRS. BORKMAN. [Coldly.] And when does this distinguished party set out, if one may ask?

MRS. WILTON. We are going at once, to-night. My covered sledge is waiting on the road, outside the Hinkels'.

MRS. BORKMAN. [Looking her from head to foot.] Aha! so that was what the party meant?

MRS. WILTON. [Smiling.] Yes, Erhart and I were the whole party. And little Frida, of course.

MRS. BORKMAN. And where is she now?

MRS. WILTON. She is sitting in the sledge waiting for us.

ERHART. [In painful embarrassment.] Mother, surely you can understand? I would have spared you all this, you and every one.

MRS. BORKMAN. [Looks at him, deeply pained.] You would have gone away from me without saying a good-bye?

ERHART. Yes, I thought that would be best; best for all of us. Our boxes were packed and everything settled. But of course when you sent for me, I [Holding out his hands to her.] Good-bye, mother.

MRS. BORKMAN. [With a gesture of repulsion.] Don't touch me!

ERHART. [Gently.] Is that your last word?

MRS. BORKMAN. [Sternly.] Yes.

ERHART. [Turning.] Good-bye to you, then, Aunt Ella.

ELLA RENTHEIM. [Pressing his hands.] Good-bye, Erhart! And live your life and be as happy, as happy as ever you can.

ERHART. Thanks, Aunt. [Bowing to BORKMAN.] Good-bye, father. [Whispers to MRS. WILTON.] Let us get away, the sooner the better.

MRS. WILTON. [In a low voice.] Yes, let us.

MRS. BORKMAN. [With a malignant smile.] Mrs. Wilton, do you think you are acting quite wisely in taking that girl with you?

MRS. WILTON. [Returning the smile, half ironically, half seriously.] Men are so unstable, Mrs. Borkman. And women too. When Erhart is done with me and I with him, then it will be well for us both that he, poor fellow, should have some one to fall back upon.

MRS. BORKMAN. But you yourself?

MRS. WILTON. Oh, I shall know what to do, I assure you. Good-bye to you all!

[She bows and goes out by the hall door. ERHART stands for a moment as though wavering; then he turns and follows her.

MRS. BORKMAN. [Dropping her folded hands.] Childless.

BORKMAN. [As though awakening to a resolution.] Then out into the storm alone! My hat! My cloak! [He goes hastily towards the door.

ELLA RENTHEIM. [In terror, stopping him.] John Gabriel, where are you going?

BORKMAN. Out into the storm of life, I tell you. Let me go, Ella!

ELLA RENTHEIM. [Holding him back.] No, no, I won't let you out! You are ill. I can see it in your face!

BORKMAN. Let me go, I tell you!

[He tears himself away from her, and goes out by the hall.

ELLA RENTHEIM. [In the doorway.] Help me to hold him, Gunhild!

MRS. BORKMAN. [Coldly and sharply, standing in the middle of the room.] I will not try to hold any one in all the world. Let them go away from me, both the one and the other! As far, as far as ever they please. [Suddenly, with a piercing shriek.] Erhart, don't leave me!

[She rushes with outstretched arms towards the door. ELLA RENTHEIM stops her.

Act Fourth

An open space outside the main building, which lies to the right. A projecting corner of it is visible, with a door approached by a flight of low stone steps. The background consists of steep fir-clad slopes, quite close at hand. On the left are small scattered trees, forming the margin of a wood. The snowstorm has ceased; but the newly fallen snow lies deep around. The fir-branches droop under heavy loads of snow. The night is dark, with drifting clouds. Now and then the moon gleams out faintly. Only a dim light is reflected from the snow.

BORKMAN, MRS. BORKMAN and ELLA RENTHEIM are standing upon the steps, BORKMAN leaning wearily against the wall of the house. He has an old-fashioned cape thrown over his shoulders, holds a soft grey felt hat in one hand and a thick knotted stick in the other. ELLA RENTHEIM carries her cloak over her arm. MRS. BORKMAN's great shawl has slipped down over her shoulders, so that her hair is uncovered.

ELLA RENTHEIM. [Barring the way for MRS. BORKMAN.] Don't go after him, Gunhild!

MRS. BORKMAN. [In fear and agitation.] Let me pass, I say! He must not go away from me!

ELLA RENTHEIM. It is utterly useless, I tell you! You will never overtake him.

MRS. BORKMAN. Let me go, Ella! I will cry aloud after him all down the road. And he must hear his mother's cry!

ELLA RENTHEIM. He cannot hear you. You may be sure he is in the sledge already.

MRS. BORKMAN. No, no; he can't be in the sledge yet!

ELLA RENTHEIM. The doors are closed upon him long ago, believe me.

MRS. BORKMAN. [In despair.] If he is in the sledge, then he is there with her, with her, her!

BORKMAN. [Laughing gloomily.] Then he probably won't hear his mother's cry.

MRS. BORKMAN. No, he will not hear it. [Listening.] Hark! what is that?

ELLA RENTHEIM. [Also listening.] It sounds like sledge-bells.

MRS. BORKMAN. [With a suppressed scream.] It is her sledge!

ELLA RENTHEIM. Perhaps it's another.

MRS. BORKMAN. No, no, it is Mrs. Wilton's covered sledge! I know the silver bells! Hark! Now they are driving right past here, at the foot of the hill!

ELLA RENTHEIM. [Quickly.] Gunhild, if you want to cry out to him, now is the time! Perhaps after all! [The tinkle of the bells sounds close at hand, in the wood.] Make haste, Gunhild! Now they are right under us!

MRS. BORKMAN. [Stands for a moment undecided, then she stiffens and says sternly and coldly.] No. I will not cry out to him. Let Erhart Borkman pass away from me, far, far away, to what he calls life and happiness. [The sound dies away in the distance.

ELLA RENTHEIM. [After a moment.] Now the bells are out of hearing.

MRS. BORKMAN. They sounded like funeral bells.

BORKMAN. [With a dry suppressed laugh.] Oho, it is not for me they are ringing to-night!

MRS. BORKMAN. No, but for me and for him who has gone from me.

ELLA RENTHEIM. [Nodding thoughtfully.] Who knows if, after all, they may not be ringing in life and happiness for him, Gunhild.

MRS. BORKMAN. [With sudden animation, looking hard at her.] Life and happiness, you say!

ELLA RENTHEIM. For a little while at any rate.

MRS. BORKMAN. Could you endure to let him know life and happiness, with her?

ELLA RENTHEIM. [With warmth and feeling.] Indeed, I could, with all my heart and soul!

MRS. BORKMAN. [Coldly.] Then you must be richer than I am in the power of love.

ELLA RENTHEIM. [Looking far away.] Perhaps it is the lack of love that keeps the power alive.

MRS. BORKMAN. [Fixing her eyes on her.] If that is so, then I shall soon be as rich as you, Ella. [She turns and goes into the house.

ELLA RENTHEIM. [Stands for a time looking with a troubled expression at BORKMAN; then lays her hand cautiously on his shoulder.] Come, John, you must come in, too.

BORKMAN. [As if wakening.] I?

ELLA RENTHEIM. Yes, this winter air is too keen for you; I can see that, John. So come, come in with me, into the house, into the warmth.

BORKMAN. [Angrily.] Up to the gallery again, I suppose.

ELLA RENTHEIM. No, rather into the room below.

BORKMAN. [His anger flaming forth.] Never will I set foot under that roof again!

ELLA RENTHEIM. Where will you go then? So late, and in the dark, John?

BORKMAN. [Putting on his hat.] First of all, I will go out and see to all my buried treasures.

ELLA RENTHEIM. [Looking anxiously at him.] John, I don't understand you.

BORKMAN. [With laughter, interrupted by coughing.] Oh, it is not hidden plunder I mean; don't be afraid of that, Ella. [Stopping, and pointing outwards.] Do you see that man there? Who is it?

[VILHELM FOLDAL, in an old cape, covered with snow, with his hat-brim turned down, and a large umbrella in his hand, advances towards the corner of the house, laboriously stumbling through the snow. He is noticeably lame in his left foot.

BORKMAN. Vilhelm! What do you want with me again?

FOLDAL. [Looking up.] Good heavens, are you out on the steps, John Gabriel? [Bowing.] And Mrs. Borkman, too, I see.

BORKMAN. [Shortly.] This is not Mrs. Borkman.

FOLDAL. Oh, I beg pardon. You see, I have lost my spectacles in the snow. But how is it that you, who never put your foot out of doors?

BORKMAN. [Carelessly and gaily.] It is high time I should come out into the open air again, don't you see? Nearly three years in detention, five years in prison, eight years in the gallery up there

ELLA RENTHEIM. [Distressed.] Borkman, I beg you

FOLDAL. Ah yes, yes, yes!

BORKMAN. But I want to know what has brought you here.

FOLDAL. [Still standing at the foot of the steps.] I wanted to come up to you, John Gabriel. I felt I must come to you, in the gallery. Ah me, that gallery!

BORKMAN. Did you want to come up to me after I had shown you the door?

FOLDAL. Oh, I couldn't let that stand in the way.

BORKMAN. What have you done to your foot? I see you are limping?

FOLDAL. Yes, what do you think, I have been run over.

ELLA RENTHEIM. Run over!

FOLDAL. Yes, by a covered sledge.

BORKMAN. Oho!

FOLDAL. With two horses. They came down the hill at a tearing gallop. I couldn't get out of the way quick enough; and so

ELLA RENTHEIM. And so they ran over you?

FOLDAL. They came right down upon me, madam, or miss. They came right upon me and sent me rolling over and over in the snow, so that I lost my spectacles and got my umbrella broken. [Rubbing his leg.] And my ankle a little hurt too.

BORKMAN. [Laughing inwardly.] Do you know who were in that sledge, Vilhelm?

FOLDAL. No, how could I see? It was a covered sledge, and the curtains were down. And the driver didn't stop a moment after he had sent me spinning. But it doesn't matter a bit, for [With an outburst.] Oh, I am so happy, so happy!

BORKMAN. Happy?

FOLDAL. Well, I don't exactly know what to call it. But I think happy is the nearest word. For something wonderful has happened! And that is why I couldn't help, I had to come out and share my happiness with you, John Gabriel.

BORKMAN. [Harshly.] Well, share away then!

ELLA RENTHEIM. Oh, but first take your friend indoors with you, Borkman.

BORKMAN. [Sternly.] I have told you I will not go into the house.

ELLA RENTHEIM. But don't you hear, he has been run over!

BORKMAN. Oh, we are all of us run over, sometime or other in life. The thing is to jump up again, and let no one see you are hurt.

FOLDAL. That is a profound saying, John Gabriel. But I can easily tell you my story out here, in a few words.

BORKMAN. [More mildly.] Yes, please do, Vilhelm.

FOLDAL. Well, now you shall hear! Only think, when I got home this evening after I had been with you, what did I find but a letter. Can you guess who it was from?

BORKMAN. Possibly from your little Frida?

FOLDAL. Precisely! Think of your hitting on it at once! Yes, it was a long letter from Frida. A footman had brought it. And can you imagine what was in it?

BORKMAN. Perhaps it was to say good-bye to her mother and you?

FOLDAL. Exactly! How good you are at guessing, John Gabriel! Yes, she tells me that Mrs. Wilton has taken such a fancy to her, and she is to go abroad with her and study music. And Mrs. Wilton has engaged a first-rate teacher who is to accompany them on the journey and to read with Frida. For unfortunately she has been a good deal neglected in some branches, you see.

BORKMAN. [Shaken with inward laughter.] Of course, of course, I see it all quite clearly, Vilhelm.

FOLDAL. [Eagerly continuing.] And only think, she knew nothing about the arrangement until this evening; at that party, you know, h'm! And yet she found time to write to me. And the letter is such a beautiful one, so warm and affectionate, I assure you. There is not a trace of contempt for her father in it. And then what a delicate thought it was to say good-bye to us by letter, before she started. [Laughing.] But of course I can't let her go like that.

BORKMAN. [Looks inquiringly at him.] How so?

FOLDAL. She tells me that they start early to-morrow morning; quite early.

BORKMAN. Oh indeed, to-morrow? Does she tell you that?

FOLDAL. [Laughing and rubbing his hands.] Yes; but I know a trick worth two of that, you see! I am going straight up to Mrs. Wilton's

BORKMAN. This evening?

FOLDAL. Oh, it's not so very late yet. And even if the house is shut up, I shall ring; without hesitation. For I must and will see Frida before she starts. Good-night, good-night! [Makes a movement to go.

BORKMAN. Stop a moment, my poor Vilhelm; you may spare yourself that heavy bit of road.

FOLDAL. Oh, you are thinking of my ankle

BORKMAN. Yes; and in any case you won't get in at Mrs. Wilton's.

FOLDAL. Yes, indeed I will. I'll go on ringing and knocking till some one comes and lets me in. For I must and will see Frida.

ELLA RENTHEIM. Your daughter has gone already, Mr. Foldal.

FOLDAL. [Stands as though thunderstruck.] Has Frida gone already! Are you quite sure? Who told you?

BORKMAN. We had it from her future teacher.

FOLDAL. Indeed? And who is he?

BORKMAN. A certain Mr. Erhart Borkman.

FOLDAL. [Beaming with joy.] Your son, John Gabriel? Is he going with them?

BORKMAN. Yes; it is he that is to help Mrs. Wilton with little Frida's education.

FOLDAL. Oh, Heaven be praised! Then the child is in the best of hands. But is it quite certain that they have started with her already?

BORKMAN. They took her away in that sledge which ran you over in the road.

FOLDAL. [Clasping his hands.] To think that my little Frida was in that magnificent sledge!

BORKMAN. [Nodding.] Yes, yes, Vilhelm, your daughter has come to drive in her carriage. And Master Erhart, too. Tell me, did you notice the silver bells?

FOLDAL. Yes, indeed. Silver bells did you say? Were they silver? Real, genuine silver bells?

BORKMAN. You may be quite sure of that. Everything was genuine both outside and in.

FOLDAL. [In quiet emotion.] Isn't it strange how fortune can sometimes befriend one? It is my, my little gift of song that has transmuted itself into music in Frida. So after all, it is not for nothing that I was born a poet. For now she is going forth into the great wide world, that I once yearned so passionately to see. Little Frida sets out in a splendid covered sledge with silver bells on the harness

BORKMAN. And runs over her father.

FOLDAL. [Happily.] Oh, pooh! What does it matter about me, if only the child! Well, so I am too late, then, after all. I must go home again and comfort her mother. I left her crying in the kitchen.

BORKMAN. Crying?

FOLDAL. [Smiling.] Yes, would you believe it, she was crying her eyes out when I came away.

BORKMAN. And you are laughing, Vilhelm?

FOLDAL. Yes, *I* am, of course. But she, poor thing, she doesn't know any better, you see. Well, good-bye! It's a good thing I have the tramway so handy. Good-bye, good-bye, John Gabriel. Good-bye, Madam.

[He bows and limps laboriously out by the way he came.

BORKMAN. [Stands silent for a moment, gazing before him.] Good-bye, Vilhelm! It is not the first time in your life that you've been run over, old friend.

ELLA RENTHEIM. [Looking at him with suppressed anxiety.] You are so pale, John, so very pale.

BORKMAN. That is the effect of the prison air up yonder.

ELLA RENTHEIM. I have never seen you like this before.

BORKMAN. No, for I suppose you have never seen an escaped convict before.

ELLA RENTHEIM. Oh, do come into the house with me, John!

BORKMAN. It is no use trying to lure me in. I have told you

ELLA RENTHEIM. But when I beg and implore you? For your own sake

[THE MAID opens the door, and stands in the doorway.

THE MAID. I beg your pardon. Mrs. Borkman told me to lock the front door now.

BORKMAN. [In a low voice, to ELLA.] You see, they want to lock me up again!

ELLA RENTHEIM. [To THE MAID.] Mr. Borkman is not quite well. He wants to have a little fresh air before coming in.

THE MAID. But Mrs. Borkman told me to

ELLA RENTHEIM. I shall lock the door. Just leave the key in the lock.

THE MAID. Oh, very well; I'll leave it. [She goes into the house again.

BORKMAN. [Stands silent for a moment, and listens; then goes hastily down the steps and out into the open space.] Now I am outside the walls, Ella! Now they will never get hold of me again!

ELLA RENTHEIM. [Who has gone down to him.] But you are a free man in there, too, John. You can come and go just as you please.

BORKMAN. [Softly, as though in terror.] Never under a roof again! It is so good to be out here in the night. If I went up into the gallery now, ceiling and walls would shrink together and crush me, crush me flat as a fly.

ELLA RENTHEIM. But where will you go, then?

BORKMAN. I will simply go on, and on, and on. I will try if I cannot make my way to freedom, and life, and human beings again. Will you go with me, Ella?

ELLA RENTHEIM. I? Now?

BORKMAN. Yes, at once!

ELLA RENTHEIM. But how far?

BORKMAN. As far as ever I can.

ELLA RENTHEIM. Oh, but think what you are doing! Out in this raw, cold winter night

BORKMAN. [Speaking very hoarsely.] Oho, my lady is concerned about her health? Yes, yes, I know it is delicate.

ELLA RENTHEIM. It is your health I am concerned about.

BORKMAN. Hohoho! A dead man's health! I can't help laughing at you, Ella! [He moves onwards.

ELLA RENTHEIM. [Following him: holding him back.] What did you call yourself?

BORKMAN. A dead man, I said. Don't you remember, Gunhild told me to lie quiet where I was?

ELLA RENTHEIM. [With resolution, throwing her cloak around her.] I will go with you, John.

BORKMAN. Yes, we two belong to each other, Ella. [Advancing.] So come!

[They have gradually passed into the low wood on the left. It conceals them little by little, until they are quite lost to sight. The house and the open space disappear. The landscape, consisting of wooded slopes and ridges, slowly changes and grows wilder and wilder.

ELLA RENTHEIM's VOICE. [Is heard in the wood to the right.] Where are we going, John? I don't recognise this place.

BORKMAN's VOICE. [Higher up.] Just follow my footprints in the snow!

ELLA RENTHEIM's VOICE. But why need we climb so high?

BORKMAN's VOICE. [Nearer at hand.] We must go up the winding path.

ELLA RENTHEIM. [Still hidden.] Oh, but I can't go much further.

BORKMAN. [On the verge of the wood to the right.] Come, come! We are not far from the view now. There used to be a seat there.

ELLA RENTHEIM. [Appearing among the trees.] Do you remember it?

BORKMAN. You can rest there.

[They have emerged upon a small high-lying, open plateau in the wood. The mountain rises abruptly behind them. To the left, far below, an extensive fiord landscape, with high ranges in the distance, towering one above the other. On the plateau, to the left, a dead fir-tree with a bench under it. The snow lies deep upon the plateau.

[BORKMAN and, after him, ELLA RENTHEIM enter from the right and wade with difficulty through the snow.

BORKMAN. [Stopping at the verge of the steep declivity on the left.] Come here, Ella, and you shall see.

ELLA RENTHEIM. [Coming up to him.] What do you want to show me, John?

BORKMAN. [Pointing outwards.] Do you see how free and open the country lies before us, away to the far horizon?

ELLA RENTHEIM. We have often sat on this bench before, and looked out into a much, much further distance.

BORKMAN. It was a dreamland we then looked out over.

ELLA RENTHEIM. [Nodding sadly.] It was the dreamland of our life, yes. And now that land is buried in snow. And the old tree is dead.

BORKMAN. [Not listening to her.] Can you see the smoke of the great steamships out on the fiord?

ELLA RENTHEIM. No.

BORKMAN. I can. They come and they go. They weave a network of fellowship all round the world. They shed light and warmth over the souls of men in many thousands of homes. That was what I dreamed of doing.

ELLA RENTHEIM. [Softly.] And it remained a dream.

BORKMAN. It remained a dream, yes. [Listening.] And hark, down by the river, dear! The factories are working! My factories! All those that I would have created! Listen! Do you hear them humming? The night shift is on, so they are working night and day. Hark! hark! the wheels are whirling and the bands are flashing, round and round and round. Can't you hear, Ella?

ELLA RENTHEIM. No.

BORKMAN. I can hear it.

ELLA RENTHEIM. [Anxiously.] I think you are mistaken, John.

BORKMAN. [More and more fired up.] Oh, but all these, they are only like the outworks around the kingdom, I tell you!

ELLA RENTHEIM. The kingdom, you say? What kingdom?

BORKMAN. My kingdom, of course! The kingdom I was on the point of conquering when I, when I died.

ELLA RENTHEIM. [Shaken, in a low voice.] Oh, John, John!

BORKMAN. And now there it lies defenceless, masterless, exposed to all the robbers and plunderers. Ella, do you see the mountain chains there far away? They soar, they tower aloft, one behind the other! That is my vast, my infinite, inexhaustible kingdom!

ELLA RENTHEIM. Oh, but there comes an icy blast from that kingdom, John!

BORKMAN. That blast is the breath of life to me. That blast comes to me like a greeting from subject spirits. I seem to touch them, the prisoned millions; I can see the veins of metal stretch out their winding, branching, luring arms to me. I saw them before my eyes like living shapes, that night when I stood in the strong-room with the candle in my hand. You begged to be liberated, and I tried to free you. But my strength failed me; and the treasure sank back into the deep again. [With outstretched hands.] But I will whisper it to you here in the stillness of the night: I love you, as you lie there spellbound in the deeps and the darkness! I love you, unborn treasures, yearning for the light! I love you, with all your shining train of power and glory! I love you, love you, love you!

ELLA RENTHEIM. [In suppressed but rising agitation.] Yes, your love is still down there, John. It has always been rooted there. But here, in the light of day, here there was a living, warm, human heart that throbbed and glowed for you. And this heart you crushed. Oh worse than that! Ten times worse! You sold it for, for

BORKMAN. [Trembles; a cold shudder seems to go through him.] For the kingdom, and the power, and the glory, you mean?

ELLA RENTHEIM. Yes, that is what I mean. I have said it once before to-night: you have murdered the love-life in the woman who loved you. And whom you loved in return, so far as you could love any one. [With uplifted arm.] And therefore I prophesy to you, John Gabriel Borkman, you will never touch the price you demanded for the murder. You will never enter in triumph into your cold, dark kingdom!

BORKMAN. [Staggers to the bench and seats himself heavily.] I almost fear your prophecy will come true, Ella.

ELLA RENTHEIM. [Going up to him.] You must not fear it, John. That is the best thing that can happen to you.

BORKMAN. [With a shriek; clutching at his breast.] Ah! [Feebly.] Now it let me go again.

ELLA RENTHEIM. [Shaking him.] What was it, John?

BORKMAN. [Sinking down against the back of the seat.] It was a hand of ice that clutched at my heart.

ELLA RENTHEIM. John! Did you feel the ice-hand again!

BORKMAN. [Murmurs.] No. No ice-hand. It was a metal hand. [He sinks right down upon the bench.

ELLA RENTHEIM. [Tears off her cloak and throws it over him.] Lie still where you are! I will go and bring help for you.

[She goes a step or two towards the right; then she stops, returns, and carefully feels his pulse and touches his face.

ELLA RENTHEIM. [Softly and firmly.] No. It is best so, John Borkman. Best for you.

[She spreads the cloak closer around him, and sinks down in the snow in front of the bench. A short silence.

[MRS. BORKMAN, wrapped in a mantle, comes through the wood on the right. THE MAID goes before her carrying a lantern.

THE MAID. [Throwing the light upon the snow.] Yes, yes, ma'am, here are their tracks.

MRS. BORKMAN. [Peering around.] Yes, here they are! They are sitting there on the bench. [Calls.] Ella!

ELLA RENTHEIM. [Rising.] Are you looking for us?

MRS. BORKMAN. [Sternly.] Yes, you see I have to.

ELLA RENTHEIM. [Pointing.] Look, there he lies, Gunhild.

MRS. BORKMAN. Sleeping?

ELLA RENTHEIM. A long, deep sleep, I think.

MRS. BORKMAN. [With an outburst.] Ella! [Controls herself and asks in a low voice.] Did he do it of his own accord?

ELLA RENTHEIM. No.

MRS. BORKMAN. [Relieved.] Not by his own hand then?

ELLA RENTHEIM. No. It was an ice-cold metal hand that gripped him by the heart.

MRS. BORKMAN. [To THE MAID.] Go for help. Get the men to come up from the farm.

THE MAID. Yes, I will, ma'am. [To herself.] Lord save us! [She goes out through the wood to the right.

MRS. BORKMAN. [Standing behind the bench.] So the night air has killed him

ELLA RENTHEIM. So it appears.

MRS. BORKMAN. strong man that he was.

ELLA RENTHEIM. [Coming in front of the bench.] Will you not look at him, Gunhild?

MRS. BORKMAN. [With a gesture of repulsion.] No, no, no. [Lowering her voice.] He was a miner's son, John Gabriel Borkman. He could not live in the fresh air.

ELLA RENTHEIM. It was rather the cold that killed him.

MRS. BORKMAN. [Shakes her head.] The cold, you say? The cold that had killed him long ago.

ELLA RENTHEIM. [Nodding to her.] Yes, and changed us two into shadows.

MRS. BORKMAN. You are right there.

ELLA RENTHEIM. [With a painful smile.] A dead man and two shadows, that is what the cold has made of us.

MRS. BORKMAN. Yes, the coldness of heart. And now I think we two may hold out our hands to each other, Ella.

ELLA RENTHEIM. I think we may, now.

MRS. BORKMAN. We twin sisters, over him we have both loved.

ELLA RENTHEIM. We two shadows, over the dead man.

[MRS. BORKMAN behind the bench, and ELLA RENTHEIM in front of it, take each other's hand.

THE END.

Henrik Ibsen - When We Dead Awaken

Index Of Contents

Characters.
PROFESSOR ARNOLD RUBEK, a sculptor.
MRS. MAIA RUBEK, his wife.
THE INSPECTOR at the Baths.
ULFHEIM, a landed proprietor.
A STRANGER LADY.
A SISTER OF MERCY.

Servants, Visitors to the Baths, and Children.

The First Act passes at a bathing establishment on the coast; the Second and Third Acts in the neighbourhood of a health resort, high in the mountains.

Act First.

[Outside the Bath Hotel. A portion of the main building can be seen to the right. An open, park-like place with a fountain, groups of fine old trees, and shrubbery. To the left, a little pavilion almost covered with ivy and Virginia creeper. A table and chair outside it. At the back a view over the fjord, right out to sea, with headlands and small islands in the distance. It is a calm, warm and sunny summer morning.

[PROFESSOR RUBEK and MRS. MAIA RUBEK are sitting in basket chairs beside a covered table on the lawn outside the hotel, having just breakfasted. They have champagne and seltzer water on the table, and each has a newspaper. PROFESSOR RUBEK is an elderly man of distinguished appearance, wearing a black velvet jacket, and otherwise in light summer attire. MAIA is quite young, with a vivacious expression and lively, mocking eyes, yet with a suggestion of fatigue. She wears an elegant travelling dress.

MAIA
[Sits for some time as though waiting for the PROFESSOR to say something, then lets her paper drop with a deep sigh.] Oh dear, dear, dear!

PROFESSOR RUBEK
[Looks up from his paper.] Well, Maia? What is the matter with you?

MAIA
Just listen how silent it is here.

PROFESSOR RUBEK

[Smiles indulgently.] And you can hear that?

MAIA

What?

PROFESSOR RUBEK

The silence?

MAIA

Yes, indeed I can.

PROFESSOR RUBEK

Well, perhaps you are right, *mein Kind*. One can really hear the silence.

MAIA

Heaven knows you can, when it's so absolutely overpowering as it is here

PROFESSOR RUBEK

Here at the Baths, you mean?

MAIA

Wherever you go at home here, it seems to me. Of course there was noise and bustle enough in the town. But I don't know how it is, even the noise and bustle seemed to have something dead about it.

PROFESSOR RUBEK

[With a searching glance.] You don't seem particularly glad to be at home again, Maia?

MAIA

[Looks at him.] Are you glad?

PROFESSOR RUBEK

[Evasively.] I -?

MAIA

Yes, you, who have been so much, much further away than I. Are you entirely happy, now that you are at home again?

PROFESSOR RUBEK

No, to be quite candid, perhaps not entirely happy

MAIA

[With animation.] There, you see! Didn't I know it!

PROFESSOR RUBEK

I have been too long abroad. I have drifted quite away from all this, this home life.

MAIA

[Eagerly, drawing her chair nearer him.] There, you see, Rubek! We had much better get away again! As quickly as ever we can.

PROFESSOR RUBEK

[Somewhat impatiently.] Well, well, that is what we intend to do, my dear Maia. You know that.

MAIA

But why not now, at once? Only think how cozy and comfortable we could be down there, in our lovely new house

PROFESSOR RUBEK

[Smiles indulgently.] We ought by rights to say: our lovely new home.

MAIA

[Shortly.] I prefer to say house, let us keep to that.

PROFESSOR RUBEK

[His eyes dwelling on her.] You are really a strange little person.

MAIA

Am I so strange?

PROFESSOR RUBEK

Yes, I think so.

MAIA

But why, pray? Perhaps because I'm not desperately in love with mooning about up here?

PROFESSOR RUBEK

Which of us was it that was absolutely bent on our coming north this summer?

MAIA

I admit, it was I.

PROFESSOR RUBEK

It was certainly not I, at any rate.

MAIA

But good heavens, who could have dreamt that everything would have altered so terribly at home here? And in so short a time, too! Why, it is only just four years since I went away

PROFESSOR RUBEK

Since you were married, yes.

MAIA

Married? What has that to do with the matter?

PROFESSOR RUBEK

[Continuing.] Since you became the Frau Professor, and found yourself mistress of a charming home, I beg your pardon, a very handsome house, I ought to say. And a villa on the Lake of Taunitz, just at the point that has become most fashionable, too. In fact it is all very handsome and distinguished, Maia, there's no denying that. And spacious too. We need not always be getting in each other's way

MAIA

[Lightly.] No, no, no, there's certainly no lack of house-room, and that sort of thing

PROFESSOR RUBEK

Remember, too, that you have been living in altogether more spacious and distinguished surroundings, in more polished society than you were accustomed to at home.

MAIA

[Looking at him.] Ah, so you think it is *I* that have changed?

PROFESSOR RUBEK

Indeed I do, Maia.

MAIA

I alone? Not the people here?

PROFESSOR RUBEK

Oh yes, they too, a little, perhaps. And not at all in the direction of amiability. That I readily admit.

MAIA

I should think you must admit it, indeed.

PROFESSOR RUBEK

[Changing the subject.] Do you know how it affects me when I look at the life of the people around us here?

MAIA

No. Tell me.

PROFESSOR RUBEK

It makes me think of that night we spent in the train, when we were coming up here

MAIA

Why, you were sound asleep all the time.

PROFESSOR RUBEK

Not quite. I noticed how silent it became at all the little roadside stations. I heard the silence, like you, Maia

MAIA

H'm, like me, yes.

PROFESSOR RUBEK

- and that assured me that we had crossed the frontier, that we were really at home. For the train stopped at all the little stations, although there was nothing doing at all.

MAIA

Then why did it stop though there was nothing to be done?

PROFESSOR RUBEK

Can't say. No one got out or in; but all the same the train stopped a long, endless time. And at every station I could make out that there were two railway men walking up and down the platform, one with a lantern in his hand, and they said things to each other in the night, low, and toneless, and meaningless.

MAIA

Yes, that is quite true. There are always two men walking up and down, and talking

PROFESSOR RUBEK

Of nothing. [Changing to a livelier tone.] But just wait till to- morrow. Then we shall have the great luxurious steamer lying in the harbour. We'll go on board her, and sail all round the coast, northward ho! right to the polar sea.

MAIA

Yes, but then you will see nothing of the country and of the people. And that was what you particularly wanted.

PROFESSOR RUBEK

[Shortly and snappishly.] I have seen more than enough.

MAIA

Do you think a sea voyage will be better for you?

PROFESSOR RUBEK

It is always a change.

MAIA

Well, well, if only it is the right thing for you

PROFESSOR RUBEK

For me? The right thing? There is nothing in the world the matter with me.

MAIA

[Rises and goes to him.] Yes, there is, Rubek. I am sure you must feel it yourself.

PROFESSOR RUBEK

Why my dearest Maia, what should be amiss with me?

MAIA

[Behind him, bending over the back of his chair.] That you must tell me. You have begun to wander about without a moment's peace. You cannot rest anywhere, neither at home nor abroad. You have become quite misanthropic of late.

PROFESSOR RUBEK

[With a touch of sarcasm.] Dear me, have you noticed that?

MAIA

No one that knows you can help noticing it. And then it seems to me so sad that you have lost all pleasure in your work.

PROFESSOR RUBEK

That too, eh?

MAIA

You that used to be so indefatigable, working from morning to night!

PROFESSOR RUBEK

[Gloomily.] Used to be, yes

MAIA

But ever since you got your great masterpiece out of hand

PROFESSOR RUBEK

[Nods thoughtfully.] "The Resurrection Day"

MAIA

- the masterpiece that has gone round the whole world, and made you so famous

PROFESSOR RUBEK

Perhaps that is just the misfortune, Maia.

MAIA

How so?

PROFESSOR RUBEK

When I had finished this masterpiece of mine [Makes a passionate movement with his hand] for "The Resurrection Day" is a masterpiece! Or was one in the beginning. No, it is one still. It must, must, must be a masterpiece!

MAIA

[Looks at him in astonishment.] Why, Rubek, all the world knows that.

PROFESSOR RUBEK

[Short, repellently.] All the world knows nothing! Understands nothing!

MAIA

Well, at any rate it can divine something

PROFESSOR RUBEK

Something that isn't there at all, yes. Something that never was in my mind. Ah yes, that they can all go into ecstasies over! [Growling to himself.] What is the good of working oneself to death for the mob and the masses for "all the world"!

MAIA

Do you think it is better, then, do you think it is worthy of you, to do nothing at all but portrait-bust now and then?

PROFESSOR RUBEK

[With a sly smile.] They are not exactly portrait-busts that I turn out, Maia.

MAIA

Yes, indeed they are, for the last two or three years, ever since you finished your great group and got it out of the house

PROFESSOR RUBEK

All the same, they are no mere portrait-busts, I assure you.

MAIA

What are they, then?

PROFESSOR RUBEK

There is something equivocal, something cryptic, lurking in and behind these busts, a secret something, that the people themselves cannot see

MAIA

Indeed?

PROFESSOR RUBEK

[Decisively.] I alone can see it. And it amuses me unspeakably. On the surface I give them the "striking likeness," as they call it, that they all stand and gape at in astonishment [Lowers his voice] but at bottom they are all respectable, pompous horse-faces, and self- opinionated donkey-muzzles, and lop-eared, low-browed dog-skulls, and fatted swine-snouts, and sometimes dull, brutal bull-fronts as well

MAIA

[Indifferently.] All the dear domestic animals, in fact.

PROFESSOR RUBEK

Simply the dear domestic animals, Maia. All the animals which men have bedevilled in their own image and which have bedevilled men in return. [Empties his champagne-glass and laughs.] And it is these double-faced works of art that our excellent plutocrats come and order of me. And pay for in all good faith, and in good round figures too, almost their weight in gold, as the saying goes.

MAIA

[Fills his glass.] Come, Rubek! Drink and be happy.

PROFESSOR RUBEK

[Passes his hand several times across his forehead and leans back in his chair.] I am happy, Maia. Really happy, in a way. [Short silence.] For after all there is a certain happiness in feeling oneself free and independent on every hand, in having at ones command everything one can possibly wish for, all outward things, that is to say. Do you not agree with me, Maia?

MAIA

Oh yes, I agree. All that is well enough in its way. [Looking at him.] But do you remember what you promised me the day we came to an understanding on, on that troublesome point

PROFESSOR RUBEK

[Nods.] - on the subject of our marriage, yes. It was no easy matter for you, Maia.

MAIA

[Continuing unruffled.] - and agreed that I was to go abroad with you, and live there for good and all and enjoy myself. Do you remember what you promised me that day?

PROFESSOR RUBEK

[Shaking his head.] No, I can't say that I do. Well, what did I promise?

MAIA

You said you would take me up to a high mountain and show me all the glory of the world.

PROFESSOR RUBEK

[With a slight start.] Did I promise you that, too?

MAIA

Me too? Who else, pray?

PROFESSOR RUBEK

[Indifferently.] No, no, I only meant did I promise to show you?

MAIA

- all the glory of the world? Yes, you did. And all that glory should be mine, you said.

PROFESSOR RUBEK

That is sort of figure of speech that I was in the habit of using once upon a time.

MAIA
Only a figure of speech?

PROFESSOR RUBEK
Yes, a schoolboy phrase, the sort of thing I used to say when I wanted to lure the neighbours' children out to play with me, in the woods and on the mountains.

MAIA
[Looking hard at him.] Perhaps you only wanted to lure me out to play, as well?

PROFESSOR RUBEK
[Passing it off as a jest.] Well, has it not been a tolerable amusing game, Maia?

MAIA
[Coldly.] I did not go with you only to play.

PROFESSOR RUBEK
No, no, I daresay not.

MAIA
And you never took me up with you to any high mountain, or showed me

PROFESSOR RUBEK
[With irritation.] - all the glory of the world? No, I did not. For, let me tell you something: you are not really born to be a mountain- climber, little Maia.

MAIA
[Trying to control herself.] Yet at one time you seemed to think I was.

PROFESSOR RUBEK
Four or five years ago, yes. [Stretching himself in his chair.] Four or five years, it's a long, long time, Maia.

MAIA
[Looking at him with a bitter expression.] Has the time seemed so very long to you, Rubek?

PROFESSOR RUBEK
I am beginning now to find it a trifle long. [Yawning.] Now and then, you know.

MAIA
[Returning to her place.] I shall not bore you any longer.

[She resumes her seat, takes up the newspaper, and begins turning over the leaves. Silence on both sides.

PROFESSOR RUBEK
[Leaning on his elbows across the table, and looking at her teasingly.] Is the Frau Professor offended?

MAIA
[Coldly, without looking up.] No, not at all.

[Visitors to the baths, most of them ladies, begin to pass, singly and in groups, through the park from the right, and out to the left.

[Waiters bring refreshments from the hotel, and go off behind the pavilion.

[The INSPECTOR, wearing gloves and carrying a stick, comes from his rounds in the park, meets visitors, bows politely, and exchanges a few words with some of them.

THE INSPECTOR
[Advancing to PROFESSOR RUBEK's table and politely taking off his hat.] I have the honour to wish you good morning, Mrs. Rubek. Good morning, Professor Rubek.

PROFESSOR RUBEK
Good morning, good morning Inspector.

THE INSPECTOR

[Addressing himself to MRS. RUBEK.] May I venture to ask if you have slept well?

MAIA

Yes, thank you; excellently for my part. I always sleep like a stone.

THE INSPECTOR

I am delighted to hear it. The first night in a strange place is often rather trying. And the Professor?

PROFESSOR RUBEK

Oh, my night's rest is never much to boast of, especially of late.

THE INSPECTOR

[With a show of sympathy.] Oh, that is a pity. But after a few weeks' stay at the Baths, you will quite get over that.

PROFESSOR RUBEK

[Looking up at him.] Tell me, Inspector are any of your patients in the habit of taking baths during the night?

THE INSPECTOR

[Astonished.] During the night? No, I have never heard of such a thing.

PROFESSOR RUBEK

Have you not?

THE INSPECTOR

No, I don't know of any one so ill as to require such treatment.

PROFESSOR RUBEK

Well, at any rate there is some one who is in the habit of walking about the park by night?

THE INSPECTOR

[Smiling and shaking his head.] No, Professor, that would be against the rules.

MAIA

[Impatiently.] Good Heavens, Rubek, I told you so this morning, you must have dreamt it.

PROFESSOR RUBEK

[Drily.] Indeed? Must I? Thank you! [Turning to the INSPECTOR.] The fact is, I got up last night. I couldn't sleep and I wanted to see what sort of night it was

THE INSPECTOR

[Attentively.] To be sure, and then?

PROFESSOR RUBEK

I looked out at the window and caught sight of a white figure in there among the trees.

MAIA

[Smiling to the INSPECTOR.] And the Professor declares that the figure was dressed in a bathing costume

PROFESSOR RUBEK

- or something like it, I said. Couldn't distinguish very clearly. But I am sure it was something white.

THE INSPECTOR

Most remarkable. Was it a gentleman or a lady?

PROFESSOR RUBEK

I could almost have sworn it was a lady. But then after it came another figure. And that one was quite dark, like a shadow.

THE INSPECTOR

[Starting.] A dark one? Quite black, perhaps?

PROFESSOR RUBEK
Yes, I should almost have said so.

THE INSPECTOR
[A light breaking in upon him.] And behind the white figure? Following close upon her?

PROFESSOR RUBEK
Yes, at a little distance

THE INSPECTOR
Aha! Then I think I can explain the mystery, Professor.

PROFESSOR RUBEK
Well, what was it then?

MAIA
[Simultaneously.] Was the professor really not dreaming?

THE INSPECTOR
[Suddenly whispering, as he directs their attention towards the background on the right.] Hush, if you please! Look there, don't speak loud for a moment.

[A slender lady, dressed in fine, cream-white cashmere, and followed by a SISTER OF MERCY in black, with a silver cross hanging by a chain on her breast, comes forward from behind the hotel and crosses the park towards the pavilion in front on the left. Her face is pale, and its lines seem to have stiffened; the eyelids are drooped and the eyes appear as though they saw nothing. Her dress comes down to her feet and clings to the body in perpendicular folds. Over her head, neck, breast, shoulders and arms she wears a large shawl of white crape. She keeps her arms crossed upon her breast. She carries her body immovably, and her steps are stiff and measured. The SISTER's bearing is also measured, and she has the air of a servant. She keeps her brown piercing eyes incessantly fixed upon the lady. WAITERS, with napkins on their arms, come forward in the hotel doorway, and cast curious glances at the strangers, who take no notice of anything, and, without looking round, enter the pavilion.

PROFESSOR RUBEK
[Has risen slowly and involuntarily, and stands staring at the closed door of the pavilion.] Who was that lady?

THE INSPECTOR
She is a stranger who has rented the little pavilion there.

PROFESSOR RUBEK
A foreigner?

THE INSPECTOR
Presumably. At any rate they both came from abroad about a week ago. They have never been here before.

PROFESSOR RUBEK
[Decidedly; looking at him.] It was she I saw in the park last night.

THE INSPECTOR
No doubt it must have been. I thought so from the first.

PROFESSOR RUBEK
What is this lady's name, Inspector?

THE INSPECTOR
She has registered herself as "Madame de Satow, with companion." We know nothing more.

PROFESSOR RUBEK
[Reflecting.] Satow? Satow?

MAIA
[Laughing mockingly.] Do you know any one of that name, Rubek? Eh?

PROFESSOR RUBEK

[Shaking his head.] No, no one. Satow? It sounds Russian or in all events Slavonic. [To the INSPECTOR.] What language does she speak?

THE INSPECTOR

When the two ladies talk to each other, it is in a language I cannot make out at all. But at other times she speaks Norwegian like a native.

PROFESSOR RUBEK

[Exclaims with a start.] Norwegian? You are sure you are not mistaken?

THE INSPECTOR

No, how could I be mistaken in that?

PROFESSOR RUBEK

[Looks at him with eager interest.] You have heard her yourself?

THE INSPECTOR

Yes. I myself have spoken to her several times. Only a few words, however; she is far from communicative. But

PROFESSOR RUBEK

But Norwegian it was?

THE INSPECTOR

Thoroughly good Norwegian, perhaps with a little north-country accent.

PROFESSOR RUBEK

[Gazing straight before him in amazement, whispers.] That too?

MAIA

[A little hurt and jarred.] Perhaps this lady has been one of your models, Rubek? Search your memory.

PROFESSOR RUBEK

[Looks cuttingly at her.] My models?

MAIA

[With a provoking smile.] In your younger days, I mean. You are said to have had innumerable models, long ago, of course.

PROFESSOR RUBEK

[In the same tone.] Oh no, little Frau Maia. I have in reality had only one single model. One and only one for everything I have done.

THE INSPECTOR

[Who has turned away and stands looking out to the left.] If you'll excuse me, I think I will take my leave. I see some one coming whom it is not particularly agreeable to meet. Especially in the presence of ladies.

PROFESSOR RUBEK

[Looking in the same direction.] That sportsman there? Who is it?

THE INSPECTOR

It is a certain Mr. Ulfheim, from

PROFESSOR RUBEK

Oh, Mr. Ulfheim

THE INSPECTOR

- the bear-killer, as they call him

PROFESSOR RUBEK

I know him.

THE INSPECTOR
Who does not know him?

PROFESSOR RUBEK
Very slightly, however. Is he on your list of patients at last?

THE INSPECTOR
No, strangely enough, not as yet. He comes here only once a year on his way up to his hunting-grounds. Excuse me for the moment

[Makes a movement to go into the hotel.

ULFHEIM'S VOICE.
[Heard outside.] Stop a moment, man! Devil take it all, can't you stop? Why do you always scuttle away from me?

THE INSPECTOR
[Stops.] I am not scuttling at all, Mr. Ulfheim.

[ULFHEIM enters from the left followed by a servant with a couple of sporting dogs in leash. ULFHEIM is in shooting costume, with high boots and a felt hat with a feather in it. He is a long, lank, sinewy personage, with matted hair and beard, and a loud voice. His appearance gives no precise clue to his age, but he is no longer young.]

ULFHEIM
[Pounces upon the INSPECTOR.] Is this a way to receive strangers, hey? You scamper away with your tail between your legs as if you had the devil at your heels.

THE INSPECTOR
[Calmly, without answering him.] Has Mr. Ulfheim arrived by the steamer?

ULFHEIM
[Growls.] Haven't had the honour of seeing any steamer. [With his arms akimbo.] Don't you know that I sail my own cutter? [To the SERVANT.] Look well after your fellow-creatures, Lars. But take care you keep them ravenous, all the same. Fresh meat-bones but not too much meat on them, do you hear? And be sure it's reeking raw, and bloody. And get something in your own belly while you're about it. [Aiming a kick at him.] Now then, go to hell with you!

[The SERVANT goes out with the dogs, behind the corner of the hotel.]

THE INSPECTOR
Would not Mr. Ulfheim like to go into the dining-room in the meantime?

ULFHEIM
In among all the half-dead flies and people? No, thank you a thousand times, Mr. Inspector.

THE INSPECTOR
Well, well, as you please.

ULFHEIM
But get the housekeeper to prepare a hamper for me as usual. There must be plenty of provender in it and lots of brandy! You can tell her that I or Lars will come and play Old Harry with her if she doesn't

THE INSPECTOR
[Interrupting.] We know your ways of old. [Turning.] Can I give the waiter any orders, Professor? Can I send Mrs. Rubek anything?

PROFESSOR RUBEK
No thank you; nothing for me.

MAIA
Nor for me.

[The INSPECTOR goes into the hotel.

ULFHEIM

[Stares at them for a moment; then lifts his hat.] Why, blast me if here isn't a country tyke that has strayed into regular tip-top society.

PROFESSOR RUBEK

[Looking up.] What do you mean by that, Mr. Ulfheim?

ULFHEIM

[More quietly and politely.] I believe I have the honour of addressing no less a person than the great Sculptor Rubek.

PROFESSOR RUBEK

[Nods.] I remember meeting you once or twice, the autumn when I was last at home.

ULFHEIM

That's many years ago, now. And then you weren't so illustrious as I hear you've since become. At that time even a dirty bear-hunter might venture to come near you.

PROFESSOR RUBEK

[Smiling.] I don't bite even now.

MAIA

[Looks with interest at ULFHEIM.] Are you really and truly a bear- hunter?

ULFHEIM

[Seating himself at the next table, nearer the hotel.] A bear-hunter when I have the chance, madam. But I make the best of any sort of game that comes in my way; eagles, and wolves, and women, and elks, and reindeer, if only it's fresh and juicy and has plenty of blood in it.

[Drinks from his pocket-flask.

MAIA

[Regarding him fixedly.] But you like bear-hunting best?

ULFHEIM

I like it best, yes. For then one can have the knife handy at a pinch. [With a slight smile.] We both work in a hard material, madam, both your husband and I. He struggles with his marble blocks, I daresay; and I struggle with tense and quivering bear-sinews. And we both of us win the fight in the end, subdue and master our material. We never rest till we've got the upper hand of it, though it fight never so hard.

PROFESSOR RUBEK

[Deep in thought.] There's a great deal of truth in what you say.

ULFHEIM

Yes, for I take it the stone has something to fight for too. It is dead, and determined by no manner of means to let itself be hammered into life. Just like the bear when you come and prod him up in his lair.

MAIA

Are you going up into the forests now to hunt?

ULFHEIM

I am going right up into the high mountain. I suppose you have never been in the high mountain, madam?

MAIA

No, never.

ULFHEIM

Confound it all then, you must be sure and come up there this very summer! I'll take you with me, both you and the Professor, with pleasure.

MAIA

Thanks. But Rubek is thinking of taking a sea trip this summer.

PROFESSOR RUBEK
Round the coast, through the island channels.

ULFHEIM
Ugh, what the devil would you do in those damnable sickly gutters, floundering about in the brackish ditchwater? Dishwater I should rather call it.

MAIA
There, you hear, Rubek!

ULFHEIM
No, much better come up with me to the mountain, away, clean away, from the trail and taint of men. You cant' think what that means for me. But such a little lady

[He stops.

[The SISTER OF MERCY comes out of the pavilion and goes into the hotel.

ULFHEIM
[Following her with his eyes.] Just look at her, do! That night-crow there! Who is it that's to be buried?

PROFESSOR RUBEK
I have not heard of any one

ULFHEIM
Well, there's some one on the point of giving up the ghost, then, in on corner or another. People that are sickly and rickety should have the goodness to see about getting themselves buried, the sooner the better.

MAIA
Have you ever been ill yourself, Mr. Ulfheim.

ULFHEIM
Never. If I had, I shouldn't be here. But my nearest friends, they have been ill, poor things.

MAIA
And what did you do for your nearest friends?

ULFHEIM
Shot them, of course.

PROFESSOR RUBEK
[Looking at him.] Shot them?

MAIA
[Moving her chair back.] Shot them dead?

ULFHEIM
[Nods.] I never miss, madam.

MAIA
But how can you possibly shoot people!

ULFHEIM
I am not speaking of people

MAIA
You said your nearest friends

ULFHEIM
Well, who should they be but my dogs?

MAIA
Are your dogs your nearest friends?

ULFHEIM

I have none nearer. My honest, trusty, absolutely loyal comrades. When one of them turns sick and miserable, bang! and there's my friend sent packing to the other world.

[The SISTER OF MERCY comes out of the hotel with a tray on which is bread and milk. She places it on the table outside the pavilion, which she enters.

ULFHEIM

[Laughs scornfully.] That stuff there, is that what you call food for human beings! Milk and water and soft, clammy bread. Ah, you should see my comrades feeding. Should you like to see it?

MAIA

[Smiling across to the PROFESSOR and rising.] Yes, very much.

ULFHEIM

[Also rising.] Spoken like a woman of spirit, madam! Come with me, then! They swallow whole great thumping meat-bones, gulp them up and then gulp them down again. Oh, it's a regular treat to see them. Come along and I'll show you and while we're about it, we can talk over this trip to the mountains

[He goes out by the corner of the hotel, MAIA following him.

[Almost at the same moment the STRANGE LADY comes out of the pavilion and seats herself at the table.

[The LADY raises her glass of milk and is about to drink, but stops and looks across at RUBEK with vacant, expressionless eyes.

PROFESSOR RUBEK

[Remains sitting at his table and gazes fixedly and earnestly at her. At last he rises, goes some steps towards her, stops, and says in a low voice.] I know you quite well, Irene.

THE LADY

[In a toneless voice, setting down her glass.] You can guess who I am, Arnold?

PROFESSOR RUBEK

[Without answering.] And you recognise me, too, I see.

THE LADY

With you it is quite another matter.

PROFESSOR RUBEK

With me? How so?

THE LADY

Oh, you are still alive.

PROFESSOR RUBEK

[Not understanding.] Alive?

THE LADY

[After a short pause.] Who was the other? The woman you had with you, there at the table?

PROFESSOR RUBEK

[A little reluctantly.] She? That was my, my wife.

THE LADY

[Nods slowly.] Indeed. That is well, Arnold. Some one, then, who does not concern me

PROFESSOR RUBEK

[Nods.] No, of course not

THE LADY

- one whom you have taken to you after my lifetime.

PROFESSOR RUBEK

[Suddenly looking hard at her.] After your? What do you mean by that, Irene?

IRENE

[Without answering.] And the child? I hear the child is prospering too. Our child survives me and has come to honour and glory.

PROFESSOR RUBEK

[Smiles as at a far-off recollection.] Our child? Yes, we called it so then.

IRENE

In my lifetime, yes.

PROFESSOR RUBEK

[Trying to take a lighter tone.] Yes, Irene. I can assure you "our child" has become famous all the wide world over. I suppose you have read about it.

IRENE

[Nods.] And has made its father famous too. That was your dream.

PROFESSOR RUBEK

[More softly, with emotion.] It is to you I owe everything, everything, Irene and I thank you.

IRENE

[Lost in thought for a moment.] If I had then done what I had a right to do, Arnold

PROFESSOR RUBEK

Well? What then?

IRENE

I should have killed that child.

PROFESSOR RUBEK

Killed it, you say?

IRENE

[Whispering.] Killed it, before I went away from you. Crushed it, crushed it to dust.

PROFESSOR RUBEK

[Shakes his head reproachfully.] You would never have been able to, Irene. You had not the heart to do it.

IRENE

No, in those days I had not that sort of heart.

PROFESSOR RUBEK

But since then? Afterwards?

IRENE

Since then I have killed it innumerable times. By daylight and in the dark. Killed it in hatred, and in revenge, and in anguish.

PROFESSOR RUBEK

[Goes close up to the table and asks softly.] Irene, tell me now at last, after all these years, why did you go away from me? You disappeared so utterly, left not a trace behind

IRENE

[Shaking her head slowly.] Oh Arnold, why should I tell you that now, from the world beyond the grave.

PROFESSOR RUBEK

Was there some one else whom you had come to love?

IRENE

There was one who had no longer any use for my love, any use for my life.

PROFESSOR RUBEK

[Changing the subject.] H'm, don't let us talk any more of the past

IRENE

No, no, by all means let us not talk of what is beyond the grave, what is now beyond the grave for me.

PROFESSOR RUBEK

Where have you been, Irene? All my inquiries were fruitless, you seemed to have vanished away.

IRENE

I went into the darkness, when the child stood transfigured in the light.

PROFESSOR RUBEK

Have you travelled much about the world?

IRENE

Yes. Travelled in many lands.

PROFESSOR RUBEK

[Looks compassionately at her.] And what have you found to do, Irene?

IRENE

[Turning her eyes upon him.] Wait a moment; let me see. Yes, now I have it. I have posed on the turntable in variety-shows. Posed as a naked statue in living pictures. Raked in heaps of money. That was more than I could do with you; for you had none. And then I turned the heads of all sorts of men. That too, was more than I could do with you, Arnold. You kept yourself better in hand.

PROFESSOR RUBEK

[Hastening to pass the subject by.] And then you have married, too?

IRENE

Yes; I married one of them.

PROFESSOR RUBEK

Who is your husband?

IRENE

He was a South American. A distinguished diplomatist. [Looks straight in front of her with a stony smile.] Him I managed to drive quite out of his mind; mad, incurably mad; inexorably mad. It was great sport, I can tell you, while it was in the doing. I could have laughed within me all the time, if I had anything within me.

PROFESSOR RUBEK

And where is he now?

IRENE

Oh, in a churchyard somewhere or other. With a fine handsome monument over him. And with a bullet rattling in his skull.

PROFESSOR RUBEK

Did he kill himself?

IRENE

Yes, he was good enough to take that off my hands.

PROFESSOR RUBEK

Do you not lament his loss, Irene?

IRENE

[Not understanding.] Lament? What loss?

PROFESSOR RUBEK

Why, the loss of Herr von Satow, of course.

IRENE

His name was not Satow.

PROFESSOR RUBEK

Was it not?

IRENE

My second husband is called Satow. He is a Russian

PROFESSOR RUBEK

And where is he?

IRENE

Far away in the Ural Mountains. Among all his gold-mines.

PROFESSOR RUBEK

So he lives there?

IRENE

[Shrugs her shoulders.] Lives? Lives? In reality I have killed him

PROFESSOR RUBEK

[Start.] Killed!

IRENE

Killed him with a fine sharp dagger which I always have with me in bed

PROFESSOR RUBEK

[Vehemently.] I don't believe you, Irene!

IRENE

[With a gentle smile.] Indeed you may believe it, Arnold.

PROFESSOR RUBEK

[Looks compassionately at her.] Have you never had a child?

IRENE

Yes, I have had many children.

PROFESSOR RUBEK

And where are your children now?

IRENE

I killed them.

PROFESSOR RUBEK

[Severely.] Now you are telling me lies again!

IRENE

I have killed them, I tell you, murdered them pitilessly. As soon as ever they came into the world. Oh, long, long before. One after the other.

PROFESSOR RUBEK

[Sadly and earnestly.] There is something hidden behind everything you say.

IRENE

How can I help that? Every word I say is whispered into my ear.

PROFESSOR RUBEK

I believe I am the only one that can divine your meaning.

IRENE

Surely you ought to be the only one.

PROFESSOR RUBEK

[Rests his hands on the table and looks intently at her.] Some of the strings of your nature have broken.

IRENE

[Gently.] Does not that always happen when a young warm-blooded woman dies?

PROFESSOR RUBEK

Oh Irene, have done with these wild imaginings! You are living! Living, living!

IRENE

[Rises slowly from her chair and says, quivering.] I was dead for many years. They came and bound me, laced my arms together behind my back. Then they lowered me into a grave-vault, with iron bars before the loop-hole. And with padded walls, so that no one on the earth above could hear the grave-shrieks. But now I am beginning, in a way, to rise from the dead.

[She seats herself again.]

PROFESSOR RUBEK

[After a pause.] In all this, do you hold me guilty?

IRENE

Yes.

PROFESSOR RUBEK

Guilty of that, your death, as you call it.

IRENE

Guilty of the fact that I had to die. [Changing her tone to one of indifference.] Why don't you sit down, Arnold?

PROFESSOR RUBEK

May I?

IRENE

Yes. You need not be afraid of being frozen. I don't think I am quite turned to ice yet.

PROFESSOR RUBEK

[Moves a chair and seats himself at her table.] There, Irene. Now we two are sitting together as in the old days.

IRENE

A little way apart from each other also as in the old days.

PROFESSOR RUBEK

[Moving nearer.] It had to be so, then.

IRENE

Had it?

PROFESSOR RUBEK

[Decisively.] There had to be a distance between us

IRENE

Was it absolutely necessary, Arnold?

PROFESSOR RUBEK

[Continuing.] Do you remember what you answered when I asked if you would go with me out into the wide world?

IRENE

I held up three fingers in the air and swore that I would go with you to the world's end and to the end of life. And that I would serve you in all things

PROFESSOR RUBEK

As the model for my art

IRENE

- in frank, utter nakedness

PROFESSOR RUBEK

[With emotion.] And you did serve me, Irene, so bravely, so gladly and ungrudgingly.

IRENE

Yes, with all the pulsing blood of my youth, I served you!

PROFESSOR RUBEK

[Nodding, with a look of gratitude.] That you have every right to say.

IRENE

I fell down at your feet and served you, Arnold! [Holding her clenched hand towards him.] But you, you, you!

PROFESSOR RUBEK

[Defensively.] I never did you any wrong! Never, Irene!

IRENE

Yes, you did! You did wrong to my innermost, inborn nature

PROFESSOR RUBEK

[Starting back.] I!

IRENE

Yes, you! I exposed myself wholly and unreservedly to your gaze [More softly.] And never once did you touch me.

PROFESSOR RUBEK

Irene, did you not understand that many a time I was almost beside myself under the spell of all your loveliness?

IRENE

[Continuing undisturbed.] And yet, if you had touched me, I think I should have killed you on the spot. For I had a sharp needle always upon me, hidden in my hair [Strokes her forehead meditatively.] But after all, after all, that you could

PROFESSOR RUBEK

[Looks impressively at her.] I was an artist, Irene.

IRENE

[Darkly.] That is just it. That is just it.

PROFESSOR RUBEK

An artist first of all. And I was sick with the desire to achieve the great work of my life. [Losing himself in recollection.] It was to be called "The Resurrection Day" figured in the likeness of a young woman, awakening from the sleep of death

IRENE

Our child, yes

PROFESSOR RUBEK

[Continuing.] It was to be the awakening of the noblest, purest, most ideal woman the world ever saw. Then I found you. You were what I required in every respect. And you consented so willingly, so gladly. You renounced home and kindred and went with me.

IRENE

To go with you meant for me the resurrection of my childhood.

PROFESSOR RUBEK

That was just why I found in you all that I required, in you and in no one else. I came to look on you as a thing hallowed, not to be touched save in adoring thoughts. In those days I was still young, Irene. And the superstition took hold of me that if I touched you, if I desired you with my senses, my soul would be profaned, so that I should be unable to accomplish what I was striving for. And I still think there was some truth in that.

IRENE

[Nods with a touch of scorn.] The work of art first, then the human being.

PROFESSOR RUBEK

You must judge me as you will; but at that time I was utterly dominated by my great task and exultantly happy in it.

IRENE

And you achieved your great task, Arnold.

PROFESSOR RUBEK

Thanks and praise be to you, I achieved my great task. I wanted to embody the pure woman as I saw her awakening on the Resurrection Day. Not marvelling at anything new and unknown and undivined; but filled with a sacred joy at finding herself unchanged, she, the woman of earth, in the higher, freer, happier region, after the long, dreamless sleep of death. [More softly.] Thus did I fashion her. I fashioned her in your image, Irene.

IRENE

[Laying her hands flat upon the table and leaning against the back of her chair.] And then you were done with me

PROFESSOR RUBEK

[Reproachfully.] Irene!

IRENE

You had no longer any use for me

PROFESSOR RUBEK

How can you say that!

IRENE

- and began to look about you for other ideals

PROFESSOR RUBEK

I found none, none after you.

IRENE

And no other models, Arnold?

PROFESSOR RUBEK

You were no model to me. You were the fountainhead of my achievement.

IRENE

[Is silent for a short time.] What poems have you made since? In marble I mean. Since the day I left you.

PROFESSOR RUBEK

I have made no poems since that day only frittered away my life in modelling.

IRENE

And that woman, whom you are now living with?

PROFESSOR RUBEK

[Interrupting vehemently.] Do not speak of her now! It makes me tingle with shame.

IRENE

Where are you thinking of going with her?

PROFESSOR RUBEK

[Slack and weary.] Oh, on a tedious coasting-voyage to the North, I suppose.

IRENE

[Looks at him, smiles almost imperceptibly, and whispers.] You should rather go high up into the mountains. As high as ever you can. Higher, higher, always higher, Arnold.

PROFESSOR RUBEK

[With eager expectation.] Are you going up there?

IRENE

Have you the courage to meet me once again?

PROFESSOR RUBEK

[Struggling with himself, uncertainly.] If we could oh, if only we could!

IRENE

Why can we not do what we will? [Looks at him and whispers beseechingly with folded hands.] Come, come, Arnold! Oh, come up to me!

[MAIA enters, glowing with pleasure, from behind the hotel, and goes quickly up to the table where they were previously sitting.]

MAIA

[Still at the corner of the hotel, without looking around.] Oh, you may say what you please, Rubek, but [Stops, as she catches sight of IRENE] Oh, I beg your pardon, I see you have made an acquaintance.

PROFESSOR RUBEK

[Curtly.] Renewed an acquaintance. [Rises.] What was it you wanted with me?

MAIA

I only wanted to say this: you may do whatever you please, but *I* am not going with you on that disgusting steamboat.

PROFESSOR RUBEK

Why not?

MAIA

Because I want to go up on the mountains and into the forests, that's what I want. [Coaxingly.] Oh, you must let me do it, Rubek. I shall be so good, so good afterwards!

PROFESSOR RUBEK

Who is it that has put these ideas into your head?

MAIA

Why he, that horrid bear-killer. Oh you cannot conceive all the marvelous things he has to tell about the mountains. And about life up there! They're ugly, horrid, repulsive, most of the yarns he spins, for I almost believe he's lying, but wonderfully alluring all the same. Oh, won't you let me go with him? Only to see if what he says is true, you understand. May I, Rubek?

PROFESSOR RUBEK

Yes, I have not the slightest objection. Off you go to the mountains, as far and as long as you please. I shall perhaps be going the same way myself.

MAIA

[Quickly.] No, no, no, you needn't do that! Not on my account!

PROFESSOR RUBEK

I want to go to the mountains. I have made up my mind to go.

MAIA

Oh thanks, thanks! May I tell the bear-killer at once?

PROFESSOR RUBEK

Tell the bear-killer whatever you please.

MAIA

Oh thanks, thanks, thanks! [Is about to take his hand; he repels the movement.] Oh, how dear and good you are to-day, Rubek!

[She runs into the hotel.]

[At the same time the door of the pavilion is softly and noiselessly set ajar. The SISTER OF MERCY stands in the opening, intently on the watch. No one sees her.

PROFESSOR RUBEK
[Decidedly, turning to IRENE.] Shall we meet up there then?

IRENE
[Rising slowly.] Yes, we shall certainly meet. I have sought for you so long.

PROFESSOR RUBEK
When did you begin to seek for me, Irene?

IRENE
[With a touch of jesting bitterness.] From the moment I realised that I had given away to you something rather indispensable, Arnold. Something one ought never to part with.

PROFESSOR RUBEK
[Bowing his head.] Yes, that is bitterly true. You gave me three or four years of your youth.

IRENE
More, more than that I gave you, spend-thrift as I then was.

PROFESSOR RUBEK
Yes, you were prodigal, Irene. You gave me all your naked loveliness

IRENE
- to gaze upon

PROFESSOR RUBEK
- and to glorify

IRENE
Yes, for your own glorification. And the child's.

PROFESSOR RUBEK
And yours too, Irene.

IRENE
But you have forgotten the most precious gift.

PROFESSOR RUBEK
The most precious? What gift was that?

IRENE
I gave you my young, living soul. And that gift left me empty within, soulless. [Looking at him with a fixed stare.] It was that I died of, Arnold.

[The SISTER OF MERCY opens the door wide and makes room for her. She goes into the pavilion.

PROFESSOR RUBEK
[Stands and looks after her; then whispers.] Irene!

Act Second.

[Near a mountain resort. The landscape stretches, in the form of an immense treeless upland, towards a long mountain lake. Beyond the lake rises a range of peaks with blue-white snow in the clefts. In the foreground on the left a purling brook falls in severed streamlets down a steep wall of rock, and thence flows smoothly over the upland until it disappears to the right. Dwarf trees, plants, and stones along the course of the brook. In the foreground on the right a hillock, with a stone bench on the top of it. It is a summer afternoon, towards sunset.

[At some distance over the upland, on the other side of the brook, a troop of children is singing, dancing, and playing. Some are dressed in peasant costume, others in town-made clothes. Their happy laughter is heard, softened by distance, during the following.

[PROFESSOR RUBEK is sitting on the bench, with a plaid over his shoulders, and looking down at the children's play.

[Presently, MAIA comes forward from among some bushes on the upland to the left, well back, and scans the prospect with her hand shading her eyes. She wears a flat tourist cap, a short skirt, kilted up, reaching only midway between ankle and knee, and high, stout lace-boots. She has in her hand a long alpenstock.

MAIA
[At last catches sight of RUBEK and calls.] Hallo!

[She advances over the upland, jumps over the brook, with the aid of her alpenstock, and climbs up the hillock.

MAIA
[Panting.] Oh, how I have been rushing around looking for you, Rubek.

PROFESSOR RUBEK
[Nods indifferently and asks.] Have you just come from the hotel?

MAIA
Yes, that was the last place I tried, that fly-trap.

PROFESSOR RUBEK
[Looking at her for moment.] I noticed that you were not at the dinner-table.

MAIA
No, we had our dinner in the open air, we two.

PROFESSOR RUBEK
"We two"? What two?

MAIA
Why, I and that horrid bear-killer, of course.

PROFESSOR RUBEK
Oh, he.

MAIA
Yes. And first thing to-morrow morning we are going off again.

PROFESSOR RUBEK
After bears?

MAIA
Yes. Off to kill a brown-boy.

PROFESSOR RUBEK
Have you found the tracks of any?

MAIA
[With superiority.] You don't suppose that bears are to be found in the naked mountains, do you?

PROFESSOR RUBEK
Where, then?

MAIA
Far beneath. On the lower slopes; in the thickest parts of the forest. Places your ordinary town-folk could never get through

PROFESSOR RUBEK

And you two are going down there to-morrow?

MAIA

[Throwing herself down among the heather.] Yes, so we have arranged. Or perhaps we may start this evening. If you have no objection, that's to say?

PROFESSOR RUBEK

I? Far be it from me to

MAIA

[Quickly.] Of course Lars goes with us, with the dogs.

PROFESSOR RUBEK

I feel no curiosity as to the movements of Mr. Lars and his dogs. [Changing the subject.] Would you not rather sit properly on the seat?

MAIA

[Drowsily.] No, thank you. I'm lying so delightfully in the soft heather.

PROFESSOR RUBEK

I can see that you are tired.

MAIA

[Yawning.] I almost think I'm beginning to feel tired.

PROFESSOR RUBEK

You don't notice it till afterwards, when the excitement is over

MAIA

[In a drowsy tone.] Just so. I will lie and close my eyes.

[A short pause.

MAIA

[With sudden impatience.] Ugh, Rubek, how can you endure to sit there listening to these children's screams! And to watch all the capers they are cutting, too!

PROFESSOR RUBEK

There is something harmonious, almost like music, in their movements, now and then; amid all the clumsiness. And it amuses me to sit and watch for these isolated moments, when they come.

MAIA

[With a somewhat scornful laugh.] Yes, you are always, always an artist.

PROFESSOR RUBEK

And I propose to remain one.

MAIA

[Lying on her side, so that her back is turned to him.] There's not a bit of the artist about him.

PROFESSOR RUBEK

[With attention.] Who is it that's not an artist?

MAIA

[Again in a sleepy tone.] Why, he, the other one, of course.

PROFESSOR RUBEK

The bear-hunter, you mean?

MAIA

Yes. There's not a bit of the artist about him, not the least little bit.

PROFESSOR RUBEK
[Smiling.] No, I believe there's no doubt about that.

MAIA
[Vehemently, without moving.] And so ugly as he is! [Plucks up a tuft of heather and throws it away.] So ugly, so ugly! Isch!

PROFESSOR RUBEK
Is that why you are so ready to set off with him, out into the wilds?

MAIA
[Curtly.] I don't know. [Turning towards him.] You are ugly, too, Rubek.

PROFESSOR RUBEK
Have you only just discovered it?

MAIA
No, I have seen it for long.

PROFESSOR RUBEK
[Shrugging his shoulders.] One doesn't grow younger. One doesn't grow younger, Frau Maia.

MAIA
It's not that sort of ugliness that I mean at all. But there has come to be such an expression of fatigue, of utter weariness, in your eyes, when you deign, once in a while, to cast a glance at me.

PROFESSOR RUBEK
Have you noticed that?

MAIA
[Nods.] Little by little this evil look has come into your eyes. It seems almost as though you were nursing some dark plot against me.

PROFESSOR RUBEK
Indeed? [In a friendly but earnest tone.] Come here and sit beside me, Maia; and let us talk a little.

MAIA
[Half rising.] Then will you let me sit upon your knee? As I used to in the early days?

PROFESSOR RUBEK
No, you mustn't, people can see us from the hotel. [Moves a little.] But you can sit here on the bench, at my side.

MAIA
No, thank you; in that case I'd rather lie here, where I am. I can hear you quite well here. [Looks inquiringly at him.] Well, what is it you want to say to me?

PROFESSOR RUBEK
[Begins slowly.] What do you think was my real reason for agreeing to make this tour?

MAIA
Well, I remember you declared, among other things, that it was going to do me such a tremendous lot of good. But, but

PROFESSOR RUBEK
But?

MAIA
But now I don't believe the least little bit that that was the reason

PROFESSOR RUBEK
Then what is your theory about it now?

MAIA

I think now that it was on account of that pale lady.

PROFESSOR RUBEK

Madame von Satow!

MAIA

Yes, she who is always hanging at our heels. Yesterday evening she made her appearance up here too.

PROFESSOR RUBEK

But what in all the world!

MAIA

Oh, I know you knew her very well indeed, long before you knew me.

PROFESSOR RUBEK

And had forgotten her, too, long before I knew you.

MAIA

[Sitting upright.] Can you forget so easily, Rubek?

PROFESSOR RUBEK

[Curtly.] Yes, very easily indeed. [Adds harshly.] When I want to forget.

MAIA

Even a woman who has been a model to you?

PROFESSOR RUBEK

When I have no more use for her

MAIA

One who has stood to you undressed?

PROFESSOR RUBEK

That means nothing, nothing for us artists. [With a change of tone.] And then, may I venture to ask, how was I to guess that she was in this country?

MAIA

Oh, you might have seen her name in a Visitor's List in one of the newspapers.

PROFESSOR RUBEK

But I had no idea of the name she now goes by. I had never heard of any Herr von Satow.

MAIA

[Affecting weariness.] Oh well then, I suppose it must have been for some other reason that you were so set upon this journey.

PROFESSOR RUBEK

[Seriously.] Yes, Maia, it was for another reason. A quite different reason. And that is what we must sooner or later have a clear explanation about.

MAIA

[In a fit of suppressed laughter.] Heavens, how solemn you look!

PROFESSOR RUBEK

[Suspiciously scrutinising her.] Yes, perhaps a little more solemn than necessary.

MAIA

How so?

PROFESSOR RUBEK

And that is a very good thing for us both.

MAIA

You begin to make me feel curious, Rubek.

PROFESSOR RUBEK

Only curious? Not a little bit uneasy.

MAIA

[Shaking her head.] Not in the least.

PROFESSOR RUBEK

Good. Then listen. You said that day down at the Baths that it seemed to you I had become very nervous of late

MAIA

Yes, and you really have.

PROFESSOR RUBEK

And what do you think can be the reason of that?

MAIA

How can I tell? [Quickly.] Perhaps you have grown weary of this constant companionship with me.

PROFESSOR RUBEK

Constant? Why not say "everlasting"?

MAIA

Daily companionship, then. Here have we two solitary people lived down there for four or five mortal years, and scarcely have an hour away from each other. We two all by ourselves.

PROFESSOR RUBEK

[With interest.] Well? And then?

MAIA

[A little oppressed.] You are not a particularly sociable man, Rubek. You like to keep to yourself and think your own thoughts. And of course I can't talk properly to you about your affairs. I know nothing about art and that sort of thing [With an impatient gesture.] And care very little either, for that matter!

PROFESSOR RUBEK

Well, well; and that's why we generally sit by the fireside, and chat about your affairs.

MAIA

Oh, good gracious, I have no affairs to chat about.

PROFESSOR RUBEK

Well, they are trifles, perhaps; but at any rate the time passes for us in that way as well as another, Maia.

MAIA

Yes, you are right. Time passes. It is passing away from you, Rubek. And I suppose it is really that that makes you so uneasy

PROFESSOR RUBEK

[Nods vehemently.] And so restless! [Writhing in his seat.] No, I shall soon not be able to endure this pitiful life any longer.

MAIA

[Rises and stands for a moment looking at him.] If you want to get rid of me, you have only to say so.

PROFESSOR RUBEK

Why will you use such phrases? Get rid of you?

MAIA

Yes, if you want to have done with me, please say so right out. And I will go that instant.

PROFESSOR RUBEK

[With an almost imperceptible smile.] Do you intend that as a threat, Maia?

MAIA

There can be no threat for you in what I said.

PROFESSOR RUBEK

[Rising.] No, I confess you are right there. [Adds after a pause.] You and I cannot possibly go on living together like this

MAIA

Well? And then?

PROFESSOR RUBEK

There is no "then" about it. [With emphasis on his words.] Because we two cannot go on living together alone, it does not necessarily follow that we must part.

MAIA

[Smiles scornfully.] Only draw away from each other a little, you mean?

PROFESSOR RUBEK

[Shakes his head.] Even that is not necessary.

MAIA

Well then? Come out with what you want to do with me.

PROFESSOR RUBEK

[With some hesitation.] What I now feel so keenly, and so painfully, that I require, is to have some one about me who really and truly stands close to me

MAIA

[Interrupts him anxiously.] Don't I do that, Rubek?

PROFESSOR RUBEK

[Waving her aside.] Not in that sense. What I need is the companionship of another person who can, as it were, complete me, supply what is wanting in me, be one with me in all my striving.

MAIA

[Slowly.] It's true that things like that are a great deal too hard for me.

PROFESSOR RUBEK

Oh no, they are not at all in your line, Maia.

MAIA

[With an outburst.] And heaven knows I don't want them to be, either!

PROFESSOR RUBEK

I know that very well. And it was with no idea of finding any such help in my life-work that I married you.

MAIA

[Observing him closely.] I can see in your face that you are thinking of some one else.

PROFESSOR RUBEK

Indeed? I have never noticed before that you were a thought-reader. But you can see that, can you?

MAIA

Yes, I can. Oh, I know you so well, so well, Rubek.

PROFESSOR RUBEK

Then perhaps you can also see who it is I am thinking of?

MAIA

Yes, indeed I can.

PROFESSOR RUBEK

Well? Have the goodness to?

MAIA

You are thinking of that, that model you once used for [Suddenly letting slip the train of thought.] Do you know, the people down at the hotel think she's mad.

PROFESSOR RUBEK

Indeed? And pray what do the people down at the hotel think of you and the bear-killer?

MAIA

That has nothing to do with the matter. [Continuing the former train of thought.] But it was this pale lady you were thinking of.

PROFESSOR RUBEK

[Calmly.] Precisely, of her. When I had no more use for her and when, besides, she went away from me, vanished without a word

MAIA

Then you accepted me as a sort of makeshift, I suppose?

PROFESSOR RUBEK

[More unfeelingly.] Something of the sort, to tell the truth, little Maia. For a year or a year and a half I had lived there lonely and brooding, and had put the last touch, the very last touch, to my work. "The Resurrection Day" went out over the world and brought me fame and everything else that heart could desire. [With greater warmth.] But I no longer loved my own work. Men's laurels and incense nauseated me, till I could have rushed away in despair and hidden myself in the depths of the woods. [Looking at her.] You, who are a thought-reader, can you guess what then occurred to me?

MAIA

[Lightly.] Yes, it occurred to you to make portrait-busts of gentlemen and ladies.

PROFESSOR RUBEK

[Nods.] To order, yes. With animals' faces behind the masks. Those I threw in gratis into the bargain, you understand. [Smiling.] But that was not precisely what I had in my mind.

MAIA

What, then?

PROFESSOR RUBEK

[Again serious.] It was this, that all the talk about the artist's vocation and the artist's mission, and so forth, began to strike me as being very empty, and hollow, and meaningless at bottom.

MAIA

Then what would you put in its place?

PROFESSOR RUBEK

Life, Maia.

MAIA

Life?

PROFESSOR RUBEK

Yes, is not life in sunshine and in beauty a hundred times better worth while than to hang about to the end of your days in a raw, damp hole, and wear yourself out in a perpetual struggle with lumps of clay and blocks of stone?

MAIA

[With a little sigh.] Yes, I have always thought so, certainly.

PROFESSOR RUBEK

And then I had become rich enough to live in luxury and in indolent, quivering sunshine. I was able to build myself the villa on the Lake of Taunitz, and the palazzo in the capital, and all the rest of it.

MAIA

[Taking up his tone.] And last but not least, you could afford to treat yourself to me, too. And you gave me leave to share in all your treasures.

PROFESSOR RUBEK

[Jesting, so as to turn the conversation.] Did I not promise to take you up to a high enough mountain and show you all the glory of the world?

MAIA

[With a gentle expression.] You have perhaps taken me up with you to a high enough mountain, Rubek but you have not shown me all the glory of the world.

PROFESSOR RUBEK

[With a laugh of irritation.] How insatiable you are, Maia.! Absolutely insatiable! [With a vehement outburst.] But do you know what is the most hopeless thing of all, Maia? Can you guess that?

MAIA

[With quiet defiance.] Yes, I suppose it is that you have gone and tied yourself to me, for life.

PROFESSOR RUBEK

I would not have expressed myself so heartlessly.

MAIA

But you would have meant it just as heartlessly.

PROFESSOR RUBEK

You have no clear idea of the inner workings of an artist's nature.

MAIA

[Smiling and shaking her head.] Good heavens, I haven't even a clear idea of the inner workings of my own nature.

PROFESSOR RUBEK

[Continuing undisturbed.] I live at such high speed, Maia. We live so, we artists. I, for my part, have lived through a whole lifetime in the few years we two have known each other. I have come to realise that I am not at all adapted for seeking happiness in indolent enjoyment. Life does not shape itself that way for me and those like me. I must go on working, producing one work after another, right up to my dying day. [Forcing himself to continue.] That is why I cannot get on with you any longer, Maia, not with you alone.

MAIA

[Quietly.] Does that mean, in plain language, that you have grown tired of me?

PROFESSOR RUBEK

[Bursts forth.] Yes, that is what it means! I have grown tired, intolerably tired and fretted and unstrung, in this life with you! Now you know it. [Controlling himself.] These are hard, ugly words I am using. I know that very well. And you are not at all to blame in this matter; that I willingly admit. It is simply and solely I myself, who have once more undergone a revolution [Half to himself] and awakening to my real life.

MAIA

[Involuntarily folding her hands.] Why in all the world should we not part then?

PROFESSOR RUBEK

[Looks at her in astonishment.] Should you be willing to?

MAIA

[Shrugging her shoulders.] Oh yes, if there's nothing else for it, then

PROFESSOR RUBEK

[Eagerly.] But there is something else for it. There is an alternative

MAIA

[Holding up her forefinger.] Now you are thinking of the pale lady again!

PROFESSOR RUBEK

Yes, to tell the truth, I cannot help constantly thinking of her. Ever since I met her again. [A step nearer her.] For now I will tell you a secret, Maia.

MAIA

Well?

PROFESSOR RUBEK

[Touching his own breast.] In here, you see, in here I have a little bramah-locked casket. And in that casket all my sculptor's visions are stored up. But when she disappeared and left no trace, the lock of the casket snapped to. And she had the key and she took it away with her. You, little Maia, you had no key; so all that the casket contains must lie unused. And the years pass! And I have no means of getting at the treasure.

MAIA

[Trying to repress a subtle smile.] Then get her to open the casket for you again

PROFESSOR RUBEK

[Not understanding.] Maia?

MAIA

- for here she is, you see. And no doubt it's on account of this casket that she has come.

PROFESSOR RUBEK

I have not said a single word to her on this subject!

MAIA

[Looks innocently at him.] My dear Rubek, is it worth while to make all this fuss and commotion about so simple a matter?

PROFESSOR RUBEK

Do you think this matter is so absolutely simple?

MAIA

Yes, certainly I think so. Do you attach yourself to whoever you most require. [Nods to him.] I shall always manage to find a place for myself.

PROFESSOR RUBEK

Where do you mean?

MAIA

[Unconcerned, evasively.] Well, I need only take myself off to the villa, if it should be necessary. But it won't be; for in town, in all that great house of ours, there must surely, with a little good will, be room enough for three.

PROFESSOR RUBEK

[Uncertainly.] And do you think that would work in the long run?

MAIA

[In a light tone.] Very well, then, if it won't work, it won't. It is no good talking about it.

PROFESSOR RUBEK

And what shall we do then, Maia, if it does not work?

MAIA

[Untroubled.] Then we two will simply get out of each other's way, part entirely. I shall always find something new for myself, somewhere in the world. Something free! Free! Free! No need to be anxious about that, Professor Rubek! [Suddenly points off to the right.] Look there! There we have her.

PROFESSOR RUBEK

[Turning.] Where?

MAIA

Out on the plain. Striding like a marble stature. She is coming this way.

PROFESSOR RUBEK

[Stands gazing with his hand over his eyes.] Does not she look like the Resurrection incarnate? [To himself.] And her I could displace and move into the shade! Remodel her. Fool that I was!

MAIA

What do you mean by that?

PROFESSOR RUBEK

[Putting the question aside.] Nothing. Nothing that you would understand.

[IRENE advances from the right over the upland. The children at their play have already caught sight of her and run to meet her. She is now surrounded by them; some appear confident and at ease, others uneasy and timid. She talks low to them and indicates that they are to go down to the hotel; she herself will rest a little beside the brook. The children run down over the slope to the left, half way to the back. IRENE goes up to the wall of rock, and lets the rillets of the cascade flow over her hands, cooling them.

MAIA

[In a low voice.] Go down and speak to her alone, Rubek.

PROFESSOR RUBEK

And where will you go in the meantime?

MAIA

[Looking significantly at him.] Henceforth I shall go my own ways.

[She descends form the hillock and leaps over the brook, by aid of her alpenstock. She stops beside IRENE.

MAIA

Professor Rubek is up there, waiting for you, madam.

IRENE

What does he want?

MAIA

He wants you to help him to open a casket that has snapped to.

IRENE

Can I help him in that?

MAIA

He says you are the only person that can.

IRENE

Then I must try.

MAIA

Yes, you really must, madam.

[She goes down by the path to the hotel.

[In a little while PROFESSOR RUBEK comes down to IRENE, but stops with the brook between them.

IRENE

[After a short pause.] She, the other one, said that you had been waiting for me.

PROFESSOR RUBEK

I have waited for you year after year without myself knowing it.

IRENE

I could not come to you, Arnold. I was lying down there, sleeping the long, deep, dreamful sleep.

PROFESSOR RUBEK

But now you have awakened, Irene!

IRENE

[Shakes her head.] I have the heavy, deep sleep still in my eyes.

PROFESSOR RUBEK

You shall see that day will dawn and lighten for us both.

IRENE

Do not believe that.

PROFESSOR RUBEK

[Urgently.] I do believe it! And I know it! Now that I have found you again

IRENE

Risen from the grave.

PROFESSOR RUBEK

Transfigured!

IRENE

Only risen, Arnold. Not transfigured.

[He crosses over to her by means of stepping-stones below the cascade.

PROFESSOR RUBEK

Where have you been all day, Irene?

IRENE

[Pointing.] Far, far over there, on the great dead waste

PROFESSOR RUBEK

[Turning the conversation.] You have not your, your friend with you to-day, I see.

IRENE

[Smiling.] My friend is keeping a close watch on me, none the less.

PROFESSOR RUBEK

Can she?

IRENE

[Glancing furtively around.] You may be sure she can, wherever I may go. She never loses sight of me [Whispering.] Until, one fine sunny morning, I shall kill her.

PROFESSOR RUBEK

Would you do that?

IRENE

With the utmost delight if only I could manage it.

PROFESSOR RUBEK

Why do you want to?

IRENE

Because she deals in witchcraft. [Mysteriously.] Only think, Arnold, she has changed herself into my shadow.

PROFESSOR RUBEK

[Trying to calm her.] Well, well, well, a shadow we must all have.

IRENE

I am my own shadow. [With an outburst.] Do you not understand that!

PROFESSOR RUBEK

[Sadly.] Yes, yes, Irene, I understand.

[He seats himself on a stone beside the brook. She stands behind him, leaning against the wall of rock.

IRENE

[After a pause.] Why do you sit there turning your eyes away from me?

PROFESSOR RUBEK

[Softly, shaking his head.] I dare not, I dare not look at you.

IRENE

Why dare you not look at me any more?

PROFESSOR RUBEK

You have a shadow that tortures me. And I have the crushing weight of my conscience.

IRENE

[With a glad cry of deliverance.] At last!

PROFESSOR RUBEK

[Springs up.] Irene, what is it!

IRENE

[Motioning him off.] Keep still, still, still! [Draws a deep breath and says, as though relieved of a burden.] There! Now they let me go. For this time. Now we can sit down and talk as we used to, when I was alive.

PROFESSOR RUBEK

Oh, if only we could talk as we used to.

IRENE

Sit there, where you were sitting. I will sit here beside you.

[He sits down again. She seats herself on another stone, close to him.

IRENE

[After a short interval of silence.] Now I have come back to you from the uttermost regions, Arnold.

PROFESSOR RUBEK

Aye, truly, from an endless journey.

IRENE

Come home to my lord and master

PROFESSOR RUBEK

To our home; to our own home, Irene.

IRENE

Have you looked for my coming every single day?

PROFESSOR RUBEK

How dared I look for you?

IRENE

[With a sidelong glance.] No, I suppose you dared not. For you understood nothing.

PROFESSOR RUBEK

Was it really not for the sake of some one else that you all of a sudden disappeared from me in that way?

IRENE

Might it not quite well be for your sake, Arnold?

PROFESSOR RUBEK

[Looks doubtfully at her.] I don't understand you?

IRENE

When I had served you with my soul and with my body, when the statue stood there finished, our child as you called it, then I laid at your feet the most precious sacrifice of all by effacing myself for all time.

PROFESSOR RUBEK

[Bows his head.] And laying my life waste.

IRENE

[Suddenly firing up.] It was just that I wanted! Never, never should you create anything again after you had created that only child of ours.

PROFESSOR RUBEK

Was it jealously that moved you, then?

IRENE

[Coldly.] I think it was rather hatred.

PROFESSOR RUBEK

Hatred? Hatred for me?

IRENE

[Again vehemently.] Yes, for you, for the artist who had so lightly and carelessly taken a warm-blooded body, a young human life, and worn the soul out of it, because you needed it for a work of art.

PROFESSOR RUBEK

And you can say that, you who threw yourself into my work with such saint-like passion and such ardent joy? that work for which we two met together every morning, as for an act of worship.

IRENE

[Coldly, as before.] I will tell you one thing, Arnold.

PROFESSOR RUBEK

Well?

IRENE

I never loved your art, before I met you. Nor after either.

PROFESSOR RUBEK

But the artist, Irene?

IRENE

The artist I hate.

PROFESSOR RUBEK

The artist in me too?

IRENE

In you most of all. When I unclothed myself and stood for you, then I hated you, Arnold

PROFESSOR RUBEK

[Warmly.] That you did not, Irene! That is not true!

IRENE

I hated you, because you could stand there so unmoved

PROFESSOR RUBEK

[Laughs.] Unmoved? Do you think so?

IRENE

- at any rate so intolerably self-controlled. And because you were an artist and an artist only, not a man! [Changing to a tone full of warmth and feeling.] But that statue in the wet, living clay, that I loved, as it rose up, a vital human creature, out of those raw, shapeless masses, for that was our creation, our child. Mine and yours.

PROFESSOR RUBEK

[Sadly.] It was so in spirit and in truth.

IRENE

Let me tell you, Arnold, it is for the sake of this child of ours that I have undertaken this long pilgrimage.

PROFESSOR RUBEK

[Suddenly alert.] For the statue's?

IRENE

Call it what you will. I call it our child.

PROFESSOR RUBEK

And now you want to see it? Finished? In marble, which you always thought so cold? [Eagerly.] You do not know, perhaps, that it is installed in a great museum somewhere far out in the world?

IRENE

I have heard a sort of legend about it.

PROFESSOR RUBEK

And museums were always a horror to you. You called them grave-vaults

IRENE

I will make a pilgrimage to the place where my soul and my child's soul lie buried.

PROFESSOR RUBEK

[Uneasy and alarmed.] You must never see that statue again! Do you hear, Irene! I implore you! Never, never see it again!

IRENE

Perhaps you think it would mean death to me a second time?

PROFESSOR RUBEK

[Clenching his hands together.] Oh, I don't know what I think. But how could I ever imagine that you would fix your mind so immovably on that statue? You, who went away from me, before it was completed.

IRENE

It was completed. That was why I could go away from you and leave you alone.

PROFESSOR RUBEK

[Sits with his elbows upon his knees, rocking his head from side to side, with his hands before his eyes.] It was not what it afterwards became.

IRENE

[Quietly but quick as lightning, half-unsheathes a narrow-bladed sharp knife which she carried in her breast, and asks in a hoarse whisper.] Arnold, have you done any evil to our child?

PROFESSOR RUBEK

[Evasively.] Any evil? How can I be sure what you would call it?

IRENE

[Breathless.] Tell me at once: what have you done to the child?

PROFESSOR RUBEK

I will tell you, if you will sit and listen quietly to what I say.

IRENE

[Hides the knife.] I will listen as quietly as a mother can when she

PROFESSOR RUBEK

[Interrupting.] And you must not look at me while I am telling you.

IRENE

[Moves to a stone behind his back.] I will sit here, behind you. Now tell me.

PROFESSOR RUBEK

[Takes his hands from before his eyes and gazes straight in front of him. When I had found you, I knew at once how I should make use of you for my life-work.

IRENE

"The Resurrection Day" you called your life-work. I call it "our child."

PROFESSOR RUBEK

I was young then, with no knowledge of life. The Resurrection, I thought, would be most beautifully and exquisitely figured as a young unsullied woman, with none of our earth-life's experiences, awakening to light and glory without having to put away from her anything ugly and impure.

IRENE

[Quickly.] Yes, and so I stand there now, in our work?

PROFESSOR RUBEK

[Hesitating.] Not absolutely and entirely so, Irene.

IRENE

[In rising excitement.] Not absolutely? Do I not stand as I always stood for you?

PROFESSOR RUBEK

[Without answering.] I learned worldly wisdom in the years that followed, Irene. "The Resurrection Day" became in my mind's eye something more and something, something more complex. The little round plinth on which your figure stood erect and solitary, it no longer afforded room for all the imagery I now wanted to add

IRENE

[Groped for her knife, but desists.] What imagery did you add then? Tell me!

PROFESSOR RUBEK

I imagined that which I saw with my eyes around me in the world. I had to include it, I could not help it, Irene. I expanded the plinth, made it wide and spacious. And on it I placed a segment of the curving, bursting earth. And up from the fissures of the soil there now swarm men and women with dimly-suggested animal-faces. Women and men as I knew them in real life.

IRENE

[In breathless suspense.] But in the middle of the rout there stands the young woman radiant with the joy of light? Do I not stand so, Arnold?

PROFESSOR RUBEK

[Evasively.] Not quite in the middle. I had unfortunately to move that figure a little back. For the sake of the general effect, you understand. Otherwise it would have dominated the whole too much.

IRENE

But the joy in the light still transfigures my face?

PROFESSOR RUBEK

Yes, it does, Irene, in a way. A little subdued perhaps, as my altered idea required.

IRENE

[Rising noiselessly.] That design expresses the life you now see, Arnold.

PROFESSOR RUBEK

Yes, I suppose it does.

IRENE

And in that design you have shifted me back, a little toned down, to serve as a background-figure, in a group.

[She draws the knife.

PROFESSOR RUBEK

Not a background-figure. Let us say, at most, a figure not quite in the foreground or something of that sort.

IRENE

[Whispers hoarsely.] There you uttered your own doom.

[On the point of striking.]

PROFESSOR RUBEK

[Turns and looks up at her.] Doom?

IRENE

[Hastily hides the knife, and says as though choked with agony.] My whole soul, you and I, we, we, we and our child were in that solitary figure.

PROFESSOR RUBEK

[Eagerly, taking off his hat and drying the drops of sweat upon his brow.] Yes, but let me tell you, too, how I have placed myself in the group. In front, beside a fountain, as it were here, sits a man weighed down with guilt, who cannot quite free himself from the earth-crust. I call him remorse for a forfeited life. He sits there and dips his fingers in the purling stream, to wash them clean, and he is gnawed and tortured by the thought that never, never will he succeed. Never in all eternity will he attain to freedom and the new life. He will remain for ever prisoned in his hell.

IRENE

[Hardly and coldly.] Poet!

PROFESSOR RUBEK

Why poet?

IRENE

Because you are nerveless and sluggish and full of forgiveness for all the sins of your life, in thought and in act. You have killed my soul, so you model yourself in remorse, and self-accusation, and penance [Smiling.] and with that you think your account is cleared.

PROFESSOR RUBEK

[Defiantly.] I am an artist, Irene. And I take no shame to myself for the frailties that perhaps cling to me. For I was born to be an artist, you see. And, do what I may, I shall never be anything else.

IRENE

[Looks at him with a lurking evil smile, and says gently and softly.] You are a poet, Arnold. [Softly strokes his hair.] You dear, great, middle-aged child, is it possible that you cannot see that!

PROFESSOR RUBEK

[Annoyed.] Why do you keep on calling me a poet?

IRENE

[With malign eyes.] Because there is something apologetic in the word, my friend. Something that suggests forgiveness of sins and spreads a cloak over all frailty. [With a sudden change of tone.] But I was a human being then! And I, too, had a life to live, and a human destiny to fulfil. And all that, look you, I let slip, gave it all up in order to make myself your bondwoman. Oh, it was self-murder, a deadly sin against myself! [Half whispering.] And that sin I can never expiate!

[She seats herself near him beside the brook, keeps close, though unnoticed, watch upon him, and, as though in absence of mind, plucks some flowers form the shrubs around them.

IRENE

[With apparent self-control.] I should have borne children in the world, many children, real children, not such children as are hidden away in grave-vaults. That was my vocation. I ought never to have served you, poet.

PROFESSOR RUBEK

[Lost in recollection.] Yet those were beautiful days, Irene. Marvellously beautiful days as I now look back upon them

IRENE

[Looking at him with a soft expression.] Can you remember a little word that you said, when you had finished, finished with me and with our child? [Nods to him.] Can you remember that little word, Arnold?

PROFESSOR RUBEK

[Looks inquiringly at her.] Did I say a little word then, which you still remember?

IRENE

Yes, you did. Can you not recall it?

PROFESSOR RUBEK

[Shaking his head.] No, I can't say that I do. Not at the present moment, at any rate.

IRENE

You took both my hands and pressed them warmly. And I stood there in breathless expectation. And then you said: "So now, Irene, I thank you from my heart. This," you said, "has been a priceless episode for me."

PROFESSOR RUBEK

[Looks doubtfully at her.] Did I say "episode"? It is not a word I am in the habit of using.

IRENE

You said "episode."

PROFESSOR RUBEK

[With assumed cheerfulness.] Well, well, after all, it was in reality an episode.

IRENE

[Curtly.] At that word I left you.

PROFESSOR RUBEK

You take everything so painfully to heart, Irene.

IRENE

[Drawing her hand over her forehead.] Perhaps you are right. Let us shake off all the hard things that go to the heart. [Plucks off the leaves of a mountain rose and strews them on the brook.] Look there, Arnold. There are our birds swimming.

PROFESSOR RUBEK

What birds are they?

IRENE

Can you not see? Of course they are flamingoes. Are they not rose-red?

PROFESSOR RUBEK

Flamingoes do not swim. They only wade.

IRENE

Then they are not flamingoes. They are sea-gulls.

PROFESSOR RUBEK

They may be sea-gulls with red bills, yes. [Plucks broad green leaves and throws them into the brook.] Now I send out my ships after them.

IRENE

But there must be no harpoon-men on board.

PROFESSOR RUBEK

No, there shall be no harpoon-men. [Smiles to her.] Can you remember the summer when we used to sit like this outside the little peasant hut on the Lake of Taunitz?

IRENE

[Nods.] On Saturday evenings, yes, when we had finished our week's work

PROFESSOR RUBEK

And taken the train out to the lake, to stay there over Sunday

IRENE

[With an evil gleam of hatred in her eyes.] It was an episode, Arnold.

PROFESSOR RUBEK

[As if not hearing.] Then, too, you used to set birds swimming in the brook. They were water-lilies which you

IRENE

They were white swans.

PROFESSOR RUBEK

I meant swans, yes. And I remember that I fastened a great furry leaf to one of the swans. It looked like a burdock-leaf

IRENE

And then it turned into Lohengrin's boat with the swan yoked to it.

PROFESSOR RUBEK

How fond you were of that game, Irene.

IRENE

We played it over and over again.

PROFESSOR RUBEK

Every single Saturday, I believe, all the summer through.

IRENE

You said I was the swan that drew your boat.

PROFESSOR RUBEK

Did I say so? Yes, I daresay I did. [Absorbed in the game.] Just see how the sea-gulls are swimming down the stream!

IRENE

[Laughing.] And all your ships have run ashore.

PROFESSOR RUBEK

[Throwing more leaves into the brook.] I have ships enough in reserve. [Follows the leaves with his eyes, throws more into the brook, and says after a pause.] Irene, I have bought the little peasant hut beside the Lake of Taunitz.

IRENE

Have you bought it? You often said you would, if you could afford it.

PROFESSOR RUBEK

The day came when I could afford it easily enough; and so I bought it.

IRENE

[With a sidelong look at him.] Then do you live out there now in our old house?

PROFESSOR RUBEK

No, I have had it pulled down long ago. And I have built myself a great, handsome, comfortable villa on the site, with a park around it. It is there that we [Stops and corrects himself.] there that I usually live during the summer.

IRENE

[Mastering herself.] So you and, and the other one live out there now?

PROFESSOR RUBEK

[With a touch of defiance.] Yes. When my wife and I are not travelling as we are this year.

IRENE

[Looking far before her.] Life was beautiful, beautiful by the Lake of Taunitz.

PROFESSOR RUBEK

[As though looking back into himself.] And yet, Irene

IRENE

[Completing his thought.] - yet we two let slip all that life and its beauty.

PROFESSOR RUBEK

[Softly, urgently.] Does repentance come too late, now?

IRENE

[Does not answer, but sits silent for a moment; then she points over the upland.] Look there, Arnold, now the sun is going down behind the peaks. See what a red glow the level rays cast over all the heathery knolls out yonder.

PROFESSOR RUBEK

[Looks where she is pointing.] It is long since I have seen a sunset in the mountains.

IRENE

Or a sunrise?

PROFESSOR RUBEK

A sunrise I don't think I have ever seen.

IRENE

[Smiles as though lost in recollection.] I once saw a marvellously lovely sunrise.

PROFESSOR RUBEK

Did you? Where was that?

IRENE

High, high up on a dizzy mountain-top. You beguiled me up there by promising that I should see all the glory of the world if only I

[She stops suddenly.

PROFESSOR RUBEK

If only you? Well?

IRENE

I did as you told me, went with you up to the heights. And there I fell upon my knees and worshipped you, and served you. [Is silent for a moment; then says softly.] Then I saw the sunrise.

PROFESSOR RUBEK

[Turning at him with a scornful smile.] With you and the other woman?

PROFESSOR RUBEK

[Urgently.] With me, as in our days of creation. You could open all that is locked up in me. Can you not find it in your heart, Irene?

IRENE

[Shaking her head.] I have no longer the key to you, Arnold.

PROFESSOR RUBEK

You have the key! You and you alone possess it! [Beseechingly.] Help me, that I may be able to live my life over again!

IRENE

[Immovable as before.] Empty dreams! Idle, dead dreams. For the life you and I led there is no resurrection.

PROFESSOR RUBEK

[Curtly, breaking off.] Then let us go on playing.

IRENE

Yes, playing, playing, only playing!

[They sit and strew leaves and petals over the brook, where they float and sail away.

[Up the slope to the left at the back come ULFHEIM and MAIA in hunting costume. After them comes the SERVANT with the leash of dogs, with which he goes out to the right.

PROFESSOR RUBEK
[Catching sight of them.] Ah! There is little Maia, going out with the bear-hunter.

IRENE
Your lady, yes.

PROFESSOR RUBEK
Or the other's.

MAIA
[Looks around as she is crossing the upland, sees the two sitting by the brook, and calls out.] Good-night, Professor! Dream of me. Now I am going off on my adventures!

PROFESSOR RUBEK
[Calls back to her.] What sort of an adventure is this to be?

MAIA
[Approaching.] I am going to let life take the place of all the rest.

PROFESSOR RUBEK
[Mockingly.] Aha! So you too are going to do that, little Maia?

MAIA
Yes. And I've made a verse about it, and this is how it goes:

[Sings triumphantly.]

I am free! I am free! I am free!
No more life in the prison for me!
I am free as a bird! I am free!
For I believe I have awakened now at last.

PROFESSOR RUBEK
It almost seems so.

MAIA
[Drawing a deep breath.] Oh, how divinely light one feels on waking!

PROFESSOR RUBEK
Good-night, Frau Maia and good luck to

ULFHEIM
[Calls out, interposing.] Hush, hush! for the devil's sake let's have none of your wizard wishes. Don't you see that we are going out to shoot

PROFESSOR RUBEK
What will you bring me home from the hunting, Maia?

MAIA
You shall have a bird of prey to model. I shall wing one for you.

PROFESSOR RUBEK
[Laughs mockingly and bitterly.] Yes, to wing things, without knowing what you are doing, that has long been quite in your way.

MAIA
[Tossing her head.] Oh, just let me take care of myself for the future, and I wish you then! [Nods and laughs roguishly.] Good-bye, and a good, peaceful summer night on the upland!

PROFESSOR RUBEK
[Jestingly.] Thanks! And all the ill-luck in the world over you and your hunting!

ULFHEIM

[Roaring with laughter.] There now, that is a wish worth having!

MAIA

[Laughing.] Thanks, thanks, thanks, Professor!

[They have both crossed the visible portion of the upland, and go out through the bushes to the right.

PROFESSOR RUBEK

[After a short pause.] A summer night on the upland! Yes, that would have been life!

IRENE

[Suddenly, with a wild expression in her eyes.] Will you spend a summer night on the upland with me?

PROFESSOR RUBEK

[Stretching his arms wide.] Yes, yes, come!

IRENE

My adored lord and master!

PROFESSOR RUBEK

Oh, Irene!

IRENE

[Hoarsely, smiling and groping in her breast.] It will be only an episode [Quickly, whispering.] Hush! do not look round, Arnold!

PROFESSOR RUBEK

[Also in a low voice.] What is it?

IRENE

A face that is staring at me.

PROFESSOR RUBEK

[Turns involuntarily.] Where! [With a start.] Ah!

[The SISTER OF MERCY's head is partly visible among the bushes beside the descent to the left. Her eyes are immovably fixed on IRENE.

IRENE

[Rises and says softly.] We must part then. No, you must remain sitting. Do you hear? You must not go with me. [Bends over him and whispers.] Till we meet again, to-night, on the upland.

PROFESSOR RUBEK

And you will come, Irene?

IRENE

Yes, surely I will come. Wait for me here.

PROFESSOR RUBEK

[Repeats dreamily.] Summer night on the upland. With you. With you. [His eyes meet hers.] Oh, Irene, that might have been our life. And that we have forfeited, we two.

IRENE

We see the irretrievable only when

[Breaks off.

PROFESSOR RUBEK

[Looks inquiringly at her.] When?

IRENE

When we dead awaken.

PROFESSOR RUBEK
[Shakes his head mournfully.] What do we really see then?

IRENE
We see that we have never lived.

[She goes towards the slope and descends.

[The SISTER OF MERCY makes way for her and follows her. PROFESSOR RUBEK remains sitting motionless beside the brook.

MAIA
[Is heard singing triumphantly among the hills.]

I am free! I am free! I am free!
No more life in the prison for me!
I am free as a bird! I am free!

Act Third.

[A wild riven mountain-side, with sheer precipices at the back. Snow-clad peaks rise to the right, and lose themselves in drifting mists. To the left, on a stone-scree, stands an old, half-ruined hut. It is early morning. Dawn is breaking. The sun has not yet risen.

[MAIA comes, flushed and irritated, down over the stone-scree on the left. ULFHEIM follows, half angry, half laughing, holding her fast by the sleeve.

MAIA
[Trying to tear herself loose.] Let me go! Let me go, I say!

ULFHEIM
Come, Come! are you going to bite now? You're as snappish as a wolf.

MAIA
[Striking him over the hand.] Let me, I tell you? And be quiet!

ULFHEIM
No, confound me if I will!

MAIA
Then I will not go another step with you. Do you hear? not a single step!

ULFHEIM
Ho, ho! How can you get away from me, here, on the wild mountain-side?

MAIA
I will jump over the precipice yonder, if need be

ULFHEIM
And mangle and mash yourself up into dogs'-meat! A juicy morsel! [Lets go his hold.] As you please. Jump over the precipice if you want to. It's a dizzy drop. There's only one narrow footpath down it, and that's almost impassable.

MAIA
[Dusts her skirt with her hand, and looks at him with angry eyes.] Well, you are a nice one to go hunting with!

ULFHEIM
Say rather, sporting.

MAIA
Oh! So you call this sport, do you?

ULFHEIM

Yes, I venture to take that liberty. It is the sort of sport I like best of all.

MAIA

[Tossing her head.] Well, I must say! [After a pause; looks searchingly at him.] Why did you let the dogs loose up there?

ULFHEIM

[Blinking his eyes and smiling.] So that they too might do a little hunting on their own account, don't you see?

MAIA

There's not a word of truth in that! It wasn't for the dogs' sake that you let them go.

ULFHEIM

[Still smiling.] Well, why did I let them go then? Let us hear.

MAIA

You let them go because you wanted to get rid of Lars. He was to run after them and bring them in again, you said. And in the meant-time. Oh, it was a pretty way to behave!

ULFHEIM

In the meantime?

MAIA

[Curtly breaking off.] No matter!

ULFHEIM

[In a confidential tone.] Lars won't find them. You may safely swear to that. He won't come with them before the time's up.

MAIA

[Looking angrily at him.] No, I daresay not.

ULFHEIM

[Catching at her arm.] For Lars, he knows my, my methods of sport, you see.

MAIA

[Eludes him, and measures him with a glance.] Do you know what you look like, Mr. Ulfheim?

ULFHEIM

I should think I'm probably most like myself.

MAIA

Yes, there you're exactly right. For you're the living image of a faun.

ULFHEIM

A faun?

MAIA

Yes, precisely; a faun.

ULFHEIM

A faun! Isn't that a sort of monster? Or a kind of a wood demon, as you might call it?

MAIA

Yes, just the sort of creature you are. A thing with a goat's beard and goat-legs. Yes, and the faun has horns too!

ULFHEIM

So, so! has he horns too?

MAIA

A pair of ugly horns, just like yours, yes.

ULFHEIM

Can you see the poor little horns *I* have?

MAIA

Yes, I seem to see them quite plainly.

ULFHEIM

[Taking the dogs' leash out of his pocket.] Then I had better see about tying you.

MAIA

Have you gone quite mad? Would you tie me?

ULFHEIM

If I am a demon, let me be a demon! So that's the way of it! You can see the horns, can you?

MAIA

[Soothingly.] There, there, there! Now try to behave nicely, Mr. Ulfheim. [Breaking off.] But what has become of that hunting-castle of yours, that you boasted so much of? You said it lay somewhere hereabouts.

ULFHEIM

[Points with a flourish to the hut.] There you have it, before your very eyes.

MAIA

[Looks at him.] That old pig-stye!

ULFHEIM

[Laughing in his beard.] It has harboured more than one king's daughter, I can tell you.

MAIA

Was it there that that horrid man you told me about came to the king's daughter in the form of a bear?

ULFHEIM

Yes, my fair companion of the chase, this is the scene. [With a gesture of invitation.] If you would deign to enter

MAIA

Isch! If ever I set foot in it! Isch!

ULFHEIM

Oh, two people can doze away a summer night in there comfortably enough. Or a whole summer, if it comes to that!

MAIA

Thanks! One would need to have a pretty strong taste for that kind of thing. [Impatiently.] But now I am tired both of you and the hunting expedition. Now I am going down to the hotel before people awaken down there.

ULFHEIM

How do you propose to get down from here?

MAIA

That's your affair. There must be a way down somewhere or other, I suppose.

ULFHEIM

[Pointing towards the back.] Oh, certainly! There is a sort of way, right down the face of the precipice yonder

MAIA

There, you see. With a little goodwill

ULFHEIM

- but just you try if you dare go that way.

MAIA

[Doubtfully.] Do you think I can't?

ULFHEIM

Never in this world if you don't let me help you.

MAIA

[Uneasily.] Why, then come and help me! What else are you here for?

ULFHEIM

Would you rather I should take you on my back?

MAIA

Nonsense!

ULFHEIM

- or carry you in my arms?

MAIA

Now do stop talking that rubbish!

ULFHEIM

[With suppressed exasperation.] I once took a young girl, lifted her up from the mire of the streets and carried her in my arms. Next my heart I carried her. So I would have borne her all through life, lest haply she should dash her foot against a stone. For her shoes were worn very thin when I found her

MAIA

And yet you took her up and carried her next your heart?

ULFHEIM

Took her up out of the gutter and carried her as high and as carefully as I could. [With a growling laugh.] And do you know what I got for my reward?

MAIA

No. What did you get?

ULFHEIM

[Looks at her, smiles and nods.] I got the horns! The horns that you can see so plainly. Is not that a comical story, madam bear-murderess?

MAIA

Oh yes, comical enough! But I know another story that is still more comical.

ULFHEIM

How does that story go?

MAIA

This is how it goes. There was once a stupid girl, who had both a father and a mother but a rather poverty-stricken home. Then there came a high and mighty seigneur into the midst of all this poverty. And he took the girl in his arms, as you did and travelled far, far away with her

ULFHEIM

Was she so anxious to be with him?

MAIA

Yes, for she was stupid, you see.

ULFHEIM

And he, no doubt, was a brilliant and beautiful personage?

MAIA

Oh, no, he wasn't so superlatively beautiful either. But he pretended that he would take her with him to the top of the highest of mountains, where there were light and sunshine without end.

ULFHEIM

So he was a mountaineer, was he, that man?

MAIA

Yes, he was, in his way.

ULFHEIM

And then he took the girl up with him?

MAIA

[With a toss of the head.] Took her up with him finely, you may be sure! Oh no! he beguiled her into a cold, clammy cage, where, as it seemed to her, there was neither sunlight nor fresh air, but only gilding and great petrified ghosts of people all around the walls.

ULFHEIM

Devil take me, but it served her right!

MAIA

Yes, but don't you think it's quite a comical story, all the same?

ULFHEIM

[Looks at her moment.] Now listen to me, my good companion of the chase

MAIA

Well, what it is now?

ULFHEIM

Should not we two tack our poor shreds of life together?

MAIA

Is his worship inclined to set up as a patching-tailor?

ULFHEIM

Yes, indeed he is. Might not we two try to draw the rags together here and there, so as to make some sort of a human life out of them?

MAIA

And when the poor tatters were quite worn out, what then?

ULFHEIM

[With a large gesture.] Then there we shall stand, free and serene as the man and woman we really are!

MAIA

[Laughing.] You with your goat-legs yes!

ULFHEIM

And you with your. Well, let that pass.

MAIA

Yes, come, let us pass, on.

ULFHEIM

Stop! Whither away, comrade?

MAIA

Down to the hotel, of course.

ULFHEIM

And afterward?

MAIA

Then we'll take a polite leave of each other, with thanks for pleasant company.

ULFHEIM

Can we part, we two? Do you think we can?

MAIA
Yes, you didn't manage to tie me up, you know.

ULFHEIM
I have a castle to offer you

MAIA
[Pointing to the hut.] A fellow to that one?

ULFHEIM
It has not fallen to ruin yet.

MAIA
And all the glory of the world, perhaps?

ULFHEIM
A castle, I tell you

MAIA
Thanks! I have had enough of castles.

ULFHEIM
- with splendid hunting-grounds stretching for miles around it.

MAIA
Are there works of art too in this castle?

ULFHEIM
[Slowly.] Well, no, it's true there are no works of art; but

MAIA
[Relieved.] Ah! that's one good thing, at any rate!

ULFHEIM
Will you go with me, then, as far and as long as I want you?

MAIA
There is a tame bird of prey keeping watch upon me.

ULFHEIM
[Wildly.] We'll put a bullet in his wing, Maia!

MAIA
[Looks at him a moment, and says resolutely.] Come then, and carry me down into the depths.

ULFHEIM
[Puts his arm round her waist.] It is high time! The mist is upon us!

MAIA
Is the way down terribly dangerous?

ULFHEIM
The mountain is more dangerous still.

[She shakes him off, goes to the edge of the precipice and looks over, but starts quickly back.]

ULFHEIM
[Goes towards her, laughing.] What? Does it make you a little giddy?

MAIA
[Faintly.] Yes, that too. But go and look over. Those two, coming up

ULFHEIM
[Goes and bends over the edge of the precipice.] It's only your bird of prey and his strange lady.

MAIA

Can't we get past them, without their seeing us?

ULFHEIM

Impossible! The path is far too narrow. And there's no other way down.

MAIA

[Nerving herself.] Well, well, let us face them here, then!

ULFHEIM

Spoken like a true bear-killer, comrade!

[PROFESSOR RUBEK and IRENE appear over the edge of the precipice at the back. He has his plaid over his shoulders; she has a fur cloak thrown loosely over her white dress, and a swansdown hood over her head.

PROFESSOR RUBEK

[Still only half visible above the edge.] What, Maia! So we two meet once again?

MAIA

[With assumed coolness.] At your service. Won't you come up?

[PROFESSOR RUBEK climbs right up and holds out his hand to IRENE, who also comes right to the top.

PROFESSOR RUBEK

[Coldly to MAIA.] So you, too, have been all night on the mountain, as we have?

MAIA

I have been hunting, yes. You gave me permission, you know.

ULFHEIM

[Pointing downward.] Have you come up that path there?

PROFESSOR RUBEK

As you saw.

ULFHEIM

And the strange lady too?

PROFESSOR RUBEK

Yes, of course. [With a glance at MAIA.] Henceforth the strange lady and I do not intend our ways to part.

ULFHEIM

Don't you know, then, that it is a deadly dangerous way you have come?

PROFESSOR RUBEK

We thought we would try it, nevertheless. For it did not seem particularly hard at first.

ULFHEIM

No, at first nothing seems hard. But presently you may come to a tight place where you can neither get forward nor back. And then you stick fast, Professor! Mountain-fast, as we hunters call it.

PROFESSOR RUBEK

[Smiles and looks at him.] Am I to take these as oracular utterances, Mr. Ulfheim?

ULFHEIM

Lord preserve me from playing the oracle! [Urgently, pointing up towards the heights.] But don't you see that the storm is upon us? Don't you hear the blasts of wind?

PROFESSOR RUBEK

[Listening.] They sound like the prelude to the Resurrection Day.

ULFHEIM

They are storm-blasts form the peaks, man! Just look how the clouds are rolling and sinking, soon they'll be all around us like a winding -sheet!

IRENE

[With a start and shiver.] I know that sheet!

MAIA

[Drawing ULFHEIM away.] Let us make haste and get down.

ULFHEIM

[To PROFESSOR RUBEK.] I cannot help more than one. Take refuge in the hut in the mean-time, while the storm lasts. Then I shall send people up to fetch the two of you away.

IRENE

[In terror.] To fetch us away! No, no!

ULFHEIM

[Harshly.] To take you by force if necessary, for it's a matter of life and death here. Now, you know it. [To MAIA.] Come, then and don't fear to trust yourself in your comrade's hands.

MAIA

[Clinging to him.] Oh, how I shall rejoice and sing, if I get down with a whole skin!

ULFHEIM

[Begins the descent and calls to the others.] You'll wait, then, in the hut, till the men come with ropes, and fetch you away.

[ULFHEIM, with MAIA in his arms, clambers rapidly but warily down the precipice.

IRENE

[Looks for some time at PROFESSOR RUBEK with terror-stricken eyes.] Did you hear that, Arnold? men are coming up to fetch me away! Many men will come up here

PROFESSOR RUBEK

Do not be alarmed, Irene!

IRENE

[In growing terror.] And she, the woman in black, she will come too. For she must have missed me long ago. And then she will seize me, Arnold! And put me in the strait-waistcoat. Oh, she has it with her, in her box. I have seen it with my own eyes

PROFESSOR RUBEK

Not a soul shall be suffered to touch you.

IRENE

[With a wild smile.] Oh no, I myself have a resource against that.

PROFESSOR RUBEK

What resource do you mean?

IRENE

[Drawing out the knife.] This!

PROFESSOR RUBEK

[Tries to seize it.] Have you a knife?

IRENE

Always, always, both day and night, in bed as well!

PROFESSOR RUBEK

Give me that knife, Irene!

IRENE

[Concealing it.] You shall not have it. I may very likely find a use for it myself.

PROFESSOR RUBEK

What use can you have for it, here?

IRENE

[Looks fixedly at him.] It was intended for you, Arnold.

PROFESSOR RUBEK

For me!

IRENE

As we were sitting by the Lake of Taunitz last evening

PROFESSOR RUBEK

By the Lake of

IRENE

- outside the peasant's hut and playing with swans and water-lilies

PROFESSOR RUBEK

What then, what then?

IRENE

- and when I heard you say with such deathly, icy coldness, that I was nothing but an episode in your life

PROFESSOR RUBEK

It was you that said that, Irene, not I.

IRENE

[Continuing.] then I had my knife out. I wanted to stab you in the back with it.

PROFESSOR RUBEK

[Darkly.] And why did you hold your hand?

IRENE

Because it flashed upon me with a sudden horror that you were dead already, long ago.

PROFESSOR RUBEK

Dead?

IRENE

Dead. Dead, you as well as I. We sat there by the Lake of Taunitz, we two clay-cold bodies and played with each other.

PROFESSOR RUBEK

I do not call that being dead. But you do not understand me.

IRENE

Then where is the burning desire for me that you fought and battled against when I stood freely forth before you as the woman arisen from the dead?

PROFESSOR RUBEK

Our love is assuredly not dead, Irene.

IRENE

The love that belongs to the life of earth, the beautiful, miraculous earth-life, the inscrutable earth-life, that is dead in both of us.

PROFESSOR RUBEK

[Passionately.] And do you know that just that love, it is burning and seething in me as hotly as ever before?

IRENE

And I? Have you forgotten who I now am?

PROFESSOR RUBEK

Be who or what you please, for aught I care! For me, you are the woman I see in my dreams of you.

IRENE

I have stood on the turn-table-naked and made a show of myself to many hundreds of men after you.

PROFESSOR RUBEK

It was I that drove you to the turn-table, blind as I then was, I, who placed the dead clay-image above the happiness of life, of love.

IRENE

[Looking down.] Too late, too late!

PROFESSOR RUBEK

Not by a hairsbreadth has all that has passed in the interval lowered you in my eyes.

IRENE

[With head erect.] Nor in my own!

PROFESSOR RUBEK

Well, what then! Then we are free and there is still time for us to live our life, Irene.

IRENE

[Looks sadly at him.] The desire for life is dead in me, Arnold. Now I have arisen. And I look for you. And I find you. And then I see that you and life lie dead, as I have lain.

PROFESSOR RUBEK

Oh, how utterly you are astray! Both in us and around us life is fermenting and throbbing as fiercely as ever!

IRENE

[Smiling and shaking her head.] The young woman of your Resurrection Day can see all life lying on its bier.

PROFESSOR RUBEK

[Throwing his arms violently around her.] Then let two of the dead, us two, for once live life to its uttermost before we go down to our graves again!

IRENE

[With a shriek.] Arnold!

PROFESSOR RUBEK

But not here in the half darkness! Not here with this hideous dank shroud flapping around us

IRENE

[Carried away by passion.] No, no, up in the light, and in all the glittering glory! Up to the Peak of Promise!

PROFESSOR RUBEK

There we will hold our marriage-feast, Irene, oh, my beloved!

IRENE

[Proudly.] The sun may freely look on us, Arnold.

PROFESSOR RUBEK

All the powers of light may freely look on us and all the powers of darkness too. [Seizes her hand.] Will you then follow me, oh my grace-given bride?

IRENE

[As though transfigured.] I follow you, freely and gladly, my lord and master!

PROFESSOR RUBEK

[Drawing her along with him.] We must first pass through the mists, Irene, and then

IRENE

Yes, through all the mists, and then right up to the summit of the tower that shines in the sunrise.

[The mist-clouds close in over the scene PROFESSOR RUBEK and IRENE, hand in hand, climb up over the snow-field to the right and soon disappear among the lower clouds. Keen storm-gusts hurtle and whistle through the air.

[The SISTER OF MERCY appears upon the stone-scree to the left. She stops and looks around silently and searchingly.

MAIA.

I am free! I am free! I am free!
No more life in the prison for me!
I am free as a bird! I am free!

[Suddenly a sound like thunder is heard from high up on the snow- field, which glides and whirls downwards with headlong speed. PROFESSOR RUBEK and IRENE can be dimly discerned as they are whirled along with the masses of snow and buried in them.

THE SISTER OF MERCY
[Gives a shriek, stretches out her arms towards them and cries.] Irene!

[Stands silent a moment, then makes the sign of the cross before her in the air, and says.

Pax vobiscum!

[MAIA's triumphant song sounds from still farther down below.

Henrik Ibsen Additional Content

Henrik Ibsen – A Biography

The Task Of The Poet, A Speech To Literary Students

Poetry Collection Of Henrik Ibsen
A Brother in Need
Burnt Ships
Gone
In the Picture Gallery

The Miner
Mountain Life
Thanks
To the Survivors
Wildflowers and Hothouse-plants
With a Water-lily

Notable Quotes Of Henrik Ibsen

Henrik Ibsen – A Biography

Henrik Johan Ibsen, the Norwegian playwright, theatre director and poet, is considered the "father" of realism, and counted among the founders of modernism in theatre. This realism marked him out as scandalous to a lot of the 19· century society whose lives he examined and revealed, though his writing is now considered some of the most poetic and his influence can be found in the writing of, among many others, George Bernard Shaw, Oscar Wilde and James Joyce.

Born to Knud Ibsen (1797-1877) and Marichen Altenburg (1799-1869) on 20· March 1828, he grew up in the small port town of Skien, in Telemark country, in a prosperous merchant family. Later he would write to critic and scholar Georg Brandes that "my parents were members on both sides of the most respected families in Skien", and that this enabled him to be on close terms with "just about all the patrician families who then dominated the place and its surroundings". Knud Ibsen's father was a ship's captain who died at sea, leaving Knud in the care of the ship-owner Ole Paus, whose success in the industry had afforded him the large estate on which Knud grew up in comfort. Other prominent members of Ibsen's ancestry include Knud's half-brothers who were variously lawyers, politicians and ship-owners, the three most affluent and influential positions in the town at the time.

Despite this heritage of ship captaincy Knud elected to become a merchant having enjoyed early commercial success with various contacts made thanks to his upbringing on the Paus estate. Indeed, his marriage to Marichen Altenburg, the daughter of a ship-owner was considered "an excellent family arrangement". Moreover, "Marichen's mother and Knud's step-father were sister and brother, and the bride and groom, who had grown up together, were practically regarded as sister and brother themselves. Marichen Altenburg was a fine catch, the daughter of one of the wealthiest merchants in the prosperous lumber town of Skien." The near-incestuous nature of his parents' marriage fascinated the young Ibsen, and he later treated the subject in his plays, most notably Rosmersholm.

Around 1835, when Ibsen was seven, the winds changed and his father's merchant business came into serious trouble. This forced the family to sell the major Altenburg building in central Skien, their most impressive property, and return to their smaller, cheaper summer house, Venstøp, outside the city. Having had no recourse but to declare bankruptcy, Knud became an embittered alcoholic, venting his "bitterness and resentment on his wife and children", though Henrik's sister Hedvig wrote of their mother "she was a quiet, lovable woman, the soul of the house, everything to her husband and children. She sacrificed herself time and again. There was no bitterness of reproach in her." Eventually Knud's half-brother, the wealthy banker and ship owner Christopher Blom Paus took pity on the family and moved them back into a town house in the city. His father's ruin clearly had a profound effect on Ibsen, for the theme of financial difficulty appears frequently throughout his work alongside moral conflicts rooted in family secrets and concealment from society. Another example of his progressive writing can be found in his unerring portrayal of, and sympathy for, the trials of woman and her helplessness, a reality he saw often from an early age at home.

At the age of fifteen, Ibsen was forced to leave school, moving to the smaller town of Grimstad in order to take an apprenticeship as a pharmacist, at which point he began writing plays. He spent three years living here in financial security, if not excess, until nine months after a dalliance with a serving-girl he found himself financially responsible for an illegitimate boy. Ibsen would dutifully supported the boy until he was well into his teens, without ever actually seeing him. Meanwhile, he went to Christiania (now Oslo) with the intention of matriculation at the University, though he soon rejected this idea after earlier failure to pass various exams encouraged him to focus on his writing. He had his first success aged twenty when his first play, the tragedy

Catilina, was published in 1850, though it was not performed at the time. He published under the pseudonym Brynjolf Bjarne, arguably to protect his dignity if the play was not well received. Later that year though he published his second play, The Burial Mound, which was performed, though it received precious little critical or public attention. Despite these apparent setbacks his determination to be a playwright prevailed and he continued to write only to be continually ignored by critics and readers alike. His early inspiration seems to have come from authors such as Henrik Wergeland, by far the most widely read Norwegian poet and playwright.

The next several years were spent in employment at Det norske Theater in Bergen, where he was involved in the production of around 150 plays in either a writing, directing or producing capacity. Five more plays were published at this time, though they too were considered unremarkable. However, despite this failure to achieve the critical success he sought, he left the theatre with a huge amount of practical experience upon which he could draw in his ensuing writing. Returning to Christiania in 1858 to become the director of the Christiania Theatre, he met Suzannah Thoresen and married her on 18 June 1858. She gave birth to Sigurd, their only child, on 23 December 1859. He later became the Norwegian Prime Minister, playing a central role in the dissolution of the union between Norway and Sweden and in currying the favour of several key statesmen for a monarchy as opposed to their current republican government. The couple's financial difficulty and the lack of state support left Ibsen disillusioned with Norway, and Ibsen resolved to leave in self-imposed exile for Sorrento in Italy in 1864. He only returned 27 years later, as the noted, controversial playwright he was to become.

The first play he wrote in Italy, Brand, in 1965, finally brought him the critical acclaim he had been waiting for, and with it came moderate financial success, affording the couple a measure of comfort which had previously been beyond their means. Ibsen followed up this success with Peer Gynt in 1867, to which the composer Edvard Grieg composed incidental music and songs, attracting a musically academic audience to the production which ultimately brought him more fame and respect as a writer. Early signs of reference to the Danish philosopher Søren Kierkegaard are apparent in Brand, yet despite Ibsen's recent reading of him, it was only until Peer Gynt that he allowed Kierkegaard to consciously inform his work. Indeed, he was initially annoyed with his friend George Brandes for comparing ideas in Brand to those of Kierkegaard, though he proceeded to read Either/Or and Fear and Trembling, both of which would inspire Peer Gynt. The success he was beginning to enjoy encouraged him to write more confidently and introduce his own beliefs and judgements into his drama, coining the term "the drama of ideas". The plays he wrote in the following years are considered his "Golden Age", and indicate the height of his influence at the heart of dramatic controversy across Europe.

Moving from Sorrento to Dresden in Germany in 1868, he spent several years writing Emperor and Galilean (1873), which he considered his greatest work at the time. A dramatisation of the life of the Roman Emperor Julian the Apostate, Ibsen considered it the cornerstone of his entire literary endeavours, though few shared this opinion. He now moved to Munich in 1875 and began writing The Pillars of Society, the first of his contemporary realist drama which was published and performed in 1877. This was followed by The Doll's House in 1879, a harsh criticism of the gender-assigned marital roles which the men and women who characterised Ibsen's society blindly assumed. The success of his scathing criticism in The Doll's House encouraged him to proceed in this vein of writing, so in 1881 his next play, Ghosts, comments on the morality of Ibsen's society in a similar manner. A plot involving a married couple, a pastor, sexual transgression and the passage of sexually transmitted diseases (syphilis) from deviant husband to naïve wife to son proved utterly scandalous. While mention of venereal disease was considered shocking enough, to illustrate the manner in which it could destroy a respectable family was utterly unacceptable. However, if Ibsen's audience considered this so intolerable, little could prepare them for his next offering, An Enemy of the People (1882), a response to the prudish critics of Ghosts in which the alienated individual (Ibsen himself, after Ghosts) is proved right in their solitude, and the mass of people are comparatively portrayed as an ignorant herd. Until then the idea that society was a trustworthy community was almost gospel, but Ibsen chose to challenge it.

Not stopping with this chastisement of the conservatism of society, he proceeded to attack the concurrent and opposing liberalism, ultimately illustrating how each of these poles were often equally self-serving. Its plot cleverly mirrors the circumstances of Ghosts's reception; a physician in a spa town discovers that the bath waters are contaminated by a local tannery and, expecting to be thanked and rewarded by the community for saving their lives and that of the town's visitors, presents his findings to the community. However, this is misconstrued as an act of sabotage on the town's tourism trade and the community declares him 'an enemy of the people', breaking his windows and forcing him out of the town. However, it is implied that the town's refusal to acknowledge this uncomfortable truth will soon herald disaster, mirroring Ibsen's disappointment at his community's rejection of his own, similar, warning. It was now to be expected that Ibsen would go after some other deeply entrenched societal construct and he did not disappoint, though his next play, The Wild Duck (1884), deals with idealistic reformers and the dangers of their eager, evangelical attitudes. His willing iconoclasm rendered him willing to examine and deconstruct any such ideological construct, even when they were as close to his own as this.

However, as his career progressed his writing became gradually more introspective, less to do with the denunciation of society's collective moral frailty and more to do with the psychological conflict of rejecting convention. His later plays, particularly Hedda Gabler (1890), and The Master Builder (1892), are clear examples of this transition, with Hedda Gabler being considered one of the most challenging and rewarding roles for actresses today, its uncompromising examination of interpersonal confrontation the main interest of the play and the driving force behind its drama. Ibsen finally returned to Norway in 1891, to find it largely different to the country he had left 27 years previously. In fact, many of the changes which Norway had undergone were due to the social evolution Ibsen encouraged through his writing; the Victorian era was faltering and modernism was beginning to invade the stage and society as a whole, thanks to Ibsen's unrelenting criticism and visionary writing. Ibsen continued to write for a few years after his return, publishing Little Eyolf in 1894, to see it performed in the Deutsches Theatre in Berlin on 12· January, 1895. Then, in 1896, he published John Gabriel Borkman, based on the attempted suicide of an army officer wrongly accused of embezzlement which Ibsen had recorded earlier in his life. Finally, in 1899 he published When We Dead Awaken, which was first performed at the Haymarket Theatre in London a few days before its publication.

His later years were plagued by ill-health and a series of paralysing strokes in March 1900 rendered him bed-ridden until his peaceful death on 23· May, 1906, in hi home at Arbins Gade 1 in Christiania. On the 22· May, his nurse assured a visitor that he was a little better, upon which Ibsen spluttered his famous last words: "On the contrary!" ("Tvertimod!"). He was buried in The Graveyard of Our Savior in central Christiania, and his gravestone remains there (now Oslo) today. In total he wrote 27 plays. The dramatic alteration to theatrical convention which Ibsen heralded was adopted by, most notably, Anton Chekhov, and others still writing today, and he is responsible for a dramatically altered perception of women, both theatrically and socially, along with the rise of modernism.

The Task Of The Poet – A Speech By Henrik Ibsen

...And what does it mean, then, to be a poet? It was a long time before I realized that to be a poet means essentially to see, but mark well, to see in such a way that whatever is seen is perceived by the audience just as the poet saw it. But only what has been lived through can be seen in that way and accepted in that way. And the secret of modern literature lies precisely in this matter of experiences that are lived through. All that I have written these last ten years, I have lived through spiritually. But no poet lives through anything in isolation. What he lives through all of his countrymen live through with him. If that were not so, what would bridge the gap between the producing and the receiving minds?

And what is it, then, that I have lived through and that has inspired me? The range has been large. In part I have been inspired by something which only rarely and only in my best moments has stirred vividly within me as something great and beautiful. I have been inspired by that which, so to speak, has stood higher than my everyday self, and I have been inspired by this because I wanted to confront it and make it part of myself.

But I have also been inspired by the opposite, by what appears on introspection as the dregs and sediments of one's own nature. Writing has in this case been to me like a bath from which I have risen feeling cleaner, healthier, and freer. Yes, gentlemen, nobody can picture poetically anything for which he himself has not to a certain degree and at least at times served as a model. And who is the man among us who has not now and then felt and recognized within himself a contradiction between word and deed, between will and duty, between life and theory in general? Or who is there among us who has not, at least at times, been egoistically sufficient unto himself, and half unconsciously, half in good faith, sought to extenuate his conduct both to others and to himself?

I believe that in saying all this to you, to the students, my remarks have found exactly the right audience. You will understand them as they are meant to be understood. For a student has essentially the same task as the poet: to make clear to himself, and thereby to others, the temporal and eternal questions which are astir in the age and in the community to which he belongs.

In this respect I dare to say of myself that I have endeavored to be a good student during my stay abroad. A poet is by nature farsighted. Never have I seen my homeland and the true life of my homeland so fully, so clearly, and at such close range, as I did in my absence when I was far away from it.

And now, my dear countrymen, in conclusion a few words which are also related to something I have lived through. When Emperor Julian stands at the end of his career, and everything collapses around him, there is nothing which makes him so despondent as the thought that all he has gained was this: to be remembered by cool and clear heads with respectful admiration, while his opponents live on, rich in the love of warm, living hearts. This thought was the result of much that I had lived through; it had its origin in a question that I had sometimes asked myself, down there in my solitude. Now the young people of Norway have come to me here tonight and given me my answer in word and song, have given me my answer more warmly and clearly than I had ever expected to hear it. I shall take this answer with me as the richest reward of my visit with my countrymen at home, and it is my hope and my belief that what I experience tonight will be an experience to "live through" which will sometime be reflected in a work of mine. And if this happens, if sometime I shall send such a book home, then I ask that the students receive it as a handshake and a thanks for this meeting. I ask you to receive it as the ones who had a share in the making of it.

Poetry Of Henrik Ibsen

Index Of Contents

A Brother In Need
Now, rallying once if ne'er again,
With flag at half-mast flown,
A people in dire need and strain
Mans Tyra's bastion.

Betrayed in danger's hour, betrayed
Before the stress of strife!
Was this the meaning that it had
That clasp of hands at Axelstad
Which gave the North new life?

The words that seemed as if they rushed
From deepest heart-springs out

Were phrases, then! the freshet gushed,
And now is fall'n the drought.
The tree, that promised rich in bloom
Mid festal sun and shower,
Stands wind-stript in the louring gloom,
A cross to mark young Norway's tomb,
The first dark testing-hour.

They were but Judas kisses, lies
In fatal wreaths enwound,
The cheers of Norway's sons, and cries
Towards the beach of Sound.
What passed that time we watched them meet,
'Twixt Norse and Danish lord?
Oh! nothing! only to repeat
King Gustav's play at Stockholm's seat
With the Twelfth Charles' sword.

"A people doomed, whose knell is rung,
Betrayed by every friend!"
Is the book closed and the song sung?
Is this our Denmark's end?
Who set the craven colophon,
While Germans seized the hold,
And o'er the last Dane lying prone
Old Denmark's tattered flag was thrown
With doubly crimsoned fold?

But thou, my brother Norsemen, set
Beyond the war-storm's power
Because thou knewest to forget
Fair words in danger's hour:
Flee from thy homes of ancient fame
Go chase a new sunrise
Pursue oblivion, and for shame
Disguise thee in a stranger's name
To hide from thine own eyes!

Each wind that sighs from Danish waves
Through Norway's woods of pine,
Of thy pale lips an answer craves:
Where wast thou, brother mine?
I fought for both a deadly fight;
In vain to spy thy prow
O'er belt and fiord I strained my sight:
My fatherland with graves grew white:
My brother, where wast thou?

It was a dream! Arise, awake
To do a nation's deed!
Each to his post, swift counsel take;
A brother is in need!
A nobler song may yet be sung
Danes, Danes, keep Tyra's hold
And o'er a Northern era, young
And rich in hope, be proudly flung
The red flag's tattered fold.

Burnt Ships
To skies that were brighter
Turned he his prows;
To gods that were lighter
Made he his vows.

The snow-land's mountains
Sank in the deep;
Sunnier fountains
Lulled him to sleep.

He burns his vessels,
The smoke flung forth
On blue cloud-trestles
A bridge to the north.

From the sun-warmed lowland
Each night that betides,
To the huts of the snow-land
A horseman rides.

Gone
The last, late guest
To the gate we followed;
Goodbye and the rest
The night-wind swallowed.

House, garden, street,
Lay tenfold gloomy,
Where accents sweet
Had made music to me.

It was but a feast
With the dark coming on;
She was but a guest
And now, she is gone.

In The Picture Gallery
With palette laden
She sat, as I passed her,
A dainty maiden
Before an Old Master.

What mountain-top is
She bent upon? Ah,
She neatly copies
Murillo's Madonna.

But rapt and brimming
The eyes' full chalice says
The heart builds dreaming
Its fairy-palaces.

The eighteenth year rolled
By, ere returning,

I greeted the dear old
Scenes with yearning.

With palette laden
She sat, as I passed her,
A faded maiden
Before an Old Master.

But what is she doing?
The same thing still, lo,
Hotly pursuing
That very Murillo!

Her wrist never falters;
It keeps her, that poor wrist,
With panels for altars
And daubs for the tourist.

And so she has painted
Through years unbrightened,
Till hopes have fainted
And hair has whitened.

But rapt and brimming
The eyes' full chalice says
The heart builds dreaming
Its fairy-palaces.

The Miner

Beetling rock, with roar and smoke
Break before my hammer-stroke!
Deeper I must thrust and lower
Till I hear the ring of ore.

From the mountain's unplumbed night,
Deep amid the gold-veins bright,
Diamonds lure me, rubies beckon,
Treasure-hoard that none may reckon.

There is peace within the deep
Peace and immemorial sleep;
Heavy hammer, burst as bidden,
To the heart-nook of the hidden!

Once I, too, a careless lad,
Under starry heavens was glad,
Trod the primrose paths of summer,
Child-like knew not care nor cummer.

But I lost the sense of light
In the poring womb of night;
Woodland songs, when earth rejoiced her,
Breathed not down my hollow cloister.

Fondly did I cry, when first
Into the dark place I burst:
"Answer spirits of the middle

Earth, my life's unending riddle!"

Still the spirits of the deep
Unrevealed their answer keep;
Still no beam from out the gloomy
Cavern rises to illume me.

Have I erred? Does this way lead
Not to clarity indeed?
If above I seek to find it,
By the glare my eyes are blinded.

Downward, then! the depths are best;
There is immemorial rest.
Heavy hammer burst as bidden
To the heart-nook of the hidden!

Hammer-blow on hammer-blow
Till the lamp of life is low.
Not a ray of hope's fore-warning;
Not a glimmer of the morning.

Mountain Life
In summer dusk the valley lies
With far-flung shadow veil;
A cloud-sea laps the precipice
Before the evening gale:
The welter of the cloud-waves grey
Cuts off from keenest sight
The glacier, looking out by day
O'er all the district, far away,
And crowned with golden light.

But o'er the smouldering cloud-wrack's flow,
Where gold and amber kiss,
Stands up the archipelago,
A home of shining peace.
The mountain eagle seems to sail
A ship far seen at even;
And over all a serried pale
Of peaks, like giants ranked in mail,
Fronts westward threatening heaven.

But look, a steading nestles, close
Beneath the ice-fields bound,
Where purple cliffs and glittering snows
The quiet home surround.
Here place and people seem to be
A world apart, alone; -
Cut off from men by spate and scree
It has a heaven more broad, more free,
A sunshine all its own.

Look: mute the saeter-maiden stays,
Half shadow, half aflame;
The deep, still vision of her gaze
Was never word to name.

She names it not herself, nor knows
What goal my be its will;
While cow-bells chime and alp-horn blows
It bears her where the sunset glows,
Or, maybe, further still.

Too brief, thy life on highland wolds
Where close the glaciers jut;
Too soon the snowstorm's cloak enfolds
Stone byre and pine-log hut.
Then wilt thou ply with hearth ablaze
The winter's well-worn tasks; -
But spin thy wool with cheerful face:
One sunset in the mountain pays
For all their winter asks.

Thanks
Her griefs were the hours
When my struggle was sore,
Her joys were the powers
That the climber upbore.

Her home is the boundless
Free ocean that seems
To rock, calm and soundless,
My galleon of dreams.

Half hers are the glancing
Creations that throng
With pageant and dancing
The ways of my song.

My fires when they dwindle
Are lit from her brand;
Men see them rekindle
Nor guess by whose hand.

Of thanks to requite her
No least thought is hers,
And therefore I write her,
Once, thanks in a verse.

To The Survivors
Now they sing the hero loud;
But they sing him in his shroud.

Torch he kindled for his land;
On his brow ye set its brand.

Taught by him to wield a glaive;
Through his heart the steel ye drave.

Trolls he smote in hard-fought fields;
Ye bore him down 'twixt traitor shields.

But the shining spoils he won,

These ye treasure as your own.

Dim them not, that so the dead
Rest appeased his thorn-crowned head.

Wildflowers And Hothouse Plants
"Good Heavens, man, what a freak of taste!
What blindness to form and feature!
The girl's no beauty, and might be placed
As a hoydenish kind of creature."

No doubt it were more in the current tone
And the tide today we move in,
If I could but choose me to make my own
A type of our average woman.

Like winter blossoms they all unfold
Their primly maturing glory;
Like pot-grown plants in the tepid mould
Of a window conservatory.

They sleep by rule and by rule they wake,
Each tendril is taught its duties;
Were I worldly-wise, yes, my choice I'd make
From our stock of average beauties.

For worldly wisdom what do I care?
I am sick of its prating mummers;
She breathes of the field and the open air,
And the fragrance of sixteen summers.

With A Water Lily
See, dear, what thy lover brings;
'Tis the flower with the white wings.
Buoyed upon the quiet stream
In the spring it lay adream.

Homelike to bestow this guest,
Lodge it, dear one, in thy breast;
There its leaves the secret keep
Of a wave both still and deep.

Child, beware the tarn-fed stream;
Danger, danger, there to dream!
Though the sprite pretends to sleep,
And above the lilies peep.

Child, thy bosom is the stream;
Danger, danger, there to dream!
Though above the lilies peep,
And the sprite pretends to sleep

Notable Quotes Of Henrik Ibsen

"A thousand words leave not the same deep impression as does a single deed."

"I don't imagine you will dispute the fact that at present the stupid people are in an absolutely overwhelming majority all the world over."

"To live is to war with trolls."

"You see, the point is that the strongest man in the world is he who stands most alone."

"The majority is never right. Never, I tell you! That's one of these lies in society that no free and intelligent man can help rebelling against. Who are the people that make up the biggest proportion of the population – the intelligent ones or the fools?"

"I believe that before all else I am a reasonable human being, just as you are–or, at all events, that I must try and become one."

"You have never loved me. You have only thought it pleasant to be in love with me."

"You see, there are some people that one loves, and others that perhaps one would rather be with."

"What is the difference in being alone with another and being alone by one's self?"

"It is the very mark of the spirit of rebellion to crave for happiness in this life"

"Was the majority right when they stood by while Jesus was crucified? Was the majority right when they refused to believe that the earth moved around the sun and let Galileo be driven to his knees like a dog? It takes fifty years for the majority to be right. The majority is never right until it does right."

"You should never wear your best trousers when you go out to fight for freedom and truth."

"Money may be the husk of many things but not the kernel. It brings you food, but not appetite; medicine, but not health; acquaintance, but not friends; servants, but not loyalty; days of joy, but not peace or happiness."

"Don't use that exotic word "ideals". We have a good enough native word: "lies"."

"I believe that before anything else I'm a human being – just as much as you are... or at any rate I shall try to become one. I know quite well that most people would agree with you, Torvald, and that you have warrant for it in books; but I can't be satisfied any longer with what most people say, and with what's in books. I must think things out for myself and try to understand them."

"The most dangerous enemy of the truth and freedom amongst us is the compact majority"

"One's life is a heavy price to pay for being born."

"The strongest men are the most alone."

"Rob the average man of his life-illusion, and you rob him of his happiness at the same stroke."

"I am in revolt against the age-old lie that the majority is always right."

"Results for "It is inexcusable for scientists to torture animals; let them make their experiments on journalists and politicians"

"It's a liberation to know that an act of spontaneous courage is yet possible in this world. An act that has something of unconditional beauty."

"Everything I touch seems destined to turn into something mean and farcical."

"People want only special revolutions, in externals, in politics, and so on. But that's just tinkering. What is really is called for is a revolution of the human mind."

"Cage an eagle and it will bite at the wires, be they of iron or of gold."

10346819R00446

Printed in Great Britain
by Amazon.co.uk, Ltd.,
Marston Gate.